THE METROPOLITAN OPERA
ENCYCLOPEDIA
A COMPREHENSIVE GUIDE TO THE WORLD OF OPERA

Edited by
DAVID HAMILTON

Contributors
Aliki Andris-Michalaros
Karen Luten
Michael Rubinovitz
Gary Schmidgall
Kenneth Stern
Debra Vanderlinde

Illustration Editor
Philip Caggiano

Executive Editor
Paul Gruber

SIMON AND SCHUSTER
New York London Toronto Sydney Tokyo

METROPOLITAN OPERA GUILD

Dedicated to the memory of
ROLAND GELATT

This publication was conceived and created by
The Metropolitan Opera Guild in collaboration with
Thames and Hudson Ltd

SIMON AND SCHUSTER

© 1987 by the Metropolitan Opera Guild, Inc.

Published by Simon and Schuster
A Division of Simon & Schuster, Inc.
Simon & Schuster Building
Rockefeller Center
1230 Avenue of the Americas
New York, New York 10020

SIMON AND SCHUSTER and colophon are registered trademarks
of Simon & Schuster, Inc.

Designed by Paul Watkins
Manufactured in the United States of America

1 3 5 7 9 10 8 6 4 2

Library of Congress Cataloging-in-Publication Data
The Metropolitan Opera encyclopedia.
    1. Opera—Dictionaries.   I. Hamilton, David,
1935 Jan. 18–
ML102.06M47   1987   782.1′03′21   87-9705
ISBN 0-671-61732-X

Table of Contents

Unless otherwise specified, all illustrations are drawn from Metropolitan Opera productions.

Preface

As its title suggests, this book aspires to be at once a guide to the world of opera, prepared under the auspices of the Metropolitan Opera Guild (a "Metropolitan *Opera Encyclopedia*"), and a compendium of information specifically related to the Metropolitan Opera, its history, repertory, and performers (a "*Metropolitan Opera* Encyclopedia"). While intended to answer a wide range of questions about this international art form, its composers and librettists and their works, its singers and conductors, designers and producers, its terms and the places where it has been most notably practiced, the book also offers, where appropriate, greater detail about their Met-related aspects (and, as the first such book compiled in the United States in some years, also a more generally American focus). Obviously, the constraints of space prevent it from completely fulfilling these dual roles, but we hope that the result will prove useful to all operagoers and listeners, not only to the millions who attend the Met or share in its performances through radio and television.

In its role as an encyclopedia of the Met, the *Encyclopedia* contains entries for all works (including operettas and other non-operatic vocal works) staged by the Metropolitan Opera since its opening in 1883, with information about the Met's productions and the singers who have appeared in them; the composers of those works; singers and conductors who have appeared prominently and frequently with the company; significant designers, stage directors, and choreographers of its productions; and its managers. (Although this policy has entailed the inclusion of some works probably never to be heard again, it seemed that a *Metropolitan Opera Encyclopedia* was the appropriate place for their interment, so to speak.)

In its broader function, the book includes entries for many additional operas (though not operettas and the like), composers, librettists, performers, and other operatic personages that a present-day listener might encounter, either in the theater or on recordings and broadcasts; brief entries on major operatic centers of America and Europe; definitions of operatic terms; and entries listing operas derived from the works of noted literary figures. A chronology lists the premieres of all the operas in the book, as well as the openings of major opera houses and events in the Met's history. To some degree, the selection of what to include in these categories has necessarily been arbitrary, involving some stabs at prophecy (for example, the recent revival of Zemlinsky's operas is noted, the steady flow of recordings of late 19th-century French opera has stimulated the inclusion of some likely candidates for future resuscitation, and the burgeoning revival of baroque opera is sampled). A special effort has been made to include data on recent singers, and on American singers not found in other operatic reference works, although restrictions of space obviously preclude exhaustive coverage in this as in other areas.

In addition, the *Encyclopedia* includes two dozen guest essays. In some of these, prominent artists discuss operas or roles with which they have been particularly associated, sharing their insights into great works and showing us the ways in which they conceptualize their approaches to performing them. In other essays, noted performers and critics consider aspects of opera and its practice, both past and present.

ON THE USE OF THE ENCYCLOPEDIA
Economy of space has been an imperative in the editing of the *Encyclopedia*, and we have endeavored not to waste words. In the entries on performers,

operas are often referred to by short titles (full titles are always given in the entries on their composers – and, of course, in the entries on the operas themselves.) Similarly, full personal names (or initials) are given only where there is a possibility of confusion. Theater names are often abbreviated, or even omitted when or where only one obvious possibility exists, and the word "theater" is omitted unless the result might be ambiguous (e.g., as in New York's "Broadway Theater"). In performer entries, three theaters are consistently cited without identifying the cities they ornament: Covent Garden (London), La Scala (Milan), and the Met. When a distinction is necessary between the theater and the company or institution performing, the latter is given in parentheses. Dates of events in pre-Revolutionary Russia are given according to the Gregorian calendar ("new style"). Place names are given in a form appropriate to the date in question, with indication of modern equivalents where desirable; standard English forms (e.g., "Vienna" rather than 'Wien") are preferred where they exist.

When the *Encyclopedia* was planned, the new *Annals of the Metropolitan Opera* were expected to be completed before our manuscript deadline, thereby furnishing us with complete, accurate computer-generated tabulations of the Met roles and performances of singers and conductors, as well as of the numbers of Met performances for each opera. In the event, refinement of the data base for that monumental work has continued long beyond the originally scheduled date, and by the time the *Encyclopedia*'s galley proofs were otherwise complete, the desired tabulations had not yet begun. Therefore, our figures for the number of Met performances of operas are based on the Met Press Department's current statistics, which include only complete performances at the Metropolitan Opera House in New York, not tour performances, partial performances in gala evenings, or the like. For singers and conductors, we have had to offer imperfect statistics or, in cases where time did not permit even approximate computation, none at all. We have accepted the figures given for singers in Robert J. Wayner's *What Did They Sing at the Met?* (3rd edition, 1981), although these include partial performances and are thus not quite comparable to our opera figures; other singers not included by Wayner, and conductors, were tabulated from the Metropolitan Opera Archives' card files, a method known to be not entirely reliable. We regret that, as a result, many of our statistics are bound to be superseded when the *Annals* are finally available; however, they certainly do reasonably represent the scope of performers' activities at the Met. Statistics include performances through the 1986–87 season.

The following notes explain features of the several types of entries.

Operas. Operas are entered under their titles in the language of composition, except for those in Slavic and Scandinavian languages, which are entered under the most standard English form; cross-references are made from familiar or alternate English titles (and occasionally foreign ones, e.g., *Coq d'Or*). In addition to identifying the composer and librettist (and, where appropriate, the libretto's literary source), each entry gives (where available) the place, date, and cast of the world premiere. (Conductors' names are sometimes absent: in early days the position did not exist as such, and even at the beginning of the present century conductors were not necessarily identified in theater programs or posters.) Where applicable, similar data are given for the United States premiere (casts are sometimes omitted when the performers are no longer familiar). The language of a performance is noted only when different from the original. For operas performed at the Met, dates and casts of Met productions follow (with the names of their designers and producers, where available), and the names of other noted Met exponents of the principal roles, as well as performance totals. (In the Met's early days, the "producer" was usually more like a traffic director than his powerful modern counterpart.) In the designer credits, a diagonal slash separates the names of set and costume designers, respectively; especially in early Met productions, many hands were sometimes involved in both categories. In "revised" productions – mostly in the 1950s – elements of previous sets were reworked by a new designer.

In the latter part of each opera entry, some characterizing observations introduce a plot summary, the degree of detail reflecting the work's prominence in the current repertory. Vocal ranges of roles mentioned in the plot summary are indicated. (In this connection, it should be noted that the relatively modern categories of mezzo-soprano and baritone are not often found in early operas, although singers of these types now often assume roles in such works; also, that many male roles in opera before 1800 were written for castratos with soprano or alto ranges, and occasionally for women singers in travesty.) Characters' proper names are generally given in the original language, although titles ("King," "Steersman") are generally translated into English; exceptions are occasionally made (especially when roles are cited in singer entries) in the interests of recognizability (e.g., "the Padre Guardiano" rather than "the Father Superior").

The following abbreviations are used in the performance listings:

c.	conductor
d.	designer
p.	producer/director

and in the plot summaries, for vocal ranges:

s	soprano
ms	mezzo–soprano
c, a	contralto, alto
t	tenor
bar	baritone
bs-bar	bass-baritone
bs	bass

Persons. Persons are entered under the most familiar professional form of their names; baptismal names, maiden names, etc., are bracketed (minor variants, such as middle names dropped in professional usage, are ignored unless they attained some general currency). Names involving particles (von, de, etc.) are entered under the short form most familiarly used ("Karajan," but "de Lucia"), with cross-references where they seem called for. Places of birth and death are given without specification of country in the case of world capitals or well-known operatic centers; the country of death is omitted if the same as the country of birth. Where a birth date is not known, a baptismal date ("bapt.") may be given instead.

Composers. The emphasis in the composer entries is on their operatic careers; where feasible, all of their major operatic works are listed. The date given for a work is the year of its first performance, usually close to the date of composition; when these are significantly different, both are given.

Librettists. Only major figures are treated in biographical detail, while entries for Authors merely list the operas entered in the *Encyclopedia* that are based on the author's work

Performers. These biographical entries have presented the greatest problems. Whereas the creators of opera have long been the object of scholarly research, lore about its performers has more often been the stamping ground of enthusiastic amateurs, and reference books are full of contradictory information about dates, teachers, debuts, and roles, sometimes provided by the subjects themselves in response to queries and interviews. Insofar as possible, our entries have been checked against opera-house annals and similar reference works. Dates given in these entries are intended to refer to years, not opera seasons; to conserve space, inclusive dates do not necessarily indicate continuous appearances in every year of a specified term; minor gaps are not indicated, though significant discontinuities are noted where possible. (In the case of conductors, inclusive dates often refer to contractual tenures, whereas singers are more often engaged a season at a time.) In English and American usage, the expression "creator of a role" refers specifically and exclusively to the singer of the role at the world premiere; in French books, however, the term is found in connection with local premieres, a discrepancy that has led to numerous misunderstandings in translation; we hope we have routed these out, and intend the term to refer only to a work's "prima assoluta."

The citations given under the heading "Bibliography" at the end of entries for important figures are restricted to a single book in English, with preference given to those that focus on the subject's operatic work over more general studies, and to recent and currently available titles. At the end of the *Encyclopedia*, a section entitled "For Further Reading" offers a guide to literature on the various aspects of opera and to reference works containing fuller bibliographies on topics both general and specific.

Places. These brief historical descriptions of operatic activity in major centers include information on famous theaters, including those presently active and their current managers.

Terms. Only specifically operatic terms, or specifically operatic significances of some general musical terms, are included; for explanations of standard musical terminology, consult *The New Harvard Dictionary of Music* or a similar work.

ACKNOWLEDGEMENTS
Many people have helped make this book possible. First, the writers who prepared the individual entries. Debra Vanderlinde contributed most of the opera entries. Michael Rubinovitz wrote those on composers, librettists, and impresarios. Gary Schmidgall was responsible for the conductors and most of the major singers, Karen Luten for the other singers. Aliki Andris-Michalaros covered designers, directors, and choreographers. The geographical entries are the work of Kenneth Stern. To all of them go heartfelt thanks – and apologies that the stringencies of space often forced

the reduction of their individual styles to an all-purpose telegraphese: I am, of course, responsible for the final form of all the entries (and entirely for the terms and authors). To the guest essayists, who took time from busy and far-ranging professional schedules, we are enormously grateful. Thanks also to Philip Caggiano, who assembled the illustrations.

Appreciation is due to many others as well. At the Metropolitan Opera, Archivist Robert Tuggle and his staff were unfailingly helpful, as were David M. Reuben and the staff of the Press Department, and James Heffernan and Winnie Klotz; Todd McConchie and Larry Mengden of the Promotion Department made available much-appreciated word-processing facilities, and Charles Riecker was a fount of valuable information. Thanks also to Darcy Dunn, Rebecca Geffner, Clarie Freimann, and Sylvia Shapero at the Metropolitan Opera Guild, as well as to Gerald Fitzgerald and Jean Uppman, who provided access to the manuscript of the forthcoming *Annals of the Metropolitan Opera*. At the Central Opera Service, we are indebted to its director, Maria F. Rich, and to John W. N. Francis, who provided ready responses, from the Service's voluminous files, to numerous pesky queries. The staff of the Music and Theater Divisions in the New York Public Library at Lincoln Center were, as always, ready and eager to assist in the search for reliable information and the picking of factual nits. Others whose help has been valuable in various ways include Edward Greenfield, Gary Lipton, Walter Price, Matthew Sprizzo, and David Wright. My friends Will Crutchfield, Andrew Porter, and Sheila Porter contributed welcome advice and support whenever needed. And the whole enterprise would not have been feasible in the time allotted without the reliable Kaypro 10 computer or the flexible Perfect Writer program.

The dedication of the book expresses a profound debt of gratitude. When he was editor of *High Fidelity*, Roland Gelatt gave me my first professional assignments as a writer, and the prospect of working with him again was one of the attractions of this joint project of the Metropolitan Opera Guild, Simon and Schuster, and Thames and Hudson. Sadly, Roland did not live to see the book's completion, but its conception and shape (notably the idea of the guest essays) owe much to his wisdom and experience, and the first groups of entries, at least, benefited from the scrutiny of his keen editorial eye. We have endeavored to keep the remainder up to his high standard, and we have been stoutly assisted in that effort by the staff of Thames and Hudson. We also appreciate the efforts of their opposite numbers at Simon and Schuster.

Finally, the book would never have reached completion without Paul Gruber, who first persuaded me to do it and endured its growing pains with patience and fortitude, furnishing wise editorial counsel and moral support when needed, and skillfully maintaining a delicate balance between the demands of production schedules and the need to get things right. In addition to overseeing the development of the guest essays and the illustrations, he also cheerfully assumed, when necessary, such various roles as researcher, writer, proofreader, word processor, and even printer of the final manuscript. It has been a constant pleasure collaborating with him, and in a significant sense this is as much his book as anyone's.

David Hamilton March 1987

A

Abbado, Claudio. Conductor; b. Milan, June 26, 1933. Studied with his father Michelangelo and at Milan Conservatory, in Vienna under Hans Swarowsky. Operatic debut, Trieste (*Love for Three Oranges*), 1958, the year of his Koussevitzky Prize. Won Mitropoulos Competition, 1963; Salzburg operatic debut, *Barbiere*, 1965; Covent Garden debut, *Don Carlos*, 1968. Met debut, Oct. 7, 1968, *Don Carlos*, to date his only appearances there. Regular appearances with London Symphony from 1966, principal conductor from 1979. At La Scala, principal conductor, 1969–71; music director, 1971–80; chief conductor, 1980–86; a tenure notable for exploration of 20th-c. repertory, on stage and in concert. Vienna State Opera debut (*Boccanegra*), 1984, led to appointment as music director (from 1986). One of the major orchestral and operatic interpreters of his generation, known for his grasp of fine details as well as structure in the Italian repertory (especially Verdi), muscular attack, and the ability to create powerful dramatic tensions while remaining scrupulously attentive to the score. His extensive recordings include cycles of Mendelssohn, Mahler, and Stravinsky, operas by Rossini and Verdi.

Abbey, Henry E. Impresario; b. Akron, Ohio, June 27, 1846; d. New York, Oct. 17, 1896. First producer of opera at the Metropolitan Opera House (1883–84), hired by the house's directors because of his proven abilities as a theatrical entrepreneur. To compete with Mapleson at the Academy of Music, Abbey spent heavily for star singers

Claudio Abbado

and spectacular scenery and costumes, while economizing on chorus and orchestra. Despite the enthusiastic reception of the opening-night *Faust* and later performances, Abbey ended the season with a personal loss variously estimated at $250,000 to $600,000. He was replaced by Leopold Damrosch and his successors, who presented seven seasons of opera in German. By 1890 the partnership of Abbey, Schoeffel, and Grau was America's most successful theater management firm, which that year gave a season of Italian opera at the Met with Patti, Albani, Nordica, and Tamagno, encouraging the boxholders to dismiss the German company in favor of the Abbey–Schoeffel–Grau Opera Company, which leased the house through the season of Abbey's death. Their roster and repertory, though basically Italian, acquired a French accent through the de Reszkes, Eames, Melba, and Calvé, and eventually incorporated German opera in the original language.

Abduction from the Seraglio, The. See *Entführung aus dem Serail, Die.*

Abgesang (Ger.). Aftersong; see *Bar.*

Abravanel, Maurice. Conductor; b. Thessaloniki, Greece, Jan. 6, 1903. A Berlin student of Kurt Weill, he conducted in Germany until 1933, then was recommended to the Met by Walter and Furtwängler. After his debut in *Samson*, Dec. 26, 1936, he led 37 perfs. of 9 works, mostly French but also *Tannhäuser* and *Lohengrin*. Music director, Utah Symphony (1947–79).

Abu Hassan. Opera in 1 act by Weber; libretto by Franz Karl Hiemer, after *The Arabian Nights.*
 First perf., Munich, Hoftheater, June 4, 1811. U.S. prem., Philadelphia, Nov. 5, 1827 (in Eng.).
 In this singspiel set in mythical Bagdad, Abu Hassan (t) and his wife Fatime (s) each claim the other dead, in order to collect funeral money to pay their debts. Revealed, their deception is forgiven, while their creditor Omar (bs) is disgraced for having sought to buy Fatime's love.

Acis and Galatea. Masque or pastoral opera by Handel; libretto by John Gay and others, after Ovid's *Metamorphoses*, xiii.
 First perf. (private), Cannons, Edgware, England, 1718. First public perf., London, Lincoln's Inn Fields, March 26, 1731: Wright, Rochetti, Leveridge. Rev. by Handel (partly in Italian, using material from his 1708 Italian serenata on the subject), London, King's, June 10, 1732. U.S. prem., N.Y., Lyceum Building, Feb. 14, 1839 (concert perf.); N.Y., Park, Nov. 21, 1842 (staged).
 A delicate score showing how skillfully Handel could adapt his musical invention to the tradition of the English masque. Enraged by the happy love of Acis (t) and Galatea (s), the giant Polyphemus (bs) kills Acis, but Galatea exerts her divine powers to make him immortal.

Ackté, Aino. Soprano; b. Helsinki, Finland, Apr. 23, 1876; d. Nummela, Aug. 8, 1944. Studied at Paris Conservatory; Opéra debut as Marguerite, 1897. Met debut in same role, Feb. 20, 1904; in her only Met season, she sang 19 perfs., including Micaela and Eva. At Covent Garden from 1907, singing first Salome there (1910). Directed Finnish National Opera, 1938–39.

Adam, Adolphe. Composer; b. Paris, July 24, 1803; d. Paris, May 3, 1856. Studied with Boieldieu at Paris

Conservatory and began composing vaudevilles in 1824. His 33 opéras comiques, beginning with *Pierre et Catherine* (1829), frequently in collaboration with librettist Scribe and soprano Miolan-Carvalho, were mostly very popular, though his three ventures into grand opera are not significant. All Adam's works are tuneful, with unerring stage instinct and strong vocal display. The best – such as *Le Chalet* (1834), *Le Postillon du Longjumeau* (1836), *Giralda* (1850), and *Si J'Étais Roi* (1852) – go further, into true musical characterization. Today his best-known works by far are not his operas but his ballets *Giselle* (1841) and *Le Corsaire* (1856), and the anthem "Cantique de Noël," known in the U.S. as "O Holy Night."

Adam, Theo. Bass-baritone; b. Dresden, Aug. 1, 1926. Sang in Dresden Kreuzchor and studied with Rudolf Dittrich, Dresden, and in Weimar; debut as Hermit (*Freischütz*), Dresden State Opera, 1949. Member, Berlin State Opera since 1952. Bayreuth debut as Ortel (*Meistersinger*), 1952; he eventually sang major Wagner roles there, notably Wotan and Sachs (1964–75). Salzburg appearances as Ochs (1969), Wozzeck (1972), and in premiere of Berio's *Re in Ascolto* (1985); Covent Garden debut as Wotan, 1967. Met debut as Sachs, Feb. 7, 1969; in 3 seasons, sang 14 perfs., also including the *Rheingold* and *Walküre* Wotans. His repertory includes such roles as Philippe II, Boris, and La Roche (*Capriccio*). Though lacking a voice of great inherent beauty, Adam has always made a powerful theatrical impression.

Adams, Suzanne. Soprano; b. Cambridge, Mass., Nov. 28, 1872; d. London, Feb. 5, 1953. Studied with Jacques Bouhy and Mathilde Marchesi, Paris. Debuts as Juliette at Paris Opéra (1895), Covent Garden (1898), and Met (Jan. 4, 1899), where she sang 52 perfs. in 4 seasons, including Euridice, Micaela, Donna Elvira, and Marguerite de Valois.

Adler, Kurt. Conductor; b. Neuhaus, Bohemia, Mar. 1, 1907; d. Butler, N.J., Sep. 21, 1977. Asst. conductor at Met (1943–45), then chorus master (1945–73), and conductor for 17 seasons (debut, Jan. 12, 1951, *Zauberflöte*); he led two dozen works, ranging from *Pagliacci* to *Parsifal*.

Adler, Kurt Herbert. Conductor and manager; b. Vienna, Apr. 2, 1905. After study in Vienna and debut at the Volksoper, appeared in European theaters and assisted Toscanini at Salzburg (1936). On staff of Chicago Opera from 1938 (debut, *Traviata*, 1940), then chorus master of San Francisco Opera (from 1943), becoming artistic director (1953–56) and general director (1956–82). After devoting himself entirely to administrative duties, he resumed conducting occasionally toward the end of his tenure. Adler adventurously broadened the company's repertory, introduced important singers to the U.S., encouraged new staging techniques, and established subsidiary companies to train young singers and explore unusual works.

Adler, Peter Herman. Conductor; b. Gablonz, Bohemia [now Jablonec, Czechoslovakia], Dec. 2, 1899. Music director, Bremen Opera (1929–32) and Kiev Philharmonia (1933–36), he came to the U.S. in 1939. Music and artistic director of NBC Television Opera (1949–59); music director, Baltimore Symphony (1959–68); director, Juilliard American Opera Center (1973–81). A pioneer of televised opera, at the Met he led *Ballo* (debut, Sep. 22, 1972) and *Manon* (1975).

Adriana Lecouvreur. Opera in 4 acts by Cilea; libretto by Arturo Colautti, after the play by Scribe and Legouvé.

First perf., Milan, Lirico, Nov. 6, 1902: A. Pandolfini, Caruso, de Luca, c. Campanini. U.S. prem., New Orleans, Jan. 5, 1907 (in Fr.). Met prem., Nov. 18, 1907: Cavalieri, Caruso, Scotti, c. Ferrari, p. Dufriche. Later Met production: Jan. 21, 1963: Tebaldi, Dalis, Corelli, Colzani, c. Varviso, d. Cristini & Parravicini, p. Merrill. Adriana has also been sung at the Met by Albanese, Caballé, Scotto. 44 perfs. in 5 seasons.

Adriana, which exemplifies Cilea's lyric adaptation of verismo conventions, has retained popularity largely because of the title role's attraction for a series of celebrated sopranos.

Paris, 1730. Adriana (s), actress with the Comédie-Française, is commencing a love affair with Maurizio (t), Count of Saxony. Through a series of intrigues, his former mistress the Princesse de Bouillon (ms) learns the identity of her rival, poisons some violets Adriana had given to Maurizio, and returns them to the actress, who believes herself rejected. When Maurizio arrives to propose marriage, she has already inhaled the poison, and dies in his arms, with her friend and admirer the theater manager Michonnet (bar) at their side.

Africaine, L' (The African Maid). Opera in 5 acts by Meyerbeer; libretto by Scribe, after the story of Vasco da Gama.

First perf., Paris, Opéra, Apr. 28, 1865: Sass, Battu, Naudin, Faure, c. Haine. U.S. prem., N.Y., Academy of Music, Dec. 1, 1865 (in Ital.). Met prem., Dec. 7, 1888 (in Ger.): Moran-Olden, Traubmann, Perotti, Robinson, Fischer, c. Seidl. d. Hoyt/Dazien, p. Habelmann. Later Met productions: Jan. 15, 1892 (in Fr.): Nordica, Pettigiani, J. de Reszke, Lassalle, E. de Reszke, c. Vianesi, p. Habelmann; Mar. 21, 1923 (in Ital.): Ponselle, Mario, Gigli, Danise, Didur, c. Bodanzky, d. Urban, p. Thewman. Sélika has also been sung at the Met by Litvinne, Bréval, Fremstad, Lehmann, Rethberg; Vasco by Tamagno, Caruso, Lauri-Volpi, Martinelli; Nélusko by Maurel, Scotti, Stracciari, de Luca. 55 perfs. in 21 seasons.

Meyerbeer's last essay in the grandiose operatic form he perfected, filled with exotic color, vocal display, and scenic effect.

Lisbon, on a ship at sea, and India; early 16th c. Vasco da Gama (t) returns from an expedition beyond the Cape of Storms with two African prisoners, Sélika (s) and Nélusko (bar), and is accused of heresy and imprisoned with them. In his absence, Vasco's beloved, Inès (s), has been promised to Don Pédro (bs). Both Inès and Sélika, also in love with Vasco, conspire for his safety; he returns with Sélika to her homeland, but is torn by regret for Inès. Sélika frees him to return with her rival; despite Nélusko's protestations of love, she commits suicide beneath the poisonous manchineel tree.

Ägyptische Helena, Die (The Egyptian Helen). Opera in 2 acts by R. Strauss; libretto by Hofmannsthal.

First perf., Dresden, State Opera, June 6, 1928: Rethberg, Rajdl, Taucher, Fazzini, Plaschke, c. Busch. U.S. & Met prem., Nov. 6, 1928: Jeritza, Fleischer, Laubenthal, Carroll, Whitehill, c. Bodanzky, d. Urban, p. Wymetal. 5 perfs. in 1 season.

Though the dramatic substance of the opera has found few defenders, the soprano writing for Helen memorably taps Strauss' vein of rhapsodic lyricism.

Egypt, after the Trojan War (1193–1184 B.C.). Menelaus (t) intends to kill his wife Helena (s) because of the bloodshed she has caused, but the sorceress Aithra (s) convinces him that Helena was never in Troy, and gives Helena a potion causing her to forget past evils. Sent to a land where the Trojan war is unknown, the couple are greeted by the desert chieftain Altair (bar) and his son Da-Ud (t), both of whom fall in love with Helena; Menelaus eventually kills Da-Ud. He and Helena drink an antidote to the forgetfulness potion and, after Aithra intervenes to head off the vengeful Altair, their life begins anew.

Aida. Opera in 4 acts by Verdi; libretto by Ghislanzoni, after the French prose of du Locle, from a plot by August Mariette.

First perf., Cairo, Opera House, Dec. 24, 1871 (not, as sometimes said, for the opening of the house or the opening of the Suez Canal): Pozzoni, Grossi, Mongini, Madini, c. Bottesini. European prem., Milan, La Scala, Feb. 8, 1872: Stolz, Waldmann, Fancelli, F. Pandolfini, c. Verdi. U.S. prem., N.Y., Academy of Music, Nov. 26, 1873. Met prem., Nov. 12, 1886 (in Ger.): Herbert-Förster, Brandt, Zobel, Robinson, c. Seidl, d. Hoyt/Schaffel, p. van Hell. Later Met prods.: Nov. 16, 1908: Destinn, Homer, Caruso, Scotti, c. Toscanini, d. Sala, Parravicini/Maison Chiappi, p. Speck; Nov. 7, 1923, Rethberg, Matzenauer, Martinelli, Danise, c. Moranzoni, d. Parravicini/E. Fox, p. Agnini; Nov. 13, 1951: Milanov, Nikolaidi, del Monaco, London, c. Cleva, d. Gérard, p. Webster; Oct. 14, 1963: Nilsson, Dalis, Bergonzi, Sereni, c. Solti, d. O'Hearn, p. Merrill; Feb. 3, 1976: L. Price, Horne, McCracken, MacNeil, c. Levine, d. Reppa/P.J. Hall, p. Dexter. Aida has also been sung at the Met by Eames, Gadski, Muzio, Ponselle, Welitsch; Radames by de Marchi, Slezak, Lauri-Volpi, Corelli; Amneris by Castagna, Barbieri, Bumbry. 651 perfs. in 87 seasons (the most of any work in the company's repertory).

One of the most popular of all operas, *Aida* combines the spectacular and exotic features of grand opera with the orchestral virtuosity of Verdi's later style and, especially in the third act, his usual vivid delineation of personal relationships.

Ancient Egypt. Aida (s), Ethiopian slave of Amneris (ms), daughter of the King of Egypt (bs), is torn by her love for the young captain Radames (t) when he is named the Egyptian commander in a new campaign against her people. Amneris, who also loves Radames, tricks Aida into revealing her love; Aida restrains herself from declaring that she is a princess in her own land. The victorious Radames is rewarded with the hand of Amneris. Amonasro (bar), Aida's father and King of Ethiopia, disguised among the Egyptian prisoners, persuades Aida to discover from Radames the route of the next Egyptian campaign. Radames' inadvertent betrayal is overheard by Amneris and the high priest Ramfis (bs), and he is sentenced to be buried alive; Aida joins him in the tomb.

BIBLIOGRAPHY: Hans Busch, *Verdi's Aida* (Minneapolis, 1978).

Aix-en-Provence. Town in southern France. Its size and proximity to operatic centers in Marseilles, Nice, and Avignon precluded establishment of a resident opera company, though French and Italian touring companies appeared in the Salle d'Opéra, constructed in 1775 and still extant. In 1948, Henri Lambert and Gabriel Dussurget, with casino director André Bigonnet, founded a summer opera festival in Aix. Most performances are held in the open-air theater (capacity 1,700) designed by A.M. Cassandre in the courtyard of the Archbishop's Palace; a few early productions were staged at Les Baux and Les Tholonets. Mozart has been central to the repertory; the initial production was *Così Fan Tutte*, conducted by Hans Rosbaud, the festival's leading musical personality until 1959. 17th- and 18th-c. operas figure prominently in the repertory, but a few contemporary works (e.g., Sauguet's *Les Caprices de Marianne*) have also been staged. Among the singers who first attracted international recognition at Aix are Berganza, Capecchi, Sciutti, Simoneau, and Stich-Randall. The current director is Louis Erlo.

Akhnaten. Opera in 3 acts by Glass; libretto by the composer, with Shalom Goldman, Robert Israel, Richard Riddell, and Jerome Robbins; vocal text drawn from original sources by Shalom Goldman.

First perf., Stuttgart, Mar. 24, 1984: Husmann, Vargas, Esswood, c. Davies. U.S. prem., Houston Opera, Oct. 12, 1984: Angel, Senn, Robson, c. DeMain.

The third of Glass' "portrait operas," based on the life of the Egyptian pharoah Akhnaten (countertenor), who ruled Egypt from 1375 B.C. to 1358 B.C. During his reign he abandons polygamy for the love of his beautiful wife Nefertiti (ms) and builds a city honoring his new god Aten. He fails to produce a male heir, and is oblivious to the suffering of his people. His family is carried off, his temple destroyed, and the old order restored.

Licia Albanese as Violetta in *La Traviata*

Albanese, Licia. Soprano; b. Bari, Italy, July 22, 1913. Trained first as a pianist, she studied voice with Giuseppina Baldassare-Tedeschi. First appeared on stage in 1934 as emergency replacement for an indisposed Butterfly, Lirico, Milan; this was also the role of her debuts in Parma (1935), at the Met (Feb. 9, 1940), and San Francisco (1941).

(continued p.18)

Aida: Triumphal Scenes at the Met

This page (top) (1908 production). Designed by Angelo Parravicini, produced by Jules Speck. Antonio Scotti, Emmy Destinn, Enrico Caruso, Giulio Rossi, Louise Homer, and Adamo Didur

(Center) (1923). Designed by Angelo Parravicini, produced by Armando Agnini

(Bottom) (1951). Designed by Rolf Gérard, produced by Margaret Webster

Opposite (top) (1963). Designed by Robert O'Hearn, produced by Nathaniel Merrill. Carlo Bergonzi, John Macurdy, Mignon Dunn, Birgit Nilsson

(bottom) (1976). Designed by David Reppa, produced by John Dexter. Leontyne Price, Cornell MacNeil, James Morris, Bonaldo Giaiotti, Marilyn Horne, James McCracken

AIDA
Leontyne Price

I find it very hard to believe it has been almost 30 years since I first stepped onto a stage as Aida. The stage was that of San Francisco's War Memorial Opera House, and I was replacing an ailing Antonietta Stella on very short notice. I had just made my debut there, in *Dialogues of the Carmelites*, and I remember Kurt Herbert Adler walking into the room and asking me if I knew Aida. I said "Yes," and went through the score once with Maestro Molinari-Pradelli, who quickly realized that I knew every single solitary note and nuance of the role, although I'd never sung it on stage before. Sometimes I think I was *born* knowing Aida.

Talking or writing about Aida is simply not easy for me; it's a little like talking to strangers about a member of one's family. The role was a very personal experience. I sang 26 different roles on stage, and I cared about all of them. (I agree with actors and directors who will tell you that it's impossible to play a role well unless you *like* the character.) But I would put Aida on a level all her own.

Let's start with the obvious, or what *seems* like the obvious. Aida is a black woman, and in the world of the opera, black artists don't have many opportunities to play black characters. That's it on a very simplistic level, but it goes far beyond that.

I used to joke that when a theater cast me as Aida they could always expect to save on make-up. (It's not that I *didn't* wear any make-up as Aida; every artist wears make-up on stage. But as Aida, I can assure you, I could get away with less than just about any of my colleagues!) It was a joke, but there was a serious statement lurking behind my attempt at humor: when I performed Aida, the color of my skin became my costume, and that gave me an incredible freedom no other role could provide. My skin was my costume – all I had to do was drape something over it! Just imagine the physical difference between roles such as Manon or Donna Anna or the Leonoras, with wigs, stays, bodices, gloves, and so forth – and Aida. I was always totally at ease when I sang the immortal phrases composed by that great master Giuseppe Verdi for his enslaved princess.

Beyond that, but still on the subject of race, the role has other very deep meanings for me. Verdi was always a great one to root for the side of the underdog, both in his personal life and in his operas. In *Nabucco* he wrote "Va, pensiero" to show the feelings of the Jews in their Babylonian captivity, and the core of *Aida* is concerned with an Ethiopian princess, in exile and servitude, facing a responsibility to her people and learning what that responsibility costs, This is something I came to understand more fully after I left the role for a time and returned to it in the 1976 Met production. At that time, the work became more profound to me, and in turn my identification with this aspect of the role helped me deepen my characterization.

There are so many reasons why I love this character. She possesses all the qualities I like about myself. She is an honest person forced into role-playing – with both Amneris and Radames – and this is terribly difficult for her. She has great strength and nobility. There's something about her that is provocative, that makes her special, which I think is not only why Amneris has chosen her to be her handmaid, but also why she immediately suspects Aida to be her rival. Why would a princess be jealous of a slave, even a beautiful slave, unless there was something very *distinctive* about that slave, something that set her apart from everyone else? We find out later in the

opera that Aida is a princess, but well before that, Amneris knows she is someone to reckon with.

Aida is usually thought of as an "epic" opera, but I think that's misleading. Certainly, there are grand scenes with everyone and the elephants dragged on, but that's only a fraction of the opera. Verdi loved to write operas where the private and public lives of the characters are contrasted, and here he uses the big scenes as a counterpoint to the intimate ones. Most of *Aida* is concerned with one-to-one relationships – Aida with her lover, with her rival, and with her father – and, while I appeared in all kinds of productions of the opera, I usually preferred those that stressed the feelings and interplay between the main characters to the more circus-like stagings.

Perhaps most important to me is the vocal content of the role. It's difficult to explain why some roles fit a voice and some do not. It goes beyond just vocal range. All I can say is that there is nothing more thrilling to a singer than to have a role where *everything* works vocally, where every phrase and every breath sounds beautiful and right in *your* voice. That is something I knew about Aida from the very beginning: that my voice was made to sing this role, above all others, that it came naturally and easily to me.

And the thrill is compounded when the music not only fits your voice, but is so exquisitely beautiful to boot! I don't think there is another opera with such a wealth of extraordinary melody, and that's saying something when you think of the other magnificent operas Verdi composed. Just Aida's music alone – from her "theme" that opens the prelude and that you hear again at her first entrance, to the "Numi, pietà" in "Ritorna vincitor," to "Ah! pietà ti prenda" in the duet with Amneris, to "O patria mia" and those two amazing duets in the Nile scene - it's all ravishing. And to me the crowning glory is "O terra, addio" in the final scene. It's a melody of unearthly beauty, which is of course what that masterful composer meant for two people who are leaving this earth.

These are the reasons why I selected *Aida* to be my last appearance on the operatic stage. My final performance, the one that was televised on "Live from the Met," was an experience I will never, ever forget for as long as I am living. Many people have asked what I was thinking during that four-minute ovation after "O patria mia." It was the most amazing moment of my life. I was determined not to break character and reveal my personal emotions, but at the same time I have *never* felt so much love in my entire life, and I really didn't know where I was. I was like a sponge, soaking up every vibration of that applause.

This noble Ethiopian princess was a rare star in the galaxy of Verdi heroines I had the joy of portraying. I am eternally grateful to Aida, because in many ways I was fulfilled, not only as an artist, but also as a human being, and with her I believe I earned my niche in the annals of operatic history.

Leontyne Price as Aida and
Simon Estes as Amonasro

Frances Alda as Cleopatra and Orville Harrold as Meiamoun in *Cleopatra's Night*

Her La Scala debut was as Lauretta (*Gianni Schicchi*), 1935; before the war, she also sang Suzel (*Amico Fritz*), Micaela, Anna (*Loreley*), and Mimi there (recording the latter opposite Gigli), and returned as Butterfly in 1951. She sang at most major Italian theaters, at Covent Garden (debut, Liù, 1937), and Chicago (debut, Micaela, 1941). By the time of her retirement from the Met in 1966, she had sung 286 perfs. of 17 roles – most notably seven Puccini heroines, but also Micaela, Susanna, Nedda, Marguerite, Violetta (72 times, the company record), Massenet's Manon, Desdemona, Nannetta (*Falstaff*), Mozart's Countess, and Adriana Lecouvreur. Toscanini chose her as Violetta and Mimi for his NBC broadcasts. A versatile singer, endowed with emotional intensity and commitment, Albanese began as a verismo specialist and broadened her repertory at the Met; by carefully limiting her excursions into more dramatic roles such as Desdemona and Tosca, she enjoyed a long career, which endured after she left the Met.

Albani [Lajeunesse], **Emma.** Soprano; b. Chambly, near Montreal, Nov. 1, 1847; d. London, Apr. 3, 1930. Studied with Duprez in Paris, Lamperti in Milan; debuts as Amina, Messina, 1870, and Covent Garden, 1871. Met debut as Gilda, Dec. 23, 1891; in her only Met season, she sang 15 perfs. as Marguerite, Desdemona, Donna Elvira, Valentine (*Huguenots*), Elsa, Eva, and Senta.

Albert, Eugen d'. Composer and pianist; b. Glasgow, Scotland, Apr. 10, 1864; d. Riga, Latvia, Mar. 3, 1932.

Studied with his father, who was ballet master at Covent Garden, and at National Training School, London, with Stainer, Prout, and Sullivan. First achieved fame as a touring piano virtuoso and protégé of Liszt, later turned to composing opera, beginning with the "musical fairy tale" *Der Rubin* (1893). *Tiefland* (1903), his first and greatest success, is representative of his international style, a combination of German Romanticism and melodious Italian verismo. *Tiefland* still makes appearances on German stages; other successes in their time, such as *Flauto Solo* (1905) and *Die toten Augen* (1916), do not.

Albert Herring. Opera in 3 acts by Britten; libretto by Eric Crozier, after de Maupassant's short story *Le Rosier de Madame Husson*.

First perf., Glyndebourne, June 20, 1947: Cross, Evans, Pears, Sharp, c. Britten. U.S. prem., Lenox, Mass., Tanglewood, Aug. 8, 1949.

A sparkling comedy written for the English Opera Group and its chamber orchestra of 12 instruments.

Loxford, a market town in East Suffolk, England, spring 1900. Lady Billows (s) and a committee of local notables are hard pressed to find a suitably chaste May Queen, so they settle on a May King, the virtuous Albert Herring (t). At the coronation, Sid (t) and Nancy (ms) spike Albert's lemonade; a bit drunk, he sets out with his prize money to find out what he's been missing. The town, upset by Albert's disappearance, fears the worst, but he shows up, somewhat dishevelled, having sampled the pleasures of alcohol and feminine companionship. He blames his mother for a repressive upbringing; the committee and authorities are indignant, and Albert's friends cheer his emancipation.

Alceste. Opera in 3 acts by Gluck; libretto by Calzabigi, after the tragedy by Euripides.

First perf., Vienna, Burgtheater, Dec. 26, 1767: Bernasconi, Tibaldi, Laschi. Rev. version, text adapted and translated into Fr. by F.L.G. Lebland du Roullet, Paris, Opéra, Apr. 23, 1776: Levasseur, Legros, Gelin. U.S. prem., Wellesley College, Mass., Mar. 11, 1938. Met. prem., Jan. 24, 1941 (in Fr.): Lawrence, Maison, Warren, c. Panizza, d. Rychtarik, p. Graf. Later Met production: Dec. 6, 1960 (in Eng.): Farrell, Gedda, Cassel, c. Leinsdorf, d. & p. Manuel. An earlier revival, on Mar. 4, 1952 (in Eng.), was the occasion of Flagstad's farewell Met appearances. 17 perfs. in 3 seasons.

A work of classic dignity and breadth, *Alceste* was published with a remarkable preface setting forth Gluck's ideals for operatic reform.

Ancient Greece. The oracle has decreed that Admète (t), King of Thessaly, must die of the illness he suffers unless a friend can be found to die in his stead. His wife Alceste (s) resolves to sacrifice herself. Admète recovers, but cannot accept the prospect of Alceste's sacrifice and joins her at the entrance to Hades. To save his king, Hercule (bar) confronts the Shades. Apollon (bar) raises Hercule to godhood and decrees that Alceste and Admète shall live because of their perfect conjugal love.

Alcina. Opera in 3 acts by Handel; libretto by Antonio Marchi, adapted from Fanzaglia's *L'Isola della Alcina*, after Ariosto's *Orlando Furioso*.

First perf., London, Covent Garden, Apr. 16, 1735: Strada, Negri, Carestini, Beard, Waltz. U.S. prem., Dallas, State Fair Music Hall, Nov. 16, 1960: Sutherland, d. & p. Zeffirelli.

Handel's last fully successful Italian opera for London is set on an island ruled by the enchantress Alcina (s), who transforms the knights who woo her into strange beasts. She has cast a spell on Ruggiero (s), who, in his infatuation for Alcina, has forgotten his own betrothed, Bradamante (c). Disguised as her brother Ricciardo, Bradamante sets off with her guardian Melisso (bs) to find Ruggiero. They are shipwrecked on Alcina's island, where a tangle of confused identities involves them with Alcina's sister Morgana (s) and her rejected suitor Oronte (t). Eventually Ruggiero is reunited with Bradamante, Morgana persuades Oronte to forgive her, Alcina loses her magical powers, and the knights are restored to human form.

Alda [Davies], **Frances.** Soprano; b. Christchurch, New Zealand, May 31, 1883; d. Venice, Sep. 18, 1952. She sang light opera in Melbourne before studying with Marchesi in Paris; debut as Manon, Opéra-Comique, 1904. Appeared at Monnaie, Brussels (1905–08), Covent Garden (1906), and at La Scala (1908) as Louise under Toscanini, who with Gatti-Casazza engaged her for their first Met season. Met debut as Gilda, Dec. 7, 1908; in 21 seasons, she sang 266 pers. of 23 roles, including Mimi, both Manons, Gounod's and Boito's Marguerites, Nannetta, Harriet (*Martha*), Desdemona, and Princess (*Marouf*). Created Roxanne in *Cyrano*, Herbert's Madeleine, and Hadley's Cleopatra. Also sang in Buenos Aires (from 1908), Boston (1909–13), and Chicago (1914–15). Married to Gatti-Casazza, 1910–28. Alda was a cultivated, musical singer with a warm lyric soprano, also noted for the sharp wit on display in her autobiography, *Men, Women, and Tenors* (1937).

Aldeburgh. Coastal town in Suffolk, England; home of Benjamin Britten from 1947 until his death in 1976 and site of an annual summer music festival, founded in 1948 by Britten, Eric Crozier, and Peter Pears. The English Opera Group, established in 1946 by Britten, Crozier, and John Piper, moved from Glyndebourne for Aldeburgh's initial season. Performances originally took place in churches and in the Jubilee Hall, expanded to 360 seats in 1960. In 1967 the festival acquired a 19th-c. malthouse in nearby Snape, and converted it into The Maltings, a theater-concert hall with excellent acoustics (capacity nearly 800); it burned on the opening night of the 1969 festival, but was reconstructed in time for the 1970 season. The repertory and the informal atmosphere have reflected Britten's personality. Aldeburgh premieres have included many of Britten's later works, as well as Berkeley's *Dinner Engagement* (1954), Walton's *Bear* (1967), and Birtwistle's *Punch and Judy* (1968). Since Britten's death, the festival has been directed by a consortium including Pears (until his death), Imogen Holst (until her death), Colin Graham, Philip Ledger, Steuart Bedford, Mstislav Rostropovich, Murray Perahia, Simon Rattle, John Shirley-Quirk, and Oliver Knussen. Since 1982, economic considerations have curtailed professional opera productions at Aldeburgh, which functions now on a more modest level.

Aleko. Opera in 1 act by Rachmaninoff; libretto by Vladimir Nemirovich-Danchenko, after Pushkin's poem *The Gypsies.*
First perf., Moscow, Bolshoi, Apr. 27, 1893: Korsov, Klementiev, Deysha-Sionitskaya, Vlasov, Shubina, c. Altani. U.S. prem., N.Y., Jolson's Theater, Jan. 11, 1926.
In Rachmaninoff's prizewinning graduation exercise at Moscow Conservatory, Aleko (bs) joins a band of gypsies. When his lover Zemfira (s), tiring of him, plans to run off with another man, Aleko kills her and is abandoned by the gypsies.

Aler, John. Tenor; b. Baltimore, Md., Oct. 4, 1949. Studied at Catholic University, Washington, D.C.; debut as Ernesto, Juilliard American Opera Center, 1977. Other debuts at Monnaie, Brussels (Belmonte, 1979), Glyndebourne (Ferrando, 1979), and N.Y.C. Opera (Ottavio, 1981). Specializes in florid lyric roles.

Alessandro Stradella. Opera in 3 acts by Flotow; libretto by Wilhelm Friedrich Riese, after the libretto for Flotow's 1837 *Stradella* by P. Duport and P.A. de Forges.
First perf., Hamburg, Stadttheater, Dec. 30, 1844. U.S. prem., Hoboken, N.J., Vauxhall Garden, Nov. 29, 1853. Met prem., Feb. 4, 1910: Gluck, Slezak, Mühlmann, c. Bendix, p. Schertel. 3 perfs. in 1 season.
From this tuneful score, based on fictitious episodes from the life of the composer, one aria, Stradella's prayer "Jungfrau Maria," has remained popular.

Alexander, John. Tenor; b. Meridian, Miss., Oct. 21, 1923. Studied with Robert Weede at Cincinnati Conservatory; debut as Faust, Cincinnati, 1952. Debuts at N.Y.C. Opera (Alfredo, 1957) and Met (Ferrando, Dec. 19, 1961). On the Met roster ever since, he is valued for his reliable and musical singing in an enormous repertory, including Bacchus (*Ariadne*), Stolzing, Hoffmann, Belmonte, Arbace and the title role (*Idomeneo*), Alfredo, and Faust. Has also appeared in Vienna, at Volksoper (*Tote Stadt*, 1967) and State Opera (Rodolfo, 1968), at Covent Garden (Pollione, 1970), San Francisco, and Boston, where he sang Don Carlos in the U.S. premiere of the original French version, 1973.

Alexander, Roberta. Soprano; b. Yellow Springs, Ohio, Mar. 3, 1949. Studied at U. of Michigan and with Herman Woltman at Royal Conservatory, Hague. Sang Pamina (Houston, 1980), Daphne (Santa Fe, 1981), Elettra in *Idomeneo* (Zurich, 1982), Mimi (Komische Oper, Berlin, 1982, and in her Covent Garden debut), Violetta, Vitellia (Netherlands Opera, 1982–83), Handel's Cleopatra (Vienna, 1985). Met debut as Zerlina, Nov. 3, 1983; she has since sung Jenůfa, Gershwin's Bess, and Mimi with the company.

Alfano, Franco. Composer; b. Posillipo, Naples, Mar. 8, 1875; d. San Remo, Oct. 27, 1954. Studied at Naples Conservatory with de Nardis and Serrao, then in Leipzig with Jadassohn. His first performed opera was *La Fonte di Enschir* (1898); a series of verismo works climaxed in the popular *Risurrezione* (1904). In *L'Ombra di Don Giovanni* (1913, rev. as *Don Juan de Manara*, 1941) and especially *La Legenda di Sakùntala* (1914–20, orchestral score lost in World War II and reconstructed as *Sakùntala*, 1952), he explored a more personal idiom combining Italian lyricism with exoticism inspired by Debussy and Strauss. In later years he composed orchestral and chamber works and songs. Between 1918 and 1950, he directed music schools in Bologna, Turin, and Pesaro. Alfano is remembered mainly for having completed Puccini's *Turandot* shortly after that composer's death in 1924.

Alfonso und Estrella. Opera in 3 acts by Schubert; libretto by Franz von Schober.
First perf., Weimar, Jan. 24, 1854: c. Liszt. U.S. prem.,

Detroit, Mich., Nov. 11, 1978 (concert perf.): Söderström, Rayam, W. Parker, Kimbrough, Lagger, c. Dorati.

Musically rich, *Alfonso* is one of Schubert's most ambitious operas, doomed by Schober's clumsy dramaturgy. Troila (bar), dethroned King of Leon, lives with his son Alfonso (t) in an idyllic valley where kindness and wisdom reign. Alfonso meets and falls in love with Estrella (s), daughter of the usurper Mauregato (bar). Adolfo (bs), Estrella's rejected suitor, attempts to overthrow Mauregato and is overcome by Alfonso. With a common enemy, Troila and Mauregato are reconciled, and Mauregato gives Estrella to Alfonso.

Allen [Lee]**, Betty.** Mezzo-soprano; b. Campbell, Ohio, Mar. 17, 1930. Studied at Hartford School of Music and with Zinka Milanov. A member of the N.Y.C. Opera in 1954 (debut, Queenie in *Show Boat*) and 1973–75; has sung in San Francisco, Boston, Santa Fe, and Houston. Mini-Met debut as Commère (*Four Saints in Three Acts*), Feb. 20, 1973. Since 1979, executive director, Harlem School of the Arts.

Allen, Peter. Broadcaster; b. Toronto, Sep. 17, 1920. After receiving a degree in English from Ohio State U., served as naval lieutenant in World War II, commanding minesweepers. He joined the staff of station WQXR, N.Y., as announcer, 1947. Asked to understudy Milton Cross on the Met broadcasts in 1973, he became the regular announcer after Cross' death, making his "debut" on Jan. 4, 1975.

Allen, Thomas. Baritone; b. Seaham, England, Sep. 10, 1944. Studied at Royal College of Music, London; debut in 1969 as Rossini's Figaro, Welsh National Opera, where he also sang Papageno, Mozart's Count and Guglielmo, and Billy Budd. At Covent Garden since 1972, Glyndebourne since 1973. Created Valerio in Musgrave's *Voice of Ariadne*, Aldeburgh, 1974. Met debut as Papageno, Nov. 5, 1981; has also sung Almaviva there.

Amahl and the Night Visitors – NBC Opera Company, 1951 world premiere. Rosemary Kuhlmann and Chet Allen

Althouse, Paul. Tenor; b. Reading, Pa., Dec. 2, 1889; d. New York, Feb. 6, 1954. Studied with Oscar Saenger, N.Y. Debut as Dimitri (*Boris*), Met, Mar. 19, 1913. Sang with Met until 1920, also 1923, 1934–1940, most often as Dimitri, Turiddu, and later as Wagnerian tenor, in 178 perfs. of 25 roles; created Lionel (*Shanewis*), François (*Madeleine*). Taught voice in N.Y.; pupils included Dalis, Steber, and Tucker.

Altmeyer, Jeannine. Soprano; b. Pasadena, Calif., May 2, 1948. Studied with Betty Olssen, Martial Singher, Lotte Lehmann, and George London. Won Met National Auditions, 1970; debut as Celestial Voice, *Don Carlos*, Sep. 25, 1971. Has sung principally in Europe, including Freia at Karajan's Salzburg Easter Festival; Sieglinde at Bayreuth, 1979. Returned to Met as Sieglinde, 1986, also singing *Walküre* Brünnhilde and Fidelio.

alto. Lowest female voice range; also known as contralto. Usual compass from F below middle C to A above the treble clef. In the 17th and 18th c., male altos (castratos, *q.v.*) were frequently the heroic protagonists of opera. Modern male voices in this range are countertenors. In modern times, true contralto voices have become rare, replaced by the mezzo-soprano (*q.v.*).

Alva, Luigi [Luis]**.** Tenor; b. Lima, Peru, Apr. 10, 1927. Studied with Rosa Morales, Lima, and later at La Scala school; debut in zarzuela *Luisa Fernanda*, Lima, 1949. European debut as Alfredo, Nuovo, Milan, 1954. Sang Paolino in *Matrimonio Segreto* at opening of Piccola Scala, Milan, 1955. La Scala debut as Almaviva, 1956. Debuts at Salzburg (1957), Covent Garden (1960), Chicago (1961). Met debut as Fenton, Mar. 6, 1964; in 8 seasons (to 1976), sang 86 perfs. of 8 roles, including Ernesto (*Pasquale*), Almaviva, Lindoro (*Italiana*), and Tamino. Also appeared in Aix, Glyndebourne, and Edinburgh, and with Vienna State Opera. The grace and musicality, spontaneity and brio of Alva's singing earned him a significant role in the revival of 18th- and early 19th-c. repertory.

Alvarez [Gouron]**, Albert.** Tenor; b. Cenon, near Bordeaux, France, May 16, 1861; d. Nice, Feb. 1, 1933. Studied voice in Paris. Debut as Faust, Ghent, 1887; debuts at Paris Opéra (Faust, 1892), Covent Garden (Leicester in de Lara's *Amy Robsart*, 1893), and Met (Roméo, Dec. 18, 1899). At the Met until 1903, somewhat in Jean de Reszke's shadow until his last season, when he appeared as Otello, Canio, Radames, and other leads. Created Nicias (*Thaïs*) and Aragui (*Navarraise*).

Alvary, Lorenzo. Bass; b. Debrecen, Hungary, Feb. 20, 1909. Studied in Milan and Berlin; debut in Vienna, 1937. American debut, Police Commissioner (*Rosenkavalier*), San Francisco, 1939. Met debut as Zuniga (*Carmen*), Nov. 26, 1942; a member of that company for 29 seasons, he sang 651 perfs., most often as Zuniga, Benoit and Alcindoro (*Bohème*), and Antonio (*Nozze*).

Alvary, Max. Tenor; b. Düsseldorf, Germany, May 3, 1856; d. near Gross-Tabarz, Thuringia, Nov. 7, 1898. Studied with Stockhausen in Frankfurt, Lamperti in Milan. As Max Anders, debut as Flotow's Alessandro Stradella, Weimar, 1879. Met debut as Don José, Nov. 25, 1885; roles included young Siegfried, Loge, Adolar (*Euryanthe*), and Alvarez (*Fernand Cortez*). Appeared at Bayreuth (Tannhäuser and Tristan, 1891) and Covent Garden (debut, young Siegfried, 1892).

Alzira. Opera in prologue and 2 acts by Verdi; libretto by Cammarano, after Voltaire's tragedy *Alzire, ou les Américains.*

First perf., Naples, San Carlo, Aug. 12, 1845: Tadolini, Fraschini, Coletti. U.S. prem., N.Y., Carnegie Hall, Jan. 17, 1968 (concert perf.): Ross, Cecchele, Quilico, c. Perlea.

The score, written quickly for a contract Verdi may have regretted, was condemned by the composer as "really ugly" and by most Verdian commentators as the worst product of the "galley years." Its best passages deserve exemption, but *Alzira* has had few revivals.

Peru, mid-16th c. Returning to his tribe after surviving torture at the hands of the Christians, the Inca chief Zamoro (t) learns that his bride Alzira (s) has been kidnapped by the Christian governor Gusmano (bar). Gusmano attempts to arrange a "peace," with the Incas in subjugation, and to keep Alzira for himself. In exchange for the release of Zamoro, who has been captured again, Alzira agrees to the marriage. At the wedding celebration, Zamoro appears in disguise and kills Gusmano.

Amadis. Opera in prologue and 5 acts by Lully; libretto by Philippe Quinault after Garcia Ordoñez de Montalvo's chivalric romance.

First perf., Paris, Opéra, Jan. 18, 1684: Moreaux, Du Mesny, Dun. U.S. prem., Cambridge, Mass., Lowell House, Mar. 15, 1951.

The first opera in which Lully and Quinault turned from ancient mythology to a medieval subject relates the adventures of Amadis (t): his reunion with his real parents, receipt of knighthood, and tests of valor, culminating in love for and reconciliation with the princess Oriane (s).

Amahl and the Night Visitors. Opera in 1 act by Menotti; libretto by the composer, inspired by Bosch's painting *The Adoration of the Magi.*

First perf., N.Y., NBC Television, Dec. 24, 1951: Kuhlman, Allan, c. Schippers; first stage perf., Bloomington, Indiana U., Feb. 21, 1952.

The first opera written for TV, and an enduring Christmas favorite in the U.S.

Biblical times. The crippled boy Amahl (s) and his mother (s), living in poverty, are visited by the Wise Men on their way to the Christ Child with gifts. In the middle of the night, the mother cannot resist stealing some of the gold they are bearing. When she is caught, she explains that she wanted it for her crippled boy, and the Wise Men tell her she may keep the riches, as Christ will build his kingdom on love. Amahl is moved to offer his crutch as a gift for the unborn King; handing it to the Wise Men, he realizes he now can walk without it. All give thanks for this miracle, and Amahl's mother allows him to accompany the Wise Men on their journey.

Amara [Armaganian], **Lucine.** Soprano; b. Hartford, Conn., Mar. 1, 1927. Studied with Stella Eisner-Eyn, San Francisco; sang in opera chorus there, 1945–46. Met debut as Celestial Voice (*Don Carlos*), Nov. 6, 1950; has sung over 450 perfs. there in more than 40 roles, including Nedda, Mimi, Donna Elvira, Butterfly, Ellen (*Grimes*), Tatiana, and Leonora (*Trovatore*).

Amato, Pasquale. Baritone; b. Naples, Mar. 21, 1878; d. Jackson Heights, N.Y., Aug. 12, 1942. After study in Naples, he made his debut there as Germont, Teatro Bellini, 1900. Within four years he had appeared at major Italian houses, Covent Garden, and other European theaters. At La Scala (1907–08), he sang many roles under Toscanini, including Golaud in the Italian premiere of *Pelléas.* After his Met debut (Germont, Nov. 20, 1908), he remained a member of the company until 1921, creating Jack Rance (*Fanciulla*), Damrosch's Cyrano, and Napoleon (*Mme. Sans-Gêne*). Other frequent roles were Tonio, Amonasro, di Luna, Barnaba, Marcello, and Manfredo (*Amore dei Tre Re*); in all, he sang 446 performances at the Met. After 1921, he appeared occasionally with American regional troupes, and celebrated the 25th anniversary of his Met debut by appearing in many of his great roles before 5,000 spectators at the Hippodrome, N.Y. Following retirement, he taught in N.Y. Amato had a voice of wide compass, with a brilliant top register; his diction, tone production, and phrasing were considered classic, and his dramatic talent ranged from the humorous to the fiercely tragic.

Amelia al Ballo (Amelia Goes to the Ball). Opera in 1 act by Menotti; libretto by the composer.

First perf., Philadelphia, Academy of Music, Apr. 1, 1937 (in Eng.): c. Reiner. Met prem., Mar. 3, 1938 (in Eng.): Dickson, Chamlee, Brownlee, Cordon, c. Panizza, d. Oenslager, p. Sachse. 6 perfs. in 2 seasons.

A lively opera buffa, set in a European city, early 20th c. When Amelia (s) is prevented from leaving for a ball by a confrontation between her husband (bar) and her lover (t), she knocks the husband unconscious, has the lover arrested, and goes to the ball with the police chief (bs).

Ameling, Elly. Soprano; b. Rotterdam, Feb. 8, 1934. Studied at Rotterdam Conservatory and with Pierre Bernac. Best known for song recitals, her rare opera appearances include Butterfly on Dutch television (1970), and Ilia (*Idomeneo*) with Netherlands Opera (1973) and Washington, D.C., Opera (1974).

Amfiparnaso, L' (roughly, The Lower Slopes of Parnassus). Madrigal comedy in prologue and 3 acts by Orazio Vecchi; libretto by Vecchi, possibly in collaboration with Giulio Cesare Croce.

First perf., probably in Modena, 1594. U.S. prem., N.Y., French Institute (concert perf.), Mar. 13, 1933.

A predecessor of opera, this madrigal cycle, scored for five voices, is an early attempt to combine farce comedy with music; its plot (a sequence of episodes related to love), character types, and use of dialect derive from commedia dell'arte.

Amico Fritz, L' (Friend Fritz). Opera in 3 acts by Mascagni; libretto by "P. Suardon" [Nicola Daspuro], after the novel *L'Ami Fritz* by Émile Erckmann and Alexandre Chatrian.

First perf., Rome, Costanzi, Oct. 31, 1891: Calvé, de Lucia, Lhérie, c. Ferrari. U.S. prem., Philadelphia, Grand Opera House, June 8, 1892. Met prem., Jan. 10, 1894: Calvé, de Lucia, Ancona, c. Bevignani, p. Parry. Later Met production: Nov. 15, 1923: Bori, Fleta, Danise, c. Moranzoni, d. Urban, p. Thewman. 5 perfs. in 2 seasons.

A story of rural charm matched by Mascagni with a pastoral score light of touch and piquant of harmony.

Alsace, late 19th c. After the wealthy middle-aged landowner Fritz (t) has bet the Rabbi David (bar) that he will never give up the bachelor life, David notices that his friend is enamored of Suzel (s), pretty daughter of one of his tenants. When David tells Fritz that he has found a young husband for Suzel, the upset Fritz leaves without a word to the girl, who loves him; she is in despair. After she appeals to him to save her from the arranged marriage, he confesses his love. David has won the bet, and gives the winnings, a vineyard, to Suzel.

Amore dei Tre Re, L' (The Love of Three Kings). Opera in 3 acts by Montemezzi; libretto by Sem Benelli, after his verse tragedy.

First perf., Milan, La Scala, Apr. 10, 1913: Villani, Ferrari-Fontana, Galeffi, de Angelis, c. Serafin. U.S. & Met prem., Jan. 2, 1914: Bori, Ferrari-Fontana, Amato, Didur, c. Toscanini, d. Sala/Mancini, p. Speck. Fiora has also been sung at the Met by Ponselle, Easton, Moore, Kirsten; Avito by Gigli, Johnson, Kullman; Manfredo by Danise, Bonelli, Weede; Archibaldo by Pinza, Lazzari; in 1941, Montemezzi conducted his work at the Met. 51 perfs. in 6 seasons.

A powerful score of symphonic cast and emotional intensity, which in its subject and medieval setting bespeaks the influence of *Tristan* in Italy.

A remote Italian castle, 10th c., 40 years after a barbarian invasion. The Italian princess Fiora (s), betrothed to prince Avito (t), has been forced to marry Manfredo (bar), son of the barbarian king Archibaldo (bs). The blind old king, who suspects her of infidelity, comes upon Fiora and Avito declaring their love to one another. Though Avito escapes unidentified, the king strangles Fiora, who has refused to reveal her lover's name. To catch her lover, Archibaldo spreads poison on the dead girl's lips. Avito passionately kisses her and dies, but Manfredo, who has forgiven her and wants to die, also kisses the poisonous lips. Archibaldo finds the body of the man he believes to be her lover and discovers it is his own son.

Amore Medico, L' (Love, the Doctor). Opera in 2 acts by Wolf-Ferrari; libretto by Enrico Golisciani, after Molière's *L'Amour Médecin*.

First perf., Dresden, Dec. 4, 1913 (in Ger.). U.S. & Met prem., Mar. 25, 1914: Bori, Cristalli, Pini-Corsi, c. Toscanini, d. Kautsky/J. Fox, p. Speck. 4 perfs. in 1 season.

An elegant pastiche comedy, set outside Paris, 17th c. The lovesick Lucinda (s) is forbidden by her father Arnolfo (bar) to marry, but her secret lover Clitandro (t), disguised as a doctor, prescribes a mock marriage to cure her. It is, of course, a real marriage, eventually blessed by Arnolfo.

Ancona, Mario. Baritone; b. Livòrno, Italy, Feb. 28, 1860; d. Florence, Feb. 22, 1931. Studied with Giuseppe Cima, Milan; debut as Scindia (*Roi de Lahore*), Trieste, 1890. La Scala debut as King (*Cid*), 1890; created Silvio (*Pagliacci*), dal Verme, Milan, 1892. London debut as Alphonse (*Favorite*), New Olympic Theatre, 1892; at Covent Garden (debut, Tonio, 1893), he sang for 17 seasons. Met debut as Tonio, Dec. 11, 1893; in 3 seasons, he sang 91 perfs. of 17 roles, including Rigoletto, Valentin, David (*Amico Fritz*), Wolfram, Mozart's Figaro, Escamillo, Tell, Amonasro, Nélusko, Telramund, Germont, and Alphonse. Appeared with Manhattan Opera (1906–08), in Boston (1913–14), Chicago (1915–16), Paris, Lisbon, Barcelona, Warsaw, and Buenos Aires. After retirement in 1916, taught in Florence. Ancona interpreted his broad repertory, from Don Giovanni to Raffaele (*Gioielli*), from Iago to Sachs, with old-fashioned elegance and an effortless technique that can still be enjoyed in his recordings.

Anders, Peter. Tenor; b. Essen, Germany, July 1, 1908; d. Hamburg, Sep. 10, 1954. Studied with Grenzenbach and Lula Mysz-Gmeiner, Berlin; sang in chorus of Reinhardt's production of *Belle Hélène*, 1931. Engagements in Heidelberg (1932), Darmstadt (1933–34), Cologne (1935–36), Hanover (1937–38), Munich (1938–40), Berlin (1940–48), and Hamburg (1948–54). Sang Tamino in Salzburg, 1941. Anders began his career as a sweet and flexible lyric tenor specializing in Mozart repertory; before his death from injuries sustained in an auto accident, he had moved into heroic roles: Florestan and Radames (Hamburg, 1949), Stolzing and Otello (Hamburg, 1950), Bacchus in *Ariadne* (Edinburgh, 1950), and Siegmund (Hamburg, 1953).

Anderson, June. Soprano; b. Boston, 1950(?). Studied with Robert Leonard, N.Y. Debut as Queen of Night, N.Y.C. Opera, Oct. 26, 1978; other roles there included Gilda, Mozart's and Bellini's Elviras, the *Hoffmann* heroines, Handel's Cleopatra. Since 1982, has sung primarily in Europe: Amina at La Scala, Lucia in Vienna, Semiramide in Rome and in concert at Covent Garden and Carnegie Hall, N.Y. (1983), *Robert le Diable* in Paris (1985).

Anderson, Marian. Contralto; b. Philadelphia, Feb. 17, 1902. After study with Giuseppe Boghetti and Frank LaForge, N.Y., she went abroad to establish her reputation, making her European debut in a London recital in 1930, and later winning accolades from Toscanini. Her formal N.Y. debut was at Town Hall, 1935. Anderson's big, velvety voice would have suited many operatic roles, had such assignments been available to black singers in her time. Known chiefly for her warm and sensitive performances of oratorio, lieder, and spirituals, late in her career she became the first black soloist to appear at the Met, singing 5 perfs. of Ulrica (*Ballo*) (debut, Jan. 7, 1955).

Andrea Chénier. Opera in 4 acts by Giordano; libretto by Illica, inspired by the life of the poet André Chénier.

First perf., Milan, La Scala, Mar. 28, 1896: Carrera, Borgatti, Sammarco, c. Ferrari. U.S. prem., N.Y., Academy of Music, Nov. 13, 1896. Met prem., Mar. 7, 1921: Muzio, Gigli, Danise, c. Moranzoni, d. J. Fox, Triangle Studios/Castel-Bert, p. Thewman. Later Met production: Nov. 16, 1954: Milanov, del Monaco, Warren, c. Cleva, d. F. Fox, p. Yannopoulos. Other Met Chéniers include Tucker, Corelli, Domingo; Maddalena has been sung by Rethberg, Tebaldi, Gérard by de Luca, Ruffo, Merrill. 110 perfs. in 22 seasons.

This impassioned verismo treatment of an historic and patriotic subject is Giordano's most successful opera.

Paris, 1789–94. At an elegant party, the poet Andrea Chénier (t) chides the wealthy Maddalena de Coigny (s) for scorning love. After the revolution, they meet again and declare their love. Carlo Gérard (bar), who as a servant in the Coigny household had desired Maddalena, is now a member of the revolutionary government, and denounces Chénier. In an attempt to save Chénier, Maddalena offers herself to Gérard; repentant, he intervenes in the proceedings, but vainly, and the poet is condemned to execution. Bribing the jailer, Maddalena changes places with a condemned female prisoner, and the lovers go to their death together.

Angel of Fire, The. See *Fiery Angel, The.*

Aniara. Opera in 2 acts by Blomdahl; libretto by Erik Lindegren, after Harry Martinson's epic poem.

Marian Anderson as Ulrica in *Un Ballo in Maschera*

First perf., Stockholm, Royal Opera, May 31, 1959: Hallin, Vikström, Ulfung, Saedén, Tyrén, c. Ehrling. N. Amer. prem., Montreal, May 31, 1967, by the Stockholm company.

In a modern idiom using electronic music, *Aniara* depicts the fate of refugees from a devastating atomic war on earth; their space craft is knocked off its course to Mars, and they must fly in space forever.

Anima Allegra (The Joyous Soul). Opera in 3 acts by Vittadini; libretto by Giuseppe Adami, after *Genio Alegre*, a comedy by the brothers Alvarez Quintero.

First perf., Rome, Costanzi, Apr. 15, 1921. U.S. & Met premiere, Feb. 14, 1923: Bori, Lauri-Volpi, Didur, c. Moranzoni, d. Rovescalli/Castel-Bert, p. Wymetal. 9 perfs. in 2 seasons.

A conservatively Puccinian score, set in Spain, c. 1830. The vivacious Consuelo (s) falls in love with Pedro (t), transforming the gloomy household of his parents.

Anna Bolena. Opera in 2 acts by Donizetti; libretto by Romani, after *Enrico VIII, ossia Anna Bolena* by Ippolito Pindemonte, which is a translation of Marie-Joseph de Chénier's *Henri VIII*; and *Anna Bolena* by Alessandro Pepoli.

First perf., Milan, Carcano, Dec. 26, 1830: Pasta, Orlandi, Laroche, Rubini, Galli. U.S. prem., New Orleans, Théâtre d'Orléans, Nov. 1839 (in Fr.).

The success of *Anna Bolena* opened the doors of Italy's opera houses to Donizetti; the 1957 La Scala production with Callas was a similar turning point in the modern revival of his Romantic tragedies.

Windsor Castle, 1536. Enrico (Henry VIII, bs) has turned from his queen, Anna Bolena (Anne Boleyn, s), to court her lady-in-waiting, Giovanna Seymour (Jane Seymour, ms). To entrap the queen and clear the way for his own marriage to Giovanna, he recalls Lord Riccardo

Percy (t), Anna's first love, from exile. Filled with emotion at encountering Anna again, Percy confesses his love and threatens to kill himself. The page Smeton (c) prevents this, but the three are arrested by Enrico. In prison, Anna refuses to admit guilt in order to save herself, and after learning that Giovanna is her rival, brings herself to forgive the other woman. Awaiting execution, Anna loses her reason, but music proclaiming the new Queen brings her to her senses, and she goes to her death forgiving the royal couple.

Ansermet, Ernest. Conductor; b. Vevey, Switzerland, Nov. 11, 1883; d. Geneva, Feb. 20, 1969. Founded Orchestre de la Suisse Romande (Geneva) in 1918 and led it until 1966. Conducted for Diaghilev's Ballets Russes, including premieres of Stravinsky's *Renard*, *Wedding*, *Soldier's Tale*. International reputation from the 1930s, especially in works of Stravinsky, Debussy, and Ravel. At Glyndebourne, led premiere of Britten's *Rape of Lucretia* (1946). Only Met appearances in 5 perfs. of *Pelléas* (debut, Nov. 30, 1962).

Antheil, George. Composer; b. Trenton, N.J., July 8, 1900; d. New York, Feb. 12, 1959. Studied composition with von Sternberg and Bloch. He moved to Berlin in 1922 and to Paris the next year, quickly becoming notorious for his percussive, ostinato-dominated piano and chamber works, notably *Ballet Mécanique* (1926). His first opera, *Transatlantic* (1927–28, libretto by the composer), was probably the first opera by an American composer to receive a full-scale production abroad (Frankfurt, 1930). Its score is jazz-influenced; the libretto, by the composer, burlesques a U.S. presidential election. In 1936, Antheil settled in Los Angeles and began to compose in a nostalgic eclectic style, combining elements ranging from classical forms to folksong quotations to remnants of his own early dissonance. Other operas (mostly one-acters) include *Helen Retires* (1930–32), *Volpone* (1950–52), *The Brothers* (1954), *Venus in Africa* (1954), *The Wish* (1955).

Anthony, Charles [Carlogero Antonio Caruso]. Tenor; b. New Orleans, La., July 15, 1929. Studied at Loyola U. with Dorothy Hulse, and after winning Met Auditions in 1952, with Picozzi and Ruisi in Rome. Since his Met debut as the Holy Fool (*Boris*), Mar. 6, 1954, he has sung over 1800 perfs. with the company, and also appeared in Dallas, Boston, and Santa Fe.

Antigonae. Opera in 1 act by Orff, setting Hölderlin's translation of Sophocles' tragedy.

First perf., Salzburg, Felsenreitschule, Aug. 9, 1949: Fischer, Fehenberger, Häfliger, Uhde, c. Fricsay, d. Neher, p. Schuh. U.S. prem., Brooklyn, Academy of Music, Apr. 21, 1968 (in concert): Borkh, Lewis, Page, Alexander, c. Scherman. U.S. stage prem., Chicago (New Opera Co.), May 14, 1983.

Orff's setting of Sophocles' tragedy relies on heightened declamation of the text over a percussive, primarily rhythmic accompaniment.

Antonicelli, Giuseppe. Conductor; b. Castrovillari, Italy, Dec. 29, 1897; d. Trieste, Mar. 10, 1980. After study in Turin, assistant conductor there; debut in Coccia (*Francesca da Rimini*). Director of Trieste Opera, 1937–43, 1950–56. During 4 Met seasons (1947–50), he led 10 Italian works (debut, *Ballo*, Nov. 10, 1947) and a recording of *Bohème*. Married to soprano Franca Somigli.

Antony and Cleopatra – World premiere, 1966. Designed and produced by Franco Zeffirelli. Justino Diaz and Leontyne Price

Antony and Cleopatra. Opera in 3 acts by Barber; libretto by Franco Zeffirelli, after Shakespeare's play.

First perf., N.Y., Met, Sep. 16, 1966: Price, Thomas, Diaz, c. Schippers, d. & p. Zeffirelli. 8 perfs. in 1 season. New version, with textual revision by Menotti, first perf., N.Y., Juilliard American Opera Center, Feb. 6, 1975: Hinds, Sherman, Hedlund, c. Conlon.

This lushly romantic score, composed for the inauguration of the new Metropolitan Opera House at Lincoln Center, was made less grandiose in the composer's revision.

The Roman Empire, 41–31 B.C. Antony (bs) leaves his mistress, the Egyptian queen Cleopatra (s), and returns to Rome, where he is pressured into marriage with Octavia, sister of Octavius Caesar (t). When Antony returns to Cleopatra, Caesar decides to wage war on him. Defeated in battle, Antony commits suicide, dying in Cleopatra's arms; to avoid being paraded in Caesar's triumph, she dies from the poisonous bite of an asp.

Aoyama, Yoshio. Producer; b. Tokyo, Jan. 9, 1903. Trained in Tokyo; has directed opera for major Japanese

Arabella – (1960). Designed by Rolf Gérard, produced by Herbert Graf. Lisa Della Casa and Martha Lipton

companies and the Met (*Madama Butterfly*, 1958). Due to his illness, the Met's 1961 *Turandot*, conceived by him, was completed by Nathaniel Merrill; he later staged *Butterfly* and *Traviata* for the Met National Company (1965–66).

Appia, Adolphe. Designer; b. Geneva, Sep. 1, 1862; d. Nyon, Feb. 29, 1928. A pupil of Liszt in Weimar and ardent admirer of Wagner's music dramas, he detested the prevailing two-dimensional "realism" of operatic production, and advocated three-dimensional, sculptural stages with abstract scenic structures that would enhance movement, with light as "the most significant plastic element on the stage." Collaborated with Toscanini on a controversial *Tristan* for La Scala (1923); his *Ring* production in Basel (1934) was cancelled after the first two operas. His theories and designs profoundly influenced later designers and directors, notably Wieland Wagner.

appoggiatura (Ital., "leaning note"). In general musical usage, a melodic note on a strong beat foreign to the prevailing harmony; usually one step above or below a harmonic note, it is resolved on the following weak beat. In 18th- and early 19th-c. opera, especially in recitatives, composers usually wrote the harmonic note on both the strong and the weak beat, and singers were expected to substitute the non-harmonic note on the strong beat. This practice fell into disuse in 20th-c. performances (the written notes being followed literally), but has recently been revived by knowledgeable musicians.

Arabella. Opera in 3 acts by R. Strauss; libretto by Hofmannsthal.

First perf., Dresden, July 1, 1933: Ursuleac, Bokor, Kremer, Jerger, c. Krauss. U.S. & Met prem., Feb. 10, 1955 (in Eng.): Steber, Gueden, Sullivan, London, c. Kempe, d. Gérard, p. Graf. Later Met production: Feb. 10, 1983: Te Kanawa, Battle, Rendall, Weikl, c. Leinsdorf, d. Schneider-Siemssen, p. Schenk. Arabella has also been sung at the Met by Della Casa; Zdenka by Rothenberger. 37 perfs. in 6 seasons.

Strauss' return to the world of *Rosenkavalier*, with lush textures, soaring vocal lines, and Mozartean overtones.

Vienna, 1860. Needing to make a profitable marriage for his beautiful daughter Arabella (s), the impoverished Count Waldner (bs) has sent her portrait to an old and wealthy friend, but is surprised when the friend's son, Mandryka (bar) arrives, eager to marry her. At a ball, Mandryka and Arabella meet, fall in love, and agree to marry. Arabella bids farewell to her other suitors, including the young officer Matteo (t), who is distraught at losing her. Arabella's sister Zdenka (s), who has been brought up as a boy to save expenses, secretly loves Matteo, and promises him a rendez-vous with Arabella, giving him a letter with a key. Mandryka overhears their exchange and, thinking himself betrayed, throws a tantrum and flirts with Fiakermilli (s), the mascot of the ball. Later, when Mandryka accuses Arabella of faithlessness, Zdenka explains that the key she gave Matteo was that of her own room. Matteo decides to turn his affections to Zdenka, and, with the confusion cleared, each sister is happily betrothed.

Aragall, Giacomo. Tenor; b. Barcelona, June 6, 1939. Studied with Francisco Puig, Barcelona; debut as Gaston (*Jérusalem*), Venice, 1963. La Scala debut as Mascagni's Fritz, 1963. The Duke of Mantua was his debut role at Verona Arena (1965), Covent Garden (1968), the Met (Sep. 19, 1968), and San Francisco (1973). Sang in 1974 San

Francisco production of *Esclarmonde*, shown at the Met in 1976; other Met roles include Rodolfo, Edgardo, and Alfredo.

Araiza, Francesco. Tenor; b. Mexico City, Oct. 4, 1950. Studied at U. of Mexico City and with Richard Holm and Erik Werba, Munich. After debut in Mexico City, joined Karlsruhe Opera in 1974. Sang with opera companies in Düsseldorf, Munich, Stuttgart, and Zurich, also at Salzburg (Ferrando, 1983). Met debut as Belmonte, Nov. 12, 1984.

Arditi, Luigi. Conductor and composer; b. Crescentino, Italy, July 16, 1822; d. Hove, England, May 1, 1903. Famous for his waltz song "Il Bacio," led a colorful world-wide career. With Marty's Havana Opera Company, conducted U.S. premieres of several Verdi works in N.Y., 1847–50. In N.Y., 1851–56, conducted opera, including opening of Academy of Music, 1854. Returned to America to tour with Mapleson (1878–94), and led three post-season Met performances featuring Patti (Apr. 1892).

Argento, Dominick. Composer; b. York, Pa., Oct. 27, 1927. Studied with Weisgall at Peabody Conservatory, Dallapiccola in Florence, and at Eastman School. On faculty of U. of Minnesota since 1958; co-founder in 1964 of Center Opera Co. (now Minnesota Opera). His operas, in a fluent, conservative style, include *The Boor* (1957), *Christopher Sly* (1963), *Postcard from Morocco* (1971), *The Voyage of Edgar Allan Poe* (1976), *Miss Havisham's Fire* (1979), and *Casanova's Homecoming* (1985).

Ariadne auf Naxos – Vienna State Opera. Sena Jurinac and Wilma Lipp

argomento (Ital., "argument"). In a printed libretto, the summary of the plot that precedes the text.

aria (Ital.). An extended, self-contained vocal solo with accompaniment. Originally simple patterned pieces with figured bass, arias soon developed more elaborate formal schemes, including the da capo aria (*q.v.*) in the 18th c. In 19th-c. Italian opera, a standard form was the double aria, comprising scena (orchestrally accompanied recitative), first aria or cantabile (usually slow and lyrical), tempo di mezzo (introducing a new plot element or a change of mood), and the cabaletta (an energetic aria, usually repeated).

aria di sortita (Ital.). See *exit aria*.

Ariadne auf Naxos (Ariadne on Naxos). Opera by R. Strauss; libretto by Hofmannsthal. Originally in 1 act, to be played after Hofmannsthal's German version of Molière's *Le Bourgeois Gentilhomme*, for which Strauss wrote incidental music.
First perf., Stuttgart, Court Theater, Oct. 25, 1912: Jeritza, Siems, Jadlowker, c. Strauss, p. Reinhardt. Revised in prologue and 1 act; first perf., Vienna, Court Opera, Oct. 4, 1916: Jeritza, Kurz, Lotte Lehmann, Környei, c. Schalk. U.S. prem., Philadelphia Civic Opera, Academy of Music, Nov. 1, 1928, c. Smallens. Met prem., Dec. 29, 1962 (prologue in Eng.): Rysanek, G. d'Angelo, Meyer, J. Thomas, c. Böhm, d. Messel, p. Ebert. Ariadne has also been sung at the Met by Della Casa, Caballé, Meier, L. Price, Harper, Norman; Bacchus by Kónya, King, Kollo; Zerbinetta by Peters, Grist, Gruberova; the Composer by Söderström, Stratas, Lear, Troyanos, Ewing. 41 perfs. in 6 seasons.
In *Ariadne*, an opera of sophisticated lyric charm, Strauss continued in the Mozartean vein he had first tapped in *Rosenkavalier*; the Prologue also puts on stage, as Strauss would do again in later operas, some of his ideas about music and drama.
Prologue: "house of a great gentleman," time unspecified, probably 18th c. An opera company and a commedia dell'arte troupe, both engaged by the owner of the house for his guests' entertainment, are shocked to learn that they must perform simultaneously, in order to finish in time for a fireworks display. A flurry of preparations follows: the Prima Donna (s) and Tenor (t), at first concerned with shortening each other's roles, are now threatened by the prospect of sharing the stage with the comedians; the latter, under the leadership of Zerbinetta (s), make plans to enliven the opera, "Ariadne." Though the Composer (ms) is distraught over the desecration of the holy art of music and the abridgement of his opera, the entertainment proceeds.
Opera: a desert island, antiquity. Ariadne (the Prima Donna of the Prologue), bewailing her abandonment by Theseus, is unmoved by the comedians, or by Zerbinetta's concentrated efforts to persuade her that there are many fish in the sea. When Bacchus (the Tenor of the Prologue) arrives, Ariadne believes him to be the god of death, but he convinces her their life together is just beginning. They depart together as Zerbinetta appears with a whispered word of approval.

Ariane et Barbe-Bleue (Ariane and Bluebeard). Opera in 3 acts by Dukas; libretto adapted from Maeterlinck's drama.
First perf., Paris, Opéra-Comique, May 10, 1907: Leblanc, Vieuille, c. Ruhlmann. U.S. & Met prem., Mar.

29, 1911: Farrar, Rothier, c. Toscanini, d. Rovescalli/ Maison Muelle, p. Speck. 7 perfs. in 2 seasons.

Dukas' only opera, based on a play written for operatic adaptation (originally destined for Grieg); influenced by *Pelléas*, but more symphonic in treatment.

Bluebeard's castle, legendary times. Bluebeard (bs) gives his beautiful new wife Ariane (ms) six keys of silver, and one of gold that she is forbidden to use. The silver keys open doors yielding huge quantities of precious gems; with the gold key Ariane boldly opens a door to a stairway, from which she hears women's voices chanting and wailing – Bluebeard's former wives, imprisoned in an underground vault. When Bluebeard tries to drag her away, her cries draw rebellious peasants, but she urges them to leave, claiming he has not harmed her. Later, in Bluebeard's absence, Ariane and her nurse explore the vault and set the wives free. When Bluebeard returns, he is captured and bound by the peasants, but Ariane tends his wounds and releases him. She attempts to free the women, inviting them to a world filled with hope, but they hesitate, and remain behind.

Arianna, L'. Opera in prologue and 8 scenes by Monteverdi; libretto by Rinuccini.

First perf., Mantua, Teatro della Corte, May 28, 1608: Andreini, Caccini, Brandi, Orlandi, Rasi.

World-famous for the expressive power of its one surviving number, the heroine's lament "Lasciatemi morire," this lost opera follows the classical story of Ariadne's abandonment by Theseus and rescue by Bacchus.

arietta (Ital.). A small aria.

Ariodante. Opera in 3 acts by Handel; libretto based on Antonio Salvi's *Ginevra, Principessa di Scozia*, after Ariosto's *Orlando Furioso*.

First perf., London, Covent Garden, Jan. 8, 1735: Strada, Negri, Carestini, Beard, Waltz. U.S. prem., N.Y., Carnegie Hall, Mar. 9, 1971: Raskin, Wise, Steffan, Stewart, Meredith, c. Simon.

The second of Handel's Ariosto operas features elaborate finales and well-integrated dances. To win the throne of Scotland, Polinesso (a), Duke of Albany, weaves an unsuccessful plot to discredit the princess Ginevra (s) in the eyes of Ariodante (a), who loves her.

arioso (Ital.). A manner of setting text, more lyrical than recitative but usually not as formal as an aria, though the term may also denote a simple one-part aria.

Arkhipova, Irina. Mezzo-soprano; b. Moscow, Dec. 2, 1925. Studied with N. Malisheva and Leonid Savransky in Moscow; joined Bolshoi Opera as Carmen, 1956. Roles include Marfa, Marina, Amneris, Eboli, and Charlotte. The preeminent Soviet mezzo, she has often toured in the West, including Carmen (Naples, 1960) and Azucena (Covent Garden, 1975).

Arlecchino (Harlequin). Opera in prologue, 1 act, and epilogue by Busoni; libretto by the composer.

First perf., Zurich, Stadttheater, May 11, 1917: Wenck, Grunert, Moissi, c. Busoni. U.S. prem., N.Y., Carnegie Hall, Oct. 11, 1951 (concert perf., in Eng.): Lipton, D. Lloyd, Brownlee, c. Mitropoulos.

Arlecchino reflects the side of Busoni's complex artistic personality that was interested in reviving the clarity and light touch of pre-Romantic Italian music, along with the dramatic qualities of the commedia dell'arte.

Bergamo 18th c. Arlecchino (speaking role) flirts with Annunziata (mute role) under the nose of her husband, the tailor Ser Matteo (bar), and uses several ruses to get rid of him. Chided by his disgusted wife Columbine (ms), Arlecchino leaves her in the hands of Leandro (t), a bombastic cavalier given to operatic outbursts in Italian. In a duel, Leandro is laid low by Arlecchino, but survives and is taken off to a hospital by Columbine, while Arlecchino elopes with Annunziata. The oblivious Matteo returns and recommences sewing and reading Dante. In an epilogue, Arlecchino suggests to the audience that they make up their own minds as to the story's moral.

Arlesiana, L' (The Girl from Arles). Opera in 3 (originally 4) acts by Cilea; libretto by Leopoldo Marenco, after Alphonse Daudet's drama *L'Arlésienne*.

First perf., Milan, Lirico, Nov. 27, 1897 (in 4 acts): Ricci de Paz, Tracey, Caruso, Arisi, c. Zuccani. Revised in 3 acts, Milan, Lirico, Oct. 22, 1898. U.S. prem., Philadelphia, Society Hill Playhouse, Jan. 11, 1962.

This verismo score with pastoral overtones features a juicy dramatic mezzo role, but is best known outside Italy for its haunting tenor lament. In Provence, Federico (t) is in love with a girl from Arles, but his mother Rosa Mamai (ms) and her godchild Vivetta (s), who loves Federico, show him letters proving that the girl has been the mistress of Metifio (bar). Federico determines to forget the girl from Arles and marry Vivetta, but when his jealous rage is stirred up by Metifio, he eventually kills himself in despair.

Armida. Opera in 3 acts by Rossini; libretto by Giovanni Federico Schmidt, after Tasso's epic *Gerusalemme Liberata*.

First perf., Naples, San Carlo, Nov. 11, 1817: Colbran, Nozzari, Ciccimarra, Benedetti, Bonoldi, Chizzola.

An opera seria exploiting the extravagant roster of virtuoso tenors Rossini enjoyed in Naples, as well as the dramatic powers of Isabella Colbran. The sorceress Armida (s) can conquer the hearts of all men except Rinaldo (t); she transports him to an enchanted island, and falls in love with him. He returns her love, but rejects her when he is made to see that he has been ensnared by magic. Other operas on the same subject were composed by Lully (1686), Haydn (1784), and Dvořák (1904); see also *Armide* (Gluck) and *Rinaldo* (Handel).

Armide. Opera in 5 acts by Gluck; libretto by Quinault, after Tasso's poem *Gerusalemme Liberata*.

First perf., Paris, Opéra, Sep. 23, 1777: Levasseur, Legros, Gélin, Arrivée. U.S. & Met prem., Nov. 14, 1910: Fremstad, Caruso, Amato, Gilly, c. Toscanini, d. Paquereau, p. Speck. 7 perfs. in 2 seasons.

Quinault's libretto for Lully's 1686 tragédie lyrique was set virtually unchanged by Gluck as a step in his conquest of Paris; the libretto's structure makes for a more fluid continuity than in his previous reform operas, and the figure of Armide is one of his greatest characterizations. During the First Crusade, the sorceress Armide (s) and Hidraot (bar), king of Damascus, intend to slay Renaud (t), general of the successful crusaders. But Armide falls in love with him instead; he is rescued from her enchantments by fellow knights.

Arne, Thomas. Composer; bapt. London, May 28, 1710; d. London, Mar. 5, 1778. First operatic success, *Rosamond* (1733), text by Joseph Addison; the music for Milton's *Comus* (1738) established his reputation. Arne's stage works, including *Eliza* (1754) and *Thomas and Sally* (1760), achieved popularity through their appealing blend of lively flowing melodies and spoken dialogue. Exceptionally, *Artaxerxes* (1762) followed Italian tradition, with dramatic recitatives and coloratura. The masque *Alfred* (1740) contained the perennial "Rule, Britannia."

Arnoldson, Sigrid. Soprano; b. Stockholm, Mar. 20, 1861; d. Stockholm, Feb. 7, 1943. Studied with her father, a tenor, and with Maurice Strakosch and Désirée Artôt; debut as Rosina, Prague, 1885. Met debut as Baucis (*Philémon*), Nov. 29, 1893; 18 perfs. in 1 season, including Micaela, Nedda, Cherubino, and Sophie (*Werther*).

Aroldo. Opera in 4 acts by Verdi; libretto by Piave, after his libretto for *Stiffelio*.
First perf., Rimini, Nuovo, Aug. 16, 1857: Lotti, Pancani, Ferri. U.S. prem., N.Y., Academy of Music, May 4, 1863.
When *Stiffelio* failed to circulate (perhaps because Italian audiences could not identify with a story about a married clergyman), Verdi recast most of its music into this form, which most commentators have found less compelling. The score retains a strong dramatic urgency.
England and Scotland, 1189–1192. Returning from the Crusades, the Saxon warrior Aroldo (t) finds that his wife Mina (s) has been seduced by the knight Godvino (t). Mina's father Egberto (bar) kills Godvino to avenge his own honor. Though Mina and Aroldo divorce, she vows her eternal love for him. Aroldo becomes a hermit and lives on the banks of Loch Lomond; when Mina and Egberto are cast ashore nearby in a storm, husband and wife are reconciled.

Aronson, Boris. Designer; b. Kiev, Ukraine, Oct. 15, 1900; d. Nyack, N.Y., Nov. 17, 1980. Studied in Kiev and Moscow. In N.Y. from 1923, designed for Yiddish Art Theater, later Broadway, including *The Crucible*, *Fiddler on the Roof*, and *Follies*; for Met, *Mourning Becomes Electra* (1967) and *Fidelio* (1970).

Arroyo, Martina. Soprano; b. New York, Feb. 2, 1936. Studied with Joseph Turnau at Hunter College and won 1958 Met Opera Auditions; professional debut as First Chorister in Pizzetti's *Assassinio*, Carnegie Hall, 1958. Met debut as Celestial Voice (*Don Carlos*), March 14, 1959. After singing small parts at the Met, she went to Europe in the mid-1960s to sing major roles at Vienna, Frankfurt, Berlin, and Zurich, returning to the Met as Aida, Feb. 6, 1965. She went on to other Verdi spinto roles, as well as Butterfly, Gioconda, Liù, Santuzza, and Elsa. Sang at Covent Garden from 1968; in 1986, as Santuzza and Aida, she returned to the Met, where she has sung over 170 perfs.

Ascanio in Alba. Festa teatrale in 2 acts by Mozart; libretto by Giuseppe Parini.
First perf., Milan, Regio Ducal, Oct. 17, 1771: Manzuoli, Falchini, Girelli-Aguilar, Tibaldi, Solzi.
One of the teen-age Mozart's earliest operatic efforts, composed for a royal wedding. Ascanio (s), to whom the Arcadian nymph Silvia (s) has been promised by his grandmother Venere (Venus, s), fortunately proves to be the man Silvia has fallen in love with in her dreams.

Ashton, Frederick. Choreographer; b. Guayaquil, Ecuador, Sep. 17, 1904. Studied with Massine and Rambert; founder, choreographer (1933–70), and director (1963–70) of what is now Royal Ballet. One of the

creators of English ballet, he also directed *Four Saints* (premiere, 1934); at Met, choreography for *Death in Venice* (1974) and *Nightingale* (1981).

Asrael. Opera in 4 acts by Franchetti; libretto by Ferdinand Fontana.
First perf., Reggio Emilia, Feb. 11, 1888. U.S. & Met prem., Nov. 26, 1890 (in Ger.): Jahn, Ritter-Götze, Dippel, c. Seidl, d. Hoyt/Dazian. 5 perfs. in 1 season.
Franchetti's first opera, which impressed Verdi and launched the composer's career, is set in Heaven, Hell, and 13th-c. Flanders, recounting the travails of the angelic lovers Asrael (t) and Nefta (s), beset by Lucifer (bs) and the sorceress Lidora (a) but eventually reunited in Heaven.

Assassinio nella Cattedrale (Murder in the Cathedral). Opera in 2 parts by Pizzetti; libretto by the composer, after Alberto Castelli's transl. of Eliot's verse drama.
First perf., Milan, La Scala, Mar. 1, 1958: Rossi-Lemeni, c. Gavazzeni. U.S. prem., N.Y., Carnegie Hall, Sep. 17, 1958 (concert perf.): Rossi-Lemeni, c. Halasz.
A late flowering of the Italian school that succeeded the verismists. In Canterbury, 1170, archbishop Tommaso (Thomas) Beckct (bs), in conflict with King Henry II over separation of church and state, is slain at prayer after refusing to make an act of submission to the King.

Assedio di Corinto, L'. See *Siège de Corinth, Le*.

Atalanta. Opera in 3 acts by Handel; libretto anonymous, after B. Valeriani's *La Caccia in Etolia*.
First perf., London, Covent Garden, May 23, 1736: Conti, Gizziello, Negri, Strada, Beard.
Produced for the wedding of Frederick, Prince of Wales, to Princess Augusta of Saxe-Gotha, the opera tells of the love of the huntress-nymph Atalanta for the shepherd-king Meleager.

Atlántida, L' (Atlantis). Scenic cantata in prologue and 3 parts by Manuel de Falla, completed by Ernesto Halffter; libretto in Catalan by the composer, after the poem by Jacint Verdaguer and other sources.
First perf., Barcelona, Nov. 24, 1961 (concert perf.); first staged perf., Milan, La Scala, June 18, 1962: Stratas, Simionato, Publisi, Halley, c. Schippers. U.S. prem., N.Y., Philharmonic Hall, Sep. 19, 1962 (concert perf., by the Met company): Farrell, Madeira, London, c. Ansermet. Rev. ed. by Halffter, 1976.
This vast epic, calling on almost prohibitive resources, relates the submersion of Atlantis, Spain's rescue by Hercules from the monster Geryon, and Columbus' discovery of the New World.

Atlantov, Vladimir. Tenor; b. Leningrad, Feb. 19, 1939. Studied with Bolotina, Leningrad Conservatory, and at La Scala school; won Tchaikovsky competition, 1966. Soloist with Kirov, Leningrad (1963–67) and Bolshoi, Moscow (from 1967), frequent appearances in Western Europe, and with the Bolshoi in N.Y., 1975. Important roles include Herman (*Queen of Spades*), Canio, Don José, Otello, and Vladimir (*Prince Igor*).

Attaque du Moulin, L' (The Attack on the Mill). Opera in 4 acts by Bruneau; libretto by Louis Gallet, after the story in Zola's *Soirées de Médan*.
First perf., Paris, Opéra-Comique, Nov. 23, 1893: Leblanc, Delna, Vergnet, c. Danbé. U.S. & Met prem., New Theater, Feb. 8, 1910: Noria, Delna, Clément,

Aufstieg und Fall der Stadt Mahagonny – (1979). Designed by Jocelyn Herbert, produced by John Dexter. Teresa Stratas and Astrid Varnay

Gilly, c. Tango, d. Burghart & Co./Freisinger, p. Speck.

This naturalistic, musically simple opera in a declamatory style, set during the Franco-Prussian War, tells of the miller Merlier (bar), who sacrifices his life to save Dominique (t), fiancé of his daughter Françoise (s).

Attila. Opera in prologue and 3 acts by Verdi; libretto by Solera, after Zacharias Werner's play *Attila, König der Hunnen.*

First perf., Venice, Fenice, Mar. 17, 1846: Loewe, Guasco, Profili, Costantini, Marini, Romanelli. U.S. prem., N.Y., Niblo's Garden, Apr. 15, 1850, with Marini as Attila.

A stirring martial drama of confrontations and strong contrasts, filled with the florid andantes and driving cabalettas that characterized Verdi's early style.

Aquileia, the Adriatic lagoons, and near Rome, mid-5th c. The troops of Attila (bs) have invaded Italy and taken Aquileia. The captured Odabella (s), whose father was killed by Attila, feigns loyalty to the Hun but secretly vows vengeance, and convinces her beloved, Foresto (t), of her determination. Despite a warning omen, Attila invites the Romans to a banquet, where Odabella saves him from being poisoned by Foresto in order to take her own vengeance. Persuaded by Odabella to spare Foresto, Attila promises to reward her by making her his bride. Foresto and Ezio (bar), the Roman envoy, do not trust Odabella's protestations, but when Attila comes upon her in their company she stabs him through the heart.

Auber, Daniel-François. Composer; b. Caen, France, Jan. 29, 1782; d. Paris, May 12 or 13, 1871. Student of Ladurner and later Cherubini. *La Bergère Châtelaine* (1820) initiated his prolific career as composer of opéras comiques, 37 of them in collaboration with Scribe. Auber tempered the buffo tradition of Rossini with French elegance and lyricism, most successfully in *Fra Diavolo* (1830). Auber's and Scribe's venture into grand opera, *La*

Muette de Portici (1828), deeply impressed Rossini and Wagner. Auber was director of the Paris Conservatory from 1842 until his death.

Auden, W(ystan) H(ugh). Librettist; b. York, England, Feb. 21, 1907; d. Vienna, Sep. 29, 1973. Leading English poet of the mid-20th c. Librettist of Britten's *Paul Bunyan* and later, with Chester Kallman, of Stravinsky's *Rake's Progress* and Henze's *Elegy for Young Lovers* and *Bassarids*.

Aufstieg und Fall der Stadt Mahagonny. Opera in 3 acts by Weill; libretto by Bertolt Brecht.

First perf., Leipzig, Neue Theater, Mar. 9, 1930: Trummer, Dannenberg, Beinert, Fleischer, Zimmer, c. Brecher. U.S. prem., N.Y., Anderson Theater, Apr. 28, 1970 (heavily adapted, in Eng.): Harris, Parsons, Porretta, de Lon, Pringle, c. Matlovsky. U.S. prem., original version, San Francisco, Feb. 18, 1972: Bybee, Neway, Kness, Manton, Mosley, c. Schneider. Met prem. (in Eng.), Nov. 16, 1979: Stratas, Varnay, Cassilly, MacNeil, Plishka, c. Levine, d. Herbert, p. Dexter. 25 perfs. in 3 seasons.

Developed from the *Mahagonny* "songspiel" (1927), the opera combines cabaret theater and Brechtian "epic opera."

Set in a gangster-movie America. Escaped convicts Leocadia Begbick (ms), Fatty (t), and Trinity Moses (bar) establish Mahagonny, a city where pleasure will reign. Among those attracted are Jenny (s) and her fellow prostitutes, and Jimmy Mahoney (t) and his friends from Alaska. After the city's close call with a hurricane, Jimmy proclaims anarchy, and Mahagonny's citizens enjoy unlimited eating, sex, sport, and drink. Only one thing is forbidden, to be short of cash; when Jimmy cannot pay for his drinks, he is imprisoned, tried, and executed. Inflation and unrest incite the citizens to demonstrate while the city burns.

Augér, Arleen. Soprano; b. Los Angeles, Sep. 13, 1939. Studied at Calif. State U. at Long Beach and with Ralph Errolle in Chicago. Debut as Queen of Night, Vienna, 1967; a member of the State Opera until 1974. Has also sung in Munich, London, Paris, Hamburg, and at N.Y.C. Opera (debut, Queen of Night, 1969). At the Met, she has sung Marzelline in *Fidelio* (debut, Oct. 2, 1978).

azione sacra (Ital.). Sacred drama, a term sometimes used for operas with religious subjects, such as Refice's *Cecilia.*

B

Baccaloni, Salvatore. Bass; b. Rome, Apr. 14, 1900; d. New York, Dec. 31, 1969. After attending Sistine Chapel choir school, studied with Giuseppe Kaschmann; debut as Rossini's Bartolo, Adriano, Rome, 1922. Sang regularly at La Scala, 1926–40, eventually specializing, at Toscanini's suggestion, in buffo roles. Foreign engagements at Covent Garden (debut, Timur in *Turandot*, 1928), Chicago (U.S. debut, Melitone in *Forza*, 1930), Buenos Aires (1931–41), Glyndebourne (Leporello, Bartolo, Osmin, Alfonso, Don Pasquale, 1936–39), and San Francisco (debut, Leporello, 1938). After his debut as Mozart's Bartolo, Dec. 7, 1940, he sang with the Met until 1962, in 297 performances of 15 roles, including both Bartolos, Don Pasquale, Leporello, Dulcamara, Varlaam, Melitone, and Gianni Schicchi, as well as character cameos such as

Benoit and Alcindoro (*Bohème*), the Sacristan (*Tosca*), and Mathieu (*Chénier*). His repertory also included Wolf-Ferrari roles such as Lunardo in *Quattro Rusteghi* (La Scala, 1938), and Verdi's *Falstaff* (San Francisco, 1944). Generally considered the finest comic bass of his time, Baccaloni was occasionally undisciplined on stage, but his jolly, portly presence was supported by polished musicianship.

Bach, Johann Christian. Composer; b. Leipzig, Sep. 5, 1735; d. London, Jan. 1, 1782. Studied keyboard with father Johann Sebastian, composition with brother Carl Philipp Emanuel in Berlin and with Padre Martini in Italy, where his first opera seria *Artaserse* was produced (Turin, 1760). After the success of *Catone in Utica* (Naples, 1761), he went to London; his *Orione* (1762) and very popular *La Clemenza di Scipione* (1778) contain few da capo arias, with chorus and orchestra assigned a greater dramatic role. In London, he met and performed keyboard improvisations with the child Mozart. In later years, he worked also in Mannheim, where the more elaborate *Temistocle* was introduced (1772).

Bacquier, Gabriel. Baritone; b. Béziers, France, May 17, 1924. Studied at Paris Conservatory; debut in Landowski's *Le Fou*, Nice, 1950. After engagements at Monnaie, Brussels (1953–56), and Opéra-Comique, Paris (1956–58), he joined the Paris Opéra in 1958 as Germont, later also singing Rigoletto, Valentin, Escamillo, Mozart roles, Boris, and Boccanegra, and creating Abdul (*Last Savage*). He appeared at Aix as Don Giovanni (1960), at Glyndebourne as Count Almaviva (1962), at Covent Garden as Almaviva, Riccardo (*Puritani*), and Scarpia (1964). U.S. debut in Chicago (1962) as High Priest (*Samson*), followed by Gluck's Orfeo. Met debut as High Priest, Oct. 17, 1964; in 15 seasons at the house, Bacquier has sung over 115 perfs. of 12 roles, notably Scarpia, Melitone, Don Pasquale, the *Hoffmann* villains, Massenet's Lescaut, Iago, Golaud, Leporello, and Rossini's Bartolo. Other U.S. engagements include Don Giovanni in Seattle (1968) and Michele (*Tabarro*) in San Francisco (1971); he has also sung Falstaff (Holland Festival, 1972). With a theatrical presence and musical intelligence comparable to Gobbi's, Bacquier has from the beginning been equally at home in comic and dramatic roles, and is much admired for his subtle and imaginative characterizations.

Gabriel Bacquier as Don Pasquale

Salvatore Baccaloni as Dr. Bartolo in *Le Nozze di Figaro*

Badea, Christian. Conductor; b. Bucharest, Romania, Dec. 10, 1947. After study at Juilliard, conducted opera at Spoleto Festival (music director 1980–86), Brussels, Netherlands Opera, English National Opera; music director of Savannah Symphony and Columbus (Ohio) Symphony (from 1983). Led European premiere of Menotti's *The Hero* (1980), and recorded Barber's *Antony and Cleopatra*.

Bahr-Mildenburg, Anna. Soprano; b. Vienna, Nov. 29, 1872; d. Vienna, Jan. 27, 1947. Studied with Rosa Papier; debut as Brünnhilde (*Walküre*), Hamburg, 1895, under Mahler, the beginning of their artistic and personal relationship. Went with Mahler in 1898 to Vienna, where she sang until 1916, returning later as guest. Specialized in Wagner (Kundry at Bayreuth, 1897–1914) and other dramatic roles, including Donna Anna, Fidelio, Norma, and Klytemnästra.

Bailey, Norman. Baritone; b. Birmingham, England, Mar. 23, 1933. Studied at Rhodes U., South Africa, later at Vienna Academy with Adolf Vogel, Josef Witt, and Patzak. Debut in Rossini's *Cambiale di Matrimonio*, Vienna Chamber Opera, 1959. Sang in Linz (1960–63), Wuppertal (1963–64), Düsseldorf (1964–67), and at Sadler's Wells (1967–71), where he won acclaim for Wagner roles in English. Hans Sachs was the role of his debuts at the N.Y.C. Opera (1975) and Met (Oct. 23, 1976). His 27 Met perfs. also included Orest, Amfortas, Jochanaan, and the *Walküre* Wotan.

Baker, Gregg. Baritone; b. Chicago, Dec. 7, 1955. Studied at Northwestern U. and with Andrew Smith. Began career on Broadway, in *The Wiz*, *Timbuktu*, and *Raisin*. Met debut as Crown (*Porgy*), Feb. 6, 1985, followed by Escamillo, and High Priest (*Samson*); Glyndebourne debut also as Crown, 1986. Repertory also includes Ford, Marcello, and Mozart's Almaviva.

Baker, Janet. Mezzo-soprano; b. Hatfield, Yorkshire, England, Aug. 21, 1933. Studied in London with Helene Isepp and Meriel St. Clair, later at Salzburg Mozarteum; operatic debut as Roza (Smetana's *Secret*) with Oxford University Opera Club (1956), followed by Gluck's Orfeo (Morley College, 1958), and Pippo in *Gazza Ladra* (Wexford, 1959). An early and continuing specialty was baroque opera, including Handel roles with Handel Opera Society (debut, *Rodelinda*, 1959) and in Birmingham (*Ariodante*, 1964; *Orlando*, 1966). Aldeburgh debut as Purcell's Dido (1962), followed by Britten's Lucretia and Nancy (*Albert Herring*) in 1964; Hermia (*Midsummer Night's Dream*) was her Covent Garden debut role (1966), and she created Kate Julian (*Owen Wingrave*) on BBC television (1971). At Glyndebourne, she first appeared in 1966 as Purcell's Dido, later in Cavalli's *Calisto* and Monteverdi's *Ritorno*. For Scottish Opera (debut, Dorabella, 1967) she sang Didon (*Troyens*), Octavian, and the Composer (*Ariadne*). Covent Garden roles included Vitellia (*Clemenza*), Walton's Cressida, and Alceste, while for the English National Opera she sang Ottavia (*Incoronazione*), Berlioz's Marguerite, Massenet's Charlotte, Handel's Giulio Cesare, and Donizetti's Maria Stuarda. Her final operatic appearances were of Gluck's Orfeo in Glyndebourne and London (1982). Baker's operatic triumphs have been in roles evoking heroism and fortitude as well as emotional warmth and intense personal involvement. Her preference for careful rehearsal and aversion to long separation from her family restricted her American career to recital and orchestral appearances.

Balanchine, George [Gyorgy Melitonovich Balanchivadze]. Choreographer; b. St. Petersburg, Jan. 22, 1904; d. New York, Apr. 30, 1983. Studied at Imperial Ballet, joined Ballets Russes (1924–29), came to U.S. in 1933. As director of American School of Ballet (from 1934) and N.Y.C. Ballet (from 1948), the most influential modern choreographer. At the Met, he staged *Orfeo* (1936), *Golden Cockerel* (1937), and *Rake* (1953), and choreographed the Polonaise in *Boris* (1974).

Balfe, Michael. Composer and singer; b. Dublin, May 15, 1808; d. Rowney Abbey, Hertfordshire, Oct. 20, 1870. Studied violin and singing in Ireland, London, and Italy; debut as Rossini's Figaro, Paris, Italien, 1828. After launching two operas in Italy, Balfe produced his first success, *The Siege of Rochelle* (1835), in London. *The Bohemian Girl* (1843), a world-wide triumph, confirmed his position in English opera with spoken dialogue. His special genius was for ballad writing; his works are rich in simple, affecting melodies with commonplace, even nonsensical lyrics.

ballabile (Ital., "danceable"). Ballet music, for orchestra or chorus with orchestra.

ballad. A narrative song, usually in several strophes sung to the same music, often with a refrain. The basis of 18th-c. English ballad opera, such songs were also introduced into 19th-c. German Romantic opera because of their folk-like character (e.g., Senta's Ballad in Wagner's *Holländer*).

Ballad of Baby Doe, The. Opera in 2 acts by Moore; libretto by the composer and John Latouche, based on the life of Baby Doe Tabor (1854–1935).
First perf., Central City, Colo., July 7, 1956: Wilson, Lipton, Krebs, Cassel, Davidson, c. Buckley.

A piece of scenic and musical Americana, using folk and folk-like tunes, with particularly effective roles for soprano and mezzo.
Colorado, and Washington, D.C., 1880–99. Elizabeth Doe (s), known as "Baby," has left her husband and gone to Leadville, Colorado, where she falls in love with Horace Tabor (bar), a wealthy man 30 years her senior. He divorces his wife Augusta (ms) and marries Baby, who is never accepted by society. Augusta warns Horace of the impending collapse of silver, but he ignores her advice and loses his fortune. His last hopes collapse with the defeat in 1896 of William Jennings Bryan, proponent of free silver. When Tabor dies, Baby Doe, who has promised never to sell his Matchless Mine, retreats there, to remain for the rest of her days.

ballad opera. An 18th-c. English musical play, made up of spoken dialogue and sung ballads or folk songs; the most notable is Pepusch's and Gay's *Beggar's Opera*.

Ballo in Maschera, Un. Opera in 3 acts by Verdi; libretto by Antonio Somma, after Scribe's libretto for Auber's *Gustave III, ou Le Bal Masqué*, based on the assassination of Gustave III of Sweden at a masked ball in 1792. (Originally called *Gustavo III* and set in late 18th-c. Sweden; changed because of censorship to late 17th-c. Boston.)
First perf., Rome, Apollo, Feb. 17, 1859: Dejean, Sbriscia, Scotti, Fraschini, Giraldone, c. Angelini. U.S. prem., N.Y., Academy of Music, Feb. 11, 1861. Met. prem., Dec. 11, 1889 (in Ger.): Lilli Lehmann, Sonntag-Uhl, Frank, Perotti, Reichmann, c. Seidl, p. Habelmann. Later Met productions: Nov. 22, 1913: Destinn, Hempel, Matzenauer, Caruso, Amato, c. Toscanini, d. Sala/Palanti, p. Speck; Dec. 2, 1940: Milanov, Andreva, Thorborg, Bjoerling, Sved, c. Panizza, d. Dobujinsky/Czettel, p. Graf; Jan. 25, 1962: Rysanek, Rothenberger, Madeira,

Rose Bampton as Sieglinde in *Die Walküre*

Bergonzi, Merrill, c. Santi, d. Maximowna, p. Rennert; Feb. 4, 1980: Ricciarelli, Blegen, Berini, Pavarotti, Quilico, c. Patané, d. Wexler/P.J. Hall, p. Moshinsky. Amelia has been sung at the Met by Gadski, Eames, Roman, Crespin, Nilsson, L. Price, Arroyo, Caballé; Oscar by Scheff, Peters, Grist; Ulrica by Homer, Castagna, Elmo, Anderson, Dunn, Forrester; Riccardo by de Marchi, Martinelli, Peerce, Tucker, Domingo, Gedda; Renato by Campanari, Scotti, Sved, Warren, MacNeil, Milnes; other conductors include Walter, Busch, Mitropoulos, Schippers. 156 perfs. in 25 seasons.

In *Ballo*, Verdi broadened the scope of his music to include French and comic-opera influences, while freeing himself increasingly from traditional forms. So finely proportioned is the score that it has generally been performed without the cuts and rearrangements often visited on Verdi's works of this period.

Riccardo (t), governor of Boston in love with Amelia (s), wife of his friend and adviser, Renato (bar), is warned by the fortune-teller Ulrica (a) that he will be killed by the next man to shake his hand – who proves to be Renato. To rid Amelia of her love for Riccardo, Ulrica recommends magic herbs gathered at midnight by the scaffold; there Amelia is interrupted by Riccardo and then by Renato, who has come to protect the governor from conspirators seeking his life. Riccardo escapes unharmed, while Renato discovers that the veiled woman he has agreed to escort to safety is his own wife. He then decides to join the conspirators. At a masked ball, the page Oscar (s) reveals his master's identity to Renato, who shoots Riccardo. He dies declaring Amelia's innocence and forgiving his enemies.

Baltsa, Agnes. Mezzo-soprano; b. Lefkas, Greece, Nov. 19, 1944. Studied in Athens, Munich, and Frankfurt; debut as Cherubino, Frankfurt, 1968; sang there until 1972. With Deutsche Oper, Berlin, from 1972, Covent

Samuel Barber, Gian Carlo Menotti, and Eleanor Steber

Garden and Vienna State Opera from 1976. Met debut as Octavian, Dec. 13, 1979; she returned in 1987 as Carmen. Other roles include Dorabella, Berlioz's Didon, Cenerentola, and Orfeo.

Bampton, Rose. Soprano, originally mezzo-soprano; b. Lakewood, near Cleveland, Ohio, Nov. 28, 1909. Studied with Horatio Connell and Queena Mario, Curtis Institute, Philadelphia; debut as Siebel (*Faust*), Chautauqua, 1929. Sang mezzo roles with Philadelphia Opera, 1929–32. Met debut as Laura (*Gioconda*), Nov. 28, 1932, with soprano debut as Leonora (*Trovatore*) in 1937; in 17 seasons, she sang 68 perfs. of 14 roles, including Sieglinde, Kundry, Donna Anna, Amneris, and Aida. Also appeared at Covent Garden (Amneris, 1937), Chicago (1937–46, including Maddalena in *Chénier*, Elsa), Colón, Buenos Aires (1942–48, including Strauss' *Daphne*), and San Francisco (1949). Admired as a sympathetic and musicianly singer, Bampton was married to conductor Wilfrid Pelletier. After retirement, she taught in N.Y. and Montreal.

banda (Ital., "band"). In operatic usage, the instrumentalists appearing on stage or behind the scenes, often comprising only winds and brass.

Bánk Bán. Opera in 3 acts by Erkel; libretto by Béni Egressy, after József Katona's tragedy.
First perf., Budapest, Mar. 9, 1861: Hollósy, Ellinger, Telek, Koszegi, c. Erkel.
The cornerstone of Hungarian national opera, set in 13th-c. Hungary, tells a tale of seduction and betrayal among the nobility.

Bar. In the music of the medieval German mastersingers, a song form consisting of two *Stollen* (strophes) and an *Abgesang* (aftersong): thus, A–A–B. Bar form is both discussed and exemplified in Wagner's opera *Meistersinger*. See also *Bogen*.

Barbaja, Domenico. Impresario; b. Milan 1778(?); d. Posillipo, near Naples, Oct. 19, 1841. The most important impresario of his day, he managed the San Carlo and Nuovo Theaters in Naples (1809–24), the Kärntnertor Theater and Theater an der Wien in Vienna (1821–28), La Scala and the Canobbiana in Milan (1826–32). He produced many works of Rossini, Bellini, and Donizetti, introduced their work to Vienna, and launched their international careers.

Barber, Samuel. Composer; b. West Chester, Pa., Mar. 9, 1910; d. New York, Jan. 23, 1981. Studied composition at Curtis Institute with Scalero; several prizes permitted travel in Europe. Showing an early interest in vocal music (Louise Homer was his aunt, and he studied singing with de Gogorza), he composed numerous songs and the soprano scena *Knoxville: Summer of 1915* (1948) before undertaking an opera. *Vanessa* (1958) achieved critical and public acclaim, and a Pulitzer Prize. Commissioned to inaugurate the Met's new opera house at Lincoln Center, *Antony and Cleopatra* (1966) was unsuccessful, its musical merits obscured by the excessively spectacular production of its librettist Franco Zeffirelli; a 1974 revision was more positively received. Barber's conservatively Romantic idiom found a ready response from many performers (including Toscanini), and his sure craftsmanship compensated for the sometimes undramatic quality of his music.

Barber of Baghdad, The. See *Barbier von Bagdad, Der*.

Barber of Seville, The. See *Barbiere di Siviglia, Il*.

Barbier, Jules. Librettist; b. Paris, Mar. 8, 1822; d. Paris, Jan. 16, 1901. Collaborator with Michel Carré on librettos of Gounod's *Faust* and *Roméo*, Meyerbeer's *Dinorah*, Thomas' *Mignon* and *Hamlet*, and Offenbach's *Hoffmann*. Although conventionalizing and sentimentalizing their often distinguished sources, these librettos proved highly effective in their day.

Barbier von Bagdad, Der (The Barber of Baghdad). Opera in 2 acts by Cornelius; libretto by the composer, after the *1,001 Nights*.

First perf., Weimar, Dec. 15, 1858: Milde, Wolf, Gaspari, Roth, c. Liszt. U.S. & Met prem., Jan. 3, 1890 (ed. Mottl): Traubmann, Kalisch, Fischer, c. & p. W. Damrosch, d. Hoyt. Later Met production: No. 7, 1925: Rethberg, Laubenthal, Bender, c. Bodanzky, d. Urban, p. Thewman. 14 perfs. in 3 seasons.

A musically and verbally sophisticated, quite un-Wagnerian comedy by an enthusiastic adherent of Wagner.

Baghdad. Nureddin (t) is hopelessly in love with Margiana (s), daughter of the Cadi Mustapha (t), and the go-between Bostana (ms) arranges an assignation, stipulating the engagement of the barber Abul Hassan (bs) to prepare him for the occasion. Abul's protracted and comic garrulity nearly causes Nureddin to miss the rendez-vous; to make matters worse, the barber proposes to accompany him to it. But when the lovers are interrupted and Nureddin must be shut up in a stifling chest, Abul's resourcefulness proves instrumental in reviving him, and eventually the Cadi consents to the union of Nureddin and Margiana.

Barbiere di Siviglia, Il (The Barber of Seville). Originally *Almaviva, ossia L'inutile precauzione* (Almaviva, or the Useless Precaution). Opera in 2 acts by Rossini; libretto by Cesare Sterbini, after Beaumarchais' play *Le Barbier de Seville*.

First perf., Rome, Argentina, Feb. 20, 1816: Giorgi-Righetti, M. Garcia Sr., Zamboni, Vitanelli, Botticelli, c. Rossini. U.S. prem., N.Y., Park, May 3, 1819 (in Eng.). Met prem., Nov. 23, 1883: Sembrich, Stagno, del Puente, Corsini, Mirabella, c. Vianesi, d. J. Fox, Schaeffer, Maeder, Thompson/Ascoli, Dazian. Later Met productions: Mar. 25, 1909: de Pasquali, Bonci, Campanari, Paterna, Didur, c. Spetrino, d. Sala, Parravicini/Maison Chiappi, p. Speck; Jan. 10, 1927: Galli-Curci, Chamlee, de Luca, Malatesta, Pinza, c. Bellezza, d. Urban, p. Agnini; Feb. 19, 1954: Peters, Valletti, Merrill, Corena, Siepi, c. Erede, d. Berman, p. Ritchard; Feb. 15, 1982: Horne, Blake, Elvira, Dara, Berberian, c. A. Davis, d. Wagner/Zipprodt, p. Cox. Figaro has been sung at the Met by Giraldoni, Amato, Ruffo, Bonelli, J.C. Thomas, Sereni, Prey, Milnes; Rosina by Patti, Hempel, Pons, Sayão, Tourel, Berger, de los Angeles, Simionato, Berganza, von Stade, Ewing, Battle; Almaviva by Campanini, Bonci, Lauri-Volpi, Tagliavini, di Stefano, Alva; Bartolo by Pini-Corsi and Baccaloni; Basilio by E. De Reszke, Chaliapin, Hines. 279 perfs. in 55 seasons.

Near the end of his life, Verdi wrote, "I cannot help believing that *The Barber of Seville*, for abundance of true musical ideas, for comic verve and for truth of declamation is the most beautiful comic opera in existence". Within the Italian repertory, only Verdi's own *Falstaff*

Il Barbiere di Siviglia – (1971). Designed by Eugene Berman, produced by Cyril Ritchard. Sherrill Milnes and Fernando Corena

challenges that assertion. Paisiello's popular earlier opera on the same subject (1782) did not long survive the success of Rossini's work.

Seville, 18th c. Rosina (a; often sung by sopranos), is kept under lock and key by her elderly guardian Dr. Bartolo (bs), who intends to marry her. Count Almaviva (t) attempts to woo her, disguised as a student named Lindoro; he enlists the aid of Figaro (bar), town barber and factotum. Don Basilio (bs), the music master, has alerted Bartolo to Almaviva's scheme, and Bartolo decides to marry her quickly. Lindoro gains entry to the house first disguised as an army officer and later as a music master, each time managing to upset the household, cause confusion, and communicate with Rosina. With Figaro's assistance, an escape plan is devised. Figaro and Almaviva come for Rosina at midnight and (after a misunderstanding fomented by Basilio is cleared up) the lovers are united, to general acquiescence and rejoicing.

Barbieri, Fedora. Mezzo-soprano; b. Trieste, Italy, June 4, 1920. Studied with Luigi Toffolo, Trieste, and Giulia Tess, Florence; debut in Florence as Fidalma (*Matrimonio Segreto*), 1940. At the Maggio Musicale, she created Dariola in Alfano's *Don Juan de Manara* (1941) and sang in revivals of Monteverdi's *Ritorno* (1942) and *Orfeo* (1943) and Pergolesi's *Flaminio* (1944). La Scala debut as Meg Page, 1942. Met debut as Eboli, Nov. 6, 1950; in 9 seasons, she sang 95 perfs. of 11 roles, including Azucena, Amneris, Laura, Carmen, and Adalgisa, adding Quickly in 1967, and, in the '70s, Cieca, Zia Principessa (*Suor Angelica*), and Zita (*Schicchi*). Also appeared at Covent Garden (with Scala, 1950; as guest, 1957–58, 1964), San Francisco (1952), Verona Arena (1955–58), and Colón, Buenos Aires (from 1947). At its peak, Barbieri's voice had breadth and power, and also the temperamental flair of the classic Italian mezzos.

Barbirolli, John. Conductor; b. London, Dec. 2, 1899; d. London, July 29, 1970. Studied at Royal Academy of Music, London, as cellist. Led standard repertory with British National Opera Co. (debut, *Roméo*, Newcastle, 1926) and at Covent Garden (1928–33, 1937, 1951–54), also in Rome (*Aida*, 1969). Music director, N.Y. Philharmonic (1937–42), Hallé Orchestra (1943–58); principal conductor, Houston Symphony (1961–64). Recorded *Butterfly* and *Otello*, many operatic excerpts.

barcarolle (Fr., Ital., **barcarola**). A Venetian boat song, or a piece constructed in imitation of one, usually in a rocking 6/8 meter.

baritone. Male voice range lying below tenor, above bass. Usual compass from G at bottom of bass clef to F above middle C. Developed as an independent category in the 19th c.; earlier, all low male voices were classified as basses. Some roles (Don Giovanni, Boris Godunov, Wotan) are sung by either baritones or basses, and the category "bass-baritone" is sometimes used.

Barrault, Jean-Louis. Actor and producer; b. Vésinet, France, Sep. 8, 1910. Student of Charles Dullin and the mime Étienne Decroux; with wife Madeleine Renaud, a central figure in French theater, notably at Théâtre Marigny (1946–56) and at Odéon (1959–68). At Met, produced *Faust* (1965) and *Carmen* (1967). Films include *Les Enfants du Paradis* (1944).

Barrientos, Maria. Soprano; b. Barcelona, Mar. 10, 1884; d. Ciboure, France, Aug. 8, 1946. Studied violin and piano, Barcelona Conservatory. Debut as Inès (*Africaine*), Novidades, Barcelona, 1899. After further study in Italy, debuts at Covent Garden (Rosina, 1903), La Scala (Dinorah, 1904), and other European opera houses. At the Met (debut, Lucia, Jan. 31, 1916), she sang 86 perfs. of 10 roles, including Gilda, Rosina, Adina (*Elisir*), the Queen (*Golden Cockerel*). After leaving the company in 1920, she concentrated on song recitals.

Barstow, Josephine. Soprano; b. Sheffield, England, Sep. 27, 1940. Studied at Birmingham U. and London Opera Centre; debut as Mimi, Opera for All, 1964. Sang with Sadler's Wells (1967–68) and Welsh National (1968–75). At Covent Garden (debut as a Niece, *Peter Grimes*, 1969), she created Denise in *Knot Garden* (1970), the Young Woman in Henze's *We Come to the River* (1976),

Fedora Barbieri as Amneris in *Aida*

The Bartered Bride – (1941). Designed by Joseph Novak, produced by Herbert Graf. Jarmila Novotná and Charles Kullman

and Gayle in *Ice Break* (1977). With Sadler's Wells, sang Jeanne (Penderecki's *Teufel von Loudon*, 1973), as well as Violetta, Natasha (*War and Peace*), and Salome. Met debut as Musetta, Mar. 28, 1977. Has also appeared at Santa Fe.

Bartered Bride, The (literally, The Sold Bride). Opera in 3 acts by Smetana; libretto by Karel Sabina.
    First perf., Prague, Provisional Theater, May 30, 1866: von Ehrenburg, Paleček, Kysela, Hynek, c. Smetana. Final revised version, Prague, Provisional, Sep. 25, 1870. U.S. prem., Chicago, Haymarket, Aug. 20, 1893. Met prem., Feb. 19, 1909 (in Ger.): Destinn, Jörn, Reiss, Didur, c. Mahler, d. Kautsky, Rottonara Bros./Lefter, p. Schertel. Later Met productions: Jan. 28, 1926 (in Ger.): Müller, Laubenthal, Meader, Bohnen, c. Bodanzky, d. Novak, p. Wymetal; Oct. 25, 1978 (in Eng.): Stratas, Gedda, Vickers, Talvela, c. Levine, d. Svoboda/Skalicky, p. Dexter. Other Met Mařenkas include Gadski, Rethberg; a 1941 revival (in Eng.), conducted by Walter, featured Novotná, Kullman, Pinza. 52 perfs. in 13 seasons.
    The Bartered Bride, which has won a place in the international repertory for its brilliant overture and profusion of spontaneous, folk-like melody, was actually the fruit of long revision on the part of the composer. It is one of the most successful scores to emerge from the eastern European flowering of nationalistic opera in the late 19th c.
    A Bohemian village, 19th c. Mařenka (s) is in love with Jeník (t), but was long ago promised by her parents, in payment of a debt, to the son of Tobias Micha (bs). When Mařenka meets Micha's son, Vašek (t), a stuttering simpleton, she flirts with him without revealing her identity, and convinces him to take an oath renouncing Mařenka. Meanwhile, Jeník accepts 300 guilder from Kečal (bs), the marriage broker who is negotiating Mařenka's betrothal, in return for renouncing his beloved to clear the way for the marriage. Jeník stipulates only that Mařenka must indeed marry the son of Micha. After argument with Mařenka, Jeník reveals that he is Micha's long-lost son by a former marriage. Mařenka learns her

sweetheart did not really betray her, and she is betrothed to the man she loves. The parents' plans are frustrated and Kečal has been outwitted, but all join in hailing the new bride and groom.

Bartók, Béla. Composer; b. Nagyszentmiklós, Hungary [now Sînnicolau Mare, Romania], Mar. 25, 1881; d. New York, Sep. 26, 1945. The greatest Hungarian composer of the 20th c., he studied with his parents, both amateur musicians, and at Budapest Academy of Music with Kessler (composition). Early influences from Strauss and Debussy were eventually submerged under Hungarian folk music, which Bartók began studying in 1904 and which led him to the harshly dissonant, rhythmically asymmetrical idiom of his maturity. However, his only opera, the one-act *Duke Bluebeard's Castle* (1911, rev. 1912, 1918), is a culmination of his early style. (The ballet *The Wooden Prince* [1917] and the pantomime-ballet *The Miraculous Mandarin* [1926] are often performed together with *Bluebeard*.) For most of his life, Bartók taught piano at Budapest Conservatory, moving to N.Y. in 1940.
BIBLIOGRAPHY: Halsey Stevens, *The Life and Music of Béla Bartók* (N.Y., and London, 1953).

Bartoletti, Bruno. Conductor; b. Sesto Fiorentino, Italy, June 10, 1926. Studied at Florence Conservatory; assisted at Teatro Comunale (debut, *Rigoletto*, 1953). Director of Maggio Musicale orchestra (1957–64); conductor at Rome Opera (1965–73). U.S. debut, Oct. 23, 1956, in *Trovatore* with Chicago Lyric, of which he became principal conductor in 1964, artistic director in 1985. Though he has conducted Berg, Shostakovich, and Prokofiev, his strengths lie in the Italian repertory, including 20th-c. composers such as Malipiero and Dallapiccola.

baryton-martin (Fr.). A high, light type of baritone voice found in French opera, named after a singer who favored falsetto effects. Debussy's *Pelléas* (ranging from C below middle C to A above) is a characteristic role for this type of voice.

bass (Fr., **basse**; Ital., **basso**). The lowest male voice range, lying below baritone. Usual compass from F below the bass clef to E or F above middle C. Today, singers with the high F are often called bass-baritones, but in the 18th c. all male voices below tenor were classified as basses. Subcategories include: basso profondo (Ital.), or deep bass; basso buffo (Ital.), or comic bass; basso cantante (Ital.; Fr., basse chantante), specializing in lyrical roles.

Bassarids, The. Opera in 1 act with an intermezzo by Henze; libretto by W.H. Auden and Chester Kallman, after Euripides' *The Bacchae*.
First perf., Salzburg, Aug. 6, 1966 (in Ger.): Hallstein, Meyer, Little, Driscoll, Melchert, Paskalis, c. Dohnányi. U.S. prem., Santa Fe, Aug. 7, 1968: Caplan, Sarfaty, Mandac, Driscoll, Bressler, Reardon, c. Henze.
Structured as a four-movement symphony, *The Bassarids* treats the conflict between social repression and sexual liberation. Pentheus (bar), King of Thebes, forbids his people to worship Dionysus (t), and is eventually torn to pieces by the god's followers, the Bassarids.

Bastianini, Ettore. Baritone; b. Siena, Italy, Sep. 24, 1922; d. Sirmione, Jan. 25, 1967. Studied with Flaminio Contini, Florence; first appeared as bass (debut, Colline, Ravenna, 1945), later singing Tiresias (*Oedipus Rex*) at La

Ettore Bastianini as Rodrigo in *Don Carlos*

Scala (1948). After further study with Rucciana Bertarini, began singing baritone roles in 1952, including Andrei in Western premiere of *War and Peace* (Florence, 1953). Met debut as Germont, Dec. 5, 1953; in 6 seasons, sang 71 perfs. of 11 roles, including Gérard (*Chénier*), Marcello, Posa, Ashton, Amonasro, and Scarpia. Returned to La Scala as Onegin (1954); debuts at Chicago (Riccardo in *Puritani*, 1956) and Covent Garden (Renato, 1962); sang Posa and di Luna under Karajan in Vienna and Salzburg (1958–63). Bastianini used his dark, powerful voice in the modern dramatic manner, if with less subtlety than Gobbi.

Bastien und Bastienne. Opera in 1 act by Mozart; libretto by Friedrich Wilhelm Weiskern, after Favart's *Les Amours de Bastien et Bastienne*, a parody of Rousseau's intermezzo *Le Devin du Village*.
First perf., Vienna, in the garden theater of Dr. Anton Mesmer's home, probably Sep. or Oct., 1768. U.S. prem., N.Y., Habelmann's Opera School, early 1905 (in Ger.).
A pastoral in singspiel style. Fearful that she been forsaken by Bastien (t), Bastienne (s) is advised by the soothsayer Colas (bs) to feign indifference, and eventually they are reconciled.

Bat, The. See *Fledermaus, Die*.

Battaglia di Legnano, La (The Battle of Legnano). Opera in 4 acts by Verdi; libretto by Cammarano, after Joseph Méry's play *La Battaille de Toulouse*.
First perf., Rome, Argentina, Jan. 27, 1849: Giuli-Borsi, Fraschini, Colini. U.S. prem., N.Y., Cooper Union (Amato Opera), Feb. 28, 1976: Robinson, Van Valkenburg, Vorhees, c. Amato.
One of Verdi's more intimate scores of the 1840s, flowing in its melodies but lacking the innovative qualities that have brought *Macbeth* and *Luisa Miller* back into circulation. At its premiere, shortly before the declaration

of a Roman republic, the nationalist subject aroused popular demonstrations.

Milan and Como, 1176. Arrigo (t) returns wounded from battle to find his sweetheart Lida (s) married to Rolando (bar), a captain in the Milanese army. Italy is invaded by Frederick Barbarossa (bs) and Arrigo enlists in the Knights of Death, who vow to die defending Milan. Lida tries to dissuade him and the two are found together by Rolando, who denounces them. Arrigo kills Barbarossa but is mortally wounded; he dies swearing to Rolando that he has not dishonored Lida.

Battistini, Mattia. Baritone; b. Rome, Feb. 27, 1856; d. Colle Baccaro, near Rieti, Nov. 7, 1928. Studied briefly with Venceslao Persichini and Eugenio Terziana before his debut as Alphonse (*Favorite*), Argentina, Rome, 1878. He travelled widely almost from the beginning of his career, including South America but never the U.S. (he was by far the most prominent singer of his time who never sang at the Met). In 1888, La Scala debut as Nélusko (*Africaine*). After his St. Petersburg debut (Hamlet, 1893), he visited Russia every season until 1914, admired for his interpretations of Onegin, Russlan, and Rubinstein's Demon. At Covent Garden (debut, Riccardo in *Puritani*, 1883), his greatest successes were in 1905–06, as Rigoletto, Valentin, Don Giovanni, Germont, and Amonasro. Late in life he appeared mostly in concerts, although in his last year he hoped to celebrate his 50th anniversary on stage by repeating his debut role.

Battistini's countrymen called him "il re dei baritoni" and "la gloria d'Italia." His high baritone extended up to A above middle C, with a complete command of timbre from villainous snarl to melting tenderness, and an unparalleled mastery of graceful and expressive ornamentation. His repertory embraced such "modern" and diverse roles as Renato (*Ballo*), Posa, Simon Boccanegra, Iago, Scarpia, Tonio, Wolfram, and Telramund, as well as the great Bellini and Donizetti parts, and he successfully appropriated the tenor role of Werther. He made some 120 recordings between 1903 and 1924, offering vivid evidence of his breath control, agility, shading, and elegance of phrasing.

Mattia Battistini as Don Carlo in *Ernani*

Ruggero Raimondi as Figaro and Kathleen Battle as Susanna in *Le Nozze di Figaro*

Battle, Kathleen. Soprano; b. Portsmouth, Ohio, Aug. 13, 1948. Studied at Cincinnati College-Conservatory, then with Franklin Bens. Sang Susanna, N.Y.C. Opera, 1976. Met debut as Shepherd, *Tannhäuser*, Sep. 18, 1978; since then, has sung over 100 perfs., including Zdenka (*Arabella*), Rosina, Despina, Zerlina, Blondchen, Susanna, and Sophie (*Werther* and *Rosenkavalier*). Has sung in Paris, Vienna, and Covent Garden, and is a noted recitalist.

Baudo, Serge. Conductor; b. Marseilles, France, July 16, 1927. Began career leading Concerts Lamoureux (1950), Paris, moving to the Opéra, 1962–65. Since 1971, music director of Lyon Orchestra; founder and artistic director of Berlioz Festival since 1979. Met debut leading *Hoffmann*, Sep. 16, 1971; in following three seasons, also conducted *Samson*, *Rigoletto*, and *Butterfly*.

Baum, Kurt. Tenor; b. Prague, Mar. 15, 1908. Studied with Garbin in Milan and Scoleri in Rome; debut in Zemlinsky's *Kreidekreis*, Zurich, 1933. Sang with German Theater, Prague (1934–39), Chicago Opera (1939–41). Joined Met as Italian Singer (*Rosenkavalier*), Nov. 27, 1941, and sang there until 1967, in roles such as Manrico, Radames, Enzo; he was the Met's first Drum Major (*Wozzeck*). Also appeared at La Scala (1948–49) and Covent Garden (1953).

Bayreuth. Town in northern Bavaria, site of the festival theater built by Wagner for the presentation of his music dramas. His attention was drawn to Bayreuth by the beautiful Margravial Opera House, designed by Carlo and Giuseppe Bibiena, which opened in 1748 and is still

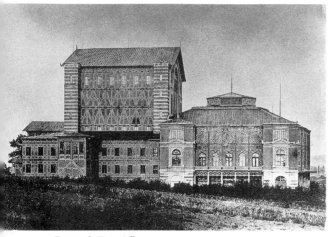

Bayreuth Festspielhaus

The orchestra pit in the Bayreuth Festspielhaus

used for performances. In Bayreuth, Wagner built a home, Villa Wahnfried, and the innovatively designed Festspielhaus, with its covered orchestra pit, superb acoustics, and unobstructed sight lines; the theater opened on Aug. 13, 1876, with *Rheingold*, inaugurating the first complete *Ring* cycle. A second festival, in 1882, presented the premiere of *Parsifal*. After Wagner's death in 1883, the festival was directed by his widow Cosima (1886–1906), her son Siegfried (1908–30), and then Siegfried's widow Winifred, with Heinz Tietjen as artistic director and Emil Preetorius as principal designer; during Winifred's regime, Bayreuth became closely associated with Hitler and Nazism, and after the war she was barred from its management. Until 1936, the festival was held in two out of every three summers, thereafter every year (no performances were given 1915–23, 1945–50).

The stigma of the Nazi connection was effectively broken by the first postwar festival, in 1951, under the management of Siegfried's sons Wieland and Wolfgang. Wieland replaced the former emphasis on realism with psychologically motivated deportment, stylized and symbolic settings, and innovative lighting techniques. Wolfgang shared the producer's assignments, and oversaw expansion of the stage and modernization of the building, enlarging the seating capacity to 1,800 while preserving Wagner's original design. Since his brother's death in 1966, Wolfgang has been sole director, and has invited producers such as Götz Friedrich and Patrice Chéreau to bring fresh approaches to the festival, which takes place annually from late July through August.

Bear, The. Opera in 1 act by Walton, libretto by Paul Dehn and the composer, after Chekhov.

First perf., Aldeburgh, June 3, 1967: Sinclair, Shaw, Lumsden, c. Lockhart. U.S. prem., Aspen, Colo., Music Festival, Aug. 15, 1968: c. L. Slatkin.

A comic score involving friendly parodies of Stravinsky and Britten, among others. Russia, 1890. Madame Popova (ms) and Smirnov (b), a creditor of her late husband, argue violently and decide to duel. While instructing Madame Popova in the use of pistols, Smirnov falls in love with her.

Beaton, Cecil. Designer; b. London, Jan. 14, 1904; d. Salisbury, Jan. 18, 1979. Fashion and portrait photographer; since 1927, designer of sets and costumes for ballet, theater, film, and opera. Met designs include ballet *Soirée* (1955), operas *Vanessa* (1958), *Turandot* (1961), and *Traviata* (1966).

Beatrice di Tenda. Opera in 2 acts by Bellini; libretto by Romani, after Carlo Tedaldi Fores' novel.

First perf., Venice, Fenice, Mar. 16, 1833: Pasta, Del Serre, Curioni, Cartegenova. U.S. prem., New Orleans, St. Charles, Mar. 5, 1842.

Bellini's penultimate opera, set in a castle near Milan, 1418. Having married Beatrice di Tenda (s) for her wealth, Filippo Maria Visconti (bar) falls in love with Agnese del Maino (c). Although Beatrice has rejected the advances of Orombello (t), whom Agnese secretly loves, Orombello testifies the opposite under torture. As she goes to the scaffold, Beatrice forgives Agnese.

Béatrice et Bénédict (Beatrice and Benedict). Opera in 2 acts by Berlioz; libretto by the composer, after Shakespeare's *Much Ado About Nothing*.

First perf., Baden-Baden, Aug. 9, 1862: Charton-Demeur, Monrose, Montaubry, c. Berlioz. U.S. prem., N.Y., Carnegie Hall (Little Orchestra Soc.), Mar. 21, 1960 (concert perf.): Jordan, Addison, Sénéchal, Thompson, c. Scherman. U.S. stage prem., Washington D.C., Opera, June 3, 1964 (in Eng.): Dussault, Newman, Porretta, Metcalf, c. Callaway.

Berlioz's elegant, witty opéra-comique version of Shakespeare's comedy does away with the darker sub-plot of the original play. When Claudio (bar) returns from the wars, he is welcomed by his beloved Hero (s), but his friend Bénédict (t) is as disdainful of marriage as Béatrice (s) is of him. After much sparring, they realize that they love each other, and a double wedding is celebrated. Berlioz adds a character named Somarone (bs), a comically pedantic band-leader.

Beaumarchais, Pierre Augustin Caron de. French dramatist (1732–99). Operas based on his writings include *Il Barbiere di Siviglia* (Rossini) and *Le Nozze di Figaro* (Mozart).

Thomas Beecham

Ludwig van Beethoven

Bedford, Steuart. Conductor; b. London, July 31, 1939. After study at Royal Academy of Music, debut at Aldeburgh Festival (*Beggar's Opera*, 1967), of which he has been an artistic director since 1973. Conducted world premiere of *Death in Venice*, and made Met debut (Oct. 18, 1974) in same work, returned in 1975–77 to lead *Figaro*.

Beecham, Thomas. Conductor; b. St. Helens, England, Apr. 29, 1879; d. London, Mar. 8, 1961. Self-taught son of a wealthy pharmaceutical manufacturer, he was in the 1910s an energetic introducer of operas new to England, and founder (1915) of the Beecham Opera Company. In 1932, founded the London Philharmonic Orchestra, artistic director (from 1932) and general director (1935–39) of Covent Garden. Spent war years in America; Met debut on Jan. 15, 1942, with double bill of Bach's *Phoebus and Pan* and Rimsky-Korsakov's *Golden Cockerel*; in 3 seasons, he led 58 perfs. of 9 works, mostly French but also *Tristan*, and *Falstaff*. Founder (1946) of the Royal Philharmonic, which he led until his death. Last operatic performances in Buenos Aires, 1958. One of the most prolific recording artists of his time, including notable complete operas (*Bohème, Carmen, Zauberflöte, Entführung, Faust*). Not fastidious or even always accurate, he was however an invariably engaging interpreter. A colorful, charismatic, witty, but often unpredictable, mercilessly outspoken man, he left an extraordinary mark upon the English musical scene and will be remembered especially for his championship of Delius and Sibelius, and his Mozart and Haydn recordings.
BIBLIOGRAPHY: Alan Jefferson, *Sir Thomas Beecham: A Centenary Tribute* (London, 1979).

Beeson, Jack. Composer; b. Muncie, Ind., July 15, 1921. Studied at Eastman School, Rochester, with Burrill Philips, Rogers, and Hanson, and privately with Bartók

while completing graduate studies at Columbia U., where he joined the faculty in 1945. His operas, in a distinctively American idiom, include *Hello Out There* (1954), *Lizzie Borden* (1965), *My Heart's in the Highlands* (after Saroyan, 1970), and *Captain Jinks of the Horse Marines* (1975).

Beethoven, Ludwig van. Composer, bapt. Bonn, Germany, Dec. 17, 1770; d. Vienna, Mar. 26, 1827. Son of a violinist, he studied during adolescence with the Bonn court organist Neefe and often played in the opera orchestra. Moving to Vienna in 1792, he studied sporadically with Haydn, Albrechtsberger, and Salieri, and quickly won fame as pianist and composer. After the rapid and innovative output of his "heroic period" (1803–08), Beethoven's productivity decreased because of musical and personal problems, including his increasing deafness. However, beginning in 1816, he developed an extraordinary late style, combining structural complexity and melodic directness. His achievements in augmenting the scale and expressive power of instrumental music served as a powerful and often daunting model for his successors.

Beethoven admired Mozart's and Cherubini's stage works, and aspired to emulate them, but his high standards of dramatic and ethical content made this difficult. *Vestas Feuer*, with libretto by Schikaneder, was abandoned in 1803 after only two scenes were completed, in favor of the subject that became *Fidelio* (1805); because of its mixture of comic and serious genres, and Beethoven's lack of theatrical experience, this required two revisions (1806, 1814) before achieving success. He composed a few arias for insertion in singspiels, as well as incidental music for Goethe's *Egmont* and several other plays, but no further operas, though such subjects as *Macbeth* and *Faust* were contemplated.
BIBLIOGRAPHY: Maynard Solomon, *Beethoven* (N.Y., 1977).

Hildegard Behrens as Elettra in *Idomeneo*

Beggar's Opera, The. Ballad opera in 3 acts, arr. and composed by Pepusch; libretto by Gay.

First perf., London, Lincoln's Inn Fields, Jan. 29, 1728: Fenton, Walker. U.S. prem., N.Y., Nassau Street, Dec. 3, 1750.

Gay's ballad opera satirized both 18th-c. politics and the forms and personalities of Italian opera. Much of the music was drawn from popular ballads of the day, and its use in the play anticipates the form of the modern musical comedy. It has been successfully revived in a variety of arrangements, the most famous of which, Brecht's and Weill's *Dreigroschenoper*, provides new melodies for all but one song.

Macheath (t) is a highwayman with a penchant for pretty women; he has seduced both Polly (s), daughter of the criminal Peachum (bs), and Lucy (s), daughter of the jailer Lockit (bar). Arrested at his favorite bordello, Macheath languishes in Newgate prison and is almost executed, but a *deus ex machina* intervenes so that the opera can have a happy ending.

Behrens, Hildegard. Soprano; b. Oldenburg, Germany, Feb. 9, 1937. After taking a law degree at U. of Freiburg, she began serious vocal study with Ines Leuwen at Freiburg Music Academy. She sang in Freiburg (debut, Countess in *Figaro*, 1971), moving in 1973 to the Deutsche Oper am Rhein; there and in Frankfurt, she added to her repertory such roles as Fiordiligi, Agathe (*Freischütz*), Elsa, Musetta, Katya Kabanova, and Marie (*Wozzeck*). Her career began to flourish in the mid-1970s, notably with a Salzburg *Salome* in 1977. She made 1976 debuts as Giorgetta (*Tabarro*) at Covent Garden and the Met (Oct. 15, 1976). She has since returned to the Met frequently as Fidelio, Donna Anna, Elettra (*Idomeneo*), Marie, Sieglinde, Isolde, Tosca, and Brünnhilde. With a bright and penetrating (though not conventionally heroic) voice, Behrens has established a reputation as an important Wagnerian soprano, and in 1983 at Bayreuth sang all three Brünnhildes for the first time. She is a vivid and engrossing theatrical personality, especially successful in roles demanding display of temperament.

Belasco, David. Playwright and producer; b. San Francisco, July 25, 1853; d. New York, May 15, 1931. Successful dramatist and actor-manager; his romantic melodramas with John Luther Long, *Madame Butterfly* (1900) and *The Girl of the Golden West* (1905), became Puccini operas; Belasco assisted in staging the latter at its Met world premiere (1910).

bel canto (Ital., "beautiful singing"). An imprecise term, generally referring to the classic Italian style of legato singing, fully supported on the breath and capable of great coloratura virtuosity; also more loosely used in reference to the early 19th-c. Italian operatic repertory epitomized by Rossini, Bellini, and Donizetti.

Bellezza, Vincenzo. Conductor; b. Bari, Italy, Feb. 17, 1888; d. Rome, Feb. 8, 1964. After a Naples debut (*Aida*, 1908) and several years touring Italy, began a long association with Teatro Colón, Buenos Aires; Covent Garden debut, (*Mefistofele*, 1926). Met debut, *Gioielli della Madonna*, Nov. 4, 1926; during 10 seasons, led 30 works in the Italian repertory, including Met premiere of *Rondine*. Reliable, unimposing, and attentive to singers, Bellezza was active mainly in Italy after 1936.

Bellincioni, Gemma. Soprano; b. Monza, Italy, Aug. 18, 1864; d. Naples, Apr. 23, 1950. Daughter and student of comic bass Cesare Bellincioni and contralto Carlotta Soroldoni; debut in dell'Orefice's *Segreto della Duchessa*, Teatro della Società Filarmonica, Naples, 1879. Further study under Luigia Ponti dell'Armi and Giovanni Corsi was followed by engagements in Spain and Portugal

Gemma Bellincioni as Santuzza and Roberto Stagno as Turiddu in *Cavalleria Rusticana*

Vincenzo Bellini

(1882), Rome (1885), and her only La Scala season (1886), when she sang Violetta, a portayal admired by Verdi; other early roles included Dinorah, Amina, and Oscar. On an 1886 tour to South America, she met tenor Roberto Stagno (1836–97), who had sung Manrico, Arturo (*Puritani*), the Duke of Mantua, Meyerbeer's Robert and Jean de Leyde, Almaviva, Ottavio, Enzo, and Lionel (*Martha*) during the Met's first season (1883–84) and later became her husband. In 1890 at the Costanzi, Rome, the couple created Turiddu and Santuzza in *Cavalleria*; Bellincioni's triumph established her as a leading interpreter of the new verismo style. Her roles now included Carmen, Boito's Margherita, and Tosca, and she created Fedora (1898). With Strauss conducting, she was the first Italian Salome (Turin, 1906) and gave over 100 performances in the role, including her farewell (Paris, 1911). Thereafter, except for 1924 appearances as Santuzza, Tosca, and Carmen in the Netherlands, she taught in Berlin (1911–15), Vienna (1931–32), and at Naples Conservatory (from 1932). Her few recordings, made in 1903 and 1905, are both fascinating and disappointing – emotionally intense but vocally uncertain.

Bellini, Vincenzo. Composer; b. Catania, Sicily, Nov. 3, 1801; d. Puteaux, near Paris, Sep. 23, 1835. Son and grandson of composers; studied with his grandfather Vincenzo Tobia Bellini and at Naples Conservatory with Giovanni Furno and Nicola Zingarelli. His first opera, *Adelson e Salvini* (Naples, 1825), was a graduation exercise. International fame came quickly with *Il Pirata* (1827), his first collaboration with Felice Romani, who was to be the librettist of six Bellini operas, including *La Sonnambula* (1831) and *Norma* (1831). Bellini's close association with the tenor Rubini also dates from 1827, that with the soprano Giuditta Pasta from 1830. Bellini lived in Milan until 1833, making his living solely from opera commissions, then went to London and Paris to supervise productions of his operas; his Parisian successes led to the commissioning of *I Puritani* (Jan. 1835), his last and greatest triumph.

In Paris, Bellini became friends with Rossini and Chopin, among many other musicians. The former's rhythmic vitality and florid writing had already strongly influenced Bellini; Chopin, in turn, based his own cantabile piano style on Bellini's concise yet highly ornamented, Romantically colored melodies. These are not only shapely enough in instrumental terms; they are also matched to the text, phrase for phrase, in a way that gave them remarkable power onstage. Although Bellini never aspired to the individual musical characterization later practiced by Verdi, the sensuality of vocal line and the withholding of the melodic climax till the end of the aria – familiar features of later Italian opera – virtually originated with him. By blurring certain formal conventions such as the distinction between recitative and aria, he imparted to his scenes a natural flow and direct emotional appeal that perfectly suited the tastes of the first generation of the Romantic era.

Other operas: *Bianca e Gernando* (1826), *La Straniera* (1829), *Zaira* (1829), *I Capuleti e i Montecchi* (1830), *Beatrice di Tenda* (1833).
BIBLIOGRAPHY: Leslie Orrey, *Bellini* (London, 1969).

Belmont, Eleanor Robson. Patron; b. Wigan, Lancashire, England, Dec. 13, 1878; d. New York, Oct. 24, 1979. A popular actress on American and British stages (Shaw wrote *Major Barbara* for her, although she never appeared in it), after her 1910 marriage to banker August Belmont she devoted herself to artistic and charitable philanthropy. The first woman member of the Met's board of directors (from 1933), in the 1950s she decisively favored the new managerial policies of Rudolf Bing. She founded the Metropolitan Opera Guild in 1936 to widen the audience for opera, and functioned as its chief executive (1936–48) and president emeritus; in 1952 she established the National Council to broaden the Met's base of support.

Bemberg, Herman. Composer; b. Paris, Mar. 29, 1859; d. Bern, July 21, 1931. Studied with Massenet and Franck at Paris Conservatory. Operas include *Le Baiser de Suzon* (1888), *Blessure d'Amour* (1903), and *Leila* (1914). The grand opera *Elaine* (1892), written for the de Reszkes and performed at Covent Garden and the Met as a favor to them, held little dramatic appeal for the public. His salon songs were recorded by Melba and others.

Beňačková (-Čápová), **Gabriela.** Soprano; b. Bratislava, Czechoslovakia, Mar. 3, 1947. Studied with Janko Blaho and Tatiana Kiesakova, Bratislava Academy; debut there as Natasha (*War and Peace*); has sung Mimi, Tatiana, Mařenka (*Bartered Bride*), and Jenůfa in Prague, and appeared in Cologne, London, and N.Y. (Czech roles with Opera Orchestra).

Bender, Paul. Bass; b. Driedorf, Germany, July 28, 1875; d. Munich, Nov. 25, 1947. Studied with Luise Reuss-Belce and Baptist Hoffmann; debut as Sarastro, Breslau, 1900. Leading bass at Munich, 1903–33. At Met, 1922–27 (debut, Ochs, Nov. 17, 1922), sang Wagner roles, Sarastro, and Cornelius' Barber. Also known for interpretations of Loewe ballads and other dramatic lieder.

benefit. A special performance, the proceeds of which are earmarked for a specific purpose. In the 18th and 19th c., singers, managers, and composers were often granted benefits in their contracts; today, the beneficiaries are usually charities, often the opera house itself or its pension or production funds.

Benois [Benua], **Nicola.** Designer; b. St. Petersburg, May 2, 1901. Studied with his father Alexandre, who designed for Diaghilev; later worked for Paris Opéra, La

Alban Berg

Scala. Principal designer at Rome Opera (1927–32) and La Scala (1936–70), also a lighting designer, stage director, painter, illustrator, and architect. For Met, designed *Siège de Corinth* (1975).

Benvenuto Cellini. Opera in 3 (originally 2) acts by Berlioz; libretto by Léon de Wailly and August Barbier, after Cellini's autobiography.

First perf., Paris, Opéra, Sep. 10, 1838: Dorus-Gras, Dérivis, Stoltz, Duprez, c. Habeneck. U.S. prem., Boston, May 3, 1975: Wells, Vickers, Reardon, Beni, c. Caldwell.

Conceived as an opéra comique, *Cellini* was eventually composed with recitatives, and later revised by Liszt and Berlioz in 1852–53 for Weimar and London; modern productions often restore elements of earlier versions, even the spoken dialogue of the original plan. The brilliant score is full of "verve and Cellinian impetuosity," according to Berlioz himself, who wondered whether he would ever find such a variety of ideas again.

Rome, 16th c. The sculptors Benvenuto Cellini (t) and Fieramosca (bar) are rivals in art and for the love of Teresa (s), daughter of the Papal treasurer Balducci (bs). After various intrigues, Cellini successfully casts his bronze of Perseus and wins Teresa's hand.

Berberian, Ara. Bass; b. Detroit, Mich. Studied with Kenneth Westerman, Themy Georgi, and Beverly Johnson; debut with Turnau Opera, Woodstock, N.Y., 1958. N.Y.C. Opera debut, 1963 (Leandro in *Love for Three Oranges*); created Henderson (Kirchner's *Lily*) there, 1977. Met debut, Sep. 25, 1979, as Zacharie (*Prophète*); over 125 perfs. there, including Mustafà (*Italiana*), Rossini's Basilio, Sparafucile, and Hermann (*Tannhäuser*). Has also appeared in San Francisco, Houston, and Santa Fe.

berceuse (Fr.). A lullaby.

Berg, Alban. Composer; b. Vienna, Feb. 9, 1885; d. Vienna, Dec. 24, 1935. Virtually all his formal musical training (1904–10) was with Schoenberg, an intensive course of study that deepened into an emotionally ambivalent father–son relationship. In May 1914, Berg saw the Vienna premiere of Büchner's play *Wozzeck* and determined to set it operatically. Three years in the Austrian Army intervened, during which Berg's experiences deepened his understanding of the play's soldier-protagonist. After the war, while earning a modest living from teaching and managing Schoenberg's contemporary-music performance society, Berg worked on *Wozzeck*, completing the orchestration in spring 1922 and publishing the vocal score himself the following year. Controversy surrounded the premiere at the Berlin State Opera (Dec. 14, 1925), as right-wing opponents of music director Kleiber accused him of promoting "anarchism" and "rubbish," but *Wozzeck* received nine more performances in Berlin that season; other successful productions followed soon after.

Bolstered by this acclaim, Berg in 1928 turned for his next opera to two plays by Wedekind that he had first read 25 years before, trimming and tightening them, as he composed, into the powerful, symmetrical libretto of *Lulu*. The music was finished in spring 1934, but political and financial concerns and a commission for a violin concerto delayed its orchestration. When he resumed this task in Aug. 1935, Berg was already ill; at his death four months later, portions of Act III remained unscored. (Because his widow refused to authorize its publication, the third act was not performed until 1979; see *Lulu*.) Berg's scores control every detail, down to the speed at which the curtain is raised or lowered, as part of elaborate and complex musical and dramatic designs involving traditional vocal and instrumental forms, networks of leitmotivic correspondences, and (in *Lulu*) a sophisticated variant of Schoenberg's 12-tone method. However, he noted with satisfaction that audiences at *Wozzeck* were unaware of the formal devices, responding instead to "the social problems of this opera." And it is the composer's sympathy for his characters, dominated by psychological and social forces beyond their control, that makes the strongest impression in his operas. Berg's non-operatic works include songs, chamber and orchestral works, and a concert aria, *Der Wein*; many of them, like the operas, conceal autobiographical references.

BIBLIOGRAPHY: George Perle, *The Operas of Alban Berg* (Berkeley, 2 vols., 1980–85).

Berganza [Vargas], **Teresa.** Mezzo-soprano; b. Madrid, Mar. 16, 1934. Studied with Lola Rodriguez Aragon; operatic debut as Dorabella, Aix, 1957. Debuts at Piccola Scala (Isolier in *Comte Ory*, 1958), Glyndebourne (Cherubino, 1958), Dallas (*Italiana*, 1958), Covent Garden (Rosina, 1960), and Chicago (Cherubino, 1962). In 2 Met seasons, she sang 15 perfs. of Cherubino (debut, Oct. 11, 1967) and Rosina. Her repertory also includes Purcell's Dido, Octavia (*Incoronazione*), Néris (*Médée*), Cenerentola, and Carmen (Edinburgh, 1977). A charming and musical artist, at her best in delicate effects; as a recitalist, she specializes in Spanish songs.

Berger, Erna. Soprano; b. Cossebaude, near Dresden, Oct. 19, 1900. Studied with Melitza Hirzel, Dresden; debut there as First Boy (*Zauberflöte*), 1925. Sang in Berlin, also at Bayreuth (1930–33) and Salzburg (1932–54).

Covent Garden debut as Marzelline (*Fidelio*), 1934. Met debut as Sophie, Nov. 21, 1949; sang with the company until 1951, notably as the Queen of Night and Gilda.

Berghaus, Ruth. Producer; b. Dresden, July 2, 1927. Began career as choreographer; associated with Berliner Ensemble (from 1964; director, 1971–77). Director, Berlin State Opera (1977–79). Noted for her aggressively symbolic productions of opera in Munich (husband Paul Dessau's *Verurteilung des Lukullus*, 1965), Frankfurt, Berlin, and elsewhere.

Berglund, Joel. Bass-baritone; b. Torsåker, Sweden, June 4, 1903. Studied with John Forsell, Stockholm Conservatory. Debut as Monterone, Stockholm, 1929; on roster there for 20 years, returning as guest until 1964. Met debut as Sachs, Jan. 9, 1946, in 4 seasons, sang 45 perfs. including Gurnemanz, the three Wotans, Jochanaan, and Kurwenal. Director of Stockholm Opera, 1949–52.

Bergonzi, Carlo. Tenor; b. Polisene, near Parma, Italy, July 13, 1924. Studied with Grandini, then at Boito Conservatory; his studies were interrupted by imprisonment for anti-Nazi activities. Began career in baritone roles, as Rossini's Figaro, Lecce, 1948; his tenor debut, as Andrea Chénier, was in Bari, 1951. At his La Scala debut (1953), he created the title role of Napoli's *Masaniello*.

Carlo Bergonzi as Riccardo in *Un Ballo in Maschera*

London debut as Alvaro, Stoll Theatre, 1953; Covent Garden debut, same role, 1962. U.S. debut as Luigi (*Tabarro*), Chicago, 1955. Met debut, Nov. 13, 1956, as Radames, which remained his most frequent role at the house; during 21 seasons there (between 1956 and 1983), he sang 249 perfs. of 21 roles, including Riccardo, Canio, Chénier, Cavaradossi, Rodolfo, Macduff, Alfredo, Manrico, Enzo, Pollione, and Nemorino. His 25th anniversary at the Met was celebrated by a gala, Dec. 4, 1981. His extensive repertory also includes Avito in *Amore dei Tre Re* (Chicago, 1955) and Boito's Faust. In the 1980s, he continued to appear in carefully selected roles (particularly in concert performances of early Verdi works), still singing with velvety tone and idiomatic phrasing.

Berini, Bianca. Mezzo-soprano; b. Trieste, Italy, Dec. 20, 1928. Debut as Suzuki, Nuovo, Milan, 1963. Met debut as Amneris, Dec. 16, 1978; other Met roles are Amneris, Santuzza, Dalila, Federica (*Luisa Miller*), Eboli, Ulrica, and Azucena. Has sung throughout Italy, and in Barcelona, Rio de Janeiro, and Paris; American appearances include Dallas, Philadelphia, San Francisco, and Baltimore.

Berio, Luciano. Composer; b. Oneglia, Italy, Oct. 24, 1925. Studied at Milan Conservatory with Ghedini, later with Dallapiccola at Tanglewood. Contacts with the Darmstadt school and his directorship (1955–60) of the Studio di Fonologia in Milan led to work with electronic music. Berio's works employ an extraordinary range of vocal and instrumental techniques, combining acoustical and electronic sounds with song, *Sprechstimme*, and inflected recitative. His stage works include *Opera* (libretto by Berio and Umberto Eco; 1970, rev. 1977), a spectacle for mixed media; *La Vera Storia* (libretto by Calvino; Milan, 1982); and *Un Re in Ascolto* (libretto by Calvino; Salzburg, 1984). Other theatrical, if not explicitly operatic, works include the chamber play *Amores* (1971) and *Recital I* (for Cathy Berberian; 1972). Berio has taught at Juilliard, Tanglewood, and Harvard.

Berlin. Politically divided city in Germany (eastern sector, capital of German Democratic Republic; western sector allied to Federal Republic of Germany). Opera was introduced to Berlin during the late 17th c.; its fortunes fluctuated according to the tastes of the court. Frederick the Great took an active part in establishing a permanent company, and during his reign the Court Opera opened on Dec. 7, 1742 with Graun's *Cleopatra e Cesare*. Though Frederick favored opera seria, opera buffa was also performed at the Potsdam palace, paving the way for singspiel (from 1771) at the Nationaltheater. Merged as the Königlich Schauspiel (1807), the two companies retained their separate identities.

The opening of the Neues Schauspielhaus, followed by the premiere of Weber's *Freischütz* (1821), was a landmark in the popularity of German opera. Spontini, music director for 22 years until succeeded by Meyerbeer (1842–48), helped establish Berlin as an operatic center; later directors were Weingartner (1891–98) and Strauss (1898–1918). In 1919 the Royal Opera became the Berlin State Opera, where under Kleiber (music director 1923–34) the adventurous repertory averaged about one world premiere a year, including *Wozzeck* (1925) and *Christophe Colomb* (1930). After the theater was destroyed during the war, performances were held in the Admiralspalast in the east zone, from 1946. Since 1955, the German State Opera has occupied the rebuilt theater on Unter den Linden

Leonard Bernstein

(capacity 1,450), presenting premieres by East German composers and a varied repertory, including Russian and Czech works; the current director is Günter Rimkus, with Otmar Suitner as chief conductor.

An important branch of the State Opera was the Kroll Opera (1927–31), occupying a theater on the Platz der Republik that had previously housed popular opera and singspiel; under Klemperer, the Kroll became renowned for its experimental productions, including a stylized *Holländer* anticipating Wieland Wagner, and *Hoffmann* with abstract sets by László Moholy-Nagy. Along with popular favorites, the repertory included Hindemith's *Cardillac*, Krenek's *Leben des Orest*, Schoenberg's *Erwartung*, Stravinsky's *Oedipus Rex*, and Weill's *Jasager*. Closed by political pressure in 1931, the theater was destroyed during the war.

West Berlin's Deutsche Oper traces its ancestry to the company established in 1912 at the new Deutsches Opernhaus (capacity 2,000), on the Bismarckstrasse in Charlottenburg. It reopened under municipal auspices as the Städtische Oper in 1925, offering an adventurous repertory (including the premiere of Weill's *Bürgschaft*, 1932) and high musical standards under conductors such as Walter, Busch, and Stiedry. After the war, the company moved to the Theater des Westens (capacity 1,529), and in 1961 relocated to a new house (capacity 2,098) on the original Bismarckstrasse site. Premieres have included Henze's *König Hirsch* (1956) and *Junge Lord* (1965). Lorin Maazel served as artistic director, 1965–71; Götz Friedrich became general manager in 1981, with Jesús López-Cobos as chief conductor.

The Komische Oper opened at East Berlin's Metropoltheater in 1947 and its theater was modernized in 1966. Under Felsenstein's direction (1947–75), it became renowned for imaginative productions of both standard and unusual repertory. Joachim Herz succeeded Felsenstein in 1976; Harry Kupfer is now opera director.

Berlioz, Hector. Composer; b. La Côte-St.-André, Isère, France, Dec. 11, 1803; d. Paris, Mar. 8, 1869. Proficient on flute and guitar as a youth, he taught himself theory. In 1821, he entered medical school in Paris, but the vitality and prestige of the opera houses, and his own passion for literature, turned his thoughts toward musical-dramatic works. Gluck's classicism and Weber's fantastic imagination made strong impressions. Abandoning medicine in 1823, he was admitted to Le Sueur's class at the Conservatory (where he later also studied with Reicha), and composed his first opera, *Estelle et Némorin*, later destroyed. *Les Francs-Juges*, a Weberesque drama of tyranny and heroism, followed in 1826; unable to get it produced, Berlioz cannibalized it for other works. He discovered his two greatest literary influences in 1827, when he saw a production of *Hamlet* (with his future wife Harriet Smithson as Ophelia) and read *Faust*. On his fourth attempt, Berlioz won the Prix de Rome and his travels in Italy (1831–32) inspired a series of colorful, Byronic works, including the opera *Benvenuto Cellini* (1834–37). Intended for the Opéra-Comique but accepted by the Opéra after expansion and revision, this brilliant, unconventional work baffled the audiences of this all-important theater, which never produced another Berlioz opera.

Travel, conducting, and journalism occupied Berlioz during the 1840s and 1850s, but gradually the idea of composing a grand opera on portions of Virgil's *Aeneid* (a favorite since his childhood) pushed these activities aside. *Les Troyens* (1856–58), though not longer or more extravagant than Meyerbeer's fashionable works, achieved no complete production in the composer's lifetime. The last three acts were given as *Les Troyens à Carthage* in 1863–64 at the Théâtre-Lyrique, to considerable acclaim, but drastic cuts in later performances further mutilated Berlioz's score and spoiled this long-awaited triumph, though the performance fees liberated him at last from the burden of daily journalism. Taking refuge from the travails of *Les Troyens*, Berlioz composed a delicate and charming opéra comique, *Béatrice et Bénédict*, in 1860–62.

Outside the mainstream of French operatic composition, Berlioz at first attracted a greater following in Germany and Russia than at home, while only in the 20th c. have his operas come to be as widely admired as his equally literary concert works.

BIBLIOGRAPHY: Jacques Barzun, *Berlioz and his Century* (N.Y., 1950, 3rd ed., 1969).

Berman, Eugene. Designer; b. St. Petersburg, Nov. 4, 1899, d. Rome, Dec. 4, 1972. Studied painting and architecture in St. Petersburg; in Paris after 1920, associated with revolt against abstract art. After 1935 in U.S., designed ballets (including *Concerto Barocco* for Balanchine, 1941) and opera. At the Met, designed sets and costumes for *Rigoletto* (1951), *Forza* (1952), *Barbiere* (1954), *Don Giovanni* (1957), and *Otello* (1963). He also designed television premiere of *Amahl* (1952) and inaugural *Così* at Piccola Scala, Milan (1956). His architecturally conceived sets are executed with an insistence on painterly surface details.

Bernstein, Leonard. Composer and conductor; b. Lawrence, Mass., Aug. 25, 1918. Studied composition with E.B. Hill and Walter Piston at Harvard, conducting with Reiner and Koussevitzky. He became assistant conductor, N.Y. Philharmonic, in 1942, later its music director (1958–69); also active as guest conductor, notably with the Vienna Philharmonic. The first American to conduct at La Scala (*Médée*, 1953), his rare operatic appearances also include Met performances of *Falstaff* (debut, Mar. 6, 1964), *Cavalleria* (1970), and *Carmen* (1972).

His theater works include the Broadway musicals *On the Town* (1944), *Wonderful Town* (1953), and *West Side Story* (1957), the operetta *Candide* (1956), the theater piece *Mass* (1971), the one-act opera *Trouble in Tahiti* (1952), and its sequel *A Quiet Place* (1983). Bernstein's music has incorporated the influences of Mahler and Stravinsky, along with a resourceful grasp of American popular idioms, in a restless search for a broadly accessible yet meaningful idiom.

Berry, Walter. Bass-baritone; b. Vienna, Apr. 8, 1929. First studied engineering, then voice with Hermann Gallos, Vienna Academy; debut as soloist in Honegger's *Jeanne d'Arc*, Vienna State Opera, 1950. Salzburg debut as Masetto, 1953; he created roles in Liebermann's *Penelope*, Egk's *Irische Legende*, and Einem's *Prozess* there. U.S. debut as Mozart's Figaro, Chicago, 1957. Met debut as Barak (*Frau*), Oct. 2, 1966; in 10 seasons, he sang 83 perfs. of 9 roles, including Ochs, Leporello, Telramund, Pizarro (*Fidelio*), Alfonso, and the *Walküre* Wotan. Covent Garden debut, also as Barak, 1976. A forceful and versatile singer, whose repertory also included Guglielmo, Papageno, Escamillo, Wozzeck, and Dr. Schön (*Lulu*). Married to mezzo Christa Ludwig, 1957–70, with whom he frequently appeared in opera and recital.

Besanzoni, Gabriella. Mezzo-soprano; b. Rome, Nov. 20, 1890; d. Rome, July 6, 1962. Studied with Hilde Brizzi and Alessandro Maggi; debut as Adalgisa, Viterbo, 1911. Sang in major Italian, Spanish, and South American theaters. Met debut as Amneris, Nov. 19, 1919; during her only season there, sang Isabella (*Italiana*), Dalila, Preziosilla, and Marina (*Boris*). A noted Carmen, role of her farewell, Rome, Caracalla, 1939.

Besuch der alten Dame, Der (The Visit of the Old Lady). Opera in 3 acts by Einem; libretto by Friedrich Dürrenmatt, after his drama.

First perf., Vienna, State Opera, May 23, 1971: Ludwig, Beirer, Wächter, Hotter, c. Stein. U.S. prem., San Francisco, Oct. 25, 1972 (in Eng.): Resnik, Cassilly, Wolansky, Yarnell, c. Peress.

This theatrically effective work explores the moral dilemma created when a wealthy woman (ms) offers a vast sum of money to her native town in return for the death of the man who seduced and abandoned her years ago.

Betrothal in a Monastery (also known as *The Duenna*). Opera in 4 acts by Prokofiev; libretto by the composer and Mira Mendelson, after Sheridan's play *The Duenna*.

First perf., Leningrad, Kirov, Nov. 3, 1946: c. Khaikin. U.S. prem., N.Y., Greenwich Mews Playhouse, June 1, 1948 (with 2 pianos, in Eng. as *The Duenna*).

Completed in 1940, its premiere was delayed by the war. Sheridan's comedy of intrigue in 18th-c. Seville was also set by Thomas Linley Sr. & Jr. (1775) and Roberto Gerhard (1951).

Bibiena. See *Galli-Bibiena*.

Bible, Frances. Mezzo-soprano; b. Jan. 26, 1927, Sacketts Harbor, N.Y. Studied with Queena Mario, Juilliard, N.Y.; 1948 debut as Shepherd (*Tosca*), N.Y.C. Opera, where she sang regularly until 1977. Created Augusta (*Ballad of Baby Doe*), Central City, 1956, and Elizabeth Proctor (*Crucible*), N.Y.C. Opera, 1961. Other roles included Cherubino, Herodias, Amneris, Adalgisa.

Billy Budd. Opera in 2 (originally 4) acts and epilogue by Britten; libretto by E.M. Forster and Eric Crozier, after Herman Melville's novel.

First perf., London, Covent Garden, Dec. 1, 1951: Pears, Uppman, Dalberg, c. Britten. U.S. prem., NBC Television, Oct. 19, 1952. U.S. stage prem., Bloomington, Indiana U., Dec. 5, 1952. Revised in 2 acts, first perf., BBC, Nov. 13, 1961 (radio perf.). First stage perf., Covent Garden, Jan. 9, 1964: R. Lewis, Kerns, Robinson, c. Solti. U.S. prem., N.Y., Carnegie Hall (American Opera Society), Jan. 4, 1966 (concert perf.): R. Lewis, Kerns, Robinson, c. Solti. U.S. stage prem., Chicago, Nov. 6, 1970: R. Lewis, Uppman, Evans, c. Bartoletti. Met prem., Sep. 19, 1978: Pears, Stilwell, Morris, c. Leppard, d. Dudley, p. Dexter. 22 perfs. in 3 seasons.

A powerful study of goodness and evil incarnate, in a musically well realized nautical setting.

On board the H.M.S. Indomitable, summer 1797. The handsome Billy Budd (bar), pressganged into service in the Royal Navy, is well-liked by all except the master-at-arms, John Claggart (bs), who envies and persecutes him, then tries to incite him to mutiny, and finally accuses him before Captain Vere (t). Called upon to defend himself, Billy is afflicted by his nervous stammer, and strikes out at Claggart, who dies of the blow. Though Captain Vere knows the truth, he must follow the law; a drumhead court condemns Billy and he is hanged at dawn.

Bing, Rudolf. Manager; b. Vienna, Jan. 9, 1902. After assisting Carl Ebert in Darmstadt (1928–30), at the Städtische Oper, Berlin (1930–33), and in Glyndebourne (from 1934; general manager, 1936–49), he became a British subject in 1946 and helped found the Edinburgh Festival (artistic director, 1947–49). General manager of the Met, 1950–72 (after Gatti-Casazza's, the longest tenure), he drew on his European experience and his new acquaintance with American stage design to bring Met

Rudolf Bing

productions up to contemporary visual standards. His aloof temperament, caustic wit, and Old World attitudes sometimes caused friction with the board of directors, artists, labor unions, and the press, but he was a well-organized and bold manager with a keen eye for talent onstage, backstage, and upstairs. With the 1955 engagement of Marian Anderson, he ended the Met's unwritten bar to black artists, and he presided over the design, building, and occupation of the new theater in Lincoln Center. As the steadily expanding Met season collided with the jet age's increased mobility for star performers, Bing at first succeeded in maintaining some semblance of a resident company, and, when this became impossible, kept up a steady flow of talent that assured, if not cohesive casts, at least many memorable performances.

BIBLIOGRAPHY: Rudolf Bing, *5000 Nights at the Opera* (N.Y., and London, 1972).

Birtwistle, Harrison. Composer; b. Accrington, England, July 15, 1934. Studied at Royal Manchester College of Music. Early influences were Stravinsky, Varèse, Webern, and medieval music. The opera *Punch and Judy* (1968) and the "dramatic pastoral" *Down by the Greenwood Side* (1969) demonstrate theatrical flair in a context of explicit violence, all the more shocking for its technical virtuosity. In *The Mask of Orpheus* (1986), the Orpheus legend is reexamined from a 20th-c. perspective, through a montage of singing and mime, acoustic and electronic forces. The "mechanical pastoral" *Yan Tan Tethera* (1986) likewise employs ritualistic elements, worked out in patterns of conflicting pulses. Birtwistle also served as music director at England's National Theatre, creating incidental music for productions by Peter Hall, notably *The Oresteia* (1981).

bis (Lat., "twice"). Used in Europe as a request for repetition, as the French word "encore" is used in the English-speaking countries.

Bishop, Henry Rowley. Composer; b. London, Nov. 18, 1786; d. London, Apr. 30, 1855. His early stage works, set pieces interspersed with dialogue, led to appointment in 1810 as music director of Covent Garden, where he wrote songs for Shakespeare's plays and arranged Mozart and Rossini operas with interpolations of his own music. *Aladdin* (1826), his only full-scale opera, was composed after he moved to Drury Lane. Many of Bishop's set pieces survived as popular melodies, notably "Home, Sweet Home," from *Clari, The Maid of Milan* (1823).

Bispham, David. Baritone; b. Philadelphia, Jan. 5, 1857; d. New York, Oct. 2, 1921. Studied with Vannuccini and Lamperti in Milan, later with William Shakespeare in London; debut as Longueville (Messager's *Basoche*), London, English Opera House, 1891; at Covent Garden, 1892–1902. Met debut as Beckmesser, Nov. 18, 1896; noted for his Wagner roles, including Wotan, Kurwenal, and Alberich, he returned frequently until 1903. A distinguished recitalist.

Bizet, Georges. Composer; b. Paris, Oct. 25, 1838; d. Bougival, near Paris, June 3, 1875. Son of a voice teacher and a pianist, he studied first with his parents, then at the Paris Conservatory (composition with Zimmerman, Halévy, and Gounod), where he won the Prix de Rome at 19. His first opera, *La Maison du Docteur* (c. 1852), was privately performed, if at all. *Le Docteur Miracle* (1857) won a competition sponsored by Offenbach and was

Georges Bizet

performed at the Bouffes-Parisiens. The Rome prize subsidized a stay in that city (1858–60), during which Bizet began several operas and completed one, the *Don Pasquale*-like *Don Procopio* (1859, first perf. 1906). Back in Paris, Bizet made a living from his skill at the piano (which Liszt lavishly praised) by turning out hack arrangements, teaching a few pupils, and accompanying rehearsals.

The sometimes overblown *Les Pêcheurs de Perles* (1863), which probably incorporates material from an earlier, withdrawn opera in an oriental setting, *La Guzla de l'Emir*, is distinguished by Bizet's facility for melody and color. Although *Pêcheurs* failed with the public and most critics (except Berlioz), its producer Carvalho commissioned another opera from Bizet. Judging from the much-edited published score, the five-act spectacular *Ivan IV* (1865, first perf. 1946) was the composer's most pretentious and least characteristic work; after many delays at the Lyrique and rejection by the Opéra, Bizet abandoned hope of a production. *La Jolie Fille de Perth* (1866) appeared at the Lyrique to better reviews, but no larger audiences; in it, Bizet's growing mastery of scoring and stagecraft only partly overcame a leaden libretto. The same may be said of *Djamileh* (1871), Bizet's first production at the Opéra-Comique; despite its failure, he was invited to compose another opera for the house. He asked for a libretto based on Mérimée's *Carmen*, and, in the meantime, sharpened his stage skills with incidental music for Daudet's play *L'Arlésienne* (1872).

Controversy surrounded *Carmen* (1874) because of the subject matter and the music's difficulty. Bizet and soprano Galli-Marié refused to water down the work's realism, despite management's fears that defiance of opéra comique conventions would alienate the theater's clientele. And so it did, at first – its 48-performance run was poorly attended – but within a year or so, soon after Bizet's death, a series of triumphant productions in Vienna and elsewhere showed that *Carmen*, far from destroying the comique genre, had infused it with new life and dramatic possibilities, a fact the Opéra-Comique recognized with a belated revival in 1883.

BIBLIOGRAPHY: Winton Dean, *Georges Bizet: His Life and Work* (London, 1948, 3rd ed. 1975).

Bjoerling [Björling], **Jussi** [Johan Jonatan]. Tenor; b. Stora Tuna, Sweden, Feb. 5, 1911; d. Stockholm, Sep. 9, 1960. Taught by his father David Björling, who with him and Jussi's two brothers formed the Björling Male Quartet (1916–26), which toured and recorded in the U.S., 1919–21. After study with John Forsell in Stockholm (1928–30), he appeared at Stockholm Opera as the Lamplighter (*Manon Lescaut*) and made his official debut there as Ottavio (both 1930). Bjoerling continued to sing regularly in Stockholm until 1939, with guest appearances in Vienna (debut, Manrico, 1936) and other Central European theaters. His American debut was in *Rigoletto*, Chicago, 1937; the next season he joined the Met as Rodolfo, Nov. 24, 1938. He appeared with the company until 1959, except for the war years, 1954–55, and 1957–59, singing 90 perfs. of 10 roles, including Manrico, Faust, Riccardo (*Ballo*), Cavaradossi, Turiddu, Puccini's Des Grieux, and Don Carlos. Other debuts at Covent Garden (Manrico, 1939), San Francisco (Rodolfo, 1940) and Florence (Manrico, 1943). After the war he sang frequently in San Francisco, and, in the later Fifties, with the Chicago Lyric (debut, Manrico, 1955). Married in 1935 to soprano Anna-Lisa Berg, he sang opposite her in *Bohème* (Stockholm, 1948) and *Roméo* (San Francisco, 1951).

Possibly the most widely admired tenor of mid-century, Bjoerling excelled in the spinto roles of Verdi and Puccini. Initially a bright, sweet lyric sound, his perfectly placed voice acquired a brilliant timbre and was capable of gentle pianissimos as well as considerable heroic thrust. His many recordings, spanning the years 1920–59, include ten complete operas as well as numerous arias and songs.

Jussi Bjoerling as Riccardo in *Un Ballo in Maschera*

Bjoner, Ingrid. Soprano; b. Kraakstad, Norway, Nov. 8, 1927. Studied at Oslo Conservatory and with Paul Lohmann in Frankfurt. Debut as Gutrune and Third Norn, Oslo Radio, 1956; stage debut as Donna Anna, Oslo, 1957. Sang at Wuppertal (1957–59). Düsseldorf (1959–61), Munich (from 1960), Bayreuth (from 1960), Covent Garden (from 1967). Met debut as Elsa, Oct. 28, 1961; sang there through 1967. Specialized in Wagner and Strauss repertory, venturing later into Turandot and several Verdi roles.

Blachut, Beno. Tenor; b. Mährische Ostrau-Wittkowitz [now Ostrava-Vitkovice, Czechoslovakia], June 14, 1913; d. Jan. 10, 1985. Studied at Prague Conservatory with Louis Kaderábek; debut as Jeník (*Bartered Bride*), Olomouc, 1939. Sang with Prague National Theater from 1941, specializing in Czech repertory. Appeared as guest artist in Amsterdam and Vienna. Known in U.S. only through recordings, including many of the first complete LPs of Czech operas.

Blake, Rockwell. Tenor; b. Plattsburgh, N.Y. Jan. 10, 1951. Studied in Plattsburgh; won first Richard Tucker award, 1978. N.Y.C. Opera debut as Count Ory, Sep. 23, 1979; later appeared in Houston (*Cenerentola*, 1980; *Donna del Lago*, 1981), Boston (*Puritani*, 1982), and Aix (*Mitridate*, 1983). Met debut as Lindoro (*Italiana*), Feb. 2, 1981; has also sung Almaviva, Ottavio, and Arturo (*Puritani*) there.

Blass, Robert. Bass; b. New York, Oct. 27, 1867; d. Berlin, Dec. 3, 1930. Studied with Julius Stockhausen, Frankfurt; debut as Heinrich (*Lohengrin*), Weimar, 1892. Met debut as Hermann (*Tannhäuser*), Dec. 24, 1900; remained there until 1910 and returned 1920–22, singing 234 perfs. of 25 roles. Also appeared in Bayreuth (1901) and Berlin (1913–19).

Blech, Leo. Conductor and composer; b. Aachen, Germany, Apr. 21, 1871; d. Berlin, Aug. 24, 1958. Studied composition with Humperdinck. Early conducting posts led to a 1906 appointment at the Berlin Court (later State) Opera, where he remained with interruptions until 1937, moving to Riga and in 1941 to Stockholm. In 1949, he returned to the Berlin Städtische Oper, celebrating his 80th birthday by conducting his operas *Das war ich* (1902) and *Versiegelt* (1908). Blech's compositions, in the post-Wagnerian tradition of Humperdinck, reveal a practitioner's knowledge of the operatic repertory. Blech appeared in N.Y. in 1923 with a touring German company at the Manhattan Opera House.

Blegen, Judith. Soprano; b. Lexington, Ky., Apr. 27, 1941. Studied with Toshiya Eto (violin) and Eufemia Giannini-Gregory (voice) at Curtis Institute, Philadelphia, and with Luigi Ricci, Rome. Operatic debut as Olympia, Nuremberg, 1965; subsequently sang Lucia, Susanna, and Zerbinetta there, and Mélisande in Spoleto, 1965. Debuts at Vienna State Opera (Rosina, 1968) and Santa Fe (Emily in Menotti's *Globolinks*, a role requiring her both to sing and play the violin, 1969). Met debut as Papagena, Jan. 19, 1970; since then, she has sung over 200 perfs. of 19 roles, including Marzelline (*Fidelio*), Zerlina, Nannetta, Sophie, Adina, Juliette, Gilda, Oscar, Blondchen, Gretel, and Adele. Debuts at Covent Garden (1975), and Paris Opéra (1977). With her radiant lyric soprano, high musical polish, and personal charm, Blegen quickly moved to the forefront of her generation. Married to Met concertmaster Raymond Gniewek.

Bliss, Anthony A. Manager; b. New York, Apr. 19, 1913. Attended Groton School, Harvard U. (B.A. 1936), and U. of Virginia (LL.B. 1940). He practised law as a member of the Wall Street firm of Milbank, Tweed, Hadley & McCloy. Son of Cornelius N. Bliss, chairman of the Met board (1938–45), he joined the board after his father's death in 1949, served on the executive committee and as president (1956–67), and persistently advocated the company's move to Lincoln Center. In 1974, following the brief tenures of Gentele and Chapin as general managers, Bliss took charge of the company's business affairs as executive director, with Levine as music director; the title of general manager was revived for him in 1981, although he continued to concern himself mainly with financial matters until his retirement in 1985. Many of his policies showed an expansionist approach to the Met's chronic financial problems: he advocated taking over the struggling N.Y.C. Opera (1956), established a Met National Company (1965) to build a wider audience and attract federal funding, and in the mid-1970s launched an ambitious program of professional marketing and fundraising. Unlike Bing, Bliss avoided public attention; his impersonal style of management, typical of the corporate world, was something new to the Met.

Blitzstein, Marc. Composer; b. Philadelphia, Mar. 2, 1905; d. Martinique, West Indies, Jan. 22, 1964. A student of Scalero at Curtis Institute, Boulanger in Paris, and Schoenberg in Berlin, Blitzstein was stimulated by Weill's *Dreigroschenoper* and Hanns Eisler's 1935 N.Y. lectures to assume a socially activist position. In his musical theater works, notably *The Cradle Will Rock* (1937) and the opera *No for an Answer* (1941), he used variations on popular commercial forms and American vernacular speech rhythms to bring his social precepts to life. After World War II, he composed the opera *Regina* (1949) and several music-theater works, and made an enormously successful English adaptation of *Dreigroschenoper* (1952). *Sacco and Vanzetti*, commissioned by the Ford Foundation for the Met, remained uncompleted at his death.

Bloch, Ernest. Composer; b. Geneva, July 24, 1880; d. Portland, Oreg., July 15, 1959. Studied composition with Rasse, Knorr, and Thuille. The influences of Strauss and Debussy, whom he met in Paris, are apparent in his early works. His only opera, *Macbeth* (1910), is reminiscent of *Pelléas*, but also of Wagner, Mussorgsky, and Dukas. In 1916, Bloch came to the U.S., where he was long active as a composer and teacher.

Blomdahl, Karl-Birger. Composer; b. Växjö, Sweden, Oct. 19, 1916; d. Kungsängen, June 14, 1968. Studied composition with Hilding Rosenberg. In the 1940s, led a movement away from the Romanticism prevalent in Sweden, towards Hindemithian "new objectivity." His first opera, *Aniara* (1959), was widely acclaimed for its eclectic blend of popular idioms and electronic sounds. The more conventional *Herr von Hancken* (1963) followed; another opera using electronics was unfinished at his death.

Bloomington. Town in Indiana, site of Indiana U. and its School of Music, established in 1921 and greatly expanded under deans Wilfred C. Bain (1947–73) and Charles H. Webb (since 1973). The Indiana U. Opera Theater was founded in 1948; its production schedule grew from one opera annually to as many as eight in the 1970s. Standard works alternate with more exotic fare

(*Poppea*, *Tamerlano*, Pizzetti's *Assassinio*), all sung in English. Performances are now given in the Musical Arts Center (capacity 1,460), which opened in 1972 with *Don Giovanni* and Eaton's *Heracles*. The faculty includes singers such as Farrell, Harshaw, King, Lipton, Rossi-Lemeni, and Zeani.

Blow, John. Composer; bapt. Newark-on-Trent, England, Feb. 23, 1649; d. London, Oct. 1, 1708. Organist of Westminster Abbey at age 20, and after 1674 associated with the Chapel Royal, where, in addition to liturgical music, his responsibilities included producing works for secular occasions. His only stage work, the masque *Venus and Adonis* (c. 1685), is an opera in miniature, synthesizing French and Italian elements, which served as a model for Purcell's *Dido and Aeneas*.

Bluebeard's Castle. See *Duke Bluebeard's Castle*.

Boatswain's Mate, The. Opera in 1 act by Ethel Smyth; libretto by the composer, after W.W. Jacobs' comedy *Captains All*.
  First perf., London, Shaftesbury, Jan. 28, 1916: Buckman, Roy, Pounds, Wynn, Ranalow, c. Smyth.
  A comic opera set in early 20th-c. England. To win the hand of Mrs. Waters (s), Harry Benn (t) hires Travers (bar) to pose as a burglar, so that Benn can rush to the lady's aid, but the lady ends up preferring Travers to Benn.

Boccaccio. Operetta in 3 acts by Suppé; libretto by "F. Zell" (Camillo Walzel) and Richard Genée.
  First perf., Vienna, Carltheater, Feb. 1, 1879. U.S. prem., Philadelphia, Chestnut St., Apr. 5, 1880 (in Eng.). Met prem., Jan. 2, 1931 (with recitatives by Bodanzky and interpolations): Jeritza, Fleischer, Telva, Kirchhoff, Schützendorf, c. Bodanzky, d. Urban, p. Wymetal. 8 perfs. in 1 season.
  A popular work from the first flowering of Viennese operetta, set in Florence in 1331, relating a fictional episode in the life of the poet Boccaccio (s), beloved by Fiammetta (s).

bocca chiusa (Ital., "closed mouth"). Humming. Off-stage choruses in opera often hum for atmospheric effect, as during the storm in *Rigoletto*.

Bockelmann, Rudolf. Bass-baritone; b. Bodenteich, near Lüneberg, Germany, April 2, 1892; d. Dresden, Oct. 9, 1958. Studied with Scheidemantel and Oscar Lassner, Leipzig. Sang in Leipzig (1921–26; debut, Herald in *Lohengrin*), Hamburg (1926–32; created title role in Krenek's *Leben des Orest*), Berlin (1932–45), and Hamburg (1946–51); also Bayreuth (1928–42), Covent Garden (1929–30, 1934–38), and Chicago (1930–32). Regarded as Schorr's only rival in major Wagner roles.

Bodanzky, Artur. Conductor; b. Vienna, Dec. 16, 1877; d. New York, Nov. 23, 1939. Studied at Vienna Conservatory and with Zemlinsky. Conducting debut, *The Geisha*, České Budějovice, 1900. Mahler's assistant in Vienna, 1902–04, he later moved to posts in Berlin, Prague, and Mannheim. A successful London *Parsifal* (1914) led to his Met appointment as successor to Hertz (debut, *Götterdämmerung*, Nov. 18, 1915). Except for a brief break in 1928, he remained for 24 seasons, until his death. Noted for his Gluck, Strauss, Meyerbeer, and Tchaikovsky operas as well as Wagner, Bodanzky led 795 perfs. of 45 operas while at the Met, including the U.S.

premieres of *Oberon, Tote Stadt, Jenůfa, Ägyptische Helena, Jonny spielt auf,* and *Shvanda,* as well as Gluck's *Iphigénie en Tauride* in Strauss' edition. His performances were fast, well-routined, dramatic rather than ruminative, and often heavily cut; he also composed recitatives to replace the spoken dialogue in *Oberon, Freischütz, Zauberflöte,* and *Fidelio.*

Boesch, Christian. Baritone; b. Vienna, July 27, 1941. Son of mezzo Ruthilde Boesch, studied at Vienna Hochschule für Musik; debut, Stadttheater, Bern, 1966. Appeared in Saarbrücken, Lucerne, and Kiel before joining Vienna Volksoper in 1975. Came to international attention as Papageno, Salzburg, 1978. Met debut as Papageno, Feb. 17, 1979; has also sung Wozzeck and Masetto there.

Bogen (Ger., "bow"). In the music of the medieval German mastersingers, a song form of the pattern A–B–A. Like the *Bar* form (*q.v.*), it plays an important role in Wagner's compositional style.

Bogianckino, Massimo. Manager; b. Rome, Nov. 10, 1922. Studied piano with Casella in Rome and Cortot in Paris. Artistic director of the Rome Opera (1963–68), Spoleto Festival (1969–72), La Scala, Milan (1972–75), Teatro Comunale, Florence (1975–83), and Paris Opéra (1983–1985). In 1985, he became mayor of Florence.

Bohème, La (Bohemia). Opera in 4 acts by Leoncavallo; libretto by the composer, after Henry Murger's novel *Scènes de la Vie de Bohème.*

First perf., Venice, Fenice, May 6, 1897: Frandin, Storchio, Beduschi, Angelini-Fornari, Isnardon, c. Pomé. Rev. as *Mimì Pinson,* in 3 acts, Palermo, Massimo, 1913. U.S. prem., N.Y., McMillin Theater (Columbia U.), Jan. 31, 1960.

One of Leoncavallo's strongest scores, doomed to obscurity by the success of Puccini's opera on the same subject. The story is similar to Puccini's, with a few additional characters and episodes. In Act II, Mimì (s) accepts a rich admirer's offer to live with him; when she returns repentant to Rodolfo (bar) in Act III, he rejects her bitterly.

Bohème, La (Bohemia). Opera in 4 acts by Puccini; libretto by Giacosa and Illica, after Henry Murger's novel *Scènes de la Vie de Bohème.*

First perf., Turin, Regio, Feb. 1, 1896: Ferrani, Pasini, Gorga, Wilmant, Mazzara, c. Toscanini. U.S. prem., Los Angeles Theater, Oct. 14, 1897. Met prem., Dec. 26, 1900: Melba, Occhiolini, Saléza, Campanari, Journet, c. Mancinelli, p. Parry. Later Met productions: Dec. 27, 1952 (in Eng.): Conner, Munsel, Tucker, Merrill, Hines, c. Cleva, p. Mankiewicz (also sung in Ital. that season, and subsequently always in Ital.); Feb. 23, 1977: Scotto, Niska, Pavarotti, Wixell, Plishka, c. Levine, d. Pizzi, p. Melano; Dec. 14, 1981: Stratas, Scotto, Carreras, Stilwell, Morris, c. Levine, d. Zeffirelli/P.J. Hall, p. Zeffirelli. Mimì has also been sung at the Met by Sembrich, Farrar, Alda, Gluck, Bori, Muzio, Galli-Curci, Rethberg, Moore, Sayão, Favero, Albanese, Kirsten, de los Angeles, Tebaldi, Freni, Moffo, Ricciarelli, Cotrubas; Rodolfo by Caruso, Bonci, Smirnov, Martinelli, McCormack, Gigli, Lauri-Volpi, Fleta, Kiepura, Bjoerling, Peerce, Tagliavini, di Stefano, Bergonzi, Gedda, Domingo; Musetta by Scheff, Schumann, Gueden, Welitsch, Söderström; Marcello by Scotti, Stracciari,

Artur Bodanzky

Amato, de Luca, Tibbett, Brownlee, Bastianini, Sereni; Colline by Rothier, Pinza, Pasero, Siepi. 631 perfs. in 80 seasons.

One of the most beloved and tuneful of all operas, a study in Puccini's lyrical distillation of verismo, in which sentiment and pathos supplant the display of violent passion. Paris, the Latin Quarter, c. 1830. In their garret on Christmas Eve, the poet Rodolfo (t) and the painter Marcello (bar) are trying to work in the bitter cold. Their fellow-lodgers return: the philosopher Colline (bs) and

(continued p.50)

La Bohème – (1930). Ezio Pinza, Millo Picco, Pompilio Malatesta, Nannette Guilford, Beniamino Gigli, Lucrezia Bori, and Giuseppe de Luca

LA BOHÈME
Luciano Pavarotti

When the editor of this encyclopedia asked me to write about the opera that has meant the most to me as a singer, I didn't have to think twice about which one to choose. I have sung over thirty roles, but to pick a favorite I must go back to the one with which I made my debut, and the one I have sung more often than any other – Rodolfo in Puccini's *La Bohème*.

Besides being the role of my first professional opera performance in Reggio Emilia in 1961, it also served for three other important debuts: at La Scala, the San Francisco Opera, and, perhaps most important, the Metropolitan Opera. I have also sung it at Covent Garden, the Vienna State Opera, the Chicago Lyric, and the Miami Opera. I always think of *La Bohème* as my first love, and since I am just a little bit superstitious, I call it my "good-luck opera."

Because I feel so close to the work and the role, it is not easy for me to analyze my feelings for it. I identify so much with Rodolfo. He is an artist and he is a romantic, and, although he is supposed to be French, by the time Puccini got through with him he became totally Italian. Above all, he is *una persona viva* – a true, living person – and that is why I never tire of playing him. His feelings are my own.

But, if pressed, I can think of three reasons why this opera appeals to me so much. First, I love that the characters are almost all struggling artists. It was not so long ago that I too was struggling to achieve recognition as an artist, and it is a feeling one never forgets. I like to believe that Rodolfo is a *wonderful* poet who will one day be celebrated but will always remember his days in the garret.

Second, I love that this opera is so full of life. These characters live in complete poverty, but attack life with the zest and optimism of the young, It's happy and terrible at the same time. Mimi and Rodolfo meet and immediately fall in love. Only later do they realize that love and life are not so simple, and, like many other lovers, they find it impossible to be apart but also impossible to stay together. All this was written ninety years ago, but I doubt if there is anyone in the audience who has not experienced these complications of life, and does not identify. That's why it is such a popular opera, and always will be.

As far as I'm concerned (I guess this is Reason Number Three), it is a perfect opera. The music perfectly suits the text. Each act has its own atmosphere and character, and each is beautifully constructed. Like all good plays, *Bohème* is like a wound-up spring: once it starts unwinding, nothing can stop it. Performing *Bohème*, you have the feeling that the music and words will carry you along until the final curtain. That is not true of many operas.

I am *always* amazed by the incredible melodic invention in this work. My favorite parts? Of course, "Che gelida manina" is very special to me – a unique aria, and not easy. I adore the duet "O soave fanciulla," but I must admit that I am usually a little tense until I have completed that first act.

Also very special to me is the little mini-aria in Act II, "Questa è Mimi," where I introduce my new love to my friends. All of Act III is heaven, and no matter how many times I sing it, I am always overwhelmed by the quartet with Mimi, Marcello, and Musetta. When all four principal roles are well cast, it is one of the greatest sounds in all of opera.

The duet with Marcello in Act IV is a great treat — the only love duet I've ever sung with a baritone! And from the moment Mimi makes her entrance in the last act, we get one wonderful melody after another — some repeated from earlier in the opera, some new, but all of them very beautiful. I have never ended a performance of the opera without feeling, like Rodolfo, totally shattered.

Of course I listened to *Bohème* many times as a young man, both in the theater and on recordings. I heard a great many performances of Rodolfo, and if you were to ask me which ones gave me the most pleasure, I would have to name Gigli, di Stefano, Bjoerling, Bergonzi, and Tucker. Their interpretations were all very different, but they all were wonderful in the role. I also love the recordings Caruso made of excerpts from the opera, and would give almost anything to have seen him perform *Bohème* on stage.

I have sung so many *Bohème*s, and, believe it or not, some of them do stand out in my memory. My debut, of course, and my Met debut, when I was so sick with flu that I don't think I could have made it to the end if Mimi had been anyone other than my beloved Mirella Freni. (For diplomatic reasons I usually don't single out favorite co-stars, but everyone knows that Mirella and I grew up together, so in her case I get away with it.)

One performance in Ankara, Turkey, was truly unique. I was the only member of the cast singing in Italian, while all of my colleagues performed in Turkish — I wish I had a recording of that one to play at parties! Also unusual was a gala Met *Bohème* in 1976. The opera wasn't in the repertory that season, but the Met brought together an exciting cast for a single performance, and without much rehearsal we had an extraordinary evening. Montserrat Caballé was my Mimi, and she astonished me when after my "Che gelida manina" she turned to me and joined the audience in applause. It may have been out of character, but she got the biggest laugh of the evening

Of course I will never forget March 15, 1977. That was when we did the famous first "Live From the Met" telecast, the one that launched opera on a new wave of popularity. Naturally, we were already nervous to be singing live on television. Then somebody told me I'd be singing in that one performance to more people than ever heard Caruso in his entire career. I wonder that I made out of my dressing room.

I've been lucky enough to work with many wonderful conductors in this opera, but my debut at La Scala with Karajan is an experience I will always treasure. Later I recorded *Bohème* with him - another wonderful time. I also sang in the opera with Carlos Kleiber at La Scala and in Vienna, and these were memorable nights for me.

I don't think I have to worry much about audiences ever getting tired of *Bohème*. It was a favorite for sixty-five years before I ever stepped on a stage, and I'm sure that a hundred years from now, all over the world, there will still be Rodolfos waiting for Mimis to come knocking on their doors. For as long as there will be opera, there will be *La Bohème*.

Mirella Freni and Luciano Pavarotti as Mimi and Rodolfo

the musician Schaunard (bar), who has managed to obtain firewood, food, and wine. Evading an attempt by the landlord Benoit (bs) to collect the rent, they set out for the Café Momus, leaving Rodolfo to finish an article. His neighbor Mimì (s), a seamstress, asks him to light her candle. Her coughing and pallor arouse his concern, her loveliness his interest; the two are soon in love. They join the others at the café, where Marcello's former sweetheart Musetta (s) stages an exhibition of pouting, singing, screaming, and other histrionics for his benefit. She gets rid of her aging admirer Alcindoro (bs) and is passionately reunited with Marcello. Both pairs of lovers have stormy relationships. Marcello and Musetta quarrel and separate; Rodolfo leaves Mimì rather than watch her tuberculosis worsen in their life of poverty. Just before she dies, Mimì returns to the garret to be with Rodolfo. She expresses her undying love for him and, after the lovers share reminiscences, she dies peacefully.

Bohemian Girl, The. Opera in 3 acts by Balfe; libretto by Alfred Bunn.

First perf., London, Drury Lane, Nov. 27, 1843: Romer, Betts, Harrison, Durnset, Borrani, Stretton. U.S. prem., N.Y., Park, Nov. 25, 1844.

A popular English opera, composed largely on Italian models, set in 19th-c. Hungary. Thaddeus (t), a noble Polish refugee, loves Arline (s), raised by a gypsy band. Accused of stealing, she is brought before Count Arnheim (bar), who recognizes her as his long-lost daughter. Despite the efforts of the vengeful Gypsy Queen (ms), Arline and Thaddeus are married.

Böhm, Karl. Conductor; b. Graz, Austria, Aug. 28, 1894; d. Salzburg, Aug. 14, 1981. While taking a law doctorate (1919) at Graz, he studied music in Vienna with Eusebius Mandyczewski and Guido Adler. After coaching in Graz, conducting there in Nessler's *Trompeter von Säckingen*, 1917. Brought by Walter to Munich (1921–27), he then held positions in Darmstadt (1927–31), Hamburg (1931–33), Dresden (1934–42), and Vienna (1943–45). His return to Vienna as music director after the theater's rebuilding in 1954 lasted only two years, and the remainder of his life was given to guest conducting, including appearances at Salzburg and Bayreuth. His Met debut was on Oct. 31, 1957, conducting *Don Giovanni*, and he returned frequently thereafter; in 16 seasons, he led 253 perfs. of German repertory (including the Met premieres of *Frau* and *Wozzeck*) and *Otello*. Noted for his economical technique and cool, understated style, he derived stylistic authority from his relationships with predecessors such as Muck and Walter, and especially with Strauss at Dresden, where Böhm conducted the premieres of *Schweigsame Frau* (1935) and *Daphne* (1938). His operatic and symphonic work is documented on recordings beginning in his Dresden years, including major operas of Mozart, Wagner, Strauss, and Berg.

Böhme, Kurt. Bass; b. Dresden, May 5, 1908. Studied with Kluge, Dresden Conservatory; debut as Caspar (*Freischütz*), Bautzen, 1929. Sang in Dresden, 1930–50, thereafter in Munich. Created Vanuzzi (*Schweigsame Frau*) in Dresden, Odysseus (Liebermann's *Penelope*) in Salzburg. Met debut as Pogner, Nov. 11, 1954; sang Wagner roles there for two seasons.

Bohnen, Michael. Bass-baritone; b. Cologne, Germany, May 2, 1887; d. Berlin, Apr. 26, 1965. Studied with Schulz-Dornburg, Cologne; after debut as Caspar

Karl Böhm

(*Freischütz*), Düsseldorf, 1910, sang in Wiesbaden. In 1914, debuts in Berlin (Gurnemanz), London (King Heinrich at Covent Garden, Ochs and Sarastro under Beecham at Drury Lane), and Bayreuth (Daland and Hunding). After war service, sang in Berlin and Vienna, also active in films (Ochs in 1925 silent *Rosenkavalier*) and operetta (*Casanova*, 1928). Met debut as Tourist/Francesco (*Mona Lisa*), Mar. 1, 1923; in 10 seasons, he sang 175 perfs. of 21 roles, including King Marke, Hagen, Wotan, Rocco, Kečal (*Bartered Bride*), Méphistophélès, and Krenek's Jonny. Sang with Städtische Oper, Berlin, 1933–45; became its administrator, 1945–47. Bohnen's potent, wide-ranging voice encompassed roles as diverse as Scarpia and Gurnemanz; his experiments with make-up and his sometimes undisciplined acting, inspired by his friend Chaliapin, were controversial.

Boieldieu, François-Adrien. Composer; b. Rouen, France, Dec. 16, 1775; d. Jarcy, Oct. 8, 1834. Studied with Charles Broche. A prolific and popular composer of opéras comiques, his first success was *La Fille Coupable* (1793). Between 1803 and 1811 he worked in St. Petersburg, then reconquered Paris with *Jean de Paris* (1812). During the 1820s, he responded to the challenge of Rossini's popularity with the Romantically atmospheric *La Dame Blanche* (1825), but was subsequently unable to match its international success.

Boito, Arrigo [Enrico]. Librettist, composer, and critic; b. Padua, Italy, Feb. 24, 1842; d. Milan, June 10, 1918. Son of a painter and a Polish countess, he studied composition (with Alberto Mazzucato) at Milan Conservatory (1853–61). On a year-long trip to Paris, Boito met Verdi and supplied the text for the cantata *Inno delle Nazioni*. Boito's interest in world literature, especially that dealing dramatically with problems of good and evil, led to the libretto (1862) of *Amleto* (Hamlet), for his school friend Franco Faccio, and the first sketches for operas about Faust and Nero. Back in Milan, he wrote poetry and music criticism characterized by idealism, wit, and sometimes belligerence, incurring Verdi's irritation. After serving briefly in Garibaldi's army in 1866, Boito completed the first version of his immensely long Faust opera, *Mefistofele*; its 1868 premiere at La Scala was a disaster. For a time Boito contented himself with writing librettos (notably Ponchielli's *Gioconda*) and making Italian translations of other operas. Eventually, a shortened and rewritten *Mefistofele* succeeded at Bologna (1875) and, eventually and gratifyingly, at La Scala (1881).

In 1870, Verdi had spurned the proposal (made through Giulio Ricordi) that he set Boito's libretto for *Nerone*. But after patient persuasion by Faccio and Ricordi, he agreed to have Boito revise the libretto of *Simon Boccanegra* for an 1881 Scala revival. Pleased with the results, Verdi forgot his past hostility and began work with Boito on *Otello*, which opened triumphantly in 1887. Their deep and satisfying working relationship continued with *Falstaff* in 1893. Though the subject of *Re Lear* was broached, the octogenarian Verdi begged off on grounds of age. The two remained friends, and Boito was with Verdi when he died in Milan in 1901. Encouraged by Verdi and Ricordi, Boito published the *Nerone* libretto in 1901 and attempted to finish the music; several times he offered the work for production and withdrew it, finally abandoning plans for a fifth act. The four-act *Nerone* was performed as a memorial at La Scala in 1924, in a version heavily edited by Toscanini and Vincenzo Tommasini.

An admirer of Wagner in the 1860s (less so later), Boito aspired to develop music drama along lofty lines, but his musical invention and technique were inadequate; between the striking and affecting moments are long stretches where spontaneous creation yields to intellectual effort. In Boito's librettos for *Otello* and *Falstaff*, he occasionally indulges his fondness for arcane vocabulary, but the tension and passion of the one, the wit and sentiment of the other, are among the most felicitous in all opera. Boito's services to Italian music extended beyond his own work, to generous encouragement of young composers such as Catalani and Puccini (although he disliked the subject of *Bohème*), wise counsel on the management of La Scala, and service on a national music education commission.

Bomarzo. Opera in 2 acts by Ginastera; libretto by Manuel Mujica Lainez, after his novel of the same name.
First perf., Washington, D.C., Opera Society, May 19, 1967: Penagos, Simon, Turner, Novoa, Torigi, c. Rudel.
A serial score anchored in formal structures derived from Renaissance music, set in 16th-c. Italy. The Duke of Bomarzo (t) drinks a potion (poisoned by a vengeful relative) to attain immortality, reviews the secret and sordid events of his life, and dies.

Bonci, Alessandro. Tenor; b. Cesena, near Rimini, Italy, Feb. 10, 1870; d. Viserba, near Rimini, Aug. 9, 1940. Studied with Pedrotti and Coen in Pesaro, delle Sedie in Paris; debut as Fenton, Parma, 1896. He appeared at La Scala in *Puritani* and *Sonnambula* (1897), and at Covent Garden as Rodolfo (1900). After singing widely in Europe, he opened the Manhattan Opera House, N.Y., in *Puritani*, 1906. Met debut as Duke of Mantua, Nov. 22, 1907; in 3 seasons, he sang 65 perfs. of 14 roles, including Rodolfo, Almaviva, Ottavio, Roberto (*Villi*), and Wilhelm Meister. After serving in the Italian Air Force, he appeared in Chicago (1919–21) and at the Costanzi, Rome (1922–23), then retired to teach in Milan. His singing was known for its elegance and agility in bel canto and lighter Verdi roles, but in N.Y. his old-fashioned fluttering timbre suffered from comparison with Caruso's more plangent tones.

Bonelli [Bunn], **Richard.** Baritone; b. Port Byron, N.Y., Feb. 6, 1887; d. Los Angeles, June 7, 1980. Studied at Syracuse U. and with Jean de Reszke in Paris; operatic debut as Valentin (*Faust*), Brooklyn Academy, N.Y., 1915. Sang in Europe, then with Chicago Opera, 1925–31. Met debut as Germont, Dec. 1, 1932; remained with the company until 1945, singing 103 perfs. of 19 roles, including Tonio, Sharpless, Wolfram, and Amonasro.

Boninsegna, Celestina. Soprano; b. Reggio Emilia, Italy, Feb. 26, 1877; d. Milan, Feb. 14, 1947. After appearing as Norina, Reggio Emilia, 1892, she studied with Virginia Boccabadati in Pesaro; second debut in *Faust*, Bari, 1897. Though she sang widely in major Verdi roles, her Met debut (Aida, Dec. 21, 1906) was followed by only three further appearances, including Santuzza; she had greater success in Boston (1909–10). Her recordings, revealing an imposing dramatic voice and temperament, have posthumously enhanced her reputation.

Bonisolli, Franco. Tenor; b. Rovereto, Italy, 1938. After private vocal study, won a Spoleto competition in 1961 and made his debut there as Ruggero (*Rondine*). U.S. debut as Alfredo, San Francisco, 1969. After his Met debut as Almaviva (Feb. 24, 1971), he also sang Nemorino, Faust, the Duke of Mantua, and Alfredo, returning as Cavaradossi in 1986. Appearances in many European theaters.

Bononcini, Giovanni. Composer; b. Modena, Italy, July 18, 1670; d. Vienna, July 9, 1747. Studied with his father, Giovanni Maria, and with G.P. Colonna. Active in Rome (1692–97), Vienna (1697–1713), and again at Rome (1714–19), his many operas in the seria genre were widely performed throughout Europe. Invited to London in 1720 as composer for the Royal Academy of Music, whose director was Handel, his *Crispo* (1722) and *Griselda* (1722) were performed with success, but political intrigue soon compromised his position. Bononcini then became the Duchess of Marlborough's private music director until 1732, when he left for Paris. His final years were spent in Vienna.

Bonynge, Richard. Conductor; b. Sydney, Australia, Sep. 29, 1930. Following study at Sydney Conservatory with Melba's accompanist Lindley Evans and in London, he became interested in bel canto vocal technique and style, working with Joan Sutherland as coach and advisor; they were married in 1954. Beginning with a Vancouver *Faust* in March 1963, he has conducted virtually all her performances. Covent Garden debut, *Puritani*, 1964. Met debut, Dec. 12, 1966, *Lucia*; has led many bel canto works there, also *Don Giovanni*, *Esclarmonde*, *Orfeo*, and *Werther*. He served as music director of the Australian Opera (1976–84); director, Vancouver Opera (1974–77). A knowledgeable student of Italian and French repertories and performance traditions, Bonynge has been instrumental in reviving and recording much operatic and ballet literature.

Boozer, Brenda. Mezzo-soprano; b. Atlanta, Ga. Studied at Fla. State U., Ga. Wesleyan, Juilliard, N.Y., and with Elena Nikolaidi; debut as Cherubino, Eastern Opera Theater, N.Y. Met debut as Hänsel, Dec. 25, 1979; other Met roles include Meg Page, the Composer, Octavian, and Orlovsky. Has also sung with Netherlands Opera (Octavian, 1980), Los Angeles Opera (Meg Page, 1982), Paris Opéra (1982).

Bordoni, Faustina. Mezzo-soprano; b. Venice, 1700; d. Venice, Nov. 4, 1781. Studied with M. Gasparini; debut in Pollarolo's *Ariodante*, Venice, 1716. She sang there until 1725, also appearing in other Italian cities, in Germany from 1723, and in Vienna from 1725. Her notable London career (debut in Handel's *Alessandro*, 1726) was marked by a lively rivalry with Cuzzoni. In 1730 she married composer Johann Adolf Hasse (1699–1783), and sang in Dresden until her farewell in 1751. Famous for her agile technique and handsome presence.

Borg, Kim. Bass; b. Helsinki, Aug. 7, 1919. Studied at Sibelius Academy, Helsinki; operatic debut, Aarhus, 1951. At Glyndebourne, sang Don Giovanni (1956) and Gremin (1968). Met debut as Mozart's Almaviva, Oct. 30, 1959; in 3 seasons, sang 36 perfs., also including Rangoni (*Boris*) and Pizarro (*Fidelio*).

Borgatti, Giuseppe. Tenor; b. Cento, Italy, Mar. 17, 1871; d. Reno, Lago Maggiore, Oct. 18, 1950. Studied with Alessandro Busi, Bologna; debut as Faust, Castelfranco Veneto, 1892. Created Andrea Chénier, La Scala, 1896. Sang Italian roles for next ten years, then became Italy's finest heldentenor, singing Siegfried and Tristan under Toscanini at La Scala. Increasing blindness forced retirement from the stage in 1914, but he sang in concert until 1928.

Borgioli, Dino. Tenor; b. Florence, Feb. 15, 1891; d. Florence, Sep. 12 or 13, 1960. Studied with Eugenio Giachetti, Florence; debut as Arturo (*Puritani*), Corso, Milan, 1914. Debuts at La Scala (Ernesto in *Don Pasquale*, 1918), Covent Garden (Edgardo, 1925), San Francisco (Cavaradossi, 1932), Chicago (Cavaradossi, 1933), and Glyndebourne (Ottavio, 1937). Met debut as Rodolfo, Dec. 31, 1934; appeared there that season only, also as Ottavio and Massenet's Des Grieux.

Bori, Lucrezia. [Lucrecia Borja y Gonzalez de Riancho]. Soprano; b. Valencia, Spain, Dec. 4, 1887; d. New York, May 14, 1960. Studied at Valencia Conservatory and with Melchiorre Vidal in Milan; debut as Micaela, Adriano, Rome, 1908. Engaged the following season at La Scala, she sang Octavian in local premiere of *Rosenkavalier*, 1911. Invited to replace an indisposed colleague as Puccini's

Lucrezia Bori as Giulietta in *Les Contes d'Hoffmann*

Manon with the visiting Met company at the Châtelet, Paris, 1910, she then made her N.Y. Met debut in the same role, Nov. 11, 1912. After a throat operation interrupted her career in 1915, she returned to the stage at Monte Carlo, 1919, and to the Met in 1921, appearing every season until her gala farewell, March 29, 1936. In 19 seasons, she sang 448 perfs. of 28 roles, notably Mimi, Violetta, Massenet's Manon, Juliette, Norina, and Fiora (*Amore dei Tre Re*); she was also the Met's first Antonia (*Hoffmann*), Lucinda (*Amore Medico*), Ah-Yoe (*Oracolo*), Snow Maiden, Despina, Mélisande, Concepcion (*Heure Espagnole*), Salud (*Vida Breve*), Magda (*Rondine*), and Mary (*Peter Ibbetson*).

Bori's clear, true voice, delicate rather than large, was capable of expressing passion as well as vulnerability and whimsical charm. During the Met's financial difficulties of the 1930s, she was active in public appeals for donations, and in 1935 was elected a director of the Metropolitan Opera Association, both the first woman and the first active artist to be so honored; she remained in this post for 25 years, until her death. She was also the first honorary chairman of the Metropolitan Opera Guild (1936–43, 1948–60; chairman, 1943–48).

Boris Godunov. Opera in prologue and 4 acts by Mussorgsky; libretto by the composer, after Pushkin's historical tragedy of the same name and Karamzin's *History of the Russian State*.

First perf., St. Petersburg, Maryinsky, Feb. 8, 1874. U.S. & Met prem., Mar. 19, 1913 (ed. Rimsky-Korsakov, in Ital.): Didur, Homer, Althouse, Bada, Rothier, de Segurola, c. Toscanini, d. Golovin, p. Speck. Later Met productions: Mar. 6, 1953 (orch. Rathaus, in Eng.): London, Thebom, Sullivan, McKinley, Hines, Baccaloni, c. Stiedry, d. (revised) Dobujinsky, p. Yannopoulos; Dec. 16, 1974 (original scoring, in Russ.): Talvela, Dunn, Theyard, Nagy, Plishka, Gramm, c. Schippers, d. Lee/P.J. Hall, p. Everding. Other noted Met Borises include Chaliapin, Pinza, Kipnis, Siepi, Hines. 180 performances in 33 seasons.

Mussorgsky's remarkable combination of historical pageant and psychological study, first completed in 1869, was revised by the composer before its (much-abridged) first performance. His colleague Rimsky-Korsakov made a new edition in 1896 (and revised it in 1908), "improving" what he considered Mussorgsky's technical weaknesses; this remained the standard performing text until recently. The orchestration of Rathaus and Shostakovich (used in Met revivals, 1960–63) are based on Mussorgsky's 1874 score.

Russia and Poland, 1598–1605. Goaded by police, the populace entreats Boris Godunov (bs) to accept the vacant throne. After his coronation, he feels pangs of guilt. In the Chudov Monastery, the monk Pimen (bs) tells the novice Grigori (t) how Boris murdered the infant Tsarevich Dimitri to clear his way to the throne. Resolving to avenge Dimitri, Grigori runs away from the monastery and joins the vagrant monks Varlaam (bs) and Missail (t); at an inn near the border, he evades the police and escapes to Lithuania. When Boris' counsellor Prince Shuisky (t) craftily excites the Tsar's guilty conscience with reports of a Pretender, Boris makes him swear that the murdered child was really Dimitri. Alone, Boris is alarmed by a chiming clock and assailed by hallucinations of the murdered child. In Poland, Grigori, declaring himself the Tsarevich Dimitri, is raising support. Urged on by the Jesuit Rangoni (bar), who hopes to convert Russia to the Roman faith, the Polish princess Marina Mnishek (ms), desirous of becoming Tsarina, plays on Dimitri's passion for her. In Moscow, the haunted Boris receives Pimen, whose tale of a miracle at the murdered Dimitri's tomb induces a seizure in the Tsar. Presenting his son Feodor (ms) as his successor, Boris dies imploring God's forgiveness. In the Kromy Forest, an unruly mob taunts one of Boris' boyars. Some boys harass a Holy Fool (t). Varlaam and Missail stir up the mob in favor of the Pretender. Arriving with his troops, the Pretender invites everyone to join him on the march to Moscow. The Holy Fool, alone, sings sadly of Russia's fate.

(Mussorgsky's original 1869 version did not include the scenes in Poland or the Kromy Forest; the death of Boris was preceded by a scene outside the Cathedral of St. Basil in Moscow, including the episode of the boys and the Holy Fool, who urges Boris to murder them as he did the infant Tsarevich. The remorseful Boris asks the man to pray for him, but is refused. This scene is often included in performances of the 1874 version.)

Borkh, Inge. Soprano; b. Mannheim, Germany, May 26, 1921. Studied acting in Vienna, singing with Muratti in Milan and at Salzburg Mozarteum; operatic debut as Czipra (*Zigeunerbaron*), Lucerne, 1940. Sang with Swiss companies until 1952; first major success as Magda Sorel in the German-language premiere of *Consul*, Basel, 1951. Sang in Munich, Vienna, Berlin, and Stuttgart. Debuts, San Francisco (Elektra, 1953), Chicago (Salome, 1956), and the Met (Salome, Jan. 24, 1958), where she also sang Elektra in 1961.

Borodin, Alexander. Composer; b. St Petersburg, Nov. 12, 1833; d. St Petersburg, Feb. 27, 1887. Illegitimate son of a prince and a wealthy young woman, Borodin early displayed gifts for chemistry and music. Without formal training in composition, he learned from the music he played and heard (especially on trips to Western Europe), and from the counsel of the ardent nationalist Balakirev, who in 1862 encouraged him to compose symphonies. Throughout his life, Borodin's musical activities had to compete with his rigorous professional schedule in medicine and chemistry, resulting in a small compositional output and many incomplete scores. His music, which often exploits a contrast of Russian and oriental idioms, is most convincing in epic and lyrical modes.

His first stage work was the pastiche *The Bogatyrs* (1867), partly adapted from composers such as Rossini and Meyerbeer. Of *The Tsar's Bride* (1868), only sketches survive. For the abandoned collaborative opéra-ballet *Mlada*, Borodin composed one act, part of it arranged and orchestrated after his death by Rimsky-Korsakov. Other parts went into the Russian historical epic *Prince Igor* (1890), at which Borodin worked sporadically during the last 18 years of his life. Still unfinished when he died at age 54 of cardiac arrest brought on by the strains of his dual career, *Igor* was completed by Rimsky-Korsakov and Glazunov.

Boston. City in Massachusetts. Though an important musical center from its foundation in 1630, Boston's Puritan heritage long restricted operatic activity; a 1750 decree against stage performances lasted until a 1794 production of Shield's ballad opera *The Farmer*. Later, Boston was visited by touring groups under the likes of Mapleson and Grau. The first resident troupe, the Boston Opera Company, established in 1908 by Henry Russell, gave 516 performances of 51 operas at the Boston Opera

Boris Godunov – (1974). Designed by Ming Cho Lee, produced by August Everding. Paul Offenkrantz, Martti Talvela, Betsy Norden, and Lenus Carlson

House (opened 1909) with international stars, flourishing until a 1914 Paris tour brought financial disaster. Later restructured as the Boston Grand Opera, it toured until 1917. The Chicago Opera visited annually, 1917–32, and the Met, 1934–86. In 1946, Boris Goldovsky founded the New England Opera Theater, earning a distinguished reputation with stagings of Gluck and Mozart operas and the U.S. premiere of *Troyens* (1955). Founded by conductor and producer Sarah Caldwell, the Opera Company of Boston (established 1958 as Opera Group, present name from 1965), has offered adventurous repertory and imaginative productions in a variety of auditoriums, including the Orpheum Theater, an old vaudeville house and cinema (the Boston Opera House was torn down in 1958); among its U.S. premieres are Nono's *Intolleranza* (1966), *Moses und Aron* (1968), *Montezuma* (1976), and *Taverner* (1986).

Boucher, Gene. Baritone; b. Tagbilaran, Bohol, Philippine Islands, Dec. 6, 1933. After private study in Jefferson City, Mo., and a musical degree at Lille (1956), won Met audition in 1958 and sang with Met Opera Studio (1962–65). Between Met debut on Sep. 28, 1965 as Master of Ceremonies (*Queen of Spades*) and retirement in 1984, he sang over 50 comprimario roles.

bouffe (Fr.). Comic, humorous.

Boughton, Rutland. Composer; b. Aylesbury, England, Jan. 23, 1878; d. London, Jan. 24, 1960. Self-taught musically, influenced by the Socialist movement and Wagner's theories, he conceived a festival to be held at Glastonbury, legendary site of Avalon, devoted to music drama after the Wagnerian model but with an English bias. Initiated in 1914, the project continued through 1927, with performances of little-known works by Purcell, Blow, and Gluck, and premieres of his own operas *The Immortal Hour* (1914), *The Round Table* (1916), *The Birth of Arthur* (1920), and *The Queen of Cornwall* (1926). His music is more traditional than Wagnerian, owing much to British folksong.

53

Boulevard Solitude. Opera in 7 scenes by Henze; libretto by the composer and Grete Weil, after the play by Walter Jockische, based on the Abbé Prévost's novel.

First perf., Hanover, Landestheater, Feb. 17, 1952: Clause, Zilliken, Buckow, c. Schüler. U.S. prem., Santa Fe, Aug. 2, 1967 (in Eng.): Brooks, Driscoll, Fortune, c. Baustian.

A modern setting of the Manon story, in which her lover Armand (t) becomes a drug addict and Manon (s) is imprisoned after her brother shoots her former protector Lilaque (t).

Boulez, Pierre. Composer and conductor; b. Montbrison, France, Mar. 26, 1925. Studied at Paris Conservatory with Messiaen (1942–45) and with René Leibowitz. At first active principally as a composer (notable works include *Le Marteau sans Maître* and *Pli selon Pli*), he increasingly involved himself in conducting 20th-c. music, including the Paris premiere of *Wozzeck* (1963). At Wieland Wagner's invitation, he came to conduct *Parsifal* (1966) at Bayreuth, where he later conducted the controversial centennial production of the *Ring* (1976). Also conducted opera at Covent Garden (*Pelléas*, 1969), and led first production of complete *Lulu*, Paris Opéra, 1979. Principal conductor, BBC Symphony (1971–74); music director, N.Y. Philharmonic (1971–78). A clear, cool, almost clinically precise musician, Boulez produces performances that are untraditional, finely measured, and sometimes more compelling intellectually than emotionally. His style is apparent in recordings of the above-named operas.

box. An enclosed subdivision of a balcony in an opera house, usually with a connecting anteroom. In many houses (including the Metropolitan Opera House before 1940), the owners of the theater retained the use of their boxes for all performances, while the impresario took the proceeds from the sale of the other seats.

Bradley, Gwendolyn. Soprano; b. New York, Dec. 12, 1952. Studied at N.C. School of the Arts, Curtis Institute, and Philadelphia Academy of Vocal Arts; debut as Nannetta (*Falstaff*), Lake George Opera, N.Y., 1976. Met debut as Nightingale (*Enfant*), Feb. 20, 1981; other roles there include Stravinsky's Nightingale, Olympia (*Hoffmann*), Blondchen, and Gilda. Has also appeared in Cleveland, Philadelphia, Central City, and Glyndebourne.

Brandt, Marianne [Marie Bischoff]. Mezzo-soprano; b. Vienna, Sep. 12, 1842; d. Vienna, July 9, 1921. Studied with Frau Marschner, Vienna, and in 1869 with Pauline Viardot-Garcia, Baden-Baden; debut as Rachel (*Juive*), Olmütz, 1867. Berlin Opera debut as Azucena, 1868; she remained with this company until 1882. Covent Garden debut as Fidelio, 1872; at Bayreuth, she created Waltraute in *Götterdämmerung* (1876) and Kundry (1882). Met debut as Fidelio, Nov. 19, 1884; in 4 seasons, she sang 160 perfs. of 18 roles, including Fidès (*Prophète*), Donna Elvira, Siebel, Adriano (*Rienzi*), and Eglantine (*Euryanthe*). Best known for Wagner roles, especially Brangäne, which she sang in *Tristan*'s Berlin, London, and N.Y. premieres. Taught in Vienna after her 1890 retirement from opera. Brandt's voice ranged from G below middle C to D above high C; her few recordings, made as late as 1905, confirm her vocal power and dramatic authority.

Branzell, Karin. Contralto; b. Stockholm, Sep. 24, 1891; d. Altadena, Calif., Dec. 14, 1974. Studied with Thekla Hofer in Stockholm, later with Louis Bachner in Berlin, Rosati in N.Y.; debut as Prince Sarvilaka in d'Albert's *Izeyl*, Stockholm, 1912. After six years in Stockholm, she joined the Berlin State Opera (1918–23). Met debut as Fricka (*Walküre*), Feb. 6, 1924; in 22 seasons (until 1942, and 1950–51), she sang 309 perfs. of 19 roles, including Wagner mezzo parts, Herodias, Amneris, Dalila, even the *Walküre* Brünnhilde. Appeared at Bayreuth (1930–31), Covent Garden (1935, 1937–38), and San Francisco (1941). After retirement, taught at Juilliard, N.Y.; her pupils included Dunn, Rankin, and Madeira. Branzell's smooth, wide-ranging voice and stately presence dominated the Wagnerian repertory until eclipsed by the more dynamic Thorborg.

bravo (Ital.). An interjection indicating approval. The feminine form is "brava," the plural "bravi" (or, if exclusively feminine in reference, "brave"); the superlatives are "bravissimo," etc.

bravura (Ital., "bravery, dash, skill"). An aria di bravura is full of difficult runs and passagework, to show off a singer's brilliance.

break. In a singer's vocal range, the point of shift between chest register and head register. In the most technically accomplished singers, the notes on either side of the break are carefully adjusted to minimize the audible tonal difference.

Brecht, Bertolt [Berthold]. Librettist; b. Augsburg, Germany, Feb. 10, 1898; d. Berlin, Aug. 14, 1956. An aggressively didactic, political playwright, who collaborated with Kurt Weill on *Dreigroschenoper*, *Happy End*, *Mahagonny* (all with substantial contributions from his assistant Elisabeth Hauptmann), and *Jasager*. His 1947 radio play *The Trial of Lucullus* was used as a libretto by Sessions and Paul Dessau.

Breil, Joseph. Composer; b. Pittsburgh, Pa., June 29, 1870; d. Los Angeles, Jan. 23, 1926. Vocal studies in Milan and Leipzig led to a brief career as provincial singer. Composed several short comic operas, as well as incidental orchestral pastiches that were used to accompany showings of D.W. Griffith's films *The Birth of a Nation* (1915) and *Intolerance* (1916). His one-act opera *The Legend* (1919) was unsuccessfully produced at the Met.

Bréval, Lucienne [Berthe-Agnès-Lisette Schilling]. Soprano; b. Männedorf, Switzerland, Nov. 4, 1869; d. Neuilly-sur-Seine, Aug. 15, 1935. Studied in Geneva and at Paris Conservatory. Debut as Sélika (*Africaine*), 1892, Paris Opéra, where she sang until 1919, creating Massenet's Grisélidis and Bloch's Lady Macbeth, as well as Fauré's Pénélope at Monte Carlo. At the Met (debut, Chimène in *Cid*, Jan. 16, 1901), in 2 seasons she also sang Sélika, Valentine (*Huguenots*), Reyer's Salammbô, and the *Siegfried* Brünnhilde.

Brice, Carol. Contralto; b. Sedalia, N.C., Apr. 16, 1918; d. Norman, Okla., Feb. 15, 1985. Studied with Francis Rogers at Juilliard School; first black artist to win Naumburg Award, 1943. Appeared in concert, recital, and Broadway musicals. At N.Y.C. Opera (debut, Addie in *Regina*, 1958), she also sang Maria (*Porgy*) and created the Contralto in Jerome Moross' *Gentlemen, Be Seated!* (1963).

Benjamin Britten

Brilioth, Helge. Tenor; b. Växjö, Sweden, May 7, 1931. Studied initially as baritone in Stockholm, at Santa Cecilia, Rome, and Salzburg Mozarteum; debut as baritone, Bartolo (Paisiello's *Barbiere*), Stockholm, 1958. After singing at Bielefeld (1962–64), returned to Stockholm for further study; tenor debut there as Don José, 1965. Later specialized in Wagnerian roles, including Siegmund (Bayreuth, 1969) and Siegfried in *Götterdämmerung* (Salzburg Easter Festival, 1970). Met debut as Parsifal, Nov. 14, 1970.

brindisi (Ital.). A drinking song.

Bristow, George. Composer; b. Brooklyn, N.Y., Dec. 19, 1825; d. New York, Dec. 13, 1898. Studied first with his father, then with Tinn (harmony) and Ole Bull (violin). Early professional activity included playing violin (in the N.Y. Philharmonic), organ, and piano, and conducting the Mendelssohn Society. A teacher in the N.Y.C. public schools, he was a strong advocate of American music and one of the first Americans to compose on native subjects, if in a basically European idiom: the opera *Rip Van Winkle* (1855) and the cantata *The Great Republic* (1872).

Britten, Benjamin. Composer; b. Lowestoft, Suffolk, England, Nov. 22, 1913; d. Aldeburgh, Dec. 4, 1976. He studied with his mother, a singer, and composed at the piano from age five. At 11, he began private study with Frank Bridge; at the Royal College of Music (from 1930), he studied piano with Harold Samuel and Arthur Benjamin, composition with John Ireland. Work in a documentary film unit, beginning in 1935, gave him experience in composing colorful music to fit the medium and the available instruments, a talent he would put to use throughout his career; a co-worker was the poet Auden, who supplied him texts, including Britten's first opera, *Paul Bunyan* (1941, withdrawn; rev. 1976). A pacifist, Britten went to the U.S. at the beginning of the war (1939–42), but returned to complete *Peter Grimes*, the premiere of which (June 7, 1945) also marked the return of the Sadler's Wells Opera to its reopened theater, and the emergence of the English musical stage's greatest exponent since Purcell.

Thereafter, opera was never far from Britten's mind. Realistically trimming his ambitions for full-scale production in England, he composed the chamber operas *The Rape of Lucretia* (1946) and *Albert Herring* (1947), accompanied by a 12-piece ensemble with piano. The English Opera Group, formed to perform these works at Glyndebourne, became the core of the first Aldeburgh Festival (1948). Though Aldeburgh had no large opera stage until the opening of the Maltings in 1967, the chamber version of *A Midsummer Night's Dream* was first heard there under the composer's baton in 1960. Britten's last opera, *Death in Venice* (1973), had its premiere at the Maltings.

Commissions account for the rest of Britten's operas, a very diverse group: for Covent Garden, both the claustrophobic *Billy Budd* (1951), with its all-male cast aboard a man-of-war, and *Gloriana* (1953), a large-scale study of Queen Elizabeth I, presented in honor of the coronation of Elizabeth II. *The Turn of the Screw* (1954), for the Venice Biennale, explores psychology and the supernatural through an intricate theme-and-variations scheme combining tonal and 12-tone elements. *Owen Wingrave* (1971), written for BBC television, makes ingenious use of video editing techniques, but has also been successfully staged. Other operatic compositions include the children's works *Let's Make an Opera* (1949, incorporating the one-act *The Little Sweep*) and *Noye's Fludde* (1957, after a Chester miracle play); a recomposition of Gay's *The Beggar's Opera* (1948); a realization of Purcell's *Dido and Aeneas* (1951); and the three "church parables" influenced by Japanese Noh drama, *Curlew River* (1964), *The Burning Fiery Furnace* (1966), and *The Prodigal Son* (1968).

Britten's musical imagination and intimate knowledge of the practicalities of theatrical performance were mutually stimulating; many of the operas were conceived for specific performers. The subjects that elicited his most vivid concern were the corruption of innocence and the plight of the misunderstood outsider (reflecting his own position as a homosexual in society), and his works almost invariably couple strong dramatic situations with ingenious structural conceptions.

BIBLIOGRAPHY: Eric Walter White, *Benjamin Britten: his Life and Operas* (London, 1970).

Brook, Peter. Producer; b. London, Mar. 21, 1925. Directed in Birmingham, Stratford, and London; director of productions, Covent Garden (1947–50). For Met, staged *Faust* (1953) and *Eugene Onegin* (1957); on Broadway, *The Visit* (1958) and *Marat/Sade* (1965). With Royal Shakespeare Company (from 1962); founded International Theatre Research Centre, Paris (1968). His controversial adaptation of Bizet's *Carmen* was seen in Paris (1981) and N.Y. (1983).

Brooks, Patricia. Soprano; b. New York, Nov. 7, 1937. Attended Manhattan School, N.Y., studied dance with Martha Graham, and appeared as an actress before deciding on a singing career. At N.Y.C. Opera (debut, Marianne in *Rosenkavalier*, 1960), she sang until 1977, with notable success in Corsaro's production of *Traviata*, also as Sophie, Gilda, and Mélisande; she created Abigail Williams in Ward's *Crucible*. Covent Garden debut as Queen (*Golden Cockerel*), 1969. Sang Lulu in Santa Fe and Houston, 1974; also appeared in Chicago, Toronto, and San Francisco.

BROADCASTING
Peter Allen

For a remarkable forty-four years, one name above all was identified with the broadcasting of opera in America: that of the original host of the Met broadcasts, Milton Cross. In a now sadly forgotten custom of the early days of radio, he repeatedly won the annual national award for clarity of speech. He was famous for the way he told the stories of the operas on the air and in his books. And he was famous for his ability to fill in during unexpected stage waits. Once, early in his career, he had to fill, with little warning, when the curtain was delayed for thirty-five minutes. From then on, he said, he came prepared, and when Giovanni Martinelli fell ill during an *Aida* broadcast, he had "six closely typewritten pages" ready. But a network studio ensemble filled the time instead, and he was mad for two weeks. We no longer "return to our studios" during emergencies, and during my first year as Cross' successor, another tenor, Carlo Bergonzi, fell ill at curtain time for a *Tosca* broadcast – but he triumphantly went on, after I had filled in for only six minutes.

When there is a need for extra talk, I feel as Milton Cross did: first priority goes to describing the scenery and costumes for the radio audience. Once there was a delay of a minute or two before the second act of *Rosenkavalier*, and, thinking of the faraway millions who had never seen the Met's splendid production, I was happy to describe the magnificent setting for the presentation of the silver rose. But the first comment I had was from a New Yorker, who had seen the production more than once, and relished having his memory of it refreshed.

The first broadcast from the Met came on December 11, 1910: it was *Cav* and *Pag*, with Destinn as Santuzza and Caruso as Canio, transmitted to the up-to-date few who had earphones. The novelty was greeted rather favorably, but nothing more was aired from the Met for twenty-one years.

Then, in the midst of the Depression, NBC offered the hard-pressed company the welcome sum of $5,000 per broadcast. The series that continues today began on Christmas Day, 1931, with Milton Cross as host, joined by Deems Taylor, who greeted an international audience in several languages, and then described the action of *Hänsel und Gretel* – over orchestral music. That feature was quickly dropped, but the broadcast was a great success and was followed by twenty-three others that first season.

Two years later, Lucky Strike became the first sponsor, followed by Listerine in 1934 and RCA in 1936. But, by 1940, after three sponsorless years, "extinction" of the broadcasts was imminent. In a last-minute rescue, the Texas Company launched the unparalleled continuing sponsorship that has proved vitally important, not only to the broadcasts, but to the Met itself. That is no exaggeration, for beyond the more than ninety million dollars Texaco has paid to date for radio and television, the broadcasts themselves have developed a nationwide audience, and that audience has contributed many additional millions of dollars to the Met.

Fund-raising for the Met (and for the nation, via War Bonds, during World War II) was accomplished largely through the popular intermission features, which were prepared, beginning in 1940, by Henry Souvaine, and later by his widow, the redoubtable Geraldine Souvaine. (She once told Rudolf Bing, "You run the Met, I run the broadcasts!") The Souvaines developed the basic intermission features – a discussion of the day's opera, background pieces, occasional singer interviews or round tables, and the Opera Quiz, which to date has drawn an estimated quarter of a million

questions from listeners. Since 1958, Edward Downes has been the quizmaster – erudite and exact, but generous with the few errors of guest experts. Outstanding intermission speakers have included Boris Goldovsky, Francis Robinson, John Culshaw, and Richard Mohr, who in 1980 also took over producing the intermissions. Special features in French are broadcast in French Canada.

Geraldine Souvaine once defined the purpose of the radio broadcasts as being "to stimulate interest in and enjoyment of opera." Interest and enjoyment have in fact been stimulated beyond any possible dream of the early broadcasters: American opera professionals have repeatedly told how important an influence the Met broadcasts have been to the remarkable growth of American opera companies. A little-realized factor behind that fertile success has been the guideline for sponsors consistently followed by Texaco, and aptly expressed by its former chairman and chief executive officer, John K. McKinley: "There is no such thing as artistic freedom if there is not economic freedom."

Although Texaco has been the sole sponsor since 1940, there have been changes in the network itself. NBC was succeeded by ABC in 1943 and by CBS in 1958. The special Texaco-Met network was set up in 1960 by G. H. Johnston. In 1980, with satellite relays gradually replacing or supplementing telephone lines, the Met's own media department took charge of the network, now more than 300 stations strong, with an audience that has reached as high as ten million.

The audience for the first telecast from the Met – the opening-night *Otello* of 1948 – was limited to New York City. But, despite some advances and occasional attempts like the Bing farewell gala in 1972, technical problems prevented satisfactory pictures until 1977, when Texaco presented "Live From the Met" on PBS with a celebrated *Bohème*. Telecasts since have ranged from familiar works like *Aida* to rarities like *Mahagonny*, and include the historic two-part Centennial Gala, which offered an unprecedented cornucopia of talent to an international audience, via the most extensive use of satellite transmission to date.

From the beginning, radio was proud to bring what had been the exclusive pleasure of the wealthy into millions of living rooms and even to coal miners underground in Canada. Today, cherished Met performances of past and present are available on videotape and laserdisc, and memorable broadcasts of the past, lovingly preserved in the deluxe Soria Series recordings, have helped raise still more millions of dollars for the Met. For opera lovers of the past, present, and future, Texaco and the Met take well-earned pride in the achievements of these broadcasts.

(*Above*) Milton Cross with Gladys Swarthout and Lawrence Tibbett.
(*Middle*) Teresa Stratas and José Carreras in the telecast of *La Bohème*.
(*Bottom*) Peter Allen

Brouwenstijn, Gré. Soprano; b. Den Helder, Holland, Aug. 26, 1915. Studied with Stroomenberg, Pelsky, and Horna, Amsterdam Music Lyceum; debut as a Lady (*Zauberflöte*), Amsterdam, 1940. Joined Netherlands Opera, 1946. Covent Garden debut as Aida, 1951; she sang Verdi roles there until 1964, including Elisabeth in Visconti *Don Carlos*, 1958. At Bayreuth, sang Elisabeth, Gutrune, Sieglinde, and Eva (1954–56); also appeared in Chicago (debut, Jenůfa, 1959) and Glyndebourne (debut, Fidelio, 1959).

Brownlee, John. Baritone; b. Geelong, Australia, Jan. 7, 1901; d. New York, Jan. 10, 1963. Encouraged by Melba, he studied with Dinh Gilly, Paris; debut as Nilakantha (*Lakmé*), Lyrique, Paris, 1926. London debut at Melba's farewell, Covent Garden, 1926; subsequently sang Mercutio, Golaud, Amonasro, Iago, and Scarpia there, and Alfonso (*Così*) and Don Giovanni at Glyndebourne (1935–39). At Paris Opéra (1927–36), sang Athanaël (*Thaïs*), Tell, Jochanaan, and lighter Wagner roles; Opéra-Comique debut as Scarpia, 1934. Met debut as Rigoletto, Feb. 17, 1937; in 21 seasons, sang 348 perfs. of 33 roles, including Papageno, Almaviva, Don Giovanni, Alfonso, Falke (*Fledermaus*), and Marcello. Also sang in Buenos Aires (1931), Chicago (1937–38, 1945), San Francisco (1940–50), and returned to Covent Garden (1949–50). President of American Guild of Musical Artists (1953–67); director (1956) and president (1966) of Manhattan School of Music. Brownlee's distinction of style made up for his somewhat dry tone, and in his later Met career he moved gracefully towards character roles.

Brüll, Ignaz. Composer and pianist; b. Prossnitz [now Prostějov], Moravia, Nov. 7, 1846; d. Vienna, Sep. 17, 1907. Studied in Vienna with Otto Dessoff. His first opera was *Die Bettler von Samarkand* (1864); his greatest success, *Das goldene Kreuz* (Berlin, 1875). A close friend of Brahms, after years of concert tours he taught piano at the Horsk School in Vienna, 1872–78.

Bruneau, Alfred. Composer; b. Paris, Mar. 3, 1857; d. Paris, June 15, 1934. Studied composition at Paris Conservatory with Massenet. Impressed by the naturalistic novels of Zola, on which he based his early operatic successes *Le Rêve* (1891) and *L'Attaque du Moulin* (1893). Zola himself wrote the text for *Messidor* (1897), *L'Ouragan* (1901), and *L'Enfant Roi* (1905), which contrast a harshly dissonant portrait of industrial society with a gentle lyricism depicting the simplicity of nature. Throughout his life, Bruneau was active as a music critic, and published several books on French music.

Bruscantini, Sesto. Bass-baritone; b. Porto Civitanova, Macerata, Italy, Dec. 10, 1919. Studied in Rome with Luigi Ricci; debut as Colline, Civitanova, 1946. La Scala debut, Geronimo (*Matrimonio Segreto*), 1949; in Rome, sang Selim in *Turco in Italia* with Callas, 1950; Mozart and Rossini at Glyndebourne, 1951–56. In Chicago (debut, Rossini's Figaro, 1961), he ventured into dramatic Verdi roles, but is best known for buffo parts such as Don Pasquale, which he continued to sing into the 1980s.

Bruson, Renato. Baritone; b. Este, Italy, Jan. 13, 1936. Studied at Padua Conservatory; debut as di Luna, Spoleto, 1961. La Scala debut in *Linda di Chamounix*, 1972. Met debut as Enrico (*Lucia*), Feb. 1, 1969, returning in the '80s; roles include di Luna, Germont, Don Carlo (*Forza*), and Posa. Specializes in Verdi and Donizetti repertory, including revivals of the latter's *Belisario* and *Gemma di Vergy*.

Buenos Aires. Capital of Argentina, and the major operatic center of South America. The city's first complete opera performance, Rossini's *Barbiere* at the Coliseo Provisional, took place in 1825. The growing population of Latin, and later German, immigrants stimulated visits by touring companies. The first Teatro Colón, opened Apr. 25, 1857, with *Traviata*, presented important Italian singers, including Patti and Tamagno. After its demolition in 1888, operatic activity centered on the Teatro de la Opera (opened 1872), which attracted notable performers, including Toscanini. The Coliseo, renamed the Teatro Argentina, was destroyed in 1872 and reopened in 1907; there, Mascagni conducted the premiere of his *Isabeau* in 1911.

The effort to make Buenos Aires an international city led to the construction of a world-class opera theater: the sumptuous new Colón (seating 2,486 plus 1,000 standing), with excellent acoustics and stage facilities, opened May 25, 1908, with *Aida*; that season, Panizza's *Aurora* was selected for performance in the first of a series of annual contests for new Argentinian works. Since its seasons coincided with the northern hemisphere's summer, the Colón was long able to attract the finest singers and conductors from both Italian and German theaters, though the growth of European summer festivals since World War II has gradually increased the competition; among those who appeared there in the past were Chaliapin and Callas, Richard Strauss and Saint-Saëns, Beecham and Weingartner. Under municipal administration since 1935, the theater's recent fortunes have reflected Argentina's volatile political climate; Carlos Montero is currently artistic director.

buffo, buffa (Ital.). Comic, humorous.

Bühne (Ger.). Stage.

Bühnenfestspiel (Ger.). Stage festival play; Wagner's term for his *Ring* cycle.

Bühnenweihfestspiel (Ger.). Stage dedication festival play; Wagner's term for *Parsifal*.

Bülow, Hans von. Conductor and pianist; b. Dresden, Jan. 8, 1830; d. Cairo, Feb 12, 1894. A student of Liszt and early partisan of Wagner, who assisted his conducting career, Bülow in 1857 married Liszt's daughter Cosima, who in 1869 finally left him for Wagner. Court conductor in Munich from 1864, where he led the premieres of *Tristan* and *Meistersinger*. He subsequently achieved a great reputation as an orchestral conductor, notably at Meiningen and Berlin, and as a piano recitalist, espousing especially the music of Beethoven and Brahms. Autocratic and temperamental, he was praised for his pursuit of high executive standards and his grasp of musical architecture. Receptive to new composers, notably Tchaikovsky, whose first piano concerto is dedicated to Bülow.

Bumbry, Grace. Mezzo-soprano and soprano; b. St. Louis, Mo., Jan. 4, 1937. Studied at Boston U., Northwestern U., and with Lotte Lehmann in Santa Barbara; debut as Amneris, Paris Opéra, 1960. In 1961, she became the first black artist to appear at Bayreuth, as Venus. Debuts at Covent Garden (Eboli, 1963), Chicago (Ulrica, 1963), and Salzburg (Lady Macbeth, 1964). Met debut as Eboli, Oct. 7, 1965. She began adding soprano roles to her repertory in 1970; her more than 170 Met perfs. include parts in both vocal categories, among them Carmen,

Amneris, Salome, Tosca, Venus, Gioconda, and Bess. Has also appeared at La Scala (Jenůfa, 1974), Vienna (Santuzza, 1970), and Rome. A versatile and enthusiastic singer, Bumbry early made her mark as a vocal and personal force.

Buona Figliuola, La (The Good Daughter). Opera in 3 acts by Piccinni; libretto by Carlo Goldoni, after Richardson's novel *Pamela*.

First perf., Rome, Dame, Feb. 6, 1760: Borghesi, Savi, de Cristofori. U.S. prem., Madison, Wisc., Jan. 6, 1967.

Piccinni's greatest success, an opera semiseria with arias in classical form alongside numbers in buffa style. The orphan Cecchina (s) and the Marquis of Conchiglia (t) are in love. Though his sister Lucinda (s) fears the girl's background will impede her own marriage, Cecchina turns out to be a baroness.

Burning Fiery Furnace, The. Parable for church performance by Britten; libretto by William Plomer, after the Old Testament, Daniel iii.

First perf., Orford Church, Suffolk, June 9, 1966: Pears, Drake, Tear, Godfrey, Shirley-Quirk. U.S. prem., Katonah, N.Y., Caramoor Festival, June 25, 1967: Velis, Metcalf, Lankston, Berberian, Pierson, c. Rudel.

The second of Britten's church parables is set in Babylon, when Nebuchadnezzar (t) was king. The Jews Shadrach (bar), Meshach (t), and Abednego (bs) are thrown into the fiery furnace for refusing to worship the Babylonian god Merodak. When the three survive untouched, the King is converted to the God of Abraham.

Burrian, Carl [Karel Burian]. Tenor; b. Rousinov, near Rakovnik, Bohemia, Jan. 12, 1870; d. Senomaty, Czechoslovakia, Sep. 25, 1924. Studied with Wallerstein, Prague; debut as Jeník (*Bartered Bride*), Brünn, 1891. Engagements in Reval, Aachen, Cologne, Hanover, Hamburg, Prague, and Budapest brought him to Dresden (1902–10), specializing in Wagner repertory and creating Herod in *Salome*. He appeared at Covent Garden in Wagner roles (1904–14) and in Bayreuth as Parsifal (1908). Met debut as Tannhäuser, Nov. 30, 1906; in 7 seasons, he sang 96 perfs. of 10 roles, including Tristan, Herod, both Siegfrieds, Siegmund, Parsifal, Loge, and Florestan. Subsequently, he joined the Vienna Opera and made guest appearances in Prague and Budapest. Admired as a musician and actor, Burrian was the most famous Tristan of his day; his records, apparently made rather casually, only partially confirm his reputation.

Burrows, Stuart. Tenor; b. Pontypridd, Wales, Feb. 7, 1933. After winning the tenor competition, Royal National Eisteddfod, 1959, he began singing in concert; operatic debut as Ismaele (*Nabucco*), Welsh National Opera, 1963. At Covent Garden from 1967 (debut, Beppe). Sang in San Francisco (from 1967), Vienna and Salzburg (1970). Met debut as Ottavio, April 13, 1971; in 9 seasons, has sung 67 perfs. of 6 roles, notably Tamino, Faust, Alfredo, and Belmonte.

Bury, John. Designer; b. Aberystwyth, Wales, Jan. 27, 1925. Chief designer, Joan Littlewood's Theatre Workshop (1946–63); head of design, Royal Shakespeare Theatre (1964–68) and National Theatre of Great Britain (since 1973). With director Peter Hall, has designed opera for Covent Garden, Glyndebourne, and the Met (*Macbeth*, 1982; *Carmen*, 1986).

Teatro Colón, Buenos Aires

Burzio, Eugenia. Soprano; b. Turin, Italy, June 20, 1872; d. Milan, May 18, 1922. Studied with Aversa and Benvenuti in Milan; debut there as Santuzza, Vittorio Emmanuele, 1903. Sang widely in Italy and South America, but not in Great Britain or U.S. At La Scala (debut, Katiusha in *Risurrezione*, 1906), she sang Catalani's Loreley and Wally, Santuzza, Aida, Gioconda, Gluck's Armide and Pacini's Saffo. Shortened by heart trouble, her career ended in 1919.

Busch, Fritz. Conductor; b. Siegen, Germany, Mar. 13, 1890; d. London, Sep. 14, 1951. Studied at Cologne Conservatory with Fritz Steinbach. Conducted at Riga, Gotha, and Aachen before becoming music director of Stuttgart Opera (1918–22) and Dresden State Opera (1922–33), where he led premieres of *Intermezzo*, *Ägyptische Helena* and *Doktor Faust*, and influential revivals of middle-period Verdi; also conducted in Bayreuth (1924). He left Germany in 1933, leading the Danish State Radio Orchestra and serving as music director of the

Simon Estes as Porgy and Grace Bumbry as Bess in *Porgy and Bess*

Glyndebourne Festival (1934–39); his finely rehearsed, stylishly played Glyndebourne recordings played a major role in the mid-century revival of Mozart's operas. Active in South America before and during World War II, Busch led the New Opera Company in N.Y. (U.S. premiere of the revised *Macbeth*, 1941), coming to the Met on Nov. 26, 1945 (*Lohengrin*); in 4 seasons, he led 69 perfs. of 9 operas in the German and Italian repertory. He returned to Glyndebourne in 1950.

Busoni, Ferruccio. Composer and pianist; b. Empoli, near Florence, Apr. 1, 1866; d. Berlin, July 27, 1924. Son of musicians (his maternal grandmother was German) and a child prodigy as pianist and conductor, he studied in Graz with Wilhelm Mayer. Soon famous as a keyboard virtuoso, he toured widely, settling in Berlin in 1894; this remained his base for most of the rest of his life, during which he composed, performed as pianist and conductor, taught, and wrote essays (notably the *Sketch for a New Esthetic of Music* (1907). Countering the turbulence of late Romanticism with the examples of Mozart and Bach, Busoni's early neo-classicism was also infused with a pianist's admiration for Lisztian virtuosity. Limited in appeal by their austere intellectuality, his operas have gradually made their way into public consciousness in recent years. After the unpublished *Sigune* (1889), he wrote his own librettos for the "fantastical comedy" *Die Brautwahl* (1912); the one-act "theatrical capriccio" *Arlecchino* (1917); the Chinese fable *Turandot* (1917); and *Doktor Faust*, unfinished at his death (perf. 1925).
BIBLIOGRAPHY: Antony Beaumont, *Busoni the Composer* (Nebraska and London, 1985).

Butt, Clara. Contralto; b. Southwick, Sussex, England, Feb. 1, 1872; d. North Stoke, Oxfordshire, Jan. 23, 1936. Studied with Daniel Rootham in Bristol, J.H. Blower at Royal Academy of Music; further lessons with Bouhy in Paris and Etelka Gerster in Berlin. Debut as Ursula in Sullivan's *Golden Legend*, London, 1892, followed by Gluck's *Orfeo*. Primarily a concert singer, she toured the U.S., 1899 and 1913, and returned to opera as Orfeo under Beecham, Covent Garden, 1920.

Byron, George Gordon, Lord. English poet (1788–1824). Operas based on his writings include Verdi's *Il Corsaro* and *I Due Foscari*.

C

cabaletta (Ital.). In early 19th-c. Italian opera, a short aria with a persistent rhythm, usually repeated (with ornamentation improvised by the singer); most often, the concluding section of a double aria, in a rapid tempo (see *aria*).

Caballé, Montserrat. Soprano; b. Barcelona, Apr. 12, 1933. After study at Barcelona Liceo with Eugenia Kemeny, Conchita Badia, and Napoleone Annovazzi, debut in *Serva Padrona* at Reus, near Barcelona. She sang in Basel (1956–58) and briefly in Bremen, then in Vienna (Salome and Donna Elvira, 1958), La Scala (Flowermaiden in *Parsifal*, 1960), and Mexico City (Massenet's *Manon*, 1962). Her international fame dates from a concert appearance as Lucrezia Borgia at Carnegie Hall, N.Y. (Apr. 20, 1965). The following summer she sang the Marschallin and Countess at Glyndebourne, and made her Met debut as Marguerite in *Faust* on Dec. 22,

Montserrat Caballé as Hélène in *Les Vêpres Siciliennes*

1965. Since then, she has returned frequently, singing over 85 perfs. as Leonora (*Trovatore*), Desdemona, Violetta, Luisa Miller, Liù, Amelia (*Ballo*), Elisabeth de Valois, Norma, Hélène (*Vêpres Siciliennes*), Mimi, Aida, Ariadne, Adriana Lecouvreur, and Tosca. At the Chicago Opera (1970) and Covent Garden (1972), her debut role was Violetta. She has appeared in most major theaters, and in many concert and radio presentations of unusual repertory, such as Spontini's *Agnese*, Bellini's *Pirata*, Donizetti's *Roberto Devereux* and *Gemma di Vergy*. Wagner she has often sung in concert, and occasionally on stage (Elisabeth, Mexico City, 1965).

At its best, Caballé's singing combines creamy tone, superb breath control, firm legato, and sympathetic musicianship. She can negotiate florid writing with facility, and commands an effortless floating pianissimo on high notes. A poised figure on stage, her communicative power is almost entirely vocal rather than thespian. Her recordings range widely, from *Lucrezia Borgia* to *Salome*, including much Verdi and Puccini as well as song and zarzuela literature. Married to Spanish tenor Bernabé Marti.

Caccini, Giulio [Giulio Romano]. Composer and singer; b. Rome or Tivoli, c. 1545; d. Florence, Dec. (buried Dec. 10), 1618. Trained as a singer and lutenist, during the 1570s and 1580s he joined in the conversations of the Florentine Camerata and composed vocal solos in recitative style. Settings of scenes by Bardi were succeeded by Peri's opera *Euridice* (1600), with songs and choruses by Caccini, and *Il Rapimento di Cefalo* (1600), by Caccini, Nibbio, Bati, and Strozzi. In 1600, Caccini set his own version of *Euridice*; it was the first published opera (1601).

cadenza (Ital., "cadence"). A virtuoso passage, interrupting the final cadence of an aria (also of an ensemble or instrumental piece) at a point indicated by a fermata sign in the printed music. Traditionally, in the 18th and 19th c., cadenzas were improvised by the soloists, even when composers wrote out conventional formulas at the appropriate points in the score; as such skills withered, and as composers rather than singers became dominant in opera, the improvised cadenza died out.

Cadman, Charles Wakefield. Composer; b. Johnstown, Pa., Dec. 24, 1881; d. Los Angeles, Dec. 30, 1946. Studied theory and conducting with Emil Paur. His interest in American Indian music led to visits to reservations, and to successful songs based on Indian music ("At Dawning" and "From the Land of the Sky-Blue Water," 1909). After giving lecture-recitals with the Omaha princess Tsianina Redfeather, he based an opera on her life, *Shanewis or The Robin Woman* (1918), successfully performed at the Met. His later operas, *The Garden of Mystery* (1925) and *A Witch of Salem* (1926), were less well received. Though Cadman used Indian melodies, he enveloped them in a conservative late-Romantic harmonic style.

Cahier, Mme. Charles (née Sara Layton-Walker). Contralto; b. Nashville, Tenn., Jan. 8, 1870; d. Manhattan Beach, Calif., Apr. 15, 1951. Studied with Jean de Reszke, Paris, and Gustav Walter, Vienna; debut in Nice, 1904. Sang with Vienna Opera, 1907–11, notably as Carmen; first perf. of Mahler's *Lied von der Erde*, Munich, 1911. At Met, sang 3 perfs. in 2 seasons, as Azucena (debut, Apr. 3, 1912), Amneris, and *Walküre* Fricka.

Caldwell, Sarah. Manager, producer, and conductor; b. Maryville, Mo., Mar. 6, 1928. Studied violin with Richard Burgin at New England Conservatory, Boston, and opera with Goldovsky. Her first production was Vaughan Williams' *Riders to the Sea* (Tanglewood, 1947), she headed the Boston U. opera workshop, 1952–60. In 1957, she founded the Opera Group of Boston (renamed Opera Company of Boston, 1965), and has been its often imaginative, sometimes indisciplined principal producer and conductor. For the N.Y.C. Opera, she staged *Junge Lord* and *Ariadne* (both 1973). The first woman to conduct at the Met (*Traviata*, 1973), she has also appeared with many leading orchestras.

Calisto, La. Opera in 3 acts by Cavalli; libretto by Giovanni Faustini, after Ovid's *Metamorphoses*, ii, 401–507.
First perf., Venice, San Apollinare, 1651. U.S. prem., Cincinnati U., Apr. 12, 1972.
Jove disguises himself as Diana (ms) in order to win her nymph Calisto (s), but Juno (s) turns Calisto into a bear, whom Jove immortalizes in the skies as Ursa Minor.

Callas [Kalogeropoulos], **Maria.** Soprano; b. New York, Dec. 2, 3, or 4, 1923; d. Paris, Sep. 16, 1977. Born to Greek immigrant parents, she went with her mother at age 13 to Athens, where she studied with Elvira de Hidalgo at the Conservatory. Student debut as Santuzza, Olympia Theater, Athens, 1939; first professional appearance, Beatrice (*Boccaccio*), Royal Opera, Athens, 1941. Other roles in Greece included Tosca, Marta (*Tiefland*), Santuzza, and Fidelio. After the war she returned to America, then made an Italian debut as Gioconda, Verona Arena, 1947, followed by dramatic Verdi and Wagner roles in other

Italian cities, until an emergency substitution as Elvira in *Puritani* (Venice, 1949) led to further florid parts. In 1949 she sang in Buenos Aires, and in 1950–52 in Mexico City. Married to Giovanni Battista Meneghini in 1949, she was billed as Maria Meneghini Callas until their separation in 1959.

At the Florence Maggio Musicale, Callas ventured into unfamiliar repertory: *Vêpres Siciliennes* and Haydn's *Orfeo* (1951), Rossini's *Armida* (1952), and Cherubini's *Médée* (1953). After a debut as a substitute Aida in 1950, she joined La Scala in 1951, where her significant revivals included Spontini's *Vestale*, Donizetti's *Anna Bolena* and *Poliuto*, and Bellini's *Pirata*; other notable productions were *Lucia* under Karajan, and *Sonnambula*, *Traviata*, and *Iphigénie en Tauride* staged (as were *Vestale* and *Anna Bolena*) by Visconti. After some cancellations in 1957–58 due to health problems, she acquired an unwarranted reputation for unreliability and wilfullness.

Norma was the role of her debuts at Covent Garden (1952), Chicago (1954), and the Met (Oct. 29, 1956). Other Chicago roles included Violetta, Lucia, Elvira (*Puritani*), Leonora (*Trovatore*), and Butterfly, 1954–55. In two Met seasons (1956–58), ended by a rift with Bing about scheduling, she also sang Tosca, Lucia, and Violetta, for a total of 18 perfs. (she returned in 1965 for two Toscas). In Dallas, she appeared as Violetta, Médée, and Lucia, 1958–59. Thereafter her operatic appearances diminished; she made several concert tours, and returned briefly to the stage as Tosca and Norma in 1964–65, in London, Paris, and N.Y. She taught master classes at the Juilliard School, N.Y. (1971–72), and made a recital tour of Europe, the U.S., and the Far East with di Stefano (1973–74) before retiring completely.

Endowed with a powerful and wide-ranging voice (up to high E-flat), Callas brought to the early 19th-c. repertory singing of a forgotten scale and power, investing "decorative" matter with intense expressivity. Her unusual breadth of phrasing and variety of color were governed by a penetrating intelligence, rigorous musicality, and spontaneity of feeling. Although her tone and technique, entailing registral inconsistencies and wiry high notes, were frequently controversial, few denied the incandescence or authority of her impersonations. Her recordings, including many complete operas – and many taken from performances – suggest, as far as possible in that medium, the power of her interpretations.
BIBLIOGRAPHY: John Ardoin and Gerald Fitzgerald, *Callas* (N.Y., and London, 1974).

Calvé [Calvet], **Emma.** Soprano; b. Decazeville, France, Aug. 15, 1858; d. Millau, Jan. 6, 1942. Studied with Jules Puget, Mathilde Marchesi, and Rosina Laborde; debut as Marguerite, Monnaie, Brussels, 1881. Appeared at the Opéra-Comique during the 1880s, and at La Scala (debut, Samara's *Flora Mirabilis*, 1887), where she had great success as Ophélie (*Hamlet*) in 1890. Santuzza eventually became her passport to fame in Italy, and she created Suzel in Mascagni's *Amico Fritz*, Rome, 1891. Calvé came to the Met as Santuzza, Nov. 29, 1893, and, returning intermittently, remained a favorite until her first retirement in 1904, singing 131 perfs., mostly of Carmen (61 times) and Santuzza (32), also Boito's Margherita and Elena, Suzel, Ophélie, and de Lara's Messaline. Later, she performed at the Manhattan Opera (1907–09), in Boston (1912) and Nice (1914), and occasionally in concert thereafter. For her, Massenet composed Anita in *Navarraise* (which she sang at the Met in 1895) and Fanny in *Sapho*. Celebrated as a tempestuous actress and exponent of veristic roles,

(continued p.64)

MARIA CALLAS
David Hamilton

As Enrico Caruso was in the eyes of the general public in the early twentieth century the quintessential operatic personality, so in recent decades has been Maria Callas. Like Caruso, she not only sang, but made news, good and bad, attracting attention not only by theatrical triumphs but with imbroglios (her walkouts comparable to Caruso's monkey-house escapade) and with publicly suffered afflictions of heart, body, and voice. Having thus won the attention of the world beyond the opera house, she, like the great Neapolitan tenor, reached through recordings an immense audience, continually augmented with ever-younger listeners who never heard her in the theater. By Callas' time, too, fame had acquired new manifestations; from the late 1950s on, a tape recorder seems to have been running every time she opened her mouth – and of course there were the trashy novels, the "*romans à skeleton clef*" with diva heroines invariably concocted from Callas facts and Callas gossip.

Some singers epitomize an existing tradition: Renata Tebaldi, for example, embodied the best tonal qualities and musical traditions of the post-verismo Italian soprano, while avoiding the expressive overvehemence of her predecessors. Others change the landscape of operatic performance. Thus, Caruso showed that the newly fashionable verismo repertory could be truly sung, not merely shouted, and his uniquely successful recordings became models for every tenor aspiring to a career in Italian opera. Callas, by contrast, revived an almost defunct literature, Italian opera from the first half of the 19th century; in her case, too, recordings carried the impact of that resuscitation far beyond the Italian theaters where most of it took place.

She didn't start out with that in mind, although her teacher was Elvira de Hidalgo, a Spanish coloratura who had sung with Battistini and Bonci, and briefly at the Met. Like Hidalgo, Callas made a precocious debut at age fifteen, and though her early concert programs ranged widely – excerpts from *Norma*, *Cenerentola*, *Thaïs* – her theatrical roles pointed to a career in the dramatic repertory. (At the Met, Edward Johnson offered her Fidelio in English and Butterfly, but she thought herself too stout for those roles.) After her Italian debut in 1947, Turandot and Isolde were her specialties – and then, in January 1949, Tullio Serafin persuaded her to fill in for the indisposed Margherita Carosio as Elvira in *Puritani*, a few days after finishing a run of Brünnhildes at La Fenice. Hidalgo's training paid off; the Callas Elvira proved "an agile creature, sensitive, vital in every note, who breathes melody filtered through a superior intelligence."

It took a while for her engagements to catch up with this extension of her repertory. Eventually, her performances of Verdi's *Vêpres Siciliennes* at the Florence Maggio Musicale led to a full-scale La Scala debut in the same role, and she came to the forefront of the "exhumation" of early nineteenth-century Italian operas, pursued especially at the Maggio Musicale. Hearing her there, the Italian critic Fedele d'Amico wrote that "In Rossini, coloratura passages could well mean ecstasy, lyrical rapture, fury; in other words, they were vehicles for dramatic expression. . . . it was not until I heard Callas in Rossini's *Armida* . . . that I really understood the true coloratura style of the golden age." And when she turned to a familiar opera such as *Lucia*, she discovered expressive potentials that infused new vitality into the prettily pathetic creature of yore; especially in the famous performances led by Karajan, Donizetti's score became a bosky nocturnal

drama, the heroine's dark-hued anguish floating over orchestral velvet and framed by Beethovenian orchestral accents.

The revival of the Rossini–Bellini–Donizetti repertory soon went beyond Callas (and still continues today, so prolific were two of these men), but there is no doubt about who gave it the decisive impetus. Thanks to the guidance of Serafin, and to her own keen intuition and fabled capacity for hard work, Callas defined a range of possibility and began its exploration. Without that example, the careers and achievements of Sutherland, Scotto, Caballé, Sills, and Horne would probably have taken different turns, as would have also the repertory of opera houses nearly everywhere.

America heard rather less of this than Italy, at least until the recordings of Callas' live performances began to circulate in the later 1960s. The commercial record companies were not yet ready for more than selections from Spontini's *Vestale* or Donizetti's *Anna Bolena* (though they gave us Callas as Nedda, Manon Lescaut, and Mimi, roles she never sang in the theater), and the American houses where she sang (Chicago, the Met, and Dallas) did not even venture *Sonnambula*. By the time they might have been prepared to mount for her something other than *Norma*, *Lucia*, or *Tosca*, the Callas career had taken a new direction; with the prospect of far better fees from concerts than from the Met, she maneuvered Bing into firing her. Then came the liaison with Onassis and the vocal crisis (which some felt was a result of her drastic and beautifying weight loss of 1953–54) that became as well a crisis of confidence. She could still perform with riveting force, but did so only sporadically.

Today, despite some video recordings (mostly from concerts), she lives more as a vocal phenomenon than as a theatrical one – though no voice was ever shot through with so much theatrical character. From Visconti and Zeffirelli, she learned to use her newly slender body, though she apparently always had a commanding presence (at a 1951 Florence *Vêpres* rehearsal, Harold Rosenthal noted "the natural dignity of her carriage, the air of quiet, innate authority which went with every movement"). I saw her in the theater only as Norma, and remember that, though her spare gestures were always vivid, they were no more vivid than the words that in a paradoxical way both rode on the vocal lines and helped to shaped them, and that this seemed to dictate the many colors the voice assumed. Hers was a fully formed theatrical art; she grew from an ugly-duckling childhood to become a creature of the theater; sadly, when the theater was no longer available to her, she found no further purpose in life.

Recently at an audition, I heard a twenty-four-year-old soprano sing Norma's "Casta diva," reproducing with infinite pains every Callas inflection – indeed, she sang, not Bellini's aria, but Callas' recording of it. Callas would have been appalled (as were all of us on the jury): that was not what she meant at all. Even when *in extremis* vocally, everything Callas did she made new, by a combination of imaginative resource and sheer hard work.

Maria Callas as Tosca, with Tito Gobbi as Scarpia at the Met in 1965

Emma Calvé as Carmen

Calvé was also highly accomplished in florid technique and deployed her silvery voice and subtle rhythmic sense for dramatic purposes without the reliance on heavy chest tones that later became standard in such roles.

Calzabigi, Raniero de. Librettist; b. Livorno, Dec. 23, 1714; d. Naples, July 1795. A Casanova-like figure first active as a librettist in Naples, he went in 1750 to Paris, where he edited Metastasio's works. In Vienna from 1761, he collaborated with Gluck on the ballet *Don Juan* and the operas *Orfeo*, *Alceste*, and *Paride ed Elena*, also working with other composers.

Cambiale di Matrimonio, La (The Marriage Contract). Opera in 1 act by Rossini; libretto by Gaetano Rossi, after Camillo Federici's comedy.

First perf., Venice, San Moïse, Nov. 3, 1810: Morandi, Ricci, Rafanelli, de Grecis. U.S. prem., N.Y., 44th Street, Nov. 8, 1937.

In this early comedy demonstrating Rossini's fresh melodic gift, the wealthy Slook (bar) offers Mill (bs) a large sum of money for a wife. Mill proposes his daughter Fanny (s), who loves Edoardo Milfort (t). Admiring the lovers' determination, Slook helps them win Mill's blessing.

Cambreling, Sylvain. Conductor; b. Amiens, France, July 2, 1948. After study in Paris under Pierre Dervaux, became in 1975 assistant to Baudo at the Lyon Orchestra, making his debut that year with the Lyon Opera (*Cenerentola*). Debuts at Paris Opéra-Comique (*Rake's Progress*, 1975) and Opéra (*Hoffmann*, 1980), and La Scala (*Lucio Silla*, 1984). From 1981, music director, Belgian National Opera. Met debut, *Roméo*, Jan. 9, 1985.

Camerata (Ital.). The group of Florentine philosophers, musicians, and amateurs who met in the salon of Count Giovanni de' Bardi in the later 16th c. and to whom is ascribed, on uncertain grounds, the intellectual stimulus for the first performances of opera.

Cammarano, Salvatore. Librettist; b. Naples, Mar. 19, 1801; d. Naples, July 17, 1852. From an important Neapolitan theatrical family, he wrote successful plays, and provided librettos for Donizetti (notably *Lucia*, *Roberto Devereux*, *Poliuto*, Verdi (*Alzira*, *Battaglia di Legnano*, *Luisa Miller*, and *Trovatore*, the latter unfinished at his death), and also for Pacini and Mercadante.

Campanari, Giuseppe. Baritone; b. Venice, Nov. 17, 1855; d. Milan, May 31, 1927. Began career as cellist, playing in La Scala Orchestra and Boston Symphony (1884–93). Studied voice in Italy and in U.S.; debut as Tonio with Hinrichs' Opera Co., N.Y., 1893. Met debut as di Luna, Nov. 30, 1894; in 14 seasons, he sang 208 perfs. of Italian repertory, Valentin, and Papageno.

Campana Sommersa, La (The Sunken Bell). Opera in 4 acts by Respighi; libretto by Claudio Guastalla, after Gerhard Hauptmann's play *Die versunkene Glocke*.

First perf., Hamburg, Stadttheater, Nov. 18, 1927 (in Ger.): Callam, Graarud, Guttmann, c. Wolff. U.S. & Met prem., Nov. 24, 1928: Rethberg, Martinelli, de Luca, c. Serafin, d. Urban, p. Wymetal. 7 perfs. in 2 seasons.

In Respighi's second mature opera, the bellcaster Enrico (t) is bewitched by the elf Rautendelein (s). When his wife Magda (s) commits suicide, the tolling of a sunken bell wakens his grief.

Campanello di Notte. Il (The Night Bell). Opera in 1 act by Donizetti; libretto by the composer, after the vaudeville *La Sonnette de la Nuit* by L.L. Brunswick, M.-B. Troin, and V. Lhérie.

First perf., Naples, Nuovo, June 1, 1836: Schütz-Oldosi, Ronconi, Casaccia. U.S. prem., N.Y., Lyceum, May 7, 1917 (in Eng.).

A light farce, today popular for student performance. The elderly apothecary Don Annibale (bs) has married beautiful Serafina (s). In various disguises, her former suitor Enrico (t) disrupts the wedding night by bothering the apothecary, who is compelled by law to answer his bell at any hour.

Campanini, Cleofonte. Conductor; b. Parma, Italy, Sep. 1, 1860; d. Chicago, Dec. 19, 1919. Studied in Parma, and began his career as deputy for Faccio and others. Led premieres of *Adriana Lecouvreur* (1902), *Siberia* (1903), and *Butterfly* (1904). Assistant conductor during the Met's inaugural season, he led *Mignon* (debut, Nov. 3, 1881), *Carmen*, *Mefistofele*, and *Sonnambula*. He remained a long time on the American operatic scene, notably as principal conductor for Hammerstein's Manhattan Opera (1906–09) and the Chicago Opera (from 1910).

Campanini, Italo. Tenor; b. Parma, Italy, June 30, 1845; d. Corcagno, near Parma, Nov. 22, 1896. Studied at Parma Conservatory with Griffini, later with Lamperti in Milan; debut as Oloferno Vitellozzo (*Lucrezia Borgia*), Parma, 1863. First Italian Lohengrin, Bologna, 1871. London debut, 1872; first Don José in London and N.Y. (both 1878). Sang Faust on opening night of Met, Oct. 22, 1883, and returned to the house, 1891–94; his 28 perfs. included Almaviva, Ottavio, Raoul (*Huguenots*), Lohengrin, Edgardo, and Boito's Faust. Brother of conductor Cleofonte.

1 *Don Giovanni* – (1957). Costume design for Don Giovanni by Eugene Berman

2 *Die Zauberflöte* – (1815). Print by Karl Friedrich Thiele, based on design by Karl Friedrich Schinkel for the Queen of Night's Act I entrance

3 *Don Giovanni* – (1943). James Melton as Don Ottavio, Zinka Milanov as Donna Anna, Bidú Sayão as Zerlina, Jarmila Novotna as Donna Elvira, Ezio Pinza as Don Giovanni, and Salvatore Baccaloni as Leporello

4 Vienna State Opera House

5 Cuvilliés Theater in Munich

6 *Lohengrin* – (1966). Act I of Wagner's opera, designed by Wieland Wagner

8 *Opposite (above). Tannhäuser* – (1977). Design by Günther Schneider-Siemssen for Act I, Scene 2
9 *Opposite (below). Tristan und Isolde* – (Bayreuth, 1886). Design by Max Brückner for Act II

7 *Lohengrin* – (1920). Design by Joseph Urban for Act I

12 (*Above*). *Der Rosenkavalier* – (1969). Reri Grist
as Sophie and Christa Ludwig as Octavian in
Act II of Richard Strauss' opera, designed by
Robert O'Hearn

13 (*Right*). *Ariadne auf Naxos* – (1984) Jessye
Norman as Ariadne in Richard Strauss' opera,
set by Oliver Messel, costume by Jane
Greenwood

10 *Opposite* (*above*). – *Das Rheingold* – (San
Francisco Opera, 1985). Entrance of the gods
into Valhalla, designed by John Conklin

11 *Opposite* (*below*). – *Die Walküre* – (1986).
Simon Estes as Wotan in Act III of Wagner's
opera, with set by Günther Schneider-
Siemssen, costumes by Rolf Langenfass

14 *Die Frau ohne Schatten* – (1966). Design by Robert O'Hearn for Act I, Scene 1 of Richard Strauss' opera

15 *Die Fledermaus* – (1986). Tatiana Troyanos (center) as Prince Orlofsky in Act II of Johann Strauss' operetta, set by Günther Schneider-Siemssen, costumes by Peter J. Hall

Campra, André. Composer; b. Aix-en-Provence, France, Dec. 4, 1660; d. Versailles, June 14, 1744. A pupil of Poitevin, he became in 1694 music director at Notre Dame in Paris, but soon turned to the stage and was induced by the success of *L'Europe Galante* (1697) and the ballet *Le Carnaval de Venise* (1699) to accept royal patronage. Successor to Lully, Campra made his greatest contributions in the genre of opéra-ballet, with works such as *Les Muses* (1703) and *Les Fêtes Vénitiennes* (1710) that combine French delicacy of orchestration with Italian melodic sophistication in the vocal lines, offering lively comic intrigues and brilliant dance music. In his tragédies lyriques, among them *Hésione* (1700), *Tancrède* (1702), and *Idoménée* (1712), Campra anticipated Rameau in his depictions of nature through orchestral interludes.

Candide. Operetta, later opera, in 2 acts by Bernstein; original libretto by Lillian Hellman, lyrics by Richard Wilbur, John Latouche, and Dorothy Parker, after Voltaire's novel.
First perf., Boston, Colonial Theater, Oct. 29, 1956: Cook, Petina, Rounseville, Adrian, Olvis, c. Krachmalnick. Second version (libretto by Hugh Wheeler, lyrics by Wilbur, Stephen Sondheim, and Latouche), Brooklyn, Academy of Music, Dec. 19, 1973: c. Mauceri. "Opera house" version, N.Y.C. Opera, Oct. 13, 1982: Mills, Costa-Greenspun, Eisler, Lankston, Harrold, c. Mauceri.
First billed as "a comic operetta," *Candide* failed on Broadway and in London, but in later revisions its mordant, accomplished score found an audience. Candide and Cunegonde, taught by Dr. Pangloss that this is "the best of all possible worlds," experience exile, war, rape, the Inquisition, and numerous betrayals in their travels, to discover at the end that they must make the best of reality and "make their gardens grow."

Caniglia, Maria. Soprano; b. Naples, May 5, 1905; d. Rome, Apr. 16, 1979. Studied with Roche, Naples Conservatory. Debut as Chrysothemis (*Elektra*), Turin, 1930. La Scala debut the same year, as Maria in Pizzetti's *Lo Straniero*; sang there until 1943 and from 1948 to 1951. Created Manuela in Montemezzi's *Notte di Zoraima* (Milan, 1931), Rosanna in Alfano's *Cyrano* (Rome, 1936), and title role of Respighi's *Lucrezia* (Rome, 1937). Met debut as Desdemona, Nov. 21, 1938; other roles in her only Met season were Aida, Alice Ford, Tosca, and Maria Boccanegra (12 perfs.). Known for Verdi and verismo roles.

Canterbury Pilgrims, The. Opera in 4 acts by De Koven; libretto by Percy W. Mackaye, after Chaucer.
First perf., Met, Mar. 8, 1917: Sundelius, Mason, Ober, Sembach, c. Bodanzky, d. Emens/Fox, p. Ordynski. 6 perfs. in 1 season.
This lightweight score was found wanting as a setting of the rather literary text, in which Chaucer (t) and his fellow pilgrims cavort on their way to Canterbury, and the Wife of Bath (ms) wins the poet's hand in marriage in a wager.

cantilena (Ital.). In the 19th c., a term referring to a sustained, flowing melodic line, or indicating such a manner of performance.

canzone (Ital., "song"). In operatic usage, a song-like musical piece that, in the dramatic situation, would actually be sung – e.g., Cherubino's "Voi che sapete" in *Nozze di Figaro*.

Capecchi, Renato. Baritone; b. Cairo, Nov. 6, 1923. Studied with Ubaldo Carrozzi, Milan; debut as Amonasro, Reggio Emilia, 1949. Sang at La Scala from 1950, at Covent Garden in 1962 and 1973. Met debut as Germont, Nov. 24, 1951; he sang with the company until 1954 and returned in 1975, for a total of 165 perfs. Created roles in Ghedini's *Billy Budd* and *Lord Inferno*, and Malipiero's *La Donna è Mobile*. Known also for his buffo parts, including Bartolo, Schicchi, Dulcamara, and Falstaff (Glyndebourne, 1977). Has staged opera at the Met (*Bohème*), San Francisco, and N.Y.C. Opera.

Capobianco, Tito. Producer; b. La Plata, Argentina, Aug. 28, 1931. Worked at Teatro Colón, Buenos Aires (1958–62); artistic director, Cincinnati Opera (1962–65) and San Diego Opera (since 1977). Productions for N.Y.C. Opera include *Giulio Cesare*, *Don Rodrigo*, and *Anna Bolena*; for Met, *Thaïs* (1978) and *Simon Boccanegra* (1984).

Caponsacchi. Opera in prologue, 3 acts and epilogue by Hageman; libretto by Arthur Goodrich, after his and Rose A. Palmer's play, in turn after Browning's poem *The Ring and the Book*.
First perf., Freiburg, Germany, Feb. 18, 1932 (in Ger., as *Tragödie in Arezzo*). U.S. & Met prem., Feb. 4, 1937: Jepson, Chamlee, Tibbett, c. Hageman, d. Novak, p. Defrère. 2 perfs. in 1 season.
Based on a 1698 Roman murder case. Despite his assertion that his wife Pompilia (s) was romantically involved with the priest Caponsacchi (t), Count Guido Franceschini (bar) is convicted of murdering her.

Cappuccilli, Piero. Baritone; b. Trieste, Nov. 9, 1929. Studied with Donaggio, Trieste; debut as Tonio, Nuovo, Milan, 1957. Only Met perf. as Germont, Mar. 26, 1960. Frequent appearances at La Scala (debut, Ashton, 1964), Covent Garden (Germont, 1967), and Chicago (from 1969). In the 1970s, he emerged as Italy's leading Verdi baritone, especially as Posa under Karajan (Salzburg, 1975) and Boccanegra under Abbado (La Scala, 1976).

Capriccio. Opera in 1 act by R. Strauss; libretto by the composer and Clemens Krauss.
First perf., Munich, Oct. 28, 1942: Ursuleac, Ranczak, Taubmann, Hotter, Hann, Höfermayer, c. Krauss. U.S. prem., N.Y., Juilliard School, Apr. 4, 1954 (in Eng.): Davy, Blankenship, Stewart, c. Waldman.
A subtle comedy about operatic composition, leaving open the classic question of words vs. music (although the lyricism of the score's most memorable pages weighs in on the side of the music). The subject derives from Salieri's short opera *Prima la Musica e poi le Parole*.
A chateau near Paris, at the time of Gluck's operatic reforms, about 1775. Countess Madeleine (s) is courted by the poet Olivier (bar) and the composer Flamand (t), who compete in arguments for the superiority of their respective arts. Does poetry or music come first in opera? It is decided that the two men should compose a work about the argument and its various supporting participants, which include Madeleine's brother the Count (bar), his lover the actress Clairon (ms), and the aggressive theater manager La Roche (bs). At the opera's close, the Countess wonders whether the question has any answer that is not trivial.

Caprices of Oxana, The. See *Vakula the Smith*.

CARMEN

Risë Stevens

It has been twenty-five years since I sang my last performance at the Metropolitan Opera. The role, of course, was Carmen. I'm not a great one for looking back – I prefer to keep my mind on the present and the future – but I know that opera buffs love to talk about the great performances of the past. Whenever I meet opera-lovers who have seen me on the stage, they invariably bring up my Carmen, although I sang many other roles as well. Ironically, Carmen was also the role that gave me the most trouble, and for years I thought it might always elude me.

My first professional engagement was in Prague, and though I sang Carmen, I was not satisfied with my performance. Then, when I came to the Met, Edward Johnson offered me *Carmen* with Sir Thomas Beecham conducting, but I told him I did not think I was ready to sing the role at the Met. Aided by the persistence of my husband, Walter Surovy, I began to work with two flamenco dancers, who taught me the dance, posture, walk, carriage, fan movements, and hand gestures, as well as how to play the castanets and tambourine. I had read the original Mérimée novel, and I worked with the baritone Martial Singher to perfect my French pronunciation. The idea of Carmen became an obsession.

I had great encouragement from Fausto Cleva, who offered me my first American Carmen, in Cincinnati. And I made the film *Going My Way*, in which I sang the "Habañera," and which was seen by more people than ever saw me in the role on stage. After another try in San Francisco, I decided I was ready to bring my Carmen to the Met, which I did on December 28, 1943. These performances firmly established me in the part, and I became the Carmen of the day.

But I was *still* not completely satisfied with my performance; I thought there was something I was missing. When Rudolf Bing became the Met's general manager, one of his innovations was to invite directors and designers from the legitimate theater to bring new life to the classic operas. He signed Tyrone Guthrie to direct a new *Carmen* and Fritz Reiner to conduct, and that is when the role became the ultimate satisfaction for me. This production was directed around me. It was the first time I had worked on Carmen with a major director, and by the time we opened, I finally felt at home in this most difficult of roles.

We started from scratch, both musically and dramatically, as if none of us had ever performed the opera before. Working with Fritz Reiner was a great experience. We went through the score with a fine-tooth comb, exploring different musical shadings and exciting tempos. We had such musical respect for one another, and this made all the difference for me.

I will never forget the thrilling effect Tony Guthrie's direction had on the entire company. We blocked and tried many alternatives for weeks on end, from early morning until midnight, breaking only for lunch and dinner. He was relentless, and I loved every minute of it, because I knew something extraordinary was going to result.

The major breakthrough, at least for an American opera production, was that every line and move was specifically motivated. There wasn't a moment left unprobed until it made sense to us, including many points which we realized we hadn't really understood previously. For example, we came up with a dramatic reason for Carmen to enter after the other cigarette girls in the first act – I had stayed behind to smuggle some tobacco.

We used the scenery, the props, even the chorus, in every way

imaginable to bring theatricality and sense to the piece. For my "Habañera," I started out at the top of a large staircase, and every time I sang "L'amour," Guthrie had a different dancer pick me up and put me on a lower step. (This business didn't stay in very long; after we opened, Mr. Bing worried that I might be dropped by a replacement dancer, and insisted that I walk down the stairs myself.)

As a result, I began to realize that my entire concept of the character was changing. Prior to this production, I had played Carmen as passive – alluring, but accepting life and whatever came to her. The more I worked on her motivations for each scene, the more I saw that she was always strongly motivated, and pursued her objectives as if by design. I think this made her much more interesting to the audience.

The crowning glory of the production was the final act. Although this usually takes place in a large square outside the arena, the production's budget had run too short for an exterior set, so we played it in Escamillo's dressing room. Richard Tucker, my wonderful Don José, made his entrance in tattered clothing, unshaven and slightly inebriated, and I first saw him as a reflection in a large mirror. He immediately plunged his knife into a large wooden trunk, a detail that caused some controversy but that added, I think, to the mounting tension.

As the scene progressed, José pursued me around the room, and in the this small dressing room I was really trapped. (This had bothered me in previous productions – in an open square, I should have been able to escape.) Tony Guthrie had my gown constructed in such a way that, as we struggled, pieces of it would rip, and I found a way to pull pins out of my hair without the audience noticing – they only saw my hair falling down as I was pursued by this madman. It became a cat-and-mouse chase, but I was very defiant. Even though I felt trapped, I played the scene as though I didn't believe José had the nerve to kill me.

Finally, he pulled the knife out of the trunk, backed me against the wall, and plunged it into my groin. (It actually went into the wall; later, Francis Robinson told me that the audience's audible gasp was from the tension that had built, and the shock of *hearing* the sound of the stabbing.) Then came the final touch of directorial genius. I staggered to a window, as if to call out, but no sound would come from my mouth. I grabbed a long red curtain for support, and as I fell the curtain ripped, twisting around me like a shroud. The audience was in shock, and there was complete silence before they exploded in applause.

Of course this production was a great success, and became the box-office attraction of the year. I sang thirty-five Carmens in one season, including the tour, which I understand is a record. And, from that time on, the Carmen that we developed was the way I played her, although I enjoyed working on my interpretation well after opening night.

I emerged from this production with very strong convictions as to how Carmen should be played. First, I believe that the role must be beautifully and musically sung, with all of the shadings and musical nuances. I interpreted Carmen as a sensuous female, with a powerful seductive quality, with not a spark of honesty, a person who prevails among thieves – a very vital, irresistible woman. With my walk and movements, I gave her a cat-like quality. Carmen must mesmerize those around her, and especially the audience, from her very first entrance. Every woman in the audience should envy her, and every man in the audience desire her. I think this is why my Carmen was a success.

Just recently, a good friend and colleague said to me, "You know, Risë, you were a damned fine Carmen." I found myself answering "Yes, I know I was."

Risë Stevens as Carmen and Richard Tucker as Don José, in a telecast of the final scene of *Carmen*

Capuleti e i Montecchi, I (The Capulets and the Montagues). Opera in 2 acts by Bellini; libretto by Romani, after his libretto for Vaccai's *Giuliette e Romeo*, in turn based on Luigi Scevola's tragedy of the same name.

First perf., Venice, Fenice, March 11, 1830: Carradori-Allan, Guiditta Grisi, Bonfigli, Antoldi. U.S. prem., New Orleans, St. Charles Theater, April 4, 1837.

An opera touched with characteristic Bellinian melody, but dominated by charged dramatic accents and vigorous rhythms. The libretto stems from a non-Shakespearean tradition, in which Giulietta's kinsman Tebaldo (t) combines the functions of Tybalt and Paris; Romeo is cast as a mezzo.

Cardillac. Opera in 3 acts by Hindemith; libretto by Ferdinand Lion, after E.T.A. Hoffmann's story *Das Fräulein von Scuderi*.

First perf., Dresden, Nov. 9, 1926: Born, Merrem-Nikisch, Hirzel, Burg, c. Busch. Rev. in 4 acts, with new libretto by the composer, first perf., Zurich, Stadttheater, June 20, 1952. U.S. prem., Santa Fe, July 26, 1967 (in Eng.): Yarick, Endich, Stewart, Reardon, c. Craft.

Hindemith's first full-length opera, embodying the "new objectivist" movement in German art. In the late 17th-c. Paris, the jeweler Cardillac, obsessed with his creations, murders those who buy them, and when found out is beaten to death by a mob.

Carelli, Emma. Soprano; b. Naples, May 12, 1877; d. Montefiascone, Aug. 17, 1928. Studied with father, composer Beniamino; debut as Giulia (Mercadante's *Vestale*), Altamura, 1895. La Scala debut, Desdemona, 1899; sang verismo heroines in Italy, Spain, Russia, and South America until 1914, then joined husband Walter Mocchi in management of Rome Opera (until 1926).

Carlson, Lenus. Baritone; b. Jamestown, N.D., Feb. 11, 1945. Studied with Dwayne Jorgenson at Moorehead State College, Minn., and Oren Brown, Juilliard; debut as Demetrius (*Midsummer Night's Dream*), Minneapolis, 1967. Mini-Met debut as Purcell's Aeneas, Feb. 23, 1973; house debut as Silvio, Oct. 25, 1974. Other Met roles include the Animal Trainer/Athlete (*Lulu*), Onegin, Escamillo, Guglielmo, Valentin, and Lescaut. At the Deutsche Oper, Berlin, he has sung Marcello, Wozzeck, and Wolfram.

Carmen. Opera in 4 acts by Bizet; libretto by Henri Meilhac and Ludovic Halévy, after the novel by Prosper Mérimée.

First perf., Paris, Opéra-Comique, Mar. 3, 1875: Galli-Marié, Chapuy, Lhérie, Bouhy, c. Deloffre. U.S. prem., N.Y., Academy of Music, Oct. 23, 1879. Met prem., Jan. 9, 1884 (in Ital.): Trebelli, Valleria, I. Campanini, del Puente, c. C. Campanini. Later Met productions: Nov. 19, 1914: Farrar, Alda, Caruso, Amato, c. Toscanini, d. Sala, J. Fox/Palanti, p. Speck; Nov. 22, 1923: Easton, Morgana, Martinelli, Mardones, c. Hasselmans, d. Urban, p. Wymetal; Jan. 31, 1952: Stevens, Conner, Tucker, Guarrera, c. Reiner, d. Gérard, p. Guthrie; Dec. 15, 1967: Bumbry, Pilou, Gedda, Diaz, c. Mehta, d. Dupont, p. Barrault; Sep. 19, 1972: Horne, Maliponte, McCracken, Krause, c. Bernstein, d. Svoboda/Walker, p. Gentele, Igesz; Mar. 10, 1986: Ewing, Malfitano, Lima, Devlin, c. Levine, d. Bury, p. P. Hall. Carmen has been sung at the Met by Lilli Lehmann, Hauk, Calvé, de Lussan, Fremstad, Gay, Jeritza, Ponselle, Castagna, Tourel, Swarthout, Resnik, Verrett, Crespin, Baltsa; Micaela by Eames, Melba, Farrar, Bori, Albanese, de los Angeles, Stratas, Freni, Lorengar, Ricciarelli; Don José by J. de Reszke, de Lucia, Maison, Jobin, Vinay, del Monaco, di Stefano, Vickers, Domingo; Escamillo by Lassalle, Ancona, E. de Reszke, Maurel, Plançon, Scotti, Journet, de Luca, Tibbett, Pinza, Warren, Singher, Merrill, London, van Dam, Morris, Ramey. 536 perfs. in 70 seasons.

An opera of incomparable melodic wealth and considerable harmonic sophistication, in which Bizet successfully expanded the range of opéra comique to encompass a tragic plot.

Spain, 1820. Outside a cigarette factory near a guardhouse in Seville, the gypsy Carmen (ms or s) is drawn to the only man who appears to ignore her, the dragoon Don José. Though he feels he should marry Micaela (s), a girl from his own village and the choice of his mother, José is distracted by Carmen's seductiveness. When she is arrested after a factory brawl, he allows the gypsy to escape and is eventually persuaded to desert the army and join her band of smugglers. But Carmen tires of him and takes up with Escamillo (bar), a bullfighter. In a confrontation outside the bullring, Carmen brazenly rejects Don José. He stabs her and collapses in remorse over her body.

carnival. The pre-Lenten season of celebration. In Italian opera houses, the "carnival season" traditionally ran from December 26 until the beginning of Lent.

Carosio, Margherita. Soprano; b. Genoa, Italy, June 7, 1908. Studied at Paganini Conservatory, Genoa. Debut as Lucia, Novi Ligure, 1927. La Scala debut as Oscar, 1929; sang there until 1952, except for war years, and created Egloge in Mascagni's *Nerone*. Other noted roles were Violetta and Adina; Italy's leading coloratura-lyric after dal Monte.

Carr, Benjamin. Composer and publisher; b. London, Sep. 12, 1768; d. Philadelphia, May 24, 1831. Apprenticed to his father, a London music publisher, he emigrated to Philadelphia in 1793 and founded Carr's Musical Repository, one of the earliest American music stores and publishing houses. Also prominent as editor, performer, and conductor, his career as composer began in London with the pastoral opera *Philander and Silvia or Love Crown'd at Last* (1792). *The Archers* was produced in N.Y. in 1796. Carr also composed many ballads and programmatic orchestral works.

Carré, Michel. Librettist; b. Paris, 1819; d. Argenteuil, June 27, 1872. He wrote the libretto of Gounod's *Mireille*, and collaborated with Jules Barbier on librettos of Gounod's *Faust* and *Roméo*, Meyerbeer's *Dinorah*, Thomas' *Mignon* and *Hamlet*, and Offenbach's *Hoffmann*.

Carreras, José. Tenor; b. Barcelona, Dec. 5, 1946. After study with Jaime Puig, at Barcelona Conservatory, and later with Juan Ruax, debut as Ismaele (*Nabucco*). Encouraged by Montserrat Caballé, he sang Gennaro in *Lucrezia Borgia* opposite her (Barcelona, 1970), won the Verdi competition in Parma (1971), and sang *Ballo* and *Lombardi* there (1972). After his N.Y.C. Opera debut as Pinkerton (1972), he sang with that company for three years, in roles such as Alfredo, Rodolfo, Edgardo, Duke of Mantua, and Cavaradossi. Debuts at San Francisco (Rodolfo, 1973) and Covent Garden (Alfredo, 1974) followed. His Met debut was as Cavaradossi (Nov. 18, 1974), and he has returned to sing more than 50 perfs. as Rodolfo (*Bohème*), Maurizio

José Carreras as Andrea Chénier

(*Adriana*), Nemorino, Rodolfo (*Luisa Miller*), Alvaro (*Forza*), and Don José. Other debuts at La Scala (Riccardo, 1975), Salzburg (Don Carlos, 1976), and Chicago (Riccardo, 1976).

At the outset of his career, Carreras' sweet, clear, and warm lyric tenor and handsome stage presence elicited comparisons with his early idol, di Stefano. He has subsequently pushed into heavier roles, especially at the urging of Karajan, for whom he sang Radames at Salzburg (1979). He is a prolific recording artist, in songs and zarzuela excerpts as well as opera, the latter including recordings of rare works such as *Juive*, *Due Foscari*, and *Corsaro*.

Carteri, Rosanna. Soprano; b. Verona, Italy, Dec. 14, 1930. Studied with Cusinati and Nino Ederle; debut as Elsa, Caracalla, Rome, 1949. Debuts at La Scala (*Buona Figliuola*, 1951), San Francisco (Mimì, 1954), Chicago (*Faust*, 1955), and Covent Garden (Mimì, 1960). Created Pizzetti's Ifigenia, 1950, and Metarosa in his *Calzare d'Argento*, 1961.

Caruso, Enrico. Tenor; b. Naples, Feb. 27, 1873; d. Naples, Aug. 2, 1921. Studied with Guglielmo Vergine and Vincenzo Lombardi in Naples, where he made his debut on Mar. 15, 1895 in Morelli's *L'Amico Francesco*. He soon won wider attention, creating Maurizio in *Adriana Lecouvreur* and Loris in *Fedora*, and singing for two seasons at la Scala (1900–02). His greatest fame was achieved in N.Y., where he sang at the Met for 18 seasons, bowing as the Duke in *Rigoletto* on Nov. 23, 1903 and singing a total of 37 roles; his 626th and last perf. was as Eléazar (*Juive*) on Christmas Eve, 1920. Caruso gradually moved from spinto to dramatic roles such as Samson and Don Alvaro, and the Met management successfully encouraged him to

extend his box-office appeal to French repertory. His most frequent roles were Canio (83 times) and Radames (63), followed by Enzo, Cavaradossi, Rodolfo (*Bohème*), Nemorino, the Duke, Lionel (*Martha*), Puccini's Des Grieux, Samson, Don José, Dick Johnson in *Fanciulla* (which he created), Massenet's Des Grieux, Alfredo, Jean de Leyde (*Prophète*), Faust, Alvaro, Raoul (*Huguenots*), Riccardo (*Ballo*), and Pinkerton. Among his excursions beyond the central repertory were Gennaro (*Lucrezia Borgia*), Fernand (*Favorite*), Elvino (*Sonnambula*), Osaka (*Iris*), Renaud (Gluck's *Armide*), and Nadir (*Pêcheurs de Perles*).

Probably the most famous tenor of all time, Caruso managed a voice of exceptional beauty with a superb technique. Plagued with unreliable high notes early in his career, in later years he avoided high C, but the remainder of the voice was unified into a plangent and unforgettable sound. His singing is documented by a famous series of recordings beginning in 1902, which contributed greatly to his celebrity (and to the success of the phonograph as a medium for opera). Over the years the timbre gradually grew more baritonal (especially after a 1909 operation for a node on his vocal cords), from 1904 on, the casual singer of the first records gives ever greater attention to polish of phrasing and tonal perfection. Gifted with a communicative ebullience, Caruso worked hard at developing his theatrical craft to encompass tragic roles such as Samson and Eléazar. His premature death resulted from the consequences of a lung ailment.
BIBLIOGRAPHY: Frances Robinson, *Caruso: A Life in Pictures* (N.Y., 1957).

Carvalho, Léon. Impresario and singer; b. Port-Louis, near Paris, Jan. 18, 1825; d. Paris, Dec. 29, 1897. While a baritone at the Opéra-Comique, he married soprano Marie Miolan. Director of the Théâtre-Lyrique (1856–68) and of the Opéra-Comique (1876–87), where a disastrous 1887 caused him to be fined and imprisoned for negligence; he was later acquitted and reinstated (1891–97).

Case, Anna. Soprano; b. Clinton, N.J., Oct. 29, 1888; d. New York, Jan. 7, 1984. Studied with Mme. Ohrstrom-Renard, N.Y. Met debut as a Page in *Lohengrin*, Nov. 20, 1909; she sang there until 1919, including first Met Sophie, 1913; her 81 perfs. also included Micaela and Aida.

Casella, Alfredo. Composer; b. Turin, Italy, July 25, 1883; d. Rome, Mar. 5, 1947. Studied with Fauré in Paris, where he encountered progressive tendencies in the arts; further stimulated by tours as pianist and conductor throughout Europe and Russia. Returning to Italy in 1915, he became an avid proponent of new music. His own work absorbed the influences of Bartók, Schoenberg, and Stravinsky; in the 1920s its fierceness was tempered by neo-classicism and by borrowings from earlier Italian music and folk song. His operatic works, all from this last period, include the full-length *La Donna Serpente* after Gozzi (1932), the one-act chamber opera *La Favola d'Orfeo* after Poliziano (1932), and the one-act mystery *Il Deserto Tentato* (1937).

Casellato-Lamberti, Giorgio. Tenor; b. Adria, Italy, July 9, 1938. Studied in Mantua; debut as Arrigo (*Vêpres*), Rome Opera, 1964. U.S. debut as Radames, Chicago, 1965. Met debut as Cavaradossi, Nov. 30, 1974; in 5 subsequent seasons, has also sung Enzo, Radames, and Turiddu.

ENRICO CARUSO
Plácido Domingo

I suppose that every profession has its paragons. Certainly every artist has
an ideal – someone whose work inspired him to try to pursue the same
muse. Painters will point to da Vinci or Goya, composers may name
Beethoven or Mozart, and a writer might say he was inspired by Tolstoy
or Shakespeare or Cervantes. Performing artists have their idols too, and if
you were to ask a conductor, an instrumentalist, a dancer, or an actor to
name an ideal, their answers would be varied, but each would have one or
two.

The same is true with tenors, but with one big difference: every tenor
has the some ideal. That is not to say there has been only one great tenor;
when I am asked to name those I admire, I usually mention several, each
for a different reason. But above all there is one giant who had everything,
and who is a god for every tenor. He is, of course, Enrico Caruso.

The fact that one man has led the list of tenors for so many years is, I
think, an extraordinary thing. Here is a singer who has been dead for over
sixty-five years. Few people are alive who heard him on stage, and certainly
no tenor now singing knows anything of his art except from recordings.
People who know nothing about opera still recognize his name, and all
who care about singing will agree that he was the best – and imagine any
two opera lovers agreeing about anything! Why should that be?

It's all there in his recordings. Put on any of his many records – he made
286 of them – and within a few minutes I think you'll see why this
admiration has continued. First there is the technique. I always think of his
voice as a tower of sound, unbroken, equal registers, with special strength
from F-natural up to top B-flat.

But if his technique were all, no one would recognize his name today,
much less his voice. Everyone admires the power of his voice, but, above
all, we love the soul of it. He gave himself completely in his interpretation
of everything he sang, and so he was able to reach many more people than
any opera singer ever had. Listen to his "Vesti la giubba," or "O tu che in
seno agli angeli," or "E lucevan le stelle." This music and these words were
in his blood, and they poured out of him as naturally as if he had written
them himself. He didn't need to think about authority or conviction – they
were *there*, in every syllable and in every breath. This is something God-
given; you cannot learn it.

Caruso was not in any way intellectual, and his approach to singing was
in many ways instinctive, but I think that the legend of Caruso as a
completely "natural," untutored voice has been exaggerated. In part, he
encouraged this image; when asked what is needed to be a great singer, he
is supposed to have said, "A big chest, a big mouth, ninety percent
memory, ten percent intelligence, lots of hard work, and something in the
heart." But again, the proof is in the recordings.

Listen to his different versions of "Celeste Aida." He recorded the aria
six times between 1901 and 1911, and it's fascinating to hear how he
changes the phrasing each time, looking for a way to make this difficult
aria work better. This is the mark of a great musician, and that is why,
throughout my career, whenever I have had a problem with a piece of
music I have turned to Caruso's recordings, and they usually have shown
me how to solve the problem.

I have many other favorites among his recordings. He made two versions
of "Una furtiva lagrima" in America, one in 1904, and another in 1911,

(*Left*) Caruso as Rodolfo
(*Below*) and off stage

after he had been singing heavier roles. Of course his voice darkened from aging, but he proved he could still easily handle Donizetti's lovely lyrical aria.

For me, his best recordings are in French: "O souverain" from *Le Cid*, "Rachel, quand du Seigneur la grace tutelaire" from *La Juive*, and the selections from *Manon* (I love the ringing intensity of "Ah fuyez, douce image"). His versions of the two arias from Leoncavallo's *Bohème* are also among my favorites.

He made three beautiful versions of the *Carmen* "Flower Song," two of them – one in French and one in Italian – in one day. Many of his recordings were made with other great singers of his time, and two that I especially admire are the *Otello* duet with Titta Ruffo (a role Caruso never attempted on stage) and the duet from *Forza* with Antonio Scotti. I've read that their voices were so well matched that when the record was first released no one could tell who was singing when, with the result that Victor for the first time printed the text of the duet on the back of the record.

Caruso recorded many pieces that were not operatic, and these are wonderful too. There are, of course, magnificent performances of Italian songs, but you'll find some surprises in his list of records – French songs, popular songs in English (like "Over There" and "The Lost Chord"), and even some beautifully sung Spanish songs. I recommend his versions of "La Partida," "Noche Feliz," and "A Granada."

While Caruso's recordings are the basis of his legacy as an artist, we are lucky also to have ample evidence of what he was like as a man. Several people close to him wrote memoirs, and many of his letters have been published. This evidence is especially important in understanding the Caruso phenomenon, because he was one of the first singers whose popularity was in part based on personality, on what he was like as a man.

Caruso was one of those down-to-earth, approachable singers who surprise their fans with their natural, unaffected behavior. He came at a time when most famous singers were viewed as aristocrats of the stage; Jean de Reszke was the darling of the Golden Horseshoe, but Caruso was a man of the Family Circle. As a result, his fame went far beyond those who normally cared about operatic singers.

We read wonderful stories about his generosity, his love for people of all kinds, his marvelous sense of humor, and his sweetness as a human being. He made friends with everyone, gave money and opera tickets to anyone who asked, and, whether singing a high B-flat to identify himself in the middle of a bank or rubbing his stomach after his twelfth curtain call to show the audience he was hungry and wanted to leave, he sounds like someone you would like to have known.

Books by his wife Dorothy and his secretary Bruno Zirato tell us first-hand how seriously he took his art – his nervousness before going on stage, his fury with anyone who did not do his job correctly, his performing habits. (Gargling salt water during performances I can understand, but that he constantly smoked cigarettes – even just before going on stage – astonishes me.) Luckily, there is enough to read about him so that the man, and not just the voice, emerges full-bodied and fascinating.

I have paid tribute to Caruso twice before in my career: once with a recording called "Domingo Sings Caruso," the second time on a live television show with Zubin Mehta and the New York Philharmonic. Both times I was very nervous, because just having your name near his is a lot to live up to. Some might listen to his records and say, "Why bother to sing?" I would rather keep him in my mind as a friendly star, a very happy source of inspiration and challenge.

Cassel, Walter. Baritone; b. Council Bluffs, Iowa, May 15, 1910. Studied with Frank La Forge, N.Y.; debut as Brétigny (*Manon*), Met, Dec. 12, 1942; N.Y.C. Opera debut as Escamillo, 1948. Returned to Met in 1955 as Scarpia, singing major roles until 1974, including Mandryka, the Dutchman, Telramund, Jochanaan, and Kurwenal, for a total of 203 perfs. Created Horace Tabor in *Ballad of Baby Doe*, Central City, 1956.

Cassilly, Richard. Tenor; b. Washington, D.C., Dec. 14, 1927. Studied at Peabody Conservatory, Baltimore, and with Hans Heinz, N.Y. Debut as Michele in *Saint of Bleecker Street* on Broadway, 1955. Appeared with N.Y.C. Opera (debut as Tchaikovsky's Vakula, 1955), later in Chicago, Hamburg, Berlin (Deutsche Oper), Covent Garden. Met debut as Radames, Jan. 20, 1973; there he has sung over 100 perfs., in roles including Tannhäuser, Tristan, Otello, Samson, Canio, Jimmy Mahoney (*Mahagonny*), Captain Vere (*Billy Budd*), and the Drum Major (*Wozzeck*).

Castagna, Bruna. Mezzo-soprano; b. Bari, Italy, Oct. 15, 1905; d. Pinamar, Argentina, July 10, 1983. Studied with Scognamiglia, Milan; debut as Marina (*Boris*), Mantua, 1922. La Scala debut as Suzuki, 1925, appearing there until 1934. Met debut as Amneris, Mar. 2, 1936, later singing Azucena, Maddalena, Santuzza, Carmen, Laura, Adalgisa, Dalila, Quickly, and Ulrica; 107 perfs. in 10 seasons. Retired to Argentina.

Castel, Nico. Tenor; b. Lisbon, Aug. 1, 1931. Studied with Carmen Hurtado in Caracas, Mercedes Llopart in Milan, and Julia Drobner, N.Y.; debut as Fenton, Santa Fe, 1958. N.Y.C. Opera debut, Oct. 20, 1965, in *Fiery Angel*. Met debut as Basilio (*Nozze*), Mar. 30, 1970; has sung Witch (*Hänsel*), Shuisky, and many other character roles with the company, and serves as staff diction coach. Has appeared in Houston, Philadelphia, Washington, Florence, Spoleto, and Lisbon.

Castelmary [de Castan], **Armand.** Baritone; b. Toulouse, France, Aug. 16, 1834, d. New York, Feb. 10, 1897. Debut at Paris Opéra, 1863; sang there until 1870, subsequently appearing in London and N.Y. Met debut as Vulcan (*Philémon*), Nov. 29, 1893; his 70 perfs. also

Cavalleria Rusticana – (1970). Designed and produced by Franco Zeffirelli

included Méphistophélès, Sparafucile, and Remigio (*Navarraise*). Died on the Met stage during a perf. of *Martha*.

castrato (Ital.). A male singer castrated before puberty to preserve the high range of his voice. Common in Italian choirs from the 16th c. (when women were forbidden to sing in church), castratos sang in the earliest operas, reached a peak of popularity in the late 17th and early 18th c., and declined after the Napoleonic invasions of Italy repressed the practice of castration. (Eunuchs were still found in the Sistine Choir in Rome until the early 20th c., and the last of them, Alessandro Moreschi, made a number of recordings.) Dominating the culture of opera seria, castrato voices had the penetrating power of male singers, placed in the range of sopranos and contraltos, and trained to a peak of virtuosic agility.

Catalani, Alfredo. Composer; b. Lucca, Italy, June 19, 1854; d. Milan, Aug. 7, 1893. Studied with Bazin in Paris and Bazzini in Milan, who brought him to Giovannina Lucca, who published his first opera *Elda* (1876; rev. as *Loreley*, 1890), as well as *Dejanice* (1883) and *Edmea* (1886). The merger of Lucca with Ricordi in 1888 placed Catalani in a position subordinate to Verdi and Puccini, but *La Wally* (1892), based on a German Romantic folk tale, was produced with some success at la Scala. Catalani's early death meant that his work, with its Romantic and Wagnerian predilections, was soon eclipsed by the raw intensity of verismo.

Caterina Cornaro. Opera in prologue and 2 acts by Donizetti; libretto by Giacomo Sacchèro, after Saint-George's libretto for Halévy's *La Reine de Chypre*.
  First perf., Naples, San Carlo, Jan. 12, 1844: Goldberg, Fraschini, Coletti, Benevento. U.S. prem., N.Y., Carnegie Hall (Opera Theater of N.J.), Apr. 15, 1973 (concert perf.): Gencer, Campora, Taddei, c. Silipigni.
  The last of Donizetti's operas to receive its premiere during his lifetime. Lusignano (bs), King of Cyprus, who covets the hand of Caterina (s), unwittingly saves the life of her betrothed, Gerardo (t); mortally wounded in battle, Lusignano commends his people to Caterina's care.

Cavalieri, Emilio de'. Composer; b. Rome, c. 1550; d. Rome, Mar. 11, 1602. Appointed in 1588 to oversee musical activities at the court of Ferdinando de' Medici in Florence, he supervised the presentation of lavish *intermedi* and was involved with the Camerata and the development of the recitative style. His principal work, *La Rappresentazione di Anima, et di Corpo* (1600), is a morality play in which recitative is interspersed with songs, madrigals, and choruses in dance rhythm.

Cavalieri, Lina. Soprano; b. Viterbo, Italy, Dec. 25, 1874; d. Florence, Feb. 7, 1944. First sang in cafés, then studied with Maddalena Mariani-Masi; debut as Mimì, San Carlo, Naples, 1900. Appeared throughout Europe, admired as much for her personal beauty as for her singing. Met debut as Fedora, Dec. 5, 1906, later singing Manon Lescaut, Tosca, Mimì, Nedda, and Adriana; 24 perfs. in 2 seasons.

Cavalleria Rusticana (Rustic Chivalry). Opera in 1 act by Mascagni; libretto by G. Targioni-Tozzetti and G. Menasci, after Giovanni Verga's short story.
  First perf., Rome, Costanzi, May 17, 1890: Bellincioni, Stagno, Salassa, c. Mugnone. U.S. prem., Philadelphia,

Grand Opera House, Sep. 9, 1891: Kört-Kronold, Guille, del Puente, c. Hinrichs. Met prem., Dec. 30, 1891 (following *Orfeo*): Eames, Valero, Camera, c. Vianesi, d. Operti, p. Habelmann. (At first Met perf. with *Pagliacci*, Dec. 22, 1893, *Pagliacci* was played first.) Later Met productions: Dec. 17, 1908: Destinn, Caruso, Amato, c. Toscanini, d. Sala, Parravicini/Maison Chiappa, p. Speck; Dec. 13, 1924: Ponselle, Tokatyan, Picco, c. Papi, d. Novak, p. Agnini; Jan. 17, 1951: Milanov, Tucker, Harvuot, c. Erede, d. Armistead/Lloyd, p. H. Busch; Nov. 7, 1958: Milanov, Zambruno, Bardelli, c. Mitropoulos, d. Gérard, p. Quintero; Jan. 8, 1970: Bumbry, Corelli, Guarrera, c. Bernstein, d. & p. Zeffirelli. Santuzza has been sung at the Met by Calvé, Muzio, Simionato; Turiddu by Tamagno, Vignas, Gigli, Lauri-Volpi, Bjoerling, del Monaco; Alfio by Scotti, de Luca, Tibbett, Warren. 391 perfs. in 68 seasons.

Cavalleria launched the verismo movement in Italian opera. The plot is brief and easy to understand, the characters and the conflicts that inflame them are drawn from ordinary life, the music is direct and impassioned.

Turiddu (t) has returned from war to find his former lover Lola (ms) married to the village carter, Alfio (bar). After seeking consolation with Santuzza (s), who is pregnant with his child, he has now rekindled his affair with Lola. Santuzza pleads with him not to abandon her, but when he scornfully rejects her, she reveals all to Alfio, who challenges his rival to a duel. Turiddu bids a tearful farewell to his mother, Mamma Lucia (a), and goes off to fight; soon a villager rushes in, crying that Turiddu has been killed.

Cavalli, Francesco. Composer; b. Crema, Italy, Feb. 14, 1602; d. Venice, Jan. 14, 1676. First instruction with his father, chapel master at Crema. In 1616, joined the choir of Saint Mark's in Venice, under the direction of Monteverdi, eventually becoming principal organist (1655) and chapel master (1668). He was a prolific composer of opera, beginning in 1639; his catalogue includes 40 works, notably *L'Ormindo* (1644), *La Calisto* (1651–52), *Serse* (1654, celebrating the wedding of Louis XIV of France), *Erismena* (1655), and *Ercole Amante* (1662, inaugurating the hall of the Tuileries). With their strophic arias and comic scenes, Cavalli's operas touched a more popular vein than the academic classicism of the earliest operas.

cavatina (Ital.). A term applied in the 18th c. to simple arias, and in the 19th c. to short, relatively slow arias; when used in 19th-c. Italian opera, however, it merely indicates the entrance aria of a principal character.

Cebotari, Maria. Soprano; b. Kishinev, Bessarabia, Feb. 10, 1910; d. Vienna, June 9, 1949. Studied with Oskar Daniel, Berlin; debut as Mimi, Dresden, 1931. Sang there until 1936, creating Aminta (*Schweigsame Frau*, 1935), later in Berlin (1936–44) and Vienna (1946–49). At Salzburg, created Lucille (*Dantons Tod*, 1947) and Iseut (Martin's *Vin Herbé*, 1948).

Cehanovsky, George. Baritone; b. St. Petersburg, Apr. 14, 1892; d. Yorktown Heights, N.Y., Mar. 25, 1986. Studied with his mother; debut as Valentin, Petrograd, 1921. Emigrated to U.S.; Met debut as Kothner (*Meistersinger*), Nov. 13, 1926; sang 40 seasons with company, 1706 perfs. of 97 roles, mostly comprimario. After retirement, served as Met's Russian diction coach. Married to soprano Elisabeth Rethberg.

Cena delle Beffe, La (The Jesters' Supper). Opera in 4 acts by Giordano; libretto by Sem Benelli, after his play (known in Eng. as *The Jest*).

First perf., Milan, La Scala, Dec. 20, 1924: Melis, Lázaro, Franci, c. Toscanini. U.S. & Met prem., Jan. 2, 1926: Alda, Gigli, Ruffo, c. Serafin, d. Urban. 8 perfs. in 2 seasons.

One of the most sadistic of verismo operas, set in Renaissance Florence. Treated brutally by the brothers Neri (bar) and Gabriello (t) because of his love for Neri's mistress Ginevra (s), Giannetto (t) maneuvers Neri into killing his own brother, who is revealed as another of Ginevra's lovers.

Cendrillon (Cinderella). Opera in 4 acts by Massenet; libretto by Henri Cain, after Charles Perrault's fairy tale.

First perf., Paris, Opéra-Comique, May 24, 1899: Giraudon, Bréjean-Silver, Emelen, Deschamps-Jehin, Fugère, c. Luigini. U.S. prem., New Orleans, French Opera House, Dec. 23, 1902.

A sweetly romantic setting of the Cinderella story, with a few added characters and episodes.

Cenerentola, La, ossia La Bontà in Trionfo (Cinderella, or The Triumph of Goodness). Opera in 2 acts by Rossini; libretto by Jacopo Ferretti, after Charles Guillaume Étienne's libretto for Isouard's *Cendrillon*; also after the fairy tale.

First perf., Rome, Valle, Jan. 25, 1817: Giorgi-Righetti, Guglielmi, de Begnis, Verni. U.S. prem., N.Y., Park, June 27, 1826: the cast included the future Maria Malibran, her mother, and her brother Manuel Garcia Jr.

In a version purged of supernatural elements, the Cinderella story is perfectly suited to Rossini's gift for stories of surprise, disguise, and confusion; the score sparkles from the overture to the dazzling rondo finale.

Salerno, unspecified time, probably 18th c. The warm-hearted Angelina, known as Cenerentola (ms), is ill-treated by her stepfather Don Magnifico (bs) and her snobbish stepsisters Tisbe (ms) and Clorinda (s). The family prepares for a visit from Prince Ramiro (t), who is searching throughout the land for a bride. He arrives disguised as his valet, and falls in love at first sight with Cenerentola, while the valet Dandini (bar), dressed as the Prince, is fawned over by the stepsisters. He invites them to a ball; Magnifico and his daughters leave Cenerentola behind. The Prince's philosopher Alidoro (bs) appears and escorts Cenerentola to the ball, where she leaves with the prince one of the twin bracelets Alidoro has given her. The next day the Prince recognizes her in spite of her clothing of rags, and makes her his princess; she ascends the throne, forgiving her cruel stepsisters and stepfather.

Cerquetti, Anita. Soprano; b. Montecosaro, near Macerata, Italy, Apr. 13, 1931. Studied in Perugia; debut as Aida, Spoleto, 1951, then sang throughout Italy. Debuts with Chicago Opera (Amelia, 1955) and La Scala (Abigaille, 1958). Retired in 1961.

Cesti, Antonio [Pietro]. Composer; b. Arezzo, Italy, bapt. Aug. 5, 1623; d. Florence, Oct. 14, 1669. Franciscan friar, studied in Rome, probably with Carissimi and Abbatini. His first operas, *Orontea* (1649) and *Il Cesare Amante* (1651), produced in Venice, established Cesti's reputation. He worked subsequently for the Habsburgs in Innsbruck and then in Vienna, where he oversaw the production of his *Il Pomo d'Oro* (1668), the most spectacular of Baroque court operas (requiring 24 sets), in the allegorical tradition of Monteverdi.

Chabrier, (Alexis-)Emmanuel. Composer; b. Ambert, Puy de Dôme, France, Jan. 18, 1841; d. Paris, Sep. 13, 1894. Despite prodigious pianistic and improvisational abilities, he prepared in Paris for a law career, studying music on the side. While holding a government position (1861–80), he pursued his artistic interests. Verlaine provided librettos for the unfinished operettas *Fisch-Ton-Kan* (1863–64) and *Vaucochard et Fils Ier* (1864). *L'Étoile* (1877) and *Une Éducation Manquée* (1879) displayed his comic and melodic gifts, as well as his skill in inventing dramatically effective dissonance. An 1879 visit to Munich to hear Wagner's *Tristan* convinced him to become a full-time composer. After the Wagnerian *Gwendoline* (1886), and the buoyant opéra comique *Le Roi Malgré Lui* (1887), he was able to complete only one act of *Briséis* before his death.

Chagall, Marc. Painter and designer; b. Vitebsk, Russia, July 7, 1887; d. St. Paul de Vence, France, Mar. 28, 1985. One of the great modern painters, he also designed ballets (including *Firebird* for Balanchine, 1949), operas (including *Zauberflöte* for the Met, 1967), and lyrical, fantastic murals for the foyer of the new Met and the ceiling of the Paris Opéra.

Chailly, Riccardo. Conductor; b. Milan, Feb. 20, 1953. Studied with his father, composer Luciano, at Verdi Conservatory, under Ferrara. U.S. opera debut, *Butterfly*, Chicago Lyric (1974). Chief conductor, Berlin Radio Symphony (from 1982); Amsterdam Concertgebouw (from 1983); music director, Comunale, Bologna (from 1986). Met debut, *Hoffmann* (Mar. 9, 1982).

Chaliapin, Feodor [Fyodor Shalyapin]. Bass; b. near Kazan, Russia, Feb. 13, 1873; d. Paris, Apr. 12, 1938. Son of poor peasants, with little formal education, at 14 he joined the chorus of a travelling opera company, in which the writer Maxim Gorky was a colleague. Debut as the Stolnik (*Halka*), Semyonov-Smarsky Company, Ufa, 1890. In 1892–93, he studied with Dmitri Usatov in Tiflis, where he sang both Valentin and Méphistophélès, then appeared in St. Petersburg with Panayev's summer company (Bertram in *Robert le Diable*, 1894) and at the Maryinsky. His first major successes came with Mamontov's company in Moscow (1896–99): Boris, Varlaam, Dosifey (*Khovanshchina*), Ivan the Terrible (*Maid of Pskov*), the Viking Guest (*Sadko*), and Holofernes (Serov's *Judith*); he also created Salieri (*Mozart and Salieri*). A 20-year association with the Bolshoi in Moscow began in 1899.

His first foreign appearances were at La Scala, 1901, including Boito's Mefistofele under Toscanini. After 1905, he sang often at Monte Carlo, where he created Massenet's Don Quichotte (1910) and appeared onstage for the last time in 1937, as Boris. In his first Met season (debut, Mefistofele, Nov. 20, 1907, followed by Méphistophélès, Basilio, and Leporello), his broad, naturalistic acting style was ill-received by critics and public. Chaliapin participated in Diaghilev's Russian seasons in Paris (including the first fully-staged *Boris* outside Russia, 1908) and Beecham's in London (1913, 1914). After the Russian Revolution, he was artistic director of the Maryinsky until his emigration to Paris in 1921; he never revisited the Soviet Union. On Dec. 9 of that year, he returned to the Met as Boris, receiving a fee of $3,000 a night (the highest paid any Met artist until the late 1960s). A member of the company every season until 1929, he sang 27 Borises, Philippe II, and the house's first Don Quichotte, for a

Feodor Chaliapin as Boris Godunov

grand total of 78 perfs.; he also sang at the Chicago Opera, 1922–24.

With a voice of commanding power and range, and a technique unconventional but remarkably secure, Chaliapin achieved a highly personal balance between the demands of declamation and musical line. Even in his voice's declining years, he was an actor of immense energy and perfectionist attention to detail, whose presence held all eyes whenever he was onstage. His characterizations, seen in many European cities during the years of his exile and disseminated by numerous recordings, influenced several generations of singers, especially in his Russian repertory. He made two films: *Tsar Ivan the Terrible* (directed by Ivanov-Gay, 1915) and *Don Quixote* (directed by Pabst, with songs by Ibert; 1933).

BIBLIOGRAPHY: Feodor Chaliapin, *Pages from My Life* (London, 1927) and *Man and Mask* (London, 1932).

chamber opera. Opera calling for small vocal and instrumental ensembles. Though retrospectively embracing the earliest Florentine operas, as well as intermezzos, ballad operas, and other works of the 18th c., the term – and the vogue of the genre – is a product of the 20th-c. reaction to Romantic extravagance.

Chamlee, Mario [Archer Cholmondeley]. Tenor; b. Los Angeles, May 29, 1892; d. Los Angeles, Nov. 13, 1966. Studied with Achille Alberti in Los Angeles; debut there as Edgardo, 1916. After army service, joined Scotti Opera Co. After Met debut as Cavaradossi, Nov. 22, 1920, returned in 1927–28 and 1935–37; roles also included Almaviva, Turiddu, both Fausts, Pinkerton, and the title role in *Caponsacchi*. Married to soprano Ruth Miller (1893–1983).

Chapin, Schuyler G. Manager; b. New York, Feb. 13, 1923. At the Longy School of Music, Cambridge, Mass.

(1940–41), Nadia Boulanger urged him to pursue a career in arts management. After working for NBC, as tour manager for Heifetz, and as a booking director with Columbia Artists, he headed the classical division of Columbia Records (1959–62). At Lincoln Center, he was vice president of creative services (1962–63) and programming (1964–69), then produced film and other projects for Leonard Bernstein (1969–71). Appointed a Met assistant manager by Gentele, after the latter's death in July 1972 he became acting general manager (1972–73), then general manager, but his contract was not renewed in 1975. Although financial and production crises kept him on the defensive, Chapin was able to carry out some of Gentele's initiatives (including the Mini-Met and the Met premiere of *Troyens*, 1973). In 1976, he became Dean of the School of the Arts at Columbia U.

BIBLIOGRAPHY: Schuyler Chapin, *Musical Chairs* (N.Y., 1977).

Charleston. City in South Carolina, and site of the first operatic performance in America: Colley Cibber's *Flora, or Hob in the Well*, Feb. 18, 1735. Visiting companies performed popular Italian opera during the 19th c., and singers such as Lind and Patti were heard in concert. Recently, Charleston has become the site of the annual Spoleto Festival U.S.A., founded in 1976 by Gian Carlo Menotti as counterpart to the festival in the Italian city of the same name. Opera performances have included unusual repertory such as Donizetti's *Furioso all'Isola di San Domingo* and Handel's *Ariodante*, controversial productions of standard works, such as Ken Russell's staging of *Madama Butterfly*, and Menotti's own works. Performances take place in the Dock Street theater and the Gaillard Municipal Auditorium. In 1987, Spiros Argiris succeeded Christian Badea as music director.

Charpentier, Gustave. Composer; b. Dieuze, Moselle, France, June 25, 1860; d. Paris, Feb. 18, 1956. Studied composition with Massenet at Paris Conservatory, and won the Prix de Rome (1887). His working-class background, fascination with Montmartre bohemian life, and strong social concerns were combined in the autobiographical "musical novel" *Louise* (1900), which mixed raw local color, feminist sympathies, and a lyrical pre-verismo musical style. In 1902, with income from festivals of his populist compositions, he founded the Conservatoire Populaire Mimi Pinson, which provided free musical instruction to working-class women. Charpentier wrote a sequel to *Louise*, the briefly successful *Julien* (1913), but his subsequent musical works remained unfinished, including the operas *L'Amour au Faubourg* (c. 1913) and *Orphée* (reportedly completed by M. Delmas in 1931).

Charpentier, Marc-Antoine. Composer; b. Paris, c. 1636; d. Paris, Feb 24, 1704. Studied with Carissimi in Rome. Composed music for Molière's company (soon to be known as the Comédie Française), including a prologue and intermezzos for *Le Malade Imaginaire* (1673). For much of Charpentier's career, royal preferment was blocked by Lully, and he concentrated on religious composition, including oratorios and sacred dramas (notably *David et Jonathas*, 1688); his only tragédie lyrique for the Paris Opéra was *Médée* (1693), equivocally received but considered by some equal to the compositions of Lully. Other stage compositions include the pastorale *Actéon* (1683–85) and the opera *Les Arts Florissants* (1685–86).

Chausson, Ernest. Composer; b. Paris, Jan. 21, 1855; d. Limay, June 10, 1899. Studied with Massenet at Paris Conservatory and privately with Franck. Attended Wagner performances in Germany, including the premiere of *Parsifal* (1882); the influence of Wagner's harmonic and orchestral techniques, as well as his use of leitmotif, are apparent in Chausson's only produced opera, *Le Roi Arthus* (1895, prod. 1903). In subsequent compositions, he moved away from Wagner; his late songs and chamber works reflect his concern for structural clarity.

Cheek, John. Bass; b. Greenville, S.C., Aug. 17, 1948. Studied at N.C. School of Arts and with Gino Bechi, Siena. Met debut as Physician (*Pelléas*), Oct. 11, 1977; his roles there include Pimen, Ferrando (*Trovatore*), Wurm (*Luisa Miller*), Klingsor, Panthée (*Troyens*), Figaro, and Monterone. N.Y.C. Opera debut as Mefistofele, 1986.

Chéreau, Patrice. Producer; b. Lézigné (Maine-et-Loire), Nov. 2, 1944. Co-director, Théâtre National Populaire (1979–81); director, Théâtre des Amandiers, Nanterre (since 1982). His radically deconstructionist and controversial operatic productions include *Hoffmann* (Paris Opéra, 1974), Bayreuth centennial *Ring* (1976), and premiere of three-act *Lulu*, Paris Opéra (1979).

Cherevichki. See *Vakula the Smith*.

Cherubini, Luigi. Composer; b. Florence, Sep. 8 or 14, 1760; d. Paris, Mar. 15, 1842. Studied in Florence, and in Milan with Sarti. After composing operas in the prevailing Neapolitan style, he went in 1784 to London, and two years later settled in Paris, where his first major success was the opéra comique *Lodoïska* (1791). This "rescue opera" proved influential for its dramatic use of ensemble and choral music, brilliant orchestration, vividly contemporary subject matter, and the introduction of character types such as the villain Dourlinsky, model for Pizarro in *Fidelio*. Despite the conservative cut of his music, Cherubini was much admired by such colleagues as Beethoven, and *Les Deux Journées* (1800) and *Faniska* (1807), also rescue operas, were widely performed. Today, only the tragedy *Médée* (1797), a powerful psychological study, holds a place in the repertory. Cherubini's later career was primarily devoted to composing sacred music, teaching, and the directorship of the Paris Conservatory (1821–41); among his students were Auber and Halévy. Other operas include *Anacréon* (1803), *Les Abencérages* (1813), and *Ali-Baba* (1833).

chest voice, chest register. The lower register of the human voice, in which the sounds appear to be produced from the chest. Chest tones are richer and heavier than those of the higher head register.

Chiara, Maria. Soprano; b. Oderzo, Italy, Nov. 24, 1942. Studied with Antonio Cassinelli (later her husband) and Maria Carbone; debut as Desdemona, Venice, Fenice, 1966. She later sang in Berlin (1971), Hamburg (1971), and at La Scala (1972). Met debut as Violetta, Dec. 16, 1977.

Chicago. City in Illinois. Operatic activity in Chicago dates from a performance of *Sonnambula* on July 29, 1850, and touring troupes subsequently made regular if brief visits. Crosby's Opera House (opened 1865, burned 1871, rebuilt 1873) was the city's first, though its usual fare was operetta. In 1889, the Metropolitan Opera brought the

(continued p.86)

THE CHORUS
David Stivender

In the "Advertisement to the First Edition" of his *Life of Johnson*, James Boswell remarked, "I have sometimes been obliged to run half over London, in order to fix a date correctly; which, when I had accomplished it, I well knew would obtain me no praise, though a failure would have been to my discredit." I often think of these words when the chorus and I are working through a particularly difficult passage. If in performance it goes smoothly, even the most discerning listener takes it for granted; if it misfires, we will likely hear that "The chorus was certainly off form last night." But of course there is no choice; what is on the page, no matter how difficult, must be made to work on the stage. This is live music.

At the Met we have a regular chorus of eighty-two members (augmented to a hundred for big operas such as *Aida* and *Boris*), and these eighty-two must come to the point where they can perform as a unit, with precision, night after night. Not only are the notes, rhythms, and words to be learned and memorized, but also what is most difficult of all to a memorizing ensemble: unanimous attacks and cutoffs. Attacking together requires knowing the cues, and the cutoffs have to be learned along with the notes and the words. A group of eighty or a hundred singers with messy cutoffs is a very noticeable group.

Of course the stage director plays an enormous part in how hard this is. In *La Sonnambula* (in my opinion the single most difficult opera for the chorus), there's not much a director can do but arrange attractive groups and allow the chorus to support the soloists (and to remember – in proper order – all those cues). In *Boris* or *Grimes*, where the chorus is a protagonist, our assignment contains large pieces of through-composed music, and fewer interjections – but the action is far more complicated; they are on the move for most of the opera, constantly adjusting their angles of vision and trying to project the sound of the choral mass into the auditorium.

What kind of singer goes to make an operatic chorister? Doubtless, few embark on a singing career with the idea of working full-time in a chorus. But only certain singers have the particular quality that says, "Listen to me. What I have to say as an individual is worth your while to listen to." For others, the alternative is not "settling" for a position in the chorus. Being a member of the Met chorus is a fulfilled – and fulfilling – career. One is working with first-class musicians and directors, wearing first-class costumes and wigs, and appearing in first-class scenery. All this matters a great deal.

And then there is the question of *esprit*. No large group of people who perform with energy and professionalism can fail to take pride in their organization. To do a run of, say, twenty *Carmen*s and retain the same energy as on opening night requires a high degree of dedication. One way to keep up that energy level is to concentrate on the details as they go by. Since we do *Carmen* season after season with a variety of soloists and conductors, the little problems that have to be solved in every score are always worked on. My personal motto for years has been Horace's *limae labor*, "the work of the file," and it is this constant filing away at details that keeps our attention during performance on the work itself, rather than straying to matters over which we have no control.

I try to eliminate problematic staging at the beginning of a new production by working closely with the director: there is no sense building pitfalls into an opera that will be performed season after season. Of course, certain difficulties are inherent in the works, and here the attention of the chorus has to be focused on the details during *every* performance. Perhaps

the most difficult are the cross-over choruses in the first and third acts of *Tannhäuser*: the men are strung out, often single file, and are required to sing unaccompanied four-part harmony of the most chromatic sort. (I can't prove it, but I have always believed that when Wagner again came to write processional choruses for men, years later in *Parsifal*, he took no chances: they are accompanied by the orchestra, sung in unison, and anchored firmly in the key of C major – in *Parsifal*, a touchstone of chromaticism!) It took us more than a decade of performances before we all felt that the *Tannhäuser* choruses were settling in. In this kind of thing, *only* the work of the file will do!

Of course the variety of types and styles of choruses is a great help, not only in learning the operas but also in performing them. I have referred to the great "choral protagonist" operas such as *Boris* and *Grimes*, but other "choral operas" are equally satisfying: Verdi's panoramic *Forza* and *Don Carlos*, and his works with choruses in a monument style (*Aida*, *Nabucco*). Then there are the operas where the chorister feels part of a clearly defined community: *Die Meistersinger* on a grand scale, *L'Elisir d'Amore* on a much smaller one. And then, of course, all those "stand up and sing" operas such as *Ernani*, which can be as exhilarating as any grander opera.

It should doubtless be emphasized that a Met chorister needs a *healthy* voice, for the job requires long hours of work on many kinds of operas. For example, in a February week in 1987, we were rehearsing a new production of *Turandot* on the main stage, going to the rehearsal room afterwards to study *Samson et Dalila* and *Parsifal*, and at night performing *Boris* and *Carmen* – all big chorus operas, all by memory, two of them complicated productions, and in four languages. Naturally, once the chorister has found his own technique for learning and memorizing, the process becomes easier, but the voice itself must always be kept in a healthy state. And it is here that an uncomplicated, sane view of daily life is necessary. On the one hand, choristers work in the closest proximity; on the other, the old theatrical adage holds, that the singer thinks with his throat: if the voice stays healthy, the daily outlook tends to remain sane, and vice versa.

These are just a few of the many thoughts that came to me while reflecting on twenty years of work with the Met chorus. One thing about the work: it is definitely not a case where familiarity breeds contempt – quite the opposite. As the years go by and we keep filing away at all those problems, we come to realize why masterpieces have turned out to be masterpieces; we know, because we are constantly dealing with them in performance. As Francis Bacon said, "Every man is a debtor to his profession." To our profession, we owe these insights.

The Met Chorus in (*above*) *Peter Grimes*, (*middle*) *Tannhäuser*, and (*below*) *Die Meistersinger* (with Gerd Brenneis, Thomas Stewart, and Ellen Shade)

Lyric Opera, Chicago

city's first *Ring* cycle. The Chicago Auditorium (designed by Louis Sullivan; capacity 4,200) opened the same year and housed touring companies until 1910, when the Chicago Grand Opera Company was formed from the remains of Hammerstein's Manhattan Opera, with Cleofonte Campanini as musical director and Mary Garden as prima donna. Garden sang in Chicago until 1931 and, as general director in the 1921–22 season, presented the world premiere of Prokofiev's *Love for Three Oranges* and ran up a deficit of over a million dollars. Solvency was restored under the leadership of utility magnate Samuel Insull, and the renamed Chicago Civic Opera performed in the Civic Opera House (opened 1929, capacity 3,593) until Insull's bankruptcy terminated the enterprise in 1932. The following decades saw several short-lived attempts to create a resident organization. In 1954 the Chicago Lyric Theater (from 1956, Lyric Opera of Chicago) was founded by Carol Fox, Lawrence Kelly, and Nicola Rescigno; the initial season featured the U.S. debut of Callas, and subsequent seasons maintained a high level of casting, if more conventional repertory. After Kelly and Rescigno left in 1956, Fox became general manager, serving until 1980, when she was succeeded by Ardis Krainik; Bruno Bartolletti has been music director since 1956. The Lyric season offers nine productions, from late September to mid-January. A smaller company, the Chicago Opera Theater, directed by Alan Stone, presents several operas in the spring.

Chookasian, Lili. Mezzo-soprano; b. Chicago, Ill., Aug. 1, 1921. Studied with Philip Manuel in N.Y., Rosa Ponselle in Baltimore; debut as Adalgisa, Little Rock, 1959. Met debut, La Cieca, Mar. 9, 1962; in over 300 perfs., she has sung 28 roles, including both Erdas, Zia Principessa (*Suor Angelica*), Frugola (*Tabarro*), Quickly, and Geneviève (*Pelléas*). Also appeared at N.Y.C. Opera (Menotti's *Medium*, 1963) and Bayreuth (Erda, 1965).

chorus. An ensemble of voices, usually singing in three or four parts, many voices to a part. Introduced into the earliest operas in emulation of the *choros* of Greek drama, it was neglected in the heyday of Italian opera seria but has otherwise usually been a central feature of musical theater.

Christie, John. Impresario; b. Eggesford, England, Dec. 14, 1882; d. Glyndebourne, July 4, 1962. Educated at Eton (where he later taught science) and Cambridge. A musical amateur briefly active in the organ-building business, in 1931 he married the lyric soprano Audrey Mildmay (1900–53), for whom he constructed a small festival theater adjacent to Glyndebourne, his manor house in Sussex. Although Christie entertained prospects of Wagner performances, what emerged in 1934 was a festival devoted to model performances of Mozart, conducted by Fritz Busch and directed by Carl Ebert. In 1954 the Glyndebourne Arts Trust was established, and since John Christie's death, his son **George Christie** (b. Glyndebourne, Dec. 31, 1934), has become the enterprise's principal administrator.

Christoff, Boris. Bass; b. Plovdiv, Bulgaria, May 18, 1914. Earned a law degree and sang with a Sofia chorus, where King Boris heard him and provided a stipend for study in Rome with Stracciari; later studies with Muratti, Salzburg, 1945. Operatic debut as Colline, Reggio Calabria, 1946. Appeared the following season at Rome and La Scala as Pimen (*Boris*), and in 1949 at Covent Garden as Boris, returning there 1958–74. Engaged to appear at the Met as Philippe II in 1950, he was barred from entry to the country under the McCarran Act, and finally made his U.S. debut as Boris, San Francisco, 1956, later also singing in Chicago (1957–63). In a career that extended to most of the world's major theaters, he never sang at the Met – or in N.Y. until a 1980 concert.

Christoff's voluminous voice, of a markedly Slavic character, was well modulated thanks to his technical command. His operatic repertory included 40 roles in six languages, including a Boris considered by many the successor to Chaliapin's, thanks to his stage presence, realistic acting, and projection of the text. He also sang and acted memorably in Verdi bass parts, especially Philippe II and Fiesco; other roles include Handel's Giulio Cesare, Gurnemanz, King Marke, Rocco, Ivan Susanin, Dosifey (*Khovanshchina*), and Khan Konchak (*Prince Igor*). His extensive discography includes much Russian opera, song, and religious music.

Christophe Colomb. Opera in 2 acts by Milhaud; libretto by Paul Claudel.

First perf., Berlin, State Opera, May 5, 1930 (in Ger.): Reinhardt, Scheidl, c. Kleiber. U.S. prem., N.Y., Carnegie Hall, Nov. 6, 1952 (concert perf., in Eng.): Dow, Harrell, c. Mitropoulos. U.S. stage prem. (Part 2 only), San Francisco, Oct. 5, 1968 (in Eng.): Todd, Monk, c. Schuller.

The first work in Milhaud's Latin-American trilogy is a religious allegory treating the events of Columbus' life in scenes connected by the use of a narrator, a chorus, and film projections.

Christopher, Russell. Bass; b. Grand Rapids, Mich., Mar. 12, 1930. After study at U. of Michigan, work at NBC music department and with Amato Opera, sang in regional companies (1960–63) and won Met Auditions (1963). A regular company member since his debut as D'Obigny (*Traviata*, Dec. 14, 1963), he has performed nearly 60 comprimario roles.

Chung, Myung-Whun. Conductor; b. Seoul, Korea, Jan. 22, 1953. After a piano debut at age seven, studied in N.Y. at Mannes under Carl Bamberger and Juilliard under Ehrling. Assistant, then associate conductor in Los

Angeles (1978–81); now principal conductor, Saarbrücken Radio Symphony. Met debut, Feb. 21, 1986, leading *Boccanegra*.

church parable. Britten's term for three chamber works intended for performance in churches, involving elements of morality play and the Japanese Noh drama. See *Curlew River*, *The Burning Fiery Furnace*, and *The Prodigal Son*.

Ciannella, Giuliano. Tenor; b. Palermo, Italy, Oct. 25, 1943. La Scala debut as Cassio, 1976; Met debut in same role, Sept. 24, 1979; other roles there have included Rodolfo, Pinkerton, Puccini's Des Grieux, Don Carlos, Macduff, and Alfredo. Appearances in Chicago (Pinkerton, 1982), San Francisco (Don José, 1984), Munich (Don Carlos, 1985), and Covent Garden (Manrico, 1986).

Cid, Le. Opera in 4 acts by Massenet; libretto by Adolphe d'Ennery, Louis Gallet, and Edouard Blau, after Corneille's drama.
First perf., Paris, Opéra, Nov. 30, 1885: Devriès, J. de Reszke, E. de Reszke, Plançon. U.S. prem., New Orleans, French Opera House, Feb. 23, 1890. Met prem., Feb. 12, 1897: Litvinne, J. de Reszke, E. de Reszke, Plançon, c. Mancinelli. 7 perfs. in 3 seasons.
An essay in Meyerbeerian grand opera, set in 12th-c. Seville. To avenge the honor of his father Don Diègue (bs), Don Rodrigue (t), "the Cid," reluctantly duels with Count Gormas (bs), father of his beloved Chimène (s). Gormas dies and the girl is torn between love and family honor, but when Rodrigue returns from battle against the Moors the lovers are reconciled.

Cigna, Gina [Ginetta Sens]. Soprano; b. Angère, Paris, Mar. 6, 1900, of Italian parents. Studied with Calvé, Darclée, and Storchio; debut as Freia, La Scala, 1927. Sang

Boris Christoff as Philippe II in *Don Carlos*

at La Scala (1929–43) and Covent Garden (from 1933). Met debut as Aida, Feb. 6, 1937, also singing the *Trovatore* Leonora, Gioconda, Norma, Donna Elvira, and Santuzza; 17 perfs. in 2 seasons.

Cilea, Francesco. Composer; b. Palmi, Italy, July 23, 1866; d. Varazza, Nov. 20, 1950. While still a student at Naples Conservatory, his opera *Gina* (1889) was produced, winning him a contract with Sonzogno. The limited success of *La Tilda* (1892) turned Cilea's attention to teaching, which he continued to do for much of his life (he was director of Naples Conservatory, 1916–36). His next two operas, *L'Arlesiana* (1897) and *Adriana Lecouvreur* (1902), were more successful, especially within Italy. *Gloria* (1907), although introduced at La Scala by Toscanini, was dropped after two performances, nor did a 1932 revision win it a place in the repertory. Notable principally for a certain short-breathed melodic charm, Cilea's successful operas borrow much of their theatrical power from their sources, and his music conspicuously lacks the urgency commanded by his verismo contemporaries. For all his craftsmanship of detail, his continuing revision of *Arlesiana* and *Adriana* even after their success indicates a certain insecurity, and they have maintained their places in the repertory through the appeal of the principal female roles to interpreters.

Cillario, Carlo Felice. Conductor; b. San Rafael, Argentina, Feb. 7, 1915. After study in Bologna and Odessa, appeared in various theaters internationally, particularly in Australia, at Stockholm Opera, and in Chicago (debut, *Forza*, 1961). In 1972–73 at the Met, he led *Sonnambula* (debut, Oct. 17, 1972), *Tosca*, and *Trovatore*, returning in 1985 for *Tosca*.

Cimara, Pietro. Conductor; b. Rome, Nov. 10, 1887; d. Oct. 1, 1967. Student of Respighi at Santa Cecilia; Rome debut, 1916; conducted at Santa Cecilia until 1927. Came to the Met in 1928 and remained 30 years, primarily as assistant conductor, leading special concerts and student performances, occasionally substituting at regular performances (debut, *Lucia*, Mar. 11, 1932).

Cimarosa, Domenico. Composer; b. Aversa, Italy, Dec. 17, 1749; d. Venice, Jan. 11, 1801. Trained in Naples, he became internationally successful as a composer of comic operas. His most important posts were as music director in St. Petersburg (1787–91) and in Vienna (1792–93), where his most famous work, *Il Matrimonio Segreto*, was presented. As well as more than 65 operas, he composed sacred and instrumental music. His sympathy for the Neapolitan republic of 1799 incurred royal displeasure that marred his final years.

Cincinnati. City in Ohio. Musical life in Cincinnati was built upon a strong foundation of German immigrants, and the chorally-oriented May Festival stimulated construction of the Music Hall, opened in 1878. From the late 19th c., touring opera companies visited, and in 1920 the Cincinnati Summer Opera Association was founded, offering a month-long season of five or six productions in an open-air band shell at the Zoological Gardens; many notable American singers attracted early attention there, especially under Fausto Cleva (music director, 1934–63). In 1972 the Music Hall (rebuilt 1971, capacity 3,600) became the home of the Cincinnati Opera Association, with performances in spring and fall as well as summer. In early years, repertory consisted mainly of standard Italian operas, but recent productions have included Weinberger's *Shvanda* and Alfano's *Risurrezione* as well as *Fanciulla del West* and *Zauberflöte*. James de Blasis is the current general director.

Cinderella. See *Cendrillon* and *Cenerentola, La*.

claque (Fr., "smack" or "clap"). A group hired by a performer or an impresario to stimulate applause; at one time virtually institutionalized in many theaters.

Clark, Richard J. Baritone; b. Tucson, Ariz., Apr. 25, 1943. Studied at Academy of Vocal Arts, Philadelphia, and Juilliard, N.Y.; debut as Monterone, San Francisco. Met debut as Monterone, Oct. 19, 1981; subsequent roles have included di Luna, Barnaba, Amfortas, Michele (*Tabarro*), Trinity Moses (*Mahagonny*), Gianciotto (*Francesca*), Kurwenal, and Germont.

Clément, Edmond. Tenor; b. Paris, Mar. 28, 1867; d. Nice, Feb. 24, 1928. Studied at Paris Conservatory with Warot; after his 1889 debut as Vincent (*Mireille*) at the Opéra-Comique, he remained on the roster until 1910, creating tenor leads in *Attaque du Moulin* (1893) and operas by Saint-Saëns. In 2 Met seasons, he sang 18 perfs. of Werther (debut, Dec. 6, 1909), Massenet's Des Grieux, Fenton, Dominique (*Attaque*), and Fra Diavolo. Also appeared with Boston Opera (1911–13), in Belgium, Spain, Portugal, and Denmark. With a not large, slightly reedy voice, Clément made his points through intense musicianship and verbal projection.

Clemenza di Tito, La (The Clemency of Titus). Opera in 2 acts by Mozart; libretto adapted by Caterino Mazzolà from a Metastasio libretto.
First perf., Prague, National Theater, Sep. 6, 1791: Marchetti-Fantozzi, Antonini, Bedini, Perini, Baglioni, Campi. U.S. prem., Mutual radio network, June 22 & 29, 1940 (concert perf.). U.S. stage prem., Tanglewood, Lenox, Mass. Aug. 4, 1952. Met prem., Oct. 18, 1984: Scotto, G. Robinson, Murray, Bybee, Riegel, Cheek, c. Levine, d. & p. Ponnelle. 22 perfs. in 2 seasons.
Mozart's return, at the moment of his highest musical attainments, to the formality of opera seria produced a swift and economical drama.
Rome, 79–81 A.D. Enraged that the emperor Tito (t) has decided to marry Berenice, Vitellia (s) persuades her admirer Sesto (s) to assassinate Tito. Tito later dismisses Berenice and plans to marry Servilia (s), but, upon learning that she loves Sesto's friend Annio (ms), renounces her and determines to wed Vitellia instead. Though Vitellia learns of the change of plans too late to halt Sesto's plot, Tito escapes death. Sesto is arrested, tried, and condemned, but Tito tears up the death warrant. After hoping to conceal her part in the plot, Vitellia ultimately confesses, to be forgiven in turn by Tito.

Cleopatra's Night. Opera in 2 acts by Hadley; libretto by Alice Leal Pollock, after Théophile Gautier's story.
First perf., N.Y., Met, Jan. 31, 1920: Alda, Harrold, c. Papi, d. Bel Geddes, p. Ordynski. 7 perfs. in 2 seasons.
A conservatively Romantic work, set in Egypt in Roman times. In return for a night of bliss in the arms of Cleopatra (s), the hunter Meïamoun (t) agrees to die at dawn.

Cleva, Fausto. Conductor; b. Trieste, May 17, 1902; d. Athens, Aug. 9, 1971. After study at Trieste and Milan

Fausto Cleva

conservatories, emigrated to U.S. in 1920, shortly after debut in *Traviata*, Carcano, Milan. Assistant conductor (1920–25, 1938–40) and chorus master (1935–38, 1940–41) at the Met. Following his Met conducting debut on Feb. 14, 1942 (*Barbiere*), he left to concentrate on work with other American companies, notably Cincinnati Summer Opera (music director, 1934–63). Returning to the Met in 1950, he conducted 677 performances of over 30 operas in the Italian and French repertories, notably *Aida*, *Chénier*, and *Gioconda*, gaining a reputation as an unprepossessing interpreter, shrewdly attentive to his singers' abilities and needs.

Cocteau, Jean. Librettist; b. Maisons-Laffitte, Paris, July 5, 1889; d. Milly-la-Forêt, Oct. 11, 1963. The *enfant terrible* of modernist French literature, Cocteau wrote librettos for Honegger's *Antigone* and Stravinsky's *Oedipus Rex*. Poulenc used his 1929 play *La Voix Humaine* as a libretto.

Colas Breugnon. Opera in 3 acts by Kabalevsky; libretto by the composer and V. Bragin, after Romain Rolland's novel.
First perf., Leningrad, Maly, Feb. 22, 1938. Revised version, Leningrad, Maryinsky, 1970.
A lyrical score in socialist-realist style, set in 16th-c. Burgundy. The sculptor Colas Breugnon (bs) responds with optimism and humor to troubles and tragedies, including the plague, the loss of his wife, and the destruction of all his works.

colla voce, colla parte (Ital., "with the voice," "with the part"). An instruction for the accompaniment to follow the singer, in a passage where freedom of rhythm is called for.

Collier, Marie. Soprano; b. Ballarat, Australia, Apr. 16, 1926; d. London, Dec. 8, 1971. Began career in musical comedy, then studied in Milan and with Joan Cross and Dawson Freer in London. Covent Garden debut as Musetta, 1956; later sang Tosca, Katerina Ismailova, and created Hecuba (*King Priam*, 1962). At Met debut, Mar.

17, 1967, created Christine Mannon in *Mourning Becomes Electra*, later singing Santuzza and Musetta; 16 perfs. in 3 seasons.

Colonnello, Attilio. Designer; b. Milan, Nov. 9, 1930. A pupil of Gio Ponti and Ernest R. Rogers, he has designed opera sets and costumes since 1956, especially for Italian theaters; his settings are elaborately architectural in concept. For the Met, designed *Lucia* (1964), *Luisa Miller* (1968), and *Trovatore* (1969).

coloratura (Ital., derived from Ger., "Koloratur"). Elaborate ornamentation of melody. Applied, by extension, to types of singers (most usually sopranos) who specialize in the execution of such writing.

Colzani, Anselmo. Baritone; b. Budrio, near Bologna, Italy, Mar. 28, 1918. Studied with Corrado Zambelli, Bologna; debut as Herald (*Lohengrin*), Comunale, 1947. Debuts at La Scala (Alfio, 1952) and San Francisco (di Luna, 1956). Met debut as Boccanegra, Apr. 7, 1960; in 16 seasons, he sang 201 perfs. of 18 roles, including Gérard, Amonasro, Jack Rance, Ashton, Scarpia, Michonnet, and Falstaff.

Combattimento di Tancredi e Clorinda, Il (The Duel of Tancredi and Clorinda). Dramatic cantata (madrigal in stage form) by Monteverdi; libretto from Torquato Tasso's *Gerusalemme Liberata*, xii.
First perf., Venice, Palazzo Mocenigo, Carnival, 1624. U.S. prem., Northampton, Mass. (Smith College), May 12, 1928.
A quasi-operatic outgrowth of Monteverdi's madrigal composition, with a Narrator (t). During the Crusades, the Christian warrior Tancredi (t) duels with and kills a Saracen in armor, unaware that it is the maiden Clorinda (s), whom he loves.

comic opera. A looser term than the French "opéra comique" or the Italian "opera buffa" (*q.v.*).

commedia dell'arte (Ital.). A form of improvised theater based on stock situations and characters (Pulcinella, Colombina, Arlecchino, *et al.*), originating in Italy in the 16th c. and popular throughout Europe. Elements and characters of the commedia dell'arte have been used by opera composers from Vecchi to Busoni and since; *Pagliacci* preserves a lower-class descendant of the form.

Compagnacci, I (The Bad Fellows). Opera in 1 act by Riccitelli; libretto by Giovacchino Forzano.
First perf., Rome, Costanzi, Apr. 10, 1923. U.S. & Met prem., Jan. 2, 1924: Rethberg, Gigli, Didur, c. Moranzoni, d. Carelli. 3 perfs. in 1 season.
Florence, April 7, 1498. A love story set against a background of the struggle between the hedonistic *Compagnacci* and the reformer Savonarola.

comprimario (Ital.). A singer of secondary roles; also used to characterize such roles.

Comte Ory, Le (Count Ory). Opera in 2 acts by Rossini; libretto by Scribe and Charles-Gaspard Delestre-Poirson.
First perf., Paris, Opéra, Aug. 20, 1828: Cinti-Damoreau, Jawureck, Nourrit, Dabadie, Levasseur, c. Habeneck. U.S. prem., N.Y., Park, Aug. 22, 1831.
Rossini's only Parisian comedy, an elegant score,

incorporates much material from *Il Viaggio a Reims*.
Touraine, during the Crusades. Through two disguises, Count Ory (t) attempts to win the Countess Adèle (s), who has sworn to shun the society of men while her brother is off on a Crusade. The Count's page Isolier (ms) also desires the girl, but their separate efforts are mutually frustrating and ultimately unsuccessful; the opera ends with their escape from the premises just as the brother returns.

Conklin, John. Designer; b. Hartford, Conn., June 23, 1937. A student of Oenslager, he designed for legitimate theater, and began operatic work in 1965, including *Turco in Italia* (1978) and *Médée* (1979) for N.Y.C. Opera, *Lulu* (1979) for Santa Fe, *Ring* (1982–85) for San Francisco, *Khovanshchina* costumes for Met (1985).

Conley, Eugene. Tenor; b. Lynn, Mass., Mar. 12, 1908; d. Denton, Tex., Dec. 18, 1981. Studied with Ettore Verna; debut as Duke of Mantua, Brooklyn Academy, 1940. Debuts in Washington, D.C. (San Carlo Co., Duke of Mantua, 1942), Chicago (Hoffmann, 1942), and at La Scala (*Puritani*, 1949). Met debut as Faust, Jan. 25, 1950; in 7 seasons, his roles also included Tom Rakewell, Rodolfo, Ottavio, Pinkerton, and Edgardo. Also appeared in San Francisco (debut, Almaviva, 1950), Stockholm, at the Opéra-Comique in Paris, and Covent Garden.

Conlon, James. Conductor; b. New York, Mar. 18, 1950. Studied with Morel at Juilliard; professional debut, *Boris*, Spoleto, 1971. Met debut, *Zauberflöte*, Dec. 11, 1976; has since led several Italian operas, *Carmen*, and *Boris*. Appearances with major orchestras and at Covent Garden. Music director, Cincinnati May Festival (from 1977), Rotterdam Philharmonic (from 1983); appointed chief conductor, Cologne Opera (effective 1989).

Connell, Elizabeth. Soprano; b. Port Elizabeth, South Africa. After study at London Opera Center and under Otakar Kraus, professional debut as mezzo (Varvara in *Katya Kabanova*, Wexford, 1972). After two years with Australian Opera, joined English National Opera (1975–80). Debuts in Bayreuth (Ortrud, 1980), Boston (Amneris, 1980), La Scala (Ortrud, 1981), and Met (Vitellia in *Clemenza*, Jan. 7, 1985).

Conner, Nadine. Soprano; b. Los Angeles, Calif., Feb. 20, 1913. Studied with Horatio Cogswell and Amado Fernandez at U. of S. Calif., Florence Easton in N.Y.; debut as Marguerite, Los Angeles, 1940. Met debut as Pamina, Dec. 22, 1941; other roles included Gilda, Rosina, Micaela, Zerlina, Mimi, Marguerite, Sophie, Violetta, and Susanna; 166 perfs. in 18 seasons.

Conrad, Barbara. Mezzo-soprano; b. Pittsburg, Tex., Aug. 11, 1945. Studied at U. of Texas, Austin. Met debut as Annina (*Rosenkavalier*), Oct. 2, 1982; later roles include Preziosilla, Maddalena (*Rigoletto*), and Maria (*Porgy*). Has appeared in Frankfurt (Azucena), Brussels (Fricka), Munich (Eboli), and Vienna (Azucena).

Conried [Cohn], **Heinrich.** Impresario; b. Bielitz, Austria, Sep. 13, 1848; d. Meran, Tyrol, Apr. 27, 1909. An actor in Vienna, he managed the Bremen municipal theater (1877) and then several N.Y. theaters, notably the Irving Place (from 1892). In 1903 his reputation for efficiency and showmanship won him the Met lease and the financial support of Otto Kahn, who was venturing

(continued p.92)

CONDUCTING
James Levine

One of the more surprising things music history tells us is how, at the Paris Opéra in Lully's time, the composer set the tempo by pounding a stick on the floor – an aural distraction it's hard for us to imagine an audience tolerating. (Not to mention the occupational hazards: Lully reputedly died from gangrene that set in after he accidentally pounded his foot instead of the floor!) Later, the first violinists of Italian opera orchestras would set the tempo by tapping their bows on their music stands.

These curious facts confirm that, long before there were conductors in the modern sense, standing in front of the orchestra and waving a baton, somebody still had to do their work. In the eighteenth century, this might be the man at the harpsichord (often the composer himself); for an ensemble or chorus, he or the first violinist or even the prompter might well wave an arm or a roll of music paper or a bow to help keep things together. In an operatic world dominated by virtuoso singers, we can bet that they too played a large role in deciding the tempo. Perhaps most important of all, since theaters then played almost exclusively new works in familiar styles, many things that today have to be consciously decided upon were then simply conventions, taken for granted: small orchestras in small theaters, at audience level rather than in sunken pits, could hear the singers and knew instinctively just where they would want to slow down, add a cadenza, speed up to make a spectacular finish.

Conductors as such began to emerge in the early nineteenth century, as new music came to be more complex, rhythmically and orchestrally. The basic eighteenth-century orchestra – strings with a small wind band, reinforced by trumpets and drums, and sometimes by trombones for special effects – pretty well balanced itself. The development of new, more flexible woodwind and brass instruments opened up a realm of possibilities that composers immediately exploited, devising sonorities both richer and more delicate: things that needed a supervisory ear to keep them together and adjust the dynamics. To think of Weber's overtures, Mendelssohn's *Midsummer Night's Dream* music without the sure hand of a full-time conductor is to realize why these composers were among the first prominent conductors.

Then came Berlioz and Wagner, who firmly established the conductor's central role in musical performance: their music, for sure, could not play itself. (They also wrote about conducting: Berlioz talks about techniques of rehearsing difficult music, Wagner about interpretation and flexibility of tempo.) And, as Verdi's style grew more complex, absorbing the spectacular mass effects of French grand opera, even Italian opera demanded a dominant conductor: the Sextet from *Lucia* can roll along and build to a plausible climax by itself, but the ensembles of *Otello* and *Falstaff* will not make any sense whatsoever without painstaking, disciplined rehearsal. This fact led to the emergence of figures such as Mariani, Faccio, and especially Toscanini. Ultimately, it was composers who made the conductor, initially a convenience, into a necessity.

Another aspect of this development was the "backwards" growth of the repertory. No longer dealing exclusively with new works, opera houses continued to play the works of Gluck and Mozart, of Beethoven and Weber alongside the latest creations. Today, an opera company deals with musical styles from at least two centuries and from many countries, and is expected to be sensitive to the musical, vocal, and expressive differences

among them; this responsibility of achieving consistency in each production, of establishing the basic conception of the work, falls primarily on the conductor.

His tools are many. Some are straightforward: the baton, of course (though some find the bare hand more expressive); the established beat patterns that represent the various musical meters; the left hand and the eyes, which cue entrances, shape dynamics, make other special points. When we get to techniques of rehearsal and preparation, we quickly shade into matters of psychology. You cannot today run an orchestra along the military lines of Szell or Toscanini; conducting is again – as it was in earlier days – something more like an extension of ensemble playing, more like democracy. The orchestra is no longer doing it because they're afraid of you and if they don't do it you'll fire them; they're doing it because they agree with what you're getting at – or, if they don't agree, they at least understand, and understand their function as part of an ensemble, a living organism. Some people respond well to very little guidance, some people respond better to lots of guidance; some people are better off when their own imagination is stimulated, others are better off relying on your imagination. Such are the subtleties that make the work fascinating.

What the conductor – any musical performer – is after, above all, is to get the music's character right. By character, I mean that thing which the composers continually express as their major priority. You never hear of them complaining about inadequate technical execution, or that the horns were cracking or the wind chords weren't together. What you hear composers complaining about is falsification of what they've written, a misunderstanding of the point, the spirit, the – whatever words you want to use – substance of the piece, of what it is all about.

Yet there's a trap here, even for the well-intentioned performer who wants to be faithful to the composer's inspiration. Some performers, with a lot of personality and temperament, produce a kind of eccentricity, a kind of distortion of the composer's piece. And others try very hard to arrive at what they think the composer wanted of them – yet what they are doing is dry as dust, and the composer didn't write a piece that is dry as dust. The rarity is people who have these elements together, who have the technique to get the idea to work, who have enough imagination, enough feeling, enough intelligence, enough perception, enough of all that human substance to be able to make contact with someone as unique as that composer – and yet have enough personality of their own to make the result vital. And this is why conducting is never-endingly fascinating and stimulating and gratifying – and frustrating.

into opera for the first time. His five-year tenure saw the debuts of Caruso, Fremstad, and Farrar, among others. More knowledgeable about publicity than about opera, he presented the first public staged *Parsifal* (1903) outside Bayreuth and the first U.S. *Salome* (withdrawn by the scandalized Met board after a single performance in 1907), and imported Humperdinck and Puccini to supervise productions of *Hänsel* (1905) and *Butterfly* (1906). The loss of many sets and costumes when the 1906 tour encountered the San Francisco earthquake and fire, and Conried's negligence in letting Oscar Hammerstein's competing Manhattan Opera House tie up the rights to important new works, combined with his failing health to force his resignation in 1908.

Consul, The. Opera in 3 acts by Menotti; libretto by the composer.

First perf., Philadelphia, Shubert, Mar. 1, 1950: Neway, Powers, Lane, MacNeil, Lishner, McKinley, Jongeyans, c. Engel.

Menotti's most successful full-length essay in his Italo-American verismo style.

An unspecified European police state, after World War II. John Sorel (bar), wanted by the police for his opposition to the regime, is hiding in the mountains at the frontier, waiting until his wife Magda (s), his child, and his mother (c) can join him. Magda's efforts to obtain visas are repeatedly frustrated by red tape at a foreign consulate, where the Secretary (ms) blocks all access to the Consul (who never appears in the opera). When Magda's child dies, John resolves to return; the desperate Magda sends word that he should not come because he will not find her alive. Upon his arrival at the Consulate, John is seized by the police; the Secretary belatedly promises help, but calls Magda minutes too late to prevent her suicide at home.

Contes d'Hoffmann, Les (The Tales of Hoffmann). Opera in prologue, 3 acts, and epilogue by Offenbach; libretto from a play by Barbier and Carré, based mainly on stories by E.T.A. Hoffmann. The standard performing version was edited and orchestrated by Guiraud and others.

First perf., Paris, Opéra-Comique, Feb. 10, 1881 (Venetian act omitted): Isaac, Ugalde, Talazac, Taskin. U.S. prem., N.Y., 5th Avenue, Oct. 16, 1882. Met prem., Jan. 11, 1913: Hempel, Fremstad, Bori, Maubourg, Macnez, Ruysdael, Didur, Gilly, Rothier, c. Polacco, d. Burghart/Comelli, p. Speck. Later Met productions: Nov. 13, 1924: Morgana, Bori (2 roles), Howard, Fleta, Wolfe, de Luca (3 roles), c. Hasselmans, d. Urban, p. Wymetal; Nov. 14, 1955: Peters, Stevens, Amara, Miller, Tucker, Singher (4 roles), c. Monteux, d. Gérard, p. Ritchard; Nov. 29, 1973: Sutherland (4 roles), Tourangeau, Domingo, Stewart (4 roles), c. Bonynge, d. Klein, p. Hebert; Mar. 8, 1982: Welting, Troyanos, Eda-Pierre, Howells, Domingo, Devlin (4 roles), c. Chailly, d. Schneider-Siemssen/Frey, p. Schenk. Other Met Hoffmanns have included Tokatyan, Jobin, Gedda, Alexander, and Kraus; Bovy, Moffo, and Malfitano have also sung all the soprano roles in the same performance; Tibbett, London, Bacquier, and Morris have done the same for the villains. Olympia has also been sung at the house by Hempel, Talley, Pons; Giulietta by Alda, Elias, Crespin; Antonia by Novotná, Steber, and Lorengar. 139 perfs. in 23 seasons.

Les Contes d'Hoffmann, Offenbach's uncompleted attempt at a full-scale opera after decades of success with opéra bouffe, contains many of the composer's most delightful songs and (especially in the Antonia act) shows him capable of pathos and sustained lyrical inspiration. The long-familiar version of the opera (in which the Munich act follows the one in Venice) is significantly corrupt; some recent productions have essayed reconstructions of the original form.

A beer-cellar in Nuremberg, 19th c. Councillor Lindorf (bar), nemesis of the poet Hoffmann (t), intercepts a note from the prima donna Stella arranging a rendezvous with Hoffmann. The latter arrives with his friend Nicklausse (ms), and is persuaded to relate the story of his three loves, each representing a different aspect of womankind, each frustrated by a different incarnation of his evil nemesis. In Paris, he falls in love with the automaton Olympia (s), built by Spalanzani (t) in collaboration with Coppélius (bar), and is in despair when Coppélius destroys her after Spalanzani attempts to cheat him of his pay for the doll's eyes. In Munich, the consumptive Antonia (s) is forbidden to sing by her father Crespel (bar), who fears the exertion would kill her as it did her mother. Antonia and Hoffmann plan to elope, but the sinister Dr. Miracle (bar) goads the girl into singing by making a portrait of her mother call to her; in a frenzy of passionate song, Antonia falls dead. In Venice, the courtesan Giulietta (s) and the sorcerer Dapertutto (bar) conspire to steal Hoffmann's reflection, which he loses by gazing into an enchanted mirror. Madly in love with Giulietta, Hoffmann kills a rival, Schlemil (bs), in a duel, but then watches her floating away in a gondola with another admirer, Pitichinaccio (t). (In Offenbach's original, he sees Giulietta succumb to Dapertutto's poison.) In the epilogue, back in the Nuremberg cellar, Hoffmann's tales are finished and he is drunk. Stella arrives, and leaves with Lindorf.

contralto. See *alto*.

Converse, Frederick. Composer; b. Newton, Mass., Jan. 5, 1871; d. Westwood, June 8, 1940. Studied composition with Paine and Chadwick in Boston and Rheinberger in Munich. Taught at the New England Conservatory and Harvard. *The Pipe of Desire* (1905) was the first American opera produced at the Met. *The Sacrifice*, produced in Boston in 1911, was better received; two later works, *Beauty and the Beast* (1913) and *The Immigrants* (1914), remain unperformed.

Cooper, Emil. Conductor; b. Kherson, Russia, Dec. 20, 1877; d. New York, Nov. 19, 1960. Studied with Nikisch in Vienna; conductor, Moscow Imperial Opera (1910–17), leading premiere of Rimsky's *Golden Cockerel* and first Moscow *Ring*. At Chicago Civic Opera (1929–32, 1939–43), he then joined the Met (debut, Jan. 26, 1944, *Gioconda*), where he led 14 operas, including house premieres of *Entführung* and *Khovanshchina*, and N.Y. premiere of *Peter Grimes* (1948).

Copland, Aaron. Composer; b. Brooklyn, N.Y., Nov. 14, 1900. Studied with Boulanger in Paris (1921–24). His ballets *Billy the Kid* (1938), *Rodeo* (1942), and *Appalachian Spring* (1944) employed variations on American folk tunes with great ingenuity and dramatic effect. During the 1940s, he wrote several memorable film scores, notably *The Heiress* (1948). Copland's first opera, *The Second Hurricane* (1937), was written for children with a chorus of parents. *The Tender Land* (1954) again drew upon American folk idioms for a midwestern pastorale, generally felt to be undramatic.

Copley, John. Producer; b. Birmingham, England, June 12, 1933. At Covent Garden since 1960, resident producer since 1972; stagings include *Benvenuto Cellini* (1976) and *Semele* (1982). U.S. debut, *Lucia* (Dallas, 1972); has also worked with San Francisco Opera, N.Y.C. Opera, Chicago Lyric, Canadian Opera, and widely in Britain and Europe.

Coq d'Or, Le. See *Golden Cockerel, The.*

Cordon, Norman. Bass-baritone; b. Washington, D.C., Jan. 20, 1904; d. Chapel Hill, N.C., Mar. 1, 1964. Studied at Nashville Conservatory and in Chicago; debut as King (*Aida*), San Carlo Co., Chicago, 1933. Met debut as Monterone, May 13, 1936; in 11 seasons, he sang 377 perfs. of 55 roles, including Commendatore (*Don Giovanni*), Colline, Sparafucile, and Méphistophélès. Also sang in Chicago (1933–35) and San Francisco (1936–39).

Corelli, Franco. Tenor; b. Ancona, Italy, Aug. 4, 1923. Studied at Pesaro Conservatory; debut as Don José, Spoleto, 1951. La Scala debut as Licinio (*Vestale*), 1954; he later sang there in *Poliuto*, *Huguenots*, and *Pirata*. Covent Garden debut as Cavaradossi, 1957. After his debut as Manrico, Jan. 27, 1961, he appeared with the Met every year until 1974 – most notably as Calaf, Cavaradossi, Enzo, Ernani, Maurizio (*Adriana Lecouvreur*), and Rodolfo. Later he undertook French roles, in new productions of *Roméo* (1967) and *Werther*. Corelli sang 263 performances with the company, and also appeared at the Berlin Städtische Oper (1961), Vienna State Opera (1963), and Paris Opéra (1970). With a handsome spinto tenor voice and movie-star looks, Corelli won a wide public following, despite complaints from critics about what they perceived as indulgences of phrasing and expression. Many of his major roles are represented on recordings.

Corena, Fernando. Bass; b. Geneva, Dec. 22, 1916; d. Lugano, Nov. 26, 1984. Studied for holy orders at Fribourg U., but turned to music professionally after winning a singing contest. Studied in Geneva (1937–38) and, after encouragement from the conductor Gui, with Enrico Romani in Milan. Spent the war years in Zurich, singing on the radio and at the Stadttheater. Formal debut as Varlaam (*Boris*), Trieste, 1947; appeared throughout Italy thereafter. Met debut as Leporello, Feb. 6, 1954, a favorite role there, along with both Bartolos, Dulcamara, Melitone, Benoit, and Don Pasquale; his final Met performance, in 1978, was his 92nd Sacristan (*Tosca*) at the house. Other roles included Falstaff, Schicchi, Alfonso (*Così*), Sulpice (*Fille du Régiment*), Mustafà (*Italiana*), and Puccini's Lescaut. Covent Garden debut as Rossini's Bartolo, 1960; at Salzburg, he sang Osmin in Strehler's production of *Entführung*, 1965. Like Baccaloni, whose successor he became at the Met, Corena began his career in standard roles (Sparafucile, Escamillo, Scarpia) but soon specialized in the buffo repertory. His Swiss background provided a broad linguistic foundation, and he was known as an ingenious and witty comedian throughout his career.

Cornelius, Peter. Composer and writer; b. Mainz, Germany, Dec. 24, 1824; d. Mainz, Oct. 26, 1874. From a theatrical family, he studied composition in Berlin with Siegfried Dehn while acquiring a rich literary background. In 1852 he joined Liszt's circle in Weimar, becoming an admirer of Wagner and Berlioz and a

Franco Corelli as Werther

prolific writer of criticism as well. After his comic opera *Der Barbier von Bagdad* (1858) failed in Weimar for political reasons, Cornelius lived in Vienna, composing *Der Cid*, successfully produced in Weimar in 1865. He then assisted Wagner in Munich and worked on a third opera, *Gunlöd*, which was never finished. Along with *Barbier von Bagdad*, his numerous lieder attest to his melodic and expressive gifts, and often to his wit as well. Although part of Wagner's circle, he retained his artistic independence.

Coronation of Poppea, The. See *Incoronazione di Poppea, L'.*

Corregidor, Der (The Magistrate). Opera in 4 acts by Wolf; libretto by Rosa Mayreder, after Alarcon's story *El Sombrero de Tres Picos.*

First perf., Mannheim, June 7, 1896: Hohenleiter, Rüdiger, Krömer. U.S. prem., N.Y., Carnegie Hall, Jan. 5, 1959 (concert perf., in Eng.): Lipton, Kelley, Thompson, c. Scherman.

Set in Andalusia, 1804, this episodic work, hampered by its libretto, includes some fine dramatic characterizations; two of Wolf's songs are interpolated. Frasquita (s), wife of the miller Tio Lucas (bar), finds the Magistrate (t) attracted to her; to win a political favor, she leads him on, arousing great confusion and suspicion in the process.

Corsaro, Frank. Producer; b. New York, Dec. 22, 1924. Studied at Yale Drama School and Actors' Studio, N.Y.; theater debut (1952). Broadway productions include *Night of the Iguana* (1961). Resident director, N.Y.C. Opera, since 1958; productions include *Traviata*, *Pelléas*, *Don Giovanni*, *Madama Butterfly*, *La Traviata*, *Makropoulos Affair*. Active with other North American companies; his Ottawa Festival production of *Rinaldo* was seen at the Met in 1984. Corsaro's productions, sometimes involving changes of time and place, are notable for their fine theatrical detail and for the intensely committed performances he generates in individual singers.

Corsaro, Il (The Corsair). Opera in 3 acts by Verdi; libretto by Piave, after Byron's poem *The Corsair.*

First perf., Trieste, Grande, Oct. 25, 1848: Barbieri-Nini, Rapazzini, Fraschini, de Bassini. U.S. prem., San Diego Opera, June 18, 1982: Plowright, Anderson, Navarrete, Raftery, c. Müller.

Così Fan Tutte – (1951). Designed by Rolf Gérard, produced by Alfred Lunt. Eleanor Steber, Blanche Thebom, Patrice Munsel

Musically typical of the dramatically charged bel canto style of Verdi's early years, though unusual in its inclusion of two leading soprano roles.

An island in the Aegean and the city of Coron, early 19th c. Corrado (t), captain of a pirate band, leads an attack on Pasha Seid (bar) and is captured and imprisoned. Gulnara (s), Seid's favorite slave, kills the Pasha to induce Corrado to escape with her to the corsairs' island. There Corrado finds that his sweetheart Medora (s), believing him dead, has poisoned herself. She dies in his arms. Corrado throws himself off a rock into the sea.

Cortez, Viorica. Mezzo-soprano; b. Bucium, Romania, Dec. 26, 1935. Studied at Iasi and Bucharest Conservatories; operatic debut as Dalila, Toulouse, 1965. Sang with Bucharest Opera, 1965–70; Covent Garden debut, 1968. Met debut as Carmen, Nov. 5, 1971, later singing the Princesse (*Adriana*), Amneris, Giulietta, and Azucena.

Cortis [Corts], **Antonio.** Tenor; b. on board ship between Oran, Algeria, and Altea, Spain, Aug. 12, 1891; d. Valencia, Apr. 2, 1952. Studied in Madrid; debut as comprimario, 1915, but soon sang major roles in Barcelona and Valencia. Principal Italian tenor at Chicago Opera, 1924–32 (debut, Nov. 5, 1924, Enzo); also appeared in San Francisco (1925–26). Roles included Cavaradossi, Calaf, Don José, and Dick Johnson.

Cosa Rara, Una (A Rare Thing). Opera in 2 acts by Vicente Martín y Soler; libretto by da Ponte, after Velez de Guevara's story *La Luna della Sierra*.

First perf., Vienna, Burgtheater, Nov. 17, 1786. U.S. professional prem., N.Y., Vineyard Opera, Apr. 11, 1986.

One of the great 18th-c. successes, which remained in the repertory until 1825; Mozart quoted a melody from its first-act finale in the supper scene of *Don Giovanni*.

Così Fan Tutte (All Women Do Thus). Opera in 2 acts by Mozart; libretto by da Ponte.

First perf., Vienna, Burgtheater, Jan. 26, 1790: Ferraresi del Bene, Villeneuve, Sardi-Bussani, Calvesi, Benucci, Bussani. U.S. & Met prem., Mar. 24, 1922: Easton, Peralta, Bori, Meader, de Luca, Didur, c. Bodanzky, d. Urban, p. Thewman. Later Met productions: Dec. 28, 1951 (in Eng.): Steber, Thebom, Munsel, Tucker, Guarrera, Brownlee, c. Stiedry, d. Gérard, p. Lunt; Jan. 29, 1982: Te Kanawa, Ewing, Battle, Rendall, Morris, Gramm, c. Levine, d. Griffin/Clancy, p. Graham. Fiordiligi has also been sung at the Met by Stich-Randall, L. Price; Ferrando by Valletti; Despina by Peters, Stratas. 91 perfs. in 15 seasons.

The last of Mozart's da Ponte operas and in some ways the most subtle and modern in its probing of human affection and allegiance. It had to await 20th-c. revival to find wide appreciation, even among operatic connoisseurs; the sporadic 19th-c. performances almost always employed disfiguring adaptations.

Naples, 18th c. Don Alfonso (bs), a cynical bachelor, makes a wager with two officers, Ferrando (t) and Guglielmo (bar), that, like other women, their fiancées – respectively, Dorabella (ms) and Fiordiligi (s) – cannot be trusted. He tells the women that their fiancés must go off to war; as they part, the lovers all vow fidelity. With the aid of Despina (s), the ladies' maid, Alfonso introduces two attractive Albanians, none other than Ferrando and Guglielmo in disguise. Each man pursues the other's fiancée with ardor, delighting in the women's initial anger and rejection. But, as they enthusiastically press their suits, the women, under the tutelage of Don Alfonso and Despina, eventually yield and Alfonso has won the bet. During a double wedding ceremony, a drum roll signals the army's return. The "Albanians" rush to hide and return in officers' uniforms. The sisters throw themselves on their lovers' mercy, but Alfonso reveals the plot, and all sing the praises of reason and tolerance.

Cossa, Dominic. Baritone; b. Jessup, Pa., May 13, 1935. Studied with Anthony Marlowe in Detroit and Robert Weede, Concord, Calif.; debut as Sharpless (*Butterfly*), N.Y.C. Opera, 1961. Sang in Europe and San Francisco (debut, 1967). Met debut as Silvio (*Pagliacci*), Jan. 30, 1970; later roles include Rossini's Figaro, Marcello, Masetto, Lescaut, and Mercutio.

Cossotto, Fiorenza. Mezzo-soprano; b. Crescentino, near Vercelli, Italy, Apr. 22, 1935. Studied at Turin Conservatory, at La Scala school, and with Ettore Campogalliani; debut as Sister Mathilde in premiere of *Carmélites*, La Scala, 1957. She continued to sing regularly in Milan, notably in *Favorite*, 1961. Her international career began in 1958, as Giovanna Seymour (*Anna Bolena*), in Wexford; debuts followed in Vienna (Maddalena, 1958), Covent Garden (Néris in *Médée*, 1959), and Chicago (*Favorite*, 1964). Met debut as Amneris, Feb. 6, 1968; her repertory there includes Laura, Eboli, Santuzza, Adalgisa, Azucena, Princesse (*Adriana*), Carmen, and Quickly. Married to bass Ivo Vinco, Cossotto progressed carefully from lighter roles to become the preeminent Italian dramatic mezzo of her day.

Cossutta, Carlo. Tenor; b. Trieste, May 8, 1932. Studied with Manfredo Miselli, Mario Melani, and Arturo Wolken, Buenos Aires; debut as Cassio, Colón, 1958; created Ginastera's Don Rodrigo there, 1964. Debuts at Chicago Opera as Cassio (1963), at Covent Garden as Duke of Mantua (1964). Met debut as Pollione, Feb. 17, 1973; 13 perfs. in 1 season. Best known for dramatic repertory, notably Otello.

Costa, Mary. Soprano; b Knoxville, Tenn., Apr. 5, 1932. Studied with Mario Chamlee and Ernest St. John Metz, Los Angeles Conservatory; debut in *Carmina Burana*, San Francisco, 1959. Met debut as Violetta, Jan. 6, 1964; other roles were Musetta, Alice Ford, Rosalinde, Manon, and Vanessa.

Cotrubas, Ileana. Soprano; b. Galati, Romania, June 9, 1939. Studied with Constantin Stroëscu in Bucharest, later at Vienna Music Academy; debut as Yniold (*Pelléas*), Bucharest, 1964. At Salzburg, debut as Second Boy (*Zauberflöte*), 1967; later sang Bastienne and Pamina there. While at Frankfurt Opera (1968–71), she made debuts at Glyndebourne (Mélisande, 1970) and Covent Garden (Tatiana, 1971). Debuts in Paris (Massenet's *Manon*, 1974), and as Mimi at Chicago (1973), La Scala (1975), and the Met (Mar. 23, 1977), where she has since sung Gilda, Violetta, Ilia (*Idomeneo*), Tatiana, and Micaela. As her list of roles suggests, Cotrubas has specialized in effects of fragile charm and pathos.

countertenor. A male singer who uses falsetto technique to sing in alto range.

Count Ory. *See Comte Ory, Le.*

couplets. In light-opera styles, a strophic song with refrain.

covered tone. A sound produced in singing when the tone is directed to the soft palate, yielding a softer, less brilliant quality; sometimes employed to facilitate technical matters even when the expressive effect is inappropriate.

Cox, Jean. Tenor; b. Gadsden, Ala., Jan. 16, 1922. Studied with William Steven, U. of Alabama; Marie Sundelius, New England Conservatory; and Willy Kirsamer and Max Lorenz, Germany. Debut as Handel's Serse, Kiel, 1954; later sang in Brunswick and Mannheim. Bayreuth debut as Steersman, 1956; later sang major roles there. Met debut as Walther, Apr. 2, 1976.

Fiorenza Cossotto as Amneris in *Aida*

Cox, John. Producer; b. Bristol, England, Mar. 12, 1935. Worked at Glyndebourne with Ebert and Rennert, in Germany with Felsenstein; operatic debut, *Ernani* (Oxford, 1957). Director of production, Glyndebourne (1971–81); administrator, Scottish Opera (1982–85), artistic director since 1985. Has directed opera in Europe and America, including *Midsummer Marriage* (San Francisco, 1984), and *Barbiere* (Met, 1982).

Crawford, Bruce. Manager; b. West Bridgewater, Mass., Mar. 16, 1929. Studied economics at U. of Penn. (B.S. 1952), then worked in advertising, becoming president of Batten, Barton, Durstine & Osborn from 1978 and chief executive officer of BBDO International from 1977. A lifelong opera fan, he joined the Met's board in 1976, served on its executive committee from 1977 (heading the television committee), became a vice-president in 1981 and president in May 1984, then accepted the position of general manager in succession to Bliss and in association with artistic director James Levine. Even before his tenure officially began (Dec. 31, 1985), he announced the elimination, after 1986, of the Met's biggest single deficit-maker (and oldest tradition), the annual spring tour.

Creech, Philip. Tenor; b. Hempstead, N.Y., June 1, 1950. Studied at Northwestern U.; sang in Chicago Symphony chorus, 1973–75. Met debut as Beppe (*Pagliacci*), Sep. 26, 1979; subsequent roles include Pedrillo (*Entführung*), Hylas (*Troyens*), Rinuccio (*Schicchi*), Edmondo (*Manon Lescaut*), and Brighella (*Ariadne*).

Cremonini, Giuseppe. Tenor; b. Cremona, Italy, Nov. 25, 1866; d. Cremona, May 9, 1903. Debut as Carlo (*Linda di Chamounix*, Genoa, 1889), then sang throughout Italy and at Covent Garden (1892). At the Met (1895–97, 1900–01), he sang over a dozen roles (debut, *Favorite*, Nov. 29, 1895), including the first U.S. Cavaradossi.

Crespin, Régine. Soprano; b. Marseilles, France, Mar. 23, 1927. At Paris Conservatory, studied with Paul Cabanel and Georges Jouatte; debut as Elsa (Mulhouse, 1950), coming to the Paris Opéra the next year in the same role. After singing for three seasons outside Paris, she returned to the Opéra as Reiza (*Oberon*), Sieglinde, the Marschallin, Elisabeth, Mme. Lidoine (*Dialogues*), Tosca, Berlioz's Marguerite and Didon. Debuts followed at Bayreuth (Kundry, 1958), Glyndebourne (Marschallin, 1959), La Scala (Pizzetti's Fedra, 1959), Vienna (Sieglinde, 1959), and Covent Garden (Marschallin, 1960). Her first American appearance came in 1962, as Tosca in Chicago, where she later sang Fidelio and Ariadne. At the Colón, Buenos Aires, beginning in 1962, she sang Fauré's Pénélope, Didon and Cassandre (*Troyens*), and Gluck's Iphigénie en Tauride. Since her Met debut as the Marschallin (Nov. 19, 1962), she has returned regularly, singing more than 100 perfs. of a dozen roles – at first, dramatic-soprano parts, including Amelia (*Ballo*), Senta, Elsa, Sieglinde, Tosca, Kundry, and the *Walküre* Brünnhilde; after 1971, mezzo repertory such as Giulietta (*Hoffmann*), Charlotte (*Werther*), Santuzza, Carmen, and Mme. de Croissy (*Dialogues*).

Though her remarkably idiomatic command of German roles first made Crespin internationally famous, she also, almost uniquely in her time, commanded the French dramatic repertory. Endowed with ample voice, a fine ear for intonation, color, and inflection, and a mastery of restrained gesture, she has been equally successful in

Régine Crespin as Madame de Croissy in *Dialogues des Carmélites*

characterizations of regal grandeur and feminine warmth. With the decline of her top register, she gracefully shifted repertory, and continues to be a valued performer (notably as Mme. de Croissy and Menotti's Medium). Her singing is well represented on records, including concert works and Offenbach operettas as well as German, French, and Italian opera.

Crimi, Giulio. Tenor; b. Paternò, Catania, Italy, May 10, 1885; d. Rome, Oct. 29, 1939. Studied with Aderno, Catania; debut as Hagenbach (*Wally*), Treviso, 1912. Covent Garden debut as Avito (*Amore dei Tre Re*), 1914; created Paolo (*Francesca da Rimini*), Turin, 1914. Met debut as Radames, Nov. 13, 1918; his 86 perfs. in 4 seasons included Rodolfo, Chénier, Turiddu, Canio, Alfredo, Milio (*Zazà*), and he created Rinuccio and Luigi (*Trittico*), 1918. Also appeared in Chicago, Milan, and Rome. Gobbi was among his pupils.

Crispino e la Comare (Crispino and the Fairy). Opera in 3 acts by F. and L. Ricci; libretto by Piave, after a comedy by S. Fabbrichesi.
First perf., Venice, San Benedetto, Feb. 28, 1850: Pecorini, Prinetti, Cambaggio. U.S. prem., N.Y., Academy of Music, Oct. 24, 1865. Met prem., Jan. 18, 1919: Hempel, Braslau, Scotti, c. Papi, d. Bianco/Musaeus. 3 perfs. in 1 season.
An old-fashioned comedy, occasionally revived as a soprano vehicle. A fairy (ms) helps Crispino (bar) become a wealthy physician, but he grows arrogant and unkind to his wife Annetta (s), almost losing his life before repenting.

Cristoforo Colombo (Christopher Colombus). Opera in 3 acts and epilogue by Franchetti; libretto by Illica.

First perf., Genoa, Carlo Felice, Oct. 6, 1892: Kaschmann, c. Mancinelli. U.S. prem., Philadelphia, Nov. 20, 1913: Ruffo.
Occasionally revived as a vehicle for a dramatic baritone; the action includes Columbus' efforts to launch his historic expedition, the actual moment of America's discovery, and his later persecution.

Crooks, Richard. Tenor; b. Trenton, N.J., June 26, 1900; d. Portola Valley, Calif., Sep. 29, 1972. Studied with Frank La Forge and Léon Rothier, N.Y.; at first concentrated on recitals and concerts (including U.S. premiere of Mahler's *Lied von der Erde* under Mengelberg, 1928). Operatic debut as Cavaradossi, Hamburg, 1927. After appearing with the Berlin State Opera, he made his American opera debut as Cavaradossi, Philadelphia, 1930. Met debut as Massenet's Des Grieux, Feb. 25, 1933; in 11 seasons, he sang 51 perfs. of 9 roles, including Alfredo, Charles (*Linda di Chamounix*), Faust, Wilhelm Meister, Roméo, and Don Ottavio. Also appeared in San Francisco (1934) and Chicago (1940–43); retired from opera in 1943. Although he had sung Lohengrin and Stolzing in Germany, at the Met Crooks concentrated on roles that exploited his finely controlled lyric singing and sweet head tones.

Crosby, John O('Hea). Impresario and conductor; b. New York, July 12, 1926. Studied with Hindemith at Yale U. and in opera workshops, especially with German director Leopold Sachse, with whom he began to evolve his ideas about establishing an opera festival. In 1957, he founded the Santa Fe Opera, which has since presented an adventurous mixture of standard repertory with lesser-known and new works every summer. From 1976 to 1985, he also served as president of the Manhattan School of Music.

Cross, Joan. Soprano; b. London, Sep. 7, 1900. Studied with Dawson Freer, Trinity College of Music; joined Old Vic chorus, 1924. Principal soprano of Sadler's Wells Opera, 1931–46, singing wide repertory; also appeared at Covent Garden from 1931. A founder of the English Opera Group (1945), she created Britten roles in *Grimes, Lucretia, Herring, Gloriana*, and *Turn of the Screw*.

Cross, Milton. Broadcaster; b. New York, Apr. 16, 1897; d. New York, Jan. 3, 1975. His early interest in singing developed into a radio career as an announcer for NBC; his specialty was music. His first opera broadcasts were from the Chicago Civic Opera, and in 1931 he was announcer for the first Met broadcast, *Hänsel*, on Christmas Day, 1931. During the next 43 years, Cross missed only two broadcasts, both following his wife's death. His well-researched commentary and brisk yet genial style won him a national following as "the Voice of the Met."

Crucible, The. Opera in 4 acts by Ward; libretto by the composer and Bernard Stambler, after Arthur Miller's play.
First perf., N.Y.C. Opera, Oct. 26, 1961: Brooks, Clements, Bible, Brown, Neate, Treigle, Ludgin, c. Buckley.
A conservative, theatrically effective opera set in Salem, Mass., 1692. The fantasies and accusations of a group of girls, some acting out of adolescent adventurousness and others out of malice, plunge Salem into a tragic series of trials and executions for witchcraft.

Cruz-Romo, Gilda. Soprano; b. Guadalajara, Mexico, Feb. 12, 1940. Studied with Angel Esquivel, Mexico City Conservatory; debut there as Ortlinde (*Walküre*), 1962. N.Y.C. Opera debut (*Mefistofele*), 1969. Met debut as Butterfly, Dec. 18, 1970, later singing Nedda, both Verdi Leonoras, Tosca, Violetta, Aida, Puccini's Manon, Suor Angelica, Desdemona, Elisabeth de Valois, Amelia (*Ballo*), Butterfly, and Violetta. Has also appeared in Chicago, Houston, Dallas, London, Milan, Paris, Vienna, and Moscow.

Cuénod, Hugues. Tenor; b. Vevey, Switzerland, June 26, 1902. Studied in Basel and Vienna; debut at Champs-Elysées, Paris, 1928. Debuts at La Scala (1951), Glyndebourne (1954), Covent Garden (1954). Known for character roles, and for interpretation of early music and French songs. Created Sellem in *Rake's Progress*, 1951. Met debut, Emperor (*Turandot*), Mar. 12, 1987.

Cunning Little Vixen, The. Opera in 3 acts by Janáček; libretto by the composer, after Rudolf Těsnohlídek's verses for drawings by Stanislav Lolek.
  First perf., Brno, Nov. 6, 1924: Hrdličková, Flögl, c. Neumann. U.S. prem., N.Y., Hunter College Playhouse (Mannes College), May 7, 1964 (in Eng.): c. Bamberger.
  A darkly vivid score that pictures the animal kingdom and also taps the psychological undercurrents of the story.
  The Moravian countryside. A forester (bs) tries to domesticate the captured vixen Sharpears (s), but she escapes by fomenting a revolt in the hen-house, takes over a badger's den, and marries the fox Goldenstripe (s), eventually meeting death at the hands of a poacher. In the glen where he first captured the vixen, the forester has a dream of nature's renewal, including a vixen cub that looks just like Sharpears.

Curlew River. Parable for church performance in 1 act by Britten; libretto by William Plomer, after the medieval Noh-play *Sumidagawa*, by Juro Motomasa.
  First perf., Orford Church, Suffolk, June 12, 1964: Pears, Shirley-Quirk, Drake, Garrard. U.S. prem., Katonah, N.Y., Caramoor Festival, June 26, 1966: Velis, Clatworthy, Berberian, c. Rudel.
  The first of Britten's church parables, a Christian transplantation of a Noh-drama about a madwomen (t) seeking her lost son.

curtain call. At the conclusion of an operatic scene or performance, the singers come before the curtain for bows, singly or in groups, depending on the practice of the theater.

Curtin (née Smith), **Phyllis.** Soprano; b. Clarksburg, W. Va., Dec. 3, 1921. Studied in Boston and sang with New England Opera Theater, 1946; N.Y.C. Opera debut, Oct. 12, 1953, as Fräulein Burstner (Einem's *Prozess*). Met debut as Fiordiligi, Nov. 4, 1961; other Met roles included Donna Anna, Rosalinde, Eva, the Countess, Ellen Orford, and Violetta. Created two Floyd heroines, Susannah (1955) and Cathy (*Wuthering Heights*, 1958). Also sang in Vienna and Glyndebourne.

Curtis–Verna, Mary. Soprano; b. Salem, Mass., May 9, 1927. Studied at Hollis College, Va., and with Ettore Verna, later her husband. Debuts as Desdemona, Lirico, Milan (1949), and La Scala (1954). N.Y.C. Opera debut as Donna Anna, 1954. Met debut as Leonora (*Trovatore*), Feb. 13, 1957; other Met roles included Aida, Tosca, Violetta, Santuzza, Elisabeth de Valois, Leonora (*Forza*), and Turandot; 72 perfs. in 10 seasons.

cut. A passage of music (or dialogue) omitted in an operatic performance. Especially in long works, composers sometimes indicate optional or possible cuts; more often, tradition has sanctified certain omissions (e.g., the tenor and baritone cabalettas in *Traviata*) or abridgements (e.g., extended cadential formulas in 19th-c. Italian operas).

Cuzzoni, Francesca. Soprano; b. Parma, c. 1698; d. Bologna, 1770. Studied with Lanzi; first known appearance, Parma, 1716. After singing in Italy, she made her London debut in Handel's *Ottone*, 1723, and sang there until 1728, creating leading roles in *Giulio Cesare*, *Tamerlano*, and many other works. She returned to London with the Opera of the Nobility (1734–36), and again in 1750–51 for a pathetic farewell. Not comparable as an actress to her great rival Bordoni, Cuzzoni was the more telling singer in doleful music.

cycle. In opera, a series of works relating a continuing story. The most celebrated example is Wagner's *Der Ring des Nibelungen*.

Cyrano de Bergerac. Opera in 4 acts by Damrosch; libretto by W.J. Henderson, after Edmond Rostand's play.
  First perf., N.Y., Met, Feb. 27, 1913: Alda, R. Martin, Amato, c. Hertz, d. Rovescalli/Maison Marie Muelle, p. Speck. 5 perfs. in 1 season.
  Damrosch's opera apparently resembled Wagner's works in length and weight of orchestration, but not in quality of inspiration. Set in Paris, c. 1640, it relates the familiar tale of Cyrano (bar), the noble knight with a large nose, and his secret love of his cousin Roxane (s); she loves the soldier Christian (t), but discovers too late that his passionate declarations and letters to her were authored by Cyrano.

D

da capo aria (from Ital., "from the top"). The dominant form of operatic aria in the 18th c. The text comprised two strophes, each set to different music, contrasting in harmony, texture, and/or dimension; after the completion of the second section, the first was repeated, often with embellishments.

Da Costa, Albert. Tenor; b. Amsterdam, N.Y., Mar. 21, 1927; d. Kolding, Denmark, Nov. 8, 1967. After study with Raymond McDermott and at Juilliard, N.Y., won Met Auditions, 1954. Met debut, Mar. 3, 1955, as Young Sailor (*Tristan*); in 8 seasons, sang 56 perfs. of 13 roles, including Dimitri (*Boris*), Erik (*Holländer*), Stolzing, Manrico, and Siegmund. Died in auto accident while pursuing a European career in Wagner roles.

Dafne. Opera in prologue and 6 scenes by Peri; libretto by Rinuccini.
  First perf., Florence, Jacopo Corsi's house, probably 1597.
  Generally accepted to be the first opera (though the music is now lost), based on the myth of Daphne. Other early operas on the same subject were written by Gagliano

(1608, libretto an altered version on Rinuccini's) and Schütz (1627, the first German opera, now lost).

Dale, Clamma. Soprano; b. Chester, Pa., July 4, 1948. Studied with Hans Heinz, Alice Howland, and Cornelius Reid, Juilliard, N.Y. Mini-Met debut as St. Theresa I (*Four Saints*), Feb. 20, 1973. N.Y.C. Opera debut as Antonia (*Hoffmann*), Sep. 30, 1975. Other roles include Musetta, Nedda, Countess, Pamina, Bess.

Dalibor. Opera in 3 acts by Smetana; libretto by Joseph Wenzig, after Czech legend.

First perf., Prague, New Town Theater, May 16, 1868: Benevicová-Milková, Lukes. U.S. prem., Chicago, Sokol Hall, Apr. 13, 1924.

First performed to celebrate the laying of the cornerstone of the National Theater, this rescue opera is associated by Czech audiences with aspirations for national liberty.

Prague, 15th c. The knight Dalibor (t) has killed the Burgrave in revenge for the killing of his friend Zdeněk and is sentenced to life imprisonment. The Burgrave's daughter Milada (s), moved to pity and then love, disguises herself as a boy and obtains work in the jail, where the two make plans for escape. But they are found out and Dalibor's sentence is changed to instant death. His supporters wait outside in readiness to attack. Dalibor comes out carrying Milada, who has been wounded, and who dies in his arms, after which he stabs himself before the captain of the guard arrives with troops. (In an alternate ending, Dalibor is executed in front of Milada, and she is killed in the rescue party's attack.)

Dalis, Irene. Mezzo-soprano; b. San Jose, Calif., Oct. 8, 1925. Studied with Edyth Walker, Paul Althouse, N.Y.; Otto Mueller, Milan; Margarete Klose, Berlin; debut as Eboli, Oldenburg, 1953. Met debut as Eboli, Mar. 16, 1957, later singing Amneris, Santuzza, Azucena, Lady Macbeth, Nurse (*Frau*), Dalila, and Wagner mezzo parts; 232 perfs. of 22 roles in 19 seasons. Also appeared in London (1958) and Bayreuth (Kundry, 1961).

Dallapiccola, Luigi. Composer; b. Pisino d'Istria, Italy, Feb. 3, 1904; d. Florence, Feb. 19, 1975. Studied composition with Frazzi at Cherubini Conservatory, Florence. Composing career encouraged by Casella. Influenced by Debussy, Busoni, and later by the 12-tone techniques of Schoenberg, Berg, and Webern, as evidenced by the eclectic *Volo di Notte* (1940). In addition to many vocal works with instruments, he composed the urgent, dramatic, wholly dodecaphonic opera *Il Prigionero* (1950); the sparer *Job* (1950), described as a "sacred representation"; and the ambitious *Ulisse* (1968), philosophical and subtly restrained. His style embodies a fruitful tension between Italian lyricism and German rigor.

Dallas. City in Texas. The Dallas Opera House opened on Oct. 15, 1883, with *Iolanthe*, but the city's operatic life long subsisted on touring companies: the Chicago Opera during the 1920s, the San Carlo during the 1930s, and the Metropolitan Opera from 1939. Dallas was put on the international operatic map in 1957 when Lawrence Kelly and Nicola Rescigno left the Chicago Lyric and established the Dallas Civic Opera; performances are held in State Fair Park Music Hall (capacity 4,100). The initial presentation was a concert by Maria Callas; the first stage performance was *Italiana in Algeri* (Nov. 21, 1957) with Simionato, designed and directed by Zeffirelli. Dallas was

subsequently the scene of the American debuts of such singers as Alva, Berganza, Dernesch, Olivero, and Sutherland. Plato S. Karayanis is now general director, and Rescigno continues as artistic director.

dal Monte, Toti [Antonietta Meneghelli]. Soprano; b. Mogliano Veneto, Italy, June 27, 1893; d. Pieve di Soligo, Treviso, Jan. 26, 1975. Studied with Barbara Marchisio, Venice; debut as Biancafiore (*Francesca*), La Scala, 1916; sang there regularly until 1939. In her only Met season, sang 3 perfs. as Lucia (debut, Dec. 5, 1924) and Gilda; also appeared in Chicago (1924–28). Although predominantly a coloratura, she was also a notable Butterfly.

Dalmorès, Charles [Henry Alphonse Boin]. Tenor; b. Nancy, Jan. 1(?), 1871; d. Los Angeles, Calif., Dec. 6, 1939. Began career as horn player and teacher, then studied singing with Daupin, Paris Conservatory; operatic debut in Rouen, 1899. Appeared at Monnaie, Brussels, 1900–06, creating Lancelot in Chausson's *Roi Arthus*, 1903. At Covent Garden (debut, Faust, 1904), he created Win-San-Luy (*Oracolo*). N.Y. debut as Faust, Manhattan Opera, 1906; other roles included José, Julien, Pelléas, Samson, Jean (*Hérodiade*), and Herod (*Salome*). After study with Franz Emmerich, sang Lohengrin in Bayreuth, 1908. Paris Opéra debut as Siegfried, 1911; appeared in Boston (1911–14) and Chicago (1910–18), where he sang Tristan, Siegmund, and Parsifal. After retirement, taught in France and U.S. A distinguished heroic tenor, who made most of his career outside his native France.

dal segno aria (from Ital., "from the sign"). A modification of the da capo aria, in which only part of the first section (from a point indicated with a symbol) was repeated.

Dame Blanche, La (The White Lady). Opera in 3 acts by Boieldieu; libretto by Scribe, after Scott's novels *Guy Mannering* and *The Monastery*.

First perf., Paris, Opéra-Comique, Dec. 10, 1825: Rigaut, Boulanger, Ponchard, Henri. U.S. prem., N.Y., Park, Aug. 24, 1827. Met prem. (and only perf.), Feb. 13, 1904 (in Ger.): Gadski, Homer, Naväl, Blass, c. Mottl, d. Emens.

An enduringly successful, freshly melodious opéra comique.

Scotland, 1759. The estate of the late Count Avenel is haunted by a "white lady" – in reality Anna (s), ward of the late Count's steward Gaveston (bs), whose plans to acquire the castle she desires to thwart. She enlists the aid of Georges Brown (t), an English officer who is the guest of tenants on the estate. Relying on funds to be provided by the "ghost" from hidden family treasure, Brown outbids Gaveston at auction, and Anna reveals that the young officer is actually the long-lost Avenel heir.

Damnation de Faust, La (The Damnation of Faust). "Dramatic legend" in 4 parts by Berlioz; libretto by the composer and Almire Gandonnière, after Gérard de Nerval's version of Goethe's drama.

First perf., Paris, Opéra-Comique, Dec. 6, 1846 (concert perf.): Duflot-Maillard, Roger, Léon, c. Berlioz. U.S. prem., N.Y., Steinway Hall, Feb. 12, 1880 (concert perf.). Met prem., Feb. 2, 1896 (concert perf.): de Vere, Lubert, Plançon, c. Seidl. Met stage prem., Dec. 7, 1906: Farrar, Rousselière, Plançon, c. Vigna, d. Fox. 5 staged perfs. in 1 season.

Berlioz never shaped this "dramatic legend" into a

stage work, as he planned to do for London in 1848; nevertheless, the score's vivid intensity has led to many operatic presentations, despite its episodic narrative. Faust (t) delights in nature and dreams of military glory, then is tempted by Méphistophélès (bs) with the promise of youth, revels with the students in Leipzig, seduces and abandons Marguerite (s). He rides to hell, while Marguerite is redeemed.

Damrosch, Leopold. Conductor; b. Posen, Germany [now Poznań, Poland], Oct. 22, 1832; d. New York, Feb. 15, 1885. A violinist and conductor in Germany, notably at Breslau, he came to N.Y. in 1871 to conduct a German choral society. He founded the Oratorio Society (1873), then the Symphony Society (1878), both of which he led until his death. A vigorous entrepreneur, he also organized the city's first music festival in 1881, and led orchestral tours in the western states. After the Met's disastrous inaugural season, he produced a German season (1884–85), conducting every performance of 11 works until, toward the season's end, he contracted pneumonia and died.

Damrosch, Walter. Conductor and composer; b. Breslau, Germany [now Wrocław, Poland], Jan. 30, 1862; d. New York, Dec. 22, 1950. Son of conductor Leopold Damrosch, whom he assisted during the Met's first German season. After his father's sudden death, he led several performances (debut, *Tannhäuser*, Feb. 11, 1885); during 8 Met seasons (1885–91, 1900–02), he led 25 operas, mostly German but also including *Prophète* and *Faust*. He organized the touring Damrosch Opera Co. (1894), led the N.Y. Symphony Society until 1928, conducted countless children's concerts, and pioneered in the broadcasting of classical music (from 1927, music advisor at NBC). His operas, in a conservative style, include *The Scarlet Letter* (1896), *Cyrano de Bergerac* (1913), and *The Man Without a Country* (1937).

d'Angelo, Gianna. Soprano; b. Hartford, Conn., Nov. 18, 1934. Studied at Juilliard, N.Y., and with de Luca and dal Monte in Italy; debut as Gilda, Caracalla, Rome, 1954. Met debut in same role, Apr. 5, 1961; 36 perfs. of 7 roles in 8 seasons, including Amina, Lucia, Rosina, and Zerbinetta. Also sang at major Italian theaters and Glyndebourne (Rosina, 1955; Zerbinetta, 1962).

d'Angelo, Louis. Bass-baritone; b. Naples, May 6, 1888; d. Jersey City, N.J., Aug. 9, 1958. Studied with Guarini, N.Y. College of Music; debut in *Fanciulla* with Savage Co., N.Y. Met debut as Wagner (*Faust*), Nov. 17, 1917; sang 1490 perfs. of 130 (mostly comprimario) roles in 30 seasons, including Zuniga, Nachtigall (*Meistersinger*), and the King (*Aida*). Created Marco (*Gianni Schicchi*), 1918.

Daniels, Barbara. Soprano; b. Cincinnati, Ohio, May 7, 1946. Studied at U. of Cincinnati; debut as Susanna, West Palm Beach, Fla., 1973. From 1974, sang in Innsbruck, Kassel, and Cologne; debuts in Washington, D.C. (Norina, 1979) and San Francisco (Zdenka in *Arabella*, 1980). Appearances at Covent Garden (1978), Paris Opéra, and Houston. Met debut as Musetta, Sep. 30, 1983; other roles are Violetta and Thérèse (*Mamelles*).

Danise, Giuseppe. Baritone; b. Salerno, Italy, Jan. 11, 1882; d. New York, Jan. 9, 1963. Studied with L. Colonnesi and A. Petillo at Naples Conservatory; debut as Alfio, Teatro Bellini, Naples, 1906. Sang in Italy, Russia, and South America. Met debut as Amonasro, Nov. 17,

1920; 312 perfs. of 29 roles in 12 seasons, including Tonio, Valentin, Gérard (*Chénier*), and Germont. Married to soprano Bidú Sayão.

Dante (Alighieri). Italian poet (1265–1321). Operas based on his writings include *Francesca da Rimini* (Zandonai) and *Gianni Schicchi* (Puccini).

Danton and Robespierre. Opera in 3 acts by Eaton; libretto by Patrick Creagh.
First perf., Bloomington, Indiana U., April 21, 1978: Anderson, Noble, c. Baldner.
This densely intricate, fast-moving opera prominently employs microtonal intervals. Set in France, 1792 and after, the plot covers the final months in the life of Danton (t), his execution at the height of the Reign of Terror, and the fall of Robespierre (bar).

Dantons Tod (Danton's Death). Opera in 2 acts by von Einem; libretto by the composer and Boris Blacher, after Georg Büchner's drama.
First perf., Salzburg, Festspielhaus, Aug. 6, 1947: Cebotari, Patzak, Witt, Schöffler, Hann, c. Fricsay. U.S. prem., N.Y.C. Opera, Mar. 9, 1966 (in Eng.): Grant, DuPree, Reardon, Beattie, c. Märzendorfer.
Einem's first opera, an expressionist score, is set in Paris, 1794; the action traces Danton's disillusionment with revolutionary government, his arrest at Robespierre's instigation, his trial and execution.

Daphne. Opera in 1 act by R. Strauss; libretto by Joseph Gregor, after the classical legend.
First perf., Dresden, Oct. 15, 1938: Teschemacher, Ralf, Kremer, c. Böhm. U.S. prem., N.Y., Brooklyn College, Oct. 7, 1960 (concert perf.): Davy, Crain, Nagy. U.S. stage prem., Santa Fe, July 29, 1964: Stahlman, Shirley, Petersen, c. Crosby.
Daphne's transformation scene calls forth Strauss' most ecstatic vein of soprano lyricism.
In a village near Mount Olympus, legendary times. Daphne (s), daughter of the fisherman Peneios (bs), loves nature more than men. Her mother Gaea (c) rebukes her for rejecting the shepherd Leukippos (t). Captivated by Daphne's beauty, the god Apollo (t) appears in human form; his passion confuses and frightens her. The jealous god kills Leukippos; when he sees her despair, he begs Zeus to give her the form of one of the trees she loves so well. She is gradually transformed into a laurel tree.

da Ponte, Lorenzo [Emmanuele Conegliano]. Librettist; b. Ceneda [now Vittorio Veneto], near Venice, Mar. 10, 1749; d. New York, Aug. 17, 1838. Converted from Judaism to Catholicism and was ordained as a priest; he was dismissed from a teaching position in Treviso for insubordination, then banished from Venice for adultery. In 1781 he became poet to Vienna's new Italian opera company. His witty, polished, compassionate librettos for Mozart's *Nozze*, *Don Giovanni*, and *Così* are among the finest ever written. Despite these and other successes, upon Joseph II's death in 1792 da Ponte was forced to leave Vienna. After a stay in London, financial difficulties forced his emigration by 1805 to N.Y., where he taught Italian (from 1825 at Columbia College), published entertaining memoirs in 1823, and witnessed the 1825 U.S. premiere of *Don Giovanni* at the Park Theatre.

Dara, Enzo. Bass; b. Oct. 13, 1938, Mantua, Italy. Studied with Bruno Sutti, Mantua; debut as Colline,

Fano, 1960. La Scala debut as Bartolo (*Barbiere*), 1970; Met debut in same role, Feb. 15, 1982. Has also appeared in Vienna, Buenos Aires, London, Moscow, and Tokyo.

Darcy, Emery. Tenor; b. Chicago, Dec. 9, 1908. Studied with Lucie Lenox (later his wife) in Chicago, Hermann Weigert and Walter Taussig in N.Y.; after debut as Malatesta (*Pasquale*), Chicago, 1932, became tenor. Met debut as Messenger (*Samson*), Dec. 6, 1940; in 13 seasons, sang 367 perfs. of 23 roles, including Froh, Melot, Parsifal, and Siegmund.

Dardanus. Opera in prologue and 5 acts by Rameau; libretto by C. Antoine Leclerc de la Bruère.
First perf., Paris, Opéra, Nov. 19, 1739. U.S. prem., N.Y., Juilliard American Opera Center, Oct. 28, 1975.
Hampered by a weak libretto, *Dardanus* is set in legendary Phrygia. Iphise (s) loves Dardanus (t) against the wishes of her father, the king of Phrygia (bs), who wants her to marry Anténor (bs). After fantastical episodes, Anténor renounces his claim and the lovers are united.

Dargomijsky, Alexander. Composer; b. Troitskoye, Tula district, Russia, Feb. 14, 1813; d. St. Petersburg, Jan. 17, 1869. Studied piano, but was essentially self-taught as a composer. Encouraged by Glinka, he modeled his first opera, *Esmeralda* (1841; libretto after Hugo's *Notre-Dame de Paris*), on the French grand-opera tradition. *Rusalka* (1856) sought simpler, more direct vocal lines and harmonies. In the unfinished *The Stone Guest*, he attempted to recreate Pushkin's inflections through "continuous melodic recitative," an experiment problematic in practice but a potent model for Mussorgsky.

Daughter of the Regiment, The. See *Fille du Régiment, La*.

David, Félicien-César. Composer; b. Cadenet, France, Apr. 13, 1810; d. St.-Germain-en-Laye, Aug. 29, 1876. Studied with Reber and Fétis at Paris Conservatory. In 1831, joined the socialist St.-Simonist movement and, upon its dispersal in 1833, travelled with members of the organization to the Near East, which inspired his enormously successful "ode-symphony," *Le Désert* (1844). This and operas such as *La Perle du Brésil* (1851) and *Lalla Ronkh* (1862), picturesque and evocative but musically conservative, influenced the Oriental operas of Bizet and Delibes.

Davies, Peter Maxwell. See *Maxwell Davies, Peter*.

Davis, Andrew. Conductor; b. Ashridge, England, Feb. 2, 1944. Studied at King's College, Cambridge, and conducting under Ferrara at Santa Cecilia, Rome. Associate conductor, New Philharmonia Orchestra (from 1973); music director, Toronto Symphony (from 1975). Operatic debut, *Capriccio*, Glyndebourne (1973); Met debut, *Salome* (Feb. 24, 1981), returning subsequently to lead *Barbiere* and *Ariadne*.

Davis, Colin. Conductor; b. Weybridge, England, Sep. 23, 1927. After study at Royal College of Music and apprentice conducting with Kalmar Orchestra (London) and Chelsea Opera Group, he made his Sadler's Wells debut (*Entführung*, 1958) and replaced Klemperer in a concert performance of *Don Giovanni* (1959). Glyndebourne debut, *Zauberflöte* (1960). Music director of Sadler's Wells Opera (1960 65), where he championed 20th-c. scores, notably Stravinsky, Weill, and Janáček.

Covent Garden debut, *Figaro* (1965); later music director (1971–86). Chief conductor, BBC Symphony (1967–71). Met debut, *Peter Grimes*, Jan. 20, 1967; the following season he led *Grimes* and *Wozzeck*, and *Pelléas* in 1971–72. First Englishman to conduct at Bayreuth (*Tannhäuser*, 1977). Principal guest conductor, Boston Symphony (1972–83); chief conductor, Bavarian Radio Symphony (since 1983). A highly successful interpreter in repertory requiring flair, brilliantly nuanced coloring, and emotional weight; his finest performances have been of Mozart, Tippett, Stravinsky, and Berlioz, whose works he has recorded extensively.

Davy, Gloria. Soprano; b. New York, Mar. 29, 1931. Studied with Belle Julie Soudent at Juilliard, where she sang the Countess in U.S. premiere of *Capriccio*, 1954; toured in *Porgy and Bess*, 1953. Noted as Aida, debut role at Nice (1957), Met (Feb. 12, 1958), Vienna (1959), and Covent Garden (1960). Other Met roles were Pamina, Nedda, and the *Trovatore* Leonora; 15 perfs. in 4 seasons.

Death in Venice. Opera in 2 acts by Britten; libretto by Myfanwy Piper, after Thomas Mann's story.
First perf., Aldeburgh Festival, June 16, 1973: Pears, Shirley-Quirk, c. Bedford. U.S. & Met prem., Oct. 18, 1974: Pears, Shirley-Quirk, c. Bedford, d. Piper/Knode, p. Graham. 9 perfs. in 1 season.
Britten's last opera, a work of spare and sometimes cryptic music and subtle, intimately personal yet almost ritualized dramaturgy.
Munich, Venice, and the Lido, 1911. Gustav von Aschenbach (t), a famous writer, is urged and tempted southward by a variety of related nemeses. In Venice, he laments his artistic exhaustion, and finds himself attracted to a young boy, Tadzio (dancer), whom he has seen with his family at the beach. The two never meet directly, but Aschenbach admits to himself with a combination of wonder and distress that he is in love with the boy. Immersed in fantasies about Tadzio's youthful beauty, he persistently ignores warnings of a cholera epidemic, and falls victim to it, dying on the beach as he watches the object of his obsession.

Debussy, Claude. Composer; b. St. Germain-en-Laye, near Paris, Aug. 22, 1862; d. Paris, Mar. 25, 1918. Studied at Paris Conservatory with Lavignac, Durand, and Guiraud. In 1880, employed by Tchaikovsky's patroness Mme. von Meck to teach her children piano, he encountered Mussorgsky's music. Other influences included Wagner, symbolist poetry, and oriental music (heard at the 1889 Paris Exposition). His mature music is characterized by fluid structure, innovative harmony, subtle coloration, and a strong sense of mood and atmosphere.
Among his abortive early dramatic projects were passages from two comedies of de Banville, *Hymnis* (c. 1882) and *Diane au Bois* (1883–86), and a scene from l'Isle Adam's *Axël* (1887–89). *Rodrigue et Chimène* (1890–92), a grand opera with libretto by Catulle Mendès, remains in an unfinished, unpublished short score. Debussy's only completed opera was a substantially verbatim setting of Maeterlinck's play *Pelléas et Mélisande* (1902), in which the shadow of Wagner was held at bay by rigorous adherence to the intonations of spoken French; restrained text-setting alternates with discreetly symphonic interludes. Debussy planned (and contracted to Gatti-Casazza for the Met) two further operas, based on Poe, *Le Diable Dans le Beffroi* (1902–11) and *La Chute de la Maison Usher* (1908–17); neither was completed, although the surviving

fragments of the latter have been reconstructed and performed.

BIBLIOGRAPHY: Robert Orledge, *Debussy and the Theatre* (Cambridge, 1982).

Deiber, Paul-Émile. Producer; b. La Broque, France, Jan. 1, 1925. Considered one of France's greatest actors after Barrault. Debut as operatic director, *Barbiere* (Paris, 1955); artistic director, Paris Opéra, 1968–71. For Met, staged *Roméo* (1967), *Norma* (1970), *Werther* (1971), *Pelléas* (1972), and *Syllabaire pour Phèdre* (Mini-Met, 1973).

De Koven, Reginald. Composer; b. Middletown, Conn., Apr. 13, 1859; d. Chicago, Jan. 16, 1920. Educated at Oxford U., studied piano and theory in Germany, singing in Florence, and operatic composition with Suppé and Delibes. His grand operas *The Canterbury Pilgrims* (1917) and *Rip Van Winkle* (1920) were performed at the Met and Chicago, respectively. His very popular operettas included *Robin Hood* (1890), source of the song "O Promise Me."

de Lara [Cohen], **Isidore.** Composer, b. London, Aug. 9, 1858; d. Paris, Sep. 2, 1935. Studied singing with Lamperti, composition with Mazzucato at Milan Conservatory and Lalo in Paris. Prolific and frequently produced in his day, he achieved transient success with *The Light of Asia* (1892), *Messalina* (1899), and *Les Trois Mousquetaires* (1921), works in the vein of Saint-Saëns and Massenet.

Delibes, Léo. Composer; b. St. Germain du Val, France, Feb. 21, 1836; d. Paris, Jan. 16, 1891. Studied with Adam at Paris Conservatory. Accompanist and chorus master at the Théâtre-Lyrique and later at the Opéra, his early stage works were operettas, including the highly successful *Deux Vieilles Gardes* (1856). After the popular and enduring ballets *Coppélia* (1870) and *Sylvia* (1876), he wrote several full-scale operatic works, including *Jean de Nivelle* (1880), the still-revived *Lakmé* (1883), and *Kassya* (unfinished; orchestrated by Massenet, perf. 1893).

Delius, Frederick. Composer; b. Bradford, England, Jan. 29, 1862; d. Grez-sur-Loing, France, June 10, 1934. During early travels to Florida, he studied musical technique with Thomas Ward, and developed a strong love of nature, a frequent theme in his compositions. Studied briefly at Leipzig Conservatory, where he was encouraged by Grieg. His first operas, *Irmelin* (1892) and *The Magic Fountain* (1895), and the later *Margot la Rouge* (1902) were unperformed in his lifetime. *Koanga* (1897) is in a verismo-oriented style; *A Village Romeo and Juliet* (1901) and *Fennimore and Gerda* (1910) are closer to his mature idiom of pastoral impressionism suffused with vernacular elements (variously black American, Nordic, or Anglo-Saxon). Disabled after 1920 by syphilis, Delius continued to compose with the help of his amanuensis Eric Fenby.

Della Casa, Lisa. Soprano; b. Burgdorf, near Bern, Switzerland, Feb. 2, 1919. Studied with Margarethe Haeser, Zurich; debut as Butterfly, Solothurn-Biel, 1941. Sang at Zurich, 1943–50; debuts at Salzburg (Zdenka in *Arabella*, 1947) and Glyndebourne (Countess, 1951). Joined Vienna State Opera, 1947. Met debut as Countess, Nov. 20, 1953; in 15 seasons, sang 155 perfs. of 11 roles, including Donna Elvira, Eva, Arabella, the Marschallin and Octavian.

Mario del Monaco as Otello

Dello Joio, Norman. Composer; b. New York, Jan. 24, 1913. Studied with Wagenaar at Juilliard and Hindemith at Tanglewood and Yale U. Influenced by 19th-c. Italian opera as well as American popular music and Gregorian chant, he combined these elements into a musical idiom suited to his preoccupation with religious themes. A series of works based on Joan of Arc began with the opera *The Triumph of St. Joan* (1950), withdrawn and reworked into a symphony; a completely new opera for television, *The Trial at Rouen* (1955), was revised for stage performance by the N.Y.C. Opera (1959) and retitled *The Triumph of St. Joan*. Other operas: *The Ruby* (1955), *Blood Moon* (1961).

del Monaco, Mario. Tenor; b. Florence, July 27, 1915; d. Mestre, near Venice, Oct. 16, 1982. Largely self-taught from recordings, he studied briefly with Melocchi at Pesaro Conservatory. Encouraged by the conductor Serafin, he won a place in the Rome Opera school, 1935. After performing opera in Pesaro, 1939, he made his formal debut as Pinkerton, Teatro Puccini, Milan, 1941, while on leave from the Italian army. Many international appearances in 1945–46: Radames at Verona Arena; Cavaradossi, Pinkerton, and Canio at Covent Garden with the Naples company; then in Mexico City, Rio de Janeiro, and Buenos Aires. U.S. debut as Radames, San Francisco, 1950. Met debut as Puccini's Des Grieux, Nov. 27, 1950; in 7 seasons (through 1959) he sang 102 perfs. of 16 roles there, most frequently Radames, followed by Otello, Don José, Canio, Chénier, Ernani, Don Alvaro, Enzo, Pollione, Samson, and others. He retired from the stage in 1973. He was buried in his Otello costume, having performed the role, by his count, 427 times.

Nature endowed del Monaco with an enormous and powerful voice, which he used with energy and a sometimes unremitting intensity; he was the most generally admired Otello of the Fifties.

Delna [Ledan], **Marie.** Contralto; b. Meudon, near Paris, Apr. 3, 1875; d. Paris, July 23, 1932. Studied with Rosine Laborde, Paris; debut as Didon (*Troyens*), Opéra-Comique, 1892. She sang there until 1898, creating Marcelline (*Attaque du Moulin*), role of her debuts at Covent Garden (1894) and the Met (Feb. 8, 1910, New Theater). At the Met itself, she also sang Gluck's Orfeo; also appeared at Paris Opéra, 1898–1901.

de los Angeles [Lopéz Garcia], **Victoria.** Soprano; b. Barcelona, Nov. 1, 1923. She studied with Dolores Frau at Barcelona Conservatory; after a 1941 debut as Mimi in that city, she continued her studies, leading to a formal stage debut in 1945 as the Countess (*Nozze*) at the Liceo. First prize in the Geneva competition (1947) led to a BBC engagement as Salud (*Vida Breve*, 1948) and debuts at the Paris Opéra (Marguerite, 1949) and La Scala (Ariadne, 1950); in Milan, she later sang Donna Anna, Agathe (*Freischütz*), Rosina, and, at the Piccola Scala, Laodice in Scarlatti's *Mitridate Eupatore*. At Covent Garden (debut, Mimi, 1950), her roles included Elsa, Santuzza, and Nedda. She came to the Met on Mar. 17, 1951 as Marguerite; in 10 seasons with the company (1951–61), she sang 103 perfs. of 13 roles, including Mimi, Manon, the Countess, Butterfly, Micaela, Eva, Mélisande, Rosina, Violetta, Desdemona, Elisabeth, and Lady Harriet in *Martha*. In 1961 she made her Bayreuth debut as Elisabeth, but thereafter restricted her operatic appearances; in the 1970s, she sang an occasional Carmen, while continuing an active recital career, specializing in Spanish and French song literature.

At the height of her powers, in the 1950s, de los Angeles offered a radiant, flexible, creamy soprano capable of precise and evocative shading; her coloratura dexterity and sound lower register enabled her to sing Rosina in the original keys. A warm and sympathetic singing actress, her operatic career was effectively curtailed by difficulties with her high register. Her discography includes notable recordings of *Bohème, Carmen, Werther, Faust, Pelléas, Manon,* and *Butterfly.*

de Luca, Giuseppe. Baritone; b. Rome, Dec. 25, 1876; d. New York, Aug. 26, 1950. Studied with Venceslao Persichini at Santa Cecilia, Rome, and also with Cotogni. Debut as Valentin (*Faust*), Piacenza, 1897. At the Lirico, Milan, he created Michonnet (*Adriana*). At La Scala (debut, Alberich, 1903), he created Gleby (Giordano's *Siberia*) and Sharpless, the role of his Covent Garden debut (1907). After singing widely in Europe, he came to the Met as Rossini's Figaro, Nov. 25, 1915, and sang there every season until 1935 in 52 roles, most often as Rigoletto, also as Germont, Ashton (*Lucia*), Puccini's Lescaut, Mercutio, Amonasro, Tonio, Plunkett, Marcello, and Sharpless, also Mozart's Figaro and Guglielmo, the *Hoffmann* villains, and Ping (*Turandot*); he created Paquiro (*Goyescas*) and Gianni Schicchi. De Luca returned to Italy in 1935 when the Met decided not to meet his fee, but returned for a few appearances as Germont, Rigoletto, and Figaro in 1940, rounding out a total of 725 perfs. He taught at the Juilliard School and celebrated the 50th anniversary of his debut in a N.Y. recital, Nov. 7, 1947.

While not particularly large, de Luca's voice was exceptionally well-produced and durable; even after his official retirement, he amazed audiences at benefits and recitals. His recordings, over a period of 45 years, document a cultivated vocal style as well as notable powers of dramatic and comic interpretation.

Victoria de los Angeles as Violetta in *La Traviata*

de Lucia, Fernando. Tenor; b. Naples, Oct. 11, 1860; d. Naples, Feb. 21, 1925. Studied with Lombardi in Naples; debut there as Faust, San Carlo, 1885. Appeared at Drury Lane, London, 1887, somewhat in the shadow of Jean de Reszke, but had greater success there in 1892–1900. He took part in the premieres of Mascagni's *Amico Fritz, I Rantzau, Silvano,* and *Iris.* He made his Met debut as Fritz, Jan. 10, 1894, singing there that season only, also as Canio, Turiddu, Don José, the Duke of Mantua, Faust, and Ottavio. De Lucia appeared often in Naples; his last stage appearance there was as Fritz, 1917, and he sang at Caruso's funeral, 1921. He taught in Naples; Thill, Maria Németh, and Gianna Pederzini were among his pupils.

With a rapid vibrato characteristic of his era, de Lucia's

Giuseppe de Luca as Rigoletto

voice was remarkably flexible; in his prime, he had difficulty with high notes, and regularly transposed arias. Though in his day a celebrated and impassioned interpreter of verismo roles, he is now often cited for his spontaneous, abundantly ornamented recordings of Rossini's Almaviva and of arias by Bellini and Donizetti. He made about 400 recordings between 1902 and 1922, which show that most of his technique and tone was preserved into his sixties.

de Lussan, Zélie. Soprano; b. Brooklyn, N.Y., Dec. 21, 1861; d. London, Dec. 18, 1949. Studied with her mother; debut as Arline (*Bohemian Girl*), Boston, 1884. Covent Garden debut as Carmen (her most famous role), 1888. Met debut as Carmen, Nov. 26, 1894; sang 32 perfs. of 8 roles in 3 seasons with the company, also including Zerlina, Nannetta, Cherubino, and Nedda.

de Marchi, Emilio. Tenor; b. Voghera, Italy, Jan. 6, 1861; d. Milan, Mar. 20, 1917. Debut as Alfredo, dal Verme, Milan, 1886; sang at Palermo, Rome, La Scala (debut, Stolzing, 1898) and Covent Garden (1901). At Costanzi, Rome, 1900, created Cavaradossi, also the role of his Met debut, Jan. 3, 1902. In 2 Met seasons, he sang 34 perfs. as Radames, Alfredo, Rodolfo, Ernani, Riccardo (*Ballo*), Turiddu, Don José, and Canio. His only known recordings are Mapleson cylinders, made at his Met perfs.

Demon, The. Opera in 3 acts by Rubinstein; libretto by Pavel Alexandrovich Viskovatov, after Lermontov's poem.

First perf., St. Petersburg, Maryinsky, Jan. 25, 1875. U.S. prem., San Francisco, Mason Opera House, Feb. 18, 1922.

Rubinstein's once-popular opera is a score of high passion and romantic melody. The Demon (bs), desiring Tamara (s), the betrothed of Prince Sinodal (t), has the prince murdered and pursues the girl even in a convent, where Sinodal, now an angel, intervenes to bring her release in death.

de Muro, Bernardo. Tenor; b. Tempio Pausania, Sardinia, Nov. 3, 1881; d. Rome, Oct. 27, 1955. Studied at Santa Cecilia, Rome, with Sbriscia and Martino; debut as Turiddu, Costanzi, Rome, 1910. La Scala debut as Folco in *Isabeau*, his most famous role, 1912. Also sang in Spain and Latin America; in N.Y., he appeared at the Hippodrome in 1933 (Manrico, Chénier) and at the Polo Grounds in 1944 for his farewell Don José.

de Paolis, Alessio. Tenor; b. Rome, Mar. 5, 1893; d. New York, Mar. 9, 1964. Studied at Santa Cecilia, Rome; debut as Duke of Mantua, Bologna, 1919. La Scala debut as Fenton, 1921. Sang lyric leads until 1932, then concentrated on character roles. Met debut as Cassio, Dec. 3, 1938; in 26 seasons, sang 1212 perfs. of 50 roles, including Goro, Shuisky, and Spoletta.

de Reszke, Édouard. Bass; b. Warsaw, Dec. 22, 1853; d. Garnek, May 25, 1917. Brother of tenor Jean and soprano Joséphine. Studied in Warsaw with Ciaffei, in Italy with Steller and Coletti; debut as Amonasro in first Paris *Aida*, Verdi conducting, Italien, 1876. After two seasons at the Italien, he sang at La Scala (1879–81), creating Ruben (Ponchielli's *Figliuol Prodigo*) and Gilberto (Gomez's *Maria Tudor*), and singing Fiesco in the newly-revised *Simon Boccanegra* (1881). Covent Garden debut as Indra (*Roi de Lahore*), 1880. During the 1890s, Édouard and Jean appeared together frequently in Paris, London, and N.Y., including the 500th *Faust* at the Opéra, 1887. Édouard joined the Met in 1891, making his U.S. debut, on tour in Chicago, as Heinrich (*Lohengrin*), Nov. 9, and his N.Y. debut as Frère Laurent, Dec. 14; he sang with the company every season until 1903, except 1892–93 and 1897–98. In 377 Met performances, his most frequent role was Méphistophélès (68 times); his 29 roles also included Marcel (*Huguenots*), King Marke, Ramfis, Boito's Mefistofele, Mozart's Almaviva, Rossini's Basilio, and Hagen. He sang Wagner first in Italian, then, after 1896, like his brother, relearned the operas in German. After his retirement from the stage at a Met gala, Apr. 27, 1903, he tried unsuccessfully to teach in London and Warsaw. He died in extreme poverty on his Polish estate amid the privations of World War I. Though considered a less conscientious singer than his brother, Édouard, with his large, rich, agile voice and enormous height, was invariably an imposing and vivid presence on stage. His few studio recordings, made in 1903, are disappointing.

de Reszke, Jean. Tenor; b. Warsaw, Jan. 14, 1850; d. Nice, Apr. 3, 1935. Studied with his mother and with Ciaffei in Warsaw, then with Cotogni in Milan. He began his career as a baritone, using the name Giovanni di Reschi at his debut, as Alphonse (*Favorite*), Fenice, Venice, 1874. The same year, he sang at Drury Lane, London. After his 1876 Paris debut as Melitone, under his own name, he left the stage for three years to study tenor roles with Sbriglia in Paris. His tenor debut (Robert le Diable, Madrid, Nov.

Édouard de Reszke as Hagen in *Götterdämmerung*

9, 1879, opposite his sister Joséphine), was unsuccessful, but his success as Jean in the Paris premiere of *Hérodiade* (Italien, 1884) led Massenet to compose Rodrigue (*Cid*) for him (Opéra, 1885). In five seasons at the Opéra, he also sang Radames, Vasco da Gama, and the title roles of *Prophète* and *Faust*, as well as the first Roméo at that house. His U.S. debut as Lohengrin took place on the Met tour in Chicago, Nov. 9, 1891; his N.Y. debut, as Roméo, followed on Dec. 14. Jean sang at the Met every season until 1901, except 1892–93, 1897–98, and 1899–1900. Among his 227 Met performances of 17 roles, Faust was the most frequent (51 times), followed by Roméo, Lohengrin, Don José, Walther, both Siegfrieds, and Vasco da Gama; he was the Met's first Otello, Rodrigue, Werther, and Des Grieux (*Manon*). His first Tristan (1895) was a landmark in the acceptance of Wagner, whose works he now sang in German, having studied the language intensively for two years. His last Met performance was in Act 2 of *Tristan* at a gala, Apr. 29, 1901. He came out of retirement to sing his first and only Canio in Paris, 1902. He taught in Paris, then in Nice; Sayão, Teyte, Saltzmann-Stevens, and Marie-Louise Edvina were among his pupils.

Jean de Reszke relied on phrasing and coloration, rather than ringing power, for his tasteful interpretations. His demonstration that the tenor roles in Wagner's music dramas could be sung smoothly made an enormous impact outside Germany. His intelligence, good looks, elegant deportment, and personal magnetism made him the idol of N.Y., London, and Paris throughout the Nineties.

His sister, soprano **Joséphine de Reszke** (b. Warsaw, June 4, 1855; d. Warsaw, Feb. 22, 1891), sang mainly at the Opéra (debut as Thomas's Ophélie, 1875; created Sita, *Roi de Lahore*, 1877) until her marriage and retirement from

Jean de Reszke as Siegfried in *Götterdämmerung*

the stage, 1885. She appeared with both her brothers in some performances of *Hérodiade*.

BIBLIOGRAPHY: Clara Leiser, *Jean de Reske and the Great Days of Opera* (N.Y., 1934, repr. 1970).

Dermota, Anton. Tenor; b. Kropa, Slovenia, June 4, 1910. Studied with Marie Radó, Vienna; debut as First Armed Man (*Zauberflöte*), State Opera, 1936. Sang primarily in Vienna and Salzburg, specializing in Mozart roles; also known for Lenski and Florestan, which he sang at reopening of Vienna State Opera, 1955.

Dernesch, Helga. Mezzo-soprano and soprano; b. Vienna, Feb. 3, 1939. Studied at Vienna Conservatory; debut as Marina (*Boris*), Bern, 1961, later singing in Wiesbaden and Cologne. After Bayreuth debut (1965), shifted to soprano parts, including Sieglinde (Covent Garden debut, 1970), Leonore, Isolde, and Brünnhilde (at Salzburg Easter Festivals, from 1969). Has since returned to mezzo roles; created Goneril in Reimann's *Lear*, Munich, 1978. Met debut as Marfa (*Khovanshchina*), Oct. 14, 1985.

de Sabata, Victor. Conductor; b. Trieste, Apr. 10, 1892; d. Santa Margherita Ligure, Dec. 11, 1967. After earning a Milan Conservatory degree (1910) and briefly devoting himself to composition, he turned to conducting, leading the premiere of *Enfant et les Sortilèges* (1923). Based at La Scala from 1929, he also conducted throughout Italy and elsewhere: Bayreuth (1939), Berlin, Vienna, and, after the war, orchestras in London, Chicago, N.Y. Music director of La Scala (1953–57), until ill health forced retirement. Because of his fiery, impulsive podium presence, he was often compared with Toscanini. A musician unafraid of excess in tempo and dynamics, he nevertheless produced compelling performances, most notably of *Tristan*, *Otello*, *Falstaff*, and other Verdi works; his recording of *Tosca* with Callas is particularly admired.

de Segurola, Andrés (Perello). Bass; b. Valencia, Spain, Mar. 27, 1874; d. Barcelona, Jan. 22, 1953. Studied in Barcelona; sang at Teatro Liceo there. Met debut as King (*Aida*), Mar. 3, 1902; in 12 seasons, sang 341 perfs. of 28 roles, including Colline (*Bohème*), Varlaam (*Boris*), and Geronte (*Manon Lescaut*), also creating Jake (*Fanciulla*) and Didier (*Madeleine*). Retired from Met in 1923, appearing in films and teaching in Hollywood.

Destinn, Emmy [Emilie Pavlina Kittlová, Ema Destinnová]. Soprano; b. Prague, Feb. 26, 1878; d. České Budějovice, Jan. 28, 1930. Studied with Marie Loewe-Destinn, whose name she adopted as a sign of gratitude; debut as Santuzza, Kroll Opera, Berlin, 1898; sang often in that city until 1908. Selected by Strauss to sing the first Salome in Berlin (1906) and Paris. At Bayreuth, sang Senta in 1901. At Covent Garden (debut, Donna Anna, 1904) she was the first Butterfly (1905) and Tatiana (1906). After her Met debut as Aida, Nov. 16, 1908, she returned until 1916 and again in 1919–21, singing 247 perfs. of 22 roles, most often as Aida, Santuzza, and Gioconda, also as Butterfly, Nedda, Eva, Mařenka (*Bartered Bride*), Alice Ford, Elisabeth, Lisa (*Queen of Spades*), Tosca, Pamina, Valentine (*Huguenots*), Amelia (*Ballo*), Leonora (*Trovatore*); she created Minnie (*Fanciulla*). She also sang in Chicago (debut, Gioconda, 1915). Just before and after World War I, she sang the title role of Smetana's patriotic *Libuše* in Prague, and spent the war under house arrest in Bohemia for her Czech nationalist views. After the war, she used the Czech form of her stage name, Ema

Destinnová, for several years, continuing to appear in concert until shortly before her death. Destinn's voluminous, warm, and flexible voice was distinctive in timbre and evenly produced throughout its range. Although especially gifted as a tragedienne, she performed a highly varied repertory of about 80 roles. The best of her recordings reveal a dramatic soprano of notable power and intensity.

deus ex machina (Lat., "the god from the machine"). A theatrical device in which a supernatural figure, lowered from above the stage, intervenes to resolve the dramatic action. By extension, any arbitrary solution to a tangled plot.

Deutekom, Christina [Stientje Engel]. Soprano; b. Amsterdam, Aug. 28, 1931. Studied with Johan Thomas and Coby Riemersma, Amsterdam Conservatory; debut as Queen of Night, Amsterdam, 1963. Sang this signature role at Met (debut, Sep. 28, 1967), La Scala, Covent Garden (1968), and Hamburg. In 3 Met seasons, she sang 15 perfs., including Donna Anna and Hélène (*Vêpres*).

Deux Journées, Les, ou Le Porteur d'Eau (The Two Days, or The Water-Carrier). Opera in 3 acts by Cherubini; libretto by Jean Nicolas Bouilly.
First perf., Paris, Feydeau, Jan. 16, 1800: Scio, Gaveux, Juliet. U.S. prem., New Orleans, St. Philippe, Mar. 12, 1811.
One of Cherubini's greatest successes in his lifetime, long popular in Germany (as *Der Wasserträger*), is set in Paris, 1647. Mikéli (bar), a water-carrier, protects Count Armand (t) and his wife Constance (s) from persecution by Cardinal Mazarin.

Devia, Mariella. Soprano; b. Chiusavecchia, Italy. Studied at Santa Cecilia, Rome; debut as Despina, Spoleto, 1972. Rome Opera debut as Lucia, 1973. Met debut as Gilda, Dec. 18, 1979; she has also sung Nannetta, Konstanze (*Entführung*), and Despina there. Appearances throughout Italy, in Brussels, Munich, Hamburg, Berlin, Dallas (Adina), Chicago (Oscar), and with Opera Orchestra of N.Y. (Lakmé).

Devil and Daniel Webster, The. Opera in 1 act by Moore; libretto by the composer, after Stephen Vincent Benét's story.
First perf., N.Y., Martin Beck, May 18, 1939.
An opera of folk-like simplicity and vigor, set in rural New Hampshire. For ten years of prosperity, farmer Jabez Stone (bs) sold his soul to the devil, who arrives to collect, disguised as the lawyer Scratch (t). Daniel Webster (bar) comes to Stone's aid, demands a trial, agrees to a jury of the dead as long as they are American, and wins an acquittal.

Devils of Loudon, The. See *Teufel von Loudon, Die*.

Devin du Village, Le (The Village Soothsayer). Opera in 1 act by Rousseau; libretto by the composer.
First perf., Fontainebleau, Oct. 18, 1752. First public perf., Paris, Opéra, Mar. 1, 1753. U.S. prem., N.Y., City Tavern, Oct. 21, 1790.
This simple pastoral embodies Rousseau's arguments in favor of Italian opera buffa style. Colette (s), abandoned by Colin (t), seeks advice from a Soothsayer (bar), who counsels pretended indifference. Told that Colette loves another, Colin woos her in earnest and the two are united.

Dialogues des Carmélites – (1977). Designed by David Reppa, produced by John Dexter

Devlin, Michael. Baritone; b. Chicago, Nov. 27, 1942. Studied at La. State U. and with Norman Treigle and Daniel Ferro, N.Y.; debut as Spalanzani (*Hoffmann*), New Orleans, 1963. N.Y.C. Opera debut, Hermit (*Don Rodrigo*), Feb. 22, 1966. Debuts at Glyndebourne (Almaviva, 1974) and Covent Garden (Don Giovanni, 1979). At the Met (debut, Escamillo, Nov. 23, 1978), he has sung the *Hoffmann* villains, Peter (*Hänsel*), the High Priest (*Zauberflöte*), and Falke (*Fledermaus*).

de Waart, Edo. Conductor; b. Amsterdam, June 1, 1941. After oboe study in Amsterdam, joined Concertgebouw in 1963. Studied conducting with Ferrara; debut in 1963 with Netherlands Radio Orchestra. Later led Netherlands Wind Ensemble (1966–71), Rotterdam Philharmonic (1967–79), San Francisco Symphony (music director, 1977–85). After conducting opera in the Netherlands (from 1970) and at Santa Fe (from 1971), debuts at Covent Garden (*Ariadne*, 1976), Bayreuth (*Lohengrin*, 1979); led San Francisco Opera *Ring* operas (1983–85). Music director, Netherlands Opera (from 1985) and Minnesota Orchestra (from 1986).

Dexter, John. Producer; b. Derby, England, Aug. 2, 1925. With English Stage Company (1957–72), produced plays by John Osborne, Arnold Wesker, Doris Lessing. Associate director of National Theatre (from 1963), his work was also seen on Broadway (including *Equus, Royal Hunt of the Sun*). First opera staging, *Benvenuto Cellini* (Covent Garden, 1966), followed by productions for Hamburg (1969–72) and Paris Opéra (1973). Director of production at the Met (1974–81), later production advisor (1981–84); his stagings there included *Vêpres Siciliennes* (1974); *Aida* (1976); *Prophète, Carmélites, Lulu, Rigoletto* (1977); *Billy Budd, Bartered Bride, Don Pasquale* (1978); *Don Carlos, Entführung, Mahagonny* (1979); and the *Parade* and *Stravinsky* triple bills (1981). Dexter's Met work included both conventional and stylized "concept" productions.

Dialogues des Carmélites (Dialogues of the Carmelites). Opera in 3 acts by Poulenc; libretto after Georges Bernanos' play, inspired by a novel of Gertrude von le Fort and a scenario of Rev. Fr. Bruckberger and Philippe Agostini.
First perf., Milan, La Scala, Jan. 26, 1957 (in Ital.): Zeani, Gencer, Ratti, Pederzini, Frazzoni, c. Sanzogno. U.S.

prem., San Francisco, Sep. 20, 1957 (in Eng.): Kirsten, L. Price, Stahlman, Turner, Thebom, c. Leinsdorf. Met prem., Feb. 5, 1977 (in Eng.): Ewing, Verrett, Norden, Crespin, Dunn, c. Plasson, d. Reppa/Greenwood, p. Dexter. Blanche has also been sung at the Met by von Stade; Mme. Lidoine by Mitchell, Norman; Mme. de Croissy by Dunn. 34 perfs. in 5 seasons.

The music of Poulenc's lyrical, religiously conservative drama leans heavily on the example of Stravinsky.

Compiègne and Paris, April 1789–summer 1792. The emotionally unstable Blanche de la Force (s) enters a Carmelite convent seeking peace. To her horror, the simple sister Constance (s) reveals an intuition that the two will die together, and the anguish of the dying prioress, Mme. de Croissy (c), aggravates Blanche's fears. When the convent is attacked by a mob, the sisters, now led by Mme. Lidoine (s), decide to accept martyrdom, but Blanche flees. As the nuns proceed serenely to the guillotine, Blanche emerges from the crowd and joins her sisters.

Diana von Solange (Diana of Solange). Opera in 5 acts by Ernest II, Duke of Saxe-Coburg-Gotha; libretto by Otto Prechtler.

First perf., Coburg, Dec. 5, 1858. U.S. & Met prem., Jan. 9, 1891: Schöller-Haag, Jahn, Dippel, Luria, C. Behrens, c. Seidl. 2 perfs, in 1 season.

This opera by a titled amateur depicts power struggles among rival claimants to the throne of the dying King Henry of Portugal in 1580.

Díaz, Justino. Bass; b. San Juan, P.R., Jan. 29, 1940. Studied at U. of Puerto Rico, New England Conservatory, and with Frederick Jagel. Debut as Ben (*Telephone*), San German, P.R., 1957. At the Met (debut, Monterone, Oct. 23, 1963), he created Barber's Antony and has sung 256 perfs. of 30 roles, including Colline, Sparafucile, Escamillo, Figaro, and Maometto (*Siège*). Appearances at Salzburg (Escamillo, 1966), Covent Garden (Escamillo, 1976), Milan, Hamburg, and Vienna. N.Y.C. Opera debut as Francesco (Ginastera's *Beatrix Cenci*), Mar. 14, 1973.

Dido and Aeneas. Opera in prologue and 3 acts by Purcell; libretto by Nahum Tate, after Virgil's *Aeneid*, iv.

First perf., London, Josiah Priest's boarding school for girls, spring(?) 1689. U.S. prem., N.Y., Town Hall, Jan. 13, 1924 (concert perf.). U.S. stage prem., N.Y., Juilliard School, Feb. 18, 1932.

Purcell's only true opera, a work of simple means and great dramatic and musical beauty. No music survives for the allegorical prologue.

Carthage, after the Trojan War. The Trojan Aeneas (t) has fallen in love with Dido (s), Queen of Carthage, who is troubled and hesitant to respond to his wooing. She is encouraged by her lady-in-waiting Belinda (s) to return Aeneas' love, for a marriage between the two would be advantageous for Carthage. In a cave, a Sorceress (ms) and her companions plan the destruction of Dido and Carthage. The queen's hunting party rests in a grove and is dispersed by the sound of thunder; Aeneas is met by one of the Sorceress' spirits disguised as Mercury (ms) and commanded to leave Carthage to found a new Troy. The evil spirits gloat over Aeneas' preparations to sail and the coming destruction of Dido and Carthage. Having learned of Aeneas' imminent departure, Dido rebuffs his brief intention of defying the god and urges him away. In her famous lament, she prepares to face death, and her people call for cupids to scatter roses on her grave.

Didur, Adamo [Adam]. Bass; b. Wola Sekowa, near Sanok, Galicia, Dec. 24, 1874; d. Katowice, Poland, Jan. 7, 1946. Studied with Walery Wysocki in Lemberg, Emmerich in Milan; debut in Rio de Janeiro, 1894. Sang in Warsaw (1899–1903) and La Scala (1904–06). Debuts in London (Colline, Covent Garden, 1905) and N.Y. (Alvise, Manhattan Opera, 1907). Met debut as Ramfis, Nov. 16, 1908; in 25 seasons, sang 690 perfs. of 54 roles, including first American Boris, Archibaldo (*Amore dei Tre Re*), Galitzky and Kontchak (*Prince Igor*), also Ramfis, Colline and Schaunard, Mozart's Figaro and Almaviva.

Diffen, Ray. Designer; b. Brighton, England, Feb. 28, 1922. Designed costumes for American Shakespeare Festival, Stratford, Conn. Resident costume designer at Met (1976–79), including *Eugene Onegin* (1977), *Adriana Lecouvreur* (1978), and *Don Carlos* (1979). Has also designed *Fledermaus* and *Aida* for Opera Company of Boston.

Di Franco, Loretta. Soprano; b. New York, Oct. 28, 1942. Studied with Maud Webber and Walter Taussig, N.Y.; while a member of Met chorus, debut as Peasant Girl (*Nozze*), Jan. 11, 1962. After winning Met National Council Auditions, 1965, solo debut as Chloë (*Queen of Spades*), Oct. 21, 1965. Subsequent Met roles, in more than 600 perfs., include Zerlina, Oscar, Lucia, Lauretta, Marcellina (*Nozze*), and Marianne (*Rosenkavalier*).

Di Giuseppe, Enrico. Tenor; b. Philadelphia, Oct. 14, 1932. Studied with Richard Bonelli, Curtis, Philadelphia, and Hans Heinz, Juilliard, N.Y.; debut as Des Grieux (*Manon*), New Orleans, 1959. Appeared with Met National Co. and N.Y.C. Opera (debut, Michele in *Saint of Bleecker Street*, 1965). Met debut as Turiddu, June 20, 1970; other Met roles are Almaviva, Werther, Alfredo, Pinkerton, Ferrando (*Così*), and Lindoro (*Italiana*).

Dimitrova, Ghena. Soprano; b. Beglej, Bulgaria, May 6, 1941. Studied with Brambarov, Sofia Conservatory, and at La Scala school; debut as Abigaille (*Nabucco*), Sofia, at age 25. Subsequent debuts at La Scala (Turandot, 1983), Salzburg (Lady Macbeth, 1984), Covent Garden (Turandot, 1984); has also sung in Buenos Aires, Verona, Vienna, and Paris. U.S. debut as Elvira (*Ernani*), Dallas, 1981; N.Y. debut, Abigaille (*Nabucco*), with Opera Orchestra (1984).

Dinorah, ou Le Pardon de Ploërmel (Ploërmel's Pardon). Opera in 3 acts by Meyerbeer; libretto by Barbier and Carré.

First perf., Paris, Opéra-Comique, Apr. 4, 1859: Cabel, Faure. U.S. prem., New Orleans, French Opera House, Mar. 4, 1861: Patti, Melchissédec, c. Prévost. Met prem., Jan. 29, 1892: van Zandt, Lassalle, c. Vianesi. Later Met production: Jan. 22, 1925: Galli-Curci, de Luca, c. Papi, d. Rovescalli/Castel-Bert. 3 perfs. in 2 seasons.

An Italianate setting of a pastoral subject. Abandoned by Hoël (bar) on their wedding day, Dinorah (s) goes mad, but a later shock restores her reason and the two are reunited.

Dippel, Andreas. Tenor; b. Kassel, Germany, Nov. 30, 1866; d. Hollywood, May 12, 1932. Studied with Zottmayr in Kassel; debut as Lionel (*Martha*), Bremen, 1887, later singing in Breslau and Vienna, 1893. Met debut as Asrael, Nov. 26, 1890; valued for his versatility, in 12 seasons he sang 191 perfs. of 41 roles, including Almaviva, Edgardo, Radames, Faust, both Siegfrieds, and Tristan. Met's administrative manager, 1908–1910; manager of Chicago Opera, 1910–13.

director. The person who supervises the stage action of an operatic performance, planning the gestures and movements of the singers and (in the case of a new production) working closely with the scenery and lighting designers. Also known as producer, especially in Europe.

Dirigent (Ger.). Conductor.

di Stefano, Giuseppe. Tenor; b. Motta Santa Anastasia, near Catania, Sicily, July 24, 1921. Studied with Adriano Torchi and Luigi Montesanto in Milan. After three years of military service, he escaped to Switzerland in 1943 and was interned as a refugee; his singing in Swiss broadcasts and concerts (1944) attracted wide attention. Debut as Massenet's Des Grieux, Comunale, Reggio Emilia, 1946; La Scala debut in same role, 1947. After his Met debut (Duke of Mantua, Feb. 25, 1948), he sang there regularly until 1952, also as Rodolfo, Faust, Rossini's Almaviva, Massenet's Des Grieux, Rinuccio (*Gianni Schicchi*), Alfredo, Nemorino, Fenton, the Italian Singer, Pinkerton, and Wilhelm Meister (*Mignon*); he returned briefly in 1955–56 as Don José and Cavaradossi, and in 1965 for a single performance as Hoffmann. San Francisco debut as Rodolfo, 1950; he sang in Mexico City (1948–52) and São Paulo (1951), often opposite Callas. In 1952 he returned to La Scala, where he remained a leading tenor for nine seasons, singing frequently with Callas and moving into heavier roles such as Canio, Turiddu, Radames, and Alvaro (*Forza*); in 1961, he created Giuliano in Pizzetti's

Giuseppe di Stefano as Faust

Calzare d'Argento. In these same years, at the Chicago Lyric (debut, Edgardo, 1954), his roles included Arturo (*Puritani*), Calaf, Don José, Riccardo (*Ballo*), and Loris (*Fedora*). British debut as Nemorino, Edinburgh, 1957; Covent Garden debut as Cavaradossi, 1961. He also appeared at the principal houses of Vienna, Berlin, Paris, and Buenos Aires. He joined Callas on the world wide concert tour (1973–74) that brought her out of retirement.

Early in his career, di Stefano was admired for his smooth and beautiful tone, with liquid pianissimos, in lyric parts. His subsequent move into spinto and dramatic parts, though not lacking in theatrical energy, was less successful, for the voice – in its prime, the most beautiful Italian tenor sound since Gigli – tended to spread, and eventually grew "fixed" and hard.

Dittersdorf, Karl Ditters von. Composer; b. Vienna, Nov. 2, 1739; d. Neuhof, Bohemia, Oct. 24, 1799. Active in Viennese court musical circles, he composed operas and operettas but his singspiels were most influential. In *Doktor und Apotheker* (1786), *Betrug durch Aberglauben* (1786), and *Die Liebe im Narrenhause* (1787), he integrated opera buffa style into the singspiel; their musical wit and vivacity served as models for this genre through the 19th c.

Djamileh. Opera in 1 act by Bizet: libretto by Louis Gallet, after Alfred de Musset's poem *Namouna*.
First perf., Paris, Opéra-Comique, May 22, 1872: Prelly, Duchesne, Pontel, c. Deloffre. U.S. prem., Boston, Opera House, Feb. 24, 1913; Marcel, Laffitte, Giaccone, c. Weingartner.
An exotic opéra comique set in Egypt. Haroun (t) habitually purchases a new mistress each month, but Djamileh (s) wins his heart by contriving to be purchased again, incognito, after her month has expired.

Dobbs, Mattiwilda. Soprano; b. Atlanta, Ga., July 11, 1925. Studied with Lotte Lehmann and Pierre Bernac; operatic debut as Stravinsky's Nightingale, Holland Festival, 1952. Sang at Glyndebourne (Zerbinetta, 1953), Covent Garden (Queen of Shemakha, Gilda, 1954). Met debut as Gilda, Nov. 9, 1956; in 8 seasons, she sang 29 perfs. of 6 roles, including Zerbinetta, Oscar, Olympia, Zerlina, and Lucia.

Docteur Miracle, Le (Dr. Miracle). Opera in 1 act by Bizet; libretto by Battu and Halévy.
First perf., Paris, Bouffes-Parisiennes, Apr. 9, 1857. U.S. prem., New Haven, Conn., Yale School of Music, July 14, 1962 (in Eng.).
Bizet's entry in an operetta contest sponsored by Offenbach. Captain Pasquin (t) poses as a charlatan doctor to gain access to Laurette (s), whose father (bar) has forbidden any contact with soldiers.

Dohnányi, Christoph von. Conductor; b. Berlin, Sep. 8, 1929. Studied at Munich Hochschule, at Florida State U. with his grandfather, composer Ernö, and at Tanglewood. Repetiteur and conductor under Solti in Frankfurt (1952–57); music director in Lübeck (1957–63), Kassel (1963–66), and Frankfurt (1968–78); artistic director and principal conductor, Hamburg (1978–84). Conducted at Chicago Opera (debut, *Holländer*, 1969). At the Met in 1972–73, he led *Falstaff* (debut, Feb. 25, 1972) and *Rosenkavalier*. Since 1984, music director, Cleveland Orchestra. Conducted premieres of Henze's *Der junge Lord* (1965) and *Bassarids* (1966). Married to the soprano Anja Silja. A leading figure of his generation, he has a reputation for vigorous, precisely articulated, and lucid performances.

Doktor Faust. Opera in 6 scenes by Busoni; libretto by the composer, after the 16th-c. German puppet-play and Marlowe's *Dr. Faustus*.

First perf., Dresden, May 21, 1925: Seinemeyer, Strack, Berg, c. Busch. U.S. prem., N.Y., Carnegie Hall (concert perf.), Dec. 1, 1964: Bjoner, Shirley, Fischer-Dieskau, c. Horenstein. U.S. stage prem., Reno, Nev., Jan. 25, 1974.

Busoni's treatment of the legend is austere, visionary, and theatrically and vocally demanding. Faust (bar) makes his pact with Mephistopheles (t), and attempts to seduce the Duchess of Parma (s) soon after her marriage to the Duke (t). She dies, but pursues him after death and tries three times to give him the corpse of their child. He finally accepts it, and attempts to revive it with his magic powers; when he falls dead, a young man rises from the child's body, going forth to accomplish all that Faust has failed to do. (The final scene, unfinished at Busoni's death, was completed by Philipp Jarnach, and more recently by Antony Beaumont.)

Domgraf-Fassbänder, Willi. Baritone; b. Aachen, Germany, Feb. 19, 1897; d. Nuremberg, Feb. 13, 1978. Studied with Jacques Stückgold and Paul Bruns in Berlin, Giuseppe Borgatti in Milan; debut as Almaviva (*Nozze*), Aachen, 1922. Member, Berlin State Opera, 1928–48. Sang Mozart roles at Glyndebourne (1934–37), also Papageno in Salzburg (1937). Father, and teacher, of mezzo Brigitte Fassbaender.

Domingo, Plácido. Tenor and conductor; b. Madrid, Jan. 21, 1941. Son of zarzuela performers, he was raised in Mexico City, where he studied piano, conducting (with Markevich), and singing (with Franco Iglesias and Carlo Morelli) at the conservatory and made his debut as Borsa (*Rigoletto*) in 1959. In 1961 he sang his first leading role (Alfredo, Monterrey) and made his U.S. debut (Edgardo, Dallas). After an engagement with the Israel National Opera (1962–65), he came to the N.Y.C. Opera (debut, Pinkerton, 1965), where he sang Ginastera's Don Rodrigo in the company's first performance at Lincoln Center (1966) and returned regularly until 1970 in Italian and French roles. 1967 brought debuts in Hamburg (Cavaradossi), Vienna (Don Carlos), and Berlin (Riccardo in *Ballo*). Although he had sung Turiddu with the Met company at Lewisohn Stadium in 1966, his formal house debut came on Oct. 8, 1968, as Maurizio (*Adriana*). He has returned every subsequent season, singing over 225 perfs. of more than 30 roles, including Canio, Cavaradossi, Pinkerton, Manrico, Calaf, Edgardo, Riccardo, Chénier, Alfredo, Radames, Ernani, Don José, Don Carlos, Faust, Rodolfo (*Luisa Miller*), Alvaro, Rodolfo (*Bohème*), Hoffmann, Arrigo, Roméo, the Duke of Mantua, Werther, Otello, Puccini's Des Grieux, Énée (*Troyens*), Paolo (*Francesca*), and Lohengrin. Subsequent debuts include Chicago (Puccini's Des Grieux, 1968), Verona Arena (Calaf, 1969), San Francisco (Rodolfo, 1969), La Scala (Ernani, 1969), Covent Garden (Cavaradossi, 1971), and Salzburg (Don Carlos, 1975). His repertory of more than 70 roles also includes Vasco (*Africaine*) and Samson, and he created the title roles of Morena Torroba's *El Poeta* (Madrid, 1980) and Menotti's *Goya* (Washington, D.C., 1986).

Beginning in the spinto repertory, Domingo has gradually embraced dramatic roles; his generous warm tone carries an appealing baritonal weight, yet can reach

Plácido Domingo as Otello

high C. His quick musical intelligence and memory have encouraged an astonishing versatility in the opera house, an even wider range (including Huon in *Oberon* and Stolzing) on recordings. A handsome stage presence and ability to take direction effectively have yielded memorable portrayals. In addition to frequent television, concert, and film appearances, he has in recent years cultivated a conducting career; at the N.Y.C. Opera, he led *Traviata* (1973) and *Tosca* (1974), and he made his Met debut in this capacity with *Bohème* (Feb. 4, 1985), followed by *Roméo*. BIBLIOGRAPHY: Plácido Domingo, *My First Forty Years* (N.Y., 1983).

Donath, Helen. Soprano; b. Corpus Christi, Tex., July 10, 1940. Studied with Paola Novikova, N.Y.; debut as Inez (*Trovatore*), Cologne, 1962. Subsequently appeared in Munich, Vienna, Salzburg, and San Francisco; repertory includes Micaela, Zerlina, Susanna, Pamina, Liù, Oscar, Eva, Sophie, and the Governess (*Turn of the Screw*). Married to conductor Klaus Donath.

Don Carlos. Opera in 5 (later 4) acts by Verdi; libretto by Joseph Méry and Camille du Locle, after Schiller's dramatic poem *Don Carlos, Infant von Spanien*; also after W.H. Prescott's *History of Philip II* and Eugène Cormon's *Philippe II Roi d'Espagne*.

First perf., Paris, Opéra, Mar. 11, 1867: Sass, Gueymard-Lauters, Morère, Faure, Obin, David, c. Hainl. U.S. prem., N.Y., Academy of Music (Havana Opera Co.), Aug. 12, 1877 (in Ital.). 2nd version in 4 acts (text rev. by Du Locle): first perf., Milan, La Scala, Jan. 10,

1884 (in Ital.): Bruschi-Chiatti, Pasque, Tamagno, Lhérie, Silvestri, Navarini, c. Faccio. 3rd version (presumably approved by Verdi), prefacing Milan version with first act of Paris version: first perf., Modena, Dec. 29, 1886 (in Ital.). Met. prem., Dec. 23, 1920 (third version, in Ital.): Ponselle, Matzenauer, Martinelli, de Luca, Didur, d'Angelo, c. Papi. Later Met productions: Nov. 6, 1950 (2nd version, in Ital.): Rigal, Barbieri, Bjoerling, Merrill, Siepi, Hines, c. Stiedry, d. Gérard, p. Webster; Feb. 5, 1979 (Modena version uncut, plus "Prelude and Introduction" to opening scene, cut by Verdi before Paris premiere; in Ital.): Scotto, Horne, Giacomini, Milnes, Ghiaurov, Morris, c. Levine, d. Reppa/Diffen, p. Dexter. Don Carlos has also been sung at the Met by Tucker, Corelli, Domingo; Elisabeth by Steber, Rysanek, Stella, Arroyo, Caballé, Millo; Eboli by Thebom, Resnik, Gorr, Verrett, Bumbry; Rodrigo by Bastianini, Hynninen; Philippe by Chaliapin, Hines, Tozzi. 129 perfs. in 20 seasons.

Verdi's most various and wide-ranging exploration of the dramatic issues (private vs. public responsibility) that fired his imagination. In its original version, it is a spacious French grand opera. The version of 1884 (still in French but planned for Italian performance, in which form it entered the repertory) is a tauter, more typically Verdian drama, rich in dark-hued melody and somber dramatic power.

France and Spain, about 1560. As part of a peace treaty, Don Carlos (t), Infante of Spain, is to marry Elisabeth de Valois of France (s). They meet and fall in love, but learn that she must instead marry Carlos' father, King Philippe II (bs). In misery, Carlos takes refuge in the monastery where his grandfather, Emperor Charles V, retired on abdication. Carlos confesses his love for the Queen to Rodrigue (bar), Marquis of Posa, who urges him to come to the aid of the oppressed Flemish. The King confides to Posa his suspicions about the Queen and Carlos, and asks him to watch them. Rejected by Carlos, Princess Eboli (ms) threatens disclosure of his forbidden passion. At an auto-da-fé, Carlos is arrested for defying his father on behalf of the Flemish. The Grand Inquisitor (bs) demands that Philippe withdraw his confidence from Posa. His suspicions roused by Eboli, Philippe discovers a portrait of Carlos in his wife's jewel case. Eboli confesses her betrayal to the Queen and is exiled. Posa has planted Carlos' incriminating papers on himself, to effect the Infante's pardon and release; in Carlos' cell, Posa is shot by the King's officers. Philippe arrives to free his son, who recoils from him. The Inquisitor cows an angry crowd, and in the confusion Eboli helps Carlos escape to the monastery, where he takes leave of Elisabeth, intending to go to Flanders. Philippe and the Inquisitor arrive, but before Carlos can be arrested the gates of the tomb open and Charles V leads Carlos back to safety.

Don Giovanni, originally *Il Dissoluto punito, ossia il Don Giovanni.* Opera in 2 acts by Mozart; libretto by Da Ponte, after Giovanni Bertati's libretto for Giuseppe Gazzaniga's *The Stone Guest*; also after the Don Juan legend.

First perf., Prague, National, Oct. 29, 1787: Saporiti, Micelli, Bassi, Baglioni, Ponziani, Lolli. U.S. prem., N.Y., Park, Nov. 7, 1817 (in Eng.). Met prem., Nov. 28, 1883: Fursch-Madi, Nilsson, Sembrich, Stagno, Kaschmann, Mirabella, Corsini, c. Vianesi, d. J. Fox, Schaeffer, Maeder, Thompson/Ascoli, Dazian. Later Met productions: Nov. 29, 1929: Corona, Rethberg, Fleischer, Gigli, Pinza, Ludikar, Rothier, c. Serafin, d. Urban, p. Wymetal; Dec. 10, 1953 ("revised"): Harshaw, Steber,

Don Carlos – Covent Garden. Designed and produced by Luchino Visconti. Tito Gobbi and Gré Brouwenstijn

Peters, Valletti, Rossi-Lemeni, Kunz, Vichey, c. Rudolf, d. Elson, p. Yannopoulos; Oct. 31, 1957: Steber, Della Casa, Peters, Valletti, Siepi, Corena, Uppman, Tozzi, c. Böhm, d. Berman, p. Graf. Don Giovanni has been sung at the Met by Maurel, Scotti, London, Raimondi, Milnes; Anna by Lilli Lehmann, Nordica, Eames, Ponselle, Rethberg, Milanov, Welitsch, L. Price, Sutherland; Elvira by Eames, Nordica, Gadski, Novotná, Schwarzkopf, Zylis-Gara; Zerlina by Farrar, Sayão, Munsel, Gueden, von Stade, Ewing; Ottavio by Bonci, Schipa, Crooks, Kullman, Peerce, Alva; Leporello by E. de Reszke, Journet, Chaliapin, Pasero, Lazzari, Baccaloni, Kipnis, Berry; other conductors include Mahler, Panizza, Walter, Szell, Reiner, and Levine. 266 perfs. in 48 seasons.

Don Giovanni – (1978). Designed by Eugene Berman, produced by Herbert Graf. Huguette Tourangeau, James Morris, Allan Monk

The oldest opera to have remained in the international repertory without significant interruption from its own era to the present, *Don Giovanni* has traditionally been seen as the greatest specimen of Mozart's dramatic genius. The emotional range of the score and the richness of the musical drama, filled with ambiguities and levels of association and meaning, have challenged each generation's greatest interpreters and seemed continually new to each generation's audiences.

In and near Seville, 17th c. Don Giovanni (bs or bar) attempts to seduce Donna Anna (s) and is set upon by her father, the Commendatore (bs). In the fight Giovanni kills the older man and escapes with his servant Leporello (bs). He next makes an attempt on the virtue of the peasant girl Zerlina (s), engaged to Masetto (bar). By the end of Act I he has accumulated a group of enraged pursuers, including Donna Elvira (s), whom he has seduced and abandoned, Anna, her fiancé Don Ottavio (t), Zerlina, and Masetto. Eluding his opponents, Giovanni finds himself in a churchyard, where a statue of the Commendatore mysteriously moves and speaks. In a show of bravado Giovanni invites the statue to dinner. To his surprise the statue accepts, arrives and ushers the unrepentant rogue to hell.

Donizetti, Gaetano. Composer; b. Bergamo, Italy, Nov. 29, 1797; d. Bergamo, Apr. 8, 1848. Studied with Mayr in Bergamo, later with Padre Mattei in Bologna. His juvenilia include several operas; the first to be staged was *Enrico di Borgogna* (1818). A Roman commission turned over to him by Mayr, the successful *Zoraide di Granata* (1822), resulted in a contract at San Carlo, Naples. Donizetti's facility and sound technical grounding enabled him to turn out as many as five operas a year, ranging from farcical one-acters to serious works, for various theaters. His first international successes, launched

Don Pasquale – (1942). Designed by Jonel Jorgulesco, produced by Désiré Defrère. Salvatore Baccaloni and Bidú Sayão

in Milan, marked the maturity of his talents: the tragedy *Anna Bolena* (1830), the comedy *L'Elisir d'Amore* (1832), and the melodramatic *Lucrezia Borgia* (1833). An 1834 Naples contract for tragic operas, plagued by censorship problems, generated *Maria Stuarda* (1834, first produced as *Buondelmonte*), *Lucia di Lammermoor* (1835), and *Roberto Devereux* (1837). Donizetti's wife died in 1837 and, to escape melancholy memories, he accepted Rossini's invitation to Paris, where in 1840 he presented the opéra comique *La Fille du Régiment* and the tragedies *La Favorite* and *Les Martyrs* (a revision of the earlier *Poliuto*), the first two highly successful. Despite declining physical and mental health (later shown to be caused by syphilis), he remained active until 1844, composing for Vienna (*Linda di Chamounix*, 1842), Paris (the buffo masterpiece *Don Pasquale* and the Meyerbeerian *Dom Sébastien*, both 1843), and Naples (*Caterina Cornaro*, 1844). His catalogue of some 65 stage works also includes *Il Campanello di Notte* (1836), *Maria di Rudenz* (1838), *Maria Padilla* (1841), and *Maria di Rohan* (1843).

Although at the beginning of his career Donizetti conformed to the formal procedures and florid style of Rossini, he found his individual voice with *Anna Bolena*; few works thereafter are without formal innovations, and he learned from contemporaries, notably Bellini and the French. While continuing to exploit the virtuosity of sopranos and contraltos, he wrote more simply for male voices than Rossini or Bellini, and began the development of the baritone voice that led to its prominence in Verdi's operas. His orchestration is spare but full of telling details, and his mastery of the swelling ensemble is attested by the celebrated sextet in *Lucia* and many other examples. At home in every genre, Donizetti excelled in Romantic tragedy and comedy with a sentimental touch, and dominated Italian opera for a decade after the death of Bellini.

BIBLIOGRAPHY: William Ashbrook, *Donizetti and His Operas* (N.Y., and Cambridge, 1982).

Donna del Lago, La (The Lady of the Lake). Opera in 2 acts by Rossini; libretto by Andrea Leone Tottola, based on Walter Scott's poem.

First perf., Naples, San Carlo, Sep. 24, 1819, with Colbran. U.S. prem., N.Y., Park, Aug. 26, 1829 (in Fr.).

Rossini's most Romantic score, with atmospheric touches looking forward to *William Tell*. Scotland, 16th c. Elena (s), "lady of the lake," loves Malcolm (a) but is promised to Rodrigo (t) and is also loved by "Uberto" – really King Giacomo V (t), who eventually pardons her father, the banished Douglas of Angus (bs), and lets her marry Malcolm.

Donna Juanita. Operetta in 3 acts by Suppé; libretto by "F. Zell" (Camillo Walzel) and Richard Genée.

First perf., Vienna, Carltheater, Feb. 21, 1880. U.S. prem., Boston, Boston Theater, May 12, 1881 (in Eng.). Met prem., Jan. 2, 1932 (with dialogue in Eng.): Jeritza, Schützendorf, c. Bodanzky, d. Urban/Palmedo, p. Niedecken-Gebhard. 6 perfs in 1 season.

A frothy operetta set in San Sebastian, Spain, during the British occupation in 1796. A French army cadet (s) disguises himself as the flirtatious Donna Juanita and helps the French capture of the city.

Donne Curiose, Le (The Inquisitive Women). Opera in 3 acts by Wolf-Ferrari; libretto by Luigi Sugana, after a play by Carlo Goldoni.

First perf., Munich, Residenz, Nov. 27, 1903 (in Ger.).

Gaetano Donizetti

U.S. & Met prem., Jan. 3, 1912: Farrar, Jadlowker, Scotti, c. Toscanini, d. Rovescalli/Caramba, p. Schertel. 8 perfs. in 2 seasons.

One of several works in which Wolf-Ferrari sought to revive opera buffa by blending its traditional elements with those of the commedia dell'arte.

Venice, 18th c. Four suspicious women contrive to spy on their husbands and sweethearts at their all-male club. Through a series of ruses, bribery, and threats, the women manage to enter the premises, only to discover the men sharing an innocent dinner. The men greet the women with shock, but ultimately share with them the secret password, "Here's to friendship."

Donnerstag. See *Licht*.

Don Pasquale. Opera in 3 acts by Donizetti; libretto by the composer and Giovanni Ruffini, after Anelli's libretto for Pavesi's *Ser Marc'Antonio*.

First perf., Paris, Italien, Jan. 3, 1843: Grisi, Mario, Tamburini, Lablache. U.S. prem., New Orleans, Jan. 7, 1845. Met prem., Jan. 8, 1900: Sembrich, Salignac, Scotti, Pini-Corsi, c. Mancinelli. Later Met productions: Feb. 23, 1935: Bori, Schipa, de Luca, Pinza, c. Panizza, d. Jorgulesco, p. Defrère; Dec. 23, 1955: Peters, Valletti, Guarrera, Corena, c. Schippers, d. Roth, p. Yannopoulos; Dec. 7, 1978: Sills, Gedda, Hagegård, Bacquier, c. Rescigno, d. Heeley, p. Dexter. Don Pasquale has also been sung at the Met by Gilibert, Baccaloni; Norina by Sayão; Ernesto by Bonci, Martini, Alva, Kraus; Malatesta by Brownlee, Merrill, Krause. 87 perfs. in 20 seasons.

In *Don Pasquale*, the last of Donizetti's long line of comic operas, the composer's bright melodic style is tinted with influences of Schubert and Mozart.

Rome, early 19th c. Don Pasquale (bs), a rich old bachelor, decides to marry in order to disinherit his nephew Ernesto (t), who has refused to marry a woman of Pasquale's choice. Ernesto is in love with a widow, Norina(s), whom Pasquale has never met. Dr. Malatesta (bar), a friend of the three, comes to the aid of the young lovers. He arranges for Pasquale to marry Norina, disguised as his sister Sofronia, just out of the convent. The sweet "Sofronia" soon becomes a hellion and makes Pasquale utterly miserable; he leaps at Malatesta's suggestion to annul the marriage. Relieved to be free again, the old man consents to the union of Norina and Ernesto.

Don Quichotte. Opera in 5 acts by Massenet; libretto by Henri Cain, after Jacques Le Lorrain's comedy *Le Chevalier de la Longue Figure*.

First perf., Monte Carlo, Feb. 19, 1910: Arbell, Gresse, Chaliapin, c. Jehin. U.S. prem., New Orleans, Jan. 27, 1912. Met prem., Apr. 3, 1926: Easton, Chaliapin, de Luca, c. Hasselmans, d. Urban, p. Thewman. 5 perfs, in 2 seasons.

This sweetly melancholy opera touches on a few episodes from Cervantes, but Dulcinée is changed into a beautiful courtesan.

Don Rodrigo. Opera in 3 acts by Ginastera; libretto by Alejandro Casona.

First perf., Buenos Aires, Teatro Colón, July 24, 1964: Bandin, Cossutta, c. Bartoletti. U.S. prem., N.Y.C. Opera, Feb. 22, 1966: Crader, Domingo, c. Rudel.

Ginastera's grandiose serial score traces the progress of Rodrigo (t), last Visigoth ruler of Spain, from his coronation to his seduction of his ward Florinda (s) and downfall.

Dooley, William. Baritone; b. Modesto, Calif., Sep. 9, 1932. Studied with Lucy Lee Call, Eastman School, Rochester, and with Vita Prestel, Munich; debut as Posa (*Don Carlos*), Heidelberg, 1957. Member of Deutsche Oper, Berlin (from 1963), where he created Cortez (*Montezuma*). Met debut as Onegin, Feb. 15, 1964; in 14 seasons, he sang 76 perfs. of 26 roles, including Amonasro, Mandryka, the *Hoffmann* villains, Orest, Telramund, and Wozzeck.

Dostoyevsky, Fyodor. Russian novelist (1821–81). Operas based on his writings include *From the House of the Dead* (Janáček) and *The Gambler* (Prokofiev).

Dow, Dorothy. Soprano; b. Houston, Tex., Oct. 8, 1920. Studied at Juilliard, N.Y.; debut in Buffalo, 1946. Created Susan B. Anthony in *Mother of Us All*, N.Y., 1947. La Scala debut as Elisabeth (*Tannhäuser*), 1950, followed by Marie (*Wozzeck*), Strauss' Danae, Gioconda, Chrysothemis, and Walton's Cressida. Sang *Erwartung* with N.Y. Philharmonic (1951), Lady Macbeth and Ariadne at Glyndebourne (1952–53), Spontini's *Agnese* in Florence (1954).

Down in the Valley. Opera in one act by Weill; libretto by Arnold Sundgaard.

First perf., Bloomington, Indiana U., July 14, 1948: Bell, Welsh, c. Hoffman.

One of the works in which Weill attempted to bridge the gap between popular and operatic musical theater. Based on an American folk song, it unfolds in a series of flashbacks, as Brack Weaver (bar) awaits execution for having killed, in self-defence, his rival for the love of Jennie Parsons (s).

Dramaturg (Ger.). In German theaters, the staff member responsible for the literary aspects of the operation, including program notes, adaptation of librettos, and the like, sometimes also for research into prospective repertory.

Semperoper, Dresden

drame lyrique (Fr.). A term applied since the later 19th c. to French serious operas in a relatively intimate style, not fitting the traditional categories of opéra comique or grand opera.

dramma giocoso (Ital.). A comic opera with serious elements, such as *Don Giovanni*.

dramma per musica (Ital.). A dramatic text written specifically for musical setting; also sometimes applied to the musical setting as well.

Dreigroschenoper, Die (The Threepenny Opera). Opera in prologue and 8 scenes by Weill; libretto by Bertolt Brecht, after Elisabeth Hauptmann's translation of Gay's *The Beggar's Opera*.

First perf., Berlin, Theater am Schiffbauerdamm, Aug. 31, 1928: Bahn, Kohl, Lenya, Valetti, Paulsen, Ponto, Gerron, c. Mackeben. U.S. prem., Philadelphia, Empire, Apr. 1, 1933 (in Eng.): Duna, Huston, Dille, Beresford, Chisholm, Weber, Heller, Evans, c. Marrow.

Weill's and Brecht's jazzy, sardonic version of *The Beggar's Opera* follows the plot of the original closely, although the action is transposed to the slums of Victorian London and the message about the vicissitudes of morality is meant to apply to Berlin in the 1920s. (Brecht picked up lyrics from Kipling and Villon as well as Gay).

Mack the Knife (t) marries Polly (s), daughter of Peachum (bar), leader of Soho's underworld. He is betrayed by his in-laws and the prostitute Jenny (s), escapes from prison with the help of Lucy (s), daughter of the corrupt police chief Tiger Brown (bar), and is recaptured. About to be hanged, he is pardoned by Queen Victoria on her coronation day.

Drei Pintos, Die (The Three Pintos). Opera in 3 acts by Weber, completed and scored by Mahler; libretto by Theodor Hell, after C.L. Seidel's story *Der Brautkampf*.

First perf., Leipzig, Jan. 20, 1888: Baumann, Rothhauser, Hübner, Hedmont, Grengg, c. Mahler. U.S. prem., St. Louis, Loretto-Hilton Theater, June 6, 1979: Woods, Camp, Rosenshein, Kays, Dickson, c. Ferden.

Put aside by Weber, this tuneful hybrid is set in old Spain. Don Pinto (bs) intends marriage to Clarissa (s), but his papers are seized while he is drunk, and two rivals in turn – the second of them Clarissa's true love, Don Gomez (t) – present themselves as Pinto.

Dresden. City in East Germany. The first German opera, Schütz's *Daphne* (1627), was staged in nearby Torgau. Dresden's first opera theater, the Kurfürstliche Opernhaus, functioned from 1667 to 1707. The Grosses Opernhaus opened in 1719 and was refurbished by Galli-Bibiena in 1750. Other houses were the Kleine Hoftheater (1755–1841), which saw the premiere of Paer's *Leonora* (1804), and the small wooden auditorium outside the Zwinger courtyard, which presented comic works and singspiel (burned 1748). A German opera company, founded in 1817 and directed by Weber until his death in 1826, eventually superseded the Italian company, which folded in 1832. The first Semper opera house opened in 1841; after the successful premiere of *Rienzi* (1842), Wagner was appointed music director, and introduced *Holländer* (1843) and *Tannhäuser* (1845) before he went into exile in 1849. In 1869 the theater burned, but was rebuilt and reopened in 1878. Under von Schuch (artistic director, 1889–1914), Reiner (1914–21), Busch (1922–33), and Böhm (1934–42), Dresden offered notable Strauss premieres, also *Cardillac* (1925) and *Doktor Faust* (1925). On Feb. 13, 1945, the Semper theater was bombed; operations moved to the town hall, and after 1948 to the Schauspielhaus. Postwar musical directors have included Keilberth (1945–50), Kempe (1950–52), Konwitschny (1953–55), and Blomstedt (1975–85); Joachim Herz is now opera director, with Hans Vonk as chief conductor. On Feb. 13, 1985, the reconstructed Semper theater (capacity 1,284) reopened with a performance of *Freischütz*.

Driscoll, Loren. Tenor; b. Midwest, Wyo., Apr. 14, 1928. Studied at Syracuse and Boston U.; debut as Dr. Caius (*Falstaff*), Boston, 1954. N.Y.C. Opera debut as Emperor (*Turandot*), 1957. With Deutsche Oper, Berlin, from 1962; created Lord Barrat (*Junge Lord*) and Dionysus (*Bassarids*). In 3 Met seasons, he sang 25 perfs. of David in *Meistersinger* (debut, Dec. 23, 1966) and Alfred in *Fledermaus*.

Dubinbaum, Gail. Mezzo-soprano; b. Brooklyn, N.Y. After private study with her mother and with Herta Glaz, won Met Auditions (Western Region) in 1981, then joined the Young Artists program, making her company debut as an Animal in *Enfant* (Dec. 6, 1982). Subsequent Met roles include Rosina, Isabella (*Italiana*), and Dorabella. Vienna State Opera debut as Rosina (1986).

Duc d'Albe, Le (The Duke of Alba). Opera in 4 acts by Donizetti (unfinished); libretto by Scribe and Charles Duvéyrier.

First perf. (completed and rev., in Ital., by Matteo Salvi et al.), Rome, Apollo, Mar. 22, 1882: Bruschi-Chiatti, Gayarré, Giraldoni. U.S. prem., N.Y., Carnegie Hall, Oct. 20, 1959 (concert perf.): Tosini, Cioni, Quilico, c. Schippers.

Begun in 1839 for the Paris Opéra but abandoned when the management changed; the libretto, set in the Netherlands in 1573, was recycled by Scribe for Verdi's *Vêpres Siciliennes*.

Dudley, William. Designer; b. London, Mar. 4, 1947. Theater debut, *Hamlet* (Nottingham, 1970); operatic debut, *Billy Budd* (Hamburg, 1972). Other productions for Welsh National Opera, Glyndebourne, Covent Garden; *Ring* cycle for Bayreuth, 1983. For the Met, *Billy Budd* (1978). Since 1981, assistant designer, National Theatre, London.

Due Foscari, I (The Two Foscari). Opera in 3 acts by Verdi; libretto by Piave, after Byron's play *The Two Foscari*.

First perf., Rome, Argentina, Nov. 3, 1844: Barbieri-Nini, Roppa, de Bassini. U.S. prem., Boston, Howard Athenaeum, May 10, 1847. Performed at the Met by the Rome Opera, July 1, 1968: Maragliano, Cioni, Zanasi, c. Bartoletti, d. Pizzi, p. de Lullo.

A somber tragedy, touched by the deep feeling for Italian history that finds its fullest expression in *Simon Boccanegra*. The role of the Doge was a favorite of many 19th-c. baritones, and contributed to the opera's wide circulation.

Venice, 1457. Francesco Foscari (bar), Doge of Venice, stoically accepts the decision of the Council of Ten to renew the exile of his son Jacopo (t), who has been unjustly accused of murder. When Jacopo's wife Lucrezia Contarini (s) appears in the Council with her two infant children, Loredano (bs), chief of the opposition, is unmoved. Jacopo dies of a broken heart as his ship leaves for Crete. Loredano influences the Council to force the Doge's resignation. The old man, who had desired to leave twice in the past but had been prevailed upon to remain and serve until his death, is disgraced and dies as he hears the bells announce his successor.

Due Litiganti, I (The Two Litigants), properly *Fra due Litiganti il Terzo Gode*. Opera in 3 acts by Giuseppe Sarti; libretto after Goldoni's *Le Nozze*.

First perf., Milan, Scala, Sep. 14, 1782. U.S. prem., N.Y., Vineyard Theater, Mar. 13, 1987. So popular in its day that Mozart had Don Giovanni's house musicians play the aria "Come un agnello" in the supper scene of *Don Giovanni*.

Duenna, The. See *Betrothal in a Monastery*.

Duesing, Dale. Baritone; b. Milwaukee, Wisc. Studied at Lawrence U. Has appeared in San Francisco (Billy Budd, Guglielmo, Belcore), Seattle (Wolfram, Marcello, Onegin), and Glyndebourne (debut, Olivier in *Capriccio*, 1976). Met debut as Harlekin (*Ariadne*), Feb. 22, 1979; other roles include Rossini's Figaro, Pelléas, and Billy Budd.

duet. A composition for two voices, of the same or different ranges, sharing equal musical interest.

Dufranne, Hector. Baritone; b. Mons, Belgium, Oct. 25, 1870; d. Paris, May 3, 1951. Studied in Brussels; debut at Monnaie as Valentin (*Faust*), 1896. 1900 debut at Opéra-Comique, Paris, where he created Golaud (*Pelléas*, 1902). Appeared with Manhattan Opera (1908–10) and Chicago Opera (1910–18, 1919–22).

Dukas, Paul. Composer; b. Paris, Oct. 1, 1865; d. May 17, 1935. Studied composition with Guiraud at Paris Conservatory. Active as a critic, and as editor of the music of Rameau, Couperin, and Beethoven, all major influences on his early compositions. Greatly impressed by Debussy's *Pelléas*, he used another symbolist Maeterlinck play as the basis for his only completed opera, *Ariane et Barbe-Bleue* (1907), which combines Wagnerian techniques with exquisite orchestral writing.

Duke Bluebeard's Castle. Opera in 1 act by Bartók; libretto by Béla Balázs, after Perrault's fairy tale.

First perf., Budapest, May 24, 1918: Haselbeck,

Kálmán, c. Tango. U.S. prem., Dallas, Fair Park Auditorium, Jan. 8, 1946 (concert perf., in Eng.): Forrai, Ligeti, c. Dorati. U.S. stage prem., N.Y.C. Opera, Oct. 2, 1952 (in Eng.): Ayars, Pease, c. Rosenstock. Met prem., June 10, 1974 (in Eng.): Verrett, Ward, c. Ehrling, d. Reppa, p. Igesz. 12 perfs. in 2 seasons.

Bartók's somber setting of the libretto's chant-like, archaic lines predates his intense involvement with Hungarian folk music.

Legendary times. Bluebeard (bs) brings his new wife Judith (ms) to his castle, a large round room with seven doors and no windows. Eager to illuminate this dark place, she asks for the keys to the doors, and, opening them, finds a torture chamber, an armory, a treasure room, a rose garden, a vision of his kingdom, and a lake of tears – all tainted with blood. The seventh door conceals the ghostly figures of his former wives, who were similarly curious; Judith must now join them. All the doors close, and Bluebeard is again alone.

Du Locle, Camille. Librettist and manager; b. Orange, France, July 16, 1832; d. Capri, Italy, Oct. 9, 1903. Co-director of the Paris Opéra-Comique (1870–74; director, 1874–76). For Verdi, he completed Méry's *Don Carlos* libretto and made an early draft of *Aida*; also librettist for Reyer's *Sigurd* and *Salammbô*.

Duncan, Todd. Baritone; b. Danville, Ky., Feb. 12, 1903. Studied at Butler U. and Columbia Teachers College. Debut as Alfio (*Cavalleria*), Aeolian Opera, N.Y., 1934. On Broadway, he created Gershwin's Porgy (1935) and Stephen Kumalo in Weill's *Lost in the Stars* (1949). Sang with N.Y.C. Opera (debut as Tonio, 1945).

Dunn, Mignon. Mezzo-soprano; b. Memphis, Tenn., June 17, 1931. Studied with Karin Branzell and Beverley Johnson, N.Y.; debut as Carmen, New Orleans, 1955. Debuts in Chicago (Maddalena, 1955) and at N.Y.C. Opera (4th Lady in *Troilus*, 1956). Met debut as Nurse (*Boris*), Oct. 29, 1958; since then, has sung over 450 perfs. of more than 50 roles, including Amneris, Marina, Azucena, Fricka, Herodias, Anna (*Troyens*), Ortrud, and Mother Marie (*Carmélites*). Has also appeared in Paris, London, and San Francisco (Brangäne, 1967).

Dunn, Susan. Soprano; b. Malvern, Ark., July 23, 1954. Studied at Hendrix College, Ark., and Indiana U.; debut as Aida, Peoria, Ill., 1982. Won several competitions in 1983, including Richard Tucker Award. Successful Carnegie Hall debut in Act I of *Walküre* (1985) led to debuts in 1986–87 in Chicago, Washington, D.C., Houston, San Francisco in several Verdi roles. Debuts in Bologna (Hélène in *Vêpres*) and at La Scala (Aida), 1986.

Dupont, Jacques. Designer; b. Chatou, France, Jan. 16, 1909; d. Paris, Apr. 21, 1978. Designed ballet productions for Paris, Royal Ballet, and Stuttgart Ballet, and operas for Paris (*Ariane et Barbe-Bleu*, *Samson*) and Aix (*Les Caprices de Marianne*, *Pelléas*). For Met, designed Barrault productions of *Faust* (1965) and *Carmen* (1967).

Duval, Denise. Soprano; b. Paris, Oct. 23, 1921. Studied at Paris Conservatory; 1947 debuts in Bordeaux, at Paris Opéra-Comique (Butterfly) and Opéra (Salomé in *Hérodiade*). Created Poulenc roles in *Mamelles*, *Carmélites*, and *Voix Humaine*. Also appeared at Glyndebourne (Mélisande, 1962–63), Edinburgh, and Vienna.

Dvořák, Antonín. Composer; b. Nelahozeves, near Kralupy, Bohemia, Sep. 8, 1841; d. Prague, May 1, 1904. After lessons with Franz Hancke, he studied with Pitsch at Prague Organ School, graduating in 1859 and pursuing a career as violist, learning the operatic repertory while playing for the Prague Provisional Theater (later National Theater), and composing. By 1877, his music had won notice, especially from Brahms, whose sponsorship brought publication and conducting engagements throughout Europe. From 1892 until 1895, he served as director of the National Conservatory of Music in N.Y., then passed his final years in Prague.

Dvořák's first operas, heavily influenced by Wagner, were unperformed at the time: *Alfred* (1870, perf. 1938) and the comedy *King and Collier* (1871). He completely rewrote the latter (perf. 1874) in a folkish style, further pursuing this simpler vein in *The Stubborn Lovers* (1874, perf. 1881), *Vanda* (1875, rev. 1879), and *The Cunning Peasant* (1878). In the tragic opera *Dmitri* (1882) and in *The Jacobin* (1887), he returned to richer textures and Wagnerian continuity. *The Devil and Kate* (1899), *Rusalka* (1900), and *Armida* (1904), the three operas that follow his American tenure, are even more symphonically conceived. Though Dvořák's operas only rarely achieve the dramatic quality of his best instrumental writing, they are always distinguished by emotional intensity, generous lyrical invention, rhythmic verve, and perfect craftsmanship.
BIBLIOGRAPHY: John Clapham, *Dvořák* (N.Y., and Newton Abbot, 1979).

Dvorsky, Peter. Tenor; b. Partizánske, Czechoslovakia, Sep. 25, 1951. Studied at Bratislava Conservatory and sang with Slovakian National Opera; after winning Tchaikovsky competition (Moscow, 1974), further study in Milan. Member, Vienna State Opera, since 1975. Met debut as Alfredo, Nov. 15, 1977; he returned in 1987 as Rodolfo.

Eames, Emma. Soprano; b. Shanghai, China, Aug. 13, 1865, of American parents; d. New York, June 14, 1952. She studied with Clara Munger in Boston and Mathilde Marchesi in Paris, where she coached Juliette and Marguerite with Gounod; debut as Juliette, Opéra, 1889; sang there for 2 seasons, creating Colombe in Saint-Saëns' *Ascanio*. After her Covent Garden debut as Marguerite, 1891, she returned in 7 seasons, until 1901. Met debut as Juliette, Dec. 14, 1891; a featured member of the company until 1909, she sang 258 perfs., appearing most often as Marguerite, followed by Tosca, Juliette, Elsa, Aida, the Countess (*Figaro*), Micaela, Elisabeth, Desdemona, Sieglinde, Eva, Leonora (*Trovatore*), Pamina, and eight other roles. After her last Met performance (Tosca, Feb. 15, 1909), she appeared only twice more in opera, as Tosca and Desdemona in Boston, Dec. 1911, though she later toured in concert, often with her second husband, baritone Emilio de Gogorza. Famous for her great personal beauty and emotional reserve, Eames effectively impersonated such dramatic roles as Tosca, in addition to the lyric parts more suited to her voice.
BIBLIOGRAPHY: Emma Eames, *Some Memories and Reflections* (N.Y., 1927, repr. 1977).

Easton, Florence. Soprano; b. Middlesbrough, England, Oct. 25, 1882; d. New York, Aug. 13, 1955. Studied

Emma Eames as Marguerite in *Faust*

with Agnes Larkcom, Royal Academy of Music, London, and Elliott Haslam, Paris; debut as Shepherd (*Tannhäuser*), Moody-Manners Co., Newcastle, 1903. She toured the U.S. with Henry Savage (1905–07); in Berlin (1908–13) and Hamburg (1913–16), sang roles such as Eva, Musetta, Sophie, Salome, and Elektra, then returned to America and sang with Chicago Opera (1915–16). Met debut as Santuzza, Dec. 7, 1917; in 13 seasons, she sang 277 perfs. of 39 roles, including Reiza (*Oberon*), Ah-Yoe (*Oracolo*), Nedda, Butterfly, Carmen, Elsa, Aida, Gioconda, Fiordiligi, the Marschallin, Lodoletta, and the *Walküre* and *Siegfried* Brünnhildes; she created Lauretta (*Schicchi*), Mother Tyl (*Oiseau Bleu*), and Aelfrida (*King's Henchmen*). She first appeared at Covent Garden in 1909, again in 1927 as Turandot and 1932 as Isolde, returned to the Met in 1936 as Brünnhilde, and sang recitals until 1943. As her career and repertory attest, Easton was a remarkably industrious and versatile artist (as well as a famously quick study), whose always professional singing perhaps lacked ultimate individuality.

Eaton, John. Composer; b. Bryn Mawr, Pa., Mar. 30, 1935. Studied composition at Princeton U. with Babbitt, Cone, and Sessions. Active as a jazz pianist, he won three Rome Prizes (1959–61) and developed the resources of electronic and microtonal music, which figure prominently in his later works. His operatic output includes *Ma Barker* (1957); *Heracles* (1972); *Myshkin* (1973), for television, after Dostoyevsky's *The Idiot; Danton and Robespierre* (1978); *The Cry of Clytemnestra* (1980); and *The Tempest* (1985). He has taught at Indiana University since 1971.

Ebert, Carl. Producer; b. Berlin, Feb. 20, 1887; d. Santa Monica, Calif., May 14, 1980. Trained as an actor under Reinhardt, he became Intendant in Darmstadt (1927–31) and general administrator and producer, Städtische Oper, Berlin (1931–33). Artistic director, Glyndebourne Festival (1934–39, 1947–59); director of opera department, U.

of So. Calif. (1948–54). Staged premiere of *Rake's Progress* (Venice, 1951). Director, Deutsche Oper, West Berlin (1956–61). His Met productions include *Macbeth* (1959), *Martha* (1961), and *Ariadne* (1962), and a re-directed *Così* (1961).

Eda-Pierre, Christiane. Soprano; b. Fort-de-France, Martinique, Mar. 24, 1932. Studied at Paris Conservatory; debut as Lucia, Paris Opéra, 1962. With that company she appeared at the Met as Mozart's Countess in 1976. Met debut as Konstanze (*Entführung*), Apr. 3, 1980; subsequently, she has sung Antonia (*Hoffmann*) and Gilda there. Has also appeared in Berlin, Hamburg, and Chicago.

Eddy, Nelson. Baritone; b. Providence, R.I., June 29, 1901; d. Miami Beach, Fla., Mar. 6, 1967. Studied with David Bispham in Philadelphia. Sang opera with Philadelphia Orchestra (including Drum Major in their N.Y. *Wozzeck*, 1931, and Gurnemanz in concert, 1932) and on radio before starring in musical films, frequently opposite Jeannette McDonald.

Edelmann, Otto. Bass; b. Brunn am Gebirge, near Vienna, Feb. 5, 1917. Studied with Lierhammer and Gunnar Graarud, Vienna Academy; debut as Mozart's Figaro, Gera, 1937. Sang in Nuremberg, 1938–40; resumed career after war, joining Vienna State Opera in 1947. Appeared at Bayreuth as Sachs (1951–52), role of his Met debut, Nov. 11, 1954; in 15 Met seasons, sang 110 perfs. of 9 roles, including Baron Ochs, Rocco, King Marke, and Wotan. Also sang in Salzburg, Edinburgh, and San Francisco.

Edgar. Opera in 3 (originally 4) acts by Puccini; libretto by Ferdinando Fontana, after Alfred de Musset's verse drama *La Coupe et les Lèvres*.

First perf., Milan, La Scala, Apr. 21, 1889: Cataneo-Caroson, Pantaleoni, Gabrielesco, Magini-Coletti, c. Faccio. Revised version in 3 acts, first perf., Ferrara, Feb. 28, 1892. U.S. prem., N.Y., Carnegie Hall (Opera Orchestra), Apr. 13, 1977 (concert perf.): Scotto, Killebrew, Bergonzi, Sardinero, c. Queler.

A score in which Puccini's mature idiom is readily identifiable, though his dramatic touch is not yet sure.

Flanders, 1302. Edgar (t) abandons Fidelia (s) for the alluring Moorish girl Tigrana (ms). Fidelia's brother Frank (bar), who also loves Tigrana, challenges Edgar to a duel and is wounded. Later, the remorseful Edgar leaves Tigrana and joins an army, where he is reconciled with Frank. At a Requiem for the supposedly dead Edgar, a monk recites his crimes, then reveals himself as Edgar; as Fidelia rushes into his arms, she is murdered by the vengeful Tigrana.

Egk [Mayer], **Werner.** Composer; b. Auchsesheim, near Donauwörth, Germany, May 17, 1901. Studied composition with Orff in Munich. After music for ballet and radio plays, he composed a radio opera, *Columbus* (1932). Until 1941 a guest conductor at the Berlin State Opera, where *Die Zaubergeige* (1935) and *Peer Gynt* (1938) were performed. Head of the German Union of Composers (1941–45), he was de-Nazified in 1947. Subsequent operas: *Circe* (1948, rev. 1966 as *17 Tage und 4 Minuten*), *Irische Legende* (1954), *Der Revisor* (1957), and *Die Verlobung in San Domingo* (1963). His fluent, colorful music, often satirical in tone, was influenced by Stravinsky and the French interwar school.

Ehrling, Sixten. Conductor; b. Malmö, Sweden, Apr. 3, 1918. Studied under Böhm in Dresden, 1941, after 1940 debut at Royal Opera, Stockholm, where he was later music director (1953–60). Music director, Detroit Symphony (1963–72); director, conducting program, Juilliard School. Met debut, Feb. 18, 1973 (*Peter Grimes*); through 1977, conducted varied repertory, including *Ring*, *Trittico*, *Boccanegra*, and Met premiere of *Bluebeard's Castle*.

Einem, Gottfried von. Composer, b. Bern, Switzerland, Jan. 24, 1918, of Austrian parents. Coach at Berlin State Opera and Bayreuth, his wartime resistance activities led to imprisonment by the Gestapo, an experience reflected in his second opera, *Der Prozess* (1953), libretto after Kafka by Einem's friend and mentor Boris Blacher. This and his first opera, *Dantons Tod* (1947), espouse an expressionistic style, indebted to Berg for organizational principles, to Stravinsky and jazz for rhythmic techniques. His later works, including *Der Zerrissene* (1964), after Nestroy, and *Kabale und Liebe* (1976), after Schiller, are in a more conservative idiom; the most successful has been *Der Besuch der alten Dame* (1971).

Einstein on the Beach. Opera in 4 acts by Glass; lyrics by the composer.

First perf., Avignon Festival, France, July 25, 1976: d. & p. Wilson. U.S. prem., N.Y., Metropolitan Opera House, Nov. 21, 1976 (same production and cast).

Glass' music, built on repetitive harmonies and rhythmic patterns, is structured around Robert Wilson's slowly shifting stage tableaux, which use four recurring visual images: trains, a trial, a spaceship, and Albert Einstein, who often observes the action while playing his violin.

Elaine. Opera in 4 acts by Bemberg; libretto by Paul Ferrier, probably after Tennyson's *Idylls of the King*.

First perf., London, Covent Garden, July 5, 1892: Melba, J. de Reszke, E. de Reszke, Plançon, c. Jehin. U.S. & Met prem., Dec. 17, 1894, with same principals, c. Mancinelli, p. Parry. 2 perfs. in 1 season.

Bemberg was one of Melba's preferred song composers, and his opera about "the lily maid of Astolat" won performances through his friendship with her and the de Reszkes.

Elder, Mark. Conductor; b. Corbridge, England, June 2, 1947. After study at Cambridge and staff posts at Glyndebourne and Covent Garden, conducted opera in Australia. Joined English National Opera in 1974; music director since 1979 (including its Met appearances in 1984), also appearing regularly with BBC Symphony and other British orchestras. Bayreuth debut, *Meistersinger*, 1981.

Elegy for Young Lovers. Opera in 3 acts by Henze; libretto by Auden and Kallman.

First perf., Schwetzingen (Bavarian State Opera), May 20, 1961 (in Ger.): Rogner, Bremert, Lenz, Fischer-Dieskau, Kohn, c. Bender. U.S. prem., N.Y., Juilliard School, Apr. 29, 1965.

A score of chilling, creatively orchestrated sensuality, set in the Austrian Alps. The egoistical poet Mittenhofer (bar) sends two young lovers up the Hammerhorn and allows them to die there, to inspire his poem (whose title is that of the opera).

Elektra. Opera in 1 act by R. Strauss; libretto by Hofmannsthal after his drama based on Sophocles' tragedy.

First perf., Dresden, Court Opera, Jan. 25, 1909: Krull, Siems, Schumann-Heink, Sembach, Perron, c. Schuch. U.S. prem., N.Y., Manhattan Opera House, Feb. 1, 1910 (in Fr.): Mazarin, Baron, Gerville-Réache, Duffault, Huberdeau, c. De la Fuente. Met prem., Dec. 3, 1932: Kappel, Ljungberg, Branzell, Laubenthal, Schorr, c. Bodanzky, d. Urban, p. Sanine. Later Met production: Oct. 28, 1966: Nilsson, Rysanek, Resnik, Nagy, Dooley, c. Schippers, d. Heinrich, p. Graf. Elektra has also been sung at the Met by Pauly, Varnay, Borkh; Chrysothemis by Resnik, Kubiak, Marton; Klytemnästra by Olszewska, Thorborg, Höngen, Madeira, Varnay, Ludwig; Orest by Hotter, Schöffler, Uhde, Stewart, Bailey; the opera has also been conducted by Leinsdorf, Reiner, Böhm, Levine. 64 perfs. in 13 seasons.

Strauss' most dissonant, brutal score utilizes extravagant musical means to generate relentless psychological pressure.

Mycenae, legendary Greece. Klytemnästra (ms) has murdered her husband Agamemnon. Their daughter Elektra (s), lives in filth in the courtyard of the palace, dreaming of the return of her brother Orest (bar), who will avenge the crime, while her mother's sleep is wracked with remorse. When strangers arrive with a report that Orest is dead, Elektra unsuccessfully begs her gentle sister Chrysothemis (s) to assist her vengeance. Left alone, she starts to dig up the axe that killed her father, which she has buried in the courtyard; one of the strangers interrupts her, and she gradually realizes that he is Orest (bar), disguised and secretly returned for vengeance. He enters the palace and kills Klytemnästra; when the latter's lover Aegisth (t) appears, Elektra, with demented joy, lights his way inside to his own death. The realization of her long-desired vengeance is too much for Elektra; dancing crazily in triumph, she falls dead.

Elias, Rosalind. Mezzo-soprano; b. Lowell, Mass., Mar. 13, 1929. Studied at New England Conservatory and in Italy with Luigi Ricci and Nazzareno de Angelis. Appeared with New England Opera, 1948–52. Met debut as Grimgerde (*Walküre*), Feb. 23, 1954; since then, has sung more than 450 perfs. of over 45 roles there, including Bersi (*Chénier*), Cherubino, Dorabella, Rosina, and Hänsel, and created Barber roles in *Vanessa* and *Antony*. Also sang Cenerentola with Scottish Opera (1970), Carmen in Vienna (1972), and Baba the Turk at Glyndebourne (1975).

Elisabetta, Regina d'Inghilterra (Elizabeth, Queen of England). Opera in 2 acts by Rossini; libretto by Giovanni Schmidt, after Carlo Federici's drama, based on Scott's novel *Kenilworth*.

First perf., Naples, San Carlo, Oct. 4, 1815: Colbran, Dardanelli, Nozzari, M. Garcia.

The first of the Neapolitan serious operas Rossini wrote for his future wife Isabella Colbran cast her as Elizabeth I. Learning that her favorite, Leicester (t), has secretly married Matilde (s), Elisabetta (s) imprisons, but eventually pardons, him.

Elisir d'Amore, L' (The Love Potion). Opera in 2 acts by Donizetti; libretto by Romani, after Scribe's libretto *Le Philtre*, first set by Auber.

First perf., Milan, Cannobiana, May 12, 1832: Heinefetter, Genero, Dabadie, Frezzolini. U.S. prem., N.Y., Park, June 18, 1838 (in Eng.). Met prem., Jan. 23, 1904: Sembrich, Caruso, Scotti, Rossi, c. Vigna, p. Schroeder. Later Met productions: Mar. 21, 1930:

Elektra – (1980). Birgit Nilsson and Leonie Rysanek

Morgana, Gigli, de Luca, Pinza, c. Serafin, d. Novak, p. Wymetal; Nov. 25, 1960: Söderström, Formichini, Guarrera, Corena, c. Cleva, d. O'Hearn, p. Merrill. Nemorino has also been sung at the Met by Bonci, Schipa, Tagliavini, di Stefano, Bergonzi, Kraus, Pavarotti, Carreras; Adina by Hempel, Sayão, Peters, Scotto, Blegen; Dulcamara by Baccaloni, Tajo, Corena. 123 perfs. in 26 seasons.

Of all Donizetti's sunny comedies the hardiest survivor, in large part because of the enduring appeal of its tenor role and its aria ("Una furtiva lagrima") to each generation's operatic leading men.

A small Italian village, 19th c. The peasant Nemorino (t) is upset by his inability to win the heart of Adina (s), a beautiful, wealthy farmowner, and further disconcerted by the efforts of a new rival, the boisterous and confident Sergeant Belcore (bar). Easy prey for the quack Dr. Dulcamara (bs), the boy buys a love potion (actually Bordeaux wine) guaranteed to win the lady's heart within twenty-four hours. He downs it and his subsequent lively drunken behavior vexes Adina; she agrees to marry Belcore right away (although postponing the actual signing of the contract). To speed the elixir's effect, Nemorino wants a second bottle, but is unable to pay for it, so he enlists in his rival's regiment for a bounty of twenty scudi. News subsequently reaches the village girls that a rich uncle has left Nemorino a fortune; he interprets their sudden attentions as evidence of the potion's efficacy. Adina, hurt at his new indifference, buys his contract from the army and, after some persuasion, expresses her true feelings to Nemorino, whereupon the two are happily united.

Ellis, Brent. Baritone; b. Kansas City, Mo., June 20, 1946. Studied with Marion Freschl and Daniel Ferro in N.Y., Luigi Ricci in Rome; debut as Maerbale in *Bomarzo*, Washington, D.C., 1966. N.Y.C. Opera debut as Ottone (*Incoronazione*), 1974. Met debut as Silvio (*Pagliacci*), Oct. 25, 1979; other roles include Rossini's Figaro, Belcore, Germont, and Ford. Has also appeared in Santa Fe (1972–81), San Francisco (1974–78), Boston (1975–82), Glyndebourne (1977–78), and Vienna (1977–79).

Elmo, Cloe. Mezzo-soprano; b. Lecce, Italy, Apr. 9, 1910; d. Ankara, Turkey, May 24, 1962. Studied with Edwige Chibaudo, Santa Cecilia, Rome, later with Rinolfi and Pedrini; debut as Santuzza, Cagliari, 1934. Appeared at La Scala, 1936–45, 1951–54. Met debut as Azucena, Nov. 19, 1947; in 2 seasons, sang 23 perfs. of 7 roles, including Ulrica, Maddalena, and Quickly.

Elvira, Pablo. Baritone; b. San Juan, P.R., Sep. 24, 1938. Studied at Casals Conservatory, Puerto Rico; debut as Rigoletto, Indiana U., 1968. Has appeared in Chicago, San Francisco, and with N.Y.C. Opera (debut, Germont, 1974). Met debut as Rigoletto, Mar. 22, 1978; other roles there include Tonio, Alfio, Lescaut, Rossini's Figaro, Ashton (*Lucia*), Don Carlo (in *Ernani* and *Forza*).

Emperor Jones, The. Opera in 1 act by Gruenberg; libretto adapted by Kathleen de Jaffa from Eugene O'Neill's drama.

First perf., N.Y., Met, Jan. 7, 1933: Besuner, Windheim, Tibbett, c. Serafin, d. Mielziner, p. Sanine. 10 perfs. in 2 seasons.

Gruenberg's theatrically effective score combines traditional spirituals with declamatory recitative over dissonant orchestral accompaniment and a persistent drumbeat. On an island in the West Indies, Brutus Jones (bar), an escaped slave become "emperor," flees into the jungle when the natives he has been ruling rebel. Exhausting his bullets on hallucinations, he shoots himself with the last.

encore (Fr., "again"). An audience exclamation requesting repetition of a musical passage. The practice of encoring operatic arias, common in earlier centuries, is now relatively rare.

L'Elisir d'Amore – (1960). Designed by Robert O'Hearn, produced by Nathaniel Merrill. Fernando Corena

Endrèze [Krackman], **Arthur.** Baritone; b. Chicago, Nov. 28, 1893; d. Chicago, Apr. 15, 1975. Studied at American Conservatory, Fontainebleau, and with Jean de Reszke, Paris; sang first in French provinces. Opéra-Comique debut, Karnac (*Roi d'Ys*), 1928; Opéra debut, Valentin, 1929; created title role in Magnard's *Guercoeur*, 1931.

Enfant et les Sortilèges, L' (The Child and the Enchantments). Opera in 2 acts by Ravel; libretto by Colette.

First perf., Monte Carlo, Mar. 21, 1925: Gauley, c. de Sabata. U.S. prem., San Francisco, Sep. 19, 1930: Mario, c. Merola. Met prem., Feb. 20, 1981: Harris, c. Rosenthal, d. Hockney, p. Dexter. 25 perfs. in 2 seasons.

An opera of exquisite imagination and restrained orchestral virtuosity.

A child (s), lazy at his lessons and tired of being good, sticks his tongue out at his mother and is scolded and confined to his room. In a temper tantrum, he smashes a teacup and pot, pricks his pet squirrel with a pen, tugs the cat's tail, stirs up the fire, rips the wall-paper, pulls the pendulum of the clock, and tears the pages of his book. He is then visited by all the animals and inanimate objects he has abused, which confront him for his misbehavior or engage in bizarre and fantastical interactions with one another. When he cries for his mother, they all attack him. In the fray, a little squirrel is hurt; when the child binds its wound, the other creatures lose their animosity, and join to help him call his mother.

Entführung aus dem Serail, Die (The Abduction from the Seraglio). Opera in 3 acts by Mozart, libretto by Gottlob Stephanie the younger, after a libretto by Christoph Friedrich Bretzner.

First perf., Vienna, Burgtheater, July 16, 1782: Cavalieri, Teyber, Adamberger, Fischer. U.S. prem., Brooklyn, N.Y., Athenaeum, Feb. 16, 1860. Met prem., Nov. 29, 1946 (in Eng.): Steber, Alarie, Kullman, Ernster, c. Cooper, d. Oenslager, p. Graf. Later Met production: Oct. 12, 1979: Moser, Burrowes, Gedda, Moll, c. Levine, d. Herbert, p. Dexter. Konstanze has also been sung in this production by Eda-Pierre, Malfitano; Belmonte by Alexander, Araiza, Burrows; Blondchen by Blegen, Battle; Osmin by Talvela. 30 perfs. in 4 seasons.

In *Entführung*, Mozart threw together a brilliantly virtuosic opera seria hero and heroine, a lively secondary couple from the world of the singspiel, and a fully drawn comic character (Osmin) whose music partakes of both styles.

16th-c. Turkey. The Spanish nobleman Belmonte (t) arrives at the palace of Pasha Selim (speaking part), where his beloved Konstanze (s), her maid Blondchen (s), and Blondchen's sweetheart Pedrillo (t) have been enslaved after capture by pirates. Konstanze has repulsed the advances of the Pasha and Blondchen those of his harem-keeper, Osmin (bs). Belmonte is engaged as an architect by the Pasha, and devises with Pedrillo an escape plan. Osmin, still smarting from Blondchen's pert rejection, apprehends the prisoners during their escape. The Pasha learns that Belmonte is the son of his archenemy Lostados, but frees the prisoners as a gesture of magnanimity.

entr'acte (Fr.). A short orchestral piece played between the acts of an opera.

entrée. In French opéra-ballet, the subdivision equivalent to an act.

Erb, Karl. Tenor; b. Ravensburg, Germany, July 13, 1877; d. Ravensburg, July 13, 1958. Self-taught, was civil servant before joining Stuttgart Opera (debut in *Evangelimann*, 1907). Appeared in Lübeck (1908–10), Stuttgart (1910–12), and Munich (1913–25), where he created Pfitzner's Palestrina (1917). A noted recitalist and Evangelist in Bach Passions, he was briefly married to soprano Maria Ivogün.

Erede, Alberto. Conductor; b. Genoa, Italy, Nov. 8, 1909. Studied in Italy and with Weingartner. Assistant to Busch and conductor at Glyndebourne (1934–39), he came to the Met with Bing (debut, *Traviata*, Nov. 11, 1950) and conducted Italian repertory until 1955, returning in 1974–75 for *Tosca* and *Turandot*. Director of Oper am Rhein (1958–62); conducted *Lohengrin* at Bayreuth (1968).

Erkel, Ferenc. Composer; b. Gyula, Hungary, Nov. 7, 1810; d. Budapest, June 15, 1893. Scion of a musical family, taught by his father, he began his career as conductor and pianist. *Bátori Mária* (1840) was influenced by contemporary French and Italian style, but *Hunyadi László* (1844) showed a significant advance in combining these influences with Hungarian-inflected recitative and indigenous dance music. Erkel continued in this direction with his best-known work, *Bánk Bán* (1861), a richly melodic nationalist opera.

Ernani. Opera in 4 acts by Verdi; libretto by Piave, after Hugo's play *Hernani*.
First perf., Venice, Fenice, Mar. 9, 1844: Loewe, Guasco, Superchi, Selva. U.S. prem., N.Y., Park, Apr. 15, 1847. Met prem., Jan. 28, 1903: Sembrich, de Marchi, Scotti, E. de Reszke, c. Mancinelli, p. Almanz. Later Met productions: Dec. 8, 1921: Ponselle, Martinelli, Danise, Mardones, c. Papi, d. Urban, p. Thewman; Nov. 23, 1956: Milanov, del Monaco, Warren, Siepi, c. Mitropoulos, d. Frances, p. Yannopoulos; Nov. 18, 1983: Mitchell, Pavarotti, Milnes, Raimondi, c. Levine, d. Samaritani/P.J. Hall, p. Samaritani. Ernani has also been sung at the Met by Bergonzi, Corelli; Elvira by L. Price, Arroyo, Millo; Don Carlo by Ruffo, de Luca, MacNeil, Sereni; Silva by Pinza, Tozzi. 64 perfs. in 11 seasons.
A fiery, quick-moving score in which the Verdian drama of "scontro" (the opposition of contrasting vocal and character types) is most sharply defined. For a century, *Ernani* was the most popular of the operas Verdi composed prior to *Rigoletto*.
Spain, early 16th c. Donna Elvira (s) is in love with Don Juan of Aragon (t), a banished nobleman turned outlaw, known as Ernani. She is also desired by Don Ruy Gomez de Silva (bs), to whom she is betrothed, and by Don Carlo (bar), King of Spain. Silva, during a celebration of his imminent wedding to Elvira, hides Ernani from the pursuing Carlo. After Carlo takes Elvira away, ostensibly for her safety, Silva challenges Ernani to a duel. The outlaw reveals the King's designs on Elvira; conceding Silva's right to vengeance, Ernani begs that it be postponed so that he may first avenge himself on the King. To prove his good faith, he gives Silva a hunting horn and promises to take his life if Silva ever sounds the horn in his hearing. Don Carlo is elected Holy Roman Emperor; Ernani and Silva are among the conspirators planning his assassination, but at Elvira's intercession Carlo pardons them, restoring Ernani's estates and blessing his marriage to Elvira. At the end of a masked ball celebrating the wedding of Ernani and Elvira, a horn is sounded. Offered by Silva the choice of dagger or poison, Ernani stabs himself, to the despair of Elvira and the satisfaction of the implacable Silva.

Ernest II, Duke of Saxe-Coburg-Gotha. Composer; b. Coburg, Germany, June 21, 1818; d. Reinhardsbrunn, Aug. 22, 1893. Like his brother, Queen Victoria's consort Albert, this member of the music-loving family composed; his opera *Diana von Solange* (1861) was performed unsuccessfully at the Met (1891) during the German years, possibly in hopes of earning Met manager Stanton a decoration.

Ero e Leandro (Hero and Leander). Opera in 3 acts by Mancinelli; libretto by Boito.
First perf., Madrid, Reale, Nov. 30, 1897. U.S. & Met prem., Mar. 10, 1899: Eames, Saléza, Plançon, c. Mancinelli. 4 perfs. in 2 seasons.
The best-known opera of one of Italy's most important conductors in the generation before Toscanini. Leandro (t) braves the Hellespont nightly for forbidden visits to his beloved Ero (s), bound to service in a watchtower. When he perishes avoiding capture in a storm, she dies of grief.

Erwartung (Expectation). Opera in 1 act by Schoenberg: libretto by Marie Pappenheim.
First perf., Prague, Neues Deutsches Theater, June 6, 1924: Gutheil-Schoder, c. Zemlinsky. U.S. prem., N.Y., Carnegie Hall, Nov. 15, 1951 (concert perf.): Dow, c. Mitropoulos. U.S. stage prem., Washington, D.C., Opera, Dec. 28, 1960: Pilarczyk, c. Craft.
A monodrama of charged expressionist intensity, in which a Woman (s) awaits her lover in the woods at night, and then stumbles upon his corpse.

Esclarmonde. Opera in prologue, 4 acts, and epilogue by Massenet; libretto by Alfred Blau and Louis de Gramont.
First perf., Paris, Opéra-Comique, May 14, 1889: Sanderson, Gilbert, Taskin, c. Danbé. U.S. prem., New Orleans, French Opera House, Feb. 10, 1893. Met prem., Nov. 19, 1976: Sutherland, Aragall, Quilico, c. Bonynge, d. Montresor, p. Mansouri. 10 perfs. in 1 season.
Massenet's most Wagnerian opera, set in medieval Byzantium and Blois. Having won the knight Roland (t) with sorcery, Esclarmonde (s) is forced to renounce him lest she lose her throne and magic powers. In a tournament, Roland wins the hand of a veiled princess, who proves to be Esclarmonde.

Esham, Faith. Soprano; b. Vanceburg, Ky. Studied in Kentucky and at Juilliard with Tourel, Beverly Johnson, and Adele Addison. Professional debut as Cherubino, N.Y.C. Opera, 1977. European debut as Nedda (*Pagliacci*), Nancy (1980), followed by debuts at Glyndebourne (Cherubino, 1981), Scala (Cherubino, 1982), Vienna State Opera (Micaela, 1984), and the Met (Dec. 27, 1986, Marzelline in *Fidelio*).

Estes, Simon. Bass-baritone; b. Centerville, Iowa, Mar. 2, 1938. Studied with Charles Kellis, U. of Iowa, and at Juilliard, N.Y. After singing opera in Germany, won Tchaikovsky competition, Moscow (1966). Appearances in Chicago, San Francisco, Boston, Philadelphia, Hamburg, Moscow, Milan. Met debut as Hermann (*Tannhäuser*), Jan. 4, 1982; has also sung Amfortas (*Parsifal*), Porgy, Amonasro, Orest, and Wotan (*Walküre*) there. At Bayreuth, has sung Dutchman (1978), Amfortas (1982).

Étoile, L' (The Star). Opera in 3 acts by Chabrier; libretto by E. Leterrier and A. Vanloo.

First perf., Paris, Bouffes-Parisiennes, Nov. 28, 1877: Paola-Marie, Stuart, Luce, c. Rocques. U.S. prem., N.Y., Broadway Theater, Aug. 18, 1890 (in Eng., music arranged by John Philip Sousa).

A lively opéra bouffe, set in an imaginary country; in a tangle of disguises and mistaken identities, King Ouf (t) loses his intended bride, Princess Laoula (s), to the peddler Lazuli (ms).

Eugene Onegin. Opera in 3 acts by Tchaikovsky; libretto by Konstantin Shilovsky and the composer, after Alexander Pushkin's poem.

First perf., Moscow, Maly, Mar. 29, 1879: student cast from the Imperial College of Music. First professional perf., Moscow, Bolshoi, Jan. 23, 1881: Verny, Usatov, Khokhlov, Abramov, c. Bevignani. U.S. prem., N.Y., Carnegie Hall, Feb. 1, 1908 (concert perf.). Met prem. (and U.S. stage prem.), Mar. 24, 1920 (in Ital.): Muzio, Martinelli, de Luca, Didur, c. Bodanzky, d. Urban/Platt, p. Ordynski. Later Met production: Oct. 28, 1957 (in Eng.): Amara, Tucker, London, Tozzi, c. Mitropoulos, d. Gérard, p. Brook. Since 1977, the opera has been sung at the Met in Russian; Onegin has also been sung there by Milnes, Mazurok, Luxon, Nucci; Tatiana by L. Price, Zylis-Gara, Kasrashvili, Kabaivanska, Kubiak, Cotrubas; Lenski by Gedda, Thomas, Shicoff; Gremin by Plishka, Talvela. 64 perfs. in 9 seasons.

This tender, impassioned series of "lyric scenes" is a repertory staple in Russia, and elsewhere Tchaikovsky's most popular opera.

A country estate and St. Petersburg, late 18th c. The impressionable Tatiana (s) falls in love at first meeting with the blasé young aristocrat Eugene Onegin (bar), and writes him an impassioned letter. When he tells her that he can offer her only friendship, she is distraught. At a ball, Onegin flirts with Tatiana's sister Olga (ms), engaged to his friend the poet Lenski (t). The enraged Lenski challenges Onegin to a duel and is killed. Some years later at a party, Onegin, disillusioned with his empty life, encounters Tatiana, now married to Prince Gremin (bs). Onegin begs her to abandon her husband and become his lover after all, but she rejects him.

Euridice. Opera in a prologue and 6 scenes by Caccini; libretto by Rinuccini.

First perf., Florence, Palazzo Pitti, Dec. 5, 1602.

Caccini's opera was published in 1600, and some of its music was incorporated into the premiere of Peri's setting of the same text that year.

Euridice. Opera in a prologue and 6 scenes by Peri; libretto by Rinuccini.

First perf., Florence, Palazzo Pitti, Oct. 6, 1600: Peri, Rasi, Brandi, p. Cavalieri. U.S. prem., Saratoga Springs, N.Y., Skidmore College, Apr. 9, 1941 (student perf., in Eng.).

The first surviving opera uses a version of the Orpheus legend in which there is no stipulation that Orpheus refrain from looking at Euridice as he leads her out of the underworld, allowing a happy ending.

Euripides. Greek dramatist (c. 483–406 B.C.). Operas based on his writings include *Alceste* (Gluck), *The Bassarids* (Henze), *Fedra* (Pizzetti), and *Iphigénie en Tauride* (Gluck).

Euryanthe. Opera in 3 acts by Weber; libretto by Helmine von Chezy, after a medieval French romance.

First perf., Vienna, Kärntnertor, Oct. 25, 1823: Sontag, Grünbaum, Haitzinger, Forti, c. Weber. U.S. & Met prem., Dec. 23, 1887: Lilli Lehmann, Brandt, Alvary, Fischer, c. Seidl, p. Habelmann. Later Met production: Dec. 19, 1914: Hempel, Ober, Sembach, Weil, c. Toscanini, d. Kautsky/Heil, p. Taylor. 9 perfs. in 2 seasons.

Weber's rich score prefigures Wagner's works, especially *Lohengrin*, but the befuddling plot has prevented it from making its way in the theater.

France, early 12th c. Lysiart (bar) wagers with Adolar (t) that he can seduce Adolar's beloved Euryanthe (s). Eglantine (ms) loves Adolar, and Euryanthe confides in her the secret of Adolar's sister's suicide. Eglantine tells Lysiart, who uses his knowledge to "prove" that he has seduced Euryanthe. When Adolar takes her into the desert to kill her, she saves him from a serpent; abandoned by him, she is rescued by the King (bs), who believes in her innocence. About to marry Lysiart, Eglantine confesses her treachery; Lysiart is taken away, and Euryanthe and Adolar are reunited.

Evangelimann, Der (The Evangelist). Opera in 2 acts by Kienzl; libretto by the composer, after Leopold Florian Meissner's story.

First perf., Berlin, Court Opera, May 4, 1895: Pierson, Götz, Sylva, Bulss, c. Muck. U.S. prem., Chicago, Great Northern Theater, Nov. 3, 1923.

This folk-like opera has retained popularity in Germany. St. Othmar, Austria, 1820 and 1850; Johannes (bar), jealous because Martha (s) loves his brother Mathias (t), has the latter expelled from the monastery and framed for arson. After 20 years in prison, Mathias returns as a street preacher and forgives his brother.

Evans, Geraint. Baritone; b. Cilfynydd, Wales, Feb. 16, 1922. After military service, he studied with Theo Hermann, Hamburg, and Fernando Carpi, Genoa. Debut as Night Watchman (*Meistersinger*), Covent Garden, 1948. Sang regularly in Glyndebourne, 1950–61, including his first Falstaff, 1957. Debuts in San Francisco (Beckmesser, 1959), La Scala (Figaro, 1960), Chicago (Lem in Giannini's *The Harvest*, 1961), Salzburg (Figaro, 1962) and Paris (Leporello, 1975). Met debut as Falstaff, Mar. 25, 1964; in 6 seasons, he sang 46 perfs. of 7 roles, including Balstrode (*Grimes*), Leporello, Wozzeck, and Beckmesser. At Covent Garden, created Flint (*Billy Budd*), Mountjoy (*Gloriana*), and Evadne and Antenor (*Troilus*). Though he sang bravura parts such as Escamillo early in his career, Evans found his niche as a resourceful singer of character roles both comic and serious.

Everding, August. Producer; b. Bottrop, Germany, Oct. 31, 1928. At Munich's Kammerspiele, worked under Hans Schweikart, later artistic director (1959–63) and Intendant (1963–73). First operatic production, *Traviata* (Munich, 1965). General manager and stage director at Hamburg State Opera (1973–77) and Bavarian State Opera (1977–82); Intendant, Bavarian State theaters (from 1982). As first postwar director at Bayreuth outside Wagner family, produced *Holländer* (1969). His Met productions are *Tristan* (1971), *Boris* (1974), *Lohengrin* (1976), and *Khovanshchina* (1985).

Ewing, Maria. Soprano; b. Detroit, Mich., Mar. 27, 1950. Studied with Eleanor Steber, at Cleveland Institute, later with Jennie Tourel; debut at Ravinia Festival, 1973. Met debut as Cherubino, Oct. 14, 1976; other Met roles include Zerlina, Blanche (*Carmélites*), Dorabella,

Composer (*Ariadne*), Rosina, and Carmen. At Glyndebourne, since 1978, has sung Dorabella, Rosina, Composer, Poppea.

Excursions of Mr. Brouček, The. Opera in 2 acts by Janáček; libretto by the composer and others, after Svatopluk Čech's novels.

First perf., Prague, Czech Theater, Apr. 23, 1920, c. Ostrcil. U.S. prem., Jan. 23, 1981, San Francisco (Opera Ensemble; in Eng.): c. Nagano.

Initially composed as two separate operas, over the period 1908–17. Prague, 1888; the first part relates Mr. Brouček's excursion to the moon; the second, his excursion to 15th-c. Prague and return to the present.

exit aria. In 18th-c. opera, most arias were at the end of scenes, the singer leaving the stage at their conclusion.

F

Fabbri, Guerrina. Contralto; b. Ferrara, Italy, 1868; d. Turin, Feb. 21, 1946. Debut as La Cieca, Viadana, 1885. Sang Azucena at Drury Lane, London, 1887. In Italy, revived *Italiana* and *Cenerentola*, 1890; La Scala debut as Lola (*Cavalleria*), 1891. At the Met, she only sang Nancy (*Martha*) on Apr. 2, 1892, and returned for a concert in 1910.

Faccio, Franco. Conductor and composer; b. Verona, Italy, Mar. 8, 1840; d. Monza, July 21, 1891. One of the first Italian musicians to achieve fame principally as a conductor, he first pursued composition; his *Hamlet*, text by Boito, was well received in 1865. Association with Verdi began in 1869, as assistant at La Scala preparing the revised *Forza*. In part responsible for the acceptance of Wagner in Italy, he led the Italian premiere of *Aida* (1877) and the premieres of *Gioconda* (1876), the revised *Boccanegra* (1881), the four-act *Don Carlos, Villi* (1885), and *Otello* (1887).

Fach (Ger., "specialty"). In opera, refers to a singer's vocal category, such as lyric soprano, dramatic tenor, basso buffo.

Falstaff – (1972). Designed and produced by Franco Zeffirelli. Geraint Evans and Renata Tebaldi

Faggioni, Piero. Producer; b. Carrara, Italy, Aug. 12, 1936. Worked under Jean Vilar and Visconti; debut as opera director, *Bohème* (Venice, 1964). He has also worked at La Scala (*Alceste*, 1972), Turin (*Fanciulla*, 1975), Vienna (*Norma*, 1977), Edinburgh (*Carmen*, 1977), Salzburg (*Macbeth*, 1984), and the Met (*Francesca da Rimini*, 1984).

Fair at Sorochintsy, The. See *Sorochintsy Fair*.

Fairy Queen, The. Semi-opera in prologue and 5 scenes by Purcell; libretto anonymously adapted (probably by Elkanah Settle) from Shakespeare's *A Midsummer Night's Dream*.

First perf., London, Dorset Garden, Apr. 1692. U.S. prem., San Francisco, Legion of Honor Palace, Apr. 30, 1932.

The score of this work, a series of arias and dances based only loosely on Shakespeare, was lost for 200 years.

Falcon, (Marie) **Cornélie.** Soprano; b. Paris, Jan. 28, 1814; d. Paris, Feb. 25, 1897. Studied with Nourrit, Paris Conservatory; debut as Alice (*Robert le Diable*), Opéra, 1832. Created Rachel (*Juive*, 1835) and Valentine (*Huguenots*, 1836); after her, this type of passionate dramatic role was christened "falcon." After an 1838 vocal breakdown, probably from overwork, she retired in 1840.

Falla, Manuel de. Composer; b. Cádiz, Spain, Nov. 2, 1876; d. Alta Gracia, Argentina, Nov. 14, 1946. Early studies in Cádiz with Broca, later with Pedrell at Madrid Conservatory. Falla's first stage works were zarzuelas. In 1907, after composing *La Vida Breve* (1905), he went to Paris and became friendly with Debussy and Ravel, whose harmonic and coloristic originality influenced his nationalistic idiom. *El Retablo de Maese Pedro* (1923), for marionettes and singers, reflected the postwar turn to reduced forces and stylistic pastiche. From 1926 until his death, Falla labored at the oratorio-like *L'Atlántida*, completed for performance by Ernesto Halffter.

falsetto. A technique of voice production whereby male singers extend their upper ranges, albeit with lighter tonal quality and less volume. Until the fourth decade of the 19th c., most operatic tenors sang high notes this way; it is the principal technique used by countertenors.

Falstaff. Opera in 3 acts by Verdi; libretto by Boito, after Shakespeare's *The Merry Wives of Windsor* and *King Henry IV*.

First perf., Milan, La Scala, Feb. 9, 1893: Zilli, Stehle, Guerrini, Pasqua, Garbin, Maurel, Pini-Corsi, c. Mascheroni. U.S. & Met prem., Feb. 4, 1895: Eames, de Lussan, Scalchi, de Vigne, Russitano, Maurel, Campanari, c. Mancinelli, p. Parry. Later Met productions: Mar. 20, 1909: Destinn, Alda, Gay, Reisenberg, Grassi, Scotti, Campanari, c. Toscanini, d. Sala, Parravicini/Maison Chiappa, p. Speck; Jan. 2, 1925: Bori, Alda, Telva, Howard, Gigli, Scotti, Tibbett, c. Serafin, d. Urban, p. Wymetal; Mar. 6, 1964: Tucci, Raskin, Resnik, Elias, Alva, Colzani, Sereni, c. Bernstein, d. & p. Zeffirelli. Falstaff has also been sung at the Met by Tibbett, Warren, Evans, Flagello, Gobbi, MacNeil, Taddei; Alice Ford by Steber, Resnik, Curtin, Tebaldi, Lear; Nannetta by Albanese, Peters, Valente, Blegen; Dame Quickly by Homer, Elmo, Barbieri, Cossotto; Fenton by di Stefano; Ford by Tibbett, Brownlee, Stewart. Other Met conductors include Beecham (in his own Eng. translation), Reiner, Levine. 107 perfs. in 17 seasons.

In *Falstaff*, the astonishing afterpiece to Verdi's long career as a tragedian, quicksilver snatches of melody and brilliantly precise instrumental touches are deployed with unmatched economical mastery, while through it all glows the warmest compassion for the foibles of the old and young alike.

Windsor, early 15th c. The seedy and bibulous Sir John Falstaff (bar) sends identical love letters to the wealthy Mistresses Alice Ford (s) and Meg Page (ms). With their friend Dame Quickly (ms) and Alice's daughter Nannetta (s), the ladies plan to accept the knight's ridiculous proposals of rendez-vous and teach him a lesson. Master Ford, learning of the knight's schemes from his friend Dr. Caius (t) — to whom he has promised Nannetta's hand — and from Falstaff's cronies, Bardolfo (t) and Pistola (bs), devises a plan to entrap the ribald, and calls on Falstaff with a fanciful commission to seduce Alice. Falstaff accepts both lures, shocking and infuriating the disguised Ford with the announcement that he already has an appointment with the lady that afternoon. Falstaff's tête-à-tête with Alice is cut short by the arrival of Ford, whose search for Falstaff turns up only Nannetta and her sweetheart Fenton (t), stealing kisses in hiding. The women have hidden Falstaff in a laundry basket, which is finally dumped out of the window into the River Thames. Notwithstanding this ignominy, Falstaff accepts the bait of another rendez-vous, meeting Alice at Herne's Oak in Windsor forest, where he finds himself surrounded by fairies and goblins (the merry wives and accomplices in disguise) who dance and thrash him into repentance. When disguises are removed, Ford discovers he has been tricked into giving Nannetta to Fenton in marriage. Falstaff finally admits that all the world is folly, and the opera ends with a brilliant fugue on that subject.

Fanciulla del West, La (The Girl of the Golden West). Opera in 3 acts by Puccini; libretto by Carlo Zangarini and Guelfo Civinini, after Belasco's play.

First perf., N. Y., Met, Dec. 10, 1910: Destinn, Caruso, Amato, c. Toscanini, d. J. Fox/Musaeus, p. Belasco. Later Met productions: Nov. 2, 1929: Jeritza, Martinelli, Tibbett, c. Bellezza, d. Novak, p. Lert; Oct. 23, 1961: L. Price, Tucker, Colzani, c. Cleva, d. Ritholz/Roth, p. Butler. Minnie has also been sung at the Met by Kirsten, Tebaldi; Dick Johnson by E. Johnson, Kónya, Corelli; Rance by Danise, Guelfi. A student matinee of *Fanciulla*, April 11, 1966, was the first performance given in the new Metropolitan Opera House at Lincoln Center. 64 perfs. in 10 seasons.

Fanciulla is an experimental opera for Puccini: it has a happy ending, a victorious heroine, a rugged masculine setting, and a strong dose of "modern" dissonance as learned from Debussy.

A California mining camp during the Gold Rush (1849–50). Minnie (s), keeper of the Polka saloon and a sort of "mother," teacher, and best friend to the miners, falls in love with a newcomer, Dick Johnson (t). She learns that he is really the bandit Ramerrez, but he expresses a desire to change his ways because of his feelings for her. After he has been shot by a posse, she hides Johnson in her cabin, but Sheriff Jack Rance (bar), also in love with Minnie, discovers him. Minnie challenges Rance to a poker game over Johnson, cheats and wins; Rance leaves without his quarry. But Johnson is soon captured and about to be hung when Minnie rides in and prays the miners to spare the man she loves. They relent, and the lovers ride off to begin a new life.

La Fanciulla del West – (1910). World premiere.
Emmy Destinn, Enrico Caruso, Pasquale Amato

Farinelli [Carlo Broschi]. Soprano castrato; b. Andria, Italy, Jan. 24, 1705; d. Bologna, Sep. 16, 1782. Studied with Porpora; debut in his teacher's *Eomene*, Rome, 1722. He sang in Italy, Vienna (from 1724), and throughout Europe, then joined the Opera of the Nobility in London (debut in *Artaserse*, 1734), singing there until 1737. Summoned by the queen of Spain to cure the depression of King Philip V, he went to Madrid, where his musical therapy was so successful that he was offered 50,000 francs a year to remain in Madrid; the singer accepted, performing every night, eventually serving as royal impresario, decorator, and stage director, and remaining in favor under Ferdinand VI. Dismissed by Carlos III in 1759, he retired to a luxurious villa near Bologna.

Farley, Carole. Soprano; b. Le Mars, Iowa, Nov. 29, 1946. Studied with William Shriner at Indiana U. and Marianne Schech in Munich. Debut as Offenbach's Hélène, N.Y.C. Opera, 1976. Met debut as Mimi, Apr. 15, 1975; she returned in 1978 as Lulu, a role she also sang with the Welsh National Opera and in Cologne and Zurich.

Farrar, Geraldine. American soprano; b. Melrose, Mass., Feb. 28, 1882; d. Ridgefield, Conn., Mar. 11, 1967. Studied with Mrs. J.H. Long in Boston, Emma Thursby in N.Y., Trabadello in Paris, and Graziani in Berlin. Debut as Marguerite (*Faust*), Berlin, 1901; Lilli Lehmann heard her there and gave her further lessons. She sang five seasons in Berlin and three in Monte Carlo (1903–06), where she created Mascagni's Amica. Met debut as Juliette, Nov. 26, 1906; she sang there for 16 consecutive seasons, singing 517 perfs. of 35 roles and creating the Goose Girl in *Königskinder*, Louise (and four associated roles) in *Julien*, Madame Sans-Gêne, and Suor Angelica. She was the Met's first Butterfly, singing the role 94 times, and she sang Carmen, Tosca, and Marguerite each 50 times or more. Other Met roles included Mimi, Massenet's Manon, Thaïs, Louise, Cherubino, Berlioz's and Boito's Marguerites, Nedda, Dukas' Ariane, and Rosaura (*Donne Curiose*).

A beautiful woman who understood the uses of publicity, Farrar sometimes overextended her essentially lyric soprano, and was most effective in roles involving coquetry and charm. She made several silent films, and was an uncommonly popular artist, especially among young women; after her farewell performance as Zazà,

Apr. 22, 1922, thousands of "Gerryflappers" gathered outside the Met in a mass demonstration of affection. She continued to give concerts, the last one in Carnegie Hall, 1931. In 1935, she acted as intermission commentator on the Met's Saturday matinee radio broadcasts.

BIBLIOGRAPHY: Geraldine Farrar, *Such Sweet Compulsion* (N.Y., 1938, repr. 1970).

Farrell, Eileen. Soprano; b. Willamantic, Conn., Feb. 13, 1920. Studied with Merle Alcock and Eleanor McLellan. Sang on radio from 1940 and in concert; Marie in concert perf. of *Wozzeck*, N.Y., 1951. Stage debut as Santuzza, Tampa, Fla., 1956; debuts in San Francisco (*Trovatore*, 1956) and Chicago (Gioconda, 1957). Met debut as Alceste, Dec. 6, 1960; in 5 seasons, she sang 34 perfs. of 5 roles, including Gioconda, Leonora (*Forza*), Maddalena (*Chénier*), and Santuzza. Taught at Indiana U., 1971–80. She frequently sang Wagner excerpts in concert, but never in the theater.

Fassbaender, Brigitte. Mezzo-soprano; b. Berlin, July 3, 1939. Studied with father, baritone Willi Domgraf-Fassbänder, Nuremberg Conservatory; debut as Nicklausse (*Hoffmann*), Munich, 1961. Appeared at Covent Garden (1971) and Salzburg (1973). Met debut as Octavian, Feb. 16, 1974; returned in 1986 as Fricka (*Walküre*). Has also appeared in Paris, Milan, and Vienna.

Faull, Ellen. Soprano; b. Pittsburgh, Pa., Oct. 14, 1918. Studied privately in Pittsburgh, then at Curtis Institute and with Joseph Regneas in N.Y.; debut as Donna Anna, N.Y.C. Opera, 1947. She sang with the company for 23 years, in roles such as Mozart's Countess, Butterfly, and Eva (*Meistersinger*), and created Abigail in *Lizzie Borden*, also appearing with many U.S. companies.

Fauré, Gabriel. Composer; b. Pamiers, France, May 12, 1845; d. Paris, Nov. 4, 1924. Studied with Niedermeyer and Saint-Saëns. Worked as organist and taught at Paris Conservatory, where his students included Ravel, Enesco, and Nadia Boulanger; director of the Conservatory, 1905–20. His own works, especially piano music and songs, became known for their harmonic subtlety and melodic clarity. *Prométhée* (1900), a tragédie lyrique with spoken interludes, was written for open-air performance by large forces; in the opera *Pénélope* (1913), brief lyrical passages are interspersed with arioso and recitative.

Faure, Jean-Baptiste. Baritone; b. Moulins, France, Jan. 15, 1830; d. Paris, Nov. 9, 1914. Studied at Paris Conservatory; debut in Massé's *Galathée*, Opéra-Comique, 1852. Covent Garden debut, 1860. Paris Opéra debut, 1861; created Nélusko (*Africaine*, 1865), Posa (1867), and Hamlet (1868) there.

Faust. Opera in 5 acts by Gounod; libretto by Barbier and Carré, after Part 1 of Goethe's drama.

First perf., Paris, Lyrique, Mar. 19, 1859: Miolan-Carvalho, Faivre, Barbot, Reynald, Balanqué, c. Deloffre. Rev. for the Paris Opéra, with recitatives and ballet, first perf., Mar. 3, 1869, with C. Nilsson as Marguerite. U.S. prem., Philadelphia, Academy of Music, Nov. 18, 1863 (in Ger.). Met prem., Oct. 22, 1883 (first perf. in the house): Nilsson, Scalchi, Campanini, del Puente, Novara, c. Vianesi, d. J. Fox, Schaffer, Maeder, Thompson/Ascoli, Dazian. Later Met productions: Nov. 17, 1917: Farrar, Delaunois, Martinelli, Chalmers, Rothier, c. Monteux, d. Urban, p. Ordynski; Nov. 16, 1953: de los Angeles,

Miller, Bjoerling, Merrill, Rossi-Lemeni, c. Monteux, d. Gérard, p. Brook; Sep. 27, 1965 (last opening night in old Met): Tucci, Baldwin, Gedda, Merrill, Siepi, c. Prêtre, d. Dupont, p. Barrault, Faust has also been sung at the Met by J. de Reszke, Caruso, Gigli, Thill, Crooks, Jobin, di Stefano, Domingo; Marguerite by Sembrich, Lilli Lehmann, Eames, Nordica, Melba, Calvé, Alda, Albanese, Kirsten, Freni; Valentin by Maurel, Scotti, Stracciari, Renaud, de Luca, Tibbett, Warren, Singher, Milnes; Méphistophélès by E. de Reszke, Plançon, Journet, Chaliapin, Bohnen, Pinza, Hines, London, Ghiaurov. 412 perfs. in 68 seasons.

In *Faust*, Gounod and his librettists bring a profound and varied drama within the pale of conventional, sentimental lyric opera; this has led to a certain amount of disfavor in recent decades, but the craftsmanship and melodic wealth of the score go far to disarm criticism. During the 1890s, *Faust* was so frequently performed at the Met that the critic W.J. Henderson dubbed the theater the "Faustspielhaus."

Germany, 16th c. Faust (t), an aged philosopher, promises his soul to the Devil, Méphistophélès (bs), in exchange for youth and the beautiful Marguerite (s). Méphistophélès obstructs the faithful Siebel (ms) in his pursuit of Marguerite and introduces her to the rejuvenated Faust, with whom she falls in love. Returning from war, her brother Valentin (bar) finds her compromised by Faust, and challenges him to a duel. Valentin is killed and Faust subsequently abandons Marguerite. She bears his child, kills it in shame, and is condemned to death. In prison she seems to have lost her senses. Faust and Méphistophélès appear at the prison and the repentant

Geraldine Farrar as Juliette in *Roméo et Juliette*

Faust tries to carry her off. She recognizes the evil spirit, renounces her love, and dies. Méphistophélès declares her condemned, but angels bear her aloft, proclaiming her salvation.

Favero, Mafalda. Soprano; b. Portomaggiore, Italy, Jan. 6, 1903; d. Milan, Sep. 3, 1981. Studied with Vezzani, Bologna Conservatory; debut as Lola (*Cavalleria*), under name Maria Bianchi, Cremona, 1926. La Scala debut as Eva (*Meistersinger*), 1928; she sang there regularly until 1943, again 1946–50. Only Met appearances were 2 perfs. as Mimi (debut, Nov. 24, 1938).

Favola d'Orfeo, La (The Fable of Orpheus). Opera in prologue and 5 acts by Monteverdi; libretto by Alessandro Striggio.

First perf. (private), Mantua, Accademia degl' Invaghiti, Feb. 1607. U.S. & Met prem., Apr. 14, 1912 (arr. Orefice, concert perf., in Eng.): Fornia, Duchêne, Weil, Witherspoon, c. Pasternack. U.S. stage prem., Northampton, Mass., Smith College, May 11, 1929 (ed. Malipiero): Kullman, c. Josten.

The eloquent directness of Monteverdi's recitatives and pastoral choruses have made this the earliest opera to establish itself as more than a curiosity in 20th-c. revival.

Legendary times. Celebrations of the coming marriage of the celebrated singer Orfeo (t) to Euridice (s) are interrupted by a messenger (c) bearing news of Euridice's death. Orfeo resolves to seek her out in Hades, and persuades Caronte (bs) to ferry him across the Styx. Plutone (bs) and Proserpina (s) are in turn persuaded to grant his plea to take Euridice back to earth, on condition that he must not look upon her until the journey is completed. He is unable to restrain himself, and looks just as they are about to emerge; Euridice sinks back into death, but Apollo (bs) consoles Orfeo with the promise that in eternity he will be able to gaze on his bride forever. (In Striggio's original version of the ending, for which no music survives, Orfeo is torn to death by Bacchantes.)

favola in musica, favola per musica (Ital., "story in music," "story through music"). A term used for the earliest operas.

Favorite, La (The Favorite). Opera in 4 acts by Donizetti; libretto by Alphonse Royer and Gustave Vaëz, with additions by Scribe, based in part on his libretto for Donizetti's *L'Ange de Nisida*.

First perf., Paris, Opéra, Dec. 2, 1840: Stolz, Duprez, Barroilhet, Levasseur, c. Habeneck. U.S. prem., New Orleans, Feb. 9, 1843. Met prem., Nov 29, 1895 (in Ital. as *La Favorita*): Mantelli, Cremonini, Ancona, Plançon, c. Bevignani, p. Parry. Later Met production: Feb. 21, 1978 (in Ital.): Verrett, Pavarotti, Milnes, Giaiotti, c. Lopez-Cobos, d. Lee/Greenwood, p. Tavernia. Léonor has also been sung at the Met by Walker; Fernand by Caruso; Alphonse by Scotti. 17 perfs. in 5 seasons.

Relationships and motivations are badly muddled by the standard Italian translation, but *Favorite* contains some of Donizetti's noblest melodies.

Castile, 1340. Although returning the affection of the novice Fernand (t), Léonor (ms) will not reveal her identity, for she is mistress of Alphonse (bar), King of Castile. After she has gained Fernand a military appointment, he saves the King's life in battle and asks for Léonor's hand as reward. Under threat of excommunication for his adulterous relationship, the King grants Fernand's wish, but Léonor is unable to warn the young

Faust – (1965). Designed by Jacques Dupont, produced by Jean-Louis Barrault. Cesare Siepi

man of the truth before the marriage. Finding he has married the King's mistress, Fernand repudiates his honors and returns to the monastery. Before Fernand takes his final vows, Léonor comes to ask forgiveness; having reawakened his passion, she collapses and dies.

Fedora. Opera in 3 acts by Giordano; libretto by Arturo Colautti, after Sardou's drama.

First perf., Milan, Lirico, Nov. 17, 1898: Bellincioni, Caruso, Menotti, c. Giordano. U.S. & Met prem., Dec. 5, 1906: Cavalieri, Caruso, Scotti, c. Vigna, d. Fox, p. Dufriche. Later Met production: Dec. 8, 1923: Jeritza, Martinelli, Scotti, c. Papi, d. Urban, p. Wymetal. 21 perfs. in 5 seasons.

One of the central works of the verismo canon, quite popular (especially in Italy) as long as the vogue lasted.

St. Petersburg, Paris, Switzerland; late 19th c. A murder mystery. The intended husband of Fedora Romanov (s) is killed by Loris Ipanov (t), whose wife had had an affair with the victim. Fedora sets in motion a scheme of vengeance, but falls in love with Loris after learning the reason behind his deed. When members of Loris' family suffer, he learns only that an unnamed woman is to blame, and swears retaliation. Fedora, realizing that the truth will eventually be discovered, poisons herself; Loris understands too late.

Fedra. Opera in 3 acts by Pizzetti; libretto by Gabriele d'Annunzio, after Euripides' *Hippolytus*.

First perf., Milan, La Scala, Mar. 20, 1915: Krusceniski, di Giovanni (Johnson), Grandini, c. Marinuzzi.

Pizzetti's first performed opera, an austere score conceived in reaction against Puccini's lush melodism. Fedra (Phaedra, s), wife of Teseo (Theseus, b), rejected by her stepson Ippolito (Hippolytus, t), hangs herself and leaves a letter falsely accusing Ippolito of dishonoring her. (Romano Romani's one-act opera on the same subject, text by Alfredo Lenozoni, was first performed in 1915 in Rome with Raisa, and sung by Ponselle at Covent Garden in 1931.)

Feen, Die. Opera in 3 acts by Wagner; libretto by the composer, after Gozzi's *La Donna Serpente*.

First perf., Munich, Hoftheater, June 29, 1888: Dressler, Mikorey, c. Fischer. U.S. prem., N.Y.C. Opera, Feb. 24,

1982 (concert perf.): Neblett, Alexander, c. Almeida.

Wagner's first opera, composed in 1833–34 but unperformed in his lifetime. Prince Arindel (t) marries the fairy Ada (s), but they must undergo many trials if they are to remain united.

Felsenstein, Walter. Producer; b. Vienna, May 30, 1901; d. Berlin, Oct. 3, 1975. Trained as an actor, he turned to directing in 1924, and staged opera in Basel (1927-29), Cologne (1932–34), and Frankfurt (1934–36), drama in Zurich (1938–40) and at Berlin's Schiller Theater (1940–44). Appointed director of Komische Oper, East Berlin, in 1947, he developed a series of meticulously rehearsed stagings incorporating realistic acting with finely calculated motivations. His most famous productions included *Orphée aux Enfers* (1948), *Carmen* (1949), *Falstaff* (1952), *Zauberflöte* (1954), *The Cunning Little Vixen* (1956), *Hoffmann* (1958), and *Otello* (1959). He also directed at La Scala, Hamburg, and Moscow, and produced a film version of *Fidelio*.

fermata. A symbol indicating that a note should be held beyond its normal duration; it often indicates the point at which a cadenza should be sung.

Fernand Cortez. Opera in 3 acts by Spontini; libretto by J.A. Esménard and V.J. Étienne de Jouy, after Alexis Piron's tragedy.

First perf., Paris, Opéra, Nov. 28, 1809: Branchu, Lainez, Laïs, Laforet, Dérivis, Bertin. U.S. & Met prem., Jan. 6, 1888 (in Ger.): Meisslinger, Niemann, Alvary, Emblad, c. Seidl, d. Hoyt/Dazian, p. Habelmann, 4 perfs. in 1 season.

In 1817, Spontini revised this stately historical opera, much admired by Berlioz and Wagner. Mexico, during the Spanish conquest. The conqueror Cortez (t) loves the Aztec princess Amazily (a), who helps him quell his men's mutiny and rescue his brother Alvarez (t) from sacrifice to the Aztec gods.

Ferne Klang, Der (The Distant Sound). Opera in 3 acts by Schreker; libretto by the composer.

First perf., Frankfurt, Aug. 18, 1912: Sellin, Gentner, c. Rottenberg.

Schreker's lush score is heavily influenced by impressionism and *fin-de-siècle* Romanticism. The young composer Fritz (t) leaves his true love Grete (s) to search for a "lost chord," rediscovers her in a Venetian bordello, and eventually dies in her arms.

Ferrani [Zanazzio], **Cesira.** Soprano; b. Turin, May 8, 1863; d. Pollone, near Biella, May 4, 1943. Studied with Antonietta Fricci; debut as Micaela, 1887, in Turin, where she created Puccini's Manon (1893) and Mimi (1896). La Scala debut as Kitzu in Franchetti's *Fior d'Alpe*, 1894; sang Mélisande there, 1908. Retired in 1909; taught in Turin.

Ferrari-Fontana, Edoardo. Tenor; b. Rome, July 8, 1878; d. Toronto, July 4, 1936. After diplomatic service in Montevideo, returned to Italy, 1908, to sing operetta. Operatic debut as Tristan, Turin, 1909; created Avito (*Amore dei Tre Re*), La Scala, 1913. Appeared with Boston Opera (1913–14), Met (debut, Jan. 2, 1914, as Avito, his only role in 2 seasons), and Chicago Opera (1915–16). Briefly married to mezzo Margaret Matzenauer.

Ferrier, Kathleen. Contralto; b. Higher Walton, Lancashire, England, Apr. 22, 1912; d. London, Oct. 8, 1953.

Studied with J.E. Hutchinson, Newcastle, and Roy Henderson, London, and sang recitals and oratorios during the war. Operatic debut at Glyndebourne, creating Britten's Lucretia (1946). Her only other stage role was Gluck's Orfeo, in Glyndebourne (1947), N.Y. (concert perf., 1949), the Netherlands (1949, 1951), and Covent Garden (1953, her last performances before her death of cancer). Also noted for her singing of the Angel in Elgar's *Dream of Gerontius* and of Mahler's *Lied von der Erde*.

Fervaal. Opera in prologue and 3 acts by d'Indy; libretto by the composer.

First perf., Brussels, La Monnaie, Mar. 12, 1897: Raunay, Imbart de la Tour, Sequin, c. Flon.

A somber, expansive score employing Wagnerian techniques in highly individual ways. In the Midi region of France, during the Saracen invasions, the wounded Celtic chief Fervaal (t) is nursed to health by the Saracen sorceress Guilhen (s), and falls in love with her. Deceived by the Druid Artagard (bar) into believing Fervaal unfaithful, Guilhen leads the Celts to their deaths.

Feuersnot (Fire Famine). Opera in 1 act by R. Strauss; libretto by Ernst von Wolzogen, after a legend in J.W. Wolf's *Sagas of the Netherlands*.

First perf., Dresden, Court Opera, Nov. 21, 1901: Krull, Scheidemantel, c. von Schuch. U.S. prem., Philadelphia, Metropolitan Opera House, Dec. 1, 1927: c. Smallens.

Strauss' first successful opera takes revenge on Munich for its hostility to Wagner and rejection of his *Guntram*. On, St. John's Eve in 12th-c. Munich, Kunrad (bar) causes all the fires of the town to die out until Diemut (s), the woman he loves (and who publicly humiliated him for his ardor) acknowledges the passion between them.

Février, Henri. Composer; b. Paris, Oct. 2, 1875; d. Paris, July 8, 1957. Studied with Fauré and Massenet at Paris Conservatory. His operas include *Le Roi Aveugle* (1906); *Monna Vanna* (1909), after Maeterlinck, played at the Met in 1914 by the Philadelphia–Chicago Opera; and *Gismonda* (1918), after Sardou, performed at the Met in 1919 by the Chicago Opera. Composed in the general style of Massenet, Février's operas have not survived in the repertory.

Fiamma, La (The Flame). Opera in 3 acts by Respighi; libretto by Claudio Guastalla, after a play by Hans Wiers-Jenssen.

First perf., Rome, Reale, Jan. 23, 1934: Cobelli, Minghetti, Tagliabue, c. Respighi. U.S. prem., Chicago, Dec. 2, 1935: Raisa, Bentonelli, Morelli, c. Hageman.

Respighi's last completed opera is a tale of witchcraft and adultery in 17th-c. Ravenna.

Fidelio, oder Die eheliche Liebe (Fidelio, or Married Love). Opera in 2 (originally 3) acts by Beethoven; libretto by Joseph von Sonnleithner, after Jean Nicolas Bouilly's play *Léonore, ou L'Amour Conjugal*.

First perf. (in 3 acts, with Leonore Overture No. 2), Vienna, an der Wien, Nov. 20, 1805: Milder, Müller, Demmer, Mayer, Rothe, c. Seyfried. Second version (rev. in 2 acts by Stefan von Breuning, with Leonore Overture No. 3), first perf., Vienna, an der Wien, Mar. 29, 1806: same cast, except Röckel as Florestan. Final version (with "Fidelio" overture in E major), first perf., Vienna, Kärntnertor, May 23, 1814: Milder, Bondra, Radichi, Vogl, Weinmüller, c. Umlauf. U.S. prem., N.Y., Park,

Sep. 9, 1839. Met prem., Nov. 19, 1884: Brandt, Kraus, Schott, Robinson, Miller, c. L. Damrosch. Later Met productions: Mar. 20, 1908: Morena, Alten, Burrian, Goritz, Blass, c. Mahler, d. Roller, p. Schertel; Jan. 22, 1927 (with recits. by Bodanzky): Larsén-Todsén, Fleischer, Laubenthal, Schorr, Bohnen, c. Bodanzky, d. Urban, p. Wymetal; Jan. 28, 1960: Lövberg, Hurley, Vickers, Uhde, Czerwenka, c. Böhm, d. Armistead, p. Graf; Dec. 16, 1970: Rysanek, Blegen, Vickers, Berry, Tozzi, c. Böhm, d. Aronson, p. Schenk. Leonore has also been sung at the Met by Lilli Lehmann, Ternina, Matzenauer, Kurt, Kappel, Ohms, Flagstad, Resnik, Nilsson, G. Jones, Behrens; Florestan by Niemann, Alvary, Urlus, Sembach, Maison, Svanholm, J. Thomas, King, McCracken; Pizarro by Whitehill, Hofmann, Schöffler, Frantz; Rocco by Fischer, E. de Reszke, List, Kipnis, Edelmann, Moll; other conductors have included Hertz, Walter, Tennstedt, Haitink. 153 perfs. in 35 seasons.

Beethoven struggled with *Fidelio*, his only opera, over a decade; vocal writing and operatic style in general did not come easily to him, in part because he insisted on a direct confrontation with the ideals of human freedom that moved him most deeply. The result is a work of high inspiration; great conductors and great sopranos of the German repertory have repeatedly reached their highest level of achievement in it.

A prison near Seville, 18th c. To free her husband Florestan (t), a nobleman imprisoned for political reasons, Leonore (s) disguises herself as a boy, "Fidelio," and is hired by the jailer Rocco (bs). Rocco's daughter Marzelline (s), enamored of Fidelio and hoping to marry him, rejects her sweetheart, the turnkey Jacquino (t). Fidelio learns that her husband is confined to the deepest dungeon, and that the prison governor Pizarro (bar) plans to murder him lest he be discovered in a pending investigation by the royal minister Don Fernando (bs). After Rocco and Fidelio have dug a grave in the dungeon, Pizarro attempts to kill Florestan, but is thwarted by Fidelio, who comes between them with the exclamation, "First kill his wife!" The arrival of Don Fernando halts the murder; Pizarro is arrested and Fernando grants Leonore the privilege of freeing her husband from his chains.

Fiery Angel, The. Opera in 5 acts by Prokofiev; libretto by the composer, after Valery Bryusov's historical novel.

First perf., Paris, French Radio, Nov. 25, 1954 (concert perf., in Fr.): Marée, Depraz, c. Bruck. First staged perf., Venice, Fenice, Sep. 29, 1955 (in Ital.): Dow, Panerai, c. Sanzogno. U.S. prem., N.Y.C. Opera, Sep. 22, 1965 (in Eng.): Schauler, Milnes, c. Rudel.

Only Act II of this opera, composed 1919–27, was heard during the composer's lifetime, at a 1928 Paris concert under Koussevitzky; parts of the urgent, dissonant music for this expressionistic tale were reused in his Third Symphony.

Germany, 16th c. The knight Ruprecht (bar) falls in love with Renata (s), who believes Count Heinrich (mute) to be the incarnation of an angel who visited her in her childhood. After inciting Ruprecht to a duel with Heinrich and nursing him back to health, Renata enters a convent, where she attracts evil spirits and is ordered to be tortured and burned by the Inquisitor (bs).

Figner [Mei-Figner, née Mei], **Medea.** Soprano; b. Florence, Apr. 4, 1859; d. Paris, July 8, 1952. Trained as mezzo in Florence; debut as Azucena, Sinalunga, 1875. Toured Italy, Spain, South America; in 1887 went with

Fidelio – (1914). Arthur Middleton, Otto Goritz, Jacques Urlus, Margaret Matzenauer, Elisabeth Schumann, Carl Braun

tenor Nikolai Figner (her husband, 1889–1904) to St. Petersburg, where (as soprano) she created Tchaikovsky's Lisa (*Queen of Spades*, 1890), and Iolanta (1892).

Figner, Nikolai. Tenor; b. Nikiforovka, near Kazan, Russia, Feb. 21, 1857; d. Kiev, Dec. 13, 1918. Studied at St. Petersburg Conservatory and with Lamperti in Italy; debut in *Philémon*, Sannazaro, Naples, 1882. Sang in Italy and South America, then in 1887 joined Imperial Opera, St. Petersburg, where he created Herman (*Queen of Spades*, 1890). Married to soprano Medea Figner.

Fille de Madame Angot, La (Mme. Angot's Daughter). Opera in 3 acts by Lecocq; libretto by L. Clairville, P. Siraudin, and V. Koning, after Maillot's vaudeville *Madame Angot*.

First perf., Brussels, Fantasies Parisiennes, Dec. 4, 1872: Desclauzas. U.S. prem., N.Y., Broadway Theater, Aug. 25, 1873. Met prem., New Theater, Dec. 14, 1909: Alda, Clément, Dutilloy, c. Tango.

An opéra bouffe set in late 18th c. Paris. Clairette (s), daughter of the late Madame Angot, who loves the satirist Ange Pitou (t) tries to extricate herself from an engagement to the hairdresser Pomponnet (bar), but ends up planning to marry the man.

Fille du Régiment, La (The Daughter of the Regiment). Opera in 2 acts by Donizetti; libretto by Jules-Henri Vernoy de Saint-Georges and Jean-François-Alfred Bayard.

First perf., Paris, Opéra-Comique, Feb. 11, 1840: Bourgeois, Boulanger, Marié de l'Isle, Henri. U.S. prem., New Orleans, Mar. 2, 1843. Met prem., Jan. 6, 1902: Sembrich, van Cauteren, Salignac, Gilibert, c. Flon. Later Met productions: Dec. 28, 1940: Pons, Petina, Jobin, Baccaloni, c. Papi, d. Jorgulesco/Czettel, p. Graf; Feb. 17, 1972: Sutherland, Resnik, Pavarotti, Corena, c. Bonynge, d. Anni/Escoffier, p. Sequi. Marie has also been sung at the Met by Hempel, Tonio by Kraus, Sulpice by Scotti. 53 perfs. in 10 seasons.

One of the composer's ever-fresh comic operas; Mendelssohn admiringly expressed the wish that he had

Emil Fischer as Hans Sachs in *Die Meistersinger von Nürnberg*

written it, and it points the way to Offenbach's opéras bouffes.

The Swiss Tyrol, about 1815. Marie (s), an orphan raised by the soldiers of the 21st Regiment as their "daughter," loves Tonio (t), a young Tyrolean who has saved her life. He enlists in the regiment in order to marry her, but she is claimed as a long-lost niece by the Marquise de Berkenfeld (c). Marie is bored by aristocratic life at the Marquise's chateau. Tonio and the regiment arrive in time to save her from a forced marriage. The Marquise admits that Marie is her illegitimate daughter and consents to her marriage with Tonio.

finale. In opera, the last number of an act, usually involving ensemble singing and choral parts, and made up of several sections, concluding with a stretta, or movement in rapid tempo.

Finta Giardiniera, La (The Feigned Garden Girl). Opera in 3 acts by Mozart; libretto revised by Marco Cottellini from the libretto (possibly by Raniero de' Calzabigi) of a 1774 opera by Anfossi.

First perf., Munich, Court Theater, Jan. 13, 1775: R. Manservisi, T. Manservisi, Consoli. U.S. prem., N.Y., Mayfair, Jan. 18, 1927 (in Eng.).

An attractive score with an improbable and convoluted plot. Searching in forgiveness for her estranged lover Belfiore (t), the marchioness Violante Onesti (s) disguises herself as the gardener girl Sandrina, but her associates suppose her to be dead, and Belfiore is arrested for murder. The various complications are brought to a happy conclusion.

Finto Stanislao, Il (The False Stanislao), see *Giorno di Regno, Un.*

fioritura (Ital., "flowering"). Coloratura passages.

Fischer, Emil. Bass; b. Brunswick, Germany, June 13, 1838; d. Hamburg, Aug. 11, 1914. Studied with his parents, both singers; debut (as tenor), Seneschal in Boieldieu's *Jean de Paris*, Graz, 1857. Appeared as baritone in Danzig (1863–70), Rotterdam (1875–80), and Dresden (1880–85). Covent Garden debut as Sachs, 1884. Met debut as King Heinrich (*Lohengrin*), Nov. 23, 1885; in 7 seasons, he sang 324 perfs. of 30 roles, including Sachs, King Marke, the *Rheingold* and *Siegfried* Wotans, and Hagen. Also appeared with Damrosch's touring company (from 1894), and sang Sachs (Act III, Scene 1) at testimonial performance, Met, 1907; taught in N.Y. until shortly before his death. For the warmth and geniality of his Sachs, Fischer was remembered and cited as the standard until the advent of Friedrich Schorr.

Fischer, Ludwig. Bass; b. Mainz, Germany, Aug. 18, 1745; d. Berlin, July 10, 1825. Studied with Anton Raaff, Mannheim. Appointed singer at Mannheim court, 1772, moving with it to Munich in 1778. Sang opera in Vienna (1780–83, creating Mozart's Osmin), Paris (1783), Prague and Dresden (1785), London (1794). Composer of the once-popular bass encore, "Im tiefen Keller."

Fischer-Dieskau, Dietrich. Baritone; b. Zehlendorf, near Berlin, May 28, 1925. Studied in Berlin with Georg Walter and Hermann Weissenborn. Served in the German army; appeared occasionally as singer while prisoner of war in Italy. Further study with Weissenborn after the war. Concert debut in Brahms' *Deutsches Requiem*, Freiburg, 1947. Operatic debut as Posa (*Don Carlos*),

Dietrich Fischer-Dieskau as Don Giovanni

Städtische Oper, Berlin, 1948; many appearances at the house thereafter. Sang in Vienna and Munich from 1949, Salzburg from 1952, Bayreuth 1954–56 as Herald (*Lohengrin*), Wolfram, Kothner, and Amfortas. Covent Garden debut as Mandryka (*Arabella*), 1965. Created Mittenhofer (*Elegy for Young Lovers*) and Reimann's Lear. Fischer-Dieskau's intelligence, poetic sensibility, and command of nuance have made him such a pre-eminent interpreter of lieder as to overshadow his operatic work, especially in the U.S. (where it is known only through recordings). But in stage roles that show off these traits (and his considerable acting ability), he has given distinguished performances. Mozart (Don Giovanni, Don Alfonso, the Speaker in *Zauberflöte*, Almaviva) and Strauss (Jochanaan, Barak in *Frau*, Olivier and the Count in *Capriccio*) are specialties, as are 20th-c. roles (Doktor Faust, Hindemith's Mathis, Berg's Wozzeck and Dr. Schön). Nor has he neglected Verdi (Renato, Falstaff) and Wagner (Kurwenal, Sachs, the *Rheingold* Wotan). He has appeared in opera and concert with his wife, the soprano Julia Varady.
BIBLIOGRAPHY: Kenneth S. Whitton, *Dietrich Fischer-Dieskau, Mastersinger: a Documented Study* (N.Y., 1981).

Fitziu [Fitzhugh], **Anna.** Soprano; b. Huntington, W. Va. 1887; d. Hollywood, Calif., Apr. 20, 1967. Studied with William Thorner, Paris; debut as Elsa, Milan, 1910. Her only 5 Met appearances were as Rosario in the world premiere of *Goyescas*, Jan. 28, 1916. Sang in Rome, Naples, Palermo, Florence, Buenos Aires, and Chicago (1917–19, 1922–25).

Flagello, Ezio. Bass; b. New York, Jan. 28, 1931. Studied with Schorr and Brownlee at Manhattan School, N.Y., Luigi Ricci in Rome; debut as Dulcamara, Empire State Festival, Ellenville, N.Y., 1955. Met debut as Jailer (*Tosca*), Nov. 9, 1957; subsequently sang Leporello, Pogner, Philippe II, and Rossini buffo roles, and created Enobarbus (*Antony and Cleopatra*), 1966; 407 perfs. of 48 roles. Has also appeared in Vienna, Milan, and Berlin.

Flagstad, Kirsten. Soprano; b. Hamar, Norway, July 12, 1895; d. Oslo, Dec. 7, 1962. Her father was a conductor, her mother a coach and pianist (and her first teacher). Further study in Oslo with Ellen Schytte-Jacobsen and in Stockholm with Dr. Gillis Bratt. Debut as Nuri (*Tiefland*), Oslo, National Theater, 1913. For the next 18 years, she sang opera, operetta, and musical comedy in Scandinavia. Her first Isolde (Oslo, June 29, 1932) led to Bayreuth engagements in small parts (1933), then as Sieglinde and Gutrune (1934), and to a Met audition to succeed Frida Leider. Her unheralded Met debut as Sieglinde, broadcast nationwide on Feb. 2, 1935, created a sensation; she sang Isolde there four days later, and her first-ever Brünnhildes (*Walküre, Götterdämmerung*) later that month, revealing herself as the pre-eminent Wagnerian soprano of her generation. That season she also sang Elsa, Elisabeth, and her first Kundry; Senta and the *Siegfried* Brünnhilde followed in 1937. Fidelio (1936) was her only non-Wagner Met role before the war. She sang the same repertory in San Francisco (1935–38) and Chicago (1937). At Covent Garden (1936–37), she sang Wagner under Reiner, Beecham, and Furtwängler. In 1941 she rejoined her husband in Nazi-occupied Norway; although she refused to sing there, her husband's brief collaboration with the Nazis later caused ill-feeling toward her in the U.S. She resumed her European career in 1947, and returned to Covent Garden in 1948 and San Francisco in 1949, but was not asked back to the Met until Bing became

Kirsten Flagstad as Isolde in *Tristan und Isolde*

Kirsten Flagstad as Fidelio

Der fliegende Holländer – Salzburg Easter Festival, 1982.
Designed by Günther Schneider-Siemssen, produced by
Herbert von Karajan

manager; in 1950–51, she showed herself still in remarkable form in *Tristan*, a *Ring* cycle, and *Fidelio*. Gluck's *Alceste* (in Eng.) was the role of her Met farewell, Apr. 1, 1952; in 9 seasons with the company, she had sung 193 perfs. of 11 roles. She sang Fidelio at Salzburg under Furtwängler, 1949–50. Her last operatic performances were as Purcell's Dido, Mermaid Theatre, London, 1953. She continued to record and sing concerts, and was director of the Norwegian National Opera, 1958–60.

When her late-blooming international career got under way, Flagstad already possessed a radiant, mature voice, plus the stamina to encompass the heaviest roles without forcing or tiring. An impeccable musician in matters of rhythm and intonation, her interpretations emphasized clarity more than passion, although she achieved considerable emotional growth in her roles. Among her 40 years' worth of recordings, the complete *Tristan* with Furtwängler is the most imposing document, though the prewar recordings show the voice in its freshest brilliance and clarity.

BIBLIOGRAPHY: Kirsten Flagstad (with Louis Biancolli), *The Flagstad Manuscript* (N.Y., 1952). Edwin McArthur, *Flagstad: A Personal Memoir* (N.Y., 1965).

Flaming Angel, The. See *Fiery Angel, The*.

Fledermaus, Die (The Bat). Operetta in 3 acts by J. Strauss; libretto by Carl Haffner and Richard Genée, after the comedy *Le Réveillon* by Meilhac and Halévy, based in turn on Roderich Benedix's comedy *Das Gefängnis*.

First perf., Vienna, an der Wien, Apr. 5, 1874: Geistinger, Hirsch, Nittinger, Szika, Rüdinger, Lebrecht, c. Strauss. U.S. prem., N.Y., Thalia Theater, Nov. 21, 1874. Met prem., Feb. 16, 1905: Sembrich, Alten, Walker, Dippel, Reiss, Greder, Goritz, c. Franko, d. J. Fox, p. Greder. Later Met productions: Dec. 20, 1950 (in Eng.): Welitsch, Munsel, Stevens, Svanholm, Tucker, Brownlee, Thompson, c. Ormandy, d. Gérard, p. Kanin; Dec. 4, 1986 (dialogue in Eng.): Te Kanawa, Blegen, Troyanos, Hagegård, Rendall, Devlin, Mazura, c. Tate, d. Schneider-Siemssen/P.J. Hall, p. Schenk.

Fledermaus typifies the conventions of the Viennese operetta as it developed in the decades surrounding the turn of the century, and its charming tunes and comic situations have made it the most successful such work to have entered the international operatic repertory.

Dr. Falke (bar) has decided to get even with his friend

Gabriel von Eisenstein (t) for a practical joke in which Falke, waking on a park bench the morning after a costume ball, dressed as a bat, found himself the laughing stock of passersby. About to leave to serve a five-day prison term for a minor offense, Eisenstein accepts Falke's invitation to attend a party given by the Russian Prince Orlovsky (ms), and postpones jail to the morrow. After the men leave, Eisenstein's wife Rosalinde (s) gives her maid Adele (s) the night off, and receives a former admirer, the singer Alfred (t), for a tête-à-tête. The prison warden Frank (bar) arrives to collect Eisenstein; taking the embarrassed Rosalinde's word that this man is her husband, he whisks Alfred off to jail. At Orlovsky's party, Falke's plot gets into full swing. Rosalinde, Adele, and Frank appear in disguise; Eisenstein flirts with Adele, who persuades him she is not his wife's chambermaid, and then with his wife, whom he does not recognize in her disguise as a Hungarian countess. The next morning in jail, more complications arise, with the amiable assistance of the drunken jailer Frosch (speaking role); Eisenstein determines to find out who was arrested in his place, while Rosalinde confronts him with the watch he had left in the hands of the "countess." Falke manages to iron things out and everyone agrees to blame the champagne.

Fleta, Miguel. Tenor; b. Albalate de Cinca, Spain, Dec. 28, 1893; d. La Coruna, May 31, 1938. Studied at Barcelona Conservatory and with Luisa Pierrich (whom he later married), Milan; debut as Paolo (*Francesca*), Trieste, 1919. Met debut as Cavaradossi, Nov. 8, 1923; in 2 seasons, he sang 31 perfs. of 9 roles, including the Duke of Mantua, Mascagni's Fritz, Radames, Canio, and Hoffmann. Created Zandonai's Romeo and Puccini's Calaf.

Fliegende Holländer, Der (The Flying Dutchman). Opera in 3 acts by Wagner; libretto by the composer, after the legend as told in Heine's *Memoirs of Herr von Schnabelewopski*.

First perf., Dresden, Court Opera, Jan. 2, 1843: Schröder-Devrient, Reinhold, Wächter, Risse, c. Wagner. U.S. prem., Philadelphia, Academy of Music, Nov. 8, 1876, (in Ital. as *Il Vascello Fantasma*): Pappenheim, Baccei, Preusser, Sullivan, c. Carlberg. Met prem., Nov. 27, 1889: Wiesner, Kalisch, Reichmann, Fischer, c. Seidl, p. Habelmann. Later Met productions: Nov. 1, 1930: Jeritza, Laubenthal, Schorr, Andrésen, c. Bodanzky, d. Soudeikine, p. Wymetal; Nov. 9, 1950: Varnay, Svanholm, Hotter, Nilsson, c. Reiner, d. Elson after Jones/Schenck, p. Graf; Mar. 8, 1979: Neblett, Lewis, van Dam, Plishka, c. Levine, d. Ponnelle/Halmen, p. Ponnelle. The Dutchman has also been sung at the Met by Lassalle, van Rooy, Janssen, London; Senta by Albani, Gadski, Ternina, Flagstad, Rysanek, Nilsson; Erik by Lorenz, Kónya; Daland by E. de Reszke. 101 perfs. in 17 seasons.

A powerfully constructed essay in Romantic German opera as Wagner inherited it from Marschner. Wagner's original intention that the opera should be played without intermissions is today often observed.

A Norwegian fishing village, 18th c. As punishment for a foolish oath, the Flying Dutchman (bar) has been doomed to sail the seas for eternity, unless he can find a woman who will remain faithful to him unto death. Once every seven years, he is permitted to come ashore in search of such a woman. Putting ashore in Norway, he encounters the sea captain Daland (bs), who, impressed by the stranger's wealth, encourages him to consider marriage with his daughter Senta (s). Though courted by Erik (t), a huntsman, she has long brooded on the legend of the

Flying Dutchman, and immediately falls in love with him when she meets him. Later he comes upon her pleading with Erik to understand her feelings, rashly concludes that she has been unfaithful, and puts out to sea in despair. Senta throws herself from a cliff, calling after him that she is faithful unto death; the Dutchman's ship sinks, and the two are seen rising transfigured to heaven.

Florence. City in Italy, and the birthplace of opera. Peri's *Dafne*, the first opera, was performed there in 1597, and 17th-c. works were sung at court theaters, including those of the Pitti Palace and the Uffizi, and in other houses. In 1656, the Accademia degli Immobili opened the Teatro della Pergola, which, altered by Antonio Galli–Bibiena in 1738 and refurbished in 1857, still stands. The dynamic impresario Alessandro Lanari became manager in 1830, and the theater staged important premieres, including Verdi's *Macbeth* (1847), and the first Italian performances of works by Mozart and Meyerbeer. The Teatro Politeama Fiorentino Vittorio Emmanuele was opened in 1864; altered in 1883 and 1960, it has been known since 1932 as the Teatro Comunale (capacity 2,500). In addition to a winter opera season (current artistic director, Bruno Bartoletti), the Comunale houses the Florence Maggio Musicale (May Festival), established in 1933. Under the direction of Guido M. Gatti, later Mario Labroca (1937–44) and Francesco Siciliani (1950–56), the Maggio presented important premieres and played a leading role in the revival of early opera and the bel canto literature. Recent artistic directors have been Luciano Berio (1984), Fedele d'Amico (1985), and Zubin Mehta (1986).

Florentinische Tragödie, Eine (A Florentine Tragedy). Opera in 1 act by Zemlinsky; libretto after Max Meyerfeld's translation of Oscar Wilde's fragmentary drama.
First perf., Stuttgart, Jan. 30, 1917: c. von Schillings. U.S. prem., N.Y., Manhattan School of Music, Apr. 22, 1982 (in Eng.).
A love triangle of passionate jealousy, with lush, Straussian scoring, set in Renaissance Florence. The merchant Simone (bar) is transformed from a passive cuckold to become the killer of Guido Bardi (t), lover of his wife Bianca (s).

Flotow, Friedrich von. Composer; b. Teutendorf, near Neu-Sanitz, Germany, Apr. 27, 1812; d. Darmstadt, Jan. 24, 1883. From an aristocratic family, he studied at Paris Conservatory with Anton Reicha and was encouraged by friends such as Gounod and Offenbach to compose operas. His first successes were comic works in collaboration with more experienced colleagues, but in 1844 he produced the independently composed, widely performed Romantic opera *Alessandro Stradella*, followed in 1847 by *Martha*, which is still in the active repertory. A dozen further operas, with frequent revisions and alternate versions in French and German, failed to repeat *Martha*'s success. Eclectic blends of opéra comique and singspiel with Italianate lyricism, Flotow's works are engaging though devoid of harmonic or structural originality.

Floyd, Carlisle. Composer; b. Latta, S. C., June 11, 1926. Studied with Ernst Bacon at Syracuse U. His opera *Susannah* (1955), in a vernacular style, has been a huge success. Later scores, musically more sophisticated and eclectic, include *Wuthering Heights* (1958); *The Passion of Jonathan Wade* (1962); *Of Mice and Men* (1970), after Steinbeck; *Bilby's Doll* (1976); and *Willie Stark* (1981).

Flying Dutchman, The. See *Fliegende Holländer, Der*

Foldi, Andrew [András Harry Földi]. Bass; b. Budapest, July 20, 1920. Studied at U. of Chicago and with Martial Singher, Richard de Young, and Maria Carpi; debut as Biondello (Giannini's *Taming of the Shrew*), Chicago, 1954. Met debut as Alberich (*Rheingold*), Feb. 22, 1975; has sung 64 perfs. of 9 roles there, including Beckmesser, both Bartolos, Dansker (*Billy Budd*), and Schigolch (*Lulu*). Has also appeared in Milan, Vienna, Naples, Munich, Glyndebourne, San Francisco, Houston, Santa Fe.

Forrester, Maureen. Contralto; b. Montreal, July 25, 1930. Studied in Montreal; recital debut there, 1953; sang with N.Y. Philharmonic, 1957; member, Bach Aria Group, 1965–74. Operatic debut as Gluck's Orfeo, Toronto, 1961; subsequently sang with N.Y.C. Opera (debut, Cornelia in *Giulio Cesare*, 1966) and San Francisco (Cieca, 1967). Met debut as Erda (*Rheingold*), Feb. 10, 1975; in 2 seasons, sang 14 perfs., including Erda (*Siegfried*) and Ulrica.

Forsell, John [Johan]. Baritone; b. Stockholm, Nov. 6, 1868; d. Stockholm, May 30, 1941. Studied in Stockholm; debut there as Rossini's Figaro, 1896. Sang at Royal Opera until 1911, and as guest until 1938, specializing in Mozart. In his only Met season, sang 11 perfs. of Telramund (debut, Nov. 20, 1909), Amfortas, Germont, Rossini's Figaro, Tonio, and Yeletzky (*Queen of Spades*). Director of Stockholm Opera, 1924–39; at Stockholm Conservatory, taught Bjoerling and Svanholm.

Forza del Destino, La (The Force of Destiny). Opera in 4 acts by Verdi; libretto by Piave, after the play *Don Alvaro, o La Fuerza del Sino* by Angel de Saavedra, Duke of Rivas.
First perf., St. Petersburg, Bolshoi, Nov. 10, 1862: Barbot, Nanticr-Didier, Tamberlik, Graziani, Angelini. Rev. version (with libretto additions by Ghislanzoni), Milan, La Scala, Feb. 27, 1869: Stolz, Benzi, Tiberini, Colonnese, Junca. U.S. prem., N.Y., Academy of Music, Feb. 24, 1865. Met prem., Nov. 15, 1918: Ponselle, Gentle, Caruso, de Luca, Mardones, c. Papi, p. Ordynski. Later Met productions: Nov. 10, 1952: Milanov, Miller, Tucker, Warren, Siepi, c. Stiedry, d. Berman, p. Graf; Jan. 17, 1975 ("revised," with Inn Scene restored): Arroyo, Casei, Vickers, MacNeil, Giaiotti, c. Levine d. Berman/P.J. Hall, p. Dexter. Leonora has also been sung at the Met by Rethberg, Tebaldi, L. Price, Farrell; Alvaro by Martinelli, del Monaco, Domingo; Carlo by Amato, Tibbett, Bastianini, Milnes; the Padre Guardiano by Pinza, Hines, Talvela, Raimondi. 166 perfs. in 25 seasons.
Spain and Italy, 18th c. While attempting to elope with Leonora di Vargas (s), Don Alvaro (t), a nobleman partly of Inca lineage, accidentally kills her father, the Marchese di Calatrava (bs). In flight, the lovers become separated, and are sought by Leonora's brother Don Carlo di Vargas (bar), who intends to kill them to avenge his father's murder and sister's dishonor. Disguised as a man, Leonora seeks refuge in a monastery, and is granted a hermitage by the abbot, the Padre Guardiano (bs). Alvaro becomes a soldier and through a series of coincidences saves Carlo's life on an Italian battlefield. Unaware of each other's true identity, the two swear eternal friendship, but Carlo later discovers a picture of Leonora among Alvaro's papers. Intent on revenge, he draws Alvaro to duel, but they are interrupted, and Alvaro retreats to a monastery. Inter-

spersed with these events are lively incidental scenes of military life, in which Verdi introduces two comic characters, a gypsy vivandière, Preziosilla (ms), and a chattering friar, Melitone (bar). Back in Spain, Carlo discovers Alvaro's retreat – the monastery of the Padre Guardiano – and again provokes a duel, in which he is mortally wounded. Calling a nearby hermit to absolve his enemy, Alvaro discovers that the hermit is Leonora, who rushes to her dying brother; stabbed by the unforgiving Carlo, she dies in the presence of the Padre Guardiano and the repentant Alvaro. (In the opera's original version, Alvaro casts himself off a precipice, cursing destiny.)

Fourestier, Louis. Conductor; b. Montpellier, France, May 31, 1892; d. Boulogne-Billancourt, Sep. 30, 1976. After a Prix de Rome tenure (1925), conducted at Paris Opéra-Comique (1927–32) and Opéra (from 1938). During two Met seasons (debut, *Lakmé*, Nov. 11, 1946), he led *Faust*, *Carmen*, *Manon*, and *Louise*. On the faculty of the Paris Conservatory (1945–63).

Fournet, Jean. Conductor; b. Rouen, France, April 14, 1913. Studied at Paris Conservatory with Gaubert; debut in Rouen, 1936. Music director, Opéra-Comique (1944–57), Netherlands Radio Orchestra (1961–68), Rotterdam Philharmonic (since 1968). Debuts in Chicago (1965) and at Met (1987) in *Samson*.

Four Saints in Three Acts. Opera in 4 acts by Thomson; libretto by Gertrude Stein.
First perf., Hartford, Conn., Avery Memorial Theatre, Feb. 8, 1934: Matthews, Wayne, Howard, Bonner, Baker, c. Smallens. Met prem., Feb. 20, 1973 (Mini-Met): Thompson, Dale, Harris, H. Price, Hendricks, c. Gagnon, d. Lee/Greenwood, p. Ailey.
Thomson's simple and melodic music, reminiscent of Baptist hymns, contrasts with Stein's plotless, surreal libretto. (The painter Maurice Grosser prepared a scenario for performance purposes, often followed.) For the premiere, Thomson cast only black singers, believing their diction to be superior – a tradition that has persisted, although not intended to be binding.
Spain, 16th c. The opera shows the daily lives of a religious community, in incidents ranging from a garden party to several heavenly visions, framed by processions and tableaux; Stein's whimsical word-plays do not necessarily relate to the action at hand.

Fox, Carol. Manager; b. Chicago, June 15, 1926; d. Chicago, July 21, 1981. Studied singing with Lazzari and Martinelli in N.Y. In 1952, she, conductor Nicola Rescigno, and businessman Lawrence Kelly founded the Lyric Theater of Chicago (later Lyric Opera of Chicago), which presented *Don Giovanni* in Feb. 1954, and the following fall offered a brilliant season, including the U.S. debut of Callas, re-establishing international opera in the city. In 1956, after a bitter power struggle, Rescigno and Kelly left to found the Dallas Civic Opera, and Fox remained general manager of the Chicago company for 25 years (1956–1981).

Fox, Frederick. Designer; b. New York, July 10, 1910. Originally an architect, influenced by Mielziner, Simonson, and R.E. Jones, he developed an original style of architectural design well suited for Broadway. For the Met, he designed *Andrea Chénier* (1954), a "revised" *Tosca* (1955), and *Simon Boccanegra* (1960).

Fra Diavolo, ou L'Hôtellerie de Terracine (Fra Diavolo, or The Inn at Terracine). Opera in 3 acts by Auber; libretto by Scribe and Germain Delavigne.
First perf., Paris, Opéra-Comique, Jan. 28, 1830: Boulanger, Prévost, Chollet, Féréol. U.S. prem., Philadelphia, Chestnut Street, Sep. 16, 1831. Met prem., Feb. 5, 1910: Alten, Maubourg, Clément, Ananian, c. Hertz, d. Fox/Musaeus, Blaschke. 3 perfs. in 1 season.
Auber's most successful opera outside France is set near Naples, 18th c. The bandit Fra Diavolo (t) is repeatedly thwarted in his attempts on the gold of a travelling English couple, and the reward for his capture enables the soldier Lorenzo (t) to marry the innkeeper's daughter Zerlina (s).

Fra Gherardo. Opera in 3 acts by Pizzetti; libretto by the composer after the 13th-c. chronicles of Salimbene de Parma.
First perf., Milan, La Scala, May 16, 1928: Cristoforeanu, Trantoul, Baccaloni, c. Toscanini. U.S. & Met prem., Mar. 21, 1929: Müller, Johnson, Pinza, c. Serafin, d. Urban, p. Agnini. 4 perfs. in 1 season.
Pizzetti's fifth opera continues the development of his arioso style. In 12th-c. Parma, Gherardo (t), a rich weaver, leaves town to atone for having compromised the orphan girl Mariola (s); he later returns as a friar and fights the corrupt authorities, but is condemned to the stake for heresy.

Francesca da Rimini. Opera in 4 acts by Zandonai; libretto by Tito Ricordi, after d'Annunzio's play.
First perf., Turin, Regio, Feb. 19, 1914: Canetti, Crimi, Cigada, c. Panizza, U.S. & Met prem., Dec. 22, 1916: Alda, Martinelli, Amato, c. Polacco, d. Sala/Caramba, p. Speck. Later Met production: Mar. 9, 1984: Scotto, Domingo, MacNeil, c. Levine, d. Frigerio/Squarciapino, p. Faggioni. 27 perfs. in 4 seasons.
A richly scored work reflecting Wagnerian and Straussian influence on the post-verismo Italians. The subject is drawn from a famous passage in Dante's *Inferno*, based on an historical event.
Ravenna and Rimini, later 13th c. Francesca (s) is promised in marriage to Gianciotto (bar), the deformed son of Malatesta, and is tricked into accepting under the impression that his fair brother Paolo (t) is the intended groom. Paolo returns Francesca's love; a third brother, Malatestino (t) also desires her but is repulsed. He betrays the lovers to Gianciotto, who kills them both.

Franchetti, Alberto. Composer; b. Turin, Italy, Sep. 18, 1860; d. Viareggio, Aug. 4, 1942. Studied with Draeseke and Rheinberger. His operas emulate the monumentality of Meyerbeer and the massive scoring of Wagner. Successful around the turn of the century were the allegorical *Asrael* (1888), and the historical *Cristoforo Colombo* (1892) and *Germania* (1902). Later works made little impression, and Franchetti is most often remembered as the composer who lost the *Tosca* libretto to Puccini.

Franci, Benvenuto. Baritone; b. Pienza, Italy, July 1, 1891; d. Rome, Feb. 27, 1985. Studied with Cotogni and Rosati, Rome; debut as Giannetto (*Lodoletta*), Costanzi, Rome, 1918. Member of La Scala (1923–26) and Rome Opera (1928–49). Created roles in Mascagni's *Piccolo Marat* (Costanzi, 1921), Giordano's *Cena delle Beffe* (Scala, 1924), Zandonai's *Cavalieri di Ekebù* (Scala, 1925). Retired in 1955. Father of conductor Carlo Franci (b. 1927).

Franci, Carlo. Conductor; b. Buenos Aires, July 18, 1927. After study at Rome Conservatory and conducting mainly orchestral repertory, he made his operatic debut in 1959 at Spoleto (*Hänsel*). With Rome Opera, conducted Rossini's *Otello* during visit to Met, June 1968. Met company debut, *Lucia* (Feb. 1, 1969); led 5 other Italian works, 1969–72.

Franck, César. Composer; b. Liège, Belgium, Dec. 10, 1822; d. Paris, Nov. 8, 1890. A child prodigy at the piano, he attended Liège and Paris Conservatories, studying theory with Leborne. The early opera *Stradella* (c. 1844) and the opéra comique *Le Valet de Ferme* (1853) were unproduced. Fruits of his later fascination with Wagnerian harmony were *Hulda* (1885) and the "lyric drama" *Ghiselle* (unfinished, completed by colleagues), performed posthumously (1894 and 1896, respectively) with little success.

Franke, Paul. Tenor; b. Boston, Dec. 23, 1920. Studied at New England Conservatory. Met debut as Youth (*Amore dei Tre Re*), Dec. 1, 1948; has subsequently performed nearly 1,500 perfs. of over 60 roles there, including Cassio, David (*Meistersinger*), and Goro.

Frantz, Ferdinand. Bass-baritone; b. Kassel, Germany, Feb. 8, 1906; d. Munich, May 26, 1959. Studied privately; debut at Ortel (*Meistersinger*), Kassel, 1927. After engagements in Halle, Chemnitz, Hamburg, joined Bavarian State Opera, Munich (1943–59). Met debut as Wotan (*Walküre*), Dec. 12, 1949; in 3 seasons, he sang 20 perfs. of 8 roles, including Pizarro (*Fidelio*) as well as Wagner baritone and bass parts. Also sang in Milan, Vienna, London, and Paris. Married to soprano Helena Braun (b. 1903), who sang one Met Brünnhilde opposite him, Dec. 21, 1949.

Franz, Paul [François Gautier]. Tenor; b. Paris, Nov. 30, 1876; d. Paris, Apr. 20, 1950. Studied with Louis Delaquerrière in Paris; debut as Lohengrin, Opéra, 1909; remained on roster until 1938, singing Énée (*Troyens*), Samson, Wagner roles, and creating Ratan-Sen in *Padmâvatî* (1923). Also sang at Covent Garden (1910–14), La Scala (1915), Buenos Aires (1918), Monte Carlo (1923).

Fraschini, Gaetano. Tenor; b. Pavia, Italy, Feb. 16, 1816; d. Naples, May 23, 1887. Studied with Moretti; debut in Pavia, 1837. Appeared at La Scala (1840) and San Carlo, Naples (1840–48), where he created Gerardo in *Caterina Cornaro* (1844). Admired by Verdi, for whom he created roles in *Alzira*, *Corsaro*, *Battaglia di Legnano*, and *Stiffelio*, 1845–50. Also sang in London (1847) and Paris (1864).

Frau ohne Schatten, Die (The Woman Without a Shadow). Opera in 3 acts by R. Strauss; libretto by Hofmannsthal, after his own story.

First perf., Vienna, State Opera, Oct. 10, 1919: Jeritza, Lehmann, Weidt, Oestvig, Mayr, c. Schalk. U.S. prem., San Francisco, Sep. 18, 1959: Lang, Schech, Dalis, Feiersinger, Yahia, c. Ludwig. Met prem., Oct. 2, 1966: Rysanek, Ludwig, Dalis, King, Berry, c. Böhm, d. O'Hearn, p. Merrill. The Empress has also been sung at the Met by Marton; the Dyer's Wife by Nilsson. 34 perfs. in 5 seasons.

A fantastic, imaginatively and exotically scored treatment of the theme of procreation as the necessary completion of love; because of its elaborate scenic and

Die Frau ohne Schatten – (1966). Designed by Robert O'Hearn, produced by Nathaniel Merrill. James King, Leonie Rysanek, Walter Berry, and Christa Ludwig

vocal demands, it only slowly found widespread performance.

A mythical time and place. The Emperor (t) has married a supernatural woman, whose spirit father has decreed that if the marriage remains childless (a state symbolized by the Empress' inability to cast a shadow), his daughter must return to the supernatural world and the Emperor be turned to stone. With her Nurse (ms), the Empress goes among men in search of a shadow. They come to the hut of the dyer Barak (bar) and his wife (s), who have no children themselves, though the wife has a shadow. She is a nagger and a complainer, and readily agrees to sell her prospects of motherhood in return for the riches the Nurse depicts for her. After witnessing Barak's shock and pain when his wife confesses what she is about to do, the Empress refuses to take the shadow at such a price. Later, seeing the couple in subterranean, supernatural punishment, and seeing her husband nearly turned to stone, she still refuses to take a shadow at the expense of another's; at that moment of resolute compassion, a shadow is granted her, and all are delivered from their sufferings.

Freischütz, Der (The Free-shooter). Opera in 3 acts by Weber; libretto by Friedrich Kind, after a Gothic legend and a story by Johann August Apel and Friedrich Laun.

First perf., Berlin, Schauspielhaus, June 18, 1821: Seidler, Eunicke, Stümer, Blume, c. Weber. U.S. prem. (in Eng.): N.Y., Park, Mar. 2, 1825. Met prem., Nov. 24, 1884: Schröder-Hanfstängl, Kraus, Udvardy, Kögel, c. L. Damrosch, d. J. Fox/Schaeffer, p. Hock. Later Met productions: Mar. 22, 1923 (with recitatives by Bodanzky): Rethberg, Mario, Taucher, Bohnen, c. Bodanzky, d. Urban/Castel-Bert, p. Thewman; Sep. 28, 1971: Lorengar, Mathis, Konya, Feldhoff, c. Ludwig, d. & p. Heinrich. Agathe has also been sung at the Met by Destinn, Gadski, Müller, Stückgold; Max by Jadlowker; Caspar by Blass. 26 perfs. in 7 seasons.

In *Freischütz*, Weber pointed the way for a whole era of German Romantic opera. The supernatural elements, the general feeling of northerliness, the inclusion of song-forms along with arias in serious contexts, the rich instrumentation all ensured *Freischütz* a lasting place in the repertory and served as examples for Marschner and the young Wagner.

Bohemia, mid-17th c. To gain the hand of Agathe (s), the forester Max (t) must win the next day's sharpshooting contest. Distraught over losing a preliminary trial, he accepts an offer from Caspar (bs) to obtain magic bullets that never miss. In spite of warnings from Agathe and her cousin Ännchen (s), Max goes to the haunted Wolf's Glen to meet Caspar. In an eerie ritual, seven magic bullets are cast, the seventh to go where Samiel, the Devil (speaking role), wills it. The next day Max finds he has only one bullet; after five bullets have been used, Caspar secretly shoots the sixth into the air, leaving Max's test at Samiel's mercy. When Max fires, both Agathe and Caspar fall, but a holy hermit (bs) restores the girl to life and Samiel claims the traitorous Caspar. Max is to pass a year's probation to prove himself worthy of Agathe.

Fremstad, Olive [Olivia Rundquist]. Mezzo-soprano and soprano; b. Stockholm, Mar. 14, 1871; d. Irvington-on-Hudson, N.Y., Apr. 21, 1951. Born to an unmarried mother, adopted by a Scandinavian-American couple, she grew up and studied piano in Minneapolis. From 1890, she studied singing with E.F. Bristol in N.Y., and appeared in Boston that year as Lady Saphir in Sullivan's *Patience*. After study with Lilli Lehmann in Berlin she made her operatic debut as Azucena, Cologne, 1895, appeared then in Munich, Vienna, Amsterdam, and Antwerp for 3 seasons, and sang contralto roles in the 1896 Bayreuth *Ring*. After study in Italy, she joined the Munich Court Opera (1900–03), singing Carmen and many other roles. Following her debut as Sieglinde, Nov. 25, 1903, she sang

Olive Fremstad as Isolde in *Tristan und Isolde*

To Mrs. to Charles Ditson
with appreciate regards
Olive Fremstad
Isolde 1914

at the Met 11 seasons (until 1914), moving into dramatic soprano parts. Among her 206 perfs. of 18 roles, the most frequent was Venus (43 times), followed by Sieglinde, Kundry, Isolde (which she sang under both Mahler and Toscanini), Elsa, and Carmen; she also sang the three Brünnhildes, Tosca, and the first U.S. perf. of Gluck's Armide. In 1907 she sang the first U.S. *Salome*, and – had the scandalized Met board not forbidden further performances – would have sung a special season of the work under Strauss later that year. She left the Met at the height of her powers, following disagreements with Gatti-Casazza, and sang with the Manhattan, Boston, and Chicago companies, giving her last operatic performance on tour with the Chicago Opera in Minneapolis, as Tosca, in 1918. Her last recital took place in N.Y., Jan. 19, 1920, after which she taught there. Fremstad made few recordings (1911–12), and these are said to be unrepresentative of her sumptuous voice and powerful dramatic temperament. The principal character of Willa Cather's novel *The Song of the Lark* is based on Fremstad.

Freni [Fregni], **Mirella.** Soprano; b. Modena, Italy, Feb. 27, 1935. Studied at Bologna Conservatory with Ettore Campogalliani; debut as Micaela, Modena, 1955. After winning the Viotti competition at Vercelli in 1957, she sang with Netherlands Opera, then at Glyndebourne (Zerlina, 1960; Susanna and Adina, 1962). Nannetta (*Falstaff*) was her debut role at both Covent Garden (1961) and La Scala (1962). She came to the Met on Sep. 29, 1965, as Mimi, returning during the Sixties, and again in the Eighties, singing more than 65 perfs. of 8 roles, including Adina, Liù, Marguerite, Juliette, Susanna, Micaela, Elisabeth de Valois, and Puccini's Manon. She also appeared at the house as Susanna and Marguerite with the visiting Paris Opéra in 1976. In Chicago, she bowed as Mimi (1965), later singing Marguerite and Tatiana. Her Salzburg career began in 1966 as Micaela, and there at Karajan's instance she first took up more dramatic roles (Desdemona, 1970; Elisabeth de Valois, 1975; Aida, 1979). Other roles have included Massenet's Manon, Violetta, Marie in *Fille*, and Amelia (*Boccanegra*).

Unlike some of her contemporaries, Freni managed the transition from lyric to spinto and even dramatic roles with care and success; the pure, clear, spinning tone has become fuller and rounder, if also less agile. Always an appealing and spontaneous performer, she has added dignity and grander passion to her original charm. Her list of recordings embodies both aspects of her career.

Frezzolini, Erminia. Soprano; b. Orvieto, Italy, Mar. 27, 1818; d. Paris, Nov. 5, 1884. Studied with her father, Giuseppe Frezzolini, who created Dulcamara (*Elisir*), then with Ronconi, Manuel Garcia, and Tacchinardi; debut as Beatrice di Tenda, Florence, 1838. At La Scala, created Verdi's Viclinda (*Lombardi*, 1843) and Giovanna d'Arco (1845). Also sang in London (1842, 1850) and N.Y. (1855).

Frick, Gottlob. Bass; b. Olbronn, Württemberg, Germany, July 28, 1906. Studied with Neudörfer-Opitz and at Stuttgart Conservatory; debut as Daland, Coburg, 1934. Appeared in Freiburg and Königsberg, then joined Dresden State Opera (1938–52), where he created Caliban in Sutermeister's *Zauberinsel* and sang Rocco, Gremin, Nicolai's Falstaff, and Wagnerian repertory. Member of Berlin Städtische Oper (1950–53) and Bavarian State Opera (from 1953). In his only Met season, he sang 12 perfs. of both Fafners (debut, *Rheingold*, Dec. 27, 1961), Hunding, and Hagen. Also performed at Covent Garden

(1951 *Ring*), Bayreuth (Pogner, 1957; *Ring*, 1960–64), and Salzburg (debut, Sarastro, 1955). The dominant Wagnerian bass of his time, Frick also used his black voice with humor as Osmin and in the bourgeois works of Lortzing; his career extended into the 1970s.

Fricsay, Ferenc. Conductor; b. Budapest, Aug. 9, 1914; d. Basel, Switzerland, Feb. 20, 1963. Student of Kodály and Bartók, he conducted in Hungary until a 1947 Salzburg debut (replacing an indisposed Klemperer in *Dantons Tod*) brought international attention. After his debut in England (1950) and directorship of the Berlin Radio Symphony (1948–52), he made his U.S. debut with the Boston Symphony (1953). Led the Bavarian State Opera (1956–58), then returned to Berlin. An intense and vigorous conductor, he was regarded as a masterful orchestral technician.

Friedenstag (Day of Peace). Opera in 1 act by R. Strauss; libretto by Joseph Gregor, based on a synopsis by Stefan Zweig.
First perf., Munich, National Theater, July 24, 1938: Ursuleac, Patzak, Hotter, Weber, c. Krauss. U.S. prem., Los Angeles, U. of So. Calif., Apr. 2, 1957 (in Eng.): c. Ducloux.
This high-minded anti-militaristic opera is, unfortunately, one of the blandest of Strauss' later works.
Set in a Catholic town besieged by Lutheran troops on the last day of the Thirty Years' War, October 24, 1648. Rather than surrender to the Lutheran commander (bs), the Catholic Commandant (bar) plans to blow up the citadel, but his wife Maria (s) persuades him to accept the Peace of Westphalia.

Friedrich, Götz. Producer; b. Nauburg, Germany, Aug. 4, 1930. Educated at Weimar Theater Institute (1949–53). At Berlin Komische Oper, assistant stage director (1953–56), assistant to Felsenstein (1957–59), and producer (1959–72). Has worked widely as guest producer; his Bayreuth productions included *Tannhäuser* (1972), *Lohengrin* (1979), and *Parsifal* (1982). Principal producer, Hamburg (1973–81) and Covent Garden (1976–81), American debut, *Wozzeck* (Houston, 1982). Intendant, Deutsche Oper, West Berlin (since 1981). His aggressively conceptualized productions usually provoke strong reactions.

Frigerio, Ezio. Designer; b. Erba, Italy, July 16, 1930. Associated with Giorgio Strehler's Piccolo Teatro di Milano as designer of sets and costumes, also collaborating with de Filippo and de Sica. Opera designs for many major houses, including La Scala (notable *Simon Boccanegra*, 1973) and the Met (*Francesca da Rimini*, 1984).

From the House of the Dead. Opera in 3 acts by Janáček; libretto by the composer, after Dostoyevsky's novel.
First perf., Brno, Apr. 12, 1930: Olšovský, Pelc, Fischer, Šíma, c. Bakala. U.S. prem., NET Television, Dec. 3, 1969: Rounseville, Lloyd, Jagel, Reardon, c. P.H. Adler.
Janáček's last opera was not completely finished at his death, and was completed by Břetislav Bakala and Osvald Chlubna. The political prisoner Petrovič (bs) arrives at a prison in Siberia, is interrogated and beaten by guards, attended by another prisoner, and eventually freed. There are two versions of the ending; the composer's original is pessimistic; Bakala and Chlubna devised a more hopeful ending for the prisoners who remain.

Mirella Freni as Manon Lescaut

Fry, William. Composer; b. Philadelphia, Aug. 19, 1813; d. Santa Cruz, V. I., Dec. 21, 1864. Active as a critic and composer of orchestral works, Fry also composed three grand operas: *Aurelia the Vestal* (1841) was unproduced, but *Leonora* (1845) and *Notre Dame of Paris* (1864) were among the first such works by an American-born composer. Despite polemical lectures and articles in which he urged American composers to establish an indigenous tradition, Fry's own works retained a strongly European flavor, particularly reminiscent of Donizetti and Bellini.

Fugère, Lucien. Baritone; b. Paris, July 22, 1848; d. Paris, Jan. 15, 1935. First sang in cabarets and at Bouffes-Parisiens; Opéra-Comique debut as Jean (*Noces de Jeannette*), 1877. Remained on roster until 1910, creating roles in more than 30 operas, including *Roi Malgré Lui* (1887), *Cendrillon* (1899), and *Louise* (1901). Roles included Papageno, Figaro, Leporello, and Rossini's Bartolo, which he sang at his 1933 farewell.

Fulton, Thomas. Conductor; b. Memphis, Tenn., Sep. 18, 1949. After study at Curtis under Rudolf and Ormandy, held staff posts at San Francisco and Hamburg Operas. Joined Met staff in 1978, conducted tour performances, and made house debut (Apr. 4, 1981, *Manon Lescaut*), returning regularly to conduct *Hänsel*, *Butterfly*, and several Verdi works. Debuts at Paris Opéra (*Robert le Diable*, 1979), Rome Opera (*Elisir*, 1986), Berlin (*Macbeth*, 1986).

Furtwängler, Wilhelm. Conductor; b. Berlin, Jan. 25, 1886; d. Baden-Baden, Nov. 30, 1954. Privately tutored, he composed several works by age 17 but soon devoted himself to conducting. Posts in Breslau, Zurich, Munich (1907–09), and Strassburg (1910–11) led to directorial positions in Lübeck (1911–15) and Mannheim (1915–20). In 1922 he began a long association with the Vienna Philharmonic and succeeded Nikisch as conductor of the Leipzig Gewandhaus Orchestra (until 1928) and Berlin Philharmonic (for life). He conducted Wagner at Bayreuth (1931, 1936–37, 1943–44) and Covent Garden (1937–38), as well as in Berlin and Vienna. After resigning all positions in 1934 when the Nazis banned Hindemith's *Mathis*, Furtwängler later resumed work in Germany, clouding his postwar career. Guest conductor (1925–27) with N.Y. Philharmonic; subsequent American appointments (to succeed Toscanini in N.Y., 1936, and Rodzinski in Chicago, 1949) were aborted because of political controversy. A deeply reflective, humanistic German musician, Furtwängler developed his interpretations in an improvisatory fashion, with considerable freedom of tempo, but the results were often profoundly compelling, notably in the works of Beethoven, Brahms, and Wagner. In addition to studio recordings of *Tristan*, *Fidelio*, and *Walküre*, his art is documented by numerous performance recordings, including two complete *Ring* cycles.

G

Gadski, Johanna. Soprano; b. Anklam, Germany, June 15, 1872; d. Berlin, Feb. 22, 1932. Studied in Stettin with Schröder-Chaloupka; debut at Kroll Opera, Berlin, in Lortzing's *Undine*, 1889; sang there and in Mainz, Bremen, and Stettin for five years. With the touring Damrosch Co., she made her N.Y. debut at the Met as Elsa, 1895, also sang Elisabeth, Eva, and Sieglinde, and created Hester Prynne in Damrosch's *Scarlet Letter*, Boston, 1896. She sang Wagner roles, Aida, and Santuzza at Covent Garden (1898–1902), and Eva at Bayreuth (1899). After her debut with resident Met company (Senta, Jan. 6, 1900), she sang there every year until 1917, except 1904–06, when she gave concerts throughout the U.S. During her Met years, she made festival appearances in Munich (1905–06) and in Salzburg as Donna Elvira (1906) and Pamina (1910). In 17 Met seasons, she gave 296 perfs. in 25 roles, including the three Brünnhildes, Eva, Elsa, Aida, Elisabeth, Isolde, Sieglinde, Santuzza, Pamina, Leonora (*Trovatore*), and Euridice. In 1917, amid war hysteria and charges of espionage against her husband, she returned to Germany, not reappearing in the U.S. until 1929, with a Wagnerian touring company organized by S. Hurok. She then formed her own company and toured for two years, until her death in an auto accident. Gadski interpreted dramatic roles, including the Italian parts that Gatti encouraged her to sing, with pure tone, a fluent line, and ample power, as attested by the many recordings she made between 1903 and 1917.

Gagliano, Marco da. Composer; b. Florence, May 1, 1582; d. Florence, Feb. 25, 1643. Chapel master of S. Lorenzo di Firenze, S. Maria del Fiore, and finally of the Medici court, his operatic setting of Rinuccini's pastorale *Dafne* was performed with great success in 1608. With Bardi and Peri, Gagliano was one of the first to compose in the *stile rappresentativo*. His only other surviving opera is *La Flora* (1628), in collaboration with Peri.

Galeffi, Carlo. Baritone; b. Malamocco, Venice, June 4, 1882; d. Rome, Sep. 22, 1961. Studied with Sbriscia; debut as Enrico (*Lucia*), Adriano, Rome, 1904. In 1910, sang in Boston and at Met (debut and only perf., Germont, Nov. 29, 1910). At La Scala (1912–38), created roles in *Amore dei Tre Re* (1913), *Parisina* (1913), and *Nerone* (1924); also roles in Mascagni's *Amica* (Monte Carlo, 1905) and *Isabeau* (Buenos Aires, 1911). Sang at Chicago Opera, 1919–21.

Gall, Yvonne. Soprano; b. Paris, Mar. 6, 1885; d. Paris, Aug. 21, 1972. Studied at Paris Conservatory; debut as Mathilde (*Guillaume Tell*), Opéra, 1908. Remained on roster until 1935; also sang at Opéra-Comique (1921–34). Appeared in Chicago (1918–21) and San Francisco (1931). Married to conductor and Paris Opéra director Henri Büsser.

Galli-Bibiena. Family of stage designers and architects in Italy, Austria, and southern Germany, 17th-18th c. **Ferdinando** (1656–1743) replaced the prevalent symmetry of stage sets with angular perspectives. His brother **Francesco** (1659–1737) emphasized a proliferation of fantastic detail. Ferdinando's son **Giuseppe** (1695–1757) designed the interior of the Margravial Opera House in Bayreuth and worked for Frederick the Great in Berlin. His son **Carlo** (1721–87) worked at Drottningholm; some of his sets are still extant there.

Galli-Curci, Amelita. Soprano; b. Milan, Nov. 18, 1882; d. La Jolla, Calif., Nov. 26, 1963. Recipient of a first prize in piano at the Milan Conservatory in 1903, she took up singing at Mascagni's suggestion, studying briefly with Carignani and Sara Dufes, but mainly self-taught. Debut as Gilda at Trani, 1906, followed by engagements elsewhere in Italy, Latin America, and Spain. After South American tours in 1915–16, she auditioned in N.Y. for Campanini, leading to a sensational U.S. debut as Gilda, Chicago, Nov. 18, 1916, and a Victor recording contract. Her roles in Chicago (1916–1924) included Rosina, Amina, Massenet's Manon, Violetta, Dinorah, Lucia, and Juliette. Although she visited N.Y. often with this company, her Met debut did not take place until Nov. 14,

Johanna Gadski as Brünnhilde in *Die Walküre*

1921, as Violetta. She was most often seen there as Rosina, Lucia, Gilda, and Violetta; her only other Met roles were the Queen (*Golden Cockerel*), Juliette, Dinorah, and a single Mimi, for a total of 68 perfs. all told. By the time of her farewell as Rosina (Jan. 24, 1930), she was in noticeable vocal difficulty; a throat tumor was removed in 1935 and, after a single Mimi in Chicago the following year, she retired for good. She was married twice: in 1910 to the artist Luigi Curci (divorced 1920), in 1921 to her accompanist Homer Samuels (1889–1956). Galli-Curci's pure, natural tone and winsome charm won her great stage success in America, and proved exceptionally adaptable to the phonograph.
BIBLIOGRAPHY: C.E. Le Massena, *Galli-Curci's Life of Song* (N.Y., 1945).

Galli-Marié [Marié de L'Isle], **Celestine.** Mezzo-soprano; b. Paris, Nov., 1840; d. Vence, Sep. 22, 1905. Studied with father; debut in Strasbourg, 1859. Sang in Toulouse (1860), Lisbon (1861), and Rouen (1862). Debut at Opéra-Comique, Paris, as Serpina (*Serva Padrona*), 1862; remained on roster until 1885, creating Mignon (1866) and Carmen (1875).

Gallo, Fortune. Impresario; b. Torremaggiore, Italy, May 9, 1878; d. New York, Mar. 28, 1970. Studied piano in Italy, then migrated to the U.S. in 1895. Managed bands and operatic touring companies (1901–1909), and in 1909 established the San Carlo Opera Company, which presented popular-priced opera throughout the U.S. until its disbanding in 1955. He also presented Pavlova and her ballet troupe (1920) and Duse's last tour (1923–24), and made the first operatic sound film, *Pagliacci* (1931).

Galvany, Marisa [Myra Beth Genis]. Soprano; b. Paterson, N.J., June 19, 1936. Studied with Armen Boyajian; debut as Tosca, Seattle, 1968. N.Y.C. Opera debut as Elisabetta (*Maria Stuarda*), 1972, later singing Médée, Anna Bolena, Santuzza, Violetta. Met debut as Norma, Mar. 12, 1979; has also sung Ortrud, Kostelnička (*Jenůfa*) and Mother (*Hänsel*) there.

Gambler, The. Opera in 4 acts by Prokofiev; libretto by the composer, after Dostoyevsky's novella.
First perf., Brussels, Monnaie, Apr. 29, 1929 (in Fr.): Leblanc, Andry, Ballard, Lense, Rambaud, Yovanovitch, c. de Thoran. U.S. prem., N.Y., 85th St. Playhouse, Apr. 4, 1957 (in Eng.).
Composed in 1917 in Prokofiev's most aggressively expressionistic manner, and revised in 1927–28, *The Gambler* was not widely produced until the 1950s.
Roulettenburg, a German spa, 1865. Alexey (t), tutor to the children of the General (bs), loves the General's stepdaughter Pauline (s), but has gambled and lost the money she has given him. The General loves Blanche (c), also broke from gambling; while waiting for his wealthy aunt Babulenka (ms) to die and leave him her fortune, he borrows money from the Marquis (t). The aunt, however, arrives at the spa in fine health, and succeeds in gambling away all her money. To prevent Pauline from marrying the Marquis, Alexey gambles again and wins. He presents the money to Pauline, who throws it back in his face; as the curtain falls, we know he will return to the tables.

Garbin, Edoardo. Tenor; b. Padua, Italy, Mar. 12, 1865; d. Brescia, Apr. 12, 1943. Studied with Selva and Orefice, Milan; debut as Alvaro (*Forza*), Vicenza, 1891. Sang in Naples, Genoa, and in Milan at both Verme and La Scala,

Amelita Galli-Curci as Lucia di Lammermoor

where he created Fenton (*Falstaff*), 1893. Toured widely, especially in verismo repertory; created Milio in *Zazà* (1900) and title role in *Giovanni Gallurese* (1905). Married to soprano Adelina Stehle.

Garcia (del Popolo), Manuel. Tenor; b. Seville, Spain, Jan. 22, 1775; d. Paris, June 9, 1832. Studied with Antonio Ripa; by 1798 he had a career as singer and composer (he

The Gambler – Bolshoi Opera. Designed by Valeri Leventhal, produced by Boris Pokrovsky

Mary Garden as Thaïs

eventually wrote over 40 operas and operettas). Sang at Paris Opéra (1808–11), then went to Italy, where he created Norfolk in Rossini's *Elisabetta* and Almaviva in *Barbiere*; he repeated the latter role in the work's Paris, London, and N.Y. premieres. Appeared in Paris, 1819–24, then produced the first season of Italian opera in N.Y. (1825–26), featuring his daughter, Maria Malibran, and the U.S. premiere of *Don Giovanni*. The most renowned teacher of his day, his pupils included Malibran, his other daughter Pauline Viardot-Garcia, Nourrit, and Méric-Lalande. His son, baritone **Manuel Garcia II** (1805–1906), studied the physiological aspects of voice, invented the laryngoscope (1855), and was a formidable teacher as well, numbering Lind, Mathilde Marchesi, Julius Stockhausen, and Santley among his students.

Gardelli, Lamberto. Conductor; b. Venice, Nov. 6, 1914. After study in Pesaro and Rome, assisted Serafin and made his debut in Rome (*Traviata*). Resident conductor, Stockholm Royal Opera (1946–55), Danish State Radio Orchestra (1955–61); music director, Budapest Opera (since 1961). U.S. debut (*Capuleti*, Carnegie Hall, 1964) led to Met appearances in *Chénier* (debut, Jan. 30, 1966) and *Rigoletto*, followed by *Butterfly* the following season. A dependable and effective exponent of the Italian repertory, Gardelli has recorded numerous operas.

Garden, Mary. Soprano; b. Aberdeen, Scotland, Feb. 20, 1874; d. Inverurie, Jan. 3, 1967. As a child, lived in Hartford, Conn., and Chicago, where she studied voice with Mrs. Robinson Duff, later working in Paris with Sbriglia, Bouhy, Trabadello, Marchesi, and Fugère. Sibyl Sanderson introduced her to Opéra-Comique director Carré, who engaged her for fall 1900; that spring, however, she replaced an indisposed colleague in the last

two acts of Charpentier's *Louise*, to instant acclaim. At the Opéra-Comique, she created Mélisande, 1902. She also appeared at the Opéra (as Ophélie), Covent Garden (as Juliette), and Monte Carlo (creating Saint-Saëns' Hélène). After her successful Manon in Paris and London, Massenet wrote *Chérubin* for her (1905). She made her N.Y. debut with Hammerstein's Manhattan Opera in the first U.S. *Thaïs*, 1907, followed by the first American Mélisande, 1908. She also re-introduced *Salome* to the U.S. (after its single 1907 performance at the Met), 1909.

A 20-year association with the Chicago Opera began with her 1910 debut as Mélisande. Garden's single season as the company's self-styled "directa" (1921–22) was artistically successful – it included Prokofiev conducting the world premiere of *Love for Three Oranges* – but financially ruinous. In Chicago she sang Tosca, Fiora (*Amore dei Tre Re*), Massenet's Cléopâtre, and the leads in the U.S. premieres of Alfano's *Risurrezione* and Honegger's *Judith*; her last performance there was in the tenor role of Jean (*Jongleur de Notre Dame*), 1931. She made occasional later operatic appearances, most often at the Opéra-Comique, where she took her final bow as Katiusha (*Risurrezione*) in 1934. She gave lecture-recitals in the U.S. (1934–35) and advised Hollywood film studios on opera sequences. Living in Scotland from 1939, she returned to the U.S. for lecture tours, 1949–55.

A versatile lyric soprano who succeeded in impressing audiences even in coloratura and spinto roles, Garden was evidently a vibrant figure on stage, the model of a singing actress. Her voice, though not large, was individual and colorful, and she phrased with great delicacy. She made relatively few recordings, of which the most important are her first: Debussy selections with the composer at the piano (1903).

BIBLIOGRAPHY: Mary Garden, with Louis Biancolli, *Mary Garden's Story* (N.Y., 1951).

Garrison, Jon. Tenor; b. Higgensville, Mo., Dec. 11, 1944. Met debut as Porter (*Death in Venice*), Oct. 18, 1974; his subsequent roles there include Edmondo (*Manon Lescaut*), Ferrando, and Tamino. Has also appeared with N.Y.C. Opera (debut as Admète in *Alceste*, 1982), and in Santa Fe, Montreal, Houston, and San Diego.

Garrison, Mabel [Martha Greiner]. Soprano; b. Baltimore, Md., Apr. 24, 1886; d. New York, Aug. 20, 1963. Studied at Peabody Conservatory and with Otto Saenger and Herbert Witherspoon, N.Y.; debut at Philine (*Mignon*), Boston, 1912. Met debut as Flowermaiden (*Parsifal*), Nov. 26, 1914; in 8 seasons, sang 74 perfs. of 16 roles, including Oscar, Rosina, Adina, Gretel, Lucia, Gilda, and the Queen of Night. Later appeared in Germany and Chicago, and taught at Smith College, Northampton, Mass.

Gasdia, Cecilia. Soprano; b. Verona, Aug. 14, 1960. Studied classics and piano in Verona, then won RAI Callas competition, 1980; debut as Giulietta (*Capuleti*), Florence, 1982, later replacing Caballé as Anna Bolena, La Scala, 1982. Paris Opéra debut in Rossini's *Moïse* (1984); U.S. debut as Gilda in concert *Rigoletto* (Philadelphia, 1985). Met debut as Juliette, Nov. 6, 1986.

Gatti-Casazza, Giulio. Manager; b. Udine, Italy, Feb. 3, 1869; d. Ferrara, Sep. 2, 1940. After studying naval engineering at Genoa U., in 1893 he took over from his father as head of the Teatro Comunale, Ferrara. Chosen by Boito to head La Scala, in ten years there (1898–1908) he and Toscanini established the highest artistic standard in Italy. The two men came together to the Met in 1908 and quickly consolidated their authority with the backing of Otto Kahn. Gatti was the first salaried manager, and the first opera specialist, to run the Met (his predecessors were principally theatrical entrepreneurs), and his tenure (until 1935) was the longest in Met history, marked, until the Depression years, by an unbroken string of venturesome yet profitable seasons, a rare – possibly unique – feat of opera management. Maintaining a cosmopolitan repertory of 40 to 50 works per season, Gatti presented world premieres of European works such as *Königskinder*, *Fanciulla*, and *Goyescas*, but also encouraged and staged American operas. Virtually all the major singers of his time appeared at the Met, and the house set world standards for staging and design. But Gatti's expansive style could not adapt to the financial restrictions of the 1930s, and he retired to Italy. He was married to the soprano Frances Alda (1910–28), then to the Met's prima ballerina Rosina Galli (from 1930).

BIBLIOGRAPHY: Giulio Gatti-Casazza, *Memories of the Opera* (N.Y., 1941).

Gavazzeni, Gianandrea. Conductor; b. Bergamo, Italy, July 27, 1909. Studied in Rome and Milan, and active as a composer until 1949. Subsequently conducted opera, especially at La Scala (artistic director, 1965–68) and Florence, also at Chicago Opera (debut, *Bohème*, 1957) and Glyndebourne (*Anna Bolena*, 1965). His only Met appearances were in *Trovatore* (debut, Oct. 11, 1976).

Gay, John. Librettist; bapt. Barnstaple, Devon, Sep. 16, 1685; d. London, Dec. 4, 1732. Librettist for Handel's *Acis and Galatea* (c. 1718) and for the hugely successful ballad opera *The Beggar's Opera* (1728); its sequel *Polly*, banned by the censors, was not heard until 1779.

Gay, Maria. Contralto; b. Barcelona, June 13, 1879; d. New York, July 29, 1943. Originally self-taught, later studied with Ada Adiny, Paris; debut as Carmen, her signature role, Monnaie, Brussels, 1902. Appeared at

Giulio Gatti-Casazza

Covent Garden (1906), La Scala (1906–07), and Buenos Aires (1907). In her only Met season, she sang 18 perfs. of Carmen (debut, Dec. 3, 1908), Quickly, Lola, Amneris, and Azucena. Sang with Boston (1910–12) and Chicago (1913–27) Operas. Married to tenor Giovanni Zenatello.

Gayarré, Julián. Tenor; b. Valle de Roncal, Spain, Jan. 9, 1844; d. Madrid, Jan. 2, 1890. Studied at Madrid Conservatory; debut in Padua, 1868. Created Enzo (*Gioconda*), La Scala, 1876. Appeared at Covent Garden, 1877–81 and 1886–87, notably as Fernand (*Favorite*) and as Sobinin in London premiere of *Life for the Tsar*. Created title role in Donizetti's *Duc d'Albe*, Rome, 1882.

Gayer [Ashkenasi], **Catherine.** Soprano; b. Los Angeles, Feb. 11, 1937. Studied at U. of Calif., Los Angeles, and in Berlin; debut as Companion (*Intolleranza*), Fenice, Venice, 1961. With Deutsche Oper, Berlin after 1961, sang many contemporary roles. Has also appeared in Vienna, Milan, Salzburg, and Covent Garden (Queen of Night, 1962).

Gazza Ladra, La (The Thieving Magpie). Opera in 2 acts by Rossini; libretto by Giovanni Gherardini, after the comedy *La Pie Voleuse* by Baudoin d'Aubigny and Caigniez.

First perf., Milan, La Scala, May 31, 1817: Giorgi-Belloc, Gallianis, Monelli, Botticelli. U.S. prem., Philadelphia, Chestnut Street, September 14, 1829 (in Fr.).

Though today only the overture is heard with frequency, the leading role in this lively comedy was a favorite of coloratura sopranos well after most other Rossini operas beyond *Barbiere* had receded in importance. In a village near Paris, the servant girl Ninetta (s) is condemned to death for stealing a silver spoon, but the timely discovery of the titular magpie's thievery spares her.

Gedda, Nicolai [Nicolai Ustinoff]. Tenor; b. Stockholm, July 11, 1925. Son of a Russian choir director and a Swedish mother (née Gedda), he studied with his father in Leipzig, in Stockholm with Carl Martin Öhmann, later in N.Y. with Paola Novikova. Debut at Stockholm Royal Opera as Chapelou (Adam's *Postillon*, 1952). He

Nicolai Gedda as Lenski in *Eugene Onegin*

immediately won international attention and bowed at La Scala (Ottavio, 1953) and the Paris Opéra (Damon in *Les Indes Galantes*, 1954), where he later sang Huon (*Oberon*), Tamino, Cassio and Faust. At Aix, he sang Vincent (*Mireille*) and Belmonte in 1954, Ferrando and Gluck's Orphée in 1955, Ottavio in 1956. His Covent Garden debut, as the Duke, came in 1954; he returned there in 1966 to sing Benvenuto Cellini. Since his Met debut as Faust (Nov. 1, 1957), he has returned regularly in 22 seasons, singing 289 perfs. of 27 roles, including Ottavio, the Italian Singer (*Rosenkavalier*), Hoffmann, Tamino, Lenski, Massenet's Des Grieux, Barinkay (*Zigeunerbaron*), Alfredo, Admète (*Alceste*), Dimitri, Pinkerton, Nemorino, Pelléas, Elvino (*Sonnambula*), Kodanda (*Last Savage*), the Duke, Don José, Roméo, Edgardo, Rodolfo, Herman (*Queen of Spades*), Henri (*Vêpres Siciliennes*), Riccardo (*Ballo*), Jeník (*Bartered Bride*), Ernesto, and Belmonte. He created Anatol in *Vanessa*, and later sang it in Salzburg. He has appeared in most major operatic centers, including Vienna (Tamino and Ottavio, 1962), Edinburgh (Berlioz's Faust, 1963), and Chicago (Alfredo, 1970).

A prodigiously versatile artist, Gedda's technical mastery enabled him to range widely through the lyric and spinto repertory, never transgressing the limits of his sturdy, sweet, firmly focused voice (he sang Lohengrin in Stockholm in 1966, but found it a strain, and thereafter abjured Wagnerian roles, even on records). A vivid and exuberant actor, he is fluent in a half-dozen languages. During a dearth of French tenors, he became most noted for his performances in that literature (notably Des Grieux, Hoffmann, Cellini, and Don José), but his Russian roles (Dimitri and Lenski) and Mozart were also distinguished, as was his Italian repertory. His vast discography includes several stylish Viennese operettas, as well as oratorios, songs, and most of his operatic roles.

Gencer, Leyla. Soprano; b. Istanbul, Oct. 10, 1924. Studied in Ankara, then with Arangi-Lombardi and Granforte, Italy; debut as Santuzza, Ankara, 1950. At La Scala, created Mme. Lidoine (*Carmélites*), 1956. Also appeared at Glyndebourne (1962–63, 1965), and Edinburgh (1969, 1972); specialized in bel canto roles.

Generalmusikdirektor (Ger.). In German theaters, the highest-ranking musical position in an operatic institution, equivalent to music director.

Generalprobe (Ger.). Dress rehearsal.

Genoveva. Opera in 4 acts by Schumann; libretto by the composer, after a draft by Robert Reinick, Tieck's tragedy *Das Leben und Tod der heiligen Genoveva*, and Hebbel's tragedy *Genoveva*.

First perf., Leipzig, Stadttheater, June 25, 1850: Mayer, Günther-Baumann, Wiedemann, Brussin, c. Reitz.

Schumann's sole operatic effort, set in medieval Trier and Strasbourg. While her husband Siegfried (bar) is on a Crusade, Genoveva (s) spurns the advances of Golo (t), who has her convicted of betraying her husband with the chaplain Drago (bs). Despite the machinations of the witch Margareta (ms), Siegfried saves his wife from execution.

Gentele, Göran. Manager and producer; b. Stockholm, Sep. 20, 1917; d. near Olbia, Sardinia, July 18, 1972. After working at the National Theater, Stockholm, as an actor and stage director, he joined the Royal Opera as producer

(1952–63) and managing director (1963–71); his productions there attracted wide attention, notably a controversial *Ballo*. Named to succeed Bing at the Met, effective June 1972, he chose Chapin as his assistant, Kubelik as music director, and (most importantly, in the event) Levine as principal conductor – the latter two positions new to the Met. He was scheduled to direct the opening *Carmen* of the 1972–73 season; after his death in an auto accident while on vacation, the production was staged from his notes.

Gérard, Rolf. Designer; b. Berlin, Aug. 9, 1909. Studied in Berlin and Paris, and designed for major European companies. The designer most frequently used by Bing at the Met, his productions included *Don Carlos* (1950), *Fledermaus* (1950), *Aida* (1951), *Così* (1951), *Carmen* (1952), *Bohème* (1952), *Faust* (1953), *Hoffmann* (1955), *Arabella* (1955), *Périchole* (1956), *Eugene Onegin* (1957), *Zigeunerbaron* (1959), *Sonnambula* (1963), and *Orfeo* (1970).

Gerhard, Roberto. Composer; b. Valls, Catalonia, Spain, Sep. 25, 1896; d. Cambridge, England, Jan. 5, 1970. Studied with Granados, Pedrell, and Schoenberg, whose dodecaphonic technique he eventually adopted. After the Republican defeat in the Spanish Civil War, he moved to England, where a BBC broadcast of his only opera, *The Duenna* (1947), brought his work to public attention. From 1950, he was a prolific composer of chamber, vocal, and orchestral pieces, including incidental music for the Royal Shakespeare Theatre, Stratford.

Germania. Opera in prologue, 2 acts, and epilogue by Franchetti; libretto by Illica.

First perf., Milan, La Scala, Mar. 11, 1902: Pinto, Caruso, Sammarco, c. Toscanini. U.S. & Met. prem., Jan. 22, 1910: Destinn, Caruso, Amato, c. Toscanini, d. Rovescalli, Sala/Hohenstein, p. Speck. 7 perfs. in 2 seasons.

This tepid example of historical verismo survived only as long as Caruso was around to sing in it. Set near Königsberg and Leipzig in the early 19th c., the action involves students opposed to the Napoleonic occupation of Germany. Before her marriage to Loewe (t), Ricke (s) has been seduced by his friend Worms (bar). Both men eventually die fighting for Germany; on his deathbed, Loewe asks his wife to forgive Worms.

Gershwin, George. Composer; b. Brooklyn, N.Y., Sep. 26, 1898; d. Hollywood, Calif., July 11, 1937. Early piano studies with Charles Hambitzer were followed, during his active career, by lessons with Edward Kilenyi, Joseph Schillinger, and others. He achieved early recognition as a composer of songs for revues and musical comedies (many with his brother Ira as librettist), notably *Lady Be Good* (1924), *Girl Crazy* (1930), and *Of Thee I Sing* (1931); these exhibit his natural gifts for melodic and rhythmic invention, wit, and original use of the vocabulary of jazz. Gershwin achieved success in the concert hall as well, with works such as *Rhapsody in Blue* (1924) and *An American in Paris* (1928).

A jazz-based operatic work, the one-act *Blue Monday Blues*, was introduced in the revue *George White's Scandals of 1922*, but withdrawn after the first night; revised in 1925 as *135th Street*, it has only historical interest. After further study, Gershwin wrote *Porgy and Bess* (1935), intended for the Met but eventually produced on Broadway; for many years, abbreviated theatrical revivals tended to play down its operatic aspects, but the original version has now won wide acceptance. Further development of Gershwin's gifts ended with his premature death of a brain tumor, while working on a film score in Hollywood.

BIBLIOGRAPHY: Charles Schwartz, *Gershwin, His Life and Music* (Indianapolis, 1973).

Gerster, Etelka. Soprano; b. Kassa (now Košice), Slovakia, June 25, 1855; d. Pontecchio, near Bologna, Aug. 20, 1920. Studied with Mathilde Marchesi, Vienna; debut as Gilda, Venice, 1876. Debuts as Amina in London, 1877, and in 1878 with Mapleson at Academy of Music, N.Y., where she also sang Elsa and Lucia. She toured widely in the U.S., and, after retiring in 1890, taught in Berlin and N.Y.

Gerville-Réache, Jeanne. Contralto; b. Orthez, France, Mar. 26, 1882; d. New York, Jan. 5, 1915. Studied with Rosine Laborde and Pauline Viardot, Paris; Opéra-Comique debut as Gluck's Orphée, 1899. Remained on roster until 1903, creating Geneviève (*Pelléas*, 1902). Later sang in Brussels, London, and with Manhattan Opera (debut as Cieca, 1907), then in Chicago, Boston, Philadelphia, and Montreal.

Gesamtkunstwerk (Ger.). The "unified work of art," Wagner's term for what he conceived as a fresh union of poetry, music, and the theatrical arts, exemplified by his mature works.

Ghiaurov, Nicolai. Bass; b. Velingrad, Bulgaria, Sep. 13, 1929. He studied privately with the composer Petko Stainov, then with Brambarov at Sofia Conservatory (1949), and won a scholarship to Moscow Conservatory; debut as Basilio (*Barbiere*), Sofia, 1955. After his Bolshoi

Nicolai Ghiaurov as Philippe II in *Don Carlos*

debut as Pimen (*Boris*), 1958, he also sang Basilio and Méphistophélès there. He has appeared regularly at La Scala since his 1960 debut as Varlaam (*Boris*), in roles including Ramfis, the Grand Inquisitor (*Don Carlos*), Créon (*Médée*), Balthasar (*Favorite*), Marcel (*Huguenots*), and Don Giovanni. He first appeared at Covent Garden in 1962 as the Padre Guardiano (*Forza*), and in the U.S. in 1963 as Méphistophélès in Chicago, where he later sang Don Giovanni, Boito's Mefistofele, Boris, Ivan Khovansky (*Khovanshchina*), and Don Quichotte. His Met debut was also in *Faust* (Nov. 8, 1965), and he has returned occasionally since, singing more than 35 perfs. as Philippe II, the Padre Guardiano, and Fiesco (*Simon Boccanegra*). His Salzburg roles have included Boris (debut, 1965), Don Giovanni, and Philippe II.

Ghiaurov's powerful, almost granitic voice brought him quick dominance of the international scene, and his easy upper register made him a successful Don Giovanni. His interpretations are musicianly and polished, and his Slavic background has made him especially authoritative in the great Russian roles.

Ghiringhelli, Antonio. Manager; b. Brunello, Italy, Mar. 5, 1903; d. Aosta, July 11, 1979. A lawyer, he supervised the reconstruction of La Scala after World War II and then became its general administrator, remaining there until 1972. During his tenure the Piccola Scala chamber-opera auditorium was built, and the company made successful visits to London, Vienna, and Moscow.

Ghislanzoni, Antonio. Librettist; b. Lecco, Italy, Nov. 25, 1824; d. Caprino Bergamasco, July 16, 1893. A singer and critic, he was librettist for Ponchielli, Gomes, and Catalani, as well as for Verdi's *Aida*.

Giacomini, Giuseppe. Tenor; b. Monselice, Padua, Sep. 7, 1940. Studied at Accademia Cesare Bollini, Padua; debut as Pinkerton, Vercelli, 1967. Sang at La Scala from 1974, in Berlin and Vienna from 1972, Hamburg from 1973. U.S. debut as Dick Johnson, Connecticut Opera, 1975. Met debut as Alvaro, Nov. 27, 1976; subsequent Met roles include Don Carlos, Macduff, Pinkerton, Canio, Cavaradossi, and Manrico.

Giacosa, Giuseppe. Librettist; b. Colleretto Parella, near Turin, Oct. 21, 1847; d. Colleretto Parella, Sep. 2, 1906. Successful author of historical and modern dramas, he was responsible for the versification of Illica's scenarios for Puccini's *Bohème*, *Tosca*, and *Butterfly*.

Giaiotti, Bonaldo. Bass; b. Ziracco, Udine, Italy, Dec. 25, 1932. Studied in Udine, Milan, and N.Y.; debut at Nuovo, Milan, 1957. U.S. debut as Rossini's Basilio, Cincinnati, 1959. Since his Met debut as the High Priest (*Nabucco*), Oct. 24, 1960, he has sung well over 300 perfs. in about 30 roles, most often Timur (*Turandot*), Ramfis, and Raimondo (*Lucia*).

Giannini, Dusolina. Soprano; b. Philadelphia, Pa., Dec. 19, 1900; d. Zurich, June 29, 1986. Studied with father, tenor Ferruccio, and with Sembrich. Operatic debut as Aida, Hamburg, 1925. Sang in Berlin, Vienna, London, and Salzburg; created Hester Prynne in brother Vittorio's *Scarlet Letter*, Hamburg, 1938. Met debut as Aida, Feb. 12, 1936; also sang Donna Anna, Santuzza, and Tosca, 12 perfs in 6 seasons. Appeared in San Francisco (from 1939) and with N.Y.C. Opera (Tosca in opening perf., Feb. 21, 1944).

Gianni Schicchi – World premiere, 1918. Designed by Pieretto Bianco and Galileo Chini, produced by Richard Ordynski

Gianni Schicchi. Opera in 1 act by Puccini: libretto by Giovacchino Forzano, suggested by an episode in Dante's *Inferno*. Part 3 of *Il trittico*.

First perf., Met, Dec. 14, 1918: Easton, Crimi, de Luca, c. Moranzoni, d. Chini/Bianco, p. Ordynski. Later Met productions: Jan. 10, 1952 ("revised," in Eng.): Peters, Hayward, Baccaloni, c. Erede, d. Armistead, p. H. Busch; June 10, 1974: Blegen, Gibbs, Guarrera, c. Ehrling, d. Reppa, p. Melano. Schicchi has also been sung at the Met by Tibbett, Tajo, Corena, Flagello, MacNeil, Bacquier, Lauretta by Albanese, Scotto, Malfitano; Rinuccio by Martini, di Stefano. 97 perfs. in 18 seasons.

Beniamino Gigli as Enzo in *La Gioconda*

Gianni Schicchi, the third panel of Puccini's *Trittico* (triptych), glints with pointed, sometimes slightly acidic wit that is reflected in pungent harmony and brightly colored orchestration. The opera portrays the crime for which Gianni Schicchi is condemned to hell in Dante's *Divine Comedy*.

Florence, 1299. The newly deceased Buoso Donati is surrounded by relatives who become distraught upon learning that his will leaves all his wealth to a monastery. Rinuccio (t) suggests that they call in the father of his sweetheart Lauretta (s), the cunning Gianni Schicchi (bar). Schicchi orders the dead man removed, and after warning the relatives of the penalty they all face if the scheme is discovered (loss of a hand and exile), climbs into bed to impersonate Buoso and dictate a new will. Each relative has tried secretly to bribe Schicchi to favor him. But when the notary arrives, Schicchi leaves the choice items to himself, and the house to Lauretta and Rinuccio. He chases the infuriated relatives out and asks the audience to applaud a verdict of "extenuating circumstances."

Gibson, Alexander. Conductor; b. Motherwell, Scotland, Feb. 11, 1926. After study in Glasgow, Salzburg (under Markevich), and Siena, joined Sadler's Wells Opera (1951), becoming in 1957 its youngest music director. In 1959, resigned to lead Scottish National Orchestra (until 1984), and in 1962 founded Scottish Opera (music director until 1987).

Gielen, Michael. Conductor; b. Dresden, July 20, 1927. Studied in Buenos Aires (assistant to E. Kleiber) and Vienna, coached and conducted in Vienna (1951–60). Principal conductor, Stockholm Royal Opera (1960–65), Cologne (1965–69), Belgian National Orchestra (1969–73), Netherlands Opera (1973–77); music director, Frankfurt Opera (1977–87), Cincinnati Symphony (1980–86), Southwest German Radio Orchestra (from 1986). A noted interpreter of contemporary works, he gave the premiere of *Soldaten* in Frankfurt and has recorded Schoenberg's *Moses*.

Gigli, Beniamino. Tenor; b. Recanati, Italy, Mar. 20, 1890; d. Rome, Nov. 30, 1957. He sang in the choir of Recanati Cathedral from age seven, and studied in Rome with Agnese Bonucci and at the Liceo Musicale with Cotogni and Rosati. After winning an international competition at Parma in 1914, he made his debut there as Enzo (*Gioconda*). Successes as Boito's Faust at Bologna under Serafin and Naples under Mascagni (both 1915), and at La Scala under Toscanini (a memorial perf. for the composer, 1918) led to a Met debut in the same role, Nov. 26, 1920. He appeared there every season until 1932, and was considered the heir to the lyric side of Caruso's repertory; his most frequent roles included Rodolfo, Enzo, Vasco da Gama (*Africaine*), Chénier, Roméo, Wilhelm Meister (*Mignon*), Massenet's and Puccini's Des Grieux, Alfredo, Edgardo, Lionel (*Martha*), the Duke of Mantua, Pinkerton, Turiddu, Cavaradossi, Ruggero (*Rondine*), and Ottavio. He left the Met in 1932 rather than accept a substantial Depression-era cut in pay, and returned to the sites of his earlier triumphs in Italy, the rest of Europe, and South America. He revisited the Met in 1939 for five performances, including two as Radames, a new role for him there; this brought his Met totals to 375 perfs. of 29 roles in 13 seasons. Notable postwar appearances included Cavaradossi, Rome Opera, 1945, and Rodolfo opposite his daughter Rina as Mimì, Covent Garden, 1946. Soon he was appearing mostly in concert, although he sang in opera in Naples and Rome until 1953. He made a farewell recital tour of the U.S. in 1955, in fading but still enchanting voice, and retired the following year.

Gigli was blessed with a once-in-a-generation voice: strong, fluent, sweet, and vital. He was no actor, and his manner was often nakedly sentimental in a way that endeared him to some listeners and not to others. His large repertory (about 60 roles) incuded a number of French parts and a highly-regarded Lohengrin. Beginning in 1933, he recorded a number of complete operas, and his hundreds of aria and song recordings span the years 1918–55.

BIBLIOGRAPHY: Beniamino Gigli, *Memoirs* (London, 1957, repr. 1977).

Gilibert, Charles. Baritone; b. Paris, Nov. 29, 1866; d. New York, Oct. 11, 1910. Studied at Paris Conservatory; Opéra-Comique debut, 1889. Appeared at Monnaie, Brussels, and Covent Garden, 1894–1909. Met debut as Duc (*Roméo*), Dec. 18, 1900; in 3 seasons, sang 20 perfs. of 18 roles including both Bartolos, Masetto, and Don Pasquale. Also appeared at Manhattan Opera, 1906–10.

Ginastera, Alberto. Composer, b. Buenos Aires, Apr. 11, 1916; d. Geneva, June 25, 1983. Studied with Palma, Gil, and André at the National Conservatory, Buenos Aires. His first theater works were the nationalistic ballets *Panambí* (1937) and *Estancia* (1941). In his operas, beginning with *Don Rodrigo* (1964), he adopted serial techniques, working within abstract musical forms. *Bomarzo* (1967) and *Beatrix Cenci* (1971) also employ aleatory procedures and avant-garde orchestral resources.

Gioconda, La (The Joyful Girl). Opera in 4 acts by Ponchielli; libretto by "Tobia Gorrio" [Arrigo Boito], after Victor Hugo's drama *Angelo, Tyran de Padoue*.

First perf., Milan, La Scala, Apr. 8, 1876: Mariani-Masi, Biancolini-Rodriguez, Barlani-Dini, Gayarré, Aldighieri, Maini, c. Faccio. U.S. & Met prem., Dec. 20, 1883: Nilsson, Fursch-Madi, Scalchi, Stagno, del Puente, Novara, c. Vianesi. Later Met productions: Nov. 15, 1909: Destinn, Homer, Meitschik, Caruso, Amato, de Segurola, c. Toscanini, d. Rota, Sala, Paravicini/Maison Chiappa, p. Speck; Nov. 8, 1924: Easton, Matzenauer, Alcock, Gigli, Danise, Mardones, c. Serafin, d. Rovescalli, Novak, p. Thewman; Sep. 22, 1966: Tebaldi, Cvejič, Dunn, Corelli, MacNeil, Siepi, c. Cleva, d. Montresor, p. Wallman. Gioconda has also been sung at the Met by Nordica, Ponselle, Cigna, Milanov, Farrell, Arroyo, Bumbry, Scotto, Marton; Laura by Ober, Branzell, Bampton, Castagna, Stevens, Thebom, Barbieri, Cossotto; Enzo by Lauri-Volpi, Martinelli, Tucker, Baum, del Monaco, Bergonzi, Domingo; Barnaba by Giraldoni, Scotti, Danise, Ruffo, de Luca, Warren, Merrill, Milnes; Alvise by Plançon, Pinza, Plishka. 201 perfs. in 37 seasons.

A theatrically vivid grand opera in a style whose chief model is middle-period Verdi, containing several famous arias and the "Dance of the Hours."

Venice, 17th c. Disguised as a fisherman, the Genoese nobleman Enzo Grimaldo (t) is in Venice in violation of his banishment. Loved by the street singer La Gioconda (s), he is himself enamored of Laura (ms), wife of the councillor Alvise Badoero (bs). Partly out of jealousy prompted by his own unrequited desire for Gioconda, the spy Barnaba (bar) denounces the disguised Enzo to the council. Enzo arranges a secret tryst with Laura on board

La Gioconda – (1966). Dance of the Hours. Designed by Beni Montresor, choreography by Zachary Solov

his ship. Gioconda comes to confront him there; recognizing Laura as the unknown woman who saved Gioconda's blind mother (c) from an angry mob who believed her a witch, she warns Laura that Alvise is coming to arrest Enzo. The grateful Laura flees; Enzo sets fire to his ship and escapes with Gioconda and his crew. Having learned of Laura's affair with Enzo, Alvise orders her to take poison; the resourceful Gioconda substitutes a sleeping potion. To win Enzo's freedom, Gioconda promises herself to Barnaba, secretly resolving to commit suicide rather than submit to him. She reunites Enzo and the revived Laura, who depart with her blessing. Barnaba arrives to claim his prize, but Gioconda has taken Laura's poison herself, and falls dead as he is about to embrace her. In impotent rage, he shouts into her ear that he has strangled her mother.

Gioielli della Madonna, I (The Jewels of the Madonna). Opera in 3 acts by Wolf-Ferrari; libretto by Enrico Golisciani and Carlo Zangarini.

First perf., Berlin, Kurfürstenoper, Dec. 23, 1911 (in Ger.): Salden, Marak, Wiedemann. U.S. prem., Chicago, Auditorium, Jan. 16, 1912: White, Bassi, Sammarco, c. Campanini. Met. prem., Dec. 12, 1925: Jeritza, Martinelli, Danise, c. Papi, d. Rovescalli, p. Wymetal. 11 perfs. in 2 seasons.

Wolf-Ferrari's sole excursion into verismo, set in Naples. The gangster Rafaele (bar) declares that for love of Maliella (s) he would dare steal the jewels on the Madonna's statue. The blacksmith Gennaro (t) overhears the girl musing on that rash offer and, desperately desiring her, carries it out himself. She gives herself to him, then confesses to Rafaele, who rejects her; after casting the jewels at Gennaro's feet, she drowns herself. Gennaro returns the jewels to the statue and stabs himself.

Giordano, Umberto. Composer; b. Foggia, Italy, Aug. 28, 1867; d. Milan, Nov. 12, 1948. Studied in Foggia and with Paolo Serrao at Naples Conservatory. His first opera, *Marina* (1888, never perf.), won Giordano a commission, but the result, *Mala Vita* (1892), was a notorious scandal due to its crude and violent story; revised as *Il Voto* (1897), it failed once more, and *Regina Diaz* (1894) was withdrawn after two performances. Despite these setbacks, Giordano composed *Andrea Chénier* (1896), a veristic adaptation of history, and won great success. Subsequent works in a similar vein, featuring intense declamation, pastiche genre scenes, and fluid but undirected harmonic motion, made steadily lesser impressions; *Fedora* (1898), *Siberia* (1903), *Marcella* (1907), the one-act *Mese Mariano* (1910), *Mme. Sans-Gêne* (1915), and *La Cena delle Beffe* (1924) are rarely performed today. His last opera, *Il Re* (1929), goes against type by featuring a coloratura soprano.

Giorno di Regno, Un (A Day's Reign); later *Il Finto Stanislao* (The False Stanislao). Opera in 2 acts by Verdi; libretto by Romani, after Alexandre Vincent Pineu-Duval's comedy *Le Faux Stanislas*.
First perf., Milan, La Scala, Sep. 5, 1840: Rainieri-Marini, Abbadia, Salvi, Ferlotti, Scalese. U.S. prem., N.Y., Town Hall (Amato Opera Co., June 18, 1960, concert perf., in Eng.).
The only conventional opera buffa in Verdi's catalogue. Its initial failure seems to have soured him on the genre for most of his life, but modern revivals have shown it stageworthy, and the score has many sparkling numbers.
Near Brest, 1733. The Cavaliere di Belfiore (bar), a young Parisian officer, poses as Stanislaus, King of Poland, to act as a decoy while the real Stanislaus attempts to secure the throne. As "King," Belfiore visits the castle of Baron Kelbar (bs) and aids the Baron's daughter Giulietta (ms) and her beloved Edoardo (t) by talking the girl's unwanted fiancé out of the marriage. Belfiore also manages to be reconciled with his own estranged beloved, the Marchesa del Poggio (s).

Giovanna d'Arco (Joan of Arc). Opera in prologue and 3 acts by Verdi; libretto by Solera, after Schiller's play *Die Jungfrau von Orleans* (although Solera maintained that his plot was original and not derived from Schiller).
First perf., Milan, La Scala, Feb. 15, 1845: Frezzolini-Poggi, Poggi, Colini. U.S. prem., Brooklyn, Academy of Music (N.Y. Grand Opera), May 14, 1976: Sellers, Inchaustegui, Andoor, c. LaSelva.
A story well-adapted to the military vein that came easily to Verdi in what he called his "galley years" – a style tempered by tender lyricism and imaginatively transparent orchestration in some of Giovanna's own music.
France, in Domrémy, Rheims, and near Rouen, 1429. King Carlo VII of France (t), considering surrender in his prolonged war with England, is persuaded to persevere by a shepherd girl, Giovanna (s), who has heard celestial voices urging her to come to France's aid. Taking up arms, she inspires the French to victory. Carlo protests his love for her; though returning his affection, she does not yield, for her "voices" urge her to avoid a mortal's love. Denounced by her father Giacomo (bar), who is suspicious of her spiritualism, she is captured by the English. But Giacomo frees her, and Giovanna is mortally wounded while leading France to another victory.

Giovanni Gallurese. Opera in 3 acts by Montemezzi; libretto by Francesco d'Angelantonio.
First perf., Turin, Vittorio Emanuele, Jan. 28, 1905. U.S. & Met prem., Feb. 19, 1925: Müller, Lauri-Volpi, Danise, c. Serafin, d. Grandi, p. Thewman. 4 perfs. in 1 season.
Montemezzi's score blends quasi-Wagnerian symphonic writing with Italianate vocal cantabile. In 17th-c. Sardinia, the outlaw Gallurese (t) saves the miller's daughter Maria (s) from abduction by the Catalan Rivegas (bar), who later kills Gallurese.

Giraldoni, Eugenio. Baritone; b. Marseilles, France, May 20, 1871; d. Helsinki, June 23, 1924. Son of baritone Leone and soprano Carolina Ferri, with whom he studied; debut as Escamillo, Barcelona, 1891. Sang in Italy, Russia, and Buenos Aires; created Scarpia, Rome, 1900. In his only Met season, sang 13 perfs. as Barnaba (debut, Nov. 28, 1904), Rigoletto, Valentin, Alfio, and Amonasro.

Girl of the Golden West, The. See *Fanciulla del West, La.*

Giulini, Carlo Maria. Conductor; b. Barletta, Italy, May 9, 1914. After study at Santa Cecilia, Rome, and with Bernardino Molinari, played viola in Rome Augusteo Orchestra and made conducting debut there in 1944. Operatic debut, *Traviata*, Bergamo, 1950. At La Scala from 1951, became principal conductor in 1953. Covent Garden debut, *Don Carlo*, 1958. After 1967, unhappy with operatic rehearsal conditions and vocal resources, he concentrated on orchestral conducting, as principal guest conductor of Chicago Symphony (1968–78), conductor of Vienna Symphony (1973–76) and Los Angeles Philharmonic (1978–86). A courtly, intense, and thoughtful perfectionist, Giulini is renowned for his finely articulated, exalted interpretations of the Italian tragic repertory and his elegant Mozart.

Giulio Cesare in Egitto (Julius Caesar in Egypt). Opera in 3 acts by Handel; libretto by Nicola F. Haym.
First perf., London, Haymarket, Feb. 20, 1724: Cuzzoni, Durastanti, Robinson, Senesino, Berenstadt. U.S. prem., Northampton, Mass., Smith College, May 14, 1927 (in Eng.).
One of the composer's most considerable dramatic scores, with moving delineations of the principal characters' deepening relationships; probably the most successful of his operas in 20th-c. revival.
Egypt, 48 B.C. Giulio Cesare (c) has defeated Pompeo (Pompey) in the battle of Pharsalia; the queen Cleopatra (s) and her brother Tolomeo (Ptolemy, c) vie for his favor. The latter has Pompeo killed, and his counselor Achilla (bs) brings the severed head to Caesar, who is infuriated at the needless murder; Pompeo's son Sesto (s) vows vengeance. Cleopatra decides to use her beauty to win Caesar's favor, and thus to triumph over her brother. Meanwhile, Tolomeo conspires with Achilla to murder

Carlo Maria Giulini

Caesar, promising Pompeo's widow Cornelia (c) as reward. After Sesto challenges Tolomeo to combat, he and Cornelia are arrested. Cleopatra visits Caesar in disguise, and they are at the point of declaring their love when word arrives that Tolomeo's troops are after Caesar's life. Cleopatra reveals her identity and implores Caesar to flee; he escapes by jumping into the harbor, and is presumed dead. To avenge Caesar, Cleopatra leads her troops against her brother, but Tolomeo is victorious and Cleopatra is imprisoned. Eventually, with the aid of the dying Achilla, who has been betrayed by Tolomeo, Caesar frees Cleopatra, Sesto kills Tolomeo, and Caesar is proclaimed Emperor.

Giuramento, Il (The Oath). Opera in 3 acts by Mercadante; libretto by G. Rossi, after Victor Hugo's drama *Angelo, Tyran de Padoue*.

First perf., Milan, La Scala, Mar. 10, 1837: Schoberlechner, Brambilla, Pedrazzi, Cartegnova. U.S. prem., N.Y., Astor Place, Feb. 14, 1848.

Mercadante plied, if less concisely, the same operatic trade as Donizetti. The plot is similar to that of *Gioconda*, drawn from the same source, but is here set in 14th-c. Syracuse, and the hero Viscardo (t) kills the heroine, Elaisa (s), wrongly believing that she has poisoned her rival Bianca (ms).

Glade, Coe. Mezzo-soprano; b. Chicago, Aug. 12, 1900; d. New York, Sep. 23, 1985. Debut as Amneris with San Carlo Opera, N.Y. 1926; she sang frequently with that company until 1948, and also with Chicago Opera (from 1928), as Laura, Azucena, and Adalgisa. Best known for Carmen, which she claimed to have sung more than 2,000 times by her retirement, 1963.

Glass, Philip. Composer; b. Baltimore, Md., Jan. 31, 1937. Studied at Juilliard with Bergsma and Persichetti, in Aspen with Milhaud, and in Paris with Boulanger. Beginning in 1966, studies in Eastern music led him to develop a radically new compositional style. Rejecting traditional Western concepts such as progressive form, melody, and harmonic movement, he has built his pieces on a "minimalist" technique of repeated modules (often arpeggios based on a simple harmonic background), gradually added to or subtracted from each other. His most important operas are the historical trilogy including *Einstein on the Beach* (1976), *Satyagraha* (1980), and *Akhnaten* (1984). Other operas include *The Panther* (1980); *The Photographer* (1982), based on the life of Eadweard Muybridge; *the CIVIL warS* (1984); and a children's opera, *The Juniper Tree* (1985).

Glinka, Mikhail. Composer; b. Novospasskoye [now Glinka], Russia, June 1, 1804; d. Berlin, Feb. 15, 1857. Son of landowners, he was exposed to folk music as a child, and to Western concert music during student years and early employment in St. Petersburg. After dabbling at composition, in 1830 he travelled to Milan and Berlin, where he undertook his only systematic compositional studies, with Siegfried Dehn. These experiences helped consolidate his talents and ambitions, and after returning to Russia in 1834 he turned to the stage; the "national heroic-tragic opera" *A Life for the Tsar* (1836) was the triumphant result, followed in 1842 by the less successful (but more original) fantasy opera *Russlan and Ludmila*. In later life he composed instrumental music and songs; sketches for a third opera, *The Bigamist*, begun in 1855, have not survived. Glinka's success in blending Italianate vocal writing and

Gloriana – Sadler's Wells Opera, 1966. Designed by Alix Stone, produced by Colin Graham. Sylvia Fisher

the pageantry of French grand opera with the materials of Russian folk music set the pattern for subsequent developments in Russian opera; his tableau-like dramaturgy, orientalism and chromaticism, and use of exotic harmonic devices strongly influence the works of Borodin, Mussorgsky, Rimsky-Korsakov, and Tchaikovsky.

BIBLIOGRAPHY: David Brown, *Mikhail Glinka: a Biographical and Critical Study* (London, 1974).

Gloriana. Opera in 3 acts by Britten; libretto by William Plomer, after Lytton Strachey's *Elizabeth and Essex*.

First perf., London, Covent Garden, June 8, 1953: Cross, Pears, c. Pritchard. U.S. prem., Cincinnati, Music Hall, May 8, 1956 (concert perf.): Borkh, Conley, c. Krips. U.S. stage prem., N.Y., Met (English National Opera), June 23, 1984: Walker, Davies, c. Elder.

This pageant-like dramatization of events from the reign of Queen Elizabeth I (s), leading to the fall from favor and execution of the Earl of Essex (t), was composed for the coronation of Elizabeth II.

Glossop, Peter. Baritone; b. Sheffield, England, July 6, 1928. Studied with Joseph Hislop; joined Sadler's Wells chorus, London, 1952, but soon assumed principal roles; on roster until 1962. Covent Garden debut as Demetrius (*Midsummer Night's Dream*), 1961; La Scala debut as Rigoletto, 1965. Met debut as Scarpia, June 5, 1971; other Met roles include Redburn (*Billy Budd*), Falstaff, Don Carlo (*Forza*), Balstrode (*Peter Grimes*), and Wozzeck. Has also appeared in Vienna, Salzburg, San Francisco.

Gluck, Alma [Reba Fiersohn]. Soprano; b. Bucharest, Romania, May 11, 1884; d. New York, Oct. 27, 1938. Studied with Arturo Buzzi-Peccia, N.Y., later with Jean de Reszke and Sembrich; debut as Sophie (*Werther*), Met, New Theater, Nov. 16, 1909; in 7 seasons, sang 57 perfs. of

14 roles, including Happy Shade (*Orfeo*), Mimi, and Nedda. From 1913, devoted herself to concerts. Married to violinist Efrem Zimbalist, mother of novelist Marcia Davenport.

Gluck, Christoph Willibald. Composer; b. Erasbach, Upper Palatinate, Germany, July 2, 1714; d. Vienna, Nov. 15, 1787. Primarily self-taught, despite occasional study in Prague and Vienna, in 1737 he joined Prince Melzi's musical establishment in Milan. His successful first opera *Artaserse* (1741) set a libretto by Metastasio in traditional opera seria style, and won him a series of Italian commissions; later he composed *La Caduta de' Giganti* and *Artamene* (both 1746) for London, *Semiramide Riconosciuta* (1748) for Vienna, *Ezio* (1750) for Prague, and *La Clemenza di Tito* (1752) for Naples. In 1750 he married and settled in Vienna, where he adapted French opéras comiques to local taste, and later composed them (notably *La Rencontre Imprévu*, 1764), The ballet-pantomime *Don Juan* (1761), his first collaboration with Calzabigi, prefigures the dramatic orchestral style exploited in their first "reform" opera, *Orfeo ed Euridice* (1762). The simplicity, clarity, and emotional directness of this work were much admired, contrasting vividly with opera seria's intricately formal librettos, rigid alternation of recitative and da capo aria, and its institutionalized license for virtuoso vocal display. Gluck wrote several further operas in traditional style before returning in *Alceste* (1767) to the reform ideals; in his 1769 preface to the score, Gluck declared that "I have striven to restrict music to its true office of serving poetry by means of expression and by following the situations of the story, without interrupting the action or stifling it with a meaningless superfluity of ornaments." After the failure of *Paride ed Elena* (1770), Gluck trained his sights on Paris, composing *Iphigénie en Aulide* (1774), a successful attempt to reform the tragédie lyrique. This was followed by French revisions of *Orfeo* (1774) and *Alceste* (1776). *Armide* (1777), a setting of Quinault's libretto for Lully, sparked one of Paris' frequent esthetic battles, the "war of the Gluckists and Piccinnists." He composed two further works for Paris, the masterful *Iphigénie en Tauride* (1779) and the unsuccessful *Echo et Narcisse* (1779), before retiring to Vienna in failing health.

A composer of genius whose technical limitations predisposed him to a noble simplicity, Gluck was ideally equipped to carry out his reform; although its components were already in the air, no work before *Orfeo* combined them so convincingly. The French operas, richer in characters and incidents, are more dramatic, and include portrayals (such as that of Armide) of remarkable psychological insight.
BIBLIOGRAPHY: Alfred Einstein, *Gluck* (London, 1936; repr. 1964).

Glückliche Hand, Die (The Lucky Hand). Opera in 1 act by Schoenberg; libretto by the composer.

First perf., Vienna, Volksoper, Oct. 14, 1924: Jerger, c. Stiedry. U.S. prem., Philadelphia, Academy of Music, Apr. 11, 1930: Ivantzoff, c. Stokowski (repeated in N.Y., Met, Apr. 22, 1930).

An allegorical treatment of the individual's isolation in industrial society, with special lighting effects conceived in coordination with the score.

Glyndebourne. Estate near Lewes, Sussex, England, site of a summer opera festival founded in 1934 by John Christie at the instigation of his wife, soprano Audrey Mildmay. The initial emphasis was on Mozart, with meticulously prepared productions of *Figaro* and *Così* conducted by Fritz Busch and directed by Carl Ebert, the dominant artistic forces at prewar Glyndebourne; Rudolf Bing served as general manager. In 1938, the repertory reached beyond Mozart to *Don Pasquale* and *Macbeth*. After World War II, the English Opera Group was in residence for two seasons, giving the premieres of *Rape of Lucretia* (1946) and *Albert Herring* (1947). Ebert directed *Orfeo* in 1947, and for several years the company presented opera at the Edinburgh festival, directed by Bing. Normal seasons at Glyndebourne resumed in 1950 under Ebert and Busch; after the latter's death the following year, Vittorio Gui was engaged as music director and introduced Rossini to the repertory. Subsequent music directors have been John Pritchard (1969–77) and Bernard Haitink (since 1977); after Ebert retired in 1959, Günther Rennert (1959–71) and John Cox (1971–82) served as head of production, and in 1984 Peter Hall was named artistic director. The repertory has broadened to embrace works by Beethoven, Cavalli, Donizetti, Henze, Janáček, Massenet, Monteverdi, Stravinsky, Strauss, and Verdi. The festival theater (original capacity 300) has twice been enlarged and now seats 800; the season runs from the end of May to early August. The Glyndebourne Touring Company, established in 1968, brings productions, with casts of younger singers, to various British cities.

Gniewek, Raymond. Violinist; b. East Meadow, N.Y., Nov. 13, 1931. Student at Eastman School (degree, 1953); member, then Concertmaster, Rochester Philharmonic. Since 1957, concertmaster of Met Orchestra. On Dec. 22, 1958, conducted part of *Manon Lescaut* when Cleva suddenly became indisposed. Married to soprano Judith Blegen.

A picnic at Glyndebourne

Tito Gobbi as Simon Boccanegra

goat's trill. A vocal ornament, usually the rapid reiteration of a single pitch.

Gobbi, Tito. Baritone; b. Bassano del Grappa, near Venice, Oct. 24, 1913; d. Rome, Mar. 5, 1984. After law study at U. of Padua, he studied singing with Giulio Crimi in Rome; debut as Rodolfo (*Sonnambula*), Gubbio, 1935. First prize in an international contest in Vienna (1936) led to debuts as Germont in two Rome houses, the Adriano (1937) and the Opera (1939), where he also sang the first Wozzeck in Italy (1942) and several world premieres of works by Italian composers; La Scala debut as Belcore (*Elisir*), 1942. His first U.S. appearance was in San Francisco (debut, Rossini's Figaro, 1948), but he was most often seen in this country with the Chicago Lyric Opera (1954–73), where his roles included Amonasro, Marcello, Rigoletto, Michele (*Tabarro*), Renato (*Ballo*), Rance (*Fanciulla*), Gérard (*Chénier*), Iago, Tonio, Mozart's Almaviva, Michonnet (*Adriana*), Falstaff, Schicchi, De Siriex (*Fedora*), Nabucco, Don Giovanni; he made his debut as director there in 1965, staging *Simon Boccanegra* with himself in the title role. He took this production to Covent Garden, where he had appeared since 1951, notably as Posa in the Visconti production of *Don Carlos* (1958). His Met debut, as Scarpia, took place Jan. 13, 1956; he returned irregularly during ten further seasons (until 1976), singing 33 perfs., 22 of them as Scarpia, also Iago, Falstaff, and a single Rigoletto, and also staging *Tosca* (1978). Gobbi was a frequent guest in most leading opera houses, and at the festivals of Florence (debut, Hidraot in *Armide*, 1941) and Salzburg (debut, Don Giovanni, 1950). In the early part of his career, he appeared in many films. A resourceful and penetrating actor and musician, Gobbi built memorable characterizations on the foundation of a voice not in itself exceptional; in his day, he was the most admired exponent of the later Verdi baritone parts – Boccanegra, Iago, and Falstaff – and (especially in collaboration with Callas) of Scarpia.
BIBLIOGRAPHY: Tito Gobbi, *Tito Gobbi: My Life* (N.Y., and London, 1979).

Godard, Benjamin. Composer; b. Paris, Aug. 18, 1849; d. Cannes, Jan. 10, 1895. Studied with Reber at Paris Conservatory. Success with salon and orchestral works encouraged him to write operas. *Jocelyn* (1888) is remembered only by the familiar "Berceuse," while the grander *Dante et Béatrice* (1890) and *Jeanne d'Arc* (1891) are long forgotten; the posthumous opéra comique *La Vivandière* (1895) had more success.

Goehr, Alexander. Composer; b. Berlin, Aug. 10, 1932. Studied at Royal Manchester College of Music and at Paris Conservatory with Messiaen. His operatic works are didactic in a Brechtian sense. *Arden Must Die* (1967) is a severely dramatic, occasionally parodistic work. *Naboth's Vineyard* (1968), *Shadow Play-2* (1970), and *Sonata about Jerusalem* (1970) together form the chamber-scaled *Triptych*, mixing Stravinskian and expressionist styles with theatrical abstraction. *Behold the Sun* (1985), based on the same historical episode as Meyerbeer's *Prophète*, abjures expressionism in favor of more traditional formalism.

Goethe, Johann Wolfgang von. German poet and dramatist (1749–1832). Operas based on his writings include *La Damnation de Faust* (Berlioz), *Faust* (Gounod), *Mefistofele* (Boito), *Mignon* (Thomas), and *Werther* (Massenet).

Goetz, Hermann. Composer, b. Königsberg, Prussia, Dec. 7, 1840; d. Hottingen, near Zurich, Dec. 3, 1876. Studied with von Bülow (piano) and Ulrich (composition). His *Die Widerspenstigen Zähmung* (1874) is considered one of the best 19th-c. German comic operas, independent of Wagnerianism, rooted in Mozartean closed forms. *Francesca von Rimini* was completed by Ernst Frank after Goetz's early death from tuberculosis.

Gogol, Nikolai. Russian author (1809–52). Operas based on his writings include *The Nose* (Shostakovich), *The Fair at Sorochinsk* (Mussorgsky), and *Vakula the Smith* (Tchaikovsky).

Goldberg, Reiner. Tenor; b. Crostau, Germany, Oct. 17, 1939. Studied with Arno Schellenberg, Dresden; debut as Armed Man (*Zauberflöte*), Saxon Regional Theater, Dresden, 1966. Joined Dresden State Opera, 1973, and Berlin State Opera, 1981. Covent Garden debut as Stolzing, 1982; N.Y. debut in concert perf. of *Guntram*, 1983. Has also appeared in Hamburg, Vienna, Leningrad.

Golden Cockerel, The. Opera in 3 acts by Rimsky-Korsakov; libretto by Vladimir Bielsky, after Pushkin's poem.
First perf., Moscow, Solodovnikov, Oct. 7, 1909: c. Cooper. U.S. & Met prem., Mar. 6, 1918 (in Fr., as *Le Coq d'Or*): Barrientos, R. Diaz, Didur, c. Monteux, d. Pogany, p. Bolm. The Queen has also been sung at the Met by Pons, Munsel; Dodon by Pinza, Cordon. 55 perfs. in 11 seasons.
Refused production by the censors, who feared it might be taken as a satire on the imperial court and the disastrous Russo-Japanese war, Rimsky-Korsakov's final opera was not performed in his lifetime. Because it calls for the singers also to dance, Fokine devised a plan, followed in early productions, whereby singers sang the roles from stage boxes and dancers mimed them.
The Astrologer (high t) gives King Dodon (bs) a Golden Cockerel (s) that will crow in case of danger; the King offers him any payment he wishes, but the

Astrologer postpones naming it. The cock crows, and when the King goes off to war he meets the beautiful Queen of Shemakha (s), who beguiles him and agrees to marry him. When they return, the Astrologer asks for the Queen as his payment for the Cockerel; Dodon kills him for his impudence, whereupon the bird pecks him to death, and the Queen vanishes.

Golden Slippers, The. See *Vakula the Smith.*

Goldene Kreuz, Das (The Golden Cross). Opera in 2 acts by Brüll; libretto by Mosenthal, after the comedy *Croix d'Or* by Brazier and Melville.
First perf., Berlin, Court Opera, Dec. 22, 1875. U.S. prem., N.Y., Terrace Garden, July 19, 1879. Met prem., Nov. 19, 1886: Seidl-Kraus, Januschowsky, Alvary, Fischer, von Milde, c. W. Damrosch, d. Hoyt. 4 perfs. in 1 season.
This amiably sentimental work enjoyed great initial success. The village of Melun, near Paris, 1812–15. To spare her brother Colas (bar) from conscription on his wedding day, Christine (s) promises her hand to any man who will go to war in his stead; eventually, she falls unwittingly in love with Gontran (t), the substitute.

Goldmark, Karl [Károly]. Composer; b. Keszthely, Hungary, May 18, 1830; d. Vienna, Jan. 2, 1915. Studied at Vienna Conservatory with Preyer. His first opera, *Die Königin von Saba* (1875), quickly achieved international popularity, blending Meyerbeerian grand opera with synagogue music and Wagnerian harmony. This eclectic style was less successful in *Merlin* (1886); the comic opera *Das Heimchen am Herd* (1896), after Dickens; and the fairy-tale opera *Ein Wintermärchen* (1908), after Shakespeare's *Winter's Tale*.

Goldoni, Carlo. Italian dramatist (1707–93). Operas based on his writings include Wolf-Ferrari's *Le Donne Curiose* and *I Quattro Rusteghi*.

Goldovsky, Boris. Producer and conductor; b. Moscow, June 7, 1908. Studied piano at Moscow Conservatory, with Schnabel in Berlin and Dohnányi in Budapest, also conducting with Reiner at Philadelphia's Curtis Institute. Head of the opera department at Boston's New England Conservatory (1942–64) and the opera workshop at Tanglewood (1946–62), where he presented the U.S. premieres of *Idomeneo, Peter Grimes*, and *Albert Herring*. Founder in 1946 of the New England Opera Theater, he also directed the Goldovsky Opera Theater, which toured opera nationwide until 1984, and has for several decades been a familiar figure on Met radio broadcasts.

Goltz, Christel. Soprano; b. Dortmund, Germany, July 8, 1912. Studied in Munich; debut as Agathe (*Freischütz*), Fürth, 1935. Member of Dresden State Opera, 1940–48, also appeared in Berlin (1947) and Vienna (from 1950). In her only Met season, she sang 6 perfs. as Salome (debut, Dec. 15, 1954); also a noted Elektra and Marie (*Wozzeck*).

Gomes, Antonio Carlos. Composer; b. Campinas, Brazil, July 11, 1836; d. Belém, Sep. 16, 1896. Early lessons with his father, a bandmaster, were followed by studies at the Conservatory in Rio, where his first operas won him a scholarship for further training at Milan Conservatory. The grand opera *Il Guarany* (1870), with a libretto after the Brazilian writer José de Alencar and a score full of local

color and melodic freshness, had great success in Europe. Later works include the grand opera *Salvator Rosa* (1874) and *Lo Schiavo* (composed in Italian but finally performed in Brazil in 1889).

Gonzalez, Dalmacio. Tenor; b. Olot, Gerona, Spain, May 12, 1945. Studied at Barcelona Conservatory, and with Gilbert Price, Arleen Augér, and Anton Dermota; debut as Ugo in Donizetti's *Parisina*, Barcelona, 1977. N.Y.C. Opera debut as Alfredo, 1979. Met debut as Ernesto (*Don Pasquale*), Mar. 26, 1980; he has also sung Nemorino, Almaviva, and Fenton there. Other appearances in Los Angeles, San Francisco, Chicago, Berlin, Barcelona, and Zurich.

Goodall, Reginald. Conductor; b. Lincoln, England, July 13, 1905. Studied at Royal College of Music, London. At Sadler's Wells Opera, conducted premiere of *Peter Grimes* (1945). At Covent Garden, staff conductor (1946–60) and repetiteur (1961–71). After 1968, conducted Wagner for Sadler's Wells/English National Opera, beginning with *Meistersinger*, followed by a highly-praised *Ring* cycle; the latter, like his subsequent *Tristan* and *Parsifal*, was recorded.

Good Soldier Schweik, The. Opera in 2 acts, with spoken prologue and epilogue, by Robert Kurka; libretto by Lewis Allan, after Jaroslav Hašek's novel.
First perf., N.Y.C. Opera, Apr. 23, 1958: Kelley, c. Rudel.
Kurka's only opera, a witty satire on war and military bureaucracy.

Goossens, Eugene. Conductor and composer; b. London, May 26, 1893; d. Hillingdon, June 13, 1962. Educated at Bruges, Liverpool, and London's Royal College of Music. Operatic debut, Stanford's *The Critic*, London, 1916. Conductor of Rochester Philharmonic (1923–31), Cincinnati Symphony (1931–46), then active in Australia (1947–56). His operas *Judith* (1929) and *Don Juan de Manara* (1939) were performed at Covent Garden.

Goritz, Otto. Baritone; b. Berlin, June 8, 1873; d. Hamburg, Apr. 11, 1929. Studied with mother, Olga Nielitz; debut as Matteo (*Fra Diavolo*), Neustrelitz, 1895. Appeared in Breslau (1898–1900) and Hamburg (1900–03). Met debut as Klingsor, Dec. 24, 1903; in 14 seasons, he sang 405 perfs. of 23 roles, including Ochs, Pizarro (*Fidelio*), Alberich, Telramund, Beckmesser, and Papageno.

Gorr, Rita [Marguerite Geirnaert]. Mezzo-soprano; b. Ghent, Belgium, Feb. 18, 1926. Studied in Ghent and Brussels; debut as Fricka (*Walküre*), Antwerp, 1949. Appeared in Strasbourg (1949–52); debuts at Paris Opéra and Opéra-Comique (1952), Bayreuth (1958), Covent Garden (1959), La Scala (Kundry, 1960). Met debut as Amneris, Oct. 17, 1962; in 4 seasons, sang 36 perfs. including Santuzza, Eboli, Azucena, and Dalila.

Götterdämmerung. See *Ring des Nibelungen, Der.*

Gounod, Charles. Composer; b. Paris, June 17, 1818; d. St. Cloud, Oct. 18, 1893. Studied privately with Reicha, and with Halévy and Le Sueur at Paris Conservatory, winning the Prix de Rome in 1839. In Italy, he was impressed by 16th-c. polyphony, and introduced to the music of Bach, Beethoven, and Mendelssohn by the

Charles Gounod

latter's sister, Fanny Hensel. At this time he composed primarily religious music, but after his return to Paris Pauline Viardot urged him to compose for the theater and appeared in his *Sapho* (1851). This was modestly successful, but the failure of *La Nonne Sanglante* (1854) proved that Meyerbeerian grand opera was not Gounod's strength. His best works resulted from his association with the Théâtre-Lyrique, beginning with the opéra comique *Le Médecin Malgré Lui*, after Molière (1858); later, the equally charming miniature *Philémon et Baucis* (1860) also found an enthusiastic audience. In *Faust* (1859), Gounod achieved his great success, treating an ambitious subject without resort to Meyerbeerian grandiosity, and creating a work of tender lyricism, vivid characterizations, and clear dramatic structure, if hardly the scope or profundity of Goethe's original. *La Reine de Saba* (1862), for the Opéra, was less well received, but Gounod returned to the Lyrique for *Mireille* (1864), with its Provençal setting and musical color, and the lyrical *Roméo et Juliette*. Gounod lived in England, 1871–74, where he became enmeshed in a liaison with a singer; his subsequent music, including the operas *Cinq Mars* (1877), *Polyeucte* (1878), and *Le Tribut de Zamora* (1880), is suffused with platitudinous religiosity. BIBLIOGRAPHY: James Harding, *Gounod* (N.Y., and London, 1973).

Goyescas. Opera in 3 scenes by Granados; libretto by Fernando Periquet y Zuaznabar.
First perf., Met, Jan. 18, 1916: Fitziu, Martinelli, de Luca, c. Bavagnoli, d. Rovescalli, p. Speck. 5 perfs. in 1 season.
A stage adaptation of Granados' piano suite of the same title (based on paintings of Goya); Paquiro (bar) and Fernando (t) duel over the love of Rosario (s).

Gozzi, Carlo. Italian dramatist (1720–1806). Operas based on his writings include *Die Feen* (Wagner), *König Hirsch* (Henze), *The Love for Three Oranges* (Prokofiev), and *Turandot* (Busoni and Puccini).

Graf, Herbert. Producer; b. Vienna, Apr. 10, 1904; d. Geneva, Apr. 5, 1973. Son of music critic Max Graf, worked as director in Münster, Breslau, and Frankfurt. Worked briefly for Philadelphia Opera, 1934; at Salzburg, staged *Meistersinger* and *Zauberflöte* for Toscanini. After his Met debut (*Samson*, 1936), he staged *Salome*, *Falstaff*, *Orfeo*, *Nozze*, *Ballo*, *Alceste*, and *Manon Lescaut* under Johnson, 14 additional works under Bing, including *Arabella*, *Wozzeck*, *Elektra*, and, with designer Eugene Berman, *Rigoletto*, *Forza*, *Don Giovanni*, and *Otello*. Manager of Zurich Opera (1960–62) and Grand Theater, Geneva (1965–72). Author of several books about opera production.

Graham, Colin. Producer; b. Hove, England, Sep. 22, 1931. With English Opera Group from 1954; director of productions (1963–75). Major positions with English National Opera (1968–83), English Music Theatre (from 1975), and Opera Theater of St. Louis (from 1978). Has produced opera for Covent Garden, Scottish Opera, Glyndebourne, BBC-TV, N.Y.C. Opera (*Voice of Ariadne*, 1977), St. Louis (*Contes d'Hoffmann*, *Viaggio a Reims*). Directed world premieres of all Britten operas after 1954 (except *Midsummer Night's Dream*). Met debut, *Death in Venice* (1974), followed by *Traviata* (1981) and *Così* (1982).

Gramm [Grambsch], **Donald.** Bass-baritone; b. Milwaukee, Wisc., Feb. 26, 1927; d. New York, July 2, 1983. Studied at Wisconsin College-Conservatory and with George Graham, later at Chicago Musical College and with Singher, Santa Barbara; debut as Raimondo (*Lucia*), 8th Street Theater, Chicago, 1944. A regular performer with N.Y.C. Opera (debut, Colline, 1952), Opera Co. of Boston (from 1958, including Schoenberg's Moses, Diaz in *Montezuma*), and Santa Fe (1960–77). Met debut as Truffaldin (*Ariadne*), Jan. 10, 1964; in 19 seasons, he sang 158 perfs. of 20 roles, including Leporello, Waldner (*Arabella*), Zuniga, Don Alfonso (*Così*), Balstrode (*Peter Grimes*), Papageno, the Doctor (*Wozzeck*), and Dr. Schön (*Lulu*). Gramm also sang in Spoleto (Leporello, 1967), Aix (Basilio, 1969), and Glyndebourne (Nick Shadow and Falstaff, 1975–76; Ochs, 1980). An extremely versatile artist, valued for his polished singing, ability to master contemporary vocal writing, and strong stage presence.

Granados, Enrique. Composer and pianist; b. Lérida, Spain, July 27, 1867; d. during sinking of S.S. Sussex in the English Channel by a German submarine, Mar. 24, 1916. After success with zarzuela composition, his piano suite *Goyescas*, inspired by the paintings of Goya, won international recognition. From it Granados derived the opera of the same title, intended for production at the Paris Opéra but eventually, because of World War I, given at the Met; during his return voyage to Europe after the premiere (1916), Granados lost his life.

grand opera. The term applied in 19th-c. France to operas on historical subjects, with prominent use of chorus and ballet, in 4 or 5 acts. Since then, applied more generally to any operas using large forces.

Granforte, Apollo [Appollinari]. Baritone; b. Legnano, near Verona, Italy, July 29, 1886; d. Milan, June 10, 1975. Studied in Buenos Aires; debut as Germont, Politeama, Rosario, Argentina, 1913. Sang in Italy from 1916, later touring in Australia and South America. La Scala debut as

Amfortas, 1922; created Menècrate (Mascagni's *Nerone*) there, 1935. Retired in 1943.

Grau, Maurice. Impresario; b. Brünn [now Brno], Moravia, 1849; d. Paris, Mar. 14, 1907. Resident in the U.S. from age 5, he studied law at Columbia U. He managed numerous celebrity tours, such as that of pianist Anton Rubinstein (1872), and formed the Kellogg Opera Co. (1873). During Henry E. Abbey's ruinous first season in the new Met (1883–84), Grau advised him on operatic matters, and they continued as a successful theater management firm, returning to the Met in 1891 with stars such as Eames and the de Reszkes. After Abbey's death in 1896, Grau took over the lease, skipped a season, and reorganized as the Maurice Grau Opera Co. (1898–1903). He also held the lease on Covent Garden, London (1896–1900), in both theaters offering a vocal "golden age." Parsimonious but shrewd, Grau catered unerringly to public taste with his "Nights of the Seven Stars." He revived the Met spring tour, on a city-by-city guaranteed-payment basis; his first 3 tours (1899–1902) visited 37 cities, 23 for the first time in Met history. He died in 1907, amid rumors that he was about to return to N.Y. as manager of the Met's arch-competitor, Hammerstein's Manhattan Opera.

Greenwood, Jane. Designer; b. Liverpool, England, Apr. 30, 1934. Has worked in both legitimate theater and opera, including N.Y.C. Opera, San Francisco, Houston, and Washington, D.C. At the Met, she designed costumes for *Syllabaire pour Phèdre*, *Dido and Aeneas* and *Four Saints* (Mini-Met, 1973), *Ariadne* (revival, 1976), *Carmélites* (1977), and *Chénier* (revival, 1977).

Giulia Grisi as Norma

Gregor, Joseph. Librettist; b. Czernowitz, Bukovina [now Chernovtsy, U.S.S.R.], Oct. 26, 1888; d. Vienna, Oct. 12, 1960. An archivist and writer, he furnished librettos for Richard Strauss' late operas *Friedenstag* (from a scenario by Stefan Zweig), *Daphne*, and *Liebe der Danae* (after a sketch by Hofmannsthal).

Greindl, Josef. Bass; b. Munich, Dec. 23, 1912. Studied with Paul Bender and Anna Bahr-Mildenburg; debut as Hunding, Krefeld, 1936. Appeared in Düsseldorf (1938–42) and Berlin, at State Opera (1942–49) and Städtische Oper (from 1949). Bayreuth debut as Pogner, 1943; sang bass roles (and Hans Sachs) there, 1951–69. In his only Met season, sang Heinrich (*Lohengrin*, debut, Nov. 15, 1952) and Pogner.

Grétry, André. Composer; b. Liège, Belgium, Feb. 8, 1741; d. Montmorency, near Paris, Sep. 24, 1813. After study in Rome, he was encouraged by Voltaire to exploit the Parisian vogue for light opera. Beginning with *Le Huron* (1768), he dominated the field of opéra comique, producing some 50 operas in 35 years, including *Le Tableau Parlant* (1769), *Zémire et Azor* (1771), and *Richard Coeur-de-Lion* (1784). Praised for clear declamation, melodic and harmonic directness and simplicity, Grétry successfully combined Italian and French models. However, in the changing musical styles of the revolutionary years he lost touch with the public.

Griffel, Kay. Soprano; b. Eldora, Iowa, Dec. 26, 1940. Studied at Northwestern U., Ill., in Berlin, and with Lotte Lehmann, Santa Barbara, as mezzo. Debut as Mercedes (*Carmen*), Chicago, 1960. Singing in German houses, she moved to soprano roles; Glyndebourne debut as Alice Ford, 1976. Met debut as Elettra (*Idomeneo*), Nov. 16, 1982; other Met roles are Arabella, Tatiana, Countess (*Figaro*), and Rosalinde.

Grillo, Joann. Mezzo-soprano; b. New York, May 14, 1936. Studied in N.Y. and Germany. N.Y.C. Opera debut as Gertrude (*Louise*), 1962. Met debut as Rosette (*Manon*), Oct. 17, 1963; her 226 perfs. there also include Carmen, Meg Page, Preziosilla, and Suzuki. Appearances abroad as Amneris (Frankfurt, 1967), Charlotte (Barcelona, 1963), and Carmen (Vienna, 1978; Paris, 1981).

Grisi, Giuditta. Mezzo-soprano; b. Milan, July 28, 1805; d. Robecco d'Oglio, near Cremona, May 1, 1840. Studied with her aunt, contralto Josephina Grassini, and at Milan Conservatory; debut in Rossini's *Bianca e Faliero*, Vienna, 1826. Appeared in Florence, Parma, Turin, and Venice, where she created Romeo in *Capuleti*, opposite her younger sister, soprano Giulia, 1830. Also appeared in London and Paris, 1832. Retired 1838.

Grisi, Giulia. Soprano; b. Milan, July 28, 1811; d. Berlin, Nov. 29, 1869. Her teachers included her sister Giuditta, Marliani in Milan, and Giacomelli in Bologna. At first she sang mezzo roles, making her debut as Emma (Rossini's *Zelmira*), Bologna, 1828. After her 1831 La Scala debut in the premiere of Strepponi's *L'Ullà di Bassora*, she also created Adalgisa in *Norma*. Unhappy at La Scala but unable to break her contract legally, she fled Italy (never to perform there again) and joined her sister in Paris at the Théâtre Italien (debut as Semiramide, 1832), where she appeared for 16 consecutive seasons, creating Elvira in *Puritani* and Norina in *Don Pasquale*, and returned in 1857 as Leonora (*Trovatore*). For her 1834 London debut, she sang Ninetta (*Gazza Ladra*), and she returned to that city nearly every year until her retirement in 1861, first at the King's (later Her Majesty's), then with the Royal Italian Opera at Covent Garden, which she opened as Semiramide (1847). In London's first *Lucrezia Borgia* (1839), she sang for the first time opposite the tenor Giovanni Mario, her companion for the rest of her life (they never married, for she had not divorced her first husband). Together they toured Russia (1849) and the U.S. (1854–55); in N.Y., she sang Lucrezia Borgia at Castle Garden and Norma at the Academy of Music. After retirement, she attempted an unsuccessful London comeback in 1866 as Lucrezia Borgia.

Giulia Grisi brought a smooth, agile voice and powerful dramatic temperament to a wide variety of roles. She knew and worked with the leading composers of her youth, and was an authoritative leading soprano in their operas, but proved able to encompass the heavier vocal demands of Meyerbeer and Verdi as well.

Grist, Reri. Soprano; b. New York, 1932. Studied in N.Y.; worked in musical comedy (including *West Side Story*, 1957) before operatic debut as Blondchen (*Entführung*), Santa Fe, 1959. N.Y.C. Opera debut in *Carmina Burana*, 1959. Appeared in Cologne (1960), at Covent Garden (1962), Salzburg (1965, 1972), Glyndebourne (1972), and Vienna (1973). Met debut as Rosina (*Barbiere*), Feb. 25, 1966, also singing Sophie, Zerbinetta, Olympia, Oscar, Norina, Adina, and Gilda; 56 perfs. in 6 seasons.

Griswold, Putnam. Bass-baritone; b. Minneapolis, Minn., Dec. 23, 1875; d. New York, Feb. 26, 1914. Studied with Randegger in London, Bouhy in Paris, Stockhausen in Frankfurt. Covent Garden debut as Leonato (Stanford's *Much Ado About Nothing*), 1901. Appeared with Berlin Opera (1904, 1906–11), then toured America as Gurnemanz with Savage's company, 1904–05. Met debut as Hagen, Nov. 23, 1911; in 3 seasons, he sang 62 perfs. of 11 roles, including Pogner, Wotan, and King Marke, and created De Guiche (*Cyrano*).

Grobe, Donald. Tenor; b. Ottawa, Ill., Dec. 16, 1929; d. Berlin, Apr. 1, 1986. Studied at Mannes School, N.Y., and with Martial Singher and Robert Weede; debut as Borsa (*Rigoletto*), Chicago, 1952. Appeared in Hanover (1957–60) and at Deutsche Oper, Berlin (from 1960), where he created Wilhelm (*Junge Lord*, 1965). Only Met appearances as Froh (debut, Nov. 22, 1968). Member of Bavarian State Opera, Munich, from 1967, and of Hamburg State Opera from 1968.

Gruberova, Edita. Soprano; b. Bratislava, Czechoslovakia, Dec. 23, 1946. Studied with Maria Medvecka in Prague, Ruthilde Boesch in Vienna; debut as Rosina, Bratislava, 1968. Has appeared in Vienna, Hamburg, Munich, Frankfurt, Glyndebourne, and Bayreuth. Met debut as Queen of Night, Jan. 5, 1977; has also sung Zerbinetta there.

Gruenberg, Louis. Composer; b. near Brest-Litovsk, Byelo-Russia, Aug. 3, 1884; d. Beverly Hills, Calif., June 19, 1964. Raised in the U.S., he studied piano and composition with Busoni in Berlin, then toured and taught in Europe. Returning to the U.S. in 1919, he advocated the incorporation of vernacular elements such as spirituals and jazz rhythms into American compositions, doing so most successfully in his opera *The Emperor*

Jones (1933). Among several other operas, the children's opera *Jack and the Beanstalk* (1931) and the radio opera *Green Mansions* (1937) had some success; others remain unperformed.

Grümmer, Elisabeth. Soprano; b. Niederjeutz, Alsace-Lorraine, Mar. 31, 1911; d. Berlin, Nov. 6, 1986. First a professional actress, studied singing with F. Schlender in Aachen; debut there as Flowermaiden (*Parsifal*), 1940. Appeared in Duisburg (1942–44), then with Berlin Städtische Oper (from 1946). Debuts at Covent Garden (Eva, 1951), Vienna and Salzburg (both 1953), Glyndebourne (1956), and Bayreuth (1957). N.Y.C. Opera debut as Marschallin, 1967. Only Met appearances as Elsa (debut, Apr. 20, 1967).

Guadagni, Gaetano. Alto, later soprano castrato; b. Lodi or Vincenza, Italy, c. 1725; d. Padua, Nov. 1792. Debut at San Moïse, Venice, 1746. After appearances at the Haymarket, London, 1748–49, Handel assigned him the alto parts in *Messiah* and *Samson*, and wrote the role of Didimus (*Theodora*) for him, 1750; while in London, Guadagni was influenced by the acting of David Garrick. He then sang in Dublin (1751–52), Paris (1754), and Lisbon (1755), where he studied with Gizziello. After engagements in Italy, he went to Vienna and created Gluck's Orfeo (1762), which he later sang in London in a pastiche version (1770). After 1776, retired to Padua, where he sang sacred music.

Guadagno, Anton. Conductor; b. Castellammare di Golfo, Italy, May 2, 1925. After study at Palermo, Santa Cecilia, and Bellini conservatories, conducted in South America and Mexico. Assistant conductor at Met (1958–59), then music director, Philadelphia Lyric Opera (1966–72), and guest conductor internationally. Met podium debut, *Ballo*, Nov. 9, 1982.

Guarrera, Frank. Baritone; b. Philadelphia, Pa., Dec. 3, 1923. Studied with Richard Bonelli, Curtis, Philadelphia; debut as Silvio, N.Y.C. Opera, 1947. La Scala debut as Zurga (*Pêcheurs*), 1948. Met debut as Escamillo, Dec. 14, 1948; in 28 seasons, he sang 429 perfs. of 34 roles, including Amonasro, Rossini's Figaro, Marcello, Don Alfonso (*Così*), Ford, Gianni Schicchi, and Germont. Has also appeared in Chicago, San Francisco, London, and Paris.

Gueden, Hilde. Soprano; b. Vienna, Sep. 15, 1917. Studied with Wetzelsberger, Vienna Conservatory; sang in operetta before operatic debut as Cherubino, Zurich, 1939. Appeared in Munich (1941–42), Rome (1942–46), Vienna (from 1946), Salzburg (1946) and at Covent Garden (1947). Met debut as Gilda, Nov. 15, 1951; in 9 seasons, she sang 102 perfs. of 13 roles, including Anne (*Rake*), Susanna, Zerlina, Zdenka, Sophie, Gilda, Mimi, Musetta, Micaela, Norina, Rosalinde (*Fledermaus*), and Euridice.

Guelfi, Giangiacomo. Baritone; b. Rome, Dec. 21, 1924. Studied with Titta Ruffo and at Centro Lirico, Florence; debut as Rigoletto, Spoleto, 1950. Appeared at La Scala from 1952, and in Rome, Naples, Venice, Hamburg, Berlin, Chicago, and Dallas. In only Met season, sang one perf. each of Scarpia (debut, Feb. 5, 1970) and Jack Rance (*Fanciulla*).

guerre des bouffons (Fr., "war of the buffoons"). A dispute (Paris, 1752–54) between the supporters of Italian opera (the *bouffons*) and those of French opera.

Guéymard, Louis. Tenor; b. Chapponay, France, Aug. 17, 1822; d. Paris, July 1880. A leading tenor at the Paris Opéra from 1848 (debut in *Robert le Diable*) until 1868, he created Arrigo (*Vêpres Siciliennes*), 1855.

Guglielmo Tell. *See Guillaume Tell.*

Gui, Vittorio. Conductor; b. Rome, Sep. 14, 1885; d. Florence, Oct. 17, 1975. Studied piano and composition at Santa Cecilia, Rome. Conducting debut in Rome (*Gioconda*, 1907), eventually going to La Scala during Toscanini regime (debut, *Salome*, 1923). Active in development of the Florence Maggio Musicale, he also conducted in Germany and Austria (Salzburg, 1935) and at Glyndebourne (1948–64; music director, 1952–64); specialized in Rossini and Mozart.

Guillaume Tell (William Tell). Opera in 4 acts (reduced to 3 in June 1831) by Rossini; libretto in French by Étienne de Jouy, Hippolyte-Louis-Florent Bis, and Armand Marrast, after Schiller's play.
First perf., Paris, Opéra, Aug. 3, 1829: Cinti-Damoreau, Nourrit, Dabadie, Levasseur. U.S. prem., N.Y., Park. Sep. 19, 1831 (in Eng.). Met prem., Nov. 28, 1884 (in Ger.): Schröder-Hanfstängl, Udvardy, Robinson, Kögel, c. W. Damrosch, d. J. Fox, Schaeffer, p. Hock. Later Met production: Jan. 5, 1923 (in Ital.): Ponselle, Martinelli, Danise, Mardones, c. Papi, d. Rota/G. Urban, p. Thewman. Tell has also been sung at the Met by Fischer, Ancona; Mathilde by Rethberg; Arnold by Tamagno, Lauri-Volpi. 24 perfs. in 8 seasons.
Rossini's last opera, an ambitious, often inspired and highly influential bid to extend his musical invention to the vast canvas of Parisian grand opera.
Switzerland, under Austrian dominion, 13th c. The patriot Tell (bar) helps a fugitive escape Austrian troops. In retaliation, the oppressors seize Melchthal (bs), father of Arnold (t), who is in love with the Hapsburg princess Mathilde (s). Mathilde wants Arnold to join the Austrians and marry her, but, learning that his father has been executed, he swears loyalty to the patriots. When Tell and his son Jemmy (s) refuse to do homage to the cap of the Austrian governor Gessler (bs), Tell is recognized as the fugitive's rescuer and forced to shoot an apple placed on Jemmy's head. He succeeds, then declares that had he failed he would have shot a second arrow at Gessler. He is arrested, but Mathilde rescues Jemmy and surrenders herself to the conspirators as hostage for Tell. Jemmy sets fire to Tell's house as a signal for the open revolt that Arnold and the other conspirators have planned. Tell is freed on the boat that was carrying him to imprisonment, as only his skill can control it in a storm; once ashore, he fells Gessler with an arrow and joins the conspirators in victory over the Austrians. As the storm clears away, all join in a prayer for the beginning of a reign of liberty.

Guiraud, Ernest. Composer; b. New Orleans, La., June 23, 1837; d. Paris, May 6, 1892. Studied with Marmontel and Halévy at Paris Conservatory. Classmate and friend of Bizet, he is best known for composing recitatives for the successful posthumous Vienna production of *Carmen* (1875). He also edited and orchestrated Offenbach's *Contes d'Hoffmann*, and taught at the Paris Conservatory, where his pupils included Dukas and Debussy. His own stage works include the opéra comique *Sylvie* (1864) and the grand opera *Frédégonde* (completed by Saint-Saëns, perf. 1895).

Gulyás, Dénes. Tenor; b. Budapest, Mar. 31, 1954. Studied at Liszt Academy and Budapest Conservatory. Debut as Alfredo, Budapest, 1978; has subsequently sung Faust, Rodolfo, and Pinkerton there. Debuts in Vienna (1978), Philadelphia (1981), and at Covent Garden (1984–85). Met debut as Singer (*Rosenkavalier*), Sep. 27, 1985; has also sung Andrei (*Khovanshchina*), Roméo, Rodolfo, and Massenet's Des Grieux there.

Guntram. Opera in 3 acts by R. Strauss; libretto by the composer.
First perf., Weimar, May 10, 1894: de Ahna, Zeller, Schwarz, Wieden, c. Strauss. U.S. prem., N.Y., Carnegie Hall (Opera Orchestra of N.Y.), Jan. 19, 1983 (concert perf.): Tokody, Goldberg, Stith, Wimberger, c. Queler.
Strauss had not yet found his distinctive theatrical voice in *Guntram*, which is burdened by an idealistic but ponderous action, set in medieval Germany. Seeking to liberate Duke Robert's people from oppression, Guntram (t) kills the tyrannical Duke (bar) in a duel; afterwards, because of his guilt at having been in love with the Duke's wife Freihild (s), he renounces her for a life of solitude.

Gutheil-Schoder, Marie. Mezzo-soprano; b. Weimar, Germany, Feb. 10, 1874; d. Ilmenau, Germany, Oct. 4, 1935. Studied in Weimar; debut there as First Lady (*Zauberflöte*), 1891. In 1900, engaged by Mahler at Vienna Opera, where she remained until 1926, singing Carmen, Elektra, Salome, and Octavian. Appeared at Covent Garden (Octavian, 1913) and Salzburg (Susanna, 1906).

Guthrie, Tyrone. Producer; b. Tunbridge Wells, England, July 2, 1900; d. Newbliss, May 15, 1971. Originally an actor, he directed for the Old Vic, London (1933–34; 1937; 1953–57) and was administrator of Old Vic/Sadler's Wells (1939–45). Founded and directed Shakespeare Festival, Stratford, Ont. (1953–57), and Guthrie Theatre, Minneapolis (1963). His first operatic staging was *Peter Grimes* (Covent Garden, 1947); at the Met, he staged *Carmen* (1952), *Traviata* (1957), and *Grimes* (1967).

Gwendoline. Opera in 2 acts by Chabrier; libretto by Catulle Mendès.
First perf., Brussels, Monnaie, Apr. 10, 1886: Thuringer, Engel, c. Dupont. U.S. prem., San Diego, Calif., Oct. 2, 1982 (in Eng.): Plowright, Norman, Raftery, c. Tauriello.
Reflecting post-Wagnerian French interest in things Nordic, set in 8th-c. Britain, when the Viking king Harald (bar) finds himself in love with Gwendoline (s), daughter of his Saxon prisoner Armel (t).

Gypsy Baron, The. See *Zigeunerbaron, Der.*

H

Habanera, La. Opera in 3 acts by Laparra; libretto by the composer.
First perf., Paris, Opéra-Comique, Feb. 26, 1908: Demellier, Salignac, Séveilhac, c. Ruhlmann. U.S. prem., Boston Opera, Dec. 14, 1910: Dereyne, Lassalle, Blanchart, Mardones, c. Caplet. Met prem., Jan 2, 1924: Easton, Tokatyan, Danise, Rothier, c. Hasselmans, d. Rovescalli, Novak/Laparra, p. Thewman. 3 perfs. in 1 season.

Laparra's briefly popular emulation of verismo, set in Castile, involves the triangle of Ramon (bar), his brother Pedro (t), and the latter's fiancée Pilar (s).

Hackett, Charles. Tenor; b. Worcester, Mass., Nov. 4, 1899; d. New York, Jan. 1, 1942. Studied in Boston and Florence; debut as Wilhelm Meister (*Mignon*), Genoa, 1914. Appeared in Europe, South America, and Chicago (1923–34). Met debut as Almaviva, Jan. 31, 1919; in 9 seasons (1919–21, 1934–39), he sang 61 perfs. of 12 roles, including Lindoro (*Italiana*), Rodolfo, Pinkerton, Roméo, and Alfredo.

Hadley, Henry. Composer and conductor; b. Somerville, Mass., Dec. 20, 1871; d. New York, Sep. 6, 1937. Studied with Chadwick at New England Conservatory, and with Mandyczewski in Vienna and Thuille in Munich. Toured as conductor in Germany, where he introduced his one-act opera *Safie* (1909). Associate conductor of the N.Y. Philharmonic (1920–27). Other operas include *Azora* (1917), produced by the Chicago Opera, and *Cleopatra's Night* (1920), produced at the Met.

Hadley, Jerry. Tenor; b. Princeton, Ill., June 16, 1952. Studied at Bradley U., U. of Illinois, and with Thomas LoMonaco; debut as Lionel (*Martha*), Sarasota, Fla., 1978. N.Y.C. Opera debut as Arturo (*Lucia*), 1979; other roles there include Tom Rakewell, Rodolfo, Nadir, Pinkerton, Massenet's Des Grieux, and Werther. Debuts in Vienna (Nemorino, 1982), Glyndebourne (Idamante, 1984), Covent Garden (Fenton, 1984), Hamburg (Rodolfo, 1986), and Met (Massenet's Des Grieux, Mar. 7, 1987).

Häfliger, Ernst. Tenor; b. Davos, Switzerland, July 6, 1919. Studied at U. of Zurich, with Patzak in Vienna and Carpi in Prague. Appeared with Zurich Opera (1943–52) and Deutsche Oper, Berlin (from 1952). Created Tiresias (*Antigonae*), Salzburg, 1949. Best known in Mozart roles (Glyndebourne, 1956–57) and as concert singer.

Hagegård, Håkan. Baritone; b. Karlstad, Sweden, Nov. 25, 1945. Studied at Royal Academy, Stockholm, and with Gobbi, Gerald Moore, and Erik Werba; debut, Stockholm, 1968, as Papageno (which he sang in Ingmar Bergman's film version). At Glyndebourne (1973–78), sang the Count (*Capriccio*), Almaviva, and Guglielmo. Since his Met debut as Malatesta (*Pasquale*), Dec. 3, 1978, he has also sung Rossini's Figaro, Wolfram, and Eisenstein at the house.

Hageman, Richard. Composer; b. Leeuwarden, Netherlands, July 9, 1882; d. Beverly Hills, Calif., March 6, 1966. Studied with his father, Maurits Hageman, and with Gevaert at Brussels Conservatory. Arriving in the U.S. in 1906 as Yvette Guilbert's accompanist, he became a conductor at the Met (1908–22) and later headed the opera department at Curtis Institute. In addition to the opera *Caponsacchi* (1932), he composed the "concert drama" *The Crucible* (1943) and many art songs, notably "Do Not Go, My Love."

Hahn, Reynaldo. Composer; b. Caracas, Venezuela, Aug. 9, 1875; d. Paris, Jan. 28, 1947. Studied at Paris Conservatory with Massenet. Best known as a composer and performer of sentimental, facile art songs, he was also a noted Mozart conductor. His first opera, *L'Île du Rêve* (1898), was performed at the Opéra-Comique, as was *La Carmélite* (1902). *Le Marchand de Venise*, after Shakespeare,

was produced at the Paris Opéra in 1935. Hahn's most appealing works are his operettas, notably *Ciboulette* (1923). In 1945–46, he was briefly director of the Opéra.

Haitink, Bernard. Conductor; b. Amsterdam, Mar. 4, 1929. After study at Amsterdam Conservatory and with Leitner, appointed assistant conductor of Netherlands Radio Orchestra (1955), then (jointly with Jochum) the youngest principal conductor of the Concertgebouw (1961); sole director, 1970–86. Principal conductor (1967–70) and artistic director (1970–79), London Philharmonic. Glyndebourne debut in 1972; music director (from 1978). Music director, Covent Garden (from 1987). Met debut, *Fidelio*, Mar. 29, 1982. A noted exponent of Mahler and Bruckner, his operatic repertory has centered upon Mozart.

Halasz, László. Conductor and manager; b. Debrecen, Hungary, June 6, 1905. Conducted in Budapest, Prague, and Vienna before making U.S. debut in St. Louis (*Tristan*, 1937), where he conducted opera until 1942. In 1943, became first director of N.Y.C. Opera, leading its inaugural performance (*Tosca*, Feb. 21, 1944). An energetic but difficult, often sarcastic administrator, he was dismissed in 1951. From 1965 to 1968, led Eastman Philharmonia (Rochester, N.Y.).

Halévy, (Jacques-François-)Fromental. Composer; b. Paris, May 27, 1799; d. Nice, Mar. 17, 1862. Studied with Cherubini at Paris Conservatory and with Méhul. His first successful stage work was *Clari* (1828), for Malibran. After several opéras comiques, he composed the grand opera *La Juive* (1835); its success and that of the opéra comique *L'Éclair* (1835) gained him entry into the Academy in 1836 and contributed to his 1840 appointment as composition professor at the Conservatory, where his pupils included Gounod and Bizet. His later works (many to librettos by Scribe) never repeated those triumphs. Skilled at local color, mass effects, and orchestration, Halévy was one of the first composers to use the new chromatic brass instruments. Other works include the operas *Charles VI* (1843) and *La Reine de Chypre* (1846), the opéras comiques *Les Mousquetaires de la Reine* (1846) and *Le Val d'Andorre*.

Halévy, Ludovic. Librettist; b. Paris, Dec. 31, 1833; d. Paris, May 7, 1908. Nephew of composer Fromental Halévy, he often collaborated with Henri Meilhac on librettos, most famously on Bizet's *Carmen*, more characteristically on operettas for Offenbach.

Halka. Opera in 4 (originally 2) acts by Moniuszko; libretto by Włodzimierz Wolski, after K.W. Wójcicki's story *Góralka*.
    First perf., Wilno, Jan. 1, 1848 (concert perf., 2-act version). First stage perf., Wilno, Feb. 28, 1854. Rev. in 4 acts, first perf., Warsaw, Jan. 1, 1858. U.S. prem., N.Y., People's Theater, June 1903 (in Russ.).
    The cornerstone of Polish national opera, a simple story of village life with a score rich in folk influences, set near the Carpathian mountains, c. 1840. Halka (s), seduced and abandoned by Janusz (t), commits suicide.

Hall, Peter. Producer; b. Bury St. Edmunds, England, Nov. 22, 1930. Worked at Arts Theatre, London (1954–56), with Royal Shakespeare Co. (managing director,

1960–68), and National Theatre, Great Britain (director, 1973–88). First operatic production, Gardner's *Moon and Sixpence* (Sadler's Wells, 1958). At Covent Garden from 1965, his productions included *Moses und Aron*, *Knot Garden*, *Eugene Onegin*, and *Tristan*. Has worked at Glyndebourne since 1970 (artistic director since 1984), staging operas by Monteverdi, Cavalli, Mozart, and Britten. Produced controversial *Ring* cycle at Bayreuth (1983). For Met, staged *Macbeth* (1982) and *Carmen* (1986).

Hall, Peter J(ohn). Designer; b. Bristol, England, Jan. 22, 1926. First designs for National Theatre, London (1959); operatic debut, costumes for *Puritani* (Massimo, Palermo, 1960). Has worked with major companies in Europe and U.S. For the Met, designed costumes for *Otello* (1972), *Boris* (1974), *Aida, Puritani, Lohengrin* (1976), *Bohème* (1981), *Ernani* (1983), *Tosca* (1985), and *Fledermaus* (1986); resident costume designer (since 1979).

Hamari, Julia. Mezzo-soprano; b. Budapest, Nov. 21, 1942. Studied in Budapest and Stuttgart; began career in concert, later singing opera, chiefly at Deutsche Oper am Rhein. Repertory includes Carmen, Dorabella, Cherubino, and Octavian. U.S. debut with Chicago Symphony, 1972. Met debut as Rosina, Nov. 2, 1984; she has also sung Despina with the company.

Hamilton, Iain. Composer; b. Glasgow, Scotland, June 6, 1922. Studied composition with Alwyn at the Royal Academy of Music. Influenced first by Bartók's chromaticism and after 1958 by Webernian serialism, his operas return to a more tonal style: *Agamemnon* (composed 1967–69), after Aeschylus; *The Royal Hunt of the Sun* (1967–69, performed 1977), after Shaffer; *The Catiline Conspiracy* (1974), after Ben Jonson; the radio opera *Tamburlaine* (1976), after Marlowe; *Anna Karenina* (1980), after Tolstoy; and *Lancelot* (1985).

Hamlet. Opera in 5 acts by Thomas; libretto by Barbier and Carré, after Shakespeare's tragedy.

First perf., Paris, Opéra, Mar. 9, 1868: Nilsson, Guéymard, Faure, Belval, c. Hainl. U.S. prem., N.Y., Academy of Music, Mar. 22, 1872: Nilsson, Cary, Brignoli, Barré. Met prem., Mar. 10, 1884 (in Ital.): Sembrich, Scalchi, Kaschmann, Mirabella, c. Vianesi. Hamlet has also been sung at the Met by Lassalle; Ophélie by van Zandt, Melba, Calvé. 7 perfs. in 5 seasons.

A conventional but thoroughly distinguished score, with a libretto that brings *Hamlet* within the pale of ordinary French Romantic opera. The plot follows Shakespeare, with simplifications and some enlargement of the role of Ophélie (s), until the end, when Hamlet (bar) ascends the throne. An alternate ending providing for the prince's death was composed for London performances.

Hammerstein, Oscar. Impresario; b. Stettin, Germany [now Szczecin, Poland], May 8, 1846; d. New York, Aug. 1, 1919. Self-taught in music, he came to N.Y., accumulated a fortune in real estate, and became active in theatrical production (including some of his own unsuccessful operettas). In 1906, he opened the Manhattan Opera House as a popular alternative to the Met, with the excellent Cleofonte Campanini as chief conductor, world-class artists such as Melba, Nordica, and Garden, and a repertory that included the U.S. premieres of *Louise* and *Pelléas*. For four years the enterprise was a sharp thorn in the Met's side, after which Hammerstein was bought out by the Met board for $1.2 million and agreed not to

George Frideric Handel

produce grand opera in N.Y. for ten years. In 1911, he opened the London Opera House, which failed within a year (it later became the Stoll Theatre); he died in N.Y. just before his decade-long ban expired.

BIBLIOGRAPHY: J.F. Cone, *Oscar Hammerstein's Manhattan Opera Company* (Norman, Okla., 1966).

Hammond, Joan. Soprano; b. Christchurch, New Zealand, May 24, 1912. Studied at Sydney Conservatory, later with Borgioli in London; debut as Giovanna (*Rigoletto*), Sydney, 1932. Appeared at Vienna Volksoper (Nedda, 1938), with Carl Rosa Co. (1942–45), Covent Garden (1948–51), and Sadler's Wells (1951, 1959). At N.Y.C. Opera, 1949, she sang Butterfly, Aida, and Tosca.

Handel, George Frideric [Georg Friederich Händel]. Composer; b. Halle, Feb. 23, 1685; d. London, Apr. 14, 1759. Studied with the organist Zachow in Halle; in 1703 he went to Hamburg, where his first operas, *Almira* and *Nero* (in German), were produced in 1705. The years 1706–10 were spent in Italy, principally in the service of Prince Ruspoli in Rome, for whom he wrote many vocal works; the operas *Rodrigo* (Florence, 1707) and *Agrippina* (Venice, 1710) were well received. After appointment as music director to the Elector of Hanover in 1710, he took (and eventually overstayed) leaves of absence to London, where *Rinaldo* (1711), staged with spectacular effects, made a great impact; *Il Pastor Fido* (1712) and *Teseo* followed. In 1714 the Elector of Hanover became George I of England, where Handel thereafter remained. While employed by Lord Burlington in London (1713–16), he composed *Silla* and *Amadigi*; the pastoral *Acis and Galatea* stems from his tenure with the Duke of Chandos (1717–18).

Handel then became involved full-time in the presentation and composition of Italian opera, initially with the Royal Academy of Music at the King's Theatre (1720–28); among the works of these years were *Giulio Cesare in Egitto*, *Tamerlano* (both 1724), and *Rodelinda* (1725), full of orchestral invention and formal innovation. In 1728, internal dissension, led to the demise of the Academy and the success of *The Beggar's Opera*, which lampooned Italian opera; Handel's works for a second Academy, formed in 1729, included *Partenope* (1730), *Sosarme* (1732), and *Orlando* (1733). The rise of the Opera of the Nobility in 1733 created ruinous competition; moving to Covent Garden in 1734, Handel produced *Ariodante* (1735), *Alcina* (1735), and *Atalanta* (1736) before the company collapsed and he suffered a stroke in 1737. Though he composed a few more operas in a lighter style, including *Serse* (1738) and *Imeneo* (1740), he focused increasingly on the composition of oratorios in English, which found a readier public, and continued to compose them until the onset of blindness in 1751. Several oratorios, including *Samson* (1743), *Semele* (1744), and *Hercules* (1745), are now sometimes staged, and his Italian operas, first revived in drastically modified versions in the 1920s, more recently in productions that accept the conventions of opera seria, are steadily revealed as a trove of richly inventive, strongly characterized dramatic music. Though always receptive to outside influences, Handel's basic style of operatic composition remained unchanged, but his resourcefulness rarely flagged, and his keen sense of contrast and color gave each of his best scores a distinctive stamp.

BIBLIOGRAPHY: Winton Dean, *Handel and the Opera Seria* (Berkeley, 1969; London, 1970).

Hänsel und Gretel. Opera in 3 acts by Humperdinck; libretto by Adelheid Wette, after the story by the Grimm brothers.

First perf., Weimar, Dec. 23, 1893: Kayser, Schubert, Tibelti, Finck, Wiedey, c. R. Strauss. U.S. prem., N.Y., Daly's Theater, Oct. 8, 1895 (in Eng.): c. Seidl. Met prem., Nov. 25, 1905: Abarbanell, Alten, Homer, Weed, Goritz, c. Hertz, d. J. Fox, p. Goldberg. Later Met productions: Nov. 5, 1927: Mario, Fleischer, Manski, Wakefield, Schützendorf, c. Bodanzky, d. Urban, p. Wymetal; Nov. 6, 1967 (in Eng.): Stratas, Elias, Dönch, Chookasian, Walker, c. Allers, d. O'Hearn, p. Merrill. Gretel has also been sung at the Met by Conner, Blegen; Hänsel by Jessner, Stevens, Elias, von Stade; the Witch by Manski, Votipka, Vehs. On Dec. 25, 1931, *Hänsel* was the first Met performance broadcast on network radio. 161 perfs. in 34 seasons.

In *Hänsel und Gretel*, Humperdinck brought Wagnerian harmony and motivic development to bear on simple folk tunes (traditional and newly invented). The opera was a brilliant and immediate success, and though it proved an unrepeatable one, it became the only German opera between *Parsifal* and *Salome* to survive in the international standard repertory.

The Harz Mountains, near the Ilsenstein peak, long ago. Hänsel (ms) and Gretel (s) have forgotten their chores as they romp and play. Gertrude, their mother (ms), scolds them and sends them to pick strawberries in the woods. Peter, their father (bar), returns and is horrified to learn where they have gone; in the forest lives a wicked witch, who bakes children in her oven and eats them. The two rush out to find their children. As evening falls, Hänsel and Gretel are lost in the forest and afraid. A friendly Sandman (s) sprinkles their eyes and after saying prayers the two fall asleep, guarded by fourteen angels through the night. A Dew Fairy (s) heralds the morning, and the children discover a candy house surrounded by a row of gingerbread children. Starting to eat, they are captured by the Gingerbread Witch (ms; sometimes sung by a man), who puts them under a magic spell, locks Hänsel up to fatten

him and orders Gretel to help with the housework. With bravery and ingenuity the two outwit the witch, break her spell, and push her into the oven where she soon becomes gingerbread herself. Gretel frees the gingerbread children, the parents arrive, and all join in a hymn of thanks.

Hans Heiling. Opera in prologue and 3 acts by Marschner; libretto by Eduard Devrient, after a folk tale.

First perf., Berlin, Court Opera, May 24, 1833: Grünbaum, Valentini, Devrient, Bader, c. Marschner.

In its legendary basis and its *Lohengrin*-like plot, an opera that influenced Wagner. In the Harz Mountains, in the 16th c., Hans Heiling (bar), son of the Queen of the Spirits (s) by a mortal father, assumes human form and falls in love with Anna (s), who rejects him when she learns his true identity.

Hanson, Howard. Composer and conductor; b. Wahoo, Nebr., Oct. 28, 1896; d. Rochester, N.Y., Feb. 26, 1981. Studied with Goetschius at Institute of Musical Art in N.Y. and Respighi in Rome. As director of Eastman School of Music, Rochester (1924–64), greatly influential in music education; as conductor, a vigorous advocate of American music. His compositions are neo-Romantic in style, influenced by Grieg and Sibelius. *Merry Mount* (1934), after Hawthorne, his only opera, was praised for its choral writing but defeated by his inexperienced stagecraft.

Harewood, Earl of (George Henry Hubert Lascelles). Manager; b. London, Feb. 7, 1923. In 1950 he founded *Opera* magazine, which he edited until 1953, then working in arts administration, as assistant artistic director, Covent Garden (1953–58); artistic director, Leeds Festival (1958–74); and director, Edinburgh Festival (1961–65). Between 1972 and 1985, he was managing

Hänsel und Gretel – (1982). Judith Blegen and Frederica von Stade

director of Sadler's Wells Opera (from 1972, English National Opera), a period of great development for the company, climaxing in its first American tour (1984). He edited three revisions of *Kobbé's Complete Opera Book* (1953, 1976, 1987).

Harmonie der Welt, Die (The Harmony of the World). Opera in 5 acts by Hindemith; libretto by the composer.
First perf., Munich, Prinzregententheater, Aug. 11, 1957: Fölser, Töpper, Holm, Metternich, c. Hindemith.
A score in the rigorously linear, firmly tonal style of Hindemith's last years. During the 30 Years' War, the astronomer Johannes Kepler (bar) and the German general Wallenstein (t), who believes in the influence of the stars, search for the principles of celestial motions and for parallels with hoped-for earthly order.

Harper, Heather. Soprano; b. Belfast, N. Ireland, May 8, 1930. Studied at Trinity College of Music, London; debut as Lady Macbeth, Oxford U., 1954. Debuts at Glyndebourne (1957), Covent Garden (Helena, *Midsummer Night's Dream*, 1962) and Bayreuth (Elsa, 1967). Met debut as Countess (*Nozze*), Feb. 26, 1977; she has also sung Ellen Orford there. Created roles in *Owen Wingrave* and *Ice Break*.

Harrell, Mack. Baritone; b. Celeste, Tex., Oct. 8, 1909; d. Dallas, Jan. 29, 1960. Studied in Texas and at Juilliard, N.Y. Won Met Auditions, 1938; debut as Biterolf (*Tannhäuser*), Dec. 16, 1939; in 12 seasons, sang 110 perfs. of 21 roles, including Kothner, Shadow (*Rake*), Jochanaan, Amfortas, and premiere of Samson (*Warrior*). At N.Y.C. Opera (debut, Germont, 1944), created Azrael in Tamkin's *Dybbuk*, 1951.

Harris, Augustus. Impresario; b. Paris, 1852; d. Folkestone, England, June 22, 1896. Originally an actor, he worked as a stage manager with various companies, including Mapleson's, and in 1879 became lessee of Drury Lane, where he gave a season of Italian opera (1887) with the de Reszkes and Battistini. The next year he moved to Covent Garden, where his seasons (1888–96) featured international stars and introduced Wagner in German to the house (including a *Ring* cycle conducted by Mahler, 1892).

Harris, Hilda. Soprano; b. Warrenton, N.C., 1930. Studied at N.C. State U., and in N.Y. Began career in Broadway musicals; European debut as Carmen, St. Gall, 1971. Appeared with N.Y.C. Opera (debut, Nicklausse, 1973) and Mini-Met (debut, St. Theresa II, *Four Saints*, Feb. 20, 1973). Met debut as Wardrobe Mistress/Schoolboy (*Lulu*), Apr. 11, 1977; has also sung Child (*Enfant*), Hänsel, Stephano, and Cherubino with the company.

Harrold, Orville. Tenor; b. Muncie, Ind., 1878; d. Darien, Conn., Oct. 23, 1933. Began career in vaudeville, then studied with Oscar Saenger, N.Y.; debut as Canio, Manhattan Opera, 1910. Appeared with Chicago Opera (1912–22). Met debut as Léopold (*Juive*), Nov. 22, 1919; in 5 seasons, sang 88 perfs. of 18 roles, including Dimitri (*Boris*), Pinkerton, Rodolfo, Parsifal, and Paul (*Tote Stadt*). His son, tenor **Jack Harrold**, sings character parts with N.Y.C. Opera (debut, Vašek, 1945).

Harshaw, Margaret. Mezzo-soprano, later soprano; b. Narbeth, Pa., May 12, 1909. Studied with Anna Schoen-

René, Juilliard, N.Y.; debut as Second Norn, Met, Nov. 25, 1942. In 21 Met seasons, she sang 286 perfs. of 39 roles, first as mezzo, from 1950 in leading Wagner soprano parts. Sang at San Francisco (debut, Amneris, 1944), Covent Garden (1953–56), and Glyndebourne (Donna Anna, 1954).

Hartmann, Rudolf. Producer; b. Ingolstadt, Germany, Oct. 11, 1900. Worked in Altenberg (1924–27), Gera (1927–28), Nuremberg (1928–34), at Berlin State Opera (1934–37) and Bavarian State Opera (1938–44), where he staged premieres of *Friedenstag* and *Capriccio*; after returning to Nuremberg (1946–52), he became Intendant in Munich (1952–67). Guest producer in most European opera houses, including Covent Garden (*Elektra*, 1953, *Ring*, 1954), Bayreuth (*Meistersinger*, 1951), Vienna State Opera, Düsseldorf–Duisburg, Mannheim, La Scala.

Háry János. Opera in prologue, 5 acts, and epilogue by Kodály; libretto by Béla Paulini and Zsolt Harsányi, after János Garay's poem.
First perf., Budapest, Oct. 16, 1926: Nagy, Palló, c. Rékai. U.S. prem., N.Y., Juilliard School, Mar. 18, 1960: c. Waldman.
The tall tales of an old soldier from the time of Napoleonic wars; the lively score, incorporating Hungarian folk tunes, is familiar from a concert suite.

Hasselmans, Louis. Conductor; b. Paris, July 15, 1878; d. San Juan, P.R., Dec. 27, 1957. Studied cello at Paris Conservatory. Conducted at Opéra-Comique (1909–11, 1919–22), Montreal (1911–13), Chicago Civic Opera (1918–19). After his Met debut (*Faust*, Jan. 20, 1922), he remained 15 seasons, leading 378 perfs. of 14 French works, including first Met *Pelléas* (1925), *Heure Espagnole* (1925), and *Don Quichotte* (1926).

Haugland, Aage. Bass; b. Copenhagen, Feb. 1, 1944, of Norwegian parents. Studied in Copenhagen; debut as Brewer (Martinů's *Comedy on the Bridge*), Oslo, 1968. Debuts at Covent Garden (Hunding, 1975), La Scala (King in *Lohengrin*, 1981), Salzburg (Rocco, 1982), and Bayreuth (Hagen, 1983). Met debut as Ochs, Dec. 13, 1979; other Met roles are Fafner, King Marke, Klingsor, and Hunding.

Hauk, Minnie [Amalia Mignon Hauck]. Soprano; b. New York, Nov. 16, 1851; d. Tribschen, near Lucerne, Switzerland, Feb. 6, 1929. Studied in New Orleans and N.Y.; debut as Amina, Brooklyn, 1866. Debuts in Paris and London, 1868; sang in Vienna (1870–73) and Berlin (1874–77). In N.Y., sang first U.S. Juliette (1867), Carmen (1878), and Manon (1885). In her only Met season, she sang 5 perfs. as Sélika (debut, Feb. 10, 1891) and Carmen.

haute-contre. A French vocal type of the 17th and 18th c., a male alto or high tenor who sang in full voice.

Hawkins, Osie. Baritone; b. Phenix City, Ala., Aug. 16, 1913. Studied in Atlanta and with Friedrich Schorr, N.Y.; debut as Donner (*Rheingold*), Met, Jan. 22, 1942. Subsequently sang 731 perfs. of 53 roles in 23 seasons with the company, including Amfortas, Wotan, Zuniga, Monterone, and Bonze (*Butterfly*); served as executive stage manager, 1963–78. Also sang with Central City Opera, Colo. and Cincinnati Summer Opera.

Haydn, Joseph. Composer; b. Rohrau, Lower Austria, Mar. 31, 1732; d. Vienna, May 31, 1809. A student of Nicola Porpora, he was employed by the Eszterházy family at Eisenstadt from 1761, and became musical director when they moved to Eszterháza in 1766. As a composer, he developed an independent, witty, expressive instrumental style; his symphonies and quartets were admired throughout Europe. During the 1790s he made two triumphant visits to London, and then composed masses and oratorios in Vienna.

A number of Haydn's operas, including most of the marionette operas popular at Eszterháza, are lost. Except for *Acide* (1763), his operatic output before 1775 was principally comic: *La Canterina* (1766), *Lo Speziale* (1768), *Le Pescatrici* (1769), *L'Infedeltà Delusa* (1773), and *L'Incontro Improvviso* (1775). At Eszterháza after 1766, he was expected to produce an extensive opera season, including works by others as well as his own operas, which increasingly incorporated serious elements of plot and musical style: *Il Mondo della Luna* (1777), *La Vera Constanza* (1779), *L'Isola Disabitata* (1779), *La Fedeltà Premiata* (1780), and *Orlando Paladino* (1782). *Armide* (1784) is an opera seria, as is *L'Anima del Filosofo* (or *Orfeo ed Euridice*), completed in 1791 for performances in London that never took place. Though lacking the theatricality of Mozart's operas, Haydn's exhibit superb musical invention and craftsmanship.

BIBLIOGRAPHY: H.C. Robbins Landon, *Haydn: Chronicle and Works,* (5 vols., Bloomington, Ind., and London, 1976–80).

head voice, head register. The highest register of the human voice, in which the sounds appear to be produced from inside the facial mask. Head tones are lighter than those of the chest register.

Hebert, Bliss. Producer; b. Faust, N.Y., Nov. 30, 1930. He has worked with major Canadian and American companies, notably Santa Fe (since 1957) and N.Y.C. Opera (1963–75); general manager, Washington, D.C., Opera Society (1960–63). Staged *Oedipus Rex* and *Nightingale* with composer conducting. For the Met, he staged *Hoffmann* (1973).

Heeley, Desmond. Designer; b. West Bromwich, England, June 1, 1931. Training at Shakespeare Memorial Theatre, Stratford (1947–52); first operatic designs for *Traviata* (Sadler's Wells, 1960). Has worked with Glyndebourne (*Puritani*, 1960), English National Opera (*Maria Stuarda*, 1973). His Met productions are *Norma* (1970), *Pelléas* (1972), *Don Pasquale* (1978), and *Manon Lescaut* (1980).

Heger, Robert. Conductor; b. Strassburg, Alsace, Aug. 19, 1886; d. Munich, Jan. 14, 1978. After study at Strassburg, Zurich, and Berlin, active in Central Europe from 1907, ultimately arriving at the Berlin State Opera in 1933. Frequent appearances in London (1925–33). After the war, at Berlin Städtische Oper (1945–50) and Munich (from 1950). Led numerous opera and operetta recordings, mainly in Munich.

Heinrich, Rudolf. Designer and producer; b. Halle, Germany, Feb. 10, 1926; d. London, Dec. 1, 1975. A protégé of Felsenstein, he designed for the Komische Oper (1953–61), and worked frequently in other theaters. For the Met, he designed *Salome* (1965), *Elektra* (1966), *Tosca* (1968), *Werther* (1970), and *Freischütz* (1971), which last he also staged.

Frieda Hempel

Heldentenor (Ger., "heroic tenor"). A tenor voice of power, tonal brilliance, and stamina, suitable for the heroes of Wagner's operas. **Heldenbariton** is the parallel term for baritones who sing roles such as Wotan in Wagner's *Ring*.

Heldy, Fanny [Marguerite Deceuninck]. Soprano; b. Ath, near Liège, Belgium, Feb. 29, 1888; d. Paris, Dec. 13, 1973. Studied at Liège Conservatory; debut at Monnaie, Brussels, 1910. Appeared in Monte Carlo, Warsaw, St. Petersburg, but principally in Paris, at Opéra-Comique (debut, Violetta, 1917) and Opéra (debut, Juliette, 1920). Sang Mélisande (1925–26) and Louise (1923) at La Scala, Manon at Covent Garden (1926).

Hempel, Frieda. Soprano; b. Leipzig, June 26, 1885; d. Berlin, Oct. 7, 1955. Studied piano at Leipzig Conservatory, then voice with Selma Nicklass-Kempner, Stern Conservatory, Berlin; formal debut as Frau Fluth (*Lustigen Weiber*), Berlin, Court Opera, 1905. Sang at Schwerin for two years, then returned to Berlin for five successful seasons (1907–12). Met debut as the Queen (*Huguenots*), Dec. 27, 1912; in seven seasons there, she sang 155 perfs. of 17 roles, including Violetta, the Queen of Night, Harriet (*Martha*), Olympia (*Hoffmann*), Adina, Marie (*Fille*), Rosina, Oscar, and Susanna. In florid Italian roles, she established herself as Sembrich's successor, but also sang Eva and Euryanthe under Toscanini. She was the first Marschallin in Berlin (1911) and in N.Y. (1913). After leaving the Met in 1919, she appeared with the Chicago Opera in San Francisco (1921), but otherwise devoted herself to concerts, including highly-publicized recitals in period costume during the Jenny Lind centennial year (1920). A fluent coloratura with a pure tone and a free and natural technique, Hempel excelled in Mozart, as her numerous recordings document.

Alfred Hertz

Hendricks, Barbara. Soprano; b. Stephens, Ark., Nov. 20, 1948. Studied at Juilliard, N.Y., and with Jennie Tourel; debut as St. Settlement (*Four Saints*), Mini-Met, Feb. 20, 1973. Has appeared at Glyndebourne (Calisto, 1974), and in Berlin (Susanna, 1978), Orange (Gilda, 1980), Paris (Juliette, 1982), Los Angeles (Nannetta, 1982). Met debut as Sophie, Oct. 30, 1986.

Henry VIII. Opera in 4 acts by Saint-Saëns; libretto by Léonce Détroyat and Armand Silvestre.

First perf., Paris, Opéra, Mar. 5, 1883: Krauss, Richard, Renaud, Lassalle, c. E. Altes. U.S. prem., N.Y., Bel Canto Opera, Apr. 20, 1974.

During Saint-Saëns' lifetime, this romantic character-ization of Henry VIII and his love for Anne Boleyn was his second most popular opera.

Henze, Hans Werner. Composer; b. Gütersloh, West-phalia, July 1, 1926. Studied at Heidelberg Church Music Institute and privately with Fortner. His early works were influenced by neo-classicism and by Bartók, but 1949 study in Darmstadt and in Paris with René Leibowitz stimulated an interest in serialism. Especially after moving to Italy in 1953, he assumed a more eclectic stance. His music has been strongly influenced by political and social concerns, increasingly so after the radical movements of 1968. His fondness for Italianate melody is joined with great richness of orchestral imagination.

Henze's first major success, *Boulevard Solitude* (1952), uses serial technique. The less strict work of his Italian period, beginning with *König Hirsch* (1956), aroused controversy in the serial-dominated German musical world, but he was widely recognized as a major theatrical composer. *Der Prinz von Homburg* (1960), after Kleist, parodies the German military; *Elegy for Young Lovers* (1961) treats the relationship of the artist to society; *Der junge Lord* (1965) satirizes bourgeois moral hypocrisy; and

The Bassarids (1966) is cast in a symphonic mold. After 1968, Henze resorted to more intimate quasi-theatrical formats, returning to the opera house with *We Come to the River* (1976) and *The English Cat* (1984).

BIBLIOGRAPHY: H.W. Henze, *Music and Politics* (Ithaca, N.Y., and London, 1982).

Herbert, Jocelyn. Designer; b. London, Feb. 22, 1917. Worked at Royal Court Theatre and National Theatre, London, including plays by Ionesco, Wesker, Beckett, and Brecht. Opera designs for Sadler's Wells (*Orfeo*, 1967), Paris Opéra (*Forza*, 1975), and Dallas (*Manon Lescaut*, 1979). Her Met productions are *Lulu* (1977), *Entführung* (1979), and *Mahagonny* (1979).

Herbert, Victor. Composer and conductor; b. Dublin, Feb. 1, 1859; d. New York, May 26, 1924. He began his career in Europe as a cellist, coming to N.Y. in 1886 with his wife, soprano Therese Förster, who had been engaged by the Met; he played cello in the Met orchestra, then began to perform as a soloist and to conduct. A prolific composer of operettas, of which the best-known are *Babes in Toyland* (1903), *The Red Mill* (1906), and *Naughty Marietta* (1910), Herbert wrote two serious operas, now forgotten: the somewhat Wagnerian *Natoma* (1911), presented by the Chicago Opera, and the lighter *Madeleine* (1914).

Hérodiade (Herodias). Opera in 4 acts by Massenet; libretto by Paul Milliet, "Henri Grémont" [Georges Hartmann], and Angelo Zanardini, after Gustave Flaubert's story.

First perf., Brussels, Monnaie, Dec. 19, 1881: Duvivier, Deschamps-Jehin, Vergnet, Manoury, Gresse, c. Dupont. U.S. prem., New Orleans, French Opera House, Feb. 13, 1892: Cagniant, Duvivier, Verhees, Guillemot, Rey.

One of Massenet's essays in a perfumed religious eroticism more popular in his day than since. The plot resembles that of Strauss' treatment, but the motivations are different; John the Baptist (t) is tormented with love for Salome (s), and the girl kills herself after Herod (bs) has the prophet executed.

Hérold, Ferdinand. Composer; b. Paris, Jan. 28, 1791; d. Paris, Jan. 19, 1833. Studied with Méhul at Paris Conservatory; awarded the Prix de Rome. His first opera, *La Gioventù di Enrico Quinto* (1815), was produced in Naples. Returning to Paris, he composed many successful *opéras comiques* in the style of Boieldieu, culminating in *Zampa* (1831) and *Le Pré aux Clercs* (1832).

Hertz, Alfred. Conductor; b. Frankfurt, Germany, July 15, 1872; d. San Francisco, Apr. 17, 1942. Came to the Met (debut, *Lohengrin*, Nov. 28, 1902) after engagements in German cities, including Breslau (1899–1902). In 13 seasons, he conducted 482 perfs. of 26 operas, including Met premieres of *Parsifal* (earning the enmity of Cosima Wagner, which reputedly prevented further engagements in Germany), *Salome*, and *Rosenkavalier*, world premieres of *Mona*, *Cyrano*. A vigorous Wagnerian, he left the Met to conduct the fledgling San Francisco Symphony (1915–30), and in 1922 initiated the Hollywood Bowl concerts.

Herz, Joachim. Producer; b. Dresden, June 15, 1924. A leading disciple of Felsenstein, whom he succeeded as Intendant of the Komische Oper, East Berlin (1977–81) after positions in Cologne (1956–57) and Leipzig (1957–77). Since 1985, chief producer, Dresden. His politically provocative productions include *Meistersinger* (opening new Leipzig opera house, 1960), *Lulu* (Komische Oper, 1979), and *Freischütz* (opening restored Semper Oper, Dresden, 1985). Has also directed for Vienna State Opera, English National Opera, Welsh National Opera, Bavarian State Opera, Paris Opéra.

Heure Espagnole, L' (The Spanish Hour). Opera in 1 act by Ravel; libretto by Franc-Nohain, after his own comedy.

First perf., Paris, Opéra-Comique, May 19, 1911: Vix, Périer, c. Ruhlmann. U.S. prem., Chicago, Auditorium, Jan. 5, 1920: Gall, Maguénat, c. Hasselmans. Met prem., Nov. 7, 1925: Bori, Tibbett, c. Hasselmans, d. Novak, p. Wymetal. 5 perfs. in 1 season.

A score of subtle Spanish flavor and French wit, set in 18th-c. Toledo. The clockmaker Torquemada (t) must make his rounds attending to the municipal clocks, which gives his wife Concepcion (s) a free day for her love affairs – but before leaving he complicates matters by allowing a customer, the muleteer Ramiro (bar), to wait in the shop until his return. Two of Concepcion's admirers arrive and each in succession hides himself in a clock; there is considerable mix-up and place-changing until eventually the woman transfers her attentions to the muleteer.

Hidalgo, Elvira de. Soprano; b. Aragón, Spain, Dec. 27, 1892; d. Milan, Jan. 21, 1980. Studied with Melchiorre Vidal, Milan; debut as Rosina, San Carlo, Naples, 1908. Met debut as Rosina, Mar. 7, 1910; also sang Amina, and returned in 1924–26 as Gilda and Lucia, for a total of 6 perfs. Appeared at La Scala (1916) and Covent Garden (1924). After 1932, taught in Athens; among her students was Maria Callas.

Hinckley, Allen. Bass; b. Gloucester, Mass., Oct. 11, 1877; d. Yonkers, N.Y., Jan. 28, 1954. Studied with Oscar Saenger, N.Y.; debut as King (*Lohengrin*), Hamburg, 1903. In 1908, debuts in Bayreuth (Hagen) and at the Met (Hunding, Nov. 18, 1908); in 4 Met seasons, sang 60 perfs. of 11 roles, including Wagner parts and Tommaso (*Tiefland*).

Hindemith, Paul. Composer; b. Hanau, near Frankfurt, Nov. 16, 1895; d. Frankfurt, Dec. 28, 1963. Studied with Arnold Mendelssohn and Bernhard Sekles at Hoch Conservatory, Frankfurt; active as a violinist. His first compositions were influenced by expressionism, but in the early twenties he assumed a neo-classical stance and became an advocate of *Gebrauchsmusik* (music for practical use, as opposed to "self-expression"). Due to Nazi harassment, he moved to America in 1940, eventually teaching at Yale U. (1941–53). A strong didactic bent led him to formulate elaborate musical theories, in the light of which he revised earlier works. In his last years he lived in Switzerland.

Hindemith's first operas set scandalous expressionist dramas, Kokoschka's *Mörder, Hoffnung der Frauen* (1921) and Stramm's *Sancta Susanna* (1922), but the music was formally rigorous, avoiding Schoenbergian complexity. *Cardillac* (1926), the one-act *Hin und Zurück* (1927), and the "Zeitoper" *Neues vom Tage* (1929) continue in this direction, while the children's opera *Wir bauen eine Stadt* (1930) exemplifies his practical music. Hindemith's response to the Nazi ascendancy was the historical allegory *Mathis der Maler* (1935, perf. 1938), banned in Germany after its attendant symphony was presented in 1934. He returned to opera after the war with the non-political *Die*

Harmonie der Welt (1957) and the one-act fantasy *The Long Christmas Dinner* (libretto by Thornton Wilder, 1961), in which several generations confront each other.
BIBLIOGRAPHY: Geoffrey Skelton, *Paul Hindemith* (N.Y., and London, 1975).

Hinds, Esther. Soprano; b. Barbados, W.I., Jan. 3, 1943. Studied in N.Y. and at Hartt College, Hartford. Debut as First Lady (*Zauberflöte*), N.Y.C. Opera, 1970; has sung Donna Elvira and Butterfly there. Appeared as Bess with Houston Opera and on Broadway; sings frequently at Spoleto Festival (Ariadne, Barber's Cleopatra).

Hines [Heinz], **Jerome.** Bass; b. Hollywood, Calif., Nov. 8, 1921. Studied with Gennaro Curci, Los Angeles, and later with Samuel Margolis, N.Y.; opera debut as Monterone, San Francisco, 1941. After working as a chemist during the war, in 1946 he won the Caruso Award and a Met debut, as the Sergeant in *Boris*, Nov. 21, 1946. Since then, he has sung more than 590 perfs. of 45 roles at the Met, including Méphistophélès, Sparafucile, Colline, Ramfis, the Grand Inquisitor, Philippe II, Gurnemanz, Sarastro, Don Basilio, and Boris. He has also sung in Edinburgh (Nick Shadow, 1953), Munich (Don Giovanni, 1954), Bayreuth (1958–61, including Wotan), and at the Bolshoi, Moscow (Boris, 1962). Composer of *I Am The Way*, an opera on the life of Christ. With a substantial voice and firm technical grounding, Hines has been a mainstay of the Met for four decades.

Hin und Zurück (There and Back). Opera in 1 act by Hindemith; libretto by Marcellus Schiffer, after an English revue sketch.

First perf., Baden-Baden, July 17, 1927: J. Klemperer, Lothar, Giebel, c. Mehlich. U.S. prem., Philadelphia, Broad Street, Apr. 22, 1928.

A brief comic opera about the cuckolded Robert (t), his wife Helene (s), and her lover, in which the action reaches

Jerome Hines as the Grand Inquisitor in *Don Carlos*

a climax with a pistol shot, after which the sequence of events is reversed until the *status quo ante* is restored.

Hippolyte et Aricie (Hippolyte and Aricie). Opera in prologue and 5 acts by Rameau; libretto by Simon Joseph Pellegrin.

First perf., Paris, Opéra, Oct. 1, 1733. U.S. prem., N.Y., Town Hall, Apr. 11, 1954 (concert perf.).

Rameau's earliest surviving opera, a work of bold dramatic contrasts, recounts the myth of Phèdre (a) and her unsuccessful attempt to come between the young lovers Hippolyte (t) and Aricie (s).

Hockney, David. Designer; b. Bradford, England, July 9, 1937. Highly original, successful artist, illustrator, and photographer. First stage design for Royal Court Theatre (*Ubu Roi*, 1966). For Glyndebourne, designed *Rake's Progress* (1975) and *Zauberflöte* (1978). For the Met, he designed two triple bills, *Parade* (1981) and *Stravinsky* (1981).

Hoffman, Grace [Goldie]. Mezzo-soprano; b. Cleveland, Ohio, Jan. 14, 1925. Studied with Schorr in N.Y., Mario Basiola in Milan, and in Stuttgart; debut in *Cavalleria*, Wagner Opera Co., N.Y., 1951. Sang in Zurich (1952–53) and Stuttgart (from 1955), also in Milan, Bayreuth, San Francisco, and London. Her only Met role was Brangäne (debut, Mar. 27, 1958).

Hoffmann, E(rnst) T(heodor) A(madeus). German author (1776–1822). Operas based on his writings include *Cardillac* (Hindemith) and *Les Contes d'Hoffmann* (Offenbach).

Hofmann, Ludwig. Bass; b. Frankfurt, Germany, Jan. 14, 1895; d. Frankfurt, Dec. 28, 1963. Studied in Frankfurt and Milan; debut in Bamberg, 1918. After engagements in Detmold, Bremen, Wiesbaden, and Berlin, joined Vienna State Opera (1935–42, guest appearances until 1955). Sang in Bayreuth (1928–42), Salzburg (1929–53), London (1932, 1939), and San Francisco (1937). Met debut as Hagen, Nov. 24, 1932; in 6 seasons, he appeared frequently in Wagner bass roles and as Sachs and Wotan.

Hofmann, Peter. Tenor; b. Marienbad, Germany [now Mariánske Lázně, Czechoslovakia], Aug. 12, 1944. Studied in Karlsruhe; debut as Tamino, Lübeck, 1972. Debuts as Siegmund in Bayreuth (1976) and San Francisco (1977). Met debut as Lohengrin, Jan. 24, 1980; has since also sung Parsifal, Siegmund, and Stolzing.

Hofmannsthal, Hugo von. Librettist; b. Vienna, Feb. 1, 1874; d. Vienna, July 15, 1929. A prodigiously gifted poet even in adolescence, he became one of Austria's leading dramatists. After Richard Strauss set his *Elektra*, Hofmannsthal wrote original librettos for Strauss' *Rosenkavalier*, *Ariadne*, *Frau ohne Schatten*, *Ägyptische Helena*, and *Arabella*. As the two met infrequently, their published correspondence is a remarkable documentation of creative collaboration; the poet's fastidious sensibility and symbolist leanings occasionally exasperating the brasher, less sensitive composer.

Hoiby, Lee. Composer; b. Madison, Wisc., Feb. 17, 1926. Studied with Menotti at Curtis Institute; a gifted pianist and recitalist. His operas, in a lyrical diatonic style, include *The Scarf* (1958), after Chekhov; *Natalia Petrovna* (1964), after Turgenev; and *Summer and Smoke* (1971), after Tennessee Williams' play.

Holloway, David. Baritone; b. Grandview, Mo., Nov. 12, 1942. Studied at U. of Kansas, in Santa Fe apprentice program, and with Luigi Ricci, Rome; debut as Belcore (*Elisir*), Kansas City, 1968. Debuts in Chicago (Billy Budd, 1970); N.Y.C. Opera (Guglielmo in *Così*, 1972). Met debut as Yamadori (*Butterfly*), Oct. 16, 1973; other roles include Schaunard, the Husband (*Mamelles*), Sharpless, and Lescaut. Resident member of the Deutsche Oper am Rhein, Düsseldorf, from 1981; also appears in Dallas, Cincinnati, Washington, D.C.

Holst, Gustav. Composer; b. Cheltenham, England, Sep. 21, 1874; d. London, May 25, 1934. Studied composition with Stanford at Royal College of Music. Fascinated by Hindu literature and philosophy, he studied Sanskrit and wrote his own libretto, after the Hindu epic *Mahabharata*, for the one-act chamber opera *Sāvitri* (1916), innovative in its subject and its austere simplicity. Other operas: *The Perfect Fool* (1923); *At the Boar's Head* (1925), based on the Falstaff episodes from Shakespeare's *Henry IV*; and the chamber opera *The Wandering Scholar* (1934). Holst's operas influenced the development of modern British opera, in particular the works of Britten and Tippett.

Homer [née Beatty], **Louise.** Contralto; b. Shadyside, near Pittsburgh, Pa., Apr. 30, 1871; d. Winter Park, Fla., May 6, 1947. Studied in Philadelphia and Boston. Married her harmony teacher, composer Sidney Homer, in 1895, and went with him to Paris, where she studied singing with Fidèle Koenig and acting with Paul Lhérie. Debut as Léonor (*Favorite*), Vichy, 1898; later sang at Covent Garden and Monnaie, Brussels. U.S. debut as Amneris with the touring Met company, San Francisco, Nov. 14, 1900; Met debut in same role, Dec. 22, 1900. During her long Met career (1900–14, 1915–19, 1927–29), Homer gave 472 perfs. in 42 roles, spanning the Italian repertory (Lola, Azucena, Maddalena, Emilia, Suzuki, Dame Quickly), French roles (Siebel, Urbain, Dalila, Fidès), and the great Wagner contralto roles (Ortrud, Brangäne, Waltraute, Fricka, and Erda). She sang Gluck's Orfeo in Paris and at the Met under Toscanini (1909), and created the Witch (*Königskinder*) the following year. During her absence from the Met, she sang in Chicago (1920–25) and San Francisco (1926). Following her Met farewell as Azucena, Nov. 28, 1929, she continued to sing recitals. Composer Samuel Barber was her nephew. Her numerous records confirm the easy power and richness of Homer's voice, which retained much of its quality to the end of her Met career.

BIBLIOGRAPHY: Anne Homer, *Louise Homer and the Golden Age of Opera* (N.Y., 1974).

Honegger, Arthur. Composer; b. Le Havre, France, Mar. 10, 1892, of Swiss parents; d. Paris, Nov. 27, 1955. Studied at Paris Conservatory with Widor and d'Indy. The "dramatic psalm" *Le Roi David* (1921) combined techniques reminiscent of Bach's oratorios with polytonal harmonies and driving rhythms, an approach continued in the Biblical opera *Judith* (1926); *Antigone* (1927), libretto by Cocteau after Sophocles; and Honegger's best-known work, the stage oratorio *Jeanne d'Arc au Bûcher* (1938). Other operas: *L'Aiglon* (1937, jointly with Ibert), and the dramatic legend *Nicolas de Flue* (1941).

Höngen, Elisabeth. Mezzo-soprano; b. Gevelsberg, Germany, Dec. 7, 1906. Studied with Weissenborn, Berlin; debut in Wuppertal, 1933, moving to Düsseldorf

Louise Homer as Amneris in *Aida*

and Dresden. Vienna State Opera debut as Ortrud, 1942, singing there until 1971, notably as Lady Macbeth and Nurse (*Frau*). In her only Met season, she sang 10 perfs. as Herodias (debut, Jan. 10, 1952), Klytemnästra, and Waltraute.

Hopf, Hans. Tenor; b. Nuremberg, Germany, Aug. 2, 1916. Studied with Paul Bender, Munich; debut as Pinkerton, Bavarian Regional Opera, 1936. Sang in Augsburg, Dresden, Oslo, and Berlin before joining Bavarian State Opera, Munich, 1949. Met debut as Walther (*Meistersinger*), Mar. 15, 1952; in 6 seasons, sang 34 perfs. in Wagnerian roles. Also appeared at Bayreuth (from 1951), Salzburg (from 1954), and London (1951–53).

Horne, Marilyn. Mezzo-soprano; b. Bradford, Pa., Jan. 16, 1934. She studied in Long Beach, Calif., with William Vennard at U. of S. Calif., and in Lotte Lehmann's master classes; opera debut in 1954 as Hata (*Bartered Bride*), Los Angeles Guild Opera, the same year she dubbed Dorothy Dandridge's voice for the film *Carmen Jones*. During three years at Gelsenkirchen, Germany (1957–60), she broadened her repertory, including soprano parts such as Mimi, Tatiana, and Marie (*Wozzeck*), the role of her San Francisco debut (1960). Debuts followed in N.Y. (concert version of *Beatrice di Tenda*, 1961), Chicago (Lora in Giannini's *The Harvest*, 1961), Covent Garden (Marie, 1964), and La Scala (Jocasta in *Oedipus Rex*, 1969), the latter immediately followed by Néocle (*Siège*). Her Met debut came on March 3, 1970, as Adalgisa opposite Sutherland, and since then she has returned regularly, singing more than 140 perfs. as Rosina, Carmen, Orfeo, Isabella (*Italiana*), Amneris, Fidès (*Prophète*), Eboli, Rinaldo, and Dalila. Her repertory also includes Rossini's

Arsace (*Semiramide*), Tancredi, and Malcolm (*Donna del Lago*), Mignon, and Vivaldi's Orlando, roles that she has recorded and sung widely in concert and on stage in Boston, Chicago, Houston, Dallas, Verona, Aix, and San Francisco.

Horne's singing is distinguished by ebullient temperament, sound musicianship, and her extraordinary command of a flexible, wide-ranging mezzo. After exploring many aspects of the repertory (even Wagnerian excerpts in concert), she gradually concentrated on the florid writing of the baroque era and of Rossini, much of which she has brought back to the repertory. A genial stage figure, she commands the audience through a combination of virtuosity, concentration, and generosity. Married, 1960–76, to the conductor Henry Lewis.

Hosenrolle (Ger., "trouser role"). A part for a woman singer impersonating a boy, such as Cherubino (*Nozze di Figaro*) or Octavian (*Rosenkavalier*).

Hotter, Hans. Bass-baritone; b. Offenbach am Main, Germany, Jan. 19, 1909. Studied with Matthäus Roemer in Munich, and worked as organist and choirmaster before making his operatic debut at Troppau (1930); he sang standard baritone roles, including the Wagnerian repertory, in Breslau (1931), Prague (1932–34), Hamburg (1934–45), and Munich, where he was a member of the company from 1937 to 1972. Closely associated with Strauss, he created the Commandant (*Friedenstag*, Munich, 1938), Olivier (*Capriccio*, Munich, 1942), and Jupiter (*Liebe der Danae*, "unofficial" premiere, Salzburg, 1944). International renown came after the war; he appeared at Covent Garden with the Vienna State Opera as Mozart's Almaviva and Don Giovanni (1947), and sang his first Hans Sachs in London, in English, in 1948. Met debut as the Dutchman, Nov. 9, 1950; in 4 seasons, he sang 35 perfs. of 13 roles, only three of which (Grand Inquisitor, Jochanaan, Orest) were non-Wagnerian. Despite his reputation in the Wagner baritone roles, Bing often cast him in bass parts, and he left in 1954. He first sang at Bayreuth in 1952; his Wotan there was admired throughout the 1950s. He also produced opera, including a complete *Ring* at Covent Garden (1961–64). A notable late interpretation was Schoenberg's (mainly spoken)

Marilyn Horne as Isabella in *L'Italiana in Algeri*

Hans Hotter as Amfortas in *Parsifal*

Moses. He retired from the operatic stage after singing the Grand Inquisitor in Vienna, Dec. 10, 1972.

Hotter's huge, warm tone and noble bearing were made to order for Wagner's grandest roles; as an actor, he commanded both breadth and detail. His ability to scale his voice down to the appropriate size and timbre also brought him considerable recognition in recital and concert work.

Houston. City in Texas. The Houston Grand Opera Association, the city's first permanent company, was established in 1955. Until 1972, Walter Herbert served as general director and principal conductor, offering annual seasons of two to five operas in the Houston Music Hall (capacity 3,300) and, from 1966, in the new Jesse H. Jones Hall for the Performing Arts (capacity 3,000). In 1973, R. David Gockley succeeded Herbert as general director, expanding the repertory and increasing both the number and quality of performances. Standard favorites are the norm in Houston, with occasional and notable exceptions such as Floyd's *Of Mice and Men*, Henze's *Junge Lord* and Massenet's *Don Quichotte*. Productions are sometimes shared with other companies (in 1986–87, Houston's *Porgy* production was widely toured); operas are usually offered with two casts, one of international level, the second comprising young American artists.

Huehn, Julius. Baritone; b. Revere, Mass., Jan. 12, 1909; d. Rochester, N.Y., June 8, 1971. Studied at Juilliard, N.Y.; Met debut as Herald (*Lohengrin*), Dec. 21, 1935; in 10 seasons, he sang 164 perfs. of 20 roles, including Wolfram, Telramund, Wotan, Gunther, Kurwenal, Amfortas, Pizarro, Jochanaan, Escamillo, and Falstaff. San Francisco debut as Kurwenal, 1937.

Hugh the Drover. Opera in 2 acts by Vaughan Williams; libretto by Harold Child.
First (professional) perf., London, His Majesty's, July 14, 1924: Lewis, Davies, Collier, c. Sargent. U.S. prem.,

Washington, D.C., Poli's Theater, Feb. 21, 1928: Montana, Davies, c. Goossens.
An attempt to revive the ballad opera in modern musical language. In early 19th-c. England, Hugh the Drover (t), having bested John the Butcher (bar) at boxing, is accused by him of spying and locked in the village stocks. Mary (s), betrothed to John against her will, unlocks Hugh; when he is cleared of treason by the army, she goes off with him.

Hugo, John Adam. Composer; b. Bridgeport, Conn., Jan. 5, 1873; d. Bridgeport, Dec. 29, 1945. Studied at Stuttgart Conservatory; active as pianist in Europe. Composer of instrumental works and the operas *The Hero of Byzanz* (student work), *The Temple Dancer* (perf. at Met, 1919), and *The Sun God*.

Hugo, Victor. French author (1802–85). Operas based on his writings include *Ernani* (Verdi), *La Gioconda* (Ponchielli), *Il Giuramento* (Mercadante), *Lucrezia Borgia* (Donizetti), and *Rigoletto* (Verdi).

Huguenots, Les (The Huguenots). Opera in 5 acts by Meyerbeer; libretto by Scribe and Émile Deschamps.
First perf., Paris, Opéra, Feb. 29, 1836: Dorus-Gras, Falcon, Flécheux, Nourrit, Dérivis, Serda, Levasseur, c. Habeneck. U.S. prem., New Orleans, Théâtre d'Orléans, Apr. 29, 1839. Met prem., Mar. 19, 1884 (in Ital.): Sembrich, Nilsson, Scalchi, Campanini, del Puente, Kaschmann, Mirabella, c. Vianesi. Later Met production: Dec. 27, 1912 (in Ital.): Hempel, Destinn, Alten, Caruso, Scotti, Rothier, Didur, c. Polacco, d. Kautsky/Heil, p. Speck. The Queen has also been sung at the Met by Melba, Adams; Valentine by Materna, Lilli Lehmann, Nordica, Bréval, Gadski; Raoul by J. de Reszke; Marcel by E. de Reszke. 66 perfs. in 17 seasons.
One of Meyerbeer's most successfully constructed and musically credible essays in the form he dominated in the second quarter of the 19th c., Parisian grand opera.
France, 1572. A marriage between the Protestant nobleman Raoul de Nangis (t) and the Catholic Valentine (s), daughter of the Count de St. Bris (bs), has been arranged to symbolize a truce between the Huguenot and Catholic factions. Raoul and his crusty old retainer Marcel (bs) dine with the Catholics, who are amused by Marcel's Huguenot battle song. Raoul is summoned by the page Urbain (s or ms) to an audience with Queen Marguerite de Valois (s), who expresses her hopes for reconciliation of the rival faiths. At the royal residence, he is introduced to Valentine, and recognizes her as a woman whose life he has saved and whom he has seen visiting the Catholic Comte de Nevers (bar) by night. Misunderstanding her purpose, which had been to break off her prior engagement with Nevers, Raoul assumes that Valentine is compromised, and instantly forswears the planned marriage, provoking consternation and renewed threats of religious hostility. The offended Catholics plan to murder Raoul, but Valentine, now married to Nevers, warns Marcel; when Raoul comes to thank her, he overhears the Catholics planning the St. Bartholomew's Day massacre. Valentine confesses her love, but Raoul must rush to save his friends. When Nevers is killed, Raoul and Valentine swear faith to each other but are themselves killed in the massacre.

Humperdinck, Engelbert. Composer; b. Siegburg, near Bonn, Germany, Sep. 1, 1854; d. Neustrelitz, Sep. 27, 1921. After study at Cologne Conservatory with Hiller,

Gernsheim, and Jensen, and in Munich with Lachner and Rheinberger, he assisted in preparing the premiere of *Parsifal* (1882), became Siegfried Wagner's music teacher, and held teaching positions in Frankfurt (1890–1900) and Berlin (1900–20). His first stage work, the fairy-tale opera *Hänsel und Gretel* (1893), was an immediate triumph, which he came close to equalling only once, when he expanded his incidental music for Rosmer's *Königskinder* (1897) into another fairy-tale opera (1910). In these works, the Wagnerian musical apparatus does not overload the freshness and naiveté of the subjects. Other operas: *Die sieben Geislein* (1895), after Grimm; *Dornröschen* (1902), after Perrault; *Die Heirat wider Willen* (1905), after Dumas; *Die Marketenderin* (1914).

Hunter, Rita. Soprano; b. Wallasey, Cheshire, England, Aug. 15, 1933. Studied in Liverpool, and with Redvers Llewellyn and Eva Turner, London; debut as Inez (*Trovatore*), Carl Rosa Co., 1956. Joined Sadler's Wells Opera, 1960; notable success as Brünnhilde in *Ring* cycle, 1970ff. Met debut as *Walküre* Brünnhilde, Dec. 19, 1972; later roles include Aida, Santuzza, Norma, and the *Götterdämmerung* Brünnhilde.

Hunyadi László. Opera in 4 acts by Erkel; libretto by Béni Egressy, after Lörinc Tóth's play *Two Lászlós*.
First perf., Budapest, Jan. 27, 1844: Pecz, Havi, Schodel, Füedi, Udvarhelyi, Molnár, c. Erkel.
Combining Romantic Hungarian music, pseudo-folk tunes, and some borrowings from Italian operatic style, this opera's story of Hungarian struggles against foreign political influence in the 15th c. made it an extremely popular nationalistic work.

Hurley, Laurel. Soprano; b. Allentown, Pa., Feb. 14, 1927. Studied with mother, a church organist; debut in *Student Prince*, N.Y., 1943. N.Y.C. Opera debut as Zerlina, 1952. Met debut as Oscar, Feb. 8, 1955; in 12 seasons, she sang 227 perfs. of 31 roles, including Zerlina, Périchole, Fiakermilli (*Arabella*), Oscar, Musetta and Mimi, Despina, Adele, and Susanna.

Hüsch, Gerhard. Baritone; b. Hanover, Germany, Feb. 2, 1901; d. Munich, Nov. 21, 1984. First trained as an actor; operatic debut as Liebenau (Lortzing's *Waffenschmied*), Osnabrück, 1923. Sang lyric baritone roles in Bremen, Cologne (1927–30), and Berlin (1930–44), also appearing at Covent Garden (1930–38) and Bayreuth (Wolfram, 1930–31). From 1932, a noted lieder singer.

Hynninen, Jorma. Baritone; b. Leppävirta, Finland, Apr. 3, 1941. Studied in Helsinki, with Luigi Ricci in Rome, and in Salzburg; debut as Silvio, Helsinki, 1970. Has appeared in Milan, Vienna, Hamburg, Munich, and Paris. Met debut as Posa (*Don Carlos*), Mar. 30, 1984; has also sung Mozart's Almaviva and Wolfram there. Artistic director of Finnish National Opera (from 1984).

I

Ibert, Jacques. Composer; b. Paris, Aug. 15, 1890; d. Paris, Feb. 5, 1962. Studied at Paris Conservatory with Vidal and Fauré. His generically diverse operas include the farce *Angélique* (1927), stylistically reminiscent of Offenbach; the opéra comique *Le Roi d'Yvetot* (1930); and the musical drama *L'Aiglon* (1937, jointly with Honegger).

Ice Break, The. Opera in 3 acts by Tippett; libretto by the composer.
First perf., London, Covent Garden, July 7, 1977: Harper, Barstow, Vaughan, Walker, McDonnell, Shirley-Quirk, c. Davis. U.S. prem., Opera Co. of Boston, May 18, 1979: Saunders, Munro, Clarey, Rayam, Gardner, Fredericks, c. Caldwell.
An idealistic contemplation of violence and hope, set in an American airport, at the present time. Lev (bs-bar) and his wife Nadia (s), their son Yuri (bar) and his girlfriend Gayle (s), the athlete Olympion (t) and his girlfriend Hannah (ms) experience reconciliations, deaths, and a race riot.

Idomeneo, Rè di Creta (Idomeneus, King of Crete). Opera in 3 acts by Mozart; libretto by Abbé Gianbattista Varesco, after Danchet's libretto for *Idomenée*, by Campra; also after the ancient legend.
First perf.: Munich, Hoftheater, Jan. 29, 1781: D. Wendling, E. Wendling, del Prato, Raaff, Panzacchi. U.S. prem., Lenox, Mass., Berkshire Festival, Aug. 4, 1947: Lenchner, Trickey, Bollinger, Laderoute, Guarrera, c. Goldovsky. Met prem., Oct. 14, 1982: Cotrubas, Behrens, von Stade, Pavarotti, Alexander, c. Levine, d. & p. Ponnelle. 23 perfs. in 2 seasons.
In *Idomeneo*, Mozart at once displayed his mastery of the opera seria forms he inherited and made bold experiments in the direction of musical continuity and large-scale organization, at the same time composing some of his most memorable arias and ensembles. Rarely performed

Idomeneo – Glyndebourne Festival, 1951. Designed by Oliver Messel, produced by Carl Ebert. Sena Jurinac, Leopold Simoneau, Birgit Nilsson

in the 19th c., rewritten in its first modern revivals (by R. Strauss and Lothar Wallerstein, Vienna, 1931, and by Wolf-Ferrari, Munich, 1931), *Idomeneo* has since World War II come to be recognized as one of Mozart's masterpieces.

Crete, mythological times. Returning victorious from the Trojan war, Idomeneo, King of Crete (t), battles a storm at sea. To save himself, he vows to sacrifice to Neptune the first person he meets upon his return. That unfortunately proves to be his son Idamante (s), who has fallen in love with the captive Trojan princess, Ilia (s). Idomeneo tries to save his son by accepting the advice of his confident Arbace (t) and ordering Idamante to take the princess Elettra (s) home to Argos. Another storm delays their departure, to Elettra's great dismay, for she desperately hopes to win Idamante's love. When a sea monster causes death and devastation throughout the land, the people of Crete demand to know the name of the person to be sacrificed. Idamante slays the monster, and, learning of his father's vow, offers himself to be sacrificed. But the Voice of Neptune (bs) intercedes and decrees that Idamante shall replace Idomeneo as king, taking Ilia as his wife. Elettra collapses in anguish.

Igesz, Bodo. Producer; b. Amsterdam, Feb. 7, 1935. Assistant stage director, Netherlands Opera (1960–61). A staff director at the Met since 1963, he staged the 1972 *Carmen* conceived by Gentele, also *Bluebeard's Castle* (1974) and many revivals. Has also worked in Santa Fe (*Bassarids*, 1968), Houston (*Forza*, 1973), and other leading theaters.

Illica, Luigi. Librettist; b. Castell'Arquato, near Piacenza, Italy, May 9, 1857; d. Colombarone, Dec. 16, 1919. A successful playwright from 1883, he wrote librettos for Smareglia, Catalani (*Wally*), Giordano (*Chénier*), and Mascagni (*Iris*). His work on Puccini's *Manon Lescaut* led to collaboration with Giuseppe Giacosa on *Bohème*, *Tosca*, and *Madama Butterfly*; Illica laid out the dramas, Giacosa wrote the verses.

imbroglio (Ital., "intrigue," "entanglement"). A scene of confusion, usually comic, supported by appropriately various and hectic music; the second-act finales of *Nozze di Figaro* and *Meistersinger* are classic examples.

Immortal Hour, The. Opera in 2 acts by Boughton; libretto adapted from plays and poems by "Fiona Macleod" [William Sharp].

First perf., Glastonbury, Assembly Rooms, Aug. 26, 1914: Lemon, Jordan, Austin, Boughton, c. Scott. U.S. prem., N.Y., Grove Street Theater, Apr. 6, 1926.

Despite lengthy London runs in the Twenties, this lush mythological opera has rarely been revived with success. Dalua (bar), Lord of Shadow, allows the mortal King Eochaidh (bar) to marry Etain (s), princess of the Fairies; after a year, the fairy prince Midir (t) comes to reclaim Etain, and Echoaidh falls dead at Dalua's touch.

impresario. In a strict sense, the organizer and manager of an opera company, hired by a theater's owners to arrange performances. More loosely, the head of any operatic enterprise.

in alt (Ital., "in the high register"). The notes above the treble staff, ranging from G up an octave or more.

Incoronazione di Poppea, L' (The Coronation of Poppea). Opera in prologue and 3 acts by Monteverdi; libretto by Gian Francesco Busenello, after Tacitus' *Annals*, xiii–xv.

First perf., Venice, Teatro Santi Giovanni e Paolo, fall 1642. U.S. prem., Northampton, Mass., Smith College, Apr. 27, 1926: c. Josten.

Monteverdi's late masterpiece, a drama of unbridled license and sensuality that 20th-c. audiences have found startlingly direct in revivals.

Rome, during Nero's rule, A.D. 62. Returning from abroad to his mistress Poppea (s), Ottone (s) discovers that the emperor Nerone (s) has taken her as his mistress. Nerone's wife Ottavia (ms) laments her humiliation, and is offered sympathy by the old philosopher Seneca (bs), who counsels her that her virtue will be rewarded. The goddess of wisdom, Pallade, warns Seneca in a vision that he risks death if he interferes, but when Nerone informs Seneca of his intention to divorce Ottavia and marry Poppea, the philosopher counsels against actions prompted by the heart that are likely to bring resentment from the people. The infuriated Nerone dismisses him; when Poppea denounces Seneca to Nerone, the ruler decides that Seneca must die. Ottone attempts a reconciliation with Poppea, but is rejected, and turns quickly to Drusilla (s), Ottavia's lady-in-waiting, who is in love with him. At his home, Seneca stoically receives Nerone's death orders, and complies by ordering his bath, where he intends to bleed to death. Ottavia commands Ottone to kill Poppea, warning that if he fails she will denounce him to Nerone. Disguised as Drusilla, Ottone attempts to kill Poppea in her sleep, but the god Amore awakens Poppea, who charges Drusilla with attempted murder. She protests her innocence, but is condemned to death, whereupon Ottone confesses and is sentenced to exile; Drusilla follows him. Nerone banishes Ottavia, and the triumphant Poppea is crowned Empress.

Indes Galantes, Les (The Elegant Indies). Opéra-ballet in prologue and 4 (originally 3) entrées by Rameau; libretto by Louis Fuzelier.

First perf., Paris, Opéra, Aug. 23, 1735. Revised in prologue and 4 entrées: first perf., Paris, Opéra, Mar. 10, 1736. U.S. prem., N.Y., Town Hall, March 1, 1961 (concert perf.): Raskin, Bressler, Shirley, Trehy, c. Dunn.

Four tales of love and rivalry, set respectively on a Turkish island, in a Peruvian desert, in Persia, and in a wood in America.

Indy, Vincent d'. Composer; b. Paris, Mar. 27, 1851; d. Paris, Dec. 2, 1931. Studied with Lavignac and at Paris Conservatory with Franck. A champion of Wagner, his first opera, *Fervaal* (1897), was strongly influenced by *Parsifal*. *L'Étranger* (1903) called for lesser forces and demonstrated a greater clarity of scoring, while the monumental *La Légende de St. Christophe* (1920) was an obstinately Romantic reaction to the modernism of Debussy and Ravel.

ingénue (Fr., "artless"). The type of naive young girl characteristic of 18th-c. French opera.

Inszenierung (Ger.). Scenic production. Also *Neuinszenierung*, new production.

Intendant (Ger.). The chief administrator of a German opera house, sometimes (but not necessarily) a musician.

intermezzo. A short comic work, performed between the acts of a serious work in the 18th c.

Intermezzo. Opera in 2 acts by R. Strauss; libretto by the composer.

First perf., Dresden, Nov. 4, 1924: Lotte Lehmann, Correck, c. Busch. U.S. prem., N.Y., Feb. 11, 1963 (concert perf.): Curtin, Bell, c. Scherman. U.S. stage prem., Philadelphia, Curtis Institute, Feb. 24, 1977.

Based on an event in the composer's life, *Intermezzo* has by some observers been thought exhibitionistic, not to mention unflattering to his wife. The music exploits a conversational style that Strauss had been developing since *Rosenkavalier*.

Grundlsee and Vienna, the 1920s. The composer Robert Storch (bar) is constantly abused by his ill-tempered wife Christine (s) because he is too gentle to stand up to her. She flirts with a young Baron (t), but threatens divorce when she opens a torrid love letter mistakenly addressed to Storch. The mistake is discovered, but Christine is only placated when Storch finally scolds her.

In the Pasha's Garden. Opera in 1 act by Seymour; libretto by H.C. Tracy, after a story by H.G. Dwight.

First perf., N.Y., Met, Jan. 24, 1935: Jepson, Jagel, Tibbett, c. Panizza, d. Kiesler, p. Wymetal Jr. 3 perfs. in 1 season.

The last of Gatti-Casazza's conservative American novelties at the Met. Near Constantinople, early 20th c. Hélène (s), wife of the Pasha (bar), hides her lover Étienne (t) in a carved chest, which her husband buries.

intonation. Tuning; the accuracy with which a singer or instrumentalist produces a precise musical pitch.

Invisible City of Kitezh, The. See *Legend of the Invisible City of Kitezh and the Maiden Fevronia, The*.

Iolanta. Opera in 1 act by Tchaikovsky; libretto by Modest Tchaikovsky, after Henrik Hertz's comedy *King René's Daughter*, after Hans Christian Andersen.

First perf., St. Petersburg, Maryinsky, Dec. 18, 1892: M. Figner, N. Figner, Sibiriakov, c. Napravnik, U.S. prem., Scarborough-on-Hudson, Garden Theater, Sep. 10, 1933.

A richly scored drama set in 15th-c. Provence. The blind princess Iolanta (s) has been protected by her father King René (bs) from awareness that she is different from anyone else. When Vaudémont (t) falls in love with her and describes the world's beauties, the King threatens him with death, but Iolanta's sight is restored.

Iphigénie en Aulide (Iphigenia in Aulis). Opera in 3 acts by Gluck; libretto by F.L.G. Leblond du Roullet, after Racine's tragedy.

First perf., Paris, Opéra, Apr. 19, 1774: Arnould, Du Plant, Legros, L'Arrivée. U.S. prem., Philadelphia, Academy of Music, Feb. 22, 1935: Tentoni, van Gordon, Bentonelli, Baklanov, c. Smallens.

Gluck's first opera for Paris, much admired (among others, by Wagner, who in 1846 prepared a much-altered performing edition) but today rarely performed.

The island of Aulis, at the beginning of the Trojan war. Having vowed to sacrifice his daughter Iphigénie (s) to Diana if a wind will bear his army safely to Troy, Agamemnon (bs) is prey to remorse. When Iphigénie arrives on the island with her mother Clytemnestra (s), believing she is to marry Achilles (t), Agamemnon tries to forestall the sacrifice, demanded by the high priest Calchas (bs). Infuriated by the impending death of his bride,

Achilles leads an attack on the Greeks, but Calchas announces that the gods will grant good weather for the voyage even without the sacrifice, and all are reconciled.

Iphigénie en Tauride (Iphigenia in Tauris). Opera in 4 acts by Gluck; libretto by Nicolas-François Guillard and F.L.G. Leblond du Roullet, after Euripides' drama.

First perf., Paris, Opéra, May 18, 1779: Levasseur, Legros, L'Arrivée, Moreau, c. Francoeur. U.S. & Met prem., Nov. 25, 1916 (in Ger., arr. R. Strauss): Kurt, Sembach, Weil, Braun, c. Bodanzky, d. Hewlett, Basing/Hewlett, p. Heythekker. 5 perfs. in 1 season.

Gluck's most resourceful and fluid opera, moving with easy mastery among recitative, aria, ensemble, choral, and orchestral textures, maintaining throughout a high level of emotional intensity.

Tauris, after the Trojan War. Iphigénie (s) has become a priestess of Diane on the island of Tauris, and is unaware that her father has been killed by her mother, who in turn has been murdered by her brother Oreste (bar). Oreste and his friend Pylade (t) arrive on the island and are taken captive, their identities unknown; the Scythian king Thoas (bar) demands that they be sacrificed. Oreste tells Iphigénie of her parents' deaths, but tells her that her brother is dead too; she wants to save him, but he, pursued by the Furies, insists that she save Pylade instead. Just as the sacrifice is about to be carried out, brother and sister recognize each other. Pylade arrives with Greek soldiers, and Diane appears to pardon Oreste.

Iris. Opera in 3 acts by Mascagni; libretto by Illica.

First perf., Rome, Costanzi, Nov. 22, 1898: Darclée, de Lucia, c. Mascagni. Revised version, Milan, La Scala, Jan. 19, 1899: Darclée, de Lucia, c. Toscanini. U.S. prem., Philadelphia, Academy of Music, Oct. 14, 1902: Farneti, Schiavazzi, c. Mascagni. Met prem., Dec. 6, 1907: Eames, Caruso, c. Ferrari, d. Fox. Later Met production: Apr. 1, 1915: Bori, Botta, c. Toscanini, d. Novak. 13 perfs. in 3 seasons.

A score combining verismo with fashionable orientalism, set in 19th-c. Japan. Osaka (t), who loves the beautiful Iris (s), has her held captive in a brothel; her blind father (bs) curses her and she drowns herself in a sewer.

Irmelin. Opera in 3 acts by Delius; libretto by the composer.

First perf., Oxford, New Theatre, May 4, 1953: c. Beecham.

In Delius' first opera, the prince Nils (t), disguised as a swineherd, finds the princess Irmelin (s), his ideal woman, at the end of a silver stream.

Isabeau. Opera in 3 acts by Mascagni; libretto by Illica.

First perf., Buenos Aires, Colón, June 2, 1911: Farneti, Saludas, Galeffi, c. Mascagni. U.S. prem., Chicago, Nov. 12, 1917: Raisa, Crimi, Rimini, c. Campanini.

A briefly popular verismo opera based on the Lady Godiva legend. Isabeau (s), forced by her father King Raimondo (bar) to ride naked through the streets, as punishment for her refusal to marry, falls in love with the forester Folco (t), who has been condemned to death for gazing on her nakedness.

Island God, The. Opera in 1 act by Menotti; libretto by the composer.

First perf., Met, Feb. 20, 1942: Varnay, Jobin, Warren, Cordon, c. Panizza, d. Rychtarik, p. Wallerstein. 3 perfs. in 1 season.

Withdrawn by the composer shortly after the premiere. On a Mediterranean island, Telea (s) leaves her husband Ilo (bar) for the fisherman Luca (t); in his despair, Ilo destroys the ancient temple he was rebuilding to an unknown God (bs).

Italiana in Algeri, L' (The Italian Girl in Algiers). Opera in 2 acts by Rossini; libretto by Anelli, originally for Luigi Mosca's 1808 opera.

First perf., Venice, San Benedetto, May 22, 1813: Marcolini, Gentili, Rosich, Galli. U.S. prem., N.Y., Richmond Hill, Nov. 5, 1832. Met prem., Dec. 5, 1919: Besanzoni, Hackett, de Luca, Didur, c. Papi, d. Pogany, p. Ordynski. Later Met production: Nov. 10, 1973: Horne, Alva, Uppman, Corena, c. Ötvos, d. & p. Ponnelle. 45 perfs. in 5 seasons.

After *Barbiere*, this sparkling score has probably been Rossini's most popular comedy in the years between his own time and ours.

Isabella (ms), an independent-minded Italian woman, has been searching far and wide for her kidnapped lover Lindoro (t). Shipwrecked and taken into captivity by Mustafà, Bey of Algiers (bs), she finds Lindoro also a captive there. With his help and that of her befuddled elderly admirer and travelling escort Taddeo (bs), Isabella contrives a plot. She flirts with the Bey, who is persuaded to bind himself to the precepts of the order of "Pappataci": eat and say nothing. Isabella has roused to action all her compatriots in the Bey's service, and as the Bey endures with difficulty what is presented as a test of his fidelity to the oath, they escape under his nose into a waiting ship.

Ivan Susanin. See *Life for the Tsar, A.*

Ivan the Terrible. See *Maid of Pskov, The.*

Ivogün, Maria [Ilse Kempner]. Soprano; b. Budapest, Nov. 18, 1891. Studied with her mother, soprano Ida von Günther, and in Vienna and Munich; debut as Mimi, Munich, 1913. Sang there until 1925, at Berlin Städtische Oper until 1934. Also appeared briefly in Chicago (Rosina, 1922) and London (1924). Specialized in coloratura parts, notably Konstanze and Zerbinetta. Taught in Berlin; pupils included Schwarzkopf and Streich.

J

Jacobin, The. Opera in 3 acts by Dvořák; libretto by Marie Červinková-Riegrová.

First perf., Prague, Czech Theater, Feb. 12, 1889. U.S. prem., Washington, D.C., Sokol Opera, Oct. 28, 1979.

Dvořák's ninth opera is set in a Czech village in 1793. Bohuš (bar), disinherited for his Jacobin leanings, returns from political exile and regains his place in the community with the help of the musician Benda (t).

Jadlowker, Hermann. Tenor; b. Riga, Latvia, July 17, 1877; d. Tel Aviv, Israel, May 13, 1953. Studied with Joseph Gänsbacher, Vienna Conservatory; debut as Gomez (Kreutzer's *Nachtlager in Granada*), Cologne, 1899. Appeared in Riga (1900–06) and Karlsruhe (1906–09). Met debut as Faust, Jan. 22, 1910; in 3 seasons, he sang 60 perfs. of 14 roles, including Rodolfo, Turiddu, Canio, Lohengrin, Max (*Freischütz*), and Pinkerton, and creating the King's Son (*Königskinder*). Also appeared in Boston

Leoš Janáček

(1909–12). Engaged by Berlin Court Opera (1911–19), he sang roles such as Otello and Parsifal, and made guest appearances, including creation of Bacchus (*Ariadne*), Stuttgart, 1912. Jadlowker retired from opera in 1919, and in 1929 returned to Riga, serving as cantor and teaching; he emigrated to Palestine in 1938. Though his records are now valued for his extraordinary command of coloratura, Jadlowker's career evinced an aspiration to compete with his heroic peers.

Jagel, Frederick. Tenor; b. Brooklyn, N.Y., June 10, 1897; d. San Francisco, July 5, 1982. Studied in N.Y. and Milan; debut as Rodolfo, Livorno, 1924 (as Federico Jeghelli). Met debut as Radames, Nov. 8, 1927; in 23 seasons, he sang 217 perfs. of 34 roles, including Pinkerton, Turiddu, Pollione, and Grimes. Also appeared in Buenos Aires (1928, 1939–41), San Francisco (Jack Rance, 1930), Chicago (Lohengrin, 1934), and at N.Y.C. Opera (Herod, 1947).

Jakob Lenz. Opera in 12 scenes by Wolfgang Rihm; libretto by Michael Fröhling, after Büchner's unfinished novella *Lenz*.

First perf., Karlsruhe, Mar. 6, 1980: Yoder, Munkittrick, Best, c. Haas. U.S. prem., Bloomington, Indiana U., July 11, 1981 (in Eng.): Smartt, Borg, Levitt, c. Baldner.

This atonal chamber opera is a study in madness, based on the life of the 18th-c. German poet Jakob Lenz (bar), who went mad and died a beggar in Moscow.

James, Henry. American novelist (1843–1916). Operas based on his writings include *Owen Wingrave* (Britten), *The Turn of the Screw* (Britten), and *The Voice of Ariadne* (Musgrave).

Janáček, Leoš. Composer; b. Hukvaldy, Moravia, July 3, 1854; d. Moravská Ostrava, Aug. 12, 1928. Studied with Skuherský in Prague, Leo Grill at Leipzig Conservatory, and Franz Krenn at Vienna Conservatory. Founded organ school in Brno, and taught at Teachers' Institute there, while composing choral, instrumental, and orchestral works as well as operas, the first of which, *Šárka* (1887), was not performed until 1925. In 1888 he began to collect and edit folk melodies, which form the musical basis of his next opera, the one-act *Beginning of a Romance*

(1891). In composing *Jenůfa* (1904), he integrated folk material more fully into his style, and abandoned the number opera. *Fate* (1905, rev. 1907) was not performed until 1934, and it was only after *Jenůfa*'s belated success in Prague (1916) and internationally that Janáček completed *The Excursions of Mr. Brouček* (1920). Now assured performances, in his final decade he composed four further operas. In part inspired by his one-sided passion for a young woman, Kamila Stösslová, three of them focus on a central female character: *Katya Kabanova* (1921), *The Cunning Little Vixen* (1924), and *The Makropoulos Affair* (1926); *From the House of the Dead* (1930) is a harrowing ensemble work based on Dostoyevsky's prison diaries. Dramatically terse, musically economical, with frequently angular and awkward vocal lines based on Janáček's own principles of stylized "speech-melody" and only sparingly blossoming into lyricism, these operas were too original for quick public acceptance. Since World War II, they have come to be valued for their directness, theatrical effectiveness, and moving assertion of the centrality of death and regeneration to human existence.

BIBLIOGRAPHY: Jaroslav Vogel, *Leoš Janáček, A Biography* (London, 1962; rev. 1981).

Janowitz, Gundula. Soprano; b. Berlin, Aug. 2, 1937. Studied at Graz Conservatory; debut as Barbarina (*Nozze*), Vienna State Opera, 1959. Sang Mozart heroines in Salzburg (1968–72), Paris (1973), and London (1976). In only Met season, sang 5 perfs. of Sieglinde (debut, Nov. 21, 1967). Has also appeared in Bayreuth (Flowermaiden, 1960), at Glyndebourne (Ilia, 1964), Munich, and Deutsche Oper, Berlin.

Janssen, Herbert. Baritone; b. Cologne, Germany, Sep. 22, 1892; d. New York, June 3, 1965. Studied with Oskar Daniel, Berlin; debut as Herod in Schreker's *Schatzgräber*, Berlin State Opera, 1922, where he remained until 1938, first singing comprimario roles, then lyric and dramatic leads, chiefly in Italian repertory. Appeared at Covent Garden, 1926–39 (Wagner roles, Prince Igor, and Orest). At Bayreuth (debut as Wolfram, 1930), he sang through 1937, in the lighter baritone roles. After a season in Buenos Aires (1938), he settled in N.Y. Met debut as Wolfram, Jan. 29, 1939; in 14 seasons, he sang 152 perfs. of 14 roles, including Gunther, Telramund, Kurwenal, Amfortas, Wotan (*Rheingold* and *Walküre*), Sachs, and Jochanaan. In San Francisco (1945–51), he also sang the Wanderer. A fine-grained lyric baritone, Janssen had less success in the heavier Wagnerian parts he assumed after Schorr's retirement.

Järvi, Neeme. Conductor; b. Tallinn, Estonia, June 7, 1937. After study at Leningrad Conservatory, became conductor of Estonian Opera Theater (1963). Won Santa Cecilia competition in 1971, thereafter active as a freelance. Met debut in *Onegin* (Mar. 21, 1979), returning for the same work in 1984 and *Khovanshchina* in 1985. Since 1984, music director of Scottish National Orchestra.

Jasager, Der (The One Who Says Yes). School opera in 2 acts by Weill; libretto by Bertolt Brecht, after the 15th-c. Japanese Noh drama *Taniko*.

First perf., Berlin, Central Institute for Education, June 23, 1930. U.S. prem., N.Y., Grand Street Playhouse, Apr. 25, 1933 (in Eng.).

A fiercely didactic opera for students. On a mountain journey to get medicine for his Mother (ms), the Boy (s) becomes ill, endangering the party; he agrees to let himself be thrown into the valley, following an old tradition, on condition that the Teacher (bar) will deliver the medicine.

Jenkins, Timothy. Tenor; b. Oklahoma City, Okla., Nov. 21, 1951. Studied at N. Texas State U.; debut as Douphol (*Traviata*), Fort Worth Opera, 1974. Met debut as Schmidt (*Mahagonny*), Dec. 10, 1979; he has since sung Parsifal, Laca (*Jenůfa*), the High Priest (*Idomeneo*), Macduff, Oedipus, and Siegmund.

Jenůfa. Opera in 3 acts by Janáček; libretto by the composer, after Gabriela Preissová's drama *Her Foster Daughter*.

First perf., Brno, Jan. 21, 1904: Kabeláčová, Svobodová, Staněk-Doubravský, Procházka, c. Hrazdira. U.S. & Met prem., Dec. 6, 1924 (in Ger.): Jeritza, Matzenauer, Öhman, Laubenthal, c. Bodanzky. Later Met production: Nov. 15, 1974 (in Eng.): Kubiak, Varnay, Vickers, Lewis, c. Nelson, d. Schneider-Siemssen, p. Rennert. 22 perfs. in 3 seasons.

The first of Janáček's mature, fully Czech-based operas, later the first of his works to establish itself on international stages, and a gripping musical and psychological drama, which seems now, despite the language barrier, nearly to have entered the international standard repertory.

A mill in the mountains, the house of the Kostelnička (or sexton's wife; s). Jenůfa (s), pregnant by Števa (t), fears he will go off as a soldier rather than marry her. Števa's stepbrother Laca (t), who loves Jenůfa himself, is jealous. When Števa appears, drunk, and treats Jenůfa coarsely, the Kostelnička, who is Jenůfa's stepmother, unaware of the pregnancy, decrees that there can be no marriage until he has stayed sober for a year. Mockingly, Laca makes advances to Jenůfa; when she rebuffs him, he scars her face with his knife, but is quickly horrified and remorseful. The Kostelnička, shaken by Jenůfa's illicit pregnancy, keeps the girl hidden before and after the infant's birth, telling others she has gone to work in Vienna as a maid. She talks to Števa about his responsibilities, but he is now engaged to the mayor's daughter, and promises nothing beyond a financial contribution to the child's well-being. Laca still loves Jenůfa; the Kostelnička, thinking the child an impediment to a possible marriage between the two, tells him that the baby is dead. After drugging Jenůfa, she takes the child away, then tells her that her baby died while she was delirious. Moved by Laca's solicitude, Jenůfa eventually agrees to marry him, but on their wedding day a child's corpse is discovered under just-melted ice. Jenůfa recognizes her child, and is immediately accused of murder; the Kostelnička, stricken, confesses to the crime. Jenůfa asks Laca to leave her, but he remains faithful to her.

Jepson, Helen. Soprano; b. Titusville, Pa., Nov. 28, 1904. Studied with Queena Mario, Curtis Institute, Philadelphia, and with Mary Garden, Paris. Sang small roles in Philadelphia (1928–30) and Montreal. Met debut as Helene (*In the Pasha's Garden*), Jan. 24, 1935; in 9 seasons, she sang 36 perfs. of 10 roles, including Violetta, Marguerite, Mélisande, Thaïs, and Nedda. Also appeared in San Francisco (*Martha*, 1935) and Chicago (*Thaïs*, 1935).

Jerger, Alfred. Bass-baritone; b. Brünn [now Brno], Moravia, June 9, 1889; d. Vienna, Nov. 18, 1976. Studied at Vienna Academy; conducted operetta in Passau, 1913. Debut as Lothario (*Mignon*), Zurich, 1917. Appeared in Munich (1919–20), Vienna (1920–64), and frequently at Salzburg, specializing in Mozart, later in character parts. Created Mandryka (*Arabella*), Dresden, 1933.

Jeritza, Maria [Mimi Jedlitzková, Marie Jedlizka]. Soprano; b. Brünn [now Brno], Moravia, Oct. 6, 1887; d. Orange, N.J., July 10, 1982. Studied in Brünn, with Auspitz in Prague, later with Sembrich in N.Y. Sang in chorus, Brünn Opera; debut as Elsa, Olmütz, 1910. Vienna debut as Elisabeth, Volksoper, 1911. Engaged by the Court Opera at the request of Emperor Franz Josef, who had heard her sing Rosalinda (*Fledermaus*) at Bad Ischl, she sang Minnie (*Fanciulla*) and Tosca to Puccini's approval, later Turandot, Salome, Octavian, the title role of *Ägyptische Helena*, and other roles ranging from Mascagni and Massenet to Wagner. She created the title role in both the 1912 and 1916 versions of *Ariadne auf Naxos*, and the Empress in *Frau ohne Schatten*, 1919, and was the first Jenůfa in both Vienna and N.Y. An important creation was Marietta (*Tote Stadt*, Hamburg, Dec. 4, 1920), also the role of her Met debut, Nov. 19, 1921; for the next 12 years, she divided her time between Vienna and N.Y. Following Farrar's retirement, Jeritza became the Met's leading prima donna. Among her 293 perfs. of 21 roles, she was most often (52 times) seen there as a flamboyant Tosca (singing "Vissi d'arte" prone on the floor), also as Elisabeth, Carmen, Santuzza, Thaïs, Elsa, Octavian, Fedora, Minnie (*Fanciulla*), and Maliella (*Gioielli*); she was the company's first Turandot and Ägyptische Helena, but left at the time of the Depression salary cuts. At the Met in Suppé's *Boccaccio* and *Donna Juanita*, and on a 1934 U.S. tour in Friml's *Music Hath Charms*, she demonstrated her light touch in operetta. After World War II she made occasional appearances, including a single Rosalinde (*Fledermaus*) at the Met, Feb. 22, 1951.

Jeritza's full and healthy voice, feminine allure, and flair for acting made her an immensely popular performer on both sides of the ocean. Unfortunately, little of her undoubted theatrical magnetism survives on her numerous studio recordings.

Jerusalem, Siegfried. Tenor; b. Oberhausen, Germany, Apr. 17, 1940. Studied in Essen and began career as bassoonist, studying singing (first as baritone) in Stuttgart, where he sang small parts, moving to Aachen and Hamburg; 1977 debuts in Bayreuth (Froh) and Berlin. Met debut as Lohengrin, Jan. 10, 1980.

Jérusalem. Opera in 4 acts by Verdi; libretto by Alphonse Royer and Gustave Vaëz. A French adaption and revision of *Lombardi* (*q.v.*).

First perf., Paris, Opéra, Nov. 22, 1847; Van Gelder, Duprez, Alizard. U.S. prem., New Orleans, Théâtre d'Orléans, Jan. 24, 1850.

Jewels of the Madonna, The. See *Gioielli della Madonna, I.*

Jobin, Raoul. Tenor; b. Quebec, Apr. 8, 1906; d. Quebec, Jan. 13, 1974. Studied in Quebec and Paris; debut as Gounod's Tybalt, Paris Opéra, 1930. Appeared at both Opéra and Opéra-Comique, 1937–57. Met debut as Massenet's Des Grieux, Feb. 19, 1940; in 10 seasons, he sang 100 perfs. of 14 roles, including Tonio (*Fille*), Faust, and Canio, and creating Luca (*Island God*). Debuts in San Francisco (*Lakmé*, 1940) and Chicago (José, 1941). Father of tenor André, who sang Pelléas at N.Y.C. Opera, 1970.

Jochum, Eugen. Conductor; b. Babenhausen, Germany, Nov. 1, 1902; d. Munich, Mar. 26, 1987. After study in Augsburg and Munich and concert debut in latter city (1926), held posts in Kiel, Mannheim, Duisburg, and Berlin (Radio Symphony). Music director of Hamburg Opera (1934–49); founded and led Bavarian Radio Orchestra (1949–74), also associated with Amsterdam Concertgebouw. Bayreuth debut, *Tristan* (1953); Chicago Opera debut, *Ariadne*, 1964.

Johnson, Edward. Tenor and manager; b. Guelph, Ontario, Aug. 22, 1878; d. Guelph, Apr. 20, 1959. After attending U. of Toronto, he studied singing in N.Y., starred in operetta (Straus' *Walzertraum* on Broadway, 1908) and concert opera (*Samson*, Worcester, Mass., 1904), and studied in Florence with Vincenzo Lombardi; operatic debut as Andrea Chénier, Padua, 1912, using the name Edoardo di Giovanni. At La Scala (debut, *Parsifal*, 1914) he created the leads in Pizzetti's *Fedra* (1915) and Montemezzi's *Nave* (1918). He sang opposite Mary Garden with the Chicago Opera (1919–22) and made his Met debut as Avito (*Amore dei Tre Re*) on Nov. 16, 1922. During 12 Met seasons, he sang 163 perfs. of 20 roles, from Roméo to Canio, and was the company's first Pelléas (1925), Fra Gherardo (1929), and Sadko (1930); he created Aethelwold (*King's Henchman*, 1927), Peter Ibbetson (1931), and Sir Gower (*Merry Mount*, 1934). By the time of his last performance in 1935, he had been named assistant general manager of the Met under Herbert Witherspoon, who died two months later; appointed to succeed him, Johnson carried out his predecessor's economy measures. His shift away from established European stars toward rising American ones was accelerated by the advent of World War II. On the financial side, Johnson's term saw the founding of the Metropolitan Opera Guild

Maria Jeritza as Fedora

(1936) and a million-dollar drive to buy the opera house from the boxholders (1940). A conservative manager who left most practical details to his assistant Edward Ziegler, Johnson retired in 1950, after which he helped organize an opera school at the Royal Conservatory of Music, Toronto.

Jolie Fille de Perth, La (The Fair Maid of Perth). Opera in 4 acts by Bizet; libretto by J.H. Vernoy de St. Georges and Jules Adenis, loosely based on Sir Walter Scott's novel.

First perf., Paris, Lyrique, Dec. 26, 1867: Devriès, Ducasse, Massy, Barré. U.S. prem., N.Y., Manhattan Opera Theatre, May 10, 1979.

An opéra comique of easy melodious charm, set in Perth, Scotland. Catherine Glover (s) believes the gypsy Mab (s or ms) has come between her and Henri Smith (t), but Mab actually helps her avoid being abducted by the Duke of Rothsay (bar or t) and eventually has a hand in the lovers' reconciliation.

Jones, Gwyneth. Soprano; b. Pontnewyndd, Wales, Nov. 7, 1936. Studied (as mezzo) in London, Siena, Zurich, and Geneva; debut as Annina (*Rosenkavalier*), Zurich, 1962. After joining Covent Garden, 1963, moved to soprano roles, including Leonora (*Trovatore*), Santuzza, Fidelio. Debuts in Vienna (Fidelio, 1966) and Bayreuth (Eva, 1968), where she later sang Senta, Kundry, Sieglinde, Elisabeth and Venus, and Brünnhilde in the 1976 *Ring*. Met debut as Sieglinde, Nov. 24, 1972; has subsequently sung 51 perfs., including Fidelio, the Marschallin, the *Walküre* Brünnhilde, Isolde, and Salome. Appearances in most major theaters, in roles including the Empress (*Frau*) and Turandot, as well as Wagnerian heroines.

Jones, Isola. Mezzo-soprano; b. Chicago, Dec. 27, 1949. Studied at Northwestern U. and in N.Y.; debut as Olga (*Onegin*), Met, Oct. 15, 1977. At the Met, she has since sung Preziosilla, Maddalena, Lola (*Cavalleria*), Giulietta (*Hoffmann*), Margret (*Wozzeck*), the Strawberry Woman (*Porgy*), and Carmen. Has also appeared with symphony orchestras of Chicago, Cleveland, and Boston.

Jones, Robert Edmond. Designer; b. Milton, N. H., Dec. 12, 1887; d. Milton, Nov. 26, 1954. After graduation from Harvard, worked under Reinhardt in Berlin (1912–13). Associated with the movement against traditional realism and stereotyped action, influenced by Appia and Gordon Craig, a close friend and collaborator of O'Neill, he relied on lighting to animate his scenes. His designs included ballets for Diaghilev, plays for Broadway, and opera; for the Met he designed Carpenter's ballet *Sky-scrapers* (1926) and the opera *Preziose Ridicole* (1930); his sketches for *Fliegende Holländer* (1950) were realized by Charles Elson.

Jongleur de Notre-Dame, Le (The Juggler of Our Lady). Opera in 3 acts by Massenet; libretto by Maurice Léna, after a story in Anatole France's *L'Étui de Nacre*.

First perf., Monte Carlo, Feb. 18, 1902: Maréchal, Renaud, Soulacroix, c. Jéhin. U.S. prem., N.Y., Manhattan Opera, Nov. 27, 1908: Garden, Renaud, Dufranne, c. Campanini.

In this sweetly reticent picture of monastic life, the title role, originally composed for a light tenor, was successfully appropriated by Mary Garden. In 14th-c. Cluny, the juggler Jean (t), a novice among monks who exercise

Edward Johnson

various well-developed talents in praise of the Virgin, pays her homage in the only way he knows: by donning his costume and doing his juggler's tricks. The brothers disapprove, but the Virgin's statue smiles and blesses him, to their astonishment.

Jonny spielt auf (Johnny Strikes Up). Opera in 2 acts by Krenek; libretto by the composer.

First perf., Leipzig, Feb. 10, 1927: Cleve, Schulthess, Horand, Spilcker, c. Brecher. U.S. & Met prem., Jan. 19, 1929: Easton, Kirchhoff, Bohnen, Schorr, c. Bodanzky, d. Urban, p. Wymetal. 7 perfs. in 1 season.

In this once successful "jazz opera," the lives of four musicians are intertwined: the composer Max (t), the opera singer Anita (s), the violin virtuoso Daniello (bar), and the jazz-band leader Jonny (bar), who steals Daniello's violin and conquers the world with his playing.

Jörn, Karl [Carl]. Tenor; b. Riga, Latvia, Jan. 5, 1873, of German parents; d. Denver, Colo., Dec. 19, 1947. Studied in Riga and Berlin; debut as Lionel (*Martha*), Freiburg,

Gwyneth Jones as the Marschallin in *Der Rosenkavalier*

1896. Sang in Zurich (1898–99), Hamburg (1899–1902), and Berlin (1902–08). Met debut as Stolzing, Jan. 22, 1909; in 6 seasons, sang 103 perfs. of 18 roles, including Tannhäuser, Jeník, Massenet's Des Grieux, Faust, and Tamino. Sang Tristan on American tour of Gadski's German Opera Co., 1928.

Journet, Marcel. Bass; b. Grasse, France, July 25, 1867; d. Vittel, Sep. 5(?), 1933. Studied with Obin and Seneghetti, Paris Conservatory; debut as Balthasar (*Favorite*), Béziers, 1891. Appeared at Monnaie, Brussels (1894–1900). Covent Garden debut as Duke of Mendoza in d'Erlanger's *Inez Mendo*, 1897; he sang regularly in London until 1907, and returned in 1927–28. Met debut as Ramfis, Dec. 22, 1900; in 8 seasons, he sang 225 perfs. of 38 roles, large and small, including Escamillo, Titurel, Sparafucile, and Colline. A member of the Paris Opéra (1908–32), he performed frequently at Monte Carlo (1912–20), Chicago (1915–18), Buenos Aires (1916–18, 1923, 1927), and La Scala, 1917–28, where he created Simon Mago (*Nerone*). Though specializing in French bass roles, Journet also sang Tonio, Scarpia, Wotan, and Hans Sachs; the year before his death, he recorded his vivid impersonation of Méphistophélès.

Juch, Emma. Soprano; b. Vienna, July 4, 1863, of American parents; d. New York, Mar. 6, 1939. Studied in Detroit; debut as Philine (*Mignon*), Her Majesty's, London, 1881. Toured in U.S. with Mapleson (1881), Thomas's American Opera Co. (1884–87), and National Opera Co. (1887–88); the latter, reorganized as Juch Grand Opera Co., toured North America (1889–91).

Juive, La (The Jewess). Opera in 5 acts by Halévy; libretto by Scribe.
First perf., Paris, Opéra, Feb. 23, 1835: Falcon, Dorus-Gras, Nourrit, Levasseur. U.S. prem., New Orleans, Feb. 13, 1844. Met prem., Jan. 16, 1885 (in Ger.): Materna, Schröder-Hanfstängl, Udvardy, Schueller, Kögel, c. L. Damrosch, d. Schaeffer. Later Met production: Nov. 22, 1919: Ponselle, Scotney, Caruso, Harrold, Rothier, c. Bodanzky, d. Urban, p. Ordynski. (On Christmas Eve, 1920, Caruso sang his last performance at the Met in this opera.) Eléazar has also been sung at the Met by Niemann, Martinelli; Rachel by Lilli Lehmann, Easton; Brogni by Fischer, Rothier, Pinza. 48 perfs. in 15 seasons.
A broad, richly filled-out score representing early Romantic Parisian opera at its finest.
Constance, Switzerland, 15th c. Rachel (s), daughter of the goldsmith Eléazar (t), learns that her lover, known to her as Samuel, is really Prince Léopold (t), married to Eudoxie (s). When Rachel reveals her relationship with him to the court, she, her father, and Léopold are condemned to death by Cardinal Brogni (bs). The Cardinal offers to spare Rachel if Eléazar will embrace Christianity, but the latter refuses. As the girl is put to death, Eléazar reveals that she was Brogni's own long-lost daughter.

Julien, ou La Vie du Poète (Julien, or The Poet's Life). Opera in prologue and 4 acts by Charpentier; libretto by the composer.
First perf., Paris, Opéra-Comique, June 4, 1913: Carré, Rousselière, c. Wolff. U.S. & Met prem., Feb. 26, 1914: Farrar, Caruso, c. Polacco, d. Paquereau, p. Speck. 5 perfs. in 1 season.
In this unsuccessful sequel to *Louise*, the ghost of Louise fails to revive Julien's faith in art.

Julius Caesar in Egypt. See *Giulio Cesare in Egitto*.

Junge Lord, Der (The Young Lord). Opera in 2 acts by Henze; libretto by Ingeborg Bachmann, after a fable from Wilhelm Hauff's *Der Scheik von Alexandria und seine Sklaven*.
First perf., Berlin, Deutsche Oper, Apr. 7, 1965: Mathis, Johnson, Graf, McDaniel, Driscoll, Hesse, Grobe, c. Dohnányi. U.S. prem., San Diego, Feb. 13, 1967 (in Eng.): Lynn, Curatillo, Turner, Toscano, Fredericks, Cole, Remo, c. Herbert.
Ambiguously, either a witty satire on manners or a black view of human nature, set to enormously proficient and lively music.
Hülsdorf-Gotha, 1830. Sir Edgar (mime), a rich English lord who has rented a house on the town square, alienates the ostentatious locals with his standoffish behavior, but his eccentric nephew Lord Barrat (t) makes a hit; he turns out to be a monkey in human clothes.

Jurinac, Sena [Stebrenka Jurinac]. Soprano; b. Travnik, Yugoslavia, Oct. 24, 1921. Studied with Milka Kostrenćić, Zagreb; debut as Mimi, Zagreb, 1942. Debuts in Vienna (Cherubino, 1945), Salzburg (Dorabella, 1947), La Scala (Cherubino, 1948), Glyndebourne (Dorabella, 1949), San Francisco (Butterfly, 1959), and Chicago (Desdemona, 1963). Especially admired for Mozart and Strauss roles, including Octavian and Composer (*Ariadne*).

K

Kabaivanska, Raina. Soprano; b. Burgas, Bulgaria, Dec. 15, 1934. Studied in Sofia and Vercelli, Italy; debut with National Opera, Sofia, 1957. Sang at La Scala (Agnese in *Beatrice di Tenda*, 1961) and Covent Garden (Desdemona, Liù, 1962–64). Met debut as Nedda, Oct. 27, 1962; in 12 seasons, she sang 72 perfs. of 12 roles, including Mimi, Elisabeth de Valois, Alice Ford, Butterfly, Leonora (*Forza*), Desdemona, and Lisa (*Queen of Spades*).

Kabalevsky, Dmitri. Composer; b. St. Petersburg, Dec. 30, 1904; d. Feb. (?), 1987. Studied composition with Miaskovsky at Moscow Conservatory. His first opera, *Colas Breugnon* (1938, rev. 1968), was in a popular style. The historical opera *Under Fire* (1943) was withdrawn, although excerpts were rewritten for *The Taras Family* (1947; rev. 1950, 1967). His last serious opera was *Nikita Vershinin* (1955), followed by the operettas *Spring Sings* (1957) and *Sisters* (1967).

Kahn, Otto. Patron; b. Mannheim, Germany, Feb. 21, 1867; d. New York, Mar. 29, 1934. A prominent banker and financier in Berlin and London, he became a member of the N.Y. banking firm Kuhn, Loeb & Co. (1893–1934) and a major patron of the city's cultural institutions. In 1907, with the Conried regime in shambles, Kahn and W.K. Vanderbilt purchased Conried's Met producing company (Kahn eventually became sole owner) and brought Gatti-Casazza and Toscanini from Milan. In 1910 Kahn bought out Oscar Hammerstein's competitive Manhattan Opera for $1.2 million. Throughout the 1920s, he unsuccessfully urged the theater's owners to build a new opera house, and eventually resigned from the board in 1931.

16 (*Right*). *Il Barbiere di Siviglia* – (1982). Ara Berberian as Basilio, Marilyn Horne as Rosina, Rockwell Blake as Almaviva, and Enzo Dara as Bartolo in Act I of Rossini's opera, set by Robin Wagner, costumes by Patricia Zipprodt

17 (*Below*). *Le Siège de Corinth* – (1975). Design by Nicola Benois for Act II, Scene 2 of Rossini's opera

18 Teatro La Fenice, c. 1835

19 (*Left*). *L'Elisir d'Amore* – Luigi Lablache as Dr. Dulcamara and Giovanni Mario as Nemorino in a production from Donizetti's time

20 (*Above*). *La Sonnambula* – (Teatro Carcano, 1831). Design by Alessandro Sanquirico for the premiere of Bellini's opera

21 Teatro alla Scala, c. 1840

22 *Il Pirata* – (La Scala, 1827). Design by Alessandro Sanquirico for the premiere

25 *Macbeth* – (1982). Sherrill Milnes as Macbeth and Renata Scotto as Lady Macbeth in Act II, Scene 3 of Verdi's opera, designed by John Bury

23 *Opposite (above)*. *La Fille du Régiment* – (1983). Alfredo Kraus as Tonio and Joan Sutherland as Marie in Act I of Donizetti's opera, set by Anna Anni, costumes by Marcel Escoffier
24 *Opposite (below)*. *Don Pasquale* – (1978). Beverly Sills as Norina and Gabriel Bacquier as Pasquale in Act III, Scene 1 of Donizetti's opera, designed by Desmond Heeley

26 *La Traviata* – (1935). Design by Jonel Jorgulesco for Act I of Verdi's opera

27 *La Traviata* – (1966). Anna Moffo as Violetta and Robert Merrill as Germont in Act II, Scene 1, designed by Cecil Beaton

28 *La Forza del Destino* – (1984). Leontyne Price as Leonora in Act II, Scene 2

29 *La Forza del Destino* – Design by Eugene Berman for Act III of Verdi's opera

30 Giuditta Pasta as Donizetti's Anna Bolena

31 Antonio Tamburini as Riccardo in Bellini's *I Puritani*

32 *Rigoletto* – (1977). Plácido Domingo as the Duke of Mantua in Act II of Verdi's opera, designed by Tanya Moiseiwitsch

33 *Lucia di Lammermoor* – (1986). Luciano Pavarotti as Edgardo in Act III, Scene 3 of Donizetti's opera, designed by Attilio Colonnello

Herbert von Karajan

Kallman, Chester. Librettist; b. Brooklyn, N.Y., Jan. 7, 1921; d. Athens, Greece, Jan. 18, 1975. Collaborator with W.H. Auden on librettos of Stravinsky's *Rake's Progress* and Henze's *Elegy for Young Lovers* and *Bassarids.*

Kammersänger, Kammersängerin (Ger., "chamber singer," male and female). Honorific title granted to singers by royal courts and governments in Germany and Austria.

Kanin, Garson. Producer and author; b. Rochester, N.Y., Nov. 24, 1912. Actor and assistant director to George Abbott (1934–35), he directed films, wrote plays, including *Born Yesterday* (1946) and screenplays (sometimes with his wife, actress Ruth Gordon). For the Met, he adapted and directed *Fledermaus* (1950).

Kapellmeister (Ger., "chapel master"). In operatic usage, a conductor, usually ranked below the music director; today, the term has overtones of pedantry.

Kappel, Gertrude. Soprano; b. Halle, Germany, Sep. 1, 1884; d. Munich, Apr. 3, 1971. Studied at Leipzig Conservatory; debut as Fidelio, 1903, in Hanover, where she remained until 1924; also appeared in London (debut, Brünnhilde, 1912), Vienna (from 1921), Salzburg (Donna Anna, 1922) and Munich (1927–31). Met debut as Isolde, Jan. 16, 1928; in 9 seasons, she sang 112 perfs. of 15 roles, including the Marschallin, Ortrud, and the first Met Elektra, 1932. Sang Isolde in San Francisco, 1933.

Karajan, Herbert von. Conductor; b. Salzburg, Apr. 5, 1908. Studied at Salzburg Mozarteum and at Vienna Academy under Schalk. Debut at Ulm (*Figaro*, 1929), where he remained until 1934, then becoming music director in Aachen (1935–37). A 1937 *Tristan* at the Berlin State Opera led to work at the Berlin Städtische Oper, and an active career in Europe. For his Nazi affiliations, barred from conducting in public between 1945 and 1947; he then worked frequently with the London Philharmonia and Vienna Symphony. In 1955, named music director of Berlin Philharmonic for life; principally with this orchestra, he has produced one of the largest and most impressive discographies in existence. Director of Salzburg Festival, 1956–60, again from 1964; director of Vienna State Opera, 1957–64. He frequently acted as stage and lighting director for his productions. In 1967, he founded the Salzburg Easter Festival (with the Berlin Philharmonic). Karajan has become a legend in his lifetime, noted for his

earnest, charismatic podium presence, complete technical mastery, and the lustrous sonorities and impeccable attacks he elicits from his players. His Met career comprises 15 perfs. of two *Ring* operas, *Walküre* (debut, Nov. 21, 1967) and *Rheingold*; his continued participation in this N.Y. reproduction of his Salzburg cycle was aborted by a company strike.

Karl V. Opera in 2 acts by Krenek; libretto by the composer.
First perf., Prague, Deutsches Theater, June 15, 1938.
This dodecaphonic opera was conceived as an explicitly anti-Nazi statement. The dying emperor Charles V (bar) meditates on the crucial events of his life: Luther's challenge, the sack of Rome, confrontations with the Pope, and Charles' denunciation as a heretic.

Kaschmann [Kašman], **Giuseppe.** Baritone; b. Lussinpiccolo [now Mali Lošinj], Istria, July 14, 1847; d. Rome, Feb. 11, 1925. Studied in Rome; debut in Zagreb, 1869. Italian debut as Alphonse (*Favorite*), Turin, 1871. Met debut as Ashton (*Lucia*), Oct. 24, 1883, returning 1895–96; in 2 seasons, he sang 43 perfs. of 12 roles, including Valentin, Don Giovanni, and Kurwenal. At Bayreuth, sang Amfortas and Wolfram, 1892; in his 60s, sang buffo parts (Bartolo, Pasquale) in Italy, and taught Baccaloni.

Katerina Ismailova. See *Lady Macbeth of Mtsensk District, The.*

Katya Kabanova. Opera in 3 acts by Janáček; libretto by the composer, after Vincenc Červinka's translation of Alexander Ostrovsky's play *The Storm.*
First perf., Brno, Nov. 23, 1921: Veselá, Hladiková, Zavřel, Šindler, Pustinská, Jeral, c. Neumann. U.S. professional prem., Bear Mountain, N.Y., Empire State Festival, Aug. 2, 1960 (in Eng.): Shuard, Doree, Petrak, Gari, Frankel, c. Halasz.
An opera of claustrophobic tension, broken by moments of great lyrical beauty; set in Kalinov, a town on the banks of the Volga, in the 1860s. Katya (s) is married to Tikhon (t), but must live also with his mother, Kabanicha (c), who harbors great hatred for her. Katya is guiltily in love with Boris (t), and succumbs to the temptation of meeting with him when her husband is away. At the height of a thunderstorm, Katya confesses to her husband and mother-in-law, then runs away; after a final meeting with Boris, she throws herself into the river.

Kavrakos, Dimitri. Bass; b. Athens, Feb. 26, 1946. Appears regularly with National Theater of Greece and Netherlands Opera. Since his Met debut as the Grand Inquisitor (*Don Carlos*), Mar. 7, 1979, his roles there have included Silva (*Ernani*), Walter (*Luisa Miller*), Ferrando (*Trovatore*), and Capulet.

Keene, Christopher. Conductor; b. Berkeley, Calif., Dec. 21, 1946. Study at U. of Calif., Berkeley; associated with Spoleto Festival from 1968 (general director, 1973; music director, 1976–80). Music director, Artpark, Lewiston, N.Y. (since 1974), Long Island Philharmonic (since 1979), N.Y.C. Opera (1983–86). N.Y.C. Opera debut, *Don Rodrigo*, 1970; Met debut, *Cavalleria* and *Pagliacci*, Sep. 24, 1971. Covent Garden debut, 1973.

Keilberth, Joseph. Conductor; b. Karlsruhe, Germany, Apr. 19, 1908; d. Munich, July 20, 1968. His operatic appointments included Karlsruhe (1935–40), Dresden State Opera (1945–49), and Bavarian State Opera (from 1951; music director, 1959–68). An important exponent of Wagner (Bayreuth, 1952–56), Strauss, Pfitzner, and the symphonies of Bruckner, he made numerous recordings, including Wagner, Strauss, and *Cardillac*.

Kellogg, Clara Louise. Soprano; b. Sumterville [now Sumter], S.C., July 9, 1842; d. New Hartford, Conn., May 13, 1916. Studied in N.Y.; debut as Gilda, Academy of Music, 1861. Appeared in Boston and in London (1867, 1872). Toured with Pauline Lucca in 1872, then formed her own English Opera Co., 1873. The first American singer to achieve broad fame in Europe, she retired in 1887.

Kelly, Michael. Tenor; b. Dublin, Dec. 25, 1762; d. Margate, England, Oct. 9, 1826. Studied in Dublin and Naples; debut as Count (*Buona Figliuola*), Dublin, 1779. Sang throughout Italy, then at Vienna Court Opera (1783–87), where he created Basilio and Curzio (*Nozze*), 1786. From 1787, sang in London and composed theater music. Retired 1811; published entertaining *Reminiscences* (1826).

Kemp [Mikley-Kemp], **Barbara.** Soprano; b. Kochem, Germany, Dec. 12, 1881; d. Berlin, Apr. 17, 1959. Studied in Strassburg; debut there as Priestess (*Aida*), 1903. Sang in Rostock and Breslau, then at Berlin Court Opera (1913–32), also in Bayreuth (Senta, 1914) and Vienna (1922–27). Met debut in title role of husband Max von Schillings' *Mona Lisa*, Mar. 1, 1923; in 2 seasons, she sang 13 perfs. of 5 roles, including Kundry, Elsa and Isolde.

Kempe, Rudolf. Conductor; b. Niederpoyritz, Germany, June 14, 1910; d. Zurich, May 12, 1976. After playing oboe in the Leipzig Gewandhaus Orchestra, conducting debut in Leipzig (*Wildschütz*, 1935), where he remained as repetiteur for several years. After the war,

Alexander Kipnis as Gurnemanz in *Parsifal*

music director at Dresden (1949–52) and Bavarian State Opera (1952–54). Regular Covent Garden appearances after 1953, especially in *Ring*. Music director, Royal Philharmonic (1960–75); shortly before his death, appointed conductor, BBC Symphony. His specialties, Wagner and Strauss, were well represented in his 22 Met perfs. (1954–56): *Tannhäuser* (debut, Jan. 26, 1955), *Meistersinger*, *Tristan*, *Arabella*, and *Rosenkavalier*. His keen attention to texture, balance, melodic continuity, and structural articulation are exemplified in recordings of *Lohengrin*, *Meistersinger*, and *Ariadne*.

Khaikin, Boris. Conductor; b. Minsk, Byelo-Russia, Oct. 16, 1904; d. Moscow, May 10, 1978. Graduated from Moscow Conservatory (1928), conducted in Stanislavsky's opera theater (1928–35). Principal conductor, Kirov Theater (from 1943), then Bolshoi (from 1954), while teaching at Leningrad and Moscow conservatories. His recordings include *Khovanshchina* and several Tchaikovsky operas.

Khovanshchina (The Khovansky Rising). Opera in 5 acts by Mussorgsky; libretto by the composer and V.V. Stassov.
First perf., St. Petersburg, Kononov Theater, Feb. 21, 1886: c. Goldstein. U.S. prem., Philadelphia, Metropolitan Opera House, Apr. 18, 1928. Met prem., Feb. 16, 1950 (ed. Rimsky-Korsakov, in Eng.): Stevens, Sullivan, Kullman, Tibbett, Weede, Hines, c. Cooper, d. Dobujinsky, p. Yannopoulos. Later Met production: Oct. 14, 1985 (ed. Shostakovich): Dernesch, Gulyas, Ochman, Monk, Haugland, Talvela, c. Järvi, d. Lee/Conklin, p. Everding. 17 perfs. in 2 seasons.
This score of gloomy strength, with imposing roles for two bass singing actors, was unfinished at Mussorgsky's death and has been completed and orchestrated by both Rimsky-Korsakov and Shostakovich.
Moscow and environs, 1682–9. In the factional struggles at the time of Peter the Great's accession to the throne, the Old Believers, led by Dosifey (bs), make common cause with the party of Prince Ivan Khovansky (bs) against Peter and his followers, led by Prince Golitsin (t). The lives of these leaders are also intertwined by the past love of Ivan's son Andrey for Marfa (ms), an Old Believer and prophetess. The Tsar prevails: Khovansky is murdered by the duplicitous boyar Shaklovity (bar), and the Old Believers, with the reunited Marfa and Andrey, immolate themselves in their forest hermitage rather than submit to religious reforms.

Kienzl, Wilhelm. Composer; b. Waizenkirchen, Austria, Jan. 17, 1857; d. Vienna, Oct. 3, 1941. A student of Rheinberger in Munich and Liszt in Weimar, his first operatic success was *Heilmar der Narr* (1892), followed by his most famous work, *Der Evangelimann* (1895), a revival of the bourgeois esthetic of Lortzing. *Der Kuhreigen* (1911) was presented at the Met in 1913 by the Philadelphia–Chicago Opera Co. as *Le Ranz des Vaches*.

Kiepura, Jan. Tenor; b. Sosnowiec, Russian Poland, May 16, 1902; d. Harrison, N.Y., Aug. 15, 1966. Studied with Leliva in Warsaw; debut as Faust, Lwów, 1924. Appeared in Vienna (Cavaradossi, 1926), Berlin, Milan (Calaf, 1928), Paris, Budapest; U.S. debut as Cavaradossi, Chicago, 1931. Met debut as Rodolfo, Feb. 10, 1938; in 3 seasons, he sang 18 perfs. of 5 roles, including Don José, Massenet's Des Grieux, the Duke of Mantua, and Cavaradossi. Made several musical films; toured in *Merry Widow* with wife, soprano Marta Eggerth.

Killebrew, Gwendolyn. Mezzo-soprano; b. Philadelphia, Pa., Aug. 26, 1939. Studied at Temple U., Philadelphia, and Juilliard, N.Y.; debut as Waltraute (*Walküre*), Met, Nov. 21, 1967. Other Met roles include Carmen and a Serving Woman (*Elektra*). Has also appeared in San Francisco, Santa Fe (Carmen, 1975), N.Y.C. Opera (debut, Ulrica, 1971), Düsseldorf, and Bayreuth.

King, James. Tenor; b. Dodge City, Kans., May 22, 1925. Studied at U. of Kansas as baritone, then as tenor with Singher, N.Y.; debut as Don José, San Francisco Spring Opera, 1961. Joined Deutsche Oper, Berlin, 1962, also appearing in Salzburg (1962), Vienna (1963), Bayreuth (1965), and London (1966). Met debut as Florestan, Jan. 8, 1966; in 11 seasons, he sang 78 perfs. of 11 roles, including Emperor (*Frau*), Siegmund, Cavaradossi, Stolzing, Don José, and Bacchus.

King Priam. Opera in 3 acts by Tippett; libretto by the composer, after Homer's *Iliad*.
First perf., Coventry, Coventry Theatre, May 29, 1962: Collier, Veasey, Elkins, R. Lewis, Godfrey, Robinson, c. Pritchard.
Tippett's most pessimistic opera retells Homer's story of Priam (bs-bar), his son Paris (t), and their roles in the Trojan War, emphasizing how individual choices affect history.

King Roger. Opera in 3 acts by Szymanowski; libretto by Jarostaw Iwaszkiewcz and the composer.
First perf., Warsaw, June 19, 1926: Mossakowski, Korwin-Szymanowska, Dobosz, Wraza, c. Młynarski.
With a richly textured score, *King Roger* takes place in 12th-c. Sicily, where a Shepherd (t) arrives at the Christian court of King Roger (bar) and Queen Roxana (s), eventually convincing them to abdicate and embrace his Dionysian religion.

King's Henchman, The. Opera in 3 acts by Taylor; libretto by Edna St. Vincent Millay.
First perf., Met, Feb. 17, 1927: Easton, Johnson, Tibbett, c. Serafin, d. Urban, p. Wymetal. 14 perfs. in 3 seasons.
The first of Taylor's Met operas, a skillful, conservative, effective score set in 10th-c. England. Aethelwold (t), sent to woo Princess Aelfrida (s) for King Eadgar of England (bar), falls in love with her, sends back word that she is not beautiful enough, and marries her himself; when his treachery is discovered, he kills himself.

Kipnis, Alexander. Bass; b. Zhitomir, Ukraine, Feb. 13, 1891; d. Westport, Conn., May 14, 1978. Studied conducting, Warsaw Conservatory (grad. 1912), and served as bandmaster in the Russian army. In Berlin, studied voice with Ernst Grenzebach at the Klindworth–Scharwenka Conservatory, and sang operetta. Operatic debut in Hamburg, 1915, sang at Wiesbaden, 1917–22. Leading bass at Berlin Charlottenburg (later Städtische) Oper (1919–29) and State Opera (1930–35), Vienna State Opera (to 1938). U.S. debut as Pogner (*Meistersinger*), with touring German Opera Co., Baltimore, 1923. Appeared in Chicago (1923–32), Buenos Aires (1926–36), Covent Garden (1927, 1929–35), and Bayreuth (1927–33). Sang Sarastro at Glyndebourne (1936) and Salzburg (1937). His belated Met debut was as Gurnemanz, Jan. 5, 1940; in 7 seasons, he sang 74 perfs. of 13 roles, including King Marke, Arkel (*Pelléas*), Hermann (*Tannhäuser*), Hagen, Hunding, Baron Ochs, and Sarastro. He performed his celebrated Boris (in Russian) only twice at that

Dorothy Kirsten as Manon Lescaut

house (1943). After his retirement from the Met and from opera in 1946, he taught singing in N.Y. Father of harpsichordist Igor Kipnis.
With one of the most majestic and smoothly produced bass voices of the century, Kipnis excelled not only in the operatic literature, but also as a lieder singer. His many recordings in both areas demonstrate a remarkable technical control as well as strong interpretive projection.

Kirchner, Leon. Composer; b. Brooklyn, N.Y., Jan. 24, 1919. Studied with Toch, Schoenberg, and Sessions; has taught at Mills College (1954–61) and Harvard (since 1961). Composer of many chamber and orchestral works, his only opera is *Lily* (after Saul Bellow's *Henderson, the Rain King*, 1977), a dramatically awkward but musically rich and vigorous score.

Kirsten, Dorothy. Soprano; b. Montclair, N.J., July 6, 1917. Studied at Juilliard School, N.Y., and (with the encouragement of Grace Moore) with Astolfo Pescia in Rome; debut as Poussette (*Manon*), Chicago, 1940. She also sang with the San Carlo Opera (debut, Micaela, Washington, D.C., 1942), N.Y.C. Opera (debut, Violetta, 1944), and San Francisco Opera (from 1947). Met debut as Mimi, Dec. 1, 1945; in her 27 seasons there, she sang 165 perfs. of 12 roles, most often Butterfly and Tosca, followed by Violetta, Minnie (*Fanciulla*), Mimi, both Manons, Marguerite, Fiora (*Amore dei Tre Re*), and Louise, in which role she had been coached by the composer. Despite an official Met farewell on New Year's Eve, 1975, she later returned occasionally. Kirsten appeared frequently on radio and television, and in several films, including *The Great Caruso* (1950). A handsome woman with a clear and well-schooled lyric voice, she was especially admired for her Puccini portrayals.

Kiss, The. Opera in 3 acts by Smetana; libretto by Eliška Krásnohorská, after the story by "Karolina Světlá" [Joanna Mužáková].

First perf., Prague, Provisional Theater, Nov. 7, 1876. U.S. prem., Chicago, Blackstone Theater, Apr. 17, 1921.

In this wistful folk tale, Vendulka (s), crediting the superstition that a kiss given a widower before his remarriage grieves the deceased wife, refuses to kiss her fiancé, the widower Lukas (t); he is indignant, but they are eventually reconciled.

Kleiber, Carlos. Conductor; b. Berlin, July 3, 1930. Though discouraged from a musical career by his father, conductor Erich, he made his debut at the Gärtnerplatz, Munich, in 1953, moving later to Zurich (1964–66) and Stuttgart (from 1966), where he specialized in Verdi, Wagner, Strauss, and *Wozzeck*. From 1968, regular conductor at Bavarian State Opera. Debuts in Vienna (1973), Bayreuth and Covent Garden (1974), U.S. (*Otello*, San Francisco, 1977). Known for his temperamental personality and lengthy rehearsal periods, Kleiber achieves interpretations of remarkable clarity and fervor, as evidenced in his recordings of *Freischütz* and *Tristan*.

Kleiber, Erich. Conductor; b. Vienna, Aug. 5, 1890; d. Zurich, Jan. 27, 1956. Trained in violin and composition in Vienna, his first important post was Darmstadt (1912–19). A brilliant Berlin debut (*Fidelio*, 1923) led immediately to directorship of the Berlin State Opera, where he conducted the world premiere of *Wozzeck*, and other new works, resigning in 1934 under Nazi pressure. Thereafter peripatetic, he conducted German opera in Buenos Aires (1937–49) and at Covent Garden (1938, 1950–53), and was director of the State Opera in East Berlin (1951–55). Known for his rigorous rehearsals, antipathy to sentimental indulgence or extreme podium exertions; his notable recordings include *Rosenkavalier* and *Figaro*.

Klein, Allen Charles. Designer; b. New York, Aug. 11, 1940. A student of Horace Armistead and Raymond Sovey. First opera designs were sets for *Don Giovanni* (Houston, 1964) and costumes for *Italiana* (San Francisco, 1964). Has worked in Santa Fe, Houston, Seattle, Vienna, and Glyndebourne. His Seattle production of *Hoffmann* was seen at the Met (1973).

Klemperer, Otto. Conductor; b. Breslau, Germany [now Wrocław, Poland], May 14, 1885; d. Zurich, July 6, 1973. A student of Pfitzner in Berlin, where he made an emergency debut leading Max Reinhardt's production of *Orphée aux Enfers*, 1906. Beginning in 1907, he held positions in Prague, Hamburg, Strassburg, Cologne, and Wiesbaden. From 1927 to 1931, music director at Kroll Opera, Berlin, presenting new works (*Oedipus Rex*, *Cardillac*) and controversial productions of repertory operas. Emigrated to U.S. in 1933, leading Los Angeles Philharmonic (1933–39) until serious illness forced a long retirement. Music director of Budapest Opera (1947–50), he eventually centered his activities on London's Philharmonia Orchestra, of which he became principal conductor in 1955, winning international acclaim as an exponent of Austro-German repertory. A 1958 accident prevented his planned Met debut in *Tristan*; at Covent Garden, he conducted and produced *Fidelio* (1961), *Lohengrin* (1962), and *Zauberflöte* (1963). A master of organic structure and rich sonority, Klemperer was not uncontroversial; his penchant for stately tempos (intensified in later years) left

Otto Klemperer

him sometimes open to charges of insufficient dramatic tension. His operatic recordings include *Fidelio*, *Holländer*, and four Mozart works.

Klobučar, Berislav. Conductor; b. Zagreb, Yugoslavia, Aug. 28, 1924. After study in Salzburg under Krauss and Matačić, became assistant at Zagreb Opera (1943–51), then conducted at Vienna Opera from 1953. General director, Graz Opera (1960–71); music director, Stockholm Opera (1972–81); principal conductor, Nice Opera (from 1983). During his only Met season, he conducted *Holländer* (debut, Jan. 13, 1968), *Walküre*, and *Lohengrin*.

Klose, Margarete. Mezzo-soprano; b. Berlin, Aug. 6, 1902; d. Berlin, Dec. 14, 1968. Studied in Berlin; debut at Ulm, 1926, as Manja in *Gräfin Mariza*. Sang in Mannheim (1928–31) and Berlin (State Opera, 1932–49, 1958–61; Städtische Oper, 1949–58). Debuts at Covent Garden (1935), Bayreuth (1936), and Rome (1939). A noted Wagner interpreter, she sang Klytemnästra, Brangäne, Fricka, and Ulrica in San Francisco, 1953.

Kluge, Die (The Wise Woman). Opera in 1 act by Orff; libretto by the composer, after the Brothers Grimm's story *Die Geschichte von dem König und der Klugen Frau*.

First perf., Frankfurt, Feb. 20, 1943: Wackers, Gonszar, c. Winkler. U.S. professional prem., San Francisco, Oct. 3, 1958 (in Eng.): L. Price, Winters, c. Ludwig.

In this primitivist fairy tale, the King (bar) has married a Wise Woman (s), but tires of her wit and sends her away with the gift of anything she may desire from the palace; when she chooses the King himself, he relents.

Knappertsbusch, Hans. Conductor; b. Elberfeld, Germany, Mar. 12, 1888; d. Munich, Oct. 25, 1965. After study in Cologne, he held posts in Leipzig (1918–19), Dessau (1920–22), and Munich (1922), where he remained until dismissed in 1936. Spent 1936–45 at the Vienna State Opera, then returned to Munich; from 1951 until his death, with few interruptions, he conducted *Parsifal* at Bayreuth. A generally conservative interpreter capable of generating dramatic excitement over long spans of time, Knappertsbusch was impatient with rehearsal and uncomfortable in the recording studio; he is best remembered by recordings of his actual performances, including two Bayreuth *Parsifals* (1951, 1962).

Knote, Heinrich. Tenor; b. Munich, Nov. 26, 1870; d. Garmisch, Jan. 12, 1953. Studied in Munich; debut there as Georg in Lortzing's *Waffenschmied*, 1892. Sang chiefly in Munich, remaining there until 1931, but also appeared in London (1901–13). Met debut as Stolzing, Dec. 3, 1904; in 3 seasons, he sang 53 perfs. of 9 roles, including Wagnerian parts and Manrico. Toured U.S. in 1923 and 1924 with German Opera Co., as Rienzi and Walther.

Knot Garden, The. Opera in 3 acts by Tippett; libretto by the composer.
First perf., London, Covent Garden, Dec. 2, 1970: Barstow, Gomez, Minton, Tear, Herincx, Carey, Hemsley, c. Davis. U.S. prem., Evanston, Ill., Northwestern U., Feb. 22, 1974: c. Rubenstein.
A descendant of Mozart's *Così*, in which two modern couples, Faber (bar) and Thea (ms), and Dov (t) and Mel (bar), wander in an emotional labyrinth, assisted by the analyst Mangus (bar).

Knussen, Oliver. Composer; b. Glasgow, Scotland, June 12, 1952. Studied in London with John Lambert and at Tanglewood with Gunther Schuller. A prodigious talent, he conducted the premiere of his Symphony No. 1 (1968) at the age of 15. His operas *Where the Wild Things Are* (1980) and *Higglety Pigglety Pop!* (1984, rev. 1985) recall the sophisticated fantasy of Ravel, in a more aggressively dissonant musical style.

Koanga. Opera in prologue, 3 acts, and epilogue by Delius; libretto by Charles Francis Keary, after George Washington Cable's novel *The Grandissimes*.
First perf., Elberfeld, Mar. 30, 1904 (in Ger.): Kaiser, Whitehill, c. Cassirer. U.S. prem., Washington, D.C., Dec. 18, 1970: Lindsey, Holmes, c. Callaway.
This score, embodying the local color Delius absorbed in Florida, is set on a plantation. The mulatto Palmyra (s) spurns the overseer (t) in favor of Koanga (bar). After she is abducted at her wedding by the overseer, the two men kill each other, and Palmyra takes her own life.

Kodály, Zoltán. Composer; b. Kecskemét, Hungary, Dec. 16, 1882; d. Budapest, Mar. 6, 1967. Studied with Koessler at Budapest Academy of Music. In collaboration with Bartók he collected, organized, and edited national folksongs, whose melodies he later used in his operas and other compositions. From 1907, he was professor at Budapest Academy; his pedagogical methods have been widely influential. *Háry János* (1926), a singspiel based on Hungarian folklore and folk music, has become familiar through an orchestral suite. Other operas: *The Spinning Room* (1932); the singspiel *Czinka Panna* (1948).

Kollo, René. Tenor; b. Berlin, Nov. 20, 1937. After singing light music, studied with Elsa Varena, Berlin, debut in triple bill of *Oedipus Rex*, *Mavra*, and *Renard*, Brunswick, 1965. Appeared in Düsseldorf (1967–71), singing Froh, Eisenstein, and Pinkerton. After Bayreuth

debut as Steersman (*Holländer*) in 1969, he gradually progressed to the heroic Wagner roles (young Siegfried, 1976; Tristan, 1981). Met debut as Lohengrin, Nov. 4, 1976; he returned in 1979 as Bacchus. Debuts at Vienna State Opera (1971), Salzburg (Lohengrin, 1974), Covent Garden (Siegmund, 1976); sang both Siegfrieds in San Francisco *Ring* (1985). Kollo's attractive stage presence has helped make convincing his appearances as a heldentenor.

Konetzni, Anny. Soprano; b. Vienna, Feb. 12, 1902; d. Vienna, Sep. 6, 1968. Studied with Erik Schmedes in Vienna and Jacques Stückgold in Berlin; debut as contralto at Vienna Volksoper, 1925. Appeared as soprano in Berlin (1931–35) and Vienna (1935–54), also London (1935) and Salzburg (Fidelio, 1936). In her only Met season, she sang 8 perfs. as Brünnhilde (debut, *Walküre*, Dec. 26, 1934), Venus, Ortrud, and Isolde. Sister of soprano Hilde (1905–80).

König Hirsch (The Stag King). Opera in 3 acts by Henze; libretto by Heinz von Cramer, after Gozzi's story.
First perf., Berlin, Städtische Oper, Sep. 23, 1956: Pilarczyk, Kónya, Neralic, c. Scherchen. Revised as *Il Re Cervo*, first perf., Kassel, 1963, c. Henze. U.S. prem., Santa Fe, Aug. 4, 1965: Allen, Shirley, Gramm, c. Baustian.
Henze's glittering, melodic fairy tale draws on 19th-c. bel-cantists for inspiration. A king (t) returns to the forest where he was raised and is metamorphosed into a stag; in this form he regains his kingdom from a usurping Governor (bs-bar).

Königin von Saba, Die (The Queen of Sheba). Opera in 4 acts by Goldmark; libretto by Salomon Mosenthal.
First perf., Vienna, Court Opera, Mar. 10, 1875: Materna, Wild, Beck. U.S. & Met prem., Dec. 2, 1885: Lilli Lehmann, Krämer-Wiedl, Stritt, Robinson, c. Seidl, d. Hoyt. 29 perfs. in 4 seasons.
Goldmark's most successful opera, full of exotic grandeur and seductive lyricism, set in Biblical times. Though betrothed to Sulamith (s), Assad (t) has fallen in love with the Queen of Sheba (ms), but King Solomon (bar) insists that the marriage go forward. Assad commits a sacrilege, is imprisoned, and upon release seeks Sulamith in the desert, but dies in her arms.

Königskinder (King's Children). Opera in 3 acts by Humperdinck; libretto by "Ernst Rosmer" [Else Bernstein-Porges].
First perf., N.Y., Met, Dec. 28, 1910: Farrar, Homer, Jadlowker, Goritz, c. Hertz, d. Burghart, Fox/Musaeus, p. Schertel. 30 perfs. in 4 seasons.
First set as speech over music (first perf., Munich, 1897), *Königskinder* initially came close to recapturing the success of *Hänsel und Gretel*. In legendary times, the Goose Girl (s), actually a princess enchanted by a Witch (c), falls in love with a Prince (t). With the help of a Fiddler (bar), she escapes and joins her lover, but the people reject her as Queen, and the two eventually die in the snow in each other's arms, poisoned by the witch.

Kónya, Sándor. Tenor; b. Sarkad, Hungary, Sep. 23, 1923. Studied in Budapest, Detmold, Rome, and Milan; debut as Turiddu, Bielefeld, 1951. Appeared in Darmstadt, Stuttgart, and Hamburg; joined Berlin Städtische Oper, 1955. Debuts as Lohengrin in Bayreuth (1958), Paris (1959), Met (Oct. 28, 1961), and Covent Garden (1963). In 14 Met seasons, he sang 212 perfs. of 21 roles, including Radames, Calaf, Pinkerton, Stolzing, Erik, Edgardo, Cavaradossi, and Max (*Freischütz*).

Kord, Kazimierz. Conductor; b. Pogórze, Poland, Nov. 18, 1930. Studied at Leningrad Academy of Music and in Cracow. Artistic director, Cracow Opera (1962–68); music director, Polish National Orchestra (1968–73); artistic director, Warsaw Philharmonic (from 1977). Since his Met debut (*Queen of Spades*, Dec. 27, 1972), he has returned in 3 subsequent seasons to lead *Così*, *Aida*, and *Boris*.

Korn, Artur. Bass; b. Wuppertal, Germany, Dec. 4, 1937. Studied in Cologne, Munich, and Vienna; debut at Cologne Opera Studio as Sam (*Ballo*), 1963. Engagements in Graz (1965–68) and Vienna (Volksoper and State Opera) from 1968; has sung in Glyndebourne (debut, Ochs, 1980) and Chicago (debut, Waldner in *Arabella*, 1984). Since his Met debut as Osmin (Mar. 12, 1984), he has also sung Mozart's Bartolo and Ochs.

Korngold, Erich. Composer; b. Brünn [now Brno], Moravia, May 29, 1897; d. Hollywood, Nov. 29, 1957. A composing prodigy who studied with Fuchs and Zemlinsky in Vienna, his pantomime *Der Schneemann* was performed at the Vienna Opera in 1910. The one-act operas *Der Ring des Polykrates* and *Violanta* followed in 1916, and then the internationally successful *Die tote Stadt* (1920). Lushly scored, with soaring vocal lines, Korngold's operas also included *Das Wunder der Heliane* (1927) and *Die Kathrin* (1939). Resident in Hollywood after 1938, he composed 19 film scores.

Korrepetitor (Ger.). Rehearser, musical coach for singers.

Köth, Erika. Soprano; b. Darmstadt, Germany, Sep. 15, 1927. Studied in Darmstadt; debut as Philine, Kaiserslautern, 1948. Appeared in Munich (from 1953), Berlin (from 1961), Salzburg (Queen of Night, 1955–63), and Bayreuth (Forest Bird, 1965–68). Specialized in coloratura repertory, notably Konstanze (*Entführung*) and Zerbinetta.

Kozlovsky, Ivan. Tenor; b. Maryanovka, near Kiev, Ukraine, Mar. 24, 1900. Studied at Kiev Conservatory; debut as Faust, Poltava, 1918. Sang in Kharkov (1924) and Sverdlovsk (1925); member of Bolshoi, Moscow, 1926–54. Best known as Lenski, Lohengrin, and Holy Fool (*Boris*); also a renowned recitalist.

Kraft, Jean. Mezzo-soprano; b. Menasha, Wis., Jan. 9, 1940. Studied with Povla Frijsh, N.Y.; N.Y.C. Opera debut as Mother (Weisgall's *Six Characters*), 1960. Met debut as Flora (*Traviata*), Feb. 7, 1970; other Met roles include Emilia, Mrs. Sedley (*Grimes*), Herodias, Ulrica, and Suzuki. Appeared in Boston, Philadelphia, Dallas, Chicago, and Santa Fe.

Krainik, Ardis. Manager; b. Manitowoc, Wis., Mar. 8, 1929. Studied voice and piano at Northwestern U., and appeared as mezzo at the Chicago Lyric Opera, where in 1954 she began an administrative career, becoming assistant manager to Carol Fox in 1960 and, upon the latter's death in 1981, general manager.

Kraus, Alfredo. Tenor; b. Las Palmas, Canary Islands, Nov. 24, 1927. Of Austrian descent, he studied in Barcelona, Valencia, and in Milan with Mercedes Llopart; first stage appearances in zarzuelas, Madrid, 1954. Formal operatic debut as Duke (*Rigoletto*), Cairo, 1956. Debuts at Covent Garden (Edgardo, 1959) and La Scala (Elvino in *Sonnambula*, 1960). U.S. debut as Nemorino, Chicago, 1962; he returned there regularly, later roles including Almaviva, Fernand (*Favorite*), Boito's and Gounod's Fausts, Gonzalve (*Heure Espagnole*), the Duke of Mantua, Nadir (*Pêcheurs*), Arturo (*Puritani*), and Massenet's Des Grieux. Met debut as the Duke, Feb. 16, 1966; his subsequent roles have been Ottavio, Edgardo, Nemorino, Ernesto (*Don Pasquale*), Alfredo, Faust, Werther, Tonio (*Fille*), and Roméo, for a total of more than 80 perfs. Equipped with an exceptional sense of style and fervent dramatic conviction, Kraus has concentrated his career in the roles for which his light, elegant tenor voice, ranging up to high D, is ideally suited; his discretion in repertory has produced a career of exceptional duration.

Krause, Tom. Baritone; b. Helsinki, Finland, July 5, 1934. Studied in Helsinki and Vienna; debut as Escamillo, Berlin Städtische Oper, 1959. Member of Hamburg company from 1962, also appearing in Bayreuth (debut, 1962), Glyndebourne (debut, Count in *Capriccio*, 1963), Salzburg (debut, Giovanni, 1968), and La Scala (1975). Met debut as Count (*Nozze*), Oct. 11, 1967; in 6 seasons, he sang 43 perfs. as Escamillo, Malatesta, and Guglielmo.

Alfredo Kraus as Edgardo in *Lucia di Lammermoor*

Krauss, Clemens. Conductor; b. Vienna, Mar.31, 1893; d. Mexico City, May 16, 1954. Made his conducting debut while chorus master at Brünn [Brno] (*Zar und Zimmermann*, 1912), advancing to director of the companies in Frankfurt (1924), Vienna (1929), Berlin (1935), and Munich (1937). His willingness to succeed men who resigned under Nazi pressure clouded his postwar career, which centered on the Vienna Opera and Philharmonic, with guest engagements in South America and at Covent Garden. A relationship with Bayreuth, begun in 1953, was aborted by his death. Remembered for his association with Strauss, he led the premieres of *Arabella*, *Friedenstag*, *Capriccio* (for which he wrote the libretto), and *Liebe der Danae*; his wife, soprano Viorica Ursuleac, took part in most of these. Equally at home in *Fledermaus* and *Wozzeck*, Krauss had a special flair for the dramatic aspects of musical theater.

Krawitz, Herman. Manager; b. New York, June 5, 1925. After graduation from City College of N.Y. and work in summer theaters, he joined the Met in 1953 as consultant on stage and labor problems, eventually becoming Bing's assistant manager for production and business (1963–72). He worked closely with architect Wallace Harrison on the planning of the new Lincoln Center theater. Since leaving the Met, he has been president of New World Records (since 1975), executive director of American Ballet Theater (1977–83), and an independent producer.

Krenek [Křenek], **Ernst.** Composer; b. Vienna, Aug. 23, 1900. Studied in Vienna, then in Berlin with Schreker; worked in theaters in Kassel and Wiesbaden as conductor and composer (1925–27). His first opera, *Der Sprung über den Schatten* (1924), uses jazz idioms in an atonal context, but in the international success *Jonny spielt auf* (1927) he adopted a more tonal framework. Eventually dissatisfied with neo-Romanticism, he turned to the 12-tone technique in *Karl V* (1933, perf. 1938), banned by the Nazis for its implicit politics. In 1938, he emigrated to the U.S. and taught widely, settling in southern California in 1947. His postwar works use electronic sounds, aleatoric techniques, and other avant-garde devices. Krenek's other operas (most to his own librettos) include *Orpheus und Eurydike* (1926); *Leben des Orest* (1930); *Pallas Athene weint* (1955); *The Bell Tower*, after Melville (1957); the mythical comic fantasy *Der goldene Bock* (1964); and the science-fiction television opera *Der Zauberspiegel* (1966).
BIBLIOGRAPHY: Ernst Krenek, *Horizons Circled* (Berkeley, 1974).

Krips, Josef. Conductor; b. Vienna, Apr. 8, 1902; d. Geneva, Oct. 13, 1974. A student of Weingartner in Vienna, he made his debut in 1921, soon becoming chorus master and repetiteur at the State Opera (1921–24), followed by posts in Dortmund and Karlsruhe and a resident conductorship in Vienna (1933–38). A major figure in Vienna and Salzburg after the war, he led the London Symphony (1950–54), Buffalo Philharmonic (1954–63), Cincinnati May Festival (1954–60), San Francisco Symphony (1963–70), and conducted opera at Chicago (debut, *Così*, 1959), Covent Garden (debut, *Don Giovanni*, 1963) and the Deutsche Oper, Berlin (from 1970). At the Met, he conducted 14 perfs. of Mozart: *Zauberflöte* (debut, Feb. 19, 1967), *Figaro* (1970), and *Don Giovanni* (1971). Chief architect of the postwar Viennese Mozart style, Krips specialized in the music of the Viennese classics.

Krull, Annie. Soprano; b. near Rostock, Germany, Jan. 12, 1876; d. Schwerin, June 14, 1947. Studied in Berlin; debut in Plauen, 1898. Member of Dresden Opera (1901–10), where she created Diemuth (*Feuersnot*), Elektra, and Ulana (*Manru*). Also sang in Mannheim (1910–12) and Weimar (1912–14).

Krusceniski [Kruszelnicka], **Salomea.** Soprano; b. Tysiv, Galicia, Sep. 23, 1872; d. Lvov, Soviet Union, Nov. 16, 1952. Studied in Lvov and later in Milan; debut in Lvov, 1892. Appeared in Warsaw and St. Petersburg (1898–1903), then in Italy; La Scala debut as Salome, 1906. Created revised *Butterfly*, Brescia, 1904, and Pizzetti's *Fedra*, Milan, 1915.

Kubelik, Rafael. Conductor; b. Býchory, near Kolin [now in Czechoslovakia], June 29, 1914. Son of violinist Jan, he studied at Prague Conservatory, and made his debut with the Czech Philharmonic (1934; music director, 1942–48); music director, Brno Opera (1939–41). Leaving Czechoslovakia after the Communist coup, he became music director, Chicago Symphony (1950–53). A 1954 Sadler's Wells production of *Katya Kabanova* led to his appointment as music director of Covent Garden (1955–58), where he led the first London performances of *Troyens* and *Jenůfa*. Music director of the Bavarian Radio Orchestra (1961–80). Appointed the Met's first music director in 1971 by Göran Gentele, he made his debut with the house's first *Troyens* (Oct. 22, 1973) and led *Götterdämmerung* later that season, but resigned in 1974 because of administrative complications and health problems. A forthright, dynamic, engaging interpreter, especially in central-European repertory.

Kubiak, Teresa. Soprano; b. Lodz, Poland, Dec. 26, 1937. Studied with Olga Olgina, Lodz; debut there as Halka, 1965. Sang in Warsaw, Glyndebourne (Lisa in *Queen of Spades*, 1971), London (1972), Vienna (1973). Met debut as Lisa, Jan. 18, 1973; in 15 seasons, she sang 46 perfs. of 14 roles, including Jenůfa, Giorgetta (*Tabarro*), Tosca, and Elisabeth.

Kullman, Charles. Tenor; b. New Haven, Conn., Jan. 13, 1903; d. New Haven, Feb. 8, 1983. Studied at Juilliard and with Salignac in Fontainebleau. Appeared in college performances of early opera, 1929; official debut as Pinkerton, Kroll, Berlin, 1931. Sang widely in Europe, also in San Francisco (1936–54) and Chicago (1940). Met debut as Faust, Dec. 19, 1935; in 25 seasons, sang 283 perfs. of 33 roles, including José, Stolzing, Pinkerton, Ottavio, Avito, and Eisenstein, later taking character parts such as Shuisky and Goro.

Kunz, Erich. Baritone; b. Vienna, May 20, 1909. Studied with Duhan and Lierhammer, Vienna; debut in Troppau, 1933. At Vienna State Opera from 1941; sang frequently at Salzburg, also Glyndebourne (Guglielmo, 1948) and Bayreuth (Beckmesser, 1951). Met debut as Leporello, Nov. 26, 1952; in 2 seasons, sang 22 perfs. of 4 roles, including Beckmesser, Faninal, and Mozart's Figaro. Also sang operetta at Vienna Volksoper.

Kupfer, Harry. Producer; b. Berlin, Aug. 12, 1935. Worked in Halle, Stralsund, and Karl-Marx-Stadt; director, National Theater, Weimar (1967–72), chief producer, Dresden Opera (1972–81), and chief producer, Komische Oper, East Berlin (since 1981). His deconstructionist productions, such as the Bayreuth *Fliegende Holländer*

(1979), reinterpret the Felsenstein tradition. Has also directed for the Komische Oper and Welsh National Opera.

Kurka, Robert. Composer; b. Cicero, Ill., Dec. 22, 1921; d. New York, Dec. 12, 1957. Son of Czech immigrants, he was primarily self-taught as a composer. In addition to orchestral and chamber works in a neo-classical style, he developed an orchestral suite into the successful opera *The Good Soldier Schweik* (perf. 1958), in an idiom influenced by Kurt Weill.

Kurt, Melanie. Soprano; b. Vienna, Jan. 8, 1880; d. New York, Mar. 11, 1941. Studied with Marie Lehmann in Vienna; debut as Elisabeth, Lübeck, 1902. Appeared in Brunswick (1905–08) and Berlin (1908–12). Met debut as Isolde, Feb. 1, 1915; in 3 seasons, sang 63 perfs. of 14 roles, including Kundry, Brünnhilde, Pamina, Fidelio, Amelia, Santuzza, and first Met Iphigénie (*Aulide*).

Kurz, Selma. Soprano; b. Bielitz, Silesia [now Biala, Poland], Oct. 15, 1874; d. Vienna, May 10, 1933. Studied in Vienna and with Marchesi, Paris; debut as Mignon, Hamburg, 1895. Sang in Frankfurt (1896–99), then joined Vienna State Opera (1899–1926), singing Gilda, Oscar, Violetta, Zerbinetta, also Tosca and Sieglinde. Also sang at Covent Garden, Monte Carlo, and Salzburg (Konstanze, 1922).

Kuznetsova, Maria. Soprano; b. Odessa, Russia, 1880; d. Paris, Apr. 26, 1966. Studied in St. Petersburg; debut as Marguerite, Maryinsky, where she created Fevronia (*Kitezh*), 1907. Debuts at Paris Opéra (Elsa, 1908), Covent Garden (Marguerite, 1909), Opéra-Comique (Massenet's Manon, 1910). Influenced by Isadora Duncan, she gave dance recitals, and created Potiphar's Wife in Strauss' ballet *Josephslegende*, 1914. Appeared with Chicago Opera (debut, Juliette, 1916) and with her own touring company in 1920s and '30s.

L

Lablache, Luigi. Bass; b. Naples, Dec. 6, 1794, of French and Irish parents; d. Naples, Jan. 23, 1858. Studied with Valesi at Conservatorio della Pietà dei Turchini, Naples; debut in Fioravanti's *La Molinara*, San Carlino, Naples, 1812, later singing in Messina and Palmero before his successful La Scala debut as Dandini (*Cenerentola*), 1821. He sang there through 1823, and returned in 1826 and 1828. A member of Barbaia's company in Vienna from 1824, he sang at Beethoven's funeral (Mozart's Requiem, 1827). He returned to Naples, appearing in operas by Bellini, Donizetti, and Rossini at the San Carlo. After his 1830 London debut as Geronimo (*Matrimonio Segreto*) at the King's Theatre (later Her Majesty's), he sang there nearly every season till 1852, remaining loyal even when most artists defected to Covent Garden in 1847; in 1836–37, he taught singing to Princess Victoria. In Paris, he sang at the Théâtre Italien from 1830 (debut as Geronimo) until 1851, creating Walton in *Puritani* (1835) and the title roles in Donizetti's *Marino Faliero* (1835) and *Don Pasquale* (1843); the latter was regarded as a classic comic impersonation. After Her Majesty's closed in 1852, he sang in St. Petersburg, but in 1854 came to Covent Garden in many of his favorite roles, such as Leporello, Rossini's Bartolo, Don Pasquale, and Balthasar (*Favorite*). Failing health caused his retirement in 1856.

Described by contemporaries as "stentorian" in power, Lablache's voice extended from low E to the E above middle C. He was a man of huge height and girth, who as Leporello customarily carried Masetto offstage under his arm. Although most famous in comic parts, he had an enormous repertory of both large and small roles, many of them dramatic, such as Enrico VIII (*Anna Bolena*) and Oroveso (*Norma*).

Labò, Flaviano. Tenor; b. Borgonovo, near Piacenza, Italy, Feb. 1, 1927. Studied in Parma and Milan; debut as Cavaradossi, Piacenza, 1954. Met debut as Alvaro (*Forza*), Nov. 29, 1957; in 8 seasons, he sang 59 perfs. of 13 roles, including Alfredo, Manrico, Radames. Also sang in Milan, Vienna, Buenos Aires, and at N.Y.C. Opera (debut, Calaf, 1959).

Lady Macbeth of Mtsensk District, The. Opera in 4 acts by Shostakovich; libretto by the composer and A. Preis, after Leskov's story.

First perf., Leningrad, Maly, Jan. 22, 1934: Sokolova, Modestov, Balashov, Zasetsky, Adrianova, c. Samosud. U.S. prem., Cleveland, Severance Hall, Jan. 31, 1935 (semi-staged): Leskaya, Ivantzoff, c. Rodzinski. Revised as *Katerina Ismailova*, first perf., Moscow, Stanislavsky/Nemirovich-Danchenko Theater, Jan. 8, 1963: Andreyeva, Yefimov, Radzievsky, Bulavin, c. Provatorov. U.S. prem., San Francisco, Oct. 23, 1964: Collier, Vickers, Ludgin, Tozzi, c. Ludwig.

This sardonic slice of realism, set to music of harsh brilliance, prompted the first official denunciation of Shostakovich, and was revised (not drastically) nearly 30 years after its composition.

Russia, 1865. Katerina (s), bored and frustrated wife of the merchant Ismailov (t), has an affair with Sergei (t), an employee of her husband's family. When her father-in-law Boris (bs) interferes she poisons him, and later throttles her husband and hides the corpse in the basement. After she marries Sergei, the murder is discovered and they are exiled to Siberia. On the way, having rejected Katerina, Sergei flirts with another woman; as they cross a bridge, Katerina seizes her and jumps with her into the river.

Lakes, Gary. Tenor; b. Dallas, Tex., Sep. 26, 1950. After study at Southern Methodist U. under Thomas Hayward, worked with William Eddy at Seattle Opera; professional debut there as Froh (*Rheingold*), 1981. After singing Florestan in Mexico City (1983), Samson at Charlotte Opera (1984), and Act I of *Walküre* in Paris (1985), Met debut as High Priest (*Idomeneo*), Feb. 4, 1986, returning the next season as Walther (*Tannhäuser*).

Lakmé. Opera in 3 acts by Delibes; libretto by Edmond Gondinet and Philippe Gille, after Pierre Loti's *Le Mariage de Loti*.

First perf., Paris, Opéra-Comique, Apr. 14, 1883: van Zandt, Frandin, Talazac, Barré, Cobalet, c. Danbé. U.S. prem., Chicago, Grand Opera, Oct. 4, 1883 (in Eng.). Met prem., Feb. 22, 1892: van Zandt, de Vigne, Montariol, Martapoura, E. de Reszke, c. Vianesi. Later Met production: Feb. 19, 1932: Pons, Swarthout, Thill, de Luca, Rothier, c. Hasselmans, d. Novak. Lakmé has also been sung at the Met by Sembrich, Barrientos; Gérald by Rousselière, Martinelli, Jagel, Jobin; Nilakantha by Journet, Rothier, Pinza. 45 perfs. in 15 seasons.

A delicately passionate opera on the favorite theme of east and west.

Giacomo Lauri-Volpi as Radames in *Aida*

India, mid-19th c. The British officer Gérald (t) becomes infatuated with Lakmé (s), daughter of the Brahmin priest Nilakantha (bs). She returns his feelings, but her father vows vengeance on the violator of his temple. To identify the stranger, Nilakantha makes Lakmé sing at the bazaar. When Gérald comes into view, the girl faints, giving away his identity. Nilakantha stabs him, but the wound is not fatal, and Lakmé tends him in a secret hut in the forest. Found by his fellow officer Frédéric (bar), Gérald is persuaded that he must return to his duty as a soldier. Sensing the change in Gérald upon her return, Lakmé eats a poison datura leaf.

Lalo, Édouard. Composer; b. Lille, France, Jan. 27, 1823; d. Paris, Apr. 22, 1892. Studied composition with Crèvecoeur at Paris Conservatory. *Fiesque* (1867), a grand opera after Schiller, was never performed. After winning attention with instrumental works, Lalo wrote the widely acclaimed *Le Roi d'Ys* (1888). *La Jacquerie* was completed after Lalo's death by Coquard and performed in 1895.

Lamperti, Francesco. Teacher; b. Savona, Italy, Mar. 11, 1811; d. Cernobbio, May 1, 1892. Studied in Lodi and at Milan Conservatory, where he later taught (1850–75); students included Albani, Campanini, Sembrich, Stolz, and Waldmann. His son **Giovanni Battista Lamperti** (1839–1910) taught in Milan, Dresden, and Berlin; students included Bispham, Schumann-Heink, and Sembrich.

Lanari, Alessandro. Impresario; b. S. Marcello di Jesi, Italy, 1790; d. Florence, Oct. 3, 1862. He began his managerial career in Lucca, 1821, but was primarily associated with the Pergola in Florence, which he man-

aged off and on, 1823–62; also active at La Scala, Milan, and La Fenice, Venice. He presented the premieres of *Norma*, *Elisir*, and *Macbeth*, also the first Italian perfs. of *Robert le Diable* (1840) and *Freischütz* (1843).

Laparra, Raoul. Composer; b. Bordeaux, France, May 13, 1876; d. Suresnes, near Paris, Apr. 4, 1943. Studied at Paris Conservatory with Massenet and Fauré. Primarily occupied as a music critic, Laparra composed several stage works based on Spanish and Basque themes, including *La Habanera* (1908), *La Jota* (1911), and *Le Joueur de Viole* (1926).

Larsén-Todsen, Nanny. Soprano; b. Hagby, Sweden, Aug. 2, 1884; d. Stockholm, May 26, 1982. Studied in Stockholm, Berlin, and Milan; debut as Agathe (*Freischütz*), Stockholm, 1906. Sang Wagner parts at La Scala (1923–24), Covent Garden (1927, 1930), and Bayreuth (1927–31). Met debut as *Götterdämmerung* Brünnhilde, Jan. 31, 1925; in 3 seasons there, she sang 49 perfs. of 10 roles, including Isolde, Kundry, Fricka, Fidelio, Rachel (*Juive*), and Gioconda.

Lassalle, Jean. Baritone; b. Lyons, France, Dec. 14, 1847; d. Paris, Sep. 7, 1909. Studied with Novelli and at Paris Conservatory; debut as St. Bris (*Huguenots*), Liège, 1869. Sang in Lille, Toulouse, and Brussels before Paris Opéra debut as William Tell, 1872. Remained on roster for 20 years, creating roles in *Roi de Lahore*, *Sigurd*, and Saint-Saëns' *Henry VIII*. Sang regularly at Covent Garden, 1879–81 and 1888–93. Met debut as Nélusko (*Africaine*), Jan. 15, 1892; in 3 seasons, he sang 79 perfs. of 15 roles, including Escamillo, Don Giovanni, Valentin, Hamlet, Telramund, Sachs, and Wolfram. Lassalle, who retired in 1901 to teach at the Paris Conservatory, was the greatest French baritone of his time, a singer of elegance comparable to his friends the de Reszke brothers.

Last Savage, The. See *Ultimo Selvaggio, L'*.

Lattuada, Felice. Composer; b. Caselle di Morimondo, Milan, Feb. 5, 1882; d. Milan, Nov. 2, 1962. Studied with Ferroni at Milan Conservatory. His operas, traditional in form and verismo in style, include *La Tempesta* (1922), after Shakespeare; *Le Preziose Ridicole* (1929); and *La Caverna di Salamanca* (1938).

Lauri-Volpi, Giacomo. Tenor; b. Lanuvio, near Rome, Dec. 11, 1892; d. Valencia, Spain, Mar. 17, 1979. Studied at Santa Cecilia, Rome, with Antonio Cotogni and later Enrico Rosati; debut as Arturo (*Puritani*), Viterbo, 1919, using the name Giacomo Rubini. Under his own name, he sang Massenet's Des Grieux opposite Storchio, Rome, 1920, then appeared in Florence and made his La Scala debut in 1922 as the Duke of Mantua, under Toscanini. This was also the role of his Met debut, Jan. 26, 1923; he sang there every season until 1933, giving 232 perfs. in 26 operas, including the first U.S. *Turandot* (1926) and the first Met *Luisa Miller* (1929). After the Duke and Calaf, his most frequent Met roles were Alfredo, Radames, Canio, Rodolfo (*Bohème*), Faust, Cavaradossi, and Pollione. During this period he also made guest appearances at Covent Garden (1925), the Paris Opéra, and the Teatro Colón; he sang Boito's Nerone at the opening of the Teatro dell'Opera, Rome (1928) and Arnold in the centenary production of Rossini's *Guillaume Tell* at La Scala (1929). In 1934 he left the financially-troubled Met; he continued to sing in public until 1959, mostly in Spain and Italy. In his 80th year, he amazed a gala audience at the Liceo, Barcelona, with his rendition of "Nessun dorma" from *Turandot*. Lauri-Volpi's ringing top notes and vigorous declamation placed him in the forefront of lyric-dramatic tenors. Between 1939 and 1957 he published five books (in Italian) of memoirs and vocal history.

Lawrence, Marjorie. Soprano; b. Dean's Marsh, near Melbourne, Australia, Feb. 17, 1909; d. Little Rock, Ark., Jan. 13, 1979. Studied with Ivor Boustead, Melbourne, and Cécile Gilly, Paris; debut as Elisabeth, Monte Carlo, 1932. At Paris Opéra (1933–36), sang Ortrud, Wagner's Brünnhilde and Reyer's Brunnhilde, Massenet's Salomé, Aida, Valentine (*Huguenots*), and created Keltis in Canteloube's *Vercingétorix*, 1933. Met debut as *Walküre* Brünnhilde, Dec. 21, 1935; in 8 seasons, she sang 59 perfs. of 11 roles, including Ortrud, Sieglinde, Strauss' Salome, the other Brünnhildes, and Alceste. Other roles included Kundry (Buenos Aires, 1936) and Carmen (Chicago, 1940). In Mexico City in 1941, she was stricken by poliomyelitis; paralyzed from the waist down, she resumed her career, chiefly as concert artist, later singing Venus (reclining on a couch) and Isolde (Met, 1943–44) and Amneris (Paris, 1946). A forceful and energetic singer (she rode Grane into the flames at the end of *Götterdämmerung*), Lawrence was first overshadowed by Kirsten Flagstad, later prevented from fulfilling the promise of her powerful voice.

Lázaro, Hipólito. Tenor; b. Barcelona, Aug. 13, 1887; d. Madrid, May 14, 1974. After singing operetta, opera debut as Fernand (*Favorite*), Novedades, Barcelona, 1910. Created leads in *Parisina* (1913), *Piccolo Marat* (1921), and *Cena delle Beffe* (1924). Met debut as Duke (*Rigoletto*), Jan. 31, 1918; in 3 seasons, sang 34 perfs. of 8 roles, including Arturo (*Puritani*), Turiddu, Daniélo (*Reine Fiammette*),

Marjorie Lawrence as Brünnhilde in *Siegfried*

and Pinkerton. Also appeared in Vienna, Buenos Aires, Budapest, and in Havana as late as 1950.

Lazzari, Carolina. Mezzo-soprano; b. Milford, Mass., Dec. 17, 1891; d. Stony Creek, Conn., Oct. 17, 1946. Studied in Milan and in the U.S. Chicago Opera debut as Giglietta (*Isabeau*), 1917, also singing Pierotto in *Linda di Chamounix*, La Cieca, Dalila. Her only Met perf. was as Amneris, Dec. 25, 1920.

Lazzari, Virgilio. Bass; b. Assisi, Italy, Apr. 20, 1887; d. Castel Gandolfo, Oct. 4, 1953. Began career in operetta, then studied with Cotogni, Rome; operatic debut as Alvise, Colón, Buenos Aires, 1914. Appeared in Boston (1917) and Chicago (1918–32). Met debut as Don Pedro (*Africaine*), Dec. 28, 1933; in 14 seasons, sang 147 perfs. of 20 roles, including Archibaldo (*Amore dei Tre Re*), Ramfis, Leporello, Alvise, Rossini's Basilio and Bartolo. Sang Leporello at Salzburg (1934–39) and Covent Garden (1939).

Lear [née Shulman], **Evelyn.** Soprano; b. Brooklyn, N.Y., Jan. 8, 1926. Studied piano and horn before vocal training with John Yard, Washington, D.C., and Sergius Kagen, Juilliard, N.Y., later with Maria Ivogün, Berlin; debut as Composer (*Ariadne*), Berlin, Städtische Oper, 1959. She made a specialty of modern roles, notably Lulu (concert perf., Vienna, 1960, staged there, 1962); created roles in operas by Klebe and Egk. At Salzburg, sang Cherubino (1962–64) and Fiordiligi (1965). Met debut as Lavinia (*Mourning Becomes Electra*), Mar. 17, 1967; in 13 seasons, she sang 67 perfs. of 10 roles, including Cherubino, the Countess, Donna Elvira, Marie (*Wozzeck*), Marschallin, Geschwitz (*Lulu*), Octavian, and Alice Ford, plus Purcell's Dido at the Mini-Met (1972). Married to baritone Thomas Stewart. Lear's vivid theatrical personality and sound musical training have combined to produce many distinctive operatic characterizations.

Lecocq, Charles. Composer; b. Paris, June 3, 1832; d. Paris, Oct. 24, 1918. Studied at Paris Conservatory with Halévy; his operetta *Le Docteur Miracle* shared a prize with Bizet's setting. His operettas were less racy, more lyrical than Offenbach's; *La Fille de Mme. Angot* (1872) and *Giroflé-Girofla* (1874) for Brussels, and *La Petite Mariée* (1875) and *Le Petit Duc* (1878) for Paris, were enormously successful in their day.

Lee, Ming Cho. Designer; b. Shanghai, Oct. 3, 1930. First professional productions for Phoenix Theater, N.Y. (1958). In addition to plays, has designed opera for N.Y.C. Opera, San Francisco, and Hamburg. His Met productions are *Boris* (1974), *Lohengrin* (1976), *Puritani* (1976), *Favorite* (1978; originally for San Francisco), and *Khovanshchina* (1985).

legato (Ital., "bound"). In vocal or instrumental technique, the smooth, uninterrupted connection of successive notes.

Legend, The. Opera in 1 act by Breil; libretto by Jacques Byrne.
First perf., N.Y., Met, Mar. 12, 1919: Ponselle, Howard, Althouse, d'Angelo, c. Moranzoni, d. Bel Geddes, p. Ordynski. 3 perfs. in 1 season.
One of the least successful of Gatti-Casazza's novelties, set in a mythical Balkan country called Muscovadia. Carmelita (s), daughter of Count Stackareff (bs), an

Evelyn Lear as the Countess Geschwitz in *Lulu*

making her last appearance at a major theater there in 1910. Her Met debut role was Carmen (Nov. 25, 1885); in 7 seasons with the company (1885–90, 1891–92, and 1898–99), she sang 203 perfs. of 25 roles. New York's first Isolde and *Siegfried* and *Götterdämmerung* Brünnhildes, she took part in the city's first complete *Ring* cycle (1889); other Met roles included Venus, Sulamith and the Queen (*Königin von Saba*), Berthe, Marguerite, Irene (*Rienzi*), Viviane (*Merlin*), Fidelio, Rachel (*Juive*), Euryanthe, Valentine (*Huguenots*), Donna Anna, Amelia (*Ballo*), Aida, Norma, Philine, Leonora (*Trovatore*), Sélika (*Africaine*), and Fricka; she also sang Elisabeth on tour. Although she broke her Berlin contract to remain in N.Y., the Kaiser arranged for her reengagement in 1891, and she returned to Bayreuth as Brünnhilde in 1896. In America, she also sang with Damrosch's touring company in 1897. She arranged Mozart performances in Salzburg (1901–13), and continued to sing concerts until 1920.

In 45 years on stage, Lehmann is reputed to have sung 170 roles. Without sacrificing her virtuoso technique (still remarkable in recordings made when she was nearly 60), she transformed herself from a coloratura into the outstanding heroic soprano of her day. A formidable, determined artist, she was one of Wagner's most ardent and persuasive disciples, as well as a notable teacher (among her students: Farrar, Fremstad, Kurt, Lubin, Telva, and Weed).

BIBLIOGRAPHY: Lilli Lehmann, *My Path Through Life* (N.Y., and London, 1914, repr. 1977).

Lilli Lehmann as Brünnhilde in *Die Walküre*

impoverished nobleman who has become a cruel bandit, kills her fiancé Stephen (t) to save her father, and loses her life as well.

Legend of the Invisible City of Kitezh and the Maiden Fevronia, The. Opera in 4 acts by Rimsky-Korsakov; libretto by V.I. Belsky, after a religious legend.

First perf., St Petersburg, Maryinsky, Feb. 20, 1907: Kuznetsova, Labinsky, Ershov, c. Blumenfeld. U.S. prem., Ann Arbor, U. of Mich., May 21, 1932 (concert perf., in Eng.). U.S. stage prem., Philadelphia, Academy of Music, Feb. 4, 1936.

Rimsky-Korsakov's next-to-last opera, based on ancient Russian legends. Miraculous invisibility spares Kitezh from the Tartars, but separates Prince Vsevolod (t) from his love Fevronia (s); they die, but are united in eternity.

Lehmann, Lilli. Soprano; b. Würzburg, Germany, Nov. 24, 1848; d. Berlin, May 17, 1929. Studied with her mother, the singer Marie Loewe, in Prague, where she made her debut as First Boy (*Zauberflöte*) in 1865, followed quickly by an emergency substitution as Pamina. Her debut role at Danzig (1868), Leipzig (1869), and the Berlin Court Opera (1869) was Marguerite de Valois (*Huguenots*); engaged in Berlin as principal soprano, she sang there until 1885, her roles including Lucia, Berthe (*Prophète*), Servilia (*Clemenza*), and Lucrezia Borgia. In the first Bayreuth *Ring* (1876), she sang Woglinde, Helmwige, and the Forest Bird. After 1884, she moved into dramatic roles, including Norma and Fidelio. In London, she bowed as Violetta at Her Majesty's (1880), and sang her first Isolde at Covent Garden (1884). After her debut as Marguerite de Valois (1882), she returned frequently to Vienna, later singing under Mahler and

Lehmann, Lotte. Soprano; b. Perleberg, Germany, Feb. 27, 1888; d. Santa Barbara, Calif., Aug. 26, 1976. Her teachers in Berlin included Mathilde Mallinger; debut as Third Boy (*Zauberflöte*), Hamburg, 1910. She progressed to larger parts, including Sophie (*Rosenkavalier*), role of her London debut (Drury Lane, 1914). In 1916, as Agathe (*Freischütz*), she began a notable career at the Vienna Court (later State) Opera, in a repertory including Suor Angelica, Massenet's Manon and Charlotte, Turandot, Tatiana, and Tosca, as well as German lyric and spinto roles. Strauss chose her to create the Composer (*Ariadne*, 1916), Dyer's Wife (*Frau*, 1919), and Christine (*Intermezzo*, 1924). Between the wars, she appeared regularly at Covent Garden; for her 1924 debut there, she sang her first Marschallin, and later roles included Ariadne, Donna Elvira, the Countess, Desdemona, and Rosalinde (*Fledermaus*). She also appeared in Buenos Aires (1922), Paris (1928–34), Chicago (frequently between 1930 and 1937), and San Francisco (1934–46). At Salzburg (1926–37), her roles included Ariadne, Fidelio (under Schalk, Krauss, Strauss, and Toscanini), and Eva (under Toscanini). Sieglinde was her Met debut role (Jan. 11, 1934); in 12 seasons between then and a Marschallin on Feb. 23, 1945, she sang 54 perfs. of 6 roles, also including Elisabeth, Eva, Elsa, and Tosca. After her last stage appearance (the Marschallin in San Francisco, Oct. 13, 1946), she continued her distinguished career as a lieder singer until a farewell N.Y. recital in 1951. Thereafter she taught in Santa Barbara, and gave master classes in London; in 1962, she shared in directing *Rosenkavalier* at the Met.

A generous and spontaneous singing actress with a creamy, vibrant voice, Lehmann excelled in portrayals of feminine warmth and humanity; despite some technical flaws (notably in breath control), her phrasing, musicianship, and verbal coloring, preserved on recordings, continue to inspire the admiration of instrumentalists as well as singers.

BIBLIOGRAPHY: Lotte Lehmann, *My Many Lives* (N.Y., 1948).

Lehnhoff, Nikolaus. Producer and designer; b. Hanover, Germany, May 20, 1939. Trained as assistant stage director, Deutsche Oper, West Berlin, also Bayreuth and Met (1963–71). First operatic staging, *Frau ohne Schatten*, Paris Opéra, 1971. Has directed for major companies in Europe, including Frankfurt, Munich, Zurich. Produced *Ring* cycle, San Francisco (1985).

Leider, Frida. Soprano; b. Berlin, Apr. 18, 1888; d. Berlin, June 4, 1975. After study in Berlin and later in Milan, she made her debut as Venus (*Tannhäuser*) in Halle, 1915. The same year, she sang her first Brünnhilde in Nuremberg, moving thereafter to Rostock (1916–18), Königsberg (1918–20), and Hamburg (1920–23), before establishing herself as principal dramatic soprano at the Berlin State Opera (1923–39), in a repertory spanning Mozart, Verdi, Wagner, and Strauss. She appeared regularly at Covent Garden (1924–38), singing the heroic Wagnerian roles, the Marschallin, Donna Anna, Leonora (*Trovatore*), and Armide, and at Bayreuth (1928–38) as Brünnhilde, Kundry, and Isolde; other engagements included La Scala (Brünnhilde in Italian-language *Ring* cycles, 1927–28), the Paris Opéra (1930–32), and the Colón, Buenos Aires (1931). With the Chicago Opera (1928–32), her roles included the *Walküre* Brünnhilde, Donna Anna, Rachel (*Juive*), Amelia (*Ballo*), Fidelio, and Schillings' Mona Lisa. In her 2 Met seasons, she sang 20 perfs. of 5 roles: Isolde (debut, Jan. 16, 1933), the three Brünnhildes, and Kundry; on tour, she also sang Venus. After her retirement from opera, she gave song recitals, produced opera in Berlin (debut, *Hänsel*, 1945), directed a studio for young singers, and taught at the Berlin Hochschule.

The dominant Brünnhilde and Isolde prior to the advent of Flagstad, Leider offered a more vibrant and spontaneous dramatic presence, a more vivid and compelling verbal utterance; if lacking the younger singer's seamless tonal clarity, her voice was rich and brilliant in sound. Her recordings of Wagnerian excerpts, often with Melchior and Schorr, testify convincingly to her powers.

Leinsdorf [Landauer], **Erich.** Conductor; b. Vienna, Feb. 4, 1912. After study in Vienna, he was a repetiteur for Walter and Toscanini in Salzburg (1934–37). At Lotte Lehmann's recommendation, he came to the Met in 1937 to assist Bodanzky, replacing him in *Walküre* for his debut (Jan. 21, 1938). At Bodanzky's death the following autumn, he took over the German repertory until 1943. While holding a series of orchestral appointments (Cleveland, 1943–44; Rochester, 1947–55; Boston, 1962–69; Berlin Radio Symphony, 1977–80), he returned frequently to the Met, and, after a brief term as music director of the N.Y.C. Opera (1956–57), served as musical consultant to Bing (1957–62). In recent years, he has been an active guest conductor. At the Met he has led more than 375 perfs. of 26 operas, centered on Mozart, Wagner, and Strauss, but also including *Orfeo*, *Pelléas*, and *Macbeth*. A professional, versatile, earnest intepreter, his performances achieve high technical finish and handsome proportions.

Lotte Lehmann as the Marschallin in *Der Rosenkavalier*

Erich Leinsdorf

leitmotif (from Ger., *Leitmotiv*, "leading motive"). A musical motive that relates to a character or idea or episode in an opera, and that recurs, often transformed, at dramatically appropriate points. The term is used principally in connection with Wagner's practice, but similar if less complex usages are found in earlier works; see *reminiscence motive*.

Leitner, Ferdinand. Conductor; b. Berlin, Mar. 4, 1921. Student in Berlin of Hindemith, Szell, and Schreker; assistant to Busch at Glyndebourne (1935); conductor at Hamburg (1945) and Munich (1946). Best known as conductor (1947–49) and music director (1950–69) at Stuttgart Opera, where he worked with Wieland Wagner on 13 productions. Principal conductor at Zurich Opera (1969–84) and, during the same period, of Hague Residentie Orchestra. Active with Chicago Opera since 1969 (debut, *Don Giovanni*).

Lemeshev, Sergie. Tenor; b. Knyazevo, Russia, July 10, 1902; d. Moscow, June 26, 1977. Studied at Moscow Conservatory and with Stanislavsky; debut in Sverdlovsk, 1926. Appeared in Harbin, Manchuria (1927–29) and Tiflis (1929–31); joined Bolshoi, Moscow, 1931. Best known for Lenski, Vladimir (*Prince Igor*), Faust, Roméo, and Duke of Mantua; also a successful concert artist.

Lemnitz, Tiana. Soprano; b. Metz, Alsace-Lorraine, Oct. 26, 1897. Studied in Metz and Frankfurt; debut as Lortzing's Undine, Heilbronn, 1920. Appeared in Aachen (1922–28), Hanover (1928–33), and Dresden (1933–34); member of Berlin State Opera, 1934–55. Repertory included Aida, Desdemona, Octavian, and Pamina. Also sang at Covent Garden (1936, 1938) and Colón, Buenos Aires (1936, 1950).

Leningrad. City in the U.S.S.R., formerly known as St. Petersburg (1703–1914) and Petrograd (1914–24). A visiting Italian company presented Francesco Araia's *La Forza dell'Amore e dell'Odio* in 1736, and others followed; Paisiello and Cimarosa later composed for the court. The Bolshoi Theater was opened in 1783 and rebuilt in 1836, reopening with Glinka's *Life for the Tsar*, a work so successful that it opened every season for years. Oct. 2, 1860 saw the opening of the important Maryinsky Theater, built by Alberto Cavos (son of Caterino Cavos, opera director, 1798–1840). The Maryinsky housed the premieres of Verdi's *Forza del Destino* (1862), Rimsky-Korsakov's *Maid of Pskov* (1873), Mussorgsky's *Boris Godunov* (1874), and Tchaikovsky's *Queen of Spades* (1890). During this time visiting companies performed at the Mikhailovsky Theater (opened 1833, rebuilt 1859).

After the 1917 revolution, the Maryinsky was called the State Academic Theater of Opera and Ballet, then in 1935 renamed the Kirov (after the leader of the Leningrad Communist Party). Its auditorium (capacity 1,621) houses both opera and ballet, with a strongly nationalistic emphasis in the repertory; M.E. Krostin is the current director, and Yuri Temirkanov the chief conductor. The Maly Theater (formerly the Mikhailovsky, capacity 1,212) has housed the premieres of Shostakovich's *Lady Macbeth of Mtsensk District* (1934) and Prokofiev's *War and Peace* (1946); its director is S.N. Potapin. The Opera Studio of the Conservatory (opened 1923, capacity 1,1718) is known for its experimental work.

Lenya, Lotte [Karoline Wilhelmine Blamauer]. Singer, actress; b. Vienna, Oct. 18, 1898; d. New York, Nov. 27, 1981. Began career as dancer in Zurich (1914–20) and Berlin (1920–22), then turned to spoken theater. After marriage to composer Kurt Weill (1926), sang in his *Mahagonny-Songspiel*, Baden-Baden, 1927. Subsequently created Jenny in his *Dreigroschenoper* (Berlin, 1928) and later works, and after his death made recordings influential in the revival of his works.

Leoncavallo, Ruggero. Composer; b. Naples, Apr. 25, 1857; d. Montecatini, Aug. 9, 1919. Studied with Ruta and Rossi at Naples Conservatory; exposed to Wagner's music, he composed the opera *Chatterton* (1876, rev. and perf. 1896). The singer Victor Maurel rescued him from a career as an itinerant pianist, bringing him to the attention of Ricordi, who took options on his operas; he worked on the libretto of Puccini's *Manon Lescaut* and composed *I Medici*, first part of a Renaissance trilogy. When Ricordi turned this down, the frustrated Leoncavallo wrote *Pagliacci* in emulation of the recently triumphant *Cavalleria*; submitted to Ricoridi's rival Sonzogno, it immediately made Leoncavallo famous (1892). Staged in 1893, the pretentious *I Medici* was poorly received. *La Bohème* (1897) was overshadowed by Puccini's treatment of the same subject, produced the year before. The sentimental comedy *Zazà* (1900), influenced by Massenet, enjoyed a small vogue. Despite his sense of raw theater, Leoncavallo lacked the technical resources to sustain his position in a period of rapid stylistic transition. Other works included the historical *Der Roland von Berlin* (1904), commissioned by the Kaiser; *Maia* (1910); *Edipo Re* (1920), premiered in Chicago; and several operettas.

Léoni, Franco. Composer; b. Milan, Oct. 24, 1864; d. London, Feb. 8, 1949. Studied at Milan Conservatory with Ponchielli. From 1892 to 1917, resident in London, where the one-act opera *L'Oracolo* (1905) proved his greatest success, becoming a vehicle for the baritone Antonio Scotti. Other operas, also in a diluted verismo style, include *Francesca da Rimini* (1914); *Le Baruffe Chiozzotte* (1920); and *La Terra del Sogno* (1920).

Leonora. Opera in 3 acts by Fry; libretto by J.R. Fry (the composer's brother), after Bulwer-Lytton's *The Lady of Lyons*.
  First perf., Philadelphia, Chestnut St., June 4, 1845.
  One of the few 19th-c. American operas, modeled closely on conservative Italian works; the action of Bulwer-Lytton's novel is transferred to Spain.

Leppard, Raymond. Conductor; b. London, Aug. 11, 1927. After study at Cambridge, conducting debut in London (1952), soon establishing a reputation in 17th- and 18th-c. repertory. Covent Garden debut, Handel's *Samson* (1959); Glyndebourne debut, *Incoronazione di Poppea* (1964), the first of his successful, textually controversial editions of Monteverdi and Cavalli operas; he has returned there frequently. Led BBC Northern Orchestra (1973–80). U.S. debut, Cavalli's *L'Egisto*, Santa Fe, 1974; Met debut, *Billy Budd*, Sep. 19, 1978. Principal guest conductor, St. Louis Symphony (from 1984); music director, Indianapolis Symphony (from 1987).

Le Roux, Xavier. Composer; b. Velletri, Italy, Oct. 11, 1863, of French parents; d. Paris, Feb. 2, 1919. Studied with Dubois and Massenet at Paris Conservatory. First opera staged, *Cléopâtre* (1890). His numerous other operas, mostly emulating the verismo style, included *Astarte* (1901); *La Reine Fiammette* (1903); *Le Chemineau* (1907); and *Le Carillonneur* (1913).

Levi, Hermann. Conductor; b. Giessen, Germany, Nov. 7, 1839; d. Munich, May 13, 1900. Son of a rabbi, he studied in Mannheim and Leipzig (1855–58), then assumed posts in Saarbrücken, Mannheim, Rotterdam, Karlsruhe (1864–72), and finally Munich (court conductor, 1872–90). An intimate of Clara Schumann and Brahms, he became a notable interpreter of Wagner's works, much admired by the composer (who sought to convert Levi to Christianity); conducted the premiere of *Parsifal* and most of its Bayreuth repetitions until 1894. Also a successful interpreter of Mozart.

Levine, James. Conductor; b. Cincinnati, Ohio, June 23, 1943. After a 1953 piano debut with the Cincinnati Symphony, he studied at Juilliard with Rosina Lhevinne (piano) and Morel (conducting), later with Serkin, Wallenstein, Rudolf, and Cleva. Assistant to Szell in Cleveland (1964–70). Director of Ravinia Festival (since 1973), Cincinnati May Festival (1974–78). Debuts at San Francisco Opera (*Tosca*, 1970), Welsh National Opera (*Aida*, 1970), and Hamburg Opera (*Otello*, 1975). Met debut in *Tosca* (June 5, 1971); named principal conductor (1973), music director (1976), and artistic director (1986). While maintaining his activities as guest conductor, accompanist for singers, and chamber musician, Levine has conducted more than 1,050 Met perfs. in an ever-growing repertory, including Mozart, Verdi, Wagner, Puccini, and Strauss operas, but also *Norma*, *Troyens*, *Carmen*, *Francesca da Rimini*, *Pelléas*, a Stravinsky triple bill, *Mahagonny*, *Porgy*, and *Lulu*. He is credited with raising the company's orchestra to the highest standards, as well as encouraging exploration of unusual repertory. His other principal operatic activities have been at Salzburg (debut, *Clemenza*, 1976) and Bayreuth (debut, *Parsifal*, 1982). An ebullient and articulate figure, Levine is admired for his carefully prepared, nuanced, and proportioned interpretations.

Levy, Marvin David. Composer; b. Passaic, N.J., Aug. 2, 1932. Studied with Philip James and Otto Luening. A moderately dissonant musical style is combined with a strong sense of theater in his operas, which include *The Tower* (1957), *Escorial* (1958), *Mourning Becomes Electra* (1967), and *The Balcony* (1978).

Lewis, Brenda. Soprano; b. Sunbury, Pa. After a debut as Esmeralda (*Bartered Bride*), Philadelphia Opera Co., she studied with Marian Freschl. Sang with New Opera Co., then with N.Y.C. Opera (debut, Santuzza, 1945) until 1967. Met debut as Musetta, Feb. 26, 1952; in 8 seasons, she sang 27 perfs. of 9 roles, including Marina, Vanessa, and Rosalinde (*Fledermaus*). Besides singing opera in San Francisco (debut, Salome, 1950), Chicago (Marie in *Wozzeck*, 1965), and Rio de Janeiro, she appeared on Broadway in *Regina* and *Rape of Lucretia*.

Lewis, Henry. Conductor; b. Los Angeles, Oct. 16, 1932. Studied at U. of So. Calif. Founder, Los Angeles Chamber Orchestra (1958); music director, Los Angeles Opera (1965–68), New Jersey Symphony (1968–76). Met debut in *Bohème* (Oct. 16, 1972); in 4 subsequent seasons, his repertory has included *Carmen*, *Roméo*, *Prophète*, and *Ballo*.

Lewis, Richard. Tenor; b. Manchester, England, May 10, 1914. Studied with Norman Allin; debut with Carl Rosa Co., 1939. Resumed career after World War II at Glyndebourne (debut, Male Chorus, *Rape of Lucretia*, 1947; he sang there until 1979) and Covent Garden (debut, Peter Grimes, 1947). Specialized in Handel, Mozart, and contemporary works; created Walton's Troilus (1954), Mark (*Midsummer Marriage*, 1955), and Achilles (*King Priam*, 1962), and sang Schoenberg's Aron and Sessions' Montezuma in Boston. Also appeared in Paris and San Francisco (debut, José, 1955).

Lewis, William. Tenor; b. Tulsa, Okla. Nov. 23, 1935. Studied at Texas Christian U. and in N.Y.; debut as Rinuccio (*Schicchi*), Fort Worth, 1953. N.Y.C. Opera debut as Alfred (*Fledermaus*), 1957. Met debut as Narraboth, Mar. 1, 1958; in his nearly 200 perfs. there, his roles have included Aegisth, Dimitri (*Boris*), Steva (*Jenůfa*), Herman (*Queen of Spades*), Rodolfo, Turiddu, Hoffmann, and Malatestino (*Francesca*). Has also sung in Dallas, Tulsa, San Antonio.

libretto (Ital., "little book"). The text of an opera; also the printed form thereof, made available to the audience for study.

Libuše. Opera in 3 acts by Smetana; libretto by Josef Wenzig, translated to Czech by Ervin Spindler.
  First perf., Prague, National Theater, June 11, 1881; c. Smetana. U.S. prem., N.Y., Carnegie Hall (Opera Orchestra), Mar. 13, 1986 (concert perf.): Benačková, Vaness, Zitek, Plishka, c. Queler.
  In this patriotic opera, which opened a new theater and commemorated an archducal marriage, the princess Libuše (s), ruler of the Czechs, adjudicates a dispute over patrimony between two brothers; when the rectitude of female rule is questioned, she chooses a wise peasant as a consort and founds a ruling dynasty.

Licht (Light). Opera cycle by Stockhausen, in progress. *Donnerstag* (Thursday), in 3 acts. First perf., Milan, La Scala, Mar. 15, 1981: Gambill, Sperry, Meriweather,

Hölle, c. Eötvös. *Samstag* (Saturday), in 4 acts. First perf., Milan, Palazzo dello Sport (La Scala company), May 25, 1984: Hölle.

Stockhausen's cycle is projected to contain seven works, one for each day of the week; electronic techniques are extensively used. *Donnerstag*, designated as "Michael's Day," traces the hero's life from childhood through a journey around the earth to his return home. *Samstag* is largely instrumental.

Liebe der Danae, Die (The Love of Danae). Opera in 3 acts by R. Strauss; libretto by Joseph Gregor.

First perf., Salzburg, Aug. 16, 1944 (public dress rehearsal); Ursuleac, Taubmann, Klarwein, Hotter, c. Krauss. Official prem., Salzburg, Aug. 14, 1952: Kupper, Gostic, Traxel, Schöffler, c. Krauss, U.S. prem., Los Angeles, U. of So. Calif., Apr. 10, 1964 (in Eng.): c. Ducloux.

Danae occasionally achieves vintage Straussian splendor. Although loved by Jupiter (bar), Danae (s) remains faithful to Midas (t) even when he is deprived of his golden touch.

Liebermann, Rolf. Manager and composer; b. Zurich, Sep. 14, 1910. Studied composition with Wladimir Vogel; his works (including the operas *Leonore 40/45*, 1952; *Penelope*, 1954; *Die Schule für Frauen*, 1955) were in a free 12-tone style. He worked in Swiss radio stations, and in 1959 became general manager of the Hamburg State Opera (artistic director, 1962–73), with a strong emphasis on contemporary works. Under his direction (1973–80), the Paris Opéra was transformed from faded provincialism to glossy internationalism.

Liebesverbot, Das (The Ban on Love). Opera in 2 acts by Wagner; libretto by the composer, after Shakespeare's *Measure for Measure*.

First perf., Magdeburg, Mar. 29, 1836: Pollert, c. Wagner.

The fruit of Wagner's infatuation with Italian opera, this was not revived, after a disastrous second performance, until 1923. In 16th-c. Palermo, the hypocritical governor Friedrich (bs) condemns Claudio (t) to death unjustly and attempts to win the favors of his sister Isabella (s) by falsely promising a pardon. Eventually, Friedrich is exposed and all are pardoned.

Liebl, Karl. Tenor; b. Wiesbaden, Germany, June 16, 1915. Studied with Paul Bender, Munich; debut in Regensburg, 1950. Subsequently appeared in Wiesbaden, Vienna, Cologne, and Berlin. Met debut as Lohengrin, Feb. 11, 1959; in 9 seasons, sang 49 perfs. of 8 roles, including Herod, Tristan, and Loge.

Liebling, Estelle. Soprano; b. New York, Apr. 21, 1880; d. New York, Sep. 25, 1970. Studied with Mathilde Marchesi, Paris; debut as Lucia, Dresden, 1898. Appeared in Paris (Opéra-Comique) and Stuttgart. In 2 Met seasons, she sang 3 perfs., as Marguerite (*Huguenots*, debut, Feb. 24, 1902), Musetta, and the First Boy (*Zauberflöte*). She taught in N.Y. for many years; among her students was Beverly Sills.

Lied (Ger.). A German song; also used as a term for simple arias.

Life for the Tsar, A. Opera in 4 acts and epilogue by Glinka; libretto by G.F. Rozen.

First perf., St. Petersburg, Bolshoi, Dec. 9, 1836: Stepanova, Petrova-Vorobyova, Leonov, Petrov, c. Cavos. U.S. prem., N.Y., Steinway Hall, Nov. 14, 1871 (abr. concert perf.). U.S. stage prem., San Francisco, Veterans Auditorium, Dec. 12, 1936.

The first great success of Russian opera, based largely on Italian models but incorporating some national color. Glinka initially called it *Ivan Susanin*, and since 1917 that title has been preferred in the Soviet Union.

Domnin, Moscow, and a Polish camp, 1613. Invading Poles seek to capture the newly elected Tsar, who is a student at a monastery. The patriotic peasant Ivan Susanin (bs) accepts their bribe and leads them astray in a forest, while his son-in-law Sobinjin (t) leads a group to warn the Tsar. When they realize they have been duped, the Poles kill Susanin, but the Tsar is safe.

Ligendza, Catarina [Katarina Beyron]. Soprano; b. Stockholm, Oct. 18, 1937. Studied in Würzburg, Vienna, and with Josef Greindl, Saarbrücken; debut as Countess (*Nozze*), Linz, 1965. Appeared in Saarbrücken (1966–69), at Deutsche Oper, Berlin (from 1969), La Scala (debut, Arabella, 1970), Bayreuth (debut, Brünnhilde, 1971), and Covent Garden (debut, Senta, 1972). Met debut as Fidelio (Feb. 25, 1971).

Ligeti, György. Composer b. Dicsőszentmárton, Transylvania [now Tîrnăveni, Romania], May 28, 1923. Studied with Farkas, Veress, and Jardányi in Budapest, where he taught until leaving Hungary in 1956. Liberated from Communist conservatism and stimulated by contact with Western colleagues, he worked with electronic sounds, aleatory and other techniques, developing a colorful style. His *Aventures* (1962) and *Nouvelles Aventures* (1965), expressive non-verbal dramas for three voices, have been staged; in 1978 his music-theater work *Le Grand Macabre* (after Ghelderode) was first performed in Stockholm.

Lighthouse, The. Opera in prologue and 1 act by Maxwell Davies; libretto by the composer.

First perf., Edinburgh Festival, Sep. 3, 1980: Mackie, Rippon, Wilson-Johnson, c. Dufallo. U.S. prem., Boston (Shakespeare Company), Nov. 2, 1983.

Based on a true story of the mysterious disappearance of three keepers of a Hebrides lighthouse in 1900. Speculating on their final hours, the opera explores the characters of the men, building tension until they (and the audience) are blinded by mysterious lights; the ambiguous ending suggests that they went mad, or were destroyed by a beast, or that they were ghosts.

Lind, Jenny [Johanna Lind-Goldschmidt]. Soprano; b. Stockholm, Oct. 6, 1820; d. Wynds Point, England, Nov. 2, 1887. While studying at the Stockholm Opera school under Isak Berg, she made stage appearances from age ten; her formal operatic debut took place in Stockholm in 1838, as Agathe (*Freischütz*); by age 21, she had also sung Euryanthe, Donna Anna, Lucia, and Norma. Evidence of strain led to a brief retirement (1841–42) and further study in Paris with Manuel Garcia the younger. She appeared throughout Europe from 1842, making debuts in Berlin (Norma, 1844), Vienna (Norma, 1846) and London (Alice in *Robert le Diable*, 1847). Hailed as the "Swedish nightingale," she sang at Her Majesty's, London, for two more years, notably as Marie (*Fille du Régiment*), Amina, Alice, and Norma. The role of Vielka in Meyerbeer's *Feldlager in Schlesien* was written for her, though she

(continued p.194)

THE LIBRETTO
William Weaver

In Florence towards the end of the sixteenth century, a group of intellectuals – writers, musicians, thinkers – invented opera, or, as they called it, *il dramma per musica*. Actually, their intention was to recreate the theater of ancient Greece, but their tales of Orpheus and Eurydice and Daphne bore little resemblance to classical tragedy. Instead, they were ideally suited to the sumptuous taste of the Medici court, for which the first works were written, and for the equally pleasure-loving court of Mantua, which quickly took up the new form of entertainment.

Those early texts, by stately poets like Alessandro Striggio and Ottavio Rinuccini, were held in high consideration, their importance equalling if not surpassing that of the music. In fact, in a number of instances, the printed texts survive, while the music – never printed – has been lost.

Opera's first composer of genius, Claudio Monteverdi, was fortunate, towards the end of his career, in finding a librettist of genius: Francesco Busenello. His text for *L'Incoronazione di Poppea*, supposedly the first opera involving historical characters rather than semi-gods, is a daring, straightforward, emotionally varied story that, in Monteverdi's simple and subtle setting, again firmly holds the stage today.

During the first part of the eighteenth century, another great librettist dominated the opera theater: Pietro Trapassi, better known by his Arcadian name, Metastasio. Since his dramas were often played without any musical setting, he was also important in the spoken theater. His neatly plotted and elegantly versified stories of noble figures torn between love and duty, rich in fanciful simile, set the taste of an age. All the leading composers of his time used Metastasio's librettos, which went on being popular well into the 19th century. Gluck's reform operas, with their librettos by Raniero de Calzabigi, were in part a reaction against Metastasio: the texts were still noble, but less complex, more human, even when the characters came from ancient mythology.

(*Above*) Lorenzo da Ponte

Beside the tradition of stately opera seria, light-hearted opera buffa also developed, especially in Naples, where the colorful local dialect was used, making even more popular the works of composers like Pergolesi and Paisiello. In Venice, the celebrated dramatist Carlo Goldoni supplied texts for Galuppi and others. Then, at the end of the 18th century, in Vienna, the Italian exile Lorenzo da Ponte excelled in both comic and serious genres, sometimes even mixing them, as in his *Don Giovanni* for Mozart, who also set da Ponte's *Così Fan Tutte* and his adaptation of Beaumarchais' *Marriage of Figaro*.

Changing literary fashions are reflected in the history of the libretto. As neo-classicism gave way to the murky wave of Romanticism, opera librettists abandoned gods and semi-gods, Greek and Roman heroes for noble bandits, villainous barons, innocent maids. The Italian critic Felice Romani, who became the leading theatrical poet of the early decades of the 19th century, was by temperament and choice a classicist, but he had to bow to the taste of the public, and he converted the grandiose dramas of Victor Hugo and other Romantics into librettos for Donizetti and Pacini, while he echoed the French pastoral, *larmoyante* style for Bellini's *Sonnambula*.

Richard Wagner dominates the German libretto of the 19th century, as he dominated the whole operatic world. For the texts of his mature operas he forged an individual style – indeed, an individual poetic – and the

(*Below, left*) Arrigo Boito
(*Below, right*) Hugo von Hofmannsthal

Wagnerian literary personality also extended its influence beyond the opera house, even into the field of interior decoration. The fanciful castles of Ludwig of Bavaria still bear witness to their Wagnerian inspiration.

While Wagner imposed his ideas on libretto forms, his Italian contemporary Giuseppe Verdi adapted existing forms to his own musical world, and rigorously bent to his will the journeyman theater poets of the day. Towards the end of his career, his encounter with Arrigo Boito lead to the Shakespearean adaptations of *Otello* and *Falstaff*, whose elegant, refined language is in contrast with the rougher melodramatic idiom of earlier texts set by Verdi.

Richard Strauss had already composed his sensationally successful *Salome* (on a text by Oscar Wilde) when he met the sensitive, introspective poet and dramatist Hugo von Hofmannsthal, whose *Elektra* – written for the spoken theater – Strauss used for an opera. Their subsequent collaboration, copiously documented, is another rare example of virtually equal partnership between librettist and composer. After Hofmannsthal's death, Strauss tried various collaborators, the last being Clemens Krauss, who supplied the text for the composer's final opera *Capriccio*. This is a staged debate between a poet and a composer, each asserting the primacy of his contribution to opera. The debate was not new: from virtually the beginning of opera's history, poets and composer have had the same argument, summarized in the title of the opera that had suggested *Capriccio*, Salieri's *Prima la Musica e poi le Parole*. In his opera, Strauss embraces neither side specifically, but the melting, seductive charm of the concluding music surely reveals the composer's bias.

Over the centuries, the position of the librettist has oscillated violently. In opera's early days, texts were written by popes (Clement IX, when he was still a cardinal) and monarchs (Catherine II of Russia). In other periods, the verses to be set to music were turned out by theater hacks or, often, patched together from previous librettos (Handel suffered particularly in this respect). Other librettists were gifted poets. But fine poetry does not always mean a good libretto: the qualities of clarity, cogency, easily grasped characterization are more important – for composer and audience – than delicately-turned phrases or striking metaphors. Even operas with jungle-like intricacy of plot (*Il Trovatore* and *La Gioconda*, to name two) can succeed, if the librettist supplies the musician with singable words, strong scenes, and those telegram-like opening verses ("Di quella pira," "Suicidio, in questo fiero momento") that establish a mood and summarize a situation.

The widely successful operas of Gian Carlo Menotti – his own librettist – have confirmed the hallmarks of a useful opera text. Virgil Thomson's wit has made theatrical sense out of Gertrude Stein's onomatopoetic prattle. And Stravinsky, commissioning the text of *The Rake's Progress* from Auden and Kallman, was rewarded with a libretto of exceptional literary worth and verbal grace. As earlier composers had used stage plays like *Salome*, *Pelléas*, and *Wozzeck* with little or even no adaptation, American composers have turned to the Broadway theater for their texts: *Regina, Mourning Becomes Electra, Summer and Smoke*. In Europe, many composers have continued the Wagner tradition of writing their own words: Dallapiccola, Iain Hamilton, Messiaen. But as the popularity of most contemporary operas is scant, the problem of the possible supremacy of words has virtually become moot, and the librettist himself may be a dying breed.

William Weaver, a leading writer on the history of opera, is author of *Verdi: A Documentary Study* and *The Golden Century of Italian Opera*.

eventually did not sing the premiere, and she created Amalia in Verdi's *Masnadieri*, 1847. In 1849, she retired from the operatic stage, and toured the U.S. under the auspices of P.T. Barnum, giving nearly a hundred recitals (1850–51). She continued to sing in recitals and oratorio until 1883, and from then until her death was on the faculty of London's Royal College of Music. By all accounts, her voice was strikingly pure, well-focused, limpid, and agile, though her dramatic temperament fell short of the demands of roles such as Norma.

BIBLIOGRAPHY: J. Bulman, *Jenny Lind* (London, 1956).

Linda di Chamounix (Linda of Chamounix). Opera in 3 acts by Donizetti; libretto by Gaetano Rossi, after *La Grâce de Dieu* by Adolphe-Philippe d'Ennery and Gustave Lemoine.

First perf., Vienna, Kärntnertor, May 19, 1842: Tadolini, Brambilla, Moriani, Varesi. U.S. prem., N.Y., Palmo's Opera House, Jan. 4, 1847. Met prem., Mar. 1, 1934: Pons, Swarthout, Crooks, de Luca, c. Serafin. 7 perfs. in 2 seasons.

Haute-Savoie and Paris, c. 1760. To protect their daughter Linda (s) from seduction by the Marquis of Boisfleury (bar), Antonio (bar) and Maddalena (c) send her to Paris. She falls in love with Carlo (t), apparently a poor painter but actually the Marquis' nephew. Though their relationship is pure, Linda lives in an apartment owned by Carlo; this leads her father to believe she is Carlo's mistress, and he curses her. The girl then hears that Carlo has married someone else, and loses her senses. Returning to Chamounix, she is reunited with Carlo, who has refused the marriage his mother had arranged.

Lindholm [Jonsson], **Berit.** Soprano; b. Stockholm, Oct. 18, 1934. Studied at Stockholm Opera school; debut as Countess (*Nozze*), Stockholm, 1963. Debuts at Covent Garden (Chrysothemis, 1966), Munich (Brünnhilde, 1967), Bayreuth (Venus, 1967), and San Francisco (1972). In her only Met season, she sang 4 perfs. as Brünnhilde in *Walküre* (debut, Feb. 20, 1975) and *Siegfried*.

Lipton, Martha. Mezzo-soprano; b. New York, Apr. 6, 1916. Studied with her mother, with Mme. Gutmann-Rice, and with Paul Reimers at Juilliard; debut as Pauline (*Queen of Spades*), New Opera Co., N.Y., 1941. N.Y.C. Opera debut, Nancy (*Martha*), 1944. Met debut as Siebel (*Faust*), Nov. 27, 1944; in 17 seasons, she sang 298 perfs. of 36 roles, including Amneris, Mercedes, Hänsel, Emilia, Mrs. Sedley (*Peter Grimes*), Maddalena, and Annina (*Rosenkavalier*).

Lisitsian, Pavel. Baritone; b. Vladikavkaz [now Ordzhonikidze], Russia, Nov. 6, 1911. Studied in Leningrad; debut at Maly Theater, 1935. Appeared with Armenian Opera, Erevan (1937–40), before joining Bolshoi, Moscow (1940–66; debut as Yeletzky in *Queen of Spades*). Other famous roles included Onegin, Germont, and Escamillo; created Napoleon in *War and Peace*. Sang 1 perf. at Met, as Amonasro, Mar. 3, 1960 – the first Soviet artist to appear there.

List [Fleissig], **Emanuel.** Bass; b. Vienna, Mar. 22, 1886; d. Vienna, June 21, 1967. After singing vaudeville in Europe and America, made operatic debut at Vienna Volksoper as Méphistophélès, 1922. Appeared with Berlin Städtische and State Operas (1925–33), at Salzburg (1931–35), Bayreuth (1933), San Francisco (1935–37), and Chicago (1935–37). Met debut as Landgraf (*Tannhäuser*),

Jenny Lind

Dec. 27, 1933; in 16 seasons, he sang 326 perfs. of 17 roles, including Ochs, Hunding, King Marke, Pogner, Hagen, Gurnemanz, and Rocco.

Liszt, Franz. Composer, pianist, and conductor; b. Raiding, Hungary, Oct. 22, 1811; d. Bayreuth, July 31, 1886. The greatest piano virtuoso of the 19th c., he studied in Vienna with Czerny and Salieri, and in Paris with Paer and Reicha. At age 13, he composed a one-act operetta, *Don Sanche* (1825); although aspiring to operatic success in later years, he never again wrote for the theater (though his oratorio *Saint Elisabeth* has been occasionally staged). His importance to operatic history rests on his popularization of operatic music through his virtuoso piano transcriptions, and on his years as music director at Weimar (1848–58), where he presented the operas of his friends Berlioz, Cornelius, and Wagner (later the husband of Liszt's daughter Cosima).

Litvinne, Félia [Françoise-Jeanne Schütz]. Soprano; b. St. Petersburg, Oct. 11, 1860 or 1861; d. Paris, Oct. 12, 1936. Studied with Viardot and Maurel in Paris; debut as Maria Boccanegra, Italien, 1883. Appeared at Academy of Music, N.Y. (1885–86) and La Scala (1889–96). In her only Met season (debut, Valentine in *Huguenots*, Nov. 25, 1896), she sang 22 perfs. of 9 roles, including Aida, Donna Anna, Chimène (*Cid*), the *Siegfried* Brünnhilde, Isolde, and Sélika (*Africaine*). Her pupils included Nina Koshetz and Germaine Lubin.

Lizzie Borden. Opera in 3 acts by Beeson; libretto by Kenward Elmslie, after a scenario by Richard Plant.

First perf., N.Y.C. Opera, Mar. 25, 1965: Lewis, Faull, Elgar, Krause, Fredericks, Beattie, c. Coppola.

The events leading up to the famous Fall River ax

murders, concentrating on the psychological tensions between Lizzie (s) and her family. In an epilogue we see Lizzie many years after the murders, clinging to her religious beliefs.

Ljungberg, Göta. Soprano; b. Sundsvall, Sweden, Oct. 4, 1893; d. Lidingö, near Stockholm, June 30, 1955. Studied in Stockholm, Berlin, and Milan. Debut as Gutrune, Stockholm, 1917; sang there till 1926, then at Berlin State Opera (1926–29). Met debut as Sieglinde, Jan. 20, 1932; in 4 seasons, she sang 33 perfs. of 13 roles, including Sieglinde, Brünnhilde, Kundry, and Salome. Created Goossens' Judith (London, 1929) and Lady Marigold Sandys in *Merry Mount* (Met, 1933).

Lloyd, Robert. Bass; b. Southend-on-Sea, England, May 2, 1940. Studied with Otakar Kraus, London; debut as Don Fernando (*Fidelio*), U. College Opera Society. Has sung at English National Opera and, since 1972, Covent Garden; roles include Guardiano, Philippe II, and Boris. Debuts in Glyndebourne (Nettuno in Monteverdi's *Ritorno*, 1972), San Francisco (Sarastro, 1975) and at Paris Opéra (Commendatore, 1975).

Lobetanz. Opera in 3 acts by Thuille; libretto by Otto Julius Bierbaum.
First perf., Karlsruhe, Feb. 6, 1898. U.S. & Met prem., Nov. 18, 1911: Gadski, Jadlowker, c. Hertz, d. Kautsky/Heil, p. Schertel. 5 perfs. in 1 season.
A light music drama in a conservative style, set in an imaginary kingdom. The wandering minstrel Lobetanz (t) wins the hand of the Princess (s) through his violin playing.

Lodoletta. Opera in 3 acts by Mascagni; libretto by Giovacchino Forzano, after the novel *Two Little Wooden Shoes* by "Ouida" [Louise de la Ramée].
First perf., Rome, Costanzi, Apr. 30, 1917: Storchio, Campioni, Molinari, c. Mascagni. U.S. & Met prem., Jan. 12, 1918: Farrar, Caruso, Amato, c. Moranzoni, d. Bianco/Palant, p. Ordynski. 8 perfs. in 2 seasons.
This minor Mascagni work is set in Holland and Paris, mid-19th c. Lodoletta (s) goes to Paris to find her lover, the painter Flammen (t); he finds her body outside his home, where she has died in the snow on New Year's Eve.

Loewe, Sophie. Soprano; b. Oldenburg, Germany, Mar. 24, 1815; d. Budapest, Nov. 28, 1866. Studied in Vienna and with Lamperti, Milan; debut in Vienna, 1832. Created Donizetti's Maria Padilla (La Scala, 1841), and two Verdi heroines at La Fenice, Venice: Elvira (*Ernani*, 1844) and Odabella (*Attila*, 1846). Also appeared in London, 1841; retired in 1848.

Lohengrin. Opera in 3 acts by Wagner; libretto by the composer, after an anonymous German epic.
First perf., Weimar, Court Theater, Aug. 28, 1850: R. von Milde, Fastlinger, Beck, F. von Milde, Höfer, c. Liszt. U.S. prem., N.Y., Stadt Theater, Apr. 3, 1871. Met prem., Nov. 7, 1883 (in Ital.): Nilsson, Fursch-Madi, Campanini, Kaschmann, Novara, c. Vianesi, d. J. Fox, Schaeffer, Maeder, Thompson/Ascoli, Dazian. Later Met productions: Feb. 2, 1921: Easton, Matzenauer, Sembach, Whitehill, Blass, c. Bodanzky, d. Urban, p. Thewman; Nov. 15, 1952 ("revised"): Steber, Harshaw, Hopf, S. Bjoerling, Greindl, d. Elson, p. Yannopoulos; Dec. 8, 1966: Bjoner, Ludwig, Kónya, Berry, Macurdy, d. Wagner, p. Wagner/Lehmann; Nov. 4, 1976: Lorengar,

Dunn, Kollo, McIntyre, Giaiotti, c. Levine, d. Lee/P.J. Hall, p. Everding. Lohengrin has also been sung at the Met by Schott, Niemann, J. de Reszke, Burrian, Slezak, Jadlowker, Urlus, Melchior, Maison, Svanholm, Thomas, King, Hofmann, Jerusalem, Domingo; Elsa by Albani, Eames, Nordica, Melba, Gadski, Ternina, Fremstad, Destinn, Jeritza, Rethberg, Müller, Lotte Lehmann, Flagstad, Varnay, Bampton, Traubel, Della Casa, Crespin, Rysanek, Grümmer, Zylis-Gara, Tomowa-Sintow, Marton; Ortrud by Brandt, Mantelli, Lilli Lehmann, Schumann-Heink, Homer, Ober, Branzell, Lawrence, Thorborg, Varnay, Dalis, Marton, Rysanek; Telramund by Bispham, Ancona, van Rooy, Schorr, Janssen, Sved; the King by E. de Reszke, Plançon, Journet; the opera has also been conducted by L. Damrosch, Seidl, Schalk, Hertz, Mottl, Bodanzky, Abravanel, Leinsdorf, Busch, Schippers, Böhm, Patanè. 393 perfs. in 69 seasons.

The quickest of Wagner's operas to find popularity outside Germany, a work of high beauty and admirable balance between the aims of the libretto and Wagner's musical means at the time he set it.

Antwerp, 10th c. King Heinrich (Henry the Fowler) of Germany (bs) finds Brabant divided by a dispute over the ducal succession: Friedrich of Telramund (bar) claims the throne, and accuses Elsa (s) of having murdered the rightful heir, her brother Gottfried. Elsa protests innocence; the King decrees that single combat between Telramund and Elsa's champion shall decide the issue. When no champion comes forward for Elsa, she narrates her dream of a shining knight, whereupon a boat drawn by a swan brings Lohengrin (t), who agrees to be her defender and consort, provided that she never inquire after his name or origin; he defeats Telramund. Banned as a traitor, the latter conspires with his wife Ortrud (ms) to undermine the mysterious knight by planting doubts in Elsa's mind. During the wedding procession, the two publicly accuse Lohengrin of having used sorcery to defeat Telramund. Later, in the bridal chamber, Elsa's curiosity mounts until she finally breaks her promise and asks the forbidden question. Telramund burst in to attack Lohengrin, who kills the intruder and then tells the court the answer to Elsa's fateful question: his name

Lohengrin – Bayreuth Festival, 1936. Designed by Emil Preetorius, produced by Heinz Tietjen

A period drawing of the "New Royal Italian Opera House, Covent Garden"

is Lohengrin, and he is a Knight of the Holy Grail, permitted to remain among men only if his identity remains secret. He bids Elsa farewell, and his swan, reappearing, is revealed as the spellbound Gottfried, the rightful duke, now restored to human form.

Lombard, Alain. Conductor; b. Paris, Oct. 4, 1940. After study at Paris Conservatory, assistant and later conductor at Lyon Opera (1961–65). Winner of Mitropoulos competition (1966); music director, Miami Philharmonic (1966–74), Strasbourg Philharmonic (1972–83), and Opéra du Rhin (1974–80), thereafter based in Paris. Met debut in ballet evening, Mar. 27, 1966, conducting world premiere of Ibert's *Concerning Oracles*; in 7 subsequent seasons, he led *Carmen, Faust, Roméo,* and *Werther.*

Lombardi alla Prima Crociata, I (The Lombards at the First Crusade). Opera in 4 acts by Verdi; libretto by Solera, after Tomasso Grossi's poem *I Lombardi alla Prima Crociata.*

First perf., Milan, La Scala, Feb. 11, 1843: Frezzolini-Poggi, Ruggeri, Guasco, Severi, Derivis, Rossi. U.S. prem., N.Y., Palmo's Opera House, Mar. 3, 1847.

Verdi's fourth opera, more Donizettian in cut than *Nabucco,* full of flowing, florid melody and occasional strokes of dramatic innovation. For Paris, Verdi revised it as *Jérusalem (q.v.).*

Milan; in and around Antioch; near Jerusalem; 1096–97. The brothers Pagano (bs) and Arvino (t) had loved the same woman, who married Arvino and bore him a daughter, Giselda (s). Exiled for trying to kill Arvino, Pagano returns and attempts the crime once more, but mistakenly kills their father, and, exiled again, becomes a hermit near Antioch. Taken prisoner by the Moslems, Giselda has fallen in love with their leader's son Oronte (t). Arvino becomes a leader of the Crusaders; journeys and battles bring him into confrontation with Giselda, who repudiates him when Oronte is mortally wounded by Lombard forces, and with his exiled brother, who is also wounded but is forgiven by Arvino as he dies.

London [Burnstein], **George.** Bass-baritone; b. Montreal, May 30, 1920; d. Armonk, N.Y., Mar. 25, 1985. After study in Los Angeles, where he made his operatic debut (under the name George Burnson) as Dr. Grenvil (*Traviata*) at the Hollywood Bowl, he came to N.Y. to study with Enrico Rosati and Paola Novikova. In 1943 he sang Monterone with the San Francisco Opera; four years later, he toured with Frances Yeend and Mario Lanza as the Bel Canto Trio, then went to Europe in 1949. A Brussels audition yielded an engagement as Amonasro at the Vienna State Opera (1949), where, after this successful debut, he sang Escamillo, the *Hoffmann* villains, Boris and Onegin (in Russian), and Don Giovanni. After appearances as Mozart's Figaro at Edinburgh (1950) and as Amfortas in Bayreuth (1951), a Met debut followed quickly (Amonasro, Nov. 13, 1951); with that company from 1951 to 1966, he sang 249 perfs. of 22 roles, including Don Giovanni, Escamillo, Boris, Scarpia, Amfortas, Wolfram, Almaviva, Méphistophélès, Mandryka, the High Priest (*Zauberflöte*), the *Hoffmann* villains, Onegin, Golaud, the Dutchman, the three Wotans, and Abdul (*Last Savage*). Further debuts at Salzburg (Almaviva, 1952), La Scala (Don Pizarro in *Fidelio,* 1952), Buenos Aires (Almaviva, Colón, 1956), and the Paris Opéra (Don Giovanni, 1962). In 1960 he became the first American to appear on the Bolshoi stage, as Boris, which he recorded in Moscow in 1964. In Wieland Wagner's Cologne *Ring* cycle of 1962–64, he sang Wotan. After his singing career was cut short in 1967 by partial paralysis of the vocal cords, he worked in arts management, staged a traditional *Ring* cycle in Seattle (1975), and directed the Opera Society of Washington, D.C. (1975–80) before retiring because of a heart ailment.

London's rich, dark bass-baritone enabled him to range widely in the repertory. With a handsome stage presence,

George London as Don Giovanni

Royal Opera House, Covent Garden

compelling in his dramatic concentration, he had a special sympathy for Slavic roles and a gift for projecting menace, mystery, and majesty; regrettably but unavoidably, the theatrical impact of his performances is only partially preserved by his recordings.

London. Capital of Great Britain. Its rich operatic tradition has featured an enduring historical tension between imported and native styles. Especially after the arrival of Handel in 1711, the upper classes favored Italian opera, a vogue that continued through the 19th c. Alongside this, English works and continental operas in translation constituted a strong counterstrain, acquiring new vitality in the 20th c.

The first theater on the site known as Covent Garden (built 1732, burned 1808) housed *The Beggar's Opera*, and some of Handel's later seasons were held there. Its successor (opened 1809, burned 1858) witnessed the premiere of *Oberon* (1826) and in 1847 became known as the Royal Italian Opera. The present theater (opened 1858, capacity 2,250), designed by Edward Barry, was the scene of an international opera season every spring until 1939 (except 1915–24); Beecham was director of the international seasons, 1932–39. Until the administration of Augustus Harris (1888–96), all works were sung in Italian, afterwards usually in the original language. In fall and winter, touring companies often occupied the house. Since 1946, a resident company has presented full-length seasons; an early policy of opera in English gradually dissipated during the 1950s. Music directors have included Rafael Kubelik (1955–58), Georg Solti (1961–71), Colin Davis (1971–86), and Bernard Haitink (from 1987); general managers have been David Webster (1946–70) and John Tooley (since 1970). *Billy Budd* (1951), *Midsummer Marriage* (1955), and *Taverner* (1972) are among the postwar premieres.

Originating in 1931 as an offshoot of the popular-priced Old Vic theatrical company, Sadler's Wells Opera presented opera in the vernacular at the north London theater of that name until moving in 1968 to the centrally located London Coliseum (capacity 2,354); in 1974, it was renamed as English National Opera. Its most important premiere was *Peter Grimes* (1945). Under the direction of Norman Tucker (1953–66), Stephen Arlen (1966–72), the Earl of Harewood (1972–85), and now Peter Jonas, it has become noted for its Wagner productions, innovative stagings, and adventurous repertory; Mark Elder is music director, David Pountney director of productions. The Sadler's Wells Theater is now the home of the New Sadler's Wells Opera, a company which specializes in operetta. Other notable companies include Opera 80, the Opera Factory, and the New Opera Company (devoted to modern works).

Other important London operatic sites include King's/Queen's Theatre (from 1837, Her/His Majesty's) in the Haymarket, which opened in 1705 with the first Italian opera staged in London, Greber's *Gli Amori d'Ergasto*, and later housed Handel's Royal Academy. The Theatre Royal, Drury Lane (present building from 1812), has had a history of opera both in English and Italian, with premieres by Balfe, Benedict, and Wallace, and later housed the Carl Rosa and Beecham companies, as also did the Lyceum Theatre (known as the English Opera House, 1816–30). Arthur Sullivan's Royal English Opera House in Cambridge Circus, unsuccessfully launched in 1891 with his *Ivanhoe*, is now the Palace Theatre.

López-Cobos, Jesús. Conductor; b. Toro, Spain, Feb. 25, 1940. Studied at U. of Madrid, then with Swarowsky in Vienna. Conducted at Deutsche Oper, Berlin (1970–75); U.S. debut, *Lucia*, San Francisco Opera (1972). Thereafter appeared at many international theaters. Music director, Deutsche Oper (from 1978) and Cincinnati Symphony (from 1986). At the Met, has conducted *Adriana Lecouvreur* (debut, Feb. 4, 1978) and *Favorite*.

Lord Byron. Opera in 3 acts and epilogue by Thomson; libretto by Jack Larson.

First perf., N.Y., Juilliard American Opera Center, Apr. 20, 1972: Hirst, Val-Schmidt, Smith, Wickenden, Carlson, c. Samuel.

Thomson's rich and lyrical opera was commissioned by the Met but never performed there. In flashbacks from Westminster Abbey, where Lord Byron (t) is mourned but ultimately refused burial, his life is examined, especially his relationships with his half-sister, wife, and lovers.

Loreley. Opera in 3 acts by Catalani; libretto by A. Zanardini and Carlo D'Ormeville.

First perf., Turin, Regio, Feb. 16, 1890: Ferni-Germano, Dexter, Durot, Stinco-Palermini, c. Mascheroni. U.S. prem., Chicago, Jan. 17, 1919: Fitziu, Macbeth, Dolci, Rimini, c. Polacco. Met prem., Mar. 4, 1922: Muzio, Sundelius, Gigli, Danise, c. Moranzoni, d. Rovescalli/Castel-Bert, p. Thewman. 8 perfs. in 2 seasons.

A rewriting of *Elda* (perf. Turin, 1880), *Loreley* has retained some popularity in Italy. On the banks of the Rhine, c. 1500, the orphan Loreley (s), rejected by Walter (t) in favor of Anna (s), promises herself to Alberich, King of the Rhine, if he will transform her into an irresistible enchantress. Now Walter loves her, but she belongs to the Rhine, into which he flings himself.

Lorengar, Pilar [Pilar Lorenza Garcia]. Soprano; b. Saragossa, Spain, Jan. 16, 1928. Studied with Angeles Ottein, Madrid, later with Carl Ebert and Hertha Klust,

Berlin; debut in zarzuelas, Madrid, 1949. 1955 debuts in Aix (Cherubino), N.Y. (Rosario in *Goyescas*, concert perf.), and Covent Garden (Violetta); sang Pamina under Beecham, Buenos Aires, 1958. Member of Deutsche Oper, Berlin, from 1959. Appeared at Glyndebourne (as Pamina and Countess, 1956–60), Salzburg (1961–64), and San Francisco (from 1964). Met debut as Donna Elvira, Feb. 11, 1966; in 12 seasons, she has sung 118 perfs. of 16 roles, including Elsa, Countess, Eva, Pamina, Agathe (*Freischütz*), and Butterfly. Lorengar's silvery soprano and sunny personality have made her a warmly sympathetic singer in the lyric repertory.

Lorenz, Max. Tenor; b. Düsseldorf, Germany, May 17, 1901; d. Salzburg, Jan. 11, 1975. Studied in Berlin; debut as Walther (*Tannhäuser*), Dresden, 1927. Member of Berlin State Opera (1933–37) and Vienna State Opera (from 1937), also sang at Covent Garden (1934, 1937) and Bayreuth (1933–39, 1952). Met debut as Stolzing, Nov. 12, 1931; in 2 prewar and 3 postwar seasons, he sang 40 perfs. of 11 roles, including Lohengrin, Erik, Tannhäuser, Siegmund, Siegfried, Parsifal, Babinsky (*Shvanda*), Herod, Tristan, and Loge.

Lortzing, Albert. Composer; b. Berlin, Oct. 23, 1801; d. Berlin, Jan. 21, 1851. Son of actors, he became an actor and singer, and taught himself composition. His practical experience in theater served him well in a series of facile singspiels, such as *Der Pole und sein Kind* (1832). Then, with *Die beiden Schützen* (1837) and *Zar und Zimmermann* (1837), he perfected a fresh style of bourgeois musical comedy, combining folk-like melody, chromatically inclined harmony, and appealing comic scenes. Later works, equally successful, included *Hans Sachs* (1840), *Der Wildschütz* (1841), *Undine* (1845), and *Der Waffenschmied* (1846).

los Angeles, Victoria de. See *de los Angeles, Victoria*.

Los Angeles. City in southern California. Though long lacking a major resident opera company, Los Angeles has been visited by touring companies since the 1880s, including those headed by Emma Abbott, Emma Juch, and Antonio Scotti, as well as Gallo's San Carlo; the Metropolitan Opera first visited in 1900, the Chicago Opera in 1913. Open-air concert performances were heard at the Hollywood Bowl from 1915. As in San Francisco, Gaetano Merola attempted to establish a resident company, and the Los Angeles Grand Opera Association, founded in 1924, gave performances in the Shrine Auditorium, 1927–32; beginning in 1935, the San Francisco Opera came south to give an annual season for 30 years. With the completion of the Dorothy Chandler Pavilion (capacity 3,250) in 1965, Los Angeles finally had a satisfactory theater for grand opera; from 1967 to 1984, the N.Y.C. Opera gave regular seasons there. Currently, two companies present opera in the city. The Los Angeles Opera Theater (director, Johanna Dordick) offers a brief season of standard repertory at the Wiltern Theater. In fall 1986, the Los Angeles Music Center Opera Association (executive director, Peter Hemmings) presented its first season at Chandler Pavilion, with international casts in a repertory consisting of *Otello*, *Salome*, *Butterfly*, and *Alcina*.

Louise. Opera in 4 acts by Charpentier; libretto by the composer.
First perf., Paris, Opéra-Comique, Feb. 2, 1900:

Rioton, Deschamps-Jehin, Maréchal, Fugère, c. Messager. U.S. prem., N.Y., Manhattan Opera House, Jan. 3, 1908: Garden, Bressler-Gianoli, Dalmorès, Gilibert, c. Campanini. Met prem., Jan. 15, 1921: Farrar, Bérat, Harrold, Whitehill, c. Wolff, d. J. Fox, Triangle Studios, p. Thewman; Mar. 1, 1930: Bori, Telva, Trantoul, Rothier, c. Hasselmans, d. Urban, p. Wymetal. Louise has also been sung at the Met by Moore, Kirsten; Julien by Maison, Jobin; the Father by Pinza, Brownlee. 37 perfs. in 9 seasons.

Though crowded with realistic details of the bustle of Paris, Charpentier's opera is at heart a romantic love story and a hymn to the city.

Paris, c. 1900. Louise (s), a working-class girl, leaves home and moves to Montmartre with the artist Julien (t). When her mother (a), who has disapproved of the liaison from the start, brings news that Louise's father (bs) is gravely ill and wishes to see her, the girl agrees, on the understanding that she will be free to go back to Julien. But, after her father's recovery, her parents refuse to let her go. Finally, during a violent argument, her father orders her to leave, and she flees, leaving him to curse the city that has robbed him of so much.

Love, Shirley. Mezzo-soprano; b. Detroit, Jan. 6, 1940. Met debut as Second Lady (*Zauberflöte*), Nov. 30, 1963; in 20 seasons, she has also sung Carmen, Dalila, Amneris, Fricka, Marina, Maddalena, Emilia, and Suzuki. Has also appeared in Chicago, Philadelphia, and in Germany, Italy, and France.

Love for Three Oranges, The. Opera in prologue and 4 acts by Prokofiev; libretto by the composer, after Gozzi's comedy.
First perf., Chicago, Dec. 30, 1921 (in Fr.): Pavlovska, Koshetz, Mojica, Dua, Dufranne, Cotreuil, c. Prokofiev.

A hard-edged musical setting of Gozzi's parodistic commedia dell'arte fairy tale. In an opera-within-an-opera, the King (bs) fears that his son the Prince (t) will die of his illness, and is told that only laughter will cure him. When other efforts fail, the witch Fata Morgana (s) appears in the Prince's room and inadvertently makes him laugh by falling. She predicts he will fall in love with three oranges, and he goes off to seek them. When he finds three gigantic oranges, each containing a princess, he disregards orders and cuts them open in the desert; two of the princesses die of thirst, but the third (s) is saved, and they eventually return home safely.

Love of Three Kings, The. See *Amore dei Tre Re, L'*.

Lubin, Germaine. Soprano; b. Paris, Feb. 1, 1890; d. Paris, Oct. 27, 1979. Studied with Litvinne and Lilli Lehmann; debut as Antonia (*Hoffmann*), Opéra-Comique, Paris, 1912. Member of Paris Opéra, 1914–44, where her roles included Fidelio, Kundry, Isolde, Octavian, Elektra, and Alceste. Appeared in Vienna (1924), Covent Garden (1939), and Bayreuth (1938–39).

Luca, Giuseppe de. See *de Luca, Giuseppe*.

Lucia, Fernando de. See *de Lucia, Fernando*.

Lucia di Lammermoor. Opera in 3 acts by Donizetti; libretto by Cammarano, after Walter Scott's novel *The Bride of Lammermoor*.
First perf., Naples, San Carlo, Sep. 26, 1835: Tacchinardi-Persiani, Duprez, Cosselli, Porto. U.S. prem.,

New Orleans, Théâtre d'Orléans, Dec. 28, 1841 (in Fr.). Met prem., Oct. 24, 1883: Sembrich, Campanini, Kaschmann, Augier, c. Vianesi, d. J. Fox, Schaeffer, Maeder, Thompson/Ascoli, Dazian. Later Met productions: Nov. 28, 1942: Pons, Peerce, Valentino, Moscona, c. St. Leger, d. Rychtarik, p. Wallerstein; Oct. 12, 1964: Sutherland, Kónya, Merrill, Giaiotti, c. Varviso, d. Colonnello, p. Wallmann. Lucia has also been sung at the Met by Patti, Melba, Tetrazzini, Hempel, Galli-Curci, dal Monte, Peters, Callas, Moffo, Scotto, Sills; Edgardo by Caruso, Martinelli, Gigli, Lauri-Volpi, Schipa, Tagliavini, Tucker, Bergonzi, Gedda, and Kraus; Enrico by Amato, de Luca, Valentino, Warren, Merrill, and Bastianini; Raimondo by Journet, Pinza, Moscona, Plishka. 308 perfs. in 65 seasons.

One of the most beautiful and popular of early Romantic operas, whose sweep and power kept it in the repertory when most of Donizetti's tragic operas were forgotten, and whose title role has attracted great sopranos in each generation.

Lucia Ashton (s) loves Edgardo of Ravenswood (t), whose family has long feuded with her own. On the eve of Edgardo's departure for France on a diplomatic mission, the lovers exchange rings and vows. Lucia's brother Enrico (bar), enraged by the discovery of her liaison with his enemy, intercepts Edgardo's letters and shows Lucia a forged one apparently proving him unfaithful. Urged by the presbyter Raimondo (bs), she unwillingly agrees to a politically advantageous marriage with Lord Arturo Bucklaw (t), to buttress her brother's shaky fortunes. As Lucia is signing the wedding contract, Edgardo bursts in and denounces her faithlessness; in a scene often omitted, Enrico challenges him to a duel. Raimondo interrupts the wedding celebration: Lucia has gone mad and murdered her new husband. The deranged girl appears, hallucinating a marriage with Edgardo. In the Ravenswoods' ancestral cemetery, Edgardo, awaiting his duel with Enrico, learns of Lucia's death and stabs himself.

Lucio Silla (Lucius Silla). Opera in 3 acts by Mozart; libretto by Giovanni da Gamerra, with alterations by Metastasio.

First perf., Milan, Regio Ducal, Dec. 26, 1772: Morganoni, de Amicis, Rauzzini, Suardi, Mienci, Onofrio. U.S. prem., Baltimore, Peabody Concert Hall, Jan. 19, 1968.

A confident opera seria set in ancient Rome. The dictator Silla (t) desires Giunia (s), and condemns her exiled lover Cecilio (s) to death for plotting against him, but Giunia's rebuke before the Senate moves him to clemency, and the lovers are reunited.

Lucrezia Borgia. Opera in prologue and 2 acts by Donizetti; libretto by Romani, after Victor Hugo's tragedy *Lucrèce Borgia*.

First perf., Milan, La Scala, Dec. 26, 1833: Méric-Lalande, Brambilla, Pedrazzi, Mariani. U.S. prem., New Orleans, American, May 11, 1843. Met prem. (and only performance), Dec. 5, 1904: de Macchi, Walker, Caruso, Scotti, c. Vigna, d. Fox.

Perhaps the most Verdian of Donizetti's serious operas, *Lucrezia*'s dark colors and charged, brilliant music have made it one of the lasting successes of the modern Donizetti revival.

Venice and Ferrara, early 16th c. Attracted to a beautiful woman at the Venice carnival, Gennaro (t) is horrified when Maffeo Orsini (ms) shows her to be the infamous Lucrezia Borgia (s). Alfonso d'Este (bs), Lucrezia's fourth husband, is jealous of her attention to

Lucia di Lammermoor – (1956). Designed by Richard Rychtarik. Maria Callas

Gennaro, unaware that he is in fact her lost son. To prove to his friends that he does not love Lucrezia, Gennaro defaces the Borgia crest and is imprisoned. Lucrezia demands the death of the offender, until she learns it is Gennaro; Alfonso gives him poison, but Lucrezia has an antidote and aids his escape. Gennaro joins his friends at a banquet where, in revenge for insults to her name, Lucrezia has poisoned the wine. Too late, she sees Gennaro, but he spurns the antidote; appalled to learn his parentage, he dies with his companions.

Ludwig, Christa. Mezzo-soprano; b. Berlin, Mar. 16, 1924. Studied with her mother, Eugenia Besalla, and with Felicie Hüni-Mihacsek in Frankfurt; debut as Orlovsky, Frankfurt, 1946, later singing in Darmstadt (1952–54) and Hanover (1954–55). Member of Vienna State Opera (from 1955), where she sang Carmen and Marie (*Wozzeck*), and created Claire Zachanassian (*Besuch der Alten Dame*), 1971. In Salzburg (from 1955), her roles included Eboli and Iphigénie (*Aulide*) as well as Mozart and Strauss. U.S. debut as Dorabella, Chicago, 1959. Met debut as Cherubino, Dec. 10, 1959; in 10 seasons, she has sung 95 perfs. of 13 roles, including the Dyer's Wife (*Frau*), Octavian, Fricka (*Walküre*), Didon (*Troyens*), Ortrud, Kundry, the Marschallin, Charlotte (*Werther*), and Klytemnästra. Also appeared at Bayreuth (Brangäne, 1966; Kundry, 1967), Covent Garden (debut, Amneris, 1969), and La Scala. Married (1957–70) to baritone Walter Berry. Encouraged by her dramatic temperament to undertake roles such as Lady Macbeth and Fidelio, Ludwig soon wisely returned to the mezzo range.

Ludwig, Leopold. Conductor; b. Witkowitz, Moravia, Jan. 12, 1908; d. Lüneburg, Apr. 24, 1979. Studied in Vienna under Paur; principal conductor, Vienna State Opera (1939–43) and Berlin Städtische Oper (1943). Music director, Hamburg Opera (1951–70), appearing during company's guest season at Met, summer 1967. U.S. debut, San Francisco Opera (*Bartered Bride*, 1958); Met company debut, *Parsifal*, Oct. 14, 1970, returning the following season for *Freischütz*.

LUCIA DI LAMMERMOOR
Joan Sutherland

People often suggest to me that Lucia must be my favorite role. After all, it was my first major bel canto role, the vehicle for my overnight success at Covent Garden on February 17, 1959, and my debut role at the Paris Opéra, La Scala, the Met, San Francisco, Chicago, Hamburg, Copenhagen, and many other theaters. And it is a role I have sung for over twenty-eight years, one that has always suited me both vocally and emotionally. I am grateful to it and love it, and after all this time I am still able to find new facets in it. But I have a confession to make: I cannot say that Lucia is my favorite role.

Actually, I'm not sure that I have one favorite role. I love to sing Norma and Violetta and Elvira, and in recent years I've had a wonderful time with Adriana Lecouvreur. I also love the challenge and variety of new roles. But the public has always demanded Lucia, and neither my husband Richard Bonynge nor I have ever tired of performing the opera. It's rather like having a pair of well-loved, comfortable old shoes.

Lucia was a talisman from the beginning. I had been performing various parts and an occasional lead at Covent Garden for seven years when Sir David Webster, then the Royal Opera's general administrator, thought it was time for me to have a major role in a new production. The board disagreed, and it was suggested that I sing a revival of *Louise*, but when I saw the decrepit sets I was crestfallen. Sir David went to bat for me, and insisted, against the board's wishes, that I be given a new *Lucia*.

Best of all, he sent Richard and me to Venice to study with Tullio Serafin, the leading Italian conductor at the time – Serafin, who had molded Rosa Ponselle and Maria Callas. We studied every afternoon with him, not only Lucia, but Amina, Norma, and Elvira. We learned so much about phrasing and breathing, and about individuality of performance. I remember that Richard was having trouble feeling the tempo of a slow passage and asked his advice. "Listen to your singer," he said, "the tempo is the one which is right for her." (What singer *wouldn't* love advice like that?) He taught us that everything in opera should be based on the drama, and that every role should be related to the dramatic context.

We were also very fortunate that Franco Zeffirelli was enlisted to stage *Lucia*. He designed the sets and costumes, and personally slaved over every detail of production, from choosing fabrics to painting scenic details. And I owe him credit for giving me my first real confidence as an actress. I had worked previously with Carl Ebert, Günther Rennert, Rudolf Hartmann, Anthony Asquith, and Tyrone Guthrie, and learned much from them, but Franco took infinite pains with great kindness on a personal level, and convinced me that I *was* Lucia. In his lovely costumes I *felt* beautiful, and they helped me to project an image of fragility and vulnerability. Since then I have been a firm believer in the importance of having beautiful costumes for every role I perform.

The result was one of the most magical productions I have ever had the joy of appearing in. (We revived the same production a few years ago, and after twenty-five years it still held up.) That night I was "discovered," and was soon asked to do Lucia and other roles all over the world.

Franco did a second production for me that year for the Paris Opéra – it was originally produced for the glorious old Teatro Massimo in Palermo, and then made slightly grander for Paris. What began as a joke became reality in that production. Lucia, having died in the penultimate scene, does

not appear in the tenor's final scene, but we often joked with Franco about Lucia rising out of the tomb, à la Giselle, in the finale, as Edgardo sings, "Bell'alma innamorata." "We'll do it for Paris," said Franco. And so out of the tomb I rose, far back on the unusually deep stage of the Opéra – behind gauzes and shrouded in a mist – a theatrical illusion that was a triumph of perspective and lighting.

But alas, after those wonderful productions our eyes were opened to reality. My first *Lucia* at La Scala was a very old production – albeit on a grand scale – and my first in the old Met had been mounted originally for Lily Pons in 1942, and was very tired by the time we got to it; San Francisco had a modernistic atrocity, and most others are best forgotten.

On the plus side, in 1971 Hamburg gave us an exciting new *Lucia* by Peter Beauvais, who really got beneath the skin of the opera and produced a hair-raising drama. The Met and La Scala both replaced their old stagings with new ones that were improvements, although rather forgettable. And in Australia *Lucia* was used to open the Sutherland-Williamson season of 1965, our first return to our homeland since leaving as students in 1950–51. These *Lucia*s have held their place in our memories with more strength than many, as they are associated with returning home and being reunited with our families, and with the warmth and affection of the Australian public. Much later, the Australian Opera made one of the most beautiful of all *Lucia*s, sensitively directed by John Copley, with all set designs by Henry Bardon and costumes by Michael Stennett. The Stennett costumes are beautiful, and I wear them whenever I sing Lucia at Covent Garden and the Met.

I've also been blessed with many wonderful colleagues in the opera. I couldn't begin to list all the great tenors who have sung Edgardo with me, but they include Plácido Domingo, Alfredo Kraus, Richard Tucker, Jan Peerce, Carlo Bergonzi, Renato Cioni, John Alexander, and Sandor Kónya. How lucky I have been to have Luciano Pavarotti as my most frequent Edgardo, first in Australia before he was famous, and later with the Metropolitan Opera. He made his American debut as Edgardo with us in 1964 in Miami, when Renato Cioni had to cancel. And, early in 1987, to celebrate my twenty-fifth anniversary at the Met, we sang three acts from three different operas together – and one of them, of course, was *Lucia*.

I must say that, even after all these performances, I never tire of Donizetti's music for the opera. His glorious melodies express every emotion, from happiness to bewilderment, melancholy, despair, and, finally, madness. Of course it's a challenge to *act* such a role, but it's so well written that if you sing the music correctly, you can't help but express what the character is feeling. The Mad Scene alone makes the role worth doing – I think it's one of the best written scenes in nineteenth-century opera, not to mention one of the most dramatic. (Richard likes to quote Albert Einstein as remarking that "madness seems to improve the art of singing.") In that one great scene, Lucia relives her entire life, singing some of the greatest music written for the soprano.

No, singing this role is never tedious for me, even if it's not my very favorite. If I do have a problem with it, it's that I am beginning to feel a bit silly playing an eighteen-year-old girl. After all, I *am* a grandmother now, and I don't think a granny is supposed to make a living by getting up in front of thousands of people, pretending to be a teen-ager! Seriously, it does bother me, but everyone tells me that I don't *look* like a granny on stage, that it's the voice they come to hear, and luckily that's still holding up.

So opera houses keep asking for *Lucia*, and I suppose I must simply consider myself lucky still to be able to sing it. It was my calling-card into so many opera-houses around the world, and by now poor mad Lucy is like a dear old friend to whom I can always return.

(*Inset*) Paul Plishka, Joan Sutherland, and Alfredo Kraus

Luisa Miller. Opera in 3 acts by Verdi; libretto by Cammarano, after Schiller's play *Kabale und Liebe*.

First perf., Naples, San Carlo, Dec. 8, 1849: Gazzaniga, Salandri, Malvezzi, de Bassini, Selva, Arati. U.S. prem., Philadelphia, Walnut St., Oct. 27, 1852 (in Eng.). Met prem., Dec. 21, 1929: Ponselle, Telva, Lauri-Volpi, de Luca, Pasero, Ludikar, c. Serafin, d. Urban, p. Lert. Later Met production: Feb. 8, 1968: Caballé, Pearl, Tucker, Milnes, Tozzi, Flagello, c. Schippers, d. Colonnello, p. Merrill. Luisa has also been sung at the Met by Maliponte, Scotto, Ricciarelli; Rodolfo by Domingo, Pavarotti, Carreras; Miller by MacNeil, Nucci. 41 perfs. in 6 seasons.

A score of melodic directness and simplicity, pointing to the new intimacy and concern for specific characterization that would blossom in *Rigoletto* and *Traviata*.

Tyrol, early 17th c. Luisa (s), daughter of Miller (bar), loves Rodolfo (t), whom she knows as a commoner called "Carlo" but who is actually the son of Count Walter (bs). Walter has planned an aristocratic match for his son with Federica (a), Duchess of Ostheim, and conspires with his steward Wurm (bs) to separate Rodolfo and Luisa. Miller is imprisoned; in return for his freedom, Wurm compels Luisa to write a letter confessing that she never loved Rodolfo and asking Wurm to elope with her. Wurm makes her swear to declare that the letter was written of her own will. When he reads the letter, Rodolfo is stricken with grief. Luisa, also grieving, plans to leave the village with her father; when Rodolfo confronts her, she defends the veracity of the letter. They both drink from a cup he has poisoned. Learning she is near death, Luisa reveals the truth. Miller appears, followed by Walter and Wurm; before he dies, Rodolfo stabs Wurm through the heart.

Lully, Jean-Baptiste [Giovanni Battista Lulli]. Composer; b. Florence, Nov. 28, 1632; d. Paris, Mar. 22, 1687. Brought to France in 1646, he became widely known for his musical skills, won the favor of the young Louis XIV, and was named court composer of instrumental music in 1653, master of music to the royal family in 1662. After composing comédies-ballets for several Molière plays, including *Le Bourgeois Gentilhomme*, in 1672 he founded the Académie Royale de Musique (later the Grand Opéra), and began to set French texts, rejecting contemporary Italianate forms in favor of dramatic recitative in strict syllabic declamation, simple aria forms, choral ensembles integral to the plot, ballets, and evocative orchestral passages; for all their formal strictness, Lully's operas achieve a dignified, elegant effect, and they dominated French operatic music for many decades. His first opera was the pastorale pastiche *Les Fêtes de l'Amour et de Bacchus* (1672), libretto by Quinault, who collaborated on ten other works; the first tragédie lyrique, *Cadmus et Hermione* (1673), was followed more or less annually, by *Alceste*, *Thésée*, *Atys*, *Isis*, *Psyché*, *Bellérophon*, *Proserpine*, *Persée*, *Phaëton*, *Amadis*, *Roland*, *Armide*, and the heroic pastorale *Acis et Galatée*. *Achille et Polyxène* (1687), begun by Lully, was completed by Collasse.

Lulu. Opera in 3 acts by Berg; libretto adapted by the composer from Frank Wedekind's plays *Erdgeist* (Earth Spirit) and *Die Büchse der Pandora* (Pandora's Box).

Acts I & II only: First perf., Zurich, Stadttheater, June 2, 1937: Hadzic, Bernhard, Baxevanos, Feher, Stig, c. Denzler. U. S. prem., Santa Fe, Aug. 7, 1963: Carroll, Bonazzi, Shirley, Gibbs, Gramm, c. Craft. Met prem., Mar. 18, 1977: Farley, Troyanos, Lewis, Gibbs, Gramm, c. Levine, d. Herbert, p. Dexter. Complete 3-act version (Act III ed. and orch. by Friedrich Cerha): first perf., Paris,

Luisa Miller – (1980). Designed by Attilio Colonnello, produced by Nathaniel Merrill. Luciano Pavarotti and Katia Ricciarelli

Opéra, Feb. 24, 1979: Stratas, Minton, Riegel, Tear, Mazura, c. Boulez; U.S. prem., Santa Fe, July 28, 1979: Shade, K. Ciesinski, Busse, Goeke, Dooley, c. Thomas; Met prem., Dec. 12, 1980: Stratas, Lear, Riegel, Little, Mazura, c. Levine. Lulu has also been sung at the Met by Migenes-Johnson. 19 perfs. in 3 seasons.

Berg's second opera, a lurid masterpiece of obsession and degradation, is at once highly structured and intensely expressive. The completion of Act III, only partly orchestrated at Berg's death, was delayed for more than 40 years by his widow.

A German city, Paris, and London, late 19th c. In the Prologue, an animal-trainer (bs) introduces his menagerie, including his prize exhibit, a destructive, irresistible femme fatale. She is Lulu (s), wife of old Dr. Goll (speaking role) and mistress of Dr. Ludwig Schön (bar), a newspaper editor, who found her in sordid surroundings and brought her up. When Dr. Goll finds the Painter (t) making love to her, he dies of a heart attack, leaving her rich. After marrying the Painter, she learns that Dr. Schön plans to wed, and determines to prevent it. After a quarrel with Lulu, Schön reveals her sordid past to the painter, who commits suicide. Manipulating Schön into marrying her, she then torments him by keeping company with her old friends, all of whom desire her: Schigolch (bs), an old swindler who may be her father; an Athlete (bar); a Student (c); the lesbian Countess Geschwitz (ms); and even Schön's son Alwa (t). The desperate Schön gives her a gun to kill herself, but she uses it on him instead. A film shows Lulu's trial and conviction for murder and her escape from prison with the help of Geschwitz, who takes her place in the cholera ward. Escaping with Alwa to Paris, Lulu narrowly avoids being sold into prostitution. Penniless, Lulu, Alwa, and Schigolch live in a London attic, where she supports them by prostitution. Geschwitz arrives from Paris, and the two women are killed by Lulu's last client, Jack the Ripper.

Lunt, Alfred. Actor and producer; b. Milwaukee, Wis., Aug. 12, 1892; d. Chicago, Aug. 3, 1977. One of America's great actors, especially teamed with his wife, Lynn Fontanne, in contemporary and classic theater works, which he occasionally also directed. Engaged by Bing to direct *Così* (1951), in which he also appeared as a servant, he returned to the Met to stage *Traviata* (1966).

Lussan, Zélie de. See *de Lussan, Zélie*.

Lustigen Weiber von Windsor, Die (The Merry Wives of Windsor). Opera in 3 acts by Nicolai: libretto by Hermann von Mosenthal, after Shakespeare's comedy.

First perf., Berlin, Court Opera, Mar. 9, 1849: c. Nicolai. U.S. prem., Philadelphia, Academy of Music, Mar. 16, 1863. Met prem. (and only perf.), Mar. 9, 1900: Sembrich, Pevny, Schumann-Heink, Dippel, Friedrichs, Bertram, c. Paur.

This tuneful comedy with juicy vocal parts has remained a favorite in German-speaking houses even after the establishment of Verdi's *Falstaff* in the repertory.

Windsor, reign of Henry IV. The episodes are essentially those used in Verdi's opera, though without the initial scene of Falstaff and his companions, without Mistress Quickly, and following Shakespeare's repeated rendez-vous of Falstaff and Mistress Ford. The principal roles are Frau Fluth (Mistress Ford, s), Frau Reich (Mistress Page, ms), Fenton (t), Herr Fluth (Mr. Ford, bar), Herr Reich (Mr. Page, bs), and Falstaff (bs).

Luxon, Benjamin. Baritone; b. Redruth, Cornwall, Mar. 24, 1937. Studied at Guildhall School, London; debut with English Opera Group, 1963. In 1972, debuts at Covent Garden and Glyndebourne; created Britten's Owen Wingrave (1971) and the Jester in Maxwell Davies' *Taverner* (1972). Met debut as Onegin, Feb. 2, 1980.

M

Maag, Peter. Conductor; b. St. Gall, Switzerland, May 10, 1919. Studied in Zurich, Basel, and Geneva, where he became assistant to Ansermet. Principal conductor, Düsseldorf (1952–54); general director, Bonn Opera (1954–59); principal conductor, Vienna Volksoper (1964–68). Chicago Opera debut, *Così*, 1961. During 3 Met seasons (debut, *Don Giovanni*, Sept. 23, 1972), he also led *Traviata*, *Norma*, and *Zauberflöte*.

Maazel, Lorin. Conductor; b. Neuilly, France, Mar. 6, 1930. After private study in Los Angeles and Pittsburgh, he made his N.Y. Philharmonic debut at age nine.. Fulbright fellow in Italy (1951); adult debut in Catania, 1953. First American to conduct at Bayreuth (*Lohengrin*, 1960; *Ring*, 1968). Met debut, *Don Giovanni* (Nov. 1, 1962), also led *Rosenkavalier* that season. Artistic director, Deutsche Oper, Berlin (1965–71), where he led 20 works, including premiere of *Ulisse*; music director, Berlin Radio Symphony (1965–75), Cleveland Orchestra (1972–82). First American director of Vienna State Opera, from 1982 until 1984, when he resigned in conflict with Austrian press and government figures. Music advisor, Pittsburgh Symphony (from 1984); appointed music director beginning 1988. In performance and on records, he has established a reputation for polished, technically precise, imaginative interpretations. His recordings include *Thaïs*, *Otello*, the first complete *Porgy*, and a Puccini series.

Macbeth. Opera in prologue and 3 acts by Bloch; libretto by Edmond Fleg, after Shakespeare.

First perf., Paris, Opéra-Comique, Nov. 30, 1910. U.S. prem., Cleveland, Karamu House, Mar. 19, 1957 (in Eng.).

Bloch's only opera, based closely on the central scenes from Shakespeare.

Macbeth. Opera in 4 acts by Verdi; libretto by Piave, after Shakespeare's tragedy.

First perf., Florence, Pergola, Mar. 14, 1847: Barbieri-Nini, Brunacci, Varesi, Benedetti. U.S. prem., N.Y., Niblo's Garden, Apr. 24, 1850. Rev. version (with ballet), first perf., Paris, Lyrique, Apr. 19, 1865 (in Fr.): Rey-Balla, Montjauze, Ismael, Petit, c. Deloffre. U.S. prem., N.Y., 44th St. (New Opera Co.), Oct. 24, 1941: Kirk, Marshall, Walters, Silva, c. F. Busch. Met prem., Feb. 5, 1959: Rysanek, Bergonzi, Warren, Hines, c. Leinsdorf, d. Neher, p. Ebert. Later Met production: Nov. 18, 1982: Scotto, Giacomini, Milnes, Raimondi, c. Levine, d. Bury, p. Hall. 53 perfs. in 7 seasons.

Verdi's veneration for Shakespeare moved him to the most daring and experimental score among his early operas. Though the uneasy coexistence of forward-looking and conventional pages was exacerbated by the 1865 revisions, *Macbeth* has won a strong place just outside the standard repertory in a series of notable 20th-c. revivals.

Scotland, and on the Anglo-Scottish border, time unspecified. Macbeth (bar) and Banquo (bs), generals of King Duncan of Scotland, hear witches hail Macbeth as Thane of Cawdor and King of Scotland, Banquo as father of future kings. News arrives that the Thane of Cawdor has been executed for treason and Macbeth appointed as his successor. At the urging of Lady Macbeth (s), her husband kills the King and takes the throne. To thwart the remaining prophecy, they set assassins on Banquo and his son Fleanzio. The latter escapes, and Banquo's ghost appears to the terrified Macbeth at a banquet. Appalled at the new King's behavior, Macduff (t), Lord of Fife, flees to England, where he joins Malcolm, Duncan's son (t). The witches warn Macbeth to beware of Macduff, that no one born of woman shall harm him – and that Banquo's progeny shall reign. With his lady, Macbeth decides that Banquo's son and Macduff's family must die. Tormented by the memory of the murders, Lady Macbeth loses her mind and dies. At the head of Malcolm's troops, Macduff (who was not born but "from his mother's womb untimely ripp'd") kills Macbeth, and the Scottish exiles hail Malcolm, Duncan's heir, as King.

McCormack, John. Tenor; b. Athlone, Ireland, June 14, 1884; d. Dublin, Sep. 16, 1945. Studied with Vincent O'Brien in Dublin and Vincenzo Sabatini in Milan; stage debut (under the name Giovanni Foli) as Mascagni's Fritz, Savona, 1906. After his Covent Garden debut (Turiddu, 1907), he appeared there regularly until 1914 in roles such as Edgardo, Elvino (*Sonnambula*), Gounod's and Boito's Fausts, and Roméo. In 1909 he sang at the San Carlo, Naples, and began his American operatic career at the Manhattan Opera, as Alfredo, followed by Edgardo, Tonio (*Fille*), Rodolfo, the Duke of Mantua, Turiddu, and Gérald (*Lakmé*). A year later, he made debuts within a single month with the Chicago (Turiddu, Nov. 7, 1910), Met (Alfredo, Nov. 29, 1910), and Boston (Turiddu, Dec. 2, 1910) companies. His Met career numbered only 6 perfs. spread over 5 seasons, also including Rodolfo, Pinkerton, and Cavaradossi. He appeared more often

John McCormack as Edgardo in *Lucia di Lammermoor*

with the Boston and Chicago companies; with the latter, he created Paul in Herbert's *Natoma* (Philadelphia, 1911). He spent the war years in America (becoming a U.S. citizen in 1917), then returned to the British Isles. At Monte Carlo, he sang Tamino in 1921, Lionel (*Martha*) and Gritzko (*Sorochintsy Fair*) in 1923, his final operatic appearances. He continued to sing recitals until 1938, and emerged from retirement during World War II for radio recitals and benefits. He made one film, *Song o' My Heart* (1929).

Although critical dissatisfaction with McCormack's undramatic stage presence probably led to his early retirement from opera, surely nobody ever regretted encountering his pliant voice, elegant phrasing, and impeccable Italianate vocalism on the operatic stage. His voluminous discography documents his art from 1904 to 1942, in opera and song, both classic and vernacular; his versions of Ottavio's "Il mio tesoro" and "O sleep" from *Semele* are among the most admired vocal recordings ever made.

BIBLIOGRAPHY: G.R. Ledbetter, *The Great Irish Tenor* (London, 1977).

McCracken, James. Tenor; b. Gary, Ind., Dec. 16, 1926. Sang on Broadway while attending Columbia U. and studying with Wellington Ezekiel; debut as Rodolfo, Central City, Colo., 1952. Met debut as Parpignol (*Bohème*), Nov. 21, 1953; after 4 seasons of small roles, he left in 1957 for Europe, where he sang dramatic roles in Bonn. He attracted wide attention as Otello with the Washington, D.C., Opera (1960), repeating this role in Zurich (1960), Vienna (1960), London (1964), and for his return to the Met (1963), where he has sung more than 410 perfs., the major roles also including Canio, Manrico, Samson, José, Radames, Calaf, Jean de Leyde (*Prophète*), and Tannhäuser. Also appeared in Salzburg (Manrico, 1963), with Boston Opera, and throughout Europe;

married to mezzo Sandra Warfield. McCracken's powerful and solidly founded tenor voice is deployed with compelling emotional intensity.

McDaniel, Barry. Baritone; b. Lyndon, Kans., Oct. 18, 1930. Studied at Juilliard School, N.Y., and Stuttgart Hochschule; recital debut, Stuttgart, 1953. Sang in Mainz, Stuttgart, Karlsruhe, and the Deutsche Oper, Berlin (from 1962), where he created the Secretary (*Junge Lord*), 1965. Only Met appearances as Pelléas (debut, Jan. 19, 1972). Specializes in 18th-c. and modern repertory.

McEwen, Terence. Manager; b. Thunder Bay, Ont., Apr. 13, 1929. Raised in Montreal, he worked in Europe for Decca Records and in 1959 became manager of its N.Y. classical division (London Records). In 1982 he succeeded Kurt Herbert Adler as general manager of the San Francisco Opera; among the events of his tenure to date are the reorganization of the company's adjunct activities as the San Francisco Opera Center, a new *Ring* cycle (1983–85), and abandonment of the unprofitable summer season.

McIntyre, Donald. Bass-baritone; b. Auckland, New Zealand, Oct. 22, 1934. Studied at Guildhall School, London; debut as Zaccaria (*Nabucco*), Welsh National Opera, Cardiff, 1959. Sang with Sadler's Wells Opera, 1960–67; Covent Garden debut as Pizarro, 1967. A Wagner specialist, he has sung regularly at Bayreuth beginning in 1968, including Wotan in the centennial *Ring*, 1976. Since his Met debut as Wotan (*Rheingold*), Feb. 15, 1975, he has sung many Wagnerian roles, also Pizarro (*Fidelio*), Orest (*Elektra*), and the High Priest (*Zauberflöte*).

James McCracken as Jean de Leyde in *Le Prophète*

Cornell MacNeil as Michele in *Il Tabarro*

Mackerras, Charles. Conductor; b. Schenectady, N.Y., Nov. 17, 1925, of Australian parents. Studied with Talich in Prague, where he first encountered the Janáček operas he conducts with such authority; at Sadler's Wells (debut, *Fledermaus*, 1948), he conducted until 1954. Appeared often at Covent Garden (debut, *Katerina Ismailova*, 1963). Principal conductor, Hamburg Opera (1966–70); music director, Sadler's Wells/English National Opera (1970–77); principal conductor, Sydney Symphony (1983–85); music director, Welsh National Opera (from 1987). Met debut, *Orfeo* (Oct. 31, 1972).

MacNeil, Cornell. Baritone; b. Minneapolis, Minn., Sep. 24, 1922. Studied with Friedrich Schorr, Hartt College of Music, Hartford. Sang in Broadway musicals, and created John Sorel in Menotti's *Consul*, Philadelphia, 1950. Debuts at N.Y.C. Opera (Germont, 1953), San Francisco (Escamillo, 1955), Chicago (Puccini's Lescaut, 1957), La Scala (Carlo in *Ernani*, 1959), and Covent Garden (Macbeth, 1964). Met debut as Rigoletto, Mar. 21, 1959; since then, he has sung more than 470 perfs. of 26 roles, including Amonasro, Nabucco, Iago, Germont, di Luna, Barnaba, Alfio, Tonio, Michele (*Tabarro*), Gianciotto (*Francesca*), Scarpia, and Trinity Moses (*Mahagonny*) with the company. He was elected president of the American Guild of Musical Artists in 1969. In MacNeil's durable career, he has moved from a suave Verdi baritone to a forceful verismo singer.

Macurdy, John. Bass; b. Detroit, Mich., Mar. 18, 1929. After studying voice with Avery Crew, interpretation with Boris Goldovsky, sang opera in New Orleans and Santa Fe. N.Y.C. Opera debut as Dr. Wilson (*Street Scene*), 1959. Met debut as Tom (*Ballo*), Dec. 8, 1962; has sung there regularly since, in more than 650 perfs. of more than 50 roles, notably the Commendatore, Crespel (*Hoffmann*), Sarastro, the First Nazarene (*Salome*), King Heinrich (*Lohengrin*), and Rocco (*Fidelio*). He created

Agrippa (*Antony*) and Ezra Mannon (*Mourning Becomes Electra*), 1967. Has also sung in Aix (Arkel, 1972), Paris (Arkel, 1973), and Milan (Pizarro in *Fidelio*, 1974).

Madama Butterfly. Opera in 3 (originally 2) acts by Puccini, libretto by Giacosa and Illica, after the drama by Belasco, based on a story by John Luther Long.

First perf. (in 2 acts) La Scala, Feb. 17, 1904: Storchio, Zenatello, de Luca, c. Campanini; revised in 3 acts, first perf., Brescia, Grande, May 28, 1904: Krusceniski, Zenatello, de Luca, c. Campanini (the standard version was only finally established for the Paris premiere, 1906). U.S. prem., Oct. 15, 1906 (in Eng.), Savage Opera Co., Washington, D.C. (beginning a No. Amer. tour of 258 perfs.). Met prem., Feb. 11, 1907: Farrar, Homer, Caruso, Scotti, c. Vigna, p. Dufriche (under Puccini's supervision). Later Met productions: Nov. 24, 1922: Easton, Perini, Martinelli, Scotti, c. Moranzoni, d. Urban, p. Wymetal; Feb. 19, 1958: Stella, Roggero, Fernandi, Zanasi, c. Mitropoulos, d. Nagasaka, p. Aoyama. Butterfly has also been sung at the Met by Destinn, Muzio, Mason, Rethberg, Albanese, de los Angeles, Kirsten, Tebaldi, L. Price, Scotto, Stratas. Met performances were suspended during World War II, but *Butterfly* has otherwise remained a staple of the repertory. 456 perfs. in 66 seasons.

An enormously popular opera, noted for its melodic beauty, exotic oriental ambience, and orchestral color. The great musical and emotional compass of the title role, growing from naive trust to confrontation with tragic loss and sacrifice, make it a pinnacle of the Italian soprano repertory.

Nagasaki, Japan, early 1900s. The geisha Cio-Cio-San, known as Madame Butterfly (s), wholeheartedly commits herself to a broker-arranged marriage with U.S. Navy lieutenant B.F. Pinkerton (t), renouncing her faith for his and enduring family denunciation on her wedding day, while he enters the union less seriously, toasting the day he will have a "real American wife." He returns to America, promising to return "when the robin nests." After three years with no word, Butterfly still hopes for his return;

(continued p.208)

Madama Butterfly – (1946). Designed by Joseph Urban. Licia Albanese and Lucielle Browning

MADAMA BUTTERFLY
Renata Scotto

I love the human drama in *Madama Butterfly*. Seeking a better life, this fifteen-year-old girl falls in love with a man who promises the world but inevitably betrays her. She sustains her dream against great odds, and courageously chooses to die rather than accept a hopeless future. The story is so modern! Cio-Cio-San could be any star-struck girl who ever fantasized about finding happiness in Hollywood or on Broadway, only to be crushed by the "real" world. Thanks to Giacomo Puccini, *Madama Butterfly* is timeless.

At nineteen, I sang my very first Cio-Cio-San in Savona, my home town. Although not much older than the geisha girl, I instinctively understood her will to succeed. I had wonderful teachers: Mafalda Favero offered a model interpretation, maestros Gianandrea Gavazzeni and Nello Santi taught me the music, and Luigi Ricci, who had worked with Puccini himself, gave me invaluable coaching sessions. Sir John Barbirolli, conductor of my first complete *Butterfly* recording, was another extraordinary Puccini interpreter. Reading the correspondence between Giacosa and Illica, I discovered how the librettists reshaped the David Belasco play. But, after many *Butterfly* performances, the composer is still my most important teacher. Search Puccini's score, and you find the meaning behind the melodies.

Butterfly is the last girl to climb up the hill overlooking Nagasaki. It's a symbolic journey for a woman who never stops fighting for happiness. Deserted by family and friends, she tells Pinkerton, "Rinegata, e felice" (I'm rejected, but happy). Following a traditional Japanese upbringing, she will do anything to please this man, even give up her religion. In the love duet, Puccini strongly contrasts this idealistic dreamer with Pinkerton, a man who wants to have his fun immediately and doesn't care about the consequences.

After three years, "Un bel dì" becomes Butterfly's credo. She insists that Pinkerton will return and take his little family back to the "gran paese," America. For both Puccini and his favorite heroine, the United States was a golden land of limitless opportunity. Refusing the chance to marry a rich Japanese suitor, Cio-Cio-San cherishes her American dream.

"What if he doesn't come back?," Sharpless asks her. The consul's question hits her like a body blow! Puccini writes one of the greatest pauses in opera, and a singing actress must fill it with a flood of feelings. No "respectable" Japanese would welcome an outcast, and Butterfly will never beg, return to the geisha house, or – even worse – become a prostitute. If hope dies, so will she.

Butterfly enjoys a short-lived triumph when she spots Pinkerton's ship entering the harbor. But after her all-night vigil she meets Kate Pinkerton and realizes that "everything is finished." For a mother, the greatest tragedy is to lose a child. Butterfly needs every bit of emotional and vocal stamina to sing the suicide scene, Puccini's overwhelming moment of truth. The tears must be in your heart, never in your throat.

Playing Cio-Cio-San, I always see the opera from her point of view. But, when making my Met directing debut in 1986, I clearly understood the many emotional colors that Puccini gave to the other characters. Pinkerton is like those servicemen who see foreign women as "baby dolls" and want a quick relationship without any emotional strings attached. Sharpless is a sensitive diplomat who knows how to deal with people of

very different backgrounds. We read all the time about shady businessmen like Goro. Everyone needs a Suzuki, that unselfish friend who remains loyal through good times and bad.

Directing another Cio-Cio-San, I make suggestions without insisting on my interpretation. If someone plays Butterfly as a fragile child bride, I disagree. She is a strong, independent woman who tries to take charge of her life. Consider other Puccini heroines: Mimi makes the first move to meet Rodolfo. Tosca fights like a tigress against Scarpia. Liù withstands torture without revealing Calaf's identity. And Minnie holds off a posse to rescue her lover. If Puccini had wanted a weak Butterfly, she would have committed hara-kiri long before Act II!

Visiting Japan, I always admire the exquisite beauty of the people and their art. But the opera is not about an actress who delicately flutters her fan, moves well in a kimono, and looks authentically oriental. Mastery of these small details is only a first step towards building a complex characterization. By Act II, the audience forgets about Japan and focuses on Butterfly's brave struggle. The setting is Nagasaki, but the feelings are universal.

In my Met staging, we respected Puccini's original intention and played the last two acts without an intermission. The long vigil scene becomes even more difficult to act! Waiting for Pinkerton, Butterfly remains absolutely motionless in front of the shoshi. The curtain falls after the humming chorus, but the suspense continues through the intermesso. The audience has a few moments to catch its breath, but Cio-Cio-San's concentration never falters. She stoically maintains that stillness until daylight streams through the shoshi.

According to tradition, Butterfly performs her ritual suicide behind a silk screen. At the Met, I played the scene in full view of the audience. Wearing a white kimono, Cio-Cio-San sits in semi-darkness, cut off from all light and human contact. After she sings a shattering farewell to her baby, we share her total separation from the outside world. A beautiful life is snuffed out, and Puccini offers us no comfort whatsoever.

Butterfly demands bel canto, not big sounds. Starting with a solid technique and a sure instinct for Puccini's phrasing, an artist discovers how to fill beautiful tones with emotional substance. That's the key to involving an audience in this great drama. After one recent *Butterfly*, the Met audience gave me a standing ovation. Crying, I thought, "Tonight, I have recreated Cio-Cio-San through words and music – and felt it!" Puccini loved his Butterfly, and so do I.

proudly displaying the son she has borne the American, she thwarts the attempts of the U.S. consul Sharpless (bar) to break the news that Pinkerton will soon arrive with his American wife. After a night-long vigil with her child and her maid Suzuki (ms), Butterfly is confronted with the truth in the person of Kate Pinkerton (s), and agrees to give up the child, if Pinkerton will come for him. Knowing she cannot endure life without honor, Butterfly bids farewell to her son and commits suicide just before Pinkerton's arrival.

Madame Sans-Gêne (Madame Free-and-Easy). Opera in 4 acts by Giordano; libretto by Renato Simoni, after the comedy by Victorien Sardou and Émile Moreau.

First perf., N.Y., Met, Jan. 25, 1915: Farrar, Martinelli, Amato, c. Toscanini, d. Rovescalli/Caramba. 14 perfs. in 4 seasons.

Exceptionally, a romantic comedy from a verismo composer; set in Paris and Compiègne, 1792 and 1811. Catherine Huebscher (s), proprietress of a laundry during the revolution and later Duchess of Danzig, twice saves the life of Count Neipperg (t), and is able to present Napoleon (bar) with an unpaid laundry bill from his days as a lieutenant.

Madeira [née Browning], **Jean.** Mezzo-soprano; b. Centralia, Ill., Nov. 14, 1918; d. Providence, R.I., July 10, 1972. Studied at Juilliard School; debut in *Martha*, Chautauqua Opera, 1943. Alternated with Powers as Menotti's Medium, European tour, 1947. After Met debut as First Norn (*Götterdämmerung*), Dec. 2, 1948, sang nearly 300 perfs. there in 41 roles, notably Carmen, Klytemnästra, and Erda. On Met roster until 1971, but after 1955 sang primarily in Europe; created Circe (*Ulisse*), Berlin, 1968.

Madeleine. Opera in 1 act by Herbert; libretto by Grant Stewart, adapted from the French of Decourcelles and Thibaut.

First perf., N.Y., Met, Jan. 24, 1914: Alda, Althouse, Pini-Corsi, c. Polacco, d. Novak. 4 perfs. in 1 season.

A slight work by the noted operetta composer, set in Paris, 1770. The pampered diva Madeleine (s) is upset when no one can dine with her on New Year's Day; eventually she dines opposite a portrait of herself.

Maderna, Bruno. Composer and conductor; b. Venice, Apr. 21, 1920; d. Darmstadt, Germany, Nov. 13, 1973. Studied composition with Malipiero at Venice Conservatory and Pizzetti at Milan Conservatory, conducting with Hermann Scherchen. He composed in an advanced serial idiom, incorporating electronic materials and aleatory procedures. His operatic output includes *Don Perlimplin*, after Lorca, for radio (1962); *Hyperion*, a "lyric in dramatic form" after Hölderlin (1964); and *Satyricon*, after Petronius (1973). Maderna conducted *Don Giovanni* at the N.Y.C. Opera (1972).

Madonna Imperia. Opera in 1 act by Alfano; libretto by A. Rossato, after one of Balzac's *Contes Drôlatiques*.

First perf., Turin, Teatro di Torino, May 5, 1927. U.S. & Met prem., Feb. 8, 1928: Müller, Jagel, Pinza, c. Serafin, d. Novak. 5 perfs. in 1 season.

A post-verismo comedy with neo-classical touches. During the Council of Constance, 1414–18, the impassioned young clerk Filippo Mala (t) wins the heart of the aristocratic courtesan Madonna Imperia (s), despite her initial disinterest and the determination of the Chancellor of Ragusa (bs) to have her for himself.

Gustav Mahler

mad scene. An episode in which a principal character goes mad. Particularly common in opera seria (e.g., Handel's *Orlando*) and in 19th-c. Italian opera (e.g., Donizetti's *Lucia*).

maestro (Ital., "master"). A title given to composers and conductors in Italy, in other countries more loosely to musicians in general. In earlier times, various combined forms described the musician in charge of a performance: the *maestro al cembalo* directed from the keyboard, the *maestro concertatore* from the podium.

Magic Flute, The. See *Zauberflöte, Die*.

Magini-Coletti, Antonio. Baritone; b. Iesi, near Ancona, Italy, 1855; d. Rome, July 21, 1912. Studied in Rome; debut as Valentin, Costanzi, 1882; sang at La Scala (1887–89, 1900–03), including Wagner roles. Created Frank in *Edgar*, 1889. In his only Met season, he sang 18 perfs. as Capulet (debut, Dec. 14, 1891), Nevers (*Huguenots*), Telramund, Pizarro (*Fidelio*), Amonasro, Escamillo, Alfio, and di Luna.

Mahagonny. See *Aufstieg und Fall der Stadt Mahagonny*.

Mahler, Gustav. Composer and conductor; b. Kalischt [now Kaliště], Bohemia, July 7, 1860; d. Vienna, May 18, 1911. Today celebrated for his symphonies and songs, he was one of the most important conductors of his day. He studied in Vienna with Fuchs and Krenn, then held positions in Kassel (1883–85), Prague (1885–86), Leipzig (1886–88; in 1888 he made a successful performing edition of Weber's unfinished *Die drei Pintos*), Budapest (1888–91), and Hamburg (1891–97). During his years as director of the Vienna Court Opera (1897–1907), his integrated productions of Mozart and Wagner in collaboration with designer Alfred Roller, his support of radical artists such as

Schoenberg, combined with Vienna's strong anti-semitic tradition, made him a figure of controversy, leading to his eventual departure for N.Y. His Met debut (*Tristan*, Jan. 1, 1908) was praised as "strikingly vital," though some found his interpretations self-indulgent and criticized his textual alterations. While at the house, he led *Don Giovanni*, *Walküre*, *Siegfried*, *Fidelio*, *Figaro*, the first American *Bartered Bride* and *Queen of Spades*. After Toscanini's arrival, Mahler accepted the conductorship of the N.Y. Philharmonic (1909–11). Victim of an incurable infection in early 1911, he returned to Vienna in May and died.

Maid of Orleans, The. Opera in 4 acts by Tchaikovsky; libretto by the composer, after V.A. Zhukovsky's translation of Schiller's tragedy.

First perf., St. Petersburg, Maryinsky, Feb. 25, 1881. U.S. prem., Reno, Nevada Opera Guild, May 13, 1976.

An opera best recalled today for the title character's famous aria of farewell. The action, set in France, 1430–31, follows Joan of Arc (ms) from her decision to take up her arms to her execution at the stake.

Maid of Pskov, The. Opera in 4 acts by Rimsky-Korsakov; libretto by the composer, after Lev Alexandrovich Mey's drama.

First perf., St. Petersburg, Maryinsky, Jan. 13, 1873: Platonova, Orlov, Petrov. Revised version, St. Petersburg, Panayevsky, Apr. 18, 1895.

Also known as *Ivan the Terrible*, this opera became a favorite vehicle for Chaliapin. In 16th-c. Russia, moved by a reunion with his long lost daughter Olga (s), Ivan the Terrible (bs) agrees to spare the city of Pskov. However, the girl is accidentally shot when her fiancé Tusha (t) attempts to rescue her.

Maria Malibran as Romeo in *I Capuleti e i Montecchi*

Maison, René. Tenor; b. Frameries, Belgium, Nov. 24, 1895; d. Mont-Doré, France, July 15, 1962. Studied at Brussels and Paris Conservatories; debut as Rodolfo, Geneva, 1920. Sang at Monte Carlo, Paris Opéra-Comique, Covent Garden, Chicago (1927–32), Buenos Aires (1934–37). Met debut as Stolzing, Feb. 3, 1936; in 8 seasons, he sang 84 perfs. of 14 roles, including Florestan, Lohengrin, Don José, Samson, and Hoffmann.

Maître de Chapelle, Le (The Choirmaster). Opera in 2 acts by Paer; libretto by Sophie Gay, after Duval's comedy *Le Souper Imprévu ou Le Chanoine de Milan*.

First perf., Paris, Opéra-Comique, Mar. 29, 1821: Boulanger, Gereol. U.S. prem., New Orleans, Castle Garden, Nov. 21, 1848. Met prem., New Theater, Dec. 9, 1909 (in Ital. as *Il Maestro di Cappella*): Gluck, Pini-Corsi, c. Podesti. 3 perfs. in 1 season.

A once-popular comedy, a vehicle for a virtuoso comic bass who must imitate all the instruments of the orchestra.

Makropoulos Affair, The. Opera in 3 acts by Janáček; libretto by the composer, after Karel Capek's drama.

First perf., Brno, Dec. 18, 1926: Čvanová, Otava, E. Olsovsky, c. Neumann. U.S. prem., San Francisco, Nov. 19, 1966 (in Eng.): Collier, Dempsey, Ludgin, c. Horenstein.

One of Janáček's powerful and unconventional examinations of a woman's psyche and fate.

Prague, the 1920s. Thanks to the effects of an elixir of life, Elena Makropoulos (s) has lived over three centuries in various guises; she is now an opera singer named Emilia Marty. Fearful that the effects of the elixir are about to end, she makes extraordinary efforts to recover its formula from among the papers of a long-standing lawsuit between Albert Gregor (t) and Baron Jaroslav Prus (bar). In the end, weary of life and no longer capable of emotion, Elena accepts her mortality; dying, she gives the formula to the girl Kristina (ms), who quickly burns it.

Malas, Spiro. Bass; b. Baltimore, Md., Jan. 28, 1933. Studied at Peabody Conservatory, Baltimore, and in N.Y.; debut as Marco (*Schicchi*), Baltimore Opera, 1959. Won Met Auditions, 1961. N.Y.C. Opera debut as Spinellocchio (*Schicchi*), 1961; toured Australia with Sutherland, 1965. Met debut as Sulpice (*Fille*), Oct. 8, 1983; subsequent roles with the company have included Zuniga (*Carmen*), Mozart's Bartolo, Frank (*Fledermaus*), and the Sacristan (*Tosca*).

Malfitano, Catherine. Soprano; b. New York, April 18, 1948. Studied at Manhattan School of Music; debut as Nannetta (*Falstaff*), Central City, Colo., 1972. Sang with Minnesota Opera, then with N.Y.C. Opera (debut, Mimi, 1974), where she remained until 1979, then joined the Met as Gretel (Dec. 24, 1979). Other Met roles include Violetta, Konstanze, Juliette, Micaela, and Massenet's Manon. Has sung widely in Europe, including Salzburg (Servilia in *Clemenza*, 1976), Vienna (Violetta, 1982) and Munich Festival (Lulu, 1985).

Malibran [née Garcia], **Maria.** Mezzo-soprano; b. Paris, Mar. 24, 1808; d. Manchester, England, Sep. 23, 1836. Elder daughter of tenor and teacher Manuel Garcia, sister of mezzo Pauline Viardot. After rigorous study with her father, she first appeared in public at age six, and made her London debut as Rosina at the King's Theatre in 1825. She took part in her father's N.Y. season (1825–26), and while in America married (briefly and unhappily) a French merchant, Eugène Malibran. Returning to Europe in 1827, she performed regularly in Paris (debut, Semiramide, Théâtre Italien, 1828) and London (Rossini's Desdemona, King's 1829). In Italy, she sang in Bologna (Bellini's Romeo, 1832), Naples (Amina, 1833), and at La Scala, where her debut role of Norma (1834) was followed by Desdemona, Amina, Romeo, and in 1835 by Adina, Rosina, and Maria Stuarda. Later London roles included Susanna (Covent Garden, 1833), Fidelio (Covent Garden, 1835), and the heroine of Balfe's *Maid of Artois* (Drury Lane, 1836). In 1836 she married the Belgian violinist Charles de Bériot, but died from the complications of a riding accident that summer, when she was pregnant. An exciting, temperamental, and troubling artist, Malibran was given to audacious improvisation; her father's efforts to extend her high notes had led to vocal unevenness alongside her great agility, and her performances are said to have varied greatly, depending on her mood and inspiration.

Malipiero, Gian Francesco. Composer; b. Venice, Mar. 18, 1882; d. Treviso, Aug. 1, 1973. Studied with Bossi in Venice and Bologna. Influenced by the French impressionists and by Monteverdi, Frescobaldi, and Vivaldi, whose works he transcribed and edited throughout his career. His vast output of stylized and symbolist operatic work, little known outside of Italy, includes the trilogy *L'Orfeide* (1925); the mystery *S. Francesco d'Assisi* (1922); *Tre Commedie Goldoniane* (1926); and *Torneo Notturno* (1931). Malipiero's nephew **Riccardo Malipiero** (b. Milan, July 24, 1914) studied with his uncle at Venice Conservatory and has composed several operas, including the 12-tone *Minnie la Candida* (1942), the opera buffa *La Donna è Mobile* (1954), and the television opera *Battono alla Porta* (1962).

Maliponte, Adriana. Soprano; b. Brescia, Italy, Dec. 26, 1942. Studied at Mulhouse Conservatory and in Como with Carmen Melis; debut as Mimi, Nuovo, Milan, 1958. Sang at La Scala, Paris Opéra and Opéra-Comique, where she created Sardula (*Last Savage*), and Covent Garden. After her Met debut as Mimi (Mar. 22, 1971), she sang 11 roles there in the early 70s, notably Micaela, Luisa Miller, and Amelia (*Boccanegra*), then returned in 1985 as Alice Ford.

Mamelles de Tirésias, Les (The Breasts of Tiresias). Opera in prologue and 2 acts by Poulenc; libretto by Guillaume Apollinaire.

First perf., Paris, Maubel Conservatory, June 3, 1947 (a week later at Opéra-Comique): Duval, Jeantet, Payen, c. Wolff. U.S. prem., Waltham, Mass., Brandeis U., June 13, 1953: Curtin, McCracken, Goss, c. Bernstein. Met prem., Feb. 20, 1981: Malfitano, Monk, Holloway, c. Rosenthal, d. Hockney, p. Dexter. 25 perfs. in 3 seasons.

Apollinaire's surrealist farce of 1917 encouraging postwar repopulation proved apt for Poulenc's irreverent operatic setting in the aftermath of World War II.

Zanzibar, an imaginary town on the French Riviera, 1910. Thérèse (s) announces her conversion to feminism, defies her husband, and opens her blouse to rid herself of her breasts (balloons, which she explodes) since they are a cause of sin. She will now be known as Tirésias, and her husband must assume the role of housewife and bear children. He does so – more than 40,000 of them in a single day – and sets to speculating on how they will make his fortune. Thérèse/Tirésias, after appearing in the guise of a fortune-teller to recommend fecundity, reveals herself and rejoins her delighted husband.

Mancinelli, Luigi. Composer and conductor; b. Orvieto, Italy, Feb. 6, 1848; d. Rome, Feb. 2, 1921. After conducting extensively in Italy (1874–86), he was chief conductor at Covent Garden (1888–1905) and the Met (1893–1903, except two seasons); his opera *Ero e Leandro* was performed at both theaters. At the Met, he led over 35 works, including Wagner as well as the first American *Tosca*.

Manon. Opera in 5 acts by Massenet; libretto by Henri Meilhac and Philippe Gille, after Abbé Prévost's novel *L'Histoire du Chevalier des Grieux et de Manon Lescaut*.

First perf., Paris, Opéra-Comique, Jan. 19, 1884: Heilbronn, Talazac, Taskin, c. Danbé. U.S. prem., N.Y., Academy of Music, Dec. 23, 1885 (in Ital.): Hauk, Giannini, del Puente, c. Arditi. Met prem., Jan. 16, 1895: Sanderson, J. de Reszke, Ancona, c. Bevignani, p. Parry. Later Met productions: Feb 3, 1909: Farrar, Caruso, Scotti, c. Spetrino, d. Rovescalli/Maison Chiappa, p. Speck; Dec. 22, 1928: Bori, Gigli, de Luca, c. Hasselmans, d. Urban, p. Wymetal; Dec. 3, 1954 ("revised"): de los Angeles, Valletti, Corena, c. Monteux, d. Meyer, p. Yannopoulos; Oct. 17, 1963: Moffo, Gedda, Guarrera, c. Schippers, d. Maximowna, p. Rennert; Feb. 6, 1987: Malfitano, Gulyás, Holloway, c. Rosenthal, d. & p. Ponnelle. Manon has also been sung at the Met by Moore,

Manon – Poster. Engraving by Antonin-Marie Chatinière (b. 1828)

Sayão, Albanese; Des Grieux by Crooks, Kullman, di Stefano. 145 perfs. in 34 seasons.

Massenet's most successful opera, marked by his typical melodic devices at their freshest and by his lively sympathy for the fully-drawn title character.

France, 1721. In Amiens, Manon (s), a young beauty with an adventurous spirit for which she is being sent away to a convent, meets the handsome Chevalier des Grieux (t) on her journey. The two fall in love and impulsively fly to Paris, where they live together. Confronted by her disapproving cousin Lescaut (bar), Des Grieux assures him that he intends to marry the girl. However, Comte des Grieux (bs), the young man's father, disapproves of their liaison and has his son abducted. Manon does not warn her lover, for she has decided to accept the tantalizing life of luxury offered her by the nobleman de Brétigny (bar). Later, when she learns that the unhappy Des Grieux has entered a seminary and is about to become an abbé, she rushes to him and with impassioned pleading wins him back. In a gambling-house altercation, Des Grieux is accused of cheating and the lovers are arrested; Des Grieux is freed by the intervention of his father, but Manon is condemned to exile. On the road to Le Havre, Manon is too weak to escape with Des Grieux; after begging his forgiveness for her excesses, the repentant Manon dies in his arms.

Manon Lescaut. Opera in 4 acts by Puccini, libretto by Marco Praga, Domenico Oliva, Illica, Giacosa, Giulio Ricordi, and Puccini, after the Abbé Prévost's novel.

First perf., Turin, Regio, Feb. 1, 1893: Ferrani, Cremonini, Moro, Polonini, c. Pomé. U.S. prem., Philadelphia, Grand Opera House, Aug. 29, 1894: Kört-Kronold, Montegriffo, Ganor, Viviani, c. Hinrichs. Met prem., Jan. 18, 1907: Cavalieri, Caruso, Scotti, Rossi, c. Vigna, d. J. Fox, p. Dufriche. Later Met productions: Nov. 23, 1949: Kirsten, Bjoerling, Valdengo, Baccaloni, c. Antonicelli, d. Krehan-Crayon, p. Graf; Mar. 17, 1980: Scotto, Domingo, Elvira, Capecchi, c. Levine, d. Heeley, p. Menotti. Manon has also been sung at the Met by Bori, Alda, Muzio, Albanese, Steber, Tebaldi, Kabaiwanska, L. Price, Zylis-Gara, Freni; Des Grieux by Martinelli, Gigli, Johnson, Tucker, del Monaco, Bergonzi. 167 perfs. in 30 seasons.

Puccini's first fully characteristic and successful work, still prized for its melodic impetus and for the arias of Manon and Des Grieux.

France, late 18th c. The Chevalier des Grieux (t) sees Manon (s) on her way to a convent, accompanied by her brother Lescaut (bar). The chevalier speaks to her, and they quickly fall in love; commandeering a carriage in which old Geronte (bs) had himself hoped to abduct the girl, they go off together to Paris. Eventually Manon, unable to resist Geronte's wealth, leaves Des Grieux. When her lover reappears, they declare renewed passion. Before they escape together, Manon pauses to gather some jewels her protector has given her; the delay results in their capture by the police Geronte has summoned. Manon is deported to New Orleans, and Des Grieux begs permission to board ship with her. In America, he helps her escape from her sentence; they go off in search of an English colony, but the exhausted girl dies in the wilderness.

Manru. Opera in 3 acts by Paderewski; libretto (in Ger.) by Alfred Nossig, after J.I. Kraszewski's novel *The Cabin Behind the Wood*.

First perf., Dresden, May 29, 1901: Krull, Anthes,

Manon Lescaut – (1959). Richard Tucker and Renata Tebaldi

Scheidemantel. U.S. & Met prem., Feb. 14, 1902: Sembrich, Scheff, Homer, Bandrowski, Bispham, c. Damrosch. 4 perfs. in 1 season.

Paderewski's only opera tells of the Galician maiden Ulana (s), who fails to overcome the inconstancy of her gypsy lover Manru (t) and drowns herself in despair.

Manski, Dorothee. Soprano; b. New York, Mar. 11, 1895; d. Atlanta, Ga., Feb. 24, 1967. Raised in Germany, she appeared in Max Reinhardt productions in Berlin. U.S. and Met debut, Nov. 5, 1927, as Witch (*Hänsel*), her most familiar role; she sang 14 consecutive seasons there, primarily in German roles, including Gutrune, Venus, Herodias, and occasional Brünnhildes. After retiring in 1941, taught at Indiana U.

Mansouri, Lotfi. Producer; b. Teheran, Iran, June 15, 1929. Opera training with Lotte Lehmann and Herbert Graf; debut, *Tosca* (Los Angeles, 1959). Staff stage director, Zurich (1960–64) and Grand Theater, Geneva (1965–74); general director, Opera Canada, Toronto (since 1977). His production of *Esclarmonde* was seen at the Met (1976).

Mantelli, Eugenia. Mezzo-soprano; b. c. 1860; d. Lisbon, March 3, 1926. After her debut as Kaled (*Roi de Lahore*), Treviso, 1883, she sang in Germany, South America, England, and Russia. Met debut as Amneris, Nov. 23, 1894; in six seasons, she sang 127 perfs. of 19 roles, including Siebel, Amneris, Urbain (*Huguenots*), Ortrud, and Azucena.

Manuguerra, Matteo. Baritone; b. Tunis, c. 1925, of Italian parents. After World War II, began vocal study at age 35 with Umberto Landi, Buenos Aires; debut as Valentin (*Faust*), Lyon, 1962. U.S. debut as Gérard (*Chénier*), Seattle, 1968. Met debut as Enrico (*Lucia*), Jan. 11, 1971; appeared there frequently in the '70s, and occasionally thereafter, as Barnaba, Alfio, Carlo (*Forza*), Amonasro, and other Italian roles.

Man Without a Country. Opera in 2 acts by W. Damrosch; libretto by Arthur Guiterman, after Edward Everett Hale's story.
First perf., N.Y., Met, May 12, 1937: Traubel, Carron, c. W. Damrosch. 5 perfs. in 2 seasons.
Damrosch's last opera. Philip Nolan (t), tried for his part in Aaron Burr's conspiracy, is sentenced to life at sea without news of his country. Regret makes him a patriot, and he dies in battle with pirates.

Maometto II. Opera in 2 acts by Rossini; libretto by Cesare della Valle, after his play *Anna Erizo*.
First perf., Naples, San Carlo, Dec. 3, 1820: Colbran, Comelli, Nozzari, Galli.
Rossini's penultimate opera for Naples, revised for Paris as *Le Siège de Corinthe*, is set in Negroponte, the Venetian colony in Greece, in the 15th c. Anna (ms), daughter of the governor, falls in love with the disguised Turkish emperor Maometto II (bs), but chooses duty over love; the Turks overrun Negroponte.

Mapleson, James H. Impresario; b. London, Mar. 4, 1830; d. London, Nov. 14, 1901. Studied violin at Royal Academy of Music and singing with Mazzucato in Milan; he appeared at Verona under the pseudonym Enrico Mariani and unsuccessfully under his own name in London. Between 1861 and 1889, he managed numerous seasons of Italian opera at various London theaters, including the Lyceum, Covent Garden, Drury Lane, and Her Majesty's. In the U.S., between 1878 and 1897, he presented seasons at the Academy of Music, N.Y., and coast-to-coast tours with stars such as Patti, with wildly varying financial success. He styled himself, without justification, "Colonel," and wrote entertaining if unreliable memoirs.

Mapleson, Lionel. Librarian; b. London, Oct. 23, 1865; d. New York, Dec. 21, 1937. Nephew of James H. Mapleson, he came to the U.S. and joined the Met orchestra as a violinist in 1889. Soon thereafter, he became the house's librarian, serving until his death, one of the company's longest tenures of service. In the early years of the century, he made experimental cylinder recordings during Met performances; those that survive were published in full by the N.Y. Public Library (1985).

Marchesi [née Graumann], **Mathilde.** Mezzo-soprano and teacher; b. Frankfurt, Germany, Mar. 24, 1821; d. London, Nov. 17, 1913. Studied with Felice Ronconi in Frankfurt, Nicolai in Vienna, and later with Garcia in Paris; concert debut in Frankfurt, 1844. A successful concert singer in Germany and London, often with baritone Salvatore Marchesi, whom she married in 1852. While based in Berlin, where she sang at the Court Opera, she made her only stage appearance, as Rosina, Bremen, 1853. She taught at Vienna Conservatory (1854–61, 1869–78), Cologne Conservatory (1865–68), and privately in Paris, where she opened her own school in 1881. Her pupils included Eames, Calvé, Gerster, Garden, Melba, and Sanderson.

Marchetti, Filippo. Composer; b. Bolognola, Macerata, Italy, Feb. 26, 1831; d. Rome, Jan. 18, 1902. Studied with Lillo and Conti at Naples Conservatory. After the success of *Gentile da Varano* (1856), he had difficulty competing with Verdi's ascendancy. Later, *Romeo e Giulietta* (1865) and the well-constructed *Ruy Blas* (1869), after Hugo, had a considerable vogue, though his final operas met with indifference.

Marchi, Emilio de. See *de Marchi, Emilio*.

Marconi, Francesco. Tenor; b. Rome, May 14, 1853; d. Rome, Feb. 5, 1916. Studied with Bartolini and Persichini in Rome; debut as Faust, Reale, Madrid, 1878. Subsequently appeared at La Scala (debut, Duke, 1880), Covent Garden (1883–84) and in Spain, Portugal, and Russia. In N.Y., sang first U.S. Otello (Academy of Music, 1888).

Marcoux, Vanni. See *Vanni-Marcoux*.

Mardones, José. Bass; b. Fontecha, Spain, 1869; d. Madrid, May 4, 1932. Studied at Madrid Conservatory; sang first in operetta. After operatic appearances in South America, Spain, and Portugal, joined Boston Opera (1909–17). Met debut as Ramfis, Nov. 12, 1917; in 9 seasons, sang 264 perfs. of 21 roles, including Sparafucile, Rossini's Basilio, Mefistofele, the Padre Guardiano, Pimen, Raimondo (*Lucia*), and Escamillo.

Maretzek [Mareček], **Max.** Impresario and conductor; b. Brünn [now Brno], Moravia, June 28, 1821; d. New York, May 14, 1897. Played violin and conducted in Europe; then came to N.Y. as conductor in 1849. Between 1849 and 1878, he managed various opera companies, at the Academy of Music, N.Y., and touring the U.S., Cuba, and Mexico; he presented the American premieres of many works, including *Traviata* and *Trovatore*.

Maria Golovin. Opera in 3 acts by Menotti; libretto by the composer.
First perf., Brussels World's Fair, U.S. Pavilion, Aug. 20, 1958: Duval, Neway, Handt, c. P.H. Adler. U.S. prem., N.Y., Martin Beck Theater, Nov. 5, 1958, with a similar cast.
Commissioned by NBC, this characteristic Menotti melodrama is set in a small frontier town, c. 1919. Maria Golovin (s), awaiting her husband's return from a prisoner-of-war camp, becomes mistress of Donato (bs-bar), a young blind man who, in a fit of jealousy, tries to kill her.

Mariani, Angelo. Conductor; b. Ravenna, Italy, Oct. 11, 1821; d. Genoa, June 13, 1873. One of the first Italians to establish professional identity as a conductor, he was closely associated with Rossini from 1843 and with Verdi from 1846. Director of Carlo Felice, Genoa (1852–73), and Comunale, Bologna (1860–73), where he led first Italian performances of *Lohengrin* (1871) and *Tannhäuser* (1872). Known for his charm, skill, insistence on rehearsal, and dedication to high standards of ensemble.

Maria Stuarda. Opera in 3 acts by Donizetti; libretto by Giuseppe Bardari, after Andrea Maffei's translation of Schiller's play *Maria Stuart*.
First perf., (censored version, as *Buondelmonte*), Naples, San Carlo, Oct. 18, 1834: Ronzi de Begnis, Delserre, Pedrazzi, Crespi. First perf., original version, Milan, La

Scala, Dec. 30, 1835. Malibran, Puzzi-Toso, Reina, Marini, Novelli. U.S. prem., N.Y., Carnegie Hall, Nov. 16, 1964 (concert perf.): Hoffman, Jordan, Traxel, Michalski, Metcalf, c. Scherman. U.S. stage prem., N.Y.C. Opera, Mar. 7, 1972: Sills, Tinsley, Stewart, Fredericks, Devlin, c. Rudel.

The opera is dominated by the spirited music for the rival queens and their dramatic (if unhistorical) confrontation.

1567, London and Northamptonshire. Leicester (t) and Talbot (bar) are concerned for Maria Stuarda (Mary Stuart, s), imprisoned in Fotheringay Castle. Although jealous of Maria's closeness to Leicester and fearful of her claim to the throne, Queen Elisabetta (Elizabeth I, s) agrees to visit her. Maria is counselled by Leicester to be submissive. Her suspicions encouraged by Cecil (bs), Elisabetta is offended by Maria's proud bearing and insults her. When Maria reacts by calling the Queen a "vile bastardess," Elisabetta threatens her with death. At Westminster, Cecil persuades Elisabetta to sign the death warrant; Leicester pleads for Maria's life, but too late. At Fotheringay, Maria prays for the forgiveness of those who have wronged her; with the distraught Leicester standing by, she walks to the block.

Mario, Giovanni. Tenor; b. Cogliari, Italy, Oct. 17, 1810; d. Rome, Dec. 11, 1883. After desertion from the army and exile for his radical politics, he studied in Paris and made his debut at the Paris Opéra in the title role of *Robert le Diable* (1838). London debut as Gennaro in *Lucrezia Borgia* (1839) at Her Majesty's opposite Grisi, who became his long-time companion and colleague. In the 1840s at the Théâtre Italien, he became the heir to Rubini's florid repertory, and later sang Manrico and Alfredo; in London in 1847 he moved from Her Majesty's to Covent Garden, where he sang regularly until his retirement (1871), adding roles such as Fernand (*Favorite*), Raoul (*Huguenots*), Eléazar (*Juive*), Tamino, the Duke of Mantua, and finally Gounod's Faust and Roméo. Though free to return to Italy after 1848, he never sang there professionally; his winters were passed in St. Petersburg (1849–53, 1866–70), Paris (1853–64), N.Y. (1854), and Madrid (1859, 1864). Graceful, sweet-toned, and agile of voice, Mario was an exceptional exponent of Rossini's Almaviva and many Donizetti and Bellini roles (taking the notes above high C in falsetto), but he mastered as well the more dramatic demands of the newer works.

Mario [Tillotson], **Queena.** Soprano; b. Akron, Ohio, Aug. 21, 1896; d. New York, May 28, 1951. First a journalist, she studied voice with Oscar Saenger and Sembrich; debut as Olympia (*Hoffmann*) with San Carlo Opera, N.Y., 1918. After her Met debut (Micaela, Nov. 30, 1922), she sang there in 17 consecutive seasons, in roles including Inès (*Africaine*), Micaela, Antonia (*Hoffmann*), Marguerite, Nedda, Gilda, Juliette, and Sophie; she was heard as Gretel in the first Met radio broadcast, Dec. 25, 1931. Also sang in San Francisco (1923–32). Married to conductor Wilfrid Pelletier (1925–36), she succeeded Sembrich at Curtis Institute, Philadelphia, 1931, and later taught at Juilliard.

marionette opera. Over the centuries, marionette theaters have occasionally presented opera, sometimes original works, such as those Haydn composed for Eszterháza. Today, the Salzburg Marionette Theater (which performs to recordings) is the best-known troupe.

Maritana. Opera in 3 acts by Wallace; libretto by Edward Fitzball, after d'Ennery's play *Don César de Bazan*.

First perf., London, Drury Lane, Nov. 15, 1845. U.S. prem., Philadelphia, Walnut Street, Nov. 9, 1846.

After *The Bohemian Girl*, this score, of considerable sweep and vigor, moved English opera even further from its ballad-opera origins. In Madrid, to win favor with the Queen, the unscrupulous Don José (bar) concocts a complicated and unsuccessful plan that involves having the gypsy singer Maritana (s) seduced by the King (bar).

Markova, Alicia [Lillian Alicia Marks]. Dancer and choreographer; b. Hackney, England, Dec. 1, 1910. Leading British ballerina in 1930s, she danced widely until her 1962 farewell, and choreographed many operas. Guest appearances at Met in opera ballets (1952–58; debut, *Fledermaus*); director, Metropolitan Opera Ballet, 1963–69.

Mârouf, Savetier du Caire (Marouf, Cobbler of Cairo). Opera in 5 acts by Rabaud; libretto by Lucien Népoty, after *The 1,001 Nights*.

First perf., Paris, Opéra-Comique, May 15, 1914: Davelli, Périer, Vieuille, c. Ruhlmann. U.S. & Met prem., Dec. 19, 1917: Alda, de Luca, Rothier, c. Monteux, d. Gros/Platt, p. Ordynski. 13 perfs. in 4 seasons.

In this picturesque comedy, the cobbler Mârouf (t or bar) leaves his cruel wife, poses as a wealthy merchant in another city, wins the Sultan's daughter (s), and with the aid of a magic genie becomes really wealthy.

Marriage of Figaro, The. See *Nozze di Figaro, Le*.

Marschner, Heinrich August. Composer; b. Zittau, near Dresden, Aug. 16, 1795; d. Hanover, Dec. 14, 1861. Studied with Schicht in Leipzig. His first success, *Heinrich IV und d'Aubigné* (1820), was produced by Weber in Dresden, where Marschner worked until 1826, moving then to Leipzig and in 1830 to Hanover. His major successes were *Der Vampyr* (1828); *Der Templer und die Jüdin*, after Scott's *Ivanhoe* (1829); and *Hans Heiling* (1833), which established his national reputation. Enlarging on Weber's heritage, Marschner incorporated into the singspiel grand finales and atmospheric interludes of considerable dramatic impact, and anticipated Wagner by experimenting with leitmotives, enlarging the dramatic role of the orchestra, and creating complex, sometimes supernatural central characters torn between good and evil.

Martha, oder Der Markt von Richmond (Martha, or The Richmond Fair). Opera in 4 acts by Flotow; libretto by "W. Friedrich" (Friedrich Wilhelm Riese), after St. Georges' ballet-pantomime *Lady Henriette, ou La Servante de Greenwich*.

First perf., Vienna, Kärntnertor, Nov. 25, 1847: Zerr, Schwarz, Ander, Formes. U.S. prem., N.Y., Niblo's Garden, Nov. 1, 1852 (in Eng.). Met prem., Mar. 14, 1884 (in Ital.): Sembrich, Trebelli, Stagno, Novara, c. Vianesi. Later Met productions: Dec. 11, 1915 (in Ital.): Hempel, Ober, Caruso, de Luca, c. Bavagnoli, p. Baudu; Dec. 14, 1923: Alda, Howard, Gigli, de Luca, c. Papi, d. Urban, p. Wymetal; Jan. 26, 1961 (in Eng.): de Los Angeles, Elias, Tucker, Tozzi, c. Verchi, d. Smith/Motley, p. Ebert, Lady Harriet has also been sung at the Met by Barrientos; Nancy by Scalchi, Mantelli, Homer, Walker; Lionel by Campanini, Valero, Bonci, Kónya; Plunkett by E. de Reszke, Plançon, Journet, Didur, Gramm. 69 perfs. in 20 seasons.

Continuously popular in Germany for its plentiful melody and sentimental tale, *Martha* was once also an international staple in Italian translation.

In and near Richmond, about 1710. For a lark, Lady Harriet (s) and her maid Nancy (c) go to Richmond Fair disguised as peasant girls and hire themselves out as servants to two young farmers, Lionel (t) and Plunkett (bs). Despite the ladies' ineptitude at cooking and spinning, their employers fall in love with them. Then the women steal away, leaving Lionel in particular heartbroken; eventually he proves to be the lost heir to the Earl of Derby, and all can be reunited.

Martin, Frank. Composer; b. Geneva, Sep. 15, 1890; d. Naarden, Nov. 21, 1974. Studied with Lauber and at Dalcroze Institute. His early music was influenced by Franck and the French impressionists, but he later adopted Schoenberg's serialism without abandoning an extended form of tonality. In addition to the occasionally staged oratorio *Le Vin Herbé* (1940) and the "oratorio-spectacle" *Le Mystère de la Nativité* (1959), Martin composed two operas: *Der Sturm*, after Shakespeare's *The Tempest* (1956) and *Monsieur de Pourceaugnac*, after Molière (1963).

Martin, Janis. Mezzo-soprano, later soprano; b. Sacramento, Calif., Aug. 16, 1939. Studied in San Francisco and N.Y.; debut as Teresa (*Sonnambula*), San Francisco, 1960, where she later sang Marina, Venus, and Meg Page. N.Y.C. Opera debut as Mrs. Grose (*Turn of the Screw*, 1962). Met debut as Flora (*Traviata*), Dec. 19, 1962; she sang for 3 seasons in mezzo parts, then returned in 1973 as Marie (*Wozzeck*), Sieglinde, and Kundry. Other appearances in Bayreuth (Magdalene and Fricka, 1968), Chicago (Tosca, 1971), Berlin (Deutsche Oper, 1971–74), Covent Garden (Marie, 1973), and La Scala (*Erwartung*, 1980).

Martin, Marvis. Soprano; b. Miami, Fla. Studied at U. of Miami and Manhattan School, N.Y. Met debut as Princess (*Enfant*), Jan. 7, 1983; subsequent roles there include the Celestial Voice (*Don Carlos*), Xenia (*Boris*), Echo (*Ariadne*), and Clara (*Porgy*). European opera debut as Ismene (*Mitridate*), Aix, 1982.

Martin, Riccardo [Hugh Whitfield Martin]. Tenor; b. Hopkinsville, Ky., Nov. 18, 1874; d. New York, Aug. 11, 1952. Studied composition with MacDowell at Columbia U., voice with Escalais and Sbriglia in Paris; debut as Gounod's Faust, Nantes, 1904. U.S. debut as Canio, San Carlo Opera, New Orleans, 1906. Met debut as Boito's Faust, Nov. 20, 1907. Sang with Met, 1907–15 (created Quintus in *Mona*, Christian in *Cyrano*) and a single perf. in 1917, also with Boston Opera (1916–17) and Chicago Opera (1920–22).

Martinelli, Giovanni. Tenor; b. Montagnana, Italy, Oct. 22, 1885; d. New York, Feb. 2, 1969. After service as clarinetist in military band and an impromptu debut in his native town as the *Aida* Messenger (1908), he studied with Giuseppe Mandolini in Milan and made his formal debut as Ernani (dal Verme, 1910). Dick Johnson (*Fanciulla*) was his passport role; he sang it for his debuts in Rome (under Toscanini), Brescia, Naples (all 1911), Genoa, Monte Carlo, and La Scala (all 1912), and also at Covent Garden (debut, Cavaradossi, 1912) and during his first U.S. engagement in Philadelphia (debut, Cavaradossi, 1913). His Met debut role was Rodolfo (Nov. 20, 1913); a mainstay of the company for 32 seasons, he sang 663 perfs. (plus 221 on tour) of 36 roles, most often as Radames (92

times), Don José, Canio, and Manrico, also as Pinkerton, Puccini's Des Grieux, Raoul (*Huguenots*), Riccardo (*Ballo*), Edgardo, Gérald (*Lakmé*), Faust, Avito (*Amore dei Tre Re*), Milio (*Zazà*), Ernani, Alvaro (*Forza*), Samson, Arnold (*Tell*), Loris (*Fedora*), Eléazar (*Juive*), Chénier, Jean de Leyde (*Prophète*), Dick Johnson, Enzo, Vasco da Gama, Pollione, and Otello. He created Lefebvre (*Mme. Sans-Gêne*) and Fernando (*Goyescas*), and was the Met's first Paolo (*Francesca*), Huon (*Oberon*), Lenski (*Onegin*), Don Carlos, Gennaro (*Gioielli*), Heinrich (*Campana Sommersa*), and Adorno (*Boccanegra*). His last complete Met perf. was *Norma* on Mar. 8, 1945; on Nov. 20, 1963, a gala honored the fiftieth anniversary of his company debut.

After World War I, Martinelli's appearances outside the U.S. were restricted; he returned to Covent Garden in 1919 and in 1937, when his Otello and Calaf were acclaimed, and appeared in Buenos Aires, Havana, Paris, rarely in Italy. In America, he sang in Boston (1914), San Francisco (1923–39), Chicago (Ravinia Park, 1924–31; Chicago Opera, 1934–44), St. Louis (1934–41), Cincinnati (Zoo Opera, 1940–45), and Philadelphia (1945–50), often trying out new roles before singing them in N.Y. (Chicago saw his first Otello, also a unique Tristan opposite Flagstad, 1939). He retired in 1950, but sang the Emperor in *Turandot* at age 82 in Seattle. Initially viewed at the Met as an overly forceful singer, Martinelli survived the inevitable comparisons with Caruso; his brilliant, forward projection and broad phrasing were best suited to the heroic roles that he gradually assumed, and the tonal tension ever-present in his later years (superfluous in lyrical roles) was put to potent dramatic use in his memorable Otello.

Martini, Nino. Tenor; b. Verona, Italy, Aug. 7, 1902; d. Verona, Dec. 9, 1976. Studied in Italy and with Zenatello,

Giovanni Martinelli as Otello

Éva Marton as Gioconda

N.Y.; U.S. operatic debut with Philadelphia Opera, 1931. After his Met debut (Duke of Mantua, Dec. 28, 1933), he sang with the company there every season until 1946, in 65 perfs.; his roles included Rodolfo, Almaviva, Alfredo, and Edgardo. Also a popular singer on radio and in films.

Martinů, Bohuslav. Composer; b. Polička, Bohemia, Dec. 8, 1890; d. Liestal, near Basel, Switzerland, Aug. 28, 1959. Studied with Suk at Prague Conservatory and Roussel in Paris. From 1941 to 1953, he lived in the U.S., teaching at Tanglewood and Princeton U., then returned to Western Europe and continued to compose in a distinctive blend of the inter-war international style and Czech folk elements. Of his prewar operas, *Comedy on the Bridge* (1937), for radio, and *Julietta* (1938), his first major stage success, are still performed. His last opera, *The Greek Passion* (1961), after Kazantzakis, was presented at the Met in 1981 by the Indiana U. School of Music.

Marton [née Heinrich], **Éva.** Soprano; b. Budapest, June 18, 1943. Studied with Endre Rösler and Jenö Sipos, Liszt Academy, Budapest; debut as Kate Pinkerton, Margareten Island festival, 1967. Member of Budapest State Opera (debut as Queen of Shemahka in *Golden Cockerel*) 1968–72, in repertory including Handel's Rodelinda, Tosca, Countess Almaviva, and Tatiana. With Frankfurt Opera (1972–77), sang Countess and Alice Ford. Debuts in Vienna (Tosca, 1973), Munich (Donna Anna, 1974), Hamburg (Empress in *Frau*, 1977), La Scala (Leonora in *Trovatore*, 1978); sang Venus and Elisabeth at Bayreuth (1977). Met debut as Eva, Nov. 3, 1976; since then, she has also sung Chrysothemis, the Empress (*Frau*), Gioconda, Elisabeth, Ortrud, Elsa, Fidelio, Tosca, and Turandot. Sang Brünnhilde in San Francisco *Ring*, 1985. In German and Italian dramatic roles, Marton has revealed an imperious voice and temperament.

Martyrs, Les. See *Poliuto*.

Mary Queen of Scots. Opera in 3 acts by Musgrave; libretto by the composer, after the play by Amelia Elguera.

First perf., Edinburgh (Scottish Opera), Sep. 6, 1977: Wilson, Hillman, Dempsey, Gardner, Dean, c. Musgrave. U.S. prem., Norfolk, Va., Mar. 29, 1978: Putnam, Garrison, Busse, Gardner, Bell, c. Mark.

This fast-moving personal drama, drawing on the traditional scenic and musical resources of grand opera, tells (with certain liberties) of Mary's fate, from her accession to the Scottish throne to her flight into England.

Masaniello. See *Muette de Portici, La*.

Mascagni, Pietro. Composer; b. Livorno, Dec. 7, 1863; d. Rome, Aug. 2, 1945. Studied at Milan Conservatory with Ponchielli and Saladino; he left after two years to play in orchestras and conduct touring operetta companies, eventually marrying and settling in Puglia as a music teacher. He composed three operas, *Pinotta* (1880, perf. 1932), *Guglielmo Ratcliff* (c. 1885, perf. 1895), and *Cavalleria Rusticana* (1890); the last, submitted by Mascagni's wife, won Sonzogno's competition for one-act operas and was produced in Rome to enormous acclaim, ushering in an international vogue for verismo. Mascagni never repeated that success, though he came closer with the lyrical pastoral *L'Amico Fritz* (1891) and with *Iris* (1899), which leavened violence with Oriental exoticism, than with the straight verismo of *Silvano* (1895). *Le Maschere* (1901), based on commedia dell'arte, failed despite (or because of) a publicity-ridden multiple premiere; the medievalizing *Isabeau* (1911) and the historical *Il Piccolo Marat* (1921) achieved some circulation, though their dependence on violent declamation in high registers has had erosive effects on all but exceptional voices. The short-breathed structure with repeated high-impact climaxes that worked so well in the brief, fast-moving *Cavalleria* was not easily adapted to other purposes. Also active as a conductor (he toured the U.S. with an opera company, 1902–03), Mascagni sided with the Fascist regime and composed the bombastic *Nerone* (1935); disgraced after World War II, he died indigent, a victim of premature success and poor judgment. Other operas: *I Rantzau* (1892), the one-act *Zanetto* (1896), *Amica* (1905), *Parisina* (1913), *Lodoletta* (1917).

Maschere, Le (The Mask). Opera in prologue and 3 acts by Mascagni; libretto by Illica.

First perf., Jan. 17, 1901, simultaneously in Milan (La Scala), Venice (Fenice), Turin (Regio), Verona (Filarmonica), Genoa (Carlo Felice), and Rome (Costanzi); a Naples premiere scheduled for the same night was postponed; in Genoa, the opera was halted by hissing.

Mascagni's essay in commedia dell'arte was over-publicized and ill-received everywhere except in Rome, where he himself conducted; revivals have encouraged a gentler verdict.

Masini, Angelo. Tenor; b. Terra del Sole, near Forlì, Italy, Nov. 28, 1844; d. Forlì, Sep. 28, 1926. Studied with Gilda Minguzzi; debut as Pollione (*Norma*), Finale Emilia, 1867. Appeared in most Italian theaters, also in London, Moscow, Cairo, St. Petersburg, Lisbon, Buenos Aires, Vienna. Sang Verdi's *Requiem* under the composer in London, Paris, and Vienna, 1875; also Radames in first

Jules Massenet

Paris *Aida*, 1876. Continued to appear on stage until 1905, but left no recordings.

Masini, Galliano. Tenor, b. Livorno, Italy, 1896; d. Livorno, Feb. 15, 1986. Studied with Laura, Milan; debut as Cavaradossi, Livorno, 1924. Sang with Rome Opera, 1930–50, and at La Scala as Turiddu in 50th-anniversary *Cavalleria* under Mascagni, also at Chicago Opera, 1937–38. In his only Met season (debut, Edgardo in *Lucia*, Dec. 14, 1938), he sang 8 perfs., including Radames, Rodolfo, and Cavaradossi.

Maskarade (Masquerade). Opera in 3 acts by Nielsen; libretto by Vilhelm Andersen, after Ludvig Holberg's play.
First perf., Copenhagen, Royal Theater, Nov. 11, 1906: c. Nielsen. U.S. prem., St. Paul, Minn., June 23, 1972: Peil, Williams, Atherton, Christesen, Ware, c. Buketoff.
A comedy in an idiom resembling the popular Danish songs in which Nielsen later specialized, set in Copenhagen, spring 1723. Leander (t) doesn't want to propose to the girl his father has chosen, because he has fallen in love with Leonora (s), whom he has met at a masked ball. But the two women turn out to be one and the same.

Masked Ball, A. See *Ballo in Maschera, Un*.

Masnadieri, I (The Robbers). Opera in 4 acts by Verdi; libretto by Andrea Maffei, after Schiller's play *Die Räuber*.
First perf., London, Her Majesty's, July 22, 1847: Lind, Gardoni, Coletti, Lablache. U.S. prem., N.Y., Winter Garden, May 31, 1860.
The violence and irony of Schiller's drama proved unsuited to London taste, and though the role of Amalia, tailored to Jenny Lind, is a fine vehicle for a florid soprano, the opera has had comparatively few revivals.
Germany, beginning of 18th c. Carlo (t), elder son of Count Massimiliano Moor (bs), has taken up with questionable company at the university; at home, his envious brother Francesco (bar) plots to win the succession. Francesco sends his brother an unforgiving letter in his father's name, driving the impulsive Carlo into forming a band of brigands. Believing Carlo dead, Massimiliano collapses and is also believed dead. Francesco, now master, tries to win the hand of Carlo's beloved, Amalia (s), but she flees and encounters Carlo in a wood. Discovering his father near death in a dungeon,

Carlo makes his men swear to avenge him. Francesco escapes, but the brigands capture Amalia, and Carlo is in despair at being revealed as an outlaw. Amalia begs Carlo to kill her rather than desert her. Unable to go back on his oath to the brigands, he stabs her and gives himself up to the authorities.

Mason, Edith [Edith Barnes]. Soprano; b. St. Louis, Mo., Mar. 22, 1893; d. San Diego, Calif., Nov. 26, 1973. After a Boston Opera debut as Nedda (1912), she studied in Europe with Enrico Bertran, Cotogni, and Clément. European debut in Nice, 1914. In 2 Met seasons (debut, Sophie, Nov. 20, 1915), she sang Micaela, Musetta, Gretel, and other roles, and returned in 1935–36. She sang Mimi at La Scala (1923), Nannetta at Salzburg (1935) under Toscanini, and appeared regularly with Chicago Opera, 1921–41; married to conductor Giorgio Polacco.

masque, mask. A form of stage entertainment in 16th- and 17th-c. England, with poetry, music, dances, costumes, and scenery. Related to French *ballet du cour* and to the later English form of semi-opera (*q.v.*).

Massenet, Jules. Composer; b. Montand, near St. Étienne, May 12, 1842; d. Paris, Aug. 13, 1912. Studied with Thomas at Paris Conservatory, while gaining practical experience as an extra percussionist at the Opéra and as a cafe pianist; Prix de Rome, 1863. Several small commissions generated minor works such as *La Grand'-Tante* (1867) and *Don César de Bazan* (1872), and Pauline Viardot's sponsorship gained attention for the "sacred drama" *Marie-Magdeleine* (1873), the first of Massenet's many portraits of women torn between hedonism and spirituality. He was, above all, eclectic and adaptable, and his 27 operas show him wooing the public with a resourceful variety of strategies. Among his most successful works, *Le Roi de Lahore* (1877) exploits Oriental exoticism, *Hérodiade* (1881) a Wagnerian mode, *Manon* (1884) 18th-c. pastiche, *Werther* (1892) Tchaikovskyan passion, *Thaïs* (1894) voluptuous religiosity, *La Navarraise* verismo violence, *Le Jongleur de Notre-Dame* (1902) medieval pastiche. At his best, Massenet combines facility, stylistic versatility, and a cunning sense of theater, but his later works, including *Ariane* (1906) and *Roma* (1912), lapse into routine: he had been overtaken by fresher voices such as Debussy and Richard Strauss. His works remained in vogue while singing actresses such as Mary Garden were on hand, and have recently aroused renewed interest among impresarios of the obscure. As a teacher, he influenced a generation of French musicians; among his students at the Conservatory after 1878 were Bruneau, Koechlin, Hahn, Schmitt, Charpentier, and Rabaud. Other operas include *Le Cid* (1885), *Esclarmonde* (1885), *Sapho* (1897), *Cendrillon* (1899), *Thérèse* (1907), *Don Quichotte* (1910).
BIBLIOGRAPHY: James Harding, *Massenet* (London, 1970).

Materna, Amalie [Amalia]. Soprano; b. St. Georgen, Austria, July 10, 1844; d. Vienna, Jan. 18, 1918. Began career in Graz (1865), and sang operetta at Karlstheater, Vienna. Vienna Court Opera debut as Sélika (*Africaine*), 1869; she remained on the roster for 25 years, creating the title role in Goldmark's *Königin von Saba* (1875). For Wagner, she sang Brünnhilde in the first Bayreuth *Ring* (1876) and the first Kundry (1882); she also sang in the first Vienna *Walküre* (1877) and *Siegfried* (1878) and in the first Berlin *Ring* cycle (1881). In her only Met season, she sang 19 perfs. as Elisabeth (debut, Jan. 5, 1885), Valentine

(*Huguenots*), Rachel (*Juive*), and the *Walküre* Brünnhilde. She reappeared in N.Y. with Damrosch's company, 1894, then taught in Vienna. One of the first of the clarion dramatic sopranos called into being by Wagner's roles.

Mathis, Edith. Soprano; b. Lucerne, Switzerland, Feb. 11, 1938. Studied in Zurich and Lucerne; debut as Boy (*Zauberflöte*), Lucerne, 1956. Sang at Cologne (1959), Berlin (Deutsche Oper, 1963), Hamburg (1960–75). Met debut as Pamina, Jan. 19, 1970; in 6 seasons, she sang 31 perfs. as Ännchen (*Freischütz*), Marzelline (*Fidelio*), Sophie, Gerhilde, and Zerlina. Frequent appearances in Glyndebourne, Salzburg, and Munich.

Mathis der Maler (Mathis the Painter). Opera in 7 scenes by Hindemith; libretto by the composer, after the life of Matthias Grünewald.

First perf., Zurich, Stadttheater, May 28, 1938: Hellwig, Funk, Stig, c. Denzler. U.S. prem., Boston U. Theater, Feb. 17, 1956 (in Eng.).

Mainz, Germany, 1524. The painter Mathis (bar) finds himself becoming involved in the Peasants' Revolt, principally through the peasants' leader Schwalb (t) and his daughter Regina (s). His patron Albrecht (t), Archbishop of Mainz, decides to renounce worldly goods and become a hermit, and Mathis in turn is tempted to renounce his painting and devote himself to the peasants' cause. In an extended dream sequence (recreating two of Grünewald's paintings), he is convinced that the best way he can serve mankind is to concentrate on his art. Regina dies, and Mathis proceeds with new inspiration.

Matrimonio Segreto, Il (The Secret Marriage). Opera in 2 acts by Cimarosa; libretto by Giovanni Bertati, after Colman's and Garrick's comedy *The Clandestine Marriage*.

First perf., Vienna, Burgtheater, Feb. 7, 1792: Bussani, Bosello, Mandini. U.S. prem., N.Y., Italian Opera

Victor Maurel as Falstaff

House, Jan. 4, 1834. Met prem., Feb. 25, 1937 (in Eng.): Bodanya, Dickson, Petina, Rasely, Huehn, L. d'Angelo, c. Panizza, d. Jorgulesco. 2 perfs. in 1 season.

The most often revived opera of Cimarosa, a score representing the gracious best of Italian opera buffa in the generation before Rossini.

Bologna, 18th c. Geronimo (bs), an old merchant, wants his daughters Carolina (s) and Elisetta (s) to marry into nobility, but Carolina has already secretly wed Paolino (t). Hoping Geronimo might accept the situation cheerfully if Elisetta were suitably matched, Carolina and Paolino arrange for Count Robinson (bs) to ask for her hand. But the Count decides he prefers Carolina and wins her father's consent; the girls' aunt Fidalma (c) mistakes Paolino's pleas for help for a proposal; and Elisetta, jealous, conspires with Fidalma to have Carolina sent off to a convent. Complications mount until the revelation of the secret marriage compels resolution.

Matzenauer, Margaret [Margarethe, Margarete]. Mezzo-soprano; b. Temesvár, Hungary [now Timişoara, Romania], June 1, 1881; d. Van Nuys, Calif., May 19, 1963. Daughter of a conductor–composer and a dramatic soprano, she studied with Georgine von Januschowsky in Graz, Antonia Mielke and Franz Emerich in Berlin, later with Ernst Preuse (her first husband) in Munich; debut as Puck (*Oberon*), Strasbourg, 1901. Member, Munich Court Opera, 1905–11; sang small roles in Bayreuth, 1911. Met debut as Amneris, Nov. 13, 1911; in 19 seasons, she sang 315 perfs. of 31 roles, including *Walküre* Brünnhilde, Dalila, Kundry, Venus, Fidès (*Prophète*), Brangäne, Azucena, Marina, Eboli, Kostelnička (*Jenůfa*), Fidelio, and Isolde. Also appeared in Boston (1912–14), Buenos Aires (1912), London (Covent Garden debut, Ortrud, 1914), and Philadelphia (Klytemnästra, 1930). After 1938, she taught in N.Y. and California; Blanche Thebom is one of her pupils. Matzenauer was a singer of great authority, whose pursuit of soprano roles apparently took a toll on her rich voice.

Mauceri, John. Conductor; b. New York, Sep. 12, 1945. After study at Yale, he conducted the Yale Symphony (1968–74); operatic debut, *Saint of Bleecker Street*, Wolf Trap, 1973. Met debut, *Fidelio*, Jan. 2, 1976. Worked at Santa Fe, San Francisco (premiere of Imbrie's *Angle of Repose*, 1976), and N.Y.C. Opera (1977–82, conducting a dozen works). Debuts in 1984 at La Scala (*Quiet Place*) and Covent Garden (*Butterfly*). Music director of Scottish Opera (from 1987).

Maurel, Victor. Baritone; b. Marseilles, June 17, 1848; d. New York, Oct. 22, 1923. Studied in Marseilles and at Paris Conservatory with Duvernoy and Vauthrot; debut in his home town in *Guillaume Tell* (1867), appearing thereafter at Paris Opéra (debut, di Luna, 1869). At his La Scala debut in 1870, he created the Cacique (*Guarany*), in 1873 also creating Cambro in Gomez's *Fosca* there. At Covent Garden, he bowed as Renato (*Ballo*) in 1873 and reappeared until 1905, in roles including Mozart's Almaviva and Figaro, Don Carlo (*Ernani*), Papageno, Wolfram, the Dutchman, Assur (*Semiramide*), Germont, and Malatesta. Touring the U.S., he sang the first American Amonasro (Philadelphia, 1873). In 1879 he returned to the Paris Opéra as Hamlet, also singing Méphistophélès and Alphonse (*Favorite*). At La Scala in 1881 he sang the title role in Verdi's revised *Boccanegra*, returning there to create Iago (1889) and Falstaff (1893); he was also the first Tonio in *Pagliacci* (dal Verme, Milan,

1892). At the Met, he made his debut as Iago (Dec. 3, 1894), and in 3 seasons sang 60 perfs. of 12 roles, most often as Falstaff, Don Giovanni, and Nevers (*Huguenots*), also as Rigoletto, Amonasro, Telramund, Mozart's Figaro, Escamillo, Valentin, Massenet's Lescaut, and Nélusko (*Africaine*). After his 1905 retirement, he opened a singing school in London, then moved to N.Y. in 1909. Though not possessed of an overpowering voice, he was accounted a skillful and thoughtful actor, and his diction and phrasing were trenchant and subtle. Originally trained as a painter, he designed sets for a 1919 Met *Mireille*.

Mauro, Ermanno. Tenor; b. Trieste, Italy, Jan. 20, 1939. Studied with George Lambert, Royal Conservatory, Toronto; debut as Manrico, Edmonton, 1962. Has sung at Covent Garden (debut, Lamplighter in *Manon Lescaut*, 1968) and with N.Y.C. Opera (debut, Calaf, 1975). Since his Met debut as Canio (Jan. 6, 1978), he has sung more than 80 perfs., in roles including Manrico, Ernani, Pinkerton, Paolo (*Francesca da Rimini*), and Des Grieux. Has also sung at La Scala and Rome (1978), San Francisco (1982), and Vienna (1983).

Mavra. Opera in 1 act by Stravinsky; libretto by Boris Kochno, after Pushkin's poem *The Little House in Kolomna*.
   First perf., Paris, Opéra, June 3, 1922 (in Fr.): Slobodskaya, Sadowen, Rosovska, Skupevsky, c. Fitelberg. U.S. prem., Philadelphia, Academy of Music, Dec. 28, 1934: Kurenko, Koretszky, Fedora, Ivantzoff, c. Smallens.
   Stravinsky's tribute to Glinka's characteristic blend of Italian and Russian styles. A small Russian town, 17th c. Parasha (s) sneaks her lover, a Hussar (t), into her house disguised as the new cook "Mavra." Discovered shaving by Parasha's mother (a), "Mavra" escapes through the window.

Maxwell Davies, Peter. Composer; b. Manchester, Sep. 8, 1934. Studied with Richard Hall at Royal Manchester College of Music where he, Birtwistle, and Goehr formed the "Manchester Group"; also with Petrassi in Rome and Sessions at Princeton. In early works, he integrated medieval musical procedures with serial techniques, leading to the opera *Taverner* (1972). For The Fires of London, the ensemble he directed until 1986, he composed the chamber operas *The Martyrdom of St. Magnus* (1977) and *The Lighthouse* (1980), as well as many shorter music-theater works, such as the expressionistic and parodistic *Eight Songs for a Mad King* (1969). His interest in music education has led to children's operas, *The Two Fiddlers* (1978) and *Cinderella* (1980).

May Night. Opera in 3 acts by Rimsky-Korsakov; libretto by the composer, after Gogol's story.
   First perf., St. Petersburg, Maryinsky, Jan. 21, 1880: c. Napravnik.
   A comedy combining nationalistic and supernatural themes, set in a small Russian village, 19th c. The love of Levko (t) and Hanna (s) is opposed by the former's father, the bumbling mayor (bs), who has his own designs on the girl. After numerous complications, the water-sprites help Levko discredit his father.

Mayr, Richard. Bass; b. Henndorf, near Salzburg, Austria, Nov. 18, 1877; d. Vienna, Dec. 1, 1935. Studied medicine, but took up singing on Mahler's advice, working with Julius Kniese in Bayreuth; operatic debut there as Hagen, 1902. Vienna Opera debut as Silva (*Ernani*), 1902; was a member of that company until his

death, creating Barak (*Frau*) in 1919. After his Met debut as Pogner (Nov. 2, 1927), he sang there for 3 seasons, in parts including Ochs (his most celebrated role), Hermann (*Tannhäuser*), and Hunding.

Mayr, Simone. Composer; b. Mendorf, Bavaria, June 14, 1763; d. Bergamo, Italy, Dec. 2, 1845. He made his career in Italy, studying with Lenzi in Bergamo and Bertoni in Venice. His early compositions were ecclesiastical, but, encouraged by Piccinni, he wrote the successful opera *Saffo* (1794), which led to numerous commissions and the production of over 60 operas, both serious and comic, during the next 30 years, including *Ginevra di Scozia* (1801), *Tamerlano* (1813), and *Medea in Corinto* (1813). Mayr enriched the Italian style with choral ensembles and evocative orchestration, influencing his pupil Donizetti.

Mazeppa. Opera in 3 acts by Tchaikovsky; libretto by V. Burenin and the composer, after Pushkin's poem *Poltava*.
   First perf., Moscow, Bolshoi, Feb. 15, 1884. U.S. prem., Boston, Opera House, Dec. 14, 1922.
   A Romantic score with touches of national color; set in the early 18th-c. Ukraine. Maria (s) marries the cossack Mazeppa (bar), who conspires to overthrow the Tsar. After her father Kochubey (bs) is executed by Mazeppa's forces and the Ukraine is devastated by the Tsar, Maria loses her mind.

Mazura, Franz. Bass-baritone; b. Salzburg, Austria, Apr. 12, 1924. Studied with Fred Husler, Detmold; debut in Kassel, 1949. After singing in Mainz, Brunswick, and Mannheim, he joined the Deutsche Oper, Berlin, in 1961. Has sung at Bayreuth since 1971, notably as Gunther, Alberich, and Klingsor. In the premiere of the 3-act *Lulu*, Paris, 1979, he sang Dr. Schön, also the role of his Met debut, Dec. 12, 1980; subsequent Met roles include Klingsor, Alberich, Gurnemanz, Creon (*Oedipus*), the Doctor (*Wozzeck*), Frank (*Fledermaus*), and Rangoni (*Boris*).

Mazurok, Yuri. Baritone; b. Krasnik, Poland, July 18, 1931. Studied with Sveshikovaya, Moscow Conservatory, and in 1963 joined Bolshoi Opera, where his roles include Onegin, Yeletsky (*Queen of Spades*), Andrei (*War and Peace*), and Rossini's Figaro. U.S. debut with Bolshoi at Met, 1975; Met debut as Germont, Sep. 20, 1978, later singing Onegin. Has sung at major European houses, including Covent Garden (debut, Renato in *Ballo*, 1975) and Vienna (Escamillo, 1979).

Mazzoleni, Ester. Soprano; b. Sebenico, Dalmatia, Mar. 12, 1883; d. May 17, 1982. Studied in Pisa and Trieste; debut as Leonora (*Trovatore*), Costanzi, Rome, 1906. La Scala debut as Isabella (Franchetti's *Cristoforo Colombo*), 1908; sang Italian premiere of *Médée* there, 1909, and inaugural Aida at Verona Arena, 1913. Taught in Palermo after retirement in 1926.

Meader, George. Tenor; b. Minneapolis, Minn., July 6, 1888; d. Hollywood, Dec. 19, 1963. Studied with Anna Schoen-René in Minnesota and Germany, and with Pauline Viardot in Paris; debut as Steersman (*Holländer*), Leipzig, 1911. At Stuttgart Opera, 1911–19, created Scaramuccio (*Ariadne*). Met debut as Victorin (*Tote Stadt*), Nov. 19, 1921; he sang there until 1931 in roles including Ferrando (*Cosi*), David (*Meistersinger*), and Mime, then turned to operetta, notably Kern's *Cat and the Fiddle*.

Médée (Medea). Opera in prologue and 5 acts by M.-A. Charpentier; libretto by Thomas Corneille.

First perf., Paris, Opéra, Dec. 4, 1693: Le Rochois, Moreau, Dun, Dumesny.

Among the earliest of many operatic treatments of the myth of Medea, this score in the tradition established by Lully has recently been revived with success.

Médée (Medea). Opera in 3 acts by Cherubini; libretto by François Benoit Hoffmann, after Corneille's tragedy.

First perf., Paris, Feydeau, Mar. 13, 1797: Scio, Legrand, Gaveaux, Dessaules. U.S. prem., N.Y., Town Hall, Nov. 8, 1955 (concert perf., in Ital.): Farrell, Hurley, McCracken, Scott, c. Gamson. U.S. stage prem., San Francisco, Sep. 12, 1958 (in Ital.): Farrell, Stahlmann, R. Lewis, Modesti, c. Fournet.

A score combining classical grandeur and psychological penetration, revived at intervals during the 19th and 20th c. for operatic actresses attracted by the compelling title role. Most modern perfs. are heavily cut, sung in Italian translation (as *Medea*), and use the recitatives composed in 1855 by Franz Lachner.

Corinth, the court of Creon, antiquity. Abandoned by Jason (t), Médée (s) arrives to wrest him back from Glauké (s), but fails. After winning permission from Créon (bs) to remain another day in Corinth despite the populace's fear of her as a sorceress, she contrives a horrible death for her rival, and with her own hand kills the children she bore Jason.

Medium, The. Opera in 2 acts by Menotti; libretto by the composer.

First perf., N.Y., Brander Matthews Theater, Columbia U., May 8, 1946: Keller, Turner, c. Luening.

A theater piece with the well-calculated impact of a good short story, set in the U.S.A., "the present" (i.e., the 1940s). Madame Flora (a), a sham medium, puts gullible customers in touch with their deceased children, with the help of her daughter Monica (s) and a mute boy, Toby. In the grip of drink and declining fortunes, she thinks something has touched her during a seance and dismisses her clients (who are unwilling to believe her scornful admissions of fakery). She throws Toby out, and, when he returns and hides, takes him for a ghost and shoots him.

Mefistofele (Mephistopheles). Opera in prologue, 4 acts, and epilogue by Boito; libretto by the composer, after Goethe's *Faust*.

First perf., Milan, La Scala, Mar. 5, 1868: Reboux, Junca, Spallazzi. Revised version, first perf., Bologna, Oct. 4, 1875: Borghi-Mamo, Campanini, Nannetti. U.S. prem., Boston, Globe Theater, Nov. 16, 1880 (in Eng.). Met. prem., Dec. 5, 1883: Nilsson, Trebelli, Campanini, Mirabella, c. Campanini, d. Fox, Schaeffer, Maeder/Thompson. Later Met production: Nov. 26, 1920: Alda, Easton, Gigli, Didur, c. Moranzoni, d. Anisfeld, p. Thewman. 45 perfs. in 11 seasons.

Boito's musically uneven, conceptually novel challenge to the operatic establishment had a great vogue after the success of the revised version, and continues to be revived as a vehicle for leading bassos.

Medieval Germany. In the prologue, Mefistofele (bs) wagers with Heaven that he can win the soul of Faust (t). The aged philosopher accepts the devil's promise of one moment's perfect joy. Restored to youth by magic, Faust seduces Margherita (s), who gives her mother a sleeping potion in order to meet him, a draught that proves eventually fatal. Abandoned by Faust, Margherita kills the child she has borne him, and dies mad in prison. Mefistofele, meanwhile, has shown Faust the revelry of a

witches' sabbath, and now transports him to ancient Greece to see Elena (Helen of Troy, s). They exchange words of love, but we last see Faust grown again old and newly repentant; he dies calling on the gospels for defense, and Mefistofele is defeated.

Mehta, Zubin. Conductor; b. Bombay, India, Apr. 29, 1936. Studied at Vienna Academy under Hans Swarowsky (1954–60). Music director of Montreal Symphony (1960–67), Los Angeles Philharmonic (1962–78), Israel Philharmonic (since 1969), N.Y. Philharmonic (since 1978). Operatic debut, *Tosca*, Montreal, 1964; Covent Garden debut, *Otello*, 1977. At Met, 1965–71, he led *Aida* (debut, Dec. 29, 1965), *Turandot*, *Otello*, *Carmen*, *Tosca*, *Trovatore*, and the premiere of *Mourning Becomes Electra*. Other operatic engagements in Vienna and Florence.

Méhul, Étienne-Nicolas. Composer; b. Givet, France, June 22, 1763; d. Paris, Oct. 18, 1817. Studied with Edelmann in Paris. He withstood the upheavals of the French Revolution better than Grétry, whose style he at first emulated. After opéras comiques such as *Euphrosine* (1790), *Le Jeune Henri* (1797), *Ariodant* (1799), *Uthal* (1806), and the very successful *Joseph* (1807), Méhul, discouraged by Napoleon's preference for Italian opera, concentrated on symphonic music. His orchestration, harmonic innovations, and use of reminiscence motives influenced Boieldieu, Beethoven, and Weber.

Meier, Johanna. Soprano; b. Chicago, Feb. 13, 1938. Studied at U. of Miami, Fla., and with John Brownlee, Manhattan School, N.Y. Debut as Countess (*Capriccio*), N.Y.C. Opera, 1969; later roles there included Louise, Donna Anna, Senta, Tosca. Since her Met debut as Marguerite, Dec. 30, 1976, she has also sung Ariadne, Senta, the Marschallin, Fidelio, Ellen Orford, Chrysothemis, Elisabeth, the *Walküre* Brünnhilde, and Isolde (the role of her 1981 Bayreuth debut).

Meier, Waltraud. Mezzo-soprano; b. Würzburg, West Germany. After debut at age 20 in Würzburg and appearances at Dortmund, Mannheim, and Buenos Aires (Fricka, 1981), her Kundry (Cologne, 1983) brought wide attention. Debuts at Bayreuth (Kundry, 1983), Paris Opéra (Brangäne, 1984), Covent Garden (Eboli, 1984). Regular member of Stuttgart Opera from 1986.

Mei-Figner, Medea. See *Figner, Medea*.

Meilhac, Henri. Librettist; b. Paris, Feb. 21, 1831; d. Paris, July 6, 1897. In tandem with Ludovic Halévy, librettist of Bizet's *Carmen* and many Offenbach operettas; he also collaborated with Philippe Gille on Massenet's *Manon*.

Meistersinger von Nürnberg, Die (The Mastersingers of Nuremberg). Opera in 3 acts by Wagner; libretto by the composer.

First perf., Munich, Court Theater, June 21, 1868: Mallinger, Diez, Nachbaur, Betz, Hölzel, Bausewein, c. von Bülow. U.S. & Met prem., Jan. 4, 1886: Seidl-Kraus, Brandt, Stritt, Krämer, Fischer, Kemlitz, Staudigl, c. Seidl, d. Hoyt/Dazian, p. van Hell. Later Met productions: Mar. 26, 1910: Gadski, Wickham, Slezak, Reiss, Soomer, Goritz, Blass, c. Toscanini, d. Burghart, p. Schertel; Nov. 9, 1923: Easton, Howard, Laubenthal, Meader, Whitehill, Schützendorf, Bender, c. Bodanzky, d. Kautsky, p. Wymetal; Nov. 11, 1954 ("revised"): Della

Die Meistersinger von Nürnberg – (1962). Designed by Robert O'Hearn, produced by Nathaniel Merrill. Sandor Kónya, Ingrid Bjoner, Karl Dönch, and Otto Wiener

Casa, Glaz, Hopf, Franke, Edelmann, Pechner, Böhme, c. Stiedry, d. Meyer, p. Yannopoulos; Oct. 18, 1962: Bjoner, Vanni, Kónya, Dickie, Wiener, Dönch, Flagello, c. Rosenstock, d. O'Hearn, p. Merrill. Eva has also been sung at the Met by Eames, Sembrich, Destinn, Hempel, Rethberg, Müller, Lotte Lehmann, Steber, de los Angeles, Lorengar, Marton; Magdalene by Schumann-Heink, Homer, Thorborg, Thebom; Walther by Dippel, Alvary, J. de Reszke, Burrian, Urlus, Lorenz, Maison, Kullman, Svanholm, Thomas, King, Hofmann; Sachs by E. de Reszke, van Rooy, Schorr, Bohnen, Janssen, Schöffler, Tozzi, Adam, Stewart, Bailey, Ridderbusch; Beckmesser by Bispham, Pechner, Kunz, Kusche; the opera has also been conducted at the Met by Mancinelli, W. Damrosch, Hertz, Bodanzky, Leinsdorf, Szell, Busch, Reiner, Kempe, Schippers. 291 perfs. in 63 seasons.

One of the peaks of Wagner's achievement, incorporating an allegory of his own struggle for his radical musical ideas within a deeply human comedy.

Nuremberg, 16th c. The Franconian knight Walther von Stolzing (t) is attracted to Eva (s), daughter of the goldsmith Veit Pogner (bs), but learns from her nurse Magdalene (ms) that Eva is to be betrothed the next day to the winner of the Mastersingers' song contest. Walther resolves to sing for her hand, but is bewildered by the guild's convoluted rules, explained to him by Magdalene's sweetheart David (t), apprentice to the cobbler Hans Sachs (bs). The Mastersingers assemble, among them the town clerk Beckmesser (bs), who also aspires to Eva's hand. Pogner announces the contest, and Walther is introduced as a candidate for memberhip. For his trial song, Beckmesser serves as marker and quickly fills his slate with marks against the singer's errors, but Sachs perceives a fresh, if unformed, poetic voice in Walther's efforts. That evening, Beckmesser, serenading Eva (actually Magdalene in disguise), is subjected by Sachs to a "marking" as stringent as Walther suffered; during the riot their altercations stimulate, the cobbler prevents Walther and Eva from eloping. The next morning, though he too loves Eva, Sachs helps Walther shape a master-song from the knight's account of his dream of love. After Beckmesser has made a fool of himself by plagiarizing the song, in the belief that it was Sachs' work, Walther wins the contest and Eva with his innovative art.

Melano, Fabrizio. Producer; b. New York, Apr. 3, 1938. Worked at Circle in the Square in N.Y., Santa Fe, and San Francisco Opera before becoming Met staff director in 1970, in charge of many revivals, also new productions of *Trittico* (1975) and *Bohème* (1977). Also works with U.S. and foreign companies.

Melba, Nellie [Helen Porter Armstrong, née Mitchell]. Soprano; b. Richmond, near Melbourne, Australia, May 19, 1861; d. Sydney, Feb. 23, 1931. After study with Pietro Cecchi and concerts in Melbourne (source of her stage name), she studied for a year in Paris with Mathilde Marchesi. Her debut as Gilda (Brussels, 1887), followed by Lakmé and Ophélie (*Hamlet*), was a great success. Her first Covent Garden appearance, as Lucia (1888), was less well received, but after her 1889 Juliette she became the house's reigning diva, returning regularly until 1926 and creating the title roles of Bemberg's *Elaine* and Saint-Saëns' *Hélène*. She also sang at the Paris Opéra (debut, Ophélie, 1889), in Monte Carlo (1891), St. Petersburg (1890–91), and Italy (Palermo, Rome, Genoa, 1892–93). Lucia was the role of her debuts at La Scala (1893) and the Met (Dec. 4, 1893); in 8 Met seasons, she sang 116 perfs. (and almost as many more on tour) of 17 roles, most frequently Marguerite, Juliette (she had prepared both roles with Gounod), Lucia, the Queen (*Huguenots*), and Gilda, also Ophélie, Nedda, Semiramide, Elisabeth, Elsa, Micaela, Elaine, Massenet's Manon, Violetta, and the Infanta (*Cid*). The first Met Mimi, she also made a single, unsuccessful appearance as the *Siegfried* Brünnhilde opposite Jean de Reszke (1896). She sang for Damrosch's touring company (1897), Hammerstein's Manhattan Opera (1907–08), and the Chicago Opera (1910, 1915–16), and made numerous international tours (especially of Australia, from 1902). After her formal farewell at Covent Garden on June 8, 1926, she sang a few further performances in Britain and Australia.

At her peak, Melba was an unparalleled vocal technician, with a clear and limpid tone, perfectly balanced scale, seamless legato, incredible accuracy and velocity in coloratura, a flawless trill, and unerring intonation. Frequently accused of a chilly perfection, she retained her tonal steadiness and beauty until her mid-60s, as attested by comparison of her 1904 recordings with those from her 1926 farewell, while sagely shifting the emphasis of her repertory from the brilliance of Lucia to the lyricism of Mimi.

BIBLIOGRAPHY: W.R. Moran, comp., *Nellie Melba: A Contemporary Review* (Westport, Conn., 1985).

Melchior, Lauritz [Lebrecht Hommel]. Tenor; b. Copenhagen, Mar. 30, 1890; d. Santa Monica, Calif., Mar. 18, 1973. Studied with Paul Bang at Copenhagen Royal Opera school; after his Copenhagen debut as Silvio (*Pagliacci*), 1913, he sang as a baritone for several seasons, until Mme. Charles Cahier encouraged him to become a tenor. Study with Vilhelm Herold led to a second debut as Tannhäuser, Copenhagen, 1918. Further work with (among others) Anna Bahr-Mildenburg preceded his first international success in Wagner, as Siegmund, Covent Garden, 1924, and his Bayreuth debut that summer as Parsifal (he sang there until 1931, in all his Wagnerian roles except Lohengrin). His repertory grew gradually: *Siegfried* (Magdeburg, 1925), *Götterdämmerung* (Bayreuth, 1927), *Lohengrin* (Hamburg, 1927), *Aida*, *Otello*, and *Prophète* (Hamburg, 1928), and *Tristan* (Barcelona, 1929). Outside Europe, he sang at the Colón, Buenos Aires (1931–43); other non-Wagnerian parts included Samson,

Canio, and Turiddu. His U.S. debut was at the Met, as Tannhäuser, Feb. 17, 1926; he appeared there in 24 seasons (omitting 1927–28), amassing a grand total of 387 performances (including 95 Tristans, in a lifetime total of 223; he never sang Stolzing or Rienzi). At the 1935 farewell gala for Gatti-Casazza, he sang Act IV of *Otello*, his only non-Wagnerian work at the Met. Covent Garden heard him as Otello and Florestan (*Fidelio*) as well as in Wagner (1926–39), as did San Francisco (1934–45); in Chicago, he sang only Wagner (1934–41). He retired from opera after a Met Lohengrin on Feb. 2, 1950, though continuing to work in films and operetta.

Universally regarded as the greatest Wagnerian tenor of the century, Melchior reigned unchallenged for nearly 25 years. His lengthy preparation afforded a strong technical underpinning, including a secure command of the transitional notes (around upper E and F) essential in Wagner's writing for tenor. His tone was brilliant and enormously powerful, yet also sweet and gentle when required; though he could be inattentive to rhythmic details and in later years tended to rush the music, his intensity and enthusiasm made him a uniquely convincing performer, despite the awkwardness of his monumental physique. While in his prime, he recorded extensively from his major roles, notably Siegmund and Siegfried.

melodrama. The practice of alternating spoken text with music, or of speaking over music. An independent genre in 18th-c. France and Germany, passages of melodrama were used in the 19th-c. German singspiel (the prison scene of *Fidelio*, the Wolf's Glen scene of *Freischütz*).

melodramma (Ital.). An operatic libretto, or the completed opera.

Nellie Melba as Juliette in *Roméo et Juliette*

Lauritz Melchior as Tristan in *Tristan und Isolde*

Melton, James. Tenor; b. Moultrie, Ga., Jan. 2, 1904; d. New York, Apr. 21, 1961. Studied with Gaetano de Luca, Vanderbilt U., and Enrico Rosati, N.Y.; operatic debut as Pinkerton, Cincinnati, 1938. After singing with San Carlo and Chicago Operas, he came to the Met (debut, Tamino, Dec. 7, 1942), where in 8 seasons he sang 58 perfs. of 7 roles, including Pinkerton, Wilhelm Meister (*Mignon*), Alfredo, and Ottavio.

Mendelssohn[-Bartholdy], **Felix.** Composer. b. Hamburg, Feb. 3, 1809; d. Leipzig, Nov. 4, 1847. Mendelssohn's completed operas, in singspiel style, were all products of his prodigious adolescence: *Die Soldatenliebschaft* (1820); *Die beiden Pädagogen* (1821); *Die wandernden Komödianten* (1822); *Der Onkel aus Boston* (1824); *Die Hochzeit des Camacho*, after Cervantes' *Don Quixote* (1825); and *Die Heimkehr aus der Fremde* (known in Eng. as *Son and Stranger*; 1829). After composing incidental music for classical drama in Berlin in the 1840s, he began the opera *Die Loreley*, completing only fragments before his death.

Menotti, Gian Carlo. Composer and stage director; b. Cadegliano, July 7, 1911. Studied at Milan Conservatory and with Rosario Scalero at Curtis Institute, where he became friends with Samuel Barber, for whose operas he wrote librettos. The success of the opera buffa *Amelia al Ballo* (1937) led to a Met performance the following year, and to an NBC commission for a radio opera, the "grotesque comedy" *The Old Maid and the Thief* (1939). His first serious opera, *The Island God* (1942), was poorly received. However, the grand guignol of *The Medium* (1946) established him as a skillful practitioner of melodrama; the opera buffa *The Telephone* (1947) is often paired with it. *The Consul* (1950), *The Saint of Bleecker Street* (1954), and *Maria Golovin* (1958) extended the veristic style in political and religious contexts, while an NBC television commission produced the popular, sentimental *Amahl and the Night Visitors* (1951), first of several children's operas. *L'Ultimo Selvaggio* (1963) continued his satirical vein; more recent historical operas include *Juana*

Robert Merrill as Germont in *La Traviata*

La Loca (1979) and *Goya* (1986). Conservative and accessible, Menotti's later work lacks the intensity and focus of his first successes. In 1958 he founded a festival in Spoleto, Italy, and in 1977 an American version thereof in Charleston, S.C.
BIBLIOGRAPHY: John Gruen, *Menotti: A Biography* (N.Y., and London, 1978).

Mercadante, Saverio. Composer; b. Altamura, near Bari, Italy, bapt. Sep. 17, 1795; d. Naples, Dec. 17, 1870. Studied composition with Zingarelli in Naples, where his first opera, *L'Apoteosi d'Ercole* (1819), was produced. Following the international success of *Elisa e Claudio* (1821), Mercadante frequently worked outside Italy; after hearing Meyerbeer's *Huguenots* in Paris, he enlarged the scale of his own work. His operas from *Il Giuramento* (1837) through *Il Reggente* (1843), rich in harmonic and orchestral imagination, influenced the young Verdi, whose works quickly overtook Mercadante's in popularity.

Meredith, Morley. Baritone; b. Winnipeg, Manitoba. Studied with W.H. Anderson in Canada, Boris Goldovsky at Tanglewood, Alfredo Martino and Melchiorre Luise. Debut as Escamillo, N.Y.C. Opera, 1957. Met debut in baritone roles of *Hoffmann*, Jan. 3, 1962; he has sung with the company in every subsequent season, in some 400 perfs. of more than 35 roles, including Zuniga, Schlemil (*Hoffmann*), the High Priest (*Zauberflöte*), Faninal, the Emperor of China (*Nightingale*), Klingsor, and the Doctor (*Wozzeck*). Has also sung in Chicago, San Francisco, Philadelphia, and Geneva.

Méric-Lalande, Henriette. Soprano; b. Dunkerque, France, 1798; d. Chantilly, Sep. 7, 1867. Studied with her father, conductor Jean-Baptiste Lalande, with Garcia in Paris, and with Bonfichi and Banderali in Milan; debut in Nantes, 1814. Sang in premieres of Meyerbeer's *Crociato in Egitto* (Venice, 1824) and Bellini's *Bianca e Gernando*

(Naples, 1826); also, at La Scala, *Pirata* (1827), *Straniera* (1829), and *Lucrezia Borgia* (1833). Appeared in Paris, Munich, Vienna, London. Retired 1836.

Merli, Francesco. Tenor; b. Milan, Jan. 27, 1887; d. Milan, Dec. 11/12, 1976. Studied with Negrini and Borghi, Milan; sang first in Buenos Aires. La Scala debut as Eliseo (Rossini's *Mosè*), 1917; he sang dramatic tenor roles there until 1942. At Covent Garden (1926–30), he sang the first London Calaf. His single Met season (debut as Radames, Mar. 2, 1932) was unsuccessful because of poor health. Retired from the stage in 1950.

Merlin. Opera in 3 acts by Goldmark; libretto by Siegfried Lipiner.
First perf., Vienna, Court Opera, Nov. 19, 1886. U.S. & Met prem., Jan 3, 1887: Lehmann, Brandt, Alvary, Fischer, c. Damrosch, d. Hoyt/Schaeffel, p. van Hell. 5 perfs. in 1 season.
In this version of the King Arthur legend, Merlin (t) is a knight of the round table with magic powers, whose powers are lost when he falls in love with the temptress Vivien (s); he is saved from perdition by her self-sacrifice.

Merola, Gaetano. Impresario and conductor; b. Naples, Jan. 4, 1881; d. San Francisco, Aug. 30, 1953. After study at Naples Conservatory, came to N.Y. as a Met assistant conductor, working later with the Savage, Hammerstein, and San Carlo companies. In 1923 he founded the San Francisco Opera, which he directed until his death, also conducting many performances. An old-fashioned impresario in the Italian mold, Merola filled principal roles with Met stars and rarely strayed beyond the standard repertory, but he built a solid public base for opera in San Francisco (if not in Los Angeles, where he founded a short-lived company, 1924–31).

Merrill, Nathaniel. Producer; b. Newton, Mass., Feb. 8, 1927. Operatic training in Europe with Graf, Rennert, Schramm; first production, Lully's *Amadis* (Boston, 1952). At the Met since 1960, he has staged *Elisir*, *Turandot*, *Meistersinger*, *Aida*, *Adriana Lecouvreur*, *Samson*, *Frau ohne Schatten*, *Hänsel*, *Luisa Miller*, *Rosenkavalier*, *Trovatore*, *Parsifal*, *Troyens*, and *Porgy*, mostly with designer Robert O'Hearn. Other productions for Vienna State Opera, Opéra du Rhin, N.Y.C. Opera, and San Francisco.

Merrill, Robert. Baritone; b. Brooklyn, N.Y., June 4, 1917. Studied with his mother, a concert singer, then with Samuel Margolis and Angelo Canarutto; debut as Amonasro, Trenton, 1943. After winning the Met Auditions of the Air, he made his debut as Germont in *Traviata* (Dec. 15, 1945), a role he sang 85 times at the Met; during 30 seasons with the company, he appeared in 551 performances (and over 200 more on tour). Selection as Germont for Toscanini's 1945 *Traviata* broadcasts gave his career a strong early impetus (he also sang Renato in *Ballo* for Toscanini, 1954). His 21 Met roles included Ashton, Escamillo, Tchelkalov (*Boris*), Valentin, Amonasro, Figaro, di Luna, Rigoletto, High Priest (*Samson*), Posa, Silvio, Tonio, Marcello, Renato, Malatesta, Barnaba, Don Carlo (*Forza*), Gérard (*Chénier*), Iago, and Scarpia. Although he devoted most of his career to the Met, Merrill also sang in San Francisco (debut, Germont, 1957) and Chicago (debut, Amonasro, 1960), and at La Fenice, Venice (1961) and Covent Garden (debut, Germont, 1967), and became a familiar performer on radio and television, in musicals and concerts. The finest American

lyric baritone of his generation, he was a remarkably consistent performer; his handsome voice was evenly and effortlessly produced, his interpretations generously scaled and musically sound.
BIBLIOGRAPHY: Robert Merrill, *Once More from the Beginning* (N.Y., 1965).

Merriman, Nan [Katherine-Ann]. Mezzo-soprano; b. Pittsburgh, Pa., Apr. 28, 1920. Studied with Alexia Bassian in Los Angeles; Hollywood; operatic debut as Cieca (*Gioconda*), Cincinnati Summer Opera, 1942. In Toscanini's NBC Symphony broadcasts, she sang Maddalena (*Rigoletto*), Orfeo (Act II), Emilia (*Otello*), and Meg Page. Noted as Dorabella at Aix (1953), Piccola Scala (1955), and Glyndebourne (1956), and as Baba (*Rake*). Retired in 1965.

Merritt, Myra. Soprano; b. Washington, D.C. After study at Peabody Conservatory and with Singher in Santa Barbara, Houston Opera debut as Clara (*Porgy*, 1982). Met debut as Shepherd (*Tannhäuser*, Jan. 21, 1982); subsequent roles include Clara, Elvira (*Italiana*), Antonia (*Hoffmann*), and Musetta.

Merry Mount. Opera in 4 acts by Hanson; libretto by Richard Stokes, after Nathaniel Hawthorne's story *The Maypole of Merry Mount*.
First perf., Ann Arbor, Michigan, Hill Auditorium (U. of Michigan), May 20, 1933 (concert perf): Corona, Jagel, J.C. Thomas, c. Hanson. Stage prem., Met, Feb. 10, 1934: Ljungberg, Johnson, Tibbett, c. Serafin, d. Mielziner, p. Wymetal, Jr. 6 perfs. in 1 season.
The choral writing in this neo-Romantic score was much admired. In a Massachusetts village, May 1625, the fiery young pastor Wrestling Bradford (bar) succumbs to an uncontrollable sexual obsession with Lady Marigold Sandys (s), bringing strife upon the community and eventually killing her and himself.

Merry Wives of Windsor, The. See *Lustigen Weiber von Windsor, Die.*

Mesplé, Mady. Soprano; b. Toulouse, France, Mar. 7, 1931. Studied with Isar-Lasson in Toulouse, Georges Jouatte and Janine Micheau in Paris; debut as Lakmé, Liège, 1953. Sang coloratura parts at Paris Opéra-Comique from 1956, at Opéra from 1958. She has sung throughout Europe and U.S., notably at Edinburgh (Lucia, 1962) and Aix. Met debut as Gilda, Sep. 25, 1973.

messa di voce (Ital.). In vocal technique, a gradual swelling of a tone followed by its diminution; a central nuance of classical technique, often requested by 18th-c. composers at the beginning of an aria or a cadenza. Not to be confused with mezza voce (*q.v.*).

Messaline. Opera in 4 acts by de Lara; libretto by Armand Silvestre and Eugène Morand.
First perf., Monte Carlo, Mar. 21, 1899: Héglon, Tamagno, Bouvet, c. Jehin. U.S. & Met prem., Jan. 22, 1902: Calvé, Alvarez, Scotti, c. Flon. 3 perfs. in 1 season.
An effective vehicle for the protagonist, de Lara's opera was otherwise deplored by reviewers. In Rome, during the reign of Claudius, the brothers Harès (bar) and Helion (t) both hate the Empress Valeria, known as Messaline (s), but fall victim to her charms and eventually lose their lives.

Messel, Oliver. Designer; b. London, Jan. 13, 1905; d. Barbados, W.I., July 13, 1978. Active as designer of sets and costumes for London's West End, Broadway, films, and ballet. He designed opera for Covent Garden and Glyndebourne, and two Met productions: *Nozze di Figaro* (1959) and *Ariadne* (1962).

Messiaen, Olivier. Composer; b. Avignon, France, Dec. 10, 1908. A student of Dukas and Dupré at Paris Conservatory, where he joined the faculty in 1942, becoming one of Europe's most influential teachers. A Roman Catholic mystic, Messiaen in his music uses elements drawn from bird song and Hindu music, complex rhythms, and serial and ostinato techniques. His only opera, *Saint François d'Assise* (1983), in eight "Franciscan scenes," is a sonorous, characteristically static summation of his style.

metaphor aria, simile aria. Principally in baroque opera, an aria with a text that compares a dramatic situation or personal emotion to some external phenomenon, such as a storm or a ferocious beast.

Metastasio [Trapassi], **Pietro.** Librettist; b. Rome, Jan. 3, 1698; d. Vienna, Apr. 12, 1782. After inheriting wealth, he became a writer, and eventually the most influential librettist of the 18th c. His first libretto was written in 1723, and *Didone Abbandonata* (1724), music by Domenico Sarro, established his name throughout Italy. He worked in Rome and Venice (1724–30), then went to Vienna, succeeding Zeno as court poet and remaining for the rest of his life. As well as numerous shorter works, his output includes 27 full-length heroic operas, many of which were set repeatedly throughout the century. Rigidly structured with an emphasis on arias, Metastasio's librettos avoided supernatural effects and elaborate stage machinery; his plots dealt with conflicts between reason and passion, depicting heroic behavior in the face of adversity.

Metternich, Josef. Baritone; b. Hermühlheim, near Cologne, Germany, June 2, 1915. Studied in Cologne, and in Berlin with Neuhaus; debut in *Lohengrin*, Berlin Städtische Oper, 1941, where he sang after the war, also appearing in Vienna, Barcelona, and London. Met debut as Carlo (*Forza*), Nov. 21, 1953; in 3 seasons, sang 22 perfs. of 8 roles, including Amonasro, Renato, di Luna, Tonio, Amfortas, Wolfram, and Kurwenal. Created Kepler (*Harmonie der Welt*), Munich, 1957.

Meyer, Kerstin. Mezzo-soprano; b. Stockholm, Apr. 3, 1928. Studied with Arne Sunnegårdh and Andrejeva von Skilondz, Stockholm Conservatory; debut as Azucena, Stockholm, 1952. Guest engagements at Salzburg (1957–58), Deutsche Oper, Berlin (1960), Glyndebourne (1961–76), Bayreuth (Brangäne, 1962–64), and Hamburg (1965–69). Met debut as Carmen, Oct. 29, 1960; in 3 seasons, her other house roles were Orfeo and the Composer (*Ariadne*). Created Agaue (*Bassarids*), Salzburg, 1966. Appointed Director of Stockholm Opera school, 1985.

Meyerbeer, Giacomo [Jakob Liebmann Meyer Beer]. Composer; b. Vogelsdorf, near Berlin, Sep. 5, 1791; d. Paris, May 2, 1864. Scion of a wealthy, cultured Jewish family, he performed in public as a pianist at age 11, and studied with Zelter and B.A. Weber in Berlin, and Abbé Vogler in Darmstadt. When his first German operas were unsuccessful, he went to Italy in 1815; six Italian operas were well received, notably *Il Crociato in Egitto* (1824), which was staged the next year in Paris to great acclaim, gaining Meyerbeer entrée to the cultured elite, among them the dramatist-librettist Scribe. Their first collaboration was *Robert le Diable* (1831), which added magic and religion to the grand-opera form of Auber and Rossini; its immense success probably stimulated Rossini's retirement from operatic composition. *Les Huguenots* (1836) was a worthy successor, a historical drama with a wealth of incident and spectacle. Meyerbeer's appointment to succeed Spontini as music director in Berlin (1842–49), where he encouraged the performance of Wagner's operas, delayed the progress of later works. His years of success were marked by constant changes of plans, contracts, and deadlines for operas. *Le Prophète*, begun in 1835, was completed by 1840 but put aside, then revised to make a stronger role for Pauline Viardot; its 1849 premiere was another triumph. *L'Africaine*, begun in 1837 but delayed by Scribe's uncooperativeness and Meyerbeer's constant revision, was produced posthumously in 1864. Meyerbeer also composed two *opéras comiques*, *L'Étoile du Nord* (1854, based on much of his 1844 singspiel for Jenny Lind, *Ein Feldlager in Schlesien*) and *Le Pardon de Ploërmel* (also known as *Dinorah*, 1859), as well as incidental music, sacred and choral works, and many songs.

Meyerbeer's grand operas, notable for their originality of subject matter, exploitation of novel instrumental possibilities, carefully researched historical and exotic color, and powerful mass effects, relied on the exceptional resources of the Paris Opéra and were carefully tailored for specific singers. The musical invention is short-breathed and rhythmically square, assembled as a mosaic of continually fresh ideas rather than through development. By the end of the 19th c., these extremely studied scores fell into disfavor, after greater composers – notably Verdi and Wagner – achieved similar effects in more inspired and spontaneous ways.

mezza voce (Ital.). With "half the voice," sung in a restrained manner.

mezzo-soprano. Female voice type lying between contralto and soprano. Usual compass from A below middle C to B-flat above the treble clef – thus, slightly shorter on the bottom than a contralto and on the top than a soprano (and not always distinguishable from them). As a category, the mezzo-soprano, like the baritone, is a development of the 19th c., and its exponents often assume roles originally placed in the upper or lower categories.

Midsummer Marriage, The. Opera in 3 acts by Tippett; libretto by the composer.

First perf., London, Covent Garden, Jan. 27, 1955: Sutherland, Leigh, Dominguez, Lewis, Lanigan, Kraus, c. Pritchard. U.S. prem., San Francisco, Oct. 15, 1983: Johnson, Greenawald, Nadler, Bailey, Davies, Herincx, c. Agler.

Tippett's first opera mixes realism with mysticism, probing the problems of contemporary relationships in a manner reminiscent of both *Zauberflöte* and *Frau ohne Schatten*.

The present. On the Midsummer day on which Mark (t) and Jenifer (s) are due to be married, she announces that she cannot go through with it until she has achieved greater self-understanding. At a mysterious clearing in the woods, they separately disappear into a cave, and are pursued by Jenifer's father King Fisher (bar), his secretary Bella (s), and her boyfriend Jack (t). After various rituals, dances, and the death of King Fisher, Jenifer and Mark emerge with a new understanding of themselves and each other, and prepare to marry.

Midsummer Night's Dream, A. Opera in 3 acts by Britten; libretto adapted by the composer and Peter Pears from Shakespeare's comedy.

First perf., Aldeburgh, Festival, June 11, 1960: Vyvyan, Cantelo, Thomas, Deller, Maran, Hemsley, Brannigan, Pears, c. Britten. U.S. prem., San Francisco, Oct. 10, 1961: Costa, Gignac, Horne, Blum, Oberlin, Thaw, Heater, Evans, Handt, c. Varviso.

Britten conjures from the chamber orchestra a remarkable variety of timbre and texture to characterize Shakespeare's three groups of characters: gods and fairies, lovers, and rustics. The plot is unchanged: Oberon (countertenor) is angry with Tytania (c), and with the help of Puck (acrobat) makes all the wrong people fall in love with one another. The rustics' play becomes a parody of grand opera, with a mad scene for Flute (t).

Mielziner, Jo. Designer; b. Paris, Mar. 19, 1901; d. New York, Mar. 15, 1976. Beginning in 1924, he designed over 300 productions of drama, opera, ballet, and musicals, ranging from *Death of a Salesman* to *Guys and Dolls*. For the Met, he designed *Emperor Jones* (1933) and *Merry Mount* (1934); a projected 1975 *Don Giovanni* was cancelled due to lack of funds.

Migenes (-Johnson), Julia. Soprano; b. New York, 1945. Began career on Broadway, and later sang Maria in *West Side Story* at Vienna Volksoper. N.Y.C. Opera debut as Annina (*Saint of Bleecker Street*), 1965. After study with Gisela Ultmann, Cologne, San Francisco debut as Musetta, 1978. Met debut as Jenny (*Mahagonny*), Dec. 10, 1979; subsequent roles include Lulu, Nedda, and Musetta. Starred in Rosi's 1984 film of *Carmen*.

Mignon. Opera in 3 acts by Thomas; libretto by Barbier and Carré, after Goethe's novel *Wilhelm Meister*.

First perf., Paris, Opéra-Comique, Nov. 17, 1866: Galli-Marié, Gabel, Achard, Bataille. U.S. prem., New Orleans, French Opera House, May 9, 1871. Met prem., Oct. 31, 1883 (in Ital.): Nilsson, Valleria, Capoul, del Puente, c. Vianesi, d. J. Fox, Schaeffer, Maeder, Thompson/Ascoli, Dazian. Later Met production: Mar. 10, 1927: Bori, Talley, Gigli, Whitehill, c. Hasselmans, d. Soudeikine, p. Wymetal. Mignon has also been sung at the Met by de Lussan, Farrar, Swarthout, Tourel, Stevens; Philine by Lilli Lehmann, Nordica, Talley, Pons, Munsel; Wilhelm Meister by Bonci, Schipa, Crooks, di Stefano. 66 perfs. in 21 seasons.

Thomas's most popular opera lacks the psychological dimensions of Goethe's novel, but offers warmth of characterization and memorable arias for each principal role.

Germany and Italy, late 18th c. Wilhelm Meister (t) buys the freedom of the young Mignon (s or ms) from a band of gypsies, who had abducted her in childhood and maltreat her. She travels with him dressed as a page, becomes devoted to him, and is jealous when the actress Philine (s) captures his attentions. Lothario (bs), a deranged minstrel befriended by Mignon (and actually her long-lost father) hears the girl wish that a castle in which Philine is performing would go up in flames, and sets fire to it. Unknown to him, Mignon has gone inside.

Wilhelm rescues her from the flames and realizes that he loves her. There are two versions of the opera's ending; Mignon recovers in the one more usually heard, but dies in the other.

Milan. City in northern Italy, and one of the world's great operatic capitals. The first opera heard in Milan was Manelli's *L'Andromeda* (1644); early performances took place in the court theater (Salone Margherita) and Teatrino della Commedia (from 1686 known as the Regio Nuovo Teatro, closed 1729). The Teatro Regio Ducal (1717–76), which replaced the Margherita (burned 1708), saw the premieres of operas by Gluck and Mozart. Other Milan theaters included the Teatro della Cannobiana (in use 1779–1894), site of the premiere of *Elisir d'Amore* (1832); the Teatro Carcano (opened 1803), where *Anna Bolena* (1830) and *Sonnambula* (1831) were introduced; the Teatro dal Verme (opened 1872), which housed the premieres of *Le Villi* (1884) and *Pagliacci* (1892); and the Teatro Lirico (opened 1894), where *Fedora* (1898) and *Adriana Lecouvreur* (1902) were first seen.

Most important is the Teatro alla Scala, built on the site of the Church of Santa Maria della Scala to a design by Giuseppe Piermarini and opened on Aug. 3, 1778 with Salieri's *Europa Riconosciuta*. From the 1820s onward, under impresarios such as Barbaja (1826–32) and Merelli (1835–50, 1861–63), it was one of Europe's leading theaters, scene of premieres from *Norma* (1831) through *Falstaff* (1893) and *Turandot* (1926). After World War I La Scala became a self-governing body; Toscanini, already twice artistic director (1898–1903, 1906–08) returned again and remained until 1929. Nearly destroyed by bombs in 1943, the theater was rebuilt according to original designs (capacity 3,000) and reopened in 1946. Subsequent artistic directors have included Antonio Ghiringhelli (1948–53), Victor de Sabata (1953–57), and Claudio Abbado (1971–80; chief conductor until 1986); currently, Cesare Mazzonis is artistic director and Riccardo Muti music director. The annual season traditionally begins on Dec. 7. In 1955, the intimate Piccola Scala (capacity 600) was opened to house small-scale operas.

Milanov [née Kunc], **Zinka.** Soprano; b. Zagreb, Croatia, May 17, 1906. Studied at Zagreb Academy and with Ternina, Maria Kostrenčić, and Fernando Carpi in Prague; debut as Leonora in *Trovatore*, Ljubljana, 1927. Sang leading roles at Zagreb Opera (1928–35), also guesting in Central Europe. After a Verdi Requiem under Toscanini at Salzburg (1937), she made her Met debut as the *Trovatore* Leonora on Dec. 17, 1937. During 24 seasons (1937–66, except for 1941–42, 1947–50) with the company, she sang 298 performances of 13 roles in the Italian dramatic repertory, including Aida (52 times), Gioconda, Amelia (*Ballo*), Donna Anna, Santuzza, Leonora (*Forza*), Norma, Maddalena (*Chénier*), Tosca, Elvira (*Ernani*), Desdemona, and Amelia (*Boccanegra*); her farewell, as Maddalena, took place on Apr. 13, 1966, in the final season at the old Met. She also appeared in Chicago (debut, Aida, 1940), San Francisco (debut, Leonora in *Forza*, 1943); at the Colón, Buenos Aires (1940–42), she sang Reiza in *Oberon*, as well as her more familiar roles. After the war in Europe, she sang at La Scala (debut, Tosca, 1950) and Covent Garden (debut, Tosca, 1956).

Milanov's powerful voice, capable of fulfilling the demands of the largest dramatic roles, also yielded caressing pianissimos; her command of broad phrasing and sensitive tonal coloring was especially telling in the great Verdi roles. Though her singing could be erratic,

La Scala, Milan

especially in intonation, and her stage deportment was old-fashioned, she conveyed her characterizations through her generous voice and temperament.

Milashkina, Tamara. Soprano; b. Astrakhan, Soviet Union, Sep. 13, 1934. Became soloist at Bolshoi Opera, 1958, while still a student of Elena Katulskaya; known for her portrayals there of Tchaikovsky heroines and Fevronia (*Kitezh*), filmed in 1966. First Soviet singer to appear at La Scala (*Battaglia di Legnano*, 1962); has sung throughout Europe and with Bolshoi at Met, 1975.

Zinka Milanov as Amelia and Jan Peerce as Riccardo in *Un Ballo in Maschera*

THE METROPOLITAN OPERA *Martin Mayer*

The Metropolitan Opera as an institution was created in 1880, not for musical performance but for the construction and maintenance of a theater, New York's Metropolitan Opera House, which opened in 1883 with unusual emphasis on what was happening before rather than behind the proscenium. The horseshoe auditorium, one of the most glamorous public spaces ever built, gave the occupants of the boxes an excellent view of each other but a somewhat less satisfactory view of the stage. The boxholders (two tiers of them, almost seventy in all, when the house was new) owned the building, and each had the sole right to occupy his box without charge for every performance in the house, operatic or otherwise. In return, they paid the expenses of the building itself, and in effect gave the facility to a separate company that received the use of the structure rent-free by the year (and could sublease it for lecture, concerts, and the like) upon its guarantee to present a stated minimum number of operatic performances with star singers approved by a board from the "real estate company."

This system survived until 1940, though it did not entirely shake down to workability until the turn of the century. In its first season, 1883–84, the house was contracted to Henry Abbey, an all-round theatrical impresario, who underestimated his expenses and overestimated his receipts (especially from a disastrous tour) though he offered nothing but familiar operas and proven stars (*Faust* with Christine Nilsson on his opening night). The next season the theater was taken over by the German–American conductor Leopold Damrosch, who designed a repertory sung entirely in German (though almost half the operas had been written in Italian or French), including three Wagner works. When Damrosch died, his son Walter took over, and the next season artistic matters were put in the hands of conductor Anton Seidl, who had been Wagner's assistant and for the remainder of the decade gave the city Wagner-dominated seasons of some austerity and great distinction, including the American premieres of *Tristan*, *Meistersinger*, and three of the *Ring* operas.

Prices were held low enough to attract the city's large and often serious-minded German immigrant community, and costs were low because German singers commanded much lower fees than their Italian or French rivals. For the only time in its history, the Met was at the cutting edge of new musical theater in New York. Until the mainspring of the German company wound down toward the end of the decade, the high-society personages in the boxes did not object. Some were serious-minded themselves, while others found the opera boxes with their private anterooms behind curtains a pleasant place to spend the latter part of the evening (and it was the latter part: the curtain rose at eight, but Mrs. Astor and her set did not arrive until nine), and did not hugely care what was on the stage so long as it was well-reputed.

In the 1890s, after a destructive fire that cost the Met a season and a rebuilding that reduced the real-estate group to the occupants of the first-tier boxes only, the lease on the theater became the possession of the redoubtable Maurice Grau, a Viennese who had been educated in New York, and who supplemented his income as an impresario with successful raids on Wall Street. Grau also secured the lease on Covent Garden, and used his power over the two richest theaters to put together casts that for a generation defined the "golden age." This period, "gay" for the rich but horribly depressed for the poor, saw the efflorescence of opera as a medium

The auditorium of the old Metropolitan Opera House

(*Overleaf*) The Metropolitan Opera House at Lincoln Center

for the entertainment of high society. It was the era of the "perfect" cast, usually headed by Jean de Reszke and Nellie Melba – but the scoffers should note that de Reszke and his brother had the artistic conscience to learn German after their establishment as superstars, so that they could sing Wagnerian roles in the original. It was in large part thanks to them that the Met became, along with Covent Garden, the first theater where operas were almost always sung in the language of their composition.

Grau's departure in 1903 was lamented as marking the end of the golden age of vocalism – and then Caruso made his American debut on the opening night of the new impresario, the megalomaniac Heinrich Conried. Conried's five years were marked by two great scandals: his staging of *Parsifal* in the teeth of opposition (up to and including lawsuits) by Wagner's widow, for the Master had reserved that work for Bayreuth in eternity, and his presentation (once) of Strauss' *Salome*, hugely offensive to, *inter alia*, J. P. Morgan, owner of the box at the center of the horseshoe, who forced its withdrawal. Among the conductors he recruited to the house was Gustav Mahler, who continued for a season after the theater's lease passed to a corporation headed by the banker Otto Kahn. The new general manager was Giulio Gatti-Casazza of Milan, who came with his partner, conductor Arturo Toscanini. In the miracle season of 1908–09, then, there were golden-age casts, new productions from the Milan ateliers, and an even money chance of finding Toscanini or Mahler presiding over the proceedings. And Toscanini expanded the audience further by offering symphonic concerts on Sunday nights.

Toscanini gave the house seven seasons, then departed. World War I cost the company its German artists and Wagner traditions, later painstakingly rebuilt by conductor Artur Bodanzky (with vast assistance in the 1930s from Lauritz Melchior and Kirsten Flagstad). In the 1920s Gatti-Casazza perfected his essentially hermetic style of running an opera house. It is not known whether he could speak English; what is certain is that he did not. Communication between opera house and public came entirely through the proscenium. Most good seats were sold far in advance by subscription, to customers who did not know what they would hear on their Monday nights. (With as many as forty-five operas in less than thirty weeks, and singers contracted for the season or the half-season, Gatti did not know more than two weeks ahead of time what he would be playing.) On the other hand, the Italian commissioned for the house its first world premieres, by Puccini and Humperdinck, and labored manfully to create an American operatic tradition, offering a new opera by an American almost every year in the 1920s. And it was in Gatti's reign that New York was given its first American star who had not first made a reputation in Europe, when Rosa Ponselle sang an opening night at the Met in her first appearance on any operatic stage anywhere.

Until the Great Depression, the Gatti years were profitable, under the special dispensation that gave the company the use of the theater without charge (at the price of the revenues from the sale of the box seats). But by 1932 the company had exhausted its reserves, and was forced to cut its seasons, cut its salaries, sell what quickly became worthless bonds to its friends, and finally launch public fund-raising campaigns. By then the Wall Street lawyer Paul Cravath had succeeded his client Otto Kahn as the executive officer of the producing company, and had made arrangements for Met performances to be broadcast on the NBC radio network (owned by the Radio Corporation of America, another Cravath client). The nationwide radio audience justified a nationwide fund-raising appeal led in large part by Mrs. August Belmont, a former actress and formidable prime mover in the world of charity. In this context, Gatti's style was a handicap, and he took, in effect, an early retirement. Cravath's first choice as his successor died before really taking office, and Edward Johnson, a Canadian-

born tenor who had already declared an interest in arts administration, became the general manager. With considerable help from Edward Ziegler (a former newspaperman who had been Gatti's number two), Johnson carried the Met through the period 1935–50. Early in his tenure, a special fund-raising campaign made it possible for the producing company to acquire the theater from the boxholders at what was a bargain price – though its rapidly deteriorating condition made it less of a bargain than had been thought.

Necessarily, these were the years for nurturing American talent, a group that included radio stars like James Melton and Nino Martini, movie stars like Grace Moore and Gladys Swarthout (and later Risë Stevens) – but also people who were nothing but great singers, like Eleanor Steber and Leonard Warren. Refugees from the war provided a superb conducting staff – Walter, Beecham, Reiner, Szell, Busch, among others. But Johnson's company led a hand-to-mouth existence, with minimal opportunity to offer new productions or new operas. With the arrival of his successor Rudolf Bing, a Viennese successfully transplanted to Britain who had founded the Edinburgh Festival, new horizons opened out. Given the worldwide primacy of the dollar, singers were available from everywhere, and substantial refurbishment of the repertory was facilitated by postwar prosperity, though the house spent in added salaries for the unionized employees more than the boom produced in added receipts, necessitating frequent and systematic fund-raising appeals. Bing stressed dramatic values, importing theater directors from Britain, France, and Broadway to do his *mise-en-scène*. Though there was a steady drumfire of complaint about a decline in vocal quality, by the 1980s we were reading commentary about a golden age of Bing. The truth was somewhere in between.

The great accomplishment of the Bing years was the move to a new theater in Lincoln Center, a large auditorium complex for the performing arts, a little more than a mile uptown from the original Met. Very successful as a machine for producing opera, with first-class manufacturing capabilities on its upper floors, and an acoustical marvel, given the necessary size of the auditorium when the economics dictated 4,000 seats, the new Met is deficient in visual elegance – which, taken with the change in the tenor of the times, has produced an audience much less formally dressed and much less socially eminent than the customers of the old house.

Bing's retirement again saw the death of a chosen successor before he could assume office, and the house passed into the hands of the arts manager Schuyler Chapin. In the uncertain economic times of the mid-1970s, Chapin's budgets were not achieved, and the board assumed control, in the person of the lawyer Anthony Bliss, who promoted the young conductor James Levine to positions of increasing artistic authority. This authority was confirmed in 1983 when it was announced that with the 1986–87 season Levine would assume overall artistic responsiblity for the company. Upon Bliss' retirement in 1985, the general manager's post devolved upon another board member, the advertising executive Bruce Crawford, whose authority would run to the business operations of a company with a budget nearing eighty million dollars a year, and whose approval Levine would need for major expenditure. The relationship sought was roughly that of Gatti-Casazza and Toscanini. What had changed, of course, was the possibility of recruiting singers for entire or even half-seasons in an age when the jet plane has given successful artists easy access to all the world's opera companies – many of them, thanks to government subsidies, richer than the Met. It may be that none of their predecessors faced challenges as daunting as those confronting Crawford and Levine.

Martin Mayer, author of *The Met*, a centennial history, and an active music critic, has also written *The Bankers*, *The Lawyers*, and *Grandissimo Pavarotti*.

Milder-Hauptmann, Anna. Soprano; b. Constantinople, Dec. 13, 1785; d. Berlin, May 29, 1838. On Schikaneder's advice, studied voice in Vienna with Tomaselli and Salieri; debut there as Juno (Süssmayr's *Spiegel von Arkadien*), 1803. Created Beethoven's Fidelio, 1805. Admired by Napoleon during an 1808 tour, she was a sensation in Gluck roles in Berlin (1812), and also sang in Russia, Sweden, Austria. Haydn reportedly described her voice as "like a house." Retired in 1836.

Milhaud, Darius. Composer; b. Aix-en-Provence, France, Sep. 4, 1892; d. Geneva, June 22, 1974. A student of Widor and Dukas at Paris Conservatory, he is one of the most industrious composers of the 20th c. (his catalogue numbers over 400 works). Milhaud's stage works are characterized by transitions between speech and song, rhythmicized but unpitched choral writing, intricate percussion passages, and polytonal harmonies. His operas include *Les Malheurs d'Orphée* (1925); *Christophe Colomb* (1930); *Maximilien* (1932); *Médée* (1939); *Bolivar* (1943; perf. 1950); *David* (1954); *La Mère Coupable*, after Beaumarchais (1965); and several chamber works and children's operas.

Miller, Jonathan. Producer; b. London, July 21, 1934. Trained as a doctor, at Cambridge he wrote and performed in *Beyond the Fringe*. Operatic debut directing Goehr's *Arden Must Die* (Sadler's Wells, 1974). His productions, combining intellectuality and theatricality, include *Cunning Little Vixen* (Glyndebourne, 1975) and *Così* (St. Louis, 1982). His *Rigoletto*, set in N.Y.'s Little Italy in the 1950s, was played at the Met by the English National Opera (1984).

Miller, Mildred. Mezzo-soprano; b. Cleveland, Ohio, Dec. 16, 1924. Studied at Cleveland Institute of Music, then with Sundelius, New England Conservatory; sang with Stuttgart and Munich operas, 1949. Met debut as Cherubino, Nov. 17, 1951; in 24 seasons, she sang 253 perfs. of 21 roles, notably also Siebel, Suzuki, Meg Page, Magdalene (*Meistersinger*), and Nicklausse (*Hoffmann*).

Millo, Aprile. Soprano; b. New York, Apr. 14, 1958. Studied wih her parents, both opera singers, and with Rita Patanè; debut as Aida, Salt Lake City, 1980. La Scala debut as Elvira (*Ernani*), 1982. Met debut as Amelia (*Boccanegra*), Dec. 3, 1984; she has since sung Elvira, Elisabeth (*Don Carlos*), Aida, and Liù there.

Mills, Erie. Soprano; b. Granite City, Ill., June 22, 1953. Studied with Karl Trump, College of Wooster, with Grace Wilson, U. of Illinois, later with Elena Nikolaidi. Debut as Ninetta (*Love for Three Oranges*), Chicago, 1979. With the N.Y.C. Opera, she has sung Cunegonde (*Candide*), Anne Trulove (*Rake*), and Marie (*Fille*); La Scala debut as Giunia (*Lucio Silla*), 1984. Other appearances in Houston, San Francisco, Washington, D.C.

Milnes, Sherrill. Baritone; b. Downers Grove, Ill., Jan. 10, 1935. Studied at Drake U. with Andrew White, and at Northwestern U. with Hermanus Baer, later with Rosa Ponselle. After a summer's study at Santa Fe (1960) he made several tours with Boris Goldovsky's company (debut as Masetto, 1960); his major debut was in Baltimore, as Gérard (*Chénier*), 1961. N.Y.C. Opera debut as Valentin, 1964, also appearing there as Ruprecht (*Fiery Angel*), John Sorel (*Consul*), and in various Italian roles through 1966 (he returned in 1982 to sing Thomas'

Hamlet). His Met debut was also as Valentin (Dec. 22, 1965), and he has returned every season since, singing more than 375 perfs. of 30 roles, notably as Verdi's Amonasro, Renato (*Ballo*), Germont, Don Carlo (*Forza*), Miller, Paolo and later Simon Boccanegra, di Luna, Carlo (*Ernani*), Iago, Posa, Rigoletto, Macbeth, and Monfort (*Vêpres*). His other Met roles include Yeletzky, Don Fernando (*Fidelio*), Jack Rance, Gérard, the Herald (*Lohengrin*), Barnaba, Donner (*Rheingold*), Rossini's Figaro, Tonio, Don Giovanni, Riccardo (*Puritani*), Scarpia, Onegin, Athanaël (*Thaïs*), and Alphonse (*Favorite*); he created Adam in *Mourning Becomes Elecktra*. He has appeared in most leading opera houses, including Chicago (debut, Posa, 1971), Covent Garden (debut, Renato, 1971).

Milnes's large, rich voice, capable of gentleness as well as bite, retains its roundness at the top of the range, equipping him particularly well for the Verdi literature, in which he has succeeded Tibbett and Warren. A forthright rather than a subtle actor, he commands the stage with easy authority. Among the most active of recording artists, he has made over 30 complete operas, as well as numerous recital discs.

Minneapolis/St. Paul. Twin cities in Minnesota. Touring opera companies visited from the 1880s, and the Metropolitan came regularly, 1945–86. The St. Paul Opera, a small, conservative troupe founded in the 1930s, closed in 1973. The Minnesota Opera was established in 1963 as an innovative company dominated by contemporary works (the initial production was Argento's *Masque of Angels*); every season includes one American or world premiere. The American premieres have included Birtwistle's *Punch and Judy* (1969) and Knussen's *Where the Wild Things Are* (1985), and the company has commissioned many works, notably Gessner's *Faust Counter Faust* (1970), Argento's *Postcard from Morocco* (1971), and Susa's *Black River* (1980). A policy of vernacular performance was abandoned in 1985 in favor of surtitles. Productions were originally presented at the Guthrie Theater and other auditoriums, but since 1984 the company is permanently housed in St. Paul's Ordway Theater. Under general director Kevin Smith and music director Joan Dornemann, it presents two or three works yearly and a summer season of American musical theater.

Minton, Yvonne. Mezzo-soprano; b. Sydney, Australia, Dec. 4, 1938. Studied with Marjorie Walker, Sydney Conservatory, then with Henry Cummings and Joan Cross, London; debut in Britten's Lucretia, City Literary Institute, London, 1964. Has sung at Covent Garden since 1965; created Thea (*Knot Garden*) there, 1970. Cologne Opera debut as Sesto (*Clemenza*), 1969; Bayreuth debut as Brangäne, 1974. Octavian was her debut role at Chicago (1970), the Met (Mar. 16, 1973; her only Met appearances), and the Paris Opéra (1976).

Miolan-Carvalho, Marie [née Félix-Miolan]. Soprano; b. Marseilles, France, Dec. 31, 1827; d. Château-Puys, near Dieppe, July 10, 1895. Studied with her father, oboist François Félix-Miolan, then with Duprez, Paris Conservatory; debut as Marie Miolan in excerpts from *Lucia* and *Juive*, Opéra, 1849. After marrying Léon Carvalho in 1853, she sang as Caroline Carvalho. At Théâtre-Lyrique, created four Gounod heroines: Marguerite (1859), Baucis (1860), Mireille (1864), Juliette (1867). A sensation as Dinorah at Covent Garden, 1859, she also appeared in Berlin and St. Petersburg, and retired in 1885.

Dimitri Mitropoulos

Mireille. Opera in 3 (originally 5) acts by Gounod; libretto by Carré, after Frédéric Mistral's poem *Mireio*.

First perf., Paris, Lyrique, Mar. 19, 1864: Miolan-Carvalho, Morini, Ismaël, c. Deloffre. U.S. prem., Chicago, Sep. 13, 1880. Met prem., Feb. 28, 1919: Barrientos, Hackett, Whitehill, c. Monteux, d. Maurel, p. Ordynski. 4 perfs. in 1 season.

Gounod is most successful with the pastoral side of this rural drama, which he altered after its initial limited success, abridging it, adding a showy waltz aria for Miolan-Carvalho, and altering the ending.

In and near Arles, mid-19th c. Mireille (s) and Vincent (t) are in love with each other, but Mireille has another suitor, the bull-tender Ourrias (bar), whom her father,

Anna Moffo as Manon

Maître Ramon (bs), prefers. She and Vincent agree to meet at a specific sanctuary if there is ever trouble in their lives. Ourrias tries to kill Vincent; in the revised version he fails, and Mireille and Vincent meet at the sanctuary, after which her father blesses their union. In the original version Ourrias kills Vincent and then drowns, while Mireille perishes of exhaustion trying to cross the desert to reach the sanctuary.

Mitchell, Leona. Soprano; b. Enid, Okla., Oct. 13, 1949. Studied at Oklahoma City U., later with Ernest St. John Metz in Los Angeles; debut as Micaela, San Francisco Spring Opera, 1972. Met debut as Micaela, Dec. 15, 1975; she has since sung Mme. Lidoine (*Carmélites*), Pamina, Leonora (*Forza*), Elvira (*Ernani*), Puccini's Manon, Liù, and Mimi there. Debuts as Liù in Geneva (1976) and Covent Garden (1980).

Mitridate, Rè di Ponto (Mithridates, King of Pontus). Opera in 3 acts by Mozart; libretto by Vittorio Amadeo Cigna-Santi, after Racine's *Mithridate*.

First perf., Milan, Regio Ducale, Dec. 26, 1770: Bernasconi, d'Ettore, Benedetti, Cicognani. U.S. prem., N.Y., Avery Fisher Hall (Mostly Mozart Festival), Aug. 15, 1985 (concert perf.): c. Schwarz.

Mozart's first opera seria, set in ancient Nymphaeum. The two sons (from former marriages) of Mitridate (t) both fall in love with the king's intended third wife, Aspasia (s). The king rejects both sons, but changes of events and hearts bring reconciliation.

Mitropoulos, Dimitri. Conductor; b. Athens, Mar. 1, 1896; d. Milan, Nov. 2, 1960. Studied in Athens, Brussels, and with Busoni in Berlin (1921–24), where he was a repetiteur under Kleiber. In 1924 returned to Athens Conservatory to lead its orchestra. Engaged in 1936 as a guest by the Boston Symphony, he settled in the U.S., becoming music director of the Minneapolis Symphony (1937–49) and the N.Y. Philharmonic (1949–58). Noted for his championship of contemporary scores (he led works such as *Elektra*, *Wozzeck*, and *Erwartung* in concert at the Philharmonic), he came to the Met in 1954 (debut, *Salome*, Dec. 15) and led a dozen operas, including *Boris*, *Tosca*, *Ballo*, *Boccanegra*, *Walküre*, *Cavalleria* and *Pagliacci*, and the premiere of *Vanessa*. At the Florence Maggio Musicale, he led *Elektra* (1950), *Fanciulla* (1954), and *Ernani* (1957); Chicago Opera debut, *Fanciulla*, 1956. His agitated, baton-less podium style was reflected in nervous, intensely expressive performances, often highly effective theatrically.

Mödl, Martha. Soprano, originally and later mezzo-soprano; b. Nuremberg, Germany, Mar. 22, 1912. Studied at Nuremberg Conservatory; debut as Hänsel, Remscheid, 1942. Sang mezzo roles at Düsseldorf, 1945–49; Covent Garden debut as Carmen, 1949. Changed to soprano register in early 1950s; after her Bayreuth debut as Kundry, 1951, she also sang Isolde and Brünnhilde there. Met debut as Brünnhilde (*Siegfried*), Jan. 30, 1957; she sang 12 perfs. there in 3 seasons, as Kundry, Isolde, and the other Brünnhildes. Returned to mezzo range, singing character roles, in 1960s. Sang in premieres of Einem's *Kabale und Liebe*, Vienna, 1976, and Reimann's *Gespenstersonate*, Berlin, 1984.

Moffo, Anna. Soprano; b. Wayne, Pa., June 27, 1932. Studied with Eufemia Giannini-Gregory, Curtis Institute, Philadelphia, later with Luigi Ricci and Mercedes Llopart,

Rome; debut as Norina (*Pasquale*), Spoleto, 1955. The next year she was seen as Butterfly on Italian television; debuts followed at Aix (Zerlina, 1956), Salzburg (Nannetta, 1957), and Chicago (Mimi, 1957). Met debut as Violetta, Nov. 14, 1959; in 17 seasons, she sang 130 perfs. of 18 roles, including Lucia, Liù, Pamina, Gilda, Adina, Massenet's Manon, Juliette, Nedda, Marguerite, and Mélisande. Also appeared in San Francisco (debut, Amina, 1960), Covent Garden (debut as Gilda, 1964), and in Vienna, Berlin, Paris, and Milan. Moffo's radiant lyric soprano, musicianship, strong feeling for the Italian idiom, and personal beauty won her instant attention among her contemporaries.

Moïse et Pharaon. See *Mosè in Egitto*.

Moiseiwitsch, Tanya. Designer; b. London, Dec. 3, 1913. Designed for Abbey Theatre (Dublin), Old Vic, Royal Shakespeare, and Guthrie Theatre. Opera productions include *Peter Grimes* (Covent Garden, 1948), Argento's *Voyage of Edgar Allan Poe* (Minnesota Opera, 1976), and, for the Met, *Grimes* (1967), *Rigoletto* (1977), and *Traviata* (1981).

Moldoveanu, Vasile. Tenor; b. Konstanza, Romania, Oct. 6, 1935. Studied in Bucharest; debut there as Rinuccio, 1966. Debuts in Stuttgart (Edgardo, 1972), Vienna (Alfredo, 1976), Munich (Rodolfo, 1976), Hamburg (Don Carlos, 1978). Met debut as Pinkerton, Feb. 6, 1979; other Met roles are Rodolfo, Turiddu, Don Carlos, Pinkerton, Puccini's Des Grieux, Gabriele Adorno, Luigi (*Tabarro*), and Henri (*Vêpres*).

Molière, Jean Baptiste Poquelin. French dramatist (1622–73). Operas based on his writings include *L'Amore Medico* (Wolf-Ferrari) and *Le Preziose Ridicole* (Lattuada).

Molinari-Pradelli, Francesco. Conductor; b. Bologna, July 4, 1911. Studied with Molinari in Rome; debut, *Elisir*, Bologna, 1939. Appeared frequently at La Scala (from 1946), Covent Garden (from 1955), San Francisco (from 1957). Between his Met debut (*Ballo*, Feb. 7, 1966) and 1973, he led 17 works, mainly Verdi and Puccini, but also *Roméo*.

Moll, Kurt. Bass; b. Buir, near Cologne, Germany, April 11, 1938. Studied at Cologne Hochschule für Musik and with Emmy Müller in Krefeld. Sang small roles with Cologne Opera while still a student, 1958–61, and made official debut as Lodovico (*Otello*), 1961. Engagements followed in Aachen (1961), Mainz (1964), Wuppertal (1965), and Hamburg (1970). Debuts in Salzburg (1970), Bayreuth (Fafner, 1974), La Scala (Marke, 1974), San Francisco (Gurnemanz, 1974), and Covent Garden (Caspar in *Freischütz*, 1975). Met debut as Landgrave (*Tannhäuser*), Sep. 18, 1978; has also sung Sparafucile, Lodovico, Rocco, Gurnemanz, Ochs, and Osmin with the company. Moll's classic German bass voice is used with fine dramatic authority; his repertory also includes Kečal (*Bartered Bride*), Daland, Ramfis, and Pogner.

Mona. Opera in 3 acts by Parker; libretto by Brian Hooker.
First perf., N.Y., Met, Mar. 14, 1912: Homer, Martin, Griswold, Witherspoon, c. Hertz, d. Paquereau, p. Taylor. 4 perfs. in 1 season.
A symphonically conceived score, with a libretto obviously indebted to *Norma*. During the Roman occupation of Britain, Mona (ms) leads a revolt that fails and kills her lover Gwynn (t), son of a Roman father (bar), erroneously believing him a traitor.

Mona Lisa. Opera in prologue, 2 acts, and epilogue by von Schillings; libretto by Beatrice Dovsky.
First perf., Stuttgart, Sep. 26, 1915: Iracema-Brügelmann, Forsell. U.S. & Met prem., Mar. 1, 1923: Kemp, Bohnen, c. Bodanzky, d. Kautsky. 6 perfs. in 2 seasons.
This grisly German verismo drama tells, in flashback form, of Mona Lisa (s) and her murder of her elderly husband (bar) after he causes the death of Giovanni (t), her former lover.

Mond, Der (The Moon). Opera in 3 acts by Orff; libretto by the composer, after the Brothers Grimm.
First perf., Munich, National Theater, Feb. 5, 1939: Patzak, c. Krauss. U.S. prem., N.Y.C. Opera, Oct. 16, 1956 (in Eng.): Kelly, c. Rosenstock.
Closer to the operatic mainstream than Orff's later stage works, this tells of four lads who steal the moon, and of how St. Peter eventually returns it to the sky.

Moniuszko, Stanislaw. Composer; b. Ubiel, near Minsk, Byelo-Russia, May 5, 1819; d. Warsaw, June 4, 1872. Studied with Freyer in Warsaw and Rungenhagen in Berlin. His opera *Halka* (1848; rev. 1858), using Polish folk rhythms and melodies, became a national institution. Among his later operas, *The Haunted Manor* (1865), another clear expression of patriotism, was suppressed by Tsarist censors after three performances. Moniuszko also composed operettas and songs based on indigenous material.

Monk, Allan. Bass-baritone; b. Mission City, B.C., Aug. 19, 1942. Studied with Elgar Higgin in Calgary and with Boris Goldovsky, N.Y.; debut as Bob (*Old Maid and the Thief*), Western Opera, San Francisco, 1967. Sang in St. Louis, Vancouver, Chicago, Hawaii, and Portland. Met debut as Schaunard (*Bohème*), Mar. 27, 1976; has since sung more than 325 perfs., including the Speaker (*Zauberflöte*), Angelotti, Wozzeck, Wolfram, Lescaut, Malatesta, Posa, Sharpless, and Ford. Created Abelard in Wilson's *Heloise and Abelard*, Canadian National Opera, 1973.

monodrama. A one-character theater work. The term is used to describe a one-character melodrama (q.v.), and was also applied by Schoenberg to his one-character opera *Erwartung*.

Montarsolo, Paolo. Bass; b. Portici, near Naples, Mar. 16, 1925. Studied at Naples Conservatory and in Munich; debut as Lunardo (*Quattro Rusteghi*), Comunale, Bologna, 1950. Sings frequently at La Scala. Met debut as Don Pasquale, Mar. 20, 1975; has also sung Rossini's Basilio and Mustafà (*Italiana*), and Mozart's Bartolo there.

Monte Carlo. Capital of Monaco. Opera became popular in this principality during the mid-19th c. To house the Monte Carlo Opera, Charles Garnier, architect of the Paris Opéra, was engaged to construct the Grand Théâtre next to the casino. This jewel-like Belle Époque theater (capacity 600) opened on Jan. 25, 1879, with Galli-Marié (the original Carmen) in the title role of Planquette's *Le Chevalier Gaston*. The list of singers who subsequently appeared in Monte Carlo included Patti, Tamagno, de Lucia, Nordica, Bonci, Melba, Caruso, and Chaliapin.

Pierre Monteux

Romanian-born impresario Raoul Gunsbourg (director, 1890–1950) made Monte Carlo into a leading operatic center, bringing Berlioz's *Damnation de Faust* to the stage (1893), and offering dozens of world premieres, including Franck's *Hulda* (1894), Fauré's *Pénélope* (1913), many of Massenet's later works, Puccini's *Rondine* (1917), and Ravel's *Enfant et les Sortilèges* (1925). Though no longer enjoying the *réclame* of earlier days, the Monte Carlo Opera, under director John Mordler, still maintains an annual season.

Montemezzi, Italo. Composer; b. Vigasio, near Verona, Italy, May 31, 1875; d. Vigasio, May 15, 1952. Studied with Saladino and Ferroni at Milan Conservatory. His first successful opera, *Giovanni Gallurese* (1905), exhibiting technical knowledge and stage sense, used Wagnerian harmonies in a vocally-oriented Italian context. His best-known work, *L'Amore dei Tre Re* (1913), has had greater success in the U.S., where he lived from 1939 to 1949 (conducting at the Met in 1940), than in Italy. Other operas: *Hellera* (1909); *La Nave* (1918); *La Notte di Zoraima* (1931); and *L'Incantesimo* (1943).

Monteux, Pierre. Conductor; b. Paris, Apr. 4, 1875; d. Hancock, Maine, July 1, 1964. Educated at Paris Conservatory (first prize, violin, 1896); conducted for Diaghilev's Ballets Russes (1911–14), including premieres of Stravinsky's *Petrushka*, *Rite of Spring*, *Nightingale*, Ravel's *Daphnis*, and Debussy's *Jeux*. For two seasons (debut, *Faust*, Nov. 17, 1917), he led the Met's French repertory: *Carmen*, *Thaïs*, *Samson*, *Mireille*, *Marouf*, and the American premiere of *Golden Cockerel*. Monteux then became music director, Boston Symphony (1920–24); second conductor, Amsterdam Concertgebouw (1924–34); founder and conductor, Paris Symphony (1929–38); music director, San Francisco Symphony (1936–52). He returned to the Met on opening night of the 1953–54 season to lead *Faust*, and also conducted *Manon*, *Carmen*, *Hoffmann*, and *Orfeo*, during 3 seasons. At the San Francisco Opera, he led *Manon* (1954). Though his mastery extended widely (he was a notable interpreter of the German classics), Monteux was particularly associated

with the French literature, which called upon his strengths: attention to nuance, coloristic brilliance, and refined phrasing. His discography includes recordings of *Manon*, *Traviata*, and *Orfeo*.

Monteverdi, Claudio. Composer; b. Cremona, May 15, 1567; d. Venice, Nov. 29, 1643. Studied with Ingegneri in Cremona; by age 25, he had published motets and madrigals and was in the employ of the Mantuan court, where he eventually became music director in 1601. By this time his work had become controversial for its harmonic daring. In 1607 his first opera, *L'Orfeo* (1607), was produced in Mantua, followed in 1608 by *L'Arianna*, of which only the protagonist's celebrated lament, "Lasciatemi morire," now survives. Unhappy in Mantua, Monteverdi sought a new position, and in 1613 was appointed music director of Saint Mark's in Venice, where he composed liturgical works, including a mass of thanksgiving (1631) for the end of the plague, and in 1632 took holy orders. During these years he also composed further madrigals, the ballet with voices *Tirsi e Clori* (1616) for Mantua, and the dramatic dialogue *Il Combattimento di Tancredi e Clorinda* (1624), and worked on several operas, the music of which has been lost. When public opera houses opened in Venice in 1637, he composed three more operas; two of these, *Il Ritorno d'Ulisse in Patria* (1641) and *L'Incoronazione di Poppea* (1642), survive, although probably in forms altered by other hands.

Monteverdi's are the earliest operas to figure prominently in the modern repertory, although they went unperformed for nearly three centuries. *L'Orfeo* draws on the same traditions of pastoral, court ballet, madrigal, and monodic recitation as other early operas, but Monteverdi, perhaps the most complete musician of his generation, surpassed all others in the vitality of his recitative, dramatic use of harmony, and theatrical power. The late works for Venice, with smaller instrumental forces, are exceptionally rich in characterization, and *Poppea* fascinates for its drama of a vicious love's triumph over virtue. BIBLIOGRAPHY: Denis Arnold and Nigel Fortune, ed., *The New Monteverdi Companion* (Boston, and London, 1985).

Montezuma. Opera in 3 acts by Sessions; libretto by G. Antonio Borgese, after the memoirs of Bernal Diaz del Castillo.

First perf., Berlin, Deutsche Oper, Apr. 19, 1964 (in Ger.): Bernard, Melchert, Dooley, Krukowski, c. Hollreiser. U.S. prem., Opera Co. of Boston, Mar. 31, 1976: Bryn-Julson, R. Lewis, Ellis, Gramm, c. Caldwell.

In Sessions's opulent, complex historical opera, Diaz (bar) recalls the 1519 landing of Spanish troops in Mexico, the love of Cortez (bar) for the beautiful Malinche (s), the Spaniards' conflict over treatment of the natives, and the death of the Aztec king Montezuma (t) at the hands of his own people.

Montreal. City in Canada. In Montreal was staged what is probably the first opera composed in North America, Joseph Quesnel's *Colas et Colinette*, on Jan. 14, 1790, at the Théâtre de Société, but that auspicious beginning had sporadic sequels. During the 19th c., touring companies gave concert performances or abridged versions at various theatres. In 1914, the Quinlan Opera company presented Canada's first *Ring* cycle, plus other Wagner and Verdi, sung in English. Metropolitan Opera visits in 1899, 1901, and 1911 (the company's first outside the U.S.) offered international casts. Short-lived native companies included

Grace Moore as Louise (film version)

the French Opera Society (1893–95), the Montreal Opera Company (1910–14), and the Canadian National Opera Society (1913–14). From 1936 to 1955, Les Variétés Lyriques included some opera in a regular operetta schedule. The other major company was the modest Opera Guild of Montreal, founded by soprano Pauline Donalda, which produced one or two works annually, 1942–69. The Montreal Symphony's operatic program, begun in 1964, was in 1971 merged with a Quebec company as L'Opéra de Québec, staging works in both cities, but this arrangement proved uneconomical and was abandoned in 1975. Now L'Opéra de Montréal presents four productions a season in the Salle Wilfrid Pelletier (seating 3,000) of the Place des Arts complex, completed in 1967; Jean-Paul Jeannotte is artistic director.

Montresor, Beni. Designer and producer; b. Bussolengo, Italy, Mar. 31, 1926. Began career in film and theater. Has designed opera for Spoleto (*Vanessa*, 1961), Glyndebourne (*Pelléas*, 1962), N.Y.C. Opera (*Zauberflöte*, 1966), and other leading theatres. Met productions: *Last Savage* (1964), *Gioconda* (1966), *Esclarmonde* (originally for San Francisco, 1976), also *Cenerentola* (National Company, 1965).

Moore, Douglas. Composer; b. Cutchogue, N.Y., Aug. 10, 1893; d. Greenpoint, N.Y., July 25, 1969. Studied at Yale U. with D.S. Smith and Parker, later with d'Indy, Boulanger, and Bloch. Most of his operas draw their subjects from rural Americana; technically accomplished, their characteristics are a dominant vocal line, dramatic librettos, and vernacular materials. They include *The Devil and Daniel Webster*, libretto by Benet after his own story (1939); *Giants in the Earth* (1951); the popular *The Ballad of Baby Doe* (1958); *The Wings of The Dove*, after James (1961); and *Carrie Nation* (1966).

Moore, Grace. Soprano; b. Nough, Tenn., Dec. 5, 1898; d. Kastrup Airport, Copenhagen (in an air accident), Jan. 26, 1947. Studied with Marafioti in N.Y., where she appeared in musicals (1921–26), and then with Richard Barthélemy, Antibes, France; operatic debut as Mimi, Met, Feb. 7, 1928; in 15 seasons, she sang 71 perfs. of 10 roles, including Micaela, Juliette, Massenet's Manon,

Louise (which she coached with Charpentier), Fiora (*Amore dei Tre Re*), and Tosca, in many of which her glamor and temperament offset vocal inconsistencies. Other debuts at Opéra-Comique (Louise, 1928), Covent Garden (Mimi, 1935), Chicago (Manon, 1937), and San Francisco (Fiora, 1941). She made films in Hollywood (notably *One Night of Love*) and France (Abel Gance's *Louise*), and published an autobiography, *You're Only Human Once* (1944).

Moranzoni, Roberto. Conductor; b. Bari, Italy, Oct. 5, 1880; d. Desio, Dec. 13, 1959. Student of Mascagni at Pesaro. Director and conductor, Boston Grand Opera (1910–17). Met debut, *Aida*, Nov. 12, 1917; in 7 seasons, he led 19 works, mainly in the Puccini and verismo repertory, including world premiere of *Trittico* and first Met *Andrea Chénier*. Appeared with Chicago Opera (1924–29), then worked in Italy until his retirement in 1947.

Morel, Jean Paul. Conductor; b. Abbéville, France, Jan. 10, 1903; d. New York, Apr. 14, 1975. Student of Pierné and Hahn in Paris; while conducting in France, taught at American Conservatory, Fontainebleau (1921–36). Teacher and conductor at Juilliard School (1949–71); N.Y.C. Opera debut in *Traviata* (Nov. 12, 1944), followed by *Carmen*, *Bohème*, *Mignon*, *Louise*. Met debut in *Périchole* (Dec. 21, 1956); in 9 seasons (1956–62, 1967–68, 1969–71), he also led *Butterfly*, *Orfeo*, and five French works.

James Morris as Dappertutto in *Les Contes d'Hoffmann*

Morell, Barry. Tenor; b. New York, Mar. 30, 1927. Studied in N.Y.; debut as Pinkerton, N.Y.C. Opera, 1955. Met debut in same role, Nov. 1, 1958; he sang there through 1969, and returned in the 1970s, for a total of 176 perfs., including Rodolfo, the Duke of Mantua, and Alfredo. Also appeared in Berlin, Vienna, London.

Morris, James. Bass-baritone; b. Baltimore, Md., Jan. 10, 1947. Studied with Rosa Ponselle, Frank Valentino, Nicola Moscona, and Anton Guadagno; debut as Crespel (*Hoffmann*), Baltimore, 1967. Met debut as King (*Aida*), Jan. 7, 1971; he first sang small roles (Monterone, the Commendatore, and the Marquis in *Forza*), then became a leading artist as Don Giovanni, 1975. He has sung more than 340 perfs. at the house, including Procida (*Vêpres*), Balthasar (*Favorite*), Colline, the Padre Guardiano, Figaro, Claggart (*Billy Budd*), the Grand Inquisitor and Philippe II (*Don Carlos*), Guglielmo (*Così*), and the *Hoffmann* villains, and has appeared widely in Europe and the U.S. Since 1984, with coaching from Hans Hotter, he has moved into the heroic Wagner roles, singing Wotan (*Walküre*) in San Francisco and Vienna (1985) to considerable acclaim.

Moscona, Nicola. Bass; b. Athens, Sep. 23, 1907; d. Philadelphia, Sep. 17, 1975. Studied with Elena Theodorini, Athens Conservatory, and sang in Greece, Egypt, and Italy; La Scala debut as Rudolfo (*Loreley*), 1939. Met debut as Ramfis, Dec. 13, 1937; in 25 seasons, he sang 485 perfs. of 33 roles, including Colline, Ramfis, Lodovico (*Otello*), Raimondo (*Lucia*), Sparafucile, and Ferrando (*Trovatore*). After retirement, taught at Academy of Vocal Arts, Philadelphia.

Moscow. Capital of the U.S.S.R. Opera was introduced here in 1731, when a visiting Italian company staged Ristori's *Calandro* and opera buffa at the Palace of Comedy. Moscow's first opera house opened in 1742 for the coronation of Empress Elizabeth. Russian works were given primarily at the Petrovsky (opened 1780, burned 1805) and Maly (opened 1824) Theaters. Most important is the Bolshoi Theater (capacity 2,000), constructed in 1825 by Bove (burned 1853, rebuilt 1856), which became the center for opera and ballet. The Bolshoi earned its reputation for spectacular productions with meticulous attention to detail, also its superb chorus, attributes that survived the Tsars and are maintained to this day. In 1897 the wealthy Savva Mamontov founded the Moscow Private Russian Opera in opposition to the Bolshoi's extravagant style, and produced both Russian and Western works, attracting important native artists and such composers as Rimsky-Korsakov; it was succeeded in 1904 by the Zimin Opera Theater, which played at the Solodovnikov Theater and Vilial Theater until 1924; Rimsky-Korsakov's *Golden Cockerel* had its first performance at the Solodovnikov in 1909. After the Revolution, the Bolshoi was initially directed by tenor Sobinov. In 1918 Stanislavsky opened the Bolshoi Theater Opera Studio, by 1928 known as the Stanislavsky Opera Theater, which stressed realism and psychological truth in operatic acting. In 1941, this company merged with one founded in 1919 by Nemirovich-Danchenko, which had performed Soviet works, to become the Stanislavsky/Nemirovich-Danchenko Theater, second after the Bolshoi and offering a more adventurous repertory; its current director is Y.P. Privegin. A Chamber Opera Theater was established in 1970, now directed by Boris Pokrovsky. The Bolshoi, however, remains Moscow's

Bolshoi Theater, Moscow

main opera company; it also performs in the 6,000-seat Palace of Congresses, and has made tours to the West in 1964 (Milan) and 1975 (New York); its current director is Stanislav Lushin, with Yuri Simonov as chief conductor.

Mosè in Egitto. Opera in 3 acts by Rossini; libretto by A.L. Tottola, after Francesco Ringhieri's *Sara in Egitto*.

First perf., Naples, San Carlo, Mar. 5, 1818: Colbran, Nozzari, Benedetti. U.S. Prem., N.Y., Masonic Hall, Dec. 22, 1832 (concert perf.). U.S. stage prem., N.Y., Italian Opera House, Mar. 2, 1835. Revised in 4 acts as *Moise et Pharaon*, libretto by Luigi Balocchi and Étienne de Jouy, first perf., Paris, Mar. 26, 1827: Cinti-Damoureau, Nourrit, Levasseur.

One of Rossini's great Neapolitan operas, written for Isabella Colbran, but most often revived for a star basso in the title role; Mosè's prayer "Dal tuo stellato soglio" (added for a Naples revival) attained independent popularity. The two versions of the opera are substantially different, but both center on the prophet's leadership of his people in captivity and conclude with the passage of the Red Sea.

Moser, Edda. Soprano; b. Berlin, Oct. 27, 1938. Studied with Hermann Weissenborn and Gerty König, Berlin Conservatory; debut as Kate Pinkerton, Städtische Oper, 1962. Has sung regularly in Vienna, Salzburg, and Hamburg. Met debut as Wellgunde (*Rheingold*), Nov. 22, 1968; also appearing there as Donna Anna, the Queen of Night, Musetta, Liù, and Konstanze (*Entführung*).

Moses und Aron (Moses and Aron). Opera in 3 acts (incomplete) by Schoenberg; libretto by the composer, after *the Old Testament*, Exodus iii, iv, xxii.

First perf., Hamburg, Northwest German Radio, Mar. 12, 1954 (concert perf.): Krebs, Fiedler, c. Rosbaud. First stage perf., Zurich, June 6, 1957: Melchert, Fiedler, c. Rosbaud. U.S. prem., Boston, Opera Co., Nov. 30, 1966: R. Lewis, Gramm, c. McConathy.

Perhaps Schoenberg's most eloquent exposition of his thought, and a troubled expression of the notion that the highest ideas are compromised by efforts to communicate them. The two completed acts were composed in 1930–32; though the brief third act was never composed, the opera's point is clear (in some performances, Act III is spoken over music by Schoenberg).

Egypt and the Sinai Desert, Biblical times. The wise but reluctant and inarticulate Moses (*Sprechstimme* role) has been chosen by God to lead the Hebrews out of Egyptian

Moses und Aron – Covent Garden. Designed by John Bury, produced by Peter Hall

bondage; his brother Aron (t) is to be his spokesman. Aron gives the people visual signs of God's power, turning Moses' rod into a serpent and healing Moses' leprous hand. Believing they will be saved from slavery, the people initially pledge loyalty to the new God. However, in the desert, when Moses is gone for 40 days, their doubts about this God grow. To calm the people and keep them from killing their priests, Aron lets them set up a Golden Calf to worship, and the people indulge in a wild orgy of lust and murder. Moses returns and destroys the idol, despairing that Aron's efforts to explain his vision to the people corrupted them. In the third act, Aron is arrested; Moses releases him, asserting that God will determine his fate, and Aron falls dead. Moses assures the people that they will be with God even as they toil in the wilderness.

Moshinsky, Elijah. Producer; b. Melbourne, Australia, Jan. 8, 1946. Worked with Royal Shakespeare Company and National Theatre. Directed opera at Covent Garden, including *Peter Grimes* (1975), *Rake* (1979), also Handel's *Samson*, repeated at Chicago Lyric and Met (1986). First Met staging, *Ballo* (1980). Has also directed for English National Opera and Australian Opera.

Mother of Us All, The. Opera in 2 (originally 3) acts by Thomson; libretto by Gertrude Stein.
First perf., N.Y., Columbia U., Brander Matthews Hall: May 7, 1947: Dow, Stich-Randall, Blakeslee, Howland, Horne, Rowe, c. Luening.
The second of Thomson's idiosyncratic, economically composed collaborations with Stein touches more directly on American life: feminist Susan B. Anthony's campaign for women's suffrage is interwoven with scenes from late 19th-c. American life, peopled by 30 other fictional and non-fictional characters.

motive. A brief but distinctive musical idea, used as a basis for development. In operatic usage, most commonly refers to the leitmotif (*q.v.*) or reminiscence motive (*q.v.*).

Motley. Trade name of team of costume and set designers organized in 1930 in England, also active in the U.S. after 1941. Operatic designs include *Beggar's Opera* (Glyndebourne tour, 1940) and *Onegin* (Sadler's Wells, 1952). For Met, designed *Trovatore* (1959), also costumes for *Simon Boccanegra* (1960) and *Martha* (1961).

Mottl, Felix. Conductor; b. Unter-St. Veit, Austria, Aug. 24, 1856; d. Munich, July 2, 1911. Studied with Bruckner in Vienna and assisted at Bayreuth in 1876 (later conducting there, from 1886). Music director at Karlsruhe (1881–1903), where he led first complete *Troyens*, and at Munich (1903–11). During his only Met season (debut, *Walküre*, Nov. 25, 1903), he helped prepare the first American *Parsifal* (actually conducted by Hertz), and led 6 works, including *Roméo* and the first Met *Zauberflöte*.

Mourning Becomes Electra. Opera in 3 acts by Levy; libretto by Henry Butler, after the play by Eugene O'Neill.
First perf., Met, Mar. 17, 1967: Lear, Collier, Milnes, Reardon, Macurdy, c. Mehta, d. Aronson, p. Cacoyannis. 11 perfs. in 2 seasons.
An angular, dramatic, largely atonal setting of O'Neill's play, re-enacting the Electra myth in a New England seaport town after the Civil War.

Moussorgsky, Modest. See *Mussorgsky, Modest.*

Mozart, Wolfgang Amadeus. Composer; b. Salzburg, Jan. 27, 1756; d. Vienna, Dec. 5, 1791. Son of the composer Leopold, his principal teacher, who exhibited him as a pianistic and musical prodigy in Munich, Vienna, Paris, and London, 1762–66. During these and subsequent travels, Wolfgang was exposed to a wide range of composers and styles, and composed the singspiel *Bastien und Bastienne* (1768), the opere buffe *La Finta Semplice* (1769), and the opera seria *Mitridate, Rè di Ponto* (1770) and *Lucio Silla* (1772); although not themselves masterpieces, they show that Mozart had already mastered the day's principal operatic styles. *La Finta Giardiniera* (1775) was composed for Munich, *Il Rè Pastore* (1775) for the Salzburg court, where he held an unrewarding position; in search of a better appointment or a major operatic commission, he travelled with his mother to Mannheim and Paris, 1777–79, but his mother died in Paris and no position was found.
Eventually a Munich commission materialized, for the opera seria *Idomeneo* (1781), Mozart's first demonstration of his full powers as a dramatic composer. That year he resigned his Salzburg post, living subsequently in Vienna on income from teaching and concerts, hoping for a court position and operatic success; in 1782 he married Constanze Weber, whose sister, soprano Aloysia, he had earlier loved. His Viennese operas were moderately successful: the singspiels *Die Entführung aus dem Serail* (1782) and *Der Schauspieldirektor*, and the first collaboration with da Ponte, the opera buffa *Le Nozze di Figaro* (1786). The latter triumphed in Prague, leading to a commission for *Don Giovanni* (1787). Despite a court appointment in 1787, Mozart's financial troubles deepened, and his prospects did not improve with the succession of the unsympathetic Leopold II as emperor, shortly after the Vienna premiere of *Così Fan Tutte* (1790).

In 1791, in failing health, Mozart composed the opera seria *La Clemenza di Tito* for Leopold's coronation as King of Bohemia, and collaborated with Emanuel Schikaneder, director of the Theater auf der Wieden, on the fantasy singspiel *Die Zauberflöte*. Other operas: the Latin intermezzo *Apollo et Hyacinthus* (1767), the "festa teatrale" *Ascanio in Alba* (1771), the serenata *Il Sogno di Scipione* (1772), the unfinished singspiel *Zaide* (1779–80), the unfinished opere buffe *L'Oca del Cairo* (1783) and *Lo Sposo Deluso* (1783); also many substitute arias for his own and others' operas.

Mozart's musical genius is evident in all his work, of which the operas comprise but a part, and the emotional range of his piano concertos and string quintets would suffice to show his exceptional human perception. His mature operas combine Italian vocal style with the formal and textural potential of the German classical instrumental style; especially in company with the wittily profound librettos of da Ponte, his music illumines mankind's weaknesses and nobility with unparalleled grace and sympathy.

BIBLIOGRAPHY: William Mann, *The Operas of Mozart* (N.Y., and London, 1977).

Mozart and Salieri. Opera in 2 acts by Rimsky-Korsakov; libretto by Pushkin.

First perf., Moscow, Solodovnikov Theater, Dec. 7, 1898: Shkafer, Chaliapin, c. Truffi. U.S. prem., Forest Park, Pa., Unity House, Aug. 6, 1933 (in Eng.).

A short, unconventional work, set directly to Pushkin's play without a librettist's intervention. Salieri (bs), disgusted by the frivolous and brilliant Mozart (t), poisons him, and then reflects on his guilt and the futility of his act.

Muck, Karl (Carl). Conductor; b. Darmstadt. Germany, Oct. 22, 1859; d. Stuttgart, Mar. 3, 1940. Without formal musical training, he worked in Zurich, Salzburg, Brünn [now Brno], and Graz before becoming principal conduc-

Wolfgang Amadeus Mozart

tor at the German Opera, Prague, in 1886. Principal conductor (from 1892) and music director (from 1908) at Berlin Opera, where he led over 1,000 performances of 100 operas. A favorite at Bayreuth, where he specialized in *Parsifal* (1901–30). His tenure at the Boston Symphony (1912–18) was cut short by anti-German sentiment. Conductor of Hamburg Philharmonic (1922–33). Noted for his arduous rehearsals and strict attentiveness to the score; Muck's recordings from *Parsifal* are among the most important documents of early 20th-c. Wagnerian performance.

Muette de Portici, La (The Mute Girl of Portici), or *Masaniello*. Opera in 5 acts by Auber; libretto by Scribe and Germain Delavigne, after an historical event.

First perf., Paris, Opéra, Feb. 29, 1828: Cinti-Damoreau, Nourrit, Dupont, c. Habeneck. U.S. prem., N.Y., Park, Nov. 9, 1829 (in Eng.). Met prem., Dec. 29, 1884 (in Ger.): Bely, Schott, Tiferro, c. L. Damrosch, d. Schoeffer. 5 perfs. in 2 seasons.

A romantic French grand opera predating Meyerbeer's domination of the form; an 1830 performance in Brussels signalled the outbreak of a local revolution.

Portici and Naples, 1647. Outraged by the betrayal of his sister, the mute girl Fénéla (dancer), at the hands of the Spanish Viceroy's son Alphonse (t), and by Spanish oppression of the Neapolitans, Masaniello (t) leads a violent uprising. Later regretting the revolutionary excesses, he helps Alphonse and his sister Elvire (s) to escape, for which he is slain by his own men. Overwhelmed by the loss of her brother, Fénéla commits suicide.

Mugnone, Leopoldo. Conductor; b. Naples, Sep. 29, 1858; d. Capodichino, Naples, Dec. 22, 1941. A leading Italian opera conductor of the verismo generation, closely associated with Puccini (world premiere of *Tosca*, Rome, 1900), he also led premiere of *Cavalleria* (1890), and appeared often in London (1905–25).

Müller, Maria. Soprano; b. Theresienstadt [now Terezin, near Litoměřice], Bohemia, Jan. 29, 1898; d. Bayreuth, Mar. 13, 1958. Studied in Prague, in Vienna with Erik Schmedes, and in N.Y. with Max Altglass; debut as Elsa, Linz, 1919. Sang in Prague (1921–23) and Munich (1923–24). Met debut as Sieglinde, Jan. 21, 1925; in 11 seasons, she sang 167 perfs. of 19 roles, including Aida, Butterfly, Eva, Sieglinde, Donna Elvira, Gutrune, and the first U.S. Amelia (*Boccanegra*). Also sang in Berlin (1926–43) and at Bayreuth (1930–44).

Munich. Capital of Bavaria, West Germany. The first theater in Germany built specifically for opera, the Opera House on the Salvatorplatz (also known as the Salvator-theater), opened in 1656 with Johann Kaspar Kerll's *Oronte*. In 1753, François Cuvilliés built the Residenz-theater (also known as Cuvilliés-Theater), which became the center for opera seria; Mozart's *Idomeneo* had its premiere there in 1781. The 19th c. saw the opening of the Theater am Isartor, where singspiel was played from 1812 to 1825, and the Hof- und Nationaltheater, designed by Karl von Fischer (opened 1818, rebuilt 1825, 1963). The latter was directed by Franz Lachner (1836–67) until King Ludwig II's patronage of Wagner brought von Bülow on the scene; Wagner's *Tristan*, *Meistersinger*, *Rheingold*, and *Walküre* were first performed in Munich (1865–70). Important later premieres include Pfitzner's *Palestrina* (1917) and Strauss' *Capriccio* (1942). Von Bülow was succeeded by an impressive list of music directors, among

The National Theater, Munich

them Levi, Mottl, Walter, Knappertsbusch, Krauss, Solti, Kempe, Fricsay, and Keilberth; the current artistic director and chief conductor is Wolfgang Sawallisch. The Prinzregententheater, modeled on the Bayreuth Festspielhaus, opened in 1901 with *Meistersinger*, and housed the Bavarian State Opera after World War II, until the destroyed Nationaltheater was rebuilt; during those years, the Staatstheater am Gärtnerplatz, opened in 1865 for comic opera, was Munich's second opera house. The refurbished Cuvilliés auditorium, disassembled and stored during World War II, was reconstructed in the Alte Residenz in 1958. Munich presents a summer opera festival, inaugurated in 1875, which concentrates on the Mozart–Strauss–Wagner repertory.

Munsel, Patrice. Soprano; b. Spokane, Wash., May 14, 1925. Studied with William Herman and Renato Bellini, N.Y.; after winning Auditions of the Air, debut at Met as Philine (*Mignon*), Dec. 4, 1943, the youngest singer ever to appear in a principal role at the house. Sang with Met until 1958, as Lucia, Rosina, Despina, Gilda, and with special success as Adele (*Fledermaus*) and Périchole. Made several European tours, and starred in the 1953 film *Melba*.

Muratore, Lucien. Tenor; b. Marseilles, France, Aug. 29, 1876(?); d. Paris, July 16, 1954. Studied at Marseilles Conservatory, but began his career as an actor, appearing occasionally with Sarah Bernhardt. Later studied voice at Paris Conservatory. Operatic debut as the King (Hahn's *Carmélite*), Opéra-Comique, 1902. Created roles in Massenet's *Ariane* and *Bacchus* at the Opéra and his *Roma* in Monte Carlo. Principal French tenor with the Boston and Chicago Operas, 1913–22, with time out for wartime service in the French Army.

Murder in the Cathedral. See *Assassinio nella Cattedrale*.

Musgrave, Thea. Composer; b. Barnton, Midlothian, Scotland, May 27, 1928. Studied at U. of Edinburgh and with Boulanger in Paris. Since the 1967 opera *The Decision*, her music has been characterized by an eclectic use of musical gesture; in her later works, the ensemble is often not strictly coordinated. Her operas include the one-act chamber opera *The Abbot of Drimoch* (1958); *The Voice of Ariadne*, after James (1974); *Mary, Queen of Scots* (1977); and two works first presented by the Virginia Opera, *A*

Christmas Carol, after Dickens (1979), and *Harriet, the Woman Called Moses* (1985).

musical comedy. A form of 20th-c. popular musical theater in the U.S. and Britain, using spoken dialogue and musical numbers in a manner similar to operetta; the musical idiom draws principally on vernacular styles, including minstrel shows, ragtime, jazz, and rock.

music drama. The term introduced by Wagner for his operas beginning with *Rheingold*; it had an implicit polemic intent, denigrating those works supposedly devoted to vocal or scenic display rather than to true drama.

music theater. A contemporary, loosely applied term for works combining music and theater in forms other than traditional opera, usually involving a high degree of theatrical stylization.

Mussorgsky, Modest. Composer; b. Karevo, Pskov district, Russia, Mar. 21, 1839; d. St Petersburg, Mar. 28, 1881. He studied piano as a child, and dabbled at composition while at military school in St. Petersburg. In 1857, he met other Russian nationalist composers, notably Balakirev, with whom he studied musical form. The next year, he resigned from the Imperial Guard to devote himself to composition; he later held civil service positions (1863–67, 1869–80). Despite an often disorganized existence (compounded by recurrent alcoholism) and a lack of formal training, he evolved in his many songs an original mode of lyrical declamation reflecting the intonations of Russian speech, and used harmony in unorthodox but often powerful ways.

In addition to works for piano, orchestra, and chorus, he worked on numerous operatic projects. *Salammbô*, after Flaubert, was abandoned in 1866 (some of the music to be re-used in *Boris*). In setting Gogol's *The Marriage*, he experimented with highly naturalistic recitative; after one act was privately performed in 1868 and criticized as extreme, this too was dropped. He achieved a more satisfactory balance of speech and music in the historical drama *Boris Godunov* (1874), his only completed opera, which transmutes elements of Meyerbeerian grand opera, into an original type of tableau dramaturgy. In 1872 Mussorgsky began another historical work, *Khovanshchina*, and in 1874 the comic opera *Sorochintsy Fair*, but neither was finished at his death. Most of Mussorgsky's works were posthumously edited by Rimsky-Korsakov, in whose versions they first achieved international circulation; he gave them a more conventional and spectacular orchestral guise, but bowdlerized much of the harmonic originality. In recent years, performances closer to the original texts have become more frequent.
BIBLIOGRAPHY: M.D. Calvocoressi, *Modest Mussorgsky* (London, 1974).

Muti, Riccardo. Conductor; b. Naples, July 28, 1941. After study at conservatories in Naples and Milan (under Votto), won 1967 Cantelli competition. Debut the next year at Florence Maggio Musicale, of which he became principal conductor (1969–80), leading important revivals, including *Africaine* and an uncut *Guillaume Tell*. U.S. debut, Philadelphia Orchestra, 1972; its music director since 1980, leading an opera in concert every season. Principal conductor (1974–79) and music director (1979–82), Philharmonia Orchestra, London. Music director, La

Modest Mussorgsky

Scala, from 1986. Regular guest in Salzburg (from 1971), also in Vienna, Paris. An admirer of Toscanini, Muti is known for his intense, polished, carefully detailed interpretations and his literalist approach to the musical text; his recordings include *Orfeo*, *Capuleti*, *Puritani*, and several Verdi works.

Claudia Muzio as Tosca

Muzio, Claudia. Soprano; b. Pavia, Feb. 7, 1889; d. Rome, May 24, 1936. Daughter of a stage director (at the Met and Covent Garden) and a chorus singer, she studied with Annetta Casaloni in Turin and Elettra Callery-Viviani in Milan; debut as Massenet's Manon, Arezzo, 1910. At La Scala (debut, Desdemona, 1913), she created Mariela in Smareglia's *L'Abisso*, 1914; though she returned there, 1925–30, and sang regularly in Rome after 1928, her career was made largely in the Americas (she sang one season at Covent Garden, 1914). After a Met debut as Tosca on Dec. 4, 1916, she remained for 6 seasons (and returned as Violetta and Santuzza in 1934), singing 152 perfs. of 15 roles, also including Puccini's Manon, Nedda, Leonora (*Trovatore*), Aida, Mimi, Berthe (*Prophète*), Fiora (*Amore dei Tre Re*), Butterfly, and Loreley; she created Giorgetta in *Tabarro*, and was the Met's first Tatiana (*Onegin*) and Maddalena (*Chénier*). Between 1919 and 1934, she sang frequently at the Colón in Buenos Aires, often also in Montevideo, Rio de Janeiro, and São Paulo, in roles that included Turandot, Norma, Wally, Elsa, the Marschallin, and Respighi's Fiamma. After leaving the Met, she joined the Chicago Opera for nine seasons, beginning with an Aida in 1922; other roles there included Monna Vanna, Boito's Margherita, and Ginevra (*Cena delle Beffe*). She sang in San Francisco, 1924–26, and returned in 1932 to open the new War Memorial Opera House as Tosca. In 1934 in Rome, she created Refic's Cecilia.

Hailed in Italy as "the Duse of song," Muzio was an intense and passionate singer of the verismo literature, resourceful in emotional coloring of the vocal line; in her Met years, she also commanded enough flexibility to deal with earlier repertory. She made many recordings in 1917–24, and a famous late series (1934–5), when her technical powers, though not her communicative ones, were in decline.

N

Nabucco (orig. *Nabucodonosor*) (Nebuchadnezzar). Opera in 3 acts by Verdi; libretto by Solera, after the play *Nabucodonosor* by Anicet-Bourgeois and Francis Cornue.

First perf., Milan, La Scala, Mar. 9, 1842: Strepponi, Ronconi, Derivis. U.S. prem., N.Y., Astor Place, Apr. 4, 1848. Met prem., Oct. 24, 1960: Rysanek, MacNeil, Siepi, c. Schippers. 9 perfs. in 1 season.

Verdi's first major success, an opera charged with the raw energy and violence (and the appeal to nationalistic sentiment) that dominated his early style.

Jerusalem and Babylon, 587 B.C. Jerusalem has been defeated by Nabucco (bar), King of Assyria, but his daughter Fenena (s) is held hostage by the Hebrews and their priest Zaccaria (bs). Ismaele (t), a Hebrew with whom she is in love, allows Fenena to escape to her father and repulses the advances of her warrior sister Abigaille (s). The Hebrews are taken captive to Babylon. Enraged by the favor shown her sister by both Ismaele and Nabucco (who has made Fenena regent), Abigaille discovers she is not Nabucco's daughter, but a child of slaves, and swears vengeance on all. Nabucco returns, declaring himself both King and God, is struck by lightning, and temporarily loses his sanity. When his reason returns, he prays for forgiveness to Jehovah, and saves the Hebrews. Abigaille poisons herself and dies repentant.

Teatro San Carlo, Naples

Nagy, Robert. Tenor; b. Lorain, Ohio, Mar. 3, 1929. Studied at Cleveland Institute of Music; debut as Giuseppe (*Traviata*), Met, Nov. 2, 1957. Since then, he has sung more than 900 perfs. with the company, from comprimario roles to Canio, Florestan, Herod (*Salome*), Emperor (*Frau*). Has also appeared with N.Y.C. Opera (debut, Luigi in *Tabarro*, 1969), and other North American companies.

Naples. Italian city. Modern scholarship tentatively dates the beginning of opera in Naples to a 1650 performance of Cavalli's *Didone*. The first permanent company, the Febi Armoncici, staged its productions in the park of the royal palace, later in the Teatro di San Bartolomeo. Naples rose as an opera center towards the end of the 17th c., when Alessandro Scarlatti was the dominant figure, and comic opera in local dialect was first seen in public in 1709. Naples' most famous theater, the San Carlo (designed by Giovanni Medrano), opened Nov. 4, 1737 with Sarro's *Achille in Sciro*, replacing the demolished San Bartolomeo as the home of opera seria. Another great period in Neapolitan musical activity was due to Domenico Barbaja, impresario of the San Carlo and Teatro del Fondo (opened 1799), for whom Rossini wrote several important works. Donizetti served as director of the royal theaters (1827–38) and was succeeded by Mercadante (until 1870), but Verdi's relationship with Naples was plagued by censorship difficulties. During the 20th c., many renowned singers and conductors have appeared at the San Carlo (capacity 1,530), rebuilt in 1816 and still in use. The season runs from December to May, and the current general manager is Francesco Canessa.

Navarraise, La (The Girl of Navarre). Opera in 2 acts by Massenet; libretto by Jules Claretie and Henri Cain, after Claretie's *La Cigarette*.

First perf., London, Covent Garden, June 20, 1894: Calvé, Alvarez, Plançon, c. Flon. U.S. & Met prem., Dec. 11, 1895: Calvé, Lubert, Plançon, c. Bevignani, p. Parry. Anita was also sung at the Met by Farrar. 9 perfs, in 2 seasons.

Massenet's essay in verismo, set near Bilbao, Spain, in the 1870s. To acquire the dowry she needs to marry Araquil (t), Anita (s) volunteers to assassinate a Carlist general; though she succeeds, Araquil has been fatally wounded, and Anita loses her reason.

Navarro, Garcia. Conductor; b. Chiva, Spain, Apr. 30, 1941. Studied conducting under Ferrara in Italy and Swarowsky in Vienna (1966–69). Principal conductor, Spanish National Orchestra (from 1972) and Stuttgart Radio Orchestra (1984–86). Covent Garden debut, *Bohème*, 1979; Met debut, *Cavalleria* and *Pagliacci*, Nov. 4, 1985.

Neblett, Carol. Soprano; b. Modesto, Calif., Feb. 1, 1946. Studied with William Vennard, Lotte Lehmann, Pierre Bernac; debut as Musetta, N.Y.C. Opera, 1969; other roles there included Marietta (*Tote Stadt*), Monteverdi's Poppea, Boito's Margherita and Elena. Also sang in Chicago (debut, Chrysothemis, 1975), and as Minnie (*Fanciulla*) in Vienna (1976) and Covent Garden (1977). Met debut as Senta, Mar. 8, 1979; other roles there include Tosca, Amelia (*Ballo*), Musetta, Puccini's Manon, and Alice Ford.

Neher, Caspar. Designer; b. Augsburg, Germany, Apr. 11, 1897; d. Vienna, June 30, 1962. Worked in Berlin with Ebert; their expressionistic *Macbeth* (1931) was recreated in Glyndebourne (1938) and at the Met (1959). Other positions in Frankfurt (1931–41) and Berlin (Deutsches Theater, 1934–44; Berliner Ensemble, 1948–57); a close friend of Brecht, he wrote the libretto for Weill's *Bürgschaft*. At Met, also designed *Wozzeck* (1959).

Neidlinger, Gustav. Bass-baritone; b. Mainz, Germany, Mar. 21, 1912. Studied with Otto Rottneper, Frankfurt; debut in Mainz, 1931. Sang at Hamburg, 1936–50, then at Stuttgart, also appearing frequently in Vienna (from 1956), and at Bayreuth (1952–75) as Kurwenal, Klingsor, Telramund, and Alberich, his most celebrated part. His only Met appearances were as Alberich in 4 perfs. of *Siegfried* (debut, Nov. 17, 1972).

Nelli, Herva. Soprano; b. Florence, Italy, Jan. 9, 1909. Came to U.S. at age 12; studied at Pittsburgh Music Institute, San Francisco. Opera debut as Santuzza, Salmaggi Opera at the Hippodrome, N.Y., 1937. Met debut as Aida, Jan. 23, 1953; she also sang Maddalena, Amelia (*Ballo*), Santuzza, Donna Anna, and both Verdi Leonoras, 1953–61. Favored by Toscanini, she participated in four of his recorded opera broadcasts: *Aida*, *Ballo*, *Falstaff*, and *Otello*.

Nelson, John. Conductor; b. San José, Costa Rica, Dec. 6, 1941, of American parents. After study at Juilliard (1963–67), conducted at N.Y.C. Opera (1972–74; debut, *Carmen*, 1972). Met debut, *Troyens*, Oct. 30, 1973; in 1974–75, led *Cavalleria*, *Pagliacci*, *Jenůfa*, and *Barbiere*. Music director, Indianapolis Symphony (1976–1987); currently director of Opera Theater of St. Louis.

Nemirovich-Danchenko, Vladimir. Manager and producer; b. Ozurgety, Georgia, Dec. 23, 1858; d. Moscow, Apr. 25, 1943. In 1898, with Stanislavsky, he founded the Moscow Art Theater, influential home of naturalistic drama productions. After the 1917 revolution, he directed the Moscow Art Theater Musical Studio, which rejected conventional operatic staging in favor of stylized movement and abstract settings;

(continued p.249)

34 (*Above*). *La Gioconda* – (1966). Design by Beni Montresor for Act II of Ponchielli's opera

35 (*Right*). *Mefistofele* – (New York City Opera, 1969). Norman Treigle as Mefistofele in Act II, Scene 2 of Boito's opera, sets by David Mitchell and costumes by Hal George

38 *Otello* – (1972). Sherrill Milnes as Iago and James McCracken as Otello in Act II of Verdi's opera, set by Franco Zeffirelli, costumes by Peter J. Hall

36 *Opposite (above)*. *Don Carlos* – (1920). Design by Joseph Urban for Act IV, Scene 1 of Verdi's opera
37 *(Below)*. *Don Carlos* – (1983). Act III, Scene 2, set by David Reppa, costumes by Ray Diffen

39 *This page (right). La Bohème* — (1981). Teresa Stratas as Mimi and José Carreras as Rodolfo in Act IV of Puccini's opera, set by Franco Zeffirelli, costumes by Peter J. Hall

40 *(Below). Manon Lescaut* — (1980). Renata Scotto as Manon in Act II of Puccini's opera, designed by Desmond Heeley

41 *Opposite (top). Madama Butterfly* — (1968). Teresa Stratas as Cio-Cio-San and Barry Morell as Pinkerton in Act I of Puccini's opera, designed by Motohiro Nagasaka

42 *(Bottom). Turandot* — (1961). Franco Corelli as Calaf and Birgit Nilsson as Turandot in the final scene of Puccini's opera, designed by Cecil Beaton

43 *Tosca* – (1985). Design by Franco Zeffirelli for Act III of Puccini's opera, showing both the roof of the Castel Sant'Angelo and (revealed later) Cavaradossi's prison cell

44 The Act I *Te Deum* with Cornell MacNeil as Scarpia in the same production, costumes by Peter J. Hall

45 *Cavalleria Rusticana* – (1970). Grace Bumbry as Santuzza and Franco Corelli as Turiddu, in a production of Mascagni's opera designed by Franco Zeffirelli

46 *Pagliacci* – (1970). Lucine Amara as Nedda in Act I of Leoncavallo's opera, designed by Franco Zeffirelli

librettos, even scores were freely altered, as in the Bizet adaptation, *Carmencita and the Soldier* (1924). Renamed the Nemirovich-Danchenko Music Theater in 1926, the studio's work, admired by Western directors such as Reinhardt and Felsenstein, was less influential in Stalin's conservative Soviet Union.

Nerone (Nero). Opera in 4 acts by Boito; libretto by the composer; unfinished, completed by Tommasini and Toscanini.
First perf., Milan, La Scala, May 1, 1924; Carena, Pertile, Galeffi, Journet, c. Toscanini. U.S. prem., N.Y., Carnegie Hall (Opera Orchestra), April 12, 1982 (concert perf.): Andrade, Cigoj, Elvira, Morris, c. Queler. U.S. stage prem., May 14, 1983, N.Y., Amato Opera.
An opera of dignity and consistency, if limited musical imagination, set in Rome, c. 60 A.D. Intrigues involving Nero (t), the sorcerer Simon Mago (bs), the tormented Asteria (s), and the Christian leader Fanuel (bar), culminate in the burning of Rome.

Nessler, Victor. Composer; b. Baldenheim, Alsace, Jan. 28, 1841; d. Strassburg [now Strasbourg], May 28, 1890. Conductor of the Carola-Theater in Leipzig from 1870, he established his reputation as a composer with *Der Rattenfänger von Hamelin* (1879), and especially *Der Trompeter von Säckingen* (1884), which won an international audience through its accessible, sentimental melodies.

Nesterenko, Evgeny. Bass; b. Moscow, Jan. 8, 1938. Studied at Leningrad Conservatory; debut as Gremin (*Onegin*), Maly, 1963. He sang there and at the Kirov until 1971, when he joined the Bolshoi, with which he sang Boris on tour at La Scala (1973), Vienna (1974), and the Met (1975). Covent Garden debut as Basilio, 1978; sang Philippe II (*Don Carlos*), La Scala, 1978.

Neues vom Tage (News of the Day). Opera in 3 (later 2) acts by Hindemith; libretto by Marcellus Schiffer.
First perf., Berlin, Kroll, June 8, 1929: Stückgold, Kalter, Cavara, Krenn, Ernster, c. Klemperer. Revised in 2 acts, first perf., Naples, San Carlo, Apr. 7, 1954. U.S prem., Santa Fe, Aug. 12, 1961 (in Eng.): Willauer, Bonazzi, Driscoll, c. Hindemith.
A satire on modern life and on journalism, which exploits the unhappiness of a young couple.

Neuinszenierung (Ger.). New production.

Neumann, Angelo. Impresario; b. Vienna, Aug. 18, 1838; b. Prague, Dec. 20, 1910. Studied singing with Stilke-Sessi; debut, Berlin, 1859. Director of Leipzig Opera (1876–1882), Bremen Opera (1882–1885), and the German Opera, Prague (1885–1910). In 1882 he formed a touring company that presented Wagner's operas, including the complete *Ring*, in London, Paris, Rome, and St. Petersburg.

Neumann, Václav. Conductor; b. Prague, Oct. 29, 1920. Studied in Prague (1940–45) and played with Smetana Quartet; conducting debut with Czech Philharmonic (1948). Won attention leading Felsenstein's production of *Cunning Little Vixen* at the Berlin Komische Oper (1956), where he remained until 1964. General director, Leipzig Opera (1964–68), Stuttgart Opera (1970–73); principal conductor, Czech Philharmonic (since 1968). Met debut, *Jenůfa*, Sep. 24, 1985.

Nevada [Wixom], **Emma.** Soprano; b. Alpha, near Nevada City, Calif., Feb. 7, 1859; d. Liverpool, June 20, 1940. Studied with Mathilde Marchesi in Vienna; debut in *Sonnambula*, London, Her Majesty's, 1880. Sang in Italy and Paris (1880–83) and in premiere of Mackenzie's *Rose of Sharon*, London, 1884. U.S. debut as Amina, Academy of Music, N.Y., 1884; alternated on tour with Patti. Sang at Covent Garden, 1887, and toured U.S. again in several later seasons.

Neway, Patricia. Soprano; b. Brooklyn, N.Y., Sep. 30, 1919. Studied at Mannes College of Music, N.Y., and with Morris Gesell (later her husband); debut as Fiordiligi, Chautauqua, 1946. Created two Menotti roles, Magda Sorel (*Consul*, Broadway, 1950) and the Mother (*Maria Golovin*, Brussels, 1958); also sang Leah in Tamkin's *Dybbuk*, her N.Y.C. Opera debut, 1951. Also sang at Aix (*Iphigénie en Tauride*, 1952) and at Paris Opéra-Comique (1952–54).

New Orleans. City in Louisiana. Operatic activity developed early because of the city's economic prosperity and mainly French population. In 1791 a French troupe arrived, led by Louis Tabary, who the next year became manager of the theater known as Le Spectacle de la Rue St. Pierre (1806–10). Other houses were the Théâtre de la Rue St. Philippe (in use 1808–32) and the more important Théâtre d'Orléans (opened 1809, rebuilt 1813, destroyed 1866) which, under Charles Boudousquié, witnessed the American premieres of *Huguenots* (1839), *Lucia* (1841), and *Prophète* (1850). The Théâtre St. Charles, though not exclusively an opera house, produced the first U.S. *Norma* and *Semiramide* (both 1836). The celebrated French Opera House, built by Boudousquié, opened Dec. 1, 1859, with *Guillaume Tell*; here, before it burned in 1919, *Le Cid* (1890) and *Samson et Dalila* (1893) had their first American hearings. In 1943, Walter Loubart founded the New Orleans Opera Association, which presented standard repertory in the New Orleans Auditorium until 1973, then moving to the more suitable New Orleans Theater for the Performing Arts (capacity 2,317). The annual season, October to December, usually includes four works, and occasionally recalls the city's operatic heritage with *Juive* or *Thaïs*; Arthur Cosenza is general manager.

New York. City in northeastern U.S. In the mid-18th c., theaters in Nassau Street, John Street, and elsewhere hosted visiting companies presenting ballad opera and opéra comique. In 1825, Italian opera was introduced at the Park Theatre (opened 1798) by a troupe headed by Manuel Garcia and his daughter Maria (later Malibran); *Barbiere* was followed by other Rossini and Mozart operas. The first theater built specifically for opera, the Italian Opera House, opened on Nov. 18, 1833, but burned in 1839. Palmo's Opera House (1844–48) and the Astor Place Opera House (1847–52) housed local premieres of works by Bellini, Donizetti, Mercadante, and Verdi. More enduring was the Academy of Music (capacity 4,600), which opened on Oct. 2, 1854 with *Norma*, starring Grisi and Mario. Annual seasons were presented until 1886 by impresarios such as Mapleson.
Built by a group of wealthy men who could not obtain boxes at the Academy, the Metropolitan Opera House (capacity 3,045, later enlarged to 3,849) opened on Oct. 22, 1883, with *Faust*, and quickly became the city's leading opera house. At first it was leased to outside managers, including Henry Abbey (1883–84), Leopold Damrosch (1884–85), Edmond C. Stanton (1885–91), Abbey, John

Academy of Music, New York

B. Schoeffel, and Maurice Grau (1891–97), Grau alone (1898–1903), and Heinrich Conried (1903–08). However, the production company founded in 1908 and managed by Giulio Gatti-Casazza (1908–35) later, during the tenure of Edward Johnson (1935–50), purchased the theater from its owners. During the regime of Rudolf Bing (1950–72), a new Metropolitan Opera House (capacity 3,800) was constructed at Lincoln Center, opening Sep. 16, 1966, with Barber's *Antony and Cleopatra*. After Bing, Göran Gentele (1972) and Schuyler Chapin (1972–75) were succeeded by Anthony A. Bliss (1975–85); current general manager is Bruce Crawford, with James Levine as artistic director. The season extends from September to April, with 7 performances weekly, as well as summer concert performances in the city's parks; an annual national tour was abandoned in 1986. The Metropolitan Opera Guild, founded by Mrs. August Belmont in 1936, publishes the magazine *Opera News* and engages in a wide range of educational and outreach programs. Unique for its size (over 110,000 members) the Guild has served as a model replicated by opera companies throughout the world.

The New York City Opera (originally the City Center Opera Company) gave its first performances at the N.Y. City Center on 56th Street in 1944, and moved in 1966 to the N.Y. State Theater (capacity 2,800) at Lincoln Center. Under directors Laszlo Halasz (1944–51), Joseph Rosenstock (1952–55), Erich Leinsdorf (1955–56), and Julius Rudel (1957–79), the company achieved a reputation for adventurous repertory and productions, while vigorously cultivating American talent. The current general director is Beverly Sills, with Sergiu Comissiona as music director; the opera season, formerly divided into fall and spring segments, now runs from July through November, with a season of American musical theater in the late winter.

Opera in New York is performed by numerous other companies, and can be heard year-round. Among the most durable are the Amato Opera Theater (founded in 1948), which concentrates on 19th-c. Italian works, and the Bel Canto Opera (founded 1969), which specializes in rare repertory. The Opera Orchestra of New York, directed and conducted by Eve Queler, offers concert performances with major stars, continuing the tradition of the American Opera Society (1951–70). Among the city's conservatories, the Juilliard American Opera Center (founded 1970) and the Manhattan School of Music present performances of virtually professional caliber.

Nicolai, Otto. Composer and conductor; b. Königsberg, Prussia, June 9, 1810; d. Berlin, May 11, 1849. Studied with Zelter and Klein in Berlin, and with Baini in Rome. Composed in Italy, his first operas, *Enrico Il d'Inghilterra* (1839) and *Il Templario* (1840), brought him only temporary success; he then worked in Vienna (1841) and Berlin (1848), where his last and best-known work, *Die lustigen Weiber von Windsor* (1849), was produced. Here Nicolai's combination of German schooling and Italianate facility found its happiest expression; regrettably, he died a few months later of a stroke.

Nicolesco [Niculescu], **Mariana.** Soprano; b. Brasov, Romania. Studied at Cluj Conservatory, with Jolanda Magnoni at Santa Cecilia, Rome; debut as Mimi, Cincinnati Opera, 1972. N.Y.C. Opera debut as Violetta, 1977, also the role of her Met debut, Oct. 11, 1978; later Met roles included Gilda, Nedda. Sang in premiere of Berio's *Vera Storia*, La Scala, 1972; has also appeared widely in Europe.

Nicolini, Ernesto [Ernest Nicolas]. Tenor; b. St. Malo, France, Feb. 23, 1834; d. Pau, Jan. 19, 1898. Studied at Paris Conservatory; debut in Halévy's *Mousquetaires de la Reine*, Opéra-Comique, 1857. Sang in Italy (1859), at Italien, Paris (1862–69), Drury Lane, London (1871), and Covent Garden (from 1872). Toured with Patti, married her in 1886.

Nielsen, Carl. Composer; b. Sortelung, near Nørre-Lyndelse, Denmark, June 9, 1865; d. Copenhagen, Oct. 3, 1931. Studied with Hartmann and Rosenhoff at Copenhagen Conservatory; conducted at the Royal Opera (1908–14). Denmark's greatest composer of the 20th c., Nielsen was primarily and most innovatively a symphonist. Before his mature style had fully developed, he composed two works for the lyric theater: the grand opera *Saul og David* (1902), with rich, oratorio-like choral writing; and *Maskarade* (1906), an opera buffa in the Danish 18th-c. style.

Niemann, Albert. Tenor; b. Erxleben, near Magdeburg, Germany, Jan. 15, 1831; d. Berlin, Jan. 13, 1917. Debut in Dessau, 1849; later studied with Schneider and Nusch, and with Duprez in Paris. Member of Berlin Opera, 1866–87. Sang first Tannhäuser in Paris version (1861), Siegmund in first complete *Ring* (Bayreuth, 1876). At the Met (debut, Siegmund, Nov. 10, 1886), he was the first American Tristan and *Götterdämmerung* Siegfried; in his 2 seasons there, he also sang Jean de Leyde (*Prophète*), Tannhäuser, Lohengrin, Florestan, Eléazar (*Juive*), and Fernand Cortez.

Nightingale, The. Opera in 3 acts by Stravinsky; libretto by the composer and Stepan Mitousoff, after Hans Christian Andersen's story.

First perf., Paris, Opéra, May 26, 1914 (in Fr., as *Le Rossignol*): Dobrovolska, Petrenko, Varfolomeyev, Andreyev, c. Monteux. U.S. & Met prem., Mar. 6, 1926 (in Fr.): Talley, Wakefield, Errolle, Didur, c. Serafin, d. Soudeikine, p. Thewman. Later Met production: Dec. 3, 1981: Bradley (danced by Makarova), Creech (danced by Dowell), Chookasian, Meredith, c. Levine, d. Hockney, p. Dexter (choreography by Ashton). 23 perfs. in 4 seasons.

Stravinsky composed the first act of this "musical fairy tale" before *Firebird*, the remainder after *Rite of Spring*; happily, the style change matches the progress of the action.

China; mythical times. Though the Nightingale (s) knows her voice is sweeter in the forest, where she sings for the Fisherman (t), than in the palace, she agrees to sing for the Emperor (bs); he is moved to tears by her song. Ambassadors from the Emperor of Japan then arrive with a mechanical nightingale, at whose song the unhappy bird flees. Offended, the Emperor bans the Nightingale and endorses the mechanical substitute, but the songstress returns to charm Death (a) away from the Emperor's bedside.

Nilsson [Svennsson], **Birgit.** Soprano; b. West Karup, Sweden, May 17, 1918. Studied with Ragnar Blennow, Ragnar Hultén, and Arne Sunnegårdh at Stockholm Opera school; debut (an emergency substitution) as Agathe (*Freischütz*), 1946. A successful Lady Macbeth under Busch (1947) led to bigger roles, including Lisa (*Queen of Spades*), Sieglinde, Senta, the *Siegfried* Brünnhilde, Aida, and Tosca, and to her first international engagement, as Elettra (*Idomeneo*) in Glyndebourne under Busch, 1951, followed by Donna Anna in Florence (1952) and Fidelio in Bad Hersfeld (1953). Her career now clearly led in Wagnerian directions; after Elisabeth and Isolde in Stockholm (1953), she made her Bayreuth debut (Elsa, 1954), and undertook the remaining Brünnhildes (Stockholm, 1954–55). Her first complete *Ring* was in 1955 in Munich, and she returned regularly to Bayreuth, 1957–70, as the festival's only Isolde, also singing Brünnhilde in the 1960s. She also appeared at Covent Garden (from 1957) and La Scala (where she opened the 1958–59 season as Turandot). Her first U.S. appearances came in 1956, as the *Walküre* Brünnhilde in San Francisco and Chicago. She joined the Met as Isolde on Dec. 18, 1959, and sang with the company regularly until 1975, returning in 1979–82 for Elektra, the Dyer's Wife (*Frau*), and concerts, for a total of more than 200 perfs. of 16 roles, most often as Turandot and Isolde, also as Brünnhilde, Fidelio, Elisabeth and Venus, Aida, Tosca, Amelia (*Ballo*), Lady Macbeth, Salome, Elektra, and Sieglinde. At the gala farewells for the old house and for Rudolf Bing, she was accorded positions of honor, and she subsequently sang Isolde's Narration at the 1983 centennial gala.

The finest heroic Wagnerian soprano of her time, Nilsson possessed a plangent, powerful, firmly integrated voice that she was able to project above Wagnerian and Straussian orchestras with almost reckless freedom and unrivalled stamina. Compared to Flagstad, her characterizations had more thrust and edge, perhaps less repose; in Italian roles, she was imposing, if not always idiomatic. Nilsson retained her vocal power and quality until a remarkable age; her finest roles are well represented on recordings from her prime, including two complete *Rings*, *Tristans*, and *Turandots*.

Nilsson, Christine. Soprano: b. Sjöabol, near Växjö, Sweden, Aug. 20, 1843; d. Stockholm, Nov. 22, 1921. Studied with Franz Berwald in Stockholm, then with Wartel, Masset, and delle Sedie in Paris; debut as Violetta, Lyrique, Paris, 1864. She created Ophélie (*Hamlet*), Paris Opéra, 1868, and appeared regularly in London at Drury Lane and Covent Garden, 1867–81. She toured widely, making her U.S. debut as Mignon, N.Y., Academy of Music, 1871, and returning to N.Y. as Marguerite in the Met's inaugural *Faust*, Oct. 22, 1883; other roles that season included Mignon, Elsa, Donna Elvira, Boito's Margherita and Elena, Gioconda, and Valentine (*Huguenots*).

Nimsgern, Siegmund. Bass-baritone; b. St. Wendel, Germany, Jan. 14, 1940. Studied in Saarbrücken; member of company there (1967–71) and of Deutsche Oper am Rhein (1971–74), thereafter singing internationally in a wide repertory. After his Met debut as Pizarro in *Fidelio* (Oct. 2, 1978), he returned in 1981 as Jochanaan (*Salome*).

Niska, Maralin. Soprano; b. San Pedro, Calif, c. 1930. Studied with Louise Mansfield and Lotte Lehmann; sang in workshops from the mid-1950s, appeared with San Diego Opera (Mimi, 1965) and Met National Co. (Susanna and other roles, 1965). N.Y.C. Opera debut as the Countess (*Nozze*), 1967; other roles there included Tosca, Turandot, Salome, and Emilia Marty (*Makropoulos Affair*). Met debut as Violetta, Mar. 17, 1970; other Met roles (through 1977) included Musetta, Tosca, Hélène (*Vêpres*), and Salome.

Nono, Luigi. Composer; b. Venice, Jan. 29, 1924. Studied with Malipiero, Maderna, and Scherchen. A member of the Resistance during World War II and a militant Communist Party member, he deploys an eclectic variety of musical techniques: serialism, electronics, and taped sounds such as factory noise and interviews with workers. His first opera, *Intolleranza 1960* (1961), describes the plight of an immigrant overwhelmed by the inhumanity of capitalism. A cooperative venture recalling the theatrical methods of Meyerhold and Brecht, *Al Gran Sole Carico d'Amore* (1975) presents the 1871 Paris Commune as a revolutionary model. *Prometeo* (1984) treats the Greek myth from a revolutionary perspective.

Norden, Betsy. Soprano; b. Cincinnati, Ohio, Oct. 17, 1945. Studied at Boston U. and began career in musical comedy; joined Met chorus in 1969, becoming soloist Jan. 27, 1972, as Peasant Girl (*Nozze*). Her subsequent roles have included Papagena, Elvira (*Italiana*), Oscar, and Constance (*Carmélites*). Debuts in Philadelphia (*Cunning Little Vixen*, 1980–81) and San Francisco (Constance, 1982–83).

Nordica [Norton], **Lillian.** Soprano; b. Farmington, Maine, May 12, 1857; d. Batavia, Java, May 10, 1914. After study with John O'Neill at New England Conservatory in Boston, she sang in concert in America (1875–77) and England (1878), then studied in Milan with Sangiovanni; debut as Donna Elvira, Manzoni, Milan, 1879. She appeared in St. Petersburg in 1880 as Philine, the Queen (*Huguenots*), and Amelia (*Ballo*), among others; Paris Opéra debut as Marguerite, 1882, also the role of her American operatic debut, at the N.Y. Academy of Music, 1883. She toured the U.S. with Mapleson (1886), and sang at Covent Garden (debut, Violetta, 1887), where she returned frequently until 1902 and created Zelika in Stanford's *The Veiled Prophet*, 1893. Her Met debut, on Dec. 18, 1891, was as Valentine (*Huguenots*); in 11 seasons there (off and on until 1910), she sang 194 perfs. (180 more on tour) in 19 roles, most often as Elsa (29 times), Isolde (24), and Valentine (24), also as Aida, the *Trovatore* Leonora, Sélika (*Africaine*), Gounod's and Berlioz's Marguerites, Susanna, Violetta, Venus, Philine (*Mignon*), Donna Anna and Donna Elvira, the three Brünnhildes, Kundry, and Gioconda. Her Wagnerian career began in the early 1890s, and in 1894 she became the first American singer to appear at Bayreuth, as Elsa; she first sang Brünnhilde with the Damrosch touring company in 1897–98, and her last operatic appearances were as Isolde, in Boston, 1913. Her repertory also included Cherubino,

(continued p.254)

NORMA
Richard Bonynge

Why is it that *Norma* has such an attraction for prima donnas? Its difficulties are legion, and no great secret has been made of them. Lilli Lehmann declared that it was more difficult to sing one Norma than three Isoldes. (She was one of the few who sang both, and she knew whereof she spoke!) Rosa Ponselle told me it was her most beloved and most difficult role, and Zinka Milanov that it was the greatest challenge of all. Even the first Norma, Giuditta Pasta, had problems with "Casta diva," and transposed it down. It's almost an impossible role, very risky, and not even that glamorous. Then why does almost every soprano with a ghost of a chance want to try it?

I suppose it's rather like mountain-climbing: they sing it because it is there. The role has always had an aura about it; most singers feel it's the greatest of all bel canto parts, so there's a tremendous temptation to give it a try. In addition, it's certainly the most intensely dramatic of the bel canto characters. This noble Druidess, living in a country conquered by the Romans, is caught in an illicit and tragic love for a Roman soldier, contemplates murdering her two children, and is finally heroically burned at the stake. The drain on the emotions of the performer is considerable, and this is both one of the attractions and one of the difficulties of the role.

Of course most of the difficulties are vocal. For one thing, it's a very long role; by the time you get through the third act, you feel like you've sung an entire opera – and you still have a long act to go. (Rather like singing *Cavalleria* as an encore after a performance of *Lucia*!) For this heroic character, Bellini envisaged a soprano capable of everything – perhaps a soprano who could never really exist. She must have power in the high, middle, and bottom registers, as well as agility for the coloratura passages. It's both a very high and a very low role. A light soprano will have trouble with the middle and bottom registers, a heavy one with the coloratura. The great Normas of this century – Ponselle, Milanov, Callas, and Sutherland – have all brought the greatest facets of their art to the role, and I doubt that any of them ever felt they had conquered every aspect.

I heard Maria Callas sing Norma in eleven performances and innumerable rehearsals. This was before her tremendous weight loss, which I believe was the beginning of her tragedy. (In shedding two-thirds of her weight, she lost a great deal of the volume and fullness of tone, and subsequently damaged her vocal cords by pressuring them to still do what she had formerly been able to do easily.) Her Norma was sublime; she got so inside the role that the emotional impact was almost unbearable. Joan had the great fortune to sing on the same stage with her – the tiny parts of Clotilde in *Norma* and the Priestess in *Aida* – and she was a great example to a young singer. She rarely marked at rehearsals, singing out constantly, for she realized that a singer must train like an athlete, and build stamina by using the voice correctly. Her Norma was not unlike her Medea, and she was always uncomfortable in the first act, but she paid great attention to the text, making every word tell.

This is particularly important in Bellini, because he took so much trouble in setting the words. I can't think of many composers who set the word as well as he, and his recitatives were written with great care. This is one of the reasons Wagner admitted to being strongly influenced by Bellini; he wrote that "Bellini is one of my predilections, because his music is so strongly felt and intimately bound up with the words."

A 19th-century engraving of the first cast of *Norma* – Domenico Donzelli as Pollione, Giulia Grisi as Adalgisa, and Giuditta Pasta as Norma

RISI PASTA

There is, of course, much else to admire about this great composer. His melodic invention is unlike that of any of his colleagues. Those marvelous long lines of melody were something very new in the early nineteenth century, and were a strong influence on many others, especially Chopin and Liszt.

Above all, he was one of the greatest composers for the human voice – to me, in fact, the greatest. He understood voices better than anyone, not only in his vocal writing, but in his orchestration. He scored to allow the voice to come out over the orchestra, and at the same time those orchestrations have great color and liveliness; they are sparse, but never underwritten. Later, in *Puritani*, they become richer (and more difficult for singers), because Rossini got to him and told him he had better change with the times. Even at the richest, compare them to Puccini's, where the orchestra doubles the voices and singers have to scream to be heard.

Joan and I had our eye on *Norma* for quite a long time before we finally performed it. We had long conversations with Ponselle, Milanov, and Callas about it, and they all advised that the role would be hers, but she was sensible enough to be terrified of it. When our old friend Irving Guttman asked her to sing it at the Vancouver Opera in 1964, she accepted, feeling it was wiser to tackle a role of such proportions away from the limelight. Irving's production was simple and real, and we had the great luck at that time to begin our association with Marilyn Horne, who was the Adalgisa in that and many of our later productions. Although Rudolf Bing asked Joan to sing Norma before Vancouver, it took her quite a while to agree, and even then she had second thoughts and did not actually sing the role at the Met until 1970. By then the time was right, and we were very glad we had waited.

Norma is a constant in Joan's repertory, and she has probably sung more performances of it than any other singer in this century. (In 1970 alone, she sang it forty times.) We both love it, and I find that Joan constantly grows in the role.

For the conductor, the most difficult aspect of this opera is keeping the drama propelled; it can be very slow and stagey, and if you let the singers indulge themselves it can last all night. The conductor must hold the drama, and shape the acts dramatically. We recently recorded the opera for the second time, with a cast including Joan, Montserrat Caballé, Luciano Pavarotti, and Samuel Ramey, and if you compare this to our 1964 recording I think you'll find that our approach is now more dramatic.

Others have expressed pessimism regarding the future of *Norma*, and it is true that there are not many singers around who can perform it well. But this has been true for the last 150 years, and I suppose will always be so. *Norma* will always be performed because singers will always want to sing it. And the best of them will succeed.

Lillian Nordica as Brünnhilde in *Die Walküre*

Ophélie (*Hamlet*), Lucia, Carmen, Desdemona, and Juliette; she sang with the Manhattan Opera (1907–08), and opened the Boston Opera House as Gioconda (1909). She died from exposure after a shipwreck on her return from an Australian tour.

Although trained in the classical florid-lyric technique and able to encompass coloratura roles, Nordica was evidently endowed with an uncommon richness and power of tone that she exploited to the full in the Wagnerian dramatic roles, joining with the de Reszkes in performances that showed these works could be sung with traditional legato line and beauty of tone. She recorded

Norma – (1970). Designed by Desmond Heeley, produced by Paul-Émile Deiber. Marilyn Horne and Joan Sutherland

toward the end of her career, but the voice appears to have overwhelmed then-current technology; however, a few "live" Mapleson cylinders (1901–03) suggest the authority and sheer power of her singing.

BIBLIOGRAPHY: Ira Glackens, *Yankee Diva: Lillian Nordica and the Golden Days of Opera* (N.Y., 1963).

Nordmo-Lövberg, Aase. Soprano; b. Maalselv. Norway, June 10, 1923. Studied with Hjaldes Ingebjart, Oslo; operatic debut as Elisabeth, Stockholm Opera, 1953. Vienna State Opera debut as Sieglinde, 1958. Met debut as Elsa, Feb. 11, 1959; in 2 seasons there, she also sang Eva, Fidelio, and Sieglinde. At Bayreuth, sang Elsa, Sieglinde, Third Norn, 1960

Norena, Eidé [Kaja Hansen-Eidé]. Soprano; b. Horten, Norway, Apr. 26, 1884; d. Lausanne, Switzerland, Nov. 19, 1968. Studied with Ellen Gulbranson in Oslo, later with Raimund von zur Mühlen; debut as Amor (*Orfeo*), Oslo, 1907. Sang in Stockholm and Oslo; debuts as Gilda at La Scala (1924), Covent Garden (1924), Paris Opéra (1925), and Chicago (1926). Met debut as Mimi, Feb. 9, 1933; she returned until 1938 as Juliette, Marguerite, Gilda, Violetta, and Antonia (*Hoffmann*).

Norfolk. City in Virginia. The Virginia Opera Association, launched in 1975 with two performances of *Bohème*, soon established itself as an adventurous, capable regional company. Without major stars but with an eye for native talent, artistic director and conductor Peter Mark leavened a repertory of standard and popular works with less well known operas such as *Capuleti*. The first U.S. performance of Musgrave's *Mary Queen of Scots* (1977) and the world premieres of her *Christmas Carol* (1979) and *Harriet, the Woman Called Moses* (1985) attracted international attention to the Virginia Opera, which now performs in Richmond as well as Norfolk.

Norma. Opera in 2 acts by Bellini; libretto by Romani, after Alexandre Soumet's play *Norma, ou L'Infanticide*.

First perf., Milan, La Scala, Dec. 26, 1831: Pasta, Giulia. Grisi, Donzelli, Negrini. U.S. prem., New Orleans, St. Charles, Apr. 1, 1836. Met prem., Feb. 27, 1890 (in Ger.): Lehmann, Frank, Kalisch, Fischer, c. Damrosch, d. Hoyt, p. Habelmann. Later Met productions: Nov. 16, 1927: Ponselle, Telva, Lauri-Volpi, Pinza, c. Serafin, d. Urban, p. Thewman; Oct. 29, 1956 ("revised"): Callas, Barbieri, del Monaco, Siepi, c. Cleva, d. Elson, p. Yannopoulos; Mar. 3, 1970: Sutherland, Horne, Bergonzi, Siepi, c. Bonynge, d. Heeley, p. Deiber. Norma has also been sung at the Met by Cigna, Milanov, Caballé, Scotto; Adalgisa by Swarthout, Tourel, Cossotto, Troyanos; Pollione by Martinelli, Alexander. 95 perfs. in 19 seasons.

Bellini's noblest and most spacious score; its title role has become a touchstone for the highest vocal, musical and dramatic achievements of the great sopranos of the Italian repertory.

Gaul during the Roman occupation. Despite her Vestal vows, the Druid high priestess Norma (s) has secretly married the Roman proconsul Pollione (t) and borne him two sons. Pollione now loves the young priestess Adalgisa (s) and wants to take her back to Rome. Adalgisa confides in Norma, who is at first sympathetic to her transgression but calls down a curse on them both when she learns the name of Adalgisa's lover. For revenge, Norma is tempted to kill Pollione's children, but cannot bring herself to do it. Resolved on suicide, she tries to entrust the children to Adalgisa, but the latter, saying she will never marry

Pollione after seeing his true nature, urges Norma to live. The two women swear eternal friendship. Attempting to abduct Adalgisa, Pollione is caught in the sacred cloister by the Druids. Norma pleads with him to return to her and threatens to denounce Adalgisa, but after summoning the Druids she instead confesses her own guilt. Asking her father Oroveso (bs) to care for the children, Norma mounts a sacrificial pyre. Witnessing her greatness of spirit, Pollione is moved to join her in death.

Norman, Jessye. Soprano; b. Augusta, Ga., Sep. 15, 1945. Studied with Carolyn Grant at Howard U., Alice Duschak at Peabody Conservatory, Pierre Bernac and Elizabeth Mannion at U. of Michigan; debut as Elisabeth, Deutsche Oper, Berlin, 1969. Appearances followed at Florence (Sélika in *Africaine*, 1971), La Scala (Aida, 1972), Covent Garden (Cassandre in *Troyens*, 1972), and Paris (*Aida* in concert, 1973). Met debut as Cassandre, Sep. 26, 1983; she has since sung Didon (*Troyens*), Jocasta (*Oedipus Rex*), Ariadne, Elisabeth, and Mme. Lidoine (*Carmélites*) with the company. Norman's sumptuous voice, musical integrity, communicative power, and statuesque stage presence have gradually found suitable stage repertory.

Nose, The. Opera in 2 acts by Shostakovich; libretto adapted from Gogol's story by Zamyatin, Ionin, Preiss, and the composer.
First perf., Leningrad, Maly, Jan. 18, 1930. U.S. prem., Santa Fe, Aug. 11, 1965 (in Eng.): Whitesides, Reardon, c. Kunzel.
Shostakovich's first opera is a madcap satire, full of fantastic and parodistic theatrical, vocal, and orchestral effects.
Major Kovalev (bar) awakes one day to find his nose missing. The nose turns up in odd places – in the barber's bread, dressed up as a high official (t); Kovalev goes to great lengths to get it back. When it is at last returned to him, it must be surgically replaced, but to Kovalev's despair the operation fails. Then, one day, the nose returns of its own accord.

Notte di Zoraima, La (The Night of Zoraima). Opera in 1 act by Montemezzi; libretto by Mario Ghisalberti.
First perf., Milan, La Scala, Jan. 31, 1931: Cobelli, Marion, Maugeri, c. Montemezzi. U.S. & Met prem., Dec. 2, 1931: Ponselle, Jagel, Basiola, c. Serafin, d. Novak/Palmedo, p. Sanine. 4 perfs. in 1 season.
Montemezzi's penultimate opera, set in Peru after the Spanish conquest. Having helped her lover Muscar (t) escape, the Inca princess Zoraima (s) stabs herself rather than submit to the Spanish leader Pedrito (bar).

Nourrit, Adolphe. Tenor; b. Montpellier, France, Mar. 3, 1802; d. Naples, Mar. 8, 1839. Though his father, tenor Louis Nourrit, discouraged his stage ambitions, he studied with Manuel Garcia; debut as Pylade (*Iphigénie en Tauride*), Paris Opéra, 1821. He created many roles there, including Néocle (*Siège de Corinthe*, 1826), Robert le Diable (1831), Arnold (*Guillaume Tell*, 1829), Eléazar (*Juive*, 1835), and Raoul (*Huguenots*, 1836). He left Paris when Duprez was engaged, and sang in Naples, where vocal and mental problems led to his death by suicide.

Novotná, Jarmila. Soprano; b. Prague, Sep. 23, 1907. Encouraged by Destinn, she studied with Hilbert Wawre, Prague; sang Rosina and Violetta in a provincial Czech theater, 1924, then Mařenka (*Bartered Bride*) and coloratura roles at Prague National Theater, 1925. After further

Jarmila Novotná as Octavian in *Der Rosenkavalier*

study in Milan, sang Gilda in Verona, 1928. Member, Berlin State Opera, 1929–33 (debut as Concepcion in *Heure Espagnole*, Kroll Opera). In 1931, Max Reinhardt staged *La Belle Hélène* and *Hoffmann* for her. At the Vienna State Opera (1933–38), she created Lehár's Giuditta; in Salzburg, she sang Mozart roles under Weingartner, Toscanini, and Walter (1935–37). Met debut as Mimi, Jan. 5, 1940; in 16 seasons, she sang 142 perfs. of 14 roles, including Euridice, Violetta, Cherubino, Manon, Mařenka, Donna Elvira, Pamina, Octavian, Antonia and Giulietta (*Hoffmann*), and Orlovsky (*Fledermaus*). Also appeared at La Scala (Alice Ford, 1937), San Francisco (debut, Butterfly, 1939), Buenos Aires and Rio de Janeiro (1943), and Chicago (Cherubino, 1945), and made films in Germany, France, and America. A great beauty and a consummate actress, Novotná's musicianship satisfied her time's most demanding conductors.

Noyes Fludde (Noah's Flood). Opera in 1 act by Britten; libretto from the Chester Miracle Play.
First perf., Orford, Parish Church (Aldeburgh Festival), June 18, 1958: Parr, Brannigan, c. Mackerras. U.S. prem., N.Y., Union Theological Seminary, Mar. 16, 1959.
A resourceful work for church performances by professionals and amateurs, depicting the building of the ark, Noah's tribulations in getting all concerned (especially the garrulous Mrs. Noah) aboard, the flood, and the deliverance.

Nozze di Figaro, Le (The Marriage of Figaro). Opera in 4 acts by Mozart; libretto by da Ponte, after Beaumarchais' play *La Folle Journée, ou Le Mariage de Figaro*.
First perf., Vienna, Burgtheater, May 1, 1786: Laschi, Storace, Bussani, Benucci, Mandini. U.S. prem., N.Y., Park, May 10, 1824 (in Eng.). Met prem., Jan. 31, 1894: Eames, Nordica, Arnoldson, Ancona, E. de Reszke, c.

(continued p.258)

LE NOZZE DI FIGARO
Frederica von Stade

The very first time I was fortunate enough to meet a saucy character named Cherubino was nearly twenty years ago, and since then I have jumped through hundreds of windows, hidden under countless chairs, and struggled and rejoiced with his wonderful, indomitable personality. It is not with hauteur that I claim his heart beats like Mozart's, but with love and gratitude, plus a dash of Peter Shaffer's marvelous *Amadeus*. I'd even go so far as to boast that the opera's overture is about Cherubino too! (When you listen to it, can't you just see him dashing about, laughing and flirting and getting into trouble?) I consider myself very lucky to have such an entertaining friend as this fourteen-year-old page.

And what is he about? Everything! The very best description I know came in a short note along with a gigantic bouquet of pale pink roses and lilies. The note said, "I wish you the joy of knowing this boy who is full of fire and passion. Your cheeks should be pink, your eyelashes long and curled, your lips bright red." The director Giorgio Strehler wrote the note, I daresay with more poetry in his phrases than I have managed, and I read it with beating heart on an opening night in Versailles many years ago.

It was my first big production of the opera, as well as Rolf Liebermann's first as general manager of the Paris Opéra, and it was opening at the magnificent Salle de l'Opéra in Versailles. Here we were, in a theater built in Mozart's time, rehearsing this masterpiece under Strehler's direction. (He's a great theater man – a real genius – with an extraordinary sense of music and rhythm and *style*.) We learned to walk the way people walked at that time, wearing costume pieces from the seventeenth and eighteenth centuries. And we worked all day, every day, for five weeks – if our union, AGMA, had been there, they'd have fallen into the Seine! Strehler created the ideal atmosphere for *Figaro*; we really felt we were in the eighteenth century, so that when I left rehearsal at the end of the day, I was always surprised to see people on the street in modern dress.

I have been in three other major productions of *Figaro*, and I've been lucky enough always to have wonderful directors – the other three were Peter Hall, Günther Rennert, and Jean-Pierre Ponnelle. They all had slightly different approaches to the opera and my role, but each seemed to work. I like trying new things with a role, and when the director has respect for the music, I know it will be right. I found myself doing Cherubino all over the world, which was wonderful. It's a marvelous role for a debut; you're protected, and don't have to carry the entire weight of the opera, but can make a great impression.

Figaro is all about relationships, and you would think that going from production to production, from one cast to another, there might sometimes be problems in making those relationships seem real to the audience. But *Figaro* is so honest and human, I've just never had the relationships *not* work. In other operas, I've had situations where there *should* be an ensemble effort, but one or more of the performers won't or can't play the game; in this work, the construction makes it hard *not* to play. The characters are so complete. I love the other Mozart operas, but I don't think it's always easy to identify with all the characters. So often they're archetypes; with Dorabella or Donna Anna or Don Ottavio, the performer must find the humanity. Not in *Figaro* – so much of the characters is in the music; the real work has already been done for us by Mozart and da Ponte.

So what else do we know about Cherubino, besides that he's full of fire

and passion and looks quite like a girl? He's involved with seven or eight other characters who are pretty passionate themselves. And that's what *Le Nozze di Figaro* is all about – life! A rather broad subject portrayed, examined, imitated, with the most extraordinary attention to detail, with the most precise consistency of behavior and with loving devotion to life's value. And all wrapped in the security of genius. I think it's wonderful to see how the greatest artists always have about them a sense of mastery, of genius and magic, with no room for chance. Then we, the audience, can relax, and feel sad or desperate or angry or joyful, knowing we are *supposed* to feel that way, that it is no accident that we do.

Please forgive me if I stray from my subject, running about like my beloved Cherubino. One of the things I love about him is the way he shows us the conflict between following our desires and doing what is expected of us (Do we *all* have that conflict? I know I do.) It's such a joy to play someone who just won't behave, who gets into constant trouble because he simply follows his instincts. Who could help identifying with that?

Then there's the aspect of being a woman playing a boy. Like any mezzo, I play lots of boys, but this one is very different from the others. Some compare him to Octavian in *Rosenkavalier*, but I think he's very different – less mature than Octavian, with much less experience. Octavian is a bit of an actor, watching himself be in love. He knows the effect he has on women, but Cherubino is just starting to figure this out. For Cherubino, I can remember picking up pointers by watching my fifteen-year-old cousins, and I try to show the incredible mood swings you see in teen-age boys. (I like playing boys, but I've come to prefer playing women. When you play women, everyone fusses over you – they make sure your costume is perfect and every hair in place. With Cherubino, you dress yourself.)

Vocally, there are lots of difficulties. I love singing Mozart, and by now singing this role should be as easy as falling off a log. But it's exposed – if you're a little to the left or right, it shows. I still have to work at it; the long, long lines, the exposure, the intricate changes of pitch all make it very hard. The words are very important, and the relationship of the words to the melody. Some Mozart arias can be sung virtually instrumentally, without paying a lot of attention to the words, but not in *Figaro*!

One of the greatest challenges of this opera is to tell the story – in under fifteen minutes or less than a thousand words. I bog down somewhere when Count Almaviva leaves with the Countess, while Cherubino and Susanna are hiding in separate closets. (I'd come to believe that rooms such as the Countess' boudoir existed only in operas, but while visiting France a few years ago we stayed in a beautiful chateau near Dijon that was full of corridors and closets and peepholes and rooms adjoining others in amazing fashion. Such rooms are very much part of the opera. One feels they are Mozart's rooms, that they are a part of his plan, and, like the opera, wonderfully indestructible.)

Figaro seems to me very modern, both in subject and style. The one and only Wolfgang Amadeus succeeded in creating a universe that will seem real forever. Here we are assured that humans will always be the same – and, best of all, that there is goodness in all. In *Figaro* there's a heart in every beat, and vice versa, and never does Mozart give up on humanity. Rather, he hugs it with music that always makes you feel better, and that joins you to your fellow human beings. With some operas, it's not always easy leaving home to go to work; with *Figaro*, I can't wait to get on stage.

Le Nozze di Figaro – (1917). Geraldine Farrar, Frieda Hempel, and Giuseppe de Luca

Bevignani, p. Parry. Later Met productions: Jan. 13, 1909: Eames, Sembrich, Farrar, Didur, Scotti, c. Mahler, d. Brioschi/Burghart, p. Schertel; Feb. 20, 1940: Rethberg, Sayão, Stevens, Pinza, Brownlee, c. Panizza, d. Jorgulesco/Czettel, p. Graf; Oct. 30, 1959: Della Casa, Söderström, Miller, Siepi, Borg, c. Leinsdorf, d. Messel, p. Ritchard; Nov. 20, 1975: Lear, Blegen, von Stade, Diaz, Brendel, c. Bedford, d. O'Hearn, p. Rennert; Nov. 22, 1985: Vaness, Battle, von Stade, Raimondi, Allen, c. Levine, d. & p. Ponnelle. Figaro has also been sung at the Met by Maurel, de Luca, Singher, Kunz, Tozzi, Evans, Morris, van Dam; the Countess by Gadski, Matzenauer, Steber, de los Angeles, Lorengar, Zylis-Gara, Te Kanawa, Söderström; Susanna by Hempel, Conner, Seefried, Peters, Gueden, Rothenberger, Raskin, Freni, Stratas, Valente; Cherubino by de Lussan, Scheff, Novotná, Elias, Ludwig, Stratas, Berganza, Lear, Ewing; the Count by Didur, London, Singher, Prey, Bacquier, Krause, Stewart, Stilwell; other conductors include Mottl, Bodanzky, Walter, Busch, Reiner, Stiedry, Rudolf, Krips, Böhm. 211 perfs. in 37 seasons.

A masterpiece of musical construction and psychological penetration, in which Mozart first brought to full realization the potential of the large-scale finale and his ability to mirror shifting emotions within a continuous musical flow.

Count Almaviva's castle near Seville, 18th c. Figaro (bs) and Susanna (s), servants respectively to the Count (bs) and Countess (s) Almaviva, are to be married. But the Count has been making advances to Susanna, who fears he may not honor his promise to abolish the hated "droit du seigneur." The page Cherubino (s) has been flirting with Susanna and the Countess; the jealous Count orders him off to the army. In the Countess' room, she and the servants hatch a plan to disguise Cherubino as Susanna and use him as bait to teach the Count a lesson. When the Count unexpectedly knocks on the door, Cherubino hides in a closet. Certain he has interrupted a rendez-vous between his wife and the page, the Count goes off for tools to break the lock; while he is gone, Susanna trades places with the page, who escapes out the window. The Count is flabbergasted to discover Susanna in the closet; further suspicions are deftly put to rest by Figaro, coached by the women. Marcellina (ms), Bartolo (bs), and Basilio (t) demand that Figaro repay a loan from Marcellina; with the discovery that she is Figaro's mother (and Bartolo is his father), this subplot is resolved. Still planning to trap the Count, Susanna at her wedding slips him an invitation to join her in the garden – an assignation accidentally revealed to Figaro. In the darkness, both Cherubino and the Count woo "Susanna" (the Countess in disguise). Catching on, Figaro exaggeratedly woos the "Countess" (Susanna in disguise), causing the furious Almaviva to summon witnesses. To his amazement and embarrassment, the real Countess then appears; he humbly begs her forgiveness.

Nucci, Leo. Baritone; b. Castiglione dei Pepoli, near Bologna, Apr. 16, 1942. Studied with Giuseppe Marchesi and Ottaviano Bizzarri; formal debut as Schaunard, Venice, 1975. After singing at La Scala and Vienna, he made his Covent Garden debut as Miller (*Luisa Miller*), 1978. Met debut as Renato (*Ballo*), Feb. 22, 1980; subsequent roles include Miller, Carlo (*Forza*), Rossini's Figaro, Onegin, Germont, Posa, Amonasro, and Sharpless. Has sung at Paris Opéra (debut, Renato, 1981) and San Francisco.

number opera. An opera composed in separate numbers – arias, duets, choruses, etc. – which are connected by spoken dialogue or recitative. The normal mode of operatic continuity until well into the 19th c., when it was increasingly superseded by through-composed music, it has been revived in modern times (e.g., Stravinsky's *Rake*).

O

obbligato (Ital., "obligatory"). Strictly speaking, a term for a solo instrumental part that cannot be omitted (e.g., the clarinet part in Sesto's aria "Parto, parto," in Mozart's *Clemenza*); however, sometimes used to refer to an optional such part.

Ober, Margarete. Contralto; b. Berlin, Apr. 15, 1885; d. Bad Sachs, Mar. 17, 1971. Studied with Benno Stolzenberg and Arthur Arndt (later her husband) in Berlin; debut as Azucena, Frankfurt, 1906. Member of Berlin Opera, 1907–45. Met debut as Ortrud, Nov. 21, 1913; she also sang other Wagner mezzo parts, Octavian, Marina, Laura, Amneris, Eglantine (*Euryanthe*), Azucena, and Katherine (*Widerspenstigen Zähmung*), but left the company when the U.S. entered World War I.

Oberon. Opera in 3 acts by Weber; libretto by James Robertson Planché, after Sotheby's translation of Wieland's poem.

First perf., London, Covent Garden, Apr. 12, 1826: Paton, Vestris, Braham, Bland, Fawcett, c. Weber. U.S. prem., N.Y., Park, Sep. 20, 1826. Met prem., Dec. 28, 1918 (with recitatives by Bodanzky): Ponselle, Gentle, Martinelli, Althouse, Reiss, c. Bodanzky, d. Urban, p. Ordynski. 13 perfs. in 3 seasons.

The full-blooded Romantic music has never escaped the burden of the unwieldy plot and the work's quasipantomimic origins, despite many attempts at adaptation.

Oberon (t) quarrels with Titania, and vows not to see her again until he finds a faithful pair of lovers. With the magical aid of Puck (s), Sir Huon (t) is sent to Baghdad to rescue Reiza (s), while his squire Sherasmin (t) rescues her attendant Fatima (s). After many adventures they return safely to Huon's home, and Oberon accepts them as proof of the possibility of fidelity.

Oberto, Conte di San Bonifacio (Oberto, Count of San Bonifacio). Opera in 2 acts by Verdi; libretto by Temistocle Solera (so described on all printed librettos, although most of the text is probably by Antonio Piazza).

First perf., Milan, La Scala, Nov. 17, 1839: Rainieri-Marini, Shaw, Salvi, Marini. U.S. prem., N.Y., Amato Opera Theater, Feb. 18, 1978.

Verdi's first opera shows cautious, sober security of style and technique rather than any great suggestion of the originality to come.

Bassano, in and near Ezzelino's castle, 1228. Leonora (s), daughter of Oberto (bs), has been seduced and promised marriage by Riccardo (t), Count of Salinguerra. But Riccardo has abandoned her and is preparing to marry Cuniza (ms), sister of Ezzelino. With the help of the sympathetic Cuniza, Leonora and Oberto confront Riccardo, and he agrees to return to Leonora; nevertheless, the vengeful Oberto challenges him to a duel and is killed.

Obraztsova, Elena. Mezzo-soprano; b. Leningrad, July 7, 1937. Studied with Grigoriev, Leningrad; debut as Marina, Bolshoi, Moscow, 1964. Appeared as Marina with the Bolshoi at the Met (1975), as Azucena in San Francisco (1975), and as Charlotte at La Scala (1976). Met debut as Amneris, Oct. 12, 1976; other Met roles (until 1980) included Carmen, Adalgisa, Charlotte, Ulrica, Santuzza, and Eboli.

Ochman, Wiesław. Tenor; b. Warsaw, Feb. 6, 1937. Studied with Gustav Serafin in Kraków, Maria Szlapák in Bytom, Sergius Nadgryzowski in Warsaw; debut as Edgardo, Bytom, 1959. He sang in Kraków, Warsaw, Berlin, Hamburg (from 1967), Glyndebourne (Lenski, Ottavio, Tamino, 1968–70), Chicago (Alfredo, 1972). Met debut as Henri (*Vêpres*), Mar. 12, 1975; he has since also sung Dimitri (*Boris*), Lenski, and Golitsin (*Khovanshchina*) there.

Oedipus Rex (King Oedipus). Opera-oratorio in 2 acts by Stravinsky; libretto by Jean Cocteau (translated into Latin by Jean Daniélou), after Sophocles' tragedy.

First perf., Paris, Théâtre Sarah Bernhardt, May 30, 1927 (concert perf.): Sadoven, Balina-Skupyevsky, Lanskoy, Zaporozhetz, Brasseur, c. Stravinsky. First staged perf., Vienna, State Opera, Feb. 23, 1928. U.S. prem., Boston, Feb. 24, 1928 (concert perf.): Matzenauer, Hackett, Gange, Leyssac, c. Koussevitzky. U.S. stage prem., Philadelphia, Apr. 10, 1931: Matzenauer, Althouse, Rudinov, Nilssen, Rudd, c. Stokowski. Met prem., Dec. 3, 1981: Troyanos, Cassilly, Mazura, Macurdy, Dowell, c. Levine, d. Hockney, p. Dexter. 16 perfs. in 2 seasons.

A bold, stirring exposition of Stravinsky's neo-classical idiom. The ritualistic, stylized action is explained before each episode by a narrator, speaking in the audience's language; the work is sung in Latin.

Ancient Thebes is devastated by plague. Creon (bs), sent by King Oedipus (t) to consult the oracle at Delphi,

Oberon – Paris Opéra. Designed by Jean-Denis Malclès, produced by Maurice Lehmann

brings word that the murderer of the king's father Laius is living undetected in Thebes; he must be punished to end the plague. Oedipus resolves to solve the mystery, and forces from the reluctant seer Tiresias (bs) the information that the king's assassin is a king. In this pronouncement Oedipus divines a conspiracy against himself, and derisively dismisses Tiresias. Queen Jocasta (ms), widow of Laius, now wife of Oedipus, urges that no faith be put in oracles; did they not falsely predict that Laius would be slain by his own son? Laius, she insists, was killed by

Oedipus Rex – Santa Fe Opera, 1961. Helen Vanni, George Shirley

robbers at a crossroad. With this information the knot begins to unravel, for Oedipus knows he once killed a stranger on the same crossroad. Next he learns that he was not the natural but the adoptive son of the parents who raised him. He has been born of whom he should not, wed whom he should not, killed whom he should not: "All is made clear," he says. Jocasta hangs herself in horror and shame; Oedipus puts out his eyes, and his people mourn his fate.

Oenslager, Donald. Designer; b. Harrisburg, Pa., March 7, 1902; d. Bedford, N.Y., June 21, 1975. Designed over 250 productions for Broadway (*Girl Crazy, Of Mice and Men*), N.Y.C. Opera (*Tosca, Rosenkavalier*), Central City (premiere of *Ballad of Baby Doe*). For the Met, he designed *Salome* (1934), *Otello* (1937), and *Entführung* (1946).

Offenbach, Jacques [Jacob]. Composer; b. Cologne, June 20, 1819; d. Paris, Oct. 5, 1880. Studied with Halévy while playing cello in the Opéra-Comique orchestra, and later toured as a virtuoso soloist; appointed conductor of the Théâtre Français in 1850. In the Exhibition year of 1855, he opened the Bouffes-Parisiens and produced works by Adam, Delibes, and others, as well as his own operettas, including *Ba-ta-clan* (1855) and *Orphée aux Enfers* (1858). After resigning the management of the Bouffes-Parisiens in 1862, he wrote for it some of his greatest international successes: *La Belle Hélène* (1864), *Barbe-Bleue* (1866), *La Vie Parisienne* (1866), *La Grande Duchesse de Gérolstein* (1867), and *La Périchole* (1868). After the Franco-Prussian War dampened the public appetite for light entertainment, Offenbach toured the U.S. (1876) and turned to his only grand opera, *Les Contes d'Hoffmann*; unfinished at his death, it was completed by Guiraud. In nearly a hundred operettas (many in one act), Offenbach's satire of contemporary politics and mores was often couched in frameworks from mythology or literature; the brio and charm (and sometimes even the satirical point) of the best of his works have survived their period, while *Hoffmann* remains a singular, if imperfect, achievement of mood and lyrical invention.

BIBLIOGRAPHY: Alexander Faris, *Jacques Offenbach* (London, 1980).

Of Mice and Men. Opera in 3 acts by Floyd; libretto by the composer, after John Steinbeck's novel and play.

First perf., Seattle, Wash., Jan. 22, 1970: Bayard, Moulson, Patrick, c. Coppola.

A score in Floyd's conservative idiom, set in the Salinas Valley, Calif., recent times. Lennie (t), a retarded farm worker, uncomprehendingly kills his boss' wife (s), who has encouraged his advances. His companion George (bar) shoots Lennie to spare him the anguish of capture and trial.

O'Hearn, Robert. Designer; b. Elkhart, Ind., July 19, 1921. Has designed for Central City, N.Y.C. Opera, Chicago Lyric, Santa Fe, Vienna State Opera, Bregenz, Hamburg. For the Met since 1960, he has designed *Elisir, Meistersinger, Aida, Samson, Frau ohne Schatten, Hänsel, Rosenkavalier, Parsifal,* and *Porgy,* all directed by Merrill.

Ohms, Elisabeth. Soprano; b. Arnhem, Netherlands, May 17, 1888; d. Marquartstein, Upper Bavaria, Oct. 16, 1974. Studied in Amsterdam, Frankfurt, and Berlin; debut in Mainz, 1921. Member, Munich Opera, 1922–36; sang Wagner and the Marschallin at Covent Garden (1928), Fidelio and Kundry at La Scala (1927–28), Kundry at

Bayreuth (1931). Met debut as Brünnhilde (*Götterdämmerung*), Jan. 17, 1930; in 3 seasons, she also sang the other Brünnhildes, Isolde, Elisabeth, Venus, Ortrud, and Kundry.

Oiseau Bleu, L' (The Blue Bird). Opera in 4 acts by Wolff; libretto by Maurice Maeterlinck.

First perf. N.Y., Met, Dec. 27, 1919: Easton, Ellis, Delaunois, Gordon, c. Wolff, d. Anisfeld, p. Ordynski. 12 perfs. in 2 seasons.

A muted, Debussyan work, set in legendary times. On Christmas Eve, Tyltyl (ms) and Mytyl (s), the woodcutter's children, are sent by a fairy (ms) on a magic journey in search of the Blue Bird, secret of man's happiness.

Olczewska, Maria [Marie Berchtenbreitner]. Mezzo-soprano; b. Ludwigsschwaige bei Donauwörth, near Augsburg, Germany, Aug. 12, 1892; d. Klagenfurt, Austria, May 17, 1969. Studied with Karl Erler, Munich; operatic debut as Page (*Tannhäuser*), Krefeld, 1917. Sang in Leipzig, Hamburg (where she created Brigitte in *Tote Stadt*), and in Vienna (from 1920); regular appearances at Covent Garden (1924–33) and in Chicago (1928–32). Met debut as Brangäne, Jan. 16, 1933; in 3 seasons, she also sang the other Wagner mezzo roles, Klytemnästra, Amneris, Azucena, and Octavian.

Olivero, Magda. Soprano; b. Saluzzo, near Turin, Italy, Mar. 25, 1912. Studied with Luigi Gerussi, Simonetto, and Ghedini in Turin; debut as Lauretta (*Schicchi*), Vittorio Emanuele, Turin, 1933. In various Italian theaters, she specialized in Puccini and other verismo parts, also Zerlina, Poppea, and Sophie (*Rosenkavalier*). She married and retired in 1941, but returned to the stage as Adriana Lecouvreur (Brescia, 1951) at Cilea's request. Thereafter, she was one of the foremost singing actresses of her day, singing verismo roles (notably Fedora, Tosca, and Minnie in *Fanciulla*) and modern works (*Medium, Voix Humaine*). Debuts in London (Mimi, 1952), Edinburgh (Adriana, 1953), Dallas (Médée, 1967). At the Met, she appeared only in 3 perfs. as Tosca, and 7 more on tour (debut, Apr. 3, 1975). Her career endured into the 1980s.

Onégin [Hoffmann], **Sigrid.** Contralto; b. Stockholm, June 1, 1889; d. Magliaso, Italy, June 16, 1943. Studied with E.R. Weiss in Munich and di Ranieri in Milan, also with Lilli Lehmann and Margarethe Siems; debut as Carmen, 1912, Stuttgart, where she created Dryade (*Ariadne*). Sang in Munich and Berlin before Met debut as Amneris, Nov. 22, 1922; in 2 seasons, her only other Met roles were Fricka and Brangäne. In Salzburg (1931–32) she sang Orfeo, in Bayreuth (1933–34), Fricka, Erda, and Waltraute.

opera. A staged drama, for the most part sung, with instrumental accompaniment.

Opera. Opera in 3 acts by Berio; libretto by the composer.

First perf., Santa Fe, Aug. 12, 1970, c. Davies. Revised version, with modified text and orchestration, Florence, Pergola, May, 1977.

Three separate actions alternate and comment on one another: the 1912 sinking of the ocean liner Titanic, scenes in a terminal hospital ward, and scenes from Striggio's *Orfeo* libretto. The music is an eclectic, wide-ranging collage of styles.

opéra-ballet (Fr.). A genre of musico-theatrical entertainment in late 17th-c. France, combining operatic and balletic forms.

opera buffa (Ital.). The genre of comic opera that arose in Italy in the 18th c.; distinguished from opera seria not only by its subject, but by its fast-moving musical textures and reliance on ensemble numbers.

opéra comique (Fr.). A French operatic genre in which the musical numbers are connected by spoken dialogue. Originally light in subject matter, the genre eventually came to involve tragic actions as well (e.g., *Carmen*).

opéra lyrique (Fr.). A style of opera cultivated in the 1850s and 1860s at the Théâtre Lyrique in Paris, involving serious subjects treated on a scale less elaborate than in grand opera; examples are Gounod's *Faust* and *Roméo*.

opera semiseria (Ital.). A genre of later 18th-c. Italian opera, combining both comic and serious elements; *Don Giovanni* is the most familiar such work.

opera seria (Ital.). The most common form of opera in the 18th c., in all countries except France. Set to librettos based on figures from ancient history, these works principally comprised da capo arias connected by recitative; later in the century, ensembles, choruses, and dances were sometimes introduced.

opera workshop. An institution or association for the instruction of amateurs or students in the skills of operatic performance, carried on through the preparation of scenes of works; primarily found in the U.S.

operetta. Originally a term denoting a short, small-scale opera, it became in the later 19th c. a distinct genre, a form of popular theater involving song, dialogue, and dance, satirical, sentimental, or farcical in manner.

Oracolo, L' (The Oracle). Opera in 1 act by Leoni; libretto by Camillo Zanoni, after C.B. Fernald's play *The Cat and the Cherub*.

First perf., London, Covent Garden, July 3, 1905: Donalda, Dalmorès, Scotti, Vanni-Marcoux, c. Messager. U.S. & Met prem., Feb. 4, 1915: Bori, Botta, Scotti, Didur, c. Polacco, d. Fox, p. Speck. 44 perfs. in 13 seasons.

A lurid verismo piece, long a vehicle for Antonio Scotti, set in the Chinese quarter of San Francisco. Chim-Fen (bar) kidnaps a rich merchant's child and offers to "find" the boy in return for the hand of Ah-Yoe (s). He murders Ah-Yoe's beloved, Win-San-Luy (t), but is himself killed by the murdered man's father, Win-Shee (bs).

orchestra pit. The enclosed, sunken area before and below the stage, occupied by the orchestra. A relatively modern development (in 18th-c. theaters, the orchestra was on the same level as the audience), the pit helped equalize the balance between singers and increasingly elaborate orchestras; the most extreme form is the covered pit that Wagner introduced at Bayreuth.

Orfeo (Monteverdi). See *Favola d'Orfeo, La*.

Orfeo ed Euridice (Orpheus and Euridice). Opera in 3 acts by Gluck; text by Raniero de Calzabigi.

First perf., Vienna, Burgtheater, Oct. 5, 1762: Bianchi, Clavaran, Guadagni. Rev. version, in Fr. as *Orphée et Euridice*, first perf., Paris, Opéra, Aug. 2, 1774: Arnould, Levasseur, Legros. U.S. prem., (possibly) Charleston, S.C., Théâtre Français, June 24, 1794, (or) N.Y., Winter Garden, May 25, 1863 (in Eng.). Met prem., Dec. 30, 1891: S. Ravogli, Bauermeister, G. Ravogli, c. Vianesi. Later Met productions: Dec. 23, 1909: Gadski, Alten, Homer, c. Toscanini, d. Paquereau; May 22, 1936: Pengelley, Stellman, Kaskas, d. Tchelitchev, p. Balanchine & Tchelitchev; Nov. 26, 1938: Jessner, Morel, Thorborg, c. Bodanzky, d. Horner/Bevan, p. Graf; Sep. 25, 1970: Tucci, Robinson, Bumbry, c. Bonynge, d. Gérard, p. Sparemblek. Orfeo has also been sung at the Met by Scalchi, Brema, Delna, Matzenauer, Stevens, Meyer, Horne. 69 perfs. in 17 seasons.

The most enduring of Gluck's reform operas, in which he drew upon not only a classical subject but also classical notions of dramatic unity and purity. In his 1774 revision, Gluck rewrote the role of Orfeo in tenor rather than alto range, and added ballet music; many modern perfs. are based on the edition prepared by Berlioz in 1859 for Pauline Viardot, essentially comprising the Paris music in the Vienna keys.

Greece, legendary times. The musician Orfeo (a or t), lamenting the death of his beloved Euridice (s), learns from Amor (s) that Zeus has taken pity: the bereaved singer may go to Hades and plead for her resurrection – on condition that, should she be released, he must not look back to gaze on her till they have safely emerged from the underworld. At the gateway to the underworld, he wins over the Furies with his fabled singing. He finds Euridice among the blessed spirits and leads her away, though averting his eyes. Ignorant of Zeus' terms, Euridice is distressed by her lover's apparent indifference, and threatens to turn back if she is thus ignored. Weakening, Orfeo turns, and his wife sinks back into the land of the dead. After Orfeo sings an eloquent lament, Amor takes pity on him and again restores Euridice to life; rejoicing and happy dances close the opera.

Orff, Carl. Composer; b. Munich, July 10, 1895; d. Munich, Mar. 29, 1982. A student of Zilcher and Kaminski in Munich, his method of music education based on rhythmic training (*Orff-Schulwerk*) has been widely adopted. His musical style, marked by pounding ostinato rhythms and simple melodies, is greatly indebted to Stravinsky's *Wedding* and *Oedipus*. The operas *Der Mond* (1939), *Die Kluge* (1943), and *Die Bernauerin* (1947) are in a vernacular style; *Antigone* (1949), *Prometheus* (1968), *Oedipus der Tyrann* (1959), and *De Temporum Fine Comoedia* (1973) emphasize starkly declamatory recitative. The "scenic cantatas" that make up *Trionfi* are often presented in opera houses: *Carmina Burana* (1937), *Catulli Carmina* (1943), and *Trionfi dell'Afrodite* (1953).

Orlando. Opera in 3 acts by Handel; libretto by Grazio Braccioli, after Ariosto's *Orlando Furioso*.

First perf., London, Haymarket, Jan. 27, 1733: Strada, Gismondi, Bertolli, Senesino, Montagnana. U.S. prem., N.Y., Carnegie Hall (Handel Opera Society), Jan. 18, 1971 (concert perf.): Williams, Bogard, Allen, Diaz, c. Simon. U.S. stage prem., Cambridge, Mass. (American Repertory Theater), Dec. 16, 1981: Bryden, Larson, Sego, Gall, Honeysucker, c. Smith.

An opera seria with pastoral touches and an adventurously composed mad scene for the hero. Orlando (a) struggles with love and madness before coming to understand that his calling in life is military valor in the defense of Christendom.

THE OPERA ORCHESTRA
Raymond Leppard

Unless he be born an opera buff, the orchestral musician tends, at least at the beginning of his professional life, to regard the prospect of playing in the pit with apprehension, even scorn. It isn't that there aren't endless interesting and exacting things to play in opera, or a wide spectrum of music to enjoy. It's the thought of being stuck down there out of sight amid the dust and debris beneath the stage, with the added dangerous possibility of things dropping down on you from time to time. It's the knowledge that most people out there in the audience have come mainly to hear the singers and see the production. The orchestra, when noticed at all, comes third in their consideration, and that's no bright prospect for a young, idealistic violinist setting out on a career.

The reality of it is strangely different. If you look at a good, well-established opera orchestra, you will find a group of players who are truly devoted to this somewhat specialized, exclusive form of music-making, and most of them, having come to the sure knowledge that they are happiest and most fulfilled where they are, would do nothing else.

Musicians in opera orchestras share certain characteristics peculiar to their calling. There is a sort of freemasonry among them, probably occasioned by the close proximity and companionship in which they play, closer by far than even the most integrated of symphony orchestras. In the confined space below the stage, they have to learn how to cope with each other on good days and bad; in temper and out of it; through good shows and bad; with each other's family problems and domestic arrangements. They are, too, among the most uxorious of musicians, for temporary internal inconstancies can be wretched with a whole opera season ahead of you.

The most distinctive characteristic of all is the way they come to know their operas so very well – better, it must be said, than some who conduct them. Collectively, they are much better judges of singing than their audience, because performing with singers gives an element of tangible experience to their judgment. You can't follow a dozen Rodolfos around a dozen *Bohème*s without learning a good deal about the human voice and the art of singing. In doing this, players also develop a flair for ensemble that is not always so evident among their colleagues in the world of the symphony orchestra. It is wonderful to hear them following the vagaries of a Faust or a Don Giovanni, breathing when the singer does, holding notes, rushing some, cradling the voice with tone and dynamics that anticipate and support without hindering. They may even think nothing of the singing, but pride in their own professional skills will make them follow even to the very brink of their respective abysses.

That skill is properly theirs – not something the conductor, however skillful and sensitive, can accomplish by himself. He can help (he can even get in the way), but he can't really integrate the voices and instruments without the special musical sensitivities of the experienced opera orchestra. It might even be said that sometimes the orchestra makes better, if less spectacular music than those on stage. Top C's are one thing and, though the canary fanciers love them, fairly silly in themselves; but a beautifully executed finale – say, to Act II of *Figaro* or *Falstaff* – by the orchestra is at an altogether different level of music-making, which, complemented by a fine ensemble of distinguished singers in a well-thought, well-rehearsed production, represents the reason why opera is such an irresistible lure to most serious musicians.

Opera orchestras, while not resenting the obscurity of their position in the pit or their third place in the pecking order when it comes to applause, do nevertheless have a constant and perhaps not unwarranted concern that some of the difficulties under which they work are not sufficiently appreciated. It is not a question of salary, for in general they are well and equitably paid. The problem comes from something the general public is scarcely aware of. Opera was never intended for repertory performance. It was conceived as a festival art form, which is to say that each work needs to be rehearsed intensively on its own, played for a number of reasonably consecutive performances, and then abandoned until such time as the process can be repeated. Performing a different opera each night puts a tremendous strain on stage and singers, and especially on the resources of the orchestra.

To rehearse a succession of operas during the day and perform others at night as the schedule dictates, with different singers, different conductors, and no real sequence of concentration, makes terrifying demands. Moreover, in simple terms of hours, there is much more work than one orchestra can encompass. So what the public thinks of as the opera orchestra is in fact at least an orchestra and a half. The organizing of the players' schedule is a horrendously difficult task, approaching the complexity of three-dimensional chess, and the man who does it is usually something of a saint and something of a double-dealer at the same time. The problems seem, and sometimes are, insoluble, and opera orchestras have reason to complain that from time to time the repertory schedule hinders them from giving their best and forces lower standards upon them. They hate it, and resent the fact that they are sometimes unfairly blamed for circumstances out of their control.

In this most dangerous of all art forms, so many elements are involved: acting, dancing, directing, designing, singing, and playing; so many things to go wrong. The miracle is that it succeeds as often as it does. When it does and a masterpiece is brought to vivid, sentient life, to be a part of it, on or behind or under the stage, is an exhilarating experience, the like of which is to be found nowhere else in art.

That's why the opera orchestra is there.

Karl Böhm leading the Met orchestra at a rehearsal of *Wozzeck*

Ormandy, Eugene [Blau, Jenö]. Conductor; b. Budapest, Nov. 18, 1899; d. Philadelphia, Mar. 12, 1985. Studied violin at Budapest Royal Academy; came to N.Y. in 1921, playing in and conducting theater orchestras. Conductor, Minneapolis Symphony (1931–36); co-conductor (1936–38) and conductor (1938–80), Philadelphia Orchestra, sustaining its reputation for virtuosity and tonal opulence. His rare operatic appearances included *Fledermaus* in Bing's first Met season (debut, Dec. 20, 1950).

Ormindo, L'. Opera in 3 acts by Cavalli; libretto by Giovanni Faustini.
First perf., Venice, San Cassiano, 1644. U.S. prem., N.Y., Juilliard School, Apr. 24, 1968.
Cavalli's seventh opera recounts the elopement of Erisbe (ms), queen of Morocco and Fez, with Ormindo (t), prince of Tunis. Ariadeno (bs), Erisbe's husband, orders the lovers poisoned, but his captain Osmano (bs) mercifully substitutes a sleeping draught, and the repentent king cedes Ormindo both his wife and throne when they awaken. Many modern perfs. have used Raymond Leppard's heavily edited version.

ornamentation. The practice of elaborating the written notes of a musical score, to emphasize individual notes, make melodies more active, vary melodic repetitions, or show off the executive abilities of a soloist. Some operatic traditions have encouraged the practice (in the baroque da capo aria and the 19th-c. Italian cabaletta, the repeated sections were expected to be ornamented), while others (those of the late 19th and early 20th c.) leave little opportunity for it.

Orphée et Euridice. See *Orfeo ed Euridice.*

Osten, Eva von der. See *von der Osten, Eva.*

O'Sullivan, John. Tenor; b. Cork, Ireland, 1878; d. Paris, Apr. 28, 1955. Studied in Paris; debut as Reyer's Sigurd, Geneva, 1911. Appeared in French provinces, then at Paris Opéra (debut, Raoul in *Huguenots,* 1914), where he appeared frequently until 1933, and was much admired for his high notes by his compatriot James Joyce – a regard shared by few other critics. Also appeared as Raoul in Parma (1922) and Covent Garden (1927), as Manrico at Verona Arena (1926), and in Chicago as Jean (*Hérodiade*) and Prinzivalle (*Monna Vanna*), 1920.

Otello. Opera in 3 acts by Rossini; libretto by Francesco Berio di Salsa, after Shakespeare.
First perf., Naples, Fondo, Dec. 4, 1816: Colbran, Nozzari, David, Ciccimarra, Benedetti. U.S. prem., N.Y., Park, Feb. 7, 1826: Malibran, Garcia.
One of Rossini's most successful serious operas, still revived occasionally right up to the time of Verdi's version, *Otello* retains little of Shakespeare's plot. Desdemona (s) has been promised to Rodrigo (t), but she loves Otello (t), who interrupts the wedding ceremony. The girl is locked away by her father Elmiro (bs). When Iago (t) convinces Otello that the girl is deceiving him with Rodrigo, Otello challenges Rodrigo to a duel. Banished, he returns secretly and kills Desdemona. Both Iago and Otello kill themselves in remorse.

Otello. Opera in 4 acts by Verdi; libretto by Boito, after Shakespeare's tragedy (in the translations of Giulio Carcano and Victor Hugo).

First perf., Milan, La Scala, Feb. 5, 1887: Pantaleoni, Tamagno, Maurel, c. Faccio. U.S. prem., N.Y., Academy of Music, Apr. 16, 1888: E. Tetrazzini, Marconi, Galassi, c. Campanini. Met prem., Jan. 11, 1892: Albani, J. de Reszke, Camera, c. Saar. Later Met productions: Nov. 17, 1909: Alda, Slezak, Scotti, c. Toscanini, d. Rota, Sala, Parravicini, p. Speck; Dec. 22, 1937: Rethberg, Martinelli, Tibbett, c. Panizza, d. Oenslager, p. Graf; Mar. 10, 1963: Tucci, McCracken, Merrill, c. Solti, d. Berman, p. Graf; Mar. 25, 1972: Zylis-Gara, McCracken, Milnes, c. Böhm, d. Zeffirelli/P.J. Hall, p. Zeffirelli. Otello has also been sung at the Met by Tamagno, Alvarez, Ralf, Vinay, del Monaco, Vickers, Domingo; Desdemona by Eames, Caniglia, Jepson, Roman, Albanese, Steber, Tebaldi, de los Angeles, Milanov, Rysanek, Caballé, Te Kanawa, Stratas, Ricciarelli, Scotto, M. Price; Iago by Maurel, Amato, Tagliabue, Sved, Warren, Gobbi, MacNeil, Bacquier, Milnes, Stewart. Other Met conductors include Mancinelli, Szell, Busch, Stiedry, Cleva, Schippers, Mehta, Levine. 174 perfs. in 31 seasons.
Verdi's penultimate opera, in which the composer's long-ripening powers of musical characterization are matched with a challenging new poetic stimulus to create a work of elevated tragic interest and symphonic grandeur.
Cyprus, late 15th c. The moor Otello (t), governor of Cyprus, returns victorious from battle with the Turkish fleet. His ensign Iago (bar), jealous of the promotion Otello has bestowed on Cassio (t), gets the latter drunk with the help of Roderigo (t), a young nobleman besotted with Otello's wife Desdemona (s). The resulting brawl provokes the angry Otello to cancel the promotion of the disgraced Cassio. Through a series of cunning manoeuvers, Iago suggests to Otello and seems to prove a liaison between Desdemona and Cassio. Recalled to Venice, the shattered Otello succumbs to his rage and strangles Desdemona in her bed. Iago's wife Emilia (ms) protests Desdemona's innocence, and word arrives that the dying Roderigo has revealed Iago's treachery. Iago escapes and the Moor kills himself.

Otto, Teo. Designer; b. Remscheid, Germany, Feb. 4, 1904, d. Frankfurt, June 6, 1968. Principal designer, Berlin State Opera (1928–33), later resident designer, Zurich Schauspielhaus (from 1933, including Brecht premieres). Designed plays and operas throughout Europe, notably at Salzburg Festival (*Freischütz,* 1954). His Met productions were *Tristan* (1959) and *Nabucco* (1960).

overture. An orchestral piece preceding the rise of the curtain on an opera (and, at times, on its individual acts); it may or may not incorporate musical material from the opera itself.

Owen Wingrave. Opera in 2 acts by Britten; libretto by Myfanwy Piper, after Henry James's story.
First perf., London, BBC Television, May 16, 1971: Harper, Baker, Pears, Luxon, Shirley-Quirk, c. Britten. First stage perf., London, Covent Garden, May 10, 1973, with largely the same cast. U.S. prem., Santa Fe, Aug. 9, 1973: Steber, Kraft, Atherton, Titus, Gramm, c. Nelson.
A harsh look at militarism's role in Britain's heritage. In late 19th-c. London, the pacifistic Owen Wingrave (bar) rejects his family's military tradition. Disinherited and spurned by his betrothed, Kate (ms), he accepts her challenge to prove he is no coward by sleeping in a haunted room, and is found dead before morning.

P

Pacini, Giovanni. Composer; b. Catania, Sicily, Feb. 17, 1796; d. Pescia, near Lucca, Italy, Dec. 6, 1867. Studied with Padre Mattei in Bologna and Furlanetto in Venice. Enormously productive (some 80 operas in 45 years), his basically Rossinian style, emphasizing energetic melody, was eclipsed in the 1830s by the popularity of Donizetti and Bellini. He returned to composition with his masterpiece, *Saffo* (1840), demonstrating a greater concern with harmony and orchestration. However, subsequent works show a stylistic retrogression.

Paderewski, Ignacy Jan. Composer and pianist; b. Kurylówka, Russian Poland, Nov. 6, 1860; d. New York, June 29, 1941. Studied composition with Kiel, piano with Leschetizky in Vienna. A greatly lionized virtuoso at the turn of the century, Paderewski composed many instrumental works; his only opera, *Manru* (1901), is in a Polish nationalist style with Wagnerian accents.

Padmâvatî. Opéra-ballet in 2 acts by Roussel; libretto by Louis Laloy, after an event in Indian history.
First perf., Paris, Opéra, June 1, 1923: Lapeyrette, Franz, Rouard, c. Gaubert.
This exotically tinted "opéra-ballet" is set in the Indian city of Chitoor, 1303. Rather than yield herself to the besieging Mogul sultan Alauddin (bar), Queen Padmâvatî (ms) stabs her husband Ratan-Sen (t), knowing she will have to die on his funeral pyre.

Paer, Ferdinando. Composer; b. Parma, Italy, June 1, 1771; d. Paris, May 3, 1839. Studied with Fortunati and Ghiretti. After successes in Italy, active as composer and administrator in Vienna (1797–1801), Prague (1801–02), Dresden (1802–06), and, initially under Napoleon's patronage, in Paris (1807–1828). Of his numerous works, many in the style of opera semiseria, still remembered are *Leonora* (1806), on the same subject as Beethoven's *Fidelio*, and the comedy *Le Maître de Chapelle* (1821).

Pagliacci (Clowns). Opera in prologue and 2 acts (originally 1) by Leoncavallo; libretto by the composer, based on a court case judged by his father.
First perf., Milan, dal Verme, May 21, 1892: Stehle, Giraud, Maurel, Ancona, c. Toscanini. U.S. prem., N.Y., Grand Opera House, June 15, 1893: Kört-Kronold, Montegriffo, Campanari, Averill, c. Hinrichs. Met prem., Dec. 11, 1893 (following *Orfeo et Euridice*): Melba, de Lucia, Ancona, de Gromzeski, c. Mancinelli, p. Parry. (1st Met perf. with *Cavalleria*, Dec. 22, 1893; *Pagliacci* opened the evening.) Later Met productions: Dec. 13, 1924: Bori, Fleta, Danise, Tibbett, c. Papi, d. Novak, p. Agnini; Jan. 17, 1951: Rigal, Vinay, Warren, Guarrera, c. Frede, d. Armistead/Lloyd, p. Leavitt; Nov. 7, 1958: Amara, del Monaco, Warren, Sereni, c. Mitropoulos, d. Gérard, p. Quintero; Jan. 8, 1970: Amara, Tucker, Milnes, Walker, c. Cleva, d. & p. Zeffirelli. Canio has also been sung at the Met by Caruso, Martinelli, Lauri-Volpi, Bergonzi, Vickers, McCracken, Domingo; Nedda by Sembrich, Farrar, Destinn, Gluck, Muzio, Rethberg, Mario, Albanese, Moffo, Stratas; Tonio by Scotti, Amato, de Luca, Ruffo, Tibbett, Merrill, MacNeil. 421 perfs. in 68 seasons.
Like its perennial partner *Cavalleria*, *Pagliacci* was a beacon for the Italian verismo school, and a hardy survivor when the school as a whole lost its vogue.

Pagliacci – (1970). Designed and produced by Franco Zeffirelli. Richard Tucker, Lucine Amara, and Sherrill Milnes

A village in Calabria, late 1860s. A prologue (sung by the baritone playing Tonio) tells the audience they are about to see a piece of real life. As the opera opens, a travelling troupe of actors arrives. Canio (t), their leader, greets the crowd and goes off to drink with the townsmen. Tonio (bar), a misshapen clown, makes advances to Canio's wife Nedda (s), who mocks him and repulses him with a whip. Later, Tonio hears her planning to run away with her lover, the young villager Silvio (bar); he alerts Canio, but Silvio escapes unidentified. During that evening's performance, the similarity of the partly improvised play to the day's events overwhelms Canio, and he demands the name of Nedda's lover. When she defies him, he stabs her to death, and then kills Silvio, who has come to her aid. Canio (originally Tonio) tells the audience that "the comedy is over."

Pagliughi, Lina. Soprano; b. New York, May 27, 1907; d. Rubicone, Italy, Oct. 1, 1980. Encouraged by Tetrazzini, studied with Gaetano Bavagnoli, Milan; debut as Gilda, Nazionale, Milan, 1927. Sang coloratura roles widely in Italy and South America until 1960, notably Lucia, Sinaide in *Mosè* (La Scala, 1937); Covent Garden debut as Gilda, 1938.

Paisiello, Giovanni. Composer; b. Roccaforzata, near Taranto, Italy, May 9, 1740; d. Naples, June 5, 1816. Studied with Durante and Abos in Naples. After producing over 50 operas in the years 1774–76, he was invited by Catherine the Great to St. Petersburg, where he remained until 1783 and composed his greatest success, *Il Barbiere di Siviglia* (1782), which held the stage until superseded by Rossini's setting. After returning to Naples, in 1802 he took positions with Napoleon and his family, falling into disgrace when the Bourbons were restored in 1815. A competitor of Cimarosa and Piccinni, the majority of his 80 operas were comic.

palco (Ital.). Box, in a theater.

Palestrina. Opera in 3 acts by Pfitzner; libretto by the composer.
First perf., Munich, Prinzregententheater, June 12, 1917: Ivogün, Erb, Feinhals, Brodersen, Bender, c. Walter. U.S. prem., Berkeley, Calif. (Symphony Orch.), May 14, 1982 (concert perf., in Eng.): c. Nagano.

Ettore Panizza

Studied in Spain and Italy; debut as Arnold (*Guillaume Tell*), Paris Opéra, 1899. Toured U.S. and Canada with troupe organized by Mascagni, 1902–03. Appeared at Colón, Buenos Aires (Manrico and Otello, 1908), and La Scala (Samson, Vasco in *Africaine*, 1910).

Papi, Gennaro. Conductor; b. Naples, Dec. 21, 1886; d. New York, Nov. 29, 1941. Studied in Naples, then worked as musical assistant in Italy, Warsaw, Buenos Aires, London, and under Toscanini at Met (1913–15; debut, *Manon Lescaut*, Nov. 16, 1916). In his Met years (1916–26, 1935–42), he conducted nearly 600 perfs. of 36 works, mostly Italian. He also worked at Chicago Opera (1926–35), St. Louis, San Francisco.

Pardon de Ploërmel, Le. See *Dinorah*.

Paride ed Elena (Paris and Helena). Opera in 5 acts by Gluck; libretto by Calzabigi.
    First perf., Vienna, Burgtheater, Nov. 3, 1770: Schindler, Kurz, Millico. U.S. prem., N.Y., Town Hall, Jan. 15, 1954 (concert perf.).
    Famous for the aria "O del mio dolce ardor," this opera's action covers Paris' wooing and winning of Helen, his reward for having chosen Venus in his celebrated judgment of female beauty.

Paris. Capital of France and from the mid-17th c. one of the foremost operatic centers. The initial opera staged in Paris remains unidentified; the first known Italian work was Sacrati's *La Finta Pazza* (1645), performed in the Salle du Petit Bourbon. Cambert's *Pomone*, regarded as the first French opera, opened the Académie de l'Opéra in 1671. The most important 18th-c. theater was the Grande Salle du Palais Royale, which from 1673 housed the Académie Royale du Musique, known also as the Opéra; operas by Lully and Rameau, Piccinni and Gluck had premieres here. The Opéra moved to several other theaters before settling in 1822 in the Rue Lepeletier (capacity 1,954), where works by Cherubini and Spontini were part of the repertory, later grand operas by Auber, Rossini, and Meyerbeer; Ciceri and Daguerre designed spectacular settings, with realistic scenery and lighting (gas lighting was introduced in 1822, electric lighting in 1849 for *Prophète*). Verdi composed for Paris (*Vêpres Siciliennes*, 1855, and *Don Carlos*, 1867), and Wagner revised *Tannhäuser* (1861) for the Opéra. In 1875, the Opéra moved to its present home in the Palais Garnier (capacity 2,131); the sumptuous theater still retains its magnificence and poor sightlines. In the reorganization of Parisian musical life in the 1970s, Rolf Liebermann became director of the Opéra (1973–80), succeeded briefly by Bernard Lefort and then by Massimo Bogianckino (until 1985); Jean-Philippe Saint-Geours is now director, with Lothar Zagrosek as music director. A new theater is currently planned at the Bastille.
    The Opéra-Comique, an offshoot of performances at the annual Paris fairs, took that name in 1715. After many vicissitudes, it achieved official status in 1807 and throughout the 19th c. presented opéras comiques by Auber, Boieldieu, Hérold, Bizet, Delibes, and Offenbach, as well as later works, such as *Louise* (1900) and *Pelléas* (1902), that did not involve spoken dialogue. In the recent reorganization, the company was temporarily disbanded, but performances of smaller works are again given in the "new" Salle Favart (opened in 1898; capacity 1,750), which also houses the École d'Art Lyrique de l'Opéra, directed by Michel Sénéchal.

Pfitzner's "musical legend" implies his kinship with Palestrina, each at the end of a long compositional tradition. Although in 1563 the Council of Trent is prepared to ban polyphony, the retired Palestrina (t) resists the urgings of Cardinal Borromeo (bar) to compose an exemplary new mass. Ghosts of the old masters encourage the weary, doubting composer, and eventually his work is acclaimed, but his son Ighino (s) has gone to Florence to join the Camerata.

Pampanini, Rosetta. Soprano; b. Milan, Sep. 2, 1896; d. Corbola, Aug. 2, 1973. Studied with Emma Molajoli, Milan; debut as Micaela, Nazionale, Rome, 1920. After further study, La Scala debut as Butterfly, 1925. Appeared at Covent Garden (1928–33), Chicago (1931–32), and Paris Opéra (1935). Best known for her Puccini roles.

Panerai, Rolando. Baritone; b. Campi Bisenzio, near Florence, Oct. 17, 1924. Studied with Frazzi, Florence Conservatory, and with Armani and Giulia Tess, Milan; debut as Pharaoh (*Mosè*), San Carlo, Naples, 1947. La Scala debut as High Priest (*Samson*), 1952. In addition to Italian repertory, sang Mozart's Figaro (Aix, 1955) and Guglielmo (Salzburg, 1958); San Francisco debut as Rossini's Figaro, 1958.

Panizza, Ettore. Conductor; b. Buenos Aires, Aug. 12, 1875; d. Milan, Nov. 27, 1967. After study at Milan Conservatory and an 1897 debut in Rome, he conducted in Italy, Spain, South America, and London (1907–14). At Turin in 1916, led world premiere of *Francesca da Rimini*. Worked at La Scala (1921–29, 1930–32) and Chicago Opera (1922–24). Succeeded Serafin in the Met's Italian wing (debut, *Aida*, Dec. 22, 1934) and remained for 8 seasons, leading 231 perfs. of 26 works, including *Salome*, *Louise*, *Boris*, the world premieres of *In the Pasha's Garden* and *Island God*, and Met premieres of *Amelia al Ballo* and *Alceste*, as well as much Verdi.

Paoli, Antonio [Ermogene Imleghi Bascaran]. Tenor; b. Ponce, P. R., Apr. 14, 1871; d. San Juan, Aug. 24, 1946.

Among the many historic Parisian theaters and companies, mention must be made of the Théâtre Italien, housed in various theaters, which during the first half of the 19th c. presented operas by Mozart, Rossini, Bellini, and Donizetti, often in world premieres, with many great vocalists. The Théâtre Lyrique, inaugurated in 1852, introduced *Faust* (1863), *Roméo* (1867), and *Pêcheurs de Perles* (1863). The Bouffes-Parisiens and Théâtre de la Gaité were among the theaters that housed Offenbach's operettas.

Parisina. Opera in 4 (later 3) acts by Mascagni; libretto by Gabriele d'Annunzio.

First perf., Milan, La Scala, Dec. 15, 1913: Poli-Randaccio, Garibaldi, Lázaro, Galeffi, c. Mascagni.

One of Mascagni's attempts to broaden his range, with a historical subject that also served Donizetti. Ugo (t), son of Nicolò d'Este (bar) by his mistress Stella dell'Assassino (ms), falls in love with his father's wife, Parisina Malatesta (s), after saving her from pirates. Nicolò sentences them both to death.

Parker, Horatio. Composer; b. Auburndale, Maine, Sep. 15, 1863; d. Cedarhurst, N.Y., Dec. 18, 1919. Studied with Chadwick and in Munich with Rheinberger; pursued a career as teacher and organist until 1894, when he was appointed a professor at Yale U. His choral works, notably the oratorio *Hora Novissima* (1893), were widely performed. Winning a competition, the opera *Mona* was heard at the Met; *Fairyland* (1915) was performed in Los Angeles. Parker's craftsmanlike work suffers from lack of individual profile.

parlando (Ital., "speaking"). A direction to the singer to use a speech-like tone quality.

Parsifal. Opera in 3 acts by Wagner; libretto by the composer, principally after Wolfram von Eschenbach's poem *Parzival*.

First perf., Bayreuth, July 26, 1882: Materna, Winkelmann, Reichmann, Hill, Scaria, c. Levi. U.S. prem., Metropolitan Opera House (Oratorio Society of N.Y.), Mar. 4, 1886 (concert perf.): Brandt, Krämer, Fischer, c. W. Damrosch. U.S. stage prem., Met, Dec. 24, 1903: Ternina, Burgstaller, van Rooy, Goritz, Blass, c. Hertz, d. Rothaug, p. Fuchs. Later Met productions: Feb. 19, 1920 (in Eng.): Matzenauer, Harrold, Whitehill, Didur, Rothier, c. Bodanzky, d. Urban/Castel-Bert, p. Ordynski; Mar. 24, 1956 ("revision"): Harshaw, Svanholm, Schöffler, Pechner, Edelmann, c. Stiedry, d. Kerz, p. Graf; Nov. 14, 1970: Ludwig, Brilioth, Stewart, Flagello, Siepi, c. Ludwig, d. O'Hearn, p. Merrill. Parsifal has also been sung at the Met by Dippel, Melchior, Vinay, Vickers, Hofmann; Kundry by Nordica, Fremstad, Leider, Flagstad, Varnay, Traubel, Mödl, Crespin, Dunn, Troyanos, Rysanek; Amfortas by Amato, Schorr, Janssen, Hotter, London, Weikl, Estes; Gurnemanz by Bohnen, List, Kipnis, Hotter, Hines, Talvela, Mazura, Moll, Sotin. The opera has also been conducted by Leinsdorf, Reiner, Böhm, Prêtre, Steinberg, Levine. 212 perfs. in 64 seasons.

Wagner's last opera, a spacious and weighty score, integrating and deepening his ideas of long-range musical construction while striking out in new, complex philosophical directions.

Near and in the Castle of the Holy Grail, Montsalvat, Spain. Amfortas (bar), king of the Grail, once yielded to the seductress Kundry (s) and thereby lost the Grail's holy spear to the sorcerer Klingsor (bs), sustaining a wound that

Paris Opéra

Opéra-Comique, Paris, in 1893

will not heal; it is prophesied that a "guileless fool" will redeem him through compassion and recover the spear. As the opera begins, Amfortas seeks comfort through healing baths, and Kundry, in her other incarnation as a wild rider serving the Grail, brings him a healing lotion. The naive youth Parsifal (t) shoots a swan and is taken to task by the Grail knight Gurnemanz (bs), who, suspecting that this may be the guileless fool, brings him to witness the Grail ceremony. Though Parsifal cannot express comprehension of what he has seen and Gurnemanz dismisses him in frustration, Klingsor realizes from a distance that the youth is indeed the potential redeemer, and orders Kundry to seduce him. Lured to the sorcerer's magic garden, at the moment of receiving Kundry's kiss Parsifal suddenly realizes how Amfortas was ensnared, and acquires compassion for his suffering. Leaping up, he rejects Kundry, who tells him that for laughing at the suffering Christ she was doomed to wander endlessly, tempting sinners to their doom. Klingsor hurls the spear at Parsifal, but it stops in the air above the youth's head and he bears it off, as Klingsor's castle and garden fall into ruin. After years of wandering, Parsifal rediscovers the realm of the Grail. Amfortas, longing for death, has refused to perform the life-extending ceremony, and the enfeebled knights await the mortal death that has already overtaken Amfortas' father Titurel (bs). Gurnemanz and Kundry

Parsifal – Bayreuth Festival, 1882. Designed by Paul von Joukowsky

Parsifal – Bayreuth Festival. Designed and produced by Wieland Wagner

bathe and anoint Parsifal, and they set out for the temple. Amfortas has promised to perform the ceremony once more, in memory of his father, but at the moment of unveiling the Grail he loses his resolve and cries out for death. Parsifal appears, touches him with the healing spear, and assumes his sacred office.

Pasatieri, Thomas. Composer; b. New York, Oct. 20, 1945. Studied with Giannini and Persichetti at Juilliard School, N.Y., and with Milhaud in Aspen. Concentrating on vocal music in a neo-Romantic style, he has composed some 15 operas, including *Black Widow* (after Unamuno, 1972), *The Seagull* (after Chekhov, 1974), *Washington Square* (after James, 1976), and a number of one-acters.

Pasero, Tancredi. Bass; b. Turin, Italy, Jan. 11, 1893; d. Milan, Feb. 17, 1983. Studied with Arturo Pessina, Turin; debut as King (*Aida*), Chiarella, Turin, 1917. La Scala debut as Philippe II (*Don Carlos*), 1926; on roster there until 1951. Met debut as Alvise (*Gioconda*), Nov. 1, 1929; in 4 seasons there, he sang 81 perfs. of 19 roles, including Ferrando (*Trovatore*), the Padre Guardiano (*Forza*), and Ramfis. Also appeared at Covent Garden (1931), Florence Maggio Musicale and Verona Arena (from 1933). Created the Miller in Giordano's *Re* (La Scala, 1929), Pizzetti's Orseolo (Florence, 1935), Babilio in Mascagni's *Nerone* (Scala, 1935).

Pasta [née Negri], **Giuditta.** Soprano; b. Saronno, Italy, Oct. 26, 1797; d. Como, Apr. 1, 1865. Studied briefly with her uncle, Filippo Ferranti, then with Bartolomeo Lotti, Giuseppe Scappa, and Davide Banderali; stage debut in Scappa's *Le Tre Eleonore*, Filodrammatici, Milan, 1816. She soon appeared in Paris (Paer's *Principe di Taranto*, Italien, 1816) and London (Cimarosa's *Penelope*, 1817), where she also sang Mozart's Cherubino, Fiordiligi, and Servilia (*Clemenza*). After further study with Scappa, she sang in Italy and returned to Paris in 1821, with sensational success, especially in the operas of Rossini, who conducted *Otello* and *Semiramide* when she returned to London in 1824; in Paris in 1825, she created Corinna in his *Viaggio a Reims*. From then, Pasta sang widely, throughout Italy, in Vienna, Berlin, Warsaw, St. Petersburg, and Moscow. In Milan, she created Donizetti's Anna Bolena, Bellini's Amina and Norma (all in 1831), and Bianca in Donizetti's *Ugo, Conte di Parigi* (1832), and in Venice, Bellini's Beatrice di Tenda (1833). She returned to London in 1833 to introduce *Norma*, again in 1837, and finally in 1850, for a disastrous final appearance in scenes from *Anna Bolena*. In London, Paris, and Milan, her salon was much sought after, and she was befriended by artists, writers, and intellectuals. She was a great favorite of Bellini, Donizetti, and Rossini; other composers who wrote roles for Pasta include Mercadante, Pacini, and Paer.

Pasta was celebrated as a vocalist who thought in terms of words as well as notes; her recitatives were riveting by their naturalness and truth of expression. The timbre was individual, immediately recognizable, and capable, within only a phrase, of soul-stirring emotion. She could execute intricate coloratura, but channeled her bravura for dramatic effect. Her originality and invention in embellishment were renowned, though she had a faulty ear and often sang flat or sharp. Her range, from low A to high E-flat (the latter only in fioritura) was not uncommon, and she experienced some of her greatest successes in pieces of moderate tessitura. An accomplished actress as well as singer, Pasta's deportment and portrayal of dignity were without peer.

pasticcio (Ital., "pastiche"). An opera assembled from parts of other works. In the 18th c., it was made feasible by the frequent settings of the same librettos and by the interchangeability of characters and situations, and was encouraged by the desire of singers to perform arias especially suited to their talents. Also, occasionally, an opera written by several composers (e.g., *Muzio Scevola*, with acts by Mattei, Bononcini, and Handel).

pastorale. A stage work evoking the bucolic life of shepherds, elements of which are found in the earliest Italian and French operas.

Pastor Fido, Il (The Faithful Shepherd). Opera in 3 acts by Handel; libretto by Rossi, after Guarini's pastoral play.

First perf., London, King's, Nov. 22, 1712: Pilotti, Margherita, Valeriano, Valentini, Barbier, Leveridge. U.S. prem., N.Y., Town Hall, Mar. 2, 1952 (concert perf.).

An early false move in Handel's operatic career, this tale of love, jealousy and fickleness among shepherds and nymphs in Arcadia, ending in a double wedding, proved too simply pastoral for London's taste in 1712.

Patanè, Giuseppe. Conductor; b. Naples, Jan. 1, 1932. Son of conductor Franco, he studied in Naples. After a debut there (*Traviata*, 1951), he worked mainly in Germany and Austria; principal conductor, Deutsche Oper, Berlin, 1962–68. U.S. debut, San Francisco, 1967. Met debut in *Gioconda* (Oct. 18, 1975), appearing regularly for 7 seasons in Italian repertory, *Carmen*, and *Lohengrin*. Currently presides over Italian repertory in Munich.

patter song. A song or aria, usually humorous in subject, in which the text is sung very rapidly; common in Italian opera buffa and in the operettas of Gilbert and Sullivan.

Patti, Adelina. Soprano; b. Madrid, Feb. 19, 1843; d. Brecon, Wales, Sep. 27, 1919. Daughter of two singers, she studied in N.Y. with her half-brother Ettore Barilli, then toured America as a prodigy. Her operatic debut was as Lucia (Academy of Music, N.Y., 1859), followed by 13 other roles, including Rosina, Elvira (*Puritani*), Zerlina, Violetta, Gilda, and Linda di Chamounix. After a London debut as Amina (*Sonnambula*) at Covent Garden in 1861,

Adelina Patti as Marie in *La Fille du Régiment*

she made triumphant appearances in Berlin (Royal Opera, 1861), Brussels (1862), Paris (Italien, 1862), and Vienna (Karlstheater, 1863); she sang in Italy in 1865–66, and the following winter in Russia. Regular Covent Garden engagements continued until 1885; Patti also appeared at La Scala (1877–78) and the Paris Opéra (1874, 1888). In 1881 she returned to the U.S. to tour with Mapleson, also singing for him at the Academy of Music in competition with the Met's initial seasons, 1883–85. In 1886, she married her frequent collaborator, tenor Ernesto Nicolini. In 1887 and 1890, under Abbey's aegis, she played the Met theater, but only joined the Met company in 1892, for a supplementary season, as Lady Harriet in *Martha* (debut, Apr. 2, 1892), Lucia, and Rosina. Her 1895 Covent Garden farewell season was followed by performances in Monte Carlo and Nice; her last U.S. tour took place in 1903–04, and her London farewell recital in 1906, but charity appearances continued until 1914.

"The reign of Patti," as it was known, lasted about half a century, by the end of which her preferred repertory, centered on such florid, highly feminine roles as Zerlina, Rosina, Lucia, Norina, and Amina, was fading behind the advent of Wagner and verismo. She successfully embraced early Verdi (notably Violetta), and even Aida (which she introduced to London in 1876), although her Carmen was judged unconvincing. Her few recordings (1905–06) find her well past her prime; though her celebrated mastery of coloratura is no longer in evidence, the legendary trill, clear and even tone, and mastery of legato line and ornament are still to be discerned. In the theater, Patti was an imaginative, mercurial, infectiously energetic performer, capable of fine variation of shading and timbre.

BIBLIOGRAPHY: Herman Klein, *The Reign of Patti* (N.Y., and London, 1920; repr. 1978).

Patzak, Julius. Tenor; b. Vienna, Apr. 9, 1898; d. Rottach-Egern, Bavaria, Jan. 26, 1974. He studied conducting in Vienna, but was self-taught as a singer; debut as Radames, Reichenberg, 1926. A member of Munich State Opera (1928–45) and Vienna State Opera (1945–59), he was best known for his Mozart roles and as Florestan (Salzburg, 1948–50), Herod, and Pfitzner's Palestrina.

Paul Bunyan. Operetta in prologue and 2 acts by Britten; libretto by W.H. Auden.

First perf., N.Y., Columbia U., May 5, 1941: Hess, Helson, Bauman, Warchoff, c. Ross. Rev. version, first perf., London, BBC, Feb. 1, 1976; stage prem., Aldeburgh, June 4, 1976.

Britten's American operetta was withdrawn a week after its premiere and revived only at the end of his life. Based on the tales of the legendary lumberman (represented by an offstage speaking voice), it bears messages of contemporary social significance.

Pauly [Pauly-Dreesen], **Rose** [Rosa Pollak]. Soprano; b. Eperjes, Hungary, Mar. 15, 1894; d. Herzlia, Israel, Dec. 14, 1975. Studied with Rosa Papier-Paumgartner, Vienna; debut as Desdemona, Vienna, 1917. Sang at Cologne (1922–27), Kroll Opera, Berlin (1927–31, including the opening *Fidelio*), and Vienna State Opera (1929–36), also La Scala (1935), Teatro Colón (1939). A celebrated Elektra (Salzburg, 1937; Met debut, Jan. 7, 1938), in 3 Met seasons she sang 9 perfs., also including Ortrud and Venus.

Paur, Emil. Conductor; b. Czernowitz [now Chernovtsy, Ukraine], Bukovina, Aug. 29, 1855; d. Mistek

Peter Pears as Aschenbach and John Shirley-Quirk as the Gondolier in *Death in Venice*

[now in Czechoslovakia], June 7, 1932. After study in Vienna, conducted in several German cities. He succeeded Nikisch at Boston Symphony in 1893, then led N.Y. Philharmonic (1899–1902). Conductor, Pittsburgh Symphony (1904–10); thereafter based in Berlin. In his only Met season (debut, *Lohengrin*, Dec. 23, 1899), he led 11 operas, including two *Ring* cycles.

Pavarotti, Luciano. Tenor; b. Modena, Oct. 12, 1935. After teaching for two years, he studied singing with Arrigo Pola in Modena and Ettore Campogalliani in Mantua, won a competition in Reggio Emilia, and made his debut there as Rodolfo, 1961. This remained his preferred debut role, at Vienna (1963), Covent Garden (1963), Naples (1964), and La Scala (1965); other early roles included the Duke of Mantua, Alfredo, Edgardo, and Pinkerton. In 1964 he sang Idamante (*Idomeneo*) at Glyndebourne; after his U.S. debut as Edgardo (Miami, 1965) and a Covent Garden *Sonnambula* (1965), both opposite Sutherland, he toured Australia with her, also singing Nemorino and Alfredo (1965). In the later 1960s he sang widely in Europe, including Tebaldo in *Capuleti* (La Scala, 1966), Tonio in *Fille* (Covent Garden, 1966), Arturo in *Puritani* (Catania, 1968), Massenet's Des Grieux (La Scala, 1969), and Oronte in *Lombardi* (Rome, 1969). In America, he bowed as Rodolfo in San Francisco (1967), at the Met (Nov. 23, 1968), in Philadelphia (1971), and Chicago (1973). He has returned to the Met nearly every season since, singing over 160 perfs. of 16 roles, including Edgardo, Alfredo, Tonio, the Duke, Riccardo (*Ballo*), Nemorino, Arturo, the Italian Singer (*Rosenkavalier*), Manrico, Fernand (*Favorite*), Cavaradossi, Rodolfo (*Luisa Miller*), Idomeneo, Ernani, and Radames. His San Fran-

cisco roles have also included Calaf and Enzo, and the competition for young singers he founded in 1981 is based at the Philadelphia Lyric Opera. He has appeared in most of the leading theaters of Europe and the Americas, and in Japan and the Soviet Union, in opera or concert.

With a sweet, bright lyric tenor, classic legato, secure upper extension, sound instincts for the Italian idiom, and an infectiously extrovert stage presence, Pavarotti early established himself as a favorite of both musicians and audiences. In the years since 1977, as his remarkable popular success as a recitalist and television celebrity has reduced the frequency of his operatic appearances, his voice has settled and darkened, and he has moved into more dramatic roles. His recordings extend beyond his stage repertory to works such as *Amico Fritz*, *Beatrice di Tenda*, and *Guillaume Tell*, as well as numerous recitals of arias and popular Italian songs.

BIBLIOGRAPHY: Martin Mayer and Gerald Fitzgerald, *Grandissimo Pavarotti* (N.Y., 1986)

Pearl Fishers, The. See *Pêcheurs de Perles, Les*.

Pears, Peter. Tenor; b. Farnham, England, June 22, 1910; d. Aldeburgh, Apr. 3, 1986. Studied in London at Royal College of Music and with Elena Gerhardt and Dawson Freer, later with Lucie Manen. His collaboration with Benjamin Britten began with a 1937 recital. Operatic debut as Hoffmann, Strand, London, 1942; member of Sadler's Wells, 1943–46, singing Almaviva, Tamino, Rodolfo, and Vašek (*Bartered Bride*) and creating Peter Grimes. In guest appearances at Covent Garden from 1947, he also sang David (*Meistersinger*), and created Vere (*Billy Budd*), Essex (*Gloriana*), and Pandarus (*Troilus*). With the English Opera Group at Glyndebourne, he created the Male Chorus (*Lucretia*) and Albert Herring; other Britten roles written for him were Quint (*Turn of the Screw*), Flute (*Midsummer Night's Dream*), the Madwoman (*Curlew River*), Sir Philip (*Owen Wingrave*), and Aschenbach (*Death in Venice*). After his Met debut as Aschenbach (Oct. 18, 1974), he returned to sing Captain Vere in 1978, a total of 16 perfs. With a highly individual technique, Pears bent his distinctively reedy voice to the service of a commanding musical and verbal intelligence.

Pêcheurs de Perles, Les (The Pearl Fishers). Opera in 3 acts by Bizet; libretto by "Eugène Cormon" [Pierre-Étienne Piestre] and Carré.

First perf., Paris, Lyrique, Sep. 30, 1863: de Maësen, Morini, Ismaël, Guyot, c. Deloffre. U.S. prem., Philadelphia, Grand Opera House, Aug. 23, 1893 (in Ital.). Met prem., Jan. 11, 1896 (Acts 1 and 2 only): Calvé, Cremonini, Ancona, Arimondi, c. Bevignani, p. Parry. Later Met production: Nov. 13, 1916: Hempel, Caruso, de Luca, Rothier, c. Polacco, d. Rota, Parravicini/Palanti, p. Speck. 4 perfs. in 2 seasons.

The score, nearly as rich in melody and originality as that of *Carmen*, is hampered by a plot generally considered one of opera's weakest.

Ceylon, tribal era. Nadir (t) joins his long estranged friend Zurga (bar) and his tribe of pearlfishers. A new priestess comes to bless the tribe's endeavors, and Nadir recognizes her as Leila (s), the woman who had been the cause of the friends' bitter quarrel long ago. Nadir and Leila renew their love, despite her vows of chastity, and are caught by the high priest Nourabad (bs). But Zurga discovers that, in the still more distant past, Leila had saved his life; he sets aside jealousy and resolves to help the couple by setting fire to the village as they escape. In the opera's original version, Zurga stands waiting amid the spreading fire; in a later version (made by various hands), he perishes at the hands of his tribesmen.

Pechner, Gerhard. Baritone; b. Berlin, Apr. 15, 1903; d. New York, Oct. 21, 1969. Debut in Berlin, 1927; sang at German Opera, Prague, 1933–39. U.S. debut in San Francisco, as Mozart's Bartolo, 1940. Met debut as Notary (*Rosenkavalier*), Nov. 27, 1941; in 25 Met seasons, he sang over 500 perfs. of 33 roles, notably Beckmesser, Alberich, Melitone (*Forza*), and the Sacristan (*Tosca*).

Peerce, Jan [Jacob Pincus Perelmuth]. Tenor; b. New York, June 3, 1904; d. New York, Dec. 15, 1984. After singing at Radio City Music Hall and on radio, studied with Giuseppe Boghetti; debut as Duke of Mantua, Baltimore, 1938. From 1938, Toscanini's regular tenor soloist, in Beethoven's Ninth Symphony and broadcasts of *Rigoletto* (Act III), *Fidelio*, *Bohème*, *Traviata*, and *Ballo*, as well as a film of Verdi's *Hymn of the Nations*, all subsequently issued on records. Debuts as the Duke in San Francisco (1941) and Chicago (1944). Met debut as Alfredo, Nov. 29, 1941; in 26 seasons, he sang 205 perfs. of 11 roles, including Edgardo, Cavaradossi, Riccardo, Rodolfo, Ottavio, Faust, and Turiddu. Sang occasionally in Europe, Soviet Union (Bolshoi, 1956), in films, and on Broadway (*Fiddler on the Roof*, 1971). Among the most reliable and musical of American artists, Peerce's mastery of vocal technique enabled him to sing impressively even in his 70s.

Pelléas et Mélisande – (1977). Designed by Desmond Heeley, produced by Paul-Émile Deiber. Teresa Stratas and Raymond Gibbs

Wilfrid Pelletier

Pelléas et Mélisande (Pelleas and Melisande). Opera in 5 acts by Debussy; libretto a slightly abridged version of Maurice Maeterlinck's play.

First perf., Paris, Opéra-Comique, Apr. 30, 1902: Garden, Gerville-Réache, Périer, Dufranne, Vieuille, c. Messager. U.S. prem., N.Y., Manhattan Opera House, Feb. 19, 1908: Garden, Gerville-Réache, Périer, Dufranne, Arimondi, c. Campanini. Met prem., Mar. 21, 1925: Bori, Howard, Johnson, Whitehill, Rothier, c. Hasselmans, d. Urban, p. Wymetal. Later Met productions: Nov. 27, 1953 ("revision"): Conner, Lipton, Uppman, Singher, Hines, c. Monteux, d. Armistead, p. Yannopoulos; Jan. 19, 1972: Blegen, Chookasian, McDaniel, Stewart, Tozzi, c. C. Davis, d. Heeley, p. Deiber. Pelléas has also been sung at the Met by Jobin, Singher, Gedda, Gibbs, Duesing; Mélisande by Jepson, Sayão, Novotná, de los Angeles, Moffo, Stratas; Golaud by Pinza, Tibbett, Brownlee, London, van Dam, Bacquier; Arkel by Kipnis; the opera has also been conducted by Leinsdorf, Cooper, Morel, Ansermet, Levine. 77 perfs. in 22 seasons.

A revolutionary advance in the approximation of opera to spoken drama, and the understated antithesis of Wagner's *Tristan* in the expression of their shared theme, the intensity of a doomed and proscribed love.

The setting is an imaginary, primitive kingdom of "Allemonde." In a forest, the prince Golaud (bar) finds the enigmatic and frightened Mélisande (s), whom he persuades to follow him. They are married, and after a time – still knowing nothing of her origins – Golaud brings her to the household of his grandfather, the king Arkel (bs). There she meets her husband's mother Geneviève (ms) and half-brother Pelléas (t); an attraction grows between Pelléas and Mélisande. Mélisande allows herself to lose her wedding ring, setting in motion a buildup of hostility and suspicion in Golaud. Eventually, he sends Yniold (treble), his son by his first wife, to spy on the pair, and though nothing incriminating emerges, his jealousy provokes him to violence against his wife. Then, shortly after the lovers have finally declared their suppressed feelings for one another, Golaud murders Pelléas. Mélisande flees, is found, and lies dying; torn by remorse, Golaud still cruelly presses her to tell whether she betrayed him with Pelléas. After saying that she has done nothing to be ashamed of, she dies.

Pelletier, Wilfrid. Conductor; b. Montreal, June 20, 1896; d. New York, Apr. 9, 1982. After study in Paris, recommended by Monteux to Met, where he became an assistant in 1917 and remained for 28 seasons; conducting debut, *King's Henchman*, Apr. 14, 1928. He rose to greater prominence in the Johnson era, leading 20 operas, mostly French, as well as Sunday concerts and Auditions of the Air. From 1942, director of Montreal Conservatory (1943–70).

Penderecki, Krzysztof. Composer; b. Dębica, Poland, Nov. 23, 1933. A student of Malawski and Wiechowicz, he first attracted international attention with orchestral and choral works based on novel, grating instrumental effects, vocal devices reminiscent of Orff, and aleatoric techniques. His operas include *Die Teufel von Loudon* (1969); *Paradise Lost* (1978), a massive setting of Milton's epic poem; and *Die schwarze Maske* (1986), based on Hauptmann's drama.

Pénélope. Opera in 3 acts by Fauré; libretto by René Fauchois.
First perf., Monte Carlo, Mar. 4, 1913: Bréval, Rousselière, Delmas, Bourbon, c. Jehin. U.S. prem., Newark, Del., U. of Del., Apr. 25, 1974.
A harmonically refined, vocally restrained version of the episode from the *Odyssey*, in which Ulysse (t) returns after his voyages to his faithful wife Pénélope (s), is recognized by the herder Eumée (bs), and drives away the arrogant suitors, led by Antinoüs (bs).

Pepusch, Johann Christoph. Composer; b. Berlin, 1667; d. London, July 20, 1752. A pupil of Klingenberg, he traveled to London c. 1700, joining the Drury Lane orchestra. Director of Lincoln's Inn Theatre (from 1713), for which he composed masques such as *Venus and Adonis* (1715) and *The Death of Dido* (1716), he is remembered as composer of the overture and arranger of the music for *The Beggar's Opera* (1728) and for its sequel *Polly* (1729).

Pergolesi, Giovanni. Composer; b. Iesi, near Ancona, Italy, Jan. 4, 1710; d. Pozzuoli, near Naples, Mar. 16, 1736. A student of Greco, Vinci, and Durante in Naples, this short-lived genius composed instrumental and sacred works as well as operas both seria and buffa. His surviving stage works are *Salustia* (1732); *Lo Frate 'Nnamorato* (1732); *La Serva Padrona* (1733), the most enduring of all comic intermezzos; *Adriano in Siria*, with its intermezzo *La Contadina Astuta* (*Livietta e Tracollo*) (1734); *L'Olimpiade* (1935); and *Il Flaminio* (1735). Posthumously, his fame attracted many false attributions, including the comedy *Il Maestro di Musica* and the song "Tre Giorni Son Che Nina."

Peri, Jacopo. Composer; b. Rome, Aug. 20, 1561; d. Florence, Aug. 12, 1633. Studied with Malvezzi at Lucca. Chapel master at the Medici court in Florence and a member of the circle around Jacopo Corsi, with whom he collaborated on music for Rinuccini's pastoral *Dafne* (1597), considered the first opera; much of the score is lost. His subsequent *Euridice* (1600), composed with Caccini, is the earliest opera known to survive. Other operas: *Lo Sposalizio di Medoro e Angelica* (1619); *La Flora* (1628, with Gagliano).

Périchole, La. Operetta in 3 acts (originally 2) by Offenbach; libretto by Meilhac and Halévy, after Mérimée's play *Le Carrosse du Saint-Sacrement*.
First perf., Paris, Variétés, Oct. 6, 1868, with Hortense Schneider. Rev. version in 3 acts, first perf., Paris, Variétés,

Apr. 25, 1874. U.S. prem., N.Y., Pike's Opera House, Jan. 4, 1869. Met prem., Dec. 21, 1956 (in Eng.): Munsel, Uppman, Ritchard, c. Morel, d. Gérard, p. Ritchard. Périchole has also been sung at the Met by Moffo and Stratas, Don Pedro by Gramm. 37 perfs. in 5 seasons.
One of Offenbach's most melodious, least satirical operettas, set in mid-19th-c. Peru. The itinerant singers Périchole (s) and her boyfriend Piquillo (t) are too poor to afford even their wedding fees. During one of his incognito jaunts through the town, the Viceroy of Peru (bar) becomes infatuated with Périchole and offers her a place at court. Tired of poverty, she accepts, leaving an apologetic note for Piquillo. Because an unmarried woman may not live within the palace precincts, the Viceroy has his men procure a husband for Périchole. By coincidence, they choose Piquillo, making him too drunk to recognize his bride; when he realizes whom he is marrying and why, he denounces Périchole (echoing Donizetti's *Favorite*) and is imprisoned. The two eventually escape and persuade the Viceroy to pardon them.

Perlea, Jonel. Conductor; b. Ograda, Romania, Dec. 13, 1900; d. New York, July 29, 1970. Studied in Munich and Leipzig, conducted in Bucharest (music director, 1934–44). After Nazi internment, worked in Italy and came to Met (debut, *Tristan*, Dec. 1, 1949) for one season, also leading *Rigoletto*, *Traviata*, and *Carmen*. In later years, taught at the Manhattan School of Music, and led concert opera performances and recordings.

pertichino (Ital., "understudy"). A secondary character who listens to narrations and other arias, occasionally interjecting questions or exclamations.

Peter Grimes – (1967). Designed by Tanya Moiseiwitsch, produced by Tyrone Guthrie. Jon Vickers

Pertile, Aureliano. Tenor; b. Montagnana, Italy, Nov. 9, 1885; d. Milan, Jan. 11, 1952. Studied with Orefice in Padua, Bavagnoli in Milan; debut as Lionel (*Martha*), Vicenza, 1911. After appearances in Italy and South America, La Scala debut as Paolo (*Francesca*), 1916. In his only Met season, he sang 11 perfs. of Cavaradossi (debut, Dec. 1, 1921), Puccini's Des Grieux, Julien (*Louise*), Turiddu, Dimitri (*Boris*), Radames, and Canio. Thereafter, he was the leading tenor at La Scala (1922–37), where his repertory also included Boito's Faust, Lohengrin, Stolzing, Edgardo, Alfredo, Osaka (*Iris*), Rodolfo, Chénier, Manrico, Riccardo, Pinkerton, Enrico (*Campana Sommersa*), Alvaro (*Forza*), Pollione, Loris (*Fedora*), Werther, Maurizio (*Adriana*), Fernand (*Favorite*), Fra Diavolo; he created Boito's Nerone (1924), Wolf-Ferrari's Sly (1927), and Mascagni's Nerone (1935). Also sang at Covent Garden (1927–31) and Colón, Buenos Aires (1923–29), and taught at Milan Conservatory after his retirement in 1946. Toscanini's preferred tenor at La Scala, Pertile achieved compelling dramatic results despite a voice of indifferent quality.

Peter Grimes. Opera in prologue, 3 acts, and epilogue by Britten; libretto by Montagu Slater, after George Crabbe's poem *The Borough*.

First perf., London, Sadler's Wells, June 7, 1945: Cross, Pears, R. Jones, c. Goodall. U.S. prem., Lenox, Mass., Berkshire Music Center, Aug. 6, 1946: Manning, W. Horne, Pease, c. Bernstein. Met prem., Feb. 12, 1948: Resnik, Jagel, Brownlee, c. Cooper, d. Novak/Schenck, p. Yannopoulos. Later Met production: Jan. 20, 1967: Amara, Vickers, Evans, c. C. Davis, d. Moiseiwitsch, p. Guthrie. Peter Grimes has also been sung at the Met by Sullivan, Ellen Orford by Stoska, Harper, Söderström; Balstrode by Harrell, Tibbett, Gramm. 41 perfs. in 7 seasons.

A rich, varied, and songfully intense score, bringing all the traditional resources of grand opera to a specifically British story and musical idiom. *Peter Grimes* stands as a late equivalent to the landmark national operas of Eastern Europe in the late 19th c.

A fishing town on the East Coast of England, around 1830. Peter Grimes (t), a fisherman, stands trial for the unexplained death of his apprentice and is acquitted, but the townspeople, distrusting his standoffish ways and inexplicable temper, widely suspect him of doing the boy in. The widowed schoolmistress Ellen Orford (s) rises to befriend Grimes and supports him in his effort to secure another apprentice. Grimes confides to Captain Balstrode (bar) his ambition to prosper as a fisherman and to marry Ellen. Ellen's own suspicions about Grimes' behavior are aroused when she discovers a tear in the new apprentice's jersey and a bruise on his neck. Later, as Grimes prepares to set out fishing, the boy slips and falls down the cliff to his death; Grimes, terrified, puts out to sea. A posse from the town invades Grimes' hut but finds nothing and departs. Grimes' disappearance makes the townspeople suspicious, and when the boy's jersey washes ashore Ellen and Balstrode believe their worst fears confirmed. Grimes wanders ashore, confused, in the fog. Ellen and Balstrode encounter him, and, finding him nearly deranged, Balstrode advises him to take his boat out to sea and sink it.

Peter Ibbetson. Opera in 3 acts by Taylor; libretto by the composer and Constance Collier, after the latter's play based on George du Maurier's novel.

First perf., N.Y., Met, Feb. 7, 1931: Bori, Telva,

Roberta Peters as the Queen of Night in *Die Zauberflöte*

Johnson, Tibbett, Rothier, c. Serafin, d. Urban, p. Wymetal. 16 perfs. in 4 seasons.

A conservatively romantic score, set in England and France, 1855–1887. Peter Ibbetson (t) accidentally kills his uncle Colonel Ibbetson (bar) upon learning that the latter is his real father, and is convicted of murder. His beloved childhood friend Mary, now Duchess of Towers (s), appears to Peter in his dreams, sustaining him through 30 years in prison.

Peters [Peterman], **Roberta.** Soprano; b. New York, May 4, 1930. Encouraged by Jan Peerce, she began vocal study at age 13 with William Herman; debut (an emergency replacement) as Zerlina, Met, Nov. 17, 1950. After that success, the Met remained the center of her operatic activities for 35 seasons, in 361 perfs. of 23 roles, including the Queen of Night, Rosina, Barbarina and Susanna (*Nozze*), Gilda, Lauretta (*Gianni Schicchi*), Despina, Sophie, the Shepherd (*Tannhäuser*), Adele (*Fledermaus*), Oscar (*Ballo*), Fiakermilli (*Arabella*), Amor (*Orfeo*), Olympia (*Hoffmann*), Norina, Lucia, Adina (*Elisir*), Zerbinetta, Kitty (*Last Savage*), Amina (*Sonnambula*), Nannetta, and Marzelline (*Fidelio*). She also sang at Covent Garden (Arline in *The Bohemian Girl* under Beecham, 1951), Salzburg (Queen of Night, 1963–64), and the Bolshoi, Moscow (Violetta, 1972), appeared in recital, television, musical comedy, and the film *Tonight We Sing*.

A piquant and charming stage presence, Peters offers a high standard of musicianship and vocal finish, and has long been one of the Met's most consistent and appealing artists. She recorded Susanna, Rosina, Lucia, and Zerbinetta under Leinsdorf, the Queen of Night under Böhm, Despina under Stiedry, Gilda under Perlea.

BIBLIOGRAPHY: Roberta Peters, *Debut at the Met* (N.Y., 1967).

Petina, Irra. Mezzo-soprano; b. St. Petersburg, 1907. Fled to China from Russian revolution, then to U.S., where she studied at Curtis Institute and appeared with Philadelphia Grand Opera. At the Met (debut as Schwertleite in *Walküre*, Dec. 29, 1933), she sang about 30 roles, large and small, notably Berta (*Barbiere*), Marcellina, Maddalena, Suzuki, also Carmen, until 1950. N.Y.C. Opera debut as Carmen (1947). Created the Old Lady (*Candide*) on Broadway, 1956.

Pfitzner, Hans. Composer; b. Moscow, May 5, 1869, of German parents; d. Salzburg, May 22, 1949. Studied with Knorr at Hoch Conservatory, Frankfurt, and with Riemann in Wiesbaden. With his first opera, *Der arme Heinrich* (1895), he was hailed as a powerful exponent of Romantic nationalism. He confirmed his anti-modernist stance with polemics against Busoni and Schoenberg, and with the opera *Palestrina* (1917), his enduring contribution to the German repertory. Other operas: *Die Rose vom Liebesgarten* (1901); *Das Christ-Elflein* (1906); *Das Herz* (1931). Out of favor with the Nazis, he spent his last years in straitened circumstances.

Philadelphia. City in Pennsylvania. Philadelphia's operatic roots go back to a 1754 production of the ballad opera *Flora, or Hob in the Wall*, and English opera became a staple at the Southwark Theatre (opened 1766). From 1827, visiting companies introduced French and Italian works, and Fry's *Leonora*, the first native grand opera, had its initial performance in 1845 at the Chestnut Street Theater. The Academy of Music, still one of the finest theaters in America (capacity 2,900), opened in 1857. To accommodate a growing public, impresarios brought European singers to the new Chestnut Street Opera House (opened 1885) and the Grand Opera House (opened 1888), where American premieres included *Cavalleria* (1891) and *Manon Lescaut* (1894). The visits of the Metropolitan Opera began in 1885 and continued until 1968 (for much of the period, the Met visited Philadelphia regularly on Tuesday nights during its New York season). In 1908 Oscar Hammerstein built the 4,000-seat Philadelphia Opera House, where his Manhattan Opera presented *Pelléas*, *Salome*, and *Elektra*; sold to the Met two years later and renamed the Metropolitan Opera House, it was little used after 1931. Later companies included the Philadelphia Civic Opera (1924–30) and the Philadelphia Grand Opera (1926–43), which gave the first U.S. *Wozzeck* (1931). The Pennsylvania Grand Opera (founded 1927), through a series of mergers, eventually in 1976 became the Opera Company of Philadelphia, which presents an annual season of five operas at the Academy of Music. Margaret Anne Everitt is general director.

Philémon et Baucis (Philemon and Baucis). Opera in 2 acts (originally 3) by Gounod; libretto by Barbier and Carré, after a legend.
First perf., Paris, Lyrique, Feb. 18, 1860: Miolan-Carvalho, Froment, Battaille, Balanqué. U.S. prem., Chicago, Auditorium, Dec. 26, 1892 (in Eng.). Met prem., Nov. 29, 1893: Arnoldson, Mauguière, Castelmary, Plançon, c. Bevignani, p. Parry. 7 perfs. in 3 seasons.
This attractive comic opera succeeded only when a superfluous central act was removed (Opéra-Comique, 1876). For their kindness to the disguised gods Jupiter (bs) and Vulcain (bar), the peasant couple Philémon (t) and Baucis (s) are restored to youth, whereupon Jupiter falls in love with Baucis.

Phoebus and Pan [properly *Der Streit zwischen Phoebus und Pan* (The Contest between Phoebus and Pan)]. Cantata by Johann Sebastian Bach.
First perf., Leipzig, 1729(?). Met prem., Jan. 15, 1942 (in Eng.): Darcy, Brownlee, c. Beecham, d. Rychtarik, p. Graf. 4 perfs. in 1 season.
Beecham augmented his stage version of this secular cantata with a ballet using music from Bach's *French Suites*. The subject is the competition for musical supremacy between Phoebus (t), god of the lyre, and the untutored Pan (bar) with his rustic pipe.

Piave, Francesco Maria. Librettist; b. Murano, Italy, May 18, 1810; d. Milan, Mar. 5, 1876. An active writer and critic, he first worked with Verdi on *Ernani*, later providing librettos for *Due Foscari*, *Macbeth*, *Corsaro*, *Stiffelio*, *Rigoletto*, *Traviata*, *Simon Boccanegra*, and *Forza*; their correspondence reveals Verdi's aggressive role in shaping the librettos. Piave also wrote librettos for Mercadante, Ponchielli, and Pacini.

Piccaver [Peckover], **Alfred.** Tenor; b. Long Sutton, Lincolnshire, England, Feb. 15, 1884; d. Vienna, Sep. 23, 1958. Raised in N.Y., studied with Rosario in Milan, and with Prohaska-Neumann in Prague after his debut as Roméo, Prague, 1907. Appeared with Vienna Opera, 1910–37, including Austrian premieres of *Fanciulla* (1913) and *Tabarro*, also at Chicago (1923–25) and Covent Garden (1924). Taught in London and at Vienna State Opera school.

Piccinni, Niccolò. Composer; b. Bari, Italy, Jan. 16, 1728; d. Passy, France, May 7, 1800. Studied with Leo and Durante in Naples. Until 1776, wrote operas for Naples and Rome, where he produced the highly successful comedy *La Buona Figliuola* (1760). In 1776, his arrival in Paris provoked the "war of the Gluckists and Piccinnists," though Gluck admired Piccinni's traditional tragédies lyriques, among them *Roland* (1778), *Atys* (1780), and *Didon* (1783). The French Revolution forced him back to Naples, where political problems led to his imprisonment; in 1798 he returned to Paris, where he died in indigence.

Piccolo Marat, Il (The Little Marat). Opera in 3 acts by Mascagni; libretto by Forzano and Targioni-Tozzetti, after Victor Martin's novel *Sous la Terreur*.
First perf., Rome, Costanzi, May 2, 1921: dalla Rizza, Lázaro, Franci, Badini, c. Mascagni.
A verismo work set in Paris during the French revolution. The Prince de Fleury (t) pretends to be a revolutionary – convincingly enough to be known as "the little Marat" – in hopes of rescuing his mother from prison. He succeeds, and they flee with his lover Mariella (s).

Pietra del Paragone, La (The Touchstone). Opera in 2 acts by Rossini; libretto by Luigi Romanelli.
First perf., Milan, La Scala, Sep. 26, 1812: Marcolini, Galli. U.S. prem., Hartford, Conn., Hartt College, May 4, 1955 (in Eng.).
One of the sparkling comedies that won Rossini his earliest fame. The wealthy Count Asdrubale (bar), desired by a number of widows, devises a test of their loyalty which only Clarice (ms), whom he loves, passes. She in turn tests his loyalty and devotion with a trick of her own.

Pilarczyk, Helga. Soprano; b. Schönigen, near Brunswick, Germany, Mar. 12, 1925. Studied with Dziobek,

Hamburg; mezzo debut as Irmentraud (*Waffenschmied*), Brunswick, 1951. Sang as soprano in Hamburg from 1953, specializing in 20th-c. works such as *Erwartung* and *Lulu*; also appeared at Covent Garden (1958), Glyndebourne (1958), La Scala (1963), Paris Opéra, and Vienna State Opera. Only Met appearances as Marie in *Wozzeck* (debut, Feb. 19, 1965).

Pilgrim's Progress, The. Opera in prologue, 4 acts, and epilogue by Vaughan Williams; libretto by the composer, after John Bunyan's allegory.

First perf., London, Covent Garden, Apr. 26, 1951: Evans, Matters, Te Wiata, Walker, c. Hancock. U.S. prem., Provo, Utah, Apr. 28, 1969.

This "morality," in the composer's characteristic blend of the mystical and the vernacular, depicts the allegorical journey of Pilgrim (bar).

Pilou, Jeannette [Joanna Pilós]. Soprano; b. Alexandria, Egypt, 1931. Studied with Carla Castellani, Milan; debut as Violetta, Milan, 1958. Met debut as Juliette, Oct. 7, 1967; in 8 seasons (through 1986), she sang 73 perfs. of 11 roles, including Mélisande, Micaela, Nedda, Marguerite, Susanna, and Mimi. Has also sung in Paris, Rome, Vienna, Hamburg, Venice, San Francisco, Chicago.

Pini-Corsi, Antonio. Baritone; b. Zara [now Zadar], Dalmatia, June 1858; d. Milan, Apr. 22, 1918. After his debut as Dandini (*Cenerentola*), Cremona, 1878, he sang buffo roles throughout Italy; La Scala debut as Rigoletto, 1893. Created Ford in *Falstaff* (1893) and Schaunard in *Bohème* (1896). Met debut as Rossini's Bartolo, Dec. 25, 1899; in 7 seasons there, he sang 180 perfs. of 23 roles,

Ezio Pinza as Figaro in *Le Nozze di Figaro*

including Don Pasquale and the Sacristan (*Tosca*), and created Happy (*Fanciulla*) and the Innkeeper (*Königskinder*).

Pinza, Ezio. Bass; b. Rome, May 18, 1892; d. Stamford, Conn., May 9, 1957. Studied with Ruzza and with Alessandro Vezzani at Bologna Conservatory; debut as Oroveso (*Norma*), Soncino, near Cremona, 1914. After military service, he sang in Rome (Costanzi, 1919–21) and Turin (1921–22), then at La Scala, where his roles included Pimen in *Boris* (debut, 1922), Pogner, Raimondo in *Lucia*, King Marke, and Rodolfo in *Sonnambula*; he created the Blind Man in Pizzetti's *Debora e Jaele* and Tigellino in Boito's *Nerone*. After singing in other Italian theaters and at the Colón, Buenos Aires (debut, Gurnemanz, 1925), he joined the Met on Nov. 1, 1926, as the Pontifex Maximus (*Vestale*). In 22 seasons with the company, he sang 587 perfs. (246 more on tour) of 51 roles, most frequently Ramfis (54 times), Don Giovanni (46), Raimondo, Basilio, Colline, Escamillo, Méphistophélès, and Mozart's Figaro, also Alvise, Sparafucile, the Padre Guardiano, Archibaldo (*Amore dei Tre Re*), Oroveso, King Dodon, Dulcamara, Lothario (*Mignon*), Fiesco (*Simon Boccanegra*), the Father (*Louise*), Boris, and Sarastro. (Though in Italy he had sung Wagner roles in translation, he decided, after a few essays, not to pursue this repertory in America, as he did not speak German.) During his Met years, Pinza also appeared at Covent Garden (debut, Oroveso, 1930; other roles included Don Magnifico in *Cenerentola* and Timur), Florence (1932–34), the Paris Opéra (Don Giovanni, 1936), and notably at Salzburg (1934–39), where he was protagonist in the first Italian-language *Don Giovanni* and sang his first Figaro. In America, he sang regularly in San Francisco (1927–48) and Chicago (1934–45, including Boito's *Mefistofele*). After retiring from opera in 1948, he appeared in musical comedy (notably *South Pacific*, 1949), films, and television.

A handsome man whose stage presence compelled equally in roles of dignity, malice, comedy, and romance, Pinza was one of the rare basses to become a charismatic star. His classic basso cantante was rich and smoothly produced over a wide range (a high F enabled him to sing baritone roles such as Escamillo), and his innate musicianship led him to phrasing of breadth and authority. More than any single singer responsible for the return of Mozart's operas to the Met repertory by mid-century, Pinza recorded no complete operas, but his major roles are well documented in excerpts from 1923 to 1952.
BIBLIOGRAPHY: Ezio Pinza, *An Autobiography* (with R. Magidoff, N.Y., 1958).

Pipe of Desire, The. Opera in 1 act by Converse; libretto by George Edward Burton.

First perf., Boston, Jordan Hall, Jan 31, 1906: Cushingchild, Deane, Townsend, c. Goodrich. Met prem., Mar. 18, 1910: Homer, Martin, Whitehill, c. Hertz, d. Fox, p. Stern. 3 perfs. in 1 season.

The first American opera given at the Met set off a pattern of conservative Romanticism; in the quasilegendary story, selfish use of the Elf King's magic pipe brings death to Iolan (t) and his lover Noia (ms).

Pique Dame. See *Queen of Spades, The.*

Pirata, Il (The Pirate). Opera in 2 acts by Bellini; libretto by Romani, after R.C. Maturin's drama *Bertram.*

First perf., Milan, La Scala, Oct. 27, 1827: Méric-Lalande, Rubini, Tamburini. U.S. prem., N.Y., Richmond Hill, Dec. 5, 1832.

A central Bellinian score, with the blend of dramatic charge and spinning lyricism that reaches its peak in *Norma*. In 13th-c. Sicily, to save her father's life, Imogene (s) must marry Ernesto (bar). Gualtiero (t), whom she loves, becomes a pirate; his men are defeated by Ernesto's, but he later kills Ernesto in a duel and is condemned to die, whereupon Imogene loses her mind.

Pirogov, Alexander. Bass; b. Novoselki, Ryazan, Russia, July 4, 1899; d. Moscow, June 26, 1964. Studied with Tyutyunik in Moscow; after singing in a choir, he became a soloist with the Zimin Free Opera, Moscow (1922–24). Bolshoi debut, 1924; sang there until 1954, notably as Russlan, Gremin, Susanin, Méphistophélès, Rossini's Basilio, and especially Boris, which he filmed in 1955.

Pizzetti, Ildebrando. Composer; b. Borgo Strinato, near Parma, Italy, Sep. 20, 1880; d. Rome, Feb. 13, 1968. Studied with Righi and Tebaldini at Parma Conservatory. His 1905 incidental music for d'Annunzio's *La Nave* led to an operatic collaboration, *Fedra* (1915); later, Pizzetti wrote many of his own librettos. His operas, including *Debora e Jaele* (1922), *Fra Gherardo (1928)*, and *Assassinio nella Cattedrale* (1958), after Eliot, feature an austere arioso style (influenced by *Pelléas* and early monody) and imaginative choral writing. Little known outside of Italy, his work after 1930 became dogmatic and repetitive.

Pizzi, Pier Luigi. Designer and producer; b. Milan, June 15, 1930. Designed for legitimate theater, especially with de Lullo; first operatic design, *Don Giovanni* (Genoa, 1951). Noteworthy productions at La Scala, Paris Opéra, Covent Garden, Munich, San Francisco. His Chicago Lyric *Bohème* was seen at the Met in 1977, his *Boccanegra* in 1984.

Plançon, Pol. Bass; b. Fumay, France, June 12, 1851; d. Paris, Aug. 11, 1914. Studied with Duprez and Sbriglia; debut as Saint-Bris (*Huguenots*), Lyon, 1877. After singing at the Gaieté-Lyrique, Paris (debut, Colonna in Duprat's *Pétrarque*, 1880), he joined the Paris Opéra as Méphistophélès in 1883, initiating a long identification with that role; he remained there for 10 seasons, singing roles such as the Grand Brahmin (*Africaine*), Oberthal (*Prophète*), Caspar (*Freischütz*), Sparafucile, Hagen (*Sigurd*), the King (*Hamlet*), and Brogni (*Juive*), and creating Don Gormas (*Cid*) and François Ier (Saint-Saëns' *Ascanio*). He appeared at Covent Garden for 14 seasons (debut, Méphistophélès, 1891), and created Friar Francis in Stanford's *Much Ado About Nothing*. His dozen Met seasons (1893–97, 1898–01, 1903–08) began as Jupiter in *Philémon* (Nov. 29, 1893), and totaled 279 perfs. (plus over 200 on tour) of 32 roles, most frequently Ramfis (34 times) and Méphistophélès (33), the King in *Lohengrin*, Capulet and Frère Laurent, Landgrave Hermann, Saint-Bris, and Balthasar (*Favorite*), also Berlioz's Méphistophélès, Escamillo, and Alvise; he was the Met's first Sarastro.

Plançon's recordings (1902–08) confirm his reputation as one of history's most polished and technically proficient basses, capable of brilliant scales, embellishments, and leaps within a generous range. He could also sustain his sleek, nearly vibrato-free voice in beautiful legato melodic lines, always shaped with musicianly care, and the wit of his Méphistophélès can still be savored.

Plishka, Paul. Bass; b. Old Forge, Pa., Aug. 28, 1941. Studied at Montclair State College and with Armen Boyajian; debut with Paterson Lyric Opera, 1961. Sang with Met National Co., 1965–67. Met debut as Monk (*Gioconda*), Sep. 21, 1967; he has since sung over 500 Met perfs. in about 50 roles, including Leporello and the Commendatore, Oroveso (*Norma*), Silva (*Ernani*), Fiesco (*Boccanegra*), Philippe II (*Don Carlos*), Varlaam, Pimen, and Boris, Frère Laurent (*Roméo*), Procida (*Vêpres*), and King Marke. La Scala debut in *Damnation de Faust*, 1974; has also sung in Hamburg, Paris, Munich, Berlin, San Francisco, and Chicago, and with Opera Orchestra of N.Y.

Plowright, Rosalind. Soprano; b. Worksop, England, May 21, 1949. Studied at Royal Manchester College of Music; debut as Miss Jessel (*Turn of the Screw*), English National Opera, 1979; other roles there include Desdemona and Elisabetta (*Maria Stuarda*). Covent Garden debut as Ortlinde, 1980; also Donna Elvira (1983), Maddalena in *Chénier* (1984). Has appeared in Frankfurt, Munich, Milan, San Diego; N.Y. debut as Strauss' Danae, Opera Orchestra, 1983.

Polacco, Giorgio. Conductor; b. Venice, Apr. 12, 1875; d. New York, Apr. 30, 1960. After study in Venice, Milan, and St. Petersburg, conducted in Europe and South America. Toured U.S. with Savage Opera Co., 1911, then joined Met (debut, *Manon Lescaut*, Nov. 11, 1912), where he headed the Italian wing (1915–17), leading U.S. premiere of *Francesca da Rimini* and Met premiere of *Oracolo*. Principal conductor, Chicago Opera, 1922–30.

Poleri, David. Tenor; b. Chestnut Hill, Pa., Jan. 10, 1921; d. Lihue, Hawaii, Dec. 13, 1967. Studied with Alberto Sciaretta; operatic debut as Faust, San Carlo Co., Chicago, 1949. N.Y.C. Opera debut as Alfredo, 1951. Created Michele (*Saint of Bleecker Street*), 1954. Sang at Edinburgh (*Forza*, 1951), Florence (*Queen of Spades*, 1952), La Scala (Michele, 1955), and Covent Garden (*Ballo*, 1956).

Poliuto. Opera in 3 acts by Donizetti; libretto by Cammarano, after Pierre Corneille's play *Polyeucte*.

Pol Plançon as Méphistophélès in *Faust*

Lily Pons as Marie in *La Fille du Régiment*

commission for *I Lituani* (1874). His greatest accomplishment was the elaborate if old-fashioned *La Gioconda* (1876), which alone among his operas maintains a place in the repertory. The subsequent melodramas *Il Figliuol Prodigo* (1880) and *Marion Delorme* (1885) achieved neither the same musical standard nor popular success. For all his skillful eclecticism, Ponchielli lacked the imagination to cut through the weighty conventions of Italian opera (as Verdi, who had himself added to their weight, was able to do in his late operas). In 1880, he became professor of composition at Milan Conservatory, where his students included Puccini and Mascagni; he also composed songs, orchestral, chamber, and instrumental works.

Ponnelle, Jean-Pierre. Producer and designer; b. Paris, Feb. 19, 1932. A student of Fernand Léger, his first operatic design was for *Boulevard Solitude* (Hanover, 1952); later worked in Berlin, Hamburg, Munich, and Stuttgart. U.S. debut designing *Carmina Burana* (San Francisco, 1958). At Düsseldorf in 1962, he staged *Tristan*, and since then generally designs and directs his productions. He has worked in most major theaters, and his Salzburg Mozart cycle, Zurich Monteverdi cycle, and La Scala *Cenerentola* have been filmed for television. Other productions include *Falstaff* for Glyndebourne (1976) and *Tristan* for Bayreuth (1981). At the Met, he has produced *Italiana* (1973), *Fliegende Holländer* (1979), *Idomeneo* (1982), *Clemenza* (1984), *Nozze* (1985), and *Manon* (1986). His productions, sometimes criticized for mannerism or irrelevance, are elaborate, sumptuously detailed, and vividly theatrical.

Pons, Lily. Soprano; b. Draguignan, near Cannes, France, Apr. 12, 1898; d. Dallas, Tex., Feb. 13, 1976. Studied piano at Paris Conservatory, voice with Albert de Gorostiaga, later with Zenatello in N.Y.; debut as Lakmé, Mulhouse, 1928. In provincial French theaters, her roles included Gretel, Cherubino, Gounod's Baucis, Blondchen, the Queen of Night, and Mimi. Brought to Gatti-Casazza's attention by Zenatello, she made an unheralded, wildly successful Met debut as Lucia (Jan. 3, 1931). In 28 seasons with the company, she sang 198 perfs. (85 more on tour) in 10 roles, most often Lucia, Lakmé, Gilda, and Rosina, also Olympia (*Hoffmann*), Philine (*Mignon*), Amina (*Sonnambula*), Linda di Chamounix, the Queen of Shemakha, and Marie (*Fille*). Her silver jubilee with the company was celebrated with a gala on Jan. 4, 1956. Pons also appeared regularly in San Francisco (from 1932; in her last season there, 1951, she essayed Violetta) and Chicago (1936–41); she sang at the Colón, Buenos Aires (1932, 1934), and in 1935 at Covent Garden (Rosina) and the Paris Opéra (Lucia, Gilda).

With her sweet, pretty voice that easily ascended to top F and her shrewd eye for fashion and theatrical glamor, the petite and fluent Pons easily won popularity. Despite a weak lower register and occasional uncertainty of intonation, her fleet coloratura and appealing manner made her an effective successor to Galli-Curci. She appeared in several movies, and sang in concert as late as 1972 (when she performed in N.Y. with her former second husband, conductor André Kostelanetz).

Ponselle [Ponzillo], **Rosa.** Soprano; b. Meriden, Conn., Jan. 22, 1897; d. Baltimore, May 25, 1981. After singing in cinema and vaudeville theaters, often with her sister, mezzo Carmela (1887–1977; 16 Met perfs., debut as Amneris, Dec. 5, 1925), she studied with Romano Romani, N.Y. Auditions for Caruso and Gatti-Casazza

First perf., Naples, San Carlo, Nov. 30, 1848: Tadolini, Baucardé, Colini. Rev. as *Les Martyrs* in 4 acts, with libretto by Scribe, first perf., Paris, Opéra, Apr. 10, 1840: Dorus-Gras, Duprez, Massol. U.S. prem., New Orleans, Mar. 24, 1846 (in Fr.).

Though first performed in the French revision, this work, like *Don Carlos*, *Favorite*, and *Dinorah*, eventually became more popular in its Italian form.

Armenia, 257 A.D. Poliuto (t), a convert to Christianity, is imprisoned. Although his wife Paolina (s) loves the Proconsul Severo (bar), she eventually joins Poliuto in martyrdom.

Polnische Jude, Der (The Polish Jew). Opera in 2 acts by Weis; libretto by Victor Léon and Richard Batka, after a novel by Émile Erckmann and Alexandre Chatrian.

First perf., Prague, German Theater, Mar. 3, 1901. U.S. & Met prem., Mar. 9, 1921 (in Eng.): Delaunois, Howard, Chamlee, Capolican, Gustafson, c. Bodanzky, d. Pogany, p. Thewman. 3 perfs. in 1 season.

Among Gatti-Casazza's least successful Met novelties. In an Alsatian village, the inn of Burgomaster Mathis (bar) is visited by a mysterious Polish Jew (bs). In a dream, Mathis confesses to the murder of a Polish Jew years earlier, and dies in his sleep.

Ponchielli, Amilcare. Composer; b. Paderno Fasolaro [now Paderno Ponchielli], near Cremona, Italy, Aug. 31, 1834; d. Milan, Jan. 17, 1886. Studied at Milan Conservatory from age nine; his composition teachers were Frasi and Mazzucato. While pursuing a career as organist and conductor, he composed several unsuccessful operas, including *I Promessi Sposi* (1856), of which an 1872 revision eventually brought him acclaim and a Ricordi

led to her operatic debut as Leonora in the Met's first *Forza*, Nov. 15, 1918. During 19 seasons with the company, she sang 258 perfs. of 22 roles, most frequently Leonora (*Forza*), Sélika (*Africaine*), Gioconda, Santuzza, and Norma, also Rachel (*Juive*), Aida, Maddalena (*Chénier*), Elvira (*Ernani*), Mathilde (*Tell*), Leonora (*Trovatore*), Fiora (*Amore*), Donna Anna, and Violetta. The Met's first Reiza (*Oberon*), Elisabeth de Valois (*Don Carlos*), Margared (*Roi d'Ys*), Julia (*Vestale*), Luisa Miller, and Zoraima (*Notte di Zoraima*), she created Carmelia in Breil's *Legend*. Among her rare operatic appearances outside the Met were three seasons at Covent Garden (debut as Norma, 1929; also Gioconda, Fiora, Traviata, and Romani's Fedra), and *Vestale* at the Florence Maggio Musicale, 1933. Her Met Carmen (1935) was poorly received, and she retired in 1937 after Johnson refused her request for a revival of *Adriana Lecouvreur*. Having married in 1936, she moved with her husband to Baltimore, where after 1951 she became involved in the direction of the Baltimore Civic Opera and in teaching; among her students were William Warfield, Sherrill Milnes, and James Morris.

As attested by recordings, Ponselle's sumptuous, vibrant voice was one of the most remarkable instruments of the century, impressively even throughout its range and capable of powerful expressive coloration. For Norma and Violetta, she acquired a battery of florid technique, and in dramatic roles projected imposing power and sweep of phrase. Unfortunately, problems with high notes after 1930 led to a restriction of her repertory and eventually to her retirement, though she continued to sing in private, and made a series of song recordings in 1954.

Popov, Vladimir. Tenor; b. Moscow, Apr. 29, 1947. Studied at Tchaikovsky Conservatory and sang with Bolshoi, Moscow (1977–81). After studying Italian repertory in Milan (1981–82), he defected to the West, making his debut in Portland in *Fanciulla* (1982). Met debut as Lenski (Sep. 26, 1984); other roles include Cavaradossi, Adorno (*Boccanegra*), Don José, Turiddu, Ernani, and Dimitri (*Boris*).

Popp, Lucia. Soprano; b. Uhorská Ves, Czechoslovakia, Nov. 12, 1939. Studied with Anna Prosence-Hrusovska at Bratislava Academy; debut as Queen of Night, Bratislava, 1963. That year, Vienna State Opera debut as Barbarina (*Nozze*), later singing Queen of Night there, and Salzburg debut as First Boy (*Zauberflöte*). Member of companies in Vienna, Munich, and Cologne (where her husband, conductor György Fischer, works); Covent Garden debut as Oscar, 1966. Met debut as Queen of Night, Feb. 19, 1967; later Met roles have been Sophie (role of her Paris Opéra debut, 1976) and Pamina. Her repertory also includes Gilda, Zerbinetta, Eva, and many Mozart parts, including Susanna (with Paris Opéra in N.Y., 1976). A superbly musical singer who has carefully moved from her coloratura beginnings to lyric roles, Popp is now poised on the edge of the German spinto repertory.

Porgy and Bess. Opera in 3 acts by Gershwin; libretto by DuBose Heyward and Ira Gershwin, after Dorothy and DuBose Heyward's play *Porgy*.

First perf., Boston, Colonial, Sep. 30, 1935: Brown, Mitchell, Elzy, Bubbles, Duncan, Coleman, c. Smallens. Met prem., Feb. 6, 1985: Bumbry, Merritt, Quivar, Williams, Estes, Baker, c. Levine, d. O'Hearn, p. Merrill. 32 perfs. in 2 seasons.

Gershwin's ambitious bid to unite American vernacular styles with the norms of opera resulted in a masterpiece, if not (to date) in the establishment of a repeatable genre.

In Catfish Row, a black neighborhood on the Charleston waterfront, 1920s. During a crap game, a fight breaks out and the belligerent Crown (bar) kills a man. He escapes, leaving his lover Bess (s) to fend for herself. She resists the blandishments of the drug dealer Sportin' Life (t), and moves in with the crippled beggar Porgy (bar). At Porgy's urging, she goes without him to a community picnic on Kittiwah Island, where Crown has been hiding out; he finds her and, unable to resist him, she stays on the island. When she reappears in Catfish Row, sick and distraught, Porgy takes her back. Later, Porgy seizes an unexpected opportunity to kill Crown as he passes the cripple's window. But he is jailed for a week when he superstitiously refuses to identify the corpse for investigators. During that time, Sportin' Life tempts the desperate Bess with "happy dust," and they leave for New York. Upon his release, Porgy sets off in search of his Bess.

portamento (Ital., "carrying"). In moving from one pitch to another, a continuous gliding movement through the intervening pitches; if used to excess, pejoratively described as "swooping" or "sliding."

Postillon de Longjumeau, Le (The Coachman of Longjumeau). Opera in 3 acts by Adam; libretto by Adolphe de Leuven and Léon Lévy.

First perf., Paris, Opéra-Comique, Oct. 13, 1836: Prévost, Ray, Clollet, Henri. U.S. prem., N.Y., Park, Mar. 30, 1840 (in Eng.).

An opéra comique popular for its flattering tenor role, a coachman who leaves his bride Madeleine (s) on their wedding night to become a star of the Paris Opéra. They are eventually reunited after she inherits a fortune.

Rosa Ponselle as Giulia in *La Vestale*

Poulenc, Francis. Composer; b. Paris, Jan. 7, 1899; d. Paris, Jan. 30, 1963. Studied piano with Viñes and, after teaching himself basic theory, harmony, and orchestration, took composition lessons with Koechlin. Influenced by Ravel and Satie, Poulenc was initially associated with the Cocteau-inspired group dubbed "Les Six"; his music, in a clearly tonal idiom, is facile, sophisticated, witty, graceful, and sometimes sentimental in the best sense. Primarily a fluent melodist, he composed many songs, as well as ballets, orchestral and chamber works, and choral music (much of it religious). Three quite different operatic subjects afforded him the opportunity to deploy these gifts and express his concern with contemporary mores and issues. The opéra bouffe *Les Mamelles de Tirésias* (1947) satirizes bourgeois familial ideals. The religious drama *Dialogues des Carmélites* (1957) expresses his personal renewal of faith, translated into the story of a young nun's response to the French Revolution. The monodrama *La Voix Humaine* (1959) is a virtuoso solo scena for singing actress.
BIBLIOGRAPHY: Francis Poulenc, *My Friends and Myself: Conversations with Francis Poulenc* (London, 1978).

Pountney, David. Producer; b. Oxford, England, Sep. 10, 1947. First operatic production, Scarlatti's *Trionfo dell'Onore* (Cambridge Opera Society, 1967). At Scottish Opera from 1971; director of productions (1976–80). Since 1982, director of productions, English National Opera. Has also worked in Australia, Italy, and Germany.

Powers, Marie. Contralto; b. Mt. Carmel, Pa., 1900(?), d. New York, Dec. 28, 1973. After study in N.Y. with Schumann-Heink and Althouse, she made a N.Y. recital debut in 1932, and in the 1940s toured with the San Carlo Opera. In 1947 she created Menotti's Madame Flora (*Medium*), which became her signature role, and in 1950 the Mother (*Consul*). N.Y.C. Opera debut in Menotti's *Old Maid and the Thief* (1948); she created Azelia in Still's *Troubled Land* (1949). Paris Opéra debut as Fricka (*Walküre*), 1951.

Prague. Capital of Czechoslovakia. During the 17th and 18th c., visiting Italian companies offered Gluck and Vivaldi operas. Occasionally a work based on a Czech subject, such as Bartolomeo Bernardi's *La Libussa* (1703), was heard. The first permanent opera house was the Estates Theater (opened 1783, from 1861 known as the Royal Provincial Theater, from 1945 the Tyl Theater), where in 1787 Mozart conducted *Figaro* and introduced *Don Giovanni*; his *Clemenza* had its first performance there in 1791. German opera dominated the repertory during the early 19th c., especially under the directorship of Weber (1813–16); some works were translated into Czech and there were occasional attempts at creating a national opera. The Provisional Theater (opened 1862) was planned as a Czech house, though the first native opera, Smetana's *Brandenburgers in Bohemia*, was not staged until 1866. The National Theater (capacity 1,598), opened June 11, 1881 with Smetana's *Libuše*, was soon destroyed by fire, and reopened Nov. 18, 1883 with the same work. It presented new Czech operas and international repertory; Tchaikovsky conducted *Eugene Onegin* there in 1888. From that year, the National had healthy competition from the New German Theater, in 1949 renamed the Smetana Theater. Performances today, in Czech, are held in both these recently renovated theaters; František Vojna is head of opera. The historically important Tyl Theater still awaits reconstruction.

Porgy and Bess – Broadway revival, 1953. Leontyne Price and Cab Calloway

Preetorius, Emil. Designer; b. Mainz, Germany, June 21, 1883; d. Munich, Jan. 27, 1973. Studied law and art in Munich; recommended to Bruno Walter by Thomas Mann, he designed *Iphigénie en Aulide* for Munich and worked in many German theaters and throughout Europe. At Bayreuth, he collaborated with director Heinz Tietjen in imposing stylized productions (1933–42).

preghiera (Ital., "prayer"). In 19th-c. Italian opera, an aria or chorus of supplication.

prelude. Term used to describe an introductory orchestral piece for an opera, beginning in the mid-19th c.; similar to an overture, but less likely to end loudly, more likely to use thematic material from the opera and to lead directly into the opera without a break.

Tyl Theater, Prague

PRODUCING OPERA
Richard Dyer

The operatic stage director, like his counterpart in the theater, is a twentieth-century invention. In earlier periods, somebody was always in charge of supervising the visual elements of operatic drama – but it was usually the composer, the librettist, the star singer, the conductor, the stage manager, even the designer. There was no profession of producers.

This system, or lack of it, continues even today in provincial theaters, and sometimes in major opera houses, particularly in the standard repertory. Someone will show the singers flown in for *Tosca* where the Madonna will be, the couch, the knife, and the parapet, and turn them loose; he will not be concerned to extract – or impose – a fresh or personal interpretation of the work.

The prominence of the producer in our time is the result of four factors. Since the repertory no longer chiefly consists of new works in productions supervised by their creators, it has become imperative to renew the standard literature by approaching it from different angles and performing it with different emphases. The increased complexity of available stage machinery also created a need for someone to coordinate the technology with the human factors. Then, too, the theatrical expectations of today's public have been formed not only by the spoken stage but by films and television, both directors' media. Finally, while earlier periods boasted constellations of commanding vocalists and conductors, ours is a more impoverished era, so today there are productions so elaborate that they can entertain an audience all by themselves.

The activities of producers tend to turn on the same axis as those of creators, and they are bounded by the same poles. Modern theater began in the contrast between the ritual drama of the mass and the rowdier exploration of the same issues on the steps of the cathedral. This basic division has continued throughout the history of theater and opera.

The letters of Verdi and the production handbooks issued by his publisher Ricordi, and the voluminous writings of Wagner provide useful points of departure for discussing the producer's role. These show how the composers of the central works of the nineteenth-century repertory expected their operas to look, to work on stage, to sound (for the placement and movement of performers has not only dramatic but acoustical consequences). Verdi concerned himself with a stylized kind of realism, Wagner with a realistic kind of stylization. Verdi was a completely practical man of the theater; Wagner's very different, and more visionary, instructions were at least equally detailed, but his "theater of the future" was very much dependent on the technology of its own time, as the composer ruefully admitted. He could write of "deeds of music made visible" – but he could also laugh at how this could dwindle to "ladies being hoisted to the roof by strings attached to their bottoms."

This basic division, or continuum, between the realistic and the visionary or stylized can be applied to most of the influential producers of the 20th century – to Stanislavsky and Meyerhold, for example, or to the key figures in postwar operatic staging, Walter Felsenstein and Wieland Wagner. At the Komische Oper in East Berlin, Felsenstein developed a detailed and realistic manner of staging that came both from Stanislavskian study of character-building and from acute awareness of musical detail. "Every eighth note, every change of tempo, every dynamic indication is a scenic direction in itself," he wrote.

Wieland Wagner, like his grandfather, would have agreed, though he went to work in a different and complementary way. Over the same years at Bayreuth, Wieland was developing a theater of myth, of Jungian archetype, of anti-realism, based on minimal stage settings, lighting schemes of the utmost suggestive complexity, and a sculptural simplicity of pose and gesture.

In our own time, a new conflict (or continuum) has developed. Along with the interest in historical performance practice, with the increasing application of musicological research to performance and the quest for authenticity, has come a corresponding interest in the theatrical styles and devices of the past, in exploring how these can illuminate old works for new audiences. These endeavors have not yet proved particularly convincing in revivals of baroque opera; imagination fails in the effort to fill in the gaps between the information available in treatises. And of course no director can reproduce the attitudes and expectations of the audience that would have filled an eighteenth-century theater.

On the other hand, some picturesque period productions of nineteenth-century operas have proved more successful, especially with conservative audiences long tried by some of the more willful excesses of the avant-garde. Such productions have also proved particularly valuable to repertory theaters, which hope to amortize the cost of a production of a standard opera by playing it for ten or even twenty years; although stylized and experimental productions may make a more immediate impact, and paradoxically a more lasting one, they date rapidly.

But there's a danger in this that the avant-garde has been quick to point out: only the most unusual picturesquely period production appeals to any emotion but nostalgia. For more than a century, the D'Oyly Carte company sought to preserve W.S. Gilbert's staging of the Gilbert and Sullivan operettas, and what was originally fresh and funny became quaint and old-fashioned – and valued for precisely that reason.

The theatrical element of any composer's vision of his own work is likely to be the most locked in its own time, the most ephemeral; photographs of old productions invariably declare their own period more immediately than they reveal their content. Pierre Boulez has pointed out that "it must surely be obvious that it is just the ability to escape from its own contingent character that constitutes the greatness of a work. Imagination can destroy and rebuild on what the work proposes, while the work itself is a heap of iron filings to be ceaselessly rearranged and reoriented by the magnet." The worst kind of staging, and a cardinal vice of opera today, is the kind that makes insufficient reference to either words or music; the magnet sends the filings flying.

The best of today's producers, on the other hand, bring all kinds of theatrical experience, historical awareness, contemporary convictions, and timeless knowledge of the heart to bear on their work. They seek to restore the elements of surprise and even of danger that marked the greatest works when they were new and that keep them alive today. Their work may draw on deep socio-political commitments, knowledge of the history of theater, familiarity with painting and sculpture; it will draw on the producer's personal experience, his observation of human nature, what he sees as the potentialities and limitations of his cast. It also, always and inevitably, must draw on the words and the music, and the third impalpable thing that the two of them have made: when everything works as it should, the eye hears what the ear has made us see.

Richard Dyer is the music critic of the *Boston Globe*.

(*Above*) Wieland Wagner and Dietrich Fischer-Dieskau at rehearsal. (*Below*) Wieland Wagner rehearsing Birgit Nilsson and Wolfgang Windgassen in *Tristan*

Prêtre, Georges. Conductor; b. Waziers, France, Aug. 14, 1924. Studied at Paris Conservatory and with Cluytens. Debut, *Roi d'Ys*, Marseilles, 1946. Opéra-Comique debut leading the first Paris *Capriccio*, 1956; remained there until 1959. Chicago Opera debut, *Thaïs*, 1959. Met debut, *Samson*, Oct. 17, 1964; in 3 seasons, he also led *Parsifal*, *Trovatore*, *Faust*, *Traviata*, and *Tristan*, returning in 1976–77 for *Faust*. Active in the Seventies at La Scala.

Prevedi, Bruno. Tenor; b. Revere, near Mantua, Italy, Dec. 21, 1928. Studied in Mantua and Milan; debut as Turiddu, Nuovo, Milan, 1959. La Scala debut in Pizzetti's *Debora e Jaele*, 1962. After singing in Berlin, Barcelona, and Florence, Met debut as Cavaradossi, Mar. 6, 1965; in 5 seasons, sang 44 perfs. of 8 roles, including Radames, Riccardo (*Ballo*), Don Carlos, Alvaro (*Forza*), Alfredo, and Manrico.

Previtali, Fernando. Conductor; b. Adria, Italy, Feb. 16, 1907; d. Rome, Aug. 1, 1985. Studied in Turin; assisted Gui at Florence Maggio Musicale (1928–36). Principal conductor, La Scala (1942–43, 1946–48); conductor, Santa Cecilia Orchestra, Rome (1953–75). As director of the Italian Radio Orchestra (1936–42, 1945–53), he was responsible for important broadcasts of rarely-heard works.

Prey, Hermann. Baritone; b. Berlin, July 11, 1929. Sang with Berlin Mozart Choir as a child, and studied with Günther Baum, Berlin Hochschule für Musik; debut as Moruccio (*Tiefland*), Wiesbaden, 1952. Appeared with Hamburg State Opera, 1953–60, singing roles in contemporary operas by Liebermann, Dallapiccola, and Henze. Debuts at Vienna (1957), Munich (1959), Salzburg (Barber in *Schweigsame Frau*, 1959), Bayreuth (Wolfram, 1965), and Covent Garden (Rossini's Figaro, 1973). In 6 Met seasons, he sang 22 perfs. of Wolfram (debut, Dec. 17, 1960), Almaviva, Papageno, and Rossini's Figaro. Prey's smooth, mellow baritone has upheld the German lyric tradition; in recent years he has added to his Mozart-centered repertory a perceptive characterization of Beckmesser (Bayreuth, 1981).

Preziose Ridicole, Le (The Ridiculous Snobs). Opera in 1 act by Lattuada; libretto by Arturo Rossato, after Molière's comedy *Les Précieuses Ridicules*.
First perf., Milan, La Scala, Feb. 9, 1929: Favero, Stignani, Kiepura, Faticanti, cond. Santini. U.S. & Met prem., Dec. 10, 1930: Bori, Swarthout, Tokatyan, Basiola, c. Bellezza, d. Jones, p. Laret. 4 perfs. in 1 season.
Lattuada here turned from verismo to neo-classical comedy. In a Paris suburb, 1650, Madelon (s) and Cathos (ms), who value artifice over true feeling, suffer a comical vengeance when their rejected lovers send the servants Mascarille (t) and Jodelet (bar) to woo them in an exaggerated style.

Price, Leontyne. Soprano; b. Laurel, Miss., Feb. 10, 1927. Studied at Central State College, Wilberforce, Ohio, and with Florence Kimball at Juilliard, N.Y. She sang St. Cecilia (*Four Saints*) at the Broadway Theater, N.Y., 1952, and Bess at the Ziegfeld, 1953, followed by an international tour. Her N.Y. recital debut (1954) was followed by a Tosca for NBC television (1955). In 1957, she made her San Francisco debut as Mme. Lidione in the U.S. premiere of *Carmélites*, followed by her first Aida; she returned there in 1958 as the *Trovatore* Leonora and the

Wise Woman in *Die Kluge*, and in 1959 as Donna Elvira. Aida was the role of her debuts in Verona, Vienna, and Covent Garden (all 1958) and at La Scala (1960); at Salzburg, she sang Donna Anna (1960–61) and Leonora in *Trovatore* (1962–63). In Chicago, she sang Liù and Thaïs in 1959, Aida and Butterfly in 1960. On Jan. 27, 1961, she came to the Met as the *Trovatore* Leonora; between then and her farewell as Aida (Jan. 3, 1985), she sang 164 perfs. in 16 roles, most frequently Aida and Verdi's two Leonoras, also Donna Anna, Elvira (*Ernani*), Amelia (*Ballo*), Butterfly, Tatiana, Fiordiligi, Puccini's Manon, Minnie (*Fanciulla*), Liù, Tosca, Pamina, and Ariadne; on the opening night of the new Lincoln Center theater in 1966, she created Barber's Cleopatra. She was married (1952–72) to bass William Warfield (b. 1920).
To the sensuously husky tone of Price's spinto soprano, a fast vibrato imparted a distinctive shimmer, and its registers and colors were well equalized and controlled. In the roles (notably Verdi) that most strongly engaged her sympathies, she was uniquely compelling in her intensity and directness of expression, and even in her less successful parts (usually quickly abandoned) she never failed to offer the audience her complete resources. Her large discography includes all of her major roles, as well as aria recitals spanning virtually the entire soprano literature; her recital career continues since her operatic retirement.

Price, Margaret. Soprano; b. Blackwood, Wales, Apr. 13, 1941. Studied at Trinity College of Music, London; debut with Welsh National Opera, 1962, as Cherubino, also the role of her Covent Garden debut in 1963, followed by other Mozart roles. With English Opera Group, sang in *Schauspieldirektor*, *Midsummer Night's Dream*, and *Acis and Galatea*, 1967. Glyndebourne debut as Angel (*Jephtha*, 1966), later singing Konstanze and Fiordiligi. Debuts in San Francisco (Pamina, 1969), Cologne (Donna Anna, 1971), and with Paris Opéra (1973); she sang the Countess and Desdemona at the Met with the Paris Opéra, 1976. Met debut as Desdemona, Jan. 21, 1985. From her initial focus on Mozart, Price has developed into an imposing if fastidious Verdi singer, in roles such as Elisabeth de Valois, Aida, and both Amelias.

Prigioniero, Il (The Prisoner). Opera in prologue and 1 act by Dallapiccola; libretto by the composer, after Villiers de l'Isle-Adam's *La Torture par l'Espérance* and Charles de Coster's *La Légende d'Ulenspiegel et de Lamme Goedzak*.
First perf., Turin, Dec. 1, 1949 (radio perf.): László, Renzi, Colombo, c. Scherchen. First stage perf.: Florence, Comunale, May 20, 1950: László, Binci, Colombo, c. Scherchen. U.S. prem., N.Y., Juilliard School, Mar. 15, 1951 (in Eng.).
An intense, pessimistic treatment of the question of human liberty; the choral writing is particularly impressive.
Saragossa, later 16th c. A prisoner of the Inquisition (bar) takes hope when his jailer (t) calls him "brother" and gives him news of Flanders' revolt. The prisoner later finds his door ajar, and fearfully makes his way out of the underground prison to a spring garden. His elation is shattered by the Inquisitor's embrace, and he realizes that the illusion of freedom has been the worst torture of all.

prima donna (Ital., "first lady"). The singer of the leading female role in an opera; more generally, the leading female singer in an operatic company. It can carry a pejorative sense of excessive temperament or arrogance.

Prince Igor. Opera in prologue and 4 acts by Borodin (completed by Rimsky-Korsakov and Glazunov); libretto by the composer, after a scenario by Vladimir Stasov based on the anonymous medieval *Tale of the Campaign of Igor*.

First perf., St. Petersburg, Maryinsky, Nov. 4, 1890: Olgina, Dolina, Melnikov, Koryakin, F. Stravinsky, Ugrinovich, c. Nápravnik. U.S. & Met prem., Dec. 30, 1915 (in Ital.): Alda, Perini, Botta, Amato, Didur, c. Polacco. 9 perfs. in 3 seasons.

A melodious and colorful score, dramatically patchy due to its protracted, unfinished gestation. The roles of Galitzky and Kontchak, who appear in different scenes, are often doubled by the same singer.

Putivl, Russia; the Polovtsi camp, 1185. Despite the evil omen of an eclipse and the trepidations of his wife Yaroslavna (s), Prince Igor (bar) sets out on a campaign against the Polovtsi, a Tartar tribe. While he is away, Yaroslavna compels her brother Prince Galitzky (bs), the governor, to restrain his riotous followers. Igor's army is defeated, and he and his son Vladimir (t) taken captive. Vladimir falls in love with Kontchakovna (ms), daughter of the Polovtsi leader Kontchak (bs). Kontchak, who admires his adversary, offers Igor freedom if he will cease waging war on him; Igor refuses and escapes. Kontchak resolves to march on Russia, keeping Vladimir as a hostage and giving him Kontchakovna to discourage him from escaping. Igor is warmly welcomed home, and determines to rally new troops.

Pritchard, John. Conductor; b. London, Feb. 5, 1921. From 1947, repetiteur at Glyndebourne, then chorus master and conductor; music director, 1969–78. Covent Garden debut in *Ballo*, 1952; led premieres of *Gloriana*, *Midsummer Marriage*, and *King Priam* there. Music director of Royal Liverpool Philharmonic (1957–63) and London Philharmonic (1962–66). U.S. debut, *Barbiere*, Chicago Lyric, 1969. Principal conductor, Cologne Opera, from 1978; music director, Monnaie, Brussels, from 1981; music director, San Francisco Opera, from 1986. Met debut, *Così*, Oct. 25, 1971; he returned in 5 subsequent seasons between 1974 and 1983 to lead *Peter Grimes*, *Don Giovanni*, *Thaïs*, *Barbiere*, *Traviata*, and *Zauberflöte*.

Probe (Ger.). Rehearsal.

Prodigal Son, The. Parable for church performance by Britten; libretto by William Plomer, after the New Testament, Luke xv: 11–32.

First perf., Orford Church, Suffolk, June 10, 1968: Pears, Tear, Shirley-Quirk, c. Britten. U.S. prem., Katonah, N.Y., Caramoor, June 29, 1969: Lankston, Velis, Clatworthy, c. Rudel.

Britten's second church parable, set in Biblical times, tells the story of the Younger Son (t), who is led by the Tempter (t) to claim his inheritance and go to the city, where he loses all. Returning home repentant, he is welcomed by his Father (bs-bar).

producer. In operatic usage (especially in Europe), the person who supervises the stage action of an operatic performance, planning the gestures and movements of the singers and (in the case of a new production) working closely with the scenery and lighting designers. In America, often called director or stage director.

Prokofiev, Sergei. Composer; b. Sontsovka, Ukraine, Apr. 23, 1891; d. Moscow, Mar. 5, 1953. A child prodigy, he studied with Glière and at St. Petersburg Conservatory with Rimsky-Korsakov and Liadov. After graduating, he composed prolifically in a dissonant, percussive style, and performed widely as a virtuoso pianist, especially in western Europe, where he lived for two decades following the Russian revolution. After his return home, his work suffered from Stalinist esthetic conservatism and political pressure, and from his failing health.

Under Glière's tutelage, Prokofiev wrote four youthful operas, and persistently pursued success in the theater, with mixed results; only recently have his "western" operas begun to achieve recognition in his native land. The 1917 revolution aborted rehearsals for *The Gambler*, and it was first heard in a 1929 revision. The satirical *The Love for Three Oranges* (1921), introduced in Chicago, was his only unequivocal success. *The Fiery Angel* (1923), a vividly expressionistic score, was not performed in its entirety during his lifetime. Though more conservative in style and subject, the Soviet operas were found controversial by the government; *War and Peace* (1946) was repeatedly revised to satisfy political demands, *The Story of a Real Man* (1948) was condemned for "formalism." Other operas: *Maddalena* (1913; perf. 1959); *Semyon Kotko* (1940); *Betrothal in a Monastery* (1946).

prompter. The musical assistant who sits in a sunken box amid the footlights at the front of the operatic stage and aids the singers' memories by calling out the first words of their lines, also sometimes relaying the conductor's beat.

Prophète, Le (The Prophet). Opera in 5 acts by Meyerbeer; libretto by Scribe.

First perf., Paris, Opéra, Apr. 16, 1849: Castellan, Viardot, Roger, Levasseur, c. Girard. U.S. prem., New Orleans, Théâtre d'Orléans, Apr. 1, 1850. Met prem., Mar. 21, 1884 (in Ital.): Valleria, Scalchi, Stagno, Mirabella, c. Vianesi, d. Fox, Schaeffer, p. Hock. Later Met productions: Feb. 7, 1918: Muzio, Matzenauer, Caruso, Mardones, c. Bodanzky, d. Urban, p. Ordynski; Jan. 18, 1977: Scotto, Horne, McCracken, Hines, c. Lewis, d. Wexler, p. Dexter. Fidès has also been sung at the Met by Brandt, G. Ravogli, Brema, Schumann-Heink, Homer, Branzell; Berthe by Lilli Lehmann, Adams, Easton; Jean de Leyde by Schott, Niemann, J. de Reszke, Alvarez, Martinelli; Zacharie by E. de Reszke, Journet, Pinza. 75 perfs. in 18 seasons.

One of Meyerbeer's most popular and influential operas, admired by Verdi among others; the large ensembles are particularly impressive, if generally foursquare.

Dordrecht and Münster, at the time of the Anabaptist rising, 16th c. The marriage of Jean de Leyde (t) and Berthe (s) is impeded by the Count Oberthal (bs), who desires the girl himself and orders her to his castle. For the sake of vengeance, Jean joins the Anabaptists, who set him up as their prophet and under his leadership capture Münster. He uses his power with increasing relish and cruelty, humiliating his mother Fidès (ms) and driving Berthe to suicide. Finally, recognizing his depravity, he willingly revels with his followers in a hall that he knows will soon be blown up; Fidès joins him in the flames.

prova (Ital.). Rehearsal.

Puccini, Giacomo. Composer; b. Lucca, Dec. 22, 1858; d. Brussels, Nov. 29, 1924. From a family of church musicians, he first studied with his uncle Fortunato Magi and with Carlo Angeloni at the Istituto Musicale Pacini in

Lucca, but a performance of *Aida* drew him toward operatic composition and he attended Milan Conservatory, working with Bazzini and Ponchielli. After going unnoticed in a Sonzogno competition, his first opera, *Le Villi* (1884), was staged at the instance of Giulio Ricordi and Boito, with considerable success. Ricordi became Puccini's mentor, and commissioned further operas; *Edgar* (1889) was a failure, but *Manon Lescaut* (1893) brought international fame. Collaboration with the librettists Illica and Giacosa, who had worked on *Manon Lescaut,* yielded three of the most popular operas in history, although each was initially controversial; *La Bohème* (1896) for its un-Romantic realism and occasional harmonic daring; *Tosca* (1900) for its sadistic violence; *Madama Butterfly* (1904) because of scandalous demonstrations at its premiere. The team broke up with Giacosa's death in 1906, and a domestic tragedy further complicated Puccini's life; his next opera did not appear for six years. In *La Fanciulla del West* (1910), Puccini incorporated Debussyan harmonies and Straussian orchestration; the result has never won wide public favor. *La Rondine* (1917), originally conceived as an operetta and launched during World War I, has a certain pallid charm, while of the atmospheric, vividly contrasted *Il Trittico* (1918), only the comedy *Gianni Schicchi*, a skillful successor to *Falstaff*, proved initially popular. Puccini's final and most ambitious opera, *Turandot* (1926), is a grandiose combination of the exotic and the grotesque; the final duet, unfinished at Puccini's death, was completed by Franco Alfano.

The failure of *Edgar* taught Puccini to take elaborate pains over his subjects and librettos, tailoring his material to match his strengths. Expressively, he was most at home with eroticism, pathos, and morbidity; dramatically, he sought simple situations, the rapid development of which he continually underlined with a cannily crafted mosaic of melodic and harmonic motives. Unlike Verdi's operas, Puccini's have little reference to larger society, dealing primarily with private emotions (the dearth of true ensembles is perhaps symptomatic).

BIBLIOGRAPHY: Mosco Carner, *Puccini: A Critical Biography*, 2nd edn. (London, 1974).

Punch and Judy. Opera in 1 act by Birtwistle; libretto by Stephen Pruslin.

First perf., Aldeburgh Festival, June 8, 1968: Hill, Morelle, Chard, Cameron, c. Atherton. U.S. prem., Minneapolis, Minnesota Opera, Feb. 12, 1970: Roche, Merriman, Sutton, c. Brunelle.

To dissonant, abrasive music, under the auspices of the Choregos (bar), the traditional puppet figures of Punch (bar), Judy (ms), the Doctor (bs), and the Lawyer (t) enact a puppet-play where Punch kills Judy and their baby in order to marry Pretty Polly (s), and eventually kills all the other characters as well.

puppet opera. See *marionette opera*.

Purcell, Henry. Composer; b. 1659; d. Westminster, London, Nov. 21, 1695. From age ten a chorister of the Chapel Royal, he was trained by Blow, Cooke, and Humfrey. Appointed composer to the King's band in 1677 and organist of Westminster Abbey in 1679, he moved in 1682 to the Chapel Royal. During the next decade, he produced odes and "welcome songs," church music, incidental music for plays, and many secular songs. In his final five years, he turned to the stage, composing the first masterpiece of English opera, *Dido and Aeneas* (1689). His most elaborate stage music is for a series of

semi-operas: *Dioclesian* (1690), *King Arthur* (text by Dryden, 1691), *The Fairy Queen* (after Shakespeare, 1692), *The Indian Queen* (text by Dryden and Howard, 1695), and *The Tempest* (after Shakespeare, c. 1695). For all Purcell's evident mastery of characterization and atmosphere, the restrictions of this genre precluded theatrical innovation and limited Purcell to ceremonial and incidental music, songs and dances, within dramatic frameworks no longer theatrically viable, despite numerous attempts at adaptation.

BIBLIOGRAPHY: F.B. Zimmerman, *Henry Purcell, His Life and Times* (Philadelphia, 2nd edn., 1983).

Puritani di Scozia, I (The Puritans of Scotland). Opera in 3 acts by Bellini; libretto by Carlo Pepoli, after the play *Têtes Rondes et Cavaliers* by Jacques-Arsène Ancelot and "Saintine" [Joseph Xavier Boniface].

First perf., Paris, Italien, Jan. 24, 1835: Grisi, Rubini, Tamburini, Lablache. U.S. prem., Philadelphia, Chestnut Street, July 22, 1843. Met prem., Oct. 29, 1883: Sembrich, Stagno, Kaschmann, Mirabella, c. Vianesi, d. J. Fox, Schaeffer, Maeder, Thompson/Ascoli, Dazian. Later Met productions: Feb. 18, 1918: Barrientos, Lazaro, de Luca, Mardones, c. Moranzoni, d. Sala, J. Fox/ Palanti, p. Ordynski; Feb. 25, 1976: Sutherland, Pavarotti, Milnes, Morris, c. Bonynge, d. Lee/P.J. Hall, p. Sequi. 25 perfs. in 4 seasons.

Bellini's last opera, in which he broke new ground in matters of continuity and large structures, while exploiting to the fullest the particular talents of a great quartet of soloists.

Plymouth, England, during the civil war, 17th c. Elvira (s), daughter of the Puritan governor Lord Gualtiero Valton (bs), loves Lord Arturo Talbo (t), a Stuart sympathizer. Though Valton has promised her hand to Sir Riccardo Forth (bar), he consents that she marry Arturo instead. On the wedding day, Valton gives Arturo a safe

Giacomo Puccini

I Puritani – (1976). Designed by Ming Cho Lee, produced by Sandro Sequi. Joan Sutherland and Luciano Pavarotti

conduct to leave the fortress with his bride. Arturo unexpectedly encounters Enrichetta (ms), widow of Charles I, held prisoner in the castle, and with his pass he escorts her out of the castle, disguised in Elvira's bridal veil; although Riccardo perceives that the woman with Arturo is not Elvira, he does not stop them. When Elvira learns Arturo has fled with another woman, she loses her reason. Months later, Arturo returns and risks his life to see her. He is arrested by the Puritans and sentenced to death, but a messenger announces the defeat of the Stuarts and a general pardon to all political prisoners. Elvira's sanity is restored and the lovers are reunited.

Pushkin, Alexander. Russian poet and dramatist (1799–1837). Operas based on his writings include *Aleko* (Rachmaninoff), *Boris Godunov* (Mussorgsky), *The Golden Cockerel* (Rimsky-Korsakov), *Mavra* (Stravinsky), *Mazeppa* (Tchaikovsky), *Mozart and Salieri* (Rimsky-Korsakov), *The Queen of Spades* (Tchaikovsky), *Rusalka* (Dargomizhsky), *Russlan and Ludmila* (Glinka), and *The Stone Guest* (Dargomijsky).

Putnam, Ashley. Soprano; b. New York, Aug. 10, 1952. Studied with Elizabeth Mosher and Willis Patterson at U. of Michigan; professional debut at Lucia, Virginia Opera, Norfolk, 1976. In 1978 she sang the title role in U.S. premiere of Musgrave's *Mary Queen of Scots*, Norfolk, and made her European debut as Musetta, Glyndebourne. N.Y.C. Opera debut as Violetta, 1978; sang both Musgrave's and Donizetti's Marys there, 1981. She sang Lucia on the 1983 Met tour, and has also appeared at Santa Fe (including Strauss' Danac, 1985) and with many other U.S. companies.

Q

Quaglio. Family of stage designers in Italy, Germany, and Austria, 17th–20th c. **Giovanni Maria** (c. 1700–1765), active in Vienna, designed Gluck's *Orfeo*; his son **Lorenzo I** (1730–1804 or 1806), in Mannheim and Munich, designed the first *Idomeneo*. From a collateral line were descended **Angelo II** (1829–1890), who designed the Munich Wagner premieres in an illusionistic historical style, and his son **Eugen** (1857–1942), who worked in Berlin.

Quartararo, Florence [Fiorenza]. Soprano; b. San Francisco, May 31, 1922. Studied with Pietro Cimini, Los Angeles; debut as Leonora (*Trovatore*), Redlands Bowl, Calif., 1945. Met debut as Micaela, Jan. 18, 1946; in 4 seasons, sang 24 perfs. of 8 roles, including Pamina, Desdemona, Violetta, and Nedda. San Francisco debut, Donna Elvira, 1947.

Quattro Rusteghi, I. (The Four Ruffians). Opera in 3 acts by Wolf-Ferrari; libretto by Giuseppe Pizzolato, after Goldoni's comedy *I Rusteghi*.
First perf., Munich, Court Opera, Mar. 19, 1906 (in Ger.): Bosetti, Matzenauer, Gever, Walter, Bender, c. Mottl. U.S. prem., N.Y.C. Opera, Oct. 18, 1951 (in Eng.): MacNeil, Mayer, Lloyd, Greenwell, Wentworth, c. Halasz.
Generally regarded as the best of Wolf-Ferrari's settings of Goldoni. In late 18th-c. Venice, Lucieta (s) and Filipeto (t), prospective bride and groom of an arranged marriage, are forbidden to meet beforehand by their tyrannical fathers, but manage to do so with the help of sympathetic relatives and friends.

Queen of Sheba, The. See *Königin von Saba, Die*.

Queen of Spades, The. Opera in 3 acts by Tchaikovsky; libretto by Modest Tchaikovsky, after Pushkin's story.
First perf., St. Petersburg, Maryinsky, Dec. 19, 1890: M. Figner, Slavina, N. Figner, Yakovlev, Melnikov, c. Nápravnik. U.S. & Met prem., Mar. 5, 1910 (in Ger.): Destinn, Meitschik, Slezak, Forsell, Didur, c. Mahler, d. Burghart & Co., p. Schertel. Later Met production: Sep. 28, 1965: Stratas, Resnik, Vickers, Walker, Reardon, c. Schippers, d. O'Hearn, p. Butler. Lisa has also been sung at the Met by Kabaivanska, Kubiak; the Countess by Thebom, Madeira; Herman by McCracken, Gedda; since 1972, the opera has been sung in Russian. 28 perfs. in 4 seasons.
Along with *Onegin*, Tchaikovsky's most popular opera: a darker and more violently emotional work, with strong roles for the principals.
St. Petersburg, late 18th c. The poor soldier Herman (t) secretly loves a girl whose identity he does not know. From his friend Tomsky (bar), he learns that the girl, Lisa (s), is of high station and is engaged to Prince Yeletzky (bar). Lisa's grandmother is the Countess (ms), once known as "the Queen of Spades" because she possesses a secret formula for winning at gambling. Herman becomes obsessed with obtaining the secret so that he can wed Lisa. After he passionately declares his love, which she returns, she gives him the key to a secret door to her apartments, reachable through the Countess' room. That night Herman comes to the old woman and begs for her secret, but when threatened with a pistol she dies of fright. Lisa sends him away, believing he cares more about the secret than about her, but later forgives him, asking him to

meet her by the river. The ghost of the Countess reveals her secret to Herman, and tells him to marry Lisa. When they meet by the river, Herman rushes away to the gambling house; in despair, Lisa throws herself into the river. At the club, Herman wins with the first two cards, and puts all his winnings on the third, an ace, but loses to Yeletzky, who has drawn the Queen of Spades. The Countess' ghost appears again; Herman curses her and kills himself.

Queler, Eve. Conductor; b. New York, Jan. 1, 1936. After study at Mannes School and privately under Rosenstock, Süsskind, and Markevich, she worked on the staffs of the N.Y.C. Opera and the Met National Company. Founder and director (since 1968) of the Opera Orchestra of N.Y., she has led concert performances of rarely-heard operas, including U.S. premieres of *Aroldo*, *Edgar*, *Nerone*, and *Guntram*. N.Y.C. Opera conducting debut, *Nozze*, Apr. 22, 1978; also active in Europe, especially Budapest.

Quiet Place, A. Opera in 3 (originally 1) acts by Bernstein; libretto by Stephen Wadsworth.

First perf., Houston, June 17, 1983: Greenawald, Kazaras, Nolen, Uppman, Ludgin, c. De Main.

Originally written as a sequel to *Trouble in Tahiti*. After Dinah's death, this work explores the relationship of her widower Sam (bar), his son Junior (bar), his daughter Dede (s), and François (t), who is Dede's husband and Junior's ex-lover. In a later, revised version, *Trouble in Tahiti* is incorporated as two flashbacks.

Quilico, Louis. Baritone; b. Montreal, Jan. 14, 1929. Studied with Martial Singher and Lina Pizzolongo (whom he married); debut as Germont, N.Y.C. Opera, 1955. Debuts at San Francisco (1955), Covent Garden (1961), Paris (1962), Met (Golaud in *Pelléas*, Feb. 10, 1972); other Met roles include Rigoletto, Iago, Tonio, Scarpia, Renato, Germont, Macbeth, Posa, Falstaff. His son, baritone Gino, has sung since 1980 with Paris Opéra.

The Rake's Progress – (1953). Designed by Horace Armistead, produced by George Balanchine. Final curtain call – opening night

Quinault, Philippe. Librettist; bapt. Paris, June 5, 1635; d. Paris, Nov. 26, 1688. A successful playwright, he married well and acquired social standing, becoming librettist for the court of Louis XIV and collaborating for 15 years with Lully on operas. The subject matter, from mythology and chivalric legends, emphasized amorous intrigue; some of his librettos were set again in the 18th c. by composers such as J.C. Bach and Gluck.

Quintero, José. Producer; b. Panama City, Panama, Oct. 15, 1924. Co-founder of Circle in the Square Theater, 1950, best known for O'Neill productions, including first U.S. staging of *Long Day's Journey Into Night* (1956). At the Met, he staged *Cavalleria* and *Pagliacci* (1958).

Quivar, Florence. Mezzo-soprano; b. Philadelphia, Mar. 3, 1944. Studied at Philadelphia Academy of Music and Juilliard American Opera Center, N.Y.; Met debut as Marina, Oct. 10, 1977; subsequent Met roles have included Jocasta, Isabella, Suzuki, Fidès (*Prophète*), Serena, and Mother Maria (*Carmélites*).

R

Raaff, Anton. Tenor; b. Gelsdorf, near Bonn, Germany, bapt. May 6, 1714; d. Munich, May 28, 1797. Studied with Ferrandini in Munich, Bernacchi in Bologna. Sang in Italy (1738–40), Bonn (1741–42), Vienna (1749), Lisbon (1753–55), Madrid (1755–59), Naples (1760–70). In 1770, appointed to court of Elector Karl Theodor, in Mannheim and later Munich, where Mozart composed *Idomeneo* (1781) for him.

Rabaud, Henri. Composer; b. Paris, Nov. 10, 1873; d. Paris, Sep. 11, 1949. Studied with Gédalge and Massenet at Paris Conservatory; later director of Paris Opéra (1914–18) and Conservatory (1922–41). The opera *Mârouf, Savetier du Caire* (1914) was influenced by Wagner's techniques and the current vogue for Orientalism. His other operas include *L'Appel de la Mer* (1924), after Synge, and *Roland et le Mauvais Garçon* (1934).

Rachmaninoff, Sergei. Composer and pianist; b. Semyonovo, Novgorod district, Russia, Apr. 1, 1873; d. Beverly Hills, Calif., Mar. 28, 1943. Studied piano with Zverev and Siloti, composition with Arensky at Moscow Conservatory; his first opera was his graduation exercise, *Aleko* (1892). Two further operas, *The Miserly Knight*, after Pushkin (1906), and *Francesca da Rimini* (1906), had little success. After the Russian Revolution, he pursued a career as piano virtuoso and composer of symphonic and keyboard works in the 19th-c. Russian Romantic tradition, broadly melodic and often deeply melancholic.

Raffanti, Dano. Tenor; b. Lucca, Italy, Apr. 5, 1948. Studied at La Scala school; debut there in Bussotti's *Nottetempo*, 1976. Sang in U.S. premiere of Vivaldi's *Orlando Furioso*, Dallas, 1980. Met debut as Alfredo, Apr. 6, 1981; subsequent Met roles include Rodolfo, Duke of Mantua, Edgardo, Goffredo (*Rinaldo*), and the *Rosenkavalier* Singer. Has also sung in Houston, San Francisco, Hamburg, and Berlin.

Raimondi, Gianni. Tenor; b. Bologna, Italy, Apr. 13, 1923. Studied with Gennaro Barra-Caracciolo; debut as

Samuel Ramey as Argante in *Rinaldo*

Duke of Mantua, Bologna, 1947. Sang in Italy, at Stoll, London, Paris Opéra, and Monte Carlo (all 1953); La Scala debut as Alfredo, 1955. Met debut as Rodolfo, Sep. 29, 1965; other Met roles were Cavaradossi and Faust. Specialized in Rossini works: *Armida* (Florence, 1952), *Mosè* (La Scala, 1958), and *Semiramide* (La Scala, 1962).

Raimondi, Ruggero. Bass; b. Bologna, Italy, Oct. 3, 1941. Studied with Campogalliani in Mantua, Teresa Pediconi and Antonio Piervenanzi at Santa Cecilia, Rome; debut as Colline, Spoleto, 1964. Sang at Fenice, Venice (1964–69); debuts at Rome (Procida, 1964), La Scala (Timur in *Turandot*, 1968), and Covent Garden (Fiesco, 1972). Since his Met debut as Silva (*Ernani*), Sep. 14, 1970, his house roles have included Oroveso, Raimondo, Ramfis, Don Giovanni, Sparafucile, Procida (*Vêpres*), Banquo, Basilio, the Padre Guardiano, and Mozart's Figaro. His Don Giovanni was also seen at Glyndebourne (1969) and in Joseph Losey's film (1978), his Escamillo in Rosi's 1984 *Carmen* film. Other roles include Méphistophélès, Boris, Don Quichotte. The leading Italian basso cantante of his generation, with an imposing stage presence to match his smooth and powerful voice.

Raisa, Rosa [Raisa Burchstein]. Soprano; b. Białystok, Russian Poland, May 23, 1893; d. Los Angeles, Sep. 28, 1963. Studied with Barbara Marchisio at Naples Conservatory; debut as Leonora (*Oberto*), Regio, Parma, 1913. With Chicago Opera (1913–36), she sang 275 perfs. of 34 roles, from Alice Ford to the Marschallin. She sang Amelia

and Nedda in Paris with Boston Opera, 1914; Covent Garden debut as Aida, 1914, returning in 1933 as Tosca. Also performed in South America, at Costanzi, Rome (1914, creating Romani's *Fedra*), and La Scala (debut, Aida, 1916), where she created Asteria in *Nerone* (1924) and Turandot (1926). Married to baritone Giacomo Rimini (1888–1952), with whom she opened a singing school in Chicago after her 1937 retirement. One of the century's foremost dramatic sopranos, with a clarion top register and imposing temperament and theatrical presence.

Rake's Progress, The. Opera in 3 acts and epilogue by Stravinsky; text by Auden and Kallman, after Hogarth's engravings.

First perf., Venice, Fenice, Sep. 11, 1951: Schwarzkopf, Tourel, Rounseville, Kraus, c. Stravinsky. U.S. & Met prem., Feb. 14, 1953: Gueden, Thebom, Conley, Harrell, c. Reiner, d. Armistead, p. Balanchine. 7 perfs. in 2 seasons.

A brilliant exercise in musical and dramatic pastiche, echoing 18th-c. language and (mostly) Mozart's music, in a series of scenes suggested by Hogarth.

18th-c. England. Into the idyllic rural world of Anne Trulove (s), her father (bs), and her sweetheart Tom Rakewell (t), comes the sinister figure of Nick Shadow (bar), announcing that Tom has inherited a fortune from an unknown uncle, and drawing him off to London, business, and a web of influence. While Anne waits at home with no word from her beloved, Tom is introduced by his "servant" Shadow to brothels and commerce. Anne seeks him out and, though rejected, remains faithful. Egged on by Nick, Tom marries the bearded Baba the Turk (ms) and stakes his fortunes on a fantastical invention supposed to turn stones into bread. Tom's profligate ways bring ruin, and his possessions are sold at auction. At the end of a year, he comes with Nick – who has emerged as an overtly Mephistophelean figure – to a cemetery, where they play cards for Tom's life. Tom wins one more chance and resolves to seek forgiveness from Anne, but the vanishing Shadow takes away his sanity. In the madhouse of Bedlam, where Anne visits him, Tom believes himself Adonis, and recognizes her only as Venus; when she leaves, he dies of grief.

Ralf, Torsten. Tenor; b. Malmö, Sweden, Jan. 2, 1901; d. Stockholm, Apr. 27, 1954. Studied with Haldis Ingebjart in Stockholm, Hertha Dehmlow in Berlin; debut as Cavaradossi, Stettin, 1930. Sang in Chemnitz (to 1933), Frankfurt (1933–35), and Dresden (1935–43), where he created Apollo (*Daphne*), 1938; appeared at Covent Garden (1935–39, 1948). Met debut as Lohengrin, Nov. 26, 1945; in 3 seasons, he sang 31 perfs. of 7 roles, including Tannhäuser, Stolzing, Parsifal, Siegmund, Otello, and Radames.

Rameau, Jean-Philippe. Composer; bapt. Sep. 25, 1683, Dijon; d. Paris, Sep. 12, 1764. Studied with his father, an organist, and briefly in Milan; after various positions as organist, he settled in Paris in 1723, writing music for popular comedies, keyboard works, and theoretical treatises. Through his patron La Pouplinière, whose private orchestra he directed, Rameau met the playwright Pellegrin, librettist of his first surviving opera, the tragédie lyrique *Hippolyte et Aricie* (1733). Despite its lukewarm reception, Rameau continued to compose for the theater, in three prolific decades producing over two dozen stage works in several genres, notably the tragédies lyriques *Castor et Pollux* (1737), *Dardanus* (1739), *Zoroastre* (1749), and *Abaris, ou Les Boréades* (1764, not perf.), the opéras-ballets *Les Indes Galantes* (1735) and *Le Temple de la Gloire* (libretto by Voltaire, 1745), and the comédie lyrique *Platée* (1745). Rameau enriched Lully's precedent with more pliant, less literal recitatives, more freely shaped arias, more expressive choruses, more elaborately gestural and pictorial dance music, and more carefully structured acts; his works have recently been revived with considerable success.

BIBLIOGRAPHY: Cuthbert Girdlestone, *Jean-Philippe Rameau: His Life and Works* (London, 2nd ed., 1969).

Ramey, Samuel. Bass; b. Colby, Kans., Mar. 28, 1942. Studied with Arthur Newman at Wichita State U., later with Armen Boyajian, N.Y.; professional debut as Zuniga (*Carmen*), at N.Y.C. Opera, 1973, where he soon sang Gounod's and Boito's devils, the *Hoffmann* villains, Attila, Enrico VIII (*Anna Bolena*), Don Giovanni, Figaro, and Don Quichotte. Glyndebourne debut as Figaro, 1976, followed by Nick Shadow, 1977; in 1978, he first appeared in Hamburg (Arkel in *Pelléas*), and in 1979 in San Francisco and Chicago (both as Colline). Debuts as Figaro at La Scala and Vienna (1981) and Covent Garden (1982). With his powerful, easily produced bass and flexible coloratura technique, Ramey has become a specialist in neglected Rossini repertory, including *Semiramide* (Aix, 1980) and *Moïse* (Paris, 1983), and regular appearances at the Pesaro Festival. Met debut as Argante (*Rinaldo*), Jan. 19, 1984; he returned in 1986–87 as Walton (*Puritani*) and Escamillo.

Randová, Eva. Mezzo-soprano; b. Kolin, Czechoslovakia. Studied at Prague Conservatory. Joined National Theater, Prague, in 1969; regular member, Stuttgart Opera, from 1971, At Bayreuth (debut as Waltraute in *Walküre*, 1973), she also sang Gutrune, Kundry, and Fricka. Met debut as Fricka on Sep. 22, 1981; returned as Venus in 1987.

range. The span of the pitches in a voice or a role; see also *tessitura*.

Rankin, Nell. Mezzo-soprano; b. Montgomery, Ala., Jan. 3, 1926. Studied with Jeanne Lorraine, Birmingham Conservatory, and Karin Branzell, N.Y. Debut as Ortrud, Zurich, 1949, later singing in Vienna and Milan. Met debut as Amneris, Nov. 22, 1951; in 19 seasons, she sang 143 perfs. of 17 roles, including Laura, Marina, Ortrud, Gutrune, Ulrica, and Azucena. Debuts as Carmen at Covent Garden (1953) and San Francisco (1955).

Rape of Lucretia, The. Opera in 2 acts by Britten; libretto by Ronald Duncan, after André Obey's play *Le Viol de Lucrèce.*

First perf., Glyndebourne (English Opera Group), July 12, 1946: Cross, Ferrier, Ritchie, Pollak, Pears, Kraus, Donlevy, Brannigan, c. Ansermet. U.S. prem., Chicago, Shubert Theater, June 1, 1947: Resnik, Kibler, Kane, Rogier, c. Breisach.

The first revelation of Britten's resourcefulness in the chamber-opera genre, eloquent despite the insistence of the framing commentary on the Christian moral.

In and near Rome, 500 B.C. A male and female chorus (t and s) narrate the story of Lucretia (c), wife of Collatinus (bs), who alone was found faithful when the Roman officers returned from the field to pay surprise visits to their spouses. Her virtue infuriates and challenges Tarquinius (bar), who rides to Rome and rapes her in her home; the next day, she kills herself for shame.

Rappold [née Winterroth], **Marie.** Soprano; b. London, c. 1873; d. N. Hollywood, Calif., May 12, 1957. Studied with Oscar Saenger, N.Y.; operatic debut as Sulamith (*Königin von Saba*), Met, Nov. 22, 1905. In 15 Met seasons, her roles included Desdemona, Elsa, Marguerite, and the *Trovatore* Leonora.

Rappresentazione di Anima e di Corpo, La (The Representation of the Soul and the Body). Stage oratorio by Cavalieri; libretto by Agostino Manni.

First perf., Rome, San Filippo Neri, Feb. 1600. U.S. prem., U. of N. Dak., Feb. 23, 1966.

An allegorical "sacra rappresentazione," one of the earliest uses of the monodic style in sacred music.

Raskin, Judith. Soprano; b. New York, June 21, 1928; d. New York, Dec. 21, 1984. Studied with Anna Hamlin, N.Y.; debut as Susanna, Ann Arbor, Mich., 1957. Sang with NBC Television Opera, including Sister Constance (*Carmélites*); N.Y.C. Opera debut as Despina, 1959. Met debut as Susanna, Feb. 23, 1962; in 11 Met seasons she sang 88 perfs. of 7 roles, including Nannetta, Pamina, and Sophie. Also sang at Glyndebourne (Zerlina, 1963–64), Santa Fe, San Francisco, Washington, and recorded Anne Trulove under Stravinsky.

rataplan. A word imitating the sound of a drum, used in music for martial situations (e.g., in Donizetti's *Fille* and Verdi's *Forza*).

Ravel, Maurice. Composer; b. Ciboure, Basses Pyrénées, France, Mar. 7, 1875; d. Paris, Dec. 28, 1937. Studied with Fauré and Gédalge at Paris Conservatory; although failing to win the Prix de Rome, even in 1905 when established as a composer, he acquired ample technique and absorbed many novel influences, from Javanese gamelan music, Russian and Spanish music, and the work of Chabrier and Satie. Working in many forms and genres, he established himself as France's greatest composer after the death of Debussy, a fastidious craftsman and prodigal inventor, a subtle master of orchestration and harmony. After 1932, he was gradually incapacitated by a brain disease.

Ravel considered many operatic projects, including Hauptmann's *Die versunkene Glocke* (later set by Respighi), but only two came to fruition, both one-act miniature masterpieces. The comic opera *L'Heure Espagnole* (1911), exploiting the Spanish vein prominent in other Ravel works, is a sophisticated amorous farce. *L'Enfant et les Sortilèges* (1925), described as a "lyric fantasy," evokes with magical sympathy a child's world of personified objects. Ravel also composed numerous songs, several successful ballets, and instrumental works.

BIBLIOGRAPHY: Arbie Orenstein, *Ravel: Man and Musician* (N.Y., 1975).

Reardon, John. Baritone; b. New York, Apr. 8, 1930. Studied at Rollins College, then with Martial Singher and Margaret Harshaw; debut as Falke, N.Y.C. Opera, 1954. Met debut as Tomsky (*Queen of Spades*), Sep. 28, 1965; in 11 seasons there, he sang 16 roles, including Mercutio, Escamillo, and Albert (*Werther*). Created roles in Moore's *Wings of the Dove* and *Carrie Nation*, Hoiby's *Summer and Smoke*, Levy's *Mourning Becomes Electra*, and Pasatieri's

Seagull, and sang many U.S. premieres, especially in Santa Fe.

Re Cervo, Il. See *König Hirsch.*

recitative. A style of setting text in imitation of natural speech, using pitches central to the singer's vocal range and reinforcing spoken accents, rhythms, and inflections; although most recitative is written in even note values, it is not intended to be delivered in a strictly metrical fashion. 18th-c. opera drew a distinction between **recitativo secco**, or "dry" recitative, accompanied only by a keyboard instrument, and **recitativo accompagnato**, or accompanied recitative, more extravagant and accompanied by expressive orchestral gestures.

Red Line, The. Opera in 2 acts by Sallinen; libretto by the composer, after a novel by Ilmari Kianto.
First perf., Helsinki, Nov. 30, 1978: Valjakka, Hynninen, Hietikkot, c. Kamu. U.S. prem., N.Y., Metropolitan Opera House (Finnish Opera), Apr. 27, 1983: Valjakka, Hynninen, Salminen, c. Kamu.
Strongly written for voices, this work tells of the Finnish farmer Topi (bar) and his wife Riika (s), beset by hunger and by a marauding bear. Political freedom does not allay their poverty, and in the end Riika finds Topi killed by the bear.

Refice, Licinio. Composer; b. Patrica, near Rome, Feb. 12, 1885; d. Rio de Janeiro, Brazil, Sep. 11, 1954. After studying composition and organ at Santa Cecilia, Rome, he was ordained in 1910 and served as music director at Santa Maria Maggiore (1911–47). As well as sacred works, he composed two religious operas in a verismo-derived idiom, *Cecilia* (1934) and *Margherita da Cortona* (1938).

Regie (Ger.). Stage direction.

Regina. Opera in 3 acts by Blitzstein; libretto by the composer, after Lillian Hellman's play *The Little Foxes.*
First perf., New Haven, Conn., Shubert, Oct. 6, 1949: Pickens, Gillette, Lewis, Thomas, Lipton, Wilderman, c. Abravanel.
A skillful "Broadway opera," set in Bowden, Ala., in 1900. Having failed to manipulate her ailing husband Horace (bs) into a business deal with her unscrupulous brothers Ben (bar) and Oscar (bar), Regina Giddens (s) coldly watches Horace suffer a heart attack, then blackmails her brothers.

régisseur (Fr.). Term used in France and Germany for an operatic producer.

regista (Ital.). Stage director.

register. A portion of the vocal range produced by a particular physical mechanism. See *chest register, head register.*

Reichmann, Theodor. Baritone; b. Rostock, Germany, Mar. 15, 1849; d. Marbach, Germany, May 22, 1903. Studied in Berlin and Prague, and with Lamperti in Milan; debut in Magdeburg, 1869. Sang in German theaters, also Covent Garden (from 1884). At Bayreuth, created Amfortas (1882), later sang Sachs (1888–89) and Wolfram (1891). Met debut as Dutchman, Nov. 27, 1889; in 2 seasons, sang 16 roles, including Don Giovanni, di Luna, Escamillo, and Wagner parts.

Fritz Reiner

Reimann, Aribert. Composer; b. Berlin, Mar. 4, 1936. Studied with Blacher and Pepping at Berlin Hochschule für Musik; active as accompanist, notably to Fischer-Dieskau. Early compositions show Webern's influence, but in 1967 he turned from serialism to more eclectic idioms. His considerable output of vocal works includes the operas *Ein Traumspiel* (1965), after Strindberg; *Melusine,* after Goll (1971); *Lear* (1978), after Shakespeare; and *Die Gespenstersonate* (1986), after Strindberg.

Reine Fiammette, La (Queen Fiammette). Opera in 4 acts by Leroux; libretto by Catulle Mendès, after his play.
First perf., Paris, Opéra-Comique, Dec. 23, 1903: Garden, Maréchal, Périer, c. Messager. U.S. & Met prem., Jan. 24, 1919: Farrar, Lázaro, Didur, c. Monteux d, Anisfeld, p. Ordynski. 4 perfs. in 1 season.
A weak derivation of the styles of Leroux's teacher Massenet and of Puccini. In 16th-c. Bologna, Queen Orlanda (the "little flame" of the title, s) and Daniélo (t), a young monk chosen to assassinate her because of her Lutheran sympathies, fall in love, but they fail to overcome a conspiracy, and are executed together.

Reiner, Fritz. Conductor; b. Budapest, Dec. 19, 1888; d. New York, Nov. 15, 1963. Studied in Budapest; debut there at Vigopera, *Carmen,* 1910. Principal conductor in Dresden (1914–21), where he worked with Strauss. Conductor, Cincinnati Symphony (1922–31). Taught at Curtis Institute (1931–34); conducted opera in Philadelphia (1932–33), at Covent Garden (1936–37), and San Francisco (1936–38). After serving as music director of Pittsburgh Symphony (1938–1948), he joined the Met (debut, *Salome,* Feb. 4, 1949) and remained for 5 seasons and 143 perfs., concentrating on the Mozart-Wagner-Strauss literature, but also leading *Carmen, Falstaff,* and the U.S. premiere of *Rake's Progress.* As music director (1953–62) of the Chicago Symphony, he raised it to an international level. Back at the Met for *Götterdämmerung* in 1963, he contracted pneumonia during the rehearsal

(continued p.292)

RECORDINGS
Roland Gelatt

For much of its first century, the Metropolitan Opera's history has been closely mirrored by recorded sound. Edison's pioneering tin-foil phonograph – first unveiled in December 1877 – actually anticipated the Met's opening by six years, but even after his primitive squawk-box became the "improved phonograph" of the 1890s, its promoters were interested in commercial applications – office dictation, coin-in-slot nickelodeons – rather than in high musical culture. As a result, no recordings survive of the stars of the Met's 1883 opening-night *Faust*. During these years, one Gianni Bettini, a semi-amateur entrepreneur, set up shop to record celebrities, but his products were evidently treated as ephemera by their purchasers and have proved elusive to subsequent collectors.

A happier fate befell the cylinders of another amateur, the Met's British-born librarian Lionel Mapleson. From 1901 until 1904, he made wax cylinders of brief snatches from actual performances on the Met stage. Though made for his private pleasure, many of Mapleson's cylinders survived, and have recently been published *in toto* on six LPs. From the outset, the sound on these first incarnations of "Live From the Met" was faint and scratchy, and the intervening eighty years have dealt harshly with the fragile originals. Still, where else can one hear Sembrich in her prime caroling Arditi's "Parla" waltz as an encore to *La Fille du Régiment*, or Nordica riding over a full Wagnerian orchestra in Brünnhilde's immolation scene?

By that time the wax cylinder was *passé*, having given way to the flat disc. The disc's overriding advantage was ease of duplication; cylinders had to be dubbed to achieve quantity, while discs could be stamped out like cookies on a baking tray. Moreover, the disc's European promoters took it seriously, and determined to build a catalogue of recordings by the greatest musical artists of the day. On March 18, 1902, they had their rendezvous with destiny in a Milan hotel room: engineers from the London-based Gramophone and Typewriter Company made ten ten-inch sides, each devoted to an operatic aria, sung by a new La Scala star, the twenty-nine-year-old Enrico Caruso. To the 1902 public, these discs were a revelation. Caruso's strong voice and slightly baritonal timbre rode over the built-in surface noise, and even on the day's inadequate reproducers his records sounded rich and vibrant. Their success persuaded nearly every singer of consequence – even the legendary, virtually retired Adelina Patti – to perform for the horn.

Celebrity recording quickly crossed the Atlantic – as did Caruso himself. In 1903, Columbia launched its Grand Opera series, Victor its Red Seal label. From this point, the Met and the phonograph industry began to run on parallel tracks. Victor took the lead in reflecting events at Broadway and Thirty-ninth Street. Although the Red Seal labels indicate no overt collaboration, the results speak for themselves: to choose just one early example, extensive excerpts were put on disc by the much-acclaimed cast of the Met's first *Butterfly* (Caruso, Farrar, Scotti) – not only the big arias and the love duet, but intervening passages as well.

A major breakthrough occurred in 1925, with the introduction of electrical recording. Before then, master discs were made in cramped studios, with the grooves engraved by the unassisted vibrations of the singer's voice (the so-called "acoustic process"); sessions could now be held in larger, more reverberant spaces, using full-sized orchestras. The documen-

(*Left*) Risë Stevens and Nadine Conner are joined by Edward Johnson at the recording of the Met's *Hänsel und Gretel*. (*Above*) Edison's original cylinder phonograph. (*Below*) Jussi Bjoerling and Birgit Nilsson record *Turandot*. (*Inset*) Robert Merrill, Carlo Bergonzi, Leontyne Price, and Reri Grist record *Un Ballo in Maschera*.

tation of Met repertory and singers continued as before: Ponselle, Martinelli, and Pinza in *Forza*, Rethberg, Lauri-Volpi, and de Luca in *Aida* – but still only excerpts. No complete opera was made for commercial release in the U.S. until after World War II. Meanwhile, European companies filled the gap, and some of their prewar albums, such as Act I of *Die Walküre* with Lotte Lehmann and Lauritz Melchior, closely paralleled Met casts.

Unknown to the general public, a source of complete opera recordings from the Met opened up in the 1930s. Beginning on Christmas Day, 1931, Met performances were regularly transmitted on the radio, and by 1940 these broadcasts were being preserved by the networks on oversize transcription discs. In due course, the Met would be able to tap this archive of "live performances" for its series of fund-raising Historic Broadcast albums.

At the end of World War II, another technological breakthrough stimulated the industry. Developed by the Germans as a superior recording medium for radio stations, magnetic tape was "liberated" by the Allies, further improved, and quickly adopted to replace the cumbersome old method of cutting directly on blank wax discs. Tape could run without interruption for a half hour or more, its fidelity was at least the equal of anything achieved on disc, and – perhaps most important – it could be edited. If a passage contained a wrong note or was otherwise blemished, the musicians simply played it again, and the corrected version was patched in place of the defective one. From the final edited tape, the master disc could then be cut under controlled laboratory conditions.

When combined with the new microgroove LP format, introduced in 1948, which played for up to 25 minutes per side (five minutes or so was the limit of the old shellac discs), tape made complete operas both easier to accomplish and more attractive in the marketplace. Columbia Records, inventors of the LP, signed a contract to record Met productions, beginning with *Hänsel und Gretel* in 1947 and including Stravinsky's *Rake's Progress* with the cast of the U.S. premiere; RCA Victor, which had many Met stars under exclusive contract, countered with its own studio productions, among them *Carmen* with Risë Stevens and *Trovatore* with Milanov, Bjoerling, and Warren.

Eventually, the high cost of working in the U.S. – and the fact that singers were becoming more peripatetic – led to the demise of New York as a capital of opera recording. It was easier and cheaper to assemble Met stars in Europe during the summer and record them with supporting local talent in Rome, Milan, Vienna, or London. Given the world-wide market, a profit could be shown even on relatively recondite repertory: early Verdi, late Puccini, Massenet, Britten. The Fifties and Sixties were the glory days of complete operas, each company exploiting its own stable of singers and conductors in their strengths (and sometimes also their weak spots).

The rest of the story is technological. The amazing improvement of the cassette medium in the 1970s provided a handy, portable alternative to the LP. The advent of the digital process in the 1980s, and the dissemination of digital recordings on laser-read compact discs, abolished wear and surface noise, expanded dynamic range, and afforded new possibilities of altering the sound as recorded.

In tandem with this closer approach to perfection, interestingly, has come a fresh emphasis on spontaneity; more and more operatic recordings stem from public performances, or at least are made in the studio in "long takes" rather than pieced together as a mosaic of correct but perhaps lifeless fragments. And the great performances of the past are rapidly finding new digital incarnations. Most significantly, operatic recording now not only mirrors the activity of the theaters; it stimulates reciprocally, building audiences for a broader repertory, whetting our appetites for live performances.

The late Roland Gelatt was author of *Music-Makers* and *The Fabulous Phonograph*.

period and died. A rigorous disciplinarian, Reiner conducted with a strong sense of line and dynamic proportion, building climaxes over long spans; his mastery of orchestral balance and color was exceptional, and is attested by numerous recordings, including *Carmen* and Strauss opera excerpts.

Reinhardt [Goldman], **Max.** Producer; b. Baden, Austria, Sep. 9, 1873; d. New York, Oct. 30, 1943. The most influential figure in German theater in the first third of the 20th c., active in Berlin from 1902 and after World War I also in Vienna. Noted for spectacles such as *The Miracle* (widely toured, 1911) and Hofmannsthal's *Jedermann* (1920) at the Salzburg Festival, which he co-founded; his Berlin operetta productions were celebrated. He assisted in staging the 1911 Dresden premiere of *Rosenkavalier*, and the *Bourgeois Gentilhomme–Ariadne* combination was written for his ensemble in gratitude. Forced to leave Germany in 1933, he produced Shakespeare's *Midsummer Night's Dream* in the Hollywood Bowl, then on film (1935).

Reiss, Albert. Tenor; b. Berlin, Feb. 22, 1870; d. Nice, France, June 19, 1940. Studied with Wilhelm Vilmar, Beno Stolzenberg, and Julius Lieban, Berlin; debut as Ivanov (*Zar und Zimmermann*), Königsberg, 1897, later singing in Posen and Wiesbaden. Met debut as Shepherd and Steersman (*Tristan*), Dec. 23, 1901; in 19 seasons there, he sang 736 perfs. of 54 roles, including the Witch (*Hänsel*), Remendado (*Carmen*), Mime, and David (*Meistersinger*), and creating Nick (*Fanciulla*) and the Broom-Maker (*Königskinder*). Sang at Covent Garden (1902–05, 1924–29) and Berlin (from 1920). Retired 1938.

Reizen, Mark. Bass; b. Zaitsevo, Russia, July 3, 1895. Studied with F. Bugamelli, Kharkov Conservatory; debut as Pimen, Kharkov, 1921. Sang at Kirov, Leningrad (1925–30) and Bolshoi, Moscow (1930–54). Best known as Boris, Dosifey (*Khovanshchina*), Susanin, the Miller (*Rusalka*), and Philippe II (*Don Carlos*). After 1954, taught and continued to sing recitals; appeared at the Bolshoi as Gremin to celebrate his 90th birthday.

Remedios, Alberto. Tenor; b. Liverpool, England, Feb. 27, 1935. Studied with Edwin Francis, Liverpool, and Clive Carey, Royal College of Music, London; debut as Tinca (*Tabarro*), Sadler's Wells, 1957; returned to English National Opera as Wagnerian tenor from 1968. Covent Garden debut as Dimitri (*Boris*), 1966. Met debut as Bacchus (*Ariadne*), Mar. 20, 1976.

reminiscence motive. A short musical idea associated with a character or idea or event in an opera, and recalled at dramatically appropriate points.

Renard. Burlesque ballet with voices in 1 act by Stravinsky; libretto by the composer, after Russian folk tales.
First perf., Paris, Opéra, May 18, 1922 (in Fr.): Fabert, Dubois, Narçon, Mahieux, c. Ansermet. U.S. prem., N.Y., Vanderbilt, Dec. 2, 1923 (concert perf., in Fr.). U.S. stage prem. N.Y., Hunter College (Ballet Society), Jan. 13, 1947 (in Eng.).
Derived from the Russian tradition of itinerant folk entertainers, *Renard*, composed in 1916, is to be played on stage by "clowns, dancers, or acrobats" with the singers placed in the orchestra. A vixen preys on the cock and nearly gets him but is foiled by the tomcat and ram, who eventually strangle her.

Renaud, Maurice. Baritone; b. Bordeaux, France, July 24, 1861(?); d. Paris, Oct. 16, 1933. Studied at Paris Conservatory and with Dupont and Gevaert, Brussels; debut at Monnaie, 1883, where he remained until 1890, singing French and Italian repertory, some Wagner, and creating the High Priest (*Sigurd*, 1884) and Hamilcar (*Salammbô*, 1890). Debut at Opéra-Comique, Paris (Karnac in *Roi d'Ys*); created Diaz's Cellini there; Opéra debut as Nélusko (*Africaine*), 1891, returning regularly until 1914. He also sang in Monte Carlo (1891–1907, creating Boniface in *Jongleur*) and at Covent Garden (1897–04). In the U.S., Renaud performed with the Manhattan Opera (1906–10), in Boston (1910–12) and Chicago (1910), in roles such as Scarpia, Athanaël (*Thaïs*), and the *Hoffmann* villains. In only 2 Met seasons, he sang 5 perfs. of Rigoletto (debut, Nov. 24, 1910) and Valentin. The leading French baritone of his day, he retired in 1912 and taught in Paris.

Rendall, David. Tenor; b. London. Studied at Royal Academy, London, and Salzburg Mozarteum; debut as Ferrando (*Così*), Glyndebourne touring troupe, 1975. Debuts at Covent Garden (Singer in *Rosenkavalier*, 1975) and N.Y.C. Opera (Rodolfo, 1978). Since his Met debut as Ernesto in *Don Pasquale* (Feb. 28, 1980), he has also sung Ottavio, Belmonte, Matteo (*Arabella*), Ferrando, Lenski, Idomeneo, Alfred (*Fledermaus*), and Tito (*Clemenza*).

Rennert, Günther. Producer; b. Essen, Germany, Apr. 1, 1911; d. Salzburg, July 31, 1978. First operatic production, *Parsifal* (Frankfurt, 1935). Principal producer at Städtische Oper, Berlin (1942–44) and Bavarian State Opera (1945), later Intendant of Hamburg State Opera (1946–56) and Bavarian State Opera (1968–76); artistic adviser, Glyndebourne (1959–67). For the Met, staged six operas: *Nabucco* (1960), *Manon* (1963), *Salome* (1965), *Zauberflöte* (1967), *Jenůfa* (1974), and *Nozze* (1975).

Rè Pastore, Il (The Shepherd King). Opera in 2 acts by Mozart; libretto by Metastasio.
First perf., Salzburg, Archbishop's Palace, Apr. 23, 1775. U.S. prem., New Haven, Conn. (Yale U.), July 7, 1971.
This static work, containing several memorable arias, is set in Sidon, after its conquest by Alexander the Great. Aminta (s), who has been raised as a shepherd, declines the throne of Sidon rather then renounce his love for the shepherdess Elisa (s), and they are allowed to reign together.

repertory, repertoire. A list of operas that a company or a singer is prepared to perform. Also, the general operatic literature. When operating on the repertory principle, an opera company rotates a number of different works during a given time period; see also *stagione*.

répétiteur (Fr.). Coach.

répétition (Fr.). Rehearsal. **Répétition générale,** dress rehearsal.

Reppa, David. Designer; b. Hammond, Ind., Nov. 2, 1926. Professional training at Met (1957–58); first design, *Nozze*, North Shore Opera, N.Y., 1960. Has also designed for Miami and San Francisco. Since 1967, resident scenic designer at Met; his productions include *Bluebeard's Castle* and *Gianni Schicchi* (1974), *Aida* (1976), *Dialogues des Carmélites* (1977), and *Don Carlos* (1979).

Regina Resnik as Klytemnästra in *Elektra*

Rescigno, Nicola. Conductor; b. New York. Studied with Pizzetti, Giannini, and Polacco, then toured U.S. with San Carlo Opera (debut, *Traviata*, Brooklyn Academy, 1943). Co-founder and artistic director, Chicago Lyric Opera (1954–56) and Dallas Opera (since 1957). A frequent guest conductor, closely associated with Callas in performances and recordings. Since his Met debut (*Don Pasquale*, Dec. 7, 1978), he has also led *Elisir*, *Italiana*, and *Traviata* there.

rescue opera. A genre of opéra comique involving the heroic last-minute rescue of a hero or heroine threatened by death or worse. Originally popular in revolutionary France, its best-known exemplar is Beethoven's *Fidelio*, based on the libretto of a French work.

Resnik, Regina. Mezzo-soprano, originally soprano; b. New York, Aug. 30, 1922. Studied at Hunter College and later with Rosalie Miller; debut as Lady Macbeth, New Opera Co., N.Y., 1942. Appearances in Mexico City (1943) and with N.Y.C. Opera (debut, Frasquita, 1944) preceded her Met debut as Leonora (*Trovatore*), Dec. 6, 1944. Until 1954, she sang soprano roles with the company, including Fidelio, Donna Anna, Ellen (*Grimes*), Alice Ford, Sieglinde, Donna Elvira, and Rosalinde (*Fledermaus*), and then switched to mezzo parts, notably Herodias, Carmen, Klytemnästra, Quickly, and the Marquise (*Fille*). In 30 seasons, she sang 242 perfs. of 38 roles, and created Delilah (*Warrior*) and the Baroness (*Vanessa*). Debuts in San Francisco (Fidelio, 1946), Bayreuth (Sieglinde, 1953), Covent Garden (Carmen, 1957), Salzburg (Eboli, 1960); sang Claire in U.S. premiere of *Besuch der alten Dame* (San Francisco, 1972). An imaginative singing actress, Resnik accomplished a difficult vocal transition to a *Fach* that proved exceptionally congenial; since the early 1970s, she has staged opera as well.

Respighi, Ottorino. Composer; b. Bologna, Italy, July 9, 1879; d. Rome, Apr. 18, 1936. Studied with Torchi and Martucci at Bologna Liceo Musicale, later in St. Petersburg. His most successful works were his evocative, lushly orchestrated symphonic poems. His less familiar stage works include *Re Enzo* (1905); *Semirama* (1910); the marionette opera *La Bella Addormentata nel Bosco* (1922); *Belfagor* (1923); *La Campana Sommersa* (1927); *Maria Egiziaca* (1932); *La Fiamma* (1934); *Lucrezia* (posthumous, 1937); and a transcription of Monteverdi's *Orfeo* (1935).

Retablo de Maese Pedro, El (Master Peter's Puppet Show). Opera in 1 act by Falla; libretto by the composer, after Cervantes' *Don Quixote*.
    First perf., Seville, San Fernando, Mar. 23, 1923 (concert perf.): Redondo, Segura, Lledo, c. Falla. U.S. prem., N.Y., Town Hall, Dec. 29, 1925.
    Intended for puppet-theater performance, with a harpsichord in the chamber-scale orchestra. While watching a puppet show, Don Quixote (bs-bar) becomes caught up in the action, takes up the cause of the underdog puppets, and in so doing destroys the show.

Rethberg, Elisabeth [Lisbeth Sättler]. Soprano; b. Schwarzenberg, Germany, Sep. 22, 1894; d. Yorktown Heights, N.Y., June 6, 1976. Studied at Dresden Conservatory with Otto Watrin; debut as Arsena (*Zigeunerbaron*), Dresden, 1915, where she remained until 1922, in roles such as Agathe (*Freischütz*), Hänsel, Sophie and Octavian, Susanna, Tosca, and the Empress (*Frau*). At Salzburg in 1922, she sang the Countess (*Nozze*) and Konstanze, later Fidelio (1933), Donna Anna (1937–39), and the Marschallin (1939). After her Met debut as Aida (Nov. 22, 1922), she remained with the company for 20 consecutive seasons, giving 270 perfs. of 30 roles, most frequently Aida (51 times), followed by Sieglinde, Eva, Elsa, and Butterfly; other roles included the Countess, Elisabeth, the *Trovatore* Leonora, Desdemona, Nedda, Sélika (*Africaine*), Amelia (*Boccanegra*), Maddalena

Elisabeth Rethberg as Rautendelein in *La Campana Sommersa*

(*Chénier*), Agathe, and Rautendelein (*Campana Sommersa*). She continued to appear in Europe, creating the title role of *Ägyptische Helena* (Dresden, 1928), and singing Aida at La Scala (1929), Rautendelein in Rome (1929), the *Walküre* Brünnhilde in Paris (1930), and the *Forza* Leonora in Florence (1934). At Covent Garden, she sang Aida and Butterfly in 1925, returning as Mimi, Elsa, Yaroslavna (*Prince Igor*), Dorotka (*Shvanda*), and the Marschallin, 1934–39. In America, she appeared frequently in San Francisco (1928–40), where her roles included Amelia (*Ballo*), Mařenka (*Bartered Bride*), Rachel (*Juive*), and Susanna, and in Chicago (1934–41). In 1957 she married Met baritone George Cehanovsky.

In the use of her beautifully clear, smoothly produced and equalized spinto soprano, Rethberg cultivated an instrumental accuracy and purity, which in N.Y. was much admired even in Italian roles, though stylistically more suited to the German romantic heroines. Despite her lack of striking dramatic individuality, her musicianship, fluency, tonal appeal, and sympathetic personality made her a popular singer.

Reyer, Ernest. Composer; b. Marseilles, France, Dec. 1, 1823; d. Le Lavandou, near Hyères, Jan. 15, 1909. Musically self-taught, he supported Berlioz and Wagner in his journalism, but their influence is oddly absent from his music. As well as two early opéras comiques and the opera *Erostrate* (1862), he had greater success with *Sigurd*, after Nordic mythology (1884), and the grandiose *Salammbô* (1890).

Rheingold, Das. See *Ring des Nibelungen, Der*.

Ricci, Federico. Composer; b. Naples, Oct. 22, 1809; d. Conegliano, Dec. 10, 1877. Studied with Zingarelli and Raimondi at Naples Conservatory, his older brother Luigi, and Bellini. Of four comedies composed with his brother, best-known is *Crispino e la Comare* (1850), while *La Prigione di Edimburgo*, after Scott (1838), and *Luigi Rolla* (1841) were his most successful independent works.

Ricci, Luigi. Composer; b. Naples, July 8, 1805; d. Prague, Dec. 31, 1859. Studied at Naples Conservatory with Furno and Zingarelli. His first major success was the opera semiseria *Chiara di Rosembergh* (1831), composed for Grisi. In addition to the comedy *Crispino e la Comare* (1850, in collaboration with his brother Federico), his opera buffa *La Festa di Piedigrotta* (1852) remained popular in the 19th c.

Ricciarelli, Katia. Soprano; b. Rovigo, Italy, Jan. 18, 1946. Studied with Iris Adami Corradetti, Venice Conservatory; debut as Mimi, Mantua, 1969. In 1970, won Parma Verdi prize and sang Leonora (*Trovatore*) there. U.S. debut as Lucrezia (*Due Foscari*), Chicago, 1972; Covent Garden debut as Mimi, 1974. Met debut as Mimi, Apr. 11, 1975; subsequently, her repertory there has included Micaela, Desdemona, Luisa Miller, and Amelia (*Ballo*). She has also appeared at La Scala, San Francisco, Rome, Paris, Munich, and Brussels; other roles include Suor Angelica and Elisabeth de Valois; her Desdemona is seen in Zeffirelli's 1986 *Otello* film.

Riccitelli, Primo. Composer; b. Campli, Italy, Aug. 9, 1875; d. Giulianova, Mar. 27, 1941. Studied at Liceo Rossini, Pesaro, with Mascagni. His operas include *Maria sul Monte* (1916); *I Compagnacci* (1923); and *Madone Oretta* (1932).

Richter, Hans. Conductor; b. Raab [now Györ], Hungary, Apr. 4, 1843; d. Bayreuth, Dec. 5, 1916. Studied in Vienna, worked as copyist for Wagner (1866–67, 1870), and assisted Bülow in Munich (1868). Debut in Vienna and appointment to Court Opera, 1875. In 1876, led first complete *Ring* in Bayreuth, where he remained a major figure until his death. In England, led Hallé Orchestra (1897–1911), London Symphony (1904–11), and first English-language *Ring* (1908).

Ricordi. Publishing house. Founded by **Giovanni Ricordi** (b. Milan, 1785; d. Milan, Mar. 15, 1853), the firm was closely associated with La Scala from 1814 and later with other Italian theaters. His son **Tito Ricordi** (b. Milan, Oct. 29, 1811; d. Milan, Sep. 7, 1888) expanded the business, opening branches in other countries and acquiring other firms before retiring in 1887 in favor of his son **Giulio Ricordi** (b. Milan, Dec. 19, 1840; d. Milan, June 6, 1912), a trained musician who played a major role in the creation of Verdi's late works and the nurturing of Puccini's talent. In 1888 the firm acquired its major competitor, the house of Lucca, including the Italian rights to Wagner's operas. Giulio's son **Tito Ricordi** (b. Milan, May 17, 1865; d. Milan, Mar. 13, 1933) lacked his ancestors' taste, alienating Puccini by his preference for Zandonai; he retired in 1919.

Ridderbusch, Karl. Bass; b. Recklinghausen, Germany, May 29, 1932. Studied at Duisburg Conservatory and with Clemens Kaiser-Bremer, Essen; debut in Münster, 1961. Sang with Essen Opera (1963–65) and Deutsche Oper am Rhein, Düsseldorf (from 1965). Debuts at Bayreuth (King in *Lohengrin*, 1967), Met (Hunding, Nov. 21, 1967), and Covent Garden (*Ring*, 1971); at the Met he also sang Fafner (*Rheingold*) and returned as Sachs in 1976.

Riders to the Sea. Opera in 1 act by Vaughan Williams; libretto from John Millington Synge's play.
First perf., London, Royal College of Music, Dec. 1, 1937: Hall, Smith-Miller, Steventon, Coad, c. Sargent. U.S. prem., Cleveland, Western Reserve U., Feb. 26, 1950.
A somberly lyrical tragedy, set on an island off the west coast of Ireland, early 20th c. Maurya (a), who has lost her husband and three sons to the sea, learns of the drowning of her fourth and then the death of the fifth; she now has nothing more to fear.

Riegel, Kenneth. Tenor; b. Womelsdorf, Pa., Apr. 19, 1938. Studied at Manhattan School of Music; debut as Alchemist in *König Hirsch*, Santa Fe, 1965. Sang with N.Y.C. Opera (1969–74; debut, Gonzalve in *Heure Espagnole*). Met debut as Iopas (*Troyens*), Oct. 22, 1973; other house roles include David, Tamino, Hoffmann, Tito, and Alwa (*Lulu*), which he sang in the 1979 Paris premiere of the complete score. In Europe, has sung works by Schreker and Zemlinsky (*Zwerg*, London, 1985).

Rienzi. Opera in 5 acts by Wagner; libretto by the composer, after Bulwer Lytton's novel.
First perf., Dresden, Court Opera, Oct. 20, 1842: Wüst, Schröder-Devrient, Tichatschek, Wächter, Dettmer, c. Reissiger. U.S. prem., N.Y., Academy of Music, Mar. 4, 1878. Met prem., Feb. 5, 1886: Lilli Lehmann, Brandt, Sylva, Robinson, Fischer, c. Seidl, p. van Hell. 13 perfs. in 3 seasons.
Wagner's spectacular youthful essay in Meyerbeerian

grand opera fairly bursts with energy, flair, and a sense of theatricality, though its original form was impracticably long and has never been performed in the theater.

Rome, mid-14th c. The Roman noble Orsini (bs) tries to abduct Irene (s), sister of the papal notary Rienzi (t). His plot is foiled by Colonna (bs), whose son Adriano (ms) loves Irene, and Rienzi leads a revolt against the patricians. After making various attempts on Rienzi's life, the nobles are killed, but the people turn against Rienzi too, and he is excommunicated. The people set fire to the Capitol, where Rienzi, who has refused to flee, is joined by Irene and Adriano; all three perish in the flames.

Righetti-Giorgi, Geltrude. Contralto; b. Bologna, Italy, 1793; d. Bologna, 1862. Studied in Bologna; debut there in 1814. In Rome, created Rosina in *Barbiere di Siviglia* (1816) and title role in *Cenerentola* (1817). Retired early, probably for health reasons, in 1822.

Rigoletto. Opera in 3 acts by Verdi; libretto by Piave, after the drama *Le Roi S'Amuse* by Hugo.

First perf., Venice, Fenice, Mar. 11, 1851: Brambilla, Mirate, Varesi, Damini. U.S. prem., N.Y., Academy of Music, Feb. 19, 1855: Frezzolini, Bignardi. Met prem., Nov. 16, 1883: Sembrich, Stagno, Guadagnini, Novara, c. Vianesi, d. J. Fox, Schaeffer, Maeder, Thompson/Ascoli, Dazian. Later Met productions: Nov. 26, 1921: Galli-Curci, Chamlee, de Luca, Rothier, c. Papi, d. Rota/Castelbert, p. Agnini; Nov. 15, 1951: Gueden, Tucker, Warren, Pernerstorfer, c. Erede, d. Berman, p. Graf; Oct. 31, 1977: Cotrubas, Domingo, Milnes, Diaz, c. Levine, d. Moiseiwitsch, p. Dexter. Rigoletto has also been sung at the Met by Ancona, Maurel, Scotti, Stracciari, Amato, Tibbett, Tagliabue, Weede, Merrill, MacNeil, Wixell, Manuguerra; Gilda by Melba, Tetrazzini, Hempel, Pons, Sayão, Peters, Moffo, Grist, Sutherland, Blegen; the Duke by Caruso, Bonci, Gigli, Lauri-Volpi, Kiepura, Bjoerling, Peerce, Tagliavini, di Stefano, Gedda, Bergonzi, Pavarotti. 450 perfs. in 78 seasons.

In the title role of *Rigoletto*, Verdi created one of his most powerful and original psychological characterizations, while the opera as a whole is perhaps his most brilliantly tuneful score.

Mantua, 16th c. Rigoletto (bar) is an embittered, hunch-backed court jester whose sole joy in life is Gilda (s), the daughter he has raised in seclusion from the world. At court he encourages the libertinism of the Duke of Mantua (t), but is cursed by Count Monterone (bar), whose daughter the Duke has seduced. The Duke, incognito, has flirted with Gilda at church, and she has fallen in love with him. The courtiers trick Rigoletto into assisting in the abduction of his own daughter (whom they believe to be his mistress), and she is seduced by the Duke. Vowing vengeance, Rigoletto hires the assassin Sparafucile (bs), using the latter's sister Maddalena (ms) as lure to the philandering, disguised Duke. But, still in love with him, Gilda contrives to take the place of her beloved Duke, and when Rigoletto comes to collect the Duke's body, he finds that the sack contains his expiring daughter. He recalls the curse and falls senseless.

Rihm, Wolfgang. Composer; b. Mar. 3, 1952, Karlsruhe, Germany. Studied with Velte and Fortner at Karlsruhe Conservatory, at Darmstadt School, with Stockhausen in Cologne, and with Klaus Huber, Wilhelm Killmayer, and Nono. His operas include *Deploration* (1974), *Dis-Kontur* (1975), *Jakob Lenz* (1980), and the theater piece *Wölfli-Szenen*.

Rigoletto – Ricordi score cover (detail)

Rimsky-Korsakov, Nikolai. Composer; b. Tikhvin, Novgorod region, Russia, Mar. 18, 1844; d. Lyubensk, near St. Petersburg, June 21, 1908. Family tradition sent him to St. Petersburg Naval Academy, but he continued early piano lessons and, encouraged by Balakirev, began composing during his naval service. He settled in St. Petersburg in 1865, heard his First Symphony conducted by Balakirev, and continued to write in the nationalist tradition founded by Glinka. In 1871, he became professor of composition and orchestration at St. Petersburg Conservatory; his students included Glazunov, Arensky, and Stravinsky. Rimsky's 1889 encounter with Wagner's *Ring*, performed in St. Petersburg by Neumann's touring company, was decisive to his career; he had already composed *The Maid of Pskov* (1873) and *May Night* (1880), but now turned his energies principally to operas. Most were on Russian subjects, especially mythological and fantastical, giving vent to his gifts for brilliant orchestral and harmonic colors: *The Snow Maiden* (1892), *Christmas Eve* (after Gogol, 1898), *Sadko* (1898), *Mozart and Salieri* (1898), *The Tsar's Bride* (1899), *The Tale of Tsar Saltan* (1900), *The Legend of the Invisible City of Kitezh* (1907), and *The Golden Cockerel* (1909). An ardent champion of his colleagues, he prepared performing editions, especially of Mussorgsky's works, that have been widely criticized for their arbitrary "improvements."
BIBLIOGRAPHY: Gerald Abraham, *Rimsky-Korsakov* (London, 1945).

Rinaldo. Opera in 3 acts by Handel; libretto by Giacomo Rossi, after a scenario by Aaron Hill based on Tasso's *Gerusalemme Liberata*.

First perf., London, Queen's, Feb. 24, 1711: Pilotti, Girardeau, Nicolini, Boschi. U.S. prem., Houston Opera, Oct. 16, 1975: Horne, Rogers, Mandac, Ramey, c. Foster. Met prem., Jan. 19, 1984: Horne, Moser, Valente, Ramey, c. Bernardi, d. Negin, p. Corsaro. 10 perfs. in 1 season.

Handel's first opera for London, a stirring and heroic

(continued p.298)

RIGOLETTO
Sherrill Milnes

Rigoletto poses the ultimate challenge to a Verdi baritone. Like Shakespeare's Richard III, the tragic comedian is both physically and emotionally deformed. While projecting Rigoletto's self-destructive obsessions, an artist must still create a sympathetic character who loves his daughter "not wisely, but too well." Singing Verdi's soaring lines and gorgeous melodies, I try to express the many passions of this tormented father.

According to conventional wisdom, a twenty-seven-year-old baritone sings Ford and Rossini's Figaro, fine-tunes his technique, and shies away from the dramatic "heavies." Wait ten years, the skeptics caution, and then try out two or three Rigolettos in a small, out-of-the-way theater. I didn't wait that long. Touring colleges and community theaters in the early Sixties, I sang forty of my first hundred *Rigoletto*s with the Boris Goldovsky company. The performing conditions were ideal for young singers; thanks to a reduced orchestra and a unit set that effectively doubled as an acoustical shell, I never pushed my voice for volume. Singing in English, I learned how to color the text and create the character. I still apply Goldovsky's lessons in stagecraft when performing Rigoletto at the Met or anywhere else in the world.

Listening to older *Rigoletto* recordings, I was impressed with Leonard Warren and Tito Gobbi. Warren had that fabulous upper extension, and crescendoed and diminuendoed through the most breathtaking phrases; the pathos and heartbreak of the character were always evident. Gobbi was a master word-painter, and one could always believe the emotion of the moment through his vocal colors. Daring to show their individuality, each of these men dug into Verdi's score and made the role his own. I work very hard to follow in their footsteps!

My first step is to make that tricky transformation into a hunchback. Rigoletto is doubly hard to sing when you are stooped over for three hours. My shorter colleagues are lucky! But, at six foot two, I have to make serious adjustments. Shouldering a foam-rubber hump on my shoulders and back, I shift the weight on to my knees. While bending deeply from side to side, I try to always maintain a good singing posture. Theater is illusion: the body might look twisted, but the voice must be supported by a powerful column of air, As I get older, my voice stays fresh – but my ankles ache more and more after each Rigoletto. It takes lots of leg lifts to stay in shape.

Rehearsing Rigoletto in street clothes, I still look and feel like Sherrill Milnes. The aging process begins in my dressing room. Applying heavy make-up before performances, I add wrinkles, crow's feet, and the foam-rubber hump, as well as a scraggly beard and a wig with a glistening bald spot. In the mirror, I see an old man who is burdened with injustice and inner conflict. Now, and only now, can I completely play the Duke's fool.

The psychological transformation swiftly follows. In the sixteenth century, a handicapped man had two career choices: become a funnyman at the local court or hit the street and beg. As the Duke of Mantua's hired hand, Rigoletto serves up the courtiers' wives, daughters, and sweethearts to his master, and he otherwise debases himself in a hundred humiliating ways. One stage director told me, "Rigoletto really loves his work." No, he *hates* it! In "Pari siamo," he compares his verbal jabs to an assassin's dagger. After work, he eagerly strips off his buffoon's cap and becomes a loving father.

A simple sadist who "loves his work" would never sing Rigoletto's achingly beautiful lines to Gilda. "You are my universe," he tell his daughter, who indeed is his only anchor in a brutal world. It helps me enormously when I can hold a lovely diva in my arms and actually *see* "the face of an angel." But if Gilda is on the plain side, I can always concentrate on the music and use my imagination.

Having endured the loss of his wife and two children, Verdi transformed his pain into many of the most moving parent-child relationships in opera. As a concerned father who has shared his three children's growing pains, I can empathize with Rigoletto's emotional attachment to Gilda. But onstage I separate Sherrill Milnes' personal life from Rigoletto's. If you take his tragedy too personally, you will never project his character beyond the footlights.

After engineering the Duke's many seductions, Rigoletto justifiably fears that his daughter might become the next victim. Monterone's curse feeds this obsession, and, as Rigoletto has always tried to shield Gilda from the real world, his fears become greater. Naturally, though, the girl can't remain a prisoner forever and, even as Rigoletto tenderly blesses his child, the Duke prepares his next conquest.

"Cortigiani, vil razza dannata" is Rigoletto's primal scream at his tormentors. "You bastards," he cries. "For years, you have humiliated me and now you steal the most important thing in my life – my daughter!" The phrases are explosive, but you must *sing* them, never yell. I work out in advance special staging details with whoever sings Marullo, the court poet. After the courtiers hurl me to the ground, I crawl on my knees to Marullo and sing, "She's in there with the Duke, isn't she?" He can turn away with a contrite look, as if to say, "I wish we could undo this situation, but it's too late." Rigoletto's last hope crumbles, and he pleads for Gilda's return with vocal sobs. The opera is filled with these nuances, and a good Rigoletto makes evey detail count.

Rigoletto now lives only to avenge his family honor. "Piangi, fanciulla." he tells Gilda, but he really weeps for his own misfortune. "Vendetta" becomes his all-consuming passion. Certain conductors would like to purify Verdi scores of all unwritten high notes. Why? A climactic high A-flat resolves the emotional tension in this scene, and the longer Rigoletto swells that sound, the better. Some stage directors ask you to rush offstage during the final measures. But Verdi freezes that moment in time, and so Rigoletto should grab Gilda's hand or arm and hold that position of "vendetta" until the curtain falls. Wise directors should forget their pet theories and stick to the score!

When the assassination plot against the Duke backfires, Rigoletto stands over his dying daughter and cries, "Poor me, what am *I* going to do now?" To the bitter end, he keeps the blinders on and shifts all blame to that terrible "maledizione." Rigoletto seems inflexible and selfish in Piave's libretto, but the music tells a more profound story. "Don't die, don't leave me!" is a piercing cry from the heart. Verdi instinctively cloaks his court jester with flesh, blood, and great humanity.

Das Rheingold – (1912). William Hinshaw, Carl Burrian, Hermann Weil, Margaret Matzenauer, Alma Gluck, and Lambert Murphy

score. The crusader Rinaldo (c), who loves Almirena (s), opposes the Saracens, led by Argante (bs). Argante's mistress, Armida (s), uses her sorcery against Rinaldo, but falls in love with him; she and Argante are eventually defeated.

Ring des Nibelungen, Der (The Nibelung's Ring). Cycle ("stage-festival play in 3 days and a preliminary evening") by Wagner; libretto by the composer.

First complete perf., Bayreuth, Aug. 13, 14, 16, 17, 1876: Materna, Schefsky, Niemann, Unger, Vogl, Schlosser, Betz, Hill, Siehr, c. Richter. First complete perf. in U.S., Met, Mar. 4, 5, 6, 11, 1889: Lilli Lehmann, Bettaque, Perotti, Alvary, Sedlmayer, Fischer, Beck, c. Seidl.

The most ambitious and complex musico-dramatic work in the European tradition, the *Ring* treats mighty themes of power and love, drawn from northern mythology but universal in significance; the cycle has often been viewed as a socio-political allegory. Wagner first worked on the subject in 1848; although he interrupted composition in 1857, between Acts II and III of *Siegfried*, resuming in 1869 when his compositional powers were more highly developed, the musical style is remarkably consistent. Each opera has a color of its own; they are linked together by motivic and harmonic associations, and all feature remarkable orchestral nature painting.

Das Rheingold (The Rhinegold); opera in 4 scenes. First perf., Munich, Sep. 22, 1869: Stehle, Seehofer, Vogl, Kindermann, Fischer, c. Wüllner. U.S. & Met prem., Jan. 4, 1889: Moran-Olden, Reil, Alvary, Fischer, Beck, c. Seidl, d. Kautsky, Doepler/Dazian, p. Habelmann. Later Met productions: Jan. 29, 1914: Fremstad, Ober, Jörn, Weil, Goritz, d. Kautsky, p. Horth; Jan. 7, 1948: Thorborg, Thebom, Lorenz, Berglund, Pechner, d. Simonson/Schenck, p. Graf; Nov. 22, 1968: Veasey, Chookasian, Stolze, Stewart, Kelemen, c. Karajan, d. Schneider-Siemssen/Wakhevitch, p. Karajan. Wotan has also been sung at the Met by van Rooy, Bohnen, Schorr, Janssen, Hotter, Uhde, London, Adam, McIntyre; Erda by Schumann-Heink, Homer, Branzell, Forrester; Loge by van Dyck, Burgstaller, Burrian, Maison, Svanholm, Vinay, Ulfung; Alberich by Bispham, Goritz, Pechner, Mazura; the opera has also been conducted by Schalk,

Hertz, Bodansky, Leinsdorf, Szell, Stiedry, Ehrling. 97 perfs. in 40 seasons.

Legendary times. Deep in the river Rhine, the Rhinemaidens (s,s,ms) celebrate the Rhinegold, explaining to the amorous Nibelung dwarf Alberich (bar) that only he who renounces love can seize the gold and fashion an all-powerful ring. Frustrated by their teasing, he curses love and makes off with the gold. On a mountainous height, Wotan (bar), head of the gods, and his wife Fricka (ms) contemplate Valhalla, the castle just built for them by the giants Fasolt (bs) and Fafner (bs). As payment, Wotan has promised the giants Freia (s), goddess of love, on whose golden apples the gods' immortality depends, but he counts on the crafty Loge (t), god of fire, to get him out of the bargain. Loge tells the giants of the wealth Alberich has acquired through the power of the ring he has forged from the Rhinegold; they agree to accept the Nibelung's hoard as an alternative to Freia, meanwhile holding her hostage. Wotan and Loge descend to Nibelheim, where Alberich has enslaved his fellow Nibelungs. The gods trick him into displaying the powers of the Tarnhelm, forged by his brother Mime (t), which bestows invisibility or altered shape on its wearer; when Alberich turns himself into a toad, Wotan captures and binds him. Forced to yield his treasure, the dwarf places a curse on the ring: may it bring destruction to whoever possesses it. The giants return, demanding enough gold to hide Freia's form; with deepest reluctance, and only after the earth goddess Erda (c) prophesies the doom of the gods, Wotan hands over the ring to complete the ransom. In a quarrel over division of the spoils, Fafner kills Fasolt. The gods move across a rainbow bridge to Valhalla, as the cynical Loge reflects on their tainted power.

Die Walküre (The Valkyrie); opera in 3 acts. First perf., Munich, Court Opera, June 26, 1870: Stehle, T. Vogl, Kaufmann, Vogl, Kindermann, Bausewein, c. Wüllner. U.S. prem., N.Y., Academy of Music, Apr. 2, 1877: Pappenheim, Canissa, Listner, Bischoff, Preusser, Blum, c. Neuendorff. Met prem., Jan. 30, 1885: Materna, Seidl-Kraus, Brandt, Schott, Staudigl, Kögel, d. Schaeffer, Maeder/Dazian, p. Hock. Later Met productions: Dec. 20, 1913: Gadski, Fremstad, Matzenauer, Urlus, Braun, Ruysdael, c. Hertz, d. Kautsky, p. Horth; Dec. 18, 1935: Lawrence, Rethberg, Meisle, Melchior, Schorr, List, c. Bodanzky, d. Jorgulesco, p. Sachse; Jan. 13, 1948: Traubel, Bampton, Thorborg, Melchior, Janssen, Székely, c. Stiedry, d. Simonson/Schenck, p. Graf; Nov. 21, 1967: Nilsson, Janowitz, Ludwig, Vickers, Stewart, Ridderbusch, c. Karajan, d. Schneider-Siemssen/ Wakhevitch, p. Karajan; Sep. 22, 1986: Behrens, Altmeyer, Fassbaender, Hofmann, Estes, Haugland, c. Levine, d. Schneider-Siemssen/Langenfass, p. Schenk. Brünnhilde has also been sung at the Met by Lilli Lehmann, Nordica, Ternina, Fremstad, Kappel, Leider, Flagstad, Varnay, Mödl, Harshaw, Crespin; Sieglinde by Lilli Lehmann, Nordica, Eames, Gadski, Ternina, Jeritza, Müller, Lotte Lehmann, Flagstad, Traubel, Varnay, Harshaw, Rysanek, Crespin; Siegmund by Niemann, van Dyck, Burgstaller, Burrian, Svanholm, Vinay; Wotan by Fischer, van Rooy, Whitehill, Bohnen, Hines; Hunding by Mayr, Kipnis, Hotter, Frick, Macurdy; the opera has also been conducted by Seidl, Schalk, Hertz, Mahler, Leinsdorf, Szell, Mitropoulos, Böhm, Steinberg, Ehrling. 339 perfs. in 70 seasons.

After the end of *Rheingold*, Wotan sought out Erda to learn more about the doom she had predicted; she bore him nine daughters, the Valkyries, who gather fallen mortal heroes to arm Valhalla. Disguised as Wälse, Wotan fathered and abandoned two mortal children, the twins Siegmund and Sieglinde; fearing that Alberich may obtain the ring from Fafner but morally unable to intervene himself, he hopes that Siegmund, hardened by heroic suffering and nominally a free agent, will win it. At the opera's beginning, the weaponless Siegmund (t), fleeing a host of foes, collapses on the hearth of a forest hut, where he is found by Sieglinde (s). Her husband Hunding (bs) returns home; Siegmund had escaped from his kinsmen, and must face Hunding in mortal combat the next day. Sieglinde drugs her husband, and shows Siegmund a sword embedded in a tree in the hut, placed there by a strange wanderer (Wotan). Siegmund takes the sword, naming it "Nothung"; recognizing their kinship – and their love – the two rush out into the spring night. In the second act, Wotan (bar) yielding to the arguments of Fricka (ms), protector of marriage vows, and realizing that the gift of the sword makes Siegmund no longer a free agent, charges Brünnhilde (s), his favorite Valkyrie daughter, to aid the betrayed Hunding. But Brünnhilde, moved by the mortals' plight and aware of her father's thwarted hopes for Siegmund, disobeys and promises Siegmund victory in the battle. Wotan himself then intervenes, shattering Nothung with his spear; Hunding kills Siegmund, and Brünnhilde flees in terror, with Sieglinde and the fragments of Nothung. On the rock where the Valkyries gather, Brünnhilde tells Sieglinde that in her womb she bears Siegmund's son, the greatest of heroes, and sends her into the wild forests to escape Wotan's wrath. The god overtakes Brünnhilde and angrily denounces her betrayal, then, in supreme regret and anguish, strips his daughter of her godhood and casts over her a magical slumber. Yielding to her pleas, he puts a ring of fire around the rock, which only the bravest mortal can cross to claim Brünnhilde as his bride.

Siegfried; opera in 3 acts. First perf., Bayreuth, Festspielhaus, Aug. 16, 1876: Materna, Jaide, Unger, Schlosser, Betz, c. Richter. U.S. & Met prem., Nov. 9, 1887: Lilli Lehmann, Brandt, Alvary, Ferenczy, Fischer, c. Seidl, d. Kautsky, p. Habelmann. Later Met productions: Dec. 4, 1913: Matzenauer, Ober, Urlus, Reiss, Griswold, c. Hertz, d. Kautsky, p. Horth; Jan. 21, 1948: Traubel, Thorborg, Svanholm, Garris, Berglund, c. Stiedry, d. Simonson/Schenck, p. Graf; Nov. 17, 1972: Nilsson, Chookasian, Thomas, Stolze, Stewart, c. Leinsdorf, d. Schneider-Siemssen/Wakhevitch, p. Weber. Siegfried has also been sung at the Met by J. de Reszke, Burgstaller, Burrian, Melchior, Windgassen; Brünnhilde by Melba, Nordica, Ternina, Gadski, Fremstad, Easton, Larsén-Todsen, Kappel, Leider, Lawrence, Flagstad, Rethberg, Varnay, Harshaw; Erda by Schumann-Heink, Homer, Matzenauer, Branzell, Forrester; the Wanderer by E. de Reszke, van Rooy, Whitehill, Bohnen, Schorr, Janssen, Edelmann, London; the opera has also been conducted by Schalk, Mottl, Mahler, Bodanzky, Serafin, Szell, Stiedry, Ehrling. 181 perfs. in 55 seasons.

Alberich's brother Mime found Sieglinde in the forest; she died giving birth to her son Siegfried, whom Mime has raised in his forest dwelling, near the cave where Fafner, now transformed by the Tarnhelm into a dragon, guards his ring and hoard. When the opera begins, Mime (t) has failed to reforge the fragments of Nothung into a sword with which Siegfried (t) can kill Fafner. Wotan, disguised as the Wanderer (bar), visits Mime and predicts that the shards will be forged by a hero, who will also kill Mime. Siegfried returns, forges the sword himself and slays Fafner (bs). Mime plans to poison him, but a taste of the dragon's blood enables Siegfried to understand the

warnings of a Forest Bird (s), and he kills Mime. At the Bird's urging, he takes the ring and Tarnhelm, and sets off to find the sleeping Brünnhilde (s). Wotan, resigned to the fall of the gods foretold by Erda (ms), attempts to bar Siegfried's path, but Nothung shatters the god's spear, and Siegfried claims the initially reluctant Brünnhilde as his bride.

Götterdämmerung (The Twilight of the Gods); opera in prologue and 3 acts. First perf., Bayreuth, Festspielhaus, Aug. 17, 1876: Materna, Weckherlin, Jaide, Unger, Gura, Hill, Siehr, c. Richter. U.S. & Met prem., Jan. 25, 1888 (Norn and Waltraute scenes omitted): Lilli Lehmann, Seidl-Kraus, Niemann, Robinson, von Milde, Fischer, c. Seidl, p. Habelmann. Later Met productions: Feb. 19, 1914: Fremstad, Fornia, Ober, Berger, Weil, Goritz, Braun, c. Hertz, d. Kautsky, p. Horth; Jan. 29, 1948: Traubel, Stoska, Thorborg, Melchior, Janssen, Pechner, Ernster, c. Stiedry, d. Simonson/Schenck, p. Graf; Mar. 8, 1974: Nilsson, Rankin, Dunn, Thomas, Stewart, Rintzler, Rundgren, c. Kubelik, d. Schneider-Siemssen/Wakhevitch, p. Weber. Brünnhilde has also been sung at the Met by Nordica, Ternina, Gadski, Larsén-Todsen, Kappel, Leider, Flagstad, Lawrence, Varnay, Mödl, Hunter; Siegfried by Alvary, J. de Reszke, Burrian, Urlus, Svanholm, Vinay, Windgassen; Waltraute by Schumann-Heink, Homer, Matzenauer; Gunther by Schorr, Hotter; Hagen by E. de Reszke, Bohnen, List, Kipnis, Frick; the opera has also been conducted by Schalk, Toscanini, Bodanzky, Leinsdorf, Szell, Ehrling. 166 perfs. in 54 seasons.

On Brünnhilde's rock, the Norns (a,ms,s), weaving the fates of men and gods, are terrified to see their thread break. Siegfried (t) and Brünnhilde (s) arise at dawn; he gives her the ring and sets out down the Rhine in search of adventure. He soon falls among the Gibichungs, Gunther (bar), Gutrune (s), and their half-brother Hagen (bs), whose father was Alberich. Hagen lays a trap, inciting Gunther to lust for Brünnhilde without revealing that Siegfried has won her, but explaining that only Siegfried can pass through the magic fire to reach her. A drug makes Siegfried forget his former love and fall under the spell of the first woman he sees: Gutrune. Gunther agrees to their marriage, provided that Siegfried will fetch Brünnhilde as a bride for Gunther. Meanwhile, the Valkyrie Waltraute (ms) urges Brünnhilde to forestall the doom of the gods by returning the ring to the Rhinemaidens, but her sister refuses to part with the token of her love. Siegfried returns, disguised by the Tarnhelm as Gunther, and tears the ring from Brünnhilde's finger. He delivers her to Gunther, but when she then sees him in his own aspect, with the ring on his finger, she cries betrayal; he does not recognize or remember her. With the wronged woman's complicity, Hagen and Gunther plot Siegfried's death. During a hunt the next day, Siegfried, his memory restored by an antidote, narrates his youthful adventures and his wooing of Brünnhilde; Gunther realizes the deception, but when Siegfried turns his back, Hagen stabs him. Later, in a fight over the ring, Hagen kills Gunther as well, but, when he tries to take the ring from the dead hero's hand, it rises in defiance. Brünnhilde, recognizing that both she and Siegfried have been betrayed and understanding now the doom that has befallen the gods, orders a funeral pyre built for Siegfried, lights it, and rides her horse into the flames, which burn the Gibichung hall. The Rhine overflows and its daughters reclaim the ring, now purged of Alberich's curse. In the heavens, Valhalla is seen ablaze; a new order of love, rather than power, is to rule the world.

Changing styles for Die Walküre, Act 1

(*Top*) (Munich, 1870). Design for the world premiere, by Angelo Quaglio

(*Left*) (Bayreuth, 1876). Model for the first complete *Ring* by Joseph Hoffmann

(*Right*) (Met, 1967). Designed by Günther Schneider-Siemssen, produced by Herbert von Karajan. Gwyneth Jones and Jon Vickers

(Right) (Bayreuth, 1979). Designed by Richard Peduzzi, produced by Patrice Chéreau. Jeannine Altmeyer and Peter Hofmann

(Below) (Met, 1986). Designed by Günther Schneider-Siemssen, produced by Otto Schenk. Peter Hofmann and Jeannine Altmeyer

BRÜNNHILDE IN
THE RING *Birgit Nilsson*

First musical impressions may be deceptive, especially when you listen to Wagner. Watching my first *Ring* cycle in Stockholm, I thought, "This is rather long. Does it ever end?" You see, even budding dramatic sopranos need ample preparation before tackling this colossal masterpiece.

When two sopranos fell sick in 1949, the Stockholm Opera asked me to sing both Sieglinde and the *Siegfried* Brünnhilde. Given fourteen sleepless nights to learn both roles, I stuggled with a mediocre maestro and a stage director who ignored my Sieglinde and flirted outrageously with the *Walküre* Brünnhilde. After one terrible rehearsal, I ran sobbing out of the theater and decided to end my career. The intendant calmed me down, and mercifully, I scored a big success in both roles. In 1954, an older Brünnhilde in Stockholm retired and I did my first *Götterdämmerung*. The next year, I dropped my Rhinemaiden roles, tearfully gave up Sieglinde, and switched to the *Walküre* Brünnhilde.

After singing the *Ring* all over the world, I learned to love Brünnhilde. Hurling out "Ho-jo-to-ho," this young goddess starts out in *Die Walküre* as a dynamic extension of Wotan's will. Discovering the bittersweet power of human love, she resolves to rescue Siegmund and Sieglinde from her father's fury. Sieglinde escapes, but the god allows his only son to be killed by Hunding and sentences Brünnhilde to a magical sleep. Fighting to the very end, she wins the right to be awakened by the world's greatest hero – Siegfried. When a great Wotan holds you in his arms and sings, "Farewell, my bravest child," it is almost impossible to blink back the tears. With Theo Adam or Thomas Stewart, the father-daughter scenes became tender, poignant, and emotionally scorching.

As comedian Anna Russell liked to remind us, the woman Siegfried wakes up is his aunt. But for Brünnhilde, this *Ring* opera is no laughing matter. Even if you sing as beautifully as ten angels, you can't compete with that incredibly vibrant "awakening" music in the orchestra. And that's only the beginning. Brünnhilde starts the scene as a goddess, shows her maternal feelings towards Siegfried, and ends the scene as a passionate lover. She never stops singing – and, believe me, no Brünnhilde looks forward to that last high C. But the public expects the note, and fortunately I never missed it.

Finally, *Götterdämmerung*, in which Brünnhilde's role is longer than in *Die Walküre* and *Siegfried* combined – and embraces the widest musical and dramatic range. Whew! The opening duet is thrilling. Wearing Siegfried's ring, Brünnhilde sends her lover off to "glorious deeds." Radiantly happy, she tosses off a high C that is somehow easier than the one in *Siegfried*. Rejecting her sister Waltraute's plea to return the ring to the Rhinemaidens, Brünnhilde holds fast to her romantic illusions. But the drugged Siegfried snatches the ring from her and brutally forces Brünnhilde back into her cave. It's always a terrifying moment in the theater.

Act II is equally hair-raising, and it is so taxing to perform. After Gunther parades his unwilling bride like a battered war trophy, the betrayed woman swears vengeance against Siegfried. Erupting like a volcano, Brünnhilde transforms her former love into red-hot hatred. Playing with her feelings, Hagen discovers Siegfried's secret: only a spear-thrust in the back will kill him.

In the Immolation Scene, Brünnhilde towers over everybody. Once again, she becomes the wise goddess, who now redeems the world through

fire and love. "No one ever loved more intensely than you did," she sings softly to her dead lover. Throwing the torch onto Siegfried's funeral pyre, she prepares to ride Grane into the flames and at last return the ring to the Rhinemaidens. The vocal line surges higher and higher, and suddenly you feel ten feet tall. It is an incomparable experience.

Although Wagner is not dangerous to your health, I had to watch my step in certain *Ring* stagings. During one Met *Götterdämmerung* rehearsal, I tumbled down a rickety staircase and dislocated my right shoulder. Exiting Siegfried's cave several nights later, I greeted my boyfriend with one arm in a sling. The public accepted this latest fad in Wagnerian fashion, and two years later my wound finally healed.

In one Florence *Siegfried*, I almost lost my clothes. My dress had just returned from the cleaner, and without suspecting that the hooks might be looser than usual, I sat up on Brünnhilde's rock and sang, "Hail to thee, sun!" Immediately, I felt the back of the robe split open all the way down to my waist. Thank goodness, Wolfgang Windgassen was my eagle-eyed Siegfried. While I desperately clutched the fabric and sang my lines, that marvelous artist threw his arms around me and refastened my hooks. I narrowly avoided unveiling Italy's first R-rated Brünnhilde!

My first Stockholm *Götterdämmerung* became a true horse opera. I forgot to bring sugar cubes, and my skittish Grane kept rearing its legs throughout the Immolation Scene. Circling back and forth, I calmly patted the animal, sang my music, and saved us both from plunging into the orchestra pit. Backstage, one fan gushed, "Your Brünnhilde was OK, but what fantastic horsemanship!" A sense of humor is a precious gift, and provided that you don't take yourself too seriously, it helps you to stay healthy – and to sing Richard Wagner's magnificent music.

I have sung Wagner in many wonderful theaters, but Bayreuth was always a special setting for my *Ring* performances. Yes, that famous covered pit can be treacherous for singers; from the auditorium, the orchestral sound appears damped, but the hood throws it towards the stage. We feel swamped by a sonic tidal wave and, while fighting this illusion, try not to push our voices over that huge orchestra. The management asked me to sing Brünnhilde on consecutive nights, but I refused, and they stretched out the schedule. You might sing a brilliant *Siegfried* duet on Tuesday night, but if you wake up exhausted, no one thanks you for Wednesday's weak *Götterdämmerung*.

But the 1965 Bayreuth *Ring* also offered two special colleagues: Wieland Wagner and Karl Böhm. Some critics questioned Böhm's almost Mozartean tempos, but the maestro knew how to shape the music with great energy and zest. "Slow" does not necessarily mean "better" in Wagner, and under Böhm's light baton singers could phrase expressively without ever running out of breath. *Ring* conductors, take note! I also profited from my performances with Herbert von Karajan, Georg Solti, and (in concert) James Levine.

Wieland gave me priceless acting lessons. "It's silly to run around, make ridiculous gestures, and contort your face like a wounded animal. You cannot compete with Wagner's music. Learn how to be still, and express your feelings with simplicity and honesty." In Wieland's superbly lit productions, we acted with our faces and with our hearts.

Rinuccini, Ottavio. Librettist; b. Florence, Jan. 20, 1562; d. Florence, Mar. 28, 1621. A musical humanist from a noble family, he collaborated with Corsi and Peri on *Dafne*, with Peri on *Euridice*, and later with Monteverdi on *Arianna*.

Rip Van Winkle. Opera in 3 acts by Bristow; libretto by J.H. Wainwright, after Washington Irving's story.

First perf., N.Y., Niblo's Garden, Sep. 27, 1855.

The music of Bristow's first opera, based on Irving's famous story of Rip and his 20-year sleep, is strongly influenced by German models, especially Mendelssohn.

Rise and Fall of the City of Mahagonny, The. See *Aufstieg und Fall der Stadt Mahagonny*.

Risurrezione (Resurrection). Opera in 4 acts by Alfano; libretto by Cesare Hanau, after Tolstoy's novel.

First perf., Turin, Vittorio Emanuele, Nov. 30, 1904: Magliulo, Scandiani, Mieli, Ceresoli, c. Serafin. U.S. prem., Chicago, Auditorium, Dec. 31, 1925 (in Fr.): Garden, Claessens, Ansseau, Baklanoff, c. Moranzoni.

A verismo score successful abroad as a vehicle for Mary Garden. In 19th-c. Russia, ruined by the events consequent on her seduction and abandonment by Prince Dmitri (t), Katiusha (s) is sentenced to Siberian servitude; though the repentant prince wins her a pardon, she rejects him, seeking redemption in renunciation.

Ritchard, Cyril. Producer; b. Sydney, Australia, Dec. 1, 1898; d. Chicago, Dec. 18, 1977. Began career in musical comedy and appeared frequently on Broadway as a skilled comedian. For the Met he directed *Barbiere* (1954, also appearing as mute servant), *Contes d'Hoffmann* (1955), *Périchole* (1956, also appearing as Don Andrès), *Nozze* (1959), and *Zigeunerbaron* (1959).

ritornello. In baroque opera, the instrumental section that introduces and recurs in an aria.

Ritorno d'Ulisse in Patria, Il (The Return of Ulysses to His Country). Opera in prologue and 5 acts by Monteverdi; libretto by G. Badoaro.

First perf., Venice, San Cassiano, Feb. 1641. U.S. prem., Washington, D.C., Opera, Jan. 18, 1974: von Stade, Walker, Stilwell, Gramm, c. Gibson.

Rediscovered in 1923, this eloquent score is now generally accepted as the work of Monteverdi.

In and around ancient Greece. Ulisse (t) has still not returned from the Trojan War, and his wife Penelope (c), surrounded by suitors, laments his absence. Unknown to her, he has found his way to Ithaca, and Minerva (s) encourages him to return to his palace. After a reunion with his son Telemaco (ms), Ulisse enters the palace disguised as a beggar. When Penelope declares she will marry the suitor who can draw Ulisse's bow, the "beggar" is the only one who can do it; he kills the suitors and is joyfully recognized by Penelope.

Robbins, Julien. Bass; b. Harrisburg, Pa., Nov. 14, 1950. Studied at Philadelphia Academy of Vocal Arts and with Nicola Moscona; debut as Samuele (*Ballo*), Philadelphia, 1976. Met debut as King (*Aida*), Oct. 29, 1979; his later Met roles include Don Fernando (*Fidelio*), Gremin, Ramfis (*Aida*), and Colline. Other appearances in Chicago, Miami, Santa Fe, and Washington.

Robert le Diable (Robert the Devil). Opera in 5 acts by Meyerbeer; libretto by Scribe and Germain Delavigne.

First perf., Paris, Opéra, Nov. 21, 1831: Dorus-Gras, Cinti-Damoreau, Nourrit, Lafond, Levasseur, c. Habeneck. U.S. prem., N.Y., Park, Apr. 7, 1834 (in Eng.). Met prem., Nov. 19, 1883 (in Ital.): Fursch-Madi, Valleria, Stagno, Capoul, Mirabella, c. Vianesi, d. J. Fox, Schaeffer, Maeder, Thompson/Ascoli, Dazian. 3 perfs. in 1 season.

The opera that established Meyerbeer's international reputation and compositional style for years to come. In 13th-c. Sicily, Robert, Duke of Normandy (t), son of Bertram (bs) – the devil in disguise (and model for Gounod's Méphistophélès) – loves Princess Isabelle of Sicily (s). However, he is repeatedly led astray by Bertram and nearly loses her, saving his soul with the aid of his foster-sister Alice (s).

Roberto Devereux. Opera in 3 acts by Donizetti; libretto by Cammarano, after Jacques-Arsène Ancelot's *Élisabeth d'Angleterre* and Romani's libretto for Mercadante's *Il Conte d'Essex*.

First perf., Naples, San Carlo, Oct. 28, 1837: Ronzi-de Begnis, Granchi, Basadonna, Barroilhet. U.S. prem., N.Y., Astor Place, Jan. 15, 1849.

England, 1598. Returned from an Irish campaign, Roberto Devereux, Earl of Essex (t), is insufficiently ardent towards Queen Elisabetta (Elizabeth I, s), who has been resisting efforts to change him with treason. Devereux secretly loves Sara (ms), who during his absence was forced to marry the Duke of Nottingham (bar). The Queen has given Devereux a ring, with her promise to come to his aid if it is presented to her; he gives it to Sara, and receives in return a blue scarf. Sentenced by the council to execution, Devereux is disarmed and searched; when the Queen sees the blue scarf embroidered with Sara's initials, she signs Devereux's death sentence, believing him to be a faithless lover as well as a traitor. In a letter, Devereux asks Sara to take the ring to the Queen; detained by her husband, she arrives too late. The Queen, who was prepared to forgive Devereux, blames Sara for the delay, orders the arrest of the Nottinghams, and prepares to abdicate.

Robinson, Anastasia. Soprano, later contralto; b. Italy, c. 1692, of English parents; d. Southampton, Apr. 1755. Studied with Sandoni and the Baroness Lindenheim, London; first appearances in private salons, then joined Handel's company. After an illness in 1718, she sang as a contralto. She created Handel's Oriana (*Amadigi*), Zenobia (*Radamisto*), Matilda (*Ottone*), Elmira (*Floridante*), Cornelia (*Giulio Cesare*), also works by Bononcini.

Robinson, Francis. Manager and broadcaster; b. Henderson, Ky., Apr. 28, 1910; d. New York, May 14, 1980. After attending Vanderbilt U., he worked in journalism and radio, then as a theatrical press representative and tour manager. From 1946, he managed the Met's tours, and under Bing became head of box office (1950–62), press director (1954–77), and assistant manager (1952–76). His personal charm and capacious memory for facts and anecdotes made him an ideal ambassador for the Met in tour cities. In 1960, he began a series of biographical intermission features on the Met radio broadcasts, and later served as host on Met telecasts; he was the author of two books, *Caruso: His Life in Pictures* (1957) and *Celebration* (1979).

Robinson, Gail. Soprano; b. Meridian, Miss., Aug. 7, 1946. Studied with Mrs. J. Norvell, Memphis State U., and with Robley Lawson; debut as Lucia, Memphis, 1967. Met debut as a Boy in *Zauberflöte*, Jan. 10, 1970; other Met roles include Rosina, Marie (*Fille*), Oscar, Gilda, Adina, Gretel, Lucia, and Ilia (*Idomeneo*). Has also sung in Hamburg, Berlin, and Munich.

Rodelinda. Opera in 3 acts by Handel; libretto by A. Salvi (originally for Perti's 1710 opera), revised by Nicola Haym.

First perf., London, Haymarket, Feb. 13, 1725: Cuzzoni, Dotti, Senesino, Pacini, Borrosini, Boschi, U.S. prem., Northampton, Mass. (Smith College), May 9, 1931 (in Eng.).

One of Handel's most consistently inspired scores, set in Milan. The conflicts created when Grimoaldo (t) attempts to usurp the throne of Bertarido (a) are resolved when Bertarido saves Grimoaldo's life. Rodelinda (s), Bertarido's wife, twice suffers the grief of believing her husband killed.

Rodzinski, Artur. Conductor; b. Spalato [now Split], Dalmatia, Jan. 1, 1892; d. Boston, Nov. 27, 1958. After study with Schalk in Vienna, debut in Lwów (*Ernani*, 1920); worked at Warsaw Opera (1921–25). Taught at Curtis Institute (1925–29); conductor, Los Angeles Philharmonic (1929–33), Cleveland Orchestra (1933–1942), including U.S. premiere of *Lady Macbeth of Mtsensk*; music director, N.Y. Philharmonic (1942–47), Chicago Symphony (1947–48). Thereafter, though in ill health, active mainly in Italy, where he led the Western premiere of *War and Peace*; *Tristan* at Chicago Lyric, 1958. A strong but difficult personality, Rodzinski was an energetic, often dramatic interpreter.

Rogers, Bernard. Composer; b. New York, Feb. 4, 1893; d. Rochester, N.Y., May 24, 1968. Studied with Farwell, Bloch, Bridge, and Boulanger; taught at Eastman School, Rochester (1929–67). His operas, in a conservative idiom, include *The Marriage of Aude* (1931); *The Warrior* (1947); and *The Veil* (1950).

Roi de Lahore, Le (The King of Lahore). Opera in 5 acts by Massenet; libretto by Louis Gallet, after the Hindu epic *Mahabharata*.

First perf., Paris, Opéra, Apr. 27, 1877: Joséphine de Reszke, Salomon, Lassalle, c. Deldevez. U.S. prem., New Orleans, French Opera House, Dec. 1883. Met prem., Feb. 29, 1924: Reinhardt, Lauri-Volpi, de Luca, c. Hasselmans, d. Anisfeld, p. Wymetal. 5 perfs. in 1 season.

One of Massenet's first international successes. In 11th-c. India, King Alim (t) is fatally wounded by Scindia (bar), his rival for the love of the priestess Sitá (s); reincarnated as a beggar, he dies again at the moment of his beloved's death.

Roi d'Ys, Le (The King of Ys). Opera in 3 acts by Lalo; libretto by Edouard Blau, after a Breton legend.

First perf., Paris, Opéra-Comique, May 7, 1888: Deschamps-Jehin, Simmonet, Talazac, Bouvet, c, Danbé. U.S. prem., New Orleans, French Opera House, Jan. 23, 1890. Met prem., Jan. 5, 1922: Ponselle, Alda, Gigli, Danise, c. Wolff, d. Urban, p. Thewman. 5 perfs, in 1 season.

A non-Wagnerian treatment of supernatural legend. The princess Margared (ms), jealous of the love of her sister Rozenn (s) and the warrior Mylio (t), opens the flood-gates to let the sea drown the city of Ys. Only when she confesses and throws herself into the sea are the waters calmed.

Roi Malgré Lui, Le (The King in Spite of Himself). Opera in 3 acts by Chabrier; libretto by Emile de Najac and Paul Burani, revised by Jean Richepin and the composer, after a comedy by François Ancelot.

First perf., Paris, Opéra-Comique, May 18, 1887: Isaac, Mézéray, Bouvet, Fugère, c. Danbé. U.S. prem., Williamstown, Mass. (Williams College), Nov. 16, 1972 (concert perf.). U.S. stage prem, N.Y., Juilliard American Opera Center, Nov. 18, 1976 (in Eng.).

The ebullience of Chabrier's music is dampened by the plot's complexities. Henri de Valois (bar), unwilling to become king of Poland in 1574, in disguise joins those plotting his downfall, but is eventually prevailed upon to remain King.

Rolandi, Gianna. Soprano; b. New York, Aug. 16, 1952. Studied with mother and at Curtis, Philadelphia; debut as Olympia, N.Y.C. Opera, 1975, later singing Lucia and Handel's Cleopatra. Since her Met debut as Sophie (Dec. 26, 1979), she has also sung Olympia, Stravinsky's Nightingale, and Zerbinetta. Debuts at Glyndebourne (1981) and Santa Fe (1982).

Roller, Alfred. Designer; b. Brünn [now Brno], Moravia, Oct. 2, 1864; d. Vienna, June 12, 1935. A member of the Vienna Sezession (1890), he was commissioned by Mahler to design *Tristan* for the Vienna Court Opera (1903) and became chief scenic artist there (1903–09, 1918–34). His 1904 Vienna *Fidelio* came to the Met with Mahler (1907); his 1905 *Don Giovanni*, using movable elements between two towers, was widely emulated. Also associated with Reinhardt and Strauss, he designed the premieres of *Rosenkavalier* (Dresden, 1911) and *Frau* (Vienna, 1919).

Roman, Stella [Florica Vierica Alma Stela Blasu]. Soprano; b. Cluj, Romania, Mar. 25, 1904. Studied in Cluj, Bucharest, and in Rome with Baldassare-Tedeschi; debut in Piacenza, 1932. La Scala debut as Empress (*Frau*), 1940. Met debut as Aida, Jan. 1, 1941; in 10 seasons, sang 75 perfs. of 12 roles, including Leonora (*Trovatore*), Desdemona, Amelia, Gioconda, and Tosca.

romance (Fr.; Ital., **romanza**; Ger., **Romanze**). Terms variously used for relatively simple, introspective arias.

Romani, Felice. Librettist; b. Genoa, Jan. 31, 1788; d. Moneglia, Jan. 28, 1865. A critic and editor in Milan, his first librettos were written in 1815 for Mayr, and he was quickly in demand throughout Italy. Prolific and versatile but notoriously lazy, Romani furnished notable librettos to Rossini (*Turco in Italia*), Donizetti (*Elisir, Anna Bolena, Lucrezia Borgia*), and especially Bellini (*Pirata, Norma, Beatrice di Tenda*). His librettos are based on previously existing works, often French plays or British Romantic novels.

Romanov, Boris. Choreographer; b. St. Petersburg, Mar. 22, 1891; d. New York, Jan. 30, 1957. Danced at Maryinsky Theater, with Pavlova, and with Diaghilev's Ballet Russes; ballet master at Teatro Colón, Buenos Aires (1928–34). At the Met, he was ballet master (1938–50) and choreographed many opera ballets.

Rome. Italian city, capital since 1871. Opera in Rome was originally staged for aristocrats in private theaters, beginning with Agazzari's *Eumelio* (1606). The Teatro Torinona (or Torre di Nona), which opened in 1670 with

Rome Opera House

Baths of Caracalla, Rome

Barbiere and Verdi's *Due Foscari* (1844) and *Battaglia di Legnano* (1849) were first heard. Later, the Teatro Costanzi (opened 1880) became the operatic center, site of the premieres of *Cavalleria* (1890) and *Tosca* (1900); refurbished and reopened in 1928 as the Teatro Reale dell'Opera, it is now called the Teatro dell'Opera. During the Fascist period it enjoyed the patronage of Mussolini, and was directed by Gino Marinuzzi (1928–34) and Tullio Serafin (1934–43); after the war, under Massimo Bogianckino (1963–68), it again earned international attention. Gianluigi Gelmetti is the current artistic director, Gustav Kuhn the music director. Since 1938, an outdoor summer season, featuring spectacular productions, is given at the Baths of Caracalla.

Roméo et Juliette. Opera in 5 acts by Gounod; libretto by Jules Barbier and Michel Carré, after Shakespeare's tragedy.

First perf., Paris, Lyrique, Apr. 27, 1867: Miolan-Carvalho, Michot, Barré, Cazaux, c. Deloffre. U.S. prem., N.Y., Academy of Music, Nov. 15, 1867 (in Ital.): Hauk, Pancani, Dominici, Medici, c. Bergman. Met prem., Dec. 14, 1891: Eames, J. de Reszke, Martapoura, E. de Reszke, c. Vianesi. Later Met productions: Jan. 13, 1911: Farrar, Smirnov, Gilly, Rothier, c. Podesti, d. Stroppa, Sala, Burghart & Co., J. Fox/Palanti; Nov. 25, 1922: Bori, Gigli, de Luca, Rothier, c. Hasselmans, d. Urban, p. Thewman; Sep. 19, 1967: Freni, Corelli, Reardon, Macurdy, c. Molinari-Pradelli, d. Gérard, p. Deiber. Roméo has also been sung at the Met by Salignac, Saléza, Alvarez, Rousselière, Johnson, Thill, Crooks, Jobin, Bjoerling, Gedda, Domingo, Kraus; Juliette by Melba, Sembrich, Adams, Ackté, Mario, Galli-Curci, Moore, Norena, Sayão, Pilou, Moffo, Blegen, Malfitano; Mercutio by Campanari, Tibbett, Brownlee, Singher; Frère Laurent by Plançon, Rothier, Pinza, Moscona, Diaz, Plishka. 196 perfs. in 37 seasons.

A melodious, well-proportioned and sentimental opera of similar cut to *Faust*, and at one time nearly as popular.

Renaissance Verona. At a masked ball given by her father Capulet (bar), Juliette (s) meets and falls in love with Roméo (t), scion of her family's enemies, the Montagues. When Juliette's cousin Tybalt (t) recognizes Roméo, the latter flees, returning to stand under Juliette's balcony. They pledge their love, and the next day are married by Frère Laurent (bs), who hopes to make peace between their families. Roméo's friend Mercutio (bar) is killed in a street fight by Tybalt; the enraged Roméo kills Tybalt in revenge and is banished from Verona. By night, the lovers exchange farewells in Juliette's bedchamber. To avert the marriage Capulet has arranged for Juliette with Paris (bar), Laurent gives her a potion that simulates death. Returning to Verona unaware of this plan, Roméo believes her dead and poisons himself in her tomb. She awakens and they are briefly reunited; learning of the poison, Juliette stabs herself and the lovers die in each other's arms.

Rondine, La (The Swallow). Opera in 3 acts by Puccini; libretto by Giuseppe Adami, translated and adapted from a German libretto by Alfred Willner and Heinz Reichert.

First perf., Monte Carlo, Mar. 27, 1917: dalla Rizza, Ferraris, Schipa, Dominici, Huberdeau, c. Marinuzzi. U.S. & Met prem., Mar. 10, 1928: Bori, Fleischer, Gigli, Tokatyan, Ludikar, c. Bellezza, d. Urban, p. Wymetal. 13 perfs. in 4 seasons.

A bittersweet, melodious score originally conceived as a Viennese operetta project; set in Second-Empire Paris.

Cavalli's *Scipione Africano*, was the first public opera house; destroyed and rebuilt a number of times until 1795, when it became known as the Teatro Apollo (demolished 1889), it housed the premieres of Verdi's *Trovatore* (1853) and *Ballo in Maschera* (1859). Other theaters included the Teatro Caprinaca (private from 1679, open to public 1695–1881), which featured first serious, later comic opera; the Teatro delle Dame (built 1717), devoted to opera seria; and the Teatro Valle (opened 1727), which had the first performance of Rossini's *Cenerentola*. In the Teatro Argentina (opened 1732, still standing), Rossini's

Magda (s), lover of the wealthy banker Rambaldo (bar), decides for adventure to go out on the town dressed as a middle-class girl, and meets Ruggero (t), a young man from the country; they fall in love and go off to live together, but when he proposes marriage she insists that she cannot bring her checkered past into his family, and returns to her former life. Meanwhile, Magda's maid Lisette (s) has also gone out for a fling, borrowing one of her mistress' fine dresses and beginning a liaison with the poet and parlor cynic Prunier (t); after a disastrous attempt to launch Lisette as an actress, they too return to the *status quo ante.*

rondo. In addition to the instrumental form, in the late 18th c. this term (often spelled *rondò*) designated an aria in two sections, respectively slow and fast, each usually repeated (Fiordiligi's "Per pietà, ben mio" in *Così* is an example).

Rorem, Ned. Composer; b. Richmond, Ind., Oct. 23, 1923. Studied with Leo Sowerby at American Conservatory, Chicago, at Northwestern U., Curtis Institute, and Juilliard in N.Y., also privately with Thomson and Copland, and with Honegger in Paris. In addition to numerous songs and other vocal works, his operas include *A Childhood Miracle* (1955), *The Robbers* (1958), *Miss Julie* (1965), and *Bertha* (1973).

Rosbaud, Hans. Conductor; b. Graz, Austria, July 22, 1895; d. Lugano, Switzerland, Dec. 29, 1962. As director of Frankfurt Radio Orchestra (1928–37) and Southwest German Radio Orchestra (Baden-Baden) from 1948 until his death, a champion of advanced contemporary repertory. He led the radio (Hamburg) and stage (Zurich)

Roméo et Juliette – (1967). Designed by Rolf Gérard, produced by Paul-Émile Deiber. Mirella Freni and Franco Corelli

Der Rosenkavalier – (1913). Frieda Hempel and Margarete Ober

premieres of Schoenberg's *Moses und Aron*, and was the first music director of the Aix-en-Provence festival, where his Mozart proved him a master of orchestral clarity and classical balance.

Roselle [Gyenge], **Anne.** Soprano; b. Budapest, Mar. 20, 1894. Trained in America, and sponsored by Scotti; debut as Musetta, Met, Dec. 4, 1920; in 2 seasons, sang 23 perfs. of 5 roles, then toured with Scotti's company as Butterfly and Tosca. After further study in Italy, sang Turandot in Dresden (1926), her signature role; sang Marie in first American *Wozzeck*, Philadelphia, 1931.

Rosenkavalier, Der (The Cavalier of the Rose). Opera in 3 acts by R. Strauss; libretto by Hofmannsthal.
First perf., Dresden, Jan. 26, 1911: Siems, Nast, von der Osten, Perron, Scheidemantel, c. Schuch, d. Roller, p. Reinhardt. U.S. & Met prem., Dec. 9, 1913: Hempel, Case, Ober, Goritz, Weil, c. Hertz, d. Kautsky & Roller, p. Hörth. Later Met productions: Feb. 6, 1956 ("revised"): Della Casa, Gueden, Stevens, Edelmann, Herbert, c. Kempe, d. Gérard, p. Graf; Jan. 23, 1969: Rysanek, Grist, Ludwig, Berry, Knoll, c. Böhm, d. O'Hearn, p. Merrill. The Marschallin has also been sung at the Met by Kurt, Easton, Lotte Lehmann, Kappel, Steber, Crespin, Schwarzkopf, Ludwig, Lear, G. Jones, Tomowa-Sintow, Te Kanawa, Söderström; Sophie by Schumann, Rethberg, Mario, Steber, Berger, Peters, Söderström, Rothenberger, Raskin, Popp, Blegen, Mathis, Battle; Octavian by Jeritza, Müller, Olszewska, Thorborg, Novotná, Töpper, Della Casa, Lear, Minton, Fassbaender, Troyanos, Baltsa; Ochs by Bender, Bohnen, Mayr, List, Kipnis, Haugland, Moll. Conductors include Bodanzky, Leinsdorf, Szell, Rudolf, Busch, Reiner, Maazel, Schippers, Levine. 251 perfs. in 41 seasons.
Rosenkavalier, fruit of Strauss' declared intention to write a "Mozart opera," poignantly blends a story of innocent youthful love with a swirl of sophisticated Viennese high and low life. The composer gave full play to his gift of sensuous writing for combined female voices,

(continued p.310)

DER ROSENKAVALIER
Elisabeth Schwarzkopf

The characters in *Rosenkavalier* are the truest human portraits you can find.
They have an impact on every individual in every group – young females,
young males, the middle-aged, old people who once were young – they are
all touched, thinking of their past or their future. My husband Walter
Legge always maintained that the Marschallin is the female equivalent of
Hans Sachs in Wagner's *Meistersinger*, and so she is in her way. The
Countess in *Capriccio* is a different thing: that opera hasn't much to do with
the development of character. You can treat it emotionally, but it isn't *real*
emotion. *Capriccio* deals with the question of a singer's profession (words or
music?), which has become the theme of my career, but *Rosenkavalier* is
about coming to grips with life.

They say the Marschallin is thirty-three, which at that time meant
"beyond repair." She is maturing mentally, learning how to come to grips
with the facts of life in a light way. That is something I had to develop.
The turning point is looking into the mirror in the Act I monologue. You
can't at that moment treat it intellectually: that is all wrong. As an educated
aristocrat, you don't let yourself go until the very end of the act. Till then,
you're looking it in the face – namely, in the mirror.

Karajan in Act I wanted me not to cry, but in my later performances I
did. The audience would realize, just at the close of the curtain, that tears
are there. Once in Vienna I had a terrible experience, when I was singing
the Marschallin opposite Irmgard Seefried doing her first Octavian. I
suddenly let myself be moved by a private thought, and I started crying,
thinking very unprofessionally. That should never happen on stage, and I
got the punishment right then and there. Mascara in those days wasn't
waterproof, and it started running, continuing right until the end of the act.
It forced me to play the Marschallin as a weeping willow, which she is not.
I hated every moment of it: "What *will* they think?" As Walter said, you
must make the public cry and not yourself.

The Marschallin came at the right time of my singing career. Sopranos
who sing Mozart also have the possibility of singing the Marschallin sooner
or later. It goes with that Countess Almaviva type of voice. She may be
one of the characters in *Rosenkavalier* taken directly from *Figaro* into
Strauss, but the development of the character is so different that I keep
them quite distinct. It was Karajan who said to me after so many
Countesses and Sophies, "Now, my dear, it is time for you to do it. You
are the type, you have the mind for it, and you have the vocal inflections
of a true lieder singer." I can hear Walter saying, too, "You need a
conductor who keeps the orchestra so far down that even a light voice can
get those inflections through." So they persuaded me.

Walter guided me in the vocal inflections. He made me listen to the
Lotte Lehmann recording over and over again, but would say, "This you
cannot take from Lehmann. You haven't got the voice for it. You haven't
got the middle for this kind of bra-less enthusiasm. In many instances you
will have to substitute elegance for enthusiasm." And that is what I did. I
also studied the behavior of aristocratic Viennese women. I think I always
had elegance in my singing, even before I met Walter, through Maria
Ivogün, my teacher, and Michael Raucheisen, her accompanist husband. It
tallied with Walter's idea of the Marschallin. He had known very well the
coloratura soprano Frieda Hempel, the first Marschallin in Berlin and at the
Met, and he knew what a light voice could do – and that I had the mind
and the acting ability for it.

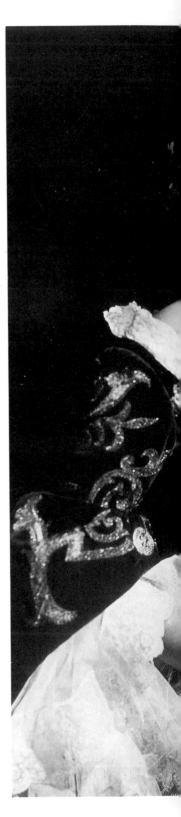

All my life, I was trained vocally, not for cutting through an orchestra, but for carrying over, and that is what made it possible to convey inflections that would never had been heard had I tried to cut through. Above all, I had the great luck to have conductors who liked my voice and inflections, and took the orchestra down so that they could be heard. Before the performances at La Scala, we rehearsed with Karajan for four weeks; he supervised everything, every piano rehearsal, which generally he would play himself. Only a few things had to be modified in the light of stage experience. I had to learn to project the private gestures suggested in Hofmannsthal's libretto, and adapt them to the distance and timing of a big house, simplifying them and slowing them down. Walter would send me notes after the first act telling me what was wrong, including hand and arm movements, too fast or too slow.

I also learned a great deal from the actress Elisabeth Bergner when we did the *Rosenkavalier* film with Karajan in Salzburg. There was only one take of each scene, and we were never shown any rushes, which was very unfair. We would then have been able to adjust details like wigs and makeup. We did the music in two three-hour sessions, and then next day we did the filming, miming and half-singing to the recording. It was Bergner who sidled up and said, "Watch the *Übergänge*" (transitions). I didn't quite know what she meant at first, but I did use it in later performances. You have to start thinking the next phrase, even though you are still in the music of the last phrase. It's difficult, cross-thinking all the time, but it works.

I sang the Marschallin under Karl Böhm in Salzburg. Apart from George Szell – the singer's conductor of all time, who never conducted *Rosenkavalier* for me – he was the easiest to work with. With Böhm, we never even had a single discussion. One never even had to look down at the conductor, and there were never any discrepancies. It was as though we had been doing it for a hundred years. With Karajan, you had to be on your toes all the time.

In *Rosenkavalier*, if you are in any way musical, you know instinctively when the changes come from conversational style to full singing. In Strauss, you cannot ever lapse into something like Mozart's *recitativo secco*, close to a speaking voice albeit on the right pitches at their right length. Strauss' conversational passages have to be sung in lieder style – they have to seem like conversations, with colorings as in lieder singing. The Marschallin's greatest moment isn't really sung at all: "Ich weiss auch nix, gar nix," before the third-act trio. Any Marschallin should be able to sing the opening of the trio *piano* as written. It is done otherwise, but it shouldn't be! Then there is "Die Zeit, die ist ein sonderbar Ding" in Act I, which with Karajan I could whisper, barely suggesting the notes.

My osprey feather, my white wig, and various other items of costume have all been imitated since my day. Also the way I went out in Act III with a hesitation over stretching my hand back to Octavian without looking. (Acting with the back can sometimes be done.) Imitation is the best compliment. But the greatest compliment I ever had was from the company of the Theater in the Josefstadt in Vienna, who saw a television performance I did in Wiesbaden; they sent me a letter saying, "We saw you, and have now learned a great deal about how to play Hofmannsthal."

and in the Marschallin he created one of opera's great, many-faceted characters.

Vienna, early 1740s. The Princess von Werdenberg, or Marschallin (s), is having an affair with the young Count Octavian Rofrano (ms). Early one morning, when the Marschallin's boorish country cousin Baron Ochs (bs) arrives unexpectedly, Octavian masquerades as a chambermaid, "Mariandel," arousing the licentious nobleman's attention. Ochs informs the Marschallin of his forthcoming marriage to Sophie von Faninal (s), and his need of a cavalier to present the traditional silver rose to her. At the Marschallin's mischievous suggestion, Octavian is chosen to bear the rose. When he presents it to Sophie, the two feel an instant mutual attraction. Finding Ochs utterly distasteful, Sophie refuses to go through with the marriage, and implores Octavian's aid. Invited by a note from "Mariandel" to a rendez-vous at an inn, Ochs is caught in an elaborate plan to make a fool of him. After much confusion, the Marschallin and Sophie's father Faninal (bar) arrive. Octavian changes to his own clothes, and the Marschallin, seeing him with Sophie, guesses what has transpired between the two. Having already sagely foreseen such a possibility, she gracefully and poignantly takes her leave of the young couple.

Rosenstock, Joseph. Conductor; b. Cracow [now in Poland], Jan. 27, 1895; d. New York, Oct. 17, 1985. After study in Vienna and posts in Germany, appeared at the Met for a season, conducting *Lohengrin* (debut, Oct. 30, 1929), *Rosenkavalier*, and *Walküre*. Conducted in Mannheim (1930–33), Berlin (1933–36), Tokyo (1937–41), and at N.Y.C. Opera (1948–52; general manager, 1952–56); returned to the Met (1961–68) and led 175 perfs. of 16 operas in the Mozart–Wagner–Strauss repertory.

Rosenthal, Manuel. Conductor; b. Paris, June 18, 1904. Studied with Ravel at Paris Conservatory (1918–23); conducted French Radio Orchestra (1934–47) and Seattle Symphony (1948–51), thereafter free-lancing and teaching. N.Y.C. Opera debut, *Oedipus Rex, Carmina Burana*, 1977. Beginning in 1981, he has led French repertory at the Met: the *Parade* triple bill (debut, Feb. 20, 1981), *Dialogues des Carmélites*, and *Manon*. In summer 1986, he returned to Seattle to conduct his first *Ring*.

Rossignol, Le. See *Nightingale, The*.

Rossi-Lemeni, Nicola. Bass; b. Istanbul, Nov. 6, 1920. Studied with mother, Xenia Macadon, and in Verona; debut as Varlaam, Fenice, Venice, 1946. At La Scala, 1947–61 (debut, Varlaam), he created Tommaso (*Assassinio*). Debuts as Boris in Buenos Aires (1949), San Francisco (1951), and Covent Garden (1952). In his only Met season, sang 11 perfs. of Méphistophélès (debut, Nov. 16, 1953), Boris, and Don Giovanni. Married to soprano Virginia Zeani.

Rossini, Gioachino. Composer; b. Pesaro, Feb. 29, 1792; d. Passy, France, Nov. 13, 1868. Son of itinerant musicians, he studied in Bologna with Padre Tesei and at the Liceo Comunale with Padre Mattei. His first operas were comic, including the one-act farces *La Cambiale di Matrimonio* (1810), *La Scala di Seta* (1812), and *Il Signor Bruschino* (1813); the longer *La Pietra del Paragone* (1812) was a major success at La Scala. In 1813, his first serious opera, *Tancredi*, and the comic *L'Italiana in Algeri*, won international notice, although *Il Turco in Italia* (1814) failed. A relationship with Naples began in 1815, when

Gioachino Rossini

Elisabetta, Regina d'Inghilterra (1815) initiated an annual series of tragic operas, increasingly elaborate in vocal style and musical structure, including *Otello, Armida, Mosè in Egitto, La Donna del Lago*, and *Maometto II*. For Rome, he composed the comic operas *Il Barbiere di Siviglia* (1816) and *La Cenerentola* (1817), for Milan the semiseria *La Gazza Ladra* (1817), for Venice his last new opera for Italy, the grandiose *Semiramide* (1823).

By now, Rossini's works had conquered Europe, and in 1824 in Paris he contracted to direct the Théâtre Italien, produce older operas, and compose new ones. At the Italien, *Il Viaggio a Reims* (1825) honored the coronation of Charles X. For the Opéra, he adapted *Maometto II* as *Le Siège de Corinthe* (1826) and *Mosè* as *Moïse et Pharaon* (1827), pruning the florid writing and emphasizing ensembles and choruses; the opéra comique *Le Comte Ory* (1828) re-cycled material from *Viaggio*. The four-act *Guillaume Tell* (1829), a broadly conceived historical pageant, substantially defined the lines of French grand opera. Then Rossini abandoned opera – whether for political, financial, artistic, or personal reasons is unknown. After years of poor health in Bologna (1836–55), he settled in Passy, outside Paris, maintained a brilliant salon, and composed the many short works known as *Sins of Old Age* (1857–68); he also composed cantatas and religious works.

A Janus-like figure who carried opera buffa into the 19th c. with new éclat, Rossini also remade the 18th-c. genre of opera seria, infusing it with new subjects from Romantic literature (his music, stronger on sentiment than passion, did not always realize their expressive implications) and defining new formal structures (especially for duets and ensembles, formerly rare in serious operas) that would dominate Italian opera until Verdi's late works. His brilliant overtures endured in the concert hall in the years when only a few of his comic operas were heard.

BIBLIOGRAPHY: Herbert Weinstock, *Rossini, A Biography* (N.Y., 1968).

Rosvaenge [Hansen], **Helge.** Tenor; b. Copenhagen, Aug. 29, 1897; d. Munich, June 19, 1972. Self-taught as a singer; a successful recital led to operatic debut as Rodolfo, Neustrelitz, 1921. He appeared in Altenburg, Basel, and Cologne before joining the Berlin State Opera, where he was the leading tenor, specializing in Italian repertory, 1930–44; returned after the war. Sang at Salzburg, 1932–38, as Singer (*Rosenkavalier*), Belmonte, Tamino, Huon (*Oberon*), and Florestan; at Bayreuth, sang Parsifal, his only Wagner part (1934, 1936). On Vienna State Opera roster, 1937–58, with occasional appearances thereafter. Created roles in Künnecke's *Die grosse Sünderin* (Berlin, 1935) and Wille's *Königsballade* (Berlin, 1939). Covent Garden debut as Florestan, 1938. Also appeared in operetta; his only U.S. appearances were recitals, 1963–64. Rosvaenge's bright if steely voice, brilliant high notes, and insistent manner dominated the Verdi tenor roles in Germany during the 1930s.

Rota [Rinaldi], **Nino.** Composer; b. Milan, Dec. 3, 1911; d. Rome, Apr. 10, 1979. Studied with Pizzetti and Casella in Rome and Scalero at Curtis Institute. His operas, popularly oriented in the directness of their tunes and situations, include *Il Cappello di Paglia di Firenze* (1955), after Labiche, and *La Visita Meravigliosa* (1970), after H.G. Wells. He wrote many film scores, notably for Federico Fellini.

Rothenberger, Anneliese. Soprano; b. Mannheim, Germany, June 19, 1924. Studied with Erika Müller in Mannheim; debut in Coblenz, 1943. Member of Hamburg State Opera (1946–54, 1958–73), singing Blondchen, Oscar, Olympia, and Lulu; also appeared in Vienna, Salzburg, Edinburgh, Milan. Met debut as Zdenka (*Arabella*), Nov. 18, 1960; in 6 seasons, she sang 47 perfs. of 7 roles, including Susanna, Oscar, Adele, and Sophie.

Rothier, Léon. Bass; b. Rheims, France, Dec. 26, 1874; d. New York, Dec. 6, 1951. Studied with Cresti, Lhérie, and Melchissèdec at Paris Conservatory; debut as Jupiter (*Philémon*), Opéra-Comique, 1899; sang there until 1903, then in Marseilles (1903–07), Nice (1907–09), and Lyon (1909–10). Met debut as Méphistophélès, Dec. 10, 1910; in 29 seasons, sang 807 perfs. of 53 roles, including Ramfis, Colline, Pimen, Zuniga, Alvise, Raimondo, Arkel, and Sparafucile; created Father Time (*Oiseau Bleu*) and Major Duquesnois (*Peter Ibbetson*).

roulade. A passage of ornamentation.

Rounseville, Robert. Tenor; b. Attleboro, Mass., Mar. 25, 1914; d. New York, Aug. 6, 1974. After singing in nightclubs and radio, studied with William Herman; debut as Pelléas, N.Y.C. Opera, 1948, remaining there until 1955 in lyric and spinto roles. Created Tom in *Rake*, Venice, 1951, and Bernstein's Candide, Broadway, 1956.

Rousseau, Jean-Jacques. Philosopher, author, and composer; b. Geneva, June 28, 1712; d. Ermenonville, near Paris, July 2, 1778. Self-taught musically, he admired Italian music and believed that through-composed opera in French was an impossibility. His surviving stage works, in a simple style, include the pastoral intermezzo *Le Devin du Village* (1752), and *Pygmalion* (1770), in which spoken dialogue is interspersed with orchestral interludes. Rousseau's *Lettre sur la Musique Française* (1753) was one of the bitterest anti-French statements in the "guerre des bouffons."

Roussel, Albert. Composer; b. Tourcoing, France, Apr. 5, 1869; d. Royan, Aug. 23, 1937. Studied with d'Indy at Schola Cantorum. Early naval experiences in Indo-China and Tunis and a honeymoon voyage to India inspired the opéra-ballet *Padmâvatî* (1923). His other theater works include ballets, incidental music, and the unsuccessful opéra-bouffe *Le Testament de la Tante Caroline* (1936).

Rousselière, Charles. Tenor; b. St. Nazaire, France, Jan. 17, 1875; d. Joue-les-Tours, May 11, 1950. Studied at Paris Conservatory; debut as Samson, Opéra, 1900. Sang there until 1912, at Opéra-Comique, 1913–19; created roles in *Pénélope* and *Julien*. In 1 Met season, sang 17 perfs. of Roméo (debut, Nov. 26, 1906), Gounod's and Berlioz's Fausts, Gérald (*Lakmé*), José, and Canio.

Rubini, Giovanni Battista. Tenor; b. Romano, near Bergamo, Apr. 7, 1794; d. Romano, Mar. 3, 1854. Studied in Bergamo, then sang as a chorister and toured briefly with a violinist; operatic debut in Generali's *Le Lagrime di una Vedova*, Pavia, 1814. He appeared in Venice and Naples (debut, Lindoro in *Italiana*, 1815), where he remained for ten years and studied further with the tenor Nozzari. An 1825 Parisian success in Rossini's *Cenerentola*, *Otello*, and *Donna del Lago* brought him European fame, and he was soon asked to create tenor leads in Bellini's *Bianca e Gernando* (1826), *Pirata* (1827), *Sonnambula* (1831), and *Puritani* (1835), and in several Donizetti works, notably *Anna Bolena* (1830) and *Marin Faliero* (1835). He sang at La Scala in 1827 (debut, Giacomo V in *Donna del Lago*) and 1829–30; his Rossini roles there included Bertrando (*Inganno Felice*), Almaviva, Aronne (*Mosè*),

Giovanni Rubini as Arturo in *I Puritani*

Giocondo (*Pietra del Paragone*), and Giannetto (*Gazza Ladra*). From 1831 until 1843, he appeared regularly at His Majesty's in London and the Italien in Paris, singing often with Grisi, Tamburini, and Lablache (the so-called "Puritani Quartet"), and later with Pasta. He retired a wealthy man in 1845.

Rubini came upon the scene at a transitional period for the tenor voice, and his combination of limpid tone and vigorous dramatic expression admirably suited the new styles of Bellini and Donizetti, while retaining the agility required for Rossini's music. Bellini's high-register writing for Rubini was originally executed in falsetto, and much of it remains beyond the reach of singers using modern techniques.

Rubinstein, Anton. Composer and pianist; b. Vikhvatinets, Podolsk district, Russia, Nov. 28, 1829; d. Peterhof, near St. Petersburg, Nov. 20, 1894. A child prodigy, he studied piano with Villoing in Moscow, composition with Delin in Berlin, and founded the Russian Musical Society (1859) and the Imperial Conservatory in St. Petersburg (1862). An adherent of the cosmopolitan strain in Russian music, he nevertheless used nationalist subjects in some of his operas, including his only success, *The Demon* (1875); other works, such as *Nero* (1879), were drawn from historical and Biblical sources.

Rudel, Julius. Conductor and manager; b. Vienna, Mar. 6, 1921. Studied at Vienna Academy and, after emigration to U.S. in 1938, at Mannes School, N.Y. Joined N.Y.C. Opera as repetiteur (conducting debut, *Zigeunerbaron*, Nov. 25, 1944); became the company's director in 1957 and remained until 1979, building a vigorous ensemble and exploring a venturesome repertory (aided by Ford Foundation grants to support American opera). Rudel has

Titta Ruffo as Figaro in *Il Barbiere di Siviglia*

also served as music director of Caramoor Festival, Wolf Trap Farm, and the Kennedy Center (1971–74), and has appeared as guest in London, Paris, Vienna, San Francisco, and Chicago. Since his Met debut in *Werther* (Oct. 7, 1978), he has returned often, leading such works as *Hoffmann*, *Entführung*, *Dialogues des Carmélites*, Handel's *Samson*, *Bohème*, and *Manon Lescaut*.

Rudolf, Max. Conductor; b. Frankfurt, Germany, June 15, 1902. Studied in Frankfurt, worked in Freiburg, Darmstadt, Prague, and Göteborg, and came to the Met as assistant conductor in 1945, remaining for 13 seasons as conductor (debut, *Rosenkavalier*, Mar. 2, 1946) and assistant manager (1950–58). Music director, Cincinnati Symphony (1958–70); on faculty of Curtis Institute (1970–73). He returned to the Met in 1973–75, amassing a total of 130 perfs., notably in the Mozart and Strauss repertory.

Ruffo, Titta [Ruffo Cafiero Titta]. Baritone; b. Pisa, June 9, 1877; d. Florence, July 6, 1953. Studied briefly with Persichini, Sparapane, and Lelio Casini, but essentially self-taught; debut as the *Lohengrin* Herald, Costanzi, Rome, 1898. He sang in Italy and South America for several seasons, his roles including Germont, Rigoletto, di Luna, Iago, and Cascart (*Zazà*). His debuts at Covent Garden (Ashton, 1903) and La Scala (Rigoletto, 1904) made no great impression, but his Cascart at the Lirico, Milan, 1904, led to important engagements, including Lisbon (where he first sang Hamlet, 1907), Monte Carlo (from 1908), the Colón, Buenos Aires (1908–31), and the Paris Opéra (1911–12). After his U.S. debut as Rigoletto in Philadelphia (1912), he sang with the Chicago Opera (1912–13) as Rigoletto, Hamlet, Tonio, Barnaba, Franchetti's Cristoforo Colombo, Rossini's Figaro, Don Giovanni, and Athanaël (*Thaïs*); he returned to Chicago in 1920 to create Leoncavallo's Edipo Re. His eight Met seasons began with Rossini's Figaro (Jan. 19, 1922), his most frequent role at the house; his 46 perfs. also included Tonio, Carlo (*Ernani*), Gérard (*Chénier*), Amonasro, Barnaba, and Neri (*Cena delle Beffe*), though never his famous Rigoletto. His final stage appearances were as Hamlet and Scarpia, Colón, 1931.

Endowed with the most imposing baritone voice of his generation, Ruffo cultivated an aggressive, dramatic style far removed from the suavity of Battistini and Ancona. Under such heavy usage, even his magnificent instrument – dark bronze in color, wide in range, with superb breath control – wore down prematurely (recognizing his own fault in this, he declined to teach). In his prime, especially as Rigoletto and Hamlet, Ruffo was a potent theatrical figure, with a mesmerizing elocutionary power to match his tonal force.

Rusalka. Opera in 4 acts by Dargomijsky; libretto by the composer, after Pushkin's dramatic poem.

First perf., St. Petersburg, Circus Theater, May 16, 1856: Bulakhova, Leonova, Petrov, Bulakhov, c. Liadov. U.S. prem., Seattle, Metropolitan Opera, Dec. 23, 1921.

An influential nationalist score. Natasha (s), daughter of a Miller (bs), is seduced and abandoned with child by the Prince (t) and becomes a water nymph (*rusalka*). Her father goes mad with grief and eventually throws the Prince in the river.

Rusalka. Opera in 3 acts by Dvořák; libretto by S. Jaroslav Kvapil, after de la Motte Fouqué's *Undine*, with additions from H.C. Andersen's *The Little Mermaid* and suggestions from Hauptmann's *The Sunken Bell*.

(continued p.321)

47 *Parade* – (1981). Design by David Hockney for the Satie ballet that opened the Met's French triple bill

50–52 *This page. Carmen* – The "Habanera" in three Met productions. (*Top*) (1967) Shirley Verrett, in a production designed by Jacques Dupont. (*Middle*) (1972) Marilyn Horne and James McCracken; set by Josef Svoboda, costumes by David Walker. (*Bottom*) (1986) Luis Lima and Maria Ewing, in a production designed by John Bury

48 *Opposite (above). La Périchole* – (1956). Design by Rolf Gérard for Act I of Offenbach's operetta.

49 (*Below*). *Les Contes d'Hoffmann* – (1982). Morley Meredith as Schlemil, Michel Sénéchal as Pitichinaccio, Anne Howells as Nicklausse, Plácido Domingo as Hoffmann, Tatiana Troyanos as Giulietta, and Michael Devlin as Dapertutto, in Act II of Offenbach's opera

53 *Porgy and Bess* – (1985). Design for Catfish Row by Robert O'Hearn

54 The Metropolitan Opera House, from a turn-of-the-century post card

55 *The Last Savage* – (1964). Design by Beni Montresor for "The Hunt" in Act I of Menotti's opera

56 *Candide* – (New York City Opera, 1982). David Eisler as Candide, John Lankston as Dr. Pangloss, Scott Reeve as Maximilian, and Erie Mills as Cunegonde, in Act 1, Scene 2 of Bernstein's opera, set by Clarke Dunham, costumes by Judith Dolan

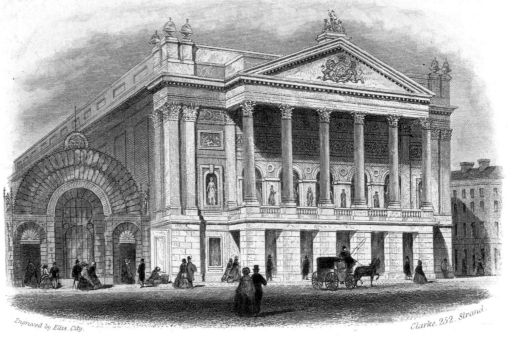

59 (*Above*). *Billy Budd* – Act II, Scene 2, the
battle scene of Britten's opera, designed by
William Dudley

60 (*Right*). *The Cunning Little Vixen* – (New
York City Opera, 1982). Gianna Rolandi as
Vixen Sharpears in Act I of Janáček's opera,
designed by Maurice Sendak

57 *Opposite* (*above*). *The Midsummer Marriage* –
(San Francisco Opera, 1983). A production
of Michael Tippett's opera, designed by
Robin Don

58 *Opposite* (*below*). The Royal Opera House,
Covent Garden

61 *Khovanshchina* – (1950). Design by Mstislav Dobujinsky for Act I of Mussorgsky's opera

62 *The Golden Cockerel* – (1945). A ballet sequence, with sets and costumes by Willy Pogany

First perf., Prague, National Theater, Mar. 31, 1901:
Maturová, Kabátová, Pták, Kliment, c. Kovařovič. U.S.
prem., Chicago, Sokol Slav Hall, Mar. 10, 1935.

A richly-colored fairy-tale score. Rusalka (s), a water
nymph, falls in love with a Prince (t); in order that she
can win him, a witch (ms) transforms her into a human
being. But he abandons her, and she is obliged to suffer
unless she avenges herself by killing him. Eventually,
regretting his betrayal, he comes to find death in her
arms.

Russlan and Ludmila. Opera in 5 acts by Glinka;
libretto by V.F. Shirkov and K.A. Bakhturin, after
Pushkin's poem.

First perf., St. Petersburg, Dec. 9, 1842. U.S. prem.,
N.Y., Town Hall, Dec. 26, 1942 (concert perf.). U.S. stage
prem., Opera Company of Boston, Mar. 5, 1977 (in Eng.):
Scovotti, Alberts, Moulson, Braun, Tozzi, c. Caldwell.

Just as *A Life for the Tsar* established the historical type of
Russian opera, this colorful fairy-tale inaugurated the
exotic, "oriental" strain.

Ludmila (s) has three suitors: the knight Russlan (bar),
the prince and poet Ratmir (a), and the cowardly warrior
Farlaf (bs). She disappears at a feast, and is promised to the
suitor who can find her. Russlan is told by the wizard Finn
(t) that Ludmila has been stolen by the evil dwarf
Chernomor, and warns him to beware the fairy Naina
(ms), who is helping Farlaf. When Russlan comes upon a
giant head whose breathing is causing a storm, he calms it
and beneath it finds a magic sword. Russlan finally kills
Chernomor and rescues Ludmila, but she has been put to
sleep by the dwarf; with a magic ring from Finn, he
awakens her.

Rysanek, Leonie. Soprano; b. Vienna, Nov. 12, 1926.
Studied at Vienna Conservatory with Alfred Jerger and
Rudolf Grossmann (her first husband); debut as Agathe
(*Freischütz*), Innsbruck, 1949. While singing at Saar-
brücken (1950–52), she appeared as Sieglinde at the first
postwar Bayreuth festival (1951), and in 1952 joined the
Bavarian State Opera, with which she made her London
debut in 1953 as Strauss' Danae. Other debuts included
Aix (Mozart's Countess, 1952), La Scala (Chrysothemis,
1954), Vienna (1954), Paris (Sieglinde, 1955), and San
Francisco (Senta, 1956), where she also sang Turandot,
Ariadne, Lady Macbeth, and the Empress (*Frau*). Her Met
debut was as the company's first Lady Macbeth (Feb. 5,
1959), and she has since returned nearly every season,
performing 239 perfs. of 20 roles, including Senta,
Chrysothemis, Elisabeth, the Marschallin, Tosca, Fidelio,
Salome, Sieglinde, Amelia (*Ballo*), Aida, Elisabeth de
Valois, Elsa and Ortrud, Kundry, Desdemona, and the
Forza Leonora; she was the Met's first Abigaille (*Nabucco*),
Ariadne, and Empress (*Frau*). A gala on Feb. 26, 1984,
celebrated her 25th anniversary with the company. She
returned frequently to Bayreuth, where her roles included
Elsa (1958), Senta (1959), Elisabeth (1964), and Kundry
(1982), as well as frequent Sieglindes. Other notable parts
include Strauss' Helena, Cherubini's Médée, and more
recently, the Kostelnička (*Jenůfa*).

Though she has sung Italian roles with some favor,
Rysanek's speciality has been the fervent, visionary,
vulnerable heroines of Wagner and Strauss. With a voice
that expands and gains in security as it ascends above the
staff, she is especially suited to the Straussian tessitura, and
her intense, spontaneous dramatic temperament has made
her one of the day's most admired operatic artists, despite
occasional vocal inequalities.

Russlan und Ludmila – Opera Company of Boston, 1977.
Edith Evans and Giorgio Tozzi

Leonie Rysanek as Senta in *Der fliegende Holländer*

S

Sadko. Opera in 7 scenes (to be divided into 3 or 5 acts) by Rimsky-Korsakov; libretto by the composer and V.I. Bielsky.

First perf., Moscow, Mamontov Private Opera, Jan. 7, 1898. U.S. & Met prem., Jan. 25, 1930 (in Fr.): Fleischer, Johnson, Ludikar, c. Serafin, d. Soudeikine, p. Lert. 16 perfs. in 3 seasons.

The most celebrated pieces in this fairy-tale opera are the songs sung by the three merchants, including the so-called "Song of India."

The wandering minstrel Sadko (t) meets and charms Volkhova (s), Princess of the Sea, who promises that he will catch golden fish, and this promise comes true. From Novgorod, where three merchants, Viking (bs), Indian (t), and Venetian (bar), sing arias describing their homelands, Sadko sets forth on a journey, where he accumulates treasure, but he is set adrift as a sacrifice to the Sea King (bs), who offers him Volkhova's hand in marriage. The tumult of their underwater wedding feast causes many ships to sink, and St. Nicholas orders Sadko back to land, turning Volkhova into the river named after her, which now connects Novgorod to the sea.

Saint Elisabeth. Oratorio by Liszt; libretto by Otto Roquette.

First perf., Budapest, Aug. 15, 1865. U.S. & Met prem., Jan. 3, 1918 (in Eng.): Easton, Matzenauer, Whitehill, c. Bodanzky, d. Urban, p. Ordynski. 5 perfs. in 1 season.

Bodanzky's stage version of Liszt's oratorio was presented at the Met when the wartime ban on German opera required fresh repertory. Elisabeth (s), daughter of a 13th-c. Hungarian king, marries Landgrave Ludwig of Thuringia (bar). After his death, she is driven from the throne by her mother-in-law Sophia (ms), and devotes herself to helping the poor.

Saint-François d'Assise. Opera in 3 acts by Messiaen; libretto by the composer.

First perf., Paris, Opéra, Nov. 28, 1983: Eda-Pierre, Riegel, van Dam, c. Ozawa. U.S. prem., Boston, Symphony Hall, Apr. 10, 1986 (concert perf. of 3 scenes): Battle, Riegel, van Dam, c. Ozawa.

An opera of great length and orchestral density, drawing on Messiaen's long-established musical procedures to portray the progress of grace in the soul of St. Francis of Assisi (bar).

St. Louis. City in Missouri. After its first operatic performance, an English version of Auber's *Muette de Portici* in 1830, touring troupes led by the likes of Arditi and Savage came and went, offering brief seasons. The Metropolitan Opera visited regularly between 1884 and 1966. The St. Louis Municipal Opera Association, organized in 1919, concentrated on operetta and musicals. In 1976, Richard Gaddes founded the Opera Theater of St. Louis, which soon emerged as a leader in regional opera. Its 1978 *Albert Herring* was widely televised, and in 1983 the company became the first from America to visit the Edinburgh Festival. The annual spring season offers operas at the Loretto-Hilton Center (capacity 924), with young American casts; performances are sung in English translation (a Mozart cycle translated by Andrew Porter is in progress). Repertory mixes familiar and unusual; world premieres have included Stephen Paulus' *The Postman*

Always Rings Twice (1982) and Delius' *Margot la Rouge* (1983), along with U.S. premieres of Prokofiev's *Maddalena* (1982) and Rossini's *Viaggio a Reims* (1986). As of 1986, the Opera Theater of Saint Louis is headed by general director Charles MacKay, music director John Nelson, and director of production Colin Graham.

Saint of Bleecker Street, The. Opera in 3 acts by Menotti; libretto by the composer.

First perf., N.Y., Broadway Theater, Dec. 27, 1954: Copeland, Lane, Poleri, c. Schippers.

Verismo formulas transplanted to New York's Little Italy, in the story of Annina (s), a sickly girl afflicted with the stigmata, and the tensions between her agnostic brother Michele (t) and his mistress Desideria (ms).

St. Paul. See *Minneapolis/St. Paul.*

Saint-Saëns, Camille. Composer; b. Paris, Oct. 9, 1835; d. Algiers, Dec. 16, 1921. A child prodigy, he made his piano debut at age ten and studied composition with Pierre Maleden and at the Paris Conservatory with Halévy. Active as an organist in Parisian churches, touring piano virtuoso, teacher (of Fauré, among others), and composer in many genres and forms, Saint-Saëns championed the music of Wagner and Liszt, and also the pre-classical repertory. His musical language and esthetic were conservative, his compositions notable for their facility of invention, craftsmanship (especially in counterpoint and orchestration), and formal ingenuity. Of his 13 operas, only one, *Samson et Dalila* (1877), is now performed with any frequency, and even this, for all its melodic and coloristic allure, has been felt to be short of the theatrical effectiveness even more conspicuously lacking in his other operas, among them *La Princesse Jaune* (1872), *Henry VIII* (1883), and *Ascanio* (1890).

BIBLIOGRAPHY: James Harding, *Saint-Saëns and His Circle* (London, 1965).

Salammbô. Opera in 5 acts by Reyer; libretto by Camille du Locle, after Flaubert's novel.

First perf., Brussels, Monnaie, Feb. 10, 1890: Caron, Sellier, Vergnet, Renaud, c. Baerwolf. U.S. prem., New Orleans, French Opera House, Jan. 25, 1900. Met prem., Mar. 20, 1901: Bréval, Saléza, Salignac, Scotti, c. Mancinelli, d. McGiehan, Emens/Castel-Bert, p. Parry. 3 perfs. in 1 season.

Though its plot recalls *Aida*, this opera is set in an austere, static style. Mathô (t), leader of mutinous Carthaginian mercenaries, loves the priestess Salammbô (s) and steals a sacred veil from her temple; when he is condemned to die by Salammbô's hand, she kills herself instead, after which he stabs himself.

Saléza, Albert. Tenor; b. Bruges, near Bayonne, France, Oct. 28, 1867; d. Paris, Nov. 26, 1916. Studied at Paris Conservatory; debut as Mylio (*Roi d'Ys*), Opéra-Comique, 1888. Sang at Paris Opéra (1892–95, including first French Otello, 1894) and Covent Garden (1898–1902, 1904). Met debut as Roméo, Dec. 2, 1898; in 4 seasons, sang 55 perfs. of 14 roles, including Rodolfo in first Met *Bohème*, 1900.

Salieri, Antonio. Composer; b. Legnago, near Verona, Aug. 18, 1750; d. Vienna, May 7, 1825. Studied in Vienna with Gassmann, whom he succeeded as Austrian court composer in 1774, becoming music director in 1788. In addition to regular works for Vienna, he composed for

Italian cities and for Paris, where *Les Danaïdes* (1784) and *Tarare* (1787) were presented to great acclaim, the latter influenced by Gluck's theories. Until his retirement in 1804, he continued to write operas, mostly in the buffo genre, among them *Falstaff* (1799).

Salignac, Thomas. Tenor; b. Générac, Gard, France, Mar. 19, 1867; d. Paris, 1945. Studied in Marseilles and Paris; debut at Opéra-Comique, 1893. Met debut as José, Dec. 11, 1896; in 6 seasons, sang 88 perfs. of 18 roles, including Almaviva, José, Ottavio, Ernesto, Faust, Edgardo, Canio, Roméo, and Alfredo. Also appeared at Covent Garden (1897–99, 1901–04).

Sallinen, Aulis. Composer; b. Salmi, Finland, Apr. 9, 1935. Studied with Merikanto and Kokkonen in Helsinki. His freely serial music has since the 1960s incorporated tonal elements, including Finnish folk material. His operas *The Horseman* (1976) and *The Red Line* (1978) have been widely admired; the allegorical *The King Goes Forth to France* was introduced at the 1984 Savonlinna festival.

Salminen, Matti. Bass; b. Turku, Finland, July 7, 1945. Studied at Sibelius Academy, Helsinki and with Luigi Ricci, Rome; sang small roles with Finnish National Opera from 1966, Philippe II in 1969. From 1972, member, Cologne Opera. Appeared at Bayreuth (debut, Hunding, 1976) and Covent Garden (debut, Fasolt, 1974). Met debut as Marke, Jan 9, 1981; has also sung Sarastro, Landgraf, and Rocco there.

Salome. Opera in 1 act by R. Strauss; libretto adapted by the composer from Hedwig Lachmann's translation of Oscar Wilde's play.
First perf., Dresden, Court Opera, Sep. 9, 1905: Wittich, Chavanne, Burrian, Perron, c. Schuch. U.S. & Met prem., Jan. 22, 1907: Fremstad, Weed, Burrian, van Rooy, c. Hertz, p. Schertel. Later Met productions: Jan. 13, 1934: Ljungberg, Manski, Lorenz, Schorr, c. Bodanzky, d. Oenslager, p. Wymetal, Jr; Feb. 3, 1965: Nilsson, Dalis, Liebl, Dooley, c. Böhm, d. Heinrich, p. Rennert. Salome has also been sung at the Met by Welitsch, Varnay, Goltz, Borkh, Rysanek, Silja, Bumbry, G. Jones; Herodias by Branzell, Thorborg, Höngen, Resnik, Dalis, Dunn, Varnay; Herod by Maison, Svanholm, Vinay, Liebl, Stolze, Ulfung; Jochanaan by Janssen, Berglund, Schöffler, Hotter, Harrell, Stewart, Bailey, Weikl. Conductors include Panizza, Szell, Reiner, Mitropoulos, Leinsdorf, Levine, A. Davis. 106 perfs. in 19 seasons.
A brilliantly orchestrated, harmonically extravagant study of sensuality, which shocked critics and audiences at the time of its premiere and has continued to thrill for the morbid vitality of the drama and music.
Galilee, c. 30 A.D. Salome (s), daughter of Herodias (ms), is fascinated by the prophet Jochanaan (John the Baptist, bar), whom her stepfather King Herod (t) has imprisoned in a cistern; though Jochanaan preaches against the king's wife Herodias, Herod is awed by the prophet and cannot bring himself to kill him. When Salome begs Jochanaan to let her run her fingers through his hair, embrace his body, and kiss his lips, she is sternly rejected and ordered to repent. Her shameless behavior causes the young captain Narraboth (t), who adores her, to kill himself. Herod lusts for his stepdaughter, who plays on his desire by exacting a promise that, if she dances for him, he will fulfill any wish she craves. She performs an exotic dance, and upon its conclusion demands

Felsenreitschule, Salzburg

Jochanaan's head. The appalled Herod balks, but Salome, gleefully supported by her mother, stands firm. The prophet is beheaded and Salome apostrophizes her prize, eventually kissing the severed head; Herod, repulsed, orders her crushed to death by his soldiers.

Saltzmann-Stevens, Minnie. Soprano; b. Blooming-ton, Ill., Mar. 17, 1874; d. Milan, Jan. 25, 1950. Studied with Jean de Reszke in Paris; debut as Brünnhilde in English *Ring*, Covent Garden, 1909. Sang other Wagner roles there (1910–13), and in Bayreuth (1911, 1913) and Chicago (1911–1914). Illness terminated her career prematurely.

Salvini-Donatelli, Fanny [Francesca Lucchi]. Soprano; b. Florence, 1815(?); d. Milan, June 1891. Debut as Rosina, Apollo, Venice, 1839. She sang in Vienna (Abigaille under Verdi's supervision, 1842–43) and at Drury Lane, London (1858). Created Violetta, Venice, Fenice, 1853; her corpulence was blamed for the opera's initial failure.

Salzburg. City in Austria, birthplace of Mozart, and since 1922 site of a major music festival, summer home of the Vienna State Opera. Intermittent festivals celebrating Mozart began in 1877, but the permanent annual festival was conceived in 1917 by Strauss, Hofmannsthal, Rein-hardt, and Schalk. Mozart operas were performed in the Stadttheater from 1922; the Festspielhaus, opened in 1924 and rebuilt in 1926 (capacity 1,200), was first used for opera in 1927 (*Fidelio* under Schalk). The German-oriented repertory was diversified in the 1930s; *Don Giovanni* was first sung in Italian in 1934, under Walter, and in 1935 Toscanini led *Falstaff* and *Fidelio*, but both these conductors departed after the 1938 Anschluss. The festival was suspended in 1945 but revived quickly; from 1948 to 1954, Furtwängler was the leading figure, and since 1957 Karajan has been the dominating force (artistic director 1957–60, 1964–present). In the postwar years, new works have been introduced at Salzburg, including Einem's *Dantons Tod* (1947), Barber's *Vanessa* (by a Met ensemble, 1958), Henze's *Bassarids* (1966), and Berio's *Re in Ascolto* (1984). The open-air Felsenreitschule, first used for drama by Reinhardt in 1926, was adapted for operatic performances after the war, and later redesigned with a roof (capacity 1,568). In 1960, the new Grosses Festspiel-haus was opened (capacity 2,371), after which the old theater was redesigned as the Kleines Festspielhaus (capac-ity 1,343); small works are performed in the former Stadttheater, renamed the Landestheater in 1941. Perfor-mances take place in late July and August. In 1967, Karajan initiated an annual Easter Festival, which includes an operatic production.

Samaritani, Pier Luigi. Designer and producer; b. Novara, Italy, Sep. 29, 1942. After assisting de Nobili, Zeffirelli, Chirico, has designed and directed at La Scala (*Luisa Miller*, 1976), Florence (*Vêpres Siciliennes*, 1978), Rome (*Thaïs*, 1979), Chicago Lyric (*Faust*, 1979), and Met (*Ernani*, 1983).

Sammarco, Mario. Baritone; b. Palermo, Sicily, Dec. 13, 1868; d. Milan, Jan. 24, 1930. Studied in Palermo and Milan; debut as Valentin, Palermo, 1888. Created Gérard (*Chénier*), Cascart (*Zazà*), and Worms (*Germania*). Sang in Russia and South America, at Covent Garden (debut, Scarpia, 1904) and Manhattan Opera, N.Y. (1907–10), in Chicago (1910–13), Boston (1910), and Philadelphia (1909–13).

Samson. Oratorio by Handel; libretto by Newburgh Hamilton, after Milton's *Samson Agonistes*.

First perf., London, Covent Garden, Feb. 18, 1743: Clive, Avolio, Cibber, Beard, Reinhold. U.S. stage prem., Dallas, Civic Opera, Nov. 5, 1976: Wells, Zoghby, Forrester, Vickers, Plishka, c. Rescigno. Met prem., Feb. 3, 1986: Mitchel, Vaness, Walker, Vickers, Macurdy, c. Rudel, d. O'Brien, p. Moshinsky.

In this oratorio, one of Handel's greatest and one of those most often transferred to the stage, the blinded hero Samson (t) is taunted by his wife Dalila (s) and the braggart Harapha (bs), but musters strength for his final feat, destruction of the Philistine temple.

Samson et Dalila (Samson and Dalila). Opera in 3 acts by Saint-Saëns; libretto by Lemaire, after the Old Testament, Judges, xiv–xvi.

First perf., Weimar, Dec. 2, 1877 (in Ger.): von Müller, Ferenczy, Milde, c. Lassen. U.S. prem., N.Y., Carnegie Hall, Mar. 25, 1892 (in Eng., concert perf.). U.S. stage prem., New Orleans, Jan. 4, 1893: Mounier, Reynaud, Hourdin. Met prem., Feb. 8, 1895: Mantelli, Tamagno, Campanari, c. Mancinelli, p. Perry. Later Met productions: Nov. 15, 1915: Matzenauer, Caruso, Amato, c. Polacco, d. Sala/Palanti, p. Speck; Dec. 26, 1936: Wettergren, Maison, Pinza, c. Abravanel, d. Koeck-Meyer Studios, p. Graf; Oct. 17, 1964: Gorr, Thomas, Bacquier, c. Prêtre, d. O'Hearn, p. Merrill. Samson has also been sung at the Met by Martinelli, Vinay, del Monaco, Tucker, Vickers; Dalila by Homer, Stevens, Thorborg, Thebom, Cossotto, Horne; the High Priest by de Luca, Warren, Singher, Quilico. 111 perfs. in 24 seasons.

The work's stately dramatic pace once made it seem apt for concert presentation, though the sensuous appeal of Dalila's arias have placed it in the stage repertory of most great mezzos.

Gaza, Old Testament times. Samson (t) arouses his Israelite brethren to rebellion, slaying the Satrap of Gaza (bs) and overwhelming the Philistine forces. But the victory is undermined by the Philistine temptress Dalila (ms), once Samson's lover, who – desiring vengeance and urged on by the High Priest of Dagon (bar) – resolves to seduce the hero and learn the secret of his superhuman strength. Ignoring the warnings of an Old Hebrew (bs), Samson succumbs to her and reveals that his powers lie with his hair; shorn, he is taken prisoner and blinded by the Philistines. They mock him as they celebrate in the temple of Dagon, but the hero's prayer for one last moment of strength is answered, and he pulls down the temple on himself and his foes.

Samstag. See *Licht*.

Sanderson, Sibyl. Soprano; b. Sacramento, Calif., Dec. 7, 1865; d. Paris, May 15, 1903. Studied with Sbriglia and Mathilde Marchesi, Paris; debut as Massenet's Manon, Hague, 1888. In Paris, created Esclarmonde (Opéra-Comique, 1889) and Thaïs (Opéra, 1894). Covent Garden debut as Manon, 1891. In 2 Met seasons, she sang 5 perfs. of Manon (debut, Jan. 16, 1895) and Juliette.

San Diego. City in southern California. From the end of the 19th c., touring companies visited; the San Diego Civic Grand Opera offered over 40 productions (1919–32), and later the San Francisco Opera brought three productions annually (1950–62). With the completion of the new Civic Theater (capacity 2,945), the San Diego Opera, under director Walter Herbert, began to offer yearly seasons of from two to five productions. Until 1973, all operas were sung in English; the mostly standard repertory was spiced with occasional events such as the U.S. premiere of Henze's *Junge Lord* (1967). Tito Capobianco, named artistic director in 1975 and general director two years later, enlarged the fall and spring seasons and presented an annual summer Verdi festival (1978–84, including early works such as *Giovanna d'Arco*, *Giorno di Regno*, and *Oberto*). Casts have featured international names, and the repertory has included the world premiere of Menotti's *La Loca* (1979) and rarities such as *Henry VIII* and *Hamlet*. In 1983, Ian Campbell succeeded Capobianco.

San Francisco. City in northern California. In 1851, shortly after the gold rush, the Pellegrini troupe, under bass Alfredo Roncovieri, performed *Sonnambula* at the Adelphi Theater. Especially after the transcontinental railway was completed in 1869, touring companies flocked to the prosperous city, and resident companies rose and fell, playing in 26 different theaters; the Civic Opera House offered 800 performances during the 1860s and 1,000 during the 1880s, and the Tivoli Opera House presented winter and summer seasons every year, 1890–1900. Abbey came in 1890 with Tamagno and Patti; in 1900 the Metropolitan Opera produced the city's initial *Ring* cycle, but its 1906 visit was abruptly terminated by the great earthquake. Beginning in 1909, the Chicago Opera and the Scotti and San Carlo companies visited the city. After a trial season in the Stanford U. stadium (1922), Gaetano Merola founded the San Francisco Opera Company in 1923; the repertory consisted mainly of standard Italian fare, with occasional French and German works, and the two-month season was timed to precede the Met's, allowing Merola to feature Met stars in his casts. The War Memorial Opera House (capacity 3,252) opened on Oct. 15, 1932 with *Tosca*, replacing the Civic Auditorium as the company's permanent base. After Merola's death in 1953, Kurt Herbert Adler became manager; under his leadership, the company ceased touring, expanded its season to four months, and often engaged international artists before they appeared in N.Y. (among them del Monaco, Gobbi, Nilsson, Rysanek, Schwarzkopf, and Tebaldi). Adler widened the repertory with operas by Cherubini, Meyerbeer, Massenet, and Janáček, and the U.S. premieres of *Dialogues des Carmélites* (1957), *Frau ohne Schatten* (1959), and *Midsummer Night's Dream* (1961). In 1961, a Spring Opera Company was founded to present popular operas with young artists (now the San Francisco Opera Center), and in 1980 a summer festival. Terence A. McEwen succeeded Adler in 1982; in 1986, John Pritchard became music director. A new *Ring* cycle was presented in summer 1985, but these seasons were subsequently discontinued; the fall season now runs from September to December.

Sanquirico, Alessandro. Designer; b. Milan, July 27, 1777; d. Milan, Mar. 2, 1849. A pupil of Paolo Landriani, he was sole designer and painter at La Scala, 1817–32. His designs for the works of Bellini, Rossini, Donizetti, Pacini, and Meyerbeer are considered the foundation of the 19th-c. grand opera tradition, reconciling rigid academicism with newer pictorial solutions.

Santa Fe. City in New Mexico. John Crosby founded the Santa Fe summer opera festival in 1957, and remains its general director. The first theater burned down in 1967, and was replaced the following year by an outdoor auditorium (with covered stage and pit). No American company has offered a wider range of contemporary repertory; its annals include the American premieres of Schoenberg's *Jakobsleiter* (1968), Hindemith's *Cardillac* (1967) and *Neues vom Tage* (1961), Berg's *Lulu* (1963; three-act version, 1979), Shostakovich's *Nose* (1965), and many Henze works, as well as the world premieres of Floyd's *Wuthering Heights* (1958), Berio's *Opera* (1970), Rochberg's *The Confidence Man* (1982), and Eaton's *The Tempest* (1985). The festival's apprentice program has nurtured many talented native singers; though the casts include some notable foreign artists, the emphasis is on Americans. The Santa Fe season runs for eight weeks in July and August.

Santi, Nello. Conductor; b. Adria, Italy, Sep. 22, 1931. Studied in Padua, where he made his debut in 1951 (*Rigoletto*); has worked extensively in Germany, Switzerland, and Austria. At the Met (debut, *Ballo*, Jan. 25, 1962), he conducted Italian repertory in 1962–65 and has returned often since 1976.

Santley, Charles. Baritone; b. Liverpool, England, Feb. 28, 1834; d. London, Sep. 22, 1922. Studied in Milan and with Garcia in London; debut as Doctor (*Traviata*), Pavia, 1857. London stage debut, Covent Garden, as Hoël (*Dinorah*), 1859; at Her Majesty's, sang first English Valentin (1863); Gounod composed "Even bravest heart" for him. Retired from opera in 1877, but sang in concert until 1911.

Sapho. Opera in 5 acts by Massenet; libretto by Henri Cain and Arthur Bernède, after Alphonse Daudet's novel.
First perf., Paris, Opéra-Comique, Nov. 27, 1897: Calve, Wyns, Lepestre, Gresse, c. Danbé. U.S. prem., N.Y., Manhattan Opera House, Nov. 17, 1909: Garden, d'Alvarez, Dalmorès, Dufranne, c. de la Fuente.
An erotically perfumed work concerning the seduction of Jean (t), an unsophisticated young man, by Fanny (s), a former artists' model attempting to rise above her past.

Sardou, Victorien. French dramatist (1831–1908). Operas based on his writings include Giordano's *Fedora* and *Madame Sans-Gêne*, and Puccini's *Tosca*.

Sarfaty, Regina. Mezzo-soprano; b. Rochester, N.Y., 1932. After study at Juilliard, appeared in Santa Fe (1957). At N.Y.C. Opera (1958–62; debut in first U.S. *Schweigsame Frau*), sang Cenerentola, Dorabella, and Stravinsky's Jocasta. Member, Frankfurt Opera (from 1963) and Zurich Opera. Recorded Baba the Turk (*Rake*) under Stravinsky.

Santa Fe Opera

Sass [Sasse, Sax], **Marie (-Constance).** Soprano; b. Ghent, Belgium, Jan. 26, 1834; d. Auteuil, near Paris, Nov. 8, 1907. Studied in Ghent, Paris, and with Lamperti in Milan; debut as Gilda, Venice, 1852. In Paris, sang at Lyrique (debut, Countess in *Nozze*, 1859) and Opéra (debut as first Elisabeth in revised *Tannhäuser*, 1860), where she created Sélika (*Africaine*), and Elisabeth de Valois (*Don Carlos*).

Sass, Sylvia. Soprano; b. Budapest, July 12, 1951. Studied at Liszt Academy, Budapest; debut as Violetta, Sofia, 1971. Debuts in Hamburg (Fiordiligi, 1975), Scottish Opera (Desdemona, 1975), Covent Garden (Giselda in *Lombardi*, 1976), and Aix (Violetta, 1976). In her only Met season, she sang Tosca (debut, Mar. 17, 1977).

Satyagraha (Love/Strength). Opera in 3 acts by Glass; libretto by Constance DeJong.
First perf., Rotterdam, Stadsschouwburg, Sep. 5, 1980: Perry, Morgan, Cummings, Hiskey, Gill, c. Ferden. U.S. prem., Lewiston, N.Y., Artpark, July 29, 1981: Perry, Nichols, Cummings, Hiskey, Miller, c. Keene.
Glass' hypnotic repetitions underpin a Sanskrit text; the scenario shows Gandhi's realization of the repression of Indians in South Africa and the development of his philosophy of civil disobedience.

Saul and David. Opera in 4 acts by Nielsen; libretto by Einar Christiansen, after the Old Testament, I Samuel.
First perf., Copenhagen, Royal Theater, Nov. 28, 1902: Dons, Lendrop, Hérold, Cornelius, Simonsen, Nissen, Müller, c. Nielsen.
In this retelling of the Biblical story, with elaborate choruses and vividly contrasted vocal writing, Saul (bar) is a complex tragic figure, who alternately loves his son's friend David (t) and envies him, gives David the hand of his daughter Mikal (s) and casts him out. Eventually Saul kills himself and David is proclaimed King.

Saunders, Arlene. Soprano; b. Cleveland, Oct. 5, 1935. Studied at Baldwin-Wallace College and in N.Y.; debut as Rosalinde (*Fledermaus*), National Opera Co., 1958. N.Y.C. Opera debut as Giorgetta (*Tabarro*), 1961; later sang in Europe, primarily at Hamburg State Opera; roles included Pamina (Glyndebourne, 1966), Louise (San Francisco, 1967), Minnie (Covent Garden, 1980); created Ginastera's Beatrix Cenci, Washington, D.C., 1971. Met debut as Eva, Apr. 2, 1976.

Savage, Henry. Impresario; b. New Durham, N.H., Mar. 21, 1859; d. Boston, Nov. 29, 1927. A real-estate broker, he acquired Boston's Castle Square Theater through a lessee's bankruptcy and put on a season of opera in English in 1895, later expanding his activities to other cities, including a 1900 season at the Met. From 1904, the Henry Savage Grand Opera Company toured English-language productions of such works as *Parsifal*, *Butterfly*, and *Fanciulla*, making a major contribution to the popularization of opera in America.

Saville, Frances. Soprano; b. San Francisco, Jan. 6, 1863; d. Burlingame, Calif., Nov. 8, 1935. Studied in Australia and with Marchesi in Paris; debut in Brussels, 1892. Sang with Carl Rosa Co., London, at Opéra-Comique, Paris, and in Berlin, Warsaw, and St. Petersburg. Met debut as Juliette, Nov. 18, 1895; in 2 seasons, sang 28 perfs. of 10 roles, including Micaela, Marguerite, Manon, Zerlina, Gutrune, Elsa, Elisabeth, and Violetta.

Sawallisch, Wolfgang. Conductor; b. Munich, Aug. 26, 1923. A graduate of Munich Conservatory (1946), he held opera positions in Aachen, Wiesbaden, and Cologne (1960–63), and orchestral posts with the Hamburg Philharmonic (1961–73), Vienna Symphony (1960–70), and Suisse Romande Orchestra (1972–80). Bayreuth debut in *Tristan*, 1957; later led *Holländer* and *Tannhäuser*. Since 1971, general director, Bavarian State Opera, Munich. A distinguished interpreter of the German–Austrian repertory, he has appeared only occasionally in the U.S.

Sayão, Bidú [Balduina de Oliveira Sayão]. Soprano; b. Rio de Janeiro, May 11, 1902. Studied in Rio and Bucharest with Elena Theodorini, and with Jean de Reszke in Nice; debut as Rosina, Costanzi, Rome (1926), followed by Gilda and Carolina (*Matrimonio Segreto*). Engagements in Rio, Lisbon, Turin, and at the Colón, Buenos Aires, in roles such as Lucia, Elvira (*Puritani*), and Norina; her La Scala debut was as Rosina (1930). In Paris she sang Juliette at both Opéra and Opéra-Comique (1931), and she returned to Rio in 1936 as Cecy (Gomes' *Guarany*). A 1935 N.Y. recital led to a concert engagement with Toscanini and a Met debut as Massenet's Manon (Feb. 13, 1937); during 16 seasons with the company, she sang 155 perfs. (plus over 70 on tour) of 12 roles, most often Mimi (31 times) and Susanna (30), also Violetta, Zerlina, Adina, Rosina, Norina, Gilda, Mélisande, Juliette, and Serpina (*Serva Padrona*). She also appeared frequently in Chicago (1941–45, and as Zerlina in Lyric Opera opening perf., 1954) and San Francisco (1946–52, where in her final season she sang Boito's Margherita). Married to impresario Walter Mocchi, later to baritone Giuseppe Danise, she retired from singing in 1957.

Sayão began as an exponent of the coloratura repertory, but at the Met she concentrated on more lyrical roles, wisely never extending herself beyond her natural resources. A skilled comedienne as well as an affectingly pathetic Violetta and Manon, she used her silvery, perfectly placed soprano with a keen ear for nuance and a carefully cultivated awareness of language and style.

Scala di Seta, La (The Silken Ladder). Opera in 1 act by Rossini; libretto by Giuseppe Maria Foppa, after François-Antoine-Eugène de Planard's play *L'Échelle de Soie*.

First perf., Venice, San Moïse, May 9, 1812: (probably) Cantarelli, Monelli, de Grecis, Tacci. U.S. prem., St. Cloud State U., Minn., Mar. 25, 1980.

In this early farce, today remembered chiefly by its

Bidú Sayão as Norina in *Don Pasquale*

sinfonia, Giulia (s) is secretly married to Dorvil (t), who climbs up to her room every night on a silken ladder. Complications arise when her guardian tries to marry her to another, but all is set right by disclosure of the secret marriage.

Scalchi, Sofia. Mezzo-soprano; b. Turin, Italy, Nov. 29, 1850; d. Rome, Aug. 22, 1922. Studied with Boccabadati; debut as Ulrica, Mantua, 1866. Sang at Covent Garden, 1868–89 (debut, Azucena). Met debut as Siebel in company's inaugural performance, Oct. 22, 1883; in 5 seasons, sang 92 perfs. of 14 roles, including Orfeo, Beppe (*Amico Fritz*), and first American Quickly.

Scarlatti, Alessandro. Composer; b. Palermo, May 2, 1660; d. Naples, Oct. 22, 1725. He lived from 1672 in Rome, but little is known of his musical education. In 1679 (apparently a reworking of a recently discovered, untitled opera of 1677–78) *Gli Equivoci nel Sembiante* was produced in Rome, then repeated successfully throughout Italy and in Austria. As music director to the Viceroy of Naples (1684–1702), he composed religious music and over 80 operas, 40 of which survive, among them *Il Pirro e Demetrio* (1694) and *La Caduta de' Decemviri* (1697). When he was assistant music director at S. Maria Maggiore in Rome (1703–08), the city had no opera, but he wrote for Venice one of his finest scores, *Il Mitridate Eupatore* (1707). Resuming his Naples position in 1708, he composed at least 11 operas, including *Il Tigrane* (1715) and *Il Trionfo d'Amore* (1718), one of his few comedies. His last operas were produced in Rome, but his vogue had passed. In Scarlatti's operas, characters and passions are stylized; he laid the foundations of baroque opera seria, and especially of the da capo aria, which he refined, increasing its expressive potential and accompanimental richness.

BIBLIOGRAPHY: Donald J. Grout, *Alessandro Scarlatti: An Introduction to His Operas* (Berkeley, 1979).

scena (Ital., "stage"). In addition to its primary meaning, refers to a subdivision of an act, articulated either by the fall of the curtain and a change of setting or by the entrance or exit of a character. In 19th-c. Italian opera, "scena" refers to the orchestrally accompanied recitative that begins a double aria; see *aria*.

scenario. An outline for a libretto, indicating the scenes, characters, and action.

Schalk, Franz. Conductor; b. Vienna, May 27, 1863; d. Edlach, Austria, Sep. 3, 1931. Student of Bruckner (and emasculator of some of his works), he conducted during the Mahler years in Vienna, where he later served as joint director with Strauss (1918–24) and on his own (1924–29). Led the premiere of *Frau ohne Schatten* and was a founder of the Salzburg Festival. During his single season at the Met (debut, *Walküre*, Dec. 14, 1898), he led six Wagner operas (including the first uncut *Ring* in the U.S.) and several concerts.

Schauspieldirektor, Der (The Impresario). Opera in 1 act by Mozart; libretto by Gottlieb Stephanie, Jr.
First perf., Vienna, Schönbrunn Palace, Feb. 7, 1786: Lange, Cavalieri, Adamberger. U.S. prem., N.Y., Stadt Theater, Nov. 9, 1870 (adapted, as *Mozart und Schikaneder*).
Mozart's attractive score for this slight spoof is often revived with freshly authored dialogue, following closely or loosely the original plot about the tribulations an impresario (speaking role) suffers at the hands of his two rival sopranos, Mme. Herz and Mme. Silberklang.

Scheff, Fritzi. Soprano; b. Vienna, Aug. 30, 1879; d. New York, Apr. 8, 1954. Studied with mother, soprano Anna Jaeger, and in Frankfurt and Munich; debut as Juliette, Frankfurt, 1896. Sang in Munich (1897–1900), and at Covent Garden (1900–03). Met debut as Marzelline (*Fidelio*), Dec. 28, 1900; in 3 seasons, sang 57 perfs. of 15 roles, including Elsa, Cherubino, Nedda, Marguerite, and Asa (*Manru*). Subsequently successful in Victor Herbert operettas, notably *Mlle. Modiste* (1906).

Scheidemantel, Karl. Baritone; b. Weimar, Germany, Jan. 21, 1859; d. Weimar, June 26, 1923. Debut as Wolfram, Weimar, 1878; later studied with Stockhausen in Frankfurt. Member, Dresden State Opera (1886–1911), where he created roles in *Feuersnot* (1901), *Manru* (1901), and *Rosenkavalier* (1911). Sang at Covent Garden (1884, 1899), Vienna (1890), and La Scala (1891); Bayreuth appearances, 1886–92.

Schenk, Otto. Producer; b. Vienna, June 12, 1930. After acting at Vienna Burgtheater and Josefstadt, directed *Don Pasquale* (Volksoper, 1961). Since 1965, chief stage director, Vienna State Opera; frequent guest director in European theaters. For the Met, he has staged *Tosca* (1968), *Fidelio* (1970), *Tannhäuser* (1977), *Contes d'Hoffmann* (1982), *Arabella* (1983), *Walküre* (1986, first installment of *Ring*) and *Fledermaus* (1986).

Schexnayder, Brian. Baritone; b. Port Arthur, Tex., Sep. 18, 1953. Studied at Juilliard, N.Y., where he sang Germont, Sharpless and Renato. Met debut as Silvio, Dec. 17, 1980; has subsequently sung Ashton, Marcello, Guglielmo (*Così*) and Puccini's Lescaut there. Paris Opéra debut as Marcello (1982–83).

Schick, George. Conductor; b. Prague, Apr. 5, 1908; d. New York, Mar. 7, 1985. Trained in Prague, came to U.S. in 1939. Associate conductor, Chicago Symphony (1950–56), then co-ordinator of NBC's opera program. On Met musical staff (1958–69), acting as replacement conductor (debut, *Rigoletto*, Feb. 18, 1959). President, Manhattan School of Music (1969–76).

Schikaneder, Emanuel [Johann Joseph Baptist]. Librettist and impresario; b. Straubing, Austria, Sep. 1, 1751; d. Vienna, Sep. 21, 1812. Actor, dancer, and eventually director of a travelling theater troupe that from 1788 occupied the Freihaus-Theater auf der Wieden in suburban Vienna, where he presented plays and operas, often to his own texts. In 1791 he collaborated with Mozart on the hugely successful *Zauberflöte*, a fantasy singspiel with Masonic elements, conceived as a vehicle for himself in the role of Papageno.

Schiller, Friedrich von. German poet and dramatist (1759–1805). Operas based on his writings include *Don Carlos* (Verdi), *Giovanna d'Arco* (Verdi), *Guillaume Tell* (Rossini), *Luisa Miller* (Verdi), *The Maid of Orleans* (Tchaikovsky), *Maria Stuarda* (Donizetti), and *I Masnadieri* (Verdi).

Schillings, Max von. Composer and conductor; b. Düren, Germany, Apr. 19, 1868; d. Berlin, July 24, 1933. Studied with Brambach at Bonn Gymnasium. General music director, Stuttgart (1911–18); director, Berlin State Opera (1919–25); in 1924 and 1931, toured U.S. with German Opera Co. His early operas *Ingwelde* (1894) and *Der Pfeifertag* (1899) were influenced by Wagnerian techniques. *Mona Lisa* (1915), his most successful work, is more veristic.

Schinkel, Karl Friedrich. Designer; b. Neuruppin, Germany, Mar. 13, 1781; d. Berlin, Oct. 9, 1841. Primarily an architect, he also painted and experimented with lighting, transparencies, dioramas, and cycloramas. Appointed state architect of Prussia in 1814, responsible for remodelling Berlin Hofoper. Designed panoramic sets for over forty operas, ballets, and plays. His ideas anticipated and influenced Wagner and Semper, as well as later European designers.

Schipa, Tito. Tenor; b. Lecce, Jan. 2, 1888; d. New York, Dec. 16, 1965. Studied with Alceste Gerunda in Lecce, then with Emilio Piccoli in Milan; debut as Alfredo, Vercelli, 1910. For five years, he sang in provincial theaters, singing parts such as Turiddu, Milio (*Zazà*), Maurizio (*Adriana*), and Cavaradossi (role of his Milan debut, dal Verme, 1912), as well as the lyric roles that would become his staples. After engagements at the Colón, Buenos Aires (1913), Costanzi, Rome, and San Carlo, Naples (1914), he made his Scala debut as Vladimir (*Prince Igor*), 1915. In 1917 at Monte Carlo, he created Ruggero (*Rondine*). Beginning in 1919, he sang regularly at Chicago Opera; his roles there, until 1932, included Almaviva, Fenton, Gérald (*Lakmé*), Carlo (*Linda*), Lionel (*Martha*), and Fra Diavolo. In San Francisco (1924–29, 1935, 1939–40), he also sang Mascagni's Fritz and Werther. He joined the Met as Nemorino on Nov. 23, 1932, and in 4 seasons sang 28 performances of 8 roles, including Don Ottavio, Alfredo, Massenet's Des Grieux, Ernesto, Edgardo, Wilhelm Meister (*Mignon*), and Elvino (*Sonnambula*). In 1929 he sang in Italy for the first time in many years, and appeared regularly at La Scala, 1932–39, returning occasionally until 1949, when he sang Paolino (*Matrimonio Segreto*). After singing Werther and Almaviva in Rome in 1952, he concentrated on recital appearances.

One of the most ingratiating of singers, with refined enunciation of text, elegant phrasing, and instinctive musicianship, Schipa held a prominent place in the light romantic Italian tenor repertory during his long and successful career. With a voice both smaller and less luscious in timbre than Gigli's, he could nonetheless project passion as well as tenderness, and was famous for his Werther and Des Grieux as well as for lighter parts.

Schippers, Thomas. Conductor; b. Kalamazoo, Mich., Mar. 9, 1930; d. New York, Dec. 16, 1977. Studied at Curtis Institute, then attracted notice as conductor of *The Consul* on Broadway in 1950, beginning a long association with Menotti (music director, Spoleto Festival, 1958–75). Conducted at N.Y.C. Opera (1952–54); in 1955, appeared with N.Y. Philharmonic, La Scala, and the Met (debut, *Don Pasquale*, Dec. 23, 1955). He returned frequently to the Met, conducting 289 perfs. of a broad repertory, including the U.S. premiere of *Last Savage*, the world premiere of *Antony and Cleopatra*, and works by Donizetti, Rossini, Bizet, Verdi, Wagner, Strauss, and Mussorgsky. Bayreuth debut, *Meistersinger*, 1963. Music director of the Cincinnati Symphony from 1970 until his early death from cancer, Schippers was a vigorous and direct interpreter, as attested by a number of operatic recordings.

Schlusnus, Heinrich. Baritone; b. Braubach am Rhein, Germany, Aug. 6, 1888; d. Frankfurt, June 18, 1952. Studied voice while working in the postal service; debut as Herald (*Lohengrin*), Hamburg, 1915. After appearing in Nuremberg (1915–17), he joined the Berlin State Opera (debut, Wolfram, 1917), where he remained on the roster until 1945, specializing in Italian repertory, notably Verdi. After study with Louis Blacher in Berlin, he began giving lieder recitals in 1918, thereafter concertizing widely. He also sang opera in Amsterdam (1919), Barcelona (1922), Bayreuth (Amfortas, 1933), and Paris (1937); his only U.S. stage appearances were in Chicago (Wolfram, 1927). With a classical voice production, Schlusnus was Germany's leading baritone between the wars. His last stage performance was as Germont in Coblenz, 1951.

Schmedes, Erik. Tenor; b. Gentofte, near Copenhagen, Aug. 27, 1868; d. Vienna, Mar. 21, 1931. Studied as baritone in Berlin and Paris; debut as Herald (*Lohengrin*), Wiesbaden, 1891. After further study, tenor debut as Siegfried, Vienna, 1898; remained there until 1924, also singing at Bayreuth (1899–1902). In his only Met season, sang 11 perfs. of Siegmund (debut, Nov. 18, 1908), Pedro (*Tiefland*), Siegfried, Tristan, and Parsifal.

Schneider-Siemssen, Günther. Designer; b. Augsburg, Germany, June 7, 1927, of Austrian parents. Studied in Munich with Preetorius and Hartmann, held positions in Munich, with Salzburg Marionettes (1952–72), and in Bremen (1954). Chief designer, Vienna State Opera, Volksoper (since 1962); frequent collaborations with Karajan in Vienna and Salzburg. His Salzburg *Ring* was re-designed for the Met (1967–72), for which he has also designed *Tristan* (1971), *Jenůfa* (1974), *Tannhäuser* (1977), *Hoffmann* (1981), *Arabella* (1983), *Walküre* (beginning new *Ring* cycle) and *Fledermaus* (both 1986).

Tito Schipa

Schnorr von Carolsfeld, Ludwig. Tenor; b. Munich, July 2, 1836; d. Dresden, July 21, 1865. Studied in Leipzig and with Eduard Devrient, Karlsruhe; debut there in small roles, 1855. As leading tenor in Dresden, 1860–65, he sang Lohengrin and Tannhäuser. Shortly after creating Tristan (Munich, 1865), Schnorr died of heart failure. He was married to soprano **Malvina Schnorr von Carolsfeld**, née Garrigues (1825–1904), a Garcia student, who created Isolde.

Schoeck, Othmar. Composer; b. Brunnen, Switzerland, Sep. 1, 1886; d. Zurich, Mar. 8, 1957. Studied at Zurich Conservatory and with Reger in Leipzig. His early works, in the Romantic tradition, include the comic opera *Don Ranudo de Colibrados* (1919) and the pantomime *Das Wandbild* (1921). Schoeck later developed a style of greater harmonic, orchestral, and psychological complexity, exemplified by the operas *Venus* (1922); *Penthesilea* (1927), considered his most dramatic work; *Massimilia Doni* (1937); and *Das Schloss Dürande* (1943).

Schoeffel, John B. Impresario; b. Rochester, N.Y., May 11, 1846; d. Boston, Aug. 31, 1918. He became Henry E. Abbey's partner during the 1870s; they were among the first to book celebrated European actors (Bernhardt, Langtry, Irving, Terry) on U.S. tours. Schoeffel apparently functioned in the firm as the budget-minded counterweight to Abbey's grandiose enthusiasms. After its financially disastrous first Met season (1883–84), the firm of Abbey, Schoeffel, and Maurice Grau became the country's most successful theatrical agency, credit for which was generally given to Schoeffel's partners. The firm returned successfully to the Met in 1891, folding after Abbey's death in 1896; in the re-organization, Schoeffel acquired the Tremont Theater in Boston, which he managed until his death.

Schoenberg, Arnold. Composer; b Vienna, Sep. 13, 1874; d. Los Angeles, Calif., July 13, 1951. Principally self-taught, with advice from Zemlinsky, he composed first in a late-Romantic style, then, fascinated by the expressive potential of post-Wagnerian chromaticism, in the oratorio *Gurrelieder* and a remarkable series of instrumental works (1901–09) gradually abandoned traditional tonality altogether. After a compositional block during World War I, he devised a new basis for musical organization, "composition with 12 tones"; most of his subsequent music used this controversial method, intended to replace the structural role of tonality. He taught in Vienna (where his students included Berg and Webern), in Berlin until forced out by the Nazis in 1933, and later in Los Angeles, where he lived from 1934 until his death.

Schoenberg composed four remarkable operas. The psychological monodrama *Erwartung* (comp. 1909) stands at the climax of his "atonal" phase, followed by the allegorical, equally expressionistic *Die glückliche Hand* (comp. 1913). Twelve-tone technique is used in the satiric opera *Von heute auf morgen* (1930) and the idealistic biblical epic *Moses und Aron*, two acts of which were completed by 1932, though Schoenberg never succeeded in writing music for the brief final act.

BIBLIOGRAPHY: H.H. Stuckenschmidt, *Arnold Schoenberg* (N.Y., and London, 1977).

Schöffler, Paul. Baritone; b. Dresden, Sep. 15, 1897; d. Amersham, England, Nov. 21, 1977. Studied with Waldemar Stägemann in Dresden and Sammarco in Milan; debut as Herald (*Lohengrin*), Dresden, 1926. Member, Dresden Opera (1926–39), Vienna State Opera (1939–70). He also sang at Covent Garden (debut, Donner, 1934), Bayreuth (debut, Sachs, 1944) and Salzburg (1938–65), where he created Einem's Danton (1947) and Jupiter in *Liebe der Danae* (1952). Met debut as Jochanaan, Jan. 26, 1950; in 9 seasons (until 1964), he sang 91 perfs. of 14 roles, including Don Giovanni, Sachs, Scarpia, Amfortas, Kurwenal, Pizarro, Orest, Grand Inquisitor, and Music Master (*Ariadne*). He sang the *Walküre* Wotan in San

Thomas Schippers

Friedrich Schorr as Hans Sachs in *Die Meistersinger von Nürnberg*

Francisco (1953) and Chicago (1956). With a firm, not quite heroic baritone and a mastery of ironic characterization, Schöffler was an effective if slightly dry Sachs and Barak (*Frau*).

Schorr, Friedrich. Bass-baritone; b. Nagyvárad, Hungary, Sep. 2, 1888; d. Farmington, Conn., Aug. 14, 1953. Studied in Vienna with Adolf Robinson; after singing the Steersman (*Tristan*) while visiting Chicago in early 1912, formal debut later that year as Wotan (*Walküre*), Graz. He sang there for four years, then moved to Prague (German Opera, 1916–18), Cologne (1918–23), and Berlin (State Opera, 1923–32), where he sang not only the Wagner roles that formed the core of his repertory, but also Barak (*Frau*), Borromeo (*Palestrina*), and Busoni's Faust. He visited N.Y. with a touring company in 1923, singing Wotan, Kurwenal, and Pizarro (*Fidelio*), and was engaged by the Met; beginning with his debut as Wolfram on Feb. 14, 1924, he sang with the company for 20 seasons, in 356 perfs. of 18 roles, most often the great Wagner parts – the *Walküre* Wotan (48 times), the Wanderer (40), and Gunther (38), Kurwenal, Hans Sachs, Telramund, Amfortas, the *Rheingold* Wotan, the Dutchman – but also Pizarro, Jochanaan (*Salome*), Faninal (*Rosenkavalier*), and the High Priest (*Zauberflöte*). He was the Met's first Orest (*Elektra*), Daniello (*Jonny spielt auf*), and Shvanda. He appeared frequently at Covent Garden, singing Wagner roles and Orest (1924–33), in Bayreuth as Wotan (1925–31), and in San Francisco (1931–38).

Without question the greatest Wagnerian bass-baritone of his time, Schorr was equally impressive in Wotan's scornful rages and Sachs's tenderness; his noble, smooth, resonant voice functioned well at all dynamic levels, and his diction was precise, authoritative, and finely colored. Extensive passages from his major roles are well preserved on recordings.

Schreier, Peter. Tenor; b. Meissen, Germany, July 19, 1935. Sang as a boy in the Dresden Kreuzchor, then studied with Polster in Leipzig and Winkler in Dresden;

Wilhelmine Schröder-Devrient

debut there as First Prisoner (*Fidelio*), 1961. Member, Berlin State Opera, since 1963, with numerous guest appearances elsewhere, including Vienna, Munich, Salzburg (debut, Tamino, 1967), La Scala (debut, 1968), and Colón, Buenos Aires (debut, 1968). In 2 Met seasons, he sang Tamino (debut, Dec. 25, 1967) and Ottavio. In addition to Mozart, his repertory includes Fenton, Almaviva, the Holy Fool (*Boris*), Lenski (*Onegin*), and Loge. Also an admired interpreter of lieder and (since 1970) a conductor.

Schreker, Franz. Composer; b. Monaco, Mar. 23, 1878, of Austrian parents; d. Berlin, Mar. 21, 1934. Studied with Fuchs in Vienna; taught composition in Vienna (from 1912) and Berlin (1920–22). In the successful *Der ferne Klang* (1912) and *Das Spielwerk und die Prinzessin* (1913), he turned from Wagnerian and Straussian models towards French impressionism. After *Die Gezeichneten* (1918) and *Der Schatzgräber* (1920), Schreker sought to remain up-to-date by turning to more radical harmony in *Irrelohe* (1924), and towards neo-classicism in *Christophorus* (1924–27), *Der singende Teufel* (1928), and *Der Schmied von Gent* (1932).

Schröder-Devrient, Wilhelmine. Soprano; b. Hamburg, Dec. 6, 1804; d. Coburg, Jan. 26, 1860. Studied with her baritone father and actress mother, later with Giuseppe Mozatti, Vienna; after appearances in drama, operatic debut as Pamina, Kärntnertortheater, 1821. The following year she sang Agathe (*Freischütz*) under Weber, and a sensational Fidelio attended by Beethoven. A member of the Dresden Court Theater, 1823–47, she created three roles for Wagner, who greatly admired her: Adriano (*Rienzi*), Senta, and Venus. In Paris (1830–32), she sang Donna Anna and Rossini's Desdemona; in London (1832–33, 1837), Euryanthe, Pamina, Amina, and Norma. Nicknamed "Queen of Tears" because she was observed weeping onstage, Schröder-Devrient overcame marked vocal deficiencies by the power of her acting and declamation.

Schubert, Franz. Composer; b. Vienna, Jan. 31, 1797; d. Vienna, Nov. 19, 1828. Studied with Ruzicka and Salieri. His genius for vocal music was revealed during adolescence in an outpouring of songs, but his works for the lyric stage were ill-fated, primarily because of ineffective librettos. Only three were performed during his lifetime: the singspiels *Die Zwillingsbrüder* (1820) and *Die Zauberharfe* (1820), and the incidental music (mostly instrumental) for *Rosamunde* (1823). His most mature stage works are the lyrical romance *Alfonso und Estrella* (1822); the singspiel *Die Verschworenen* (1823); and the opera *Fierabras* (1823). Other operas: *Des Teufels Lustschloss* (1814), *Adrast* (1817–19, unfinished); *Der vierjährige Posten* (1815); *Fernando* (1815); *Claudine von Villa Bella*, after Goethe (1815); *Die Freunde von Salamanka* (1815).

Schubert, Richard. Tenor; b. Dessau, Germany, Dec. 15, 1885; d. Oberstaufen, Oct. 12, 1959. Studied in Dresden; debut as baritone, Strassburg, 1909; second debut as tenor, Nuremberg, 1911. Sang Wagner roles in Wiesbaden (1913–17) and Hamburg (1917–35), where he created Paul (*Tote Stadt*), 1920. Also appeared in Vienna (1920–29) and Chicago (1921–22).

Schuch, Ernst von. Conductor; b. Graz, Austria, Nov. 23, 1846; d. Kötzschenbroda, Germany, May 10, 1914. A figure in Dresden musical life from 1872, he became general director in 1889, built a world-class ensemble, and was entrusted by Strauss with the premieres of *Feuersnot*, *Salome*, *Elektra*, and *Rosenkavalier*. During a brief visit to the Met in 1900, he led several concerts (debut, Mar. 29) and a single performance of *Lohengrin*.

Schuller, Gunther. Composer; b. New York, Nov. 22, 1925. Early career as horn player (Cincinnati Symphony, Met orchestra) and soloist; taught composition at Yale and Tanglewood. President of New England Conservatory, Boston (1967–77). An active proponent of "third stream" music, fusing contemporary jazz and art styles. His operas include *The Visitation* (1966), incorporating jazz elements, and a fairy tale for children, *The Fisherman and His Wife* (1970). Has conducted opera, including *Erwartung*, *Ariadne*, and *Rake* (San Francisco, 1968–70).

Schumann, Elisabeth. Soprano; b. Merseburg, Germany, June 13, 1885; d. New York, Apr. 23, 1952. Studied with Natalie Hänisch in Dresden, Marie Dietrich in Berlin, and Alma Schadow in Hamburg; debut as Shepherd (*Tannhäuser*), Hamburg, 1909. Member of Hamburg Opera (1909–19) and Vienna State Opera (1919–37). During her only Met season, she sang 45 perfs. of 10 roles, including Sophie (debut, Nov. 20, 1914), Musetta, Papagena, Gerhilde, Gretel, and Marzelline (*Fidelio*). At Salzburg, 1924–36, she sang Despina, Susanna, Serpina (*Serva Padrona*), and Zerlina under Strauss, Schalk, and Weingartner; her Covent Garden roles, 1924–31, included Eva, Blondchen, and Adele (*Fledermaus*). She moved to the U.S. in 1938, teaching and continuing to appear in recital. With a light, silvery voice and great personal charm, Schumann was inimitable in her special repertory.

Schumann, Robert. Composer; b. Zwickau, Saxony, June 8, 1810; d. Endenich, near Bonn, July 29, 1856. One of the great figures of German Romantic music, Schumann composed prolifically in several genres, notably piano music and songs. His stage works were confined to the opera *Genoveva* (1852), crippled by his inexperience in the theater, and incidental music for Byron's *Manfred* (1852).

Schumann-Heink [née Rössler], **Ernestine.** Contralto; b. Lieben, near Prague, June 15, 1861; d. Hollywood, Nov. 17, 1936. Studied with Marietta von Leclair in Graz, later with Franz Wüllner and G.B. Lamperti; operatic debut as Azucena, Dresden, 1878. After four years there, she moved to Hamburg (1882–98), where her roles included Amneris, Orfeo, Orsini (*Lucrezia Borgia*), Ulrica, Adriano (*Rienzi*), Carmen, and Quickly in the first German *Falstaff*. She first appeared in London in a *Ring* cycle under Mahler (1892), returning to Covent Garden (1897–1900) as Magdalene (*Evangelimann*), Ortrud, the Prologue in *Ero e Leandro*, and other roles. In Bayreuth, 1896–1914, she sang Erda, Waltraute, Magdalene, Mary (*Holländer*), the First Norn, and the offstage alto solo in *Parsifal*. At the Met, she sang 157 perfs. in 14 scattered seasons (1899–1932), beginning as Ortrud on Jan. 9, 1899; her 17 roles included most of her Bayreuth parts, also Fricka, Flosshilde (*Rheingold*), Brangäne, and Fidès (*Prophète*). Her last Met appearance, at age 70, was as Erda (*Siegfried*), Mar. 11, 1932. She continued to sing in Europe, and created Klytemnästra (*Elektra*), Dresden, 1909; in America she also appeared in Chicago (1911–12) and Boston (debut, Azucena, 1913). Beginning in 1904, she increasingly concentrated on recitals, and eventually became a beloved popular figure, in musical comedy, radio, and films.

Only the earliest of Schumann-Heink's recordings convey the full extent of her range (almost three octaves, from low D to high B) and technical command in coloratura and trilling, but even the last of them attest to her dramatic and communicative powers, her ability to project words with authority, color, and expressivity, and her imposing musicianship.

BIBLIOGRAPHY: M. Lawton, *Schumann-Heink: The Last of the Titans* (N.Y., 1928, reprinted 1977).

Ernestine Schumann-Heink as Waltraute in *Götterdämmerung*

Schütz, Heinrich. Composer; b. Köstritz, near Gera, Germany, bapt. Oct. 9, 1585; d. Dresden, Nov. 6, 1672. Studied with Giovanni Gabrieli in Venice. The leading 17th-c. German composer of sacred music, from 1617 he was music director to the Elector of Saxony. Only stage works: the first German opera, *Dafne* (1627), which set a translation of Rinuccini's libretto for Peri's *Dafne*; and the opéra-ballet *Orpheus und Eurydice* (1638); the music of both is lost.

Schützendorf, Gustav. Baritone; b. Cologne, Germany, 1883; d. Berlin, Apr. 27, 1937. Studied in Cologne and Milan; debut as Don Giovanni, Krefeld, 1905. Sang in Munich (1914–20) and Berlin (State Opera, 1920–22). Met debut as Faninal, Nov. 17, 1922; in 13 seasons, sang 321 perfs. of 34 roles, including Beckmesser, Alberich, Klingsor, and Papageno. Brother of baritone Leo; married to sopranos Delia Reinhardt and Grete Stückgold.

Schützendorf, Leo. Baritone; b. Cologne, Germany, May 7, 1886; d. Berlin, Dec. 18, 1931. Studied in Cologne; debut in Düsseldorf, 1908. Appeared in Krefeld (1909–12), Darmstadt (1913–17), Wiesbaden (1917–19), and Vienna (1919–20). At Berlin State Opera (1920–29), sang such roles as Ochs, Alberich, Sparafucile, and Boris, and created Wozzeck. Brother of baritone Gustav.

Schwanda der Dudelsackpfeifer. See *Shvanda the Bagpiper*.

Schwarz, Joseph. Baritone; b. Riga, Latvia, Oct. 10, 1880; d. Berlin, Nov. 10, 1926. Studied in Berlin and Vienna; debut as Amonasro, Linz, 1900. Sang in Riga, Graz, St. Petersburg, at Vienna Volksoper (from 1906) and Court Opera (1909–15; debut as di Luna). Member of Berlin Court/State Opera (1915–20, 1924–26); also appeared in Chicago (1921–25; debut as Rigoletto), Paris Opéra (1923), and Covent Garden (1925).

Schwarzkopf, Elisabeth. Soprano; b. Jarotschin [now Jarocin], Russian Poland, Dec. 9, 1915. Studied in Berlin as alto with Lula Mysz-Gmeiner, later as soprano with Maria Ivogün; debut as Flowermaiden (*Parsifal*), Städtische Oper, Berlin, 1938. She sang there until 1942, in roles such as Oscar (*Ballo*), Adele (*Fledermaus*), and Zerbinetta, then moved to the Vienna State Opera, with which she visited London in 1947 as Donna Elvira and Marzelline (*Fidelio*). With the resident Covent Garden company, 1947–53, she sang Sophie, Violetta, Pamina, Mimi, Eva, Susanna, Gilda, Butterfly, and Manon (all in English). In Salzburg (1947–64), she perfected what became her core repertory: the Countess (*Nozze*), Donna Elvira, Alice Ford, Fiordiligi, and the Marschallin; at La Scala (1948–63), she also sang Elisabeth, Elsa, Mélisande, Marguerite, and Iole in Handel's oratorio *Hercules*. With the Scala company she created Anne Trulove (*Rake's Progress*), Venice, 1951, that summer also appearing at Bayreuth as Eva and Woglinde. Her American debut, as the Marschallin, was in San Francisco (1955), where she sang Mařenka (*Bartered Bride*) as well as her more familiar roles; in 1959, she sang Mozart operas in Chicago. The Marschallin was the role of her debuts at the Paris Opéra (1962) and the Met (Oct. 13, 1964), where her only 2 seasons comprised 9 Marschallins, one Elvira. She retired from opera after a 1972 Brussels *Rosenkavalier*, and from concerts after a 1975 farewell tour. Since then she has conducted master classes in Europe and America.

Schwarzkopf began her career as a coloratura, moved gradually to lyric parts, and eventually specialized in a small group of roles that she refined to a high degree of subtle artifice and nuance. Her careful (if, for some, too self-conscious) attention to detail and effect, remarkable musical and dramatic intelligence, and carefully controlled and husbanded voice made her one of the most admired artists of the postwar years. She is well represented by recordings of her major roles, produced by her husband Walter Legge, for many years principal producer for EMI.

Schweigsame Frau, Die (The Silent Woman). Opera in 3 acts by Strauss; libretto by Stefan Zweig, after Ben Jonson's *Epicoene*.

First perf., Dresden, June 24, 1935: Cebotari, Sack, Kremer, Ahlersmeyer, Plaschke, c. Böhm. U.S. prem., N.Y.C. Opera, Oct. 7, 1958 (in Eng.): Carroll, Moody, Alexander, Beattie, Ukena, c. Adler.

This extravagantly if inventively composed opera descends from the same ancient plot line as *Don Pasquale*.

A suburb of London, c. 1780. Sir Morosus (bs), a retired admiral, cannot bear noise; his barber (bar) encourages him to reorganize his household by marrying a silent woman, and offers to find one. Morosus' nephew Henry (t) arrives; his uncle is outraged to learn that Henry has joined a travelling operatic troupe and married the singer Aminta (s). Disinheriting Henry, Morosus orders the barber to find a silent wife. The barber and Henry arrange a fake marriage between Morosus and Aminta, disguised as "Timida" – who immediately after the wedding becomes very noisy, making Morosus miserable. Eventually the plot is revealed and Morosus, welcoming the return of peace and quiet, forgives all.

Sciutti, Graziella. Soprano; b. Turin, Italy, Apr. 17, 1927. Studied at Santa Cecilia, Rome; debut as Lucy (*Telephone*), Aix, 1951. Specialized in 17th- and 18th-c. repertory, also Rossini. Opened Piccola Scala, Milan, as Carolina (*Matrimonio Segreto*), 1955; Covent Garden debut as Oscar, 1956. Also appeared at Glyndebourne, Salzburg, San Francisco.

Scotney, Evelyn. Soprano; b. Ballarat, Australia, July 11, 1896; d. London, Aug. 5, 1967. A Melba protegée, studied with Marchesi in London; debut as Frasquita, Boston, 1912, later singing Lucia, Gilda, and Violetta. In her 2 Met seasons, she sang 16 perfs. of the Princess in *Juive* (debut, Nov. 22, 1919), the Queen of Shemakha, and Lucia.

Scott, Walter. Scottish novelist (1771–1832). Operas based on his writings include *La Dame Blanche* (Boieldieu), *La Donna del Lago* (Rossini), *Elisabetta, Regina d'Inghilterra* (Rossini), *La Jolie Fille de Perth* (Bizet), and *Lucia di Lammermoor* (Donizetti).

Scotti, Antonio. Baritone; b. Naples, Jan. 25, 1866; d. Naples, Feb. 26, 1936. Studied in Naples with Ester Triffani-Paganini and Vincenzo Lombardi; debut there as Cinna (*Vestale*), Circolo Filarmonico, 1889. He then sang classic roles such as Alphonse (*Favorite*) and Carlo (*Ernani*) at the Manzoni, Milan (1890), the Argentina, Rome (1891), in Madrid (1891–92) and Buenos Aires (from 1892), also in Russia and throughout Italy. La Scala debut as Hans Sachs (1898), followed by Falstaff, both under Toscanini; thereafter he sang mainly in England and America. At Covent Garden (debut, Don Giovanni,

1899), he sang regularly until 1910 and again in 1913–14, and created Chim-Fen (*Oracolo*). Don Giovanni was also his debut role at the Met (Dec. 27, 1899), where he appeared for 34 consecutive seasons in 832 perfs. (and nearly 350 more on tour) of 36 roles, most frequently as Scarpia (156 times), Sharpless (119), Marcello (107), also Tonio and Chim-Fen; other roles included Nevers (*Huguenots*), Valentin, Escamillo, Rigoletto, Amonasro, Malatesta (*Don Pasquale*), Iago, Germont, Almaviva, Belcore, de Siriex (*Fedora*), Puccini's and Massenet's Lescauts, Falstaff, and Count Gil (*Segreto*). He appeared occasionally in his most celebrated roles in Boston (1911–14), Chicago (1910), Ravinia (1919), and San Francisco (1927), and organized the (financially disastrous) Scotti Grand Opera Co., which toured the U.S. and Canada, 1919–22. His 25th Met season was celebrated with a gala *Tosca* in 1924, and he made his farewell as Chim-Fen on Jan. 20, 1933.

At first a classic Italian baritone with a smooth, flexible, nuanced delivery, Scotti concentrated increasingly on verismo parts as his voice waned, and became perhaps the most celebrated Italian operatic actor of his day; at the Met, he dominated such roles as Scarpia for over three decades (only 11 *Tosca*s during his Met career did not feature Scotti!)

Scotto, Renata. Soprano; b. Savona, Feb. 24, 1934. Studied in Milan as a mezzo with Emilio Ghirardini and then as a soprano with Mercedes Llopart; debut while still a teenager as Violetta, Savona. After her formal debut in the same role (Nuovo, Milan, 1953), she came to La Scala in 1954 as Walter (*Wally*), but then worked in Trieste, Rome (Sophie in *Werther*, 1955), and at La Fenice, Venice (Micaela, 1956), and the Stoll, London (1957). At Edinburgh in 1957, she attracted attention when she replaced Callas as Amina (*Sonnambula*) with the Scala company, which she then rejoined in roles such as Adina, Mimi, Antonida (*Life for the Tsar*), Gretel, Elvira (*Puritani*), Nannetta, Marguerite, and Butterfly. Debuts followed at

Antonio Scotti as Scarpia in *Tosca*

Anton Seidl

Chicago (Mimi, 1960), Covent Garden (Butterfly, 1962), and the Met (Butterfly, Oct. 13, 1965). She has since returned regularly to the Met, appearing in more than 230 perfs. of 25 roles, initially lighter lyric-spinto and coloratura repertory (Lucia, Adina, Violetta, Gilda, Amina, and Mimi), then, from 1974, increasingly heavier fare: Hélène (*Vêpres*), the three heroines of Puccini's *Trittico* (a Met first), the *Trovatore* Leonora, Berthe (*Prophète*), Musetta, Adriana Lecouvreur, Desdemona, Luisa Miller, Elisabeth de Valois, Gioconda, Puccini's Manon, Norma, Lady Macbeth, Francesca da Rimini, and Vitellia (*Clemenza*). In the 1970s in other theaters, she sang parts such as Bellini's Straniera, Donizetti's Maria di Rohan and Anna Bolena, and Verdi's Giselda (*Lombardi*). In 1986, she directed *Butterfly* at the Met and made her house farewell in that opera on Jan. 17, 1987.

As a lyric-coloratura, Scotto was in the classic Italian tradition, with a lovely tone, excellent technique, innate musicality, and theatrical command. Though the increasing weight of her roles took its toll on the voice, her exceptional musical intelligence, dramatic intensity, and feeling for the idiom compensated to some extent for the tonal losses. Many of her roles are represented in recordings from her prime.

BIBLIOGRAPHY: Renata Scotto, *More Than a Diva* (N.Y., 1984).

Scribe, Eugène. Librettist; b. Paris, Dec. 25, 1791; d. Paris, Feb. 20, 1861. A prolific and vastly successful playwright in his day, he also dominated French opera through his collaborations with Auber (*Muette de Portici, Fra Diavolo*), Meyerbeer (*Robert le Diable, Huguenots, Prophète, Africaine*), Boieldieu (*Dame Blanche*), and Halévy (*Juive*); for Verdi, he reworked his libretto for Donizetti's unfinished *Duc d'Albe* into *Vêpres Siciliennes*.

Seattle. City in Washington state. The first opera performed here was *Carmen*, by the touring Metropolitan Opera in 1899. Various troupes visited subsequently, and short-lived attempts were made to create permanent organizations, such as the Standard Grand Opera Company (1914) and the Northwest Grand Opera Association (1950s). In 1964, the Seattle Opera Association was established by Glynn Ross, who became its general manager and stage director; housed in the Opera House (formerly the Civic Auditorium, refurbished in 1962, capacity 3,100), the company began modestly with four

performances of *Carmen* and *Tosca*, eventually emerging as a leader in regional opera. In addition to standard works, Seattle has presented the world premieres of Floyd's *Of Mice and Men* (1970) and Pasatieri's *Black Widow* (1972). Seattle confirmed its place on the operatic map in 1975, with the inauguration of annual summer festivals devoted to the *Ring* cycle (in both German and English). In 1983, Speight Jenkins succeeded Ross; in 1984 he retired the old *Ring* production, introducing a controversial new staging (in German with surtitles) in 1986.

Seefehlner, Egon. Manager; b. Vienna, June 3, 1912. Assistant director at the Vienna State Opera under Böhm and Karajan (1951–61), he became director (1961–72), then general manager (1972–75) of the Deutsche Oper, Berlin. He later returned to Vienna as general director (1975–82, 1984–86).

Seefried, Irmgard. Soprano; b. Köngetried, Germany, Oct. 9, 1919. As a child, studied with her father, with Albert Meyer at Augsburg Conservatory, and later with Paola Novikova; debut as Priestess (*Aida*), Aachen, 1940. She remained in Aachen until 1943, then joined the Vienna State Opera (debut, Eva in *Meistersinger*, 1943); the following year, she sang the Composer (*Ariadne*) in a performance honoring Strauss' 80th birthday. She remained a member of the Vienna company, making her London debut with them in 1947 as Fiordiligi and Susanna, also appearing at Salzburg (from 1946, notably as Pamina) and La Scala (debut, Susanna, 1949). In her only Met season, she sang 5 perfs. of Susanna (debut, Nov. 20, 1953). Other appearances in Chicago (1961, 1964), Aix (1963), and Stuttgart (Marie in *Wozzeck*, 1966). A vibrant, spontaneous performer with a warm soprano and sympathetic musicianship.

Segreto di Susanna, Il (The Secret of Susanna). Opera in 1 act by Wolf-Ferrari; libretto by Enrico Golisciani.

First perf., Munich, Court Opera, Dec. 4, 1909 (in Ger.): c. Mottl. U.S. prem., N.Y., Metropolitan Opera House (Chicago Opera Co.), Mar. 14, 1911: White, Sammarco, c. Campanini. Met prem., Dec. 13, 1912: Farrar, Scotti, c. Polacco, p. Speck. 11 perfs. in 4 seasons.

Modeled on the two-character intermezzos of the baroque period; set in a Piedmontese drawing room, 1840. The countess Susanna (s) smokes in secret; her husband Count Gil (bar) catches the scent and suspects her of entertaining a lover. Disclosure of her clandestine habit sets all at ease.

Segurola, Andrés (Perello) de. See *de Segurola, Andrés (Perello)*.

Seidl, Anton. Conductor; b. Pest [now Budapest], Hungary, May 7, 1850; d. New York, Mar. 28, 1898. After study in Leipzig, he assisted in preparations for the 1876 Bayreuth *Ring*. Conducted in Leipzig (1875–83) and Bremen (1883–85), then came to the Met (debut, *Lohengrin*, Nov. 23, 1885) to replace the late Leopold Damrosch, and in 11 seasons conducted 340 perfs., including the American premieres of *Meistersinger, Tristan*, and all the *Ring* operas except *Walküre*, as well as *Königin von Saba*. In 1891, with the return of Italian opera to the Met, he became conductor of the N.Y. Philharmonic, returning to the opera house for German repertory until his premature death. One of the major early Wagnerians, much admired for his authority and his contributions to N.Y. musical life.

Seinemeyer, Meta. Soprano; b. Berlin, Sep. 5, 1895; d. Dresden, July 19, 1929. Studied in Berlin; debut in *Orphée aux Enfers*, Charlottenburg Opera, 1918; remained there until 1925. Sang Eva and Elisabeth in N.Y. with touring German company, 1923. With Dresden State Opera (1925–29), especially noted as Maddalena (*Chénier*) and Leonora (*Forza*). Sang Wagner roles at Covent Garden, 1929.

Sellars, Peter. Producer; b. Pittsburgh, Pa., 1958. Directed theater while at Harvard, and in 1980 staged *Don Giovanni* for New Hampshire Symphony. Subsequent productions include Handel's *Orlando* (Cambridge, Mass., 1981), *Mikado* (Chicago Lyric, 1983), *Così* (Ipswich, Mass., 1984), Maxwell Davies' *Lighthouse* (Boston, 1983), and *Giulio Cesare* (Purchase, N.Y., 1985). The *enfant terrible* of American opera, his productions are perceptive, tendentious, and controversial.

Sembach [Semfke], **Johannes.** Tenor; b. Berlin, Mar. 9, 1881; d. Bremerhaven, June 20, 1944. Studied in Vienna and with Jean de Reszke in Paris; debut, Vienna, 1900. Sang in Vienna (until 1905) and Dresden (1905–13), creating Aegisth (*Elektra*). Met debut as Parsifal, Nov. 26, 1914; in 5 seasons (1915–17, 1921–22), he sang 91 perfs. of 14 roles, including Tamino, Loge, Siegmund, Tristan, and Adolar (*Euryanthe*).

Sembrich, Marcella [Prakseda Marcelina Kochańska]. Soprano; b. Wiśniewczyk, Galicia, Feb. 15, 1858; d. New York, Jan. 11, 1935. Studied violin and piano with her father, later at Lvov Conservatory with Wilhelm Stengel (whom she eventually married) – and in Vienna, and singing in Milan with G.B. Lamperti, later also with F. Lamperti; debut as Elvira (*Puritani*), Athens, 1877. Debuts as Lucia followed in Dresden (1878), Milan (dal Verme, 1879), and at Covent Garden (1880), where for 5 seasons she sang coloratura repertory, including Dinorah, Konstanze, Catherine (*Étoile du Nord*), Gilda, and Violetta. She also appeared in Russia (1880–98), Spain, Paris, and Berlin. She made her Met debut as Lucia on the theater's second night (Oct. 24, 1883), followed by Elvira, Violetta, Amina, Gilda, Rosina, Zerlina, Lady Harriet (*Martha*), Ophélie (*Hamlet*), Marguerite (*Huguenots*), and Juliette. She returned in 1898 to sing 10 more seasons, for a total of 253 perfs. (185 more on tour) of 25 roles, most often Violetta (33 times), Rosina (32), Lucia (25), and Mimi (21). The Met's first Frau Fluth (*Lustigen Weiber*), Queen of Night, Marie (*Fille*), Ulana (*Manru*), Elvira (*Ernani*), Adina, and Rosalinde (*Fledermaus*), Sembrich also sang Susanna, Norina, Marguerite, Lakmé, Eva, and Nedda at the house, and retired after a gala on Feb. 6, 1909. She sang recitals until 1917, and taught at the Curtis and Juilliard schools; her pupils included Antoine, Giannini, Gluck, and Mario.

A completely accomplished florid soprano in the tradition of Patti, with a range from middle C to high F, a fluent technique, and great expressivity, Sembrich was also a distinguished recitalist. Her musical achievements were not limited to singing; at the 1884 Met benefit for Abbey, she played two movements from a de Bériot violin concerto, and encored it with a Chopin selection on the piano.

Semele. Opera in 3 acts by Handel; libretto after William Congreve's for John Eccles' 1706 opera.

First perf., London, Covent Garden, Feb. 10, 1744: Duparc, Young, Beard. U.S. stage prem., Evanston, Ill., Northwestern U., Jan. 1959: c. Johnson.

Marcella Sembrich as Marguerite de Valois in *Les Huguenots*

Hovering between opera and oratorio, this brilliant work has proved stageworthy in modern revivals. The love of Jupiter (t) for Semele (s) comes to an end when, at the insidious urging of Juno (ms), the girl demands to see her lover in his godly guise; when he complies, his glory burns her to death.

semi-opera. An English dramatic genre of the years around 1700, incorporating elaborate musical scenes for minor characters, although the principals did not sing. Most of Purcell's theater work was devoted to this genre.

Semiramide. Opera in 2 acts by Rossini; libretto by Rossi, after Voltaire's tragedy *Sémiramis*.

First perf., Venice, Fenice, Feb. 3, 1823: Colbran, Mariani, Sinclair, Galli. U.S. prem., New Orleans, St. Charles, May 19, 1837. Met prem., Jan. 12, 1894: Melba, Scalchi, Guetary, E. de Reszke, c. Mancinelli, p. Parry. 5 perfs in 2 seasons.

Among the best of the grand, wide-ranging, and virtuosic serious operas that Rossini composed for Isabella Colbran, his first wife.

Ancient Babylon. Semiramide (s), Queen of Babylon, has killed her husband Nino with the help of Prince Assur (bs), who wants her hand and the throne. But she is drawn to the handsome young commander Arsace (c), unaware that he is really her son. Arsace, himself unaware of his relation to the queen until it is revealed to him by the high priest Oroe (bs), loves the princess Azema (s). When Semiramide announces her intention to marry Arsace, the ghost of Nino appears amid thunder and lightning to declare that Arsace will be king, but not before crimes are expiated and a victim sacrificed. The ghost bids Arsace return later to the tomb; Assur follows him, intent on murdering the commander. Semiramide, who has learned the youth's true identity, also follows, to protect him. In the darkness of the tomb, Arsace kills Semiramide with the thrust meant for Assur; Nino's murder is expiated, and Arsace ascends the throne with Azema. (A revised version evades the matricide by having Arsace kill Assur.)

Sendak, Maurice. Illustrator and designer; b. Brooklyn, N.Y., June 10, 1928. A brilliant and successful illustrator and author of children's books, notably *Where the Wild Things Are* and *Higglety Pigglety Pop!*, made into operas by Knussen. Sendak has also designed sets and costumes for *Zauberflöte* (Houston, 1981), *Cunning Little Vixen* (N.Y.C. Opera, 1981), and *Love for Three Oranges* (Glyndebourne, 1982).

Sénéchal, Michel. Tenor; b. Tavery, France, Feb. 11, 1927. Studied at Paris Conservatory; debut at Monnaie, Brussels, 1950. Sang Rameau's *Platée*, Aix, 1956. France's leading specialist in character parts, he made his Met debut in the four tenor roles in *Hoffmann*, Mar. 8, 1982, and has since sung Basilio (*Nozze*) and Guillot (*Manon*).

Senesino [Francesco Bernardi]. Alto castrato; b. Siena (hence his nickname), c. 1680; d. Siena(?), c. 1759. Studied with Bernacchi, Bologna; from 1707, he sang in Genoa, Naples, Venice, and Bologna. Appeared in Dresden (1717–19), where Handel heard him and hired him to sing in London for the Royal Academy (1720–28, 1730–32). After his debut at the King's Theatre in Bononcini's *Astarto*, he created roles in Handel's *Ottone, Flavio, Giulio Cesare, Tamerlano, Rodelinda, Scipione, Alessandro, Admeto, Riccardo, Siroe, Tolomeo, Poro, Ezio, Sosarme,* and *Orlando*. Notoriously temperamental, he quarreled with Handel and in 1733 joined the rival Opera of the Nobility, remaining there until 1736, when he returned to Italy.

Tullio Serafin

After appearances in Florence (1737–39) and Naples (1740), he retired to Siena. One of the greatest castratos, and the most highly regarded by London audiences.

Sequi, Sandro. Producer; b. Rome, Nov. 10, 1935. Since his first operatic production, Respighi's *Lucrezia* (Venice, 1961), he has worked in most European and American theaters. His Met stagings are *Fille du Régiment* (1972), *Siège de Corinth* (1975), and *Puritani* (1976); his Rome Opera production of Rossini's *Otello* was seen at Lincoln Center (1968).

Serafin, Tullio. Conductor; b. Rottanova di Cavarzere, Venice, Dec. 8, 1878; d. Rome, Feb. 2, 1968. After study at Milan Conservatory, a debut in Ferrara (1898), and several Italian posts, he became principal conductor at La Scala (1909–14, 1917–18). At the Met (debut, *Aida*, Nov. 3, 1924), in 10 seasons he conducted 504 perfs.: in addition to Italian repertory (including the U.S. premieres of *Turandot* and *Simon Boccanegra*), he led American works (premieres of *King's Henchman, Peter Ibbetson, Emperor Jones,* and *Merry Mount*) and *Siegfried*. After leaving the Met, he was artistic director of Rome's Teatro Reale (1934–43), where he led the first Italian *Wozzeck*. He returned to America to conduct at the N.Y.C. Opera (debut, *Tosca*, 1952) and the Chicago Opera (1955–58). He remained active until his eighties at various Italian theaters and in the recording studio. Much admired for his astute guidance of singers (including Ponselle, Callas, and Sutherland), Serafin was an authoritative keeper of Italian operatic tradition well into the modern era.

Serban, Andrei. Producer; b. Bucharest, Romania, 1943(?). Active in Bucharest student theater, he came to the U.S. to direct at La Mama, N.Y. (*Arden of Feversham* and *Ubu*, 1970), then assisted Peter Brook in Paris. Has staged opera in Nancy (*Zauberflöte*, 1979), for Welsh National and Covent Garden (*Turandot*, 1983). At N.Y.C. Opera, staged *Alcina* (1983) and *Norma* (1985).

serenata (Ital., "serenade"). In addition to its primary meaning, refers in the 18th c. to a short vocal work composed to celebrate a special occasion, presented with scenery but no action; Handel's *Acis and Galatea* is an example.

Sereni, Mario. Baritone; b. Perugia, Italy, Mar. 25, 1928. Studied at Santa Cecilia, Rome, and in Siena; debut as a Guest (*Stone Guest*), Florence, Comunale, 1954. Met debut as Gérard, Nov. 9, 1957; has since sung over 380 perfs. of 26 roles, including Germont, Marcello, Sharpless, Amonasro, and Belcore (*Elisir*). Also appeared in Buenos Aires, London, Vienna, Chicago, Houston and Dallas.

Serov, Alexander. Composer and critic; b. St. Petersburg, Jan. 23, 1820; d. St. Petersburg, Feb. 1, 1871. Primarily self-taught as a composer, he made his living as an acerbic critic whose writings supported the camp of Liszt and Wagner; however, his stage compositions were influenced more by Gounod, middle Verdi, and Meyerbeer. Most successful were the heroic *Judith* (1863); the historical drama *Rogneda* (1865); and *The Power of Evil* (1871), after a realistic drama by Ostrovsky.

Serse (Xerxes). Opera in 3 acts by Handel; text from Niccolò Minato's libretto for Cavalli's 1654 opera, revised in 1694 for Bononcini.

First perf., London, Haymarket, Apr. 15, 1738:

Francesina, Caffarelli, Montagnana. U.S. prem., North-ampton, Mass. (Smith College), May 12, 1928 (in Eng.): Garrison, Kullman, Marsh, c. Josten.

Blending comic and seria elements, this opera includes what is surely Handel's most famous operatic aria, "Ombra mai fù" (incorrectly known as "Handel's Largo"). In Ancient Persia, the king Serse (s) is betrothed to Amastre (a), but falls in love with Romilda (s) after hearing her sing; after various intrigues fail, all return to their original partners at the end.

Serva Padrona, La (The Maidservant turned Mistress). Intermezzo in 2 acts by Pergolesi; libretto by G.A. Federico.

First perf., Naples, San Bartolomeo, Aug. 28, 1733 (between the acts of Pergolesi's opera seria *Il Prigionier Superbo*): Monti, Corrado. U.S. prem., Baltimore, New Theater, June 14, 1790 (in Fr.). Met prem., Feb. 23, 1935: Fleischer, d'Angelo, c. Bellezza, p. Defrère. Later Met production: Dec. 9, 1942: Sayão, Baccaloni, c. Breisach, d. Rychtarik/Schenck, p. Wallerstein. 6 perfs. in 2 seasons.

This charming score has survived to represent a genre of comedy that spawned dozens if not hundreds of examples; the two-character cast of soprano and bass (sometimes with a mute third player) was standard. Serpina (s) is engaged as the housemaid of Uberto (bs), but with the help of her fellow-servant Vespone (mute) manipulates her master into marrying her.

Sessions, Roger. Composer; b. Brooklyn, N.Y., Dec. 28, 1896; d. Princeton, N.J., Mar. 16, 1985. Studied at Harvard U., at Yale U. with Horatio Parker, and privately with Ernest Bloch. A distinguished proponent of international modernism, his style evolved from neo-classicism to a complex, extended tonality, and in the Fifties to serialism; his students included Babbitt, Kirchner, Diamond, and Imbrie. His two operas, *The Trial of Lucullus* (1947) and *Montezuma* (1964), are uncompromising in style and seriousness.

Setti, Giulio. Chorus master and conductor; b. Treviglio, Italy, Oct. 3, 1869; d. Turin, Oct. 2, 1938. After study in Milan and posts in Italy, Cairo, Cologne, and Buenos Aires, he came to the Met with Toscanini in 1908 as chorus master, remaining until 1935. He frequently led Sunday-evening concerts (including the Verdi *Messa da Requiem*), but only three regular performances (debut, *Barbiere*, Feb. 12, 1922).

Seymour, John Laurence. Composer; b. Los Angeles, Calif., Jan. 18, 1893. Studied with Pizzetti in Italy and d'Indy in Paris. Initially a playwright, he turned to composing operas, including *Ramona* (1970) and *Olanta, el Jefe Kolla* (1977); his one-act *In the Pasha's Garden*, originally titled *The Eunuch*, was presented at the Met in 1935.

Shade, Ellen. Soprano; b. New York, Feb. 17, 1944(?). Studied in N.Y. at Juilliard Opera Center and with Cornelius Reid; debut as Liù, Frankfurt, 1972. In Chicago (debut, Emma in *Khovanshchina*, 1976), she sang Ilia (*Idomeneo*) and created Eve in Penderecki's *Paradise Lost*. Met debut as Eva, Apr. 21, 1976. N.Y.C. Opera debut as Donna Elvira, 1981.

Shade, Nancy. Soprano; b. Rockford, Ill. Studied at DePauw and Indiana U. and with Vera Scammon; debut as Leonora (*Trovatore*), Louisville, 1967. N.Y.C.

Opera debut as Musetta, 1971. Sang Manon Lescaut in Spoleto (1973), Giorgetta (*Tabarro*) at Covent Garden (1974), Lulu in Santa Fe (1979) and Frankfurt (1984–85), Marie (*Soldaten*) in Lyon (1983).

Shakespeare, William. English dramatist (1564–1616). Operas based on his writings include *Antony and Cleopatra* (Barber), *Béatrice et Bénédict* (Berlioz), *The Fairy Queen* (Purcell), *Falstaff* (Verdi), *Hamlet* (Thomas), *Das Liebesverbot* (Wagner), *Die lustigen Weiber von Windsor* (Nicolai), *Macbeth* (Verdi and Bloch), *A Midsummer Night's Dream* (Britten), *Otello* (Rossini and Verdi), *Roméo et Juliette* (Gounod), and *Der Widerspenstigen Zähmung* (Goetz).

Shalyapin, Fyodor. See *Chaliapin, Feodor*.

Shane, Rita. Soprano; b. New York. Studied at Barnard College and with Beverly Peck Johnson; debut as Olympia (*Hoffmann*), Chattanooga, 1964. N.Y.C. Opera debut as Donna Elvira, 1965; in 1979, she created the protagonist in Argento's *Miss Havisham's Fire* there. Sang at La Scala, Vienna, Munich. Met debut as Queen of Night, Mar. 22, 1973; in 8 seasons, she sang 46 perfs., including Berthe (*Prophète*), Oscar (*Ballo*), and Violetta.

Shanewis. Opera in 2 acts by Cadman; libretto by Nelle Richmond Eberhardt.

First perf., N.Y., Met, Mar. 23, 1918: Sundelius, Braslau, Howard, Althouse, c. Moranzoni, d. J. Fox, Bel Geddes/Bel Geddes. 8 perfs. in 2 seasons.

Set in California and Oklahoma, early 20th c., this opera reflects Cadman's fascination with American Indian music. Shanewis (c), a beautiful Indian girl, wins the heart of the architect Lionel (t), unaware that he is engaged to Amy (s), daughter of her benefactress Mrs. Everton (ms).

Shicoff, Neil. Tenor; b. New York, June 2, 1949. Studied with his father, a cantor, and at Juilliard, N.Y.; professional debut as Rinuccio (*Schicchi*), Met, Oct. 15, 1976; subsequent roles there include Duke, Lenski, Werther, Hoffmann, and Massenet's Des Grieux. Debuts in Chicago (Rodolfo, 1979), San Francisco (Edgardo, 1981), Paris (Roméo, 1981). Has appeared in Florence, Hamburg, London, Zurich, Munich, Houston, and Santa Fe.

Shirley, George. Tenor; b. Indianapolis, Ind., Apr. 18, 1934. Studied with Thelmy Georgi in Washington and Cornelius Reid in N.Y.; debut as Eisenstein (*Fledermaus*), Woodstock, N.Y., 1959. N.Y.C. Opera debut as Rodolfo, 1961; created Romilayu in Kirchner's *Lily* there, 1977. Met debut as Ferrando (*Così*), Oct. 24, 1961; in 12 seasons, sang 189 perfs. of 27 roles, including Tamino, Ottavio, Alfredo, Pinkerton, Roméo, Almaviva. Appeared at Glyndebourne (Tamino, 1966), Covent Garden (Ottavio, 1967; Pelléas, 1969), La Scala, and Santa Fe.

Shirley-Quirk, John. Bass-baritone; b. Liverpool, England, Aug. 28, 1931. Studied with Roy Henderson and sang in St. Paul's Cathedral Choir; operatic debut as Doctor (*Pelléas*), Glyndebourne, 1962. Joined English Opera Group, 1964; created roles in Britten's church parables, *Death in Venice*, and *Owen Wingrave*. In 2 Met seasons, he sang 17 perfs. of the Traveller and associated roles in *Death in Venice* (debut, Oct. 18, 1974), the Speaker (*Zauberflöte*), and the Music Master (*Ariadne*).

Shostakovich, Dmitri. Composer, b. St. Petersburg, Sep. 25, 1906; d. Moscow, Aug. 9, 1975. Studied with Maximilian Steinberg at Petrograd Conservatory; having attracted attention with his irreverent First Symphony (1926), he became an active member of the Leningrad avant-garde, notably with the satirical opera. *The Nose* (1930). *Lady Macbeth of Mtsensk District* (1934), a naturalistic treatment of adultery, murder, and suicide, in an adventurous musical style influenced by Mahler and Berg, was initially successful, but became in 1936 the target of violent official attacks. Forced to make a public apology, Shostakovich agreed to conform to the canons of socialist realism, but thereafter virtually abandoned serious operatic composition (an opera after Gogol's *The Gamblers*, begun in 1941, was never completed), concentrating primarily on symphonic and chamber music, and later also song. After the demise of Stalinism, he revised *Lady Macbeth* under its alternate title, *Katerina Izmailova* (perf. 1963), and composed *Moscow, Cheremushki* (1959), a musical comedy about public housing. He also made new orchestrations of Mussorgsky's *Boris Godunov* (1940) and *Khovanshchina* (1959). For all the significance of Shostakovich's contributions to the concert hall, the stifling of his theatrical talent constitutes one of the century's major musical tragedies.
BIBLIOGRAPHY: Eric Roseberry, *Shostakovich, His Life and Times* (N.Y., 1982).

Shvanda the Bagpiper. Opera in 2 acts by Weinberger; libretto by Miloš Kareš, after Tyl's folk tale.
First perf., Prague, National Theater, Apr. 27, 1927: c. Ostrčil. U.S. & Met prem., Nov. 7, 1931 (in Ger.): Müller, Branzell, Laubenthal, Schorr, c. Bodanzky, d. Urban/Palmedo, p. Niedecken-Gebhard. 5 perfs. in 1 season.
A fairy-tale opera of melodic charm and orchestral ingenuity. The Papageno-like bagpiper Shvanda (bar) falls under the influence of the robber Babinsky (t); his adventures take him to the kingdom of the Ice Queen (ms) and then to hell, whence Babinsky rescues him by winning a card game with the bored devil. In the end, the piper is reunited with his beloved Dorotka (s).

Cesare Siepi as Figaro in *Le Nozze di Figaro*

Siège de Corinth, Le (The Siege of Corinth). Opera in 3 acts by Rossini; libretto by Luigi Balocchi and Alexandre Soumet, after the libretto for *Maometto II*.
First perf., Paris, Opéra, Oct. 9, 1826: Cinti-Damoreau, Frémont, L. Nourrit, A. Nourrit, Dérivis. U.S. prem., N.Y., Italian Opera House (in Ital., as *L'Assedio di Corinto*), Feb. 6, 1835. Met prem., Apr. 7, 1975 (in Ital.): Sills, Theyard, Verrett, Diaz, c. Schippers, d. Benois, p. Sequi. 13 perfs. in 2 seasons.
Rossini's first French opera is a reworking of *Maometto II* (q.v.), involving much new music, orchestral refinements and an adaptation to French vocal style. The subsequent performing history of the opera – mostly in Italian translation – is complicated by conflation of the earlier work with the later.

Siegfried. See *Ring des Nibelungen, Der.*

Siems, Margarethe. Soprano; b. Breslau, Germany [now Wrocław, Poland]; Dec. 30, 1879; d. Dresden, Apr. 13, 1952. Studied in Dresden with Orgeni; debut at German Theater, Prague, 1902. She sang there until 1908, then at Dresden Court Opera (1908–20) and Berlin State Opera (1920–26). Her wide repertory included Lucia, Philine, Violetta, Aida, Mimi, Butterfly, Elisabeth, and Isolde; she created Strauss' Chrysothemis, Marschallin, and Zerbinetta. Covent Garden debut as London's first Marschallin, under Beecham, 1913. Beginning in 1920, she taught in Berlin, Dresden and Breslau; one of her pupils was Sigrid Onégin.

Siepi, Cesare. Bass; b. Milan, Feb. 10, 1923. Studied at Milan Conservatory; debut as Sparafucile, Schio, 1941. In 1946 he appeared at La Fenice (debut, Silva in *Ernani*) and in a La Scala summer season as Ramfis, Sparafucile, and the Padre Guardiano, and sang Zaccaria (*Nabucco*) in the first production in the rebuilt Scala. He remained with the company until 1950, in roles including Raimondo, the Old Hebrew (*Samson*), the Grand Inquisitor, Pogner, Lothario (*Mignon*), and Balthasar (*Favorite*), sang in Toscanini's Boito commemoration (1948), created Nonno Innocenzo (Pizzetti's *L'Oro*), and later returned as Fiesco (1955), Don Giovanni (1956), and Mefistofele (1958). His Met debut was as Philippe II on Bing's first opening night (Nov. 6, 1950), and he remained with the company for 23 seasons, singing 379 perfs. (plus nearly 100 on tour) of 18 roles, most frequently Mozart's Don Giovanni (71 times) and Figaro (56), also Méphistophélès, Basilio, Colline, the Padre Guardiano, Ramfis, Alvise, Boris, Oroveso (*Norma*), Silva, Zaccaria, and Fiesco; in 1970 he sang his first Wagner role in German, Gurnemanz. Other debuts during his Met years included Salzburg (Don Giovanni, 1953), San Francisco (Padre Guardiano, 1954), and Covent Garden (Don Giovanni, 1962). He also sang in musical comedy (including *Bravo Giovanni*, 1962), and continued to appear in opera in the 1980s, including Rodolfo in *Sonnambula* (Seattle, 1984) and Roger in *Jérusalem* (Parma, 1985).
Siepi's poised, rich, evenly produced voice could also command an edge of authority, his musicianship has always been of the first rank, and his handsome stature and bearing were matched with a lively, direct stage manner. His recordings include his famous Mozart roles, a Verdi Requiem under Toscanini, and a notable performance of Archibaldo (*Amore dei Tre Re*).

Signor Bruschino, Il. Opera in 1 act by Rossini; libretto by Giuseppe Foppa, after a French comedy by de Chazet and Ourry.

Beverly Sills as Violetta in *La Traviata*

First perf., Venice, San Moïse, late Jan. 1813: Pontiggia, Berti, Raffanelli, de Grecis. U.S. & Met prem., Dec. 9, 1932: Fleischer, Tokatyan, de Luca, Pinza, c. Serafin, d. Urban, Novak. 4 perfs. in 1 season.

A light farce set in 18th-c. Italy. Florville (t) and Sofia (s) wish to marry, but her guardian Gaudenzio (bs) has promised her to the son of old Signor Bruschino (bar). Florville impersonates the son, and the lovers manage to marry before the confusion clears.

Sigurd. Opera in 4 acts by Reyer; libretto by Camille du Locle and A. Blau.

First perf., Brussels, Monnaie, Jan. 7, 1884: Caron, Deschamps-Jehin, Jourdain, Devriès, Renaud, c. Dupont. U.S. prem., New Orleans, French Opera House, Dec. 24 1891.

A broadly lyrical but harmonically plain treatment of the Sigurd (Siegfried) story from the Younger Edda, popular in France at the height of the vogue for mythic-Nordic subjects that flourished there in Wagner's wake.

Silbersee, Der. Opera in 3 acts by Weill; libretto by Georg Kaiser.

First perf., Leipzig, Altes Theater, Feb. 18, 1933: Berndt, Carstens, Siedel, Golling, Sattler, c. Brecher (and simultaneously in Erfurt and Magdeburg). U.S. prem., N.Y.C. Opera, Mar. 20, 1980 (in Eng., adapted by Hugh Wheeler and Lys Symonette): Hynes, Bonazzi, Grey, Neill, Harrold, c. Rudel.

This "winter's tale" attempts to develop Weill's popular manner into a style comparable to that of *Zauberflöte*; as Hitler had become chancellor while it was in rehearsal, it was quickly banned. The policeman Olim (t) shoots the needy robber Severin (t), then feels sympathy for him, and they find a new, rewarding basis for true friendship.

Silja, Anja. Soprano; b. Berlin, Apr. 17, 1940. Studied with her grandfather, Egon van Rijn; debut as Rosina, Berlin Städtische Oper, 1956. Sang in Brunswick, Stuttgart, and at Bayreuth (debut as Senta, 1960, later singing Elsa, Eva, and Elisabeth). Since her Met debut as Fidelio (Feb. 26, 1972), she has returned to sing Salome and Marie (*Wozzeck*). Married to conductor Christoph von Dohnányi.

Sills, Beverly [Belle Silverman]. Soprano; b. Brooklyn, N.Y., May 25, 1929. As a child prodigy she sang frequently on radio, and studied with Estelle Liebling from age seven; operatic debut as Frasquita (*Carmen*), Philadelphia Civic Opera, 1946. She toured with the Charles Wagner Co., made a San Francisco debut as Elena (*Mefistofele*) in 1953, and eventually joined the N.Y.C. Opera as Rosalinde (*Fledermaus*), 1955. Over some two decades, she gradually became this company's unofficial prima donna; her roles there included Philine (*Mignon*), the Merry Widow, Moore's Baby Doe and Milly Theale (*Wings of the Dove*), Louise, Donna Anna, Marguerite, the *Hoffmann* heroines, Handel's Cleopatra, Konstanze, the Queen of Night, the *Trittico* heroines, the Queen (*Golden Cockerel*), Massenet's Manon, Lucia, Donizetti's Tudor queens (in *Roberto Devereux*, *Anna Bolena*, and *Maria Stuarda*), Elvira (*Puritani*), Marie (*Fille*), Lucrezia Borgia, Rosina, Louise, Adele (*Fledermaus*), and Fiorilla (*Turco in Italia*), and she created the Coloratura in Weisgall's *Six Characters*. After her 1966 success as Cleopatra, she attracted international engagements, including Vienna (Queen of Night, 1967), La Scala (Pamira in Rossini's *Siège*, 1969), and Covent Garden (Lucia, 1970). For many seasons she appeared frequently with Sarah Caldwell's Opera Company of Boston. Although she sang Donna Anna with the Met company at Lewisohn Stadium in July 1966, her formal debut with the company came only on Apr. 7, 1975, as Pamira; in 5 seasons, she sang 46 perfs. of 5 roles, including Violetta, Lucia, Thaïs, and Norina. In 1979 she succeeded Julius Rudel as director of the N.Y.C. Opera; her last operatic performances took place there that year in Menotti's *La Loca*, a role she had earlier created in San Diego, and she made a formal farewell at a City Opera gala on Oct. 27, 1980.

Solidly trained and endowed with superb musicianship, Sills sang for many years as a lyric-coloratura before her special talents in the bel canto repertory were widely recognized. Her combination of stage sense and technical facility produced rewarding results in both tragic pathos and effervescent comedy. Regrettably, most of her recordings were made after her vocal prime; *Giulio Cesare* probably gives the best account of her engaging, involving vocalism.

BIBLIOGRAPHY: Beverly Sills, *Bubbles* (N.Y., 1976).

Silveri, Paolo. Baritone; b. Ofena, near Aquila, Italy, Dec. 28, 1913. Studied in Florence and at Santa Cecilia, Rome; debuts as bass, Schwarz (*Meistersinger*), Rome, 1939, and as baritone, Germont, Rome, 1944. Sang at Covent Garden (1947–49) and La Scala (1949–55). Met debut as Don Giovanni, Nov. 20, 1950; in 3 seasons, sang 34 perfs. of 13 roles, including Posa and Rigoletto. Sang Otello, Dublin, 1959, then reverted to baritone roles.

simile aria. See *metaphor aria*.

Simionato, Giulietta. Mezzo-soprano; b. Forlì, Italy, May 12, 1910. Studied with Ettore Locatello in Rovigo and Guido Palumbo in Padua; debut as Lola (*Cavalleria*), Montagnana, 1928. Sang in premiere of Pizzetti's *Orsèolo*, Florence, 1935, and made her La Scala debut as Maddalena (*Rigoletto*), 1936. She sang regularly at La Scala, 1939–66, working her way from small roles to leads, notably

Mignon, Isabella (*Italiana*), Charlotte (*Werther*), Cenerentola, Carmen, Léonor (*Favorite*), Giovanna Seymour (*Anna Bolena*), and Valentine (*Huguenots*). She also appeared at Edinburgh (1947). Covent Garden (1953, 1963–65), San Francisco (1953), Chicago (1954–61), and Salzburg (1957–63). In 3 Met seasons, she sang 20 perfs. as Azucena (debut, Oct. 26, 1959), Rosina, Amneris, and Santuzza. Her farewell performance was as Servilia (*Clemenza*), Piccola Scala, 1966. Intense in tragedy, ebullient in comedy, Simionato was the most versatile Italian mezzo of her generation.

Simon Boccanegra. Opera in prologue and 3 acts by Verdi; libretto by Piave, with additions by G. Montanelli, after the play by Antonio Garcia Gutiérrez.

First perf., Venice, Fenice, Mar. 12, 1857: Bendazzi, Negrini, Giraldone, Echevarria, Vercellini. Rev. version, with textual changes by Boito: Milan, La Scala, Mar. 24, 1881: D'Angeri, Tamagno, Maurel, E. de Reszke, Salvati. U.S. & Met prem., Jan. 28, 1932: Müller, Martinelli, Tibbett, Pinza, Frigerio, c. Serafin, d. Parravicini, p. Sanine. Later Met productions: Mar. 1, 1960: Curtis-Verna, Tucker, Warren, Tozzi, Flagello, c. Mitropoulos, d. Fox/Motley, p. Webster; Nov. 23, 1984: Tomowa-Sintow, Moldoveanu, Milnes, Plishka, Glossop, c. Levine, d. unidentified, p. Capobianco. Boccanegra has also been sung at the Met by Guarrera, Colzani, MacNeil, Wixell; Amelia by Rethberg, Varnay, Tebaldi, Milanov, Maliponte, Millo; Adorno by Bergonzi, Shirley; Fiesco by Pasero, Székely, Hines, Siepi, Ghiaurov, Plishka. 87 perfs. in 14 seasons.

Simon Boccanegra, an opera dearer to Verdi's heart than it was popular with the public of his day, has come into its own only with the 20th-c. Verdi revival. It is his most

Giulietta Simionato as Santuzza in *Cavalleria Rusticana*

Simon Boccanegra – (1939). Designed by Camillo Parravicini. Lawrence Tibbett

somber work, and the great Council Chamber scene added in 1881 is the threshold to *Otello*.

In and near Genoa, mid-14th-c. At the urging of plebeians Paolo (bar) and Pietro (bs), Simon Boccanegra (bar) agrees to be nominated as Doge, hoping this will make possible his marriage with Maria, daughter of the patrician Jacopo Fiesco (bs), who has refused Boccanegra as son-in-law even though Maria has borne him a daughter. Left in the care of an old woman, the child has disappeared. After learning that Maria has died, Boccanegra is elected Doge.

25 years pass. Under the name of Andrea, Fiesco lives with his adopted ward, Amelia Grimaldi (s), who loves the nobleman Gabriele Adorno (t). Visiting Amelia to ask her to marry Paolo, Boccanegra learns that she was an orphan, and realizes that she is his daughter Maria. He then denies her hand to Paolo, who conspires with Pietro to have her abducted. When Adorno kills the plebeian abductor, the quarreling factions invade the Council Chamber, and Boccanegra quiets them with an eloquent plea for peace. Gabriele and Fiesco are detained. Paolo urges them to murder Boccanegra; Fiesco refuses, but Gabriele, led to believe that Simon is Amelia's lover, attempts the crime. Amelia intervenes, and Gabriele, learning the true relationship of Simon and Amelia, helps put down a revolt against Boccanegra. However, Paolo has already poisoned Boccanegra; before he dies, the Doge confronts Fiesco and reveals Amelia's identity; tearfully, the two pardon one another. Simon dies blessing the lovers, and names Gabriele his successor.

Simoneau, Léopold. Tenor; b. St.-Flavien, near Quebec, May 3, 1918. Studied with Salvator Issaurel in Montreal, later with Paul Althouse, N.Y.; debut as Hadji (*Lakmé*), Variétés Lyriques, Montreal, 1941. Paris debuts in 1949 at Opéra-Comique (Vincent in *Mireille*) and Opéra (Tamino); sang in Aix (from 1950) and Glyndebourne (Idamante, 1951), especially Mozart roles.

(continued p.342)

SINGING
Will Crutchfield

Joan Sutherland

"What was it, then," Franz Werfel asked rhetorically in recounting the history of opera by way of introduction to a collection of Verdi's letters, "that brought this heady success to the new kind of art? It was the *human voice*, especially the Italian voice."

The importance of song in life, history, and myth is too manifestly great for this to be surprising – in spite of which many musicians through the years have felt, or at least expressed, surprise at the role played in the world of opera by love of the human voice raised in song. There is among Robert Schumann's critical writings a delightful vignette of "Florestan" (the hotheaded side of the composer's imaginary double persona) hysterically berating himself for having been moved to tears – and, worse yet, observed in it – by hearing a simple Donizetti aria beautifully sung. We look back with incredulity at the apparent fact that Adelina Patti was thought as important a representative of operatic art as Verdi, and Farinelli a more important practitioner of it than any composer whose music he ever sang.

But singing – especially Italian singing – has always held a primacy, at once celebrated and embattled, among the various performing arts that contribute to opera, and for many years it held a parity with the genius of the composer. Werfel's formulation is fair. The headiness, the special thrill in the theater that caps broader appreciation and mature understanding, the excitement that provokes ovations and folly – this is not all of a full response to opera, but it is an essential part, and it comes essentially from the singing.

The technique of it, at the highest level, is as marvelous an attainment as the arts, sciences, or athletics have ever challenged their aspirants to acquire. It consists in the development of the voice's physical capacity to meet the demands of music and to respond to the artistic intentions of the singer. This involves the management of breath; the fine-tuning of multiple muscular coordinations that are as yet only imperfectly understood by physiology and insusceptible to direct volitional manipulation; the mastery of various more or less mechanical feats of vocalization that may be called upon in a given score; the implanting of a mental image of the desired tone quality (ideally, the cultivation within normative parameters of a timbre personal to the singer, instantly recognizable) – and the integration of all these into a routine that will hold up through the stresses, passions, distractions, exhaustion and exhilaration of public performance.

Much of the foregoing is redefined from generation to generation, but the highest achievements as they are understood at any given time have always compelled wonderment, and earned adulation. When such achievements (even if their realization is flawed or incomplete) are allied with a powerful artistic will, an inspired imagination, and a repertory either of new music or of old music newly understood and reinterpreted, then the singer can genuinely be said to figure in opera as a creative as well as a recreative force.

The very embattlement of singing's special position has its own role in opera's history. The power of vocal art and its secure constituency among the public have allowed it to serve as a point of attack for the champions of operatic change. To a significant degree, the history of opera has been shaped by a creative friction between singing (along with the features of operatic composition and administration conducive to its freest exercise) and the other evolving elements of opera, in which the latter have gradually

Montserrat Caballé

encroached on vocal prerogatives, while the art of singing, in turn, has adapted and evolved creatively in response.

This unquestioned movement of history has given rise to the popular oversimplification – all too often perpetuated by thoughtless modern scholars – of the virtuous and serious composer laboring under the yoke of the capricious singer who cared nothing for art. Perhaps this is partly explicable by the consideration that while anecdotes about singers' excesses and failures to understand innovation survive easily, their positive contribution – the actual singing – was lost with each generation until the invention of the phonograph. But the composers and audiences of opera's heyday did not fail to esteem that positive contribution at its true worth. The fact is that Italian operatic music quite legitimately makes its impact through the interaction of deep structure, melody, and surface detail. The first is the composer's province; the third was, for the bulk of Italian opera's history, almost entirely the singer's; in melody the two arts touched and intertwined. This equilibrium has historically been somewhat different in German and French music; where an Italian composer will often confide the crux of his musical argument to an unaccompanied vocal phrase, a clinching high note, a burst of coloratura or a line of recitative, other composers have been far likelier to count on resources of harmony, structure, scoring, or even scenic effect. Since operatic change has historically been driven by dramatic and non-Italian concepts, vocal values have tended to be thought dispensable in a time of reform.

But this dynamic can be observed within, not just against, the sphere of vocal art. Again and again, opera has moved forward through the collaboration of a composer with a great singer or group of singers willing to let fall some of the disciplines and niceties of singing in pursuit of a new musical and dramatic vision. For singing is both technique and inspiration, both music and drama, both tone and word. The artists who have risked re-imagining vocalism and triumphed have been among the most thrilling performers of opera's history. Schröder-Devrient, Pasta, Tamagno, Caruso, Chaliapin, Callas and others like them have left a creative legacy, a vision of artistic possibilities to be explored by their successors on the stage and drawn on by composers in turn.

Part of the challenge such artists pose is to safeguard the technical values and refinements, in the face of the fact that so much that is thrilling in opera has been associated with the willingness to relax those standards. And it is for that reason that we honor, somewhat differently but no less deeply, another kind of singer, not the pioneer but the paragon, whose art encompasses the advances that have been made and balances them with high aspiration to the disciplines of vocalism, and whose understanding of service to music and drama is embodied in an ideal of beauty. At their best, at different times, singers as diverse as Farinelli, Lind, Patti, Jean de Reszke, Tibbett, Schorr, and Ponselle – among many others – have been thought of in such terms. Some of them may have had failings or foibles, but we sense in them also noble dedication to a high calling, and operatic posterity returns not just the echo of the "heady success" they won in life, but heartfelt gratitude.

Will Crutchfield, a music critic for *The New York Times*, has written widely about operatic singing and performance practice.

His only Met appearances were 5 perfs. of Ottavio (debut, Oct. 18, 1963). Also appeared in Chicago, Buenos Aires, Milan, Vienna. Married to soprano Pierrette Alarie.

Simonson, Lee. Designer; b. New York, June 26, 1888; d. Yonkers, N.Y., Jan. 23, 1967. Studied painting in Paris (1908–12), influenced by Reinhardt and Diaghilev. A founding director of, and principal designer for, Theater Guild, Simonson's designs involved simplified, monumental playing spaces. In 1948, designed sets and costumes for Met *Ring* production.

Singher, Martial. Baritone; b. Oloron Ste. Marie, France, Aug. 14, 1904. Studied with André Gresse at Paris Conservatory and with Juliette Fourestier; debut as Oreste (*Iphigénie en Tauride*), Amsterdam, 1930. At the Paris Opéra (1930–41; debut, Athanäel in *Thaïs*), sang Verdi and light Wagner roles, and created Bassanio in Hahn's *Marchand de Venise*, 1935; also sang at Opéra-Comique. Met debut as Dappertutto, Dec. 10, 1943; in 12 seasons, until 1959, he sang 149 perfs. of 19 roles, including the other *Hoffmann* villains, Escamillo, Valentin, both Pelléas and Golaud, Figaro and Almaviva (*Nozze*), Mercutio, and the High Priest (*Samson*). Also sang in Buenos Aires (1936–43), Chicago (1944–45), and San Francisco (debut, Mercutio, 1947). Since retirement from the stage, has taught; his students include Altmeyer, Blegen, Gramm, King, Quilico, Reardon, and Valente. With a lean, clear, voice, Singher was an elegant interpreter, especially in French repertory.

Singspiel (Ger.). A German operatic genre in which the musical numbers are connected by spoken dialogue. An essentially popular genre, common in the 18th and early 19th c., though sometimes more elevated plots were involved, as in Mozart's *Entführung*.

Sinopoli, Giuseppe. Conductor and composer; b. Venice, Nov. 2, 1946. Studied composition with Maderna and Stockhausen, conducting with Swarowsky. His works, in a post-expressionist style, include an opera, *Lou Salomé* (1981). Since his operatic conducting debut (*Aida*, La Fenice, Venice, 1978), he has appeared widely, especially in Verdi and Puccini. Principal conductor, Philharmonia Orchestra, London (from 1984); Bayreuth debut, *Tannhäuser*, 1985; Met debut, *Tosca* (Mar. 11, 1985).

Sitzprobe (Ger., "sitting rehearsal"). The first full musical rehearsal of an opera, without staging, the singers seated.

Slezak, Leo. Tenor; b. Schönberg [now Šumperk], Moravia, Aug. 18, 1873; d. Egern am Tegernsee, Bavaria, June 1, 1946. Studied with Adolf Robinson, later with Jean de Reszke; debut as Lohengrin, Brünn, 1896. After singing briefly in Berlin (1898–99) and Breslau (1900–01), he joined the Vienna Court Opera in 1901, where he dominated the heavier tenor repertory until the 1920s. He made guest appearances widely in Europe and Russia, including debuts at Covent Garden (Lohengrin, 1900) and La Scala (Tannhäuser, 1905); he returned to London in 1909 as Radames and Otello, the latter a part he had first sung at the Vienna Volksoper earlier that year and which also served for his Met debut, Nov. 17, 1909. In his 4 Met seasons, he sang 72 perfs. of 10 roles, most often Otello (18 times), Tannhäuser (15), and Manrico (12), also Radames, Stradella, Herman (*Pique Dame*), Stolzing, Lohengrin, Tamino, and Faust. At the Boston Opera, he sang Otello

and Manrico in 1910. After 1913, he sang mainly in Vienna and Germany, including operetta appearances (including Offenbach's *Barbe-Bleu*, Berlin, 1929). His last performance in opera was as Canio in 1933, after which he continued to appear as a comedian in Austrian films.

Slezak's voice, like his physique, was huge, and occasionally uneven in production, but his excellent diction, musical phrasing, and warmth of temperament made him a memorable performer. His charm and wit are on display in his memoirs, the first entitled (in German) *My Complete Works*, its sequel *The Broken Promise*. His son Walter appeared in films, musicals, and operettas – and at the Met as Zsupán (*Zigeunerbaron*), 1959.
BIBLIOGRAPHY: Leo Slezak, *Songs of Motley* (N.Y., 1938).

Slippers, The. See *Vakula the Smith.*

Smareglia, Antonio. Composer; b. Pola, Istria, May 5, 1854; d. Grado, near Trieste, Apr. 15, 1929. Studied with Faccio at Milan Conservatory. Influenced by the early style of Wagner, his *Il Vassallo di Szigeth* (1889) was introduced in Vienna under Richter, and *Cornil Schut* (1893) in Dresden under Schuch. *Nozze Istriane* (1895), in a tempered verismo style, was briefly popular in Germany.

Smetana, Bedřich. Composer; b. Litomyšl, Bohemia, Mar. 2, 1824; d. Prague, May 12, 1884. Son of an amateur musician, he studied with Josef Proksch. In 1856 he founded a music school in Göteborg, Sweden, but returned to Prague in 1861, sensing opportunity in the rising nationalistic artistic ferment. In 1866 the newly-established Provisional Theater performed his first operas, *The Brandenburgers in Bohemia* and the folk comedy *The Bartered Bride*, with texts by the nationalist poet Karel Sabina. These won Smetana recognition as Bohemia's

Leo Slezak as Otello

leading composer, and he became principal conductor of the Provisional Theater (1866–74). The patriotic legend *Dalibor* (1868) was accused of Wagnerism. *The Two Widows* (1874) and *The Secret* (1878) are sympathetic, lyrical treatments of Czech life. The festival opera *Libuše* (1881), a spectacular historical pageant, opened the National Theater. Although Smetana's health and hearing deteriorated after 1874, he completed a final opera, *The Devil's Wall* (1882), before his death. Smetana drew musical influences from such figures as Gluck, Meyerbeer, Verdi, and Wagner, and only learned the Czech language in the 1850s, but his conscious effort to celebrate his people's history and legends forged a style of musical richness and dramatic mastery.

BIBLIOGRAPHY: John Clapham, *Smetana* (London, 1972).

Smirnov, Dmitri. Tenor; b. Moscow, Nov. 19. 1882; d. Riga, Apr. 27, 1944. Studied in Moscow, later in Paris and Milan; debut as Gigi (Esposito's *Camorra*), Hermitage, Moscow, 1903. Member of Bolshoi (1904–10) and Maryinsky (1907–17). Appeared in West from 1908, notably in Paris and Monte Carlo. In his 2 Met seasons, he sang 12 perfs. of the Duke of Mantua (debut, Dec. 30, 1910), Roméo, Rodolfo, and Alfredo. After 1917, based in Paris.

Smith, Oliver. Designer; b. Waupun, Wis., Feb. 13, 1918. A student of architecture, he designed for the Ballets Russes and American Ballet Theater, Broadway (including *My Fair Lady*, *Candide*), and films (including *Bandwagon*). His Met productions were *Traviata* (1957) and *Martha* (1961).

Smyth, Ethel. Composer; b. Marylebone, London, Apr. 22, 1858; d. Woking, May 9, 1944. Studied at Leipzig Conservatory with Reinecke, and privately with Herzogenberg. Her operas include *Fantasio* (1898; libretto in German by the composer); the one-act *Der Wald* (1902); *Les Naufrageurs* (The Wreckers, 1906, libretto in French by the composer), first presented in Leipzig; the comic *The Boatswain's Mate* (1916); the one-acters *Fête Galante* (1923) and *Entente Cordiale* (1925). Technically skilled, her music has been faulted for stylistic uncertainty.

Snegourochka. See *Snow Maiden, The*.

Snow Maiden, The (Snegourochka). Opera in prologue and 4 acts by Rimsky-Korsakov; libretto by the composer, after Alexander Ostrovsky's drama.
First perf., St Petersburg, Maryinsky, Feb. 10, 1882: c. Naprávník. U.S. prem., Seattle, Jan. 5, 1922. Met prem., Jan. 23, 1922 (in Fr.): Bori, Delaunois, Harrold, Laurenti, Rothier, c. Bodanzky, d. Anisfeld, p. Thewman. 9 perfs. in 2 seasons.
One of Rimsky-Korsakov's most consistently realized fairy-tale operas. To remain safe from the sun's warmth, the Snow Maiden (s), daughter of Spring and Winter, must renounce love, but she eventually wants to be loved by Misgir (bar). Her mother (ms) grants her wish, but the warmth of love melts her, and Misgir drowns himself.

Sobinov, Leonid. Tenor; b. Yaroslavl, Russia, June 7, 1872; d. Riga, Oct. 14, 1934. Studied in Moscow and Milan; debut in Moscow with touring Italian troupe, 1894. Debuts at Bolshoi (Sinodal in *Demon*, 1897) and Maryinsky (Lenski, 1901). Sang at La Scala (Ernesto, 1904), Monte Carlo (from 1907), and Madrid (1908). Director of Bolshoi, 1917–18 and 1921.

Sodero, Cesare. Conductor; b. Naples, Aug. 2, 1886; d. New York, Dec. 16, 1947. Studied in Naples and came to the U.S. in 1907. After positions with Edison's recording company, NBC, and the San Carlo Opera, conducted Italian repertory at the Met (debut, *Aida*, Nov. 28, 1942), leading 188 perfs. of 13 works before his death.

Söderström, Elisabeth. Soprano; b. Stockholm, May 7, 1927. Studied with Andrejeva von Skilondz and at Royal Academy, Stockholm; debut as Mozart's Bastienne, Drottningholm, 1947. Member of Royal Opera, Stockholm, since 1949. Debuts at Salzburg (Ighino in *Palestrina*, 1955), Glyndebourne (Composer in *Ariadne*, 1957), and Covent Garden (with Stockholm company, as Daisy Doody in *Aniara*, 1960). Met debut as Susanna, Oct. 30, 1959; in 4 seasons, she sang Marguerite, the Composer, Musetta, Adina (*Elisir*), Rosalinde (*Fledermaus*) and Sophie (*Rosenkavalier*), returning in 1983–87 as Ellen Orford, the Countess (*Nozze*), and the Marschallin. A repertory embracing Nero (*Incoronazione*), Fidelio, Mélisande, Sophie, Octavian, and the Marschallin, Frau Storch in *Intermezzo*, the Countess in *Capriccio*, Jenůfa, Elena Makropoulos, Marie (*Wozzeck*), and Elizabeth in *Elegie* attests to the musicianship and commitment of this exceptionally versatile and winning singer.

Soldaten, Die (The Soldiers). Opera in 4 acts by Zimmermann; libretto by the composer, after Jakob Lenz's drama.
First perf., Cologne, Feb. 15, 1965: Gabry, de Ridder, Brokmeier, Nicolai, c. Gielen. U.S. prem., Opera Co. of Boston, Jan. 22, 1982: Hunter, Cochran, Evans, c. Caldwell.
Zimmermann's serial opera uses dance, jazz, film, electronic music, and circus, with many events taking place simultaneously. It tells the story of Marie (s), a young girl who, though in love with Stolzius (bar), allows herself to be seduced by Baron Desportes (t), has several other lovers, and eventually becomes a prostitute.

Solera, Temistocle. Librettist; b. Ferrara, Italy, Dec. 25, 1815; d. Milan, Apr. 21, 1878. Began literary career as poet, then collaborated with Verdi on *Oberto*, *Nabucco*, *Lombardi*, *Giovanna d'Arco*, and *Attila*; he also composed operas to his own librettos, with little success.

Solov, Zachary. Choreographer; b. Philadelphia, Feb. 15, 1923. Danced with Littlefield Ballet, American Ballet Theater, and on Broadway. Ballet master for Met (1951–58), he choreographed many productions, including *Aida* (1951), *Gioconda* (1952), *Faust* (1953), and *Samson* (1964).

Solti, Georg. Conductor; b. Budapest, Oct. 21, 1912. A student of Dohnányi, Bartók, and Kodály at Liszt Institute (Budapest), he served as repetiteur in Budapest and assistant to Toscanini in Salzburg (1936–37); Budapest debut, *Nozze*, 1938. After spending war years in Switzerland, became music director of Bavarian State Opera (1946–52), general director in Frankfurt (1952–61), and music director at Covent Garden (1961–71), raising the company to international standards; music advisor, Paris Opéra (1971–73). Other appearances in San Francisco (debut, *Elektra*, 1953), Glyndebourne (*Don Giovanni*, 1954), Chicago Opera (debut, *Salome*, 1956), Salzburg (from 1956), and the Met (debut, *Tannhäuser*, Dec. 17, 1960), where during 3 seasons he led *Aida*, *Boris*, *Don Carlos*, *Otello*, and *Tristan*. Since 1969, music director of the Chicago Symphony; other affiliations with Orchestre de Paris (1972–75) and London Philharmonic Orchestra (1979–83). Solti's tense, precisely articulated, vigorous interpretations first achieved international celebrity through recordings, notably the first complete *Ring* cycle on disc, with the Vienna Philharmonic (1958–65).

Somers, Harry. Composer; b. Toronto, Sep. 11, 1925. Studied composition with Weinzweig at Toronto Conservatory and with Milhaud. Composing in an eclectic style, he has explored novel vocal and aleatoric techniques. The historical opera *Louis Riel* (1967) mixes English, French and Cree languages appropriately to the dramatic situation, and also corresponding musical styles, including electronic sounds. Other works: the chamber operas *The Fool* (1956) and *Enkidu* (1977); and *Improvisation* (1968), a "theater piece."

Somigli, Franca [Marion Bruce Clark]. Soprano; b. Chicago, Mar. 17, 1901; d. Trieste, May 14, 1974. Studied with Storchio in Milan; debut as Mimi, Rovigo, 1927. She sang dramatic roles (Fedora, Salome) in major Italian theaters, made her Chicago Opera debut as Maddalena (*Chénier*) in 1934, and sang Alice Ford under Toscanini, Salzburg, 1936. In her only Met season, she sang 3 perfs. of *Butterfly* (debut, Mar. 8, 1937) and Mimi. Married to conductor Giuseppe Antonicelli.

Sonnambula, La (The Sleepwalker). Opera in 2 acts by Bellini; libretto by Romani, after Scribe's ballet-pantomime *La Sonnambule*.
First perf., Milan, Carcano, Mar. 6, 1831: Pasta, Rubini, Mariani. U.S. prem., N.Y., Park, Nov. 13, 1835 (in Eng.). Met. prem., Nov. 14, 1883: Sembrich, Campanini, Novara, c. Campanini, d. J. Fox, Schaeffer, Maeder, Thompson/Ascoli, Dazian. Later Met productions: Mar. 16, 1932: Pons, Gigli, Pinza, c. Serafin, d. Urban, p. Sanine; Feb. 21, 1963: Sutherland, Gedda, Tozzi, c. Varviso, d. Gérard, p. Butler. Amina has also been sung at the Met by van Zandt, Peters, Scotto; Elvino by Caruso, Lauri-Volpi; Rodolfo by Plançon, Flagello. 55 perfs. in 12 seasons.
The purest expression of Bellini's pathetic or pastoral vein, a score of tender cantilenas and brilliant, joyous allegros.
A Swiss village, early 19th c. At the celebration of their engagement, Amina (s) and Elvino (t) receive compliments from a stranger, who is really Count Rodolfo (bs), lord of the castle. His attentions to Amina upset Elvino. The innkeeper Lisa (s), also enamored of Elvino, visits Rodolfo in his room, but runs off upon hearing a noise, dropping her handkerchief. When Amina enters, sleepwalking, Rodolfo leaves, but she lies down and is found there asleep by villagers who come to greet the Count. Elvino cannot believe Rodolfo's story about her sleepwalking; leaving Amina distraught, he breaks the engagement and decides to wed Lisa – but then, learning that her handkerchief was found in Rodolfo's room, rejects her too. Finally, when Amina is seen sleepwalking on the roof of the mill, Elvino realizes the truth, awakens her, and wins her forgiveness.

Sontag [Sonntag], **Henriette.** Soprano; b. Coblenz, Germany, Jan. 3, 1806; d. Mexico City, June 17, 1854. Studied at Prague Conservatory; debut there in Boieldieu's *Jean de Paris*, 1821. In Vienna, created Euryanthe (1823) and soprano solos in Beethoven's Ninth and *Missa Solemnis* (1824). She sang in Berlin (1825), Paris (1826),

London (1828), retired in 1830, reappeared in 1849, and died during an American tour.

Sonzogno, Edoardo. Publisher, impresario; b. Milan, Apr. 21, 1836; d. Milan, Mar. 14, 1920. Head of the publishing firm of Sonzogno, founded in the late 18th c., he acquired the Italian rights for popular French operas, and in 1883 established a competition for new operas; among the winners was the young, unknown Pietro Mascagni, who received the 1889 award for *Cavalleria*. Sonzogno promoted the verismo school, publishing Mascagni, Giordano, Leoncavallo, and Cilea. In 1875, he managed a season at the Teatro San Redegonda, Milan, and in 1894 opened the Teatro Lirico Internazionale in Milan.

Sooter, Edward. Tenor; b. Salina, Kans., Dec. 8, 1934. Studied at U. of Kansas and Hamburg Musikhochschule; debut as Florestan, 1966. Subsequently sang in Cologne, Essen, Hanover, Mainz. Met debut as Florestan, Feb. 7, 1980; he has since sung Otello, Tannhäuser, Énée (*Troyens*), Tristan, Stolzing, and Lohengrin there.

Sophocles. Greek dramatist (c. 496–406 B.C.). Operas based on his writings include *Antigonae* (Orff), *Elektra* (R. Strauss), and *Oedipus Rex* (Stravinsky).

soprano. The highest female voice range, with many subcategories. The range of dramatic sopranos usually reaches from G below middle C to C above the treble clef ("high C"), lyric sopranos from B-flat below middle C to high C, spintos from A below middle C to high C, and light or coloratura sopranos, whose top notes reach F above C, occasionally even higher.

Soria, Dario. Recording executive, arts manager; b. Rome, May 21, 1912; d. New York, Mar. 28, 1980. Member of an Italian banking family, he came to N.Y. in 1939, worked in broadcasting during the war, and later imported Italian opera recordings to America. After founding and directing the Cetra-Soria label (1948–53) and the Angel label (1953–58), he joined RCA to produce the deluxe Soria Series. From 1970 to 1980, Soria was managing director of the Metropolitan Opera Guild, and produced the Met's historic broadcast recordings.

Sorochintsy Fair. Unfinished opera by Mussorgsky; libretto by the composer, after Gogol's story *Evenings on a Farm near Dekanka*.
First perf., St. Petersburg, Comedy Theater, Dec. 30, 1911. U.S. & Met prem., Nov. 29, 1930 (ed. Tcherepnin, in Ital.): Müller, Bourskaya, Jagel, Pinza, c. Serafin, d. Soudeikine, p. Lert. 5 perfs. in 1 season.
Various hands (also including Liadov, Cui, and Shebalin) have made performing editions of this fragmentary score, which draws upon Ukrainian folk material. Gritzko (t) and Parassia (s) are refused permission to marry by the latter's disapproving stepmother (ms), but discovery of the stepmother's illicit affair undermines her authority and the lovers are united.

Sosarme, Rè di Media. Opera in 3 acts by Handel; libretto by Antonio Salvi.
First perf., London, King's, Feb. 15, 1732: Strada, Senesino, Bagnolesi, Bertolli, Montagnana.
Originally set in Portugal, moved to Asia Minor when the opera was half completed, the plot deals with the rivalry of two brothers for the throne of their father.

Sotin, Hans. Bass; b. Dortmund, Germany, Sep. 10, 1939. Studied at Dortmund Conservatory; debut as Police Commissioner (*Rosenkavalier*), Essen, 1962. Joined Hamburg State Opera, 1964; has also appeared at Bayreuth (from 1972), Vienna State Opera (from 1973), Covent Garden (1974). Met debut as Sarastro, Oct. 26, 1972; has also sung Wotan (*Walküre*), Hunding, Fafner, and Gurnemanz there.

soubrette. A female role whose primary characteristics are shrewdness and pertness (e.g., Susanna in *Nozze di Figaro*, Adele in *Fledermaus*).

Souez [Rains], **Ina.** Soprano; b. Windsor, Ontario, June 3, 1908. Studied in Denver and Milan; debut as Mimi, Ivrea, 1928. Covent Garden debut as Liù, 1929. Sang at Glyndebourne from 1934 as Donna Anna and Fiordiligi, with Stockholm Opera (1939) and New Opera Co., N.Y. (Fiordiligi, 1945). Later sang with Spike Jones' band.

souffleur (Fr.). Prompter.

Souliotis [Suliotis], **Elena.** Soprano; b. Athens, May 28, 1943. Studied in Buenos Aires and Milan; debut as Santuzza, San Carlo, Naples, 1964. American debut as Elena (*Mefistofele*), Chicago Lyric, 1965. Debuts in 1966 in Florence (Luisa Miller), N.Y. (Anna Bolena, concert), and La Scala (Abigaille). Also sang at Covent Garden and Colón, Buenos Aires.

Soyer, Roger. Bass; b. Paris, Sep. 1, 1939. Studied at Paris Conservatory; debut at Paris Opéra, 1962, where he has sung Ferrando (*Trovatore*), Procida (*Vêpres*), Méphistophélès. Appearances in Milan, Vienna, Munich, and Aix; at the Met, he sang 4 perfs. as Don Giovanni (debut, Nov. 16, 1972).

Spielleiter (Ger.). Stage director.

Spieloper (Ger.). A 19th-c. German comic-opera genre, successor to the singspiel, with spoken dialogue; its leading exponent was Lortzing.

Spieltenor (Ger., "acting tenor"). A German type of character tenor, who plays roles in which acting is of predominant importance.

spinto (Ital., "pushed"). A lyric voice with the capacity to "push" into somewhat more dramatic roles.

Spohr, Louis. Composer; b. Brunswick, Germany, Apr. 5, 1784; d. Kassel, Oct. 22, 1859. After an early career as violin virtuoso, became a conductor, active in Vienna, Frankfurt, and Kassel. Substantially self-taught as a composer, his first major opera was *Faust* (1816), a Romantic opera utilizing reminiscence motives – a technique further developed in *Zemire und Azor* (1819), which includes a theme of redemption through sacrificial love anticipating Wagner. *Jessonda* (1823) enchanted audiences by its Oriental subject and chromatic harmony, but these and later operas were eclipsed by the advent of Wagner.

Spoleto. City in Umbria, Italy. In 1958, Gian Carlo Menotti established the annual Festival of Two Worlds in Spoleto. Intended principally to give experience to young artists, the Festival has also attracted internationally renowned singers and conductors. Luchino Visconti

Georg Solti

staged several operas (*Macbeth* in 1958), Menotti and Roman Polanski have also functioned as stage directors, and a 1967 *Don Giovanni* featured designs by Henry Moore. Thomas Schippers was music director until 1970; his successors have been Christopher Keene, Christian Badea, and (since 1987) Spiros Argiris. The festival repertory has included such unusual works as Donizetti's *Furioso all'Isola di San Domingo*, Gagliano's *Dafne*, Salieri's *Prima la Musica e poi le Parole*, Prokofiev's *Fiery Angel*, and Henze's *Prinz von Homburg,* as well as Menotti's own works. The festival takes place in late June and early July; opera performances are given in the Teatro Caio Melisso (rebuilt 1830) and Teatro Nuovo (opened 1864). Rafaello de Banfield is currently artistic director.

Spontini, Gaspare. Composer; b. Maiolati, near Iesi, Italy, Nov. 14, 1774; d. Maiolati, Jan. 24, 1851. After study at Conservatorio della Pietà dei Turchini, Naples, he composed comic operas in Italy with moderate success before going to Paris in 1802. There he attracted the patronage of the Empress Josephine, and achieved a triumph with *La Vestale* (1807), a work in the tradition of Gluck. His status as a major figure was confirmed by the historical pageant *Fernand Cortez* (1809). Briefly director of the Théâtre Italien (1810–12), after the Restoration Spontini was appointed court composer by Louis XVIII, but in 1820, he moved to Berlin as general music director for his admirer Friedrich Wilhelm III. In part because of the triumph of Weber's *Freischütz* and the growth of German nationalism, his tenure there was tempestuous. His later works won little attention outside of Berlin, and after his patron's death in 1840, Spontini returned under lifelong pension to Paris, then retired to his native village. An influence on Berlioz and Wagner, Spontini enlivened the statuesque tradition of tragédie lyrique with Italian lyricism, rhythmic intensity, and melodramatic coups de théâtre; his sense of overall structure was often superior to the quality of his musical invention.

Sprechgesang, Sprechstimme (Ger., "speech-song," "speaking voice"). A vocal style halfway between speech and song, suggesting but not sustaining pitches. First employed by Humperdinck in *Königskinder*, but most prominently exploited by Schoenberg.

STAGE DESIGN
Dale Harris

Opera, initially a mutation of lavish court entertainments such as *Le Ballet Comique de la Reine* (1581), was born in palatial circumstances, and took its tone from the ceremonies attendant upon autocratic rule. Solemn, leisurely, and elaborate, the first operas professed a kinship with Greek tragedy, but unhesitatingly subordinated drama to spectacle, in large measure because the magnificence with which they were presented redounded to the glory of their sponsors.

Despite the opulence that characterized operatic scenery and costumes during the seventeenth and early eighteenth centuries, the most important aspect of the production was the machinery, which was often of remarkable complexity. In Cesti's *Il Pomo d'Oro* (1667), written for the wedding of the Austrian Emperor Leopold I and designed by Lodovico Burnacini, the noble audience witnessed a succession of marvels, including a battle at sea and an eagle that flew down from Mount Olympus to present the titular Golden Apple to the new Austrian empress.

With the spread of Enlightenment ideas during the eighteenth century, supernatural wonders gave way to earthly splendor. Both at court and in the growing number of public opera houses, architectural vistas based on classical prototypes affirmed the elevated and generalized view of human behavior that underlay the vocal feats of opera seria. Ferdinando Galli-Bibiena and his numerous progeny perfected the art of illusionistic scene painting, usually of buildings observed from a sharply angular perspective and designed to create an impression of suprahuman monumentality consonant with the themes of the operas.

The cult of sensibility that developed among the increasingly powerful middle classes during the course of the eighteenth century shifted the esthetic emphasis in opera from formal beauty to dramatic expressivity. To satisfy the change in the audience's expectations, a new scenic pictorialism came into vogue, based on the landscapes of Claude. Its most notable exponents were the Galliari brothers, who, working as a team, provided the sets for many of the reform operas, including Gluck's *Alceste* (1767), in which the new humanism found an eloquent voice.

The tendency toward a more natural and dramatic style of operatic discourse was given impetus during this period by the popularity of opera buffa, a genre in close touch with ordinary daily life. However, the interiors, in which opera buffa was for the most part played, lacked verisimilitude, since the limitations of contemporary stage lighting did not allow the set to be enclosed until the second decade of the nineteenth century. The improvements in lighting that took place in the years between 1817, when gas was first used in the theater, and 1881, when electricity began to sweep all other forms of stage illumination aside, immeasurably extended the range of illusionism.

Immediately affected by these developments was Romantic opera, which demanded greater specificity of setting – geographical, historical, and atmospheric – than had been required before. The leading exponent of the Romantic style was Alessandro Sanquirico, chief designer at La Scala from 1817 to 1832, who determined the visual style of grand opera in the first part of the century. Primarily architectural, his sets, like those for *La Gazza Ladra* (1817), combined scrupulous illusionism with calculated exaggerations of scale and proportion intended to engage the audience's emotions and lend plausibility to operatic license.

(*Above*) One of Burnacini's designs for *Il Pomo d'Oro*. (*Below*) A sketch for a stage setting by Giuseppe Bibiena

By the mid-nineteenth century, leadership in operatic production had passed to the Paris Opéra, where Romantic illusionism was modified by a bourgeois dedication to realistic detail, increasingly based on scrupulous historical research. The designs of Piere Cicéri – e.g., for Meyerbeer's *Robert le Diable* – and of his many pupils established the approach to operatic presentation all over the world. Even the music dramas of Wagner, mythic in subject and ritualistic in structure, were staged in accordance with the precepts of literalism in use at the Opéra, regardless of whether the characters were gods, the settings fantastic, and the situations visionary.

A reaction against realism began to gather force in the 1890s, at a time when composers like Debussy were in full flight from the Wagnerian esthetic. Adolphe Appia sought ways to present Wagner's later works in terms of their poetical intentions rather than their plots. His method required the elaborate play of lighting on abstract, dun-colored, three-dimensional sets, in order to remove the productions as far as possible from the constraints of representationalism.

Though Appia himself had little luck in realizing his ideas in the theater, his theories had important consequences. Under Mahler, the Vienna Court Opera presented key works – including *Tristan*, *Fidelio*, and *Don Giovanni*, all designed by Alfred Roller – with an interpretive freedom that significantly deepened their meaning.

Nevertheless, despite a great deal of subsequent experimentation in operatic staging, especially in Germany during the Weimar Republic, Appia's theories did not come into their own until after World War II, when Wieland Wagner introduced them to Bayreuth with such artistic success that the majority of operatic productions in Europe henceforth took on a non-representational cast. For the past three decades, European opera houses have accepted the proposition that illustrationism is less true to the essential achievement of the composer and librettist than imaginative interpretation, even when this departs wildly from the milieu prescribed in the text.

As a result, operatic design in Europe tends to be more a commentary upon the intentions of composer and librettist than an attempt to realize those intentions. Sometimes, indeed, staging an opera today involves an act of near-autonomous creativity. While some sections of the audience are plainly at odds with this tendency to elevate production over the written text, the current shortage of operatic stars makes novel ideas of staging the chief point of interest in many European houses.

United States operagoers, more conservative than their European counterparts, have largely rejected the trend to unceasing experimentation. Instead, they favor the kind of spectacular realism typified by the designs of Franco Zeffirelli, which blend monumentality, vivid pictorialism, and sensationalist literalism with such theatrical force that the audience often feels less dramatically involved than scenically awed. However, the recent success of David Hockney's imaginative and painterly approach to operatic design suggest that a shift to a poetical, non-illusionistic style of presentation might be at hand.

Dale Harris is a music critic for the *New York Post*, dance critic for the *Wall Street Journal*, and writes for *Opera Quarterly* and *Opera News*. A professor of literature at Sarah Lawrence and of art history at Cooper Union, he is also a popular lecturer.

Stabile, Mariano. Baritone; b. Palermo, Sicily, May 12, 1888; d. Milan, Jan. 11, 1968. Studied with Cotogni at Santa Cecilia, Rome; debut as Marcello, Biondo, Palermo, 1909. He sang in Italy, Spain, and Latin America for some years before Toscanini chose him as Falstaff for the reopening of La Scala, 1921; he eventually sang this role more than 1,000 times. Among his other roles at La Scala (until 1955) were Gérard, Scarpia, Iago, Malatesta, and Don Giovanni, later Beckmesser, Dulcamara, and Prosdocimo (*Turco*); he created the title role in Respighi's *Belfagor* (1923). In England, he sang at Covent Garden (1926–31), Glyndebourne (1936–39), and the Cambridge Theatre, London (1946–49); he also appeared in Chicago (1924) and in Salzburg (1931–39). Essentially a character baritone, Stabile won favor in *cantante* roles through his canny acting and superior declamation.

Stabreim (Ger., "initial rhyme"). Alliteration, used prominently by Wagner in the librettos of his *Ring* cycle.

stagione (Ital.). Season. The *stagione* principle of scheduling an opera season is based on the intensive preparation and performance of a single work at a time. See also *repertory*.

Stanislavsky, Konstantin. Producer; b. Moscow, Jan. 17, 1863; d. Moscow, Aug. 7, 1938. Founder, with Nemirovich-Danchenko, of Moscow Art Theater (1898), which presented the work of Chekhov and Gorky, and where he developed new theories of naturalistic acting and staging, requiring total identification of actor with stage character. In 1918, he established the Bolshoi Theater Opera Studio (later the Stanislavsky Opera Theater), to renovate opera traditions; among the studio productions were *Werther* (1921), *Eugene Onegin* (1922), *Matrimonio Segreto* (1925), *Tsar's Bride* (1926), *Boris* (1929), and *Don Pasquale* (1936).

Eleanor Steber as Donna Anna in *Don Giovanni*

Stanton, Edmund C. Manager; b. Stonington, Conn., Aug. 5, 1854; d. Bournemouth, England, Jan. 1901. Executive secretary of the board of directors of the Metropolitan Opera Company, he was named, following the death of Leopold Damrosch in 1885, as general manager, and presided over six seasons of opera in German (1885–91), with Anton Seidl as *de facto* music director. However, once the later works of Wagner had been introduced to N.Y. and thoroughly explored, Stanton and Seidl were unable to extend the repertory of their Germanophone troupe in rewarding directions; the novelties of 1890–91 (Franchetti's *Asrael*, Smareglia's *Vassallo di Szigeth*, and Ernest II of Saxe-Coburg-Gotha's *Diane von Solange*) exasperated the N.Y. public, and the Met was turned over to Abbey and Grau.

Stapp, Olivia. Soprano; b. New York, May 30, 1940. Studied in N.Y.; N.Y.C. Opera debut as Carmen, 1972; later sang Norma there. Met debut as Lady Macbeth, Dec. 7, 1982; has also sung Tosca with the company. Debuts at Paris Opéra (Lady Macbeth, 1982), La Scala (Turandot, 1983); has also appeared in San Francisco, Chicago, and Hamburg.

Steber, Eleanor. Soprano; b. Wheeling, W. Va., July 17, 1916. Studied with her mother, then at New England Conservatory with William Whitney and in N.Y. with Paul Althouse; formal debut as Senta, Commonwealth Opera (Boston), 1936. After winning the Met Auditions of the Air, she made her debut as Sophie in *Rosenkavalier* (Dec. 7, 1940); in 22 seasons, she sang 287 perfs. of 33 roles, most often in Mozart: the Countess in *Figaro* (35 times), Donna Anna (27), Fiordiligi (23), Donna Elvira, Pamina and the First Lady (*Zauberflöte*). Other roles in her wide repertory included Violetta, the Marschallin, Eva, Elsa, and Rosalinde (*Fledermaus*); she was the Met's first Konstanze, Arabella, and Marie (*Wozzeck*), and created Barber's Vanessa. Other appearances in San Francisco (debut, Micaela, 1945), Edinburgh (the Countess, with Glyndebourne Opera, 1947), Florence (Minnie in *Fanciulla*, Maggio Musicale, 1954), Chicago (debut, Donna Anna, 1954), and Salzburg (Vanessa, 1958). Since retirement from the stage, she has taught at the Cleveland Institute and the Juilliard School. A singer of versatility, energy, and spontaneity, Steber was much admired for her luminous tone and musical phrasing.

Stehle(-Garbin), Adelina. Soprano; b. Graz, Austria, 1860; d. Milan, Dec. 24, 1945. Studied in Milan; debut as Amina, Broni, 1881. In 1890, joined La Scala, where she created Nannetta (*Falstaff*) and Walter in *Wally*. Sang verismo roles in Berlin, Vienna, St. Petersburg, and the Americas. Married to tenor Edoardo Garbin.

Stein, Gertrude. Librettist; b. Allegheny, Pa., Feb. 3, 1874; d. Neuilly, France, July 27, 1946. As an expatriate writer in Paris, she wrote prolifically in a jargon largely ignored by critics and public. For Virgil Thomson she wrote two librettos, obscure in import but admirably suited for music, *Four Saints in Three Acts* and *The Mother of Us All*.

Steinberg, William [Hans Wilhelm]. Conductor; b. Cologne, Germany, Aug. 1, 1899; d. May 16, 1978. Studied in Cologne and assisted Klemperer at the city's opera; appointed principal conductor there in 1924, moving later to Prague and Frankfurt and guest-conducting at the Berlin Opera. In 1936, co-founder of the

Thomas Stewart as Wotan in *Das Rheingold*

Palestine Orchestra. Sponsored in America by Toscanini, he became music director of the Buffalo Philharmonic (1945–52), Pittsburgh Symphony (1952–76), and Boston Symphony (1969–72). At the Met, he led *Aida* (debut, Jan. 2, 1965), *Vanessa*, and *Walküre*, and returned in 1973–74 for *Parsifal*.

Stella, Antonietta. Soprano; b. Perugia, Italy, Mar. 15, 1929. Studied in Perugia; debut as Leonora (*Forza*), Rome Opera, 1951. Debuts at La Scala (Desdemona, 1954), Covent Garden (Aida, 1955), and the Met (Aida, Nov. 13, 1956), where in 4 seasons she sang 54 perfs. of 8 roles, including Butterfly, Leonora (*Trovatore*), Tosca, Elisabeth de Valois, Violetta, and Amelia (*Ballo*).

Stevens [Steenberg], **Risë.** Mezzo-soprano; b. New York, June 11, 1913. Studied with Anna Schoen-René at Julliard; debut in *Bartered Bride*, Little Theatre Opera, N.Y., 1931. After further study with Marie Gutheil-Schoder and Herbert Graf, she sang in Prague (1936), later in Cairo and Buenos Aires. At Glyndebourne, she sang Dorabella and Cherubino, 1939. Her Met debut was as Mignon (Dec. 17, 1938); during her 23 consecutive seasons with the company, she sang 220 perfs. (over 100 more on tour) of 15 roles, most frequently Carmen (75 times) and Octavian (50), Mignon, and Dalila, also Cherubino, Orfeo, Laura, Orlovsky (*Fledermaus*), Marina, Hänsel, and Giulietta (*Hoffmann*). She made 1940 debuts in San Francisco (Cherubino) and Chicago (Octavian), appeared at the Paris Opéra as Octavian (1949), created Erodiade in Mortari's *Figlia del Diavolo* at La Scala (1954), and returned to Glyndebourne as Cherubino (1955). She made several films (notably *Going My Way*, with Bing Crosby), served as director of the Met National Company (1965–67) and president of the Mannes College of Music (1975–78), and is advisor to the Met's young artists development program.

With a warm, full, beautifully schooled mezzo, Stevens evaded early attempts to cast her in Wagner, and eventually focussed on a group of distinctive roles that gave full play to her personal glamor, cultivated musicianship, and skilled stagecraft.

Stewart, Thomas. Baritone; b. San Saba, Tex., Aug. 29, 1928. Studied with Mack Harrell, Juilliard, N.Y.; debut there as student, as La Roche in U.S. premiere of *Capriccio*, 1954. N.Y.C. Opera debut as Commendatore, 1954; he sang bass roles there and in Chicago (debut, Baptista in Giannini's *Taming of the Shrew*, 1954), before going to Europe in 1956 with his wife, soprano Evelyn Lear. A member of the Berlin Städtische Oper (1957–64), he also sang at Covent Garden (Escamillo, 1960), Bayreuth (1960–72, in all principal baritone roles), and Paris Opéra (Gunther, 1962). Met debut as Ford (*Falstaff*), Mar. 9, 1966; in 14 seasons, he sang 169 perfs. of 23 roles, including Wotan, Amfortas, Kurwenal, Golaud, Almaviva, Jochanaan, the *Hoffmann* villains, Iago, Sachs, and Balstrode (*Grimes*). In San Francisco, he sang the U.S. premiere of Reimann's *Lear*, 1981. With a handsome if not quite heroic baritone, this intelligent, well-schooled singer made a strong mark, especially in the Wagner repertory.

Stich-Randall, Teresa. Soprano; b. West Hartford, Conn., Dec. 24, 1927. Studied at Hartford Conservatory and Columbia U., where she created Henrietta M. (*Mother of Us All*), N.Y., 1947. Under Toscanini, sang Priestess (*Aida*, 1949) and Nannetta (1950) with NBC Symphony. European debut at Maggio Musicale, Florence, as Mermaid (*Oberon*), 1952. Sang in Vienna (from 1952), Aix (1953–71), Chicago (from 1955). In 4 Met seasons, she sang 17 perfs. as Fiordiligi (debut, Oct. 24, 1961) and Donna Anna. The first American singer to be named an Austrian *Kämmersängerin*.

Stiedry, Fritz. Conductor; b. Vienna, Oct. 11, 1883; d. Zurich, Aug. 8, 1968. Study in Vienna led him, with Mahler's help, to an assistantship in Dresden (1907–08). After several central European positions, became principal conductor at Berlin Opera (1914–23), Vienna Volksoper (1924–25), and Berlin Städtische Oper (1928–33). Coming to N.Y. after four years in Russia, he directed the New Friends of Music concert series, conducted the Chicago Opera (1945–46), and joined the Met in 1948 (debut, *Siegfried*, Nov. 15), where he remained for 12 seasons, conducting 257 perfs., concentrating on Mozart and Wagner, but also including the middle Verdi works he had earlier espoused in Germany.

Stiffelio. Opera in 3 acts by Verdi; libretto by Piave, after the play *Le Pasteur, ou L'Évangile et le Foyer* by Émile Souvestre and Eugène Bourgeois.

First perf., Trieste, Grande, Nov. 16, 1850: Gazzaniga-Malaspina, Fraschini, Colini, Dei. U.S. prem., Brooklyn, Academy of Music (N.Y. Grand Opera), June 4, 1976: French, Taylor, Lambrinos, Sher, c. LaSelva.

A tense psychological drama, coming on the heels of *Rigoletto, Stiffelio* was believed lost until 1968 because most scores were destroyed after 1857, when Verdi remade it into *Aroldo* (*q.v.*).

Austria, Count Stankar's castle by the river Salzbach [*sic*], early 19th c. The evangelical preacher Stiffelio (t) breaks up a fight between his father-in-law Count Stankar (bar) and the nobleman Raffaele (t), and then learns of the adulterous liaison between the latter and his own wife, Lina (s). Stiffelio gives her a divorce, after which she confesses that she still loves him, and insists that she was betrayed into adultery. Stankar kills Raffaele. In a church service, Stiffelio forgives his wife by reading aloud the story of the woman taken in adultery.

Stignani, Ebe. Mezzo-soprano; b. Naples, July 11, 1903; d. Imola, Oct. 5, 1974. Studied with Agostino Roche, Naples Conservatory; debut as Amneris, San Carlo, Naples, 1925. At La Scala (debut, Eboli, 1926), she was a leading mezzo until 1956, her roles including Ännchen (*Freischütz*), Gutrune, Laura, Preziosilla, Ortrud, Azucena, Brangäne, Adalgisa, Rubria (*Nerone*), Léonor (*Favorite*), Dalila, Ulrica, Orfeo, Rosa Mamai (*Arlesiana*), and creating the Voice in Respighi's *Lucrezia*. At the first Florence Maggio Musicale, 1933, she sang Fenena (*Nabucco*) and the High Priestess (*Vestale*), and in 1940, Arsace (*Semiramide*). She also sang at Covent Garden, Paris, Lisbon, Barcelona, and the Colón, Buenos Aires (from 1927). In the U.S., Stignani sang opera in San Francisco (1938, 1948) and Chicago (1955), and concerts in N.Y. With a voice of extraordinary range, power, and richness, Stignani was the dominant Italian mezzo between the wars, whose grand and committed singing overshadowed her undramatic stage presence.

stile rappresentativo (Ital., "representational style"). The term applied by the earliest opera composers to the style of sung recitative, in "representation" of speech.

Still, William Grant. Composer; b. Woodville, Miss., May 11, 1895; d. Los Angeles, Dec. 3, 1978. Early career as performer and arranger for W.C. Handy; studied at Oberlin Conservatory, privately with Varèse, and with Chadwick at New England Conservatory of Music. First American black to win recognition for serious composition, he worked in a folk-derived neo-Romantic vein. His operas include *Troubled Island* (1941), *A Bayou Legend* (1941, perf. 1974), *Minette Fontaine* (1958, perf. 1984), and *Highway 1, U.S.A.* (1960), as well as the still unperformed *Blue Steel* (1934), *Costaso* (1950), *Mota* (1951), and *The Pillar* (1956).

Stilwell, Richard. Baritone; b. St. Louis, Mo., May 6, 1942. Studied at Indiana U. and with Daniel Ferro in N.Y.; operatic debut as Pelléas, N.Y.C. Opera, 1970. Appeared at Glyndebourne (Almaviva and Monteverdi's Ulisse, 1973), Covent Garden (1974); created roles in Pasatieri's *Seagull* (1974) and *Inez di Castro* (1976). Met debut as Guglielmo, Oct. 15, 1975; has also sung Rossini's Figaro, Billy Budd, Malatesta, Pelléas, Marcello, and Mozart's Almaviva with the company.

Stivender, David. Chorus master and conductor; b. Milwaukee, Wis., Sep. 6, 1933. After graduation from Northwestern U., assistant conductor at Chicago Lyric (1961–65). At the Met, assistant chorus master from 1962, chorus master from 1973, credited with raising the chorus' quality to the highest standards. Podium debut with the company, Jan. 3, 1978 (*Trovatore*); has since led other Verdi works in N.Y. and on tour.

Stockhausen, Karlheinz. Composer; b. Burg Mödrath, near Cologne, Germany, Aug. 22, 1928. Studied at Cologne Musikhochschule; at the 1951 Darmstadt summer school, he was influenced by serialism and the music of Messiaen, with whom he studied in Paris. Stockhausen's career has been marked by Wagnerian ambition and theorizing, and by unceasing innovation, passing through serial, electronic, aleatoric, and environmental phases; many of his works have a strong theatrical

component. His major composition for the opera house is the cycle *Licht* (1977–), of which *Samstag* (1977) and *Donnerstag* (1981) have been performed to date.

Stokowski, Leopold. Conductor; b. London, Apr. 18, 1882; d. Nether Wallop, Sep. 13, 1977. Studied at Royal College of Music (London), Oxford, Berlin, Munich, and Paris. Debut concerts in Paris (1908) and London (1909) led to engagement with Cincinnati Symphony (1909–12) and an historic tenure with the Philadelphia Orchestra (1912–38), where he cultivated a sumptuous orchestral sound and vigorously promoted new music (including U.S. premiere of Berg's *Wozzeck*). After 1938, he held various positions in the U.S. and abroad, founding the American Symphony Orchestra in N.Y. in 1962. In his only Met appearances, Stokowski conducted *Turandot* (debut, Feb. 24, 1961), and also took part in the 1966 Farewell Gala for the old house. A pioneer of recordings, his "symphonic syntheses" from the Wagner operas were once as prominent and controversial as his Bach transcriptions, but opera did not figure prominently in his career, which continued into his nineties.

Stoltz, Rosine [Victoire Noel]. Mezzo-soprano; b. Paris, Feb. 13, 1815; d. Paris, July 28, 1903. Stage debut, Monnaie, Brussels, 1832. At Paris Opéra (debut, 1837), she created roles in works by Halévy, Auber, Berlioz (Ascanio in *Cellini*) and Donizetti (Léonor in *Favorite*, Zaida in *Dom Sebastian*). Later sang in Lisbon, Vienna, Turin, and Brazil.

Stolz, Teresa [Teresina (Terezie) Stolzová]. Soprano; b. Elbekosteletz [now Kostelec nad Labem], Bohemia, June 5, 1834; d. Milan, Aug. 23, 1902. Studied at Prague Conservatory, with Luigi Ricci in Trieste, and Lamperti in Milan; debut in Tiflis, 1857, also appearing in Constantinople and Odessa before Italian debut in Turin, 1863. Italian successes in Verdi roles brought her to the attention of conductor Angelo Mariani, to whom she was for a time engaged. La Scala debut as Giovanna d'Arco, 1865; she sang Elisabeth de Valois in Italian premiere of *Don Carlos*, Bologna (1867), Leonora in Verdi's revision of *Forza* (1869), the first Italian Aida (1872), and created the soprano solo in Verdi's Requiem (1874). During this time, she may have been romantically involved with Verdi. Also noted for her interpretations of Alice (*Robert le Diable*), and Rachel (*Juive*), Stolz, who retired in 1879, was apparently the ideal Verdi soprano, a powerful and impassioned singer.

Stolze, Gerhard. Tenor; b. Dessau, Germany, Oct. 1, 1926; d. Garmisch-Partenkirchen, Mar. 11, 1979. Studied in Dresden and Berlin; debut as Moser (*Meistersinger*), Dresden, 1949. Appeared at Bayreuth (1951–69), Berlin State Opera (1953–61), Covent Garden (debut, 1960), specializing in character roles. In 3 Met seasons, he sang 15 perfs. as Loge (debut, Nov. 22, 1968), Herod, and Mime (*Siegfried*).

Stone Guest, The. Opera in 3 acts by Dargomijsky; libretto after Pushkin's dramatic poem.
   First perf., St. Petersburg, Maryinsky, Feb. 28, 1872. U.S. prem., N.Y., Marymount Manhattan Theater (Chamber Opera Theater), Feb. 25, 1986: c. Kin.
   An experiment in arioso/parlando writing; orchestrated by Rimsky-Korsakov after the composer's death. In this version of the story, Don Juan (t) returns from exile

and decides to seduce Donna Anna (s), widow of the Commander he has murdered. He jokingly invites the status of the Commander to Anna's house; the statue (bs) accepts and, as in Mozart, dooms the Don with his handclasp.

Storace, Nancy [Ann (Anna) Selina Storace]. Soprano; b. London, Oct. 27, 1765; d. London, Aug. 24, 1817. Studied with Rauzzini and Sacchini, Venice; debut in Rauzzini's *Le Ali d'Amore*, 1776. Sang in Florence (1780), Parma (1781), Milan (1782), then in Vienna (from 1783), where she created Mozart's Susanna, 1786. Returned to England, 1787; retired 1808.

Storchio, Rosina. Soprano; b. Venice, May 19, 1872; d. Milan, July 24, 1945. Studied at Milan Conservatory; debut as Micaela, dal Verme, 1892. After singing in smaller theaters, La Scala debut as Sophie (*Werther*), 1895, returning (1902–06) as Linda di Chamounix, Euryanthe, Norina, Wally, Susanna, and Violetta, and later as Amina, Mimi, Massenet's Manon, and Mignon. She created Leoncavallo's Musetta (1897) and Zazà (1900), Stefana in Giordano's *Siberia* (1903), Butterfly (1904), and Mascagni's Lodoletta (1917). Appearances in Barcelona (1898–1923) and Buenos Aires (1904–14); in the U.S., she sang only with the Chicago Opera in 1921 (Butterfly, Linda, Violetta), including a single Butterfly on tour in N.Y. A singing actress of personality, fragility, and intimacy, much admired by Puccini and Toscanini.

Story of A Real Man, The. Opera in 3 (originally 4) acts by Prokofiev; libretto by the composer and Mira Mendelson, after Boris Polevoj's story.
First perf. (private), Leningrad, Kirov, Dec. 3, 1948. Revised version, first public perf., Moscow, Bolshoi, Oct. 7, 1960: Kibkalo, c. Ermler.
Prokofiev's unsuccessful bid to overturn the Stalinist condemnation of his music in 1948, is set in 1942, during the War. The Russian aviator Alexei (bar) is shot down behind German lines, and loses his legs as a result of his injuries, but pulls himself out of spiritual and physical defeat, learning to walk and dance on wooden legs.

Stracciari, Riccardo. Baritone; b. Casalecchio di Reno, near Bologna, Italy, June 26, 1875; d. Rome, Oct. 10, 1955. After singing in an operetta chorus, studied with Ulisse Masetti, Bologna Conservatory; operatic debut as Marcello, Bologna, 1900. He appeared in Lisbon (1901), Genoa (1903–04), Milan (La Scala, 1904–06), and at Covent Garden (1905) before his Met debut as Germont, Dec. 1, 1906; in 2 seasons there, he sang 5 perfs. of 11 roles, including Ashton, Amonasro, Valentin, Sharpless, Rigoletto, Marcello, and di Luna. Subsequent appearances in Paris (Opéra, 1909), Madrid (Real, 1909–10), Buenos Aires (Colón, 1913), Chicago (1917–1919), and San Francisco (1925). Stracciari's 1929 complete recordings of *Rigoletto* and Rossini's *Barbiere* document his imposing baritone, assured technique, and command of style. Though he began teaching in 1926 (in Naples and later in Rome), he did not retire from the stage until 1944; among his students were Sved and Christoff.

Strakosch, Maurice [Moritz]. Impresario; b. Gross-Seelowitz [now Židlochovice], Moravia, 1825; d. Paris, Oct. 9, 1887. Studied piano with Sechter in Vienna, then toured Europe and America, where he settled as a teacher and from 1851 managed the concerts of his sister-in-law,

Teresa Stratas as Lulu

Adelina Patti. After presenting Italian opera in N.Y. (1857) and Chicago (1859), he returned to Europe, later offering seasons in Paris (1873–74) and at Rome's Teatro Apollo (1884–85).

Straniera, La (The Foreigner). Opera in 2 acts by Bellini; libretto by Romani, after d'Arlincourt's novel *L'Etrangère*.
First perf., Milan, La Scala, Feb. 14, 1829: Méric-Lalande, Unger, Reina, Tamburini, Spiagi. U.S. prem., N.Y., Italian Opera House, Nov. 10, 1834.
Still relatively neglected, but rich in Bellini's typical long, fluid melodies. In 14th-c. Brittany, Arturo (t), betrothed to Isoletta (ms), has fallen in love with the reclusive "straniera," Alaide (s). When Arturo flees from his wedding, the Prior (bs) reveals that Alaide is Queen Agnès of France; realizing the impossibility of his love, Arturo kills himself.

Stratas, Teresa [Anastasia Strataki]. Soprano; b. Toronto, May 26, 1938. After singing in nightclubs and theaters from age 12, she studied at Toronto under Irene Jessner, then at the U. of Toronto with Barbini and Geiger-Torel; debut as Mimi, Canadian Opera, 1958. A winner of the Met Auditions of the Air, she made her company debut as Poussette (*Manon*), Oct. 28, 1959, soon graduating from small parts to Micaela and a notable success as Liù (1961). She has since sung more than 250 perfs. of more than 35 roles at the Met, most frequently Mimi, Nedda, Zerlina, Lisa (*Queen of Spades*), Mařenka (*Bartered Bride*), and Jenny (*Mahagonny*), also the Composer (*Ariadne*), Sardulla (*Last Savage*), Cherubino, Périchole, Gretel, Susanna, Despina, Desdemona, Mélisande, and Lulu, which she also sang at the 1979 Paris Opéra premiere of the complete 3-act version. Her Covent Garden debut was as Mimi (1961), and at La Scala she created the role of Isabella in Falla's *Atlántida* (1962). Her Despina was seen at Salzburg in 1969. Her Violetta is seen in Zeffirelli's film of

Traviata (1983), and she made her Broadway debut in the musical *Rags* (1986).

One of the most distinctively personal and theatrically intense artists of her time, Stratas has evolved a repertory of idiosyncratic portrayals ranging from the coloratura to the spinto repertory, that exploit her wide-ranging, intriguingly colored voice, superior musicianship, and dramatic temperament.

Strauss, Johann, Jr. Composer; b. Vienna, Oct. 25, 1825; d. Vienna, June 3, 1899. His father, a successful conductor and composer of dance music, discouraged his son's musical ambitions, but Johann Jr. studied with Joseph Drechsler and at age 19 conducted a program of his own and his father's waltzes, launching a triumphant career. His prolific output and frequent international tours (including the U.S., 1872) with his own orchestra earned him the title of "The Waltz King." Stimulated by the Viennese success of Offenbach's works (and Suppé's emulations of them), the directors of the Theater an der Wien urged Strauss, who had already composed the operetta *Indigo und die Vierzig Räuber* (1871), to write for their theater. *Die Fledermaus* (1874), thanks to its excellent libretto, inspired melodies, and peculiarly Viennese blend of sentiment and hedonism, achieved universal popularity. *Der Zigeunerbaron* (1885), with its piquant Hungarian accent, was also successful, but Strauss' uncritical acceptance of poor librettos crippled such musically rich scores as *Eine Nacht in Venedig* (1884), *Ritter Pázmán* (1892), and *Wiener Blut* (1899, completed by A. Müller, Jr.).
BIBLIOGRAPHY: Egon Gartenberg, *Johann Strauss: The End of An Era* (University Park, Pa., 1974).

Strauss, Richard. Composer; b. Munich, June 11, 1864; d. Garmisch-Partenkirchen, Bavaria, Sep. 8, 1949. Son of Munich Opera's principal hornist, he composed from age six and studied musical theory with F.W. Meyer in Munich. Having learned conducting under von Bülow, he held positions in Munich and Weimar, directed the Berlin Court Opera (1898–1910), and co-directed the Vienna State Opera (1919–1924). Originally influenced as a composer by Brahms, he became a disciple of Liszt and Wagner, and in the 1890s his harmonically adventurous, orchestrally luxuriant symphonic poems attracted international attention. Early in the new century, he began to devote his energies principally to opera.

Strauss' heavily Wagnerian first opera, *Guntram* (1894), failed drastically in Munich; he later responded with *Feuersnot* (1901), a thinly-disguised satire of the city's conservatism. To *Salome* (1905) he brought a dazzling orchestral palette and volatile harmonic language, and followed this *succès de scandale* with *Elektra*, an even more dissonant exploration of morbid psychology, after a play by Hugo von Hofmannsthal, who then became Strauss' librettist and turned him in a more conservative direction. *Der Rosenkavalier* (1911), a warm comedy of 18th-c. Vienna, was composed as a sumptuous pastiche, including anachronistic waltz rhythms. More specifically neoclassical, *Ariadne auf Naxos* (1912) combined opera seria and commedia dell'arte, with a chamber orchestra in the pit. The remaining operas with Hofmannsthal were *Die Frau ohne Schatten* (1919), a fantasy-allegory on a Wagnerian scale; *Die ägyptische Helena* (1928), a ponderous gloss on mythology; and *Arabella* (1933), a return to a Viennese milieu. For the autobiographical *Intermezzo* (1924), Strauss wrote his own libretto. After Hofmannsthal's death, the advent of the Nazis doomed a collaboration with the Jewish writer Stefan Zweig, begun in *Die*

Richard Strauss

schweigsame Frau (1935); thereafter, Strauss tolerated Joseph Gregor's platitudinous librettos for *Friedenstag* (1938), *Daphne* (1938), and *Die Liebe der Danae* (1944). *Capriccio* (1942), an opera about opera, marks the beginning of his Indian summer as a composer.

Strauss' remarkable fluency and craftsmanship, evident in all his operas, occasionally led him into banality, even in *Salome*, *Elektra*, and *Rosenkavalier*; the later operas frequently descend to note-spinning, from which they are sometimes redeemed by the writing for soprano voice, inspired by Strauss' wife, the singer Pauline de Ahna. His restlessness when lacking a libretto to set may account for his acceptance of Hofmannsthal's symbolic density and Gregor's turgidity; at least he seized whatever musico-theatrical opportunities their work offered him.
BIBLIOGRAPHY: Norman Del Mar, *Richard Strauss: A Critical Commentary on His Life and Works* (3 vols., Philadelphia, and London, 1962–72).

Stravinsky, Feodor. Bass; b. Novïy Dvor, Russia, June 20, 1843; d. St. Petersburg, Dec. 4, 1902. Studied at St. Petersburg Conservatory; debut as Rodolfo (*Sonnambula*), Kiev, 1873. Member of Maryinsky, St. Petersburg, 1876–1901, creating roles in Tchaikovsky's *Mazeppa* (1884) and Rimsky-Korsakov's *Sadko* (1898). Father of Igor.

Stravinsky, Igor. Composer; b. Oranienbaum [now Lomonosov], Russia, June 17, 1882; d. New York, Apr. 6, 1971. Studied with Rimsky-Korsakov, who arranged performances that led to an association with Diaghilev; the ballets *The Firebird* (1910), *Petrushka* (1911), and *The Rite of Spring* (1913) made a sensational impact in western Europe with their color and rhythmic violence. An exile from Russia after 1917, Stravinsky lived in France, performing as pianist and conductor, and turned in his concert and theater works from Russian subjects to a chameleon-like neo-classicism. After 1939, he lived in the U.S., and during the 1950s, in another transformation, adopted Schoenberg's serial technique.

Constantly involved with some form of theater, Stravinsky undertook opera only occasionally. His first, *The Nightingale* (1914), moves from Debussyism to dissonant chinoiserie. The one-act burlesque *Renard*

(1922) is modeled on Russian folk theater, while the opera buffa *Mavra* (1922), his last stage work in Russian, recalls the Russo-Italian style of Glinka. The opera-oratorio *Oedipus Rex* (1927), with Latin text, invokes Handelian and Verdian models in a stylized context. At the apex of his neo-classic period stands the full-length *The Rake's Progress* (1951), a mannered and moving evocation of 18th-c. opera.

BIBLIOGRAPHY: Eric Walter White, *Stravinsky: The Composer and His Works* (Berkeley, and London, 2nd ed., 1979).

Street Scene. Opera in 2 acts by Weill; libretto by Langston Hughes, after Elmer Rice's play.

First perf., Philadelphia, Shubert Theater, Dec. 16, 1946: Jeffries, Stoska, Sullivan, c. Abravanel.

A work conceived for Broadway, but musically continuous in the traditional manner of opera. On a street of N.Y. tenements during hot June days, "everyday life" culminates in a murder and a young woman's resolve to leave and seek a better life elsewhere.

Strehler, Giorgio. Producer; b. Barcolo, Trieste, Aug. 14, 1921. First an actor, he directed from 1941 and with Paolo Grassi founded the Piccolo Teatro di Milano (1947), which became Italy's foremost art theater. First operatic productions, *Traviata* and *Love for Three Oranges*, in 1947 at La Scala, center of his activity, though he also works in other European opera houses.

Streich, Rita. Soprano; b. Barnaul, Russia, Dec. 18, 1920, of German and Russian parents. Studied with Berger, Ivogün, and Domgraf-Fassbänder; debut as Zerbinetta, Aussig, 1943. Sang in Berlin (State Opera, 1946–51; Städtische Oper, from 1951) and Vienna (from 1953); also in London (1954), San Francisco (Sophie, 1957), Glyndebourne (Zerbinetta, 1958), and Chicago (Susanna, 1960).

Strepponi, Giuseppina. Soprano; b. Lodi, Italy, Sep. 8, 1815; d. Sant'Agata, near Busseto, Nov. 14, 1897. Studied at Milan Conservatory; debut (?) at Adria, 1834. Sang in Trieste (1835) and Vienna (Amina and Adalgisa, 1835). At La Scala, 1839, she sang Lucia, Elvira (*Puritani*), and Adina,

Max Rudolf, Fritz Reiner, Igor Stravinsky, and George Balanchine

Suor Angelica – World premiere, 1918. Geraldine Farrar

urged the production of Verdi's *Oberto*, and created Abigaille (*Nabucco*). Also created title role in Donizetti's *Adelia*, Rome, 1841. Married Verdi in 1859.

stretta (Ital., "narrow"). Applied to a final, climactic section in faster tempo, especially in an operatic finale.

subscription. A method of ticket sales, in which a number of performances (e.g., all Monday evenings or all opening nights) are grouped together and sold as a package, often at a discount.

Suliotis, Elena. See *Souliotis, Elena.*

Sullivan, Arthur. Composer; b. Lambeth, London, May 13, 1842; d. London, Nov. 22, 1900. Studied at Royal Academy of Music with Bennett and at Leipzig Conservatory with Hauptmann and Rietz. Composer of oratorios, orchestral works, and one grand opera, *Ivanhoe* (1891), his reputation rests on operettas written with librettist W.S. Gilbert, blending satire, burlesque, and sentimentality. Among them are *H.M.S. Pinafore* (1878), *The Pirates of Penzance* (1879), *Patience* (1881), *Iolanthe* (1882), *The Mikado* (1885), and *Ruddigore* (1887). In them, Sullivan draws upon a variety of operatic models, as well as on his flair for matching music to Gilbert's brilliant words.

Sullivan, Brian. Tenor; b. Oakland, Calif., Aug. 9, 1917; d. Lake Geneva, Switzerland, June 17, 1969. Studied at U. of So. California; debut as Almaviva, Long Beach, 1940. Appeared on Broadway (*Street Scene*) and in films. Met debut as Grimes, Feb. 23, 1948; in 12 seasons, he sang 122 perfs. of 20 roles, including Admète (*Alceste*), Tamino, José, and Lohengrin. Sang Avito (*Amore dei Tre Re*) in San Francisco (1952), Don Carlos in Chicago (1957).

Suor Angelica (Sister Angelica). Opera in 1 act by Puccini; libretto by Giovacchino Forzano. Part 2 of *Il Trittico*.

First perf., N.Y., Met, Dec. 14, 1918: Farrar, Perini, c.

Moranzoni, d. Stroppa, p. Ordynski. Later Met production: Dec. 19, 1975: Cruz-Romo, Chookasian, c. Ehrling, d. Reppa, p. Melano. Angelica has also been sung at the Met by Scotto, Zylis-Gara; the Princess by Dalis, Barbieri. 43 perfs. in 5 seasons.

Composed for female voices only and including Puccini's only significant role for mezzo-soprano, this religious confection has received the weakest response of the *Trittico* operas.

The cloister of a convent near Siena, 17th c. Angelica (s), daughter of a wealthy family, has entered a convent after bearing a child out of wedlock. Her aunt, the Princess (ms), visits and asks her to sign away her share of the family fortune. When Angelica inquires about her son, she is brusquely told that he is dead. The distraught Angelica takes poison, and in her dying moments has a vision of the Virgin Mary bringing her baby to her.

supertitles. A system of projecting vernacular translations of foreign operatic texts on a screen above the stage opening. Also known as "surtitles," "supratitles," and (erroneously) as "subtitles," the latter properly reserved to the translations at the bottom of the screen used in films and operatic telecasts.

Supervia, Conchita. Mezzo-soprano; b. Barcelona, Dec. 9, 1895; d. London, Mar. 30, 1936. Studied at Colegio de las Damas Negras, Barcelona; debut in Stiattesi's *Blanca de Beaulieu*, with touring troupe, Colón, Buenos Aires, 1910. She sang Carmen in Bari, Octavian in Rome premiere of *Rosenkavalier*, Costanzi, 1911, and Carmen at opening of Liceo, Barcelona, 1912; in Chicago (1915–16), she sang Charlotte (*Werther*), Mignon, and Carmen. La Scala debut as Hänsel, 1926; she also sang Octavian, Cherubino, and Concepcion (*Heure Espagnole*) there. As the heroines of Rossini's then nearly forgotten *Italiana* and *Cenerentola*, and in the original mezzo version of his Rosina, she had great successes in Paris (1929–30), Florence (1930, 1933), and Covent Garden (1934–35). Though Supervia's pronounced vibrato troubled some listeners, she was, in both passion and mirth, one of the most vivid of singers. She died of complications following childbirth.

Suppé, Franz. Composer, b. Spalato [now Split], Dalmatia, Apr. 18, 1819, of Austrian parents; d. Vienna, May 21, 1895. A student of Sechter and Seyfried in Vienna, he became a conductor and composer of operettas for various Viennese theaters. After 1865, at the Theater in der Leopoldstadt, he came under the influence of Offenbach, whose manner he blended with the sentiment characteristic of Viennese operetta, in such successes as *Die schöne Galatea* (1865), *Boccaccio* (1879), and *Donna Juanita* (1880).

surtitles. See *supertitles.*

Sutherland, Joan. Soprano; b. Sydney, Nov. 7, 1926. Studied in Sydney with her mother, a mezzo, and with John and Aida Dickens, later with Clive Carey, Royal College of Music, London; operatic debut as Goossens' Judith, Sydney, 1951. Covent Garden debut as the First Lady (*Zauberflöte*) in 1952; in the next seven years, she sang such varied roles as Amelia (*Ballo*), Agathe (*Freischütz*), Aida, the *Hoffmann* heroines, Eva, Gilda, Pamina, and the Israelite Woman (*Samson*), and created Jenifer (*Midsummer Marriage*). In 1954 she married the pianist Richard Bonynge, who directed her towards the florid soprano repertory and in the 1960s became her favored conductor. An Alcina with the Handel Opera Society (1957) demonstrated her exceptional talent for such music, confirmed by her first Lucia at Covent Garden in 1959, the start of her international career. In 1960, she made debuts as Lucia at the Massimo, Palermo, and the Paris Opéra, as Alcina at La Fenice, Venice, and Dallas; the following year, she sang Elvira (*Puritani*) in Palermo and Glyndebourne, made her N.Y. debut in a concert version of *Beatrice di Tenda*, and bowed as Lucia at La Scala, Chicago, and the Met (Nov. 26, 1961). Since then she has returned frequently to the Met, singing more than 215 perfs. of 13 roles, most often Lucia (33), Amina (27), and Marie in *Fille* (26), also Norma, Elvira, Violetta, the *Hoffmann* heroines, Donna Anna, Esclarmonde, and Gilda; the 25th anniversary of her Met debut was celebrated with a gala on Jan. 11, 1987. At Covent Garden after 1959, her roles included the Queen of Night and Alcina; at La Scala, she sang Beatrice di Tenda, Marguerite de Valois, and Semiramide; and she has sung in most of the world's great theaters, with special attention to her native Australia.

Combining vocal power and flexibility to a degree unknown since Melba, Sutherland is one of the great coloratura technicians in operatic history; with flawless intonation, fearless attack, brilliant staccato, firmly defined runs and roulades, she revived the esthetic potential of full-throated florid singing. Though occasionally sacrificing precision of diction to beauty of tone, her command of cantilena lines and her exuberance in cabalettas offered their own rewards. Fortunately, she recorded all of her leading roles while in her prime, and also a few operas she did not sing on stage, including *Turandot* and *Suor Angelica.*
BIBLIOGRAPHY: B. Adams, *La Stupenda* (Sydney, 1981).

Svanholm, Set. Tenor; b. Västerås, Sweden, Sep. 2, 1904; d. Saltsjö-Duvnäs, near Stockholm, Oct. 4, 1964. Studied as baritone with John Forsell; debut as Silvio (*Pagliacci*), Stockholm, 1930. After further study, tenor debut there as Radames, 1937; he remained with the company until 1956, singing Wagner parts, also José, Otello, Énée, Idomeneo, and Grimes. He sang Tannhäuser in Salzburg (1938) and Milan (1942), also appearing in Vienna and Bayreuth (both Siegfrieds, Erik, 1942). In 1946, he sang in Rio de Janeiro (Tristan and Siegmund), San Francisco (Lohengrin, returning through 1951), and Chicago (Tristan). Met debut as the young Siegfried, Nov. 15, 1946; in 10 seasons, he sang 105 perfs. of 17 roles, including Wagner heldentenor repertory, Herod, Eisenstein (*Fledermaus*), Florestan, and Aegisth (*Elektra*). Also sang at Covent Garden (1948–54). Administrator of Royal Opera, Stockholm (1956–63). Svanholm's handsome presence enhanced his always reliable and musical, if somewhat dry, singing.

Sved, Alexander [Sándor Svéd]. Baritone; b. Budapest, May 28, 1904; d. Budapest, June 9, 1979. After debut as di Luna, Budapest, 1928, studied with Sammarco and Stracciari in Milan. Sang at Vienna State Opera (1935–39), Covent Garden (1936), and La Scala (debut, Macbeth, 1938). Met debut as Renato (*Ballo*), Dec. 2, 1940; in 8 seasons, sang 60 perfs. of 12 roles, including Scarpia, Telramund, Escamillo, Alfio, and Amonasro. In 1950 he returned to Budapest, where he sang until 1956.

Svoboda, Josef. Designer; b. Caslav, Czechoslovakia, May 10, 1920. Since 1948, leading designer for National Theater, Prague, also working in opera, ballet, and films. His innovative use of lighting, projections, and film at the

Prague Laterna Magika has been applied to many opera productions, including Nono's *Intolleranza* (Venice, 1961) and *Wozzeck* (La Scala, 1971). For the Met, he designed *Carmen* (1972), *Vêpres Siciliennes* (1974), and *Bartered Bride* (1978).

Swarthout, Gladys. Mezzo-soprano; b. Deepwater, Mo., Dec. 25, 1900; d. Florence, July 7, 1969. Studied at Bush Conservatory, Chicago; debut as Shepherd (*Tosca*), Chicago Civic Opera, 1924, appearing the following year as Carmen at Ravinia. Met debut as Cieca, Nov. 15, 1929; in 13 seasons, she sang 162 perfs. of 22 roles, including Carmen, Stephano (*Roméo*), Niejata (*Sadko*), Lola, Siebel, Frédéric (*Mignon*), Maddalena, Mrs. Deane (*Peter Ibbetson*), and Mallika (*Lakmé*); she created Plentiful Tewke (*Merry Mount*), 1934. She also sang Carmen in Chicago (1939) and San Francisco (1941), and made several films. She retired to Florence in 1954, after suffering a severe heart attack. Swarthout's warm and cultivated mezzo was much admired, though a placid temperament kept her from the first rank of operatic performers.

Syllabaire pour Phèdre (Spelling-book for Phaedra). Opera in prologue and 1 act by Ohana; libretto by Raphaël Cluzel.

First perf., Paris, Théâtre de la Musique, Feb. 5, 1968: c. Constant. U.S. prem., N.Y., Mini-Met, Feb. 17, 1973: Williams, c. Dufallo, d. Lee/Greenwood, p. Deiber.

A contemporary work based on the Greek myth of Phèdre (ms), wife of Theseus, who fell in love with her stepson Hippolytus. The text is sung, spoken, screamed, and distorted on magnetic tape, while the actors and singers are immobile.

Székely, Mihály. Bass; b. Jászberény, Hungary, May 8, 1901; d. Budapest, Mar. 22, 1963. Studied in Budapest; debut as Hermit (*Freischütz*), Municipal Theater, Budapest, 1923. He joined the Budapest Opera (debut, Ferrando in *Trovatore*, 1923), remaining on roster until his death. Met debut as Hunding, Jan. 17, 1947; in 3 seasons, sang 29 perfs. of 7 roles, including Fafner, Sparafucile, Fiesco, and King Marke. Also appeared at Glyndebourne (Osmin, Sarastro, 1957–61) and in Paris (Boris, 1957).

Szell, George. Conductor; b. Budapest, June 7, 1897; d. Cleveland, Ohio, July 29, 1970. A child prodigy as pianist, he was conducting by the age of 16, and joined the Berlin Opera staff in 1915. Later operatic posts were in Darmstadt, Düsseldorf, Berlin (1924–29), and Prague (1929–37). After conducting in Glasgow (1937–39), he came to America and was active at the Met from 1942 to 1946 (and briefly in 1953–54), leading 76 perfs. of *Salome* (debut, Dec. 9, 1942), *Rosenkavalier*, *Boris*, *Don Giovanni*, *Tannhäuser*, *Meistersinger*, the *Ring*, and *Otello*. For the rest of his life, he was music director of the Cleveland Orchestra (1946–70), raising it to international stature. Szell's musical personality was marked by meticulous discipline and the highest standards of orchestral craftsmanship.

Szymanowski, Karol. Composer; b. Tymoszówka, Ukraine, Oct. 6, 1882; d. Lausanne, Switzerland, Mar. 29, 1937. Studied composition with Naskowski and harmony with Zawirski. Poland's leading 20th-c. composer, he was co-founder in 1901 of "Young Poland in Music." His first opera, the one-act *Hagith* (1922), influenced by Strauss and Ravel, established his reputation. He became director of Warsaw Conservatory in 1926, the year of the premiere of his ambitious historical opera *King Roger* (1926).

T

Tabarro, Il (The Cloak). Opera in 1 act by Puccini; libretto by Adami, after Didier Gold's tragedy *La Houppelande*. Part 1 of *Il Trittico*.

First perf., N.Y., Met, Dec. 14, 1918: Muzio, Crimi, Montesanto, c. Moranzoni, d. Stroppa, p. Ordynski. Later Met productions: Jan. 5, 1946: Albanese, Jagel, Tibbett, c. Sodero, d. Novak, p. Graf; Dec. 19, 1975: Kubiak, Theyard, MacNeil, c. Ehrling, d. Reppa, p. Melano. Giorgetta has also been sung at the Met by Behrens, Scotto; Michele by Amato, Sved. 46 perfs. in 6 seasons.

The *grand guignol* of this brooding, sometimes impressionistic score inaugurates the contrasts of Puccini's *Trittico*.

A barge on the Seine, late 19th c. Michele (bar) lives on his barge with his wife Giorgetta (s), who is bored with their life together. Suspecting that she has taken a lover, Michele lies in wait to discover him. It turns out to be Luigi (t), one of his hired hands. Michele strangles him. Giorgetta comes on deck and her husband offers her comfort, as of old, under his warm cloak. He draws it aside to reveal Luigi's corpse.

tableau (Fr., "picture"). In French opera, the equivalent of "scene." In general usage, a temporarily "frozen" stage picture, as at the climax of an ensemble or finale.

Taddei, Giuseppe. Baritone; b. Genoa, Italy, June 26, 1916. Studied in Rome; debut as Herald (*Lohengrin*), Rome Opera, 1936. He sang there until drafted in 1942;

Il Tabarro – World premiere, 1918. Claudia Muzio and Giulio Crimi

after release from German imprisonment, a Vienna concert won him a State Opera contract (1946–48), singing Rigoletto, Amonasro, and both Figaros. London debut at Cambridge Theatre, 1947, as Scarpia and Rigoletto; at Salzburg, 1948, sang Mozart's Figaro. He performed regularly at La Scala (1948–51, 1955–61) in roles such as Papageno, Pizarro (*Fidelio*), Malatesta, and the *Hoffmann* villains, also singing Wagner roles elsewhere in Italy. Debuts in San Francisco (Macbeth, 1957) and Chicago (Barnaba, 1959); at Covent Garden (1960–67), he sang Macbeth, Rigoletto, and Iago. He made a triumphant, if belated, Met debut as Falstaff, Sep. 25, 1985. A versatile singer and resourceful actor, equally effective in dramatic and comic roles.

Tagliabue, Carlo. Baritone; b. Mariano Comense, Italy, Jan. 13, 1898; d. Monza, Apr. 5, 1978. Studied in Milan; debut as Amonasro, Lodi, 1922. Sang frequently at La Scala, 1929–58; created Basilio (*Fiamma*), Rome, 1934. Met debut as Amonasro, Dec. 2, 1937; in 2 seasons, sang 36 perfs. of 9 roles, including Rigoletto, Marcello, Alfio, Iago, Germont, and di Luna. Also sang in Buenos Aires (1934), London (Rigoletto, 1938), and San Francisco (Gérard, 1938).

Tagliavini, Ferruccio. Tenor; b. Barco, Reggio Emilia, Italy, Aug. 14, 1913. Studied with Brancucci in Parma, Amedeo Bassi in Florence; debut as Rodolfo, Florence, 1938. At La Scala (1942–53), his roles included Elvino (*Sonnambula*), Mascagni's Fritz, and Werther. In 1946, toured South America and made U.S. debut in Chicago as Rodolfo, also the role of his Met debut, Jan. 10, 1947; in 9 seasons (to 1954, and 1961–62), he sang 69 perfs. of 8 roles, including Almaviva, Alfredo, Edgardo, Duke of Mantua, Nemorino, and Cavaradossi. He sang in San Francisco (1948–49, returning as Boito's Faust, 1952) and at Covent Garden (1950, 1955–56). Married to soprano Pia Tassinari (b. 1909), he retired from opera in 1965, occasionally concertizing thereafter. With velvety pianissimos and caressing legato, Tagliavini seemed the heir apparent to Gigli, but in spinto parts he resorted to forcing his tone.

taille (Fr.). Tenor voice.

Taillon, Jocelyne. Mezzo-soprano; b. Doudeville, France, May 19, 1941. Studied with Suzanne Balguerie and Lubin, Grenoble Conservatory; debut as Nurse (*Ariane et Barbe-Bleue*), Bordeaux, 1968. Member of Paris Opéra; at Glyndebourne, sang Geneviève in *Pelléas*, 1969. At the Met, she has sung La Cieca (debut, Nov. 29, 1979), Geneviève, Anna (*Troyens*), Quickly, and Erda.

Tajo, Italo. Bass; b. Pinerolo, Italy, Apr. 25, 1915. Studied in Turin; debut at Teatro Regio there, as Fafner (*Rheingold*), 1935. Sang at Glyndebourne (1935), Rome (1942), La Scala (1941–56), Chicago (1946), San Francisco (1948–56). Met debut as Basilio, Dec. 28, 1948; remained on roster until 1950, in roles including Mozart's Figaro, Gianni Schicchi, Dulcamara; returned in 1976 to sing Alcindoro, Benoit, Sacristan, and Don Pasquale.

Tales of Hoffmann, The. See *Contes d'Hoffmann, Les.*

Talley, Marion. Soprano; b. Nevada, Mo., Dec. 20, 1907; d. Los Angeles, Jan. 3, 1983. Studied with Frank LaForge, N.Y., then in Italy. Debut as Gilda, Met, Feb. 17, 1926; in 4 seasons, sang 53 perfs. of 7 roles, including Lucia, Olympia, Philine, and Stravinsky's Nightingale. Sang Gilda in Chicago (1933).

Francesco Tamagno as Otello

Talvela, Martti. Bass; b. Hiitola, East Karelia, Finland, Feb. 4, 1935. Studied with Taunokaivela at Lahti Academy of Music and with Carl Martin Öhman, Stockholm; debut as Sparafucile, Stockholm, 1961. The following year, he joined the Deutsche Oper, Berlin, and made his Bayreuth debut as Titurel, returning through 1970. Salzburg debut as Commendatore, 1968; he returned in 1978 as Sarastro. Met debut as Grand Inquisitor (*Don Carlos*), Oct. 7, 1968; subsequently he has sung more than 100 perfs. there, including Hunding, Fasolt, Boris, the Padre Guardiano, Gremin, Kečal (*Bartered Bride*), Gurnemanz, Osmin, and Sarastro. He has also appeared at Chicago (Daland, 1969), Covent Garden (*Ring*, 1970), and the Paris Opéra. From 1972, director of Savonlinna Festival in Finland. A singer of imposing stature and vocal weight.

Tamagno, Francesco. Tenor; b. Turin, Italy, Dec. 28, 1850; d. Varese, Aug. 31, 1905. Studied with Pedrotti and sang as chorister, Regio, Turin; debut in brief role of Nearco (*Poliuto*). After further study, first major role was Riccardo (*Ballo*), Palermo, 1874, then he sang at La Fenice (Pery in *Guarany*, and Poliuto, 1874–75) and the Barcelona Liceo (Ernani, 1875–76). At La Scala (debut, Vasco in *Africaine*, 1877), his roles included Don Carlos, Raoul (*Huguenots*), and Boito's Faust, and he created Fabiano in Gomes' *Maria Tudor* (1879), Adorno in the revised *Boccanegra* (1881), Didier in Ponchielli's *Marion Delorme* (1885), and – the climax of his career – Verdi's Otello (1887). He sang throughout the Italian and Hispanic world in the classic heroic roles and also in verismo works, including Puccini's *Edgar* (Madrid, 1892), Leoncavallo's *Medici* (premiere, dal Verme, Milan, 1893), and Chénier (St. Petersburg, 1898). Otello was his passport outside Latin theaters, in London (Lyceum, 1889, and Covent Garden, 1895), N.Y. (with a touring company at the Met, 1891), and Paris (Opéra, 1897). He sang only one season with the resident Met company, in 24 perfs. as Arnold in *Guillaume Tell* (debut, Nov. 21, 1894), Edgardo, Manrico, Radames, Otello, Jean de Leyde, Vasco, Samson, and Turiddu. He returned to Covent Garden in 1901 as Radames and Hélion (*Messaline*), and made his last appearances in 1904, in Rome and Naples.

Tamagno's trumpet-like voice, able to carry over an orchestra in full cry and declaim forcefully at the top of the staff, was a new phenomenon, and it incited Italian composers from Verdi onwards to a kind of writing that eventually took a toll on the grace and fluency of less plentifully endowed tenors. An imposing actor, his emotional and declamatory intensity is still audible in recordings, notably the excerpts from *Otello*.

Tamberlik [Tamberlick], **Enrico**. Tenor; b. Rome, Mar. 16, 1820; d. Paris, Mar. 13, 1889. Studied in Rome, Naples, and Bologna; debut as Tebaldo (*Capuleti*), Fondo, Naples, 1841. Covent Garden debut as Masaniello, 1850; sang there regularly until 1864. Appeared in Paris, Madrid, Buenos Aires, and St. Petersburg, where he created Verdi's Alvaro (*Forza*), 1862.

Tamburini, Antonio. Baritone; b. Faenza, Italy, Mar. 28, 1800; d. Nice, France, Nov. 8, 1876. Debut in Generali's *Contessa di Colle*, Cento, 1818. Sang throughout Italy, 1824–32, then appeared frequently in London and Paris until 1843. Created Ernesto (*Pirata*), Valdeburgo (*Straniera*), Riccardo (*Puritani*), and many Donizetti roles, notably Malatesta (*Pasquale*).

Tamerlano. Opera in 3 acts by Handel; libretto by Agostino Piovene, adapted by Nicola F. Haym.
First perf., London, King's Theater, Oct. 31, 1724: Cuzzoni, Dotti, Senesino, Pacini, Borosini, Boschi. U.S. prem., Bloomington, Indiana U., Jan. 26, 1985 (in Eng.): c. Bradshaw.
One of Handel's most rigorously characterized dramas, unusual in its starring role for tenor (Bajazet, the captive Turkish ruler). The plot treats conflicting loves and loyalties among the allies and vanquished foes of the Tartar emperor Tamerlano (a), who is ultimately pressed to a grant of clemency.

Taming of the Shrew, The. See *Widerspenstigen Zähmung, Die*.

Tancredi. Opera in 2 acts by Rossini; libretto by Gaetano Rossi, after Voltaire's *Tancrède* and Tasso's *Gerusalemme Liberata*.
First perf., Venice, Fenice, Feb. 6, 1813: Malanotte, Manfredini, Toldran, Bianchi, Marchesi. U.S. prem., N.Y., Park, Dec. 31, 1825: Malibran, Barbieri, Garcia, Crivelli, Angrisani, c. Étienne.
Rossini's first triumph in serious opera effectively defined the forms that would prevail for a generation in Italian opera. In Syracuse, besieged by Saracens, Tancredi (a) returns in time to prevent the marriage of his beloved Amenaide (s) to Orbazzano (bs), who then intercepts a letter apparently proving Amenaide a traitor. Tancredi champions her, she is cleared, and they are united.

Taneyev, Sergei. Composer; b. Vladimir district, Russia, Nov. 25, 1856; d. Dyudkovo, near Moscow, June 19, 1915. Studied at Moscow Conservatory with Hubert and Tchaikovsky, and taught there from 1878, becoming director in 1885 but resigning in 1889 to concentrate on composition. Erudite and highly skilled, especially in counterpoint, Taneyev wrote one opera, the ambitious epic *Oresteia*, after Aeschylus (1895), modeled on French grand opera; its complexity is generally considered to outrun its inspiration.

Tannhäuser und der Sängerkrieg auf Wartburg (Tannhäuser and the Song Contest at the Wartburg). Opera in 3 acts by Wagner; libretto by the composer.
First perf., Dresden, Oct. 19, 1845; J. Wagner, Schröder-Devrient, Tichatschek, Mitterwurzer, Dettner, c. Wagner. Rev. version with ballet, first perf. Paris, Opéra, Mar. 13, 1861 (in Fr.): Saxe, Tedesco, Niemann, Morelli, Cazaux, c. Dietsch. U.S. prem. (first Wagner opera perf. in U.S.), N.Y., Stadt Theater, Apr. 4, 1859: Siedenburg, Pickaneser, Pickaneser, Lehmann, Graff, c.

Tannhäuser – (1977). Designed by Günther Schneider-Siemssen, produced by Otto Schenk. Bernd Weikl, John Macurdy, Leonie Rysanek

Bergmann. Met prem., Nov. 17, 1884 (Dresden version): Seidl-Kraus, Slach, Schott, Robinson, Kögel, c. L. Damrosch, d. staff/Ascoli. Later Met productions: Feb. 1, 1923 (Paris version): Jeritza, Matzenauer, Taucher, Whitehill, Bender, c. Bodanzky, d. Kautsky, p. Thewman; Dec. 26, 1953 (Dresden version): Harshaw, Varnay, Vinay, London, Hines, c. Szell, d. Gérard, p. Graf; Dec. 22, 1977 (Paris version): Rysanek, Bumbry, McCracken, Weikl, Macurdy, c. Levine, d. Schneider-Siemssen/Zipprodt, p. Schenk. Tannhäuser has also been sung at the Met by Niemann, Alvary, van Dyck, Kraus, Knote, Burrian, Jörn, Slezak, Urlus, Melchior, Lorenz, Ralf, Svanholm; Elisabeth by Materna, Melba, Eames, Gadski, Ternina, Farrar, Destinn, Fremstad, Easton, Rethberg, Müller, Lotte Lehmann, Flagstad, Traubel, Varnay, de los Angeles, Nilsson, Zylis-Gara, Marton, Norman; Venus by Lilli Lehmann, Nordica, Homer, Fremstad, Branzell, Thorborg, Lawrence, Thebom, Dunn, Nilsson, Troyanos, Randová; Wolfram by Ancona, Kaschmann, Bispham, van Rooy, Schorr, Tibbett, Janssen, Prey, Stewart; the Landgrave by Fischer, Plançon, Bohnen, Mayr, Pinza, List, Kipnis, Moll; the opera has also been conducted by Seidl, Mancinelli, Hertz, Mottl, Abravanel, Leinsdorf, Busch, Kempe, Solti. 311 perfs. in 60 seasons.

The most traditionally conceived of the Wagner operas that survive in current repertory, arranged in set pieces, though in some details looking forward to later developments (reflected in the Paris additions).

Near Eisenach, early 13th c. The knight minstrel Tannhäuser (t), who has succumbed to the forbidden pleasures of the mountain of Venus (s), now invokes the Virgin's aid to escape them. Encountering his erstwhile comrades, he is persuaded by Wolfram (bar) to return in the name of his beloved Elisabeth (s). In the Wartburg's hall of song, Elisabeth and her father the Landgrave (bs) await the assembly of the knights for a contest of minstrelsy. As the contest proceeds, however, Tannhäuser is seized by a frenzied scorn for the pale love songs he hears, and rises to hymn the voluptuary delights of the Venusberg, to the horror of all around; only Elisabeth begs for pity on his behalf. The Landgrave decrees that Tannhäuser must make a pilgrimage to Rome and seek absolution from the Pope. Much later, Wolfram encounters the shaken Tannhäuser, who has been told in Rome that he who has tasted the Venusberg's joys is as likely to be pardoned as the Pope's wooden staff is to burst into flower. He has resolved to abandon hope and to return to Venus, but a funeral procession, bearing the bier of Elisabeth who has died of grief for Tannhäuser, comes from the Wartburg, and a band of pilgrims brings the Papal staff, now in blossom: Elisabeth's interceding prayers have won Tannhäuser's salvation.

Tate, Jeffrey. Conductor; b. Farnham, Surrey, England, Apr. 28, 1943. After graduation from Cambridge, served as coach and assistant at Covent Garden (1970–77), Cologne (1977–79), and the Met (from 1979), where his conducting career began (debut, *Lulu*, Dec. 26, 1980), in works ranging from Mozart to Weill, as well as both Strausses. Principal guest conductor, Geneva Opera (from 1983) and Covent Garden (from 1986).

Tauber, Richard. Tenor; b. Linz, May 16, 1891; d. London, Jan. 8, 1948. Studied conducting and composition at Frankfurt Conservatory, singing with Carl Beines in Freiburg; debut as Tamino, Chemnitz, 1913. Contracted to the Dresden Opera (debut, Alphonse in *Muette*, 1913), where he sang until 1922, in roles of Mozart, Puccini, Lortzing and other light German and French composers. A member of the Vienna State Opera (1922–28, 1932–38), he also sang Ottavio and Belmonte in Salzburg (1922, 1926). Concurrently a member of the Berlin State Opera (1923–33), he returned to Dresden in 1926 as the first German Calaf. A Viennese engagement in Lehár's *Frasquita* (1922) opened a lucrative additional career, and operettas, notably Lehár's *Land des Lächelns* (1929) and *Giuditta* (1934), were tailored specifically for him. Tauber also conducted operettas, composed his own (including *Old Chelsea*, 1942), and starred in films (including *Blossom Time*, 1934). After the Nazi takeover of Austria, he sang at Covent Garden (Mozart, and Jeník in *Bartered Bride*, 1938–39), and became a British subject in 1940. In the U.S., he gave recital tours from 1931, and sang in a Broadway adaptation of *Land des Lächelns* (1946). His last appearance was at Covent Garden in 1947, as Ottavio with the visiting Vienna State Opera; a week later, a cancerous lung was removed, and he died within a few months. He was married to soprano Carlotta Vanconti, later to actress Diana Napier, who published a memoir in 1949.

To whatever music he performed, Tauber brought the skills of a fully-trained, refined musician and a canny vocal technician able to manage spinto roles with a light lyric tenor that never lost its flexibility. He sang (and recorded) reams of popular music with great elegance and charming mannerisms, yet his operatic singing remained a model of style, polish, imagination, and communicative warmth.

Taverner. Opera in 2 acts by Maxwell Davies; libretto by the composer.

First perf., London, Covent Garden, July 12, 1972: Knight, Bowman, Ulfung, Lanigan, Luxon, Herincx, c. Downes. U.S. prem., Boston, Mar. 9, 1986: R. Freni, Gall, Moulson, Valesco, Oke, Herincx, c. Caldwell.

An intellectually and musically rigorous exploration of the theme of religious conviction vs. opportunism, in the figure of the medieval English composer John Taverner (t), who is tried for heresy and released by the intervention of Cardinal Wolsey (t) but later becomes a bigoted Protestant, giving up musical composition.

Taylor, Deems. Composer; b. New York, Dec. 22, 1885; d. New York, July 3, 1966. Studied with Oscar Coon. Active as music critic, author, and commentator on the first Met radio broadcasts, Taylor composed in a facile and eclectic late-Romantic style. His first two operas, *The King's Henchman* (1927) and *Peter Ibbetson* (1931), commissioned by the Met, were initially well received but have not endured. Other operas: *Ramuntcho* (1942); *The Dragon* (1958).

Tchaikovsky, Peter Ilyich. Composer; b. Kamsko-Votkinsk, Vyatka province, Russia, May 7, 1840; d. St. Petersburg, Nov. 6, 1893. Studied piano from childhood; after abandoning a clerical career in 1863, studied composition with Nikolai Zaremba and Anton Rubinstein, then taught at Moscow Conservatory (1866–78). He withdrew his first opera, *The Voyevoda* (1869), after five performances and re-used much of its music in *The Oprichnik* (1874), a Meyerbeerian historical drama incorporating Russian folk songs. The comedy *Vakula the Smith* (1876) achieved a modest success. After 1876, the patronage of the wealthy Nadezhda von Meck freed Tchaikovsky from financial worries, although an ill-advised marriage in 1877 left enduring psychic scars on the morbidly sensitive (and homosexual) composer; while convalescent in Western Europe, he composed *Eugene Onegin* (1879), loosely constructed "lyrical scenes" that owe their power to Tchaikovsky's identification with the heroine Tatiana. Another Meyerbeerian essay, *The Maid of Orleans* (1881), and two nationalistic works, *Mazeppa* (1884) and *The Enchantress* (1887), were unsuccessful. The eerie and melodramatic *The Queen of Spades* (1890) was followed by the one-act fairy tale *Iolanta* (1892). Trained in a Western tradition by Rubinstein but also sympathetic to the Russian nationalists, Tchaikovsky gradually found his own way between the two poles. He worked earnestly at operas that did not consistently engage his strongest sympathies, but his encounters with appropriate situations and characters brought forth music of great lyrical and theatrical power. His other works include ballets, six symphonies, concertos, tone poems, and songs.

BIBLIOGRAPHY: John Warrack, *Tchaikovsky* (N.Y., and London, 1973).

Tebaldi, Renata. Soprano; b. Pesaro, Feb. 1, 1922. Studied with Brancucci and Campogalliani in Parma, Carmen Melis in Pesaro; debut as Elena (*Mefistofele*), Rovigo, 1944. She quickly reached Milan, in Toscanini's 1946 concert for the reopening of La Scala; at that theater until 1955, her roles included Eva, Boito's and Gounod's Marguerites, Wally, and Tatiana. In 1948, Violetta introduced her to Naples (where other roles included Elisabeth, Giovanna d'Arco, Refice's Cecilia, and Amazily in *Fernand Cortez*) and Rome (where she sang Casavola's Salammbô and the Countess in *Nozze*). At the Florence Maggio Musicale, 1948–53, she sang Elsa, Pamira (*Siège*), Spontini's Olympie, and Mathilde (*Tell*). She was first heard outside Italy as Donna Elvira in Lisbon (1949) and as Desdemona at Covent Garden on a Scala tour (1950). After her American debut in San Francisco (*Aida*, 1950), she sang regularly in Rio de Janeiro, 1951–54. At the Met (debut, Desdemona, Jan. 31, 1955), in 17 seasons she sang 210 perfs. of 14 roles, most often Tosca (36 times), Mimì (31), and Gioconda (25), also Desdemona, Adriana Lecouvreur, Maddalena (*Chénier*), Manon Lescaut, Amelia (*Boccanegra*), Violetta, Butterfly, Alice Ford, Leonora (*Forza*), Minnie (*Fanciulla*), and Aida. She also appeared at the Chicago Lyric (from 1955), Paris

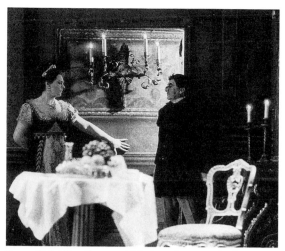

Renata Tebaldi as Tosca and Mariano Caruso as Spoletta in *Tosca*

Opéra (1959), Vienna State Opera (from 1959), and Deutsche Oper, Berlin (1962), and in Tokyo and Osaka (1961). Other roles were Suzel in *Amico Fritz* (Parma, 1945), Handel's Cleopatra (Pompeii, 1950), and Fedora (Chicago, 1960). She retired from opera in 1973, and from concerts in 1976.

Tebaldi's radiant spinto voice and warm personality made her a central figure in postwar Italian opera. She combined a high standard of musicianship and vocal quality with a sympathetic stage presence, and was capable of considerable dramatic vitality when in the company of stimulating colleagues, although her studio recordings tend to emphasize the placid side of her art.

Kiri Te Kanawa as Arabella

Te Kanawa, Kiri. Soprano; b. Gisborne, New Zealand, Mar. 6, 1944. After winning a Melbourne competition in 1966, she studied at London Opera Centre and with Vera Rosza; professional debut as Carmen, Northern Opera, Newcastle-upon-Tyne, 1968. She appeared as Idamante in *Idomeneo* (Chelsea Opera Group, 1968) and Elena in *Donna del Lago* (Camden Festival, 1969) before her 1971 Covent Garden debut as a Flowermaiden (*Parsifal*). The Countess (*Nozze*) became her first success, at Santa Fe and Covent Garden (1971), in Lyon and San Francisco (1972), and later at Glyndebourne (1973–74). She also sang Desdemona (Scottish Opera, 1972), Micaela, Amelia (*Boccanegra*), and Donna Elvira (all at Covent Garden, 1973) before her Met debut, on three hours' notice, as Desdemona (Feb. 9, 1974). She returned to the Met through 1976 as Donna Elvira and the Countess, and since 1982 as Fiordiligi, Arabella, the Marschallin, Violetta, the Israelite Woman (*Samson*), and Rosalinde (*Fledermaus*). Other debuts in Paris (Elvira, 1975), Houston (Arabella, 1977), La Scala (Amelia in *Boccanegra*, 1978), Salzburg (Countess, 1979), and Vienna (Desdemona, 1980). At Covent Garden since 1974, she has also sung Marguerite, Mimi, and Tatiana; other roles include Pamina (San Francisco, 1975), Violetta (Sydney, 1978), and Tosca (Paris, 1982).

With her creamy, mellifluous lyric soprano, Te Kanawa immediately attracted attention as one of the day's notable talents; her tonal splendor, well matched by her personal beauty and poise on stage, is featured in many recordings.

Telemann, Georg Philipp. Composer; b. Magdeburg, Germany, Mar. 14, 1681; d. Hamburg, June 25, 1767. Self-taught by studying the works of eminent contemporaries, he became the most prolific and cosmopolitan composer of the 18th c. Composing in all genres and styles, he bridged late baroque and early classical periods. He directed the Hamburg Opera (1722–38), where most of his operas were produced – notably the intermezzo *Pimpinone* (1728), which anticipated Pergolesi's *Serva Padrona* in its opera buffa style.

Telephone, The. Opera in 1 act by Menotti; libretto by the composer.

First perf., N.Y., Heckscher, Feb. 18, 1947: Cotlow, Kwartin, c. Barzin.

A descendant of the old Italian intermezzo, with the telephone taking the place of the traditional mute comedian. Lucy (s) spends most of her time on the telephone; her boyfriend Ben (bar), who is waiting to propose to her, has no recourse but to go to a phone booth and call her.

Telva [Toucke], Marion. Mezzo-soprano; b. St. Louis, Mo., Dec. 26, 1897; d. Norwalk, Conn., Oct. 23, 1962. Studied in N.Y.; debut as Musician (*Manon Lescaut*), Met, Dec. 31, 1920; in 12 seasons, sang 416 perfs. of 55 roles, including Adalgisa, Marina, Lola, Laura and Cieca, Magdalene, and Brangäne. Sang Amneris, Suzuki, and Maddalena (*Chénier*), San Francisco, 1928.

Temple Dancer, The. Opera in 1 act by Hugo; libretto by Jutta Bell-Ranske.

First perf., N.Y., Met, Mar. 12, 1919: Easton, Kingston, c. Moranzoni, d. J. Fox/Musaeus. 3 perfs. in 1 season.

One of the Met's most short-lived American experiments. In the Temple of Mahadeo, a Hindu Temple Dancer (s) falls in love with a man of another faith (t); to help him, she tries to steal the temple's jewels.

tempo di mezzo (Ital.). In the 19th-c. Italian double aria, the section between the two arias, in which a new plot element or a change of mood is introduced.

Tender Land, The. Opera in 3 (originally 2) acts by Copland; libretto by Horace Everett.

First perf., N.Y.C. Opera, Apr. 1, 1954: Carlos, Crain, Gainey, Treigle, c. Schippers. Rev. in 3 acts, 1955.

A romantic pastoral set in the American midwest, early 1930s. Heady with the celebration of her graduation from high school, Laurie Moss (s) becomes attracted to Martin (t), a drifter farmhand, and plans to elope with him. He thinks better of the idea and leaves without her, but the girl sets out on her own.

Tennstedt, Klaus. Conductor; b. Merseburg, Germany, June 6, 1926. Studied at Leipzig Conservatory; from 1948, principal conductor at Halle. After operatic positions in Dresden (1958–62) and Schwerin (1962–71), left East Germany, appearing widely with orchestras. Principal guest conductor, Minnesota Orchestra (1979–82); music director, London Philharmonic (from 1983). Met debut, *Fidelio* (Dec. 14, 1983).

tenor. The highest natural male voice range. Usual range from C below middle C to C above middle C. Among the subcategories are the heroic or dramatic tenor (Ger., Heldentenor; Ital., tenore di forza), lyric tenor (Ital., tenore di grazia), and the light tenor (Ger., Spieltenor; Ital., tenor buffo; Fr., ténor-bouffe or trial).

Ternina, Milka. Soprano; b. Vezisce, near Zagreb, Dec. 19, 1863; d. Zagreb, May 18, 1941. Studied with Ida Winterberg, Zagreb, and with Gänsbacher, Vienna Conservatory; debut as Amelia (*Ballo*), Zagreb, 1882. She appeared in Leipzig (1883–84), Graz (1884–86), and

Luisa Tetrazzini as Lucia di Lammermoor

Bremen (1886–90), before joining the Munich Opera (1890–99), where her repertory included Valentine (*Huguenots*), Elisabeth, Fidelio, later Isolde and Brünnhilde. American debut in Boston, with Damrosch's touring company, as Brünnhilde and Isolde, 1896. At Covent Garden, 1898–1906, besides Wagner and Fidelio, she was London's first Tosca; she sang Kundry in Bayreuth, 1899. Met debut as Elisabeth, Jan. 27, 1900; in 4 seasons, she sang 74 perfs. of 15 roles, including Isolde, Santuzza, Fidelio, Brünnhilde, Elsa, Sieglinde, and the first U.S. Tosca and Kundry. A singer of fabled power and temperament, she was forced to retire in 1906 by a paralysis of facial muscles; among her students in Zagreb was Zinka Milanov.

Teseo. Opera in 5 acts by Handel; libretto by Nicola Haym, after the French of Philippe Quinault.

First perf., London, Queen's Theatre, Jan. 10, 1713: Pellegrini, Urbani, Pilotti-Schiavonetti, de l'Épine, Gallia, Barbier. U.S. prem., Boston (Early Music Festival), May 30, 1985: Wong, Rickards, Armstrong, Nelson, Armistead, Minter, c. McGegan.

Handel's third London opera featured spectacular scenery and stage machinery. The plot concerns the frustrated love of the sorceress Medea (s) for Teseo (s), her unsuccessful plots to separate him from his beloved Agilea (s), and his eventual recognition as the long-lost son of King Egeo (a).

tessitura (Ital., "texture"). The portion of a role's vocal range most consistently exploited, as distinct from its total compass. In Purcell's *Dido*, both Dido and Belinda require the same range, but Dido's music lies principally in the lower two-thirds of that range, Belinda's in the upper two-thirds.

Tetrazzini, Luisa. Soprano; b. Florence, June 28, 1871; d. Milan, Apr. 28, 1940. Studied with her elder sister, soprano Eva, and in Florence with Contrucci and Ceccherini; debut as Inès (*Africaine*), Pagliano, Florence, 1890. She sang at the Argentina, Rome (1890–91), and in Italian provincial theaters, toured extensively in South America (1893–95), Spain (1897), eastern Europe (1899–1903), and Mexico (1903–06), and made her U.S. debut in San Francisco (1906). International success eluded her until her London debut as Violetta in Covent Garden's 1907 fall season; she also sang Lucia and Gilda, and returned in the prestigious spring seasons until 1912, inheriting the more altitudinous reaches of Melba's repertory, including Rosina, Marguerite de Valois (*Huguenots*), Leila (*Pêcheurs*), and Amina. When Conried failed to exercise an option for her N.Y. debut, Hammerstein presented her at the Manhattan Opera in 1908 as Violetta, Lucia, Gilda, Annetta (*Crispino*), and Dinorah, in two later seasons as Rosina, Elvira (*Puritani*), Marie (*Fille*), and Lakmé. In her sole Met season, she sang just 8 perfs. as Lucia (debut, Dec. 27, 1911), Gilda, and Violetta. She also appeared in Boston (1911–14) and Chicago (1911–13), sang for Italian troops during the war, and thereafter appeared only in concerts, the last in London in 1934.

Tetrazzini's mastery of coloratura technique was formidable, and her voice, except for a clouded patch in the lower range, was firm and bright. A plump stage figure, she convinced in comedy through personal charm and rhythmic brilliance, and her singing carried the day in more serious roles. While in her prime she recorded many arias and songs, but, wiser than many colleagues, left no audible souvenirs of the later years.

BIBLIOGRAPHY: Luisa Tetrazzini, *My Life of Song* (London, 1921, repr. 1977).

Teufel von Loudon, Die (The Devils of Loudon). Opera in 3 acts by Penderecki; libretto by the composer, after John Whiting's dramatization of Aldous Huxley's book.

First perf., Hamburg, June 20, 1969: Troyanos, Hiolski, c. Czyz. U.S. prem., Santa Fe, Aug. 14, 1969: Davidson, Reardon, c. Skrowaczewski.

Based on historical events in 17th-c. France, set to aptly abrasive music. The prioress Jeanne (s) and her Ursuline nuns claim to be possessed by the devil, whom they identify as the worldly priest Grandier (bar); he is tortured and burned at the stake.

Teyte, Maggie [Margaret Tate]. Soprano; b. Wolverhampton, England, Apr. 17, 1888; d. London, May 26, 1976. Studied with Jean de Reszke, Paris; debut in *Myriame et Daphne*, an Offenbach pastiche, Monte Carlo, 1907. Sang Mélisande, Opéra-Comique, Paris, 1908, coached with Debussy. Also appeared with Beecham Opera Co. (1910–11), Chicago Opera (debut, Cherubino, 1911), Boston Opera (1914–17; debut, Mimi), and British National Opera (1922–23). N.Y.C. Opera debut as Mélisande, 1947; also noted as recitalist in French song.

Thaïs. Opera in 3 acts by Massenet; libretto by Louis Gallet, after Anatole France's novel.

First perf., Paris, Opéra, Mar. 16, 1894: Sanderson, Alvarez, Delmas, Delpouget, c. Taffanel. U.S. prem., N.Y., Manhattan Opera House, Nov. 25, 1907: Garden, Dalmorès, Renaud, Mugnoz, c. Campanini. Met prem., Feb. 16, 1917: Farrar, Botta, Amato, Rothier, c. Polacco, d. Bianco, p. Speck. Later Met productions: Dec. 14, 1922: Jeritza, Harrold, Whitehill, d'Angelo, c. Hasselmans, d. Urban, p. Wymetal; Jan. 18, 1978: Sills, Gibbs, Milnes, Morris, c. Pritchard, d. Toms, p. Capobianco. 48 perfs. in 9 seasons.

Massenet's familiar idioms of melodic invention and aria construction, matched to his preferred theme of religious eroticism.

In and near Alexandria, 4th c. A.D. The monk Athanaël (bar) believes that he must save the beautiful courtesan Thaïs (s) from her life of sin and debauchery. His friend Nicias (t), who has bought her favors for a week, helps Athanaël speak to her at a banquet, where he tries to convert her. He succeeds in persuading her to take up the holy life in a convent, but afterwards himself finds no peace; he is in love with Thaïs, and haunted by her memory. He goes to the convent to profess his love, only to find her dying.

Thebom, Blanche. Mezzo-soprano; b. Monessen, Pa., Sep. 19, 1918. Studied with Matzenauer and Edyth Walker; debut as Brangäne, with Met in Philadelphia, Nov. 28, 1944. Met debut in same role, Dec. 14, 1944; in 22 seasons, she sang 236 perfs. of 26 roles, including Wagner roles, Marina, Herodias, and Orlovsky. Sang in Chicago (debut, Brangäne, 1946), San Francisco (1947–59; debut, Amneris), Glyndebourne (Dorabella, 1950), and Covent Garden (Didon in *Troyens*, 1957).

Thill, Georges. Tenor; b. Paris, Dec. 14, 1897; d. Paris, Oct. 17, 1984. Studied with André Gresse at Paris Conservatory, Fernando de Lucia in Naples; debut as Nicias (*Thaïs*), Paris Opéra, 1924. He remained on the Opéra roster until 1940, singing Faust, Duke of Mantua, Radames, Werther, Canio, Admète (*Alceste*), Énée (*Troyens*), Parsifal, Tannhäuser, Arnold (*Guillaume Tell*),

and creating the title role in Canteloube's *Vercingétorix*. Sang Calaf at Verona Arena (1928), La Scala (1929), and Colón, Buenos Aires (1929). In his 2 Met seasons, he sang 10 perfs. of Roméo (debut, Mar. 20, 1931), Faust, Radames, Gérald (*Lakmé*), and Sadko. Appeared throughout France, at Monte Carlo (from 1929) and Covent Garden (debut, Samson, 1928), and in films, notably Abel Gance's *Louise*. He retired from the stage in 1953, from singing in 1956. Though he made little impression in N.Y., Thill was France's greatest tenor between the wars, brilliantly wedding Italianate polish with the Gallic idiom.

Thomas, Ambroise. Composer; b. Metz, Aug. 5, 1811; d. Paris, Feb. 12, 1896. Studied at Paris Conservatory with Le Sueur and won the Prix de Rome in 1832. At first he composed opéras comiques in the tradition of Auber, with graceful melodies and delicate orchestration. His greatest successes sprang from emulation of Gounod's Goethe and Shakespeare operas: *Mignon* (1866) has retained a place in the international repertory, the more grandiose *Hamlet* (1868) has not. Appointed professor of composition at the Conservatory in 1856, he became director in 1871, a tenure of rigid academic conservatism. Other operas: *Le Caïd* (1849); *Le Songe d'une Nuit d'Été* (1850, not after Shakespeare's play).

Thomas, Jess. Tenor; b. Hot Springs, S. Dak., Aug. 4, 1927. Studied at Stanford U. and later in Germany; debut as Faninal's Major-Domo, San Francisco, 1957. Sang widely in Germany from 1958; Bayreuth debut as Parsifal, 1961. Met debut as Stolzing, Dec. 11, 1962; in 12 seasons, sang 97 perfs. of 15 roles, including major Wagner parts, Florestan, and Samson. Created Caesar (*Antony*) at opening of new Met, 1966, and sang Stolzing at reopening of Munich National Theater (1963) and at Covent Garden (1969).

Thomas, John Charles. Baritone; b. Meyersdale, Pa., Sep. 6, 1891; d. Apple Valley, Calif., Dec. 13, 1960. Studied at Peabody, Baltimore, and sang in musical comedy; operatic debut as Amonasro, Washington, D.C., 1924. Sang at Monnaie, Brussels (1925–28), Covent Garden (debut, Valentin, 1928), San Francisco (debut, Jochanaan, 1930), and Chicago (1930–42; debut, Tonio). Met debut as Germont, Feb. 2, 1934; in 9 seasons, sang 35 perfs. of 9 roles, including Rossini's Figaro and Athanaël (*Thaïs*).

Thomas, Theodore. Conductor, impresario, administrator; b. Esens, Germany, Oct. 11, 1835; d. Chicago, Jan. 4, 1905. A central figure in the dissemination of European art music in 19th-c. America, Thomas toured widely with his own orchestra, founded the Cincinnati May Festival (1873) and Chicago Symphony (1891), and conducted the N.Y. Philharmonic (1877–91). Director of the American Opera Company (1885–87), an early, unsuccessful attempt to propagate opera in English with American singers.

Thompson, Arthur. Baritone; b. New York, Dec. 27, 1942. After study at Manhattan School, Hartt College of Music, and Juilliard, entered Met Opera Studio (1966–71). Professional debut as Papageno, Chautauqua (1964). Formal Met debut as the Mandarin (*Turandot*), Sep. 24, 1970. Since then he has sung over 50 comprimario roles there. Covent Garden debut as Mel (*Knot Garden*), 1987.

TOURING
Roberta Peters

Imagine for a moment that you are an opera singer, a member of the Metropolitan Opera's company on its annual spring tour. It's 1954, you've been in and out of eight or nine cities, practically living on the train since you left New York five weeks ago. Now you're pulling into St. Louis, or maybe it's Des Moines or maybe Lafayette, for another one-night stand. You've enjoyed the train ride with your colleagues, played countless games of cards, and laughed at as many stories, but you know that within hours you must go through a piano rehearsal in your hotel ballroom, and later step onto a stage you've never seen, to give your all as Gilda or Rosina or Zerlina.

Now you're getting off the train and worrying about how far your dressing room will be from the stage and how far your hotel will be from the theater, and you don't quite know where your makeup case is, but you step onto the station platform and suddenly hear applause and shouting. You look up and realize, this crowd is here for *us!* And there are streamers and photographers and people are handing you bouquets and there's a band playing, and here is the mayor of St. Louis or Des Moines or Lafayette welcoming you to his city. And all this helps you realize that it may be your eighth city and your hundredth Gilda, but for the music lovers in the town, it is the *only* performance, and you're going to give them the best *Rigoletto* they've ever heard.

That may give you some idea of what it was like to be on the Met tour in the 1950s. The Met has toured its productions around the country since the company started in 1883, and its most recent tour, in 1986, was the 98th time the company took to the road. For all those years, with only a few interruptions, the Met left home in the spring and brought grand opera to scores of cities all over the United States and Canada. For years, it was the only way people living outside New York, Chicago, or San Francisco could experience live opera. It was certainly the only way they could see the *stars* of opera; while there were wonderful touring troupes like the San Carlo or those run by Charles Wagner and Boris Goldovsky, giving invaluable experience to young American singers, the Met was for many years the only major company with international singing stars to leave its home theater and play on the road.

I think this was very important for the singers as well as the audiences. My early career was directed by Sol Hurok, who certainly knew the value of touring, and he convinced me that the best way to become known to the public outside New York was to perform on the road as often as I could. I did a lot of television too, but in those days television was a matter of an aria here and a song there; few complete operas were televised until the late 1970s, and the audience could hardly form an opinion from one "Una voce poco fa" on the Ed Sullivan Show.

It's also important for an artist to learn how audiences differ, and that can only be done outside New York. I'm a New Yorker and will always adore this city, but it's a tough town to perform in. Audiences in New York see so much, and can be quite jaded about opera and singers. It's a real education to go outside New York, where people don't get so much live music. It isn't that they are unknowledgeable, or necessarily easy; I played before some opera lovers who were old enough to have heard my roles sung by Bori, Galli-Curci, Pons, and Sayão, and were about to judge how Peters measured up. But when you play for people who have been

(*Top*) At the train station (*l. to r.*): Madelaine Chambers, Theodor Uppman, Emilia Cundari, Sandra Warfield, James McCracken, Fritz Stiedry, Lucine Amara, Giorgio Tozzi, and Roberta Peters. (*Middle*) Zinka Milanov, Osie Hawkins, Risë Stevens, Lodovico Oliviero, William Hargrave, and Wellington Ezekiel. (*Below*) On the platform: Martha Lipton, Désiré Defrère, Dorothy Kirsten, Frances Greer, Herta Glaz, Alessio de Paolis, Irene Jessner, Mario Berini, Marks Levine, and Mae Frohman. On the tracks: Dezsö Ernster, Frank St. Leger, Edward Johnson, Jan Peerce, Gerhard Pechner, Giacomo Vaghi, and tour director Francis Robinson

waiting a year for the Met to come to town, you are their treat for the year, and they never let you forget it.

I toured nineteen times with the Met, and always looked forward to it. The camaraderie was wonderful, especially in the days of the train tour. When we sang in New York, everyone in the house was friendly, but we were all in our separate operas, and if a fellow artist was not in your cast, the most contact you might have was a "hello" as you passed at the stage door. But on tour we were together on the train for five or six weeks, and everyone was part of the family. Then, when we got to our destination, we would meet so many wonderful people – there are relationships begun on the Met tour that I've maintained to this day. It was a lovely way to work.

It took two complete special trains to carry us all, with eighteen sleeping cars and twenty-two baggage cars. I traveled with my mother until I married, and then with my husband. By the time I started, the days of divas with their private railway cars were long gone; I've seen pictures of Lillian Nordica's car, and I'm sure it must have been an extraordinary way to travel. But we would have staterooms, and in the cities we'd have a good choice of hotels, so we were usually quite comfortable. This is important, as on the road most artists spend as much time in their rooms as they can; it's the only quiet place they have to rest and prepare for the performance.

There were, of course, many difficulties as well. Performing conditions were not always terrific, as we played in theaters that varied widely in size and in the quality of their facilities. We rarely could take the New York sets, and never got to rehearse on stage. Often, our dressing rooms were makeshift and nowhere near the stage. (I remember a *Don Giovanni* in Cleveland when Fernando Corena, dressing several floors away from the stage, got stuck in the elevator and missed an entrance. The rest of us improvised madly, which is not so easy in Mozart, singing Fernando's music as well as our own until he showed up.)

But we got through many such mishaps because every one of the three hundred people who traveled with the company was a seasoned professional, ready to deal with any possible situation that might arise. And we were organized by pros, unsung heroes such as Frank Paola, Arge Keely, and Florence Guarino. Above all, there was always our dear, beloved Francis Robinson, a unique unflappable, generous *gentleman*.

For me, the tour changed immeasurably when we began to travel by air. The European festivals, taking place at the same time as the tour, were always a strong temptation to the artists. When we stopped traveling by train, people began coming and going, fitting in as many performances around the world as they could. We lost a lot of fine artists that way, and I think the quality of performances was affected too, as well as the pleasure of touring. In many ways, the jet plane was the death knell of the tour.

I'm very sad to see the demise of the tour as we knew it. I know there are terrible financial problems, but I still feel we'd be able to make it if we went out with the best artists and productions. The Met is trying to solve the problems, and I'm confident that they'll find some way to resume touring, even if it's a modification of what we once did.

I owe so much to the Met tour. If it hadn't existed, I would never have had the chance to sing on stage with Jussi Bjoerling, a singer I idolized and with whom I shared only one performance, a *Rigoletto* in Cleveland. The tour helped me to polish many of my roles, and helped us all to learn how to adapt and still give a solid performance. I hate to think that the younger artists will not have this experience, not to mention that the audiences around the country will have to do without the Met. Television is wonderful, but there is nothing like a *live* performance – that's where real communication takes place. The Met tour was a way for the company to reach out to the country and communicate in person, and touring is essential if we want to keep opera alive in America.

Thomson, Virgil. Composer; b. Nov. 25, 1896. Studied at Harvard with Edward Burlingame Hill, A.T. Davison, and S. Foster Damon (who introduced him to the works of Satie and Gertrude Stein), and later in Paris with Nadia Boulanger. He lived in Paris, 1925–40, met Stein in 1926, and set her dada libretto for *Four Saints in Three Acts* (1928, perf. 1934) using diatonic harmonies, hymn tunes and chants, and popular dance rhythms. Appointed chief music reviewer for the N.Y. *Herald Tribune* in 1940, he wrote with distinction and elegance for 14 years, while continuing to compose. From this period dates his second collaboration with Stein, *The Mother of Us All* (1947), which again incorporates American popular styles in ingenious and theatrical juxtapositions. Thomson's most ambitious opera, *Lord Byron* (1961–68; perf. 1972), a more broadly lyrical and emotional score, has yet to be fully appreciated.
BIBLIOGRAPHY: Virgil Thomson, *Virgil Thomson* (N.Y., 1977).

Thorborg, Kerstin. Mezzo; b. Venjan, Sweden, May 19, 1896; d. Falun, Apr. 12, 1970. Studied at Royal Conservatory, Stockholm; debut at Royal Opera there in small roles, 1923. She appeared in Sweden until 1930, in roles such as Ortrud, Amneris, and Geneviève (*Pelléas*), then held engagements in Nuremberg (1930–32), Berlin (Städtische Oper, 1932–35), and Vienna (State Opera, 1935–38). In Salzburg, 1935–37, she sang Brangäne, Orfeo, Mercedes (*Corregidor*), and Eglantine (*Euryanthe*); her Covent Garden roles (1936–39) included Klytemnästra as well as Wagner. Met debut as Fricka (*Walküre*), Dec. 21, 1936; in 13 seasons, she sang 243 perfs. of 19 roles, including Brangäne, Erda (*Siegfried*), Venus, Octavian, Orfeo, Ortrud, Waltraute, Marina, Ulrica, Amneris, Kundry, Azucena, and Herodias. Also sang in Buenos Aires (1933), San Francisco (1938, 1943), and Chicago (1942–45). Admired for her vital stage presence and heroic voice, Thorborg was the Met's mezzo counterpart to Flagstad and Melchior.

Threepenny Opera, The. See *Dreigroschenoper, Die.*

through-composed (Ger., *durchkomponiert*). In song and aria composition, a through-composed setting responds specifically and progressively to the events or emotions invoked by the words (by contrast with strophic setting, which employs musical repetitions corresponding to the patterning of the verse). In connection with an opera, "through-composed" may also refer to a work in which the musical texture is substantially continuous, rather than interrupted by recitative or dialogue (see *number opera*).

Thuille, Ludwig. Composer; b. Bozen, Tyrol [now Bolzano, Italy], Nov. 30, 1861; d. Munich, Feb. 5, 1907. Studied with Pembour at Innsbruck and Rheinberger at Königliche Musikschule, Munich, where he taught from 1883, influencing a generation of composers, including Bloch. Of his three operas, in a richly-orchestrated late-Romantic style of considerable harmonic invention, only the second, *Lobetanz* (1898), was produced internationally.

Tibbett [Tibbet], **Lawrence.** Baritone; b. Bakersfield, Calif., Nov. 16, 1896; d. New York, July 15, 1960. After acting and singing in operetta, he studied in Los Angeles with Basil Ruysdael, later in N.Y. with Frank LaForge; operatic debut as Amonasro, Los Angeles, 1923. Within a

Kerstin Thorborg as Brangäne in *Tristan und Isolde*

week of his Met debut as Lovitsky in *Boris* (Nov. 24, 1923), he graduated to Valentin, and his Ford opposite Scotti's Falstaff in 1925 was greatly applauded. In 27 seasons with the company (1923–50), he sang 384 perfs. (163 more on tour) in 49 roles, most frequently as Germont (35 times), Rigoletto (22), Amonasro (19), and Scarpia (19), also as Valentin, the *Lohengrin* Herald, Tonio, Wolfram, Iago, Golaud (*Pelléas*), Krenek's Jonny, and the *Hoffmann* villains; he created Eadgar (*King's Henchman*), Colonel Ibbetson, the Emperor Jones, and Wrestling Bradford (*Merry Mount*), and was the Met's first Simon Boccanegra, Balstrode (*Peter Grimes*), and Ivan Khovansky (*Khovanshchina*). He also appeared in San Francisco (1927–49), Chicago (1936–46), and Cincinnati (1943–46), and sang Jochanaan in New Orleans (1949). In 1937 he toured Europe, singing at Covent Garden (debut, Scarpia; created title role in Goossens' *Don Juan de Manara*), Stockholm, the Paris Opéra, Prague, Budapest, and Vienna; after the war, he sang Rigoletto in Rome (1946) and Johannesburg (1947). He appeared in early musical films (notably *New Moon*, 1930) and, after retiring from the Met, on Broadway (including *Fanny*, 1956) and on television.

To his firmly focused, smoothly produced, timbrally flexible baritone, Tibbett joined a natural actor's superb diction and theatrical command; though he avoided the 19th-c. florid repertory and the heroic Wagner roles, he was a compelling performer whose glamour enhanced the appeal of several American operas. His theatrical powers remained intact after a throat ailment in 1940 impaired his vocal suavity.
BIBLIOGRAPHY: Lawrence Tibbett, *The Glory Road* (N.Y., 1933; repr. 1977).

Tichatschek, Josef. Tenor; b. Ober-Weckelsdorf, Saxony [now Teplice, Czechoslovakia], July 11, 1807; d. Blasewitz, near Dresden, Jan. 18, 1886. Studied in Vienna;

Lawrence Tibbett as Iago in *Otello*

joined chorus of Kärntnertor Theater, 1830. Sang in Graz, Vienna, then made Dresden debut as Auber's Gustave III, 1837; remained there 33 years, creating Wagner's Rienzi (1842) and Tannhäuser (1845).

Tiefland (Lowland). Opera in prologue and 2 (originally 3) acts by d'Albert; libretto by Rudolf Lothar, after a Catalan play, *Terra Baixa*, by Angel Guimera.

First perf., Prague, Neues Deutsches Theater, Nov. 15, 1903. Revised in prologue and 2 acts, first perf., Magdeburg, Jan. 6, 1905. Met prem., Nov. 23, 1908: Destinn, Schmedes, Feinhals, c. Hertz. 4 perfs. in 1 season.

The most successful German emulation of verismo, still performed in Germany. The Pyrenees and Catalonia, 19th c. To conceal his liaison with the orphaned Marta (s), the brutal Sebastiano (bar) marries her off to the naive shepherd Pedro (t). After realizing that Pedro has been duped, Marta falls in love with him; he strangles Sebastiano and takes her back to the mountains.

Tietjens, Therese. Soprano; b. Hamburg, July 17, 1831; d. London, Oct. 3, 1877. Studied in Hamburg and Vienna; debut as Lucrezia Borgia, Hamburg, 1849. Appeared in Frankfurt (1850–56) and Vienna (1856–59), then in London (1858–77), where her vast repertory at Drury Lane and Covent Garden included Médée, Fidelio, Leonora (*Forza*), Marguerite, and Ortrud. Also appeared in Paris, Naples; toured U.S. in 1875.

Tippett, Michael. Composer; b. London, Jan. 2, 1905. Studied with Charles Wood, C.H. Kitson, later with R.O. Morris at Royal College of Music, and worked as an educator. Director of music at Morley College, 1940–51, he first received wide recognition in 1944 for the pacifistic oratorio *A Child of Our Time*. Despite (or because of) a late start in music, he developed an independent style, incorporating elements from pre-classical music (modal-

ity, cross-rhythmed counterpoint) and vernacular styles along with traditional forms. After 1951, he concentrated on composition, including song cycles, choral, chamber, and orchestral works.

His four operas are distinguished by their profound concern with the nature of man and his society. *The Midsummer Marriage* (1955) is a quest opera drawing on Jungian psychology, its plot reminiscent of Mozart's *Zauberflöte*, expansively lyrical, richly colored in harmony and orchestration. *King Priam* (1962), after Homeric myth, is more starkly declamatory and pessimistic. *The Knot Garden* (1970) and *The Ice Break* (1977) treat individual human relations in modern settings, invoking the blues as a symbol of reconciliation.

BIBLIOGRAPHY: Ian Kemp, *Tippett: The Composer and his Works* (N.Y., and London, 1984).

Titus, Alan. Baritone; b. New York, Oct. 28, 1945. Studied with Aksel Schiøtz at Colorado School of Music, Hans Heinz at Juilliard, N.Y.; debut in *Bohème*, Washington, D.C., 1969. Created Celebrant in Bernstein's *Mass* (Washington, 1971) and Archie Kramer in *Summer and Smoke* (St. Paul, 1971), the role of his N.Y.C. Opera debut; European debut as Pelléas, Amsterdam, 1973; has sung widely in Europe and America. Met debut as Harlekin (*Ariadne*), Mar. 20, 1976.

Tokatyan, Armand. Tenor; b. Plovdiv, Bulgaria, Feb. 12, 1896, of Armenian parents; d. Pasadena, Calif., June 12, 1960. Studied in Milan and Vienna; operatic debut in *Manon Lescaut*, dal Verme, Milan, 1921. Toured U.S. with Scotti Opera Co. Met debut as Lucio (*Anima Allegra*), Feb. 14, 1923; in 20 seasons, sang 237 perfs. of 38 roles, including Almaviva, Rodolfo, José, Hoffmann, Faust, Enzo, Alfredo, and Roméo. Also appeared in San Francisco (debut, Luigi in *Tabarro*, 1923), Berlin, Vienna, and London (Calaf, 1934).

Tolstoy, Leo. Russian writer (1828–1910). Operas based on his writings include *Risurrezione* (Alfano) and *War and Peace* (Prokofiev).

Tomowa-Sintow, Anna. Soprano; b. Stara Zagora, Bulgaria, Sep. 22, 1941. Studied with Zlatew-Tscherkin and Katja Zpiridonowa, Sofia Conservatory; debut as Tatiana (*Onegin*), Sofia, 1965. Member of Leipzig Opera (debut, Abigaille, 1967), singing Arabella, Desdemona, Butterfly, and Violetta, and of Berlin State Opera (debut, Countess Almaviva, 1972). She participated in premiere of Orff's *De Temporum Fine Comoedia*, Salzburg, 1973, and has sung at the Easter Festival there. Debuts at Bavarian State Opera, Munich, and San Francisco (both Donna Anna, 1974), Covent Garden (Fiordiligi, 1975), Vienna State Opera (Mozart's Countess, 1977), and Met (Donna Anna, Apr. 3, 1978), where she has also sung Elsa, Aida, the Marschallin, and Amelia (*Boccanegra*). With her creamy spinto, this musical singer has made an impressive career, initially under the auspices of Karajan.

tonadilla (Sp., "little song"). A short, simple 18th-c. Spanish operatic genre, which began as a solo appendix to a larger work and grew to incorporate additional characters and more elaborate action.

Tooley, John. Manager; b. Rochester, Kent, June 1, 1924. After study at Cambridge, served as secretary of Guildhall School (1952–55), then joined Covent Garden, becoming assistant general administrator in 1960 and

Arturo Toscanini

succeeding David Webster as general administrator ten years later. Active in organizing international co-operation among major opera houses, he introduced the Covent Garden "prom" performances aimed at younger audiences.

Toronto. City in Ontario, Canada. The first full-scale opera in Toronto was an 1853 *Norma* at the Royal Lyceum, with Rosa Devries in the title role and Luigi Arditi conducting. Touring companies such as the National Opera Company and Kellogg Opera Company appeared regularly at the Royal Lyceum Theater (1848–74) and Grand Opera House (1874–83). In 1867, George Holman's English Opera Company leased the Royal Lyceum until 1873 and presented nearly 35 different works. The Metropolitan Opera first visited in 1899, and returned in the 1950s. In the interim, opera was limited to sporadic efforts, until the establishment in 1946 of the Royal Conservatory Opera, which led to a formal season in 1950 and the founding, in 1959, of the Canadian Opera Company, directed by Herman Geiger-Torel. Based at the O'Keefe Center (capacity 3,167) since 1961, the company has produced standard repertory and also premieres of Canadian operas such as Healey Willan's *Deirdre* (1966) and Charles Wilson's *Héloïse and Abelard* (1972). The roster has often included native singers such as Forrester, Quilico, Stratas, and Vickers. In 1976, Geiger-Torel died and was succeeded by Lotfi Mansouri as general director; the company now presents 12 operas in its year-round season.

Tosca. Opera in 3 acts by Puccini; libretto by Illica and Giacosa, after the play by Sardou.
    First perf., Rome, Costanzi, Jan. 14, 1900: Darclée, de Marchi, Giraldoni, c. Mugnone. U.S. & Met prem., Feb. 4, 1901: Ternina, Cremonini, Scotti, c. Mancinelli, p. Parry. Later Met productions: Nov. 19, 1917: Farrar, Martinelli, Scotti, c. Moranzoni, d. Sala (Acts I, II); Dec. 8, 1955 ("revised"): Tebaldi, Tucker, Warren, c.

Mitropoulos, d. Fox, p. Yannopoulos; Oct. 4, 1968: Nilsson, Corelli, Bacquier, c. Molinari-Pradelli, d. Heinrich, p. Schenk; Mar. 11, 1985: Behrens, Domingo, MacNeil, c. Sinopoli, d. Zeffirelli/P.J. Hall, p. Zeffirelli. Tosca has also been sung at the Met by Eames, Cavalieri, Fremstad, Destinn, Muzio, Jeritza, Lotte Lehmann, Caniglia, Moore, Welitsch, Kirsten, Albanese, Milanov, Callas, L. Price, Rysanek, Crespin, Olivero, Caballé, Marton; Cavaradossi by Caruso, Martin, Bonci, McCormack, Gigli, Lauri-Volpi, Fleta, Kiepura, Peerce, Bjoerling, Tagliavini, del Monaco, di Stefano, Bergonzi, Carreras, Pavarotti; Scarpia by Amato, de Luca, Danise, Tibbett, Sved, London, Gobbi, Merrill, Bastianini, Wixell, Milnes. 503 perfs. in 69 seasons.
    Tosca is a taut, brilliant melodrama in which Puccini's melodic gift and his sense of effective if violent theater are both at their peak.
    Rome, June 1800. In the church of Sant'Andrea della Valle, the painter Mario Cavaradossi (t) assists the escaped political prisoner Cesare Angelotti (bs), offering a hiding place at his villa. Hearing them conversing behind closed doors, Cavaradossi's lover, the singer Floria Tosca (s), suspects him of an affair, and the sadistic chief of police, Scarpia (bar), searching for Angelotti, plays on her jealousy and love. He has the painter arrested and tortured; Tosca, unable to bear her lover's cries of pain, reveals Angelotti's hiding place. Scarpia tells her she can save Cavaradossi by giving herself to him. She accepts; Scarpia arranges for what he says will be a mock execution. As he turns to embrace Tosca, she stabs him with a knife from his supper table. At the Castel Sant'Angelo, Tosca tells Cavaradossi of the plan, but when she rushes to her lover after the firing squad has gone, he is dead; Scarpia has tricked her. The murder of Scarpia has been discovered, and as the soldiers come for her Tosca leaps to her death from the battlements.

Toscanini, Arturo. Conductor; b. Parma, Italy, Mar. 25, 1867; d. New York, Jan. 16, 1957. Studied at Parma (cello, piano, composition, 1876–85); during engagement as cellist with touring company in Rio de Janeiro, he made an unscheduled debut as replacement conductor (*Aida*, June 30, 1886). Conducted in Italy, becoming music director in Turin (1895–98) and then at La Scala under Gatti-Casazza (1898–1903, 1906–08); championed the works of Catalani and Wagner and led premieres of *Pagliacci* and *Bohème*. He came to Met with Gatti (debut, *Aida*, Nov. 16, 1908) and, during 7 seasons, led 367 perfs. of 30 operas, adding to his Italian repertory *Tristan*, *Meistersinger*, *Götterdämmerung*, *Carmen*, *Orfeo*, as well as the Met premieres of *Armide*, *Boris*, *Ariane et Barbe-Bleu*, *Villi*, *Amore dei Tre Re*, and the world premiere of *Fanciulla del West*. Leaving in 1915 over disagreements with Gatti about artistic conditions, he free-lanced in Italy during the war and then became artistic director of a reorganized La Scala (1920–29). Conducted the N.Y. Philharmonic (1928–36), while conducting opera at Bayreuth (1930–31, the first non-German to conduct there) and Salzburg (1934–37). His anti-Fascism led to his withdrawal from activity in Germany, Italy, and Austria; in N.Y., beginning in 1937, he directed the NBC Symphony Orchestra in radio concerts, retiring in 1954. During his later years at NBC, he conducted a number of operas in concert form, later issued on records.
    The most influential conductor of the 20th c., Toscanini was a man of extraordinary energy, concentration, rigor, and occasional tyrannical violence, as unsparing to himself as to others. His perfectionist insistence on fidelity to the

score and on the integrity of the musical and theatrical aspects of opera was revolutionary in the somewhat casual atmosphere of Italian opera houses at the end of the 19th c., but necessary for adequate realization of the works of Wagner and late Verdi; it eventually became a world-wide standard for operatic performance.

BIBLIOGRAPHY: Harvey Sachs, *Toscanini* (1978).

Tosi, Francesco. Castrato and teacher; b. Cesena, Italy, c. 1653; d. Faenza, Apr. 1732. Studied with his father; sang in Italy and Germany. Settled in London, 1692, giving frequent concerts and teaching. Admired as a singer, he is best remembered for his 1723 treatise on vocal technique, translated into English as *Observations on the Florid Song.*

Tote Stadt, Die (The Dead City). Opera in 3 acts by Korngold; libretto by "Paul Schott" [Korngold and his father Julius], after Georges Rodenbach's novel *Bruges la Morte* and play *La Mirage.*

First perf., Dec. 4, 1920, simultaneously in Hamburg (Munchow, Schubert, Degler, c. Pollak) and Cologne (J. Klemperer, Schröder, Renner, c. Klemperer). U.S. & Met prem., Nov. 19, 1921: Jeritza, Harrold, Leonhardt, c. Bodanzky, d. Kautsky, p. Thewman. 10 perfs. in 2 seasons.

A macabre, overheated late-Romantic score, set in late 19th-c. Bruges. Grieving over his late wife Marie, Paul (t) meets the dancer Marietta (s), who reminds him of Marie. In an extended "dream vision," he has a series of experiences with Marietta which enable him to end his mourning.

Tourel [Davidovich], **Jennie.** Mezzo-soprano; b. Vitebsk, Bielorussia, June 22, 1900(?); d. New York, Nov. 23, 1973. Studied with Reynaldo Hahn and Anna El Tour, Paris; debut as Second Scholar in Moret's *Lorenzaccio,* Chicago, 1930. In Paris, sang with Russian Opera (1931) and Opéra-Comique (from 1933). Met debut as Mignon, May 15, 1937; in 4 seasons, sang 14 perfs. of 4 roles, including Rosina, Adalgisa, and Carmen (which she also sang at N.Y.C. Opera, 1944). Created Baba the Turk (*Rake*), Venice, 1951. Noted recitalist.

Tozzi, Giorgio [George]. Bass; b. Chicago, Ill., Jan. 8, 1923. Studied with Giacomo Rimini, Rosa Raisa, and John Daggett Howell in Chicago; debut as Tarquinius in Britten's *Lucretia,* Broadway, 1948, later appearing in musicals in London. In study with Giulio Lorandi, Milan, made transition from baritone to bass; debuts followed at Nuovo, Milan (Rodolfo in *Sonnambula,* 1950) and La Scala (Stromminger in *Wally,* 1953). Met debut as Alvise (*Gioconda*), Mar. 19, 1955; in 21 seasons he sang 399 perfs. of 37 roles, including Ramfis, Sparafucile, Pimen and Boris, Mozart's Figaro, Gremin, Rossini's Basilio, Philippe II, Arkel, Daland, Pogner and Sachs, and Rocco, and created the Doctor in *Vanessa* (1958). In San Francisco (debut, Ramfis, 1955), he also sang Calkas (*Troilus*), Kečal (*Bartered Bride*), and Archibaldo (*Amore dei Tre Re*). Endowed with a fine bass and a firm grasp of the Italian style, Tozzi was an uncommonly assured and communicative singer.

transposition. Performance of music at a pitch higher or lower than written, usually to accommodate the capacities of singers. A common and feasible practice in number operas, it becomes more difficult in through-composed works.

Helen Traubel as Brünnhilde in *Die Walküre*

Traubel, Helen. Soprano; b. St. Louis, Mo., June 20, 1899; d. Santa Monica, Calif., July 28, 1972. Studied from age 13 with Louise Vetta Karst, sang in concert; operatic debut as Mary Rutledge in premiere of Damrosch's *Man Without a Country,* Met, May 12, 1937. She returned two seasons later as Sieglinde, and in 16 seasons with the company sang 133 perfs. (and 43 on tour) of 10 roles, all Wagnerian except for her debut role and three late appearances as the Marschallin: the three Brünnhildes (a total of 66 times), Isolde (34), Elisabeth, Elsa, and Kundry. She also sang in Chicago (1937–1946, including the Damrosch work), and San Francisco (1945–47); abroad, she was heard in opera only in Latin America. She left the Met in 1953, when Bing disapproved of her comedy appearances in television and nightclubs, and worked in films, television, and on Broadway (*Pipe Dream,* 1955).

The finest American Wagnerian soprano of her generation, imposing in both physical and vocal presence, Traubel possessed a massive and clarion voice with a warm timbre. Her principal effect was of majestic poise, but, as her recordings reveal, she was also capable of expressive coloring.

travesti (Fr., "disguised"). A role in which a male character, usually a boy, is played by a woman, such as Cherubino (*Nozze di Figaro*) or Octavian (*Rosenkavalier*).

Traviata, La (The Strayed One). Opera in 3 acts by Verdi; libretto by Piave, after the play *La Dame aux Camélias* by Alexandre Dumas *fils.*

First perf., Venice, Fenice, Mar. 6, 1853: Salvini-Donatelli, Graziani, Varesi. U.S. prem., N.Y., Academy of Music, Dec. 3, 1856. Met prem., Nov. 5, 1883: Sembrich, Capoul, del Puente, c. Vianesi, d. J. Fox, Schaeffer, Maeder, Thompson/Ascoli, Dazian. Later Met productions: Nov. 14, 1921: Galli-Curci, Gigli, de Luca, c. Moranzoni, d. Urban/Castel-Bert, p. Thewman; Dec. 16, 1935: Bori, Crooks, Tibbett, c. Panizza, d. Jorgulesco, p. Defrère; Feb. 21, 1957: Tebaldi, Campora, Warren, c. Cleva, d. O. Smith/Gérard, p. Guthrie; Sep. 24, 1966: Moffo, Prevedi, Merrill, c. Prêtre, d. Beaton, p. Lunt; Mar. 17, 1981: Cotrubas, Domingo, MacNeil, c. Levine, d. Moiseiwitsch, p. Graham. Violetta has also been sung at the Met by Nordica, Melba, Farrar, Tetrazzini, Hempel, Ponselle, Muzio, Sayão, Novotná, Albanese, Steber, Kirsten, de los Angeles, Callas, Sutherland, Caballé, Sills; Alfredo by de Lucia, Caruso, Bonci, McCormack, Smirnov, Lauri-Volpi, Schipa, Kullman, Peerce, Tucker, Tagliavini, di Stefano, Valletti, Gedda, Bergonzi, Pavarotti, Kraus, Carreras; Germont by Ancona, Campanari, Scotti, Stracciari, Amato, Danise, Bastianini, Sereni, Milnes, Wixell, Mazurok. 506 perfs. in 79 seasons.

The first full expression of the kind of intimate character-drama that Verdi had explored in *Luisa Miller*. Though its premiere was not a triumph, *Traviata* has been a beloved favorite of the public and of nearly every soprano of the Italian repertory from its first successful revival to the present.

Paris and environs, 1850. The courtesan Violetta (s) finds herself falling in love with Alfredo Germont (t), a young man from Provence. Renouncing her life in the whirl of Paris society, she moves to the country with her new lover. Giorgio Germont (bar), Alfredo's father, asks Violetta to renounce his son, so that Alfredo's sister may make a respectable marriage untainted by scandal. Violetta, who knows she suffers from consumption, fears that the separation will kill her, but agrees to leave Alfredo, and returns to her former protector, Baron Douphol (bar). At a party, the distraught Alfredo denounces Violetta and is challenged to a duel by Douphol, in which the Baron is wounded. Germont eventually tells his son of Violetta's sacrifice. Alfredo rushes to her sickbed and the lovers are briefly reunited before Violetta dies.

Treigle, Norman. Bass-baritone; b. New Orleans, La., Mar. 6, 1927; d. New Orleans, Feb. 16, 1975. Studied with Elizabeth Wood, New Orleans; debut there as Lodovico (*Otello*), 1947. After singing with local companies, he made his N.Y.C. Opera debut as Colline in 1953 and remained on the roster until 1972; as the company's principal bass, his repertory included Figaro, Don Giovanni, Gounod's and Boito's devils, Boris, Schicchi, King Dodon (*Golden Cockerel*), the *Hoffmann* villains, Handel's Julius Caesar, and Olin Blitch (*Susannah*). Treigle created roles in Floyd's *Passion of Jonathan Wade* (N.Y., 1962), *The Sojourner and Mollie Sinclair* (Raleigh, 1963), and *Markheim* (New Orleans, 1966). After leaving the City Opera, he sang in Europe; Covent Garden debut as Méphistophélès, 1973. Despite a wiry voice, Treigle was a compelling singing actor, especially in roles invoking irony and villainy.

tremolo (Ital.). A "trembling" of the voice, usually in a pejorative sense, referring to excessive vibrato that obscures the pitch.

trial. In French opera, a category of very light tenor with minimal voice but exceptional acting ability; named after Antoine Trial (1737–1795) of the Opéra-Comique.

Trial of Lucullus, The. Opera in 1 act by Sessions; libretto by Bertolt Brecht, translated by H.R. Hays.

First perf., Berkeley, Calif., Wheeler Auditorium, Apr. 18, 1947: c. Sessions.

Sessions's eloquent anti-war opera is based on a radio play later also set by the German composer Paul Dessau. The deceased Roman conqueror Lucullus (bar) stands trial in the Court of Justice of the Dead for his life's activities.

Tristan und Isolde (Tristan and Isolde). Opera in 3 acts by Wagner; libretto by the composer, after Gottfried von Strassburg's *Tristan*.

First perf., Munich, Court Theater, June 10, 1865: M. Schnorr von Carolsfeld, Deinet, L. Schnorr von Carolsfeld, Mitterwurzer, Zottmayer, c. von Bülow. U.S. & Met prem., Dec. 1, 1886: Lilli Lehmann, Brandt, Niemann, Robinson, Fischer, c. Seidl, d. Hoyt, p. van Hell. Later Met productions: Nov. 27, 1909: Gadski, Homer, Burrian, Amato, Blass, c. Toscanini, d. Fortuny/Maison Chiappa, p. Schertel; Nov. 20, 1920 (in Eng.): Matzenauer, Gordon, Sembach, Whitehill, Blass, c. Bodanzky, d. Urban, p. Thewman; Dec. 18, 1959: Nilsson, Dalis, Liebl, Cassel, Hines, c. Böhm, d. Otto, p. Graf; Nov. 18, 1971: Nilsson, Dunn, Thomas, Stewart, Macurdy, c. Leinsdorf, d. Schneider-Siemssen, p. Everding. Tristan has also been sung at the Met by J. de Reszke, Urlus, Melchior, Svanholm, Vinay, Vickers; Isolde by Nordica, Ternina, Fremstad, Kappel, Leider, Flagstad, Traubel, Varnay, Harshaw, Mödl, Jones, Behrens; Brangäne by Schumann-Heink, Matzenauer, Branzell, Olszewska, Thorborg, Thebom, Dunn, Troyanos; Kurwenal by Kaschmann, Bispham, von Rooy, Amato, Schorr, Janssen, Berglund, Hotter; King Marke by E. de Reszke, Urlus, Pinza, List, Kipnis, Székely, Hotter, Tozzi, Salminen; the opera has also been conducted by Schalk, Hertz, Mottl, Mahler, Beecham, Busch, Perlea, Reiner,

Tristan und Isolde – (1977). Designed by Günther Schneider-Siemssen, produced by August Everding. Birgit Nilsson and Jess Thomas

Stiedry, Kempe, Solti, Levine. 343 perfs. in 66 seasons.

The most radical of Wagner's operas in its surrender to the power of music, as also in the originality of its treatment of chromatic harmony, *Tristan*'s influence spread far beyond the world of music.

On board his ship, Tristan (t) and his faithful retainer Kurwenal (bar) are bringing the proud Irish princess Isolde (s) to her destined husband (and Tristan's uncle), King Marke of Cornwall (bs). Isolde, whose lover Tristan once slew, regrets not having slain him in turn when he was sick and in her power; now, she resolves to kill herself and him with poison. But her companion Brangäne (s) substitutes a love potion; assuming they are about to die, Tristan and Isolde pour forth their long-repressed passion, only to discover that they must live on, as the ship arrives in Cornwall. Later they meet for a night of love while the court goes hunting, but their opportunity proves to have been a trap laid by Tristan's jealous friend Melot (t); the King finds them and reproaches them bitterly. Tristan asks Isolde whether she is willing to follow him wherever he goes; when she assents, he attacks Melot, allowing himself to be wounded. In his castle in Brittany, he awakes from delirium and learns that Kurwenal has sent for Isolde to heal him. When her approach is imminent, he tears the bandages from his wounds and dies as she reaches his side; transfigured by love, she dies on his body.

Trittico, Il. Puccini's "triptych" of contrasting operas; see *Tabarro, Il*; *Suor Angelica*; and *Gianni Schicchi*.

Troilus and Cressida. Opera in 3 acts by Walton; libretto by Christopher Hassall, after Chaucer's poem.

First perf., London, Covent Garden, Dec. 3, 1954: László, Lewis, Pears, Kraus, c. Sargent. U.S. prem., San Francisco, Oct. 7, 1955: Kirsten, Lewis, McChesney, Weede, c. Leinsdorf.

A Romantic score molded onto the richly ornate language of Hassall's libretto. The Trojan Cressida (s) yields to her Greek captor Prince Diomede (bar) after messages from her lover Troilus (t) have been intercepted. When Troilus arrives and is killed, Cressida takes her own life.

Trojans, The. See *Troyens, Les*.

Trompeter von Säckingen, Der. Opera in 4 acts by Nessler; libretto by Rudolf Bunge, after Joseph Victor von Scheffel's poem, inspired by a folk tale.

First perf., Leipzig, Stadttheater, May 4, 1884: Jahns, Marion, Schelper, c. Nikisch. U.S. prem., N.Y., Thalia Theater, Jan. 2, 1886. Met prem., Nov. 23, 1887: Seidl-Kraus, Ferenczy, Robinson, c. Seidl, d. Hoyt. 11 perfs. in 2 seasons.

This melodious, sentimental score is set in Germany and Rome after the 30 Years' War. Maria (s), betrothed to the nobleman Damian (t), falls in love with Werner Kirchhof (bar), a commoner who has taught her to play the trumpet. Though separated by her father, the two are eventually reunited in Rome, where Werner has become a choirmaster.

Troubled Island. Opera in 3 acts by William Grant Still; libretto by Langston Hughes.

First perf., N.Y.C. Opera, Mar. 31, 1949: Powers, Weede, c. Halasz.

One of the first operas by a black composer to be performed by a leading company. Haiti, Napoleonic era. Jean Jacques Dessalines (bar), who has led a successful revolt of Haitian slaves against the French, becomes emperor and rejects his faithful wife Azelia (ms) for another woman, who assists his enemies in an uprising that leads to his assassination.

Trouble in Tahiti. Opera in 1 act by Bernstein; libretto by the composer.

First perf., Waltham, Mass., Brandeis, June 12, 1952: Tangeman, Atkinson, c. Bernstein.

Bernstein's jazzy, satiric opera can be performed by itself or as part of the later *A Quiet Place*. In their perfect suburban home, Dinah (ms) and Sam (bar) attempt to live up to the standard of happiness offered on television commercials; deeply unhappy and unable to communicate with one another, they dream of a movie-inspired Tahiti where they will find peace.

trouser role. A part for a woman singer impersonating a boy, such as Cherubino (*Nozze di Figaro*) or Octavian (*Rosenkavalier*).

Trovatore, Il (The Troubadour). Opera in 4 acts by Verdi; libretto by Cammarano (completed by Bardare following Cammarano's death in 1852), after the play *El Trovador* by Gutiérrez.

First perf., Rome, Apollo, Jan. 19, 1853: Penco, Goggi, Baucarde, Guicciardi, c. Angelini. U.S. prem., N.Y., Academy of Music, May 2, 1855. Met prem., Oct. 26, 1883: Valleria, Trebelli, Stagno, Kaschmann, c. Vianesi, d. J. Fox, Schaeffer, Maeder, Thompson/Ascoli, Dazian. Later Met productions: Feb. 20, 1915: Destinn, Ober, Martinelli, Amato, c. Toscanini, d. Sala, Fox; Dec. 12, 1940: Greco, Castagna, Bjoerling, Valentino, c. Calusio, d. Horner/Schenck, p. Graf; Oct. 26, 1959: Stella, Simionato, Bergonzi, Warren, c. Cleva, d. Motley, p. Graf; Mar. 6, 1969: L. Price, Bumbry, Domingo, Milnes, c. Mehta, d. Colonnello, p. Merrill. Manrico has also been sung at the Met by Tamagno, Caruso, Slezak, Lauri-Volpi, Baum, del Monaco, Corelli, Tucker, McCracken, Pavarotti; Leonora by Lilli Lehmann, Nordica, Eames, Gadski, Muzio, Ponselle, Rethberg, Milanov, Arroyo, Caballé, Scotto; Azucena by Homer, Matzenauer, Thorborg, Harshaw, Elmo, Dalis, Verrett, Cossotto; di Luna by Stracciari, de Luca, Danise, Bonelli, Bastianini, Merrill, Wixell. 335 perfs. in 68 seasons.

Trovatore is Verdi's richest essay using the operatic forms and customs he inherited from Donizetti and developed over the first decade of his career, while the music of Azucena points toward the dramatic experiments of his later works.

Spain, 15th c. A melodrama of love and vengeance with a bizarre and confusing plot, in which Count di Luna of Aragon (bar) and Manrico of Biscay (t) are enemies in a civil war, rivals for the hand of Duchess Leonora (s), and – unknown to both them – brothers. Many of the relevant events take place before the curtain rises and are related in narrative arias by di Luna's retainer Ferrando (bs) and the gypsy Azucena (ms), whom Manrico believes to be his mother and whose own mother was burned for witchcraft by di Luna's father. Ultimately both Azucena and Manrico are imprisoned by the Count. In exchange for Manrico's freedom, Leonora offers herself to di Luna; when he accepts, she surreptitiously takes poison and goes to tell Manrico he is free. Di Luna interrupts them, sees her dying, and orders Manrico beheaded. Azucena, witnessing the execution, proclaims that her mother has been avenged and reveals to di Luna that he has killed his own brother.

TRANSLATION
Andrew Porter

In 1711, while Handel's *Rinaldo*, his first London opera, was enjoying its run at the Queen's Theatre, Addison wrote an essay on opera, in *The Spectator*, and remarked at the start: "There is no question but our great-Grandchildren will be very curious to know the Reason why their Forefathers used to sit together like an Audience of Foreigners in their own Country, and to hear whole Plays acted before them in a Tongue which they did not understand." Addison was wrong: those great-grandchildren and their great-grandchildren were – for the most part – not at all curious but continued themselves to enjoy operas sung in tongues that they did not understand. For the most part, but not entirely: there have always been champions, too, of opera sung in the native language of the audience. Most opera composers have been of their company – have wanted their words to be understood.

Lully's *Armide*, first heard in Paris in 1686, appeared in Rome four years later as *Armida*, "tradotta dal francese, senza mutar le note." This seems to have been the first singing translation. Others soon followed. During the early eighteenth century, as Pergolesi's *La Serva Padrona* made its triumphant progress through Europe, it was translated into language after language. Mozart's Italian operas were early provided and published with German translations. Opera in the original and opera in vernacular translation flourished side by side, and continued to do so. When Verdi's *Falstaff* (1893) appeared, it was published in Italian, English, German, and French editions.

One can make historical generalizations only with the proviso that there are constantly important exceptions. The eighteenth-century court troupes (outside France) sang, one might say, chiefly in Italian, being largely stocked with Italian singers, while the popular and touring troupes sang in the language of the country. In the nineteenth century, as national schools of opera (and of singing) developed, foreign operas tended more often to be translated into the national language. Beethoven's *Fidelio* followed on a series of Cherubini operas translated, for Vienna, into German. In London, Giuditta Pasta sang Bellini's *Norma* in Italian, but Maria Malibran sang his *Sonnambula* in English.

This flexibility reflects the always unstable balance between the merits of opera in the original and opera in the vernacular. On occasion, particular companies settled for performing in particular languages. In 1847, Covent Garden became the Royal Italian Opera and thereafter for many years almost everything in the international seasons was sung in Italian – including *Il Flauto Magico*, *I Maestri Cantori*, and *Mirella* (*Mireille*). But also in 1847, one of the many attempts to found an English National Opera began, at Drury Lane; the music director was Berlioz, and the prima donna was Julie Dorus-Gras, Meyerbeer's first Alice and Marguerite de Valois, who sang Lucia in English. When the first American grand opera, Fry's *Leonora* (1845), was done in New York, at the Academy of Music in 1858, it was in Italian translation. But from 1884 to 1891, the Met sang all its operas in German, including *Faust*, *Die Huguenotten*, and *Carmen*. In Paris, foreign operas (*Tannhäuser*, *Il Trovatore*) were translated for performances at the Opéra, Opéra-Comique, and Théâtre-Lyrique, while the Théâtre-Italien provided Italian opera in the original. In Britain and America, there was plenty of opera in English in addition to the international performances that have prominence in the annals and histories.

During the first half of the twentieth century, a pattern emerged. In

The Met program page for the February 28, 1902 performance of *Die Zauberflöte*, or *Il Flauto Magico*, as it was performed in Italian

Italy, Germany, and France – in most of Europe – operas from abroad were generally translated into the language of the audience, and a star like Geraldine Farrar was proud of her ability to communicate directly with her listeners in whatever language. But at Covent Garden and in the big houses of America, opera in the original became the norm (with the exception of French operas sung by mainly Italian singers, which were often translated into Italian). The chorus – witness Chaliapin's live-from-Covent-Garden recordings and the Mapleson cylinders from the Met – learned its roles in Italian, whatever the language of the principals.

After World War II, when Covent Garden reopened, it was as a "national" house. Singers like Flagstad, Schwarzkopf, and Hotter relearned their roles in English translations in order to make them vivid to English audiences. But gradually "internationalism" took over there, as it did also in Milan, Paris, Vienna, Munich, and most of the larger houses. Such performances as Callas' Italian Isolde, Hotter's Graf Almaviva in *Figaros Hochzeit*, and Welitsch's English Salome became rare. Today's stars tend to know their roles in one language only – the original – wherever they may be singing. Dr. Johnson's famous phrase "an exotic and irrational entertainment" – his description of not opera but, specifically, Italian opera in London – has become more generally applicable. American regional companies – Houston, Seattle – that once twinned "international" and "national' presentations of their productions now offer both first and second casts in original-language performances.

The reason is not a sudden worldwide increase in audiences' linguistic skills. It lies in opera's increased internationalism, fostered by jet travel, the commercial importance of recordings (and now videos), and the abandonment of stable local companies in favor of international star assemblies. Reinforcing the move toward original-language opera is a notion that if today's stars (unlike those of the past) sing only in the original, then those who sing in translation must necessarily be lesser lights. But opera in translation is far from dead; in Britain, the English National Opera, committed to opera in English, attracts more than forty percent of that country's operatic audience.

The arguments for and against translation are too familiar to need restatement. There is no agreement except on an ideal: ideally, an opera is sung in the language of its composition by singers who command that language and to an audience which understands it. Once operas and their performers cross national borders, compromise is inevitable: original sound is sacrificed to verbal comprehensibility, or vice versa. Hard-and-fast rules are inappropriate. Each production of each work is a special case, and the decision on whether or not to translate must depend on the nature of the work itself, on the kind of production intended, on the singers available, on the acoustics of the theater, on whether or not a good translation exists. When all factors have been weighed, even a macaronic performance may on occasion be justified: Berlin was able to enjoy Caruso's Rodolfo framed in its German-language *Bohème* production.

Plot summaries, bilingual librettos, and now the provision of supertitles can mitigate the disadvantages of verbal incomprehension; translations more faithful to musical values can help to overcome the objection, "But it sounds so awful." Wise opera-goers see the merits of both systems and enjoy the complementary experiences. Enthusiasts – whether performers or listeners – master as many tongues as possible and move toward that ideal in which both words and music, unaltered, are fully understood.

Andrew Porter, music critic of *The New Yorker*, has made many admired English translations of operas by Mozart, Verdi, Wagner, and others.

Tatiana Troyanos as the Composer in *Ariadne auf Naxos*

Troyanos, Tatiana. Mezzo-soprano; b. New York, Sep. 12, 1938. Studied with Hans Heinz, Juilliard, N.Y.; debut as Hippolyta (*Midsummer Night's Dream*), N.Y.C. Opera, 1963. After singing Marina, Cherubino, and Jocasta (*Oedipus Rex*) with this company, she spent ten years in Hamburg (debut, Preziosilla, 1965), in roles including Dorabella, Baba (*Rake*), and Elisetta (*Matrimonio Segreto*); she created Jeanne (*Teufel von Loudon*). Debuts followed at Aix (Composer in *Ariadne*, 1966), Covent Garden and Salzburg (both Octavian, 1969), Washington, D.C. (Handel's Ariodante, 1971), Chicago (Charlotte in *Werther*,

Les Troyens – (1983). Jessye Norman and Allan Monk

1971), Boston (Romeo in *Capuleti*, 1975), and La Scala (Adalgisa, 1977). Met debut as Octavian, Mar. 8, 1976; there she has sung more than 160 perfs., her roles including the Composer, Amneris, Geschwitz (*Lulu*), Santuzza, Venus, Charlotte, Hänsel, Eboli, Kundry, Brangäne, Adalgisa, Didon and Cassandre (*Troyens*), Jocasta, Giulietta (*Hoffmann*), Sesto (*Clemenza*) and Orlovsky (*Fledermaus*). A committed singer with a rich, flexible mezzo, Troyanos has proved one of the Met's most versatile singers.

Troyens, Les (The Trojans). Opera in 5 acts by Berlioz; libretto by the composer, after Virgil's *Aeneid*.

First perf. (Part II only), Paris, Lyrique, Nov. 4, 1863: Charton-Demeur, Dubois, Monjauze, Cabel, Petit, c. Deloffre. First complete perf., Karlsruhe, Dec. 6–7, 1890 (in Ger.): c. Mottl. U.S. prem., Boston, Opera House, Mar. 27, 1955 (abr. version): c. Goldovsky. Met prem., Oct. 22, 1973: Part I: Verrett, Blegen, Vickers, Quilico; Part II: Verrett, Dunn, Vickers, Riegel, Macurdy; c. Kubelik, d. Wexler, p. Merrill. Énée has also been sung at the Met by Domingo, W. Lewis; Cassandre by Norman; Didon by Ludwig, Troyanos, Norman. 20 perfs. in 2 seasons.

A vast work, whose scope and demands frustrated all attempts to have it mounted in its entirety within the composer's lifetime (Berlioz finally divided it into two parts and accepted half a loaf) and for many years thereafter. Its passionate distillation of what thrilled Berlioz in the classics has made its recent revivals stirring experiences.

Part I, *La Prise de Troie* (The Capture of Troy). After more than nine years of fighting, the Trojans believe the Greeks have retreated, leaving behind a bizarre wooden horse. Only Cassandre (s) and the priest Laocoön foresee doom. The Trojan warrior Énée (Aeneas, t) arrives with news that Laocoön has been devoured by a sea monster, suggesting that the Goddess Pallas is offended and must be placated by bringing the horse to her temple. This is eagerly done, with only Cassandre still prophesying doom, disbelieved even by her lover Chorèbe (bar). At night, the ghost of Hector (bs) tells Énée that Troy has fallen, and commands him to go to Italy and found a new empire. Énée then learns from Panthée (bs) of the destruction of Troy by Greek soldiers disgorged from the horse, and he rushes off to battle. In the temple of Vesta, Cassandre informs the Trojan women of Énée's escape. Chorèbe is dead, and at her urging the women drive away those who will not commit suicide rather than accept dishonor at the hands of the Greeks.

Part II, *Les Troyens à Carthage* (The Trojans at Carthage). The widowed queen Didon (Dido, ms) of Carthage is counselled by her sister Anna (c) to remarry for the good of Carthage and herself, but the Queen cannot forget her husband. Énée, incognito, and the Trojan survivors arrive and are welcomed. Didon's minister Narbal (bs) announces an invasion by the Numidians; Énée reveals his identity and leads his men to repel them, asking Didon to care for his son Ascagne (s). Didon and Énée fall in love, but the god Mercury recalls Énée to his destiny in Italy. Though heartsick, Énée orders his men to their boats. Didon, furious that Énée will not forsake his gods for her, vows vengeance on the Trojans. A great funeral pyre is built overlooking the harbor, piled with remembrances of Énée. Didon prophesies vengeance on his descendants by her people, and kills herself with his sword, but a vision of Rome triumphant rises above her pyre.

Tsar's Bride, The. Opera in 3 acts by Rimsky-Korsakov; libretto from Lev Aleksandrovich Mey's drama, with scenes added by I. F. Tumenev.

First perf., Moscow, Private Russian Opera, Nov. 3, 1899. U.S. prem., Seattle, Jan. 6, 1922.

A grisly tale of power relationships in Czarist Russia. Gryaznoy (bar), a member of the Tsar's guard, uses a love potion to win the heart of Marfa (s), fiancée of the boyar Lykov (bs). But it is really a slow poison arranged by Lyubasha (ms), whom Gryaznoy has seduced. Marfa is chosen by Ivan the Terrible as his bride, but soon dies of the poison; when Lyubasha confesses, Lykov kills her.

Tucci, Gabriella. Soprano; b. Rome, Aug. 4, 1929. Studied at Santa Cecilia, Rome; debut as Leonora (*Forza*), Spoleto, 1951. Sang Mimi at La Scala (1959), Aida and Tosca at Covent Garden (1960), Maddalena (*Chénier*) and Desdemona in San Francisco (1959). Met debut as Butterfly, Oct. 29, 1960; in 13 seasons, sang 167 perfs. of 20 roles, including Aida, both Verdi Leonoras, Alice Ford, Marguerite, Euridice and Violetta. Also appeared in Vienna, Berlin, Buenos Aires, and Moscow.

Tucker, Richard [Rubin Ticker]. Tenor; b. Brooklyn N.Y., Aug. 28, 1913; d. Kalamazoo, Mich., Jan. 8, 1975. Studied with Paul Althouse; debut as Alfredo, Salmaggi Opera, Jolson Theater, N.Y., 1943. His Met career began as Enzo on Jan. 25, 1945, and endured for 30 seasons, during which he sang 499 perfs. (plus 225 more on tour) of 30 roles, most frequently Rodolfo (39 times), Don José (36), and Enzo (27), also the Duke of Mantua, Gabriele (*Boccanegra*), Cavaradossi, Alvaro (*Forza*), Riccardo (*Ballo*), Alfredo, Turiddu, Edgardo, Puccini's Des Grieux, Don Carlos, Ferrando (*Così*), Chénier, Hoffmann, Manrico, Radames, Rodolfo (*Luisa Miller*), Canio, Lenski, Lionel (*Martha*), Calaf, and Samson. At his 25th-anniversary gala in 1970, he was partnered by Sutherland, Tebaldi, and Price. He also sang in Chicago (Chicago Opera, 1946; San Carlo, 1947; Lyric Opera, 1957–64), San Francisco (1954–55), and with other American companies. His European debut, as Enzo at the Verona Arena (1947), was also Callas' Italian debut; he sang at Covent Garden (1957–58), Vienna (1958), the Colón, Buenos Aires (from 1960) and in several Italian theaters, including Rome and La Scala (1969). Although he sang Eléazar (*Juive*) in concert in N.Y. (1964) and on stage in New Orleans (1973) and Barcelona (1974), a planned Met production was thwarted by his death; he is the only singer whose funeral was held on the Met stage.

Tucker's distinctively vibrant sound, almost relentless intensity of projection, and musical perfectionism made him the leading American tenor of his generation. His career was notable for its carefully orchestrated progression through the spinto repertory to dramatic roles, and for his constant readiness to learn from colleagues, conductors, and directors. His numerous recordings preserve many of his major roles, some of them in duplicate.

BIBLIOGRAPHY: James A. Drake, *Richard Tucker* (N.Y., 1984).

Tudor, Anthony. Choreographer; b. London, Apr. 4, 1908; d. New York, Apr. 19, 1987. Dancer and choreographer in London in the 1930s, he joined Ballet Theater in N.Y. as staff choreographer (1939–49). For the Met, he choreographed *Fledermaus* (1950), *Tannhäuser* (1953), and *Alceste* (1960), and served as ballet director (1957–63).

Richard Tucker as Des Grieux in *Manon Lescaut*

Turandot. Opera in 2 acts by Busoni; libretto by the composer, after Carlo Gozzi's play.

First perf., Zurich, Stadttheater, May 11, 1917: Encke, Smeikal, Richter, Saeger-Pieroth, c. Busoni. U.S. prem., N.Y., Avery Fisher Hall (Little Orchestra Society), Oct. 10, 1967 (concert perf.): Kuhse, c. Scherman. U.S. stage prem., Hartford, Nov. 15, 1986: Craig, c. Gilgore.

Antiquity, the Far East. Based on the same source as Puccini's opera, but without some of the latter's alterations; the character of Liù is absent, and Adelma (ms), confidante of Turandot (s), reveals the name of the unknown prince (t). The score is an economical, sophisticated contrast to Puccini's.

Turandot. Opera in 3 acts by Puccini; libretto by Giuseppe Adami and Renato Simoni, after Schiller's adaptation of the play *Turandotte* by Carlo Gozzi; also possibly after *The Arabian Nights*. Last scene completed by Franco Alfano after Puccini's death, and abridged by Toscanini (recently, Alfano's full version has been used occasionally).

First perf., Milan, La Scala, Apr. 25, 1926: Raisa, Zamboni, Fleta, Walter, c. Toscanini. U.S. & Met prem., Nov. 16, 1926: Jeritza, Attwood, Lauri-Volpi, Ludikar, c. Serafin, d. Urban, p. Wymetal. Later Met productions: Feb. 24, 1961: Nilsson, Moffo, Corelli, Giaiotti, c. Stokowski, d. Beaton, p. Aoyama, Merrill; Mar. 12, 1987: Marton, Mitchell, Domingo, Plishka, c. Levine, d. Zeffirelli/Anna, Saligeri, p. Zeffirelli. Turandot has also been sung at the Met by Easton; Liù by Albanese, Stratas, Freni; Calaf by Tucker, Thomas, McCracken; Timur by Pinza. 108 perfs. in 14 seasons.

Puccini's most exotic opera, in scoring and dramaturgy. The arias of Liù and Calaf immediately became popular favorites, while the long scene of the riddles is one of Puccini's most telling dramatic confrontations. The strenuous tessitura of the title role make it one of Italian opera's most formidable challenges to dramatic sopranos.

Peking, legendary times. Turandot (s), Princess of

Peking, will marry the suitor who can solve three riddles; anyone who fails is beheaded. Spellbound by her beauty, Calaf (t), exiled Prince of Tartary, is determined to win her, despite the protestations of his father, the exiled King Timur (bs), and the faithful slave girl Liù (s), who is herself in love with Calaf. Calaf stuns the Princess by answering the riddles correctly, but she still refuses to marry him. He poses his own riddle for her: if she can guess his name before dawn, he will forfeit his life. Threatened with torture if she will not reveal the name, Liù kills herself rather than betray Calaf. Alone with Turandot after the suicide, Calaf tears off the princess' veil, kisses her passionately, and reveals his name, giving her the opportunity to take his life. She summons her court and announces the stranger's name: Love.

Turco in Italia, Il (The Turk in Italy). Opera in 2 acts by Rossini; libretto by Romani.
First perf., Milan, La Scala, Aug. 14, 1814: Maffei-Festa, David, Galli, Pacini. U.S. prem., N.Y., Park, Mar. 14, 1826: Malibran, Garcia, Garcia Jr., Crivelli.
One of Rossini's early comic successes, and one of the first successful entries in the modern Rossini revival. In 18th-c. Naples, a poet (bs) in search of an operatic plot provides an amusing frame for the story of Fiorilla (s), her boring husband Don Geronio (bs), her handsome admirer Don Narciso (t), the visiting Turk (bs) who captures her fancy, and Zaida (ms), the Turk's former lover and Fiorilla's rival for his attention. A comedy of intrigues and disguises ends with apologies and reunions all round.

Turin. Italian city. Operatic activity in Turin began in the 18th c., centered in the Teatro Carignano (opened 1710) and the more important Teatro Regio, which opened Apr. 9, 1740 with Francesco Feo's *Arsace* and subsequently staged a repertory of both comic and serious works by such composers as Jommelli, Traetta, and Piccinni. Though less influential than Milan, Venice or Naples, Turin nonetheless attracted leading 18th- and 19th-c. singers for its short seasons. In 1895, Toscanini (music director, 1895–98, 1905–06) led the first Italian performance of *Götterdämmerung*. Notable premieres at the Regio included *Manon Lescaut* (1893), *Bohème* (1896) and *Francesca da Rimini* (1914). The Teatro de Torino (1925–31), under Guido M. Gatti and Vittorio Gui, revived Rossini and Gluck operas, and saw the first Italian performances of *Ariadne* and *Heure Espagnole*. In 1936, the Regio was gutted by fire and the Teatro di Torino was later damaged by war; opera was transferred to the inadequate Teatro Nuovo. Reconstructed as a completely modern structure, the Teatro Regio reopened Apr. 10, 1973, with a production of *Vêpres* directed by Callas and di Stefano. It offers annual seasons, under the artistic direction of Piero Rattalino.

Turner, Claramae. Contralto; b. Dinuba, Calif., Oct. 28, 1920. Studied in San Francisco and N.Y.; debut as offstage Voice (*Amore dei Tre Re*), San Francisco, 1942. Met debut as Marthe (*Faust*), Nov. 16, 1946; in 4 seasons, sang 75 perfs. of 14 roles, including Zita (*Schicchi*) and Amneris. Created Baba in Menotti's *Medium*, 1946, role of her 1952 debut with N.Y.C. Opera, where she sang until 1969.

Turner, Eva. Soprano; b. Oldham, England, Mar. 10, 1892. Studied with Dan Rootham in Bristol, at Royal Academy of Music, London, and later with Albert Richards Broad; debut as Page (*Tannhäuser*), Carl Rosa Co., 1916. She sang with Carl Rosa until 1924, her roles

including Tosca, Aida, Brünnhilde, Fidelio, and Butterfly. Recommended to Toscanini by Panizza, Turner made her La Scala debut as Freia (*Rheingold*), 1924, thereafter singing widely in Italy, especially as Turandot (which she first sang in Brescia, 1926), and in South America. During 11 seasons at Covent Garden (1928–48), she was heard as Turandot, Aida, Santuzza, Sieglinde, Isolde, Agathe, and Amelia (*Ballo*). Turner also appeared in Chicago (1928–29, 1938), and sang Mascagni's Isabeau in Verona (1929) and Rome (1930). After retirement, she taught at U. of Oklahoma (1950–59) and then at Royal Academy of Music, London. One of England's greatest singers, with a clarion voice and strong dramatic instincts, Turner made most of her career in Italy.

Turn of the Screw, The. Opera in prologue and 2 acts by Britten; libretto by Myfanwy Piper, after Henry James' novella.
First perf., Venice, Fenice, Sep. 14, 1954: Vyvyan, Cross, Dyer, Mandikian, Pears, Hemmings, c. Britten. U.S. prem., N.Y., Kaufmann Concert Hall, YMHA (N.Y. College of Music), Mar. 19, 1958.
The score's structure, with the many scenes embedded in a series of variations on a theme, is a virtuosic embodiment of the image suggested in the title; the aura of mysterious depravity in the original is well preserved by the evocative music.
In and around Bly, an English country house, mid-19th c. A new governess (s) comes to care for Miles (treble) and Flora (s), whose uncle and guardian has made it a condition that the governess assume total responsibility and refer nothing to him. Both children behave strangely, and Miles is dismissed from his school; with the help of information from the housekeeper, Mrs. Grose (s), the governess gradually realizes that the children are under the influence of two ghosts: Peter Quint (t), the former manservant, and her own predecessor Miss Jessel (s), who had given herself to Quint. The Governess resolves to fight them for the children's souls rather than flee, and eventually elicits from Miles a cry naming his supernatural tormentor – but the boy falls dead the next instant.

Twilight of the Gods, The. See *Ring des Nibelungen, Der*.

Tynes, Margaret. Soprano; b. Saluda, Va., Sep. 11, 1929. Studied in N.Y., and with Tullio Serafin, Italy. N.Y.C. Opera debut as Fata Morgana (*Love for Three Oranges*), 1952. Sang in Bologna (Lady Macbeth), Spoleto (Salome), Vienna, Prague, Budapest. At the Met, she sang 3 perfs. as Jenůfa (debut, Nov. 30, 1974).

U

Uhde, Hermann. Bass-baritone; b. Bremen, Germany, July 20, 1914; d. Copenhagen, Oct. 10, 1965 (during a perf.). Studied in Bremen; debut there as Titurel, 1936. Sang in Freiburg and Munich, Bayreuth (1951–57, 1960) and Salzburg (where he created Creon in *Antigonae*, 1949). Met debut as Telramund, Nov. 18, 1955; in 6 seasons, sang 60 perfs. of 12 roles, including Grand Inquisitor, Amfortas, and first Met Wozzeck.

Ulfung, Ragnar. Tenor; b. Oslo, Feb. 28, 1927. Studied in Oslo and Milan; debut in Oslo. Sang in Bergen and Göteborg; joined Stockholm Opera, 1958. Debuts in

Sante Fe (1966), San Francisco (1967), Chicago (1971), and Milan (1972). Met debut as Mime (*Siegfried*), Dec. 12, 1972; has also sung Fatty (*Mahagonny*), Herod, Captain (*Wozzeck*), Mime, and Loge. Created title role in Maxwell Davies' *Taverner*, London, 1972.

Ulisse (Ulysses). Opera in prologue and 2 acts by Dallapiccola; libretto by the composer, after Homer's *Odyssey*.

First perf., Berlin, Deutsche Oper, Sep. 29, 1968: Gayer, Hillebrecht, Madeira, Driscoll, Melchert, Saedén, c. Maazel.

Dallapiccola's last and most ambitious opera, using the tale of Ulysses to raise questions of man's quest for meaning and peace.

Ultimo Selvaggio, L' (The Last Savage). Opera in 3 acts by Menotti; libretto by the composer.

First perf. Paris, Opéra-Comique, Oct. 21, 1962 (in Fr.): Mesplé, Maliponte, Molese, Bacquier, Depraz, c. Baudo. U.S. and Met prem., Jan. 23, 1964 (in Eng): Peters, Stratas, Gedda, London, Flagello, c. Schippers, d. Montresor, p. Menotti. 10 perfs. in 2 seasons.

A satirical opera buffa in a traditional style., set in India and Chicago in modern times. As part of an elaborate scheme to marry his daughter to the Indian prince Kodanda (t), the father of Kitty (s), an American college girl, arranges for her to capture and tame Abdul (bar), a "prehistoric man" (hired by the father to play the part). The plan backfires when she falls in love with the "savage," while Kodanda marries the servant girl Sardula (s).

Theodor Uppman as Billy Budd

Unger [Ungher], **Caroline.** Contralto; b. Stuhlweissenburg [now Székesfehérvár, Hungary], of Austrian parents, Oct. 28, 1803; d. Florence, March 23, 1877. Studied in Milan and with Aloysia Lange and Johann Michael Vogl, Vienna; debut as Dorabella, Vienna, 1824. Sang in first perfs. of Beethoven's *Missa Solemnis* and Ninth Symphony, 1824. In Italy, created roles in Donizetti's *Parisina, Belisario, Maria di Rudenz,* and Bellini's *Straniera.* Also sang in Paris (1833) and Dresden (1841).

Unger, Georg. Tenor; b. Leipzig, Mar. 6, 1837; d. Leipzig, Feb. 2, 1887. Debut in Leipzig, 1867. He was coached by Julius Hey for the role of Siegfried, Bayreuth, 1876. Sang in Leipzig till 1881.

Uppman, Theodor. Baritone; b. San Jose, Calif., Jan. 12, 1920. Studied at Curtis in Philadelphia, Stanford U., and U. of S. Calif.; concert debut as Pelléas, San Francisco Symphony, 1947. Debuts with N.Y.C. Opera (1948) and Met (Nov. 27, 1953) in same role. In 24 Met seasons, he sang 312 perfs. of 14 roles, including Masetto, Papageno, Paquillo (*Périchole*), Sharpless, Harlekin (*Ariadne*), Ping, and Guglielmo. Created Billy Budd (London, 1951), Floyd's Jonathan Wade (N.Y.C. Opera, 1962), and Bill in Bernstein's *Quiet Place* (Houston, 1983).

Urban, Joseph. Designer; b. Vienna, May 26, 1872; d. New York, July 10, 1933. Worked under Roller in Vienna, came to U.S. in 1912 as chief designer for Boston Opera, then moved to N.Y., working on Broadway, especially for Ziegfeld. Principal designer for the Met from 1917 until his death, in over 50 productions, including *Faust, Don Carlos, Norma, Parsifal, Don Giovanni, Louise, Pelléas, Sonnambula, Juive, Lohengrin,* and *Hoffmann.* An eclectic virtuoso, his innovations included plastic three-dimensional scenery and swinging platform stages. His daughter Gretl designed the costumes for many of his productions.

Urlus, Jacques. Tenor; b. Hergenrath, near Aachen, Germany, Jan. 9, 1867, of Dutch parents; d. Noordwijk, Netherlands, June 6, 1935. Studied with Hugo Nolthenius, Utrecht, and Anton Averkamp, Amsterdam, but substantially self-taught as a singer; debut as Beppe (*Pagliacci*), Amsterdam, 1894. Engagements with Netherlands Opera (1894–99) and Leipzig (1900–14), where he began specializing in Wagnerian repertory. Sang at Munich Festival (1909), Covent Garden (1910, 1914, 1924), Bayreuth (Siegmund, 1911–12), and Boston (1912–14). Met debut as Tristan, Feb. 8, 1913; in 5 seasons, he sang 98 perfs. of 10 roles, including Siegmund, Lohengrin, Stolzing, Tannhäuser, Siegfried, Parsifal, Tamino, and Florestan. Returned to U.S. in 1923 with touring German company; sang opera until 1932. The greatest Wagerian tenor before Melchior, Urlus projected his dark and authoritative tenor with comparable force and conviction.

Ursuleac, Viorica. Soprano; b. Czernowitz, Bukovina [now Chernovtsy, U.S.S.R.], Mar. 26, 1894; d. Ehrwald, Austria, Oct. 23, 1985. Studied in Vienna; debut as Charlotte (*Werther*), Zagreb, 1922. Sang in Vienna (Volksoper, 1924–26; State Opera, 1930–34), Berlin (1935–37), and Munich (1937–44). Created Strauss' Arabella, Maria (*Friedenstag*), Countess (*Capriccio*), and Danae (1944). Married to conductor Clemens Krauss.

V

Vakula the Smith. Opera in 4 acts by Tchaikovsky; libretto by Yakov Polonsky, after Gogol's story *Christmas Eve*.

First perf., St. Petersburg, Maryinsky, Dec. 6, 1876. Revised as *Cherevichki* (The Little Shoes), Moscow, Bolshoi, Jan. 31, 1887. U.S. prem., N.Y., Metropolitan Opera House (touring Russian company), May 26, 1922.

Tchaikovsky's most nationalistic stage work, in the tradition of Glinka, was composed as an entry in an opera contest. In the West, it is also known as *The Caprices of Oxana* and *The Golden Slippers*.

Vakula (t), son of the witch Solokha (ms), tries to pay court to Oxana (s), but is hindered by a vengeful Devil (bar) and by Oxana's drunken father Chub (bs). To win her, he flies to St. Petersburg on the devil's back to procure a pair of leather boots belonging to the Tsarina and desired by Oxana. (In Russian, the revised version is entitled *Cherevichki*, the name for the high-heeled leather boots).

Valdengo, Giuseppe. Baritone; b. Turin, Italy, May 24, 1914. Studied in Turin; debut as Rossini's Figaro, Parma, 1936. Appeared at La Scala (1941–43), N.Y.C. Opera (debut, Sharpless, 1946), San Francisco (debut, Valentin, 1947). Met debut as Tonio, Dec. 19, 1947; in 7 seasons, he sang 90 perfs. of 17 roles, including Marcello, Germont, Mozart's Almaviva, and Belcore. With NBC Symphony under Toscanini, sang Iago, Amonasro, and Falstaff (1947–50).

Valente, Benita. Soprano; b. Delano, Calif., Oct. 19, 1934. Studied with Lotte Lehmann in Santa Barbara, Calif. and Singher at Curtis, Philadelphia; debut as Pamina, Freiburg, 1962. Later sang in Nuremberg, Cincinnati, Santa Fe, Pittsburgh, Frankfurt, and Zurich. Met debut as Pamina, Sep. 22, 1973; has also sung Nannetta, Susanna, Almirena (*Rinaldo*), Violetta, Ilia (*Idomeneo*), and Gilda there.

Valentini (-Terrani), Lucia. Mezzo-soprano; b. Padua, Italy, Aug. 28, 1948. Studied at Padua Conservatory; debut in *Cenerentola*, Brescia. Sang this and other Rossini parts at La Scala (1973), Chicago, Covent Garden, and Colón, Buenos Aires. Only Met appearances as Isabella in *Italiana* (debut, Nov. 16, 1974). Sang Quickly (*Falstaff*) under Giulini, Los Angeles, 1982.

Valentino, Frank (Francesco) [Francis Dinhaupt]. Baritone; b. Denver, Colo., Jan. 6, 1907. Studied at Denver Conservatory and in Milan; debut as Germont, Parma, 1927. Sang at La Scala (1938–40) and Glyndebourne (Macbeth, 1938–39). Met debut as Ashton (*Lucia*), Dec. 9, 1940; in 21 seasons, he sang 284 perfs. of 26 roles, including Marcello, Alfio, Sharpless, Rigoletto, Germont, and di Luna. Also appeared in San Francisco, 1943–52.

Valero, Fernando. Tenor; b. Seville, Spain, 1854; d. St. Petersburg, 1914. Studied with Vidal and Tamberlik; debut as Lorenzo (*Fra Diavolo*), Real, Madrid, 1878. La Scala debut as Faust, 1883; also sang Turiddu there, 1891. Debuts as José in St. Petersburg (1884) and Covent Garden (1890). In his only Met season, sang 11 perfs. of Turiddu (debut, Dec. 30, 1891), José, Lionel (*Martha*), and the Duke of Mantua.

Valkyrie, The. See *Ring des Nibelungen, Der.*

Valleria [Lohman; Schoening], **Alwina.** Soprano; b. Baltimore, Md., Oct. 12, 1848; d. Nice, France, Feb. 17, 1925. Studied with Arditi in London; operatic debut as Linda di Chamounix, St. Petersburg, 1871. La Scala debut as Isabelle (*Robert le Diable*), 1873; sang there until 1876, and frequently in London from 1873. N.Y. debut as Marguerite, Academy of Music, 1879. In Met's opening season, sang 14 perfs. as Leonora in *Trovatore* (debut, Oct. 26, 1883), Micaela, Philine (*Mignon*), Berthe (*Prophète*), and Isabelle.

Valletti, Cesare. Tenor; b. Rome, Dec. 18, 1922. Studied with Tito Schipa; debut as Alfredo, Bari, 1947. Sang in Rome (*Matrimonio Segreto*, 1947–48), Palermo (Almaviva, 1949), Naples (Elvino in *Sonnambula*, 1949), and at the Eliseo, Rome (Narciso in *Turco*, 1950). After London debut with La Scala company as Fenton, 1950, he sang Nemorino, Vladimir (*Prince Igor*), Lindoro (*Italiana*), and Filipeto (*Quattro Rusteghi*) in Milan. He sang Alfredo opposite Callas in Mexico City (1951) and at Covent Garden (1958), and Werther in San Francisco (1953). His 7 Met seasons included 80 perfs. of Ottavio (debut, Dec. 10, 1953), Almaviva, Massenet's Des Grieux, Ferrando, Ernesto, Alfredo, Alfred (*Fledermaus*), and Tamino. Also appeared at Florence Maggio Musicale (Giacomo in *Donna del Lago*, 1958; Idamante in *Idomeneo*, 1962; Giannetto in *Gazza Ladra*, 1965), Salzburg (Ottavio, 1960), and Caramoor Festival, N.Y. (Nero in *Poppea*, 1968). With his welcome combination of elegance and intensity, Valletti was an important factor in the postwar revival of the early 19th-c. repertory.

Vallin(-Pardo), Ninon [Eugénie Vallin]. Soprano; b. Montalieu-Vercien, France, Sep. 8 or 9, 1886; d. Lyon, Nov. 22, 1961. Studied with Mme. Mauvarnay at Lyon Conservatory and Méyriane Héglon in Paris. She first sang in concert, and was chosen by Debussy to create the offstage voice of Érigone in *Martyre de Saint Sébastien* (1911); he accompanied her in recital (1914). Stage debut in 1912 as Micaela at Opéra-Comique, where she remained until 1916 and returned frequently thereafter. From 1916, she appeared regularly at Colón, Buenos Aires, and also performed at La Scala (1916–17, in *Mignon*, *Segreto di Susanna* and *Mârouf*), the Paris Opéra (debut, 1920) and San Francisco (1934). Her roles included Mimi, Louise, Marguerite, Massenet's Manon, Charlotte, Thaïs, Juliette, Alceste, Mignon, and Zerlina. Retired after singing Countess Almaviva and Carmen in Monte Carlo, 1943, and taught near Lyon. One of the most versatile and stylish French sopranos, with a rounder, warmer voice than many of the breed.

Vampyr, Der (The Vampire). Opera in 2 acts by Marschner; libretto by Wilhelm August Wohlbrück, after John Polidori's story.

First perf., Leipzig, Stadttheater, Mar. 29, 1828: Röckert, Devrient, c. Marschner. U.S. prem., Boston, New England Conservatory, Apr. 9, 1980 (in Eng.).

An influential Romantic setting of a supernatural tale. Lord Ruthven (t), a vampire, is restored to life on condition that he find Satan three virgin brides in as many years. Thwarted by his third target – Malvina (s), beloved of Aubry (bar), who helped him regain his life – he sinks back to hell.

Vancouver. City in British Columbia, Canada. Though sporadic performances took place during the late 19th c. at the Vancouver Opera House (opened 1891), only in 1960 did a resident company begin operations; the Vancouver Opera Association's first production was *Carmen*. Irving Guttman became artistic director in 1961 and developed an annual season at the Queen Elizabeth Theatre (capacity 2,820), occasionally featuring singers of international stature: Sutherland and Horne sang their first *Norma* here (1963). Richard Bonynge, who made his conducting debut in Vancouver (*Faust*, 1963), succeeded Guttman as artistic director in 1974, developed the opera orchestra (before 1977, players were recruited from the Vancouver Symphony), and expanded the season to four productions, but his emphasis on unusual repertory brought financial difficulties. Hamilton McClymont, general manager from 1978, returned the repertory to popular favorites. Brian McMaster is now artistic director.

van Dam, José [Joseph Van Damme]. Bass; b. Brussels, Aug. 25, 1940. Studied with Frederic Anspach, Brussels Conservatory; debut as Basilio, Liège, 1960. Paris Opéra debut as Voice of Mercury (*Troyens*), 1961; he sang small roles there and at the Opéra-Comique before going to Geneva (1965–67), where he took part in the premiere of Milhaud's *Mère Coupable*, 1966. Debut with Deutsche Oper, Berlin, in 1967; his repertory with this company included Paolo (*Boccanegra*), Leporello, Don Alfonso, and Attila. Escamillo was the role of his debuts at Santa Fe (1967), San Francisco (1970), Covent Garden (1973), and the Met (Nov. 21, 1975). At the latter house, he has also sung Golaud, Colline, the Dutchman, Wozzeck, Mozart's Figaro, and Jochanaan. He has appeared at Salzburg, Aix, and Athens, and created Messiaen's Saint François. A vigorous and engaging performer with an unusually wide range, van Dam effectively embraces some baritone roles.

van Dyck [van Dijck], **Ernest.** Tenor; b. Antwerp, Belgium, Apr. 2, 1861; d. Berlaer-lez-Lierre, Aug. 31, 1923. Studied in Paris; debut there as Lohengrin, Théâtre Eden, 1887. Bayreuth debut as Parsifal, 1888; sang there until 1912. At Vienna Opera (1888–1900), created Werther, 1892. Met debut as Tannhäuser, Nov. 29, 1898; in 4 seasons, he sang 37 perfs. of 7 roles, including Loge, Lohengrin, Siegmund, Tristan, and Massenet's Des Grieux. Also appeared in London (1891) and Brussels (1894).

Vaness, Carol. Soprano; b. Los Angeles, July 27, 1952. Studied at Calif. Poly. U. and Calif. State U., Northridge; professional debut as Vitellia (*Clemenza*), San Francisco, 1977. N.Y.C. Opera debut in same role, 1979; other roles there were Frau Fluth (*Lustigen Weiber*), Leila (*Pêcheurs*), and Mimi. Glyndebourne debut as Donna Anna, 1982. Met debut as Armida (*Rinaldo*), Feb. 14, 1984; subsequent roles there include Vitellia, Fiordiligi, Elettra (*Idomeneo*), the Countess (*Nozze*), and the Israelite Woman (*Samson*). With Australian Opera, 1985, sang Violetta and Amelia (*Ballo*).

Vanessa. Opera in 3 acts by Barber; libretto by Menotti. First perf., Met, Jan. 15, 1958: Steber, Elias, Resnik, Gedda, Tozzi, c. Mitropoulos, d. Beaton, p. Menotti. 15 perfs. in 3 seasons.
A lushly conservative score, well-suited to the libretto, set in a country mansion in northern Europe, c. 1905. Having waited 20 years for her lover's return, the beautiful Vanessa (s) learns from his son Anatol (t), who arrives in his stead one wintry night, that he is dead. Anatol seduces Vanessa's niece Erika (ms), but marries

Vanessa and moves with her to Paris; Erika is left with the realization that it is now her turn to re-enact Vanessa's long wait.

Vanni-Marcoux [Jean Émile Diogène Marcoux]. Bass-baritone; b. Turin, Italy, June 12, 1877; d. Paris, Oct. 22, 1962. Studied at Paris Conservatory; debut as Sparafucile, Turin, 1894. Paris Opéra debut as Méphistophélès, 1908; remained with company till 1947. Also sang at Covent Garden (1905–12), Boston (1912–14; debut, Golaud), Chicago (1913, 1926–32; debut, Scarpia), and La Scala (Boris, 1922).

van Rooy, Anton. Baritone; b. Rotterdam, Jan. 1, 1870; d. Munich, Nov. 28, 1932. Studied with Julius Stock-hausen, Frankfurt; debut as the three Wotans at Bayreuth, 1897. He sang these roles there every season until 1902, plus Sachs (1899) and the Dutchman (1901–02). Berlin debut, 1898; at Covent Garden, he appeared regularly in all the leading Wagner parts, 1898–1908, 1912–13. Met debut as Wotan (*Walküre*), Dec. 14, 1898; in 9 seasons, he sang 183 perfs. of 13 roles, including Wagner repertory, also Jochanaan, Escamillo, and Valentin. For his part in the Met's unauthorized *Parsifal* (1903), he was banished from Bayreuth. After leaving the Met, he sang in Frankfurt until retirement in 1913. Van Rooy's breadth of declamation and (in his prime) fine high baritone made him the greatest Wotan of his day.

van Zandt, Marie. Soprano; b. New York, Oct. 8, 1858; d. Cannes, Dec. 31, 1919. Studied with her mother and with Lamperti, Milan; debut as Zerlina, Turin, 1879. London debut as Amina, Her Majesty's, 1879. Sang at Opéra-Comique, Paris, 1880–85, creating Délibes' Lakmé, 1881. U.S. debut as Amina on Met tour, Chicago, 1891; in her only Met season, sang 12 perfs. of Amina (N.Y. debut, Dec. 21, 1891), Dinorah, Zerlina, Ophélie (*Hamlet*), Lakmé, and Mignon.

Vanzo, Alain. Tenor; b. Monte Carlo, Apr. 2, 1928. Studied with Rolande Darcoeur in Paris; debut as Pirate (*Oberon*), Paris Opéra, 1954. Appears regularly at Opéra and Opéra-Comique, as Duke, Don Ottavio, Edgardo, Des Grieux, Werther, Cellini. Has also sung at Covent Garden (1961–63), Wexford, and as Faust with Paris Opéra in U.S.

Varady, Julia. Soprano; b. Oradea, Romania, Sep. 1, 1941. Studied in Bucharest; joined Cluj Opera, 1963. Has sung in Italy, Frankfurt, Berlin, Paris, Cologne, Munich; is known for Mozart roles. At the Met, she sang 6 perfs. of Donna Elvira (debut, Mar. 10, 1978). Created Cordelia in Reimann's *Lear*. Married to baritone Dietrich Fischer-Dieskau.

Varesi, Felice. Baritone; b. Calais, France, 1813; d. Milan, Mar. 13, 1889. Debut in Donizetti's *Furioso all'Isola di San Domingo*, Varese, 1834. Sang throughout Italy (La Scala, 1841–42) and frequently in Vienna, where he created Antonio (*Linda di Chamounix*); for Verdi, he created Macbeth, Rigoletto, and Germont.

Varnay, Astrid. Soprano; b. Stockholm, Apr. 25, 1918. Studied with her mother, a soprano, and with Paul Althouse in N.Y., later with Hermann Weigert, whom she married in 1944; debut (without rehearsal) as Sieglinde, Met, Dec. 6, 1941. The next week she sang her first Brünnhilde (*Walküre*), and remained with the company until 1956, in all the Wagnerian soprano roles plus Kundry, Venus, and Ortrud, also the Marschallin, Elektra, Amelia (*Boccanegra*), Santuzza, and Salome, and creating Telea (*Island God*). In Chicago, she sang Sieglinde (1944), Amneris, and the Grandmother in Banfield's *Lord Byron's Love Letter* (1955); her San Francisco roles (1946–51) included Fidelio and Gioconda. She first undertook Italian parts in Mexico City (1948), and in 1951 sang the *Trovatore* Leonora (Covent Garden) and Lady Macbeth (Florence Maggio Musicale), but the focus of her European career was set that summer by her success at the first postwar Bayreuth festival. One of Wieland Wagner's favorite singers, she appeared in every festival until 1967, usually as Brünnhilde, also as Isolde, Ortrud, Sieglinde, Gutrune, Senta, the Third Norn, and Kundry. She bowed as Isolde at the Paris Opéra (1956) and La Scala (1957), created Jocasta in Orff's *Oedipus* (Stuttgart, 1959), and sang Elektra at Salzburg (1964–65). She then turned to character portrayals in the mezzo range, including Claire (Einem's *Besuch*) and the Nurse (*Frau*). She returned to the Met in 1974 as the Kostelnička (*Jenůfa*), later also singing Klytemnästra, Herodias, and Begbick (*Mahagonny*), and bringing her Met career totals to 158 perfs. of 24 roles in 19 seasons.

Though her gleaming, wide-ranging voice was unevenly produced (perhaps as a consequence of her early start in heavy roles), Varnay was one of the most compelling of Wagnerian singers, offering an exceptional dimension of psychological complexity, which also made her a memorable Elektra.

Varviso, Silvio. Conductor; b. Zurich, June 20, 1924. After study in Zurich, operatic positions in Basel (1950–62), Stockholm (1965–78), Stuttgart (1972–80), and Paris (since 1980). Met debut in *Lucia*, Nov. 26, 1961; returning during 6 later seasons, he has conducted 14 operas, mainly in the Italian repertory, but including *Fledermaus*, *Meistersinger*, and *Walküre*.

Vassallo di Szigeth, Il (The Vassal of Szigeth). Opera in 3 acts by Smareglia; libretto by Illica and F. Pozza.
First perf., Vienna, Court Opera, Oct. 4, 1889 (in Ger.). U.S. & Met prem., Dec. 12, 1890 (in Ger.): Schöller-Haag, Dippel, Fischer, Reichmann, c. Seidl, d. Hoyt/Dazian, p. Habelmann. 4 perfs. in 1 season.
Smareglia's opera, which points tentatively in Wagnerian directions, is set in Hungary, 1200. Miklus (bar) has seduced the wife of his vassal Rolf (bar), who after Miklus' death avenges himself on his master's sons.

vaudeville (Fr.). Once a popular song, later used in 18th-c. opéra comique, eventually referring particularly to a final number in which each principal character sings a stanza (as in Mozart's *Entführung*); later, it referred to popular variety shows.

Vaughan Williams, Ralph. Composer; b. Down Ampney, Gloucestershire, England, Oct. 12, 1872; d. London, Aug. 26, 1958. Studied at Cambridge U., Royal College of Music, and privately with Bruch in Berlin and Ravel in Paris. Initially inspired by study of folklore, his highly personal nationalist idiom is best exemplified by his nine symphonies. His operas have been less widely recognized, though their seriousness is unquestionable; they include *Hugh the Drover* (1914), *Sir John in Love* (1929), *The Poisoned Kiss* (1936), *Riders to the Sea* (1937), and *The Pilgrim's Progress*, after Bunyan (1951, incorporating the one-act *Shepherds of the Delectable Mountains*, 1922).

Astrid Varnay as Elektra

Vecchi, Orazio. Composer; b. Modena, Italy, bapt. Dec. 6, 1550; d. Modena, Feb. 19, 1605. Music director at cathedrals of Salò (1581–84) and Modena (1584–86), he composed much church music, but his best-known work is *L'Amfiparnaso* (1597), a witty madrigal comedy with a commedia dell'arte plot; a precursor of opera, it is occasionally staged today.

Velis, Andrea. Tenor; b. New Kensington, Pa., June 7, 1932. Studied in Pittsburgh and at Santa Cecilia, Rome; debut in Pittsburgh, 1954. Since his Met debut as Joe in *Fanciulla* (Oct. 3, 1961), he has sung over 1560 perfs. of more than 50 comprimario roles there, including Remendado, Spoletta, Valzacchi, Bardolfo, Roderigo, the Holy Fool (*Boris*), the Witch (*Hänsel*), the character parts in *Hoffmann*, Mime, and M. Triquet (*Onegin*).

Velluti, Giovanni Battista. Soprano castrato; b. Montolmo [now Corridonia], Ancona, Italy, Jan. 28, 1781; d. Sambruson di Dolo, Venice, Jan. 22, 1861. Studied in Bologna and Ravenna; debut in Forlì, 1801. The last of the great operatic castratos, he sang throughout Europe, and created Arsace in Rossini's *Aureliano in Palmira* (La Scala, 1813) and Armando in Meyerbeer's *Crociato in Egitto* (Venice, 1824).

Veltri, Michelangelo. Conductor; b. Buenos Aires, Aug. 16, 1940. Studied in Buenos Aires and later in Milan with Panizza. Music director, Liceo, Barcelona (from 1966); debuts at La Scala (*Don Carlos*, 1970), Covent Garden (1984), San Francisco (1986). At the Met (debut *Rigoletto*, Nov. 10, 1971), he led Italian repertory in 1971–72 and 1979–80, as well as tour performances (1977–83).

Vendice, William. Conductor; b. Petaluma, Calif., Nov. 24, 1948. Studied at San Francisco State College (degree, 1972), worked as assistant conductor in Santa Fe (1973–76, 1979) and at Hamburg Opera (1974–75). Since 1976, on Met conducting staff; debut, *Barbiere*, Apr. 16, 1983; has also led *Porgy* and *Italiana*.

Venice. Italian city in the Veneto region. Venice's first operatic performance was Monteverdi's now-lost *Proserpina Rapita* (1630), at the Palazzo Mocenigo Dandolo. The Teatro San Cassiano, formerly a private theater, opened as the world's first public opera house in 1637 with Mannelli's *Andromeda*, and later introduced Monteverdi's *Ritorno d'Ulisse* (1641). The ensuing rage for opera quickly led to the opening of numerous theaters, including the Teatro San Giovanni e San Paolo (1639–1748), where Monteverdi's *Incoronazione* was first played (1642); the Teatro San Moïse (1640–1818); the Teatro San Salvatore (1661, known today as the Teatro Goldoni); the Teatro San Giovanni Gristosomo (1678, from 1835 the Teatro Malibran, in which small-scale operas are still performed); and the Teatro San Benedetto (1755, renamed Teatro Rossini in 1868, currently a cinema), where *Italiana in Algeri* (1813) was first heard. Most important has been the Teatro La Fenice (opened May 16, 1792 with Paisiello's *I Giuochi d'Agrigento*, burned 1836, rebuilt 1837, refurbished 1854 and 1938), considered by many to be the world's most beautiful opera house. La Fenice's premieres include *Semiramide* (1823), *Capuleti* (1830), *Ernani* (1844), *Rigoletto* (1851), *Traviata* (1853), and *Simon Boccanegra* (1857). Since World War II, in connection with Venetian festivals of contemporary music, La Fenice has housed the premieres of *Rake's Progress* (1951), *Turn of the Screw* (1954), and Nono's *Intolleranza* (1961). Italo Gomez is currently artistic director.

Venus and Adonis. Masque in prologue and 3 acts by Blow; librettist unknown.

First perf., London, site unknown, c. 1684. U.S. prem., Cambridge, Mass., Lowell House, Mar. 11, 1941.

Blow's only dramatic composition, a masque for court use (with participation by one of the King's mistresses). Venus (s), Adonis (bar) and Cupid (s) comment on love, pleasure and constancy; urged by Venus to remember that "absence kindles new desire," Adonis goes to the hunt and is fatally wounded.

Vêpres Siciliennes, Les (The Sicilian Vespers). Opera in 5 acts by Verdi; libretto by Scribe and Charles Duveyrier, after their libretto for Donizetti's *Le Duc d'Albe*.

First perf., Paris, Opéra, June 13, 1855: Cruvelli, Gueymard, Bonnehée, Obin. U.S. prem., N.Y., Academy of Music, Nov. 7, 1859 (in Ital.), c. Muzio. Met prem., Jan. 31, 1974 (in Ital.): Caballé, Gedda, Milnes, Diaz, c. Levine, d. Svoboda/Skalicky, p. Dexter. Hélène has also been sung at the Met by Deutekom, Niska, Scotto; Henri by Domingo, Ochman; Monfort by MacNeil, Elvira; Procida by Plishka, Raimondi. 31 perfs. in 3 seasons.

The first of Verdi's two full-scale essays in Parisian grand opera. He transferred his long-standing dramatic preoccupations – love in conflict with familial and patriotic feelings – to a more spacious, slower-unfolding frame of action, while enriching his musical language with French models.

Palermo, 1282 (based on an historical event during the French occupation of Sicily: on March 30, 1282, as the church bells tolled vespers, the French were massacred by the Sicilians). Henri (t), a young Sicilian, and Duchess Hélène (s) plan an uprising along with Jean Procida (bs), a Sicilian revolutionary who has obtained arms and support

from Spain. But the tyrant governor Montfort (bar) discovers that Henri is his own illegitimate son and reveals to the horrified Sicilian his true paternity. Out of filial duty, Henri interposes himself when Hélène and other conspirators attempt to assassinate Montfort. The betrayed Sicilians are taken captive and Hélène repudiates Henri, but forgives him when she learns of his dilemma. Henri wins his father's pardon for the conspirators and consent to his marriage with Hélène. But Procida sees in the wedding feast the best opportunity to take the French oppressors by surprise. As Montfort declares the couple man and wife, the bells ring out and the Sicilians massacre the unarmed French.

Verchi, Nino. Conductor; b. Trieste, Feb. 21, 1921; d. Milan, July 4, 1978. After study in his native city, repetiteur in Italian theaters; assistant at La Scala (1947–52). Debut in *Consul*, Trieste, 1952. During 3 Met seasons (debut *Cavalleria* and *Pagliacci*, Oct. 31, 1959), he led 8 Italian works.

Verdi, Giuseppe. Composer; b. Roncole, near Busseto, Italy, Oct. 9 or 10, 1813; d. Milan, Jan. 27, 1901. Son of a tavern-keeper, he studied piano from age three, and composition with Ferdinando Provesi in Busseto and Vincenzo Lavigna in Milan. The modest success of *Oberto* (1839) at La Scala led to publication by Ricordi and a commission for three more works. Though the opera buffa *Un Giorno di Regno* (1840) failed, *Nabucco* (1842) was an international success; its portrayal of oppressed Hebrews was understood as a political statement, and Verdi's name (as acronym for "Vittorio Emmanuele, Re d'Italia") became synonymous with the movement to free and unify Italy. In the hectic decade that followed, he wrote several operas in the same vein: *I Lombardi alla Prima Crociata* (1843), *Attila* (1846), and *La Battaglia di Legnano* (1849). *Ernani* (1844), *I Due Foscari* (1844), *Giovanna d'Arco* (1845), and especially *Macbeth* (1847) and *Luisa Miller* (1849) reveal the growth of his ability to embody character and situation in music, and his willingness to alter established forms to match his dramatic purposes.

Giuseppe Verdi

In Paris in 1847, Verdi began a lifelong, stabilizing relationship with the soprano Giuseppina Strepponi; they were married in 1859. Three vastly different, enormously successful masterpieces, *Rigoletto* (1851), *Il Trovatore* (1853), and *La Traviata* (1853), allowed him to restrict his work to attractive commissions. In *Les Vêpres Siciliennes* (1855), *Simon Boccanegra* (1857), *Un Ballo in Maschera* (1859), *La Forza del Destino* (1863), *Don Carlos* (1867), and *Aida* (1871), he explored conflicts between public and personal responsibility, often on the grandest of scales. Having apparently abandoned operatic composition to become a gentleman farmer in Sant'Agata, near Busseto, Verdi was eventually enticed by Strepponi, Ricordi, and Boito to set the latter's libretto for *Otello* (1887), a triumph of dramatic pacing, flexible musical structure, and meticulous workmanship. Verdi and Boito then collaborated on *Falstaff* (1893), a miraculously wise, witty, quicksilver comedy. Other operas: *Alzira* (1845), *I Masnadieri* (1847), *Il Corsaro* (1848), and *Stiffelio* (1850, rewritten as *Aroldo*, 1857); also a Requiem (1874), four *Sacred Pieces* (1898), a string quartet (c. 1873), and songs.

Beginning as an adaptable, practical man of the theater, Verdi increasingly insisted on his own conditions (including the inviolability of his scores), tyrannized his librettists, and broadened the span of his musical architecture. The trajectory from the surging melodies of his early operas to the intricate tracery of *Falstaff* is one of the longest traversed by any composer; although German-oriented criticism once viewed it as "progress," all of Verdi's styles are now regarded with admiration.
BIBLIOGRAPHY: Julian Budden, *The Operas of Verdi* (N.Y., and London, 3 vols., 1973–81).

verismo (Ital., "realism"). A style of opera that arose in Italy in the 1890s, deriving from literary naturalism and emphasizing contemporary settings, lower-class subjects, violent passions and actions.

Vernon, Richard. Bass; b. Memphis, Tenn. Studied at Memphis State U.; debut as Pimen (*Boris*), Memphis, 1972. Joined Houston Opera Studio, 1977, appearing in *Otello, Aida, Falstaff*; debuts with Washington Opera (1979) and Pittsburgh Opera (1980). Met debut as an Animal (*Enfant*), Feb. 20, 1981; he has since sung more than 200 perfs., including the Commendatore and Titurel.

Verona. Italian city. Though not a major musical center such as Venice or Milan, Verona had an active operatic life during the 18th and 19th c. The major theater was the beautiful Teatro Filarmonico, designed by Francesco Galli-Bibiena, opened Jan. 6, 1732 with Vivaldi's *Fida Ninfa*. The Filarmonico (burned 1749, reopened 1754, bombed 1945) was host to numerous great singers and gave first performances of works by Cimarosa and Traetta. Verona figures on the international scene today because of the summer open-air performances in the Roman arena (capacity 25,000, constructed 1st c. A.D.). Established by tenor Giovanni Zenatello, who first managed them with his wife, mezzo Maria Gay, and impresario Ottone Rovato, the arena opened with *Aida* on Aug. 10, 1913. Performances have continued annually, except during the war years (1915–18 and 1940–45). Spectacular productions of grand operas (*Aida, Turandot, Gioconda*) are its mainstay, though the Arena di Verona has successfully staged more intimate works (*Bohème, Traviata*). Carlo Perucci is currently artistic director.

Verrett [-Carter], **Shirley.** Mezzo-soprano, later soprano; b. New Orleans, La., May 31, 1931. Studied with Anna Fitziu and Hall Johnson in Los Angeles, and with Marion Székely-Fresski, Juilliard, N.Y.; while still at Juilliard, she sang Britten's Lucretia (Yellow Springs, Ohio, 1957) and made her N.Y.C. Opera debut as Irina (*Lost in the Stars*), 1958. Her European debut was in Nabokov's *Rasputins Tod*, Cologne, 1959, and she was much praised as Carmen at Spoleto, 1962, an impersonation later seen at the Bolshoi, Moscow (1963), N.Y.C. Opera (1964), La Scala (1966), Met (her debut role, Sep. 21, 1968), and Covent Garden (1973). At the Met, she has sung more than 100 perfs., in both mezzo and soprano roles, including Eboli, Azucena, Cassandre and Didon (*Troyens*), Judith (*Bluebeard's Castle*), Néocle (*Siège de Corinth*), Adalgisa and Norma, Mme. Lidoine (*Carmélites*), Tosca, and Léonor (*Favorite*). She has also sung in San Francisco (Sélika, 1972), Milan (Lady Macbeth, 1974), Boston, Paris, and Vienna. Verrett has taken advantage of her wide-ranging voice to move beyond the normal mezzo repertory, and her vibrant temperament has produced portrayals of memorable intensity.

Versiegelt (Sealed). Opera in 1 act by Blech; libretto by Richard Batka and Pordes-Milo, after a story by Rauppach.
First perf., Hamburg, Nov. 4, 1908. U.S. & Met prem., Jan. 20, 1912: Gadski, Alten, Weil, Jadlowker, Goritz, c. Hertz, d. Fox, p. Schertel. 4 perfs. in 1 season.
A comedy by a prominent conductor, set in a country town, 1830. The Mayor (bar), his daughter (s), her lover (t), and an old bachelor (bar) are successively imprisoned in an antique wardrobe.

Vespri Siciliani, I. See *Vêpres Siciliennes, Les*.

Vestale, La (The Vestal Virgin). Opera in 3 acts by Spontini; libretto by Étienne de Jouy.
First perf., Paris, Opéra, Dec. 15, 1807: Branchu, Maillard, Lainé, Lays, Dérivis, c. Rey. U.S. prem., New Orleans, Théâtre d'Orléans, Feb. 17, 1828. Met prem., Nov. 12, 1925 (in Ital.): Ponselle, Matzenauer, Johnson, de Luca, Mardones, c. Serafin, d. Urban, p. Wymetal. 8 perfs. in 2 seasons.
A spacious score integrating the Gluckian traditions of the Paris Opéra with Italianate lyricism. In ancient Rome, the young general Licinius (t) is in love with Julia (s), bound to chastity as a priestess of Vesta. He seeks her out in the temple, and during their encounter she allows the sacred flame to go out. As she is about to be executed for betrayal of her vows, lightning strikes the altar and relights the flame.

Viaggio a Reims, Il (The Voyage to Rheims). Opera in 1 act by Rossini; libretto by Luigi Balocchi, based in part on Mme. de Staël's novel *Corinne, ou l'Italie*.
First perf., Paris, Italien, June 19, 1825: Pasta, Schiasetti, Cinti, Mombelli, Donzelli, Bordogni, Zucchelli, Pellegrini, Graziani, Levasseur. U.S. prem., St. Louis, Mo., June 12, 1986.
Composed for the coronation of Charles X of France, dismembered and partly reused in *Conte Ory*, reconstructed in 1984. Travellers to the coronation find their trip thwarted (and their amorous intrigies interrupted) by the unavailability of coach horses, but are consoled by the promise of post-coronation festivities in Paris.

Vianesi, Augusto [Auguste]. Conductor; b. Legnano, Nov. 2, 1837; d. New York, Nov. 4, 1908. After training

Aida at the Arena di Verona

in Paris and conducting in N.Y., Russia, and London, he returned to N.Y. for the opening season of the Metropolitan Opera House (debut, *Faust*, Oct. 22, 1883), leading 15 other works, including first American *Gioconda*. Chief conductor, Paris Opéra (1887–91). Returned to Met in 1891–92 to lead 17 works, including first Met *Cavalleria*, then taught singing in N.Y.

Viardot [née Garcia], **Pauline.** Mezzo-soprano; b. Paris, July 18, 1821; d. Paris, May 18, 1910. Daughter of Manuel Garcia and sister of Maria Malibran, she studied singing with her mother, composition with Reicha, piano with Liszt; operatic debut as Rossini's Desdemona, London, 1839, followed quickly by a Paris debut in the same role. The next year she married the French writer Louis Viardot; their home became a center of Parisian intellectual life. She toured Russia in 1843, and sang at Covent Garden, 1849–55, in roles including Amina, Donna Anna, Romeo (*Capuleti*), Valentine, Adina, Rachel (*Juive*), Papagena, Rosina, and Azucena. At the Paris Opéra, she triumphed in 1849 as Fidès (*Prophète*), composed for her by Meyerbeer, and in 1851 created Gounod's Sapho. At

Shirley Verrett as Néocle in *Le Siège de Corinthe*

Pauline Viardot

the Théâtre Lyrique, a production of Gluck's *Orphée*, in an edition prepared for her by Berlioz, ran for 138 perfs. (1859–63). An 1860 revival of *Fidelio* more clearly exposed the worn condition of her voice; her rare appearances after 1863 included the premieres of Brahms' *Rhapsodie* (1870) and Massenet's *Marie-Magdeleine* (1878). She composed songs and operettas, taught (her pupils included Aglaja Orgeni and Marianne Brandt), and befriended and encouraged composers such as Massenet and Fauré. Turgenev, who fell in love with her in 1843, was a member of the Viardot household until his death in 1883, though their relationship was probably platonic.

A powerful musical tragedienne rather than a virtuoso of florid technique, Viardot knew how to conceal the defects of her artificially extended mezzo, and her great artistry won her the admiration of most composers and critics.
BIBLIOGRAPHY: April Fitzlyon, *The Price of Genius: A Biography of Pauline Viardot* (London, 1964).

vibrato (Ital., "vibrated"). A fluctuation of pitch (and sometimes of volume) employed by singers to enrich their sound. Though a feature of traditional operatic singing technique, it is not a necessary part of singing, and may be abandoned for special effects (see *voce bianca*). An excessive vibrato is called a tremolo (or, more colloquially, a wobble).

Vickers, Jon. Tenor; b. Prince Albert, Saskatchewan, Oct. 29, 1926. Studied with George Lambert, Royal Conservatory, Toronto; debut as Duke (*Rigoletto*), Toronto, 1952. He sang Don José and the Male Chorus (*Lucretia*) at Stratford, Ont. (1956), then made his Covent Garden debut as Riccardo (*Ballo*), 1957; he sang regularly with that company until 1969, his roles including Énée (*Troyens*), Radames, Don Carlos, Handel's Samson, Jason (*Médée*), Canio, Florestan, and Peter Grimes. He made his Bayreuth debut as Siegmund in 1958, and returned in 1964 as Parsifal. Canio was the role of his Met debut (Jan. 17, 1960), and he has returned in more than 20 subsequent seasons, for more than 225 perfs. of 16 roles, most often as Florestan, Siegmund, Otello, and Peter Grimes, also Don José, Herman (*Queen of Spades*), Vašek (*Bartered Bride*), Énée (*Troyens*), Parsifal, the Samsons of both Saint-Saëns and Handel, Don Alvaro, Laca (*Jenůfa*), and Tristan. Other debuts in San Francisco (Radames, 1959), Chicago (Siegmund, 1961), La Scala (Florestan, 1960), and Salzburg (Don José, 1966; later Tristan and Otello).

Despite his imposing voice and physique, Vickers declined to sing Siegfried and Tannhäuser, but his intense conviction and involvement in his roles – almost invariably troubled figures rejected by society – have combined with his mastery of expressive vocalism (diction, tone color, phrasing) to create some of the most gripping and idiosyncratic portrayals in recent operatic experience.

Vida Breve, La (The Short Life). Opera in 2 acts by Falla; libretto by Carlos Fernández Shaw.
First perf., Nice, Apr. 1, 1913 (in Fr.): Grenville, Devriès, Cotreuil, c. Miranne. U.S. & Met prem., Mar. 6, 1926: Bori, Tokatyan, d'Angelo, c. Serafin, d. Urban/Thurlow, p. Wymetal. 4 perfs. in 1 season.
Shaped by verismo and Spanish folk music, set in Granada. Learning that her wealthy lover Paco (t) is marrying another, the gypsy Salud (s) denounces him at the wedding, then falls dead at his feet.

vi-de. Optional or possible cuts in a score are marked with "vi-" at the beginning of the omitted passage, "-de" at the end.

Vienna. Capital of Austria, and a major operatic center from the mid-17th c. Ludovico Bartolaia's *Il Sidonio* (1633) was probably the first opera given in the city, followed by Cavalli's *Egisto* (1643). Opera was primarily a court function; Cesti's *Pomo d'Oro* (1668) was composed for the marriage of the musically sophisticated Leopold I to Infanta Margherita, and librettists Zeno and Metastasio worked in Vienna, as did designer Giuseppe Galli-Bibiena. In 1748, the Theater bei der Hofburg (or Burgtheater) opened with Gluck's *Semiramide Riconosciuta*; he later became music director and composed ten works for Vienna. Mozart's *Entführung* (1782), *Nozze* (1786) and *Così* (1790) had their premieres at the Burgtheater, as did Cimarosa's *Matrimonio Segreto* (1792). The Theater auf der Wieden (built 1787, closed 1801) produced the first *Zauberflöte* (1791). Beethoven's *Fidelio* (1805) was first heard at the Theater an der Wien (opened 1801, built by Schikaneder), which later housed operetta, including the premiere of *Fledermaus*; renovated in 1961 and reopened 1962, it is presently the home of the Vienna Festival, held annually in June. Another house of importance was the Theater am Kärntnertor (opened 1708), site of the premieres of several Salieri works, the final version of *Fidelio* (1814), *Euryanthe* (1823), *Linda di Chamounix* (1842), and *Martha* (1847); in 1861, Wagner conducted the first local performance of *Lohengrin* there. The reconstruction of central Vienna in the later 19th c. incorporated a new theater on the Ring to house the Court Opera

Jon Vickers as Otello

(capacity 2,260), opening May 25, 1869 with *Don Giovanni*. A particularly brilliant period was the music directorship of Mahler (1897–1907), when performance standards were greatly improved. In 1918, the Court Opera became the State Opera, a year later producing the premiere of *Frau ohne Schatten*; inter-war music directors included Schalk (1918 29; jointly with Strauss, 1920–24), Krauss (1929–34), Weingartner (1934–36), and Walter (1936–38). After the State Opera was bombed in 1943, performances were given in the Volksoper (opened 1898) and the Theater an der Wien; in the postwar years the performances of Mozart were particularly admired. Today the Volksoper is Vienna's second house, offering more popularly priced operas and operettas as well as musicals; Karl Dönch is its director. Rebuilt and reopened on Nov. 5, 1955, with a performance of *Fidelio*, the State Opera retains its position as one of the world's great opera theaters, although its management has been fraught with politics and intrigue; music directors have included Böhm (1954–56), Karajan (1956–64), Maazel (1982–84), and currently Abbado.

Village Romeo and Juliet, A. Opera in prologue and 3 acts by Delius; libretto by C.F. Keary, after a story in Gottfried Keller's *Leute von Seldwyla*.

First perf., Berlin, Komische Oper, Feb. 21, 1907 (in Ger.): Padilla, Merkel, Egener, c. Cassirer. U.S. prem., Washington, D.C., Opera, Apr. 26, 1972: Wells, Stewart, Reardon, c. Callaway.

This wistful descendant of *Tristan* combines lushly orchestrated chromaticism and the melodic accents of Celtic folk melody.

The village of Seldwyla, Switzerland, mid-19th c. Two farmers feud over a strip of land between their farms, which belongs rightfully (though not legally) to the Dark Fiddler (bar). Because of the feud, the children Sali (treble, then t) and Vreli (s) are forbidden to play together or speak with one another, but they meet secretly and fall in love. Meanwhile, the farmers exhaust their funds and goods paying for their lawsuits. One day, when Vreli's father comes upon the children together and drags his daughter away, Sali knocks him down, and he loses his mind. Sali must then sell their house, and the two impoverished lovers commit suicide by taking a barge to the middle of the river and sinking it.

Villi, Le (The Willis). Opera in 2 (originally 1) acts by Puccini; libretto by Ferdinand Fontana, after a popular folk legend, and perhaps after Adam's ballet *Giselle*.

First perf., Milan, dal Verme, May 31, 1884: Caponetti, d'Andrade, Pelz, c. A. Panizza. Revised version in 2 acts, first perf., Turin, Regio, Dec. 26, 1884. U.S. & Met prem., Dec. 17, 1908: Alda, Bonci, Amato, c. Toscanini, d. Sala, Parravicini, p. Speck. 5 perfs. in 1 season.

Puccini's first opera, an entry in a publisher's contest of one-act works, contains arias that look forward to his personal melodic style.

The Black Forest, olden times. Roberto (t) abandons his betrothed, Anna (s), and she dies of grief. Her spirit joins the Willis, ghosts who prey on faithless lovers; urged on by the vengeful prayers of her father Guglielmo (bar), she appears to the returning Roberto and lures him into a wild dance of death.

Vinay, Ramon. Tenor and baritone; b. Chillán, Chile, Aug. 31, 1912. Studied in Mexico City; baritone debut there as Alphonse (*Favorite*), 1931; tenor debut there as Don José, 1943, role of his debuts at N.Y.C. Opera (1945)

Vienna State Opera, before and after World War II

and Met (Feb. 22, 1946). In 16 Met seasons as tenor, he sang 121 perfs. of 14 roles, including Canio, Tristan, Samson, Herod, and Otello – his signature role, which he sang under Toscanini (NBC Symphony, 1947), at La Scala (1947), Salzburg (1951), Covent Garden (1955), and Paris (1958). Sang Tristan, Parsifal, Siegmund, and Tannhäuser in Bayreuth (1952–57). After 1962, resumed baritone roles (Telramund in Bayreuth, 1962; a single Met perf. as Rossini's Bartolo, 1966).

Violanta. Opera in 1 act by Korngold; libretto by Hans Müller.

First perf., Munich, Court Opera, Mar. 28, 1916: Krüger, Gruber, Brodersen, c. Walter. U.S. & Met prem., Nov. 5, 1927: Jeritza, Kirchhoff, Whitehill, c. Bodanzky, d. Urban, p. Wymetal. 4 perfs. in 1 season.

A lushly Romantic score, set in 15th-c. Venice. Violanta (s) lures Alfonso (t), seducer of her sister, to her home so that her husband Simone (bar) can murder him; falling in love with Alfonso, she throws herself between the men and is killed by her husband's dagger.

Virgil. Roman poet (70–19 B.C.). Operas based on his writings include *Dido and Aeneas* (Purcell) and *Les Troyens* (Berlioz).

Visconti, Luchino. Producer and designer; b. Milan, Nov. 2, 1906; d. Rome, Mar. 17, 1976. An amateur musician, he worked as assistant to Jean Renoir in Paris (1936), and directed films and theater in Italy. His first operatic production was *Vestale* (La Scala, 1955), with Maria Callas, whom he later directed in *Sonnambula*, *Traviata*, *Anna Bolena*, and *Iphigénie en Tauride*. Also active at Spoleto (*Macbeth*, 1958), Covent Garden (*Don Carlos*, 1958), and Vienna (*Falstaff*, 1966). Visconti's stagings were marked by a strong sense of historical style (he occasionally used 19th-c. sets from warehouses) and psychological intensity.

Vishnevskaya, Galina. Soprano; b. Leningrad, Oct. 25, 1926. After appearances in operetta (from 1944), studied with Vera Garina, Leningrad, and in Bolshoi youth group, Moscow; operatic debut as Tatiana, Bolshoi, 1953. Her repertory there included Fidelio, Kupava (*Snow Maiden*), Cherubino, Butterfly, Aida, Lisa (*Queen of Spades*), Natasha (*War and Peace*), Alice Ford, Marguerite, Violetta, Liù, *Voix Humaine*, Desdemona, Marfa (*Tsar's Bride*), Tosca, Rachmaninov's Francesca, Polina (*Gambler*), Lady Macbeth, and the premieres of several Soviet operas; she also made a film of *Katerina Ismailova*. Guest appearances at the Met as Aida (debut, Nov. 6, 1961) and Butterfly, also at Covent Garden (Aida, 1962) and La Scala (Liù, 1964). After she and her husband, cellist and conductor Mstislav Rostropovich, left the U.S.S.R. in 1974 and settled in the U.S., she reappeared at the Met as Tosca in 1975. Her operatic performances combined veristic intensity with acting that Western audiences sometimes found old-fashioned.

Visit of the Old Lady, The. See *Besuch der alten Dame, Der*.

Vittadini, Franco. Composer; b. Pavia, Italy, Apr. 9, 1884; d. Pavia, Nov. 30, 1948. Studied at Milan Conservatory; from 1924 until his death, director of Istituto Musicale, Pavia. Of his operas, only *Anima Allegra* (1921), with its finely crafted Spanish local color, achieved international attention. Other works: the operas *Nazareth* (1925) and *La Sagredo* (1930), ballets, and religious music.

Vivaldi, Antonio. Composer; b. Venice, Mar. 4, 1678; d. Vienna, July 28, 1741. Studied with his father Giovanni Battista Vivaldi and entered the priesthood in 1703, teaching violin at the Ospedale della Pietà, Venice. After 1718, while retaining his ties with the Pietà and with Venetian theaters, he travelled frequently. Unlike his instrumental music, Vivaldi's extensive operatic output still awaits broad revival; of some 46 known works, only 21 scores survive, among them *Tito Manlio* (1720), *Orlando Furioso* (1727), *La Fida Ninfa* (1732), and *L'Olimpiade* (1734).

voce bianca (Ital., "white voice"). Singing with a "straight," vibrato-less tone; often used to convey an impression of illness (e.g., the dying Violetta and Mimi).

Vogl, Heinrich. Tenor; b. Munich, Jan. 15, 1845; d. Munich, Apr. 21, 1900. Studied in Munich; debut there as Max (*Freischütz*), 1865, remaining on roster till his death. Created Loge (1869) and Siegmund (1870) in Munich; sang in Bayreuth (1876–97), Berlin (1881), London (1882). In his only Met season, he sang 24 perfs. of Lohengrin (debut, Jan. 1, 1890), Tannhäuser, Tristan, Loge, Siegmund and both Siegfrieds. Married soprano Therese Thoma (1845–1921), who created Sieglinde.

Voice of Ariadne, The. Opera in 3 acts by Musgrave; libretto by Amalia Elguera, after Henry James' story *The Last of the Valerii*.

First perf., Aldeburgh Festival, June 11, 1974: Gomez, Wilkens, Allen, Drake, c. Musgrave. U.S. prem., N.Y.C. Opera, Sep. 30, 1977: Clarey, Walker, Holloway, Jamerson, c. Musgrave.

Composed for the English Opera Group, this formally and melodically fluent opera is set in Rome in the 1870s. On the estate of the Count (bar) and his American wife (s), the pedestal of a statue of Ariadne is found. The Count hears Ariadne's voice (tape) calling to Theseus and falls in love with his vision of Ariadne, but eventually realizes that it is the Countess he seeks.

Voix Humaine, La (The Human Voice). Opera in 1 act by Poulenc; libretto by Jean Cocteau.

First perf., Paris, Opéra-Comique, Feb. 6. 1959: Duval, c. Prêtre. U.S. prem., N.Y., Metropolitan Museum of Art, Feb. 21, 1960: Duval, c. Prêtre.

A monodrama created for Denise Duval, in the role of a woman talking on the telephone to a lover who is ending their affair.

Völker, Franz. Tenor; b. Neu-Isenburg, Germany, Mar. 31, 1899; d. Darmstadt, Dec. 5, 1965. Studied in Frankfurt; debut there as Florestan, 1926. Sang in Vienna (1931–36), Berlin (1933–43), Munich (1936–37, 1945–52), Covent Garden (1934, 1937), and at Salzburg (1931–39) and Bayreuth (1933–42) festivals. Best known for Lohengrin, Parsifal, Siegmund, and Emperor (*Frau*), but also sang Mozart.

Volo di Notte (Night Flight). Opera in 1 act by Dallapiccola; libretto by the composer, after Saint-Exupéry's novel *Vol de Nuit*.

First perf., Florence, Pergola, May 18, 1940: Fiorenza, Danco, Pauli, Melandri, Valentino, c. Previtali. U.S. professional prem., N.Y., Manhattan School of Music, Mar. 10, 1967.

Dallapiccola's first opera, notably influenced by Berg. In a Buenos Aires airline office, c. 1930, the director, Rivière (bs-bar), plans dangerous night flights, undeterred by the loss of one of his planes. His attitude gradually wins the respect of his colleagues.

Voltaire (François Marie Arouet de). French author (1694–1788). Operas based on his writings include *Alzira* (Verdi), *Candide* (Bernstein), *Semiramide* (Rossini), and *Tancredi* (Rossini).

von der Osten, Eva. Soprano; b. Helgoland, Germany, Aug. 19, 1881; d. Dresden, May 5, 1936. Studied with August Iffert in Dresden; debut as Urbain (*Huguenots*), 1902, in Dresden, where she remained until 1927, creating Octavian (1911) and singing the first Dresden Tatiana, Ariadne, Kundry, and Dyer's Wife (*Frau*). The first London Octavian and Ariadne (1912–13), she toured the U.S. with German Opera Co. (1922–24) as Isolde and Sieglinde. Married to bass Friedrich Plaschke (1875–1951), who also created major Strauss roles in Dresden.

Von heute auf morgen (From Today Till Tomorrow). Opera in 1 act by Schoenberg; libretto by "Max Blonda" [Gertrud Schoenberg].

First perf., Frankfurt, Feb. 1, 1930: Gentner-Fischer, Ziegler, c. Steinberg. U.S. prem., Santa Fe, July 26, 1980 (in Eng.): Shearer, Stone, c. Manahan.

Schoenberg's only comic opera, a satire on "modernity." A Husband (bar) and Wife (s) return from a party, each having become infatuated with one of the guests; an argument develops, but eventually they realize they love each other and pledge mutual fidelity.

von Stade, Frederica. Mezzo-soprano; b. Somerville, N.J., June 1, 1945. Studied with Sebastian Engelberg, Paul Berl, and Otto Guth, Mannes College, N.Y.; debut as Third Boy (*Zauberflöte*), Met, Jan. 10, 1970. After singing some 20 smaller roles, including Suzuki, Lola (*Cavalleria*), Wowkle (*Fanciulla*), and Nicklausse (*Hoffmann*), in 3 seasons, she went to Europe, where her career advanced quickly, notably as Cherubino in Paris, Glyndebourne (both 1973), and Salzburg (1974). She sang Mélisande in Santa Fe (1972), Penelope (*Ritorno d'Ulisse*) in Washington, D.C. (1974), at the N.Y.C. Opera (1976), and Glyndebourne (1979), Rosina at Covent Garden (1975), Octavian in Houston (1975) and at the Holland Festival (1976), and Elena (*Donna del Lago*) in Houston (1981). Since 1973, her Met repertory has included Hänsel, Cherubino, Octavian, Rosina, Zerlina, Adalgisa, and Idamante (*Idomeneo*). A singer much admired for her smooth mezzo, polished technique, and refined musicality.

Votipka, Thelma. Mezzo-soprano; b. Cleveland, Ohio, Dec. 20, 1906; d. New York, Oct. 24, 1972. Studied at Oberlin College; sang the Countess (*Figaro*) with American Opera Company (1927), and appeared in Chicago (1929–30), and San Francisco (1938–47, 1952). Met debut as Flora (*Traviata*), Dec. 16, 1935; in 29 seasons, she sang 1029 perfs. of 40 comprimario roles, including the Witch (*Hänsel*), Marthe (*Faust*), Frasquita (*Carmen*), and Marianne (*Rosenkavalier*).

W

Wächter, Eberhard. Baritone; b. Vienna, July 9, 1929. Studied with Elisabeth Radó, Vienna; debut as Silvio, Volksoper, 1953. Joined State Opera in 1954. Appeared at Covent Garden (Almaviva, 1956), Salzburg (Arbace in *Idomeneo*, 1956), Bayreuth (Amfortas, 1958), Paris (Wolfram, 1959), La Scala and Chicago (both Almaviva, 1960). At the Met, he sang 3 perfs. of Wolfram (debut, Jan. 25, 1961).

Wagner [née Liszt], **Cosima.** Manager; b. Bellaggio, on Lake Como, Dec. 24, 1837; d. Bayreuth, Apr. 1, 1930. Daughter of Liszt and Countess Marie d'Agoult, she married the conductor Hans von Bülow in 1857. In the 1860s she began a liaison with Richard Wagner, father of her daughters Isolde and Eva; their son Siegfried was born after she joined Wagner at Tribschen in 1868. Her 1870 divorce from von Bülow was followed quickly by marriage to Wagner. After his death, she assumed control of the Bayreuth festival, dedicating herself to a rigid implementation of her husband's wishes as she interpreted them; she succeeded in establishing the festival as a permanent institution, though at the cost of some artistic fossilization. In 1906, in ill health, she turned the management over to Siegfried, but remained a palpable presence until her death.

Richard Wagner

Wagner, Richard. Composer; b. Leipzig, May 22, 1813; d. Venice, Feb. 13, 1883. Studied with C.G. Müller and C.T. Weinlig in Leipzig. His early instrumental works were much influenced by Beethoven, his first opera *Die Feen* (1833–34; perf. 1888) by Weber and Marschner. The unsuccessful *Das Liebesverbot* (1836) was colored by his encounters with French and Italian opera while musical director in Magdeburg (1834–36). In 1836, he married actress Minna Planer. After positions in Königsberg (1837) and Riga (1837–38), he lived in Paris (1839–42), completing the grand opera *Rienzi* and the somber Romantic tragedy *Der fliegende Holländer*. Accepted on Meyerbeer's recommendation, *Rienzi* triumphed in 1842 at Dresden, leading to Wagner's appointment as music director. *Holländer* (1843) and the more pessimistic *Tannhäuser* (1845) met with increasing puzzlement, while Wagner's reforming zeal, extravagance, and association with political radicals terminated plans to present *Lohengrin* (perf. 1850). When participation in the 1849 Dresden uprising brought a warrant for his arrest, he fled Germany.

In Swiss exile, after setting forth ideas about operatic reform in essays, notably *Opera and Drama* (1851), Wagner expanded a planned opera on the Siegfried myths into a four-evening cycle, *Der Ring des Nibelungen*, and composed music for more than half of it before breaking off to write *Tristan und Isolde*, a Romantic love tragedy of epoch-making harmonic originality and expressive power, and the genial historical comedy *Die Meistersinger von Nürnberg*. An 1860 amnesty allowed him to return to Germany; Paris performances of *Tannhäuser* in 1861, though ill-received, confirmed his international stature. Beginning in 1864, the patronage of Ludwig II of Bavaria, a fanatical admirer, brought about the premieres, in Munich, of *Tristan* (1865), *Meistersinger* (1868), and (against Wagner's wishes) *Rheingold* (1869) and *Walküre* (1870). In the 1860s he began a relationship with Cosima, Liszt's daughter and von Bülow's wife; after Minna's death and Cosima's divorce, they were married in 1870.

Resumed in 1869 and completed in 1874, the *Ring* received its premiere in 1876, in a specially built festival theater in Bayreuth, but the exertions of raising money for this permanently damaged Wagner's health. His final opera, *Parsifal*, was presented at the second Bayreuth festival in 1882, and he died the following winter in Italy.

In the last half of the 19th c., Wagner was a dominant figure in European culture, not only as composer, but as prophet of an all-embracing theatrical mode (the *Gesamt-kunstwerk*) and even as social philosopher. A gifted journalist and polemicist, he was his own librettist, and also the first modern interpretive conductor. Among his compositional innovations were the pervasive use of leitmotifs, the expansion (and vivid pictorial use) of the orchestra as well as its increasing domination of opera's musical texture, the exploration of chromatic harmony and polar tonalities, and the extension of musical structures to span entire operas. His liberties with other men's money and wives and with the facts of his own life, as well as his anti-Semitism, have kept him a controversial figure. BIBLIOGRAPHY: Ernest Newman, *The Wagner Operas* (N.Y., 1949); London, 1949, as *Wagner Nights*.

Wagner, Robin. Designer; b. San Francisco, Aug. 31, 1933. First designs for Golden Gate Opera Workshop (1953) for *Don Pasquale*, *Amahl*, and *Zanetto*. In addition to Broadway musicals (notably *Hair*, *A Chorus Line*, *Dreamgirls*), he has designed ballet and opera, including *Barbiere* (Met, 1982).

Wagner, Siegfried. Composer and conductor; b. Tribschen, near Lucerne, Switzerland, June 6, 1869; d. Bayreuth, Aug. 4, 1930. Son of Richard and Cosima Wagner (and inspiration of his father's *Siegfried Idyll*, 1870), he studied with Julius Kniese and Humperdinck, first conducted at Bayreuth in 1896, began to stage opera there in 1901, and in 1908 succeeded his mother as festival director. He composed 15 music dramas in a conservative late-Romantic idiom; among those staged were *Der Bärenhäuter* (1899), *Der Kobold* (1904), and *Der Schmied von Marienburg* (1923).

Wagner, Wieland. Producer and designer; b. Bayreuth, Jan. 5, 1917; d. Munich, Oct. 17, 1966. Son of Siegfried Wagner, he studied painting and music, and designed sets for Lübeck and Altenberg, then for Bayreuth (*Parsifal*, 1937; *Meistersinger*, 1943) and Nuremberg. With his brother Wolfgang, directed the Bayreuth festival (1951–66), sharing production and design. Wieland's productions there were *Parsifal* (1951), the *Ring* (1951, 1965), *Tristan* (1952, 1962), *Tannhäuser* (1954, 1961), *Meistersinger* (1956, 1963), *Lohengrin* (1958), and *Fliegende Holländer* (1959). He also worked in other theaters, including Stuttgart and Berlin, producing works of Gluck, Verdi, Bizet, and Strauss. Influenced by Appia, his productions abolished Bayreuth's tradition of stylized realism in favor of spare sets, subtle lighting, and psychological symbolism. His production of *Lohengrin* for the Met was posthumously realized by his assistant, Peter Lehmann (1966).

Wagner, Wolfgang. Producer, designer, and manager; b. Bayreuth, Aug. 30, 1919. Son of Siegfried Wagner and brother of Wieland Wagner, he studied theater management and direction with Preetorius in Berlin. With Wieland, he directed the Bayreuth festival from 1951, serving primarily as business manager but also designing and producing operas, in a style similar to Wieland's if less

Bruno Walter

imaginative and perceptive. His productions included *Lohengrin* (1953, 1967), *Holländer* (1955), *Tristan* (1957), the *Ring* (1960, 1970), *Meistersinger* (1968, 1981), *Parsifal* (1975), and *Tannhäuser* (1985). After Wieland's death in 1966, Wolfgang became sole director; since 1969, he has invited other producers to work at Bayreuth, keeping it in the forefront of theatrical innovation.

Wald, Der (The Forest). Opera in 1 act by Smyth; libretto by the composer.

First perf., Berlin, Opernhaus, Apr. 9, 1902: c. Muck. U.S. & Met prem., Mar. 11, 1903: Gadski, Reuss-Belce, Anthes, Bispham, c. Hertz. 2 perfs. in 1 season.

The only opera by a woman performed by the Met to date, a symbolist tale of sorcery and sacrifice of life for love, deep in the forest.

Walker, Edyth. Mezzo-soprano, later soprano; b. Hopewell, N.Y., Mar. 27, 1867(?); d. New York, Feb. 19, 1950. Studied with Aglaja Orgeni, Dresden; debut as Fidès (*Prophète*), Berlin, 1894. Member, Vienna Court Opera, 1895–1903. Debuts as Amneris at Covent Garden (1900) and Met (Nov. 30, 1903); in 3 Met seasons, sang 64 perfs. of 16 roles, including Brünnhilde, Léonor (*Favorite*), Ortrud, Nancy (*Martha*), Brangäne, and Fricka. Appeared in Hamburg (1906–12), Bayreuth (Kundry and Ortrud, 1908), and Munich (1912–17).

Walker, Sarah. Mezzo-soprano; b. Cheltenham, England, Mar. 11, 1945. Studied with Vera Rozsa, Royal College of Music, London; debut as Diana/Giove (*Calisto*), Glyndebourne, 1970. Has appeared at Aldeburgh, and with Scottish, English National, and Royal Operas, in roles including Charlotte (*Werther*), Baba (*Rake*), Didon (*Troyens*), and Britten's Gloriana. Met debut as Micah (Handel's *Samson*), Feb. 3, 1986. Also a noted recitalist.

Walküre, Die. See *Ring des Nibelungen, Der*.

Wallace, Vincent. Composer; b. Waterford, Ireland, Mar. 11, 1812; d. Château de Haget, Vieuzos, Hautes-Pyrénées, Oct. 12, 1865. After an early career as piano and violin virtuoso, touring as far as Asia and South America, his first opera, the eclectic *Maritana* (1845), was a major success. Among his later works, only the spectacular *Lurline*, commissioned by the Paris Opéra in 1847 but not staged until 1860 (at Covent Garden), came near to repeating his initial triumph.

Wallmann, Margherita. Producer; b. Vienna, June 22, 1904. Originally a dancer, she was choreographer for the Salzburg Festival (1933–39) and ballet director in Vienna (1934–39), and later worked extensively at La Scala as director, including *Alceste* (1954), *Norma* (1955), and *Ballo* (1957) with Callas. For the Met, she staged *Lucia* (1964) and *Gioconda* (1966).

Wally, La. Opera in 4 acts by Catalani; libretto by Illica, after Wilhelmine von Hillern's *Die Geyer-Wally*.
    First perf., Milan, La Scala, Jan. 20, 1892: Darclée, Stehle, Suagnes, Pessina, c. Mascheroni. U.S. & Met prem., Jan. 6, 1909: Destinn, L'Huilier, Martin, Amato, c. Toscanini, d. Sala/Parravicini, p. Speck. 4 perfs. in 1 season.
    A prominent work of the verismo era, though not typical of that school; set in the Tyrol, c. 1800. Her love for Hagenbach (t) unrequited, Wally (s) arranges to have him murdered, then forgives him in time to rescue him. When Hagenbach returns to proclaim that he now loves her, the two are killed in an avalanche.

Walter, Bruno [Bruno Walter Schlesinger]. Conductor; b. Berlin, Sep. 15, 1876; d. Beverly Hills, Calif., Feb. 17, 1962. After study in Berlin, and a position in Cologne (debut, 1894), he worked with Mahler in Hamburg (1894) and in Vienna (1901–13), and led the posthumous premieres of Mahler's *Lied von der Erde* (1911) and Ninth Symphony (1912). Music director, Munich Opera (1913–22; world premiere of *Palestrina*); conductor, Leipzig Gewandhaus (1929–33); active at Berlin Opera (1925–29), Salzburg (from 1925), Covent Garden (1924–31), and Vienna (1935–38). Came to the U.S. in 1939, guest-conducting widely. Met debut, *Fidelio*, Feb. 14, 1941, returning through 1946 in a repertory including Mozart, *Orfeo*, *Forza*, and *Ballo*, and again in 1950–51 for *Fidelio*, and 1955–56 for *Zauberflöte*, for a total of 79 perfs. Walter's interpretations, not always ideally disciplined, were notable for their emotional warmth and affectionate phrasing. His operatic recordings include Act I of *Walküre* and numerous aria accompaniments.

Walton, William. Composer; b. Oldham, Lancashire, England, Mar. 29, 1902; d. Ischia, Bay of Naples, Mar. 8, 1983. Studied with Hugh Allen at Oxford U. Though he began his career as an *enfant terrible*, Walton's concert music grew steadily more serious and conservative. His two operas are the traditionally Romantic grand opera *Troilus and Cressida* (1954) and the one-act comedy *The Bear* (1967). Walton also wrote several cinema scores, notably for the Shakespeare films of Laurence Olivier.

War and Peace. Opera in 5 acts by Prokofiev; libretto by the composer and Mira Mendelson, after Tolstoy's novel.
    First perf., Moscow, Writer's Club, Oct. 16, 1944 (concert perf.). First stage perf., Leningrad, Maly, June 12, 1946 (first 8 scenes only), c. Samosud. First perf., final version: Leningrad, Maly, Mar. 31, 1955, c. Grikurov. U.S. prem., N.Y., NBC Television Opera, Jan. 13, 1957 (in Eng.): Scott, Cunningham, Meredith, Smith, c. Adler. U.S. stage prem., Opera Co. of Boston, May 8, 1974: Saunders, Moulson, Carlson, Gramm, c. Caldwell.
    An ambitious attempt to capture the scope of Russia's most celebrated panoramic novel in the musical style of Soviet realism. The opening scenes depict Peace: the love of Prince Andrei Bolkonsky (bar) and Natasha Rostova (s), the postponement of their marriage, and the attempt of the dissolute Anatol Kuragin (t) to elope with Natasha, foiled by Count Pierre Bezukhov (t). Napoleon's 1812 invasion of Russia ensues: the battle of Borodino, the Russian war council at which General Kutuzov (bs) orders a retreat from Moscow, the burning of the city by its inhabitants, the brief reunion of Natasha and the dying Andrei, Pierre's imprisonment by the French and his rescue by partisans.

Ward, Robert. Composer; b. Cleveland, Ohio, Sep. 13, 1917. Studied at Eastman School, Rochester, with Rogers, Royce, and Hanson, and at Juilliard, N.Y. Taught at Juilliard and Columbia U., worked in music publishing, and was president of N.C. School of the Arts. His operas include *The Crucible* (1961), *The Lady from Colorado* (1964), and *Claudia Legare* (after Ibsen, 1978).

Warren [Warrenoff], **Leonard.** Baritone; b. New York, Apr. 21, 1911; d. New York, Mar. 4, 1960. Studied with Sidney Dietsch while singing in Radio City Music Hall chorus, and, after winning the Met Auditions in 1938, briefly with Pais and Picozzi in Milan; debut as Paolo (*Boccanegra*), Met, Jan. 13, 1939. In 22 seasons with the company, he became its leading "Italian baritone," singing 416 perfs. (plus over 200 on tour) of 26 roles, most often Rigoletto (56 times), Amonasro (37), Iago (33), di

Leonard Warren as Simon Boccanegra

Luna (32), and Tonio (30), also Germont, Barnaba, Don Carlo (*Forza*), Scarpia, Ashton, Renato (*Ballo*), Valentin, Rangoni (*Boris*), Escamillo, Gérard (*Chénier*), and Carlo (*Ernani*); he was the Met's first Macbeth, and created Ilo (*Island God*). Three nights after appearing in a new production of *Simon Boccanegra*, he collapsed and died on stage during the battle scene of *Forza*. Although his career was devoted principally to the Met, Warren also sang in Rio de Janeiro (1942), San Francisco (1943–56), Chicago (1944–46), Mexico City (1948), and at La Scala (debut, Rigoletto, 1953, also Iago), and in 1958 he toured the Soviet Union.

Warren's voluminous baritone enjoyed an easy upper extension (even beyond high A) that made the tessitura of Verdi's baritone roles especially congenial, and he acquired a fine control of soft singing and useful agility. At first an awkward stage figure, he worked conscientiously to improve his acting, and became a compelling performer as well as a reliable one, whose loss while still in his prime was a serious blow to the Met. Recordings preserve a number of his most famous roles, notably Rigoletto, di Luna, Tonio, and Macbeth.

Warrior, The. Opera in 1 act by Rogers; libretto by Norman Corwin, after the Old Testament, Judges, xvi.

First perf., N.Y., Met, Jan. 11, 1947: Resnik, Harrell, c. Rudolf, d. Leve/Schenck, p. Graf. 2 perfs. in 1 season.

Originally a radio drama with music, this conservative score tells the story of Samson and Delilah, from Samson's capture through the destruction of the temple.

Washington, D.C. Capital of the United States. Until the present generation, Washington depended on touring companies for its opera, there being neither a suitable theater nor public support for a permanent company. The Opera Society of Washington was established in 1956, and offered brief seasons at the Lisner Auditorium of George Washington University (capacity 1,500), including the U.S. premieres of *Erwartung* and *Bomarzo*, and Stravinsky's *Oedipus Rex* conducted by the composer. With the opening of the opera house (capacity 2,200) in the Kennedy Center for the Performing Arts in 1971, the company (now known as the Washington Opera) found a suitable home; the first production was Ginastera's *Beatrix Cenci*, commissioned for the occasion. Subsequent American premieres have included *Village Romeo and Juliet* (1972) and *Ritorno d'Ulisse* (1974). Directors have been Ian Strasfogel (1972–76), George London (1976–80), and Martin Feinstein (since 1980). The season, comprising eight productions, runs from October to February; some works are given in the Kennedy Center's more intimate Terrace Theater (capacity 500). The opera house has also accommodated visiting international companies, such as La Scala and the Paris Opéra (1975).

Water Carrier, The. See *Les Deux Journées*.

Watson [née McLamore], **Claire.** Soprano; b. New York, Feb. 3, 1927; d. Utling, Germany, July 16, 1986. Studied at Eastman School, Rochester, and with Elisabeth Schumann and Sergius Kagen, N.Y.; debut as Desdemona, Graz, 1951. Sang with Frankfurt (1956–58) and Bavarian State (from 1958) Operas. Debuts at Covent Garden (1958) and Glyndebourne (1960) as Marschallin; also sang in Berlin, Salzburg (Mozart's Countess, 1966), Chicago, San Francisco.

Weber(-Lange), Aloysia. Soprano; b. Mannheim, Germany, c. 1759–61; d. Salzburg, June 8, 1839. Early liaison

with Mozart, whom she met in 1777 and toured with in recital. He composed several arias to suit her remarkable range and agility, and she created Mme. Herz in *Schauspieldirektor*. She sang in Munich (1778) and Vienna (1779–92). Mozart eventually married her younger sister Constanze, while Aloysia married the painter Joseph Lange.

Weber, Carl Maria von. Composer; b. Eutin, near Lübeck, Nov. 18(?), 1786; d. London, June 5, 1826. Son of the music director of an itinerant theater company, his early musical education was haphazard yet practical; he studied with Michael Haydn, Kalcher, and later with Abbé Vogler. He composed his first staged opera, *Das Waldmädchen* (1800), while still an adolescent. After holding several theatrical appointments, travelling, and concertizing, he became music director in Prague (1813–16) and Dresden (from 1816), where he invigorated the companies, broadened the repertories, and began to formulate ideas about German opera that anticipate Wagner's. These he put into practice in *Der Freischütz* (1821), which, besides defining a new identity for German opera, became an international success, leading to commissions from Vienna for *Euryanthe* (1823) and from Covent Garden for *Oberon* (1826). Despite problems in their librettos (the former's is woefully inept, the latter's a product of the British tradition of "semi-opera"), both are scores of great musical richness, extending *Freischütz*'s use of reminiscence motives, chromatic harmony, and formal elaboration, pointing toward such later works as *Lohengrin*. Already racked with tuberculosis when he accepted the London commission, Weber died only weeks after conducting the premiere of *Oberon*. Other operas include *Abu Hassan* (singspiel, 1811) and *Die drei Pintos* (1820–21, unfinished; completed by Mahler).

BIBLIOGRAPHY: John Warrack, *Carl Maria von Weber* (N.Y., and Cambridge, 2nd ed., 1976).

Weber, Ludwig. Bass; b. Vienna, July 29, 1899; d. Vienna, Dec. 9, 1974. Studied in Vienna; debut at Volksoper, 1920. Sang in Düsseldorf, Cologne, Munich, then joined Bavarian State Opera (1933); with Vienna State Opera (1945–60). Appeared frequently at Covent Garden (from 1936), Salzburg (1939–47) and Bayreuth (1951–58). Best known for Mozart, Wagner (notably Gurnemanz), and Baron Ochs.

Webster, David. Manager; b. Dundee, Scotland, July 3, 1903; d. London, May 11, 1971. As a student at Liverpool U., he produced several operas. During years in business, he was chairman of the Liverpool Philharmonic (1940–45). He then became general administrator of the Royal Opera House, Covent Garden, comprising the Sadler's Wells Ballet (later the Royal Ballet) and a new resident opera company, which acquired international stature during Webster's tenure (until 1970), especially under music director Solti.

Webster, Margaret. Producer; b. New York, Mar. 15, 1905; d. London, Nov. 13, 1972. Appeared as actress from 1925, and directed plays from 1935; especially noted for Shakespeare productions in U.S. and Britain. Bing brought her to the Met for *Don Carlos* (1950), *Aida* (1951), and *Simon Boccanegra* (1960). For N.Y.C. Opera, she staged *Troilus and Cressida* (1955), *Macbeth* (1957), and *Taming of the Shrew* (1958).

Wechsler, Gil. Lighting designer; b. Brooklyn, N.Y., Feb. 5, 1942. Studied with Herman Krawitz and Donald

Oenslager; worked as lighting designer with Harkness Ballet, Stratford (Ont.) Shakespeare Festival, and Chicago Lyric. Since 1977, resident lighting designer at the Met; beginning with *Carmélites*, he has designed the lighting for every new production and most revivals.

Weed, Marion. Soprano; b. Rochester, N.Y., 1870; d. Rochester, N.Y., June 23, 1947. Studied with Lilli Lehmann and sang Wagner roles in Hamburg, Cologne, and Bayreuth (small parts, 1896–99). Met debut as *Walküre* Brünnhilde, Nov. 28, 1903; in 5 seasons, sang 70 perfs. of 17 roles, including Kundry, Gertrude (*Hänsel*), Orlovsky (*Fledermaus*), Ortrud, Freia, and Venus.

Weede [Wiedefeld], **Robert.** Baritone; b. Baltimore, Md., Feb. 11, 1903; d. Walnut Creek, Calif., July 9, 1972. Studied at Eastman School and in Milan, and sang at Radio City Music Hall, N.Y., from 1933. Met debut as Tonio, May 15, 1937; in 10 seasons, sang 21 perfs. of 8 roles, including Scarpia and Manfredo (*Amore dei Tre Re*). Debuts as Rigoletto in Chicago (1939), San Francisco (1940), and N.Y.C. Opera (1948). On Broadway, created Tony in Loesser's *The Most Happy Fella* (1956).

Weikl, Bernd. Baritone; b. Vienna, July 29, 1942. Studied in Mainz and Hanover; debut, Hanover, 1968. Member of Hamburg State Opera from 1973; appeared at Bayreuth (from 1973, including Sachs). Met debut as Wolfram, Dec. 22, 1977; has since sung Amfortas, Jochanaan, Mandryka (*Arabella*), and Don Fernando (*Fidelio*) there.

Weil, Hermann. Baritone; b. Mühlburg, near Karlsruhe, Germany, May 29, 1877; d. Blue Mountain Lake, N.Y., July 6, 1949. Studied in Frankfurt; debut as Wolfram, Freiburg, 1901. Appeared widely in Germany, especially in Stuttgart; sang at Covent Garden (Jochanaan, 1913) and Bayreuth (1911–12, 1924–25). Met debut as Kurwenal, Nov. 17, 1911; in 6 seasons, sang 115 perfs. of 16 roles, including Gunther, Sachs, Faninal, Telramund, Wotan, and Wolfram. Sang with Boston Opera, 1912–14; returned to N.Y. with touring German companies in 1919 and 1923.

Weill, Kurt. Composer; b. Dessau, Mar. 2, 1900; d. New York, Apr. 3, 1950. Son of a cantor, he studied with Albert Bing in Dessau, later with Humperdinck, Jarnach, and Busoni. Attracted by Berlin's avant-garde intellectual milieu, he abandoned post-Romantic musical complexity and experimented with jazz idioms and parody in the one-act operas (texts by Georg Kaiser) *Der Protagonist* (1926) and *Der Zar lässt sich photographieren* (1928). Collaboration with the didactic poet and social critic Bertolt Brecht produced the "songspiel" *Mahagonny* (1927), the internationally popular *Die Dreigroschenoper* (1928), and the children's opera *Der Jasager* (1930); the "songspiel" was later expanded to a full-length opera, *Aufstieg und Fall der Stadt Mahagonny* (1930). Its reception suffered from the increasingly uncongenial political climate, as did the socially compassionate operas *Die Bürgschaft* (text by Caspar Neher, 1932) and *Der Silbersee* (text by Kaiser, 1933). Weill fled to Paris in 1933, and then settled in the U.S. with his wife, singer Lotte Lenya, mastered Broadway's musical idiom, and composed successful musical comedies, as well as the operas *Street Scene* (1947) and *Down in the Valley* (1948). Weill's ambivalent position between "art" and "commerce" has troubled many critics, but the originality and force of his best work are hardly in doubt.

BIBLIOGRAPHY: Douglas Jarman, *Kurt Weill, An Illustrated Biography* (Bloomington, Ind., and London, 1982).

Weinberger, Jaromír. Composer; b. Prague, Jan. 8, 1896; d. St. Petersburg, Fla., Aug. 8, 1967. Studied in Prague with Křička and Hoffmeister and in Leipzig with Reger. His first opera, *Shvanda the Bagpiper* (1927), was widely successful. The ambitious *Wallenstein*, after Schiller (1937), was produced in Vienna just before the Anschluss forced Weinberger to flee to the U.S., where he was unable to adapt and committed suicide at the age of 71. Other operas: *Die geliebte Stimme* (1931); *The Outcasts of Poker Flat*, after Bret Harte (1932).

Weingartner, Felix. Conductor; b. Zara [now Zadar], Dalmatia, June 2, 1863; d. Winterthur, Switzerland, May 7, 1942. A protégé of Liszt, his operatic positions included directorship of the Berlin Opera (1891–98), Vienna Opera (1908–11, again briefly in 1935–36), and Vienna Volksoper (1919–24). In the U.S., he conducted at the Boston Opera (1911–14). A frequent guest conductor in London, Hamburg, and elsewhere, Weingartner was noted for the classical poise and sobriety of his interpretations, especially of the Beethoven symphonies.

Weis, Karel. Composer; b. Prague, Feb. 13, 1862; d. Prague, Apr. 4, 1944. Studied at Prague Conservatory, and at Prague Organ School with Fibich. Early career as organist, conductor, and archivist of Bohemian folk music. His operas include *Viola* (1892), after Shakespeare's *Twelfth Night*; the successful *Der polnische Jude* (1901); and *Der Sturm auf die Mühle*, after Zola (1912); these works are in the nationalist tradition of Smetana and Dvořák.

Weisgall, Hugo. Composer; b. Eibenschütz, Moravia [now Ivančice, Czechoslovakia], Oct. 13, 1912. In 1920, emigrated to U.S., where he was educated, studying composition at Peabody Conservatory, Baltimore, and with Sessions and Scalero. His highly literate operas, in a personal idiom evolving from neo-classicism and Bergian expressionism, include *The Tenor*, after Wedekind (1952); *The Stronger*, after Strindberg (1952); *Six Characters in Search of an Author*, after Pirandello (1959); *Purgatory*, after Yeats (1961); *The Gardens of Adonis*, after Shakespeare and Obey (1959, rev. 1977–81); *Athaliah*, after Racine (concert perf., 1964); *Nine Rivers from Jordan* (1968); and *Jennie, or The Hundred Nights*, after Mishima (1976).

Welitsch [Veličkova], **Ljuba.** Soprano; b. Borisovo, Bulgaria, July 10, 1913. Studied with Gyorgy Zlatov in Sofia, later with Theodor Lierhammer in Vienna; debut in small part in *Louise*, Sofia, 1934. Engagements followed in Graz (1937–41), Hamburg (1941–42), and at the Vienna Volksoper (1942–44), where she first sang Salome, which became her signature role. A regular member of the Vienna State Opera from 1946, her roles included Butterfly, Nedda, Puccini's Manon and Minnie, Elisabeth, Desdemona, Fiordiligi, and Chrysothemis. At Covent Garden with the Vienna company in 1947, she sang Salome and Donna Anna, returning to sing Aida, Lisa (*Queen of Spades*), and Tosca with the resident company. She sang Donna Anna at Salzburg (1946, 1950) and with the Glyndebourne company at Edinburgh (1948; also Amelia in *Ballo*, 1949). Her U.S. debut was as Salome at the Met, Feb. 4, 1949; in 4 seasons with the company, she appeared 52 times, most often as Salome, Donna Anna, and Rosalinde (*Fledermaus*), also as Aida, Tosca, and a single, flamboyant Musetta. She continued to appear at the Vienna State Opera, mostly in character parts, until her final operatic appearance in Egk's *Revisor*, 1959, and made a second career as an actress in theater, films, and television. She returned to the Met in 1972 for a dozen perfs. in the non-singing role of the Duchess of Crakentorp (*Fille*), 1972.

Welitsch's silvery soprano, with its soaring top register, and her fiery temperament seemed tireless in her first Met seasons, but her prodigal use of these exceptional resources surely shortened her career, though producing some of the most memorable operatic impersonations of the immediate postwar years. Her relatively few recordings convey something of the impact of her potent theatrical presence.

Welting, Ruth. Soprano; b. Memphis, Tenn., May 11, 1949. Studied in N.Y. and with Luigi Ricci, Rome, and Janine Reiss, Paris; debut as Blondchen, N.Y.C. Opera, 1971. Met debut as Zerbinetta, Mar. 20, 1976; other Met roles include Sophie, Princess (*Enfant*). Has sung Fairy Godmother (*Cendrillon*) in Ottawa (1979) and Washington (1980), and appeared in Santa Fe, San Francisco, Covent Garden.

Werther. Opera in 4 acts by Massenet; libretto by Édouard Blau, Georges Hartmann, and Paul Milliet, after Goethe's novel *The Sorrows of Young Werther*.

First perf., Vienna, Court Opera, Feb. 16, 1892 (in Ger.): Renard, Forster, van Dyck, Neidl, c. Massenet. U.S. prem., Chicago, Auditorium (Met tour), Mar. 29, 1894: Eames, Arnoldson, J. de Reszke, Martapoura, c. Mancinelli. Met prem., Apr. 19, 1894, with same cast. Later Met production: New Theater, Nov. 16, 1909: Farrar, Gluck, Clément, Gilly, c. Tango, d. Burghart & Co.; p. Stern (house premiere, Feb. 28, 1910, with same cast); Feb. 19, 1971: Ludwig, Blegen, di Giuseppe, Reardon, c. Lombard, d. Heinrich, p. Deiber. Werther has also been sung at the Met by Corelli, Domingo, Kraus; Charlotte by Elias, Crespin, Obraztsova, Troyanos. 36 perfs. in 7 seasons.

One of Massenet's strongest and most economically constructed scores, with a fine balance of lyrical outpouring and dramatic urgency that captures a large measure of Goethe's famous portrait of a young man's love, obsession, and despair.

Near Frankfurt, c. 1780. The young poet Werther (t) visits Charlotte (ms), daughter of the Magistrate of Wetzlar, and falls in love with her. Though stunned to learn that she is betrothed to another man, he becomes obsessed with the idea that his destiny is to be united with her. He dissembles with her fiancé Albert (bar), who understands what he thinks are Werther's past feelings and welcomes him as a friend. The cheerful admiration of Charlotte's younger sister Sophie (s) does not rouse Werther from his melancholy. He resolves to go abroad, but while away thinks constantly of Charlotte, writing her a series of poetic, impassioned letters. She, meanwhile, cannot forget the intense young man, and realizes that her feelings for him are strong. Werther returns and, in a passionate encounter, wrings an admission of love from the anguished Charlotte before she recovers her composure and insists that he leave her. Albert, returning to find Charlotte distraught, suspects what has transpired. When a message arrives from Werther asking for the loan of Albert's pistols for a voyage, the latter grimly consents. Werther shoots himself; too late, Charlotte rushes to his side, and they exchange words of love as Werther dies.

Ljuba Welitsch as Salome

Wexler, Peter. Designer; b. New York, Oct. 31, 1936. Has designed for American Shakespeare Festival, Broadway, N.Y.C. Opera (*Lizzie Borden*, 1965), also Houston and Savonlinna Festival, Finland. His Met productions include *Troyens* (1973), *Prophète* (1977), and *Ballo* (1980).

Where the Wild Things Are. Opera in 1 act by Oliver Knussen; libretto by Maurice Sendak, after his book.

First perf., Brussels, Monnaie, Nov. 28, 1980: Manning, c. Zollmon. U.S. prem., N.Y., Avery Fisher Hall (N.Y. Philharmonic), June 7, 1984 (concert perf.): Beardsley, c. Mehta. U.S. stage prem., Minnesota Opera, Sep. 27, 1985: Beardsley, c. Zukerman.

Sendak's much-loved children's tale has become an opera with affinities to Mussorgsky and Ravel. Sent to bed without dinner because of misbehavior, the boy Max (s) travels to a lush forest and cavorts with wild monsters over which he has dominion, then escapes to sail home.

White, Willard. Bass; b. Jamaica, West Indies, Oct. 10, 1946. Studied with Beverly Johnson and Giorgio Tozzi, Juilliard, N.Y.; debut as Colline, N.Y.C. Opera, 1974, later also singing Giorgio (*Puritani*), Créon (*Médée*), and Osmin with this company. Sang Father (*Treemonisha*) in Houston; has also appeared with San Francisco Opera and Spring Opera, and at Glyndebourne (*Porgy*, 1986).

Whitehill, Clarence. Baritone; b. near Parnell, Iowa, Nov. 5, 1871; d. New York, Dec. 18, 1932. Studied in Chicago, with Giraudet and Sbriglia in Paris, and later with Stockhausen in Frankfurt; debut as Donner, Monnaie, Brussels, 1898. Sang at Opéra-Comique, Paris (1899), Bayreuth (1904–09), Covent Garden (1905), and Paris Opéra (1909). Met debut as Amfortas, Nov. 25, 1909; in 19 seasons, he sang 317 perfs. of 26 roles, including Wagner parts, Golaud, Escamillo, and Athanaël (*Thaïs*). Created Delius' Koanga, Elberfeld, 1904. Also sang at Chicago Opera (1911–17).

Wolfgang Windgassen as Siegfried

Widerspenstigen Zähmung, Der (The Taming of the Shrew). Opera in 4 acts by Goetz; libretto by Joseph Viktor Widmann, after Shakespeare's comedy.

First perf., Mannheim, Oct. 11, 1874: Ottiker, Schlosser. U.S. prem., N.Y., theater unknown, 1886. Met prem., Mar. 15, 1916: Rappold, Ober, Sembach, Whitehill, Goritz, c. Bodanzky. d. Sievert, p. Heythekkar. 2 perfs. in 1 season.

In the pre-Wagnerian tradition of Nicolai, an opera much admired by Shaw, among others). In renaissance Padua, so that Lucentio (t) may marry Bianca (s), Petruchio (bar) agrees to marry her termagant older sister Katharina (ms), and succeeds in wooing and taming her.

Wilde, Oscar. British writer (1854–1900). Operas based on his writings include *Eine florentinische Tragödie* (Zemlinsky), *Salome* (R. Strauss), and *Der Zwerg* (Zemlinsky).

Wildschütz, Der (The Poacher). Opera in 3 acts by Lortzing; libretto by the composer, after A. von Kotzebue's play *Der Rehbock*.

First perf., Leipzig, Dec. 31, 1842. U.S. prem., Brooklyn, Theater-Lokale des Herrn Flossman, Mar. 1856.

A popular work in the German bourgeois tradition. The schoolmaster Baculus (bs), caught accidentally poaching on the lands of the Count (bar), is assisted by the Count's sister (s), who in the guise of a schoolboy offers to disguise herself as Baculus' fiancée Gretchen and intercede with the Count. Amazingly, all is finally resolved.

Williams, Camilla. Soprano; b. Danville, Va., Oct. 18, 1922. Studied at Virginia State College, in Philadelphia and N.Y. Debut as Butterfly, N.Y.C. Opera, 1946; with the company until 1954, also singing Nedda, Mimi, Aida. In Vienna, sang Annina (*Saint of Bleecker Street*), 1955. Repertory also included Marguerite, Ilia (*Idomeneo*), and Aida; she was Bess in first complete recording of *Porgy*.

William Tell. See *Guillaume Tell*.

Windgassen, Wolfgang. Tenor; b. Annemasse, French Savoy, June 26, 1914, of German parents; d. Stuttgart, Sep. 8, 1974. Studied with his father Fritz, a leading tenor, then at Stuttgart Conservatory with Maria Ranzow and Alfons Fischer; debut as Alvaro (*Forza*), Pforzheim, 1941. After the war, he was a regular member of the Stuttgart Opera, 1945–72, specializing first in lighter repertory (Hoffmann, Tamino, the Lortzing operas), then moving into the Wagnerian roles that became the center of his career. International attention came with his Parsifal in the first postwar Bayreuth festival, and he sang there every summer until 1970, in all the major tenor roles, most frequently Siegfried and Tristan. He also sang at La Scala (debut, Florestan, 1952), the Paris Opéra (debut, Parsifal, 1954), and Covent Garden (debut, Tristan, 1954), where he was the regular Siegfried in *Ring* cycles through 1966. His Met career consisted of 6 perfs. as Siegmund (debut, Jan. 22, 1957) and the two Siegfrieds; in his prime, the Met offered too few Wagner performances to entice him, and he sang only once more in America, as Tristan opposite Nilsson in San Francisco, 1970. That same year, he took up operatic production, and was director of the Stuttgart Opera, 1972–74.

The leading heldentenor of the postwar generation, Windgassen offered a leaner sound than Melchior, and matched it to Wagner's demands with canny economy. An intelligent, musicianly artist with a secure technique and attractive tone, he became a lively and convincing actor under Wieland Wagner's tutelage. His portrayals are well preserved on numerous recordings.

Winkelmann [Winckelmann], **Hermann.** Tenor; b. Brunswick, Germany, Mar. 8, 1849; d. Vienna, Jan. 18, 1912. Studied in Paris and Hanover; debut as Manrico, Sondershausen, 1875. Created Wagner's Parsifal, Bayreuth, 1882. Sang Tristan, Lohengrin, Tannhäuser in London, 1882; member, Vienna Court Opera, 1883–1906, in roles such as Florestan, Masaniello, Pollione, Dalibor. In the U.S., he sang in Theodore Thomas' 1884 Wagner festivals.

Winters, Lawrence. Baritone; b. King's Creek, S.C.; Nov. 12, 1915; d. Hamburg, Sep. 24, 1965. Studied at Howard U. and with Todd Duncan; after debut as Amonasro, N.Y.C. Opera, 1948, remained with company until 1956. Debut at Hamburg State Opera in same role, 1952; sang Porgy in first complete recording of Gershwin's opera. Also sang in Berlin, San Francisco (King in *Kluge*, 1958).

Witherspoon, Herbert. Bass and manager; b. Buffalo, N.Y., July 21, 1873; d. New York, May 10, 1935. Studied with Stoeckel at Yale, later with Bouhy in Paris and Lamperti in Berlin; operatic debut as Ramfis, Savage's company, N.Y., 1898. Met debut as Titurel (*Parsifal*), Nov. 26, 1908; during 8 Met seasons, he sang most prominently in German roles. After 1916, he taught, becoming president of the Chicago Musical College (1925–29). As manager of the Chicago Civic Opera (1930–31), his stringent economies failed to save the ailing company. He directed the Cincinnati Conservatory of Music (1933–34), then taught at Juilliard, N.Y., and in 1935 was named Gatti-Casazza's successor as Met general manager. On the eve of departure for Europe in search of talent, he died of a heart attack in the theater; his assistant, Edward Johnson, became general manager.

Wittrisch, Marcel. Tenor; b. Antwerp, Belgium, Oct. 1, 1901, of German parents; d. Stuttgart, June 3, 1955.

Studied in Munich and Leipzig, also Milan; debut as Konrad (*Hans Heiling*), Halle, 1925. Sang in Brunswick (1927–29), Berlin (1929–44), Stuttgart (1950–55), also at Covent Garden (Tamino and Alfred in *Fledermaus*, 1931) and Bayreuth (Lohengrin, 1937).

Wixell, Ingvar. Baritone; b. Luleå, Sweden, May 7, 1931. Studied in Stockholm; operatic debut as Silvio, Stockholm Opera, 1955. Remained with that company until joining the Deutsche Oper, Berlin, 1967, also singing at Covent Garden and Glyndebourne. Created Pentheus (*Bassarids*), Salzburg, 1966. Met debut as Rigoletto, Jan. 29, 1973; subsequent roles have been Boccanegra, Germont, Amonasro, Marcello, Renato, and Scarpia.

Woitach, Richard. Conductor; b. Binghamton, N.Y., July 27, 1935. Graduate of Eastman School, Rochester. Assistant conductor at Met (1959–68); from 1973, resident associate conductor. Since his debut (*Butterfly*, Sep. 18, 1974), he has led many performances in N.Y. and on tour.

Wolf, Hugo. Composer; b. Windischgraz, Styria [now Slovenj Gradec, Yugoslavia], Mar. 13, 1860; d. Vienna, Feb. 22, 1903. Studied with Fuchs at Vienna Conservatory. Music critic for the *Wiener Salonblatt* (1883–87), he resigned to devote himself entirely to composition, primarily of subtly crafted art songs. His only completed opera, *Der Corregidor* (1895), lacked dramatic substance and was unsuccessful; only 600 measures of *Manuel Venegas* were completed before Wolf's calamitous nervous breakdown in 1897.

Wolff, Albert. Conductor and composer; b. Paris, Jan. 19, 1884; d. Paris, Feb. 20, 1970. At the Opéra-Comique, repetiteur (1906), conductor (1911), and music director (1921–24 and briefly in 1945). At the Met, he succeeded Monteux in the French repertory (1919–22), leading 74 perfs., including the premiere of his own *Oiseau Bleu*. Active in Paris for the remainder of his career, leading important premieres, including *Mamelles de Tirésias*.

Wolff, Beverly. Mezzo-soprano; b. Atlanta, Ga., Nov. 6, 1928. Studied in Atlanta and Philadelphia; debut as Dinah (*Trouble in Tahiti*), CBS TV, 1952. N.Y.C. Opera debut in same role, 1958; she returned to the company in 1963 as Cherubino, later singing Siebel, Carmen, Sesto (*Giulio Cesare*), and Sara (*Roberto Devereux*). Created Moore's Carry Nation, 1966, Lawrence, Kans.

Wolf-Ferrari, Ermanno. Composer; b. Venice, Jan. 12, 1876; d. Venice, Jan. 21, 1948. Son of a Bavarian painter and an Italian mother, he studied with Rheinberger and became a protégé of Boito in Milan during the 1890s. His first opera, *Cenerentola* (1900), failed in Venice, but its revision was well received in Germany, where all his subsequent prewar operas, though composed to Italian texts, were first heard. The comic operas after Goldoni, *Le Donne Curiose* (1930) and *I Quattro Rusteghi* (1906), are brilliant pastiches of 18th-c. music, as are the one-act *Il Segreto di Susanna* (1909) and *L'Amore Medico*, after Molière. By contrast, *I Gioielli della Madonna* (1911) is a full-blown, even vulgar verismo opera. Wolf-Ferrari suffered a nervous collapse during World War I and composed little until the mid-1920s. His postwar comedies, including *Gli Amanti Sposi* (1925), *Sly* (1927), and *La Vedova Scaltra* (1931), were not widely performed, and in his last years he composed only instrumental music.

Wozzeck – (1984). Hildegard Behrens and Christian Boesch

Wozzeck. Opera in 3 acts by Berg; libretto by the composer, after Georg Büchner's drama.

First perf., Berlin, State Opera, Dec. 14, 1925: Johanson, L. Schützendorf, c. Kleiber. U.S. prem., Philadelphia, Academy of Music, Mar. 19, 1931: Roselle, Ivantzoff, c. Stokowski. Met prem., Mar. 5, 1959 (in Eng.): Steber, Uhde, c. Böhm, d. Neher, p. Graf. Wozzeck has also been sung at the Met by Evans, Glossop, van Dam, Monk; Marie by Pilarczyk, Lear, Silja, Behrens; the opera has also been conducted by Davis and Levine. 39 perfs. in 7 seasons.

An intense expressionist score, combining highly disciplined formal structure with freely conceived contextual atonality.

The soldier Wozzeck (bar) is the subject of manipulative experiments by the Doctor (bs) and confusing preachments and exhortations by the Captain (t). With his common-law wife Marie (s), he has had a son, to whose support he contributes the money he receives for participating in the Doctor's experiments. Wozzeck begins to have hallucinations, and his discovery that the frustrated Marie has begun an affair with the Drum Major (t) plunges him deeper into a frenzied state of agitation. After seeing the pair together at a dancing hall, he leads the unsuspecting Marie into a wood and cuts her throat. He throws the knife into a pool and flees but is compelled to return to the scene in fearful search of the weapon; he walks into the pool and drowns himself. Marie's body is found, and neighbor children tell her little son that his mother is dead.

Wunderlich, Fritz. Tenor; b. Kusel, Palatinate, Germany, Sep. 26, 1930; d. Heidelberg, Sep. 17, 1966. Studied with Margarethe von Winterfeldt in Freiburg; a school performance of Tamino (1954) led to his professional debut as Eislinger (*Meistersinger*), Stuttgart, 1955. After two years there, he joined the Frankfurt Opera (1958–60), and moved to the Bavarian State Opera, Munich, in 1960; from 1962, he also appeared in Vienna. His repertory included Mozart, Alfredo, Lenski, Jeník (*Bartered Bride*), Leukippos (*Daphne*), and Palestrina; he created Tiresias in Orff's *Oedipus* (1959) and Christoph in Egk's *Verlobung in San Domingo* (1963). Salzburg debut as Henry (*Schweigsame Frau*), 1960; he later sang Tamino and Belmonte there. Covent Garden debut as Ottavio (1965). Scheduled to make his Met debut as Ottavio on Oct. 8, 1966, he died after a fall down stairs. The best German lyric tenor of his day (also at home in operetta), Wunderlich produced his suavely beautiful voice with flair and musicality.

Y

Yannopoulos, Dino [Konstantin]. Producer; b. Athens, Dec. 15, 1919. Assisted Graf in Salzburg (1937) and directed opera and drama in Athens (1940–45). His many Met productions include *Tabarro* (1946), *Boris* and *Don Giovanni* (1953), *Chénier* and *Meistersinger* (1954), *Norma* and *Ernani* (1956), and *Rosenkavalier* (1964). Other productions for Montreal Opera Guild, Teatro Colón, Buenos Aires, San Francisco, and N.Y.C. Opera. Since 1977, director, Academy of Vocal Arts, Phil.; director, Corfu Festival.

Yaw, Ellen Beach. Soprano; b. Boston, Erie County, N.Y., Sep. 14, 1869; d. Covina, Calif., Sep. 9, 1974. Studied in U.S. and with Marchesi in Paris; debut in St. Paul, Minnesota, 1894. Despite her remarkable high register and ability to trill in thirds, Yaw's operatic career was limited to relatively few appearances in Europe and America, including a single Met *Lucia* (Mar. 21, 1908). In London, she created Sultana in Sullivan's *Rose of Persia* (1899).

Yeend, Frances. Soprano; b. Vancouver, Wash., Jan. 28, 1918. Studied at Washington State U.; debut as Nedda, Spokane, Wash. Sang Ellen in U.S. premiere of *Grimes*, Tanglewood, 1946. N.Y.C. Opera debut, Violetta, 1948; with company until 1959, in roles including Countess (*Nozze*), Micaela, Marguerite, and Eva. Met debut as Chrysothemis, Feb. 13, 1961; in 3 seasons, sang 8 perfs. of 3 roles, including Violetta and Gutrune. Also sang at Edinburgh (1951), Covent Garden (Mimi, 1953), and Verona Arena (Turandot, 1958).

Z

Zaide. Opera (unfinished) in 2 acts by Mozart; libretto by Johann Andreas Schachtner, after Franz Joseph Sebastiani's singspiel *Das Serail*.

First perf., Frankfurt, Jan. 27, 1866 (completed by Gollmick and Anton André). U.S. prem., Lenox, Mass., Tanglewood, Aug. 8, 1955 (in Eng.): Cardillo, Lussier, H. Boatwright, Zulick, c. Caldwell.

Probably begun and abandoned in 1779; in this singspiel, with its rescue story of Europeans imprisoned in the Near East prefiguring *Entführung*, Mozart tried out some of the musical ideas he would refine in the later opera.

Zampa. Opera in 3 acts by Hérold; libretto by A. Honoré Joseph Mélesville.

First perf., Paris, Opéra-Comique, May 3, 1831. U.S. prem., Boston, Tremont Theater, July 26, 1833.

A dashing opéra comique with a once-famous overture, set in 17th-c. Sicily. The pirate Zampa (bar) attempts to steal Camilla (s), betrothed of Alfonso (t, actually Zampa's brother), but is thwarted when a marble statue, inhabited by the ghost of his brokenhearted former sweetheart, drags him away.

Zampieri, Mara. Soprano; b. Padua, Italy, May 24, 1941. Studied at Padua Conservatory; debut in Pavia. Scala debut as Amalia (*Masnadieri*), 1977, followed by other Verdi roles. In Vienna, sang in *Giuramento* (1979),

Attila (1980), and *Macbeth* (1982). Covent Garden debut as Tosca, 1984. Also appears in Munich, Berlin, Buenos Aires, San Francisco.

Zancanaro, Giorgio. Baritone. Debut in *Puritani*, Teatro Nuovo, Milan; Scala debut as Ford, 1981. Met appearances as Renato in *Ballo* (debut, Oct. 26, 1982) and di Luna. Sings regularly at Vienna State Opera, also appears in Frankfurt, Rome, Hamburg, Paris, Zurich, and London.

Zandonai, Riccardo. Composer; b. Sacco di Rovereto, Trentino, Italy, May 28, 1883; d. Pesaro, June 12, 1944. Studied with Mascagni at Pesaro Liceo Musicale. Introduced in 1907 by Boito to Giulio Ricordi, who launched *Il Grillo del Focolare* (1908), hoping to find in Zandonai the successor to Puccini. The veristic *Conchita*, after Louÿs (1911; presented in N.Y. by the Chicago–Philadelphia Company, 1913) and the archaizing *Francesca da Rimini* (1914) were widely performed at first. Other operas: *Giulietta e Romeo* (1922), *I Cavalieri di Ekebù* (1925).

Zanelli [Morales], **Renato.** Baritone, later tenor; b. Valparaíso, Chile, Apr. 1, 1892; d. Santiago, Mar. 25, 1935. Studied in Chile; debut as Valentin, Santiago, 1916. Met debut as Amonasro, Nov. 19, 1919; in 4 seasons, sang 13 perfs. of 6 roles, including Tonio, King Dodon, Valentin, Don Carlo (*Forza*), and di Luna. After further study, tenor debut as Raoul (*Huguenots*), San Carlo, Naples, 1924; sang Wagner parts and Otello in Italy, London, and Buenos Aires.

Zar lässt sich photographieren, Der (The Tsar Has his Picture Taken). Opera in 1 act by Weill; libretto by Georg Kaiser.

First perf., Leipzig, Neues Theater, Feb. 18, 1928: Kögel, Janowska, Horand, c. Brecher. U.S. prem., N.Y., Juilliard School, Oct. 27, 1949 (in Eng.).

A satire on anarchist conspiracies, with popular-music elements. During a trip to Paris, the Tsar (bar) unwittingly outsmarts his would-be assassins.

Zar und Zimmermann (Tsar and Carpenter). Opera in 3 acts by Lortzing; libretto by the composer, after the play *Le Bourgmestre de Sardam* by A.H.J. Mélesville, J.T. Merle, and E.C. de Boirie.

First perf., Leipzig, Stadttheater, Dec. 22, 1837: Günther, Frau Lortzing, A. Lortzing, Richter, Berthold. U.S. prem., N.Y., Astor Place, Dec. 9, 1851. Met prem., New Theater, Nov. 30, 1909: Alten, Mattfeld, Reiss, Jörn, Whitehill, Goritz, c. Hertz, p. Schertel. 3 perfs. in 1 season.

This engaging bourgeois comedy remains popular in Germany. In 1698, Tsar Peter the Great (bar), disguised as "Peter Michaelov" and working in the shipyards of Saardam, Holland, befriends another Russian, Peter Ivanov (t), leading to complexities of love and mistaken identity.

zarzuela. A type of Spanish operetta, dating back to the 17th c., combining music and spoken dialogue.

Zauberflöte, Die (The Magic Flute). Opera in 2 acts by Mozart; libretto by Schikaneder, after a fairy tale by Wieland.

First perf., Vienna, auf der Wieden, Sep. 30, 1791: with Schikaneder as Papageno, Josefa Hofer as the Queen of Night. U.S. prem., N.Y., Park, Apr. 17, 1833. Met prem., Mar. 30, 1900 (in Ital.): Eames, Sembrich, Dippel,

Campanari, Plançon, c. Mancinelli, p. Baudo. Later Met productions: Nov. 23, 1912: Destinn, Parks, Slezak, Goritz, Lankow, c. Hertz, d. Kautsky/Heil, p. Schertel; Nov. 6, 1926: Rethberg, Talley, Laubenthal, Schützendorf, Bender, c. Bodanzky d. Soudeikine, p. Thewman; Dec. 11, 1941 (in Eng.): Novotná, Bok, Kullman, Brownlee, Kipnis, c. Walter, d. Rychtarik, p. Graf; Feb. 23, 1956 (in Eng.): Amara, Peters, Sullivan, Uppman, Hines, c. Walter, d. Horner, p. Graf; Feb. 19, 1967: Lorengar, Popp, Gedda, Prey, Hines, c. Krips, d. Chagall, p. Rennert. Pamina has also been sung at the Met by Gadski, Steber, Raskin, Zylis-Gara, Valente, Popp; the Queen of Night by Hempel, Berger, Deutekom; Tamino by Tucker, Valletti, Shirley, Schreier, Burrows, Alva; Papageno by Harrell, Reardon, Boesch, Duesing; Sarastro by E. de Reszke, Pinza, Tozzi, Siepi, Macurdy, Sotin. 202 perfs. in 30 seasons.

Mozart's joyous and mysterious singspiel with its blend of simple song and more complex forms from the buffa and seria operatic genres, was a cornerstone in the edifice of early Romantic opera, and a guiding inspiration to Beethoven and Weber.

An eastern country, legendary times. Prince Tamino (t) is saved from a serpent by the Three Ladies (s, s, a) of the Queen of Night (s), who show him a portrait of the Queen's daughter Pamina (s). Tamino is enchanted. The Queen promises the prince her daughter's hand if he will rescue her from Sarastro (bs), who is described as an evil sorcerer. Accompanied by Papageno (bar), a birdcatcher in the Queen's employ, Tamino sets out. They take along a magic flute and glockenspiel, with instructions that three genii (child trebles) will also guide their way. The two become separated; Papageno finds Pamina in the power of the Moor Monostatos (t) and helps her attempt an escape; Tamino enters a temple where he learns of the Queen's evil nature and of Sarastro's noble order, which he resolves to join. Tamino resists all the temptations posed by the trials of initiation, but leaves Pamina bewildered and grieving when he maintains the required silence in her presence. Although Papageno endures his trials with complaints and succumbs to most of the temptations, he too is rewarded with a sweetheart, Papagena (s). With Pamina at his side, Tamino emerges victorious from his final trials. The Queen and her ladies, foiled in their attempt to storm the temple, sink into the earth. In a grand ceremony, Sarastro proclaims the triumph of light over the powers of darkness.

Zazà. Opera in 4 acts by Leoncavallo; libretto by the composer, after the play by C. Simon and P. Berton.

First perf., Milan, Lirico, Nov. 10, 1900: Storchio, Garbin, Sammarco, c. Toscanini. U.S. prem., San Francisco, Tivoli Opera House, Nov. 27, 1903. Met prem., Jan. 16, 1920: Farrar, Crimi, Amato, c. Moranzoni, d. J. Fox, p. Ordynski. 20 perfs. in 3 seasons.

A vivid verismo score, full of juicy writing for the principals, set in and around Paris, 1900. Having won the affections of Milio Dufresne (t) on a wager, the music-hall actress Zazà (s) falls in love with him, but is led by her partner Cascart (bar) to discover that Milio is married and loves his wife.

Zeffirelli, Franco. Producer and designer; b. Florence, Feb. 12, 1923. First an actor, then designer and assistant to Visconti for plays and films (1949–52), his first operatic work was at La Scala, designing *Italiana* (1953), then designing and directing *Cenerentola* (1954). Covent Garden debut, *Lucia* (1959) with Sutherland; U.S. debut, at

Dallas Opera, *Traviata* with Callas (1958). For the Met, he has staged *Falstaff* (1964), *Antony and Cleopatra* (for which he served as librettist, 1966), *Cavalleria* and *Pagliacci* (1970), *Otello* (1972), *Bohème* (1981), *Tosca* (1985), and *Turandot* (1987). His many films include the operas *Traviata*, *Cavalleria*, *Pagliacci*, and *Otello*. A dominant figure in Italian opera who works at all the leading theaters; grandiose scale and authenticity of detail are hallmarks of his highly picturesque productions.

Zeitoper (Ger.). A term used in Germany in the 1920s to refer to operas with aggressively "up-to-date" subject matter (e.g., Krenek's *Jonny spielt auf*).

Zemlinsky, Alexander von. Composer and conductor; b. Vienna, Oct. 14, 1871; d. Larchmont, N.Y., Mar. 15, 1942. Studied with Fuchs at Vienna Conservatory; composition teacher of Schoenberg and Korngold. Conducted at Vienna Volksoper (1906–08) and Court Opera (1908–11), Deutsches Landestheater, Prague (1911–27), and Kroll Opera, Berlin (1927–32); emigrated to U.S. after the Anschluss (1938). Zemlinsky's operas, in an expressionistic tonal idiom, include *Kleider machen Leute* (1910, rev. 1922); *Eine florentinische Tragödie* (1917); *Der Zwerg* (1922); and *Der Kreidekreis* (1933). His music has been widely revived in the Eighties.

Zenatello, Giovanni. Tenor; b. Verona, Italy, Feb. 22, 1876; d. New York, Feb. 11, 1949. Studied as baritone with Zannoni, Verona, later with Moretti, Milan; debut as Silvio (*Pagliacci*), Belluno, 1898. In 1899, at Fondo, Naples, he replaced an indisposed colleague as Canio, and thereafter sang as a tenor, eventually reaching La Scala (1902–07), where his roles included the Fausts of Berlioz and Gounod, Riccardo (*Ballo*), Walter (*Loreley*), José, and Radames; he created Vassili (Giordano's *Siberia*, 1903), Pinkerton (both Milan and Brescia versions), and Ricci (Cilea's *Gloria*). Sang at Colón, Buenos Aires (1903–10), and Covent Garden (1905–09, 1926). At Manhattan Opera, debut as Enzo (*Gioconda*), 1907; later roles included Canio and Otello. On the 1909 Met tour he sang Radames, Faust, and Pinkerton, replacing the indisposed Caruso, but never appeared with the company in N.Y. He also sang in Boston (1910–17) and Chicago (1912–13). In 1913, he sang Radames at opening of Verona Arena, which he later managed. In N.Y., he and his wife, mezzo Maria Gay, taught pupils including Lily Pons and Nino Martini. Despite his baritonal beginnings, Zenatello's dramatic tenor had a ringing top and remained a powerful instrument until his retirement from the stage in 1928.

Zeno, Apostolo. Librettist; b. Venice, Dec. 11, 1668; d. Venice, Nov. 11, 1750. He wrote his first libretto in 1695, *Gl'Inganni Felici* for Pollarolo, and eventually became court poet at Vienna (1718–29), where he wrote 18 librettos, mostly for the music of Antonio Caldara, before retiring, to be succeeded by Metastasio. He simplified the plots and regularized the forms of opera seria, usually drawing his subjects from ancient history.

Ziegler, Edward. Manager; b. Baltimore, Mar. 25, 1870; d. New York, Oct. 25, 1947. A journalist and critic, he advised Otto Kahn on artistic ventures, becoming in 1916 administrative secretary of the Met. From 1920 until 1945, he was the company's assistant general manager, in charge of administrative and financial operations; during the Depression years, he devised the economy measures that kept the Met afloat. Little known to the public,

Ziegler was the indispensable right hand of managers Gatti-Casazza and Johnson.

Zigeunerbaron, Der (The Gypsy Baron). Operetta in 3 acts by J. Strauss; libretto by Ignaz Schnitzer, after Maurus Jókai's story *Saffi*.

First perf., Vienna, Theater an der Wien, Oct. 24, 1885: Collin, Hartmann, Reisser, Streitmann, Girardi, c. J. Strauss. U.S. prem., N.Y., Casino Theater, Feb. 15, 1886 (in Eng.). Met prem., Feb. 15, 1906: Alten, Rappold, Homer, Dippel, Goritz, c. Franko, d. J. Fox, p. Conried. Later Met production: Nov. 25, 1959 (in Eng.): Della Casa, Hurley, Resnik, Gedda, W. Slezak, c. Leinsdorf, d. Gérard, p. Ritchard. 10 perfs. in 2 seasons.

Strauss' most ambitious operetta has a strong infusion of Hungarian idiom to match the setting, but also a plot of numbing complications. Returning to claim his castle and lands, Baron Barinkay (t) finds them occupied by gypsies. He falls in love with the gypsy girl Saffi (s), who is discovered to be a princess.

Zimmermann, Bernd Alois. Composer; b. Bliesheim, near Cologne, Germany, Mar. 20, 1918; d. Königsdorf, near Cologne, Aug. 10, 1970. Studied composition with Lemacher, Jarnach, Fortner, and Leibowitz. In addition to many instrumental works, he composed *Die Soldaten* (1965), considered by many the most important German opera since Berg, a work based on his technique of "collage," or eclectic and simultaneous musical quotation. At the time of his suicide, another opera, *Medea*, remained unfinished.

Zipprodt, Patricia. Designer; b. Evanston, Ill., Feb. 24, 1925. Has designed costumes for Broadway (*Fiddler on the Roof*, *Cabaret*, and *Pippin*), American Ballet Theater,

television (*Glass Managerie*), and film (*The Graduate*). For the Met, costumes for *Tannhäuser* (1977) and *Barbiere* (1982).

Zschau, Marilyn. Soprano; b. Chicago, Feb. 9, 1944. Studied at Juilliard School and with John Lester in Montana; toured with Met National Company (1965–66). Debut at Vienna Volksoper as Marietta (*Tote Stadt*), 1967; State Opera debut as Composer (*Ariadne*), 1971. N.Y.C. Opera debut as Minnie (*Fanciulla*), 1978; other roles there included Butterfly and Odabella (*Attila*). Met debut as Musetta (Feb. 4, 1985), later singing Tosca. La Scala debut, Dyer's Wife in *Frau* (1986).

Zwerg, Der (The Dwarf). Opera in 1 act by Zemlinsky; libretto by Georg Klaren, after Oscar Wilde's story *The Birthday of the Infanta*.

First perf., Cologne, May 29, 1922: c. Klemperer.

Zemlinsky's macabre opera has recently been revived with success, using a modified libretto and Wilde's title. The spoiled Infanta Donna Clara (s) is given an ugly Dwarf (t) as a birthday present, and although she treats him as a toy, he falls in love with her. When he sees himself in a mirror for the first time, he dies of a broken heart; the Infanta is annoyed that her toy has broken.

Zylis-Gara, Teresa. Soprano; b. Vilna, Poland [now Vilnius, U.S.S.R.], Jan. 23, 1935. Studied in Lódź; debut in *Halka*, Kraków, 1957. Sang in Germany; debuts at Glyndebourne (Octavian, 1966), Covent Garden (Violetta, 1968), in Paris (1966) and Salzburg (1968). Met debut as Donna Elvira, Dec. 17, 1968; later roles there included Desdemona, Tatiana, Suor Angelica, Fiordiligi, Elsa, Elisabeth, the Marschallin, and Manon Lescaut.

Franco Zeffirelli's production of *Turandot* (1987). Éva Marton, Plácido Domingo, and Hugues Cuénod

A Chronology of Opera
For Further Reading
Sources of Illustrations

A Chronology of Opera

1594 *L'Amfiparnaso* (Vecchi), probably in Modena

1597 *Dafne* (Peri), Florence

1600 Feb.: *La Rappresentazione di Anima e di Corpo* (Cavalieri), Rome
Oct. 6: *Euridice* (Peri), Florence

1602 Dec. 5: *Euridice* (Caccini), Florence

1607 Feb.: *La Favola d'Orfeo* (Monteverdi), Mantua

1608 Jan.: *La Dafne* (Gagliano), Mantua
May 28: *L'Arianna* (Monteverdi), Mantua

1624 *Il Combattimento di Tancredi e Clorinda* (Monteverdi), Venice

1627 Apr. 23: *Dafne* (Schütz), first German opera, Torgau

1637 Feb. or Mar.: Teatro San Cassiano, Venice, first public opera house, opens with Mannelli's *Andromeda*

1641 Feb.: *Il Ritorno d'Ulisse in Patria* (Monteverdi), Venice

1642 Autumn: *L'Incoronazione di Poppea* (Monteverdi), Venice

1644 *L'Ormindo* (Cavalli), Venice

1651 *La Calisto* (Cavalli), Venice

1671 Mar. 3: Académie de l'Opéra, Paris, opens with Perrin's and Cambert's *Pomone*, first French opera

1672 Nov. 15: Lully opens Académie Royale de Musique (Opéra), Paris, with his *Les Fêtes de l'Amour et de Bacchus*

c.1684 *Venus and Adonis* (Blow), London

1684 Jan. 18: *Amadis* (Lully), Paris

1689 Spring (?): *Dido and Aeneas* (Purcell), London

1692 Apr.: *The Fairy Queen* (Purcell), London

1693 Dec. 4: *Médée* (M.-A. Charpentier), Paris

1705 Apr. 9: Queen's Theatre, Haymarket, opens with Greber's *Gli Amori d'Ergasto*, first Italian opera in London

1711 Feb. 24: *Rinaldo* (Handel), London.

1712 Nov. 22: *Il Pastor Fido* (Handel), London

1713 Jan. 10: *Teseo* (Handel), London

1724 Feb. 20: *Giulio Cesare in Egitto* (Handel), London
Oct. 31: *Tamerlano* (Handel), London

1725 Feb. 13: *Rodelinda* (Handel), London

1728 Jan. 29: *The Beggar's Opera* (Pepusch), London

1731 Mar. 26: *Acis and Galatea* (Handel), London (first public perf.)

1732 Feb. 15: *Sosarme, Rè di Media* (Handel), London
Dec. 7: First theater at Covent Garden, London, opens

1733 Jan. 27: *Orlando* (Handel), London
Aug. 28: *La Serva Padrona* (Pergolesi), Naples
Oct. 1: *Hippolyte et Aricie* (Rameau), Paris

1735 Jan. 8: *Ariodante* (Handel), London
Apr. 16: *Alcina* (Handel), London
Aug. 23: *Les Indes Galantes* (Rameau), Paris

1736 May 23: *Atalanta* (Handel), London

1737 Nov. 4: Teatro San Carlo, Naples, opens with Sarro's *Achille in Sciro*

1738 Apr. 15: *Serse* (Handel), London

1739 Nov. 19: *Dardanus* (Rameau), Paris

1740 Apr. 9: Teatro Regio, Turin, opens with Feo's *Arsace*

1742 Dec. 7: Berlin Court Opera opens with Graun's *Cleopatra e Cesare*

1743 Feb. 18: *Samson* (Handel), London

1744 Feb. 10: *Semele* (Handel), London

1748 May 14: Theater bei der Hofburg (Burgtheater), Vienna, opens with Gluck's *Semiramide Riconosciuta*

1753 Oct. 12: Residenztheater (Cuvilliés-Theater), Munich, opens with Ferrandini's *Catone in Utica*
Mar. 1: *Le Devin du Village* (Rousseau), Paris

1760 Feb. 6: *La Buona Figliuola* (Piccinni), Rome

1762 Oct. 5: *Orfeo ed Euridice* (Gluck), Vienna

1767 Dec. 26: *Alceste* (Gluck), Vienna

1768 Sep. or Oct.: *Bastien und Bastienne* (Mozart), Vienna

1770 Nov. 3: *Paride ed Elena* (Gluck), Vienna
Dec. 26: *Mitridate, Rè di Ponto* (Mozart), Milan

1771 Oct. 17: *Ascanio in Alba* (Mozart), Milan

1772 Dec. 26: *Lucio Silla* (Mozart), Milan

1774 Apr. 19: *Iphigénie en Aulide* (Gluck), Paris

1775 Jan. 13: *La Finta Giardiniera* (Mozart), Munich
Apr. 23: *Il Rè Pastore* (Mozart), Salzburg

1777 Sep. 23: *Armide* (Gluck), Paris

1778 Aug. 3: Teatro alla Scala, Milan, opens with Salieri's *Europa Riconosciuta*

1779 May 18: *Iphigénie en Tauride* (Gluck), Paris

1781 Jan. 29: *Idomeneo* (Mozart), Munich

1782 July 16: *Die Entführung aus dem Serail* (Mozart), Vienna
Sep. 14: *I Due Litiganti* (Sarti), Milan

1786 Feb. 7: *Der Schauspieldirektor* (Mozart), Vienna
May 1: *Le Nozze di Figaro* (Mozart), Vienna
Nov. 17: *Una Cosa Rara* (Martin y Soler), Vienna

1787 Oct. 29: *Don Giovanni* (Mozart), Prague

1790 Jan. 26: *Così Fan Tutte* (Mozart), Vienna

1791 Sep. 6: *La Clemenza di Tito* (Mozart), Prague
Sep. 30: *Die Zauberflöte* (Mozart), Vienna

1792 Feb. 7: *Il Matrimonio Segreto* (Cimarosa), Vienna
May 16: Teatro La Fenice, Venice, opens with Paisiello's *I Giuochi d'Agrigento*

1797 Mar. 13: *Médée* (Cherubini), Paris

1800 Jan. 16: *Les Deux Journées* (Cherubini), Paris

1805 Nov. 20: *Fidelio* (Beethoven), Vienna

1807 Dec. 15: *La Vestale* (Spontini), Paris

1809 Sep. 18: Second theater at Covent Garden, London, opens
Nov. 28: *Fernand Cortez* (Spontini), Paris

1810 Nov. 3: *La Cambiale di Matrimonio* (Rossini), Venice

1811 June 4: *Abu Hassan* (Weber), Munich

1812 May 9: *La Scala di Seta* (Rossini), Venice
Sep. 26: *La Pietra del Paragone* (Rossini), Milan

1813 late Jan.: *Il Signor Bruschino* (Rossini), Venice
Feb. 6: *Tancredi* (Rossini), Venice
May 22: *L'Italiana in Algeri* (Rossini), Venice

1814 Aug. 14: *Il Turco in Italia* (Rossini), Milan

1815 Oct. 4: *Elisabetta, Regina d'Inghilterra* (Rossini), Naples

1816 Feb. 20: *Il Barbiere di Siviglia* (Rossini), Rome
Dec. 4: *Otello* (Rossini), Naples

1817 Jan. 25: *La Cenerentola* (Rossini), Rome
May 31: *La Gazza Ladra* (Rossini), Milan
Nov. 11: *Armida* (Rossini), Naples

1818 Oct. 12: Hof- und Nationaltheater, Munich, opens
Mar. 5: *Mosè in Egitto* (Rossini)

1819 Sep. 24: *La Donna del Lago* (Rossini), Naples

1820 Dec. 3: *Maometto II* (Rossini), Naples

1821 Mar. 29: *Le Maître de Chapelle* (Paer), Paris
June 18: *Der Freischütz* (Weber), Berlin

1823 Feb. 3: *Semiramide* (Rossini), Venice
Oct. 25: *Euryanthe* (Weber), Vienna

1825 June 19: *Il Viaggio a Reims* (Rossini), Paris
Nov. 29: First performance of Italian opera in the United States,
Il Barbiere di Siviglia, Park Theatre, New York
Dec. 10: *La Dame Blanche* (Boieldieu), Paris

1826 Apr. 12: *Oberon* (Weber), London
Oct. 9: *Le Siège de Corinth* (Rossini), Paris

1827 Oct. 27: *Il Pirata* (Bellini), Milan

1828 Feb. 29: *La Muette de Portici* (Auber), Paris
Mar. 29: *Der Vampyr* (Marschner), Leipzig
Aug. 20: *Le Comte Ory* (Rossini), Paris

1829 Feb. 14: *La Straniera* (Bellini), Milan
Aug. 3: *Guillaume Tell* (Rossini), Paris

1830 Jan. 28: *Fra Diavolo* (Auber), Paris
Mar. 11: *I Capuleti e i Montecchi* (Bellini), Venice
Dec. 26: *Anna Bolena* (Donizetti), Milan

1831 Mar. 6: *La Sonnambula* (Bellini), Milan
May 3: *Zampa* (Hérold), Paris
Nov. 21: *Robert le Diable* (Meyerbeer), Paris
Dec. 26: *Norma* (Bellini), Milan

1832 May 12: *L'Elisir d'Amore* (Donizetti), Milan

1833 Mar. 16: *Beatrice di Tenda* (Bellini), Venice
May 24: *Hans Heiling* (Marschner), Berlin
Nov. 18: Italian Opera House, New York, opens with *La Gazza Ladra*
Dec. 26: *Lucrezia Borgia* (Donizetti), Milan

1835 Jan. 24: *I Puritani di Scozia* (Bellini), Paris
Feb. 23: *La Juive* (Halévy), Paris
Sep. 26: *Lucia di Lammermoor* (Donizetti), Naples
Dec. 30: *Maria Stuarda* (Donizetti), Milan

1836 Feb. 29: *Les Huguenots* (Meyerbeer), Paris
Mar. 29: *Das Liebesverbot* (Wagner), Magdeburg
June 1: *Il Campanello di Notte* (Donizetti), Naples
Oct. 13: *Le Postillon de Longjumeau* (Adam), Paris
Dec. 9: *A Life for the Tsar* (Glinka), St. Petersburg

1837 Mar. 10: *Il Giuramento* (Mercadante), Milan
Oct. 29: *Roberto Devereux* (Donizetti), Naples
Dec. 22: *Zar und Zimmermann* (Lortzing), Leipzig

1838 Sep. 10: *Benvenuto Cellini* (Berlioz), Paris

1839 Nov. 17: *Oberto* (Verdi), Milan

1840 Feb. 11: *La Fille du Régiment* (Donizetti), Paris
Apr. 10: *Les Martyrs* (Donizetti), Paris.
Sep. 5: *Un Giorno di Regno* (Verdi), Milan
Dec. 2: *La Favorite* (Donizetti), Paris

1842 Mar. 9: *Nabucco* (Verdi), Milan
May 19: *Linda di Chamounix* (Donizetti), Vienna
Oct. 20: *Rienzi* (Wagner), Dresden
Dec. 9: *Russlan and Ludmila* (Glinka), St. Petersburg
Dec. 31: *Der Wildschütz* (Lortzing), Leipzig

1843 Jan. 2: *Der fliegende Holländer* (Wagner), Dresden
Jan. 3: *Don Pasquale* (Donizetti), Paris
Feb. 11: *I Lombardi alla Prima Crociata* (Verdi), Milan
Nov. 27: *The Bohemian Girl* (Balfe), London

1844 Jan. 12: *Caterina Cornaro* (Donizetti), Naples
Jan. 27: *Hunyadi László* (Erkel), Budapest
Feb. 3: Palmo's Opera House, New York, opens with *I Puritani*
Mar. 9: *Ernani* (Verdi), Venice
Nov. 3: *I Due Foscari* (Verdi), Rome
Dec. 30: *Alessandro Stradella* (Flotow), Hamburg

1845 Feb. 15: *Giovanna d'Arco* (Verdi), Milan
June 4: *Leonora* (Fry), Philadelphia
Aug. 12: *Alzira* (Verdi), Naples
Oct. 19: *Tannhäuser* (Wagner), Dresden
Nov. 15: *Maritana* (Wallace), London

1846 Mar. 17: *Attila* (Verdi), Venice
Dec. 6: *La Damnation de Faust* (Berlioz), Paris

1847 Mar. 14: *Macbeth* (Verdi), Florence
July 22: *I Masnadieri* (Verdi), London
Nov. 22: Astor Place Opera House, New York, opens with *Ernani*
Nov. 25: *Martha* (Flotow), Vienna

1848 Jan. 1: *Halka* (Moniuszko), Wilno
Oct. 25: *Il Corsaro* (Verdi), Trieste

1849 Jan. 27: *La Battaglia di Legnano* (Verdi), Rome
Mar. 9: *Die lustigen Weiber von Windsor* (Nicolai), Berlin
Apr. 16: *Le Prophète* (Meyerbeer), Paris
Dec. 8: *Luisa Miller* (Verdi), Naples

1850 Feb. 28: *Crispino e la Comare* (F. and L. Ricci), Venice

June 25: *Genoveva* (Schumann), Leipzig
Aug. 28: *Lohengrin* (Wagner), Weimar
Nov. 16: *Stiffelio* (Verdi), Trieste

1851 Mar. 11: *Rigoletto* (Verdi), Venice

1853 Jan. 19: *Il Trovatore* (Verdi), Rome
Mar. 6: *La Traviata* (Verdi), Venice

1854 Jan. 24: *Alfonso und Estrella* (Schubert), Weimar
Oct. 2: Academy of Music, New York, opens with *Norma*

1855 June 13: *Les Vêpres Siciliennes* (Verdi), Paris
Sep. 27: *Rip Van Winkle* (Bristow), New York

1856 Feb. 25: Academy of Music, Philadelphia, opens with *Il Trovatore*
May 16: *Rusalka* (Dargomijsky), St. Petersburg
Sep. 1: Present Bolshoi Theater, Moscow, opens

1857 Mar. 12: *Simon Boccanegra* (Verdi), Venice
Apr. 9: *Le Docteur Miracle* (Bizet), Paris
Apr. 25: First Teatro Colón, Buenos Aires, opens with *La Traviata*
Aug. 16: *Aroldo* (Verdi), Rimini

1858 May 15: Royal Opera House, Covent Garden, London, opens with *Les Huguenots*
Dec. 5: *Diana von Solange* (Ernest II, Duke of Saxe-Coburg-Gotha), Coburg
Dec. 15: *Der Barbier von Bagdad* (Cornelius), Weimar

1859 Feb. 17: *Un Ballo in Maschera* (Verdi), Rome
Mar. 19: *Faust* (Gounod), Paris
Apr. 4: *Dinorah* (Meyerbeer), Paris

1860 Feb. 18: *Philémon et Baucis* (Gounod), Paris

1861 Mar. 9: *Bánk Bán* (Erkel), Budapest

1862 Aug. 9: *Béatrice et Bénédict* (Berlioz), Baden-Baden
Nov. 10: *La Forza del Destino* (Verdi), St. Petersburg

1863 Sep. 30: *Les Pêcheurs de Perles* (Bizet), Paris
Nov. 4: *Les Troyens à Carthage* (Berlioz), Paris

1864 Mar. 19: *Mireille* (Gounod), Paris

1865 Apr. 28: *L'Africaine* (Meyerbeer), Paris
June 10: *Tristan und Isolde* (Wagner), Munich
Aug. 15: *Saint Elisabeth* (Liszt), Budapest

1866 May 30: *The Bartered Bride* (Smetana), Prague
Nov. 17: *Mignon* (Thomas), Paris

1867 Mar. 11: *Don Carlos* (Verdi), Paris
Apr. 27: *Roméo et Juliette* (Gounod), Paris
Dec. 26: *La Jolie Fille de Perth* (Bizet), Paris

1868 Mar. 5: *Mefistofele* (Boito), Milan
Mar. 9: *Hamlet* (Thomas), Paris
May 16: *Dalibor* (Smetana), Prague
June 21: *Die Meistersinger von Nürnberg* (Wagner), Munich
Oct. 6: *La Périchole* (Offenbach), Paris

1869 May 25: Opera House on the Ring (later State Opera), Vienna, opens with *Don Giovanni*
Sep. 22: *Das Rheingold* (Wagner), Munich

1870 June 26: *Die Walküre* (Wagner), Munich

1871 Dec. 24: *Aida* (Verdi), Cairo

1872 Feb. 28: *The Stone Guest* (Dargomijsky), St. Petersburg
May 22: *Djamileh* (Bizet), Paris
Dec. 4: *La Fille de Madame Angot* (Lecocq), Brussels

1873 Jan. 13: *The Maid of Pskov* (Rimsky-Korsakov), St. Petersburg

1874 Feb. 8: *Boris Godunov* (Mussorgsky), St. Petersburg
Apr. 5: *Die Fledermaus* (J. Strauss), Vienna
Oct. 11: *Der Widerspenstigen Zähmung* (Goetz), Mannheim

1875 Jan. 5: Salle Garnier, new home of Paris Opéra, opens with *La Juive*
Jan. 25: *The Demon* (Rubinstein), St. Petersburg
Mar. 3: *Carmen* (Bizet), Paris
Mar. 10: *Die Königin von Saba* (Goldmark), Vienna
Dec. 22: *Das goldene Kreuz* (Brüll), Berlin

1876 Apr. 8: *La Gioconda* (Ponchielli), Milan
Aug. 13: First Bayreuth festival opens with *Das Rheingold*
Aug. 16: *Siegfried* (Wagner), Bayreuth
Aug. 17: *Götterdämmerung* (Wagner), Bayreuth
Nov. 7: *The Kiss* (Smetana), Prague
Dec. 6: *Vakula the Smith* (Tchaikovsky), St. Petersburg

1877 Apr. 27: *Le Roi de Lahore* (Massenet), Paris
Nov. 28: *L'Étoile* (Chabrier), Paris
Dec. 2: *Samson et Dalila* (Saint-Saëns), Weimar

1879 Jan. 25: Grand Théâtre, Monte Carlo, opens with Planquette's *Le Chevalier Errante*
Feb. 1: *Boccaccio* (Suppé), Vienna
Mar. 29: *Eugene Onegin* (Tchaikovsky), Moscow

1880 Jan. 21: *May Night* (Rimsky-Korsakov), St. Petersburg
Feb. 21: *Donna Juanita* (Suppé), Vienna
Nov. 27: Teatro Costanzi (later Teatro dell'Opera), Rome, opens with *Semiramide*

1881 Feb. 10: *Les Contes d'Hoffmann* (Offenbach), Paris
Feb. 25: *The Maid of Orleans* (Tchaikovsky), St. Petersburg
June 11: National Theater, Prague, opens with premiere of *Libuše* (Smetana)
Dec. 19: *Hérodiade* (Massenet), Brussels

1882 Feb. 10: *The Snow Maiden* (Rimsky-Korsakov), St. Petersburg
Mar. 22: *Le Duc d'Albe* (Donizetti), Rome
July 26: *Parsifal* (Wagner), Bayreuth

1883 Mar. 5: *Henry VIII* (Saint-Saëns), Paris
Apr. 14: *Lakmé* (Delibes), Paris
Oct. 22: Metropolitan Opera House, New York, opens with *Faust*

1884 Jan. 7: *Sigurd* (Reyer), Brussels
Jan. 19: *Manon* (Massenet), Paris
Feb. 15: *Mazeppa* (Tchaikovsky), Moscow
May 4: *Der Trompeter von Säckingen* (Nessler), Leipzig
May 31: *Le Villi* (Puccini), Milan

1885 Oct. 24: *Der Zigeunerbaron* (J. Strauss), Vienna
Nov. 30: *Le Cid* (Massenet), Paris

1886 Feb. 21: *Khovanshchina* (Moussorgsky), St. Petersburg
Apr. 10: *Gwendoline* (Chabrier), Brussels
Nov. 19: *Merlin* (Goldmark), Vienna

1887 Feb. 5: *Otello* (Verdi), Milan
May 18: *Le Roi Malgré Lui* (Chabrier), Paris

1888 Jan. 20: *Die drei Pintos* (Weber, comp. Mahler), Leipzig
Feb. 11: *Asrael* (Franchetti), Reggio Emilia
May 7: *Le Roi d'Ys* (Lalo), Paris
June 29: *Die Feen* (Wagner), Munich

1889 Feb. 12: *The Jacobin* (Dvořák), Prague
Apr. 21: *Edgar* (Puccini), Milan
May 14: *Esclarmonde* (Massenet), Paris
Oct. 4: *Il Vassalo di Szigeth* (Smareglia), Vienna

1890 Feb. 10: *Salammbô* (Reyer), Brussels
Feb. 16: *Loreley* (Catalani), Turin
May 17: *Cavalleria Rusticana* (Mascagni), Rome
Nov. 4: *Prince Igor* (Borodin), St. Petersburg
Dec. 6–7: *Les Troyens* (Berlioz), Karlsruhe (first complete perf.)
Dec. 19: *The Queen of Spades* (Tchaikovsky), St. Petersburg

1891 Oct. 31: *L'Amico Fritz* (Mascagni), Rome

1892 Jan. 20: *La Wally* (Catalani), Milan
Feb. 16: *Werther* (Massenet), Vienna
May 21: *Pagliacci* (Leoncavallo), Milan
July 5: *Elaine* (Bemberg), London
Aug. 27: Metropolitan Opera House destroyed by fire
Oct. 6: *Cristoforo Colombo* (Franchetti), Genoa
Dec. 18: *Iolanta* (Tchaikovsky), St. Petersburg

1893 Feb. 1: *Manon Lescaut* (Puccini), Turin
Feb. 9: *Falstaff* (Verdi), Milan
Apr. 27: *Aleko* (Rachmaninoff), Moscow
Nov. 23: *L'Attaque du Moulin* (Bruneau), Paris
Nov. 27: Rebuilt Metropolitan Opera House reopens with *Faust*
Dec. 23: *Hänsel und Gretel* (Humperdinck), Weimar

1894 Mar. 16: *Thaïs* (Massenet), Paris
May 10: *Guntram* (R. Strauss), Weimar
June 20: *La Navarraise* (Massenet), London

1895 May 4: *Der Evangelimann* (Kienzl), Berlin

1896 Feb. 1: *La Bohème* (Puccini), Turin
Mar. 28: *Andrea Chénier* (Giordano), Milan
June 7: *Der Corregidor* (Wolf), Mannheim

1897 Mar. 12: *Fervaal* (d'Indy), Brussels
May 6: *La Bohème* (Leoncavallo), Venice
Nov. 27: *Sapho* (Massenet), Paris
Nov. 27: *L'Arlesiana* (Cilea), Milan
Nov. 30: *Ero e Leandro* (Mancinelli), Madrid

1898 Jan. 7: *Sadko* (Rimsky-Korsakov), Moscow
Feb. 6: *Lobetanz* (Thuille), Karlsruhe
Nov. 17: *Fedora* (Giordano), Milan
Nov. 22: *Iris* (Mascagni), Rome
Dec. 7: *Mozart and Salieri* (Rimsky-Korsakov), Moscow

1899 Mar. 21: *Messaline* (de Lara), Monte Carlo
May 24: *Cendrillon* (Massenet), Paris
Nov. 3: *The Tsar's Bride* (Rimsky-Korsakov), Moscow

1900 Jan. 14: *Tosca* (Puccini), Rome
Feb. 2: *Louise* (Charpentier), Paris

Nov. 10: *Zazà* (Leoncavallo), Milan

1901 Jan. 17: *Le Maschere* (Mascagni), in six Italian cities
Mar. 3: *Der polnische Jude* (Weis), Prague
Mar. 31: *Rusalka* (Dvořák), Prague
May 29: *Manru* (Paderewski), Dresden
Nov. 21: *Feuersnot* (R. Strauss), Dresden

1902 Feb. 18: *Le Jongleur de Notre-Dame* (Massenet), Monte Carlo
Mar. 11: *Germania* (Franchetti), Milan
Apr. 9: *Der Wald* (Smyth), Berlin
Apr. 30: *Pelléas et Mélisande* (Debussy), Paris
Nov. 4: *Adriana Lecouvreur* (Cilea), Milan
Nov. 28: *Saul and David* (Nielsen), Copenhagen

1903 Nov. 15: *Tiefland* (D'Albert), Prague
Nov. 23: Metropolitan Opera opens redecorated theater with
Rigoletto; debut of Enrico Caruso
Nov. 27: *Le Donne Curiose* (Wolf-Ferrari), Munich
Dec. 23: *La Reine Fiammette* (Leroux), Paris

1904 Jan. 21: *Jenůfa* (Janáček), Brno
Feb. 17: *Madama Butterfly* (Puccini), Milan
Mar. 30: *Koanga* (Delius), Elberfeld
Nov. 30: *Risurrezione* (Alfano), Turin

1905 Jan. 28: *Giovanni Gallurese* (Montemezzi), Turin
July 3: *L'Oracolo* (Leoni), London
Sep. 9: *Salome* (R. Strauss), Dresden

1906 Jan. 31: *The Pipe of Desire* (Converse), Boston
Mar. 19: *I Quattro Rusteghi* (Wolf-Ferrari), Munich
Nov. 11: *Maskarade* (Nielsen), Copenhagen
Dec. 3: Manhattan Opera House, New York, opens with *I Puritani*

1907 Feb. 20: *The Legend of the Invisible City of Kitezh and the Maiden
Fevronia* (Rimsky-Korsakov), St. Petersburg
Feb. 21: *A Village Romeo and Juliet* (Delius), Berlin
May 10: *Ariane et Barbe-Bleue* (Dukas), Paris

1908 Feb. 26: *La Habanera* (Laparra), Paris
May 25: New Teatro Colón, Buenos Aires, opens with *Aida*
Nov. 4: *Versiegelt* (Blech), Hamburg
Nov. 16: Metropolitan Opera opens with *Aida*, under new general
manager Giulio Gatti-Casazza, with Arturo Toscanini as principal
conductor

1909 Jan. 25: *Elektra* (R. Strauss), Dresden
Oct. 7: *The Golden Cockerel* (Rimsky-Korsakov), Moscow
Dec. 4: *Il Segreto di Susanna* (Wolf-Ferrari), Munich

1910 Feb. 19: *Don Quichotte* (Massenet), Monte Carlo
Nov. 30: *Macbeth* (Bloch), Paris
Dec. 10: *La Fanciulla del West* (Puccini), New York, Met
Dec. 28: *Königskinder* (Humperdinck), New York, Met

1911 Jan. 26: *Der Rosenkavalier* (Strauss), Dresden
May 19: *L'Heure Espagnole* (Ravel), Paris
June 2: *Isabeau* (Mascagni), Buenos Aires
Dec. 23: *I Gioielli della Madonna* (Wolf-Ferrari), Berlin
Dec. 30: *Sorochintsy Fair* (Mussorgsky), St. Petersburg

1912 Mar. 14: *Mona* (Parker), New York, Met
Aug. 18: *Der ferne Klang* (Schreker), Frankfurt

Oct. 5: *Ariadne auf Naxos* (Strauss), Stuttgart

1913 Feb. 27: *Cyrano de Bergerac* (Damrosch), New York, Met
Mar. 4: *Pénélope* (Fauré), Monte Carlo
Apr. 1: *La Vida Breve* (Falla), Nice
Apr. 10: *L'Amore dei Tre Re* (Montemezzi), Milan
Aug. 10: First operatic performance in Verona Arena: *Aida*
Dec. 4: *L'Amore Medico* (Wolf-Ferrari), Dresden
Dec. 15: *Parisina* (Mascagni), Milan

1914 Jan. 24: *Madeleine* (Herbert), New York, Met
Feb. 19: *Francesca da Rimini* (Zandonai), Turin
May 15: *Mârouf* (Rabaud), Paris
May 26: *The Nightingale* (Stravinsky), Paris
Aug. 26: *The Immortal Hour* (Boughton), Glastonbury

1915 Jan. 25: *Madame Sans-Gêne* (Giordano), New York, Met
Mar. 20: *Fedra* (Pizzetti), Milan
Sep. 26: *Mona Lisa* (von Schillings), Stuttgart

1916 Jan. 18: *Goyescas* (Granados), New York, Met
Jan. 28: *The Boatswain's Mate* (Smyth), London
Mar. 28: *Violanta* (Korngold), Munich

1917 Jan. 30: *Eine florentinische Tragödie* (Zemlinsky), Stuttgart
Mar. 8: *The Canterbury Pilgrims* (De Koven), New York, Met
Mar. 27: *La Rondine* (Puccini), Monte Carlo
Apr. 30: *Lodoletta* (Mascagni), Rome
May 11: *Turandot* and *Arlecchino* (Busoni), Zurich
June 12: *Palestrina* (Pfitzner), Munich

1918 Mar. 23: *Shanewis* (Cadman), New York, Met
May 24: *Duke Bluebeard's Castle* (Bartók), Budapest
June 4: *Julien* (Charpentier), Paris
Dec. 14: *Il Trittico* (Puccini), New York, Met

1919 Mar. 12: *The Legend* (Breil), and *The Temple Dancer* (Hugo), New York, Met
Oct. 10: *Die Frau ohne Schatten* (R. Strauss), Vienna
Dec. 27: *L'Oiseau Bleu* (Wolff), New York, Met

1920 Jan. 31: *Cleopatra's Night* (Hadley), New York, Met
Apr. 23: *The Excursions of Mr Brouček* (Janáček), Prague
Dec. 4: *Die tote Stadt* (Korngold), Hamburg and Cologne

1921 Apr. 15: *Anima Allegra* (Vittadini), Rome
May 2: *Il Piccolo Marat* (Mascagni), Rome
Nov. 23: *Katya Kabanova* (Janáček), Brno
Dec. 30: *The Love for Three Oranges* (Prokofiev), Chicago

1922 May 18: *Renard* (Stravinsky), Paris
May 29: *Der Zwerg* (Zemlinsky), Cologne
June 3: *Mavra* (Stravinsky), Paris
Aug. 14: First operatic performance at Salzburg Festival, *Don Giovanni*

1923 Mar. 23: *El Retablo de Maese Pedro* (Falla), Seville
Apr. 10: *I Compagnacci* (Riccitelli), Rome
June 1: *Padmâvatî* (Roussel), Paris

1924 May 1: *Nerone* (Boito), Milan
June 6: *Erwartung* (Schoenberg), Prague
July 14: *Hugh the Drover* (Vaughan Williams), London
Oct. 14: *Die glückliche Hand* (Schoenberg), Vienna

Nov. 4: *Intermezzo* (R. Strauss), Dresden
Nov. 6: *The Cunning Little Vixen* (Janáček), Brno
Dec. 20: *La Cena delle Beffe* (Giordano), Milan

1925 Mar. 21: *L'Enfant et les Sortilèges* (Ravel), Monte Carlo
May 21: *Doktor Faust* (Busoni), Dresden
Aug. 13: Opening of Salzburg Festspielhaus
Dec. 14: *Wozzeck* (Berg), Berlin

1926 Apr. 25: *Turandot* (Puccini), Milan
June 19: *King Roger* (Szymanowski), Warsaw
Oct. 16: *Háry János* (Kodály), Budapest
Nov. 9: *Cardillac* (Hindemith), Dresden
Dec. 18: *The Makropoulos Affair* (Janáček), Brno

1927 Feb. 10: *Jonny spielt auf* (Krenek), Leipzig
Feb. 17: *The King's Henchman* (Taylor), New York, Met
Apr. 27: *Shvanda the Bagpiper* (Weinberger), Prague
May 5: *Madonna Imperia* (Alfano), Turin
May 30: *Oedipus Rex* (Stravinsky), Paris
July 17: *Hin und Zurück* (Hindemith), Baden-Baden
Nov. 18: *La Compana Sommersa* (Respighi), Hamburg
Nov. 19: Kroll Opera, Berlin, opens with *Fidelio*

1928 Feb. 18: *Der Zar lässt sich photographieren* (Weill), Leipzig
May 16: *Fra Gherardo* (Pizzetti), Milan
June 6: *Die ägyptische Helena* (Strauss), Dresden
Aug. 31: *Die Dreigroschenoper* (Weill), Berlin

1929 Feb. 9: *Le Preziose Ridicole* (Lattuada), Milan
Apr. 29: *The Gambler* (Prokofiev), Brussels
June 8: *Neues vom Tage* (Hindemith), Berlin

1930 Jan. 18: *The Nose* (Shostakovich), Leningrad
Feb. 1: *Von Heute auf Morgen* (Schoenberg), Frankfurt
Mar. 9: *Aufstieg und Fall der Stadt Mahagonny* (Weill), Leipzig
Apr. 12: *From the House of the Dead* (Janáček), Brno
May 5: *Christophe Colomb* (Milhaud), Berlin
June 23: *Der Jasager* (Weill), Berlin

1931 Jan. 20: First performance by Vic–Wells Opera at Sadler's Wells
Theatre, London: *Carmen*
Jan. 31: *La Notte di Zoraima* (Montemezzi), Milan
Feb. 7: *Peter Ibbetson* (Taylor), New York, Met
Dec. 25: first radio broadcast of a Met performance: *Hänsel und Gretel*

1932 Feb. 18: *Caponsacchi* (Hageman), Freiburg
Oct. 15: War Memorial Opera House, San Francisco, opens with
Tosca

1933 Jan. 7: *The Emperor Jones* (Gruenberg), New York, Met
Feb. 18: *Der Silbersee* (Weill), Leipzig
Apr. 22: First Maggio Musicale Fiorentino opens with *Nabucco*
May 20: *Merry Mount* (Hanson), Ann Arbor
July 1: *Arabella* (Strauss), Dresden

1934 Jan. 22: *The Lady Macbeth of Mtsensk District* (Shostakovich),
Leningrad
Jan. 23: *La Fiamma* (Respighi), Rome
Feb. 8: *Four Saints in Three Acts* (Thomson), Hartford
May 28: First Glyndebourne festival opens with *Così Fan Tutte*

1935 Jan. 24: *In the Pasha's Garden* (Seymour), New York, Met

June 24: *Die schweigsame Frau* (Strauss), Dresden
Sep. 30: *Porgy and Bess* (Gershwin), Boston
Dec. 16: Metropolitan Opera opens under new manager Edward Johnson, with *La Traviata*

1937 Mar. 28: Mrs August Belmont incorporates the Metropolitan Opera Guild
Apr. 1: *Amelia al Ballo* (Menotti), Philadelphia
May 12: *The Man Without a Country* (Damrosch), New York, Met
May 25: First Metropolitan Opera Auditions of the Air
June 2: *Lulu* (Berg) (Acts I & II), Zurich
Dec. 1: *Riders to the Sea* (Vaughan Williams), London

1938 Feb. 22: *Colas Breugnon* (Kabalevsky), Leningrad
May 28: *Mathis der Maler* (Hindemith), Zurich
June 15: *Karl V* (Krenek), Prague
July 24: *Friedenstag* (Strauss), Munich
Oct. 15: *Daphne* (Strauss), Dresden

1939 Feb. 5: *Der Mond* (Orff), Munich
May 18: *The Devil and Daniel Webster* (Moore), New York

1940 May 18: *Volo di Notte* (Dallapiccola), Florence

1941 May 5: *Paul Bunyan* (Britten), New York

1942 Feb. 20: *The Island God* (Menotti), New York, Met
Oct. 28: *Capriccio* (R. Strauss), Munich

1943 Feb. 20: *Die Kluge* (Orff), Frankfurt

1944 Feb. 21: New York City Opera opens first season with *Tosca*
Aug. 16: *Die Liebe der Danae* (R. Strauss), Salzburg (public rehearsal)

1945 June 7: *Peter Grimes* (Britten), London

1946 May 8: *The Medium* (Menotti), New York
June 12: *War and Peace* (Prokofiev), Leningrad (partial stage perf.)
July 12: *The Rape of Lucretia* (Britten), Glyndebourne
Nov. 3: *Betrothal in a Monastery* (Prokofiev), Leningrad
Dec. 16: *Street Scene* (Weill), Philadelphia

1947 Jan. 11: *The Warrior* (Rogers), New York, Met
Feb. 18: *The Telephone* (Menotti), New York
Apr. 18: *The Trial of Lucullus* (Sessions), Berkeley
May 7: *The Mother of Us All* (Thomson), New York
June 3: *Les Mamelles de Tirésias* (Poulenc), Paris
June 20: *Albert Herring* (Britten), Glyndebourne
Aug. 6: *Dantons Tod* (Einem), Salzburg

1948 June 7: First opera performance at Aldeburgh festival, *Albert Herring*
July 14: *Down in the Valley* (Weill), Bloomington
Nov. 29: First opera telecast from the Met: opening-night *Otello*
Dec. 3: *The Story of A Real Man* (Prokofiev), Leningrad

1949 Mar. 31: *Troubled Island* (Still), New York
Aug. 9: *Antigonae* (Orff), Salzburg
Oct. 6: *Regina* (Blitzstein), New Haven, Conn.
Dec. 1: *Il Prigioniero* (Dallapiccola), Turin

1950 Mar. 1: *The Consul* (Menotti), Philadelphia
Nov. 6: Met opens under new manager Rudolf Bing with *Don Carlos*

1951 Apr. 26: *The Pilgrim's Progress* (Vaughan Williams), London
Sep. 11: *The Rake's Progress* (Stravinsky), Venice
Dec. 1: *Billy Budd* (Britten), London

Dec. 24: *Amahl and the Night Visitors* (Menotti), NBC Television

1952 Feb. 17: *Boulevard Solitude* (Henze), Hanover
June 12: *Trouble in Tahiti* (Bernstein), Waltham

1953 May 4: *Irmelin* (Delius), Oxford
June 8: *Gloriana* (Britten), London

1954 Feb. 5: Lyric Opera of Chicago presents first production, *Don Giovanni*
Mar. 12: *Moses und Aron* (Schoenberg), Hamburg (concert perf.)
Apr. 1: *The Tender Land* (Copland), New York
Sep. 14: *The Turn of the Screw* (Britten), Venice
Nov. 25: *The Fiery Angel* (Prokofiev), Paris (concert perf.)
Dec. 3: *Troilus and Cressida* (Walton), London
Dec. 27: *The Saint of Bleecker Street* (Menotti), New York

1955 Jan. 27: *The Midsummer Marriage* (Tippett), London

1956 July 7: *The Ballad of Baby Doe* (Moore), Central City
Sep. 23: *König Hirsch* (Henze), Berlin
Oct. 29: *Candide* (Bernstein), Boston

1957 Jan. 26: *Dialogues des Carmélites* (Poulenc), Milan
July 3: Santa Fe Opera opens with *Madama Butterfly*
Aug. 11: *Die Harmonie der Welt* (Hindemith), Munich
Nov. 21: Dallas Civic Opera presents first opera, *L'Italiana in Algeri*

1958 Jan. 15: *Vanessa* (Barber), New York, Met
Mar. 1: *Assassinio nella Cattedrale* (Pizzetti), Milan
Apr. 23: *The Good Soldier Schweik* (Kurka), New York
June 5: First Spoleto festival opens with *Macbeth*
June 18: *Noyes Fludde* (Britten), Orford, England
Aug. 20: *Maria Golovin* (Menotti), Brussels

1959 Feb. 6: *La Voix Humaine* (Poulenc), Paris
May 31: *Aniara* (Blomdahl), Stockholm

1960 June 11: *A Midsummer Night's Dream* (Britten), Aldeburgh
July 26: Neues Festspielhaus, Salzburg, opens with *Der Rosenkavalier*

1961 May 20: *Elegy for Young Lovers* (Henze), Schwetzingen
Oct. 26: *The Crucible* (Ward), New York
Nov. 24: *L'Atlantida* (de Falla), Barcelona

1962 May 29: *King Priam* (Tippett), Coventry
Oct. 21: *L'Ultimo Selvaggio* (Menotti), Paris

1964 Apr. 19: *Montezuma* (Sessions), Berlin
June 12: *Curlew River* (Britten), Orford
July 24: *Don Rodrigo* (Ginastera), Buenos Aires

1965 Feb. 15: *Die Soldaten* (Zimmermann), Cologne
Mar. 25: *Lizzie Borden* (Beeson), New York
Apr. 7: *Der junge Lord* (Henze), Berlin

1966 Feb. 22: New York City Opera's first performance at New York
State Theater, Lincoln Center, *Don Rodrigo*
Apr. 16: Farewell performance at old Metropolitan Opera House
June 9: *The Burning Fiery Furnace* (Britten), Orford
Aug. 6: *The Bassarids* (Henze), Salzburg
Sep. 16: Opening performance at new Metropolitan Opera House in
Lincoln Center: world premiere of Barber's *Antony and Cleopatra*

1967 Mar. 17: *Mourning Becomes Electra* (Levy), New York, Met

June 3: *The Bear* (Walton), Aldeburgh
June 28: "The Met in the Parks" concert series inaugurated with *La Bohème*

1968 Feb. 5: *Syllabaire pour Phèdre* (Ohana), Paris
June 8: *Punch and Judy* (Birtwistle), Aldeburgh
June 10: *The Prodigal Son* (Britten), Orford
Sep. 29: *Ulisse* (Dallapiccola), Berlin

1969 June 20: *Die Teufel von Loudon* (Penderecki), Hamburg

1970 Jan. 22: *Of Mice and Men* (Floyd), Seattle
Aug. 12: *Opera* (Berio), Santa Fe
Dec. 2: *The Knot Garden* (Tippett), London

1971 May 16: *Owen Wingrave* (Britten), BBC Television
May 23: *Der Besuch der alten Damen* (Einem), Vienna

1972 Apr. 20: *Lord Byron* (Thomson), New York
July 12: *Taverner* (Maxwell Davies), London
Sep. 19: Met opens with *Carmen*, under acting general manager Schuyler Chapin

1973 June 16: *Death in Venice* (Britten), Aldeburgh

1974 June 11: *The Voice of Ariadne* (Musgrave), Aldeburgh

1975 May 29: Met opens tour of Japan
Oct. 14: Met opens with *Boris Godunov*, under executive director Anthony A. Bliss

1976 July 25: *Einstein on the Beach* (Glass), Avignon

1977 Mar. 15: First "Live from the Met" telecast: *La Bohème*
July 7: *The Ice Break* (Tippett), London
Sep. 6: *Mary Queen of Scots* (Musgrave), Edinburgh

1978 Apr. 21: *Danton and Robespierre* (Eaton), Bloomington
Nov. 30: *The Red Line* (Sallinen), Helsinki

1979 Feb. 24: *Lulu* (Berg) (3-act version), Paris

1980 Mar. 6: *Jakob Lenz* (Rihm), Karlsruhe
Sep. 3: *The Lighthouse* (Maxwell Davies), Edinburgh
Sep. 5: *Satyagraha* (Glass), Rotterdam
Nov. 28: *Where the Wild Things Are* (Knussen), Brussels

1981 Mar. 15: *Donnerstag* (Stockhausen), Milan

1983 June 17: *A Quiet Place* (Bernstein), Houston
Oct. 22: Metropolitan Opera Centennial Gala
Nov. 28: *Saint-François d'Assise* (Messiaen), Paris

1984 Mar. 24: *Akhnaten* (Glass), Stuttgart
May 25: *Samstag* (Stockhausen), Milan

1986 Jan. 1: Bruce Crawford becomes general manager of the Met
Sep. 22: Met opens with new production of *Die Walküre*, under artistic director James Levine

For Further Reading

The reader in search of enlightenment about opera, its creators and performers, its forms and history, can turn to a variety of books and reference tools. A basic starting point is *The New Grove Dictionary of Music and Musicians*, edited by Stanley Sadie (20 vols., Washington, D.C., and London, 1980), available in most libraries; in addition to articles on composers, performers, general subjects, and specific terms, *The New Grove* includes extensive bibliographies covering research in all languages. Its younger relative, *The New Grove Dictionary of American Music*, edited by H. Wiley Hitchcock and Stanley Sadie (4 vols., N.Y., and London, 1986), expands and brings up to date *New Grove's* treatment of American topics. In a single volume, *The New Harvard Dictionary of Music*, edited by Don Michael Randel (Cambridge, Mass., and London, 1986), provides excellent coverage of musical terms, topics, and works, but no personal entries. *Baker's Biographical Dictionary of Musicians*, edited by Nicolas Slonimsky (7th ed., N.Y., 1984), also in one volume, is devoted entirely to personal entries. A more compact survey of both musical subjects and persons will be found in *The Oxford Dictionary of Music*, by Michael Kennedy (N.Y., and Oxford, 1985).

The standard single-volume history of opera is Donald Jay Grout's *A Short History of Opera*, (2nd ed., N.Y., and London, 1965), with a voluminous bibliography. Alfred Loewenberg's *Annals of Opera: 1597–1940* (3rd ed., Totowa, N.J., 1978) comprises a chronological listing of works in the order of their premieres, plus additional information about first performances in other countries and cities. Patrick J. Smith's *The Tenth Muse* (N.Y., 1970; repr. 1975) is a historical study of the opera libretto. Joseph Kerman's *Opera as Drama* (N.Y., 1956), opinionated and thoughtful, is still the most stimulating introduction to operatic esthetics. Richard Traubner's *Operetta: A Theatrical History* (Garden City, N.Y., 1983) surveys that genre. And *The Concise Oxford Dictionary of Opera*, by John Warrack and Harold Rosenthal (2nd ed., 1979), is a convenient general reference work with different emphases than the present book, particularly strong on historical matters and on opera in Great Britain and Eastern Europe.

The standard guides to operas and their stories are *The New Kobbé's Complete Opera Book*, edited and revised by the Earl of Harewood (3rd ed., London, 1987), and *The Metropolitan Opera Stories of the Great Operas*, by John W. Freeman (N.Y., and London, 1984). Two admirable and growing series are devoted to the illumination of individual works: the *Cambridge Opera Handbooks* (N.Y., and Cambridge) and the *Opera Guides*, edited by Nicholas John in collaboration with the English National Opera and the Royal Opera (N.Y., and London); the latter include librettos and English translations as well as historical essays.

The most comprehensive reference work about singers in English, *A Concise Biographical Dictionary of Singers*, by K.J. Kutsch and Leo Riemens, translated by Harry Earl Jones (Philadelphia, N.Y., and London, 1969), is unfortunately unreliable in detail (more recent editions of its German original, *Unvergängliche Stimmen*, incorporate important corrections). The two volumes of *The Record of Singing* (London, and N.Y., 1977–79), by Michael Scott, contain gossipy biographies and provocative evaluations of singers who recorded before 1914 and from 1914 to 1925, respectively; J. B. Steane's *The Grand Tradition: Seventy Years of Singing on Record, 1900–1970* (N.Y., and London, 1974), more sympathetic in tone, has less biographical information. Also useful is Robert H. Cowden's *Concert and Opera Singers: A Bibliography of Biographical Materials* (Westport, Conn., and London,

1985). *Who's Who in Opera* (N.Y., 1976), edited by Maria F. Rich, covers not only singers but other opera professionals.

For the Met, the basic work is William H. Seltsam's *Metropolitan Opera Annals* (N.Y., 1947), with its supplements, the first two compiled by Seltsam (N.Y., 1957, 1968), the third by Mary Ellis Peltz and Gerald Fitzgerald (Clifton, N.J., 1978), containing complete casts of all the company's home performances, along with excerpts from reviews; a new and vastly more comprehensive edition, under the title *Annals of the Metropolitan Opera*, is currently in preparation. That will contain, among other things, the Met's tour performances, currently available up to 1956 in Quaintance Eaton's *Opera Caravan* (N.Y., 1957; repr. 1978). Irving Kolodin's *The Metropolitan Opera: 1883–1966: A Candid History* (N.Y., 1966), is principally a season-by-season review of the company's performances in the old Met at Broadway and Thirty-Ninth Street. Martin Mayer's *The Met: One Hundred Years of Grand Opera* (N.Y., and London, 1983) adopts a more synoptic point of view, and benefits from access to the Met's archives. Useful tabulations of the Met careers of noted singers will be found in Robert J. Wayner's *What Did They Sing at the Met?* (3rd ed., N.Y., 1981), and the company's commercial studio recordings are documented in Frederick P. Fellers' *The Metropolitan Opera on Record* (Westport, Conn., and London, 1984).

Histories of other major American companies, with performance annals, include: *The New York City Opera* (N.Y., and London, 1981), by Martin L. Sokol; *The Boston Opera Company* (N.Y., 1965; repr. 1980), by Quaintance Eaton; *The San Francisco Opera, 1922–1978* (Sausalito, Calif., 1978), by Arthur J. Bloomfield; *Opera in Chicago* (N.Y., 1966), by Ronald Davis; and *Lyric Opera of Chicago* (Chicago, 1979), by Claudia Cassidy. Comparable British works are Harold Rosenthal's *Two Centuries of Opera at Covent Garden* (London, 1958) and John Julius Norwich's *Fifty Years of Glyndebourne: An Illustrated History* (London, 1985). Similar publications exist for some continental theaters, and their "annals" sections can usually be deciphered even by those who don't read the languages; an excellent "Bibliography of Opera House Annals," by Thomas G. Kaufman, was published in *The Donizetti Society Journal*, No. 5 (1984).

Opera on Record, edited by Alan Blyth (3 vols., London, 1979–84), contains surveys of the recordings of major operas (both complete sets and excerpts, available and out-of-print), primarily by British critics. To locate discographies of composers and performers, consult Michael H. Gray and Gerald D. Gibson, *Bibliography of Discographies: Volume 1, Classical Music, 1925–1975* (N.Y., and London, 1977).

Finally, there are the periodicals that keep the opera world abreast of itself. These include the Metropolitan Opera Guild's biweekly (in season)/ monthly (out of season) *Opera News*; the *Bulletin* published by that invaluable clearing-house of information, the Central Opera Service; and the British monthly *Opera*, founded by the Earl of Harewood and long edited by the late Harold Rosenthal.

Sources of Illustrations

Angel/EMI, courtesy of: 87, 142, 180

© 1987 Beth Bergman: 15 (bottom), 28, 29 (bottom), 32, 35 (top), 38 (top), 42, 53, 59 (bottom), 60, 70 (bottom), 80, 84–5, 93, 105, 108, 109 (bottom), 116, 120, 133, 137 (top), 139, 159 (bottom), 167 (bottom), 173, 175 (top), 182, 187 (top), 200–1, 202, 204 (bottom), 205 (top), 206–7, 215, 241 (bottom), 247, 256–7, 270, 271 (bottom), 272, 285, 293 (top), 296–7, 300 (bottom right), 317 (bottom), 319 (bottom), 338, 340–1, 351, 357, 368, 372, 392, 395

Phil Brodatz: 48–9

Columbia University, Rare Book and Manuscript Library: 68 (bottom), 242 (top)

© 1987 Erika Davidson: 71 (bottom), 172 (top), 176 (bottom right), 238, 315 (bottom)

Deutsche Grammophon: 126 (bottom)

Erwin Döring: 112

Edison National Historic Site: 291 (top)

English National Opera (Zoë Dominic): 143

Fred Fehl: 386

Festspiele Bayreuth: 36 (bottom – Siegfried Lauterwasser), 268 (bottom), 280–1 (Wilhelm Rauh)

Yveta Synek Graff, courtesy of: 164

James Heffernan: 16–7 (bottom), 41, 95, 96, 117, 153, 157, 234 (bottom), 244 (top), 287, 301 (bottom), 359 (bottom), 382

© 1982 David Hockney, courtesy of Petersburg Press, New York/London: 313

International Foundation Mozarteum, Salzburg: 237

Robert Jacobson, courtesy of: 314 (top)

Siegfried Lauterwasser: 128, 177

Harvey Lloyd: 123

Alec MacWeeney: 131

The Metropolitan Museum of Art, The Elisha Whittelsey Collection, The Elisha Whittelsey Fund, 1954. (54.602.1.14): 66 (top)

Metropolitan Opera Archives: 24 (bottom – Louis Mélançon), 47 (bottom), 62–3 (Mélançon), 68 (top – Mélançon), 78–9 (top), 140 (top – White Studios, bottom – Herman Mishkin), 144, 155, 175 (bottom), 188, 204 (top), 205 (bottom), 220 (Mélançon), 245 (bottom – Mélançon), 255, 273 (Mélançon), 278 (Mishkin), 284, 307 (bottom – Mélançon), 312, 316 (bottom), 326, 337 (Mélançon), 339 (top – Carlo Edwards), 348 (Mélançon), 349 (Mélançon), 353 (bottom – Sedge Leblang), 365, 370–1, 378, 391

Metropolitan Opera Guild, Education Department: 72 (bottom – William Harris), 169 (top – Harris), 172 (bottom – Wist Thorpe), 174 (bottom – Frank Dunand), 176 (bottom left – Thorpe), 242 (bottom – Harris), 243 (Dunand), 244 (bottom – Thorpe), 245 (top – Dunand), 248 (Dunand), 265 (Dunand), 314 (bottom – Harris), 315 (top, middle – Dunand), 319 (top – Thorpe)

Metropolitan Opera Guild/*Opera News*: 11, 13, 14, 18 (White Studios), 20,

23 (Sedge Leblang), 25 (Rudolf Pittner), 29 (top), 30, 31, 33 (top), (bottom – Leblang), 34 (Leblang), 35 (bottom), 36 (top), 38 (bottom), 39, 40, 43, 44, 45, 47 (top), 50, 52 (Herman Mishkin), 55, 56–7 (top, bottom), 59 (top), 64, 66 (bottom), 67, 69 (top), 71 (top – Louis Mélançon), 74–5, 78–9 (bottom), 82 (Mishkin), 86, 90–1, 94 (Leblang), 101, 102 (top – Mélançon, bottom – Mishkin), 103, 104, 107 (Mélançon), 110, 111, 114, 121, 122, 125 (White Studios), 126 (top), 127, 132 (Mishkin), 134, 135, 136 (Mishkin), 137 (bottom), 147, 148, 152, 156, 159 (top – Aimé Dupont), 160 (Leblang), 161, 166 (White Studios), 167 (top), 169 (bottom), 170 (bottom left), 174 (top), 178, 179, 185, 186, 187 (bottom), 189, 192–3, 194, 196 (top), (bottom – Leblang), 197, 199 (Frank Lerner), 208, 209, 210, 211 (Mélançon), 214, 216, 217, 221, 222 (Mélançon), 225 (bottom), 226–9, 231 (top), (bottom – Mélançon), 233, 234 (top), 235, 239 (top), (bottom – Mishkin), 240, 241 (top), 246, 250, 252–3, 254 (top), 258 (White Studios), 259 (top), (bottom – Tony Perry), 263, 266, 267, 269, 271 (top), 275, 276, 277, 279, 286 (Leblang), 289, 290 (top), 293 (bottom –Mishkin), 295, 298, 300 (top, bottom left), 302–3 (Mélançon), 306, 307 (top – White Studios), 308–9, 310, 311, 316 (top), 317 (top), 318 (bottom), 320 (bottom), 321 (bottom), 323, 325, 328, 329, 330, 331, 332, 333, 334 (Dupont), 335 (Mishkin), 342 (Mishkin), 345, 346–7, 353 (top – White Studios), 355 (White Studios), 356, 359 (top), 360, 362–3, 364, 366, 367, 373 (Mélançon), 379, 381 (top, bottom right), 383, 385, 387 (Mélançon), 390

Museo Teatrale alla Scala (Milan): 170 (top, bottom right), 171, 176 (top), 225 (top)

Steven Mark Needham: 56–7 (middle)

New York Public Library: 69 (bottom), 195, 268 (top)

Opera Company of Boston: 321 (top)

E. Piccagliani: 339 (bottom)

Private Collection: 320 (top)

RCA: 88, 290–1 (bottom)

Gary Renaud: 24 (top)

Royal Opera, Covent Garden: 77 (Clive Barda), 109 (top – Houstan Rogers), 145 (Rogers), 236 (Donald Southern)

San Francisco Opera/Ron Scherl: 70 (top), 318 (top)

Vernon Smith: 15 (top), 147, 254 (bottom)

Christian Steiner: 381 (bottom left)

Robert L. B. Tobin, courtesy of: 65, 72 (top)

Robert Tuggle Collection: 352

© 1980 Unitel: 301 (top)

Theodor Uppman, courtesy of: 375